Organizational Behaviour

Concepts, Controversies, Applications

Eighth
Canadian
Edition

Organizational Behaviour

Concepts, Controversies, Applications

Eighth Canadian Edition

Nancy Langton
University of British Columbia

Stephen P. Robbins
San Diego State University

Timothy A. Judge
University of Notre Dame

EDITORIAL DIRECTOR: Anne Williams
PORTFOLIO MANAGER: Karen Townsend
MARKETING MANAGER: Darcey Pepper
CONTENT MANAGER: John Polanszky
PROJECT MANAGER: Jessica Mifsud
CONTENT DEVELOPER: Jennifer Murray
MEDIA EDITOR: Rachel Stuckey
MEDIA DEVELOPER: Kelli Cadet

PRODUCTION SERVICES: Cenveo® Publisher Services
PERMISSIONS PROJECT MANAGER: Joanne Tang
PHOTO PERMISSIONS RESEARCH: iEnergizerAptara®, Ltd
TEXT PERMISSIONS RESEARCH: iEnergizerAptara®, Ltd
INTERIOR AND COVER DESIGN: Anthony Leung
COVER IMAGE: © Echo3005 / Shutterstock
VICE-PRESIDENT, CROSS MEDIA AND PUBLISHING SERVICES: Gary Bennett

Pearson Canada Inc., 26 Prince Andrew Place, Don Mills, Ontario M3C 2T8.

9780134645858

1 18

Library and Archives Canada Cataloguing in Publication

Robbins, Stephen P., 1943–, author Organizational behaviour: concepts, controversies, applications / Nancy Langton (University of British Columbia), Stephen P. Robbins (San Diego State University), Timothy A. Judge (University of Notre Dame) — 8th Canadian ed.

Includes index.
ISBN 978-0-13-464585-8

1. Organizational behavior—Textbooks. 2. Management—Textbooks. I. Langton, Nancy, author II. Judge, Tim, author III. Title.

QE28.2.T37 2011   550   C2010-905691-4

BRIEF CONTENTS

CONTENTS

PREFACE

Welcome to the eighth Canadian edition of *Organizational Behaviour*. Since its arrival in Canada, *Organizational Behaviour* has enjoyed widespread acclaim across the country for its rich Canadian content and has quickly established itself as the leading text in the field.

Organizational Behaviour, Eighth Canadian edition, is truly a Canadian product. While it draws upon the strongest aspects of its American cousin, it expresses its own vision and voice. It provides the context for understanding organizational behaviour (OB) in the Canadian workplace and highlights the many Canadian contributions to the field. Indeed, it goes a step further than most OB texts prepared for the Canadian marketplace. Specifically, it asks, in many instances:

- How does this theory apply in the Canadian workplace of today?

- What are the implications of the theory for managers and employees working in the twenty-first century?

- What are the implications of the theory for everyday life? OB, after all, is not something that applies only in the workplace.

This text is sensitive to important Canadian issues. Subject matter reflects the broad multicultural flavour of Canada and also highlights the roles of women and visible minorities in the workplace. Examples reflect the broad range of organizations in Canada: large, small, public and private sector, unionized and non-unionized.

Organizational Behaviour continues to be a vibrant and relevant text because it's a product of the Canadian classroom. It is used in Canada by the first author and her colleagues. Thus, there is a "front-line" approach to considering revisions. We also solicit considerable feedback from OB instructors and students throughout the country. While we have kept the features of the previous edition that adopters continue to say they like, there is also a great deal that is new.

Key Changes to the Eighth Canadian Edition

The eighth edition was designed to evolve with today's students. There are more relevant examples, updated theory coverage, and a continued emphasis on providing the latest research findings. Based on reviews from numerous instructors and students across Canada, we have found that many potential users want chapters that have the right balance of theory, research, and application material, while being relevant to student learning.

- *NEW* feature in every chapter! *Career Objectives* offers advice in a question-and-answer format to help students think through issues they may face in the workforce today.

- *NEW Opening Vignette* in every chapter brings current business trends and events to the forefront.

- *NEW* **key terms presented in bold** throughout the text highlight new vocabulary pertinent to today's study of organizational behaviour.

- *NEW* **photos and captions** in every chapter link the chapter content to contemporary real-life worldwide situations to enhance the student's understanding of hands-on application of concepts.

- *NEW* These features are either **completely new or substantially updated** within each chapter as applicable to reflect ongoing challenges in business worldwide and focus the student's attention on new topics:

  - *Learning Objectives*

  - *Exhibits*

  - *Point/Counterpoint*

- *NEW* The following end-of-chapter material is either **completely new or substantially revised and updated** for each chapter to bring the most contemporary thinking to the attention of students:

  - *Summary*

  - *OB at Work: For Review*

  - *OB at Work: For Managers*

  - *Experiential Exercise*

  - *Ethical Dilemma*

  - *Case Incidents*

Chapter-by-Chapter Changes
Chapter 1: What Is Organizational Behaviour?

- Revised *Learning Outcomes*

- New *Opening Vignette* (Target's failure in Canada)

- New research in The Importance of Interpersonal Skills

- New research in Big Data

- New feature! *Career Objectives* (What Do I Say About My Termination?)

- New *Point/Counterpoint* (The Battle of the Texts)

- New *Experiential Exercise* (Managing the OB Way)

- New *Ethical Dilemma* (There's a Drone in Your Soup)

- Updated *Case Incident* (Apple Goes Global)

- New *Case Incident* (Big Data for Dummies)

Chapter 2: Perception, Personality, and Emotions

- New *Opening Vignette* (Michele Romanow)

- New section in The Myers-Briggs Type Indicator

- New research and discussion in The Big Five Personality Model

- New sections on Big Five personality trait research: Conscientiousness, Emotional Stability, Extraversion, Openness to Experience, and Agreeableness

- New research in The Dark Triad

- New major section: Other Traits (on traits that are socially undesirable)

- New research and discussion in Moral Emotions

- New research and discussion in Choosing Emotions: Emotional Labour
- New section: Emotion Regulation Techniques
- New feature! *Career Objectives* (So What If I'm a Few Minutes Late to Work?)
- New *Point/Counterpoint* (Sometimes Yelling Is for Everyone's Good)
- New *Case Incident* (The Power of Quiet)
- New *Case Incident* (Tall Poppy Syndrome)

Chapter 3: Values, Attitudes, and Diversity in the Workplace

- New *Opening Vignette* (Ladies Learning Code)
- New research in What Causes Job Satisfaction?
- New section: Job Conditions
- New section: Personality
- New section: Pay
- New section: Life Satisfaction
- New major section: Counterproductive Work Behaviour (CWB)
- New feature! *Career Objectives* (Is It Okay to Be Gay at Work?)
- New *Point/Counterpoint* (Millennials Have Inflated Images of Themselves Compared to Their Parents)
- New *Ethical Dilemma* (Tell-All Websites)
- New *Case Incident* (Job Crafting)
- New *Case Incident* (Walking the Walk)

OB on the Edge: Stress at Work

- New *Opening Vignette* (workspaces are not for eating)
- Updated list of The Most and Least Stressful Jobs
- New research in Causes of Stress
- New research and discussion in Organizational Approaches

Chapter 4: Theories of Motivation

- Revised *Learning Outcomes*
- New *Opening Vignette* (Lee Valley Tools)
- New research and discussion in Maslow's Hierarchy of Needs Theory
- New international research and discussion in McClelland's Theory of Needs
- New feature! *Career Objectives* (Why Won't He Take My Advice?)
- New research and discussion in Self-Determination Theory
- New Global Implications section: Justice
- New *Ethical Dilemma* (The New GPA)

Chapter 5: Motivation in Action

- New *Opening Vignette* (G Adventures)
- New research and discussion in Job Rotation
- New section and research in Relational Job Design
- New research in Flextime
- New feature! *Career Objectives* (How Can I Get Flextime?)
- New research and discussion in Telecommuting
- New international research and discussion in Employee Involvement and Participation
- New research in Participative Management
- New research in Representative Participation
- New international research and new discussion in How to Pay: Rewarding Individual Employees through Variable-Pay Programs
- New research in Merit-Based Pay
- New international research in Bonuses
- New research in Profit-Sharing Plans
- New research in Employee Stock Ownership Plans
- New material and international research in Flexible Benefits: Developing a Benefits Package
- New research in Intrinsic Rewards: Employee Recognition Programs
- New *Case Incident* (Pay Raises Every Day)

Chapter 6: Groups and Teamwork

- New *Opening Vignette* (Summerlunch+)
- New research and discussion in Why Have Teams Become So Popular?
- New discussion in Problem-Solving Teams
- New research in Cross-Functional Teams
- New research in Virtual Teams
- New research and discussion in Multiteam Systems
- New international research in Climate of Trust
- New material in Composition (of teams)
- New research and discussion in Personality of Members
- New section: Cultural Differences
- New section: Positive Norms and Group Outcomes
- New section: Negative Norms and Group Outcomes
- New section: Team Identity
- New section: Team Cohesion
- New international research and discussion in Mental Models

- New international research and discussion in Conflict Levels
- New feature! *Career Objectives* (Can I Fudge the Numbers and Not Take the Blame?)
- Revised *Ethical Dilemma* (Dealing with Shirkers)
- New *Case Incident* (Intragroup Trust and Survival)

OB on the Edge: Trust

- Revised section: What Can Leaders Do to Increase Trust?
- New discussion in Building Team Trust
- New major section: The Need to Prevent Lying

Chapter 7: Communication

- Revised *Learning Outcomes*
- New *Opening Vignette* (Slack)
- New research in Downward Communication
- New research and discussion in The Grapevine
- New major section: Modes of Communication
- New section: Oral Communication
- New section: Meetings
- New section: Videoconferencing and Conference Calling
- New section: Telephone
- New section: Written Communication
- New section: Letters
- New section: PowerPoint
- New research in Social Media
- New section: Apps
- New research in Blogs
- New feature! *Career Objectives* (Isn't This Disability Too Much to Accommodate?)
- New *Ethical Dilemma* (BYOD)
- Updated *Case Incident* (Organizational Leveraging of Social Media)

Chapter 8: Power and Politics

- Revised *Learning Outcomes*
- New *Opening Vignette* (Jian Ghomeshi)
- New international research and discussion in Sexual Harassment
- New research in Impression Management
- New feature! *Career Objectives* (Should I Become Political?)
- New *Experiential Exercise* (Comparing Influence Tactics)

Chapter 9: Conflict and Negotiation

- New *Opening Vignette* (GM Canada and Unifor)
- New international research in Personal Variables
- New major section: Negotiating in a Social Context
- New research and discussion in Gender Differences in Negotiation
- New research in Conflict Resolution and Culture
- New feature! *Career Objectives* (How Can I Get a Better Job?)
- Revised *For Managers*
- New *Point/Counterpoint* (Pro Sports Strikes Are Caused by Greedy Owners)
- New *Case Incident* (Disorderly Conduct)

OB on the Edge: Workplace Bullying

- New *Opening Vignette* (The Vancouver School Board)
- New research in Workplace Violence
- New research in the box Do You Have a Bad Boss?
- Updated statistics in What Are the Effects of Incivility and Toxicity in the Workplace?

Chapter 10: Organizational Culture

- Revised *Learning Outcomes*
- New *Opening Vignette* (Hyatt Hotels)
- New discussion in What Is Organizational Culture?
- New section: Culture and Sustainability
- Updated research in Culture and Innovation
- New section: Strengthening Dysfunctions
- New research in Barriers to Acquisitions and Mergers
- New feature! *Career Objectives* (How Do I Learn to Lead?)
- New *Experiential Exercise* (Greeting Newcomers)
- New *Ethical Dilemma* (Culture of Deceit)
- New *Case Incident* (The Place Makes the People)
- New *Case Incident* (Active Cultures)

Chapter 11: Leadership

- New *Opening Vignette* (Kelly Lovell)
- New international research in Trait Theories: Are Leaders Different from Others?
- New research in What Is Charismatic Leadership?
- New research in Transactional and Transformational Leadership

- New research in How Transformational Leadership Works
- New section: Transformational vs. Charismatic Leadership
- New research in Servant Leadership
- New feature! *Career Objectives* (How Can I Get My Boss to Be a Better Leader?)
- New *Experiential Exercise* (What Is Leadership?)
- New *Ethical Dilemma* (Smoking Success)
- New *Case Incident* (Leadership Mettle Forged in Battle)

Chapter 12: Decision Making, Creativity, and Ethics

- New *Opening Vignette* (TD Bank)
- New sections created with new research and discussion: Intelligence and Creativity, Personality and Creativity, Expertise and Creativity, and Ethics and Creativity
- New section: Creative Environment
- New international research and discussion in Four Ethical Decision Criteria
- New feature! *Career Objectives* (How Can I Make My Job Better?)

OB on the Edge: Spirituality in the Workplace

- New *Opening Vignette* (The Good Spirit)
- New research in Spirituality and Mindfulness
- New discussion in Achieving a Spiritual Organization

Chapter 13: Organizational Structure

- Updated *Learning Outcomes*
- New *Opening Vignette* (Precision Nutrition)
- New section: Boundary Spanning
- New section: The Functional Structure
- New section: The Divisional Structure
- New section: The Team Structure
- New section: The Circular Structure
- New section: Institutions
- New feature! *Career Objectives* (What Structure Should I Choose?)
- New *Experiential Exercise* (The Sandwich Shop)
- New *Ethical Dilemma* (Post-Millennium Tensions in the Flexible Organization)

Chapter 14: Organizational Change

- New *Opening Vignette* (Cirque du Soleil)
- New discussion in Forces for Change

- New research in Appreciative Inquiry

- New research in Resistance to Change

- New section: Managing Paradox

- New international research in Sources of Innovation

- New research in What Is a Learning Organization?

- New feature! *Career Objectives* (How Do I Fire Someone?)

- New *Experiential Exercise* (Strategizing Change)

- New *Case Incident* (Sprucing Up Walmart)

Pedagogical Features

The pedagogical features of *Organizational Behaviour: Concepts, Controversies, Applications*, Eighth Canadian edition, are designed to complement and reinforce the textual material. This text offers the most complete assortment of pedagogy available in any OB book on the market.

- The text is developed in a "story-line" format that emphasizes how the topics fit together. Each chapter opens with a list of learning outcomes related to a main example that threads through the chapter. The opening vignette is carried throughout the chapter to help students apply a real-life example to the concepts they are learning. The learning outcome questions appear in the margin of the text, to indicate where they are addressed. In "For Review" at the end of each chapter, students can discover whether they have achieved these learning outcomes.

- **OB Is for Everyone** in the chapter-opener highlights the integrated questions that students will encounter throughout each chapter. Right from the start, these questions encourage students to think about how OB applies to everyday lives.

- A "Big Idea/Lessons Learned" feature appears at the beginning and end of each chapter. These resources are designed to work hand-in-hand. At the beginning of the chapter, a "Big Idea" item appears in the margin which is meant to give readers a big-picture view of the topic at hand. Then, at the end of the chapter a "Lessons Learned" appears in the margin to recap the key takeaways from the chapter.

- NEW! **Career Objectives** is a new feature that offers advice in a question-and-answer format to help students with issues that they could face in the workforce today.

- Exclusive to the Canadian edition, **OB in the Street**, **OB in the Workplace**, **Focus on Ethics**, **Focus on Diversity**, and **Focus on Research** help students see the links between theoretical material and applications.

- **OB in Action** features provide tips for using the concepts of OB in everyday life, such as Managing Virtual Teams, Reducing Team Conflict, Using Social Media Responsibly, and Reducing Biases and Errors in Decision Making.

- To help instructors and students readily spot significant discussions of **Research Findings**, we have included a research icon to indicate where these discussions appear. **Focus on Research** provides additional links to related research. Marking research discussions so clearly helps emphasize the strong research foundation that underlies OB.

- We have continued to integrate a series of relevant and helpful questions throughout the chapters to encourage students to think about how OB applies to their everyday lives and engage students in their reading of the material. These questions first appear as a bullet list in the chapter opener, under the heading **OB Is for Everyone,** and then appear throughout each chapter.

- The **Global Implications** section addresses and highlights how OB principles vary across cultures.

- **Summary** provides a review of the key points of the chapter, while the **Snapshot Summary** provides a study tool that helps students to see the overall connections among concepts presented within each chapter.

- Each chapter concludes with **OB at Work**, a set of resources designed to help students apply the lessons of the chapter. Included in **OB at Work** are the following features:

    - **For Review** poses a series of questions that are linked to the learning outcomes identified in the chapter opener.

    - **For Managers** outlines ways that managers can apply OB in the workplace.

    - **For You** outlines how OB can be used by individuals in their daily lives.

    - **Point/Counterpoint** promotes debate on contentious OB issues. This feature presents more focused arguments.

    - **Breakout Group Exercises**, **Experiential Exercise**, and **Ethical Dilemma** are valuable application exercises for the classroom. The many new exercises included here are ones that we have found particularly stimulating in our own classrooms. Our students say they like these exercises *and* they learn from them.

    - **Case Incidents** (two per chapter) deal with real-world scenarios and require students to exercise their decision-making skills. Each case enables an instructor to quickly generate class discussion on a key theme within the chapter.

    - **From Concepts to Skills** provides a wide range of applications for students. The section begins with a practical set of tips on topics such as reading emotions, setting goals, and solving problems creatively, which demonstrate real-world applications of OB theories. These tips are followed by the features *Practising Skills* and *Reinforcing Skills*. *Practising Skills* presents an additional case or group activity to apply the chapter's learning outcomes. *Reinforcing Skills* asks students to talk about the material they have learned with others, or to apply it to their own personal experiences.

- Exclusive to the Canadian edition, **OB on the Edge** (following each part) takes a close look at some of the hottest topics in the field: work-related stress, trust, behavioural pathologies that can lead to workplace bullying, and spirituality in the workplace. Since this is a stand-alone feature, these topics can be introduced at the instructor's discretion.

- Our reviewers have asked for more cases, and more comprehensive and integrated cases. To address this request, we have included 10 **Additional Cases** that feature a variety of challenges and organizations. All of these cases require students to apply material from a variety of chapters.

Supplements

MyLab Management

MyLab Management is an online study tool for students and an online homework and assessment tool for faculty. MyLab Management lets students assess their understanding through auto-graded tests and assignments, develop a personalized study plan to address areas of weakness, and practise a variety of learning tools to master management principles. New and updated MyLab Management resources include the following:

- *Personal Inventory Assessment (PIA)*. Students learn better when they can connect what they are learning to their personal experience. PIA is a collection of online exercises designed to promote self-reflection and engagement in students, enhancing their ability to connect with concepts taught in principles of management, organizational behaviour, and human resource management classes. Assessments can be assigned by instructors, who can then track students' completions. Student results include a written explanation along with a graphic display that shows how their results compare to the class as a whole. Instructors will also have access to this graphic representation of results to promote classroom discussion.

- *Updated Personalized Study Plan*. As students work through MyLab Management's Study Plan, they can clearly see which topics they have mastered—and, more importantly, which they need to work on. Each question has been carefully written to match the concepts, language, and focus of the text, so students can get an accurate sense of how well they've understood the chapter content.

- *MediaShare*. Consisting of a curated collection of videos and customizable, auto-scored assignments, MediaShare helps students understand why they are learning key concepts and how they will apply those in their careers. Instructors can also assign favorite YouTube clips or original content and employ MediaShare's powerful repository of tools to maximize student accountability and interactive learning, and provide contextualized feedback for students and teams who upload presentations, media, or business plans.

- *NEW Mini-Simulations*. New Mini-Simulations walk students through key business decision-making scenarios to help them understand how management decisions are made. Students are asked to make important decisions relating to core business concepts. At each point in the simulation, students receive feedback to help them understand the implications of their choices in the management environment. These simulations can now be assigned by instructors and graded directly through MyLab Management.

- *Learning Catalytics*. Learning Catalytics is a "bring your own device" student engagement, assessment, and classroom intelligence system. It allows instructors to engage students in class with a variety of question types designed to gauge student understanding.

- *Assignable Mini-Cases and Video Cases*. Instructors have access to a variety of case-based assessment material that can be assigned to students, with multiple-choice quizzes or written-response format in MyLab Management's Writing Space.

- *Lesson Presentations*. Students can study key chapter topics and work through interactive assessments to test their knowledge and mastery of concepts. Each presentation allows students to explore through expertly designed steps of reading, practising, and testing to ensure that students not only experience the content but also truly engage with each topic. Instructors also have the ability to assign quizzes, projects, and follow-up discussion questions relating to the online lessons to further develop the valuable learning experiences from the presentations.

- *Dynamic Study Modules.* These study modules allow students to work through groups of questions and check their understanding of foundational management topics. As students work through questions, the Dynamic Study Modules assess their knowledge and only show questions that still require practice. Dynamic Study Modules can be completed online using a computer, tablet, or mobile device.

- *Pearson eText:* MyLab Management also includes an eText version of *Organizational Behaviour*, including a complete Glossary and Index. This dynamic, online version of the text is integrated throughout MyLab Management to create an enriched, interactive learning experience for students. Users can create notes, highlight text in different colours, create bookmarks, zoom, and click hyperlinked words and phrases to view definitions and go directly to weblinks. The Pearson eText allows quick navigation to key parts of the eText using a table of contents and provides full-text search.

Most of the following materials are available for download from a password-protected section of Pearson Canada's online catalogue (http://www.pearsoncanada.ca/highered). Navigate to your text's catalogue page to view a list of those supplements that are available. Contact your local sales representative for details and access.

- *Instructor's Resource Manual.* Each chapter of the Instructor's Resource Manual includes a chapter outline, learning outcomes, chapter synopsis, study questions, suggested teaching plan, annotated lecture outlines, answers to questions found under OB at Work's *For Review,* a summary and analysis of *Point/Counterpoint* features, comments on end-of-chapter exercises, notes on the *Case Incidents* and *From Concepts to Skills,* and key terms.

- *Computerized Test Bank.* The Test Bank contains over 1800 items, including multiple-choice, true/false, and discussion questions that relate not only to the body of the text but to *From Concepts to Skills, Point/Counterpoint,* and case materials. For each question, we have provided the correct answer, a reference to the relevant section of the text, a difficulty rating, and a classification (recall/applied). Pearson's computerized test banks allow instructors to filter and select questions to create quizzes, tests, or homework. Instructors can revise questions or add their own, and may be able to choose print or online options. These questions are also available in Microsoft Word format.

- *PowerPoint Presentation.* A ready-to-use PowerPoint slideshow designed for classroom presentation. Use it as is, or edit content to fit your individual classroom needs.

- *Image Gallery.* This package provides instructors with images to enhance their teaching.

Learning Solutions Managers. Pearson's Learning Solutions Managers work with faculty and campus course designers to ensure that Pearson technology products, assessment tools, and online course materials are tailored to meet your specific needs. This highly qualified team is dedicated to helping schools take full advantage of a wide range of educational resources, by assisting in the integration of a variety of instructional materials and media formats. Your local Pearson Education sales representative can provide you with more details on this service program.

Acknowledgments

A number of people worked hard to give this eighth Canadian edition of *Organizational Behaviour* a new look.

I received incredible support for this project from a variety of people at Pearson Canada. The three people who worked hardest to keep this project on track were Jennifer Murray, Content Developer, Claudia Forgas, Production Editor, and Jessica Mifsud, Project Manager. All three were extremely supportive and helpful. Jennifer supplied a number of great ideas for examples and vignettes, never complained when I was late with chapters, and she provided much needed cheerfulness at some of the most difficult parts of this project. I can't thank her enough for her dedication to the task.

Claudia Forgas was the Production Editor for the project. Claudia has worked on a number of my projects and still continues to amaze for how well she makes sure everything is in place and written clearly. Claudia provided a wealth of support, great ideas, and goodwill throughout the production process. Turning the manuscript into the text you hold in your hands could not have happened without her inspired leadership. She was extremely diligent about checking for consistency throughout the text and performed a number of helpful fact-checking activities. Her keen eyes helped to make these pages as clean as they are. I am grateful for the opportunity to work with her again.

There are a variety of other people at Pearson who also had a hand in making sure that the manuscript would be transformed into this book and then delivered to you. To all of them I extend my thanks. I know the Pearson sales team will do everything possible to make this book successful.

I also want to acknowledge my divisional secretary, Nancy Tang, who helps keep me on track in a variety of ways. I could not ask for a better, more dedicated, or more cheerful assistant. She really helps keep things together.

In our continuing effort to improve the text, we have conducted many reviews to elicit feedback over the years and editions. Many thanks to several students from the Northern Alberta Institute of Technology (NAIT) who provided us with suggestions for improving the text. The students are Barb Kosak, Prudence Musinguzi, Andres Sarrate, and Robert Tucci. Student input helps keep the material fresh and alive.

Finally, I want to acknowledge the many reviewers of this text for their detailed, helpful comments. I appreciate the time and care that they put into their reviewing. The reviewers include Nancy Breen (Nova Scotia Community College), Sabrina Deutsch Salamon (York University), Harold Ekstein (George Brown College), Leah Hamilton (Mount Royal University), Shari Ann Herrmann (Kwantlen Polytechnic University), Puneet Luthra (Seneca College), Jody Merritt (University of Windsor), John Predyk (Vancouver Island University), Wayne Rawcliffe (University of British Columbia), Sandra Steen (University of Regina), and Sujay Vardhmane (George Brown College).

ABOUT THE AUTHORS

Nancy Langton   received her Ph.D. from Stanford University. Since completing her graduate studies, Dr. Langton has taught at the University of Oklahoma and the University of British Columbia. Currently a member of the Organizational Behaviour and Human Resources division in the Sauder School of Business, UBC, she teaches at the undergraduate, MBA, and Ph.D. levels and conducts executive programs on attracting and retaining employees, time management, family business issues, as well as women and management issues. Dr. Langton has received several major three-year research grants from the Social Sciences and Humanities Research Council of Canada, and her research interests have focused on human resource issues in the workplace, including pay equity, gender equity, and leadership and communication styles. Her articles on these and other topics have appeared in such journals as *Administrative Science Quarterly*, *American Sociological Review*, *Sociological Quarterly*, *Journal of Management Education*, and *Gender, Work and Organizations*. She has won Best Paper commendations from both the Academy of Management and the Administrative Sciences Association of Canada.

Dr. Langton routinely wins high marks from her students for teaching. She has been nominated many times for the Commerce Undergraduate Society Awards, and has won several honourable mention plaques. She has also won the Sauder School of Business's most prestigious award for teaching innovation, The Talking Stick. The award was given for Dr. Langton's redesign of the undergraduate organizational behaviour course as well as the many activities that were a spin-off of these efforts. She was also part of the UBC MBA Core design team that won the Alan Blizzard award, a national award that recognizes innovation in teaching. More recently, she was acknowledged by the Sauder School of Business for her development of the Sauder Africa Initiative, which took her to Kenya with UBC students to help young people in the slums of Nairobi write business plans.

In Dr. Langton's "other life," she engages in the artistry of quiltmaking, and one day hopes to win first prize at *Visions*, the juried show for quilts as works of art. More recently, she has been working at mastering the art of photography, creating abstract art using segments of real objects. When she is not designing quilts or taking photographs, she is either reading novels recommended by her book club colleagues or studying cookbooks for new ideas. All of her friends would say that she makes the best pizza from scratch in all of Vancouver, and one has even offered to supply venture capital to open a pizza parlour.

Stephen P. Robbins

Education

Ph.D., University of Arizona

Professional Experience

Academic Positions: Professor, San Diego State University, Southern Illinois University at Edwardsville, University of Baltimore, Concordia University in Montreal, and University of Nebraska at Omaha.

   Research: Research interests have focused on conflict, power, and politics in organizations; behavioural decision making; and the development of effective interpersonal skills.

   Books Published: World's best-selling author of textbooks in both management and organizational behaviour. His books have sold more than 5 million copies and have been translated into 20 languages; editions have been adapted for Canada, Australia, South Africa, and India, such as these:

- *Essentials of Organizational Behavior*, 14th ed. (Pearson, 2017)
- *Management*, 14th ed. with Mary Coulter (Pearson, 2017)
- *Fundamentals of Human Resource Management*, 11th ed., with David DeCenzo (Wiley, 2012)
- *Prentice Hall's Self-Assessment Library 3.4* (Prentice Hall, 2010)
- *Fundamentals of Management*, 9th ed., with David DeCenzo and Mary Coulter (Pearson, 2014)
- *Supervision Today!* 8th ed., with David DeCenzo and Robert Wolter (Pearson, 2014)
- *Training in Interpersonal Skills: TIPS for Managing People at Work*, 6th ed., with Phillip Hunsaker (Prentice Hall, 2012)
- *Managing Today!* 2nd ed. (Prentice Hall, 2000)
- *Organization Theory*, 3rd ed. (Prentice Hall, 1990)
- *The Truth About Managing People*, 4th ed. (Pearson FT Press, 2014)
- *Decide and Conquer: Make Winning Decisions and Take Control of Your Life* (Financial Times/Prentice Hall, 2004)

Other Interests

In his "other life," Dr. Robbins actively participates in masters' track competition. After turning 50 in 1993, he won 18 national championships and 12 world titles. He is the current world record holder at 100 metres (12.37 seconds) and 200 metres (25.20 seconds) for men 65 and over.

Timothy A. Judge

Education

Ph.D., University of Illinois at Urbana-Champaign

Professional Experience

Academic Positions: Franklin D. Schurz Chair, Department of Management, Mendoza College of Business, University of Notre Dame; Visiting Distinguished Adjunct Professor of King Abdulaziz University, Saudi Arabia; Visiting Professor, Division of Psychology & Language Sciences, University College London; Matherly-McKethan Eminent Scholar in Management, Warrington College of Business Administration, University of Florida; Stanley M. Howe Professor in Leadership, Henry B. Tippie College of Business, University of Iowa; Associate Professor (with tenure), Department of Human Resource Studies, School of Industrial and Labor Relations, Cornell University; Lecturer, Charles University, Czech Republic, and Comenius University, Slovakia; Instructor, Industrial/Organizational Psychology, Department of Psychology, University of Illinois at Urbana-Champaign.

Research: Dr. Judge's primary research interests are in (1) personality, moods, and emotions; (2) job attitudes; (3) leadership and influence behaviours; and (4) careers (person–organization fit, career success). Dr. Judge has published more than 145 articles on these and other major topics in journals such as *Journal of Organizational Behavior*, *Personnel Psychology*, *Academy of Management Journal*, *Journal of Applied Psychology*, *European Journal of Personality*, and *European Journal of Work and Organizational Psychology*.

Fellowship: Dr. Judge is a fellow of the American Psychological Association, the Academy of Management, the Society for Industrial and Organizational Psychology, and the American Psychological Society.

Awards: In 1995, Dr. Judge received the Ernest J. McCormick Award for Distinguished Early Career Contributions from the Society for Industrial and Organizational Psychology. In 2001, he received the Larry L. Cummings Award for mid-career contributions from the Organizational Behavior Division of the Academy of Management. In 2007, he received the Professional Practice Award from the Institute of Industrial and Labor Relations, University of Illinois. In 2008, he received the University of Florida Doctoral Mentoring Award. And in 2012, he received the Editorial Board of the *European Journal of Work and Organizational Psychology* (EJWOP) best paper of the year award.

Other Books Published: H. G. Heneman III, T. A. Judge, and J. D. Kammeyer-Mueller, *Staffing Organizations*, 8th ed. (Mishawaka, IN: McGraw-Hill Education, 2014).

Other Interests

Although he cannot keep up (literally!) with Dr. Robbins' accomplishments on the track, Dr. Judge enjoys golf, cooking and baking, literature (he's a particular fan of Thomas Hardy and is a member of the Thomas Hardy Society), and keeping up with his three children.

1 What Is Organizational Behaviour?

How can people skills help you run a successful business?

LEARNING OUTCOMES

After studying this chapter, you should be able to:

1. Demonstrate the importance of interpersonal skills in the workplace.
2. Define *organizational behaviour* (OB).
3. Understand the value of systematic study to OB.
4. Identify the major behavioural science disciplines that contribute to OB.
5. Demonstrate why few absolutes apply to OB.
6. Identify workplace challenges that provide opportunities to apply OB concepts.
7. Describe the three levels of analysis in this book's OB model.

REUTERS/Ben Nelms

In 2011, American retail giant Target bought the leases of the entire Zellers chain, with the goal to open 124 locations in Canada during 2013.[1] There was much excitement among Canadian consumers who had been to Target in the States, and who wished something like it existed in Canada. Target was very successful in the United States, and apparently thought it could bring that success easily to Canada.

The first stores were set to open in March 2013. Almost from the beginning things did not go well. The shelves were often empty, and the items advertised for sale in weekly flyers were nowhere to be found. Consumers became frustrated almost from the start. In the rush to get stores opened, new staff did not receive enough training, the software for monitoring stock supplies was not working properly, and the company had not adequately assessed how quickly the company would be able to adjust to having a Canadian presence.

The challenges that organizations such as Target face illustrate several concepts you will learn about as you study the field of organizational behaviour. Let's take a look, then, at what organizational behaviour is.

 **OB** IS FOR **EVERYONE**

- Does job satisfaction really make a difference?
- Why do some people do well in organizational settings while others have difficulty?
- Do you know what a "typical" organization looks like?
- What people-related challenges have you noticed in the workplace?
- Why should you care about understanding other people?
- Are you ready to take on more responsibility at work?

THE BIG IDEA

OB helps managers and employees make sense of the workplace and also applies to work in groups of all kinds.

1 Demonstrate the importance of interpersonal skills in the workplace.

The Importance of Interpersonal Skills

Until the late 1980s, business school curricula emphasized the technical aspects of management, focusing on economics, accounting, finance, and quantitative techniques. Course work in human behaviour and people skills received less attention. Since then, however, business schools have realized the significant role interpersonal skills play in determining a manager's effectiveness. In fact, a survey of over 2100 CFOs across 20 industries indicated that a lack of interpersonal skills is the top reason why some employees fail to advance.[2]

Incorporating OB principles into the workplace can yield many important organizational outcomes. For one, companies known as good places to work in 2017—such as Toronto-based Royal Bank of Canada (RBC); St. John, New Brunswick-based Irving Oil; Bedford, Nova Scotia-based Clearwater Seafoods; Winnipeg-based Aboriginal Peoples Television Network; Regina-based SaskTel; Calgary-based Agrium, and Vancouver-based West Fraser Timber[3]—have been found to generate superior financial performance.[4] Second, developing managers' interpersonal skills helps organizations attract and keep high-performing employees, which is important since outstanding employees are always in short supply and are costly to replace. Third, there are strong associations between the quality of workplace relationships and employee job satisfaction, stress, and turnover. One very large survey of hundreds of workplaces and more than 200 000 respondents showed that social relationships among co-workers and supervisors were strongly related to overall job satisfaction. Positive social relationships were also associated with lower stress at work and lower intentions to quit.[5] Further research indicates that employees who relate to their managers with supportive dialogue and proactivity find that their ideas are endorsed more often, which improves workplace satisfaction.[6] Fourth, increasing the OB element in organizations can foster social responsibility awareness. Accordingly, universities have begun to incorporate social entrepreneurship education into their curriculum in order to train future leaders to address social issues within their organizations.[7] This is especially important because there is a growing need for understanding the means and outcomes of corporate social responsibility, known as CSR.[8]

Edward Regan/The Globe and Mail/The Canadian Press

Indigo CEO Heather Reisman has the interpersonal skills required to succeed in management. Communication and leadership skills distinguish managers such as Reisman, who rise to the top of their profession.

We understand that in today's competitive and demanding workplace, managers can't succeed on their technical skills alone. Succeeding in the workplace also takes good people skills. This book has been written to help managers and employees develop those people skills. To learn more about the kinds of people skills needed in the workplace, see the *Experiential Exercise* on page 29 and *From Concepts to Skills—Developing Interpersonal Skills* on pages 32–35.

> Does job satisfaction really make a difference?

Defining Organizational Behaviour

2 Define *organizational behaviour* (OB).

> As Target tried to deal with the failure of running its new stores in Canada, problems within the organization became increasingly obvious.[9] While the Target Canada president was optimistic throughout, he and his team suffered from groupthink. The CEO, based in Minneapolis, Minnesota, did not want to pay rent on empty stores longer than necessary. This put pressure on senior management to keep going, rather than slow down and try to solve very real problems. "Nobody wanted to be the one person who stopped the Canadian venture," says a former employee. "It wound up just being a constant elephant in the room."
>
> Better knowledge of organizational behaviour might have helped management adjust to some of the problems Target was facing in Canada. Let's look at what organizational behaviour is.

Organizational behaviour (often abbreviated as OB) is a field of study that looks at the impact that individuals, groups, and structure have on behaviour within organizations for the purpose of applying such knowledge toward improving an organization's effectiveness. Because the organizations studied are often business organizations, OB is often applied to topics such as job satisfaction, absenteeism, employment turnover, productivity, human performance, and management. OB also examines the following core topics, although debate exists about their relative importance:[10]

- Motivation
- Leader behaviour and power
- Interpersonal communication
- Group structure and processes
- Attitude development and perception
- Change processes
- Conflict and negotiation
- Work design

Much of OB is relevant beyond the workplace. The study of OB can cast light on the interactions among family members, students working as a team on a class project, the voluntary group that comes together to do something about reviving the downtown area, the parents who sit on the board of their children's daycare centre, or even the members of a lunchtime pickup basketball team.

> Why do some people do well in organizational settings while others have difficulty?

organizational behaviour A field of study that investigates the impact of individuals, groups, and structure on behaviour within organizations; its purpose is to apply such knowledge toward improving an organization's effectiveness.

organization A consciously coordinated social unit, composed of a group of people, that functions on a relatively continuous basis to achieve a common goal or set of goals.

What Do We Mean by *Organization*?

An **organization** is a consciously coordinated social unit, composed of a group of people, that functions on a relatively continuous basis to achieve a common goal or set of goals. Manufacturing and service firms are organizations, and so are schools, hospitals, churches, military units, retail stores, police departments, volunteer organizations, start-ups, and local, provincial, and federal government agencies. Thus, when we use the term *organization* in this book, we are referring not only to large manufacturing firms but also to small mom-and-pop stores, as well as to the variety of other forms of organization that exist. Small businesses with less than 100 people made up 98 percent of the employers in Canada in 2015, and they employed 70 percent of the private sector workforce. Only 0.3 percent of businesses have more than 500 employees, and they employ just under 10 percent of the workforce. Most of these large organizations are in the public sector.[11]

The examples in this book present various organizations so that you can gain a better understanding of the many types of organizations that exist. The college or university you attend is every bit as much a "real" organization as is Lululemon Athletica, Air Canada, or the Vancouver Canucks. A small for-profit organization that hires unskilled workers to renovate and build in the inner city of Winnipeg is as much a real organization as is London, Ontario-based EllisDon, one of North America's largest construction companies. Therefore, the theories we cover should be considered in light of the variety of organizations you may encounter. We try to point out instances where the theory may be less applicable (or especially applicable) to a particular type of organization. For the most part, however, you should expect that the discussions in this book apply across the broad spectrum of organizations. Throughout, we highlight applications to a variety of organizations in our feature *OB in the Workplace*.

> Do you know what a "typical" organization looks like?

OB Is for Everyone

It might seem natural to think that the study of OB is for leaders and managers of organizations. However, many organizations also have informal leadership opportunities. In organizations in which employees are asked to share in a greater number of decision-making processes rather than simply follow orders, the roles of managers and employees are becoming blurred.[12] For instance, employees in some retail operations are asked to make decisions about when to accept returned items rather than defer the decision to the manager.

OB is not just for managers and employees. Entrepreneurs and self-employed individuals may not act as managers, but they certainly interact with other individuals and organizations as part of their work. OB applies equally well to all situations in which you interact with others: on the basketball court, at the grocery store, in school, or in church. In fact, OB is relevant anywhere that people come together and share experiences, work on goals, or meet to solve problems. To help you understand these broader connections, you will find a feature called *OB in the Street* throughout the book.

3 Understand the value of systematic study to OB.

Complementing Intuition with Systematic Study

Whether you have explicitly thought about it before or not, you have been "reading" people almost all your life by watching their actions and interpreting what you see, or by trying to predict what people might do under different conditions. The casual approach to reading others can often lead to erroneous predictions, but using a systematic approach can improve your accuracy.

Underlying the systematic approach in this text is the belief that behaviour is not random. Rather, we can identify fundamental consistencies underlying the behaviour of all individuals and modify them to reflect individual differences.

These fundamental consistencies are very important. Why? Because they allow predictability. Behaviour is generally predictable, and the *systematic study* of behaviour is a means to making reasonably accurate predictions. When we use the term **systematic study**, we mean looking at relationships, attempting to attribute causes and effects, and basing our conclusions on scientific evidence—that is, on data gathered under controlled conditions and measured and interpreted in a rigorous manner.

Evidence-based management (EBM) complements systematic study by basing managerial decisions on the best available scientific evidence. For example, we want doctors to make decisions about patient care based on the latest available evidence, and EBM argues that managers should do the same, thinking more scientifically about management problems. A manager might pose a question, search for the best available evidence, and apply the relevant information to the question or case at hand. You might wonder what manager would not base decisions on evidence, but the vast majority of management decisions are made "on the fly," with little to no systematic study of available evidence.[13]

Systematic study and EBM add to **intuition**, or those "gut feelings" about what makes others (and ourselves) "tick." Of course, the things you have come to believe in an unsystematic way are not necessarily incorrect. Jack Welch (former CEO of General Electric) noted, "The trick, of course, is to know when to go with your gut." But if we make *all* decisions with intuition or gut instinct, we are likely working with incomplete information—like making an investment decision with only half the data about the potential for risk and reward.

Relying on intuition is made worse because we tend to overestimate the accuracy of what we think we know. Surveys of human resource managers have also shown that many managers hold "common-sense" opinions regarding effective management that have been flatly refuted by empirical evidence.

We find a similar problem in chasing the business and popular media for management wisdom. The business press tends to be dominated by fads. As a writer for *The New Yorker* put it, "Every few years, new companies succeed, and they are scrutinized for the underlying truths they might reveal. But often there is no underlying truth; the companies just happened to be in the right place at the right time."[14] Although we try to avoid it, we might also fall into this trap. It's not that the business press stories are all wrong; it's that without a systematic approach, it's hard to separate the wheat from the chaff.

Big Data

It's difficult to believe now, but not long ago companies treated online shopping as a virtual point-of-sale experience: Shoppers browsed websites anonymously, and sellers tracked sales data only on what customers bought. "Big data"—the extensive use of statistical compilation and analysis—didn't become possible until computers were sophisticated enough to both store and manipulate large amounts of information. Gradually, as a result, online retailers began to track and act upon information about customer preferences that was uniquely available through the Internet shopping experience, information that was far superior to data gathered in simple in-store transactions. This enabled them to create more targeted marketing strategies than ever before. See the *Case Incident—Big Data for Dummies* on pages 31–32 to learn more about how organizations use big data.

The bookselling industry is a case in point: Before online selling, brick-and-mortar bookstores could collect data about book sales only to create projections about consumer interests and trends. With the advent of Amazon, suddenly a vast array of information about consumer preferences became available for tracking: what customers bought, what they looked at, how they navigated the site, and what

systematic study Looking at relationships, attempting to attribute causes and effects, and drawing conclusions based on scientific evidence.

evidence-based management (EBM) The basing of managerial decisions on the best available scientific evidence.

intuition An instinctive feeling not necessarily supported by research.

they were influenced by (such as promotions, reviews, and page presentation). The challenge for Amazon then was to identify which statistics were *persistent,* giving relatively constant outcomes over time, and *predictive,* showing steady causality between certain inputs and outcomes. The company used these statistics to develop algorithms to forecast which books customers would like to read next. Amazon then could base its wholesale purchase decisions on the feedback customers provided, both through these passive collection methods and through solicited recommendations for upcoming titles.

Big data has been used by technology companies like Google and Facebook, who rely on advertising dollars for revenue and thus need to predict user behaviour. Companies like Netflix and Uber similarly use big data to predict where and when customers may want to use their virtual services, although their revenue comes from subscribers to their services. Insurance firms predict behaviour to assess risks, such as the chance of traffic accidents, in order to set customer premiums.

Online retailers like eBay and Amazon, which market tangible products through online platforms, also rely on big data to predict what will sell. For organizations like Nielsen Holdings, which tracks television and radio watching, the results of data analyses *are* the product they sell. Still other organizations collect big data but do not directly use it. These are often organizations whose primary business is not online. Think of the loyalty cards you carry around (Starbucks, Tim Hortons, Indigo-Chapters). These companies sell their data to vendors who stock shelves, and they use the data to identify trends and new market possibilities.[15] Sometimes even technology companies simply sell their data; Twitter sells 500 million tweets a day to four data assimilation companies.[16]

It is good news for the future of business that researchers, the media, and company leaders have identified the potential of data-driven management and decision making. A manager who uses data to define objectives, develop theories of causality, and test those theories can determine which employee activities are relevant to the objectives.[17] Big data has implications for correcting management assumptions and increasing positive performance outcomes. Increasingly, it is applied toward making effective decisions (Chapter 12) and managing human resources. It is quite possible that the best use of big data in managing people will come from organizational behaviour and psychology research, where it might even help employees with mental illnesses monitor and change their behaviour.[18]

We must keep in mind that big data will always be limited in predicting behaviour, curtailing risk, and preventing catastrophes. In contrast to the replicable results we can obtain in the sciences through big data analytics, human behaviour is often capricious and predicated on innumerable variables. Otherwise, our decision making would have been taken over by artificial intelligence by now! But that will never be a worthy goal.[19] Management is more than the sum of data.

We are not advising that you throw your intuition, or all the business press, out the window. Nor are we arguing that research is always right. Researchers make mistakes, too. What we are advising is to use evidence as much as possible to inform your intuition and experience. That is the promise of OB.

Throughout this book, the *Focus on Research* feature will highlight some of the careful studies that form the building blocks of OB.

If understanding behaviour were simply common sense, we would not observe many of the problems that occur in the workplace, because managers and employees would know how to behave. Unfortunately, as you will see from examples throughout this book, many employees and managers exhibit less-than-desirable behaviour in the workplace. With a stronger grounding in OB, you might be able to avoid some of these mistakes.

OB is even being adopted by other disciplines, as *OB in the Street* shows.

OB IN THE STREET
Is OB Just for the Workplace?

Can finance learn anything from OB? It may surprise you to learn that, increasingly, other business disciplines are employing OB concepts.[20] Marketing has the closest overlap with OB. Trying to predict consumer behaviour is not that different from trying to predict employee behaviour. Both require an understanding of the dynamics and underlying causes of human behaviour, and there is a lot of correspondence between the disciplines.

What is perhaps more surprising is the degree to which the so-called hard disciplines are using soft OB concepts. Behavioural finance, behavioural accounting, and behavioural economics (also called *economic psychology*) all have grown in importance and interest in the past several years.

On reflection, the use of OB by these disciplines should not be so surprising. Your common sense will tell you that humans are not perfectly rational creatures, and in many cases, our actions don't conform to a rational model of behaviour. Although some elements of irrationality are incorporated into finance, accounting, and economics, researchers find it increasingly useful to draw from OB concepts.

For example, investors have a tendency to place more weight on private information (information that only they, or a limited group of people, know) than on public information, even when there is reason to believe that the public information is more accurate. To understand this phenomenon, finance researchers use OB concepts. In addition, behavioural accounting research might study how feedback influences auditors' behaviour, or the functional and dysfunctional implications of earnings warnings on investor behaviour.

The point is that while you take separate courses in various business disciplines, the lines between them are increasingly being blurred as researchers draw from common disciplines to explain behaviour. We think that this is a good thing because it more accurately matches the way managers actually work, think, and behave. . . . .

Disciplines That Contribute to the OB Field

4 Identify the major behavioural science disciplines that contribute to OB.

One of the major problems Target Canada had was making sure that items were on the shelves, available for customers to purchase.[21] Products often went out of stock because of issues with the company's new inventory management software. However, the problem turned out to be more than just a software issue.

Business analysts responsible for making sure that stock was available were judged on the percentage of their products that were in stock at any given time. If their percentage of in-stock number was low, they would receive a call from a vice-president who would demand an explanation. Some analysts discovered that they could turn off a software feature that notified distribution centres to ship more product. By disabling this feature, the vice-presidents would not know stock was low, which meant the analysts would not be criticized. However, once this feature was fully activated, and analysts could no longer turn it off on their own, the company could finally see the low in-stock percentages.

The analysts may have been acting rationally by covering up the shortages so that they would not get into trouble with their managers, but this was short-term thinking because it was ultimately harmful to the stores. What might Target Canada have learned from OB to do a better job of managing communications and incentives for the analysts?

The Building Blocks of OB

OB is an applied behavioural science that builds upon contributions from a number of behavioural disciplines: mainly psychology, social psychology, sociology, and anthropology. Psychology's contributions have been primarily at the individual, or micro, level of analysis, while the other three disciplines have contributed to our understanding of macro concepts, such as group processes and organization. Exhibit 1-1 presents an overview of the major contributions of behavioural science to the study of OB.

Psychology

Psychology seeks to measure, explain, and sometimes change the behaviour of humans and other animals. Contributors to the knowledge of OB are learning theorists, personality theorists, counselling psychologists, and, most important, industrial and organizational psychologists.

Early industrial and organizational psychologists studied the problems of fatigue, boredom, and other working conditions that could impede efficient work performance. More recently, their contributions have been expanded to include learning, perception, personality, emotions, training, leadership effectiveness, needs and motivational forces, job satisfaction, individual decision making, performance appraisal, attitude measurement, employee selection techniques, work design, and work stress.

Social Psychology

Social psychology, generally considered a branch of psychology, blends concepts from both psychology and sociology to focus on people's influence on one another. One

EXHIBIT 1-1 Toward an OB Discipline

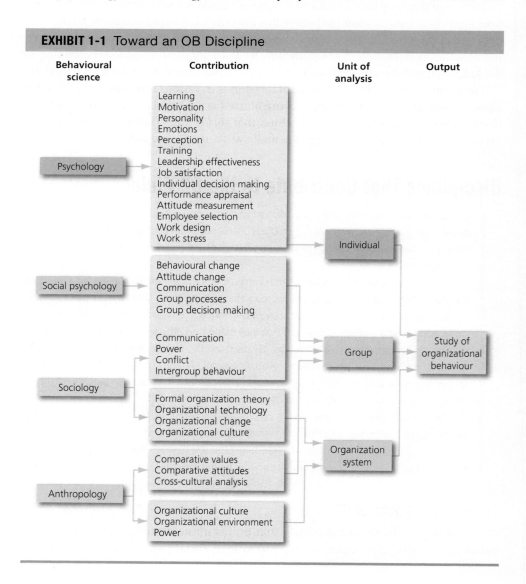

major study area is *change*—how to implement it and how to reduce barriers to its acceptance. Social psychologists also contribute to measuring, understanding, and changing attitudes; identifying communication patterns; and building trust. Finally, they have made important contributions to our study of communication, intergroup behaviour, power, and conflict.

Sociology

While psychology focuses on the individual, sociology studies people in relation to their social environment or culture. Sociologists have contributed to OB through their study of group behaviour in organizations, particularly formal and complex organizations. Perhaps most important, sociologists have studied organizational culture and change, formal organizational theory and structure, organizational technology, communication, power, and conflict.

Anthropology

Anthropology is the study of societies to learn about human beings and their activities. Anthropologists' work on cultures and environments has helped us understand differences in fundamental values, attitudes, and behaviour among people in different countries and within different organizations. Much of our current understanding of organizational culture, organizational climate, and differences among national cultures is the result of the work of anthropologists or those using their methodologies.

The Rigour of OB

Whether you want to respond to the challenges of the Canadian workplace, manage well, or guarantee satisfying and rewarding employment for yourself, it pays to understand organizational behaviour. OB provides a systematic approach to the study of behaviour in organizations. Underlying this systematic approach is the belief that behaviour is not random. It stems from and is directed toward some end that the individual believes, rightly or wrongly, is in his or her best interest.

OB Has Few Absolutes

Laws in the physical sciences—chemistry, astronomy, physics—are consistent and apply in a wide range of situations. They allow scientists to generalize about the pull of gravity or to confidently send astronauts into space to repair satellites. Human beings are complex, and few, if any, simple and universal principles explain organizational behaviour. Because we are not all alike, our ability to make simple, accurate, and sweeping generalizations about ourselves is limited. Two people often act very differently in the same situation, and the same person's behaviour changes in different situations. For example, not everyone is motivated by money, and people may behave differently at a religious service than they do at a party.

5 Demonstrate why few absolutes apply to OB.

OB Takes a Contingency Approach

Just because people can behave differently at different times does not mean, of course, that we cannot offer reasonably accurate explanations of human behaviour or make valid predictions. It does mean, however, that OB must consider behaviour within the context in which it occurs—a strategy known as a **contingency approach**. In other words, OB's answers depend upon the situation. For example, OB scholars would avoid stating that everyone likes complex and challenging work (the general concept). Why? Because not everyone wants a challenging job. Some people prefer routine over varied work, or simple over complex tasks. A job that is appealing to one person may not appeal to another, so the appeal of the job is contingent on the person who holds it. Often, we'll find both general effects (money does have some ability to motivate most of us) and contingencies

contingency approach An approach taken by OB that considers behaviour within the context in which it occurs.

(some of us are more motivated by money than others, and some situations are more about money than others). We will best understand OB when we realize how both (general effects, and the contingencies that affect them) often guide behaviour.

Consistent with the contingency approach, *Point/Counterpoint* debates are provided in each chapter. These debates are included to highlight the fact that within OB there are disagreements. Through the *Point/Counterpoint* format, you will gain the opportunity to explore different points of view, discover how diverse perspectives complement and oppose each other, and gain insight into some of the debates currently taking place within the OB field. *Point/Counterpoint* on page 28 debates the quality of evidence offered by popular books and academic research studies on organizational behaviour.

<table>
<tr><td>**6**</td><td>Identify workplace challenges that provide opportunities to apply OB concepts.</td></tr>
</table>

Challenges and Opportunities in the Canadian Workplace

In the United States, Target prides itself on its corporate culture of being a "fast, fun, and friendly" place to work.[22] Target hires people it thinks will fit well into the environment, and the company worries less about new employees having experience. "Target's motto was they could train you for the job, but they couldn't train culture," says a former employee. New employees in the United States go through an extensive development program, and are assigned a mentor.

When Target Canada had to hire quickly to staff more than 120 stores within one year, former employees say that the company did succeed in hiring people with the right personalities. However, there was no time to train them. Most received a few weeks of training at best. According to one employee, "Everyone was stretched thin. We didn't have the manpower to get everything done in the time frame that was laid out."

Target was not ready to move to Canada, and the results were costly. Within two years of opening its first store, the company announced bankruptcy for the Canadian operation, and shuttered all of its stores.

Understanding OB has never been more important for managers. Take a quick look at the dramatic changes in organizations. The typical employee is getting older; the workforce is becoming increasingly diverse; and global competition requires employees to become more flexible and cope with rapid change.

As a result of these changes and others, employment options have emerged. Exhibit 1-2 details some of the options individuals may find offered to them by organizations or for which they would like to negotiate. Under each heading in the exhibit, you will find a grouping of options from which to choose—or combine. For instance, at one point in your career you may find yourself employed full time in an office in a localized, non-union setting with a salary and bonus compensation package, while at another point you may wish to negotiate for a flextime, virtual position and choose to work from overseas for a combination of salary and extra paid time off.

In short, today's challenges bring opportunities for managers to use OB concepts. In this section, we review some of the most critical issues confronting managers for which OB offers solutions—or at least meaningful insights toward solutions.

> What people-related challenges have you noticed in the workplace?

Economic Pressures

When the US economy plunged into a deep and prolonged recession in 2008, virtually all other large economies around the world followed suit. Canada fared much better

EXHIBIT 1-2 Employment Options

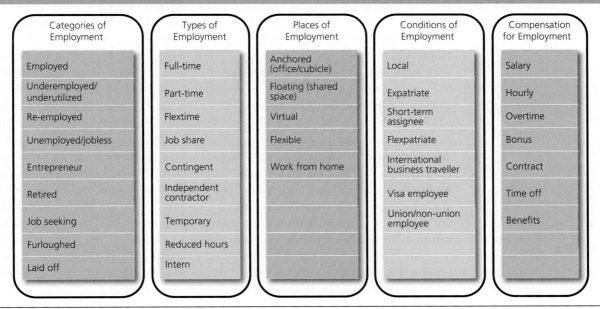

Categories of Employment	Types of Employment	Places of Employment	Conditions of Employment	Compensation for Employment
Employed	Full-time	Anchored (office/cubicle)	Local	Salary
Underemployed/underutilized	Part-time	Floating (shared space)	Expatriate	Hourly
Re-employed	Flextime	Virtual	Short-term assignee	Overtime
Unemployed/jobless	Job share	Flexible	Flexpatriate	Bonus
Entrepreneur	Contingent	Work from home	International business traveller	Contract
Retired	Independent contractor		Visa employee	Time off
Job seeking	Temporary		Union/non-union employee	Benefits
Furloughed	Reduced hours			
Laid off	Intern			

Sources: J. R. Anderson, "Action Items: 42 Trends Affecting Benefits, Compensation, Training, Staffing and Technology," *HR Magazine*, January 2013, p. 33; M. Dewhurst, B. Hancock, and D. Ellsworth, "Redesigning Knowledge Work," *Harvard Business Review*, January–February 2013, pp. 58–64; E. Frauenheim, "Creating a New Contingent Culture," *Workforce Management*, August 2012, pp. 34–39; N. Koeppen, "State Job Aid Takes Pressure off Germany," *Wall Street Journal*, February 1, 2013, p. A8; and M. A. Shaffer, M. L. Kraimer, Y.-P. Chen, and M. C. Bolino, "Choices, Challenges, and Career Consequences of Global Work Experiences: A Review and Future Agenda," *Journal of Management*, July 2012, pp. 1282–1327.

than the United States, but still faced widespread layoffs and job losses, and those who survived the axe were often asked to accept pay cuts. When times are bad, as they were during the recession, managers are on the front lines with employees who are asked to make do with less, and who worry about their futures, and who sometimes must be fired. The difference between good and bad management can be the difference between profit and loss or, ultimately, between business survival and failure.

Managing employees well when times are tough is just as hard as when times are good—if not harder. In good times, understanding how to reward, satisfy, and retain employees is at a premium. In bad times, issues such as stress, decision making, and coping come to the forefront.

Continuing Globalization

Organizations are no longer constrained by national borders. Samsung, the largest South Korean business conglomerate, sells most of its products to organizations in other countries. Burger King is owned by a Brazilian firm. McDonald's sells hamburgers in more than 118 countries on six continents. All major automobile makers now manufacture cars outside their borders; Honda builds cars in Alliston, Ontario, Ford in Brazil, Volkswagen in Mexico, and both Mercedes and BMW in South Africa. Apple has also moved almost all of its manufacturing overseas, as discussed in *Case Incident—Apple Goes Global* on page 31.

In recent years, businesses in Canada have faced tough competition from those in the United States, Europe, Japan, and China, as well as from other businesses within our borders. To survive, they have had to reduce costs, increase productivity, and improve quality. A number of Canadian companies have found it necessary to merge in order to survive. For instance, Rona, the Boucherville, Quebec-based home improvement store, bought out Lansing, Revy, and Revelstoke in recent years to defend its turf against the

Atlanta, Georgia-based Home Depot. Then as a counteroffensive, Lowe's bought out Rona in 2016, hoping to take market share from Home Depot.[23]

Some employers have outsourced jobs to other countries where labour costs are lower to remain profitable. For instance, Toronto-based Dell Canada's technical service lines are handled by technicians working in India. Toronto-based Wall & Associates, a full-service chartered accounting and management consulting firm, outsources document management to Uganda. Employees in Uganda are willing to work for $1 an hour to sort and record receipts. While these wages might seem low, on average, Ugandans make only $1 a day.

Twenty or 30 years ago, national borders protected most firms from foreign competitive pressures. This is no longer the case. Trading blocs such as the North American Free Trade Agreement (NAFTA) and the European Union (EU) have significantly reduced tariffs and barriers to trade, and North America and Europe no longer have a monopoly on highly skilled labour. The Internet has also enabled companies to become more globally connected by opening up international sales and by increasing the opportunities to carry on business across borders. Even small firms can bid on projects in different countries and compete with larger firms via the Internet.

Even in your own country, you will find yourself working with bosses, peers, and other employees born and raised in different cultures. As multinational corporations develop operations worldwide, as companies develop joint ventures with foreign partners, and as employees increasingly pursue job opportunities across national borders, managers and employees must become capable of working with people from different cultures. To be successful, managers and employees need to know the cultural practices of the workforce in each country where they do business. The ever-changing global competitive environment means that not only individuals but also organizations have to become increasingly flexible by learning new skills, new ways of thinking, and new ways of doing business.

Understanding Workforce Diversity

An important challenge for organizations is *workforce diversity*, a concept that recognizes the heterogeneous nature of employees in the workplace. Whereas globalization focuses

Montreal-based Bombardier, a leading aerospace and transportation company in the world, takes globalization seriously as part of its strategy. It helped build a bullet train for Italy, using Japanese technology, and has designed award-winning trams for a number of European cities.

Dcphoto/Alamy Stock Photo

on differences among people from different countries, workforce diversity addresses differences among people within given countries. **Workforce diversity** acknowledges that the workforce consists of women and men; many racial and ethnic groups; individuals with a variety of physical or psychological abilities; and people who differ in age, sexual orientation, and demographic characteristics. We discuss workforce diversity in Chapter 3.

One workforce diversity challenge in Canadian workplaces is the mix of generations—members of the Baby Boom, Generation X, and Millennials—who work side by side. Due to their very different life experiences, they bring different values and different expectations to the workplace.

> Why should you care about understanding other people?

We used to assume that people in organizations who differed from the stereotypical employee would somehow simply fit in. We now recognize that employees don't set aside their cultural values and lifestyle preferences when they go to work. The challenge for organizations, therefore, is to accommodate diverse groups of people by addressing their different lifestyles, family needs, and work styles.[24]

The *Focus on Diversity* feature found throughout this book highlights diversity matters that arise in organizations. Our first example looks at Regina-based SaskTel, which values having a diverse workforce.

FOCUS ON DIVERSITY

SaskTel Is a Top Diversity Employer

Does workforce diversity make business sense?   Regina-based SaskTel was named one of Canada's Best Diversity Employers in 2014 because of its commitment to diversity.[25] It has diversity programs for women, people with disabilities, visible minorities, and Indigenous people. While the company received this award for a number of reasons, its work with Indigenous people is particularly outstanding. Indigenous people are well represented in the SaskTel workplace: 10 percent of its employees and 8.1 percent of its managers are Indigenous. Indigenous people currently represent 15 percent of the Saskatchewan population, and that number is expected to grow to 21 to 24 percent in 20 years.

The number of Indigenous employees at SaskTel speaks to the effectiveness of the company's Indigenous recruitment strategy, which was intended to increase the number of Indigenous employees and address SaskTel's chronic labour shortages in information and communications technologies. SaskTel partners with First Nations bands, tribal councils, and Indigenous employment agencies.

SaskTel also keeps a database of Indigenous-owned and -operated businesses, which it consults when it is looking for new suppliers and partners.

SaskTel is not just a good employer. It also tries to be a good community member. Several years ago it started an initiative to bring Internet and wireless coverage to the 28 First Nations communities in Saskatchewan. "We have always believed in the importance of all Saskatchewan people benefitting from having access to the most powerful and extensive communications network available," said Don McMorris, MPP and cabinet minister responsible for SaskTel. "With increased access to technology, residents of these communities will be able to take advantage of numerous educational and business opportunities that were not available to them before."

SaskTel strives to have a workforce that is as diverse as its customers—a goal the company finds makes good sense not only for the community but also for its own future. . . . .

workforce diversity The mix of people in organizations in terms of gender, race, ethnicity, ability, sexual orientation, age, and demographic characteristics such as education and socio-economic status.

Evy Mages/The Washington Post/Getty Images

A Whole Foods Market customer learns how to grind flour with the help of the store's cooking coach, whose job is to provide information about cooking ingredients, methods, and techniques. Cooking coaches embody the best of the retailer's customer-responsive culture of serving people with competency, efficiency, knowledge, and flair.

Customer Service

Today, the majority of employees in developed countries work in service jobs, including 78 percent in Canada.[26] Service employees include technical support representatives, fast-food counter workers, sales clerks, nurses, automobile repair technicians, consultants, financial planners, and flight attendants. The shared characteristic of their jobs is substantial interaction with an organization's customers. OB can increase the success of these interactions by showing how employee attitudes and behaviour influence customer satisfaction.

Many an organization has failed because its employees failed to please customers. Management needs to create a customer-responsive culture. OB can provide considerable guidance in helping managers create cultures that establish rapport with customers, put customers at ease, show genuine interest, and are sensitive to a customer's individual situation.[27]

People Skills

Throughout the chapters of this text, we will present relevant concepts and theories that can help you explain and predict the behaviour of people at work. You will also gain insights into specific people skills that you can use on the job. For instance, you will learn how to design motivating jobs, improve your listening skills, and create more effective teams.

Networked Organizations

Networked organizations allow people to communicate and work together even though they may be thousands of kilometres apart. Independent contractors can telecommute via computer and change employers as the demand for their services changes. Software programmers, graphic designers, systems analysts, technical writers, photo researchers, book and media editors, and medical transcribers are just a few examples of people who can work from home or other nonoffice locations.

The manager's job is different in a networked organization. Motivating and leading people and making collaborative decisions online require different techniques than when individuals are physically present in a single location. As more employees do their jobs by linking to others through networks, managers and employees must develop new skills. OB can provide valuable insights to help with improving those skills.

Social Media

As we will discuss in Chapter 7, social media in the business world is here to stay. Despite its pervasiveness, many organizations continue to struggle with employees' use of social media in the workplace, which presents both a challenge and an opportunity for OB. Employees have been fired for tweeting unflattering comments about their employer. How much should HR look into a candidate's social media presence? Should a hiring manager read the candidate's Twitter feeds, or just do a quick perusal of her Facebook profile? We will discuss this issue later in the text.

Once employees are on the job, many organizations have policies about accessing social media at work—when, where, and for what purposes. But what about the impact of social media on employee well-being? One recent study found that subjects who woke up in a positive mood and then accessed Facebook frequently found their mood decreased during the day. Moreover, subjects who checked Facebook frequently over a two-week period reported a decreased level of satisfaction with their lives.[28] These are issues that organizations have to deal with.

Enhancing Employee Well-Being at Work

Employees are increasingly frustrated as the definition of the workplace has expanded to include anywhere a laptop or smartphone can go. However, even if employees work flexible hours at home or from half a continent away, managers need to consider their well-being at work.

One of the biggest challenges to maintaining employee well-being is the new reality that many workers never get away from the virtual workplace. Communication technology allows employees to do their work at home, in their cars, or on the ski slopes at Whistler—but it also means many feel like they are never really part of a team. It is hard for employees to get a sense of belonging if they are working alone. Another challenge is that organizations are asking employees to be available in off-work hours via cellphones and email. According to one study, one in four employees shows signs of burnout, and two in three report high stress levels and fatigue.[29] These findings may actually underestimate how common employee burnout is because many employees maintain "always on" access for their managers through email and texting. Finally, employee well-being is challenged by heavy outside commitments. Employees who are single parents or have dependent parents have even more significant challenges in balancing work and family responsibilities, for instance.

As a result of their increased responsibilities in and out of the workplace, employees want jobs that give them flexibility in their work schedules so they can better manage work–life conflicts.[30] In fact, 56 percent of men and women in a recent study reported that work–life balance was their definition of career success—more than money, recognition, and autonomy.[31] Most college and university students say that attaining a balance between personal life and work is a primary career goal; they want "a life" as well as a job. Organizations that don't help their people achieve work–life balance will find it increasingly difficult to attract and retain the most capable and motivated employees. As you will see in later chapters, the field of OB offers a number of suggestions for designing workplaces and jobs that can help employees deal with work–life conflicts. *OB in the Workplace* looks at how Habañero helps its employees manage work–life balance.

OB IN THE WORKPLACE

Habañero's Employees Help Set Policies

What do empowered employees do?   Steven Fitzgerald, president of Vancouver-based IT firm Habañero Consulting Group, believes in empowering his employees.[32] Employees share human resources duties by mentoring each other, encouraging career development, and making sure everyone understands their jobs.

Fitzgerald knows that an "all work and no play" ethic is not a good way to define the business. As a result, he gives his employees autonomy, telling them they will be "judged on the quality of their work—not the number of hours they put in." Habañero allows telecommuting and flextime, and does not track sick days.

More recently, Fitzgerald's employees noted that Habañero's invoicing model, which was based on a target number of billable hours per month, contradicted the company's commitment to work–life balance. The employees worked with management to develop a new model of project-based billing that was more consistent with a truly flexible workplace, while still maintaining profitability. Fitzgerald is pleased with how empowerment has worked for Habañero. He says that knowing what employees want and acting on that knowledge can help you "attract people who are engaged for the right reasons."

Creating a Positive Work Environment

A real growth area in OB research is **positive organizational scholarship** (also called *positive organizational behaviour*), which studies how organizations develop human strengths, foster vitality and resilience, and unlock potential. Researchers in this area argue that too much of OB research and management practice has been targeted toward identifying what is wrong with organizations and their employees. In response, they try to study what is *good* about organizations.[33] Some key independent variables in positive

Noah Berger/Reuters

positive organizational scholarship An area of OB research that concerns how organizations develop human strengths, foster vitality and resilience, and unlock potential.

Twitter employees rave about their company's culture, which creates a positive work environment where smart and friendly colleagues learn; share values, ideas, and information; and work together to help the company grow and succeed. At Twitter's San Francisco headquarters, employees like Jenna Sampson, community relations manager, enjoy free meals, yoga classes, and a rooftop garden.

OB research are engagement, hope, optimism, and resilience in the face of strain. Researchers hope to help practitioners create positive work environments for employees.

Positive organizational scholars have studied a concept called "reflected best self"— asking employees to think about situations in which they were at their "personal best" to understand how to exploit their strengths. The idea is that we all have things at which we are unusually good, yet too often we focus on addressing our limitations and too rarely think about how to exploit our strengths.[34]

Although positive organizational scholarship does not deny the negative (such as critical feedback), it does challenge researchers to look at OB through a new lens and pushes organizations to think about how to use their employees' strengths rather than dwell on their limitations. One aspect of a positive work environment is the organization's culture, the topic of Chapter 10. Organizational culture influences employee behaviour so strongly that organizations have begun to employ a culture officer to shape and preserve the company's personality.[35]

Ethical Behaviour

In an organizational world characterized by cutbacks, expectations of increasing productivity, and tough competition, it's not surprising that many employees feel pressured to cut corners, break rules, and engage in other questionable practices. Increasingly they face **ethical dilemmas and ethical choices**, in which they are required to identify right and wrong conduct. Should they "blow the whistle" if they uncover illegal activities taking place in their company? Do they follow orders with which they don't personally agree? Do they "play politics" to advance their careers?

Ethics is the study of moral values or principles that guide our behaviour and inform us whether actions are right or wrong. Ethical principles help us "do the right thing," such as not padding expense reports, or not phoning in sick to attend the opening of *Avengers 2: Age of Ultron*.

As we show in Chapter 11, the study of ethics does not come with black and white answers. What constitutes good ethical behaviour has never been clearly defined, and, in recent years, the line differentiating right from wrong has blurred. We see people all around us engaging in unethical practices—elected officials pad expense accounts or take bribes; corporate executives inflate profits to cash in lucrative stock options; and university administrators look the other way when winning coaches encourage scholarship athletes to take easy courses.

Nonetheless, individuals who strive hard to create their own set of ethical values will more often do the right thing. Moreover, companies that promote a strong ethical mission encourage employees to behave with integrity, and provide strong ethical leadership that can influence employee decisions to behave ethically.[36] Classroom training sessions in ethics have also proven helpful in maintaining a higher level of awareness of the implications of employee choices as long as the training sessions are given on an ongoing basis.[37] The *Ethical Dilemma* on page 30 asks you to consider whether it's ever appropriate to engineer corporate opportunities to your personal advantage. What are the ethics about receiving "gifts" from clients?

Throughout this book, you will find references to ethical and unethical behaviour. The *Focus on Ethics* feature will provide you with thought-provoking illustrations of how ethics is treated in various organizations.

Coming Attractions: Developing an OB Model

We conclude this chapter by presenting a general model that defines the field of OB, and stakes out its parameters, concepts, and relationships. By studying the model, you will have a good picture of how the topics in this text can inform your approach to organizational issues and opportunities.

ethical dilemmas and ethical choices Situations in which individuals are required to define right and wrong conduct.

ethics The study of moral values or principles that guide our behaviour and inform us whether actions are right or wrong.

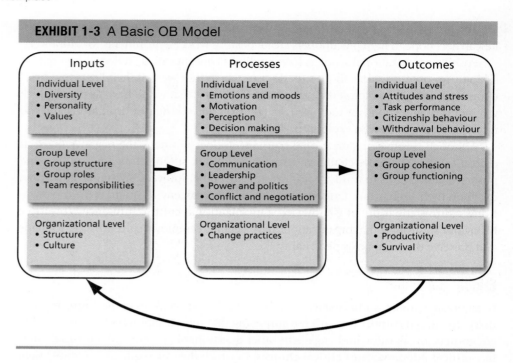

EXHIBIT 1-3 A Basic OB Model

Inputs

Individual Level
- Diversity
- Personality
- Values

Group Level
- Group structure
- Group roles
- Team responsibilities

Organizational Level
- Structure
- Culture

Processes

Individual Level
- Emotions and moods
- Motivation
- Perception
- Decision making

Group Level
- Communication
- Leadership
- Power and politics
- Conflict and negotiation

Organizational Level
- Change practices

Outcomes

Individual Level
- Attitudes and stress
- Task performance
- Citizenship behaviour
- Withdrawal behaviour

Group Level
- Group cohesion
- Group functioning

Organizational Level
- Productivity
- Survival

---

7 Describe the three levels of analysis in this book's OB model.

An Overview

A **model** is an abstraction of reality, a simplified representation of some real-world phenomenon. Exhibit 1-3 presents the skeleton of our OB model. It proposes three types of variables (inputs, processes, and outcomes) at three levels of analysis (individual, group, and organizational). In the chapters that follow, we will consider the individual level, group behaviour, and the organizational system. The model illustrates that inputs lead to processes, which lead to outcomes; we will discuss interrelationships at each level of analysis. Notice that the model also shows that outcomes can influence inputs in the future, which highlights the broad-reaching effect OB initiatives can have on an organization's future.

Inputs

Inputs are the variables like personality, group structure, and organizational culture that lead to processes. These variables set the stage for what will occur in an organization later. Many are determined in advance of the employment relationship. For example, individually diverse characteristics, personality, and values are shaped by a combination of an individual's genetic inheritance and childhood environment. Group structure, roles, and team responsibilities are typically assigned immediately before or after a group is formed. Finally, organizational structure and culture are usually the result of years of development and change as an organization adapts to its environment and builds up customs and norms.

model An abstraction of reality. A simplified representation of some real-world phenomenon.

input Variables that lead to processes.

processes Actions that individuals, groups, and organizations engage in as a result of inputs and that lead to certain outcomes.

Processes

If inputs are like the nouns in OB, processes are like the verbs. **Processes** are actions that individuals, groups, and organizations engage in as a result of inputs and that lead to certain outcomes. At the individual level, processes include emotions and moods, motivation, perception, and decision making. At the group level, they include communication, leadership, power and politics, and conflict and negotiation. Finally, at the organizational level, processes include change practices.

Outcomes

Outcomes are the key variables that you want to explain or predict, and that are affected by some other variables. What are the primary outcomes in OB? Scholars have emphasized individual-level outcomes such as attitudes and stress, task performance, citizenship behaviour, and withdrawal behaviour. At the group level, cohesion and functioning are the dependent variables. Finally, at the organizational level, we look at overall productivity and survival. Because these outcomes will be covered in all the chapters, we will briefly discuss each here so you can understand the "goal" of OB.

Attitudes and Stress

Employee **attitudes** are the evaluations employees make, ranging from positive to negative, about objects, people, or events. For example, the statement, "I really think my job is great," is a positive job attitude, and "My job is boring and tedious" is a negative job attitude. **Stress** is an unpleasant psychological process that occurs in response to environmental pressures.

Some people might think that influencing employee attitudes and stress is purely soft stuff and not the business of serious managers, but as we will show, attitudes often have behavioural consequences that directly relate to organizational effectiveness. The belief that satisfied employees are more productive than dissatisfied employees has been a basic tenet among managers for years, although only now has research begun to support it. Ample evidence shows that employees who are more satisfied and treated fairly are more willing to engage in the above-and-beyond citizenship behaviour so vital in the contemporary business environment. For more information on the causes and consequences of stress as well as coping mechanisms, see *OB on the Edge—Stress at Work* on pages 116–123.

Task Performance

The combination of effectiveness and efficiency at doing your core job tasks is a reflection of your level of **task performance**. If we think about the job of a factory worker, task performance could be measured by the number and quality of products produced in an hour. The task performance of a teacher would be the level of education that students obtain. The task performance of a consultant might be measured by the timeliness and quality of the presentations they offer to the client. All these types of performance relate to the core duties and responsibilities of a job and are often directly related to the functions listed on a formal job description.

Obviously, task performance is the most important human output contributing to organizational effectiveness, so in every chapter we devote considerable time to detailing how task performance is affected by the topic in question.

Organizational Citizenship Behaviour

The discretionary behaviour that is not part of an employee's formal job requirements, and that contributes to the psychological and social environment of the workplace, is called **organizational citizenship behaviour (OCB)**, or simply citizenship behaviour. Recent research has also looked at expanding the work on OCB to team behaviour.

Successful organizations have employees who will do more than their usual job duties—who will provide performance that is *beyond* expectations. In today's dynamic workplace, where tasks are increasingly performed by teams and flexibility is critical, employees who engage in "good

> Are you ready to take on more responsibility at work?

outcomes Key factors that are affected by some other variables.

attitudes Positive or negative feelings about objects, people, or events.

stress An unpleasant psychological process that occurs in response to environmental pressures.

task performance The combination of effectiveness and efficiency at doing your core job tasks.

organizational citizenship behaviour (OCB) Discretionary behaviour that is not part of an employee's formal job requirements, but that nevertheless promotes the effective functioning of the organization.

citizenship" behaviours help others on their team, volunteer for extra job activities, avoid unnecessary conflicts, respect the spirit as well as the letter of rules and regulations, and gracefully tolerate the occasional work-related impositions and nuisances.

Organizations want and need employees who will do those things that are not in any job description. Evidence indicates that organizations that have such employees outperform those that don't.[38] As a result, OB is concerned with organizational citizenship behaviour.

Withdrawal Behaviour

We have already mentioned behaviour that goes above and beyond task requirements, but what about behaviour that in some way is below task requirements? **Withdrawal behaviour** is the set of actions that employees take to separate themselves from the organization. There are many forms of withdrawal, ranging from showing up late or failing to attend meetings to absenteeism and turnover.

Employee withdrawal can have a very negative effect on an organization. The cost of employee turnover alone has been estimated to run into the thousands of dollars, even for entry-level positions. Absenteeism also costs organizations significant amounts of money and time every year. For instance, a recent survey found the average direct cost to employers for absenteeism in Canada is $16.6 billion.[39] In Sweden, an average of 10 percent of the country's workforce is on sick leave at any given time.[40]

It's obviously difficult for an organization to operate smoothly and attain its objectives if employees fail to report to their jobs. The workflow is disrupted, and important decisions may be delayed. In organizations that rely heavily on assembly-line production, absenteeism can be considerably more than a disruption; it can drastically reduce the quality of output or even shut down the facility. Levels of absenteeism beyond the normal range have a direct impact on any organization's effectiveness and efficiency. A high rate of turnover can also disrupt the efficient running of an organization when knowledgeable and experienced personnel leave and replacements must be found to assume positions of responsibility. Research indicates that, in general, turnover is significantly harmful for organizational performance.[41]

All organizations, of course, have some turnover. Turnover rates vary greatly by country and, in part, reflect the economy of that country. If the "right" people are leaving the organization—the marginal and submarginal employees—turnover can actually be positive. It can create an opportunity to replace an underperforming individual with someone who has higher skills or motivation, open up increased opportunities for promotions, and bring new and fresh ideas to the organization. In today's changing world of work, reasonable levels of employee-initiated turnover improve organizational flexibility and employee independence, and they can lessen the need for management-initiated layoffs. Thus, while it is reasonable to conclude that high turnover often indicates high employee withdrawal (and thus has a negative effect on organizational performance), zero turnover is not necessarily the goal; it's also important for organizations to assess which employees are leaving, and why. Millennials have nearly double the turnover rates of Gen-Xers. According to a recent Gallup poll, 60 percent are open to new job opportunities and in 2016, 21 percent of millennials changed jobs.[42]

So why do employees withdraw from work through counterproductive behaviours or quitting? As we will show later in the text, reasons include negative job attitudes, emotions, moods, and negative interactions with co-workers and supervisors. Despite these large turnover numbers for millennials, Vancouver-based Hootsuite CEO, Ryan Holmes, does not see all of this as bad. He welcomes turnover in his company, because some of it simply reflects people moving into other jobs in the

withdrawal behaviour The set of actions employees take to separate themselves from the organization.

CAREER OBJECTIVES

What Do I Say About My Termination?

I got fired! When prospective employers find out, they will never hire me. Is there anything I can say to turn this around?

—Matt

Dear Matt:

Under this dark cloud, there are some silver linings: (1) firing, or involuntary termination, happens to just about everyone at least once in a career; and (2) there is a worldwide job shortage of skilled workers. You might be amazed to know that, historically, individuals have changed jobs an average of 11 times over their early careers (from age 18 to 44). In fact, you can probably expect to stay in a job for less than three years, which means you will have a lot of jobs in your lifetime.

Therefore, you should not feel hopeless; you are likely to find your next job soon. ManpowerGroup's recent survey of over 37 000 employers in 42 countries found that 36 percent of organizations have talent shortages, the highest percentage in 7 years.

Still, we know you are worried about how to present the facts of your involuntary termination to prospective employers. If you give a truthful, brief account of the reason for your termination, you can position yourself well. Here are some additional suggestions:

- *Remember your soft skills count; in fact, they top the lists of employer requirements for all industries.* According to Chuck Knebl, a communications manager for the job placement company WorkOne, use your résumé and cover letter, interviews, and thank-you notes to showcase your communication skills. Employers report they are also looking for a teamwork attitude, positivity, personal responsibility, and punctuality, so use every opportunity to demonstrate these traits.
- *Although your soft skills count, don't forget your technical skills; employers agree they are equally important.* Knebl advises you to use your résumé to list your technical abilities and be prepared to elaborate upon request. Need some more skills? Job training has been shown to be helpful and can sometimes be free through colleges and unemployment offices.
- *Emphasize your ongoing training and education, especially as they relate to new technology; top performers*

are known to be continuous learners. Also, if you have kept up with recent trends in social media, show it, but don't go on about your friend's tweet to Rihanna.

Best wishes for your success!

Sources: Bureau of Labor Statistics, United States Department of Labor, Employment Projections, http://www.bls.gov/emp/ep_chart_001. htm; G. Jones, "How the Best Get Better and Better," *Harvard Business Review* (June 2008): 123–127; ManpowerGroup, "The Talent Shortage Continues/2014," http://www.manpowergroup. com/wps/wcm/connect/0b882c15-38bf-41f3-8882-44c33d0e2952/2014_Talent_Shortage_WP_US2.pdf?MOD=AJPERES; J. Meister, "Job Hopping Is the 'New Normal' for Millennials: Three Ways to Prevent a Human Resource Nightmare," *Forbes* (August 14, 2012), http://www. forbes.com/sites/jeannemeister/2012/08/14/job-hopping-is-the-new-normal-for-millennials-three-ways-to-prevent-a-human-resource-nightmare/; and N. Schulz, "Hard Unemployment Truths about 'Soft' Skills," *Wall Street Journal*, September 19, 2012, A15.

company. In fact, he says that management made a goal "that 20% of our employees, or around 200 people in total, aren't in the same seat by the end of 2017."[43]

Group Cohesion

Although many outcomes in our model can be conceptualized as individual-level phenomena, some relate to the way groups operate. **Group cohesion** is the extent to which members of a group support and validate one another at work. In other words, a cohesive group is one that sticks together. When employees trust one another, seek common goals, and work together to achieve these common ends, the group is cohesive; when employees are divided among themselves in terms of what they want to achieve and have little loyalty to one another, the group is not cohesive.

group cohesion The extent to which members of a group support and validate one another while at work.

Ample evidence shows that cohesive groups are more effective.[44] These results are found both for groups studied in highly controlled laboratory settings and for work teams observed in field settings. This finding fits with our intuitive sense that people tend to work harder in groups that have a common purpose. Companies attempt to increase cohesion in a variety of ways ranging from brief icebreaker sessions to social events such as picnics, parties, and outdoor adventure team retreats. Throughout the text we will try to assess whether these specific efforts are likely to increase group cohesiveness. We will also consider how to enhance cohesion by picking the right people to be on the team in the first place.

Group Functioning

In the same way that positive job attitudes can be associated with higher levels of task performance, group cohesion should lead to positive group functioning. **Group functioning** refers to the quantity and quality of a group's work output. In the same way that the performance of a sports team is more than the sum of individual players' performance, group functioning in work organizations is more than the sum of individual task performances.

What does it mean to say that a group is functioning effectively? In some organizations, an effective group is one that stays focused on a core task and achieves its ends as specified. Other organizations look for teams that are able to work together collaboratively to provide excellent customer service. Still others put more of a premium on group creativity and the flexibility to adapt to changing situations. In each case, different types of activities will be required to get the most from the team.

Productivity

The highest level of analysis in OB is the organization as a whole. An organization is productive if it achieves its goals by transforming inputs into outputs at the lowest cost. Thus **productivity** requires both **effectiveness** and **efficiency**.

A hospital is *effective* when it successfully meets the needs of its clientele. It is *efficient* when it can do so at a low cost. If a hospital manages to achieve higher output from its present staff by reducing the average number of days a patient is confined to bed or increasing the number of staff–patient contacts per day, we say the hospital has gained productive efficiency. A business firm is effective when it attains its sales or market share goals, but its productivity also depends on achieving those goals efficiently. Popular measures of organizational efficiency include return on investment, profit per dollar of sales, and output per hour of labour.

Service organizations must include customer needs and requirements in assessing their effectiveness. Why? Because a clear chain of cause and effect runs from employee attitudes and behaviour to customer attitudes and profitability. For example, a recent study of six hotels in China indicated that negative employee attitudes decreased customer satisfaction and ultimately harmed the organization's profitability.[45]

Survival

The final outcome we will consider is **organizational survival**, which is simply evidence that the organization is able to exist and grow over the long term. The survival of an organization depends not just on how productive the organization is, but also on how well it fits with its environment. A company that is very productively making goods and services of little value to the market is unlikely to survive for long, so survival also relies on perceiving the market successfully, making good decisions about how and when to pursue opportunities, and successfully managing change to adapt to new business conditions.

Having reviewed the input, process, and outcome model, we will group topics based on whether we study them at the individual, group, or organizational level. We will deal with inputs, processes, and outcomes at all three levels of analysis, but we group the

group functioning The quantity and quality of a work group's output.

productivity The combination of the effectiveness and efficiency of an organization.

effectiveness The degree to which an organization meets the needs of its clientele or customers.

efficiency The degree to which an organization can achieve its ends at a low cost.

organizational survival The degree to which an organization is able to exist and grow over the long term.

EXHIBIT 1-4 The Plan of the Book

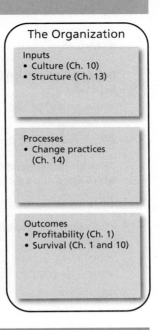

The Individual

Inputs
- Personality (Ch. 2)
- Values (Ch. 3)
- Diversity in Organizations (Ch. 3)

Processes
- Perception (Ch. 2)
- Emotions and moods (Ch. 2)
- Motivation (Ch. 4 and 5)
- Decision making (Ch. 6)

Outcomes
- Attitudes (Ch. 3)
- Stress (OB on the Edge: Stress at Work)
- Task performance (all)
- Citizenship behaviour (all)
- Withdrawal behaviour (all)

The Group

Inputs
- Group structures (Ch. 6)
- Group roles (Ch. 6)
- Team responsibilities (Ch. 6)

Processes
- Communication (Ch. 7)
- Power and politics (Ch. 8)
- Conflict and negotiation (Ch. 9)
- Leadership (Ch. 11)

Outcomes
- Group cohesion (Ch. 6)
- Group functioning (Ch. 6)

The Organization

Inputs
- Culture (Ch. 10)
- Structure (Ch. 13)

Processes
- Change practices (Ch. 14)

Outcomes
- Profitability (Ch. 1)
- Survival (Ch. 1 and 10)

chapters as shown in Exhibit 1-4 to correspond with the typical ways that research has been done in these areas. For example, it is easier to understand one unified presentation about how personality leads to motivation, which leads to performance, than to jump around levels of analysis. Because each level builds on the one that precedes it, after going through them in sequence you will have a good idea of how the human side of organizations functions.

Summary

Organizational behaviour (OB) investigates the impact that individuals, groups, and organizational structure have on behaviour within an organization, and it applies that knowledge to make organizations work more effectively. Specifically, OB focuses on how to improve productivity; reduce absenteeism, turnover, and deviant workplace behaviour; and increase organizational citizenship behaviour and job satisfaction. The essential points of OB that you should keep in mind as you study this topic are listed in Exhibit 1-5.

LESSONS LEARNED
- OB is for everyone.
- OB draws upon a rigorous multidisciplinary research base.

EXHIBIT 1-5 The Fundamentals of OB

- OB considers the multiple levels in an organization: individual, group, and organizational.

- OB is built from the wisdom and research of multiple disciplines, including psychology, sociology, social psychology, and anthropology.

- OB takes a systematic approach to the study of organizational phenomena. It is research-based.

- OB takes a contingency approach to the consideration of organizational phenomena. Recommendations depend on the situation.

SNAPSHOT SUMMARY

The Importance of Interpersonal Skills

Defining Organizational Behaviour
- What Do We Mean by *Organization*?
- OB Is for Everyone

Complementing Intuition with Systematic Study
- Big Data

Disciplines That Contribute to the OB Field
- The Building Blocks of OB
- The Rigour of OB

OB Has Few Absolutes
- OB Takes a Contingency Approach

Challenges and Opportunities in the Canadian Workplace
- Economic Pressures
- Continuing Globalization
- Understanding Workforce Diversity
- Customer Service
- People Skills
- Networked Organizations
- Social Media
- Enhancing Employee Well-Being at Work

- Creating a Positive Work Environment
- Ethical Behaviour

Coming Attractions: Developing an OB Model
- An Overview
- Inputs
- Processes
- Outcomes

MyLab Management

 PERSONAL INVENTORY ASSESSMENT

Study, practise, and explore real business situations with these helpful resources:

- **Study Plan:** Check your understanding of chapter concepts with self-study quizzes.
- **Online Lesson Presentations:** Study key chapter topics and work through interactive assessments to test your knowledge and master management concepts.
- **Videos:** Learn more about the management practices and strategies of real companies.
- **Simulations:** Practise management decision-making in simulated business environments.

OB at Work

for **Review**

1. What is the importance of inter-personal skills in the workplace?

2. What is organizational behaviour (OB)?

3. Why is systematic study of value to OB?

4. What are the major behavioural science disciplines that contribute to OB?

5. Why are there so few absolutes in OB?

6. What workplace challenges provide opportunities to apply OB concepts?

7. What are the three levels of analysis in this book's OB model?

for **Managers**

- Resist the inclination to rely on generalizations; some provide valid insights into human behaviour, but many are erroneous. Get to know the person, and understand the context.

- Use metrics rather than "hunches" to explain cause-and-effect relationships.

- Work on your interpersonal skills to increase your leadership potential.

- Improve your technical skills and conceptual skills through training and staying current with OB trends such as big data.

- OB can improve your employees' work quality and productivity by showing you how to empower your employees, design and implement change programs, improve customer service, and help your employees balance work–life conflicts.

for **You**

- As you journey through this course in OB, bear in mind that the processes we describe are as relevant to you as an individual as they are to organizations, managers, and employees.

- When you work together with student teams, join a student organization, or volunteer time to a community group, know that your ability to get along with others has an effect on your interactions with the other people in the group and the achievement of the group's goals.

- If you are aware of how your perceptions and personality affect your interactions with others, you can be more careful in forming your initial impression of others.

- By knowing how to motivate others who are working with you, how to communicate effectively, and when to negotiate and compromise, you can get along in a variety of situations that are not necessarily work-related.

THE BATTLE OF THE TEXTS

POINT

Walk into your nearest major bookstore and you will see a large section of books devoted to management whose topics we apparently need to know about:

- *The Secret* (Berrett-Koehler, 2014)
- *Turn the Ship Around!* (Portfolio, 2013)
- *The Way You Do Anything Is the Way You Do Everything* (Wiley, 2014)
- *Leadership Safari* (Best Seller, 2014)
- *Business Is a Baby* (Amazon Digital Services, 2014)
- *Think Like a Freak* (William Morrow, 2014)
- *Spiraling Upward* (Amazon Digital Services, 2015)
- *Refire! Don't Retire* (Berrett-Koehler, 2015)
- *Top Dog* (Amazon Digital Services, 2015)

Popular books on OB often have cute titles and are fun to read, but they make the job of managing people seem like it's just a matter of having a good slogan and five easy steps. If you dig into the texts, you will find that most are based on the author's opinions rather than substantive research. Most become popular, in part, because people largely agree with the opinions they are reading and enjoy the author's writing style. Often, the writers are presentation speakers or consultants whose real business is in delivering ideas to you. When the author is a veteran from the business world, it is doubtful that one person's experience translates into effective management practice for everyone. Even when the authors are numbers-oriented, as are the "Freak" authors Steven Levitt and Stephen Dubner, their conclusions for management are not management-research based. So why do we base our own management philosophies on these books when, with a little effort, we can access knowledge produced from thousands of scientific studies on human behaviour in organizations?

OB is a complex subject. Few, if any, simple statements about human behaviour are generalizable to all people in all situations. Would you try to apply leadership insights you got from a book about *Star Wars* or *Breaking Bad* to managing software engineers in the twenty-first century? Surely not. Neither should we try to apply leadership insights that are not based on research about the type of workplaces in which we function.

COUNTERPOINT

People want to know about management—the good, the bad, and the ugly. People who have experience or high interest write books about the topics that interest readers. When books become popular, we know people are finding good results by applying the author's management ideas. Isn't it better to learn about management from people in the trenches, as opposed to the latest obscure references from the "Ivory Tower"? Many of the most important insights we gain from life aren't necessarily the product of careful empirical research studies.

"Fluffy" management guides sometimes do get published, and once in a while they become popular. But do they outnumber the esoteric research studies published in scholarly journal articles every year? Far from it; sometimes it seems that for every popular business text, there are thousands of scholarly journal articles. Many of these articles can hardly be read by individuals in the workplace—they are buried in academic libraries, riddled with strange acronyms and "insider" terms, and light on practical application. Often they apply to specific management scenarios, so they are even less generalizable. For example, a few recent management and OB studies were published in 2015 with the following titles:

- *Transferring Management Practices to China: A Bourdieusian Critique of Ethnocentricity*
- *Cross-Cultural Perceptions of Clan Control in Korean Multinational Companies: A Conceptual Investigation of Employees' Fairness Monitoring Based on Cultural Values*
- *The Resistible Rise of Bayesian Thinking in Management: Historical Lessons from Decision Analysis*
- *A Model of Rhetorical Legitimation: The Structure of Communication and Cognition Underlying Institutional Maintenance and Change*

We don't mean to poke fun at these studies, but our point is that all ways of creating knowledge can be criticized. Popular books can add to our understanding of how people work and how to best manage them; we shouldn't assume they are not of value. There is no one right way to learn the science and art of managing people in organizations. The most enlightened managers gather insights from multiple sources: their own experience, research findings, observations of others, and, yes, the popular business press. Authors and academics have an important role to play, and it isn't fair to condemn business books with catchy titles.

BREAKOUT **GROUP** EXERCISES

Form small groups to discuss the following topics, as assigned by your instructor.

1. Consider a group situation in which you have worked. To what extent did the group rely on the technical skills of the group members vs. their interpersonal skills? Which skills seemed most important in helping the group function well?

2. Identify some examples of "worst jobs." What conditions of these jobs made them unpleasant? To what extent were these conditions related to behaviours of individuals?

3. Develop a list of "organizational puzzles," that is, behaviour you have observed in organizations that seemed to make little sense. As the term progresses, see if you can begin to explain these puzzles, using your knowledge of OB.

EXPERIENTIAL EXERCISE

Managing the OB Way

Divide the class into groups of approximately four members each. Each group should consider the following scenario:

You will assume the role of a special committee of district managers at a large pharmaceutical company. Your committee will be meeting to discuss some problems. The process set up by the company is as follows:

1. Each committee member should first review the problem privately and formulate independent ideas for what might be done.

2. At the start of the meeting, each member should spend one minute addressing the group.

During the meeting, the committee must reach a consensus on both the best solution and supporting rationale to each problem. How this is done is entirely up to the committee members, but you must come up with a consensus decision and not a majority opinion achieved by voting.

Here is the problem your committee is to consider:
The company has no specific policy regarding facial hair. Tom, a pharmaceutical sales rep with a little more than a year's experience and an average (but declining) sales record, has grown a very long and ragged beard that detracts significantly from his appearance. His hobby is playing bass in an amateur bluegrass band, and he feels that a ragged beard is an important part of the act. Tom says his beard is a personal fashion statement that has to do with his individual freedom.

There have been numerous complaints about Tom's appearance from both doctors and pharmacists. The manager has talked to him on many occasions about the impact his appearance could have on his sales. Nevertheless, Tom still has the beard.

The manager is concerned about Tom's decreasing sales as well as the professional image of the sales force in the medical community. Tom says his sales decrease has nothing to do with his beard. However, sales in the other territories in the district are significantly better than they were last year.

When the groups have reached their consensus decisions, the following questions will serve for class discussion:

1. What do you think are the concerns for the company regarding Tom's facial hair? Should they care about his appearance?

2. What was your group's consensus decision regarding the issue with Tom's facial hair?

3. Suppose Tom told you he grew a beard as part of his personal religion. Do you think that announcement would change how you talk to Tom about the issue?

ETHICAL **DILEMMA**

There's a Drone in Your Soup

It is the year 2020, and drones are everywhere. Alibaba quadcopters have been delivering special ginger tea to customers in Beijing, Shanghai, and Guangzhou for years; Amazon's octocopters finally deliver packages in most major cities within 30 minutes without knocking down pedestrians; and college students everywhere welcome late-night nachos from Taco Bell Tacocopters. Indoor drones are still in the pioneering phase—backyard enthusiasts are building tiny versions, but no large-scale commercial efforts have been put toward indoor utility drones. That's all about to change.

You work for a multinational technology corporation on a sprawling, 25-acre headquarters campus, with offices in 2 million square feet of interior space in one large building and four additional smaller (but still large) buildings. The official Head of Interior Spaces is your boss; you're the leader of the Consideration of New Things team. In a meeting with your team, your boss says, "I've just heard from my friend at Right To Drones Too (R2D2) that his group has perfected their inside drone. It's small and light but can carry up to 10 pounds. It includes a camera, a speaker, and a recorder."

Your team expresses surprise; no one even knew an inside utility drone was under development, and governments worldwide are still haggling over regulations for drones. Your boss goes on enthusiastically, "I've seen the little drones, and I think you'll be impressed—not only can they scoot across the quad, but they can fetch things off tables, grab me a latté, attend meetings for me, check over your shoulders to see what you're working on . . . anything! They're really accurate, agile, and super quiet, so

you'll barely even know they're around. My friend wants us to have the first 100 drones here for free, and he's willing to send them over tomorrow! I figure we can hand them out randomly, although of course we'll each have one."

Your boss sits back, smiling and expecting applause. You glance at your team members and are relieved to see doubt and hesitation on their faces.

"Sounds, uh, great," you reply. "But how about the team takes the afternoon to set the ground rules?"

Questions

1. How might the R2D2 drones influence employee behaviour? Do you think they will cause people to act more or less ethically? Why?

2. Who should get the drones initially? How can you justify your decision ethically? What restrictions for use should these people be given, and how do you think employees, both those who get drones and those who don't, will react to this change?

3. How will your organization deal with sabotage or misuse of the drones? The value of an R2D2 drone is $2500.

4. Many organizations already use electronic monitoring of employees, including sifting through website usage and email correspondence, often without the employees' direct knowledge. In what ways might drone monitoring be better or worse for employees than covert electronic monitoring of web or email activity?

CASE INCIDENTS

Apple Goes Global

It was not long ago that products from Apple, perhaps the most recognizable name in electronics manufacturing around the world, were made entirely in the United States.[46] This is not so anymore. Now, almost all of the approximately 70 million iPhones, 30 million iPads, and 59 million other Apple products sold yearly are manufactured overseas. This change represents more than 20 000 jobs directly lost by US workers, not to mention more than 700 000 other jobs given to foreign companies in Asia, Europe, and elsewhere. The loss is not temporary. As the late Steve Jobs, Apple's iconic co-founder, told US President Obama, "Those jobs aren't coming back."

Vancouver-based Lululemon Athletica has also transferred many jobs out of Canada to countries such as Cambodia and Bangladesh. When the company first started in 1998, all of its factories were located in Canada. By 2007, only 50 percent of the factories were in Canada and now that figure is only 3 percent.

At first glance, the transfer of jobs from one workforce to another would seem to hinge on a difference in wages, but Apple shows this is an oversimplification. In fact, some say paying US wages would add only $65 to each iPhone's expense, while Apple's profits average hundreds of dollars per phone. Rather, and of more concern, Apple's leaders believe the intrinsic characteristics of the labour force available to them in China—which they identify as flexibility, diligence, and industrial skills—are superior to those of the North American labour force. Apple executives tell of shorter lead times and faster manufacturing processes in China that are becoming the stuff of company legend. "The speed and flexibility is breathtaking," one executive said. "There's

no American plant that can match that." Another said, "We shouldn't be criticized for using Chinese workers. The US has stopped producing people with the skills we need."

The perception of an overseas advantage might suggest that the North American workforce needs to be better led, better trained, more effectively managed, and more motivated to be proactive and flexible. If Canadian and US workers are less motivated and less adaptable, it's hard to imagine how that does not spell trouble for the future of the North American workforce.

There is an ongoing debate whether companies such as Lululemon and Apple serve as examples of the failure of North America to maintain manufacturing plants at home or whether these companies should best be viewed as examples of global ingenuity.

Questions

1. What are the pros and cons for local and overseas labour forces for companies going global? What are the potential political implications for country relationships?

2. Do you think Apple is justified in drawing the observations and conclusions expressed in the case? Why or why not? Do you think it is good or harmful to the company that its executives have voiced these opinions?

3. How could managers use increased worker flexibility and diligence to increase the competitiveness of their manufacturing sites? What would you recommend?

Big Data for Dummies

Do you need big data? Maybe the question is better phrased as: Can you afford not to use big data? The age of big data is here, and to ignore its benefits is to run the risk of missed opportunities.[47]

Organizations using big data are quickly reaping rewards, as a survey of 2022 managers worldwide indicated recently. In fact, 71 percent of respondents agreed that organizations using big data will gain a "huge competitive advantage." These managers also saw the need for big data: 58 percent responded that they never, rarely, or

only sometimes have enough data to make key business decisions. Furthermore, they've witnessed the benefits: 67 percent agreed that big data has helped their organization to innovate. So why did only 28 percent find that their access to useful data significantly increased in a year?

According to Amy Braverman, a principal statistician who analyzes NASA's spacecraft data, the problem is in interpreting the new kinds and volumes of data we are able to collect. "This opportunistic data collection is leading to entirely new kinds of data that aren't well suited to the existing statistical and data-mining methodologies," she said. IT and business leaders agree: In a recent survey, "determining how to get value" was identified as the number one challenge of big data.

With strong need combatting the high hurdle for usability, how should a company get started using big data? The quick answer seems to be to hire talent. But not just anyone will do. Here are some points to ponder when hiring data professionals:

1. **Look for candidates with a strong educational background in analytics/statistics.** You want someone who knows more than you do about handling copious amounts of data.

2. **The ideal candidates will have specific experience in your industry or a related industry.** "When you have all those PhDs in a room, magic doesn't necessarily happen because they may not have the business capability," said Andy Rusnak, a senior executive at Ernst & Young.

3. **Search for potential candidates from industry leader organizations that are more advanced in big data.**

4. **Communication skills are a must.** Look for a candidate "who can translate PhD to English," says SAP Chief Data Scientist David Ginsberg. He adds, "Those are the hardest people to find."

5. **Find candidates with a proven record of finding useful information from a mess of data, including data from questionable sources.** You want someone who is analytical *and* discerning.

6. **Look for people who can think in 8- to 10-week periods, not just long term.** Most data projects have a short-term focus.

7. **Test candidates' expertise on real problems.** Netflix's Director of Algorithms asks candidates, "You have this data that comes from our users. How can you use it to solve this particular problem?"

Questions

1. Let's say you work in a metropolitan city for a large department store chain and your manager puts you in charge of a team to find out whether keeping the store open an hour longer each day would increase profits. What data might be available to your decision-making process? What data would be important to your decision?

2. What kinds of data might we want in OB applications?

3. As Braverman notes, one problem with big data is making sense of the information. How might a better understanding of psychology help you sift through all this data?

FROM CONCEPTS TO SKILLS

Developing Interpersonal Skills

We note in this chapter that having a broad range of interpersonal skills to draw on makes us more effective organizational participants. So what kinds of interpersonal skills does an individual need in today's workplace?

Robert Quinn, Kim Cameron, and their colleagues have developed a model known as the "Competing Values Framework" that can help us identify some of the most useful skills.[48] They note that the range of issues organizations face can be divided along two dimensions: internal–external and flexibility–control. This idea is illustrated in Exhibit 1-6. The internal–external dimension refers to the extent that organizations focus on one of two directions: either inwardly, toward employee needs and concerns and/or production processes and internal systems; or outwardly, toward such factors as the marketplace, government regulations, and the changing social, environmental, and technological conditions of the future. The flexibility–control dimension refers to the competing demands of organizations to stay focused on doing what has been done in the past versus being more flexible in orientation and outlook.

Because organizations face the competing demands shown in Exhibit 1-6, it becomes obvious that managers and employees need a variety of skills to help them function within the various quadrants at different points in time. For instance, the skills needed to operate an efficient assembly-line process are not the same as those needed to scan the external environment or to create opportunities in anticipation of changes in the environment. Quinn and his

EXHIBIT 1-6 Competing Values Framework

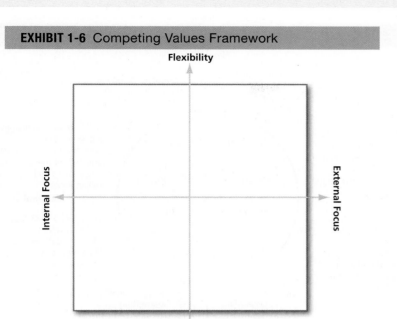

Source: Adapted from K. Cameron and R. E. Quinn, *Diagnosing and Changing Organizational Culture: Based on the Competing Values Framework*, 2006, ISBN: 9780787982836, Fig 3.1, pg. 35. Copyright © John Wiley & Sons.

colleagues use the term *master manager* to indicate that successful managers learn and apply skills that will help them manage across the range of organizational demands; sometimes moving toward flexibility and other times moving toward control, and sometimes being more internally focused and other times being more externally driven.[49]

As organizations increasingly cut their layers, reducing the number of managers while also relying more on the use of teams in the workplace, the skills of the master manager apply as well to the employee. In other words, considering the Competing Values Framework, we can see that both managers and individual employees need to learn new skills and new ways of interpreting their organizational contexts. Continuing to use traditional skills and practices that worked in the past is not an option. The growth in self-employment also indicates a need to develop more interpersonal skills, particularly for anyone who goes on to build a business that involves hiring and managing employees.

Exhibit 1-7 outlines the many skills required of today's manager. It gives you an indication of the complex roles that managers and employees fill in the changing workplace. The skills are organized in terms of four major roles: maintaining flexibility, maintaining control, maintaining an external focus, and maintaining an internal focus. Identifying your own strengths and weaknesses in these skill areas can give you a better sense of how close you are to becoming a successful manager.

On the flexibility side, organizations want to inspire their employees toward high-performance behaviour. Such behaviour includes looking ahead to the future and imagining possible new directions for the organization. To do these things, employees need to think and act like mentors and facilitators. It is also important to have the skills of innovators and brokers. On the control side, organizations need to set clear goals about productivity expectations, and they have to develop and implement

EXHIBIT 1-7 Skills for Mastery in the New Workplace

Source: R. E. Quinn, *Beyond Rational Management* (San Francisco: Jossey-Bass, 1988), p. 86. Copyright © John Wiley & Sons.

systems to carry out the production process. To be effective on the production side, employees need to have the skills of monitors, coordinators, directors, and producers. The *Experiential Exercise* on page 29 helps you better understand how closely your views on the ideal skills of managers and leaders match the skills needed to be successful in the broad range of activities that managers and leaders encounter.

At this point, you may wonder whether it's possible for people to learn all of the skills necessary to become a master manager. More important, you may wonder whether we can change our individual style, say from more controlling to more flexible. Here is what Peggy Kent, chair, former president, and CEO of Century Mining Corporation (a mid-tier Canadian gold producer), said about how her managerial style changed from controlling to more flexible over time: "I started out being very dictatorial. Everybody in head office reported to me. I had to learn to trust other executives so we could work out problems together."[50] So, while it is probably true that each of us has a preferred style of operating, it is also the case that we can develop new skills if that is something we choose to do.

Practising Skills

As the father of two young children, Marshall Rogers thought that serving on the board of Marysville Daycare would be a good way to stay in touch with those who cared for his children during the day.[51] But he never dreamed that he would become involved in union–management negotiations with daycare-centre employees.

Late one Sunday evening, in his ninth month as president of the daycare centre, Rogers received a phone call from Grace Ng, a union representative of the Provincial Government Employees' Union (PGEU). Ng informed Rogers that the daycare employees would be unionized the following week. Rogers was stunned to hear this news. Early the next morning, he had to present his new marketing plan to senior management at

Techtronix Industries, where he was vice-president of marketing. Somehow he made it through the meeting, wondering why he had not been aware of the employees' unhappiness, and how this action would affect his children.

Following his presentation, Rogers received documentation from the Labour Relations Board indicating that the daycare employees had been working to unionize themselves for more than a year. Rogers immediately contacted Xavier Breslin, the board's vice-president, and together they determined that no one on the board had been aware that the daycare workers were unhappy, let alone prepared to join a union.

Hoping that there was some sort of misunderstanding, Rogers called Emma Reynaud, the Marysville supervisor. Reynaud attended most board meetings, but had never mentioned the union-organizing drive. Yet Reynaud now told Rogers that she had actively encouraged the other daycare employees to consider joining the PGEU because the board had not been interested in the employees' concerns, had not increased their wages sufficiently over the past two years, and had not maintained communication channels between the board and the employees.

All of the board members had full-time jobs elsewhere, and many were upper- and middle-level managers in their own companies. They were used to dealing with unhappy employees in their own workplaces, although none had experienced a union-organizing drive. Like Rogers, they had chosen to serve on the board of Marysville to stay informed about the day-to-day events of the centre. They had not really thought of themselves as the centre's employer, although, as board members, they represented all the parents of children enrolled at Marysville. Their main tasks on the daycare-centre board had been setting fees for the children and wages for the daycare employees. The board members usually saw the staff members several times a week, when they picked up their children, yet the unhappiness represented by the union-organizing drive was surprising to all of them. When they met at an emergency board meeting that evening, they tried to evaluate what had gone wrong at Marysville.

Questions

1. If you were either a board member or a parent, how would you know that the employees taking care of your children were unhappy with their jobs?

2. What might you do if you learned about their unhappiness?

3. What might Rogers have done differently as president of the board?

4. In what ways does this case illustrate that knowledge of OB can be applied beyond your own workplace?

Reinforcing Skills

1. Talk to several managers you know and ask them what skills they think are most important in today's workplace. Ask them to specifically consider the use of teams in their workplace, and what skills their team members most need to have but are least likely to have. How might you use this information to develop greater interpersonal skills?

2. Talk to several managers you know and ask them what skills they have found to be most important in doing their jobs. Why did they find these skills most important? What advice would they give a would-be manager about skills worth developing?

2 Perception, Personality, and Emotions

Can a manager with a hard-driving personality attract employees who have the same kind of drive?

How does someone become a successful entrepreneur?[1] Some say it's a process of elimination—when people find through trial and error that there is no job that fits them, they create their own; the more trial and error, the more likely the person will become successful. Others say success comes from a lengthy process of nurturing and mentoring. Still others say it's about having the right stuff—the right personality.

Michele Romanow, co-founder of Buytopia.ca, an online marketplace for goods and services, would say that her success is from all of the above: personality, nurturing/mentoring, and experience. First, while working on her civil engineering degree at Queen's, she realized that she

Michael Nagle/Bloomberg/Getty Images

was not pursuing the life she wanted. Instead, she recognized that she wanted to become an entrepreneur, which she did in her fourth year of university, in 2008. She opened the Tea Room (a zero-waste café) on campus and operated it while earning her MBA. She has long since graduated, but the Tea Room is still run by the Queen's student government.

Second, Romanow was nurtured by her parents. When she was debating whether to leave a corporate job at Sears to launch Buytopia, her parents urged her to do so. They recognized that Romanow was meant to be a successful entrepreneur. Third, Romanow learned from the personal experience of both her business successes and failures. She did not let her failures reduce her enthusiasm for entrepreneurship, though. "I think entrepreneurship is, in many ways, luck and timing as well. I think it's really important to look at where the economy is going and where the growth and trends are. You gotta have an online strategy. You certainly have to have a website," said Romanow.

Romanow is passionate about entrepreneurship. At 32, she is the youngest dragon on *Dragons' Den*, a Canadian television program that now has spinoffs in 28 countries. The program gives her the opportunity to provide insight and support to entrepreneurs of the future.

All of our behaviour is somewhat shaped by our perceptions, personalities, emotions, and experiences. In this chapter, we consider the role that perception plays in affecting the way we see the world and the people around us. We also consider how personality characteristics affect our attitudes toward people and situations. We then consider how emotions shape many of our work-related behaviours.

OB IS FOR EVERYONE

- What causes people to have different perceptions of the same situation?
- Can people be mistaken in their perceptions?
- Have you ever misjudged a person? Do you know why?
- Can perception really affect outcomes?
- Are people born with their personalities?
- Ever wonder why the grocery clerk is always smiling?

THE BIG IDEA

Individual differences can have a large impact on how groups and organizations function.

1 Define *perception*, and explain the factors that influence it.

Perception

Perception is the process by which we organize and interpret impressions to give meaning to our environment. However, what we perceive can be substantially different from objective reality. We often disagree about what is real. For example, all employees in a firm may view it as a great place to work—favourable working conditions, interesting job assignments, good pay, excellent benefits, understanding and responsible management—but, as most of us know, it's very unusual to find universal agreement.

Perception is important to organizational behaviour (OB) because people's behaviour is based on their perception of what reality is, not on reality itself. *The world as it is perceived is the world that is behaviourally important.* In other words, our perception becomes the reality from which we act. To understand what all of us have in common in our interpretations of reality, we need to begin with the factors that influence our perceptions.

> What causes people to have different perceptions of the same situation?

Factors That Influence Perception

A number of factors shape and sometimes distort perception. These factors can reside in the *perceiver*; in the object, or *target*, being perceived; or in the *situation* in which the perception is made. Exhibit 2-1 summarizes the factors that influence perception.

The Perceiver

When you ("the perceiver") look at a target, your interpretation of what you see is heavily influenced by your personal characteristics—attitudes, motives, interests, past experiences, and expectations. In some ways, we hear what we want to hear[2] and we see what we want to see—not because it's the truth, but because it conforms to our

EXHIBIT 2-1 Factors That Influence Perception

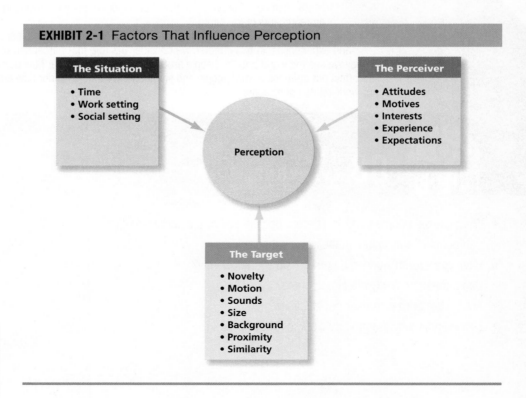

perception The process by which individuals organize and interpret their impressions in order to give meaning to their environment.

thinking. For instance, recent research indicated that supervisors perceived employees who started work earlier in the day as more conscientious and therefore as higher performers; however, supervisors who were night owls *themselves* were less likely to make that erroneous assumption.[3] Some perceptions created by attitudes like these can be counteracted by objective evaluation, but others can be insidious. Consider, for instance, observer perceptions of a recent shooting in New York. There were two eyewitnesses—one said a police officer chased and shot a fleeing man; the other said a handcuffed man lying on the ground was shot. Neither perceived the situation correctly: The man was actually attempting to attack a police officer with a hammer when he was shot by another officer.[4]

The Target

A target's characteristics also affect what we perceive. Because we don't look at targets in isolation, the relationship of a target to its background influences perception. For instance, we can perceive women, Indigenous people, Asians, or members of any other group that has clearly distinguishable characteristics as alike in other unrelated ways as well. Often, these assumptions are harmful, as when people who have criminal records are prejudged in the workplace even when it is known they were wrongly arrested.[5] Sometimes differences can work in our favour, though, such as when we are drawn to targets that are different from what we expect. For instance, in a recent study participants respected a professor wearing a T-shirt and sneakers in the classroom more than the same professor dressed traditionally. The professor stood out from the norm for the classroom setting and was therefore perceived as an individualist.[6]

The Situation

Context matters too. The time at which we see an object or event can influence attention, as can location, light, heat, or any number of situational factors. For example, at a nightclub on Saturday night, you may not notice someone "decked out." Yet that same person so attired for your Monday morning management class would certainly catch your attention. Neither the perceiver nor the target changed between Saturday night and Monday morning, but the situation changed.

People are usually not aware of the factors that influence their view of reality. In fact, people are not even that perceptive about their *own* abilities.[7] Thankfully, awareness and objective measures can reduce our perception distortions. For instance, when people are asked to ponder specific aspects of their ability, they become more realistic in their self-perceptions.[8] Let's next consider *how* we make perceptions of others.

> Can people be mistaken in their perceptions?

Perceptual Errors

Perceiving and interpreting why others do what they do takes time. As a result, we develop techniques to make this task more manageable. These techniques are frequently valuable—they allow us to make accurate perceptions rapidly and provide valid data for making predictions. Many of our perceptions of others are formed by first impressions and small cues that have little supporting evidence. This is particularly troublesome— but common—when we infer another person's morality. Research indicates we form our strongest impressions based on what we perceive about another's moral character, but our initial information about this can be sketchy and unfounded.[9] Some of the errors that distort the perception process are attribution theory, selective perception, halo effect, contrast effects, and stereotyping.

CAREER OBJECTIVES

So What If I'm a Few Minutes Late to Work?

I'm often late to work; something always comes up at the last minute. But my boss is such a jerk about it! He's threatening to install a time clock. This is so insulting—I'm in management, I'm a professional, I'm on salary, and I do the work! Please tell me how to talk some sense into him.

—Renée

Dear Renée:

This issue seems to be very frustrating to you, and we'd like to help you eliminate that dissatisfaction. Let's start by analyzing why you and your boss think differently on the issue. You and he certainly perceive the situation differently—he sees your lateness as a violation, and you see it as a natural occurrence. In many other jobs, precise timing may not be expected, valued, or needed. Perhaps your boss is trying to highlight the value he places on punctuality. Or maybe he sees your lateness as unethical behaviour that cheats your organization of your valuable work time.

According to Ann Tenbrunsel, Director of the Institute for Ethical Business Worldwide, the way we look at our decisions changes our perception of our behaviours. You view your tardiness as something that just happens, not part of a decision process. What if you looked at your tardiness as a daily ethical decision? Your organization has a start time to which you agreed as a condition of your employment, so coming in late is a deviation from the standard. There *are* actions you can take throughout your early morning that control your arrival time. So, by this model, your behaviour is unethical.

Your situation is not uncommon; we all have moral blind spots, or situations with ethical ramifications we don't see. Also, as we said earlier, other organizations may not care about your arrival time, so it's not always an ethical situation. But for situations where ethics are in play, research indicates punishment doesn't work. Reframing the decisions so we see the ethical implications does work. Try these steps to gain insight:

- *Look at the motives for your decisions during your morning routine.* Can you see where you make choices?
- *Consider your past actions.* When you think back about your early-morning decisions, do you find yourself justifying your delays? Justification signals that our decisions might be suspect.
- *Look at the facts.* How do the reasons for your past delays reflect attitudes you have unconsciously acted on?

If you can see the ethical aspect of your daily lateness, you can work to meet the expectation. Think briefly about the ethics of your morning choices when you first wake up, and you'll be much more likely to be on time.

———

Sources: C. Moore and A. E. Tenbrunsel, "'Just Think About It'? Cognitive Complexity and Moral Choice," *Organizational Behavior and Human Decision Processes* 123, no. 2 (2014), pp. 138–49; A. Tenbrunsel, Ethical Systems, www.ethical-systems.org/content/ann-tenbrunsel, accessed May 7, 2015; Review and podcast of *Blind Spots: Why We Fail to Do What's Right and What to Do about It,* May 4, 2015, http://press.princeton.edu/titles/9390.html, accessed May 7, 2015.

The opinions provided here are of the authors only. The authors are not responsible for any errors or omissions, or for the results obtained from the use of this information. In no event will the authors or their related partnerships or corporations thereof, be liable to you or anyone else for any decision made or action taken in reliance on the opinions provided here.

 Explain attribution theory, and list the three determinants of attribution.

Attribution Theory

Attribution theory tries to explain the ways we judge people differently, depending on the meaning we attribute to a given behaviour.[10] For instance, consider what you think when people smile at you. Do you think they are cooperative, exploitative, or competitive? We assign meaning to smiles and other expressions in many different ways.[11]

Basically, the theory suggests that when we observe what seems like atypical behaviour by an individual, we try to make sense of it. We consider whether the individual is responsible for the behaviour (the cause is internal), or whether something outside the individual caused the behaviour (the cause is external). *Internally* caused behaviours are those an observer believes to be under the personal behavioural control of another individual. *Externally* caused behaviours are what we imagine the situation forced the individual to do. For example, if a student is late for class, the instructor might attribute his lateness to partying into the wee hours of the morning and then oversleeping. This would be an internal attribution. But if the instructor assumes that a traffic jam occurred on the student's regular route to school, he or she is making an external attribution.

attribution theory The theory that when we observe what seems like atypical behaviour by an individual, we attempt to determine whether it is internally or externally caused.

In trying to determine whether behaviour is internally or externally caused, we rely on three rules about the behaviour: (1) distinctiveness, (2) consensus, and (3) consistency. Let's discuss each of these in turn.

Distinctiveness   **Distinctiveness** refers to whether an individual acts similarly across a variety of situations. Is the student who arrives late for class today also the one who is always goofing off in team meetings and not answering urgent emails? If the behaviour is unusual, we are likely to give it an external attribution. If it's not, we will probably judge the behaviour to be internal.

Consensus   If everyone who is faced with a similar situation responds in the same way, we can say the behaviour shows **consensus**. The tardy student's behaviour would meet this criterion if all students who took the same route to school were also late. From an attribution perspective, if consensus is high, you would probably give an external attribution to the student's tardiness. But if other students who took the same route made it to class on time, you would attribute the cause of lateness for the student in question to an internal cause.

> Have you ever misjudged a person? Do you know why?

Consistency   Finally, an observer looks for **consistency** in a person's actions. Does the person respond the same way over time? If a student is usually on time for class, being 10 minutes late will be perceived differently from the student who is late for almost every class. The more consistent the behaviour, the more we are inclined to attribute it to internal causes.

Exhibit 2-2 summarizes the key elements in attribution theory. It illustrates, for instance, how to evaluate an employee's behaviour on a new task. To do this, you might note that employee Emma generally performs at about the same level on other related tasks as she does on her current task (low distinctiveness). You see that other employees frequently perform differently—better or worse—than Emma does on that current task (low consensus). Finally, if Emma's performance on this current task is

EXHIBIT 2-2 Attribution Theory

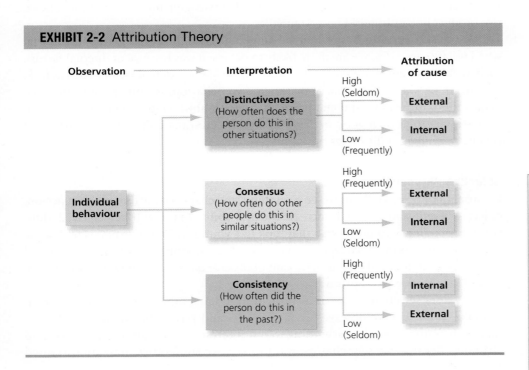

distinctiveness A behavioural rule that considers whether an individual acts similarly across a variety of situations.

consensus A behavioural rule that considers whether everyone faced with a similar situation responds in the same way.

consistency A behavioural rule that considers whether the individual has been acting in the same way over time.

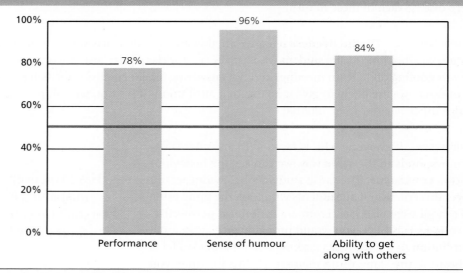

EXHIBIT 2-3 Percentage of Individuals Rating Themselves Above Average on Each Attribute

Source: Based on C. Merkle and M. Weber, *True Overconfidence—The Inability of Rational Information Processing to Account for Overconfidence* (March 2009). Available at SSRN: http://ssrn.com/abstract=1373675.

consistent over time (high consistency), you or anyone else who is judging Emma's work is likely to hold her primarily responsible for her task performance (internal attribution).

How Attributions Get Distorted Errors or biases distort attributions. When we judge the behaviour of other people, we tend to underestimate the influence of external factors and overestimate the influence of internal, or personal, factors.[12] This **fundamental attribution error** can explain why a sales manager attributes the poor performance of his or her sales agents to laziness rather than acknowledging the impact of the innovative product line introduced by a competitor.

We use **self-serving bias** when we judge ourselves, however.[13] This means that when we are successful, we are more likely to believe it was because of internal factors, such as ability or effort. When we fail, however, we blame external factors, such as luck. In general, people tend to believe that their own behaviour is more positive than the behaviour of those around them. Research suggests, however, that individuals tend to overestimate their own good behaviour, and underestimate the good behaviour of others.[14] Exhibit 2-3 illustrates this point.

Selective Perception

Because it's impossible for us to see everything, any characteristic that makes a person, object, or event stand out will increase the probability that it will be perceived; thus, you are more likely to notice cars that look like your own. It also explains why some people may be reprimanded by their manager for doing something that goes unnoticed when other employees do it. Since we cannot observe everything going on about us, we engage in **selective perception**.

How does selectivity work as a shortcut in judging other people? Since we cannot take in all that we observe, we take in bits and pieces. But we do not choose randomly; rather, we select according to our interests, background, experience, and attitudes. Because we see what we want to see, we sometimes draw unwarranted

fundamental attribution error The tendency to underestimate the influence of external factors and overestimate the influence of internal factors when making judgments about the behaviour of others.

self-serving bias The tendency for individuals to attribute their own successes to internal factors while putting the blame for failures on external factors.

selective perception People's selective interpretation of what they see based on their interests, background, experience, and attitudes.

conclusions from an ambiguous situation. Selective perception led the Law Society of British Columbia to discriminate against lawyers who suffer from a mental illness, as *Focus on Diversity* shows.

FOCUS ON DIVERSITY

Law Society's Question About Mental Health Challenged

Should employees be required to reveal that they have a mental illness? In July 2011, the BC Human Rights Tribunal ruled that the Law Society of British Columbia had discriminated against a lawyer with a mental disability.[15] The lawyer, Peter Mokua Gichuru, was awarded almost $100 000 by the tribunal.

Gichuru's problems started when he began applying for work as an articling student and had to fill out a law society admission program form with the following question: "Have you ever been treated for schizophrenia, paranoia, or a mood disorder described as a major affective illness, bipolar mood disorder, or manic depressive illness?" He answered "yes."

Gichuru had been suffering from bouts of depression for almost five years and was on antidepressants when he was faced with the law society's question. He felt that his articles were delayed because he answered truthfully about his mental health. He also felt that his difficulties in keeping his articling positions and finding others were a result of his answer to the question.

In making its determination, the tribunal found that the law society, while acting in good faith, went beyond what was necessary to determine the fitness of someone to practise law. The law society changed the question related to mental health history on the admission form as a result of Gichuru's appeal. It now reads:

Based upon your personal history, your current circumstances, or any professional opinion or advice you have received, do you have any existing condition that is reasonably likely to impair your ability to function as a lawyer or articled student? If the answer is "yes" to the question above, please provide a general description of the impairment.

Those who answer "yes" to this new question are followed on a case-by-case basis, but the information is kept confidential and is not disclosed to potential employers. While Gichuru still has some concerns about the use of the information, he testified that it "is a dramatic improvement . . . and that on its face it does not discriminate between so-called physical and mental illnesses." ....

Halo Effect

When we draw a general impression of an individual on the basis of a single characteristic, such as intelligence, likeability, or appearance, a **halo effect** operates.[16] The halo effect is easy to demonstrate. If you knew someone was, say, gregarious, what else would you infer? You probably would not say the person was introverted, right? You might assume the person was loud, happy, or quick-witted, when in fact gregarious does not include those other attributes. As managers, we need to be careful not to draw inferences from small clues.

Contrast Effects

There is an old saying among entertainers: "Never follow an act that has children or animals in it." Why? Audiences love children and animals so much that you will look bad in comparison.

This example demonstrates how **contrast effects** can distort perceptions. We don't evaluate a person in isolation. Our reaction is influenced by other people we have recently encountered.

halo effect Drawing a general impression of an individual on the basis of a single characteristic.

contrast effects The concept that our reaction to one person is often influenced by other people we have recently encountered.

Sean Kilpatrick/The Canadian Press

Ottawa-based A Tribe Called Red is a Canadian experimental electronic group with three musicians who come from Ontario Indigenous reserves. The trio has been meeting with Indigenous groups in various parts of the world to explore Indigenous music. They are welcoming those who want more from music than colonialism to help build Halluci Nation, a collective of artists and activists.

In a series of job interviews, for instance, a candidate is likely to receive a more favourable evaluation if preceded by mediocre applicants, and a less favourable evaluation if preceded by strong applicants. Thus, interviewers can make distortions in any given candidate's evaluation as a result of her or his place in the interview schedule.

Stereotyping

When we judge someone on the basis of our perception of the group to which he or she belongs, we are using the shortcut called **stereotyping**.

We rely on generalizations every day because they help us make decisions quickly. They are a means of simplifying a complex world. It's less difficult to deal with an unmanageable number of stimuli if we use **heuristics** (judgment shortcuts in decision making) or stereotypes. For example, it does make sense to assume that Tre, the new employee from accounting, is going to know something about budgeting or that Allie from finance will be able to help you figure out a forecasting problem. Stereotypes can be so deeply ingrained and powerful that they influence life-and-death decisions. One study showed that, controlling for a wide array of factors (such as aggravating or mitigating circumstances), the degree to which black defendants in murder trials looked "stereotypically black" essentially doubled their odds of receiving a death sentence if convicted.[17] Another study found that students tended to assign higher scores for leadership potential and effective leadership to whites than to minorities, supporting the stereotype of whites as better leaders.[18]

One of the problems of stereotypes is that they *are* widespread and often useful generalizations, despite the fact that they may not contain a shred of truth when applied to a particular person or situation. So we have to check ourselves to make sure we are not unfairly or inaccurately applying a stereotype in our evaluations and decisions. Stereotypes are an example of the warning, "The more useful, the more danger from misuse."

It should be obvious by now that our perceptions, many of which are near-instantaneous and without conscious deliberation, colour our outlook. Sometimes they have little impact on anyone, but more often our perceptions greatly influence our decisions.

stereotyping Judging someone on the basis of one's perception of the group to which that person belongs.

heuristics Judgment shortcuts in decision making.

Jason D'Souza/CBC Radio-Canada

Muslim women in Canada often experience discrimination in being hired, or how their co-workers treat them, when they wear a hijab. In some cases, co-workers of Muslim women have been surprised when they returned to work following maternity leave. The co-workers assumed that Muslim women would be expected by their husbands to stay at home to raise children rather than work.

The first step toward increasing the effectiveness of organizational decision making is to understand the perception process on an individualized level, discussed next.

RESEARCH FINDINGS: Stereotyping

A variety of recent studies show that even today we believe Germans are better workers, Italians and African Americans are more loyal, Jews and Chinese are more intelligent, and Japanese and English are more courteous.[19] What is surprising is that positive stereotypes are not always positive.

Men are commonly believed to have stronger math abilities than women. One study shows that when this stereotype is activated before men take a math test, their performance on the test actually goes down. Another study found that the belief that white men are better at science and math than women or visible minorities caused white men to leave science, technology, engineering, and math majors. Finally, a study used basketball to illustrate the complexity of stereotypes. Researchers provided evidence to one group of undergraduates that whites were better free-throw shooters than blacks. Another group was provided evidence that blacks were better free-throw shooters than whites. A third group was given no stereotypical information. The undergraduates in all three groups then shot free throws while observers watched. The people who performed the worst were those in the negative stereotype condition (black undergraduates who were told whites were better and white undergraduates who were told blacks were better). However, the positive stereotype group (black undergraduates who were told blacks were better and white undergraduates who were told whites were better) also did not perform well. The best performance was turned in by those in the no stereotypical information group. In short, we are more likely to "choke" when we identify with positive stereotypes because they induce pressure to perform at the stereotypical level.

Why Do Perception and Judgment Matter?

People in organizations are always judging one another. Managers must appraise their employees' performances. We evaluate how much effort our co-workers are putting into their jobs. When a new person joins a work team, the other members immediately "size her up." Individuals even make judgments about people's virtues based on whether they exercise, as a study by McMaster University professor Kathleen Martin Ginis showed.[20] In many cases, judgments have important consequences for the organization. A recent study found that in organizations that did not seem to value innovation, employees who wanted to see change were often afraid to speak out due to fear of negative perceptions from co-workers who valued the status quo.[21] Another recent study found that positive employee perceptions of an organization have a positive impact on retention, customer loyalty, and financial outcomes.[22] A study noted that individuals who misperceive how well they have done on a task (positively or negatively) tend to prepare less and to perform poorly in subsequent tasks.[23]

> Can perception really affect outcomes?

Let's briefly look at a few of the most obvious applications of judgment shortcuts in the workplace: employment interviews, performance expectations, and performance evaluations.

Employment Interviews

It's fair to say that few people are hired without undergoing an interview. But interviewers make perceptual judgments that are often inaccurate[24] and draw early impressions that quickly become entrenched. Research shows we form impressions of others within a tenth of a second based on our first glance.[25] Most interviewers' decisions change very little after the first four or five minutes of an interview. As a result, information that comes out early in the interview carries greater weight than information that comes out later, and a "good applicant" is probably characterized more by the absence of unfavourable characteristics than by the presence of favourable ones. Our individual intuition about a job candidate is not reliable in predicting job performance, so collecting input from multiple independent evaluators can be predictive.[26]

Performance Expectations

People attempt to validate their perceptions of reality even when they are faulty.[27] The terms **self-fulfilling prophecy** and *Pygmalion effect* describe how an individual's behaviour is determined by others' expectations. If a manager expects big things from her people, they are not likely to let her down. Similarly, if she expects only minimal performance, they will likely meet those low expectations. Expectations become reality. The self-fulfilling prophecy has been found to affect the performance of students, soldiers, and even accountants.[28]

Performance Evaluations

Performance evaluations very much depend on the perceptual process.[29] An employee's future is closely tied to the appraisal—promotion, pay raises, and continuation of employment are among the most obvious outcomes. Although the appraisal can be objective (for example, a salesperson is appraised on how many dollars of sales are generated in his territory), many jobs are evaluated subjectively. Subjective evaluations, although often necessary, are problematic because all the errors we have discussed thus far—selective perception, contrast effects, halo effect, and so on—affect them. Ironically, sometimes performance ratings say as much about the evaluator as they do about the employee!

As you can see, perception plays a large role in how people are evaluated. Personality, which we review next, is another major factor affecting how people relate to and evaluate one another in the workplace.

self-fulfilling prophecy A concept that proposes a person will behave in ways consistent with how he or she is perceived by others.

Personality

3 Describe personality, the way it is measured, and the factors that shape it.

> By her own acknowledgment, Michele Romanow is a risk taker.[30] She said that Buytopia was late to launch a daily deal site. "We were a year behind our major competitors. We had competitors that had already raised $60 million." That did not stop her from trying though. Romanow's philosophy about launching businesses is that "You can't be scared when it isn't perfect. You've just got to launch it. You'll figure it out."
>
> One of Romanow's strong personality traits is that she is a high self-monitor. She thinks that a dream job is about having control: "Control over the types of problems you take on, and your approach to those problems. Control over the culture you build." In other words, Romanow is a proactive person. She does not wait for things to happen, she makes them happen.
>
> While working at Buytopia, Romanow and her partners developed a mobile couponing app called SnapSaves, that allowed consumers to get rebates from manufacturers by emailing their receipts. Romanow realized the company needed investors in order to grow. She and her partners ended up selling the app to Groupon, and it was renamed Groupon Snap. As part of the acquisition, she promised that she would work with Groupon for a year and a half at its headquarters in the United States. As soon as that time was up, she moved back to Canada, to work on her next start-up.
>
> Romanow can take these risks because she is open to experiences, one of the Big Five personality traits that we discuss below. How do one's personality attributes influence OB?

Understanding the impact of individual personalities on OB is important. Why are some people quiet and passive, while others are loud and aggressive? Are certain personality types better adapted to certain jobs? Before we can answer these questions, we need to address a more basic one: What is personality?

What Is Personality?

When we speak of someone's personality, we use many adjectives to describe how they act and seem to think; in fa t, participants in a recent study used 624 distinct adjectives to describe people they knew.[31] As organizational behaviourists, however, we organize personality characteristics by overall traits, describing the growth and development of a person's personality.

Defining Personality

For our purposes, we define **personality** as the sum of the ways in which an individual reacts to and interacts with others. We most often describe personality in terms of measurable traits that a person exhibits.

Measuring Personality

Personality assessments have been increasingly used in diverse organizational settings. In fact, many large companies use them,[32] including Xerox, McDonald's, and Lowe's,[33] and schools such as DePaul University have begun to use personality assessments in their admissions process.[34] A 2017 study by professors from Western University, University of Guelph, University of PEI, and University of York, along with colleagues from elsewhere, suggested that based on their research, medical schools should start using personality tests for admission decisions. Personality seemed to predict clinical performance more accurately that either grades or medical exam scores.[35]

The most common means of measuring personality is through self-report surveys, with which individuals evaluate themselves on a series of factors, such as "I worry a lot about the future." In general, when people know that their personality scores are going

personality The sum total of ways in which an individual reacts to and interacts with others.

to be used for hiring decisions, they rate themselves as about half a standard deviation more conscientious and emotionally stable than if they are taking the test just to learn more about themselves.[36] Another problem is accuracy: A candidate who is in a bad mood when taking the survey may have inaccurate scores.

Observer-rating surveys provide an independent assessment of personality. Here, a co-worker or another observer does the rating. Although the results of self-reports and observer-rating surveys are strongly correlated, research suggests that observer ratings predict job success better than self-ratings alone.[37] However, each can tell us something unique about an individual's behaviour in the workplace. A combination of self-reports and observer-reports predicts performance better than any one type of information. The implication is clear: Use both observer ratings and self-report ratings of personality when making important employment decisions.

Personality Determinants

An early debate in personality research centred on whether an individual's personality is predetermined at birth or is the result of the individual's environment. Clearly, there is no simple answer. Personality appears to be a result of both; however, research tends to support the importance of heredity over environment.

Heredity refers to those factors that were determined at conception. Physical stature, facial attractiveness, gender, temperament, muscle composition and reflexes, energy level, and biological rhythms are either completely or substantially influenced by your biological parents' biological, physiological, and inherent psychological makeup. The heredity approach argues that the ultimate explanation of an individual's personality is a person's genes.

> Are people born with their personalities?

This is not to suggest that personality never changes. People's scores on dependability tend to increase over time, as when young adults start families and establish careers. However, strong individual differences in dependability remain; everyone tends to change by about the same amount, so their rank order stays roughly the same. Furthermore, personality is more changeable in adolescence and more stable among adults.[38]

Personality Traits

The early work on personality tried to identify and label enduring characteristics that describe an individual's behaviour, including shy, aggressive, submissive, lazy, ambitious, loyal, and timid. Those characteristics, when they are exhibited in a large number of situations and are relatively enduring, we call **personality traits**.[39] The more consistent the characteristic and the more frequently it occurs in diverse situations, the more important that trait is in describing the individual.

Throughout history, people have sought to understand what makes individuals behave in myriad ways. Many of our behaviours stem from our personalities, so understanding the components of personality helps us predict behaviour. Important theoretical frameworks and assessment tools help us categorize and study the dimensions of personality.

The most widely used and best known personality frameworks are the Myers-Briggs Type Indicator (MBTI) and the Big Five Personality Model. Both describe a person's total personality through exploration of the facets of personality. Other frameworks, such as the Dark Triad, explain certain aspects, but not the total, of an individual's personality. We discuss each below, but let's begin with the dominant frameworks.

personality traits Enduring characteristics that describe an individual's behaviour.

The Myers-Briggs Type Indicator

The **Myers-Briggs Type Indicator (MBTI)** is the most widely used personality-assessment instrument in the world.[40] It's a 100-question personality test that asks people how they usually feel or act in particular situations. On the basis of their answers, individuals are classified as extraverted or introverted (E or I), sensing or intuitive (S or N), thinking or feeling (T or F), and judging or perceiving (J or P). These terms are defined as follows:

 Describe the Myers-Briggs Type Indicator personality framework and its strengths and weaknesses.

- *Extraverted/introverted.*   Extraverted individuals are outgoing, sociable, and assertive. Introverts are quiet and shy. E/I measures where we direct our energy when dealing with people and things.

- *Sensing/intuitive.*   Sensing types are practical and prefer routine and order. They focus on details. Intuitives rely on unconscious processes and look at the "big picture." This dimension looks at how we process information.

- *Thinking/feeling.*   Thinking types use reason and logic to handle problems. Feeling types rely on their personal values and emotions.

- *Judging/perceiving.*   Judging types want control and prefer their world to be ordered and structured. Perceiving types are flexible and spontaneous.

These classifications together describe 16 personality types by identifying one trait from each of the four pairs. To illustrate, let's look at three examples:

- *INTJs are visionaries.*   They usually have original minds and great drive. They are skeptical, critical, independent, determined, and often stubborn.

- *ESTJs are organizers.*   They are realistic, logical, analytical, decisive, and have a natural head for business or mechanics. They like to organize and run activities.

- *ENTPs are conceptualizers.*   They are innovative, individualistic, versatile, and attracted to entrepreneurial ideas. They tend to be resourceful in solving challenging problems, but may neglect routine assignments.

The MBTI is used in a variety of organizational settings. Evidence is mixed as to whether the MBTI is a valid measure of personality; however, much of the evidence is against it.[41]

One problem with the MBTI is that the model forces a person into either one type or another (that is, you are either introverted or extraverted). There is no in-between. Another problem is with the reliability of the measure: When people retake the assessment, they often receive different results. An additional problem is in the difficulty of interpretation. There are levels of importance for each of the MBTI facets, and separate meanings for certain combinations of facets, all of which require trained interpretation that can leave room for error. Finally, results from the MBTI tend to be unrelated to job performance. The MBTI can thus be a valuable tool for increasing self-awareness and providing career guidance. But because results tend to be unrelated to job performance, managers should consider using the Big Five Personality Model, discussed next, as the personality selection test for job candidates.

5 Identify the key traits in the Big Five Personality Model.

The Big Five Personality Model

The MBTI may lack valid supporting evidence, but an impressive body of research supports the **Big Five Personality Model**. The model proposes that five basic personality dimensions underlie all others and encompass most of the significant variation in human personality.[42] Test scores of these traits do a very good job of

Myers-Briggs Type Indicator (MBTI) A personality test that taps four characteristics and classifies people into 1 of 16 personality types.

Big Five Personality Model A personality-assessment model that taps five basic dimensions.

predicting how people behave in a variety of real-life situations,[43] and remain relatively stable for an individual over time, with some daily variations.[44] The Big Five personality traits are:

- *Conscientiousness.* The **conscientiousness** dimension is a measure of reliability. A highly conscientious person is responsible, organized, dependable, and persistent. Those who score low on this dimension are easily distracted, disorganized, and unreliable.

- *Emotional stability.* The **emotional stability** dimension taps a person's ability to withstand stress. People with emotional stability tend to be calm, self-confident, and secure. High scorers are more likely to be positive and optimistic and experience fewer negative emotions; they are generally happier than low scorers. Emotional stability is sometimes discussed as its converse, neuroticism. Low scorers (those with high neuroticism) are hypervigilant and vulnerable to the physical and psychological effects of stress. Those with high neuroticism tend to be nervous, anxious, depressed, and insecure.

- *Extraversion.* The **extraversion** dimension captures our comfort level with relationships. Extraverts tend to be gregarious, assertive, and sociable. They are generally happier and are often ambitious.[45] They experience more positive emotions than do introverts, and they more freely express these feelings. On the other hand, introverts (low extraversion) tend to be more thoughtful, reserved, timid, and quiet. Read more about introverts and extraverts in *Case Incident—The Power of Quiet* on pages 75–76.

- *Openness to experience.* The **openness to experience** dimension addresses the range of interests and fascination with novelty. Open people are creative, curious, and artistically sensitive. Those at the low end of the category are conventional and find comfort in the familiar.

- *Agreeableness.* The **agreeableness** dimension refers to an individual's propensity to defer to others. Agreeable people are cooperative, warm, and trusting. You might expect agreeable people to be happier than disagreeable people. They are, but only slightly. When people choose organizational team members, agreeable individuals are usually their first choice. In contrast, people who score low on agreeableness are cold and antagonistic.

Researchers at the University of Toronto have recently created a "fake proof" personality test to measure the Big Five personality traits.[46] Professor Jordan Peterson, one of the researchers, noted that it is common for people to try to "make themselves look better than they actually are on these questionnaires. . . . This sort of faking can distort the predictive validity of these tests, with significant negative economic consequences. We wanted to develop a measure that could predict real-world performance even in the absence of completely honest responding."[47]

Exhibit 2-4 shows the characteristics for the high and low dimensions of each Big Five personality trait.

6 Demonstrate how the Big Five personality traits predict behaviour at work.

conscientiousness A personality factor that describes the degree to which a person is responsible, dependable, persistent, and achievement-oriented.

emotional stability A personality dimension that characterizes someone as calm, self-confident, and secure (positive) vs. nervous, depressed, and insecure (negative).

extraversion A personality factor that describes the degree to which a person is sociable, talkative, and assertive.

openness to experience A personality factor that describes the degree to which a person is imaginative, artistically sensitive, and curious.

agreeableness A personality factor that describes the degree to which a person is good-natured, cooperative, and trusting.

[[◉]] **RESEARCH FINDINGS:** The Big Five

There are many relationships between the Big Five personality dimensions and job performance,[48] and we are learning more about them every day. Let's explore one trait at a time, beginning with the strongest predictor of job performance—conscientiousness.

Conscientiousness As researchers recently stated, "Personal attributes related to conscientiousness and agreeableness are important for success across many jobs,

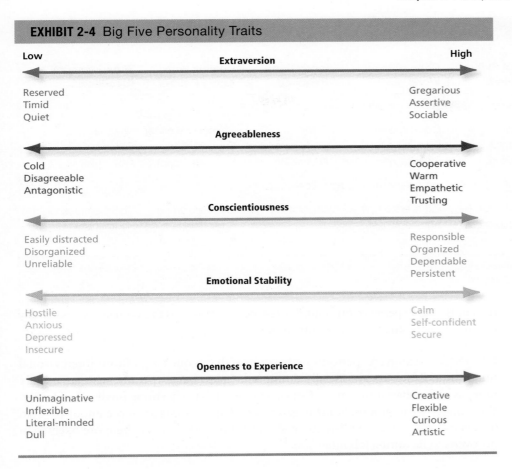

EXHIBIT 2-4 Big Five Personality Traits

spanning across low to high levels of job complexity, training, and experience."[49] Employees who are more conscientious provide better service.[50] Employees who score higher in conscientiousness develop higher levels of job knowledge, probably because highly conscientious people learn more (conscientiousness may be related to grade point average).[51] Higher levels of job knowledge then contribute to higher levels of job performance.[52] Conscientious people are also more able to maintain their job performance when faced with abusive supervision, according to a recent study in India.[53]

Like any trait, conscientiousness has pitfalls. Highly conscientious individuals can prioritize work over family, resulting in more conflict between their work and family roles (termed *work–family conflict*).[54] They may also become too focused on their own work to help others in the organization,[55] and they don't adapt well to changing contexts. Furthermore, conscientious people may have trouble learning complex skills early in the training process because their focus is on performing well rather than on learning. Finally, they are often less creative, especially artistically.[56]

The Big Five have also been found to be related to characteristics needed for specific jobs. This is illustrated in Exhibit 2-5.

Although conscientiousness is the trait most consistently related to job performance, the other Big Five personality traits are also related to aspects of performance and have other implications for work and for life. Exhibit 2-6 summarizes the discussion.

Emotional Stability Of the Big Five personality traits, emotional stability is most strongly related to life satisfaction, job satisfaction, and low stress levels. People with high emotional stability can adapt to unexpected or changing demands in the workplace.[57] At the other end of the spectrum, neurotic individuals, who may be unable to cope with these

EXHIBIT 2-5 Jobs in Which Certain Big Five Personality Traits Are More Relevant

Detail Orientation Required	Social Skills Required	Competitive Work	Innovation Required	Dealing with Angry People	Time Pressure (Deadlines)
Jobs scoring high (the traits listed below should predict behaviour in these jobs)					
Air traffic controller	Clergy	Coach/scout	Actor	Correctional officer	News analyst
Accountant	Therapist	Financial manager	Systems analyst	Telemarketer	Editor
Legal secretary	Concierge	Sales representative	Advertising writer	Flight attendant	Airline pilot
Jobs that score high make these traits more relevant to predicting behaviour					
Conscientiousness (+)	Extraversion (+) Agreeableness (+)	Extraversion (+) Agreeableness (−)	Openness (+)	Extraversion (+) Agreeableness (+) Neuroticism (−)	Conscientiousness (+) Neuroticism (−)

Note: A plus (+) sign means individuals who score high on this trait should do better in this job. A minus (−) sign means individuals who score low on this trait should do better in this job.

demands, may experience burnout.[58] These people also tend to experience work–family conflict, which can affect work outcomes.[59]

Extraversion Extraverts perform better in jobs that require significant interpersonal interaction. Extraverts are socially dominant, "take charge" people, who are usually more assertive than introverts.[60] Extraversion is a relatively strong predictor of leadership emergence in groups. Some negatives are that extraverts are more impulsive than introverts; they are more likely to be absent from work and may be more likely than introverts to lie during job interviews.[61]

EXHIBIT 2-6 How the Big Five Personality Traits Influence OB

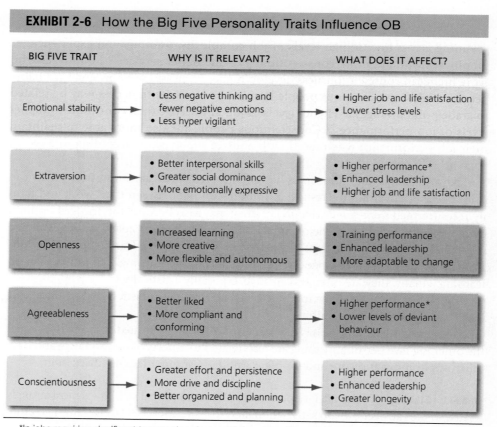

*In jobs requiring significant teamwork or frequent interpersonal interactions.

Captured Value

Courtesy of Shopify

It's unusual for one person to be the CEO of a company and yet another person be the public face of the organization. But that is how it works for Ottawa-based Shopify's CEO Tobias Lütke and COO Harley Finkelstein (shown here). This arrangement works for the two because Lütke is an introvert, while Finkelstein is an extravert. Finkelstein says the two men play to their individual strengths, which makes for a stronger company.

Openness to Experience   Open people are more likely to be effective leaders—and more comfortable with ambiguity and change. They cope better with organizational change and are more adaptable. While openness is not related to initial performance on a job, individuals higher in openness are less susceptible to a decline in performance over a longer time period.[62] Open people also experience less work–family conflict.[63]

Agreeableness   Agreeable individuals are better liked than disagreeable people, which explains why they tend to do better in interpersonally oriented jobs such as customer service. They are also more compliant and rule abiding, less likely to get into accidents, and more satisfied in their jobs. They also contribute to organizational performance by engaging in organizational citizenship behaviour (OCB).[64] Disagreeable people, on the other hand, are more likely to engage in counterproductive work behaviours (also referred to as CWBs), as are people low in conscientiousness.[65] Low agreeableness also predicts involvement in work accidents.[66] Lastly, agreeableness is associated with lower levels of career success (especially earnings), perhaps because highly agreeable people consider themselves less marketable and are less willing to assert themselves.[67]

Research indicates the Big Five traits have the most verifiable links to important organizational outcomes, but they are not the only traits a person exhibits, nor the only ones with OB implications. Let's discuss some other traits, known collectively as the Dark Triad.

The Dark Triad

With the exception of neuroticism, the Big Five personality traits are what we call socially desirable, meaning that we would be glad to score high on them. Researchers have found three other socially *undesirable* traits, which we all have in varying degrees, are also relevant to organizational behaviour: Machiavellianism, narcissism, and psychopathy. Owing to their negative nature, researchers have labelled these three traits the **Dark Triad**—though they do not always occur together.[68] See *Case Incident—Tall Poppy Syndrome* on page 76 for a discussion of how negative traits can be manifested in the workplace.

The Dark Triad may sound sinister, but these traits are not clinical pathologies hindering everyday functioning. They might be expressed particularly strongly when an individual is under stress and unable to moderate any inappropriate responses. Sustained high levels of dark personality traits can cause individuals to derail their careers and personal lives.[69]

Machiavellianism

Hao is a young bank manager in Shanghai. He has received three promotions in the past four years and makes no apologies for the aggressive tactics he has used. "My name means clever, and that's what I am—I do whatever I have to do to get ahead," he says. Hao would be termed Machiavellian.

The personality characteristic of **Machiavellianism** (often abbreviated to *Mach*) is named after Niccolò Machiavelli, who wrote in the sixteenth century on how to gain and use power. An individual high in Machiavellianism is pragmatic, maintains emotional distance, and believes that ends can justify means. "If it works, use it" is consistent with a high-Mach perspective. High Machs manipulate more, win more, are persuaded less by others but persuade others more than do low Machs.[70] They are more likely to act aggressively and engage in other counterproductive work behaviours as well. Surprisingly, Machiavellianism does not significantly predict overall job performance.[71] High-Mach employees, by manipulating others to their advantage, win in the short term at a job, but they lose those gains in the long term because they are not well-liked.

Machiavellianism tendencies may have ethical implications. One study showed that high-Mach job seekers were not positively affected by knowing that a potential employer engaged in a high level of corporate social responsibility (CSR),[72] suggesting that high-Mach people may care less about sustainability issues. Another 2012 study found that Machs' ethical leadership behaviours were less likely to translate into followers' work engagement because followers "see through" these behaviours and realize it is a case of surface acting.[73]

Narcissism

Sabrina likes to be the centre of attention. She often looks at herself in the mirror, has extravagant dreams about her future, and considers herself a person of many talents. Sabrina is a narcissist. The trait is named for the Greek myth of Narcissus, a youth so vain and proud he fell in love with his own image. In psychology, **narcissism** describes a person who has a grandiose sense of self-importance, requires excessive admiration, and is arrogant. Narcissists often have fantasies of grand success, a tendency to exploit situations and people, a sense of entitlement, and a lack of empathy.[74] However, narcissists can be hypersensitive and fragile people.[75] They also may experience more anger.[76]

While narcissism seems to have little relationship to job effectiveness or OCB,[77] it is one of the largest predictors of increased counterproductive work behaviour in individualistic cultures—but not in collectivist cultures that discourage self-promotion.[78] Narcissists commonly think they are overqualified for their positions.[79] When they

Dark Triad A group of negative personality traits consisting of Machiavellianism, narcissism, and psychopathy.

Machiavellianism The degree to which an individual is pragmatic, maintains emotional distance, and believes that ends can justify means.

narcissism The tendency to be arrogant, have a grandiose sense of self-importance, require excessive admiration, and have a sense of entitlement.

receive feedback about their performance, they often tune out information that conflicts with their positive self-perception, but they will work harder if rewards are offered.[80] A recent study found that the easiest way to identify a narcissist is to ask them. The researchers used the following question, with the note, to ask people whether they were narcissists:

> To what extent do you agree with this statement: "I am a narcissist." (Note: The word "narcissist" means egotistical, self-focused, and vain.) Participants rated themselves on a scale of 1 (not very true of me) to 7 (very true of me).

One of the study's authors noted that people who respond positively probably are more narcissistic than those who do not. "People who are narcissists are almost proud of the fact," said Brad Bushman.[81]

On the bright side, narcissists may be more charismatic than others.[82] They also might be found in business more often than in other fields (see OB Poll). They are more likely to be chosen for leadership positions, and medium ratings of narcissism (neither extremely high nor extremely low) are positively correlated with leadership effectiveness.[83] Some evidence suggests that narcissists are more adaptable and make better business decisions than others when the issue is complex.[84] Furthermore, a study of Norwegian bank employees found those scoring high on narcissism enjoyed their work more.[85]

Special attention has been paid to narcissistic CEOs who make more acquisitions, pay higher premiums for those acquisitions, respond less clearly to objective measures of performance, and respond to media praise by making even more acquisitions.[86] Research using data compiled over 100 years has shown that narcissistic CEOs of baseball organizations generate higher levels of manager turnover, although members of external organizations see them as more influential.[87]

Narcissism and its effects are not confined to CEOs or celebrities. Like the effects of Machiavellianism, those of narcissism vary by context, but are evident in all areas of life.

Does business school reinforce narcissism in the classroom? The results of a study that compared the level of narcissism in Millennial business and psychology students appear in Exhibit 2-7.

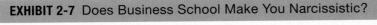

EXHIBIT 2-7 Does Business School Make You Narcissistic?

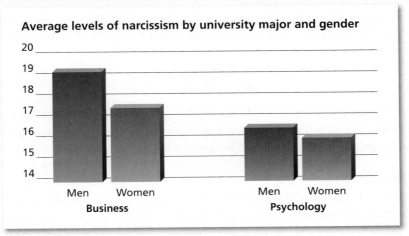

Average levels of narcissism by university major and gender

Source: Based on J. W. Westerman, J. Z. Bergman, S. M. Bergman, and J. P. Daly, "Are Universities Creating Millennial Narcissistic Employees? An Empirical Examination of Narcissism in Business Students and Its Implications," *Journal of Management Education* 36 (2012), pp. 5–32.

Psychopathy

Psychopathy is part of the Dark Triad, but in OB, it does not connote clinical mental illness. In the OB context, **psychopathy** is defined as a lack of concern for others and a lack of guilt or remorse when actions cause harm.[88] Measures of psychopathy attempt to assess the motivation to comply with social norms, impulsivity, willingness to use deceit to obtain desired ends, and disregard, that is, lack of empathetic concern, for others.

The literature is not consistent about whether psychopathy is important to work behaviour. One review found little correlation between measures of psychopathy and job performance or counterproductive work behaviours.[89] Another study found that antisocial personality, which is closely related to psychopathy, was positively related to advancement in the organization but unrelated to other aspects of career success and effectiveness.[90] Still other recent research suggests that psychopathy is related to the use of hard influence tactics (threats, manipulation) and bullying work behaviour (physical or verbal threatening).[91] The cunning displayed by people who score high on psychopathy may thus help them gain power in an organization but keep them from using that power toward healthy ends for themselves or their organizations.

Other Traits

The Dark Triad is a helpful framework for studying the three dominant dark-side traits in current personality research, and researchers are exploring other traits as well. One emerging framework incorporates five additional aberrant compound traits based on the Big Five. First, *antisocial* people are indifferent and callous toward others. They use their extraversion to charm people, but they may be prone to violent counterproductive work behaviours and risky decision making. Second, *borderline* people have low self-esteem and high uncertainty. They are unpredictable in their interactions at work, are inefficient, and may have low job satisfaction. Their low self-esteem can lead to clinical depression.[92] Third, *schizotypal* individuals are eccentric and disorganized. In the workplace, they can be highly creative, although they are susceptible to work stress. Fourth, *obsessive-compulsive* people are perfectionists and can be stubborn, yet they attend to details, carry a strong work ethic, and may be motivated by achievement. Fifth, *avoidant* individuals feel inadequate and hate criticism. They can function only in environments requiring little interaction.[93]

Personality traits have both positive and negative aspects. The degree of each trait—the Big Five, the Dark Triad, and others—in a person, and the combination of traits, matter a great deal to organizational outcomes. It would be easy to make quick management decisions based on our observations, but it is important to keep discussions on personality in perspective and to consider other theories.

Other Personality Attributes That Influence OB

As we've discussed, studies of traits have much to offer to the field of OB. Now we will look at other attributes that are powerful predictors of behaviour in organizations: core self-evaluation, self-monitoring, and proactive personality.

Core Self-Evaluation

Core self-evaluations (CSEs) are bottom-line conclusions individuals have about their capabilities, competence, and worth as a person. People who have positive CSEs like themselves and see themselves as effective, capable, and in control of their environment. Those with negative CSEs tend to dislike themselves, question their capabilities, and view themselves as powerless over their environment.[94]

People with positive CSEs perform better than others because they set more ambitious goals, are more committed to their goals, and persist longer at attempting to

psychopathy The tendency for a lack of concern for others and a lack of guilt or remorse when one's actions cause harm.

core self-evaluation Bottom-line conclusions individuals have about their capabilities, competence, and worth as a person.

Donato Sardella/WireImage/Getty Images

Blake Mycoskie, founder of TOMS Shoes, is confident, capable, and effective. His high core self-evaluations enabled him to realize his dream of a company that uses profits to give shoes to children in need.

reach these goals. People who have high CSEs provide better customer service, are more popular co-workers, and may have careers that begin on a better footing and ascend more rapidly over time.[95] They perform especially well if they feel their work provides meaning and is helpful to others.[96] Therefore, people with high CSEs may thrive in organizations with a high level of CSR.

Self-Monitoring

Zoe is always in trouble at work. Although she is competent, hard-working, and pro-ductive, she receives average ratings in performance reviews, and seems to have made a career out of irritating her bosses. Zoe's problem is that she is politically inept and unable to adjust her behaviour to fit changing situations. As she said, "I'm true to myself. I don't remake myself to please others." Zoe is a low self-monitor.

Self-monitoring refers to an individual's ability to adjust his or her behaviour to external, situational factors.[97] High self-monitors show considerable adaptability in adjusting their behaviour to external situational factors. They are highly sensitive to external cues and can behave differently in varying situations, sometimes presenting striking contradictions between their public personae and their private selves. Low self-monitors like Zoe cannot disguise themselves in the same way. They tend to display their true dispositions and attitudes in every situation. High behavioural consistency exists between who they are and what they do.

Research suggests that high self-monitors tend to pay closer attention to the behav-iour of others and are more capable of conforming than are low self-monitors.[98] High self-monitor employees show less commitment to their organizations, but receive better performance ratings and are more likely to emerge as leaders.[99] High self-monitoring managers tend to be more mobile in their careers and receive more promotions (both internal and cross-organizational) and are more likely to occupy central positions in an organization.[100]

According to research, we can accurately judge others' personalities a few seconds after meeting them, as *Focus on Research* shows.

self-monitoring A personality trait that measures an individual's ability to adjust behaviour to external, situational factors.

FOCUS ON RESEARCH
First Impressions Count

How accurate are first impressions of people's personalities? Research indicates that individuals can accurately appraise others' personalities only a few seconds after first meeting them, or sometimes even from a photo.[101] This "zero acquaintance" approach[102] shows that regardless of the way in which people first meet someone, whether in person or online, their first judgments about the other's personality have validity. In one study, for example, individuals were asked to introduce themselves, on average, in 7.4 seconds. Observers' ratings of those individuals' extraversion were significantly correlated with the individuals' self-reported extraversion. Other research suggests personalities can be surmised from online profiles at zero acquaintance as well.[103] One study even found that participants were able to determine the personality traits of individuals at the ends of the trait spectrum from viewing only photos.

Some traits, such as extraversion, are easier to perceive than others upon initial acquaintance, but less obvious traits like self-esteem are also often judged fairly accurately by others. Even being forced to make intuitive, quick judgments rather than deliberate evaluations does not seem to undermine the accuracy of the appraisals.

Situations make a difference in the accuracy of the judgments for some personality traits. For example, although neuroticism is perhaps the most difficult trait to detect accurately, a recent study found neuroticism could be judged much more accurately when the situation made the individual react nervously. This makes sense when you consider that some situations activate or draw out a trait much more readily than others. Almost everybody looks calm when they are about to fall asleep!

The moderate accuracy of "thin slices" helps explain the moderate validity of employment interviews. Specifically, research shows that interviewers make up their minds about candidates within two minutes of first meeting them. While this is hardly an ideal way to make important employment decisions, the research on personality shows that these judgments do have some level of validity. It is important to keep in mind, however, that though we can ascertain people's personalities quickly, we should still keep an open mind and suspend judgment. There is always more to people than first meets the eye.

Proactive Personality

Did you ever notice that some people actively take the initiative to improve their current circumstances or create new ones? These people have a **proactive personality**.[104] People with a proactive personality identify opportunities, show initiative, take action, and persevere until meaningful change occurs compared to others who generally react to situations. Proactives have many behaviours that organizations desire. They have higher levels of job performance[105] and do not need much oversight.[106] They are receptive to changes in job demands and thrive when they can informally tailor their jobs to their strengths. Proactive individuals often achieve career success.[107]

Proactive personality may be important for work teams. One study of 95 R & D teams in 33 Chinese companies revealed that teams with high-average levels of proactive personality were more innovative.[108] Proactive individuals are also more likely to exchange information with others in a team, which builds trust relationships.[109] Like other traits, proactive personality is affected by the context. One study of bank branch teams in China found that if a team's leader was not proactive, the benefits of the team's proactivity became dormant or, worse, was suppressed by the leader.[110] In terms of pitfalls, one study of 231 Flemish unemployed individuals found that proactive individuals abandoned their job searches sooner. It may be that proactivity includes stepping back in the face of failure.[111]

proactive personality A person who identifies opportunities, shows initiative, takes action, and perseveres until meaningful change occurs.

Situation Strength Theory

Imagine you are in a meeting with your department. How likely are you to walk out, shout at someone, or turn your back on everyone? Probably highly unlikely. Now imagine working from home. You might work in your pyjamas, listen to loud music, or take a catnap.

Situation strength theory proposes that the way personality translates into behaviour depends on the strength of the situation. By *situation strength*, we mean the degree to which norms, cues, or standards dictate appropriate behaviour. Strong situations show us what the right behaviour is, pressure us to exhibit it, and discourage the wrong behaviour. In weak situations, conversely, "anything goes," and thus we are freer to express our personality in behaviour. Thus, personality traits better predict behaviour in weak situations than in strong ones.

Researchers have analyzed situation strength in organizations in terms of four elements:[112]

1. **Clarity,** or the degree to which cues about work duties and responsibilities are available and clear. Jobs high in clarity produce strong situations because individuals can readily determine what to do. For example, the job of janitor probably provides higher clarity about each task than the job of nanny.

2. **Consistency,** or the extent to which cues regarding work duties and responsibilities are compatible with one another. Jobs with high consistency represent strong situations because all the cues point toward the same desired behaviour. The job of acute care nurse, for example, probably has higher consistency than the job of manager.

3. **Constraints,** or the extent to which individuals' freedom to decide or act is limited by forces outside their control. Jobs with many constraints represent strong situations because an individual has limited individual discretion. Bank examiner, for example, is probably a job with stronger constraints than forest ranger.

4. **Consequences,** or the degree to which decisions or actions have important implications for the organization or its members, clients, suppliers, and so on. Jobs with important consequences represent strong situations because the environment is probably heavily structured to guard against mistakes. A surgeon's job, for example, has higher consequences than a foreign-language teacher's.

Some researchers have speculated organizations are, by definition, strong situations because they impose rules, norms, and standards that govern behaviour. These constraints are usually appropriate. For example, we would not want an employee to feel free to engage in sexual harassment, follow questionable accounting procedures, or come to work only when the mood strikes.

Beyond the basics, though, it is not always desirable for organizations to create strong situations for their employees for a number of reasons. First, the elements of situation strength are often determined by organization rules and guidelines, which adds some objectivity to them. However, the perception of these rules influences how the person will respond to the situation's strength. For instance, a person who is usually self-directed may view step-by-step instructions (high clarity) for a simple task as a lack of faith in his ability. Another person who is a rule-follower might appreciate the detailed instructions. Their responses (and work attitudes) will reflect their perception of the situation.[113]

Second, jobs with myriad rules and tightly controlled processes can be dull or demotivating. Imagine that all work was executed with an assembly-line approach. Some people may prefer the routine, but many prefer having some variety and freedom. Third, strong situations might suppress the creativity, initiative, and discretion prized by some organizational cultures. One recent study, for example, found that in

situation strength theory
A theory indicating that the way personality translates into behaviour depends on the strength of the situation.

weak organizational situations, employees were more likely to behave proactively in accordance with their values.[114] Finally, work is increasingly complex and interrelated globally. Creating strong rules to govern diverse systems might be not only difficult but also unwise. In sum, managers need to recognize the role of situation strength in the workplace and find the appropriate balance.

Emotions

Each of us has a range of personality characteristics, but we also bring with us a range of emotions. Given the obvious role that emotions play in our everyday life, it might surprise you to learn that, until very recently, the topic of emotions was given little or no attention within the field of OB.[115] Why? Generally, because emotions in the workplace were historically thought to be detrimental to performance. Although managers knew emotions were an inseparable part of everyday life, they tried to create organizations that were emotion-free. Researchers tended to focus on strong negative emotions—especially anger—that interfered with an employee's ability to work effectively. (*Point/Counterpoint* on page 73 considers whether organizations should encourage the expression of negative emotions at work.)

Thankfully, this type of thinking is changing. Certainly some emotions, particularly when exhibited at the wrong time, can reduce employee performance. Other emotions are neutral, and some are constructive. Employees do bring their emotions to work every day, so no study of OB would be complete without considering their role in workplace behaviour.

7 Differentiate between emotions and moods.

What Are Emotions and Moods?

Let's look at three terms that are closely intertwined: *affect, emotions,* and *moods.* **Affect** is a generic term that covers a broad range of feelings people experience, including both emotions and moods.[116] **Emotions** are intense feelings that are directed at someone or something.[117] **Moods** are less intense feelings than emotions and often (although not always) arise without a specific event acting as a stimulus.[118]

Exhibit 2-8 shows the relationships among affect, emotions, and moods.

As the exhibit shows, *affect* is a broad term that encompasses emotions and moods. Second, there are differences between emotions and moods. Emotions are more likely to be caused by a specific event and are more fleeting than moods. Also, some researchers

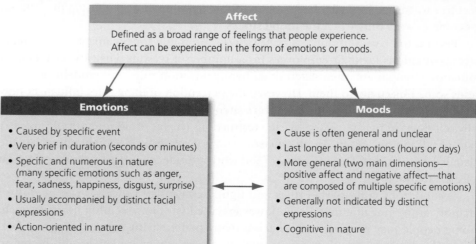

EXHIBIT 2-8 Affect, Emotions, and Moods

Affect

Defined as a broad range of feelings that people experience. Affect can be experienced in the form of emotions or moods.

Emotions
- Caused by specific event
- Very brief in duration (seconds or minutes)
- Specific and numerous in nature (many specific emotions such as anger, fear, sadness, happiness, disgust, surprise)
- Usually accompanied by distinct facial expressions
- Action-oriented in nature

Moods
- Cause is often general and unclear
- Last longer than emotions (hours or days)
- More general (two main dimensions— positive affect and negative affect—that are composed of multiple specific emotions)
- Generally not indicated by distinct expressions
- Cognitive in nature

affect A broad range of feelings that people experience.

emotions Intense feelings that are directed at someone or something.

moods Feelings that tend to be less intense than emotions and that lack a contextual stimulus.

speculate that emotions may be more action-oriented—they may lead us to some immediate action—while moods may be more cognitive, meaning that they may cause us to think or brood for a while.[119]

Affect, emotions, and moods are separable in theory; in practice the distinction is not always defined. When we review the OB topics on emotions and moods, you may see more information about emotions in one area and moods in another. This is simply the state of the research. *OB in the Street* discusses how our perception of emotions can affect our romantic relationships.

From Concepts to Skills on pages 77–78 gives you some insight into reading the emotions of others.

OB IN THE STREET
How Perception Causes Fights in Relationships

What happens if you think your partner is neglecting you? A study found that how people perceive the emotions of their romantic partner during a conflict affected their overall view of and reactions to the conflict.[120] The researchers studied the arguments that 105 university students had during an eight-week period. They looked at two types of emotions: "hard" (asserting power) and "soft" (expressing vulnerability). They also looked at two types of perceptions: "perceived threat" (perception that the partner is being hostile, critical, blaming, or controlling) and "perceived neglect" (perception that the partner does not seem committed to or invested in the relationship).

The researchers found that when a person sees his or her partner react with hard emotion, that person perceives a threat to control, power, and status in the relationship. When a person sees his or her partner show little emotion, or less soft emotion than desired, that person perceives partner neglect. The perceived threat and neglect increase the person's own hard and soft emotions.

One of the study's co-authors explained the results as follows: "[W]hat you perceive your partner to be feeling influences different types of thoughts, feelings and reactions in yourself, whether what you perceive is actually correct. . . . If a person perceives the other as angry, they will perceive a threat so they will respond with a hard emotion like anger or blame. Likewise, if a person is perceived to be sad or vulnerable, they will perceive a neglect and will respond [with] either flat or soft [emotions]." . . . .

Moral Emotions

We may tend to think our internal emotions are innate. For instance, if someone jumped out at you from behind a door, wouldn't you feel surprised? Maybe you would, but you might also feel any of the other five universal emotions—anger, fear, sadness, happiness, or disgust—depending on the circumstance. Our experiences of emotions are closely tied to our interpretations of events.

Researchers have been studying what are called **moral emotions**; that is, emotions that have moral implications because of our instant judgment of the situation that evokes them. Examples of moral emotions include sympathy for the suffering of others, guilt about our own immoral behaviour, anger about injustice done to others, and contempt for those who behave unethically.

Another example is the disgust we feel about violations of moral norms, called *moral disgust*. Moral disgust is different from disgust. Say you stepped in cow dung by mistake—you might feel disgusted by it, but not moral disgust—you probably would not make a moral judgment. In contrast, say you watched a video of a police officer making

moral emotions Emotions that have moral implications.

a sexist or racist slur. You might feel disgusted in a different way because it offends your sense of right and wrong. In fact, you might feel a variety of emotions based on your moral judgment of the situation.[121]

Interestingly, research indicates that our responses to moral emotions differ from our responses to other emotions.[122] When we feel moral anger, for instance, we may be more likely to confront the situation that causes it than when we just feel angry. However, we cannot assume our emotional reactions to events on a moral level will be the same as someone else's. Moral emotions are learned, usually in childhood,[123] and thus they are not universal like innate emotions. Because morality is a construct that differs among cultures, so do moral emotions. Therefore, we need to be aware of the moral aspects of situations that trigger our emotions and make certain we understand the context before we act, especially in the workplace.

You can think about this research in your own life to see how moral emotions operate. Consider a time when you have done something that hurt someone else. Did you feel angry or upset with yourself? Or think about a time when you have seen someone else treated unfairly. Did you feel contempt for the person acting unfairly, or did you engage in a cool, rational calculation of the justice of the situation? Most people who think about these situations have some sense of an emotional stirring that might prompt them to engage in ethical actions like donating money to help others, apologizing and attempting to make amends, or intervening on behalf of those who have been mistreated. In sum, we can conclude that people who are behaving ethically are at least partially making decisions based on their emotions and feelings.

Emotions can be fleeting, but moods can endure . . . for quite a while. In order to understand the impact of emotions and moods in organizations, we next classify the many distinct emotions into broader mood categories.

8 Show the impact of emotional labour on employees.

Choosing Emotions: Emotional Labour

If you have ever had a job working in retail sales or waiting on tables in a restaurant, you know the importance of projecting a friendly demeanour and smiling. Even though there were days when you did not feel cheerful, you knew management expected you to be upbeat when dealing with customers. So you faked it. Every employee expends physical and mental labour by putting body and mind into the job. But jobs also require **emotional labour**, an employee's expression of organizationally desired emotions during interpersonal transactions at work.[124] Emotional labour is a key component of effective job performance. We expect flight attendants to be cheerful, funeral directors to be sad, and doctors emotionally neutral. At the least, your managers expect you to be courteous, not hostile, in your interactions with co-workers.

> Ever wonder why the grocery clerk is always smiling?

The way we experience an emotion is obviously not always the same as the way we show it. To analyze emotional labour, we divide emotions into *felt* or *displayed emotions*.[125] **Felt emotions** are our actual emotions. In contrast, **displayed emotions** are those that the organization requires employees to show and considers appropriate in a given job. They are not natural; they are learned.

Effective managers have learned to be serious when giving an employee a negative performance evaluation and look calm when they are berated by their bosses, because the organization expects these displays. Of course, there are no display rules for many workplace situations. Does your employer dictate what emotions you display when you are, say, heading out for lunch? Probably not. Many workplaces have explicit display rules, but usually only for interactions that matter, particularly between employees and customers. Regarding employee and customer interactions, you might expect that the more an employer dictates salespeople's emotional displays, the higher the sales.

emotional labour When an employee expresses organizationally desired emotions during interpersonal interactions.

felt emotions An individual's actual emotions.

displayed emotions Emotions that are organizationally required and considered appropriate in a given job.

Actually, employees under very high or very low display rules do not perform as well in sales situations as employees who have moderate display rules and a high degree of discretion in their roles.[126]

Displaying fake emotions requires us to suppress real ones. **Surface acting** is hiding one's inner feelings and emotional expressions in response to display rules. For example, when an employee smiles at a customer even when he does not feel like it, he is surface acting. **Deep acting** is trying to modify one's true inner feelings based on display rules. A health care provider trying to genuinely feel more empathy for her patients is deep acting.[127] Surface acting deals with one's *displayed* emotions, and deep acting deals with one's *felt* emotions. Research in the Netherlands and Belgium indicated that surface acting is stressful to employees, while **mindfulness** (learning to objectively evaluate one's emotional situation in the moment) is beneficial to employee well-being.[128]

Displaying emotions we don't really feel is exhausting. Surface acting is associated with increased stress and decreased job satisfaction.[129] Surface acting on a daily basis can also lead to emotional exhaustion at home, work–family conflict, and insomnia.[130] On the other hand, deep acting has a positive relationship with job satisfaction and job performance.[131] We also experience less emotional exhaustion with deep acting. So, it is important to give employees who engage in surface acting a chance to relax and recharge. A study that looked at how cheerleading instructors spent their breaks from teaching found those who used the time to rest and relax were more effective after their breaks.[132] Instructors who did chores during their breaks were only about as effective after their break as they were before. Another study found that in hospital work groups where there were heavy emotional display demands, burnout was higher than in other hospital work groups.[133] Although much of the research on emotional labour shows negative consequences for those displaying false positive emotions, one study suggests that as people age, engaging in positive emotions and attitudes, even when the circumstances warrant otherwise, actually enhances emotional well-being.[134] The *Experiential Exercise* on page 74 asks you whether you can detect when someone is lying.

Why Should We Care About Emotions in the Workplace?

We have seen that emotions and moods are an important part of our personal and work lives. But how do they influence our job performance and satisfaction? **Affective events theory (AET)** proposes that employees react emotionally to things that happen to them at work, and this reaction influences their job performance and satisfaction.[135] Say you just found out your company is downsizing. You might experience a variety of negative emotions, causing you to worry that you will lose your job. Because it is out of your hands, you feel insecure and fearful, and spend much of your time worrying rather than working. Needless to say, your job satisfaction will also be down.

Work events trigger positive or negative emotional reactions, to which employees' personalities and moods predispose them to respond with greater or lesser intensity.[136] People who score low on emotional stability are more likely to react strongly to negative events, and our emotional response to a given event can change depending on mood. Finally, emotions influence a number of performance and satisfaction variables, such as OCB, organizational commitment, level of effort, intention to quit, and workplace deviance.

In sum, AET offers two important messages.[137] First, emotions provide valuable insights into how workplace events influence employee performance and satisfaction. Second, employees and managers should not ignore emotions or the events that cause them, even when they appear minor, because they accumulate. Emotional intelligence is another framework that helps us understand the impact of emotions on job performance, so we will look at that next.

surface acting Hiding one's inner feelings to display what is expected.

deep acting Trying to modify one's true inner feelings to match what is expected.

mindfulness Objectively and deliberately evaluating the emotional situation in the moment.

affective events theory (AET) A model that suggests that workplace events cause emotional reactions on the part of employees, which then influence workplace attitudes and behaviours.

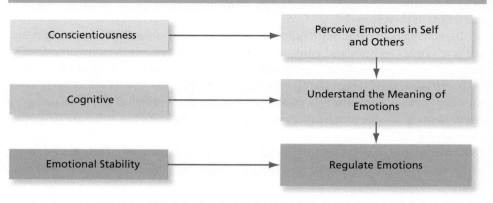

EXHIBIT 2-9 A Cascading Model of Emotional Intelligence

```
Conscientiousness  ──────►  Perceive Emotions in Self
                                      and Others
                                          │
                                          ▼
Cognitive          ──────►  Understand the Meaning of
                                      Emotions
                                          │
                                          ▼
Emotional Stability ─────►        Regulate Emotions
```

⑨ Contrast the evidence for and against the existence of emotional intelligence.

Emotional Intelligence

Diane is an office manager. Her awareness of her own and others' emotions is almost zero. She is moody and unable to generate much enthusiasm or interest in her employees. She does not understand why employees get upset with her. She often overreacts to problems and chooses the most ineffectual responses to emotional situations.[138] Diane has low emotional intelligence. **Emotional intelligence (EI)** is a person's ability to (1) perceive emotions in the self and others, (2) understand the meaning of these emotions, and (3) regulate his or her own emotions accordingly in a cascading model, as shown in Exhibit 2-9. People who know their own emotions and are good at reading emotional cues—for instance, knowing why they are angry and how to express themselves without violating norms—are most likely to be effective.[139] *Focus on Research* looks at the issue of whether smiles are infectious. You may be surprised to learn the extent to which your mood can affect the mood of others.

FOCUS ON RESEARCH
Smile, and the Work World Smiles with You

Can you make another person smile?   It is true that a smile usually creates an unconscious return smile from the person smiled at.[140] However, anyone who has ever smiled at an angry manager knows that a smile does not always have a positive effect. In truth, the giving and withholding of smiles is an unconscious power play of office politics.

New research on the "boss effect" suggests that the amount of power and status a person feels over another person dictates who will smile. Subordinates generally smile more often than their bosses smile back at them. However, the perception of power is complex and varies by national culture: In a recent study, Chinese workers reflexively smiled only at bosses who had the power to give them negative job evaluations, while US participants smiled most to managers perceived to have higher social power. Other researchers found that when individuals felt powerful, they usually did not return even a high-ranking individual's smile. Conversely, when people felt powerless, they returned everyone's smiles.

While we think of smiling as a choice, smiling (or concealing a smile) is often unconscious. Researchers are finding that social pressure affects neurobiology. "It shapes your neural architecture," said cognitive neuroscientist Sook-Lei Liew. Smile reactions are, therefore, partially involuntary; when smiling is a product of our attitudes, it can become an unconscious process. Thus, "your feelings about power and status seem to dictate how much you are willing to return a smile to another person," cognitive neuroscientist Evan Carr affirmed. ....

emotional intelligence (EI) The ability to detect and to manage emotional cues and information.

A comprehensive study reviewed and analyzed most of the previous studies on EI and concluded that EI is strongly and positively correlated with job performance—emotionally intelligent people are better workers.[141] One study that used functional magnetic resonance imaging (fMRI) technology found that executive MBA students who performed best on a strategic decision-making task were more likely to incorporate emotion centres of the brain into their choice process. The students also de-emphasized the use of the more cognitive parts of their brains.[142] One simulation study showed that students who were good at identifying and distinguishing among their own feelings were able to make more profitable investment decisions.[143]

Although the field is progressing in its understanding of EI, many questions have not been answered. One relates to proving what EI may predict. For example, while evidence indicates that EI has some correlation with job performance, the correlation is not high, and it is explained to a large degree by traits such as emotional stability. A second question is about the reliability of EI testing. For example, part of the reason EI has only a modest correlation with job effectiveness is that it is hard to measure—mostly it is measured with self-report inventories, which of course are often far from objective!

Thus, assessing exactly how EI should be used in the workplace is unclear, as *Focus on Ethics* shows.

FOCUS ON ETHICS
An Ethical Choice

Should managers use emotional intelligence tests? Should EI tests be used to select the best job candidate?[144] Here are some ethical considerations:

- *No commonly accepted test exists.* For instance, researchers have recently used the Mayer-Salovey-Caruso Emotional Intelligence Test (MSCEIT), the Trait Emotional Intelligence Questionnaire, and the Situational Judgment Test of Emotional Intelligence (SJT of EI) in studies. Researchers feel EI tests may need to be culturally specific because emotional displays vary by culture; thus, the interpretation of emotional cues differs. For example, a recent study in India comparing the EI scores for Indian and North American executives using the Emotional Competence Inventory (ECI-2) test found the results similar but not the same, suggesting the need for modification.

- *Applicants may react negatively to taking an EI test in general, or to parts of it.* The face recognition test, for example, may seem culturally biased to some if the subject photos are not diverse. Also, participants who score high on EI tests tend to consider them fair; applicants who score lower may not perceive the tests to be fair and can thus view the hiring organizations unfavourably—even if they score well on other assessments.

- *EI tests may not be predictive of performance for all types of jobs.* In a study of 600 Romanian participants, results indicated that EI was valid for salespeople, public servants, and CEOs of public hospitals, but these were all roles requiring significant social interaction. EI tests may need to be tailored for each position category or not be used when the position description does not warrant.

- *It remains somewhat unclear what EI tests are actually measuring.* They may reflect personality or intelligence, in which case other measures might be better. Also, mixed EI tests may predict job performance, but many of these tests include personality constructs and measures of general mental ability.

- *Not enough research exists on how EI affects counterproductive or desirable work behaviours.* It may not be prudent to test and select applicants who are rated high on EI when we are not yet certain that everything about EI leads to desired workplace outcomes.

These concerns suggest that EI tests should be avoided in hiring decisions. However, because research has indicated that EI does predict job performance to some degree, managers should not be too hasty to dismiss them altogether. Rather, those wishing to use EI in hiring decisions should be aware of these issues to make informed and ethical decisions about not only whom to hire but also how to hire. . . . .

Negative Workplace Emotions

Negative emotions can lead to a number of deviant workplace behaviours. Anyone who has spent much time in an organization realizes that people often engage in voluntary actions that violate established norms and threaten the organization, its members, or both. These actions are called *counterproductive work behaviours*.[145] They can be traced to negative emotions and can take many forms. People who feel negative emotions are more likely than others to engage in short-term deviant behaviour at work, such as gossiping or surfing the Internet,[146] though negative emotions can also lead to more serious forms of counterproductive work behaviour.

For instance, envy is an emotion that occurs when you resent someone for having something you don't, and strongly desire—such as a better work assignment, larger office, or higher salary. It can lead to malicious deviant behaviours. An envious employee could undermine other employees and take all the credit for things others accomplished. Angry people look for other people to blame for their bad mood, interpret other people's behaviour as hostile, and have trouble considering others' points of view.[147] It's not hard to see how these thought processes, too, can lead directly to verbal or physical aggression.

Managing emotions in the workplace becomes important both to ward off negative behaviour and to encourage positive behaviour in those around us. Some managers have even hired happiness coaches for their employees, as discussed in *Ethical Dilemma* on pages 74–75.

You may be surprised to learn the extent to which your mood can affect the mood of others. A recent study in Pakistan found that anger correlated with more aggressive counterproductive work behaviours such as abuse against others and production deviance, while sadness did not. Interestingly, neither anger nor sadness predicted workplace withdrawal, which suggests that managers need to take employee expressions of anger seriously; employees may stay with an organization and continue to act aggressively toward others.[148] Once aggression starts, it's likely that other people will become angry and aggressive, so the stage is set for a serious escalation of negative behaviour. Managers therefore need to stay connected with their employees to gauge emotions and emotional intensity levels.

Emotion Regulation

10 Identify strategies for emotion regulation and their likely effects.

Have you ever tried to cheer yourself up when you are feeling down or calm yourself when you are feeling angry? If so, you have engaged in *emotion regulation*.[149] The central idea behind emotion regulation is to identify and modify the emotions you feel. Recent research suggests that emotion management ability is a strong predictor of task performance for some jobs and organizational citizenship behaviours.[150] Therefore, in our study of OB, we are interested in *whether* and *how* emotion regulation should be used in the workplace. We begin by identifying which individuals might naturally employ it.

Emotion Regulation Techniques Researchers of emotion regulation often study the strategies people may employ to change their emotions. One technique we have discussed in this chapter is surface acting, or literally "putting on a face" of appropriate response to a given situation. Surface acting does not change emotions, though, so the regulation effect is minimal and the result of daily surface acting leads to exhaustion and fewer OCBs.[151] Perhaps due to the costs of creatively expressing what we don't feel, individuals who vary their surface-acting response may have lower job satisfaction and higher levels of work withdrawal than those who consistently give the same responses.[152]

Deep acting, another strategy we have covered, is less psychologically costly than surface acting because the employee is actually trying to experience the emotion. Emotion regulation through deep acting can have a positive impact on work outcomes.

For example, a recent study in the Netherlands and Germany found that individuals in service jobs earned significantly more direct pay (tips) after they received training in deep acting.[153]

One technique of emotion regulation is *emotional suppression*, or suppressing initial emotional responses to situations. This response seems to facilitate practical thinking in the short term. However, it appears to be helpful only when a strongly negative event would elicit a distressed emotional reaction in a crisis situation.[154] For example, a soldier in battle may suppress initial emotional distress after a shooting and thus be able to make clearer decisions about how to proceed. A portfolio manager might suppress an emotional reaction to a sudden drop in the value of a stock and therefore be able to clearly decide how to plan. Suppression used in crisis situations appears to help an individual recover from the event emotionally, while suppression used as an everyday emotion regulation technique can take a toll on mental ability, emotional ability, health, and relationships.[155]

Thus, unless we are truly in a crisis situation, acknowledging rather than suppressing our emotional responses to situations, and re-evaluating events after they occur yield the best outcomes.[156] *Cognitive reappraisal*, or reframing our outlook on an emotional situation, is one way to effectively regulate emotions.[157] Cognitive reappraisal ability seems to be the most helpful to individuals in situations where they cannot control the sources of stress.[158] A recent study illustrates the potentially powerful effect of this technique. Israeli participants were shown anger-inducing information about the Israeli–Palestinian conflict; after they were primed to reappraise the situation they showed more willingness to consider conciliatory measures toward Palestine and less support for aggressive tactics against Palestinians, not just immediately after the study but up to five months later. This finding suggests that cognitive reappraisal may allow people to change their emotional responses, even when the subject matter is as highly emotionally charged as the Israeli–Palestinian conflict.[159] Mindfulness also has been shown to increase the ability to shape our behavioural responses to emotions.[160] When people become non-judgmentally aware of the emotions they are experiencing, they are better able to look at situations separately from their emotions.

Another technique with potential for emotion regulation is *social sharing* or venting. Research shows that the open expression of emotions can help the individuals regulate their emotions, as opposed to keeping emotions "bottled up." Social sharing can reduce anger reactions when people can talk about the facts of a bad situation, their feelings about the situation, or any positive aspects of the situation.[161] Caution must be exercised, though, because expressing your frustration affects other people. In fact, whether venting emotions helps the "venter" feel better depends very much upon the listener's response. If the listener does not respond (many refuse to respond to venting), the venter actually feels worse. If the listener responds with expressions of support or validation, the venter feels better. Therefore, if we are going to vent to a co-worker, we need to choose someone who will respond sympathetically. Venting to the perceived offender rarely improves things and can result in heightening the negative emotions.[162]

[[ ]] RESEARCH FINDINGS: Emotion Regulation

While emotion regulation techniques can help us cope with difficult workplace situations, research indicates that the effect varies. A recent study in Taiwan found that participants who worked for abusive supervisors reported emotional exhaustion and work withdrawal tendencies, but to different degrees based on the emotion regulation strategies they employed. Employees who used suppression techniques suffered greater emotional exhaustion and work withdrawal than employees who used cognitive reappraisal. This suggests that more research on the application of techniques needs to be done to help employees increase their coping skills.[163]

Thus, while there is much promise in emotion regulation techniques, the best route to a positive workplace is to recruit positive-minded individuals and to train leaders to manage their moods, job attitudes, and performance.[164] The best leaders manage emotions as much as they do tasks and activities. The best employees can use their knowledge of emotion regulation to decide when to speak up and how to express themselves effectively.[165] With computers now being programmed to read emotions, as *OB in the Workplace* indicates, it may be harder to hide emotions at work in the future.

OB IN THE WORKPLACE

Affective Computing: Reading Your State of Mind

Can computers really recognize a user's emotions? The Massachusetts Institute of Technology (MIT) Media Lab is currently programming computers to use 24 facial points from which they can infer an emotion.[166] What if computers could be made emotionally intelligent to help a person get past frustration into productivity? What if managers could automatically receive reports on virtual employees' emotions? What if sensors could help employees stay well by providing feedback on their emotional reactions to stress?

Affective computing can provide managers with in-the-moment help. At MIT's lab, a tiny traffic light, visible only to the wearer, flashes yellow when a listener's face indicates lack of engagement in the conversation and red for complete disengagement. These cues could help a manager who is delivering important safety information to an employee, for instance. The MIT team has also developed wristbands that sense emotional states and activity levels. They could help managers work with employees who are on the Asperger's or autism spectrum. "With this technology in the future, we'll be able to understand things . . . that we weren't able to see before, things that calm them, things that stress them," said Rosalind Picard, the team's director.

With this possibility comes responsibility, of course. Obvious ethical issues will only grow with the technology's increasing sophistication. Employees may not want computers to read their emotions either for their managers' use or for automatic feedback. "We want to have some control over how we display ourselves to others," said Nick Bostrom of the University of Oxford's Future of Humanity Institute.

Organizations will eventually have to decide when it is appropriate to read employees' emotions, as well as which emotions to read. In the meantime, according to affective computing experts, people are still the best readers of emotions from facial cues. Perhaps managers can get to know their employees' state of mind by paying closer attention to those cues.

GLOBAL IMPLICATIONS

In considering potential global differences in this chapter's concepts, let's look at the four areas that have attracted the most research: (1) perception, (2) attributions, (3) personality, and (4) emotions.

Perception

Several studies have examined how people observe the world around them.[167] In one study, researchers showed East Asian and US subjects a photo with a focal object (like a train) with a busy background and tracked their eye movements. They found that the US subjects were more likely to look at the focal object, whereas the East Asian subjects were more likely to look at the background. Thus, the East Asians appeared to focus more on the context or environment than on the most important object in it. As one of the researchers concluded, "If people are seeing different things, it may be because they are looking differently at the world."[168]

Perceptual differences across cultures have been found to be rooted in the brain's architecture. Using an fMRI device to scan subjects' brains, one researcher found that when Singaporeans were shown pictures where either the foreground or background was varied, their brains were less attuned to new foreground images and more attuned to new background images than were the brains of US subjects.[169] This finding suggests that perception is not universal, and that the cultural tendency to focus on either an object/person or a context is part of the "hard wiring" of our brains.

Finally, culture affects what we remember as well. When asked to remember events, US subjects recall more about personal details and their own personal characteristics, whereas Asians recall more about personal relationships and group activities.[170]

As a set, these studies provide striking evidence that Eastern and Western cultures differ in one of the deepest aspects of organizational behaviour: how we see the world around us.

Attributions

The evidence on cultural differences in perception is mixed, but most studies suggest that there *are* differences across cultures in the attributions people make.[171] In one study, Asian managers were more likely to lay blame on institutions or whole organizations when things went wrong, whereas Western observers believed individual managers should be the focus of blame or praise.[172] That probably explains why Canadian and US newspapers prominently report the names of individual executives when firms do poorly, whereas Asian media provide more coverage of how the firm as a whole has failed. This tendency to make group-based attributions also explains why individuals from Asian cultures, which are more collectivistic in orientation, are more likely to use group stereotypes.[173]

Self-serving biases may be less common in East Asian cultures, but evidence suggests that they still operate there.[174] Studies suggest that Chinese managers assess blame for mistakes using the same distinctiveness, consensus, and consistency cues Western managers use.[175] It may just take more evidence for Asian managers to conclude someone else should be blamed.

Personality

The five personality traits identified in the Big Five model appear in almost all cross-cultural studies.[176] These studies have included a wide variety of diverse cultures—such as China, Israel, Germany, Japan, Spain, Nigeria, Norway, Pakistan, and the United States. However, a study of illiterate Indigenous people in Bolivia suggested the Big Five framework may be less applicable when studying the personalities of small, remote groups.[177]

Emotions

People vary in the degree to which they experience emotions. In China, for example, people report experiencing fewer positive and negative emotions than people in other cultures, and the emotions they experience are less intense than what other cultures report. Compared with mainland Chinese, Taiwanese are more like Canadian employees in their experience of emotions: On average, Taiwanese report more positive and fewer negative emotions than their Chinese counterparts.[178] People in most cultures appear to experience certain positive and negative emotions, but the frequency of their experience and their intensity vary to some degree.[179] Exhibit 2-10 illustrates the percentage of people who experience emotions on a daily basis across cultures.

EXHIBIT 2-10 Emotional States Cross-Culturally

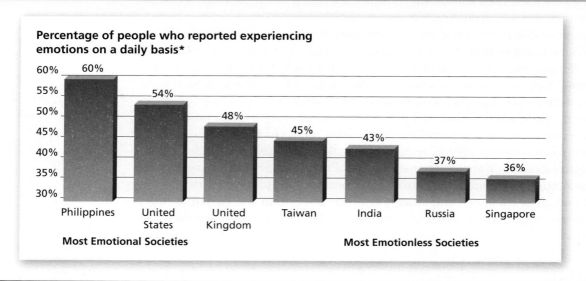

Percentage of people who reported experiencing emotions on a daily basis*

Most Emotional Societies — Most Emotionless Societies

*Respondents in 150+ countries worldwide over two years were asked whether they experienced five positive emotions (well-rested, treated with respect, enjoyment, smiling and laughing, learning or doing something interesting) and five negative emotions (anger, stress, sadness, physical pain, worry) daily.

Source: J. Clifton, "Singapore Ranks as Least Emotional Country in the World," *Gallup World*, November 21, 2012, http://www.gallup.com/poll/158882/singapore-ranks-least-emotional-country-world.aspx.

A recent study suggested that people do not interpret emotions the same way across cultures from vocalizations. While vocalizations (such as sighs or screams) conveyed meaning in all cultures, the specific emotions people perceived varied. For example, Himba participants (from northwestern Namibia) did not agree with Western participants that crying meant sadness or a growl meant anger.[180] In addition, cultures have norms that govern emotional expression, so the way we *experience* an emotion is not always the same as the way we *show* it. For example, people in the Middle East and Canada recognize a smile as indicating happiness, but in the Middle East a smile is also often interpreted as a sign of sexual attraction, so women have learned not to smile at men. In collectivist countries, people are more likely to believe another's emotional displays have something to do with the relationship between them, while people in individualistic cultures don't think others' emotional expressions are directed at them.

Summary

Individuals base their behaviour not on the way their external environment actually is, but rather on the way they see it or believe it to be.

Personality matters to OB. It does not explain all behaviour, but it sets the stage. Emerging theory and research reveal how personality matters more in some situations than others. The Big Five Personality Model has been a particularly important advancement, although the Dark Triad and other traits matter as well. Moreover, every trait has advantages and disadvantages for work behaviour. No perfect constellation of traits is ideal in every situation. Personality can help you understand why people (including yourself!) act, think, and feel the way they do, and the astute manager can

LESSONS LEARNED

- People act on the basis of their perception of reality.
- Personality attributes provide a framework for predicting behaviour.
- People who are good at reading the emotions of others are generally more effective in the workplace.

put that understanding to use by taking care to place employees in situations that best fit their personalities.

Emotions and moods are similar in that both are affective in nature. They are also different—moods are more general and less contextual than emotions. The time of day, stressful events, and sleep patterns are some of the factors that influence emotions and moods. OB research on emotional labour, affective events theory, emotional intelligence, and emotion regulation helps us understand how people deal with emotions. Emotions and moods have proven relevant for virtually every OB topic we study, with implications for managerial practice.

SNAPSHOT SUMMARY

Perception
- Factors That Influence Perception
- Perceptual Errors
- Why Do Perception and Judgment Matter?

Personality
- What Is Personality?
- Measuring Personality

- Personality Determinants
- Personality Traits
- The Dark Triad
- Other Personality Attributes That Influence OB
- Situation Strength Theory

Emotions
- What Are Emotions and Moods?

- Moral Emotions
- Choosing Emotions: Emotional Labour
- Why Should We Care About Emotions in the Workplace?

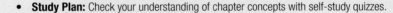

MyLab Management

Study, practise, and explore real business situations with these helpful resources:
- **Study Plan:** Check your understanding of chapter concepts with self-study quizzes.
- **Online Lesson Presentations:** Study key chapter topics and work through interactive assessments to test your knowledge and master management concepts.
- **Videos:** Learn more about the management practices and strategies of real companies.
- **Simulations:** Practise management decision-making in simulated business environments.

OB at Work

for **Review**

1. What is perception? What factors influence our perception?

2. What is attribution theory? What are the three determinants of attribution? What are the implications of attribution theory for explaining organizational behaviour?

3. What is personality? How do we typically measure it? What factors determine personality?

4. What is the Myers-Briggs Type Indicator? What are its strengths and weaknesses?

5. What are the key traits in the Big Five Personality Model?

6. How do the Big Five personality traits predict behaviour at work?

7. What is the difference between emotions and moods?

8. What impact does emotional labour have on employees?

9. What is the evidence for and against the existence of emotional intelligence?

10. What are some strategies for emotion regulation and their likely effects?

for **Managers**

- Consider screening job candidates for the Big Five personality traits your organization finds most important. Other traits, such as core self-evaluation or narcissism, may be relevant as well.

- Know that the MBTI has been widely criticized. Yet, it may be helpful for training and development; it can also help employees better understand themselves and one another, open up communication in work groups, and possibly reduce conflicts.

- Behaviour follows perception, so to influence behaviour at work, assess how people perceive their work. Often behaviours we find puzzling can be explained by understanding the initiating perceptions.

- Recognize that emotions are a natural part of the workplace and good management does not mean creating an emotion-free environment.

- To foster effective decision making, creativity, and motivation in employees, model positive emotions and moods as much as is authentically possible.

- Regulate your intense emotional responses to an event by recognizing the legitimacy of the emotion and being careful to vent only to a supportive listener who is not involved in the event.

- Don't ignore co-workers' and employees' emotions; don't assess others' behaviour as if it were completely rational. As one consultant said, "You can't divorce emotions from the workplace because you can't divorce emotions from people."[181] Understanding emotions and moods will significantly improve your ability to explain and predict others' behaviour.

for **You**

- The discussion of perception might get you thinking about how you view the world. When we perceive someone as a troublemaker, for instance, that may be only a perception and not a real characteristic of the person. It is always good to question your perceptions, just to be sure that you are not reading something into a situation that is not there.

- One important thing to consider when looking for a job is whether your personality will fit the organization to which you are applying. For instance, let's say that you are considering working for a highly structured company. If you, by nature, are much less formal, then that company may not be a good fit for you.

- Sometimes personalities get in the way when working in groups. You may want to see if you can figure out ways to get personality differences to work in favour of group goals.

- Emotions need not always be suppressed when working with others. While emotions can sometimes hinder performance, positive emotions can motivate you and those around you.

SOMETIMES YELLING IS FOR EVERYONE'S GOOD

POINT

Anger is discussed throughout this chapter for a reason: It's an important emotion.[182] There are benefits to expressing anger. For one, research indicates that only employees who are committed to their organizations tend to express their anger, and generally only to leaders who created the situation. This type of expression of anger could lead to positive organizational change. Second, suppressed anger can lower job satisfaction and lead to feelings of hopelessness.

Even with these findings, we hear a lot about not responding emotionally to work challenges. Work cultures teach us to avoid showing any anger at all, lest we be seen as poor workers or, worse, unprofessional or even deviant or violent. While, of course, there are times when the expression of anger is harmful or unprofessional, we have taken this view so far that we now teach people to suppress perfectly normal emotions, and to ignore the effectiveness of some emotional expression.

Emerging research shows that suppressing anger takes a terrible internal toll on individuals. One Stanford University study found, for example, that when individuals were asked to wear a poker face during the showing of a movie clip depicting the atomic bombings of Japan during World War II, they were much more stressed in conversations after the video. Other research shows that college students who suppress emotions like anger have more trouble making friends and are more likely to be depressed, and that employees who suppress anger feel more stressed by work.

For the good of organizations and their employees, we should encourage people not to hold back their emotions, but to share them constructively.

COUNTERPOINT

Yes, anger is a common emotion. But it's also a toxic one for the giver and the receiver. Angry outbursts can compromise the heart and contribute to diabetes, among other ill effects. The experience of another's anger and its close correlate, hostility, is also linked to many counterproductive behaviours in organizations. The US Bureau of Labor Statistics estimates that 16 percent of fatal workplace injuries result from workplace violence. That is why many organizations have developed counteractive techniques—to blunt the harmful effects of anger in the workplace.

To reduce outcomes, many companies develop policies that govern conduct such as yelling, shouting profanities, and making hostile gestures. Others institute anger management programs. For example, one organization conducted mandatory in-house workshops that showed individuals how to deal with conflicts in the workplace before they boil over. The director who instituted the training said it "gave people specific tools for opening a dialogue to work things out." MTS Systems, a Minnesota engineering firm, engages an outside consulting company to conduct anger management programs for its organization. Typically, MTS consultants hold an 8-hour seminar that discusses sources of anger, conflict resolution techniques, and organizational policies. This is followed by one-on-one sessions with individual employees that focus on cognitive behavioural techniques to manage their anger. The outside trainer charges around $10 000 for the seminar and one-on-one sessions. The financial cost, though, is worth it for the emotional benefits the participants receive. "You want people to get better at communicating with each other," says MTS manager Karen Borre.

In the end, everyone wins when organizations seek to diminish both the experience and the expression of anger at work. The work environment becomes less threatening and stressful to employees and customers. Employees are likely to feel safer, and the angry employee is often helped as well.

BREAKOUT **GROUP** EXERCISES

Form small groups to discuss the following topics, as assigned by your instructor. Each person in the group should first identify 3–5 key personal values.

1. Think back to your perception of this course and your instructor on the first day of class. What factors might have affected your perceptions of what the rest of the term would be like?

2. Describe a situation where your perception turned out to be wrong. What perceptual errors did you make that might have caused this to happen?

EXPERIENTIAL EXERCISE

Who Can Catch a Liar?

We mentioned earlier in the chapter that emotion researchers are highly interested in facial expressions as a window into individuals' emotional worlds.[183] Research has also studied whether people can tell someone is lying based on signs of guilt or nervousness in their facial expressions. Let's see who is good at catching liars, but first consider this: How good you are at detecting lies by others is related to your own mood. You are actually less likely to correctly detect a lie if you are in a happy mood. *Hint:* If you are in a negative mood, concentrate mostly on the message itself (Does it seem plausible?); if you are in a positive mood, concentrate more on the nonverbal cues (such as fidgety or calm behaviour).

Split up into teams and follow these instructions.

1. Randomly choose someone to be the team organizer. Have this person write down on a piece of paper "T" for truth and "L" for lie. If there are, say, six people in the group (other than the organizer), then three people will get a slip with a "T" and three a slip with an "L." It's important that all team members keep what is on their paper a secret.

2. Each team member who holds a T slip needs to come up with a true statement, and each team member who holds an L slip needs to come up with a false statement. Try not to make the statement so outrageous that no one would believe it (for example, "I have flown to the moon").

3. The organizer will have each member make his or her statement. Group members should then examine the person making the statement closely to try to determine whether he or she is telling the truth or lying. Once each person has made his or her statement, the organizer will ask for a vote and record the tallies.

4. Each person should now indicate whether the statement was the truth or a lie.

5. How good was your group at catching the liars? Were some people good liars? What did you look for to determine whether someone was lying?

ETHICAL **DILEMMA**

Happiness Coaches for Employees

We know there is considerable spillover from personal unhappiness to negative emotions at work.[184] Moreover, those who experience negative emotions in life and at work are more likely to engage in counterproductive behaviours with customers, clients, or fellow employees.

Increasingly, organizations such as American Express, UBS, and KPMG are turning to happiness coaches to address this spillover from personal unhappiness to work emotions and behaviours.

Srikumar Rao is a former college professor who has the nickname "the happiness guru." Rao teaches people to analyze negative emotions to prevent them from becoming overwhelming. If your job is restructured, for example, Rao suggests avoiding negative thoughts and feelings about it. Instead, he advises, tell yourself it could turn out well in the long run, and there is no way to know at present.

Beyond reframing the emotional impact of work situations, some happiness coaches attack the negative emotional spillover from life to work (and from work to life). A working mother found that a happiness talk by Shawn Achor helped her stop focusing on her stressed-out life and instead look for chances to smile, laugh, and be grateful.

In some cases, the claims made by happiness coaches seem a bit trite. Jim Smith, who labels himself "The Executive Happiness Coach," asks: "What if I told you that there are secrets nobody told you as a kid—or as an adult, for that matter—that can unlock for you all sorts of positive emotional experiences? What if the only thing that gets in the way of you feeling more happiness is—YOU?! What if you can change your experience of the world by shifting a few simple things in your life, and then practising them until they become second nature?"

If employees leave their experiences with a happiness coach feeling happier about their jobs and their lives, is that not better for everyone? Says one individual, Ivelisse Rivera, who felt she benefited from a happiness coach, "If I assume a negative attitude and complain all the time, whoever is working with me is going to feel the same way."

But what if you cannot afford a happiness coach and your employer does not want to foot the bill? Recent research suggests a do-it-yourself opportunity to increase your good mood at home. The key is to lend a helping hand. If you help others at work, you may find that later at home, after you have had a chance to relax and reflect, your mood will be improved.

Questions

1. Do you think happiness coaches are effective? How might you assess their effectiveness?

2. Would you welcome happiness training in your workplace? Why or why not?

3. Under what circumstances—if any—is it ethically appropriate for a supervisor to suggest a happiness coach for a subordinate?

CASE INCIDENTS

The Power of Quiet

If someone labelled you an "introvert" how would it make you feel?[185]

Judging from research on social desirability, most of us would prefer to be labelled extraverts. Normal distributions being what they are, however, half the world is more introverted than average. Earlier in the chapter we discussed the upside of introversion, but in many ways, it's an extravert's world. So says Susan Cain in her best-selling book *Quiet*.

Cain makes three arguments:

1. **We see ourselves as extraverts.** Introversion is generally seen as undesirable, partly because extraverts like being in charge and are more apt to shape environments to fit their wishes. "Many of the most important institutions of contemporary life are designed for those who enjoy group projects and high levels of stimulation."

2. **Introversion is driven underground.** Thanks to social norms and structures, introverts often are

forced to be "closet introverts"—acting according to an extraverted ideal, even if that is not their personality at heart. Think about it. If someone comments, "You're awfully quiet," they nearly always assume an underlying problem, as if not being quiet is the norm.

3. **Extraversion is not all it's cracked up to be.** Because introversion is suppressed, we cause the introverts of the world distress and fail to capitalize on the many virtues of introversion. We may overlook the quiet, thoughtful introvert when choosing a leader, we may quell creativity by doing most of our work in groups, and we may mistake appearance for reality ("Don't mistake assertiveness or eloquence for good ideas," Cain writes). Society may unwittingly push people to take risks more than is warranted, to act before they think, and to focus on short-term rewards above all else. Introverts prefer quiet conditions to concentrate on difficult tasks.

Cain is not anti-extravert. She simply thinks we should encourage people to be who they truly are, and that means valuing extraversion *and* introversion. Research indicates happy introverts are every bit as happy as happy extraverts. Cain concludes, "The next time you see a person with a composed face and soft voice, remember that inside her mind she might be solving an equation, composing a sonnet, designing a hat. She might, that is, be deploying the powers of quiet."

Questions

1. Would you classify yourself as introverted or extraverted? How would people who know you describe you?

2. Would you prefer to be more introverted, or more extraverted, than you are? Why?

3. Do you agree with Cain's arguments? Why or why not?

Tall Poppy Syndrome

". . . the tall poppy syndrome, where the successful are cut down to the same size as everyone else, quick smart. You're not supposed to stand out for intelligence, achievement, or, worst of all, wealth."

—*Peter Hartcher*

You may be wondering what poppies have to do with the workplace.[186] It's a reasonable question. The allegory behind tall poppy syndrome goes back centuries, but the emotions of envy and resentment toward strong performers—and the desire to "cut them down to size"—are timeless. So is the reality—evidence indicates that individuals whose performance and status rise above the rest (the tall poppies) sometimes find their careers are decapitated by jealous co-workers (the shorter poppies) who undermine their efforts. Tall poppies are more likely to be victimized by group members, and group members are often pleased if a tall poppy is "brought down" by outsiders.

Tall poppy syndrome seems to be motivated by the observer's personality traits, emotions, and perception of justice. When individuals believe the high achiever is undeserving of his or her status, or conversely when individuals believe they deserve a higher status than they have been given (called relative deprivation), resentment and envy are heightened. The degree of tall poppy syndrome also seems to relate to the traits of the people who judge their co-workers. People who have lower self-esteem and who do not value power and achievement tend to think high performers are undeserving and should fall. Finally, the general likeability of the achiever seems to influence the emotions of observers. If achievers are popular, part of the in-group, work hard, and exhibit high moral character, observers are less likely to feel resentful and wish them ill.

Tall poppy syndrome may be universal, but there are cultural differences. Research has shown that in collectivistic societies like Japan, students in a study were more inclined to cut down a high performer because they resented distinguishing one person more than the rest of the group. In contrast, students from the individualistic United States were more likely to reward high achievers than were Australian students because the Americans did not feel the same degree of envy.

To the extent that it cuts down those with legitimate achievements, there is nothing good about tall poppy syndrome when high performers are victimized and work performance is limited to a common denominator. Both the high performer and the organization can employ some countermeasures aimed at lessening the emotional reactions of observers. For one, high performers can demonstrate humbleness and humility. This may allow them to boost the performance of co-workers, who then no longer feel resentful of their success. Second, managers can increase work group identity for the co-workers, so they see the success of one individual as the success of the group, rather than as an injustice.

Questions

1. Have you observed tall poppy syndrome in your workplace or school? Which traits seemed to bother the observers the most?

2. In what specific ways do you think high performers can mitigate feelings of envy and resentment? Give examples.

FROM CONCEPTS TO SKILLS

Reading Emotions

Understanding another person's felt emotions is very difficult. But we can learn to read others' displayed emotions.[187] We do this by focusing on verbal, nonverbal, and paralanguage cues.

The easiest way to find out what someone is feeling is to ask them. Saying something as simple as "Are you okay? What's the problem?" can often provide you with the information to assess an individual's emotional state. But relying on a verbal response has two drawbacks. First, almost all of us conceal our emotions to some extent for privacy and to reflect social expectations. So we might be unwilling to share our true feelings. Second, even if we want to verbally convey our feelings, we may be unable to do so. As we noted earlier, some people have difficulty understanding their own emotions and, hence, are unable to express them verbally. So, at best, verbal responses provide only partial information.

Let's say you are talking with a co-worker. Does the fact that his back is rigid, his teeth clenched, and his facial muscles tight tell you something about his emotional state? It probably should. Facial expressions, gestures, body movements, and physical distance are nonverbal cues that can provide additional insights into what a person is feeling. The facial expressions shown in Exhibit 2-11, for instance, are a window into a person's feelings. Notice the difference in facial features: the height of the cheeks, the raising or lowering of the brow, the turn of the mouth, the positioning of the lips, and the configuration of muscles

EXHIBIT 2-11 Facial Expressions and Emotions

Each picture portrays a different emotion. Try to identify them before looking at the answers.

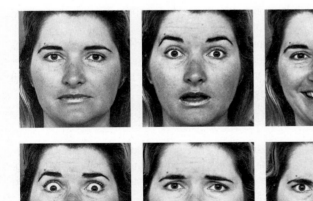

Top, left to right: neutral, surprise, happiness. Bottom: fear, sadness, anger.

Source: Paul Ekman, PhD/Paul Ekman Group, LLC.

around the eyes. Even something as subtle as the distance at which someone chooses to position him- or herself from you can convey how much intimacy, aggressiveness, repugnance, or withdrawal that person feels.

When you speak with someone, you may notice a sharp change in the tone of her voice and the speed at which she speaks. You are tapping into the third source of information on a person's emotions—paralanguage. This is communication that goes beyond the specific spoken words. It includes pitch, amplitude, rate, and voice quality of speech. Paralanguage reminds us that people convey their feelings not only in what they say, but also in how they say it.

Practising Skills

Part A. Form groups of 2. Each person is to spend a couple of minutes thinking of a time in the past when he or she was emotional about something. Examples might include being upset with a parent, sibling, or friend; being excited or disappointed about an academic or athletic achievement; being angry with someone over an insult or slight; being disgusted by something someone has said or done; or being happy because of something good that happened. Do not share this event with the other person in your group.

Part B. Now you will conduct 2 role plays. Each will be an interview. In the first, 1 person will play the interviewer and the other will play the job applicant. The job is for a summer management internship with a large retail chain. Each role play will last no longer than 10 minutes. The interviewer is to conduct a normal job interview, except you are to continually rethink the emotional episode you envisioned in part A. Try hard to convey this emotion while, at the same time, being professional in interviewing the job applicant.

Part C. Now reverse positions for the second role-play. The interviewer becomes the job applicant and vice versa. The new interviewer will conduct a normal job interview, except that he or she will continually rethink the emotional episode chosen in part A.

Part D. Spend 10 minutes analyzing the interview, with specific attention focused on these questions: What emotion(s) do you think the other person was conveying? What cues did you pick up? How accurate were you in reading those cues?

Reinforcing Skills

1. Watch the actors in an emotion-laden film, such as *Death of a Salesman* or *12 Angry Men*, for clues to the emotions they are exhibiting. Try to determine the various emotions projected and explain how you arrived at your conclusion.

2. Spend a day specifically looking for emotional cues in the people with whom you interact. Did paying attention to emotional cues improve communication?

3 Values, Attitudes, and Diversity in the Workplace

Ladies Learning Code was developed to teach adult women how to code. Will endeavours like this improve the diversity in technology jobs?

LEARNING OUTCOMES

After studying this chapter, you should be able to:

1. Contrast Rokeach's terminal and instrumental values.

2. Describe Hofstede's value dimensions for assessing cultures.

3. Identify unique Canadian values.

4. Understand the three components of an attitude.

5. Describe key attitudes that affect organizational performance.

6. Summarize the main causes of job satisfaction.

7. Identify the main consequences of job satisfaction.

8. Identify four employee responses to job dissatisfaction.

9. Describe how organizations can manage diversity effectively.

10. Identify the benefits of cultural intelligence.

Tara Walton/Toronto Star/Getty Images

Donald Trump's travel ban for citizens from seven predominantly Muslim countries sparked an outcry from many Canadians.[1] Justin Trudeau tweeted, "To those fleeing persecution, terror & war, Canadians will welcome you, regardless of your faith. Diversity is our strength."

Canadian tech companies, including Black-Berry, Hootsuite, and Shopify, also spoke out, and executives and employees signed an online letter calling on the federal government to issue visas to individuals affected by the ban. The tech community felt that diversity was the strength of their industry, thus their strong support.

However, tech companies are not as diverse as they imagine and they are sometimes criticized for their hostile environments toward women. One of Uber's former female engineers wrote a scathing review of the treatment of women in Uber's engineering department. There is also concern that fewer women go into the STEM subjects (Science, Technology, Engineering, and Mathematics), making them less likely to end up in the technology sector.

Toronto-based Ladies Learning Code is training women and youth to become more engaged with technology (founders Melissa Crnic, Heather Payne, Breanna Hughes, and Laura Plant are shown here). The company was founded in 2011 by four young women who decided to run workshops for women who wanted to learn to code. Their mission statement makes their values clear: "We are a not-for-profit organization with the mission to be the leading resource for women and youth to become passionate builders—not just consumers—of technology by learning technical skills in a hands-on, social, and collaborative way."

In this chapter, we look carefully at how values influence behaviour and consider the relationship between values and attitudes. We also examine two significant issues that arise from our discussion of values and attitudes: how to enhance job satisfaction and manage workforce diversity.

OB IS FOR EVERYONE

- How do countries differ in their values?
- Are Millennials really different from their elders?
- What things affect your job satisfaction?
- Are you comfortable working with people from other cultures?

THE BIG IDEA

Values affect our behaviours and attitudes, and can have a big impact on how people with different backgrounds get along in the workplace.

Values

Is capital punishment right or wrong? Is a person's desire for power good or bad? The answers to these questions are value-laden.

Values represent basic convictions that "a specific mode of conduct or end-state of existence is personally or socially preferable to an opposite or converse mode of conduct or end-state of existence."[2] They contain a judgmental element in that they carry an individual's ideas as to what is right, good, or desirable. Values have both content and intensity attributes. The content attribute says a mode of conduct or end-state of existence is *important*. The intensity attribute specifies *how important* it is. When we rank an individual's values in terms of their intensity, we discover that person's **value system**. All of us have a hierarchy of values according to the relative importance we assign to values such as freedom, pleasure, self-respect, honesty, obedience, and equality.[3]

Values tend to be relatively stable and enduring.[4] Most of our values are formed in our early years—with input from parents, teachers, friends, and others. As children, we were told that certain behaviours or outcomes are *always* desirable or *always* undesirable. There were few grey areas. It is this absolute or "black-or-white" characteristic of values that more or less ensures their stability and endurance. If we question our values, they may change, but more often they are reinforced. There is also evidence linking personality to values, implying our values may be partly determined by genetically transmitted traits.[5] Open people, for example, may be more politically liberal, whereas conscientious people may place a greater value on safe and ethical conduct. Below we examine two frameworks for understanding values: Milton Rokeach's terminal and instrumental values, and Kent Hodgson's general moral principles.

① Contrast Rokeach's terminal and instrumental values.

Rokeach Value Survey

Milton Rokeach created the Rokeach Value Survey (RVS), which consists of two sets of values, each containing 18 individual value items. One set, called **terminal values**, refers to desirable end-states of existence. These are the goals that individuals would like to achieve during their lifetime. They include

- A comfortable life (a prosperous life)
- An exciting life (a stimulating, active life)
- A sense of accomplishment (lasting contribution)
- Equality (brotherhood, equal opportunity for all)
- Inner harmony (freedom from inner conflict)
- Happiness (contentedness)

The other set, called **instrumental values**, refers to preferable modes of behaviour, or means for achieving the terminal values. They include

- Ambitious (hard-working, aspiring)
- Broad-minded (open-minded)
- Capable (competent, effective)
- Courageous (standing up for your beliefs)
- Imaginative (daring, creative)
- Honest (sincere, truthful)[6]

Each of us places value on both the ends (terminal values) and the means (instrumental values). A balance between the two is important, as well as an understanding of how to strike this balance.

values Basic convictions that a specific mode of conduct or end-state of existence is personally or socially preferable to an opposite or converse mode of conduct or end-state of existence.

value system A hierarchy based on a ranking of an individual's values in terms of their intensity.

terminal values Goals that individuals would like to achieve during their lifetime.

instrumental values Preferable ways of behaving.

Hodgson's General Moral Principles

Ethics is the study of moral principles that guide our behaviour and inform us whether actions are right or wrong. Thus, ethical principles are related to moral judgments about right and wrong.

In recent years, there has been concern that individuals are not grounded in moral principles. It is believed that this lack of moral roots has resulted in a number of business scandals, such as those at WorldCom, Enron, Hollinger International, and even in the sponsorship scandal of the Canadian government. We discuss the issue of ethics further in Chapter 12.

Management consultant Kent Hodgson has identified seven general moral principles that individuals should follow when making decisions. He calls these "the Magnificent Seven" and suggests that they are universal values that managers should use to make *principled, appropriate,* and *defensible* decisions.[7] They are presented in *OB in Action—The Magnificent Seven Principles.*

Assessing Cultural Values

> As it develops its many workshops, Ladies Learning Code is committed to recognizing the diversity of Canada.[9] Ladies Learning Code believes that "girls, people with disabilities, Indigenous youth and newcomers [should be] given equal opportunity to build our future." This belief reflects a dominant value of Canada as a multi-cultural country. The approach to diversity is very different in the United States, which considers itself a melting pot with respect to different cultures. What do you know about the values of people from other countries? What values make Canadians unique?

Unlike personality, which is largely genetically determined, values are learned. They are passed down through generations and vary by cultures. As researchers have sought to understand cultural value differences, two important frameworks that have emerged are from Geert Hofstede and the GLOBE studies.

Hofstede's Framework for Assessing Cultures

One of the most widely referenced approaches for analyzing variations among cultures was developed in the late 1970s by Geert Hofstede.[10] He surveyed more than 116 000 IBM employees in 40 countries about their work-related values, and found that managers and employees vary on five value dimensions of national culture:

- *Power distance.* **Power distance** describes the degree to which people in a country accept that power in institutions and organizations is distributed unequally. A high rating on power distance means that large inequalities of power and wealth exist and are tolerated in the culture, as in a class or caste system that discourages upward mobility. A low power-distance rating characterizes societies that stress equality and opportunity.

- *Individualism vs. collectivism.* **Individualism** is the degree to which people prefer to act as individuals rather than as members of groups and believe in individual rights above all else. **Collectivism** emphasizes a tight social framework in which people expect others in groups of which they are a part to look after them and protect them.

- *Masculinity vs. femininity.* Hofstede's construct of **masculinity** is the degree to which the culture favours traditional masculine roles, such as achievement, power, and control, as opposed to viewing men and women as equals. A

OB IN ACTION

The Magnificent Seven Principles

→ *Dignity of human life.* The lives of **people are to be respected**.

→ *Autonomy.* All persons are **intrinsically valuable** and have the **right to self-determination**.

→ *Honesty.* **The truth should be told** to those who have a right to know it.

→ *Loyalty.* **Promises, contracts,** and **commitments** should be **honoured**.

→ *Fairness.* **People should be treated justly.**

→ *Humaneness.* Our **actions ought to accomplish good**, and we should **avoid doing evil**.

→ *The common good.* Actions should accomplish **the greatest good for the greatest number** of people.[8]

 2 Describe Hofstede's value dimensions for assessing cultures.

---

ethics The study of moral values or principles that guide our behaviour and inform us whether actions are right or wrong.

power distance A national culture attribute that describes the extent to which a society accepts that power in institutions and organizations is distributed unequally.

individualism A national culture attribute that describes the degree to which people prefer to act as individuals rather than as members of groups.

collectivism A national culture attribute that describes a tight social framework in which people expect others in groups of which they are a part to look after them and protect them.

masculinity A national culture attribute that describes the extent to which the culture favours traditional masculine work roles of achievement, power, and control. Societal values are characterized by assertiveness and materialism.

high masculinity rating indicates the culture has separate roles for men and women, with men dominating the society. A high **femininity** rating means the culture sees little differentiation between male and female roles and treats women and men equally in all respects.

- *Uncertainty avoidance.* The degree to which people in a country prefer structured over unstructured situations defines their **uncertainty avoidance**. In cultures that score high on uncertainty avoidance, people have an increased level of anxiety about uncertainty and ambiguity, and use laws and controls to reduce uncertainty. Cultures low on uncertainty avoidance are more accepting of ambiguity and are less rule-oriented, take more risks, and more readily accept change.

- *Long-term vs. short-term orientation.* This more recent addition to Hofstede's typology measures a society's long-term devotion to traditional values. People in a culture with **long-term orientation** look to the future and value thrift, persistence, and tradition. In a culture with **short-term orientation**, people value the here and now; they accept change more readily and don't see commitments as impediments to change.

More recently, Hofstede has added a sixth dimension, based on studies he has conducted over the past 10 years.[11]

- *Indulgence vs. restraint.* This newest addition to Hofstede's typology measures society's devotion (or lack thereof) to indulgence. Cultures that emphasize **indulgence** encourage "relatively free gratification of basic and natural human desires related to enjoying life."[12] Those that favour **restraint** emphasize the need to control the gratification of needs.

How do different countries score on Hofstede's dimensions? Exhibit 3-1 shows the ratings for the countries for which data are available. For example, power distance is higher in Malaysia than in any other country. Canada is tied with the Netherlands as one of the top five individualistic countries in the world, falling just behind the United States, Australia, and Great Britain. Canada also tends to be short term in orientation and is low in power distance (people in Canada tend not to accept built-in class differences among people). Canada is also relatively low on uncertainty avoidance, meaning that most adults are relatively tolerant of uncertainty and ambiguity. Canada has a much higher score on masculinity in comparison with Sweden and Norway, although its score is lower than that of the United States. Guatemala is the most collectivistic nation. The country with the highest masculinity rank by far is Japan, and the country with the highest femininity rank is Sweden. Greece scores the highest in uncertainty avoidance, while Singapore scores the lowest. Hong Kong has one of the longest-term orientations; Pakistan has the shortest-term orientation.

> How do countries differ in their values?

femininity A national culture attribute that sees little differentiation between male and female roles; women are treated as the equals of men in all respects.

uncertainty avoidance A national culture attribute that describes the extent to which a society feels threatened by uncertain and ambiguous situations and tries to avoid them.

long-term orientation A national culture attribute that emphasizes the future, thrift, and tradition.

short-term orientation A national culture attribute that emphasizes the here and now and accepts change more readily.

indulgence A national culture attribute that emphasizes the gratification of basic needs and the desire to enjoy life.

restraint A national culture attribute that emphasizes the importance of controlling the gratification of needs.

RESEARCH FINDINGS: Hofstede

Research across 598 studies with more than 200 000 respondents has investigated the relationship of Hofstede's cultural values and a variety of organizational criteria at both the individual and national levels of analysis.[13] Overall, the five original cultural dimensions were found to be equally strong predictors of relevant outcomes. The researchers also found that measuring individual scores resulted in much better predictions of most outcomes than assigning all people in a country the same cultural values. In sum, this research suggests that Hofstede's value framework may be a valuable way of thinking about differences among people, but we should be cautious about assuming that all people from a country have the same values.

EXHIBIT 3-1 Hofstede's Cultural Values by Nation

Country	Power Distance		Individualism versus Collectivism		Masculinity versus Femininity		Uncertainty Avoidance		Long- versus Short-Term Orientation	
	Index	Rank	Index	Rank	Index	Rank	Index	Rank	Index	Rank
Argentina	49	35–36	46	22–23	56	20–21	86	10–15		
Australia	36	41	90	2	61	16	51	37	31	22–24
Austria	11	53	55	18	79	2	70	24–25	31	22–24
Belgium	65	20	75	8	54	22	94	5–6	38	18
Brazil	69	14	38	26–27	49	27	76	21–22	65	6
Canada	39	39	80	4–5	52	24	48	41–42	23	30
Chile	63	24–25	23	38	28	46	86	10–15		
Colombia	67	17	13	49	64	11–12	80	20		
Costa Rica	35	42–44	15	46	21	48–49	86	10–15		
Denmark	18	51	74	9	16	50	23	51	46	10
Ecuador	78	8–9	8	52	63	13–14	67	28		
El Salvador	66	18–19	19	42	40	40	94	5–6		
Finland	33	46	63	17	26	47	59	31–32	41	14
France	68	15–16	71	10–11	43	35–36	86	10–15	39	17
Germany	35	42–44	67	15	66	9–10	65	29	31	22–24
Great Britain	35	42–44	89	3	66	9–10	35	47–48	25	28–29
Greece	60	27–28	35	30	57	18–19	112	1		
Guatemala	95	2–3	6	53	37	43	101	3		
Hong Kong	68	15–16	25	37	57	18–19	29	49–50	96	2
India	77	10–11	48	21	56	20–21	40	45	61	7
Indonesia	78	8–9	14	47–48	46	30–31	48	41–42		
Iran	58	29–30	41	24	43	35–36	59	31–32		
Ireland	28	49	70	12	68	7–8	35	47–48	43	13
Israel	13	52	54	19	47	29	81	19		
Italy	50	34	76	7	70	4–5	75	23	34	19
Jamaica	45	37	39	25	68	7–8	13	52		
Japan	54	33	46	22–23	95	1	92	7	80	4
Korea (South)	60	27–28	18	43	39	41	85	16–17	75	5
Malaysia	104	1	26	36	50	25–26	36	46		
Mexico	81	5–6	30	32	69	6	82	18		
The Netherlands	38	40	80	4–5	14	51	53	35	44	11–12
New Zealand	22	50	79	6	58	17	49	39–40	30	25–26
Norway	31	47–48	69	13	8	52	50	38	44	11–12
Pakistan	55	32	14	47–48	50	25–26	70	24–25	0	34
Panama	95	2–3	11	51	44	34	86	10–15		
Peru	64	21–23	16	45	42	37–38	87	9		
Philippines	94	4	32	31	64	11–12	44	44	19	31–32
Portugal	63	24–25	27	33–35	31	45	104	2	30	25–26
Singapore	74	13	20	39–41	48	28	8	53	48	9
South Africa	49	35–36	65	16	63	13–14	49	39–40		
Spain	57	31	51	20	42	37–38	86	10–15	19	31–32
Sweden	31	47–48	71	10–11	5	53	29	49–50	33	20
Switzerland	34	45	68	14	70	4–5	58	33	40	15–16
Taiwan	58	29–30	17	44	45	32–33	69	26	87	3
Thailand	64	21–23	20	39–41	34	44	64	30	56	8
Turkey	66	18–19	37	28	45	32–33	85	16–17		
United States	40	38	91	1	62	15	46	43	29	27
Uruguay	61	26	36	29	38	42	100	4		
Venezuela	81	5–6	12	50	73	3	76	21–22		
Yugoslavia	76	12	27	33–35	21	48–49	88	8		
Regions:										
Arab countries	80	7	38	26–27	53	23	68	27		
East Africa	64	21–23	27	33–35	41	39	52	36	25	28–29
West Africa	77	10–11	20	39–41	46	30–31	54	34	16	33

Scores range from 0 = extremely low on dimension to 100 = extremely high.

Note: 1 = highest rank. LTO ranks: 1 = China; 15–16 = Bangladesh; 21 = Poland; 34 = lowest.

Source: Geert Hofstede, Gert Jan Hofstede, Michael Minkov, *Cultures and Organizations, Software of the Mind*, Third Revised Edition, McGraw-Hill 2010, ISBN 0-07-166418-1.

The GLOBE Framework for Assessing Cultures

Begun in 1993, the Global Leadership and Organizational Behavior Effectiveness (GLOBE) research program is an ongoing cross-cultural investigation of leadership and national culture. Using data from 825 organizations in 62 countries, the GLOBE team identified nine dimensions on which national cultures differ.[14] Some dimensions—such as power distance, individualism/collectivism, uncertainty avoidance, gender differentiation (similar to masculinity vs. femininity), and future orientation (similar to long-term vs. short-term orientation)—resemble the Hofstede dimensions. The main difference is that the GLOBE framework added dimensions, such as humane orientation (the degree to which a society rewards individuals for being altruistic, generous, and kind to others) and performance orientation (the degree to which a society encourages and rewards group members for performance improvement and excellence).

Which framework is better, Hofstede's or the GLOBE? That is hard to say, and each has its supporters. We give more emphasis to Hofstede's dimensions here because they have stood the test of time and the GLOBE study confirmed them. For example, a review of the organizational commitment literature shows that both the Hofstede and GLOBE individualism/collectivism dimensions operated similarly. Specifically, both frameworks showed that organizational commitment (which we discuss later in the chapter) tends to be lower in individualistic countries.[15] Both frameworks have a great deal in common, and each has something to offer.

3 Identify unique Canadian values.

Values in the Canadian Workplace

Studies have shown that when individual values align with organizational values, the results are positive. Individuals who have an accurate understanding of the job requirements and the organization's values adjust better to their jobs and have greater levels of satisfaction and organizational commitment.[16] In addition, shared values between the employee and the organization lead to more positive work attitudes,[17] lower turnover,[18] and greater productivity.[19]

Individual and organizational values do not always align. Moreover, within organizations, individuals can have very different values. Two major factors lead to a potential clash of values in the Canadian workplace: generational differences and cultural differences.

Let's look at the findings and implications of generational and cultural differences in Canada.

Generational Differences

Research suggests that generational differences exist in the workplace among the Baby Boomers (born between the mid-1940s and the mid-1960s), Generation Xers (born between the mid-1960s and the late 1970s), and the Millennials (born between 1979 through 1994).[20] Exhibit 3-2 highlights the different work values of the three

EXHIBIT 3-2 Dominant Work Values in Today's Workforce			
Cohort	Entered the Workforce	Approximate Current Age	Dominant Work Values
Baby Boomers	1965–1985	Mid-40s to mid-60s	Success, achievement, ambition, dislike of authority; loyalty to career
Generation Xers	1985–2000	Late 20s to early 40s	Work–life balance, team-oriented, dislike of rules; loyalty to relationships
Millennials	2000 to present	Under 30	Confident, financial success, self-reliant but team-oriented; loyalty to both self and relationships

Sue Cavallucci

When Robert Dutton, former president and CEO of Boucherville, Quebec-based Rona, started working at the company, senior managers often were his grandfather's age, while he was a young Baby Boomer. After working over 30 years at Rona, Dutton noticed that Millennials were starting to make up a larger portion of Rona's dealers. Dutton started the group Young Rona Business Leaders to help develop the Millennial talent that will be the future of Rona.[21]

generations, and indicates when each entered the workforce. Because most people start working between the ages of 18 and 23, the eras also correlate closely with employee age.

Generation Xers are squeezed in the workplace between the much larger Baby Boomer and Millennial groups. With Millennials starting to climb the ladder in organizations, and Boomers continuing to hold on to their jobs rather than retire, the impact of having these two large generations—one younger and one older—in the workplace is gaining attention. Bear in mind that our discussion of these generations presents broad generalizations, and you should certainly avoid stereotyping individuals on the basis of these general-

> Are Millennials really different from their elders?

izations. There are individual differences in values. For instance, there is no law that says a Baby Boomer cannot think like a Millennial. Despite these limitations, values do change over generations.[22] We can gain some useful insights from analyzing values this way to understand how others might view things differently from ourselves, even when they are exposed to the same situation. The *Point/Counterpoint* on page 110 considers whether Millennials have a more inflated view of themselves as compared with their parents.

An understanding that individuals' values differ but tend to reflect the societal values of the period in which they grew up can be a valuable aid in explaining and predicting behaviour. The change in the demographic composition of the workplace will definitely have an impact. Millennials edged out the Baby Boomers to become the largest cohort in the Canadian workplace in 2016.[23]

RESEARCH FINDINGS: Generational Differences

Although it's fascinating to think about generational values, remember that these classifications lack solid research support. Early research was plagued by methodological problems that made it difficult to assess whether differences actually exist. Reviews suggest many of the generalizations are either overblown or incorrect.[24] Differences across generations often don't support popular conceptions of how generations differ. One study that used an appropriate longitudinal design did find the value placed on leisure has increased over generations from the Baby Boomers to the Millennials and work centrality has declined, but research did not find that Millennials had more altruistic work values.[25] Generational classifications may help us understand our own and other generations better, but we must also appreciate their limits. A new generation will be coming to the workplace soon, and researchers suggest that this new generation may be the cause of revolution in the workplace. *OB in the Street* looks at Generation Z.

OB IN THE STREET

Generation Z: Coming to Your Workplace Soon

Will the next generation of employees be radically different from their older siblings? Ann Makosinski, just 16 years old and from Victoria, is already trying to start her own company.[26] A friend from the Philippines was having trouble getting homework done and failed a grade because she did not have access to electricity to study at night. Makosinski won Google's annual international science fair in 2013 with her battery-free "Hollow Flashlight," which is powered by body heat.

Makosinski is part of Generation Z, the group that comes after the Millennials, and was born starting in 1995. The oldest are in their early 20s and just starting to enter the workplace. Makosinski's cohort is described by researchers as "educated, industrious, collaborative and eager to build a better planet," exactly what she is already doing.

Sparks & Honey, a New York City advertising agency, found that 60 percent of Gen Zers want jobs that have a social impact compared with 31 percent of Millennials. They are the first generation to have digital access from the crib, making them extremely comfortable in that world. While their parents feel anxious about how multitasking might affect thinking, Gen Zers see it as a natural action.

It's probably too early to define where Gen Z will go, but Makosinski is representative of her generation thus far. "I'm just very glad I've been able to inspire a few people," she says. "I think that's what really changed my life, now I'm more conscious of my actions and how I spend my time."

Cultural Differences

Canada is a multicultural country: In 2011, 20.6 percent of its population was foreign-born.[27] It is projected that in 2036 that number will be between 24.5 percent and 30 percent.[28] This figure compares with 12.9 percent for the United States in 2013.[29] In 2011, 46 percent of Toronto's population, 40 percent of Vancouver's population, and 22.6 percent of Montreal's population were made up of immigrants.[30] The 2011 Census found that 20 percent of Canada's population spoke a language other than the country's two official languages at home. This is expected to increase to between 26.1 percent and 30.6 percent in 2036. In Vancouver and Toronto, this rate was 31 percent and 32 percent, respectively, so nearly one-third of the population of those two cities does not speak either English or French as a first language.[31] In Canada, of those who speak other languages, the dominant languages are Punjabi, Chinese (not specified), Cantonese, and Spanish.[32] These figures indicate the very different cultures that are part of the Canadian fabric of life.

Although we live in a multicultural society, some tension exists among people from different races and ethnic groups. In a recent poll, 25 percent of Canadians reported that they had experienced racism. Hate crimes directed mostly at Muslims, Arabs, and West Asians rose 5 percent between 2014 and 2015, with 1362 criminal incidents reported.[33]

Attitudes

The attitudes of management are reflected in how employees handle their jobs.[34] The tech industry is hard on women, and at least at Uber, the sexist attitude of its CEO bubbled through the company. In an interview in 2014, then-CEO Travis Kalanick referred to Uber as "Boob-er" because it helped him attract women. It is therefore not surprising that many of his senior managers ignored women who complained about sexual harassment. Kalanick was forced to resign in June 2017. In this section we discuss how attitudes affect behaviour.

Attitudes are evaluative statements—either positive or negative—about objects, people, or events. They reflect how we feel about something. When I say, "I like my job," I am expressing my attitude about work. Typically, researchers have assumed that attitudes have three components: cognition, affect, and behaviour.[35] Let's look at each.

The statement "My pay is low" is the **cognitive component** of an attitude—a description of or belief in the way things are. It sets the stage for the more critical part of an attitude—its **affective component**. Affect is the emotional or feeling segment of an attitude and is reflected in the statement "I'm angry over how little I'm paid." Affect can lead to behavioural outcomes. The **behavioural component** of an attitude describes an intention to behave in a certain way toward someone or something, as in "I'm going to look for another job that pays better."

Viewing attitudes as having three components—cognition, affect, and behaviour—helps us understand their complexity and the potential relationship between attitudes and behaviour. For example, imagine that you realized someone has just treated you unfairly. You are likely to have feelings about that, occurring virtually instantaneously with the realization. Thus, cognition and affect are intertwined.

Exhibit 3-3 illustrates how the three components of an attitude are related. In this example, an employee did not get a promotion he thought he deserved. The employee's attitude toward his supervisor is illustrated as follows: The employee thought he deserved the promotion (cognition), he strongly dislikes his supervisor (affect), and he has complained and taken action (behaviour). Although we often think cognition causes affect, which then causes behaviour, in reality these components are difficult to separate.

4 Understand the three components of an attitude.

EXHIBIT 3-3 The Components of an Attitude

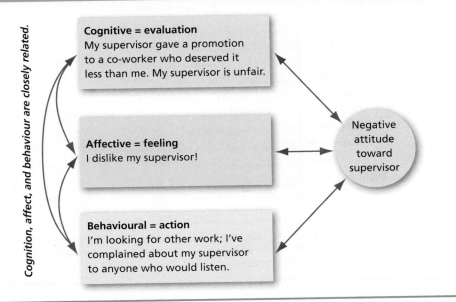

Cognition, affect, and behaviour are closely related.

Cognitive = evaluation
My supervisor gave a promotion to a co-worker who deserved it less than me. My supervisor is unfair.

Affective = feeling
I dislike my supervisor!

Behavioural = action
I'm looking for other work; I've complained about my supervisor to anyone who would listen.

Negative attitude toward supervisor

attitudes Positive or negative feelings about objects, people, or events.

cognitive component The opinion or belief segment of an attitude.

affective component The emotional or feeling segment of an attitude.

behavioural component An intention to behave in a certain way toward someone or something.

In organizations, attitudes are important because they affect job behaviour.[36] Employees may believe, for example, that managers, auditors, and engineers are in a conspiracy to make them work harder for less money. This may then lead to a negative attitude toward management when an employee is asked to stay late to help on a special project.

Employees may also be negatively affected by the attitudes of their co-workers or clients. *From Concepts to Skills* on pages 114–115 looks at whether it's possible to change someone's attitude, and how that might happen in the workplace.

A person can have thousands of attitudes, but OB focuses our attention on a limited number of work-related attitudes that tap positive or negative evaluations that employees hold about aspects of their work environments.[37] Next we consider five important attitudes that affect organizational performance: job satisfaction, organizational commitment, job involvement, perceived organizational support, and employee engagement.

5 Describe key attitudes that affect organizational performance.

Job Satisfaction

When people speak of employee attitudes, they usually mean **job satisfaction**, a positive feeling about a job resulting from an evaluation of its characteristics.[38] A survey conducted by Hays Canada in 2016 found that Canadians are not all that satisfied: 47 percent said they were unhappy with their job.[39] A person with high job satisfaction holds positive feelings about the work, while a person with low satisfaction holds negative feelings. Because OB researchers give job satisfaction high importance, we will review this attitude in detail.

6 Summarize the main causes of job satisfaction.

What Causes Job Satisfaction?

Think about the best job you have ever had. What made it great? Chances are you liked the work you did and the people with whom you worked. Interesting jobs that provide training, variety, independence, and control satisfy most employees.[40] A recent European study indicated that job satisfaction is positively correlated with life satisfaction, in that your attitudes and experiences in life spill over into your job approaches and experiences.[41] Exhibit 3-4 shows what jobs people feel provide the worst job satisfaction.

What things affect your job satisfaction?

EXHIBIT 3-4 The Worst Jobs for Job Satisfaction*

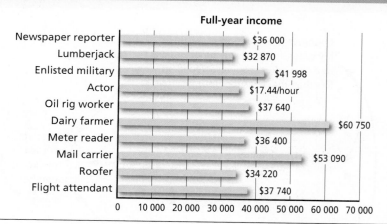

*Based on physical demands, work environment, income, stress, and hiring outlook.

Sources: L. Weber, "Best and Worst Jobs," *Wall Street Journal*, April 11, 2012, in the CareerCast.com Jobs Rated report, p. B6; and K. Kensing, "The Worst Jobs of 2013," *CareerCast.com*, 2013, http://www.careercast.com/jobs-rated/worst-jobs-2013.

job satisfaction A positive feeling about a job resulting from an evaluation of its characteristics.

EXHIBIT 3-5 Average Job Satisfaction Levels by Facet

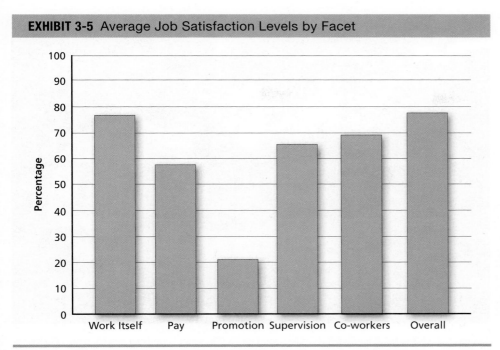

The facets of job satisfaction levels can vary widely. As shown in Exhibit 3-5, people have typically been more satisfied with their jobs overall, the work itself, and their supervisors and co-workers than they have been with their pay and promotion opportunities.

The reasons can differ greatly. Let's discuss some characteristics that likely influence job satisfaction, starting with job conditions.

Job Conditions Generally, interesting jobs that provide training, variety, independence, and control satisfy most employees. Interdependence, feedback, social support, and interaction with co-workers outside the workplace are also strongly related to job satisfaction, even after accounting for characteristics of the work itself.[42] As you may have guessed, managers also play a big role in employees' job satisfaction. Employees who feel empowered by their leaders experience higher job satisfaction, one study of a large Hong Kong telecommunications corporation found.[43] Research in Israel suggested that a manager's attentiveness, responsiveness, and support increase the employee's job satisfaction.[44]

Thus, job conditions—especially the intrinsic nature of the work itself, social interactions, and supervision—are important predictors of job satisfaction. Although each is important and their relative value varies across employees, the intrinsic nature of the work is most important.[45]

Personality As important as job conditions are to job satisfaction, personality also plays an important role. People who have positive **core self-evaluations (CSEs)**—who believe in their inner worth and basic competence—are more satisfied with their jobs than people with negative CSEs. Additionally, in the context of career commitment, CSE influences job satisfaction as people with high levels of both CSE and career commitment may realize particularly high job satisfaction.[46]

Pay You have probably noticed that pay comes up often when people discuss job satisfaction. Pay does correlate with job satisfaction and overall happiness for many people, but the effect can be smaller once an individual reaches a standard level of comfortable living. Money does motivate people, as we will discover in Chapter 4. But what motivates us is not necessarily the same as what makes us happy.

core self-evaluation (CSE)
Bottom-line conclusions individuals have about their capabilities, competence, and worth as a person.

Carlos Osorio/Toronto Star/Getty Images

Toronto-based Real Food for Real Kids makes food for 15 000 school-aged children each day. Co-founders Lulu Cohen-Farnell and David Farnell believe that making sure their employees connect with the work that they do increases motivation and reduces turnover of the caterers.

7 Identify the main consequences of job satisfaction.

Job Satisfaction and Productivity

As several studies have concluded, happy workers are more likely to be productive workers. Some researchers used to believe the relationship between job satisfaction and job performance was a myth. But a review of more than 300 studies suggested the correlation between job satisfaction and job performance is quite strong, even across international contexts.[47] Individuals with higher job satisfaction perform better, and organizations with more satisfied employees tend to be more effective than those with fewer.

Job Satisfaction and Organizational Citizenship Behaviour

In Chapter 1, we defined **organizational citizenship behaviour (OCB)** as discretionary behaviour that is not part of an employee's formal job requirements, and is not usually rewarded, but that nevertheless promotes the effective functioning of the organization.[48]

It seems logical to assume that job satisfaction should be a major determinant of an employee's OCB.[49] OCBs include people talking positively about their organizations, helping others, and going beyond the normal expectations of their jobs. Evidence suggests job satisfaction *is* moderately correlated with OCB; people who are more satisfied with their jobs are more likely to engage in citizenship behaviour.[50]

Why does job satisfaction lead to OCB? One reason is trust. Research in 18 countries suggests that managers reciprocate employees' OCB with trusting behaviours of their own.[51] Individuals who feel their co-workers support them are also more likely to engage in helpful behaviours than those who have antagonistic co-worker relationships.[52] Personality matters, too. Individuals with certain personality traits (agreeableness and conscientiousness, see Chapter 2) are more satisfied with their work, which in turn leads them to engage in more OCB.[53] Finally, individuals who receive positive feedback on their OCB from their peers are more likely to continue their citizenship activities.[54]

organizational citizenship behaviour (OCB) Discretionary behaviour that is not part of an employee's formal job requirements, but that nevertheless promotes the effective functioning of the organization.

Job Satisfaction and Customer Satisfaction

As we noted in Chapter 1, employees in service jobs often interact with customers. Because service organization managers should be concerned with pleasing customers, it's reasonable to ask: Is employee satisfaction related to positive customer outcomes?

Service firms like Air Canada understand that satisfied employees increase customer satisfaction and loyalty. As front-line employees who have regular customer contact, the airline's ticket agents are friendly, upbeat, and responsive while greeting passengers and helping them with luggage check-in and seat assignments.

For front-line employees who have regular contact with customers, the answer is yes. Satisfied employees increase customer satisfaction and loyalty.[55]

A number of companies are acting on this evidence. Online shoe retailer Zappos is so committed to finding customer service employees who are satisfied with the job that it offers a $2000 bribe to quit the company after training, figuring the least satisfied will take the cash and go.[56] Employees are empowered to "create fun and a little weirdness" and are given unusual discretion in making customers satisfied, and it works: Of the company's more than 24 million customers, 75 percent are repeat buyers. Therefore, for Zappos, employee satisfaction has a direct effect on customer satisfaction.

Life Satisfaction

Until now, we have treated job satisfaction as if it were separate from life satisfaction, but they may be more related than you think.[57] Research in Europe indicated that job satisfaction is positively correlated with life satisfaction, and your attitudes and experiences in life spill over into your job approaches and experiences.[58] Furthermore, life satisfaction decreases when people become unemployed, according to research in Germany, and not just because of the loss of income.[59] For most individuals, work is an important part of life, and therefore it makes sense that our overall happiness depends in no small part on our happiness in our work (our job satisfaction).

How Employees Can Express Dissatisfaction

What happens when employees like their jobs, and when they dislike their jobs? One theoretical model—the exit–voice–loyalty–neglect framework—is helpful in understanding the consequences of dissatisfaction. Exhibit 3-6 illustrates the framework's four responses, which differ along two dimensions: constructive/destructive and active/passive. The responses are as follows:[60]

- **Exit.** Actively attempting to leave the organization, including looking for a new position as well as resigning. This action is destructive from the point

 Identify four employee responses to job dissatisfaction.

---

exit Dissatisfaction expressed by actively attempting to leave the organization.

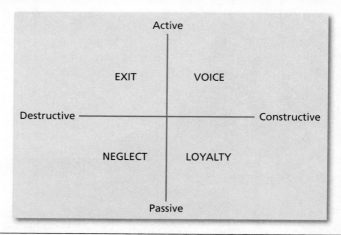

EXHIBIT 3-6 Responses to Job Dissatisfaction

Source: "When Bureaucrats Get the Blues: Responses to Dissatisfaction among Federal Employees" by Caryl Rusbult, David Lowery. *Journal of Applied Social Psychology 15*, no. 1, p. 83. Copyright © 1985, John Wiley and Sons.

of view of the organization. Researchers study individual terminations and *collective turnover*, the total loss to the organization of employee knowledge, skills, abilities, and other characteristics.[61]

- **Voice.** Actively and constructively attempting to improve conditions, including suggesting improvements, discussing problems with superiors, and undertaking union activity.

- **Loyalty.** Passively but optimistically waiting for conditions to improve, including speaking up for the organization in the face of external criticism and trusting the organization and its management to "do the right thing."

- **Neglect.** Passively allowing conditions to worsen, including chronic absenteeism or lateness, reduced effort, and increased error rate. This action is destructive from the point of view of the organization.

Exit and neglect behaviours are linked to performance variables such as productivity, absenteeism, and turnover. But this model expands employee responses to include voice and loyalty—constructive behaviours that allow individuals to tolerate unpleasant situations or improve working conditions.

This model helps us understand various situations. For instance, union members often express dissatisfaction through the grievance procedure or through formal contract negotiations. These voice mechanisms allow them to continue in their jobs while acting to improve the situation. The *Ethical Dilemma* on page 112 provides additional ways that employees can voice their views about their workplaces.

As helpful as this framework is, it's quite general. We will next address counterproductive work behaviour, a behavioural response to job dissatisfaction.

Counterproductive Work Behaviour (CWB)

Substance abuse, stealing at work, undue socializing, gossiping, absenteeism, and tardiness are examples of behaviours that are destructive to organizations. They are indicators of a broader syndrome called **counterproductive work behaviour (CWB)**, also termed deviant behaviour in the workplace, or simply employee withdrawal.[62] Like other behaviours we have discussed, CWB doesn't just happen—the behaviours often

voice Dissatisfaction expressed by actively and constructively attempting to improve conditions.

loyalty Dissatisfaction expressed by passively waiting for conditions to improve.

neglect Dissatisfaction expressed by passively allowing conditions to worsen.

counterproductive work behaviour (CWB) Actions that actively damage the organization, including stealing, behaving aggressively toward co-workers, or being late or absent.

follow negative and sometimes longstanding attitudes. Therefore, if we can identify the predictors of CWB, we may lessen the probability of its effects.

Generally, job dissatisfaction predicts CWB. People who are not satisfied with their work become frustrated, which lowers their performance[63] and makes them more likely to commit CWB.[64] Other research suggests that, in addition to vocational misfit (being in the wrong line of work), lack of fit with the organization (working in the wrong kind of organizational culture) also predicts CWBs.[65] Our immediate social environment also matters. One German study suggests that we are influenced toward CWB by the norms of our immediate work environment, such that individuals in teams with high absenteeism are more likely to be absent themselves.[66] CWB can, furthermore, be a response to abusive supervision from managers, which then increases the abuse, starting a vicious cycle.[67]

One important point about CWB is that dissatisfied employees often choose one or more of these specific behaviours due to idiosyncratic factors. One worker might quit. Another might use work time to surf the Internet or take work supplies home for personal use. In short, workers who don't like their jobs "get even" in various ways. Because those ways can be quite creative, controlling only one behaviour with policies and punishments leaves the root cause untouched. Employers should seek to correct the source of the problem—the dissatisfaction—rather than try to control the different responses.

According to UK research, sometimes CWB is an emotional reaction to perceived unfairness, a way to try to restore an employee's sense of equity exchange.[68] It therefore has complex ethical implications. For example, is someone who takes a box of markers home from the office for his children acting ethically? Some people consider this stealing. Others may want to look at moderating factors such as the employee's contribution to the organization before they decide. Does the person generously give extra time and effort to the organization, with little thanks or compensation? If so, they might see CWB behaviour as part of an attempt to "even the score."

As a manager, you can take steps to mitigate CWB. You can poll employee attitudes, for instance, and identify areas for workplace improvement. If there is no vocational fit, the employee will not be fulfilled,[69] so you can screen for that. Tailoring tasks so a person's abilities and values can be exercised should increase job satisfaction and reduce CWB.[70] Furthermore, creating strong teams, integrating supervisors with them, providing formalized team policies, and introducing team-based incentives may help lower the CWB "contagion" that lowers the standards of the group.[71]

Absenteeism   We find a consistent negative relationship between satisfaction and absenteeism, but the relationship is moderate to weak.[72] Generally, when numerous alternative jobs are available, dissatisfied employees have high absence rates, but when there are few alternatives, dissatisfied employees have the same (low) rate of absence as satisfied employees.[73] Organizations that provide liberal sick leave benefits are encouraging all their employees—including those who are highly satisfied—to take days off. You can find work satisfying yet still want to enjoy a three-day weekend if those days come free with no penalties.

Turnover   The relationship between job satisfaction and turnover is stronger than between satisfaction and absenteeism.[74] Overall, a pattern of lowered job satisfaction is the best predictor of intent to leave. Turnover has a workplace environment connection too. If the climate within an employee's immediate workplace is one of low job satisfaction leading to turnover, there will be a contagion effect. This suggests managers consider the job satisfaction (and turnover) patterns of co-workers when assigning workers to a new area.[75]

The satisfaction–turnover relationship is affected by alternative job prospects. If an employee accepts an unsolicited job offer, job dissatisfaction is less predictive of turnover because the employee more likely left in response to "pull" (the lure of the other job) than "push" (the unattractiveness of the current job). Similarly, job dissatisfaction is more likely to translate into turnover when other employment opportunities are plentiful. Furthermore, when employees have high "human capital" (high education, high ability), job dissatisfaction is more likely to translate into turnover because they have, or perceive, many available alternatives.[76] Employees' embeddedness—connections to the job and community—can help lower the probability of turnover, particularly in collectivist (group-oriented) cultures.[77] Embedded employees seem less likely to want to consider alternative job prospects.

Organizational Commitment

In **organizational commitment** an employee identifies with a particular organization and its goals, and wishes to remain a member.[78] Most research has focused on emotional attachment to an organization and belief in its values as the "gold standard" for employee commitment.[79]

Professor John Meyer at the University of Western Ontario and his colleagues have identified and developed measures for three types of commitment:[80]

- **Affective commitment**. An individual's emotional attachment to an organization and a belief in its values. For example, a PetSmart employee may be affectively committed to the company because of its involvement with animals.

- **Normative commitment**. The obligation an individual feels to stay with an organization for moral or ethical reasons. An employee spearheading a new initiative may remain with an employer because she feels she would "leave the employer in the lurch" if she left.

- **Continuance commitment**. An individual's perceived economic value of remaining with an organization. An employee may be committed to an employer because she is paid well and feels it would hurt her family to quit.

A positive relationship appears to exist between organizational commitment and job productivity, but it is a modest one.[81] A review of 27 studies found that the relationship between commitment and performance is strongest for new employees, and considerably weaker for more experienced employees.[82] Interestingly, research indicates that employees who feel their employers fail to keep promises to them feel less committed, and these reductions in commitment, in turn, lead to lower levels of creative performance.[83] And, as with job involvement, the research evidence demonstrates negative relationships between organizational commitment and both absenteeism and turnover.[84] Read the *Ethical Dilemma* on page 112 to see how social forums tell both employees and employers about organizational commitment.

Different forms of commitment have different effects on behaviour. One study found managerial affective commitment was more strongly related to organizational performance than was continuance commitment.[85] Another study showed that continuance commitment was related to a lower intention to quit but an increased tendency to be absent and lower job performance. These results make sense in that continuance commitment is not really a commitment at all. Rather than an allegiance (affective commitment) or an obligation (normative commitment) to an employer, a continuance commitment describes an employee "tethered" to an employer simply because nothing better is available.[86]

Job Involvement

Related to job satisfaction is **job involvement**,[87] the degree to which people identify psychologically with their job and consider their perceived performance level

organizational commitment The degree to which an employee identifies with a particular organization and its goals, and wishes to maintain membership in the organization.

affective commitment An individual's emotional attachment to and identification with an organization, and a belief in its values.

normative commitment The obligation an individual feels to stay with an organization.

continuance commitment An individual's calculation to stay with an organization based on the perceived costs of leaving the organization.

job involvement The degree to which a person identifies with a job, actively participates in it, and considers performance important to self-worth.

Developing the talents of women is a strategic diversity imperative for business success at Nissan Motor Company in Japan. Attracted by Nissan's commitment to equality for women in the workplace and to developing their careers, Li Ning of China decided to join the company after graduating from Tokyo University.

important to their self-worth.[88] Employees with high job involvement strongly identify with and really care about the kind of work they do. Another closely related concept is **psychological empowerment**, or employees' beliefs in the degree to which they influence their work environment, their competence, the meaningfulness of their job, and their perceived autonomy.[89]

Research suggests that empowerment initiatives need to be tailored to desired behavioural outcomes. Research in Singapore found that good leaders empower their employees by fostering their self-perception of competence—through involving them in decisions, making them feel their work is important, and giving them discretion to "do their own thing."[90]

Perceived Organizational Support

Perceived organizational support (POS) is the degree to which employees believe the organization values their contributions and cares about their well-being. An excellent example is R & D engineer John Greene, whose POS is sky-high because when he was diagnosed with leukemia, CEO Marc Benioff and 350 fellow salesforce.com employees covered all out-of-pocket costs for his care, staying in touch with him throughout his recovery. No doubt stories like this one are part of the reason salesforce.com was number eight of *Fortune*'s 100 Best Companies to Work For list in 2015.[91]

People perceive their organization as supportive when rewards are deemed fair, when employees have a voice in decisions, and when employees view their supervisors as supportive.[92] POS is a predictor, but there are some cultural influences. POS is important in countries where power distance is lower. In low power-distance countries like Canada, people are more likely to view work as an exchange rather than a moral obligation, so employees look for reasons to feel supported by their organizations. In high power-distance countries like China, employee POS perceptions are not as deeply based on demonstrations of fairness, support, and encouragement.

psychological empowerment Employees' belief in the degree to which they affect their work environment, their competence, the meaningfulness of their job, and their perceived autonomy in their work.

perceived organizational support (POS) The degree to which employees believe an organization values their contribution and cares about their well-being.

Employee Engagement

Employee engagement is an individual's involvement with, satisfaction with, and enthusiasm for the work he or she does. To evaluate employee engagement, we might ask employees whether they have access to resources and the opportunities to learn new skills, whether they feel their work is important and meaningful, and whether their interactions with co-workers and supervisors are rewarding.[93] Highly engaged employees have a passion for their work and feel a deep connection to their company; disengaged employees have essentially "checked out"—putting time but not energy or attention into their work.[94] Calgary-based Vista Projects, an engineering procurement and construction management firm, consults with its employees for engagement ideas. Doing so has resulted in educational initiatives, opportunities for company owner-ship, and time off for religious holidays.[95] To encourage engagement, the president of Charlottetown, PEI-based Holland College visits the college's 13 sites routinely to give employees an opportunity to raise concerns.[96] Read *Case Incident—Job Crafting* on pages 112–113 to see how one individual proactively improved her employee engagement.

Engagement becomes a real concern for most organizations because surveys indicate that few employees—between 17 percent and 29 percent— are highly engaged by their work. A 2016 survey of Canadians conducted by the Conference Board of Canada found that only 27 percent of employees are highly engaged.[97] A 2013 poll by Gallup, conducted in 142 countries, found that only 13 percent of employees worldwide are engaged at work.[98] Most are disengaged: 63 percent are not engaged, and 24 percent are actively disengaged. Oakville, Ontario-based Ford Canada recently contracted with Charles "the Butler" MacPherson to help its employees develop more engaged customer service relationships, as *OB in the Workplace* illustrates.

OB IN THE WORKPLACE

Minding Manners, Helping Customers

Can a butler help salespeople engage more with their customers?   Ford Canada recently hired Charles "the Butler" MacPherson to provide customer service training sessions to employees.[99] His first stop was Ottawa, and then 23 more Ford locations across Canada.

MacPherson's role is to help employees in Ford's service departments engage more with their customers so that customers receive more personalized service. MacPherson explained why he was comfortable helping salespeople: "Whether you're serving food or whether you're presenting someone a proposal on a repair in the car, you still have to be able to do it in the same way about making sure that you're at ease, that we're listening to you, that you're able to speak your thoughts."

Ford Canada's national consumer experience manager, Gemma Giovinazzo, is enthusiastic about developing more engaged employees. "We know, based on statistical research, that a highly engaged employee will lead to a highly engaged customer. Highly engaged employees will bend over backwards for the company and its customers. In such a culture, there is no 'this is just my job; I am only going to do that.'"

Ford believes its investment in employees will also lead to more loyal customers. . . . . .

employee engagement An individual's involvement with, satisfaction with, and enthusiasm for the work he or she does.

Engagement levels determine many measurable outcomes. A study of nearly 8000 business units in 36 companies found that units whose employees reported high-average levels of engagement achieved higher levels of customer satisfaction, were more productive, brought in higher profits, and experienced lower levels of turnover and accidents than at other business units.[100] Molson Coors, for example, found engaged employees were five times less likely to have safety incidents, and when an accident did occur it was much less serious and less costly for the engaged employee than for a disengaged one ($63 per incident versus $392). Caterpillar set out to increase employee engagement and recorded a resulting 80 percent drop in grievances and a 34 percent increase in highly satisfied customers.[101]

Promising findings have earned employee engagement a following in many business organizations and management consulting firms. However, the concept generates active debate about its usefulness, partly because of difficulty in identifying what creates job engagement. The two top reasons for job engagement that participants in one study gave recently were (1) having a good manager they enjoy working for and (2) feeling appreciated by their supervisor.[102] However, most of their other reasons didn't relate to the job engagement construct.[103] Another study in Australia found that emotional intelligence is linked to employee engagement.[104] Other research suggested that engagement fluctuates partially due to daily challenges and demands.[105]

One review of the job engagement literature concluded, "The meaning of employee engagement is ambiguous among both academic researchers and among practitioners who use it in conversations with clients." Another reviewer called engagement "an umbrella term for whatever one wants it to be."[106] Research on engagement has set out to identify the dimensions of employee engagement, but the debate is far from settled. For now, we can see that job engagement, in its various incarnations, yields important organizational outcomes.

Some critics note that engagement may have a "dark side," as evidenced by positive relationships between engagement and work–family conflict.[107] Individuals might grow so engaged in their work roles that family responsibilities become an unwelcome intrusion. Further research exploring how engagement relates to these negative outcomes may help clarify whether some highly engaged employees might be getting "too much of a good thing."

Managing Diversity in the Workplace

In the spring of 2017, *CBC News* decided to find out how much diversity there really is within the technology sector.[108] It asked 31 Canadian tech companies about their data-gathering process regarding employee diversity and whether the companies would share their data. Two companies agreed to share data: Clearpath Robotics and Wealthsimple, an investing app. Toronto-based Hubba said it was in the process of collecting data.

Judging from *CBC News'* findings, it is not surprising that diversity is not handled well in tech companies. If companies do not collect statistics on their employees to help management understand diversity issues, it's hard to know whether improvement is needed. Diversity consultants suggest that collecting data is not enough, however. "Reports done well should be part of a company's larger diversity and inclusion strategy—one that, like any problem a business faces, requires data so that it can be understood and goals can be set for improvement."

Ladies Learning Code expects to be a part of the solution for the tech industry's low diversity numbers. The company has at least one chapter in every province, and in six years it has run 904 workshops that in total have reached more than 21 000 adult learners and more than 19 000 youth learners. The workshops are starting to make a difference, "[f]rom the woman who completely reinvented her career through our programs, to the young girl who created a game for her visually impaired sister when there were none, to the teen who aced her AP CS class and is now on her way to university to major in computer science."

In this section we discuss why managing diversity well matters.

Although much has been said about diversity in age, race, gender, ethnicity, religion, and disability status, experts now recognize that these demographic characteristics are just the tip of the iceberg.[109] Demographics mostly reflect **surface-level diversity**, not thoughts and feelings, and can lead employees to perceive one another through stereotypes and assumptions. However, evidence has shown that people are less concerned about demographic differences if they see themselves as sharing more important characteristics, such as personality and values, that represent **deep-level diversity**.[110]

To understand the difference between surface- and deep-level diversity, consider an example. Luis and Carol are managers who seem to have little in common. Luis is a young, recently hired male from a Punjabi-speaking neighbourhood in Vancouver with a business degree. Carol is an older woman from rural Alberta who started as a customer service trainee after secondary school and worked her way up the hierarchy. At first, these co-workers may notice their surface-level differences in education, ethnicity, regional background, and gender. However, as they get to know one another, they may find they are both deeply committed to their families, share a common way of thinking about important work problems, like to work collaboratively, and are interested in international assignments. These deep-level similarities can overshadow the more superficial differences between them, and research suggests they will work well together.

Many organizations have attempted to incorporate workforce diversity initiatives into their workplaces to improve relations among co-workers. Toronto-based Corus Entertainment is one such company. Corus' policy on diversity states the following:

> Corus is committed to promoting an equitable work environment based on the merit principle. Corus is also committed to conducting business and providing services in the communities where we operate in a manner that respects the dignity and independence of all employees and customers, including those with varying abilities.
>
> Our collective commitment to respect and nurture a diverse and accessible work environment promotes Accountability, Innovation, Initiative, Teamwork and Knowledge across the organization.[111]

Corus' statement on diversity is typical of statements found in company annual reports and employee information packets to signal corporate values to those who interact with the company. Some corporations choose to signal the value of diversity because they think it is an important strategic goal. Other organizations recognize that the purchasing power of diverse groups is substantial.

When companies design and then publicize statements about the importance of diversity, they are essentially producing value statements. The hope, of course, is that the statements will influence the behaviour of members of the organization, particularly since preference for people who are ethnically like ourselves may be ingrained in us at an early age. For example, researchers from Concordia University and the University of Montreal found that Asian Canadian and French Canadian preschoolers preferred to interact with kids of their own ethnic group.[112]

Little research indicates that values can be changed successfully. Because values tend to be relatively stable, workplaces try to address diversity issues through education aimed at changing attitudes. See *Case Incident—Walking the Walk* on pages 113–114 to learn about diversity at Google.

Effective Diversity Programs

Joan Vogelesang, who was CEO of Montreal-based animation software company Toon Boom, says that Canadian companies don't make use of the diversity in the employees they have. She thinks Canadian companies need to look beyond imperfect English and cultural customs when hiring. When she worked at Toon Boom, most of her executive team were first-generation immigrants. Her employees could speak 20 languages among them. "Two . . . staff members [could] speak Japanese. You can hardly do business in Japan if you don't speak it," she says.[113]

9 Describe how organizations can manage diversity effectively.

surface-level diversity Differences in easily perceived characteristics, such as gender, race, ethnicity, age, or disability, that do not necessarily reflect the ways people think or feel but that may activate certain stereotypes.

deep-level diversity Differences in values, personality, and work preferences that become progressively more important for determining similarity as people get to know one another better.

CAREER OBJECTIVES

Is It Okay to Be Gay at Work?

I'm gay, but no one at my workplace knows it. How much should I be willing to tell? I want to be sure to have a shot at the big positions in the firm.

—Ryan

Dear Ryan:

Unfortunately, you are right to be concerned. Here are some suggestions:

- *Look for an inclusive company culture.* Apple CEO Tim Cook said, "I've had the good fortune to work at a company that loves creativity and innovation and knows it can only flourish when you embrace people's differences. Not everyone is so lucky." Recent research has focused on discovering new methods to counteract a discrimination culture in the United States, the United Kingdom, and Australia.

- *Choose your moral ground.* Do you feel you have a responsibility to "come out" to help effect social change? Do you have a right to keep your private life private? The balance is a private decision. A recent study by the US Human Rights Campaign indicated that only half of LGBT employees nationwide disclose their status.

- *Consider your future in top management.* Corporate-level leaders are urged to be open with peers and employees. As Ernst & Young global vice chairperson Beth Brooke said about her decades of staying closeted, the pressure to be "authentic" adds stress if you are keeping your gay status a secret.

- *Weigh your options.* The word from people at the top who are gay (some who have come out and others who have not) is mixed. Brooke said, "Life really did get better" after she announced her status in a company-sponsored video. Mark Stephanz, a vice chairman at Bank of America Merrill Lynch, agreed, remarking that "most people still deal with you the same way they always do." Yet Deena Fidas, deputy director for the largest LGBT civil rights group in the United States, reported that being gay in the workplace is still "far from being a 'nonissue.'"

- *Be aware of international and national laws.* Sadly, some nations and states are intolerant. You will need to study the laws to be sure you will be safe from repercussions when you reveal your status.

So, think about your decision from both an ethical and a self-interested point of view. Your timing depends not only on what you think are your ethical responsibilities, but also on your context—where you work, the culture of your organization, and the support of the people within it. Thankfully, globalization is ensuring that the world becomes increasingly accepting and fair.

Good luck in your career!

Sources: M. D. Birtel, "'Treating' Prejudice: An Exposure-Therapy Approach to Reducing Negative Reactions Toward Stigmatized Groups," Psychological Science (November 2012): 1379–86; L. Cooper and J. Raspanti, "The Cost of the Closet and the Rewards of Inclusion," Human Rights Campaign report (May 2014), http://hrc-assets.s3-website-us-east-1.amazonaws.com//files/assets/resources/Cost_of_the_Closet_May2014.pdf; N. Rumens and J. Broomfield, "Gay Men in the Police: Identity Disclosure and Management Issues," Human Resource Management Journal (July 2012): 283–98; and A. M Ryan and J. L. Wessel, "Sexual Orientation Harassment in the Workplace: When Do Observers Intervene?" Journal of Organizational Behavior (May 2012): 488–509.

Vogelesang's description of diversity as a competitive advantage speaks to the need for a variety of diversity programs in recruiting and selection policies, as well as training and development practices.

Effective, comprehensive workforce programs encouraging diversity have three distinct components. First, they teach employees about the legal framework for equal employment opportunity and encourage fair treatment of all people, regardless of their demographic characteristics. Second, they teach employees how a diverse workforce will be better able to serve a diverse market of customers and clients. Third, they foster personal development practices that bring out the skills and abilities of all workers, acknowledging how differences

> Are you comfortable working with people from other cultures?

in perspective can be a valuable way to improve performance for everyone.[114] A study by researchers at the University of Toronto Scarborough found that focusing on the positive benefits of diversity, rather than telling people what they should and should not do, was more likely to reduce people's prejudices toward other groups.[115] The *Experiential Exercise* on page 111 considers what it feels like to be targeted or excluded based on demographic status.

Most negative reactions to employment discrimination are based on the idea that discriminatory treatment is unfair. Regardless of race or gender, people are generally in favour of diversity-oriented programs if they believe the policies ensure everyone has a fair opportunity to show their skills and abilities.

Organizational leaders should examine their workforce to determine whether the **protected groups** covered by Canada's Employment Equity Act (women, people with disabilities, Aboriginal people, and visible minorities) have been underutilized. If groups of employees are not proportionally represented in top management, managers should look for any hidden barriers to advancement. They can often improve recruiting practices, make selection systems more transparent, and provide training for those employees who have not had adequate exposure to necessary work-related experiences in the past. Exhibit 3-7 presents examples of what some of the leading companies are doing as part of their diversity initiatives.

Management should also clearly communicate the company's diversity policies and their rationale to employees so they can understand how and why certain practices are followed. Communications should focus as much as possible on qualifications and job performance; emphasizing that certain groups need more assistance could well backfire.

To ensure the top-level management team represents the diversity of its workforce and client base, Safeway implemented the Retail Leadership Development (RLD) program, a formal career development program. This program is open to all employees, so it is inclusive, but women and underrepresented racial or ethnic groups are particularly

protected groups The four groups designated by the Employment Equity Act as the beneficiaries of employment equity (women, people with disabilities, Aboriginal people, and visible minorities).

Rob Latour/REX/Shutterstock/The Canadian Press

Toronto-based AccessNow founder Maayan Ziv speaks up about the need for more diversity in the technology sector. AccessNow lets its users know whether buildings are accessible throughout many places in the world. She says that when she builds events, she want them to be inclusive, and asks herself about that: "Is it inclusive? Is the messaging inclusive? Does it support other people's perspectives being brought to the table?" Ziv believes that having people surrounded with people who are different than themselves helps improve the perspectives that can be shared.[116]

EXHIBIT 3-7 Practices Used by a Selected Sample of Canada's Most Welcoming Places to Work, 2017

Company (Location)	Industry	Number of Employees	Diversity Activities
Jazz Aviation (Dartmouth, NS)	Aviation	4266	Has an LGBTA employee resource group and launched a Safe Space campaign to promote an inclusive work environment
Cameco Corp. (Saskatoon)	Mining	3040	Works with Women in Mining and the Mining Human Resource Council to research employment barriers faced by women in the mining industry
Telus (Vancouver)	Telecommunications	23 328	Maintains "Eagles," a dedicated resource group to provide professional development and networking opportunities for Indigenous employees
CIBC (Toronto)	Commercial bank	36 215	Updated its board of directors' goal for the representation of women to no less than 30 percent
Manitoba Hydro (Winnipeg)	Hydroelectric power generation	6001	Provides work placements to grade 12 high school students with intellectual disabilities
Ontario Public Service (OPS) (Toronto)	Government support	62 080	Launched the Accessibility@Source campaign to help staff integrate accessibility considerations into everything they do
Sodexo Canada (Burlington, ON)	Food services	5961	Offers internships to Vancouver Community College students with intellectual disabilities, in partnership with the Vancouver School Board's Life Skills Program
Northwest Territories Government (Yellowknife)	Government services	5950	Established a Diversity and Inclusion Unit, composed of a manager of diversity and inclusion, an Indigenous HR specialist, and two workforce diversity officers
Agrium Inc. (Calgary)	Agricultural products and fertilizer manufacturing	3440	Piloted a Women's Leadership Development program to develop women candidates with high potential for senior management positions

Source: Based on D. Jermyn, "Canada's Best Diversity Employers," March 28, 2017, https://www.theglobeandmail.com/report-on-business/careers/top-employers/canadas-best-diversity-employers-welcome-new-voices/article34434138/.

encouraged to participate. Interested individuals take tests to determine whether they have management potential. Safeway managers are charged with providing promising RLD participants with additional training and development opportunities to ensure they have the skills needed for advancement, and are given performance bonuses if they meet concrete diversity goals. The RLD program has increased the number of white women store managers by 31 percent since its inception, and the number of women-of-colour store managers by 92 percent.[117] *OB in the Street* looks at what corporate boards in Canada can do to recruit more diverse members.

Just because a company's managers value diversity does not mean that all employees will share that value. Consequently, even if they are required to attend diversity training, employees may exhibit negative attitudes toward individuals because of their gender or ethnicity. Additionally, what attitudes are appropriately displayed outside of the workplace may be questioned by some employers.

Cultural Intelligence

Consider the cases of an Italian COO who can't motivate his Indian employees at a technology company in Mumbai, an Israeli consultant in the US having difficulty giving

 Identify the benefits of cultural intelligence.

OB IN THE STREET
Adding Diversity to Boards of Directors

Why should corporate boards pay more attention to diversity? The Canadian Board Diversity Council together with KPMG recently published a study on the boards of 450 of the Financial Post 500 (FP500) companies.[118] The study found that women held 15 percent of board seats on the FP500 companies; visible minorities held 5.3 percent; persons with disabilities held 2.9 percent; and Aboriginal people (including First Nations, Inuit, and Métis) held 8 percent. With the exception of Aboriginal representation, the numbers were far fewer than the representation of these categories in society at large. Pamela Jeffery, founder and president of the council, called the results "disappointing."

Does the lack of diversity hurt the bottom line? Accounting firm Ernst & Young found that the lack of diversity on boards can make it difficult for companies to innovate. Directors who sat on FP500 boards that had more women, visible minorities, or Aboriginal diversity believed that the boards made better decisions because the diversity led to better discussions with more perspectives. Board members expressed some frustration about finding new directors and reported that "their own networks are almost exclusively made up of white men."

The council does not favour using quotas to change the situation. Instead, it recommends that with the large wave of retirements from boards expected in the next several years, FP500 boards should use rigorous, transparent recruiting processes "to replace one of every three retiring directors with a director of a diverse background." ....

feedback, and a Korean software firm CEO working in Shanghai who cannot retain his Chinese employees. The Italian COO knows his Indian employees expect a more authoritarian style than he is used to; the Israeli knows her feedback should be softer, rather than so blunt; and the Korean knows that Chinese bosses are more paternalistic than Korean ones. That is because they have cultural intelligence.[119]

Management professors Christopher Earley of the London School of Business and Elaine Mosakowski of the University of Colorado at Boulder introduced the idea of **cultural intelligence (CQ)** to suggest that people vary in how they deal with other cultures. CQ is defined as "the seemingly natural ability to interpret someone's unfamiliar and ambiguous gestures in just the way that person's compatriots and colleagues would, even to mirror them."[120]

Earley and Mosakowski suggest that CQ "picks up where emotional intelligence leaves off." Those with CQ try to figure out whether a person's behaviour is representative of all members of a group or just that person. Thus, for example, a person with high CQ who encounters two German engineers would be able to determine which aspects of the engineers' conduct are explained by the fact of being an engineer, by being German, or by behaviour that is simply particular to the individual. A recent study found that CQ is particularly helpful to expatriates on international assignment because the ability to be confident about and interested in being in new cultural environments makes it easier to adjust to the demands of foreign assignments.[121]

RESEARCH FINDINGS: Cultural Intelligence

According to researchers, "cultural intelligence resides in the body [the physical] and the heart [the emotional/motivational], as well as the head [the cognitive]."[122] Individuals who have high *cognitive* CQ look for clues to help them identify a culture's shared understandings. Specifically, an individual does this by looking for consistencies in behaviours across a variety of people from the same cultural background. Individuals with high *physical* CQ learn the customs and gestures of those from other cultures and therefore act more like them. This increases understanding, trust, and openness

cultural intelligence (CQ) The ability to understand someone's unfamiliar and ambiguous gestures in the same way as would people from that person's culture.

among people of different cultures. One study found that job candidates who used some of the mannerisms of recruiters who had different cultural backgrounds from themselves were more likely to receive job offers than those who did not do so.[123] Those with high *emotional/motivational* CQ believe that they are capable of understanding people from other cultures, and will keep trying to do so, even if faced with difficulties in doing so.

Based on their research, Earley and Mosakowski have discovered that most managers fall into the following CQ profiles:[124]

- *Provincial.* They work best with people of similar background, but have difficulties working with those from different backgrounds.

- *Analyst.* They analyze a foreign culture's rules and expectations to figure out how to interact with others.

- *Natural.* They use intuition rather than systematic study to understand those from other cultural backgrounds.

- *Ambassador.* They communicate convincingly that they fit in, even if they do not know much about the foreign culture.

- *Mimic.* They control actions and behaviours to match others, even if they do not understand the significance of the cultural cues observed.

- *Chameleon.* They have high levels of all three CQ components. They could be mistaken as being from the foreign culture. According to research, only about 5 percent of managers fit this profile.

Exhibit 3-8 can help you assess your own CQ.

EXHIBIT 3-8 Measuring Your Cultural Intelligence

Rate the extent to which you agree with each statement, using the following scale:

1 = strongly disagree
2 = disagree
3 = neutral
4 = agree
5 = strongly agree

_____ Before I interact with people from a new culture, I ask myself what I hope to achieve.
_____ If I encounter something unexpected while working in a new culture, I use this experience to figure out new ways to approach other cultures in the future.
_____ I plan how I'm going to relate to people from a different culture before I meet them.
_____ When I come into a new cultural situation, I can immediately sense whether something is going well or something is wrong.

Total _____ ÷ 4 = **Cognitive CQ**

_____ It's easy for me to change my body language (for example, eye contact or posture) to suit people from a different culture.
_____ I can alter my expression when a cultural encounter requires it.
_____ I modify my speech style (for example, accent or tone) to suit people from a different culture.
_____ I easily change the way I act when a cross-cultural encounter seems to require it.

Total _____ ÷ 4 = **Physical CQ**

_____ I have confidence that I can deal well with people from a different culture.
_____ I am certain that I can befriend people whose cultural backgrounds are different from mine.
_____ I can adapt to the lifestyle of a different culture with relative ease.
_____ I am confident that I can deal with a cultural situation that is unfamiliar.

Total _____ ÷ 4 = **Emotional/motivational CQ**

Interpretation: Generally, an average of less than 3 would indicate an area calling for improvement, while an average of greater than 4.5 reflects a true CQ strength.

Source: P. C. Earley and E. Mosakowski, "Cultural Intelligence," *Harvard Business Review* 82, no. 10 (October 2004), pp. 139–146. Reprinted by permission of *Harvard Business Review*.

Cultural intelligence may not be enough, however. Remember the Italian COO, the Israeli consultant, and the Korean CEO from the start of this section? Recent research suggests that they lack **cultural code-switching**—"the ability to modify behaviour in specific situations to accommodate varying cultural norms."[125] It can be difficult to act against the norms you're accustomed to when acting in new environments. Being culturally fluent means being able to learn the norms of the new environment and to feel comfortable applying them.

GLOBAL IMPLICATIONS

Although a number of topics were covered in this chapter, we review only three in terms of their application beyond Canada and the United States. First, we consider whether job satisfaction is simply a US concept. Second, we examine whether employees in Western cultures are more satisfied with their jobs than people from other cultures. Finally, we look at international differences in how diversity is managed.

Is Job Satisfaction a North American Concept?

Most of the research on job satisfaction has been conducted in the United States and Canada. So, is job satisfaction just relevant to those countries? The evidence strongly suggests it is *not*; people in other cultures can and do form judgments of job satisfaction. Moreover, similar factors seem to cause, and result from, job satisfaction across cultures: We noted earlier that pay is positively, but relatively weakly, related to job satisfaction. This relationship appears to hold in other industrialized nations as well.

Are Employees in Western Cultures More Satisfied with Their Jobs?

There are some cultural differences in job satisfaction. Exhibit 3-9 provides the results of a global study of job satisfaction levels of employees in 15 countries, with the highest levels in Mexico and Switzerland. Do employees in these cultures have better jobs? Or are they simply more positive (and less self-critical)? Conversely, the lowest score in

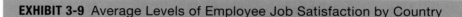

EXHIBIT 3-9 Average Levels of Employee Job Satisfaction by Country

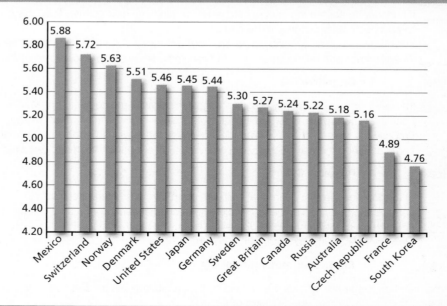

Source: Based on J. H. Westover, "The Impact of Comparative State-Directed Development on Working Conditions and Employee Satisfaction," *Journal of Management & Organization*, July 2012, pp. 537–554.

cultural code-switching The ability to modify behaviour in specific situations to accommodate varying cultural norms.

the study was for South Korea. Autonomy is low in South Korea, and businesses tend to be rigidly hierarchical. Do these factors make for low job satisfaction?[126] It is difficult to discern all the factors influencing the scores, but considering how businesses are responding to changes brought on by globalization may give us clues.

The amount of exposure the culture gets to diverse ways of life may affect job satisfaction in South Korea. The country has the highest percentage of wireless Internet broadband subscriptions of any country (100 percent, or 100 subscriptions per every 100 people), which indicates that people have access to worldwide contemporary business practices. South Korean employees may therefore know about autonomy, merit-based rewards, and benefits for workers in other countries that are unavailable to them. In contrast, Mexico, which has one of the highest job satisfaction scores, has the lowest percentage of Internet subscriptions (7.7 percent).[127] The higher job satisfaction rate in Mexico could still indicate that it has better jobs or that employees are more satisfied in lesser jobs because there is not as much opportunity for exposure to outside contemporary influences. As you can see, higher job satisfaction may somewhat reflect employee acceptance of the culture's business practices, whether the practices are traditional or cutting-edge. There are also many other potential contributing factors.

Does organizational commitment vary cross-nationally? A recent study explored this question and compared the organizational commitment of Chinese employees with that of Canadian and South Korean employees.[128] Although results revealed that the three types of commitment—normative, affective, and continuance—are present in all three cultures, they differ in importance. In addition, the study found that Canadians and South Koreans are closer to each other in values than either is with the Chinese. Normative commitment (an obligation to remain with an organization for moral or ethical reasons) and affective commitment (an emotional attachment to the organization and belief in its values) were highest among Chinese employees. Continuance commitment (the perceived economic value of remaining with an organization) was *lower* among Chinese employees than among Canadian, British, and South Korean employees.

Is Diversity Managed Differently across Cultures?

Besides the mere presence of diversity in international work settings, international differences exist in how diversity is managed. Each country has its own legal framework for dealing with diversity, and these frameworks are a powerful reflection of the diversity-related concerns of each country. Many countries require specific targets and quotas for achieving employment equity goals, whereas the legal framework in Canada specifically forbids their use. The types of demographic differences considered important for diversity management also vary across countries. For example, South Africa protects blacks through the Equal Employment Act; China has "preferential policies" that require ethnic minorities and women be appointed to top government positions; Israel has a class-based policy to promote women, Arabs, blacks, and people with disabilities; India has a policy of reservation to reserve jobs for underrepresented castes; Sri Lanka has the Standardization policy to help those in areas with lower rates of education; Malaysia's New Economic Policy (NEP) provides advantage for the majority group, the Malays, who have lower income; Germany's Basic Law has an affirmative action plan for women and those with handicaps; and Russia has quotas for women and ethnic minorities.

Summary

Why is it important to know an individual's values? Values often underlie and explain attitudes, behaviours, and perceptions. Values tend to vary internationally along dimensions that can predict organizational outcomes; however, an individual may or may not hold values that are consistent with the values of the national culture.

LESSONS LEARNED

- Values represent basic convictions about what is important, right, and good.
- Attitudes tend to predict behaviours.
- Job satisfaction leads to better performance.

Managers should be interested in their employees' attitudes because attitudes influence behaviour and indicate potential problems. Creating a satisfied workforce is hardly a guarantee of successful organizational performance, but evidence strongly suggests that managers' efforts to improve employee attitudes will likely result in positive outcomes, including greater organizational effectiveness, high customer satisfaction, and increased profits.

Diversity management must be an ongoing commitment that crosses all levels of the organization. Policies to improve the climate for diversity can be effective, so long as they are designed to acknowledge all employees' perspectives.

SNAPSHOT SUMMARY

Values
- Rokeach Value Survey
- Hodgson's General Moral Principles

Assessing Cultural Values
- Hofstede's Framework for Assessing Cultures
- The GLOBE Framework for Assessing Cultures

Values in the Canadian Workplace
- Generational Differences
- Cultural Differences

Attitudes
- Job Satisfaction
- Organizational Commitment
- Job Involvement

- Perceived Organizational Support
- Employee Engagement

Managing Diversity in the Workplace
- Effective Diversity Programs
- Cultural Intelligence

MyLab Management

 PERSONAL INVENTORY ASSESSMENT

Study, practise, and explore real business situations with these helpful resources:

- **Study Plan:** Check your understanding of chapter concepts with self-study quizzes.
- **Online Lesson Presentations:** Study key chapter topics and work through interactive assessments to test your knowledge and master management concepts.
- **Videos:** Learn more about the management practices and strategies of real companies.
- **Simulations:** Practise management decision-making in simulated business environments.

OB at Work

for Review

1. What is the difference between Rokeach's terminal and instrumental values?

2. What are Hofstede's value dimensions for assessing cultures?

3. What values are unique to Canadian culture?

4. What are the three components of an attitude? Are these components related or unrelated?

5. What are the key attitudes that affect organizational performance? In what ways are these attitudes alike? What is unique about each?

6. What causes job satisfaction? For most people, is pay or the work itself more important?

7. What outcomes does job satisfaction influence? What implications do the consequences of job satisfaction have for management?

8. What are the four employee responses to job dissatisfaction?

9. How can organizations manage diversity effectively?

10. What are the benefits of cultural intelligence?

for Managers

- Of the major job attitudes—job satisfaction, job involvement, organizational commitment, perceived organizational support (POS), and employee engagement—remember that an employee's job satisfaction level is the best single predictor of behaviour.

- Pay attention to your employees' job satisfaction levels as determinants of their performance, turnover, absenteeism, and withdrawal behaviours.

- Measure employee job attitudes objectively and at regular intervals in order to determine how employees are reacting to their work.

- To raise employee job satisfaction, evaluate the fit between the employee's work interests and the intrinsic parts of the job, then create work that is challenging and interesting to the employee.

- Consider the fact that high pay alone is unlikely to create a satisfying work environment.

- Understand your organization's anti-discrimination policies thoroughly and share them with your employees.

- Look beyond readily observable biographical characteristics and consider the individual's capabilities before making management decisions; remain open and encouraging for individuals to disclose any hidden disabilities.

- Fully evaluate what accommodations a person with disabilities will need and then fine-tune a job to that person's abilities.

- Seek to understand and respect the unique biographical characteristics of each employee; a fair but individual-oriented approach yields the best performance.

for You

- You will encounter many people who have values different from yours in the classroom and in various kinds of activities in which you participate, as well as in the workplace. Try to understand value differences, and to figure out ways to work positively with people who are different from you.

- We indicated that a moderate number of Canadians are very satisfied with their jobs, and we mentioned the sources of some of the satisfactions. We also identified some of the reasons people are dissatisfied with their jobs. This information may help you understand your own feelings about whether you are satisfied with your job.

- You may be able to use some of the information on attitudes to think about how to better work with people from different cultures. An understanding of how cultures differ may provide insight when you observe people doing things differently from the way you do them.

MILLENNIALS HAVE INFLATED IMAGES OF THEMSELVES COMPARED TO THEIR PARENTS

POINT

Millennials have some great virtues: As a group, they are technologically savvy, socially tolerant, and engaged.[129] They value their quality of life as equal to their career, seeking a balance between home and work. In these ways, Millennials surpass their Baby Boomer parents, who are less technologically adept, less tolerant, more localized, and who have a history of striving to get ahead at all costs.

Several large-scale, longitudinal studies found Millennials are more likely than Baby Boomers to have seemingly inflated views of themselves. More Millennials rate themselves as above average on attributes such as academic ability, leadership, public-speaking ability, and writing ability. Millennials are also more likely to agree they would be "very good" spouses (56 percent, compared to 37 percent among 1980 graduates), parents (54 percent; 36 percent for 1980 graduates), and employees (65 percent; 49 percent for 1980 graduates).

Cliff Zukin, a senior faculty fellow at Rutgers University, believes the reason is in the childhood upbringing of Millennials. "This is the most affirmed generation in history," he says. "They were raised believing they could do anything they wanted to, and that they have skills and talents to bring to a job setting." Jean M. Twenge, author of *Generation Me*, agrees. "People were not saying, 'Believe in yourself' and 'You are special' in the '60s."

Narcissism is bad for society, and particularly bad for the workplace. "[Narcissists] tend to be very self-absorbed; they value fun in their personal and their work life," one administrator said. "I can't expect them to work on one project for any amount of time without getting bored."

COUNTERPOINT

Wasn't "The Me Generation" generations ago? Honestly, every generation thinks they are better than the ones that come after! "You can find complaints [about the younger generation] in Greek literature, in the Bible," Professor Cappelli of the Wharton School observed. "There's no evidence Millennials are different. They're just younger." While Millennials are the 20-somethings of today, what *is* universally true is that young people share certain characteristics . . . *because* they are young.

A recent study shows the similarity between how Millennials and Baby Boomers thought about themselves at the same stage of life. As college freshmen, 71 percent of Millennials thought they were above average academically, and 63 percent of Baby Boomers thought the same thing when they were college freshmen. Similarly, 77 percent of Millennials believed they were above average in the drive to achieve, versus 68 percent for Baby Boomers. In other words, "Every generation is Generation Me."

In some ways, Millennials may be less narcissistic than Baby Boomers today. As one manager observed, "[Millennials] don't have that line between work and home that used to exist, so they're doing Facebook for the company at night, on Saturday or Sunday. We get incredible productivity out of them." Millennials also may be more altruistic. For example, 29 percent of Millennials believe individuals have a responsibility to remain involved in issues and causes for the good of all, while only 24 percent of Baby Boomers feel the same level of responsibility.

Rather than comparing different generations, it is more accurate to compare people at one life stage with others at the same life stage. Research supports that people in their 20s tend to be more narcissistic than people in their 50s. Since Millennials are in their 20s, and many of their parents are in their 50s, Millennials are no more narcissistic than Baby Boomers were in their youth.

BREAKOUT **GROUP** EXERCISES

Form small groups to discuss the following topics, as assigned by your instructor. Each person in the group should first identify 3 to 5 key personal values.

1. Identify the extent to which values overlap in your group.

2. Try to uncover with your group members the source of some of your key values (for example, parents, peer group, teachers, church).

3. What kind of workplace would be most suitable for the values that you hold most closely?

EXPERIENTIAL EXERCISE

Feeling Excluded

This 6-step exercise takes approximately 20 minutes.

Individual Work (Steps 1 and 2)

1. All participants are asked to recall a time when they have felt uncomfortable or targeted because of their demographic status. Ideally, situations at work should be used, but if no work situations come to mind, any situation will work. Encourage students to use any demographic characteristic they think is most appropriate, so they can write about feeling excluded on the basis of race, ethnicity, gender, age, disability status, religion, or any other characteristic. They should briefly describe the situation, what precipitated the event, how they felt at the time, how they reacted, and how they believe the other party could have made the situation better.

2. The instructor asks the students to then think about a time when they might have either deliberately or accidentally done something that made someone else feel excluded or targeted because of their demographic status. Once again, they should briefly describe the situation, what precipitated the event, how they felt at the time, how the other person reacted, and how they could have made the situation better.

Small Groups (Steps 3 and 4)

3. Once everyone has written their descriptions, divide the class into small groups of not more than 4 people. If at all possible, try to compose groups that are somewhat demographically diverse, to avoid intergroup conflicts in the class review discussion. Students should be encouraged to discuss their situations and consider how their experiences were similar or different.

4. After reading through everyone's reactions, each group should develop a short list of principles for how they personally can avoid excluding or targeting people in the future. Encourage them to be as specific as possible, and also ask each group to find solutions that work for everyone. Solutions should focus on both avoiding these situations in the first place and resolving them when they do occur.

Class Review (Steps 5 and 6)

5. Members of each group are invited to provide a very brief summary of the major principles of how they have felt excluded or targeted, and then describe their group's collective decisions regarding how these situations can be minimized in the future.

6. The instructor should lead a discussion on how companies might be able to develop comprehensive policies that will encourage people to be sensitive in their interactions with one another.

ETHICAL **DILEMMA**

Tell–All Websites

"Arrogant, condescending, mean-spirited, hateful . . . and those traits describe the nicest people at Netflix," writes one anonymous employee.[130] "Management is awful . . . good old boys club," writes a Coca-Cola market development manager. And the reviews keep rolling in; Coca-Cola has 1600 employee reviews and some companies, like Google, have double that number on Glassdoor, one of the websites that allows employees to rate their employers.

Websites like Glassdoor are thriving; employees increasingly join the forums and seem to relish the chance to speak freely. Ryan Janssen, former CEO of Memo (an app that allowed users to talk honestly about work), said that apps such as Whisper give bosses access to candid feedback they can't get otherwise. "The employee's natural reaction [when managers ask for feedback directly] is to tell you what you want to hear," he said. There is certainly truth to this—studies indicate that employees "put on a happy face" for their bosses. When people know their posts are not anonymous, "people put on this weird, fake professional face," Janssen added.

Organizations are aware that employees watch what they say when they can be identified, and many have used anonymous job attitude surveys for this reason. Still, evaluations from these surveys are often more glowing, and less detailed, than anonymous website feedback. Some organizations have therefore altered the frequency and scope of surveys to obtain more depth. Others have their own intranet platforms to solicit concerns and complaints.

Beyond the personally unethical aspect of posting scathing denouncements about people or organizations online—sharing details with the world that you would not share in person—issues of organizational ethics come into play. While some companies try to discourage employees from anonymously venting on websites and apps, such mandates may violate the employees' right to free speech. And how anonymous are anonymous posts? Posts on Glassdoor and other forums eliminate a person's name, but can't bosses sometimes determine which subordinate posted the comments? Managers everywhere need to decide how much management sleuthing is ethical, and what consequences, if any, can be forced on subordinates for anonymous posts.

Questions

1. Do you think employees have a right to say what they want to about their organizations online, as opposed to in private?

2. How would you react if you learned one of your employees posted unflattering comments about you as a manager? Would your reaction be any different if the employee posted unflattering comments about you as a person?

3. Do you feel it is acceptable to post comments anonymously, or do you think people should include their names? Why or why not?

CASE INCIDENTS

Job Crafting

Consider for a moment a midlevel manager, Fatima, who seems to be doing well.[131] She consistently meets her required benchmarks and goals, has built successful relationships with colleagues, and has been identified by senior management as having "high potential." But she isn't satisfied in her job. For example, she is interested in understanding how social media may be used in marketing efforts at all levels of the organization, but her job does not allow her to work on this. She wants to quit and find something that better suits her passions, but in her economic situation, this may not be an option. So she has decided to proactively reconfigure her current job.

Fatima is part of a movement toward job "crafting," which is the process of deliberately reorganizing your job so that it better fits your motives, strengths, and passions. How did Fatima craft her job? She first noticed that she was spending too much of her time monitoring her team's performance and answering questions, and not enough time working on the creative projects that inspired her. She then considered how to modify her relationship with her team so that her activities incorporated her passion for social media strategies, while the team's activities centred on developing new marketing. She also identified members of her team who might be able to help her implement her new strategies and directed her interactions with these individuals toward her new goals. As a result, not only did her engagement in her work increase, but she also developed new ideas that were recognized and advanced within the organization. In sum, she found that by actively and creatively examining her work, she was able to shape her job into one that is truly satisfying.

As you may have noted, Fatima exhibited a proactive personality—she was eager to develop her own options and find her own resources. Proactive individuals are often self-empowered and are, therefore, more likely to seek workable solutions when they are not satisfied. Research leads us to believe Fatima will be successful in her customized job and that she will experience increased well-being. To the extent possible, then, all employees should feel encouraged to be proactive in creating their best work situations.

Questions

1. Should organizations work to create jobs that are satisfying to individual employees?

2. Are the principles of job crafting described here relevant to your job or studies? Why or why not?

3. Are there any potential drawbacks to the job crafting approach? If so, how can they be minimized?

Walking the Walk

Do you want to work for Google?[132] In some ways, who wouldn't? Sunny California, fabulous campus, free organic meals, perks galore . . . oh, and challenging work with some of the brightest minds in the field. By all accounts, Google is a class act, a symbol of modernization.

Does Google want you to work for it? Ah, that is the question. Eric Schmidt, a former Google CEO, and Jonathan Rosenberg, a former Google senior product manager, say Google searches for a certain type of person: a "smart creative." They say smart creatives are "a new kind of animal"—and the secret ingredient to Google's success.

Do you think you are a smart creative? Are you an impatient, outspoken, risk taker who is easily bored? Do you change jobs frequently? Are you intellectually flexible? Do you have technical know-how, business knowledge, and creativity? Do you think analytically? According to Schmidt and Rosenberg, answering yes to these questions makes you a smart creative. As you can see, being a smart creative is not all positive. But it will get you hired at Google.

One last question: Are you male or female? Google may be a symbol of the modernization of the work*place*, but perhaps not of the work*force*. The Google workforce, with 48 600 individuals, is a man's world—70 percent male overall. On the technical side, a full 83 percent of the engineering employees are male. In the management ranks, 79 percent of the managers are male. On the executive level, only three of the company's 36 executives are women.

Google officials say they are aware of the lack of diversity, but that their diversity initiatives have failed. However, others report that sexist comments go unchecked and there is a frat-house atmosphere. In fact, an interviewer at an all-company presentation insultingly teased a man and woman who shared an office, asking them, "Which one of you does the dishes?"

Thankfully, Google has begun to put its smart creatives to work on new thoughts about diversity. With the help of social psychology research, the company sent all employees through training on unconscious bias—our reflexive tendency to be biased toward our own groups—to force people to consider their racist and sexist mindsets. So far, the training seems to be making a bigger difference than former initiatives, but the firm has a long way to go. Laszlo Bock, Google's top HR executive, said, "Suddenly you go from being completely oblivious to going, 'Oh my god, it's everywhere.'"

Critics are skeptical that Google and other large technology firms will ever count women in their ranks in numbers that reflect the population, though research continues to indicate that men and women are highly similar employees. Once Google has achieved greater diversity than it currently has, perhaps its executives can begin to work on the pay differentials: A recent Harvard study indicated that women computer scientists receive 89 percent of the pay men earn for the same jobs.

Questions

1. Does this article change your perception of Google as an employer? How?

2. Why do you think men at Google continue to hire mainly men?

3. Would you do anything to address diversity issues at Google if you worked there? What might you try?

FROM CONCEPTS TO SKILLS

Changing Attitudes

Can you change unfavourable employee attitudes? Sometimes! It depends on who you are, the strength of the employee's attitude, the magnitude of the change, and the technique you choose to try to change the attitude.

People are most likely to respond to changes suggested by someone who is liked, credible, and convincing. If people like you, they are more apt to identify and adopt your message. Credibility implies trust, expertise, and objectivity. So you are more likely to change someone's attitude if that person views you as believable, knowledgeable about what you are saying, and unbiased in your presentation. Finally, successful attitude change is enhanced when you present your arguments clearly and persuasively.

It's easier to change a person's attitude if he or she is not strongly committed to it. Conversely, the stronger the belief in the attitude, the harder it is to change it. Also, attitudes that have been expressed publicly are more difficult to change because doing so requires admitting having made a mistake.

It's also easier to change attitudes when the change required is not very significant. To get a person to accept a new attitude that varies greatly from his or her current position requires more effort. It may also threaten other deeply held attitudes.

Practising Skills

All attitude-change techniques are not equally effective across situations. Oral persuasion techniques are most effective when you use a positive, tactful tone; present strong evidence to support your position; tailor your argument to the listener; use logic; and support your evidence by appealing to the person's fears, frustrations, and other emotions. But people are more likely to embrace change when they can experience it. The use of training sessions where employees share and personalize experiences, and practise new behaviours, can be a powerful stimulant for change. Consistent with self-perception theory, changes in behaviour can lead to changes in attitudes.

Form groups of 2. Person A is to choose any topic that he or she feels strongly about and state his or her position on the topic in 30 words or less. Person B's task will be to try to change Person A's attitude on this topic. Person B will have 10 minutes to make his or her case. When the time is up, the roles are reversed. Person B picks the topic and Person A has 10 minutes to try to change Person B's attitude.

Potential topics (you can choose either side of a topic) include the following: politics; the economy; world events; social practices; or specific management issues, such as that organizations should require all employees to undergo regular drug testing, there is no such thing as organizational loyalty anymore, the customer is always right, or layoffs are an indication of management failures.

Questions

1. Were you successful at changing the other person's attitude? Why or why not?

2. Was the other person successful at changing your attitude? Why or why not?

3. What conclusions can you draw about changing the attitudes of yourself and others?

. . . .

1. Try to convince a friend or relative to go with you to see a movie or play that you know he or she does not want to see.

2. Try to convince a friend or relative to try a different brand of toothpaste.

. . . .

Reinforcing Skills

Grinvalds/iStock/Getty Images

Stress @Work

Mackenzie Sharpe hardly ever left his desk.[1] He was too busy. So eating lunch at his desk was a regular part of his working life. He was worried when his employer, Vancouver-based CBRE, instituted a new policy: Workspaces were not for eating. "I was concerned that I'd be distracted if I had to get up and move to a lunch room just to have a nibble," says Mr. Sharpe, a senior sales associate.

CBRE introduced the policy because studies indicated that this type of workplace behaviour leads to stress.

Sharpe came to appreciate the policy within several months. "I feel more productive, because I realize when you're eating at your desk, you're not necessarily working at full attention to what you're doing," he says.

While not a common policy in Canada, Lisa Fulford-Roy, CBRE's managing director of workplace strategy, thinks it was the right thing to do. "We want people to take a break from their screens, relax, and connect with colleagues in an informal setting. Ultimately, we expect it will help lower stress and increase productivity."

Ashley O'Neill, vice-president of corporate strategy at CBRE, considers this new policy a wellness issue. She doesn't think eating at one's desk really saves anyone any time. The policy is meant to promote physical and mental well-being. She also says it has benefited CBRE. "Since the move, we have recorded substantially more multidiscipline business solutions being successfully executed for our clients—and that is a win on every front."

Are We Overstressed?

Stress appears to be a major factor in the lives of many Canadians. A recent survey conducted by Statistics Canada found that Canadians experience a great deal of stress, with those from Quebec topping the list.[2] The survey also found that women were more stressed than men. The inset *Stressed Quite a Lot, 2013* reports the findings.

The impact of stress on the Canadian economy is huge, costing an estimated $50 billion in lost productivity in 2016, with two-thirds of that coming from depression,[3] and considerably more than that in medical costs.

An additional problem is that employees are working longer hours than ever, according to Professor Linda Duxbury of Carleton University's Sprott School of Business and Professor Chris Higgins of the Richard Ivey School of Business at the University of Western Ontario. Their survey of more than 24 000 Canadians found that almost two-thirds of Canadians work more than 45 hours a week, a significant increase from 20 years ago.[4] Canadian businesses have cut the number of employees over time, but not the amount of work. Duxbury notes that "Organizations are fooling themselves if they think they're getting increased productivity by expecting those who they have left to do more."[5]

Jobs and Stress Levels

How do jobs rate in terms of stress? The inset *The Most and Least Stressful Jobs* on page 118 shows how selected occupations ranked in an evaluation of 250 jobs. Among the criteria used in the rankings were overtime, quotas, deadlines, competitiveness, physical demands, environmental conditions, hazards encountered, initiative required, stamina required, win–lose situations, and working in the public eye.

What Is Stress?

Stress is a dynamic condition in which an individual is confronted with an opportunity, demand, or resource related to what the individual desires and for which the outcome is perceived to be both uncertain and important.[7] This definition is complicated. Let's look at its components more closely.

Although stress is typically discussed in a negative context, it also has a positive value.[8] In response to stress, your nervous system, hypothalamus, pituitary, and adrenal glands supply you with stress hormones to cope. Your heartbeat and breathing accelerate to increase oxygen, while your muscles tense for action.[9] This is a time when stress offers potential gain. Consider, for example, the superior performance that an athlete or stage performer gives in "clutch" situations. Such individuals often use stress positively to rise to the occasion and perform at or near their maximum. Similarly, many professionals see the pressures of heavy workloads and deadlines as positive challenges that enhance the quality of their work and the satisfaction they get from their job. However, when the situation is negative, stress is harmful and may hinder your progress by elevating your blood pressure uncomfortably

Stressed Quite a Lot[6]

Canada	Males (%) 21.3	Females (%) 24.6
Newfoundland and Labrador	13.7	16.5
Prince Edward Island	12.8*	22.7
Nova Scotia	18.7	20.6
New Brunswick	19.3	20.8
Quebec	23.8	27.1
Ontario	21.6	25.5
Manitoba	19.3	20.9
Saskatchewan	19.1	20.1
Alberta	18.7	23.6
British Columbia	21.1	23.1
Yukon	16.9	23.8
Northwest Territories	12.6*	21.0

*Use with caution.

Note: Population aged 15 and older who reported experiencing quite a lot or extreme stress most days of their lives.

and creating an erratic heart rhythm as you struggle to speak and think logically.[10]

Researchers have argued that *challenge stressors*—or stressors associated with workload, pressure to complete tasks, and time urgency—operate quite differently from *hindrance stressors*—or stressors that keep you from reaching your goals (red tape, office politics, confusion over job responsibilities). Early evidence suggests that challenge stressors produce less strain than hindrance stressors.[11]

Researchers have sought to clarify the conditions under which each type of stress exists. It appears that employees who have a stronger affective commitment to their organization can transfer psychological stress into greater focus and higher sales performance, whereas employees with low levels of commitment perform worse under stress.[12] When challenge stress increases, those with high levels of organizational support have higher role-based performance, but those with low levels of organizational support do not.[13]

More typically, stress is associated with *demands* and *resources*. Demands are responsibilities, pressures, obligations, and even uncertainties that individuals face in the workplace. Resources are things within an individual's control that can be used to resolve the demands. For example, when you write an exam, you feel stress because you confront opportunities and performance pressures. To the extent that you can apply resources to the demands on you—such as being prepared for the exam—you will feel less stress.

Overall, social support may be more important on an ongoing basis than any other factor in coping with stress. According to recent research, people with emotional support may feel lower stress levels, less depressed from stress, and more likely to make lifestyle changes that may reduce stress.[15] Overall, under the demands–resources perspective, having resources to cope with stress is just as important in offsetting it as demands are in increasing it.[16]

Causes of Stress

Workplace stress can arise from a variety of factors:

- *Environmental factors.* Just as environmental uncertainty influences the design of an organization's structure, it also influences stress levels among employees in that organization. Indeed, uncertainty is the biggest reason people have trouble coping with organizational changes.[17] Three common types of environmental uncertainty are economic, political, and technological. Changes in the business cycle create *economic uncertainties*. When the economy is contracting, for example, people become increasingly anxious about their job security. *Political uncertainties* don't tend to create as much stress among North Americans as they do for employees in countries such as Haiti or Venezuela. The obvious reason is that the United States and Canada have stable political systems, in which change is typically implemented in an orderly manner. Because innovations can make an employee's skills and experience obsolete in a very short time, keeping up with new computer programs, robotics, automation, and similar forms of *technological change* are also a threat to many people at work that causes them stress.

- *Organizational factors.* There is no shortage of factors within an organization that can cause stress. Pressures to avoid errors or complete tasks in a limited time, work overload, a demanding and insensitive boss, and unpleasant co-workers are a few examples. We have categorized these factors around task, role, and interpersonal demands.

The Most and Least Stressful Jobs

How do jobs rate in terms of stress? According to 2017 research by CareerCast.com, the top 10 most and least stressful jobs are as follows:[14]

Ten Most Stressful Jobs

1. Enlisted military personnel
2. Firefighter
3. Airline pilot
4. Police officer
5. Event coordinator
6. Newspaper reporter
7. Senior corporate executive
8. Public relations coordinator
9. Taxi driver
10. Broadcaster

Ten Least Stressful Jobs

1. Diagnostic medical sonographer
2. Compliance officer
3. Hair stylist
4. Audiologist
5. University professor
6. Medical records technician
7. Jeweller
8. Operations research analyst
9. Pharmacy technician
10. Medical laboratory technician

- *Task demands* relate to a person's job. They include the design of the individual's job (including its degree of autonomy, task variety, and automation), working conditions, and the physical work layout. The single factor most consistently related to stress in the workplace is the amount of work that needs to be done, followed closely by the presence of looming deadlines.[18] Working in an overcrowded room or in a visible location where noise and interruptions are constant can also increase anxiety and stress.[19] As customer service grows ever more important, emotional labour becomes a source of stress.[20] Do you think you could put on a happy face while working at Starbucks or WestJet when you are having a bad day?

- *Role demands* relate to pressures placed on a person as a function of the particular role he or she plays in the organization.

- *Interpersonal demands* are pressures created by other employees. Some pressures are expected, but a rapidly growing body of research has shown that negative co-worker and supervisor behaviours, including fights, bullying, incivility, racial harassment, and sexual harassment, are especially strongly related to stress at work.[21] Interpersonal mistreatment can have effects at a physiological level, with one study finding that unfair treatment in a controlled setting triggered the release of cortisol, a hormone involved in the stress-reaction process.[22] Furthermore, individuals who believe they are experiencing a social climate of discrimination

from multiple sources over time have higher levels of psychological strain, even after accounting for differing baseline levels of well-being.[23] Social exclusion, perhaps as a form of interpersonal mistreatment, can also be a significant source of psychological strain. One study found that experiences of ostracism may have even more negative effects than experiences of interpersonal conflict.[24]

- *Personal factors.* The typical individual may work between 40 and 50 hours a week. But the experiences and problems that people encounter in the other 120-plus nonwork hours can spill over to the job. The final category of sources of stress at work includes factors of an employee's personal life: family issues and personal economic problems.

  - Most people hold *family* and personal relationships dear. *Family issues*, even good ones, can cause stress that significantly impacts individuals. Family issues are often closely related to work–life conflict.

  - Regardless of income level, some people are poor money managers or have wants that exceed their earning capacity. People who make $100 000 per year seem to have as much trouble handling their finances as those who earn $20 000—although recent research indicates that those who make under $50 000 per year do experience more stress.[25] The *personal economic* problems of overextended financial resources create stress and take attention away from work.

When we review stressors individually, it's easy to overlook that stress is an additive phenomenon—it builds

up.[27] Each new and persistent stressor adds to an individual's stress level. A single stressor may seem relatively unimportant in and of itself, but if it is added to an already high level of stress, it can be too much. To appraise the total amount of stress an individual is under, we have to sum up all of the sources and severity levels of that person's stress. Since this cannot be easily quantified or observed, managers should remain aware of the potential stress loads from organizational factors in particular. Many employees are willing to express their perceived stress load at work to a caring manager.

Consequences of Stress

Stress shows itself in a number of ways, such as high blood pressure, irritability, difficulty in making routine decisions, changes in appetite, accident proneness, and the like. These symptoms fit into three general categories: physiological, psychological, and behavioural symptoms.[28]

FACTBOX

How employees explained why they were stressed at work in a recent survey:

- 59 percent said they feel stressed and on edge.
- 67 percent said that their job expectations are too demanding.
- 60 percent reported problems of trust between employees and management at their workplace.
- 56 percent said their workplace culture isn't positive.[26]

- *Physiological symptoms.* Most early research concerned with stress was directed at physiological symptoms because most researchers in this area were specialists in the health and medical sciences. Their work led to the conclusion that stress could create changes in metabolism, increase heart and breathing rates, increase blood pressure, cause headaches, and induce heart attacks. Evidence now clearly indicates that stress may have harmful physiological effects. A long-term study conducted in the United Kingdom found that job strain was associated with higher levels of coronary heart disease.[29] Still another study conducted with Danish human services workers found that higher levels of psychological burnout at the work-unit level were related to significantly higher levels of sickness absence.[30] Many other studies have shown similar results linking work stress to a variety of indicators of poor health.

- *Psychological symptoms.* Job dissatisfaction is an obvious cause of stress. But stress also shows itself in other psychological states—for instance, tension, anxiety, irritability, boredom, and procrastination. One study that tracked physiological responses of employees over time found that stress due to high workloads was related to lower emotional well-being.[31] Jobs that make multiple and conflicting demands or in which there is a lack of clarity as to the person's duties, authority, and responsibilities increase stress and dissatisfaction.[32] Similarly, the less control people have over the pace of their work, the greater their stress and dissatisfaction. Jobs that provide a low level of variety, significance, autonomy, feedback, and identity create stress and reduce satisfaction and involvement in the job.[33] Not everyone reacts to autonomy in the same way, however. For those with an external locus of control, increased job control increases the tendency to experience stress and exhaustion.[34]

- *Behavioural symptoms.* Research on behaviour and stress has been conducted across several countries and over time, and the relationships appear relatively consistent. Behaviourally related stress symptoms include reductions in productivity, increases in absence and turnover, changes in eating habits, increased smoking or consumption of alcohol, rapid speech, fidgeting, and sleep disorders.[35] More recently, stress has been linked to aggression and violence in the workplace.

Why Do Individuals Differ in Their Experiences of Stress?

Some people thrive on stressful situations, while others are overwhelmed by them. What differentiates people in terms of their ability to handle stress? What individual difference variables moderate the relationship between *potential* stressors and *experienced* stress? At least four variables—perception, job experience, social support, and personality—are relevant.

- *Perception.* Individuals react in response to their *perception* of reality rather than to reality itself. Perception, therefore, moderates the relationship between a potential stress condition and an employee's reaction to it. Layoffs may cause one person to fear losing his job, while another sees an opportunity to get a large severance allowance and start her own business. So stress potential does not lie in objective conditions; instead it lies in an employee's interpretation of those conditions.

- *Job experience.* Experience on the job tends to be negatively related to work stress. Two explanations have been offered.[36] First is selective withdrawal. Voluntary turnover is more probable among people who experience more stress. Therefore, people who remain with the organization longer are those with more stress-resistant traits or those who are more resistant to the stress characteristics of the organization. Second, people eventually develop coping mechanisms to deal with stress. Because this takes time, senior members of the organization are more likely to be fully adapted and should experience less stress.

- *Social support.* Collegial relationships with co-workers or supervisors can buffer the impact of stress.[37] This is among the best-documented relationships in the stress literature. Social support helps ease the negative effects of even high-strain jobs.

- *Personality.* Stress symptoms expressed on the job may originate in the person's personality.[38] Perhaps the most widely studied *personality trait* in research on stress is neuroticism, which we discussed in Chapter 2. As you might expect, neurotic individuals are more prone to experiencing psychological strain.[39] Evidence suggests that neurotic individuals are more likely to find stressors in their work environments, so they believe their environments are more threatening. They also tend to select less adaptive coping mechanisms, relying on avoidance as a way of dealing with problems rather than attempting to resolve them.[40]

Workaholism is a personality characteristic related to stress levels. Workaholics are people obsessed with their work; they put in an enormous

number of hours, think about work even when not working, and create additional work responsibilities to satisfy an inner compulsion to work more. In some ways, they might seem like ideal employees. That is probably why when most people are asked in interviews what their greatest weakness is, they reflexively say, "I just work too hard." However, working hard is different from working compulsively. Workaholics are not necessarily more productive than other employees, despite their extreme efforts. The strain of putting in such a high level of work effort eventually begins to wear on the person, leading to higher levels of work–life conflict and psychological burnout.[41]

How Do We Manage Stress?

Next we discuss ways that individuals can manage stress, and the programs organizations use to help employees manage stress.

Individual Approaches

An employee can and should take personal responsibility for reducing his or her stress level. Individual strategies that have proven effective include time-management techniques, physical exercise, relaxation techniques, and a close social support network.

● *Time-management techniques.* Many people manage their time poorly. The well-organized employee, like the well-organized student, can often accomplish twice as much as the person who is poorly organized. A few of the more well-known time-management techniques are (1) maintaining to-do lists, (2) scheduling activities based on priorities, not what you can accomplish, (3) doing the hard tasks first,

and (4) blocking out distraction-free time to accomplish tasks. These time-management skills can help minimize procrastination by focusing efforts on immediate goals and boosting motivation even in the face of tasks that are less enjoyable.[42]

● *Physical activity.* Physicians have recommended noncompetitive physical exercise, such as aerobics, walking, jogging, swimming, and riding a bicycle, as a way to deal with excessive stress levels. These activities decrease the detrimental physiological responses to stress and allow us to recover from stress more quickly.[43]

● *Relaxation techniques.* Individuals can teach themselves to reduce tension through relaxation techniques such as meditation, hypnosis, and deep breathing. The objective is to reach a state of deep relaxation, in which you focus all your energy on the release of muscle tension.[44] Deep relaxation for 15 or 20 minutes a day releases tension and provides a pronounced sense of peacefulness, as well as significant changes in heart rate, blood pressure, and other physiological factors. A growing body of research shows that simply taking breaks from work at routine intervals can facilitate psychological recovery and reduce stress significantly and may improve job performance, and these

effects are even greater if relaxation techniques are employed.[45]

● *Social support.* Having friends, family, or colleagues to talk to provides an outlet when stress levels become excessive. Expanding your social support network provides you with someone to listen to your problems and to offer a more objective perspective on the situation.

The inset *Tips for Reducing Stress* offers additional ideas for managing stress.

Organizational Approaches

Montreal-based CGI, a global IT company, delivers a comprehensive corporate wellness program to its 68 000 employees worldwide through its Health Portal. Calgary-based Devon Energy built The Well, a 1400-square-metre wellness and fitness facility. Employees can use the state-of-the-art facility to "improve overall wellness, increase energy levels, reduce absenteeism, and effectively recruit and retain staff. The Manitoba Teachers' Society created a wellness program based on teacher input. The program helps teachers manage stress, and allows them to find time to take care of themselves. Balance initiatives include chair massages, smoothie delivery, a regular magazine, and learning opportunities on health and wellness topics."[46]

Tips for Reducing Stress

- Spend time with supportive friends or family.
- Talk yourself through it.
- Make sure to get enough sleep.
- Engage in exercise, hobbies, positive thinking, and relaxation techniques such as meditation or yoga.[47]

Most firms that have introduced wellness programs have found significant benefits. A recent joint study conducted by Sun Life Financial and the Richard Ivey School of Business found that in companies with wellness programs, employees missed 1.5 to 1.7 fewer days due to absenteeism. This resulted in estimated savings of $251 per employee per year.[48] While many Canadian businesses report having wellness initiatives, only 24 percent have "fully implemented wellness strategies" (which includes multi-year goals and an evaluation of results), according to a recent survey.[49]

So what can organizations do to reduce employee stress? In general, strategies to reduce stress include improved employee selection, placement of employees in appropriate jobs, realistic goal setting, designing jobs with employee needs and skills in mind, increased employee involvement, improved organizational communication, offering employee sabbaticals, and, as mentioned, establishment of corporate wellness programs.

Certain jobs are more stressful than others, but individuals also differ in their response to stressful situations. We know, for example, that individuals with little experience or an external locus of control tend to be more prone to stress. Selection and placement decisions should take these facts into consideration. Although management should not restrict hiring to only experienced individuals with an internal locus of control, such individuals may adapt better to high-stress jobs and perform those jobs more effectively. Similarly, *training* can increase an individual's self-efficacy and thus lessen job strain.

Individuals perform better when they have specific and challenging goals and receive feedback on how well they are progressing toward them. Goals can reduce stress as well as provide motivation.[50] Employees who are highly committed to their goals and see purpose in their jobs experience less stress because they are more likely to perceive stressors as challenges rather than hindrances. Specific goals that are perceived as attainable clarify performance expectations. Additionally, goal feedback reduces uncertainties as to actual job performance. The result is less employee frustration, role ambiguity, and stress.

Redesigning jobs to give employees more responsibility, more meaningful work, more autonomy, and increased feedback can reduce stress because these factors give the employee greater control over work activities and lessen dependence on others. Of course, not all employees want jobs with increased responsibility. The right design for employees with a low need for growth might be less responsibility and increased specialization. If individuals prefer structure and routine, more structured jobs should also reduce uncertainties and stress levels.

Role stress is detrimental to a large extent because employees feel uncertain about goals, expectations, how they will be evaluated, and the like. By giving employees a voice in the decisions that directly affect their job performance, management can increase employee control and reduce role stress. So managers should consider *increasing employee involvement* in decision making because evidence clearly shows that increases in employee empowerment reduce psychological strain.[51]

Increasing formal organizational communication with employees reduces uncertainty by lessening role ambiguity and role conflict. Given the importance that perceptions play in moderating the stress-response relationship, management can also use effective communication as a means to shape employee perceptions. Remember that what employees categorize as demands, threats, or opportunities at work are merely interpretations, and those interpretations can be affected by the symbols and actions communicated by management.

Some employees need an occasional escape from the frenetic pace of their work. In recent years, companies such as American Express, Intel, General Mills, Microsoft, Morningstar, DreamWorks Animation, and Adobe Systems have begun to provide extended voluntary leaves.[52] These *sabbaticals*—ranging in length from a few weeks to several months—allow employees to travel, relax, or pursue personal projects that consume time beyond normal vacation weeks. Proponents say that these sabbaticals can revive and rejuvenate employees who might be headed for burnout.

Our final suggestion is to offer organizationally supported wellness programs. These typically provide workshops to help people quit smoking, control alcohol use, lose weight, eat better, and develop a regular exercise program; they focus on the employee's total physical and mental condition.[53] A meta-analysis of 36 programs designed to reduce stress (including wellness programs) showed that interventions to help employees reframe stressful situations and use active coping strategies appreciably reduced stress levels.[54] Most wellness programs assume that employees need to take personal responsibility for their physical and mental health and that the organization is merely a means to that end. The inset *Toward Less Stressful Work* offers additional ideas.

F A C E O F F

When organizations provide on-site daycare facilities, they are filling a needed role in parents' lives, and making it easier for parents to attend to their job demands rather than worry about child-care arrangements.

When employees expect organizations to provide child care, they are shifting their responsibilities to their employers, rather than keeping their family needs and concerns private. Moreover, it is unfair to offer child-care benefits when not all employees have children.

RESEARCH EXERCISES

1. Look for data on stress levels in other countries. How do these data compare with the Canadian data presented in the *Factbox*? Are the sources of stress the same in different countries? What might you conclude about how stress affects people in different cultures?

2. Find out what three Canadian organizations in three different industries have done to help employees manage stress. Are there common themes in these programs? Did you find any unusual programs? To what extent are these programs tailored to the needs of the employees in those industries?

YOUR PERSPECTIVE

1. Think of all the technical avenues enabling employees to be connected 24/7 to the workplace: email, texting, company intranets. A generation ago, most employees could go home after a day at work and not be "on call." What are the positive benefits of this change? What are the downsides? As an employee facing the demand to "stay connected" to your workplace, how would you try to maintain a balance in your life?

2. How much responsibility should individuals take for managing their own stress? To what extent should organizations become involved in the personal lives of their employees when trying to help them manage stress? What are the pros and cons for whether employees or organizations take responsibility for managing stress?

WANT TO KNOW MORE?

If you want more tips on detecting stress and coping with it, the Canadian Heart & Stroke Foundation has created a helpful brochure: **http://www.heartandstroke.ca/-/media/pdf-files/canada/health-information-catalogue/en-stress-test-v3-0.ashx**. The site also offers tips on reducing stress. You can also take a work–life balance quiz at the Canadian Mental Health Association website (**www.cmha.ca/mental_health/work-life-balance-quiz/**) and read more on the effects of mental illness and stress.

Toward Less Stressful Work

- Avoid high-stress jobs—such as stockbroker, customer service/complaint worker, police officer, waiter, medical intern, secretary, and air traffic controller—unless you are confident in your ability to handle stress.

- If you do experience stress at work, try to find a job that has plenty of control (so you can decide how to perform your work) and supportive co-workers.

- Lack of money is the top stressor reported by people under age 30, so pursue a career that pays you well but does not have a high degree of stress.[55]

4 Theories of Motivation

Lee Valley Tools founder Leonard Lee decided to become an entrepreneur at age 40. He wanted his employees to act as entrepreneurs too. How did he use motivation to build a very successful tool store?

LEARNING OUTCOMES

After studying this chapter, you should be able to:

1. Describe the three key elements of motivation.
2. Evaluate the applicability of early theories of motivation.
3. Apply the key tenets of expectancy theory to motivating employees.
4. Demonstrate the differences among goal-setting theory, self-efficacy theory, and reinforcement theory.
5. Describe why equity and fairness matter in the workplace.
6. Demonstrate how organizational justice is a refinement of equity theory.
7. Apply the predictions of self-determination theory to intrinsic and extrinsic rewards.
8. Discuss the ethics behind motivation theories.
9. Summarize the essence of what we know about motivating employees.

Jonathan Hayward/The Canadian Press

A pproaching age 40, Leonard Lee was tiring of working for the federal government.[1] Though his grandmother felt he had won the lottery by getting a government job, Lee was not so sure. He was tired of the bureaucratic decision making, for one thing, and was troubled by the fact that some of his colleagues did not really seem motivated by their jobs. "But what was driving me crazy were the number of people who would say, 'I have 17 years, eight months, two weeks, two days, and seven hours before I retire.'"

Lee looked for something else to do, and he and his wife started a small mail-order business, selling cast-iron barrel stove kits. After doing this successfully for two years, Lee's confidence built up, and he quit his government job to launch Lee Valley Tools. At first it was a catalogue business. Then a long postal strike almost ruined the business. So Lee opened a retail store, and then continued to open stores over the years. An investment partner explained why he had helped Lee start his business: "He was always full of energy, full of beans, full of ideas . . . he was constantly churning up new ideas and continued to do that right up until the end."

In other words, Leonard Lee was very motivated in whatever he did: He found too much responsibility in government work, without enough authority. Due largely to his personal motivation, there are now 19 Lee Valley stores from Halifax to Victoria, all family-owned.

What motivates people? In this chapter, we review the basics of motivation, assess motivation theories, and provide an integrative understanding of how the different theories apply to motivating employees in organizations.

OB IS FOR EVERYONE

- Are managers manipulating employees when they link rewards to productivity?
- Why do some managers do a better job of motivating people than others?
- How important is fairness to you?
- What can you do if you think your salary is unfair?

THE BIG IDEA

Successfully motivating individuals requires identifying their needs and making it possible for them to achieve those needs.

1 Describe the three key elements of motivation.

What Is Motivation?

Motivation is one of the most frequently researched topics in organizational behaviour (OB).[2] A 2013 Gallup poll suggests that employees are not motivated. Seventy percent of Canadian employees are not engaged in their work, and another 14 percent are actively disengaged.[3] In a 2014 survey, 89 percent of employees reported wasting time at work every day, and 62 percent said they waste between 30 and 60 minutes each day. How? Surfing the Internet came in first with 26 percent of respondents (Google, Facebook, and LinkedIn were the most popular time distractors); "too many meetings/conference calls and dealing with annoying co-workers tied for second place with 24% each."[4]

Motivation is the process that accounts for an individual's intensity, direction, and persistence of effort toward reaching a goal.[5]

The three key elements in our definition are intensity, direction, and persistence. *Intensity* describes how hard a person tries. This is the element most of us focus on when we talk about motivation. However, high intensity is unlikely to lead to favourable job-performance outcomes unless the effort is channelled in a *direction* that is beneficial. Therefore, we consider the quality of effort as well as its intensity. Finally, the effort requires *persistence*. This measures how long a person can maintain effort. Motivated individuals stay with a task long enough to achieve their goal.

Many people incorrectly view motivation as a personal trait—something some people have and others don't. Along these lines, Douglas McGregor proposed two distinct views of human beings. **Theory X**, which is basically negative, suggests that employees dislike work, will attempt to avoid it, and must be coerced, controlled, or threatened with punishment to achieve goals. **Theory Y**, which is basically positive, suggests that employees like work, are creative, seek responsibility, and will exercise self-direction and self-control if they are committed to the objectives.[6]

Our knowledge of motivation tells us that neither theory alone fully accounts for employee behaviour. What we know is that motivation is the result of the interaction of the individual and the situation. Certainly, individuals differ in their basic motivational drive. But the same employee who is quickly bored when pulling the lever on a drill press may enthusiastically pull a slot machine lever in Casino Windsor for hours on end. You may read the latest bestseller at one sitting, yet find it difficult to concentrate on a textbook for more than 20 minutes. It's not necessarily you—it's the situation. So as we analyze the concept of motivation, keep in mind that the level of motivation varies both *among* individuals and *within* individuals at different times.

You should also realize that what motivates people will also vary among individuals and situations. Motivation theorists talk about **intrinsic motivators** and **extrinsic motivators**. Extrinsic motivators come from outside the person and include such things as pay, bonuses, and other tangible rewards. Intrinsic motivators come from a person's internal desire to do something due to such things as interest, challenge, and personal satisfaction. Individuals are intrinsically motivated when they genuinely care about their work, look for better ways to do it, and are energized and fulfilled by doing it well.[7] The rewards the individual gets from intrinsic motivation come from the work itself rather than from external factors such as increases in pay or compliments from the boss.

Are individuals primarily intrinsically or extrinsically motivated? Theory X suggests that people are almost exclusively driven by extrinsic motivators. However, Theory Y suggests that people are more intrinsically motivated.

Intrinsic and extrinsic motivation may reflect the situation, however, rather than individual personalities. For example, suppose that your mother has asked you or your brother to take her to a meeting an hour away. You may be willing to drive her, without any thought of compensation, because it will make you feel good to do something for her. That is intrinsic motivation. But if you have a love–hate relationship with your brother, you may insist that he buy you lunch for helping out. Lunch would then be an

motivation The intensity, direction, and persistence of effort a person shows in reaching a goal.

Theory X The assumption that employees dislike work, will attempt to avoid it, and must be coerced, controlled, or threatened with punishment to achieve goals.

Theory Y The assumption that employees like work, are creative, seek responsibility, and will exercise self-direction and self-control if they are committed to the objectives.

intrinsic motivators A person's internal desire to do something due to such things as interest, challenge, and personal satisfaction.

extrinsic motivators Motivation that comes from outside the person and includes such things as pay, bonuses, and other tangible rewards.

extrinsic motivator—something that came from outside yourself and motivated you to do the task. Later in the chapter, we review the evidence regarding the significance of extrinsic vs. intrinsic rewards, and also examine how to increase intrinsic motivation. Meanwhile, you might consider whether you can motivate yourself through self-talk, an idea considered in *Focus on Research*.

FOCUS ON RESEARCH
Talking to Yourself Can Be a Powerful Self-Motivator

How does internal dialogue affect our motivation? In the children's book *The Little Engine That Could*, the title character says, "I think I can, I think I can," motivating itself to do the job through positive self-talk. In a 2010 study, researchers examined whether this type of talk is the best way to motivate oneself, or whether it is better to ask, "Can I do this?"[8]

Subjects were asked to spend one minute either "wondering whether they would complete a task or telling themselves they would." Then they were asked to complete some puzzles. Subjects who asked themselves whether they would complete the task were more successful than those who said they would. Several similar studies were conducted, and the results of each of them indicate that intrinsic motivation increased when subjects asked themselves a question about performance.

These findings suggest that asking yourself whether you will go to the gym three times next week will be more effective than telling yourself that you will go to the gym three times next week. One of the authors of the study summarized the results as follows: "The popular idea is that self-affirmations enhance people's ability to meet their goals. It seems, however, that when it comes to performing a specific behaviour, asking questions is a more promising way of achieving your objectives." . . . .

Needs Theories of Motivation

People vary in what they need to motivate themselves. Some need external support and guidance, while others are motivated intrinsically, relying on themselves.[9] One of the things that motivated Leonard Lee, founder of Lee Valley Tools, was sourcing and designing tools for his customers—in other words, meeting the needs of other people. When Lee heard that an Ottawa-based plastic surgeon was using Lee Valley woodworking knives, he started a new company to sell medical instruments.

The company made a number of specialized tools for the medical profession. Though he eventually sold the rights to these tools, his son Robin Lee said that his father "was most proud of and most disappointed by" the medical company because "selling to the Canadian medical system proved frustrating." That said, Leonard Lee ran the business for almost 16 years.

In this section we discuss how needs can be used to motivate others.

Theories of motivation generally fall into two categories: needs theories and process theories. *Needs theories* describe the types of needs that must be met to motivate individuals. *Process theories* help us understand the actual ways in which we and others can be motivated. There are a variety of needs theories, including Maslow's hierarchy of needs, Herzberg's motivation–hygiene theory (sometimes called the *two-factor theory*), and McClelland's theory of needs. We briefly review these to illustrate the basic properties of needs theories.

Needs theories are widely criticized for not standing up to scientific review. However, you should know them because (1) they represent a foundation from which contemporary theories have grown, and (2) practising managers still regularly use these theories and their terminology in explaining employee motivation.

2 Evaluate the applicability of early theories of motivation.

Maslow's Hierarchy of Needs Theory

The best known theory of motivation is Abraham Maslow's **hierarchy of needs**.[10] Maslow hypothesized that within every human being there exists a hierarchy of five needs:

- *Physiological.* Includes hunger, thirst, shelter, sex, and other bodily needs.
- *Safety.* Includes security and protection from physical and emotional harm.
- *Social.* Includes affection, belongingness, acceptance, and friendship.
- *Esteem.* Includes internal esteem factors such as self-respect, autonomy, and achievement; and external esteem factors such as status, recognition, and attention.
- *Self-actualization.* Includes growth, achieving one's potential, and self-fulfillment. This is the drive to become what one is capable of becoming.

Recently, a sixth need has been proposed as the highest level—intrinsic values—which is said to have originated from Maslow, but it has yet to gain widespread acceptance.[11]

Although no need is ever fully met, a substantially satisfied need no longer motivates. Thus, as each need becomes substantially satisfied, the next need becomes dominant. This is what Maslow means by moving up the steps of the hierarchy. So if you want to motivate someone, according to Maslow, you need to understand what level of the hierarchy that person is currently on and focus on satisfying needs at or above that level. Exhibit 4-1 identifies Maslow's hierarchy of needs on the left, and then illustrates how these needs are applied in the workplace.[12]

Maslow separated the five needs into higher and lower orders. Physiological and safety needs, where people start, are **lower-order needs**; social (belonging), self-esteem, and **self-actualization** are **higher-order needs**. Higher-order needs are satisfied internally (within the person), whereas lower-order needs are mainly satisfied externally (by rewards such as pay, union contracts, and tenure).

Maslow's theory has received long-standing wide recognition, particularly among practising managers. It's intuitively logical and easy to understand, even though little research supports the theory. Maslow himself provided no empirical evidence, and some research has validated it.[13] Unfortunately, however, most research does not, especially when the theory is applied to diverse cultures,[14] with the possible exception of physiological needs.[15] But old theories, especially intuitively logical ones, die hard. It is thus important to be aware of the prevailing public acceptance of the hierarchy when discussing motivation.

Two-Factor Theory

Believing that an individual's relationship to work is basic and that attitude toward this work can very well determine success or failure, Frederick Herzberg wondered, "What do people want from their jobs?" He asked people to describe, in detail, situations in which they felt exceptionally *good* or *bad* about their jobs. The replies people gave when they felt good about their jobs significantly differed from when they felt bad, which led Herzberg to his **two-factor theory**—also called *motivation–hygiene theory*, but this term is not used much today.[16]

As Exhibit 4-2 shows, intrinsic factors, such as achievement, recognition, the work itself, responsibility, advancement, and growth, seem to be related to job satisfaction. Respondents who felt good about their work tended to attribute these factors to their

hierarchy of needs theory A hierarchy of five needs—physiological, safety, social, esteem, and self-actualization—in which, as each need is substantially satisfied, the next need becomes dominant.

lower-order needs Needs that are satisfied externally, such as physiological and safety needs.

self-actualization The drive to become what a person is capable of becoming.

higher-order needs Needs that are satisfied internally, such as social (belonging), self-esteem, and self-actualization needs.

two-factor theory A theory that relates intrinsic factors to job satisfaction and associates extrinsic factors with dissatisfaction. Also called the *motivation–hygiene theory*.

EXHIBIT 4-1 Maslow's Hierarchy of Needs Applied to the Workplace

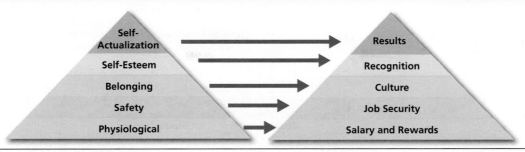

Source: C. Conley, *Peak: How Great Companies Get Their Mojo from Maslow* (San Francisco: Jossey-Bass, 2007). ISBN: 978-0787988616. Copyright © John Wiley & Sons.

situations. On the other hand, dissatisfied respondents tended to cite extrinsic factors, such as company policy and administration, supervision, interpersonal relations, and work conditions.

The data suggest that the opposite of satisfaction is not dissatisfaction, as was traditionally believed. Removing dissatisfying characteristics from a job does not necessarily make the job satisfying. As illustrated in Exhibit 4-3, Herzberg proposed a dual

EXHIBIT 4-2 Comparison of Satisfiers and Dissatisfiers

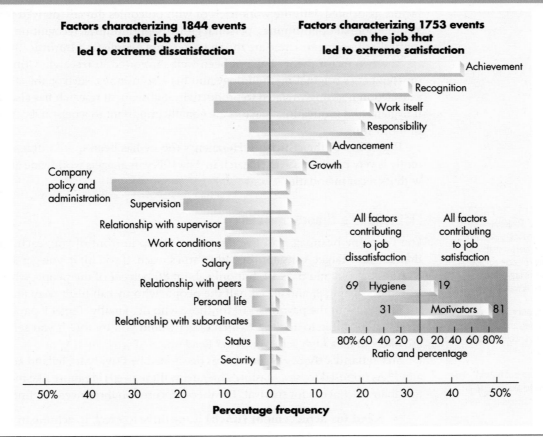

Source: Harvard Business Review. An exhibit from Frederick Herzberg, "One More Time: How Do You Motivate Employees?" *Harvard Business Review* 81, no. 1 (January 2003), p. 90.

EXHIBIT 4-3 Contrasting Views of Satisfaction and Dissatisfaction

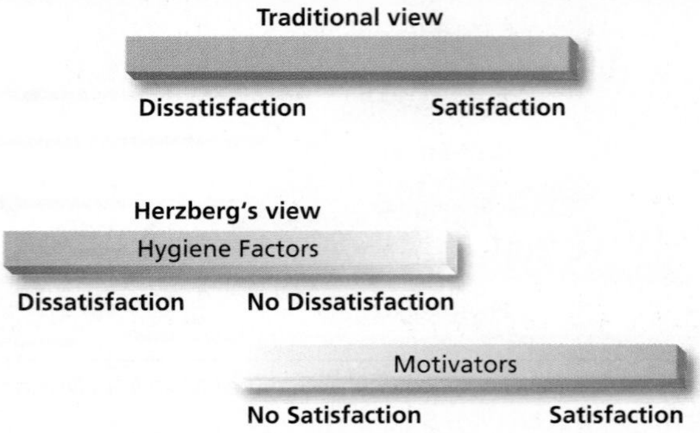

Traditional view

Dissatisfaction   Satisfaction

Herzberg's view
Hygiene Factors

Dissatisfaction   No Dissatisfaction

Motivators

No Satisfaction   Satisfaction

continuum: The opposite of "Satisfaction" is "No Satisfaction," and the opposite of "Dissatisfaction" is "No Dissatisfaction."

Under two-factor theory, the factors that lead to job satisfaction (motivators) are separate and distinct from those that lead to job dissatisfaction (hygiene factors). Therefore, managers who seek to eliminate factors that create job dissatisfaction may bring about peace but not necessarily motivation. They will be placating rather than motivating their employees. Conditions such as quality of supervision, pay, company policies, physical work conditions, relationships with others, and job security are **hygiene factors**. When they are adequate, people will not be dissatisfied; but neither will they be satisfied. If we want to *motivate* people in their jobs, we should emphasize factors associated with the work itself or with outcomes directly derived from it, such as promotional opportunities, personal growth opportunities, recognition, responsibility, and achievement. These are the characteristics people find intrinsically rewarding.

The two-factor theory has not been well supported in research. Criticisms centre on Herzberg's original methodology and his assumptions, such as the statement that satisfaction is strongly related to productivity. Subsequent research has also shown that if hygiene and motivational factors are equally important to a person, both are capable of motivating.

Regardless of the criticisms, Herzberg's theory has been quite influential and currently is very much in use in research in Asia.[17] Few managers worldwide are unfamiliar with its recommendations.

McClelland's Theory of Needs

You have one beanbag, and five targets are set up in front of you, each farther away than the last. Target A sits almost within arm's reach. If you hit it, you get $2. Target B is a bit farther out and pays $4, but only about 80 percent of the people who try can hit it. Target C pays $8, and about half the people who try can hit it. Very few people can hit Target D, but the payoff is $16 for those who do. Finally, Target E pays $32, but it's almost impossible to achieve. Which target would you try for? If you selected C, you are likely to be a high achiever. Why? Read on.

McClelland's theory of needs was developed by David McClelland and his associates.[18] As opposed to, say, Maslow's hierarchy, these needs are more like motivating factors than strict needs for survival. The theory focuses on three needs, defined as follows:

- **Need for achievement (nAch)** is the drive to excel, to achieve in relation to a set of standards, and to strive to succeed.

- **Need for power (nPow)** is the need to make others behave in a way that they would not have behaved otherwise.

hygiene factors Factors—such as company policy and administration, supervision, and salary—that, when adequate in a job, placate employees. When these factors are adequate, people will not be dissatisfied.

McClelland's theory of needs Achievement, power, and affiliation are three important needs that help explain motivation.

need for achievement (nAch) The drive to excel, to achieve in relation to a set of standards, and to strive to succeed.

need for power (nPow) The need to make others behave in a way that they would not have behaved otherwise.

- **Need for affiliation (nAff)** is the desire for friendly and close interpersonal relationships.

McClelland and subsequent researchers focused most of their attention on nAch. High achievers perform best when they perceive their probability of success as 0.5—that is, a 50–50 chance.[19] They dislike gambling with high odds because they get no achievement satisfaction from success that comes by pure chance. Similarly, they dislike low odds (high probability of success) because then there is no challenge to their skills. They like to set goals that require stretching themselves a little.

Relying on an extensive amount of research, we can predict some relationships between achievement need and job performance. First, when jobs have a high degree of personal responsibility, feedback, and an intermediate degree of risk, high achievers are strongly motivated. Second, a high need to achieve does not necessarily make someone a good manager, especially in large organizations. People with a high achievement need are interested in how well they do personally and not in influencing others to do well. Third, needs for affiliation and power tend to be closely related to managerial success. The best managers may be high in their need for power and low in their need for affiliation.[20]

McClelland's theory has research support, particularly cross-culturally (when cultural dimensions including power distance are taken into account).[21] The concept of the need for achievement has received a great deal of research attention and acceptance in a wide array of fields, including organizational behaviour, psychology, and general business.[22] Therefore, in this text we utilize the concept descriptively. The need for power also has research support, but it may be more familiar to people in broad terms than in relation to the original definition.[23] We will discuss power much more in Chapter 13. The need for affiliation is well established and accepted in research. Although it may seem like an updated version of Maslow's social need, it is actually quite separate. Many people take for granted the idea that human beings have a drive toward relationships, so none of us may completely lack this motivation. However, recent research of Cameroonian and German adults suggests we may be constrained by our personalities to the extent that we are high in neuroticism. Agreeableness supports our pursuit of affiliation, while extraversion has no significant effect.[24]

The degree to which we have each of the three needs is difficult to measure, and therefore the theory is difficult to put into practice. It is more common to find situations in which managers aware of these motivational drivers label employees based on observations made over time. Therefore, the concepts are helpful, but not often used objectively.

Alexandra Greenhill, co-founder and CEO of myBestHelper, is a high achiever. She has been named one of Vancouver's Top 40 under 40 and has also won a Cartier Women's Initiative Award, which is an international award for female entrepreneurs. myBestHelper is a website where people who need care providers (such as nannies, tutors, or babysitters) can connect with people who are looking to provide care. Greenhill, who was writing computer code at an early age, is also a family physician and has helped the BC Medical Association with its work on electronic medical records. She envisions that myBestHelper will be in every major city in Canada within five years.

Summarizing Needs Theories

The needs theories we have just reviewed all propose a similar idea: Individuals have needs that, when unsatisfied, will result in motivation. For instance, if you have a need to be praised, you may work harder at your task in order to receive recognition from your manager or other co-workers. Similarly, if you need money and you are asked to do something (within reason) that offers money as a reward, you will be motivated to complete that task.

Where needs theories differ is in the types of needs they consider and whether they propose a hierarchy of needs (where some needs have to be satisfied before others) or simply a list of needs. Exhibit 4-4 illustrates the relationship among the three needs theories that we discussed, and Exhibit 4-5 indicates whether the theory proposes a hierarchy of needs, and the contribution of and empirical support for each theory.

need for affiliation (nAff) The desire for friendly and close interpersonal relationships.

CAREER OBJECTIVES

Why Won't He Take My Advice?

The new guy in the office is nice enough, but he's straight out of college, and I have 20 years of experience in the field. I'd like to help him out, but he won't take it no matter how I approach him. Is there anything I can do to motivate him to accept my advice? He badly needs a few pointers.

—James

Dear James:

It's great that you want to help, and surely you have wisdom to offer. But let's start with this: When is the last time you took someone else's advice? Chances are it's easier for you to remember the last time you *did not* take someone's advice than when you did. That is because we want success on our own terms, and we don't like the idea that a ready answer was out there all along (and we missed it). "When somebody says, 'You should do something,' the subtext is: 'You're an idiot for not already doing it,'" said psychologist Alan Goldberg. "Nobody takes advice under those conditions." So under what conditions *do* people take advice?

There are two parts to the motivation equation for advice: what your co-worker wants to hear, and how you can approach him. For the first part, keep this rule in mind: He wants to hear that whatever decisions he has made are brilliant. If he hears anything different from that, he is likely to tune you out or keep talking until you come over to his side.

For the second part, your co-worker's motivation to accept and, more importantly, act on advice has a lot to do with how you approach him. Are you likely to "impart your wisdom to the younger generation?" Anything like "I wish I had known this when I was just starting out like you" advice will likely have him thinking you (and your advice) are out of date. Are you going to give "if I were you, I would do this" advice? He may resent your intrusion. According to research, what is most likely to work is a gentle suggestion, phrased as a request. Ravi Dhar, a director at Yale, said, "Interrogatives have less reactance and may be more effective." You might say, for instance, "Would you consider trying out this idea?"

Take heart, the problem is not that we don't like advice—we do, as long as we seek it. According to research, we are more motivated toward advice when we are facing important decisions, so good timing may work in your favour. When he does ask, you may suggest that he write down the parameters of his choices and his interpretations of the ethics of each decision. Researcher Dan Ariely has found that we are much more motivated to make morally right decisions when we have considered the moral implications in a forthright manner. In this way, your co-worker may motivate himself to make the right decisions.

Keep trying!

_____

Sources: D. Ariely, "What Price for the Soul of a Stranger?" *Wall Street Journal,* May 10–11, 2014, p. C12; J. Queenan, "A Word to the Wise," *Wall Street Journal*, February 8–9, 2014, pp. C1–C2; and S. Reddy, "The Trick to Getting People to Take the Stairs? Just Ask," *Wall Street Journal,* February 17, 2015, p. R4.

EXHIBIT 4-4 Relationship of Various Needs Theories

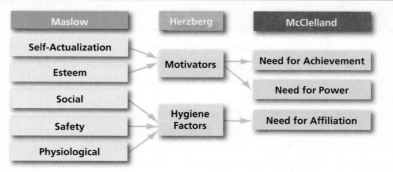

EXHIBIT 4-5 Summarizing the Various Needs Theories

Theory	Maslow	Herzberg	McClelland
Is there a hierarchy of needs?	The theory argues that lower-order needs must be satisfied before one progresses to higher-order needs.	Hygiene factors must be met if a person is not to be dissatisfied. They will not lead to satisfaction, however. Motivators lead to satisfaction.	People vary in the types of needs they have. Their motivation and how well they perform in a work situation are related to whether they have a need for achievement, power, or affiliation.
What is the theory's impact/ contribution?	The theory enjoys wide recognition among practising managers. Most managers are familiar with it.	The popularity of giving employees greater responsibility for planning and controlling their work can be attributed to this theory (see, for instance, the job characteristics model in Chapter 5). It shows that more than one need may operate at the same time.	The theory tells us that high-need achievers do not necessarily make good managers, since high achievers are more interested in how they do personally.
What empirical support/ criticisms exist?	Research has not validated the hierarchical nature of needs. However, a 2011 study found that the needs are universally related to individual happiness.	It is not really a theory of motivation: It assumes a link between satisfaction and productivity that was not measured or demonstrated.	It has mixed empirical support, but the theory is consistent with our knowledge of individual differences among people. Good empirical support exists on needs for achievement in particular.

What can we conclude from needs theories? We can safely say that individuals do have needs, and that they can be highly motivated to achieve those needs. The types of needs, and their importance, vary by individual, and probably vary over time for the same individual as well. When rewarding individuals, you should consider their specific needs. Obviously, in a workplace, it would be difficult to design a reward structure that could completely take into account the specific needs of every employee.

Process Theories of Motivation

Lee Valley Tools has a long history of paying its employees fairly.[25] Senior managers are paid no more than 10 times the lowest-paid employee. Twenty-five percent of pre-tax profits are divided evenly among all employees who have been with the company for at least two years. Leonard Lee believed that work was more than just about the money. He once counselled graduating university students: "If you do work you love, it's much easier to excel than it is if you are working primarily for money. It is also easier to be more creative."

Treating employees fairly and empowering them are some of the ways that organizations can motivate their employees.

EXHIBIT 4-6 How Does Expectancy Theory Work?

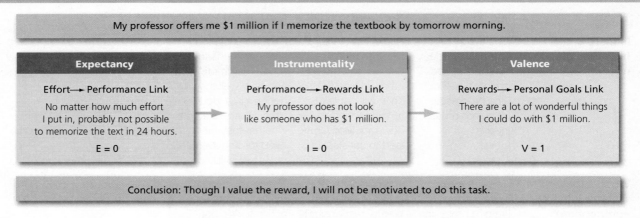

Process theories go beyond individual needs and focus on the broader picture of how one motivates oneself and others. Process theories include expectancy theory, goal-setting theory (and its application, management by objectives), self-efficacy theory, and reinforcement theory.

3 Apply the key tenets of expectancy theory to motivating employees.

Expectancy Theory

One of the most widely accepted explanations of motivation is Victor Vroom's **expectancy theory**.[26] Although it has critics, most of the evidence supports the theory.[27]

Expectancy theory says that employees will be motivated to exert a high level of effort when they believe the following:

- That the effort will lead to good performance
- That good performance will lead to organizational rewards, such as salary increases and/or intrinsic rewards
- That the rewards will satisfy employees' personal goals

The theory focuses on the three relationships (expectancy, instrumentality, and valence) illustrated in Exhibit 4-6 and described in the following pages. This exhibit also provides an example of how you might apply the theory.

Effort–Performance Relationship

The effort–performance relationship is commonly called **expectancy**. It answers the question: *If I give a maximum effort, will it be recognized in my performance appraisal?* For many employees, the answer is no. Why? Their skill level may be deficient, which means that no matter how hard they try, they are not likely to be high performers. The organization's performance appraisal system may be designed to assess nonperformance factors such as loyalty, initiative, or courage, which means more effort will not necessarily result in a higher evaluation. Another possibility is that employees, rightly or wrongly, think the boss does not like them. As a result, they expect a poor appraisal, regardless of effort. These examples suggest that people will only be motivated if they perceive a link between their effort and their performance. Expectancy can be expressed as a probability, and ranges from 0 to 1. To further provoke your thoughts on this matter, the *Ethical Dilemma* on pages 158–159 asks you to consider how grade inflation has affected the meaning of grades.

expectancy theory The theory that individuals act based on their evaluation of whether their effort will lead to good performance, whether good performance will be followed by a given outcome, and whether that outcome is attractive.

expectancy The belief that effort is related to performance.

Performance–Rewards Relationship

The performance–rewards relationship is commonly called **instrumentality**. It answers the question: *If I get a good performance appraisal, will it lead to organizational rewards?* Many organizations reward things besides performance. When pay is based on factors such as having seniority, being cooperative, or "kissing up" to the boss, employees are likely to see the performance–rewards relationship as weak and demotivating. Instrumentality ranges from −1 to +1. A negative instrumentality indicates that high performance reduces the chances of getting the desired outcome. An instrumentality of 0 indicates that no relationship exists between performance and receiving the desired outcome.

> Are managers manipulating employees when they link rewards to productivity?

Rewards–Personal Goals Relationship

The rewards–personal goals relationship is commonly called **valence**. It answers the question: *If I am rewarded, are the rewards attractive to me?* The employee works hard in the hope of getting a promotion but gets a pay raise instead. Or the employee wants a more interesting and challenging job but receives only a few words of praise. Or the employee puts in extra effort to be relocated to the Paris office but instead is transferred to Singapore. Unfortunately, many managers are limited in the rewards they can distribute, which makes it difficult to tailor rewards to individual employee needs. Moreover, some managers incorrectly assume that all employees want the same thing. They overlook the motivational effects of differentiating rewards. In either case, employee motivation may be lower because the specific need the employee has is not being met through

> Why do some managers do a better job of motivating people than others?

The performance–reward relationship is strong at Mary Kay Cosmetics, which offers a rewards and recognition program based on the achievement of personal goals set by each salesperson. These independent consultants are posing in front of Mary Kay Career Cars, one of many rewards that motivate Mary Kay's salesforce.

China Photos/Getty Images

instrumentality The belief that performance is related to rewards.

valence The value or importance an individual places on a reward.

OB IN THE WORKPLACE

Stock Analyst Recommendations and Valence

Could rewards obscure making accurate recommendations? Stock analysts make their living trying to forecast a stock's future price; the accuracy of their buy, sell, and hold recommendations is what keeps them in work or gets them fired.[28] Nevertheless, analysts place few sell ratings on stocks, although in a steady market, by definition, as many stocks are falling as are rising.

Expectancy theory provides an explanation: Analysts who place a sell rating on a company's stock have to balance the benefits they receive by being accurate against the risks they run by drawing that company's ire. What are these risks? They include public rebuke, professional blackballing, and exclusion from information. Their valence for this is –1. When analysts place a buy rating on a stock, they face no such trade-off because, obviously, companies love it when analysts recommend that investors buy their stock. Expectancy theory suggests that the expected rewards and their desirability is higher for buy ratings than sell ratings, and that is why buy ratings vastly outnumber sell ratings.

the reward structure. Valence ranges from −1 (very undesirable reward) to +1 (very desirable reward). *OB in the Workplace* shows that valence can drive stock analysts to place more buy ratings than sell ratings.

Expectancy Theory in the Workplace

Does expectancy theory work? Although it has its critics,[29] most of the research evidence supports the theory.[30] Research in cross-cultural settings has also indicated support for expectancy theory.[31]

Exhibit 4-7 gives some suggestions for what a manager can do to increase the motivation of employees, using insights from expectancy theory. To appreciate how expectancy theory might apply in the workplace, see this chapter's *Case Incident—Wage Reduction Proposal* on page 160 for an example of what happens when expected rewards are withdrawn.

The Importance of Providing Performance Feedback

People do better when they get feedback on how well they are progressing toward their goals because it helps identify discrepancies between what they have done and what they want to do—that is, feedback guides behaviour. But all feedback is not equally potent. Self-generated feedback—with which employees are able to monitor their own progress or receive feedback from the task process itself—is more powerful than externally generated feedback.[32] Recent research has also shown that people monitor

EXHIBIT 4-7 Steps to Increasing Motivation, Using Expectancy Theory

Improving Expectancy	Improving Instrumentality	Improving Valence
Improve the ability of the individual to perform.	Increase the individual's belief that performance will lead to reward.	Make sure that the reward is meaningful to the individual.
• Make sure employees have skills for the task. • Provide training. • Assign reasonable tasks and goals.	• Observe and recognize performance. • Deliver rewards as promised. • Indicate to employees how previous good performance led to greater rewards.	• Ask employees what rewards they value. • Give rewards that are valued.

their progress differently depending on how close they are to goal accomplishment. When they have just begun pursuing a goal, they derive motivation from believing that the goal is attainable, so they exaggerate their level of progress in order to stay motivated. However, when they are close to accomplishing their goal, they derive motivation from believing a discrepancy still exists between where they are currently and where they would like to be, so they downplay their progress to date to signal a need for higher effort.[33]

Effective feedback—where the employee perceives the appraisal as fair, the manager as sincere, and the climate as constructive—can lead the employee to respond positively and become determined to correct his or her performance deficiencies.[34] Thus, the performance review should be more like a counselling activity than a judgment process, allowing the review to evolve out of the employee's own self-evaluation. For more tips on performance feedback, see *OB in Action—Giving More Effective Feedback*.

Goal-Setting Theory

You have heard the phrase a number of times: "Just do your best. That's all anyone can ask for." But what does "do your best" mean? Do we ever know whether we have achieved that vague goal? Might we do better with specific goals? Research on **goal-setting theory**, proposed by Edwin Locke, reveals the impressive effects of goal specificity, challenge, and feedback on performance.

The research on goal-setting theory by Locke and his colleague, Professor Gary Latham at the University of Toronto, shows that intentions to work toward a **goal** are

OB IN ACTION
Giving More Effective Feedback

Managers can use the following tips to give more effective feedback:

→ Relate feedback to existing performance **goals** and clear **expectations**.

→ Give **specific** feedback tied to observable behaviour or measurable results.

→ Channel feedback toward **key result areas**.

→ Give feedback as **soon** as possible.

→ Give positive feedback for **improvement**, not just final results.

→ Focus feedback on **performance**, not personalities.

→ Base feedback on **accurate** and **credible** information.[35]

4 Demonstrate the differences among goal-setting theory, self-efficacy theory, and reinforcement theory.

Co-founders Anthony Thomson (left) and Vernon Hill (right) launched their first Metro Bank in London, England, with a long-term goal of adding 200 new branches and capturing up to 10 percent of London's banking market. Metro Bank challenges employees to reach this high goal by giving customers exceptionally friendly, convenient, and flexible service.

Toby Melville/Reuters

goal-setting theory A theory that says that specific and difficult goals, with feedback, lead to higher performance.

goal What an individual is trying to accomplish.

a major source of work motivation.[36] Goals tell an employee what needs to be done and how much effort is needed.[37] *Point/Counterpoint* on page 157 considers the benefits of goal setting.

How do managers make goal-setting theory operational? That is often left up to the individual. Some managers set aggressive performance targets—what General Electric calls "stretch goals." Some senior executives, such as Procter & Gamble's former CEO Robert McDonald and Best Buy's president and CEO Hubert Joly, are known for demanding performance goals. But many managers don't set goals. When asked whether their job had clearly defined goals, only a minority of employees in a survey said yes.[38]

A more systematic way to utilize goal setting is with **management by objectives (MBO)**, an initiative most popular in the 1970s but still used today. MBO emphasizes participatively set goals that are tangible, verifiable, and measurable.[39] Progress on goals is periodically reviewed, and rewards are allocated on the basis of this progress.

Four ingredients are common to MBO programs: goal specificity, participation in decision making (including the setting of goals or objectives), an explicit time period, and performance feedback.[40] Many elements in MBO programs match the propositions of goal-setting theory.

You will find MBO programs in many business, health care, educational, government, and nonprofit organizations.[41] A version of MBO, called Management by Objectives and Results (MBOR), has been used for 30 years in the governments of Denmark, Norway, and Sweden.[42] However, the popularity of these programs does not mean they always work.[43] When MBO fails, the culprits tend to be unrealistic expectations, lack of commitment by top management, and inability or unwillingness to allocate rewards based on goal accomplishment.

How Does Goal Setting Motivate?

According to Locke, goal setting motivates in four ways (see Exhibit 4-8):[44]

- *Goals direct attention.* Goals indicate where individuals should direct their efforts when they are choosing among things to do. For instance, recognizing that an important assignment is due in a few days, goal setting may encourage you to say no when friends invite you to a movie this evening.

- *Goals regulate effort.* Goals suggest how much effort an individual should put into a given task. For instance, if earning a high mark in accounting is more important to you than earning a high mark in organizational behaviour, you will likely put more effort into studying accounting.

- *Goals increase persistence.* Persistence represents the effort spent on a task over time. When people keep goals in mind, they will work hard on them, even in the face of obstacles.

- *Goals encourage the development of strategies and action plans.* Once goals are set, individuals can develop plans for achieving those goals. For instance, a goal to become more fit may include plans to join a gym, work out with friends, and change eating habits.

In order for goals to be effective, they should be "SMART." SMART stands for

- **Specific:** Individuals know exactly what is to be achieved.
- **Measurable:** The goals proposed can be tracked and reviewed.
- **Attainable:** The goals, even if difficult, are reasonable and achievable.
- **Results-oriented:** The goals should support the vision of the organization.
- **Time-bound:** The goals are to be achieved within a stated time.

management by objectives (MBO) An approach to goal setting in which specific measurable goals are jointly set by managers and employees; progress on goals is periodically reviewed; and rewards are allocated on the basis of this progress.

EXHIBIT 4-8 Locke's Model of Goal Setting

Goals motivate by . . . → Directing attention / Regulating effort / Increasing persistence / Encouraging the development of strategies and action plans → Task performance

Source: Adapted from E. A. Locke and G. P. Latham, *A Theory of Goal Setting and Task Performance* (Englewood Cliffs, NJ: Prentice Hall, 1980).

From Concepts to Skills on pages 160–161 presents additional ideas on how to effectively engage in goal setting.

Although goal setting has positive outcomes, it's not unequivocally beneficial. For example, some goals may be *too* effective.[45] When learning something is important, goals related to performance may cause people to become too focused on outcomes and ignore the learning process. Nor are all goals equally effective. For rote tasks with quantifiable standards of productivity, goals that reward quantity can be highly motivating. For other jobs that require complex thinking and personal investment, goals and rewards for quantity may not be effective.[46] Finally, individuals may fail to give up on an unattainable goal, even when it might be beneficial to do so.

Research has found that people differ in the way they regulate their thoughts and behaviours during goal pursuit.[47] Generally, people fall into one of two categories, although they could belong to both. Those with a **promotion focus** strive for advancement and accomplishment and approach conditions that move them closer toward desired goals. Those with a **prevention focus** strive to fulfill duties and obligations and avoid conditions that pull them away from desired goals. Aspects of this concept are similar to the avoidance side of the approach-avoidance framework. Although both strategies work toward goal accomplishment, the manner in which they get there is quite different. As an example, consider studying for an exam. You could engage in promotion-focused activities such as reading class materials, or you could engage in prevention-focused activities such as refraining from doing things that would get in the way of studying, such as playing video games.

You may ask, "Which is the better strategy?" The answer depends on the outcome you are striving for. While a promotion (but not a prevention) focus is related to higher levels of task performance, organizational citizenship behaviour, and innovation, a prevention (but not a promotion) focus is related to safety performance. Ideally, it's probably best to be both promotion *and* prevention oriented.[48] Keep in mind a person's job satisfaction will be more heavily impacted by low success when that person has an avoidance (prevention) outlook,[49] so set achievable goals, remove distractions, and provide structure for these individuals.[50]

Goal-setting theory is consistent with expectancy theory. The goals can be considered the effort–performance link—in other words, the goals determine what must be done. Feedback can be considered the performance–reward relationship, where the individual's efforts are recognized. Finally, the implication of goal setting is that

Lilly Singh, born in Scarborough, Ontario, has her own YouTube channel. She started it in 2013, and by spring 2017 she had 11.5 million subscribers, putting her in the top 75 channels. By any measure, she has been wildly successful with her videos. Singh is also promotion focused; she is driven to do still more because of her accomplishments. As she explains, "I think once you get successful and you love what you do so much and get opportunities—I think that's why movie stars continue to make so many movies. It's because success is the most addictive drug, you get addicted to this idea that: 'No, I want more. I want more experiences. I want more of this.'" So she keeps driving ahead.

promotion focus A self-regulation strategy that involves striving for goals through advancement and accomplishment.

prevention focus A self-regulation strategy that involves striving for goals by fulfilling duties and obligations.

the achievement of the goals will result in intrinsic satisfaction (and, of course, may be linked to external rewards).

Self-Efficacy Theory

The basic premise of **self-efficacy theory**, also known as *social cognitive theory* or *social learning theory*, is that individuals' beliefs in their ability to perform a task influence their behaviour.[51] The higher your self-efficacy, the more confidence you have in your ability to succeed in a task. So, in difficult situations, people with low self-efficacy are more likely to lessen their effort or give up altogether, while those with high self-efficacy will try harder to master the challenge.[52] Self-efficacy can create a positive spiral in which those with high efficacy become more engaged in their tasks and then, in turn, increase performance, which increases efficacy further.[53] One recent study introduced a further explanation, in that self-efficacy was associated with a higher level of focused attention, which led to increased task performance.[54]

Feedback influences self-efficacy; individuals high in self-efficacy also seem to respond to negative feedback with increased effort and motivation, while those low in self-efficacy are likely to lessen their effort after negative feedback.[55] Changes in self-efficacy over time are related to changes in creative performance as well.[56] How can managers help their employees achieve high levels of self-efficacy? By bringing goal-setting theory and self-efficacy theory together.

Goal-setting theory and self-efficacy theory don't compete: They complement each other. As Exhibit 4-9 shows, employees whose managers set difficult goals for them will have a higher level of self-efficacy, and set higher goals for their own performance. Why? Setting difficult goals for people communicates your confidence in them.

The researcher who developed self-efficacy theory, Albert Bandura, proposes four ways self-efficacy can be increased:[57]

- *Enactive mastery.* Gaining relevant experience with the task or job. If you have been able to do the job successfully in the past, then you are more confident that you will be able to do it in the future.

- *Vicarious modelling.* Becoming more confident because you see someone else doing the task. For example, if your friend loses weight, then it increases your confidence that you can lose weight, too. Vicarious modelling is most effective when you see yourself as similar to the person you are observing.

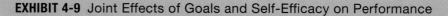

EXHIBIT 4-9 Joint Effects of Goals and Self-Efficacy on Performance

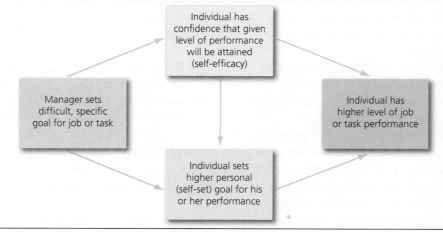

Source: Based on E. A. Locke and G. P. Latham, "Building a Practically Useful Theory of Goal Setting and Task Motivation: A 35-Year Odyssey," *American Psychologist*, September 2002, pp. 705–717.

self-efficacy theory Individuals' beliefs in their ability to perform a task influence their behaviour.

- *Verbal persuasion.* Becoming more confident because someone convinces you that you have the skills necessary to be successful. Motivational speakers use this tactic.

- *Arousal.* An energized state, so the person gets "psyched up" and performs better. But if the task is something that requires a steady, lower-key perspective (say, carefully editing a manuscript), arousal may in fact hurt performance even as it increases self-efficacy because we might hurry through the task.

Intelligence and personality are absent from Bandura's list but they too can increase self-efficacy.[58] People who are intelligent, conscientious, and emotionally stable are so much more likely to have high self-efficacy that some researchers argue that self-efficacy is less important than prior research would suggest.[59] They believe it is partially a by-product in a smart person with a confident personality.

The best way for a manager to use verbal persuasion is through the *Pygmalion effect,* a term based on a Greek myth about a sculptor (Pygmalion) who fell in love with a statue he carved. The Pygmalion effect is a form of *self-fulfilling prophecy* in which believing something can make it true. Here, it is often used to describe "that what one person expects of another can come to serve a self-fulfilling prophecy."[60] An example should make this clear. In studies, teachers were told their students had very high IQ scores when, in fact, they spanned a range from high to low. Consistent with the Pygmalion effect, the teachers spent more time with the students they *thought* were smart, gave them more challenging assignments, and expected more of them—all of which led to higher student self-efficacy and better achievement outcomes.[61] This strategy has been used in the workplace too, with replicable results and enhanced effects when leader-subordinate relationships are strong.[62]

What are the OB implications of self-efficacy theory? Well, it's a matter of applying Bandura's sources of self-efficacy to the work setting. Training programs often make use of enactive mastery by having people practise and build their skills. In fact, the reason training works is because it increases self-efficacy, particularly when the training is interactive and feedback is given after training.[63] Individuals with higher levels of self-efficacy also appear to reap more benefits from training programs and are more likely to use their training on the job.[64]

Reinforcement Theory

Goal-setting is a cognitive approach, proposing that an individual's purposes direct his or her actions. **Reinforcement theory**, in contrast, takes a behaviouristic view, arguing that reinforcement conditions behaviour. The two theories are clearly at odds philosophically. Reinforcement theorists see behaviour as environmentally caused. You need not be concerned, they would argue, with internal cognitive events; what controls behaviour is reinforcers—any consequences that, when immediately following responses, increase the probability that the behaviour will be repeated.

Reinforcement theory ignores the inner state of the individual and concentrates solely on what happens when he or she takes some action. Because it does not concern itself with what initiates behaviour, it is not, strictly speaking, a theory of motivation. But it does provide a powerful means of analyzing what controls behaviour, and this is why we typically consider it in discussions of motivation.[65]

Operant conditioning theory, probably the most relevant component of reinforcement theory for management, argues that people learn to behave to get something they want or to avoid something they don't want. Unlike reflexive or unlearned behaviour, operant behaviour is influenced by the reinforcement or lack of reinforcement brought about by its consequences. Therefore, reinforcement strengthens a behaviour and increases the likelihood it will be repeated.[66]

B.F. Skinner, one of the most prominent advocates of operant conditioning, demonstrated that people will most likely engage in desired behaviours if they are positively

reinforcement theory A theory that says that behaviour is a function of its consequences.

reinforced for doing so; rewards are most effective if they immediately follow the desired behaviour; and behaviour that is not rewarded, or is punished, is less likely to be repeated. The concept of operant conditioning was part of Skinner's broader concept of **behaviourism**, which asserts that behaviour follows stimuli in a relatively unthinking manner. Skinner's form of radical behaviourism rejects feelings, thoughts, and other states of mind as causes of behaviour. In short, people learn to associate stimulus and response, but their conscious awareness of this association is irrelevant.[67]

You can see illustrations of operant conditioning everywhere. For instance, a commissioned salesperson who wants to earn a high income must generate high sales in her territory. Of course, the linkage can also teach individuals to engage in behaviours that work against the best interests of the organization. Assume that your boss says that if you will work overtime during the next three-week busy season, you will be compensated for it at the next performance appraisal. However, when performance appraisal time comes, you find that you are given no positive reinforcement for your overtime work. The next time your manager asks you to work overtime, you will probably decline!

Methods of Shaping Behaviour

Behaviour can be shaped in four ways: through positive reinforcement, negative reinforcement, punishment, and extinction.

Following a response with something pleasant is called *positive reinforcement*. Following a response with the termination or withdrawal of something unpleasant is called *negative reinforcement*. *Punishment* is causing an unpleasant condition in an attempt to eliminate an undesirable behaviour. Eliminating any reinforcement that is maintaining a behaviour is called *extinction*. Exhibit 4-10 presents examples of each type of reinforcement. Negative reinforcement should not be confused with punishment: Negative reinforcement strengthens a behaviour because it takes away an unpleasant situation.

Schedules of Reinforcement

While consequences have an effect on behaviour, the timing of those consequences or reinforcements is also important. The two major types of reinforcement schedules are *continuous* and *intermittent*. A **continuous reinforcement** schedule reinforces the desired behaviour each and every time it is demonstrated. Take, for example, the case of someone who has historically had trouble arriving at work on time. Every time he is not tardy, his manager might compliment him on his desirable behaviour. In an intermittent schedule, on the other hand, not every instance of the desirable behaviour is reinforced, but reinforcement is given often enough to make the behaviour worth repeating. Evidence indicates that the intermittent, or varied, form of reinforcement tends to promote more resistance to extinction than does the continuous form.[68]

behaviourism A theory that argues that behaviour follows stimuli in a relatively unthinking manner.

continuous reinforcement A desired behaviour is reinforced each and every time it is demonstrated.

EXHIBIT 4-10 Types of Reinforcement	
Reinforcement Type	**Example**
Positive reinforcement	A manager praises an employee for a job well done.
Negative reinforcement	An instructor asks a question and a student looks through her lecture notes to avoid being called on. She has learned that looking busily through her notes prevents the instructor from calling on her.
Punishment	A manager gives an employee a two-day suspension from work without pay for showing up drunk.
Extinction	An instructor ignores students who raise their hands to ask questions. Hand-raising becomes extinct.

EXHIBIT 4-11 Schedules of Reinforcement

Reinforcement Schedule	Nature of Reinforcement	Effect on Behaviour	Example
Continuous	Reward given after each desired behaviour	Fast learning of new behaviour but rapid extinction	Compliments
Fixed-interval	Reward given at fixed time intervals	Average and irregular performance with rapid extinction	Weekly paycheques
Variable-interval	Reward given at variable time intervals	Moderately high and stable performance with slow extinction	Pop quizzes
Fixed-ratio	Reward given at fixed amounts of output	High and stable performance attained quickly but also with rapid extinction	Piece-rate pay
Variable-ratio	Reward given at variable amounts of output	Very high performance with slow extinction	Commissioned sales

An **intermittent reinforcement** schedule can be of a ratio or interval type. Ratio schedules depend on how many responses the subject makes. The individual is reinforced after giving a certain number of specific types of behaviour. Interval schedules depend on how much time has passed since the previous reinforcement. With interval schedules, the individual is reinforced on the first appropriate behaviour after a particular time has elapsed. A reinforcement can also be classified as fixed or variable. When these factors are combined, four types of intermittent schedules of reinforcement result: **fixed-interval schedule**, **variable-interval schedule**, **fixed-ratio schedule**, and **variable-ratio schedule**.

Exhibit 4-11 summarizes the five schedules of reinforcement and their effects on behaviour.

Although reinforcers such as pay can motivate people, the process is much more complicated than stimulus–response. In its pure form, reinforcement theory ignores feelings, attitudes, expectations, and other cognitive variables known to affect behaviour. Reinforcement is undoubtedly an important influence on behaviour, but few scholars are prepared to argue that it's the only one. The behaviours you engage in at work and the amount of effort you allocate to each task are affected by the consequences that follow. If you are consistently reprimanded for outproducing your colleagues, you will likely reduce your productivity. But we might also explain your lower productivity in terms of goals, inequity, or expectancies.

Responses to the Reward System

Lee Valley Tools' system of paying its employees fairly has paid off in a number of ways.[69] The turnover rate is low. Employees feel empowered because they are encouraged to take action to solve customer problems. They don't have to check in with the boss, they are simply expected to do the right thing. Founder Leonard Lee disliked the nature of his previous job that gave him responsibility but no authority, so he changed that dynamic for his employees. Even customers appreciate the sense of fairness that echoes through the store, and how the employees share in the profits. "That's something that our customers comment on a lot. They appreciate shopping here because they know the money is not all being funnelled to the top," says Peter Gowdy, assistant manager at Lee Valley Tools' store on King Street in downtown Toronto.

5 Describe why equity and fairness matter in the workplace.

intermittent reinforcement A desired behaviour is reinforced often enough to make the behaviour worth repeating, but not every time it is demonstrated.

fixed-interval schedule The reward is given at fixed time intervals.

variable-interval schedule The reward is given at variable time intervals.

fixed-ratio schedule The reward is given at fixed amounts of output.

variable-ratio schedule The reward is given at variable amounts of output.

To a large extent, motivation theories are about rewards. The theories suggest that individuals have needs and will exert effort in order to have those needs met. The needs theories specifically identify those needs. Goal-setting and expectancy theories portray processes by which individuals act and then receive desirable rewards (intrinsic or extrinsic) for their behaviour.

Three additional process theories ask us to consider how individuals respond to rewards. Equity theory suggests that individuals evaluate and interpret rewards. Fair process goes one step further, suggesting that employees are sensitive to a variety of fairness issues in the workplace that extend beyond the reward system but also affect employee motivation. Self-determination theory examines how individuals respond to the introduction of extrinsic rewards for intrinsically satisfying activities.

Equity Theory

Ainsley is a student working toward a bachelor's degree in finance. In order to gain some work experience and increase her marketability, she has accepted a summer internship in the finance department at a pharmaceutical company. She is quite pleased with the pay: $15 an hour is more than other students in her cohort receive for their summer internships. At work she meets Josh, a recent graduate of the same university working as a middle manager in the same finance department. Josh makes $30 an hour.

On the job, Ainsley is a go-getter. She is engaged, satisfied, and always seems willing to help others. Josh is the opposite. He often seems disinterested in his job and thinks about quitting. When pressed one day about why he is unhappy, Josh cites his pay as the main reason. Specifically, he tells Ainsley that, compared with managers at other pharmaceutical companies, he makes much less. "It isn't fair," he complains. "I work just as hard as they do, yet I don't make as much. Maybe I should go work for the competition."

> How important is fairness to you?

How could someone making $30 an hour be less satisfied with his pay than someone making $15 an hour and be less motivated as a result? The answer lies in **equity theory** and, more broadly, in principles of organizational justice. According to equity theory, employees compare what they get from their job (their "outcomes," such as pay, promotions, recognition, or having a bigger office) to what they put into it (their "inputs," such as effort, experience, and education). They take the ratio of their outcomes to their inputs and compare it to the ratio of others, usually someone similar, such as a co-worker or someone doing the same job. This idea is illustrated in Exhibit 4-12. If we believe our ratio is equal to those with whom we compare ourselves, a state of equity exists and we perceive our situation as fair.

To Whom Do We Compare Ourselves?

The referent that an employee selects when making comparisons adds to the complexity of equity theory.[70] There are four referent comparisons that an employee can use:

- *Self-inside.* An employee's experiences in a different position inside his or her current organization.

- *Self-outside.* An employee's experiences in a situation or position outside his or her current organization.

- *Other-inside.* Another individual or group of individuals inside the employee's organization.

- *Other-outside.* Another individual or group of individuals outside the employee's organization.

Employees might compare themselves with friends, neighbours, co-workers, or colleagues in other organizations. Alternatively, they might compare their present job with

equity theory A theory that asserts that individuals compare their job inputs and outcomes with those of others and then respond to eliminate any inequities.

EXHIBIT 4-12 Equity Theory

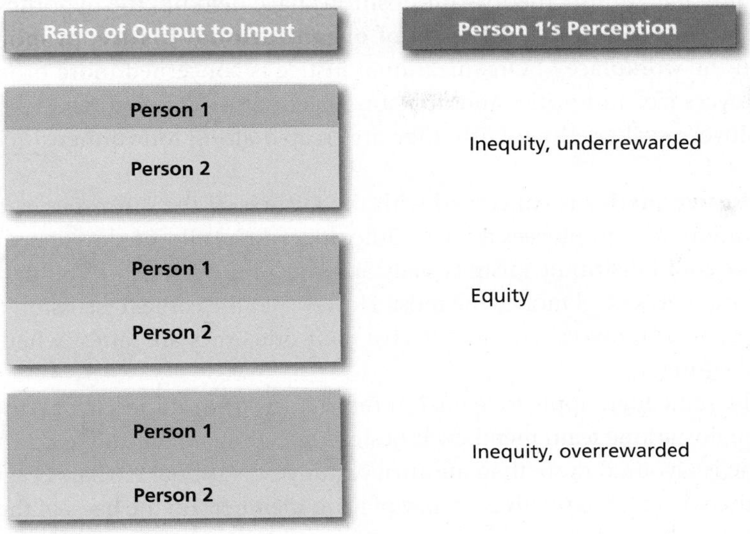

previous jobs they have had. Which referent an employee chooses will be influenced by the information the employee holds about referents, as well as by the attractiveness of the referent. *Case Incident—Equity and Executive Pay* on page 159 considers whether executive compensation is equitable when compared with the pay of the average worker.

What Happens When We Feel Treated Inequitably?

Based on equity theory, employees who perceive an inequity will make one of six choices.[71]

- *Change their inputs* (exert less effort if underpaid, or more if overpaid).
- *Change their outcomes* (individuals paid on a piece-rate basis can increase their pay by producing a higher quantity of units of lower quality).
- *Adjust perceptions of self* ("I used to think I worked at a moderate pace, but now I realize I work a lot harder than everyone else.")
- *Adjust perceptions of others* ("Mike's job isn't as desirable as I thought.")
- *Choose a different referent* ("I may not make as much as my brother-in-law, but I'm doing a lot better than my Dad did when he was my age.")
- *Leave the field* (quit the job).

> What can you do if you think your salary is unfair?

RESEARCH FINDINGS: Inequitable Pay

Equity theory has support from some researchers, but not from all.[72] There are some concerns with the propositions. First, inequities created by overpayment do not seem to significantly affect behaviour in most work situations. So don't expect an employee who feels overpaid to give back part of her salary or put in more hours to make up for the inequity. Although individuals may sometimes perceive that they are overrewarded, they restore equity by rationalizing their situation ("I'm worth it because I work harder than everyone else"). Second, not everyone is equally equity-sensitive, for various reasons, including feelings of entitlement.[73] A few actually prefer outcome–input ratios lower than the referent comparisons. Predictions from equity theory are not likely to be very accurate with these "benevolent types."[74]

6 Demonstrate how organizational justice is a refinement of equity theory.

Fair Process and Treatment

Although not all of equity theory's propositions have held up, the hypothesis served as an important precursor to the study of **organizational justice**, or more simply fairness, in the workplace.[75] Organizational justice is concerned more broadly with how employees feel authorities and decision makers at work treat them. For the most part, employees evaluate how fairly they are treated along four dimensions, shown in Exhibit 4-13.

Distributive justice is concerned with the fairness of the outcomes, such as pay and recognition, that employees receive. Outcomes can be allocated in many ways. For example, we could distribute raises equally among employees, or we could base them on which employees need money the most. However, as the earlier discussion on equity theory suggests, employees tend to perceive their outcomes are fairest when they are distributed equitably.

Does the same logic apply to teams? At first glance, it would seem that distributing rewards equally among team members is best for boosting morale and teamwork—that way, no one is favoured more than another. A study of National Hockey League teams suggests otherwise. Differentiating the pay of team members on the basis of their inputs

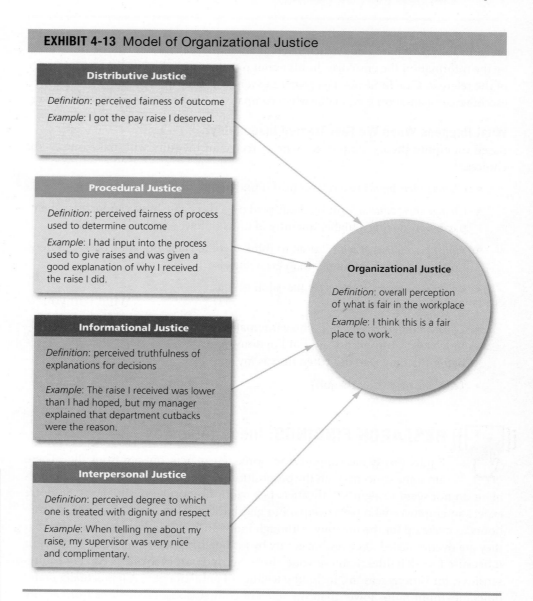

EXHIBIT 4-13 Model of Organizational Justice

Distributive Justice

Definition: perceived fairness of outcome
Example: I got the pay raise I deserved.

Procedural Justice

Definition: perceived fairness of process used to determine outcome
Example: I had input into the process used to give raises and was given a good explanation of why I received the raise I did.

Informational Justice

Definition: perceived truthfulness of explanations for decisions
Example: The raise I received was lower than I had hoped, but my manager explained that department cutbacks were the reason.

Interpersonal Justice

Definition: perceived degree to which one is treated with dignity and respect
Example: When telling me about my raise, my supervisor was very nice and complimentary.

Organizational Justice

Definition: overall perception of what is fair in the workplace
Example: I think this is a fair place to work.

organizational justice An overall perception of what is fair in the workplace, composed of distributive, procedural, informational, and interpersonal justice.

distributive justice Perceived fairness of the amount and allocation of rewards among individuals.

(how well they performed in games) attracted better players to the team, made it more likely they would stay, and increased team performance.[76]

The way we have described things so far, it would seem that individuals assess distributive justice and equity in a rational, calculative way as they compare their outcome–input ratios to those of others. But the experience of justice, and especially of injustice, is often not so cold and calculated. Instead, people base distributive judgments on a feeling or an emotional reaction to the way they think they are being treated relative to others, and their reactions are often "hot" and emotional rather than cool and rational.[77]

Although employees care a lot about *what* outcomes are distributed (distributive justice), they also care about *how* they are distributed. While distributive justice looks at *what* outcomes are allocated, **procedural justice** examines *how* outcomes are allocated.[78] What makes procedures more or less fair? There are several factors. For one, employees perceive that procedures are fairer when they are given a say in the decision-making process. Having direct influence over how decisions are made, or at the very least being able to present your opinion to decision makers, creates a sense of control and makes us feel empowered (we discuss empowerment more in Chapter 8). Employees also perceive that procedures are fairer when decision makers follow several "rules." These include making decisions in a consistent manner (across people and over time), avoiding bias (not favouring one group or person over another), using accurate information, considering the groups or people their decisions affect, acting ethically, and remaining open to appeals or correction.

If outcomes are favourable and individuals get what they want, they care less about the process, so procedural justice does not matter as much when distributions are perceived to be fair. It's when outcomes are unfavourable that people pay close attention to the process. If the process is judged to be fair, then employees are more accepting of unfavourable outcomes.[79] Why is this the case? It's likely that employees believe that fair procedures, which often have long-lasting effects, will eventually result in a fair outcome, even if the immediate outcome is unfair. Think about it. If you are hoping for a raise and your manager informs you that you did not receive one, you will probably want to know how raises were determined. If it turns out that your manager allocated raises based on merit, and you were simply outperformed by a co-worker, then you are more likely to accept your manager's decision than if raises were based on favouritism. Of course, if you get the raise in the first place, then you will be less concerned with how the decision was made.

Beyond outcomes and procedures, research has shown that employees care about two other types of fairness that have to do with the way they are treated during interactions with others. The first type is **informational justice**, which reflects whether managers provide employees with explanations for key decisions and keep them informed of important organizational matters. The more detailed and candid managers are with employees, the more fairly treated those employees feel.

Although it may seem obvious that managers should be honest with their employees and not keep them in the dark about organizational matters, many managers are hesitant to share information. This is especially the case with bad news, which is uncomfortable for both the manager delivering it and the employee receiving it. Explanations for bad news are beneficial when they take the form of excuses after the fact ("I know this is bad, and I wanted to give you the office, but it wasn't my decision") rather than justifications ("I decided to give the office to Sam, but having it isn't a big deal").[80]

The second type of justice relevant to interactions between managers and employees is **interpersonal justice**, which reflects whether employees are treated with dignity and respect. Compared with the three other forms of justice we have discussed, interpersonal justice is unique in that it can occur in everyday interactions between

procedural justice The perceived fairness of the process used to determine the distribution of rewards.

informational justice The degree to which employees are provided truthful explanations for decisions.

interpersonal justice The degree to which employees are treated with dignity and respect.

managers and employees.[81] This quality allows managers to take advantage of (or miss out on) opportunities to make their employees feel fairly treated. Many managers may view treating employees politely and respectfully as too "soft," choosing more aggressive tactics out of a belief that doing so will be more motivating. Although displays of negative emotions such as anger may be motivating in some cases,[82] managers sometimes take this too far.

How much does justice really matter to employees? A great deal, as it turns out. When employees feel fairly treated, they respond in a number of positive ways. All four types of justice discussed in this section have been linked to higher levels of task performance and organizational citizenship behaviours (such as helping co-workers) as well as lower levels of counterproductive behaviours (such as shirking job duties). Distributive and procedural justice are more strongly associated with task performance, while informational and interpersonal justice are more strongly associated with organizational citizenship behaviour. Even more physiological outcomes, such as how well employees sleep and the state of their health, have been linked to fair treatment.[83]

Why does justice have these positive effects? Fair treatment enhances commitment to the organization and makes employees feel it cares about their well-being. In addition, employees who feel fairly treated trust their supervisors more, which reduces uncertainty and fear of being exploited by the organization. Finally, fair treatment elicits positive emotions, which in turn prompts behaviours like organizational citizenship behaviour.[84] The *Experiential Exercise* on page 158 helps you understand how managers can foster fairness in the workplace based on the four types of organizational justice.

Despite all attempts to enhance fairness, perceived injustices are still likely to occur. Fairness is often subjective; what one person sees as unfair, another may see as perfectly appropriate. In general, people see allocations or procedures favouring themselves as fair.[85] So, when addressing perceived injustices, managers need to focus their actions on the source of the problem. In addition, if employees feel they have been treated unjustly, having opportunities to express their frustration has been shown to reduce their desire for retribution.[86]

How can an organization affect the justice perceptions and rule adherence of its managers? This depends upon the motivation of each manager. Some managers are likely to calculate justice by their degree of adherence to the justice rules of the organization. These managers will try to gain greater subordinate compliance with behavioural expectations, create an identity of being fair to their employees, or establish norms of fairness. Other managers may be motivated in justice decisions by their emotions. When they have a high positive affect and/or a low negative affect, these managers are most likely to act fairly.

It might be tempting for organizations to adopt strong justice guidelines in attempts to mandate managerial behaviour, but this isn't likely to be universally effective. In cases where managers have more rules and less discretion, those who calculate justice are more likely to act fairly, but managers whose justice behaviour follows from their affect may act more fairly when they have greater discretion.[87]

Self-Determination Theory

7 Apply the predictions of self-determination theory to intrinsic and extrinsic rewards.

"It's strange," said Marcia. "I started work at the Humane Society as a volunteer. I put in 15 hours a week helping people adopt pets. And I loved coming to work. Then, three months ago, they hired me full-time at $11 an hour. I'm doing the same work I did before. But I'm not finding it as much fun."

Does Marcia's reaction seem counterintuitive? There is an explanation for it. It's called **self-determination theory**, which proposes that people prefer to feel they have control over their actions, so anything that makes a previously enjoyed task feel more like an obligation than a freely chosen activity will undermine motivation.[88] The theory is widely used in psychology, management, education, and medical research.

self-determination theory A theory of motivation that is concerned with the beneficial effects of intrinsic motivation and the harmful effects of extrinsic motivation.

Much research on self-determination theory in OB has focused on **cognitive evaluation theory**, which hypothesizes that extrinsic rewards will reduce intrinsic interest in a task. When people are paid for work, it feels less like something they *want* to do and more like something they *have* to do. Self-determination theory also proposes that in addition to being driven by a need for autonomy, people seek ways to achieve competence and positive connections to others. A large number of studies support self-determination theory.[89] Its major implications relate to work rewards.

Extrinsic vs. Intrinsic Rewards

Historically, motivation theorists have generally assumed that intrinsic motivators are independent of extrinsic motivators. That is, the stimulation of one would not affect the other. But cognitive evaluation theory suggests otherwise. It argues that when extrinsic rewards are used by organizations as payoffs for superior performance, the intrinsic rewards, which are derived from individuals doing what they like, are reduced.

What does self-determination theory suggest about providing rewards? It suggests that some caution in the use of extrinsic rewards to motivate is wise, and that pursuing goals from intrinsic motives (such as a strong interest in the work itself) is more sustaining to human motivation than are extrinsic rewards. Similarly, cognitive evaluation theory suggests that providing extrinsic incentives may, in many cases, undermine intrinsic motivation.

For example, if a computer programmer values writing code because she likes to solve problems, a bonus for writing a certain number of lines of code every day could feel coercive, and her intrinsic motivation would suffer. She would be less interested in the task and might reduce her effort. She may or may not increase her number of lines of code per day in response to the extrinsic motivator. In support, a recent meta-analysis confirms that intrinsic motivation contributes to the quality of work, while incentives contribute to the quantity of work. Although intrinsic motivation predicts performance whether or not there are incentives, it may be less of a predictor when incentives are tied to performance directly (such as with monetary bonuses) rather than indirectly.[90]

A more recent outgrowth of cognitive evaluation research is **self-concordance**, which considers how strongly people's reasons for pursuing goals are consistent with their interests and core values.[91] Across cultures, if individuals pursue goals because of intrinsic interest, they are more likely to attain goals, are happier when they do, and are happy even if they do not.[92] Why? Because the process of striving toward goals is fun whether or not the goal is achieved. Recent research reveals that when people do *not* enjoy their work for intrinsic reasons (those who work because they feel obligated to do so) can still perform well, although they experience higher levels of strain as a result.[93] In contrast, people who pursue goals for extrinsic reasons (money, status, or other benefits) are less likely to attain goals and less happy even when they do. Why? Because the goals are less meaningful to them.[94]

What does all of this mean? For individuals, it means you should choose your job for reasons other than extrinsic rewards. For organizations, it means managers should provide intrinsic as well as extrinsic incentives. Managers need to make the work interesting, provide recognition, and support employee growth and development. Employees who feel that what they do is within their control and a result of free choice are likely to be more motivated by their work and committed to their employers.[95]

Increasing Intrinsic Motivation

Our discussion of motivation theories and our discussion of how to apply motivation theories in the workplace has focused more on improving extrinsic motivation. Professor Kenneth Thomas of the Naval Postgraduate School in Monterey, California, developed a model of intrinsic motivation that draws from the job characteristics model

cognitive evaluation theory Offering extrinsic rewards (for example, pay) for work effort that was previously rewarding intrinsically will tend to decrease the overall level of a person's motivation.

self-concordance The degree to which a person's reasons for pursuing a goal are consistent with the person's interests and core values.

(see Chapter 5) and cognitive evaluation theory.[96] He identified four key rewards that increase an individual's intrinsic motivation:

- *Sense of choice.* The opportunity to select what one will do and perform the way one thinks best. Individuals can use their own judgment to carry out the task.

- *Sense of competence.* The feeling of accomplishment for doing a good job. Individuals are more likely to feel a sense of accomplishment when they carry out challenging tasks.

- *Sense of meaningfulness.* The opportunity to pursue worthwhile tasks. Individuals feel good about what they are doing and believe that what they are doing matters.

- *Sense of progress.* The feeling of accomplishment that one is making progress on a task, and that it is moving forward. Individuals feel that they are spending their time wisely in doing their jobs.

Thomas also identified four sets of behaviours managers can use to build intrinsic rewards for their employees:

- *Leading for choice.* Empowering employees and delegating tasks.

- *Leading for competence.* Supporting and coaching employees.

- *Leading for meaningfulness.* Inspiring employees and modelling desired behaviours.

- *Leading for progress.* Monitoring and rewarding employees.

Exhibit 4-14 describes what managers can do to increase the likelihood that intrinsic rewards are motivational.

8 Discuss the ethics behind motivation theories.

Motivation for Whom?

An ongoing debate among organizational behaviour scholars is, Who benefits from the theories of motivation?[97] Some argue that motivation theories are only intended to help managers get more productivity out of employees, and are little concerned with employees beyond improvements in productivity. Thus, needs theories, process

---

EXHIBIT 4-14 Building Blocks for Intrinsic Rewards

Leading for Choice	Leading for Competence
• Delegated authority	• Knowledge
• Trust in workers	• Positive feedback
• Security (no punishment) for honest mistakes	• Skill recognition
• A clear purpose	• Challenge
• Information	• High, noncomparative standards
Leading for Meaningfulness	**Leading for Progress**
• A noncynical climate	• A collaborative climate
• Clearly identified passions	• Milestones
• An exciting vision	• Celebrations
• Relevant task purposes	• Access to customers
• Whole tasks	• Measurement of improvement

Source: From Intrinsic Motivation at Work: Building Energy and Commitment. Copyright © K. Thomas. 1997. Berrett-Koehler Publishers Inc., San Francisco, CA. All rights reserved. www.bkconnection.com.

theories, and theories concerned with fairness could be interpreted not as ways to help employees get what they want or need, but rather as means to help managers get what they want from employees. In his review of "meaningful work" literature, professor Christopher Michaelson of New York University Stern finds that researchers propose that organizations have a moral obligation to provide employees with "free choice to enter, honest communication, fair and respectful treatment, intellectual challenge, considerable independence to determine work methods, democratic participation in decision making, moral development, due process and justice, nonpaternalism, and fair compensation."[98]

Michaelson suggests that scholars concerned with meaningful work should focus on the conditions of the workplace and improving those conditions. He also suggests that researchers have a moral obligation to make workplaces better for employees. While productivity may be a by-product of better work conditions, the important thing is for employers to treat employees well, and to consider the needs of employees as an end in itself. By contrast, he argues, mainstream motivation theory does not consider the moral obligation of employers to their employees, but it does consider ways to ensure employees are more productive.

While this debate is not easily resolved, and may well guide the elaboration of motivation theories in years to come, it does inspire a provocative analysis of why employers provide the workplace conditions they do.

Job Engagement

When Joseph reports to his job as a hospital nurse, it seems that everything else in his life goes away, and he becomes completely absorbed in what he is doing. His emotions, thoughts, and behaviour are all directed toward patient care. In fact, he can get so caught up in his work that he isn't even aware of how long he's been there. As a result of this total commitment, he is more effective in providing patient care and feels uplifted by his time at work.

Joseph has a high level of **job engagement**, the investment of an employee's physical, cognitive, and emotional energies into job performance.[99] Practising managers and scholars have become interested in facilitating job engagement, believing factors deeper than liking a job or finding it interesting drives performance. Studies attempt to measure this deeper level of commitment.

The Gallup organization has been studying the extent to which employee engagement is linked to positive work outcomes for millions of employees over the past 30 years.[100] They have found there are far more engaged employees in highly successful organizations than in average ones, and groups with more engaged employees have higher levels of productivity, fewer safety incidents, and lower turnover. Academic studies have also found positive outcomes. For instance, one review found higher levels of engagement were associated with task performance and citizenship behaviour.[101]

What makes people more likely to be engaged in their jobs? One key factor is the degree to which an employee believes it is meaningful to engage in work. This is partially determined by job characteristics and access to sufficient resources to work effectively.[102] Another factor is a match between the individual's values and those of the organization.[103] Leadership behaviours that inspire workers to a greater sense of mission also increase employee engagement.[104]

One of the critiques of the concept of engagement is that the construct is partially redundant with job attitudes like satisfaction or stress.[105] However, engagement questionnaires usually assess motivation and absorption in a task, quite unlike job satisfaction questionnaires. Engagement may also predict important work outcomes better than traditional job attitudes.[106] Other critics note there may be a "dark side" to engagement, as evidenced by positive relationships between engagement and work–family conflict.[107] It is possible individuals might grow so engaged in their work roles

job engagement The investment of an employee's physical, cognitive, and emotional energies into job performance.

that family responsibilities become an unwelcome intrusion. Also, an overly high level of engagement can lead to a loss of perspective and, ultimately, burnout. Further research exploring how engagement relates to these negative outcomes may help clarify whether some highly engaged employees might be getting "too much of a good thing."

9 Summarize the essence of what we know about motivating employees.

Putting It All Together

While it's always dangerous to synthesize a large number of complex ideas into a few simple guidelines, the following suggestions summarize the essence of what we know about motivating employees in organizations:

- *Recognize individual differences.* Employees have different needs and should not be treated alike. Managers should spend the time necessary to understand what is important to each employee and then align goals, level of involvement, and rewards with individual needs.

- *Use goals and feedback.* Employees should have challenging, specific goals, as well as feedback on how well they are doing in pursuit of those goals.

- *Allow employees to participate in decisions that affect them.* Employees should contribute to a number of decisions that affect them: setting work goals, choosing their own benefits packages, solving productivity and quality problems, and the like. Doing so can increase employee productivity, commitment to work goals, motivation, and job satisfaction.

- *When giving rewards, be sure that they reward desired performance.* Rewards should be linked to the type of performance expected. It's important that employees perceive a clear linkage. How closely rewards are actually correlated to performance criteria is less important than the perception of this relationship. If individuals perceive this relationship to be low, the results will be low performance, a decrease in job satisfaction, and an increase in turnover and absenteeism.

- *Check the system for equity.* Employees should be able to perceive rewards as equating with the inputs they bring to the job. At a simplistic level, this means that experience, skills, abilities, effort, and other obvious inputs should explain differences in performance and, hence, pay, job assignments, and other obvious rewards.

GLOBAL IMPLICATIONS

Most current motivation theories were developed in the United States and Canada.[108] Goal-setting and expectancy theories emphasize goal accomplishment as well as rational and individual thought—characteristics consistent with Canadian and American culture. Let's look at several motivation theories and consider their cross-cultural transferability.

Needs Theories

Maslow's needs theory says people start at the physiological level and progress up the hierarchy to safety, social (belonging), self-esteem, and self-actualization needs. This hierarchy, if it applies at all, aligns with Canadian and US culture. In Japan, Greece, and Mexico, where uncertainty-avoidance characteristics are strong, security needs would be on top of the hierarchy. Countries that score high on nurturing characteristics—Denmark, Sweden, Norway, the Netherlands, and Finland—would have social needs on top.[109] Group work will motivate employees more when the country's culture scores high on the nurturing criterion.

The view that a high achievement need acts as an internal motivator presupposes two cultural characteristics—willingness to accept a moderate degree of risk (which excludes countries with strong uncertainty-avoidance characteristics) and concern with performance (which applies to countries with strong achievement characteristics). This combination is found in Anglo-American countries such as the United States, Canada, and Great Britain[110] and much less so in Chile and Portugal.

Goal-Setting Theory

Setting specific, difficult, individual goals may have different effects in different cultures. Most goal-setting research has been done in the United States and Canada, where individual achievement and performance are most highly valued. To date, research has not shown that group-based goals are more effective in collectivistic than in individualistic cultures. There is evidence that in collectivistic and high power-distance cultures, achievable moderate goals can be more highly motivating than difficult ones.[111] Finally, assigned goals appear to generate greater goal commitment in high rather than low power-distance cultures.[112] Much more research is needed to assess how goal constructs might differ across cultures.

Equity Theory and Fairness

Equity theory has gained a strong following in Canada and the United States because the reward systems assume that employees are highly sensitive to equity in reward allocations and equity is meant to closely tie pay to performance.

Meta-analytic evidence shows individuals in both individualistic and collectivistic cultures prefer an equitable distribution of rewards over an equal division (everyone gets paid the same regardless of performance).[113] Across nations, the same basic principles of procedural justice are respected, and workers around the world prefer rewards based on performance and skills over rewards based on seniority.[114] However, in collectivistic cultures employees expect rewards to reflect their individual needs as well as their performance.[115] Other research suggests that inputs and outcomes are valued differently in various cultures.[116] Some cultures emphasize status over individual achievement as a basis for allocating resources. Materialistic cultures are more likely to see cash compensation and rewards as the most relevant outcomes of work, whereas relational cultures will see social rewards and status as important outcomes. International managers must consider the cultural preferences of each group of employees when determining what is "fair" in different contexts.

Justice

Across nations, the same basic principles of procedural justice are respected in that employees around the world prefer rewards based on performance and skills over rewards based on seniority.[117] However, inputs and outcomes are valued differently in various cultures.[118]

We may think of justice differences in terms of Hofstede's cultural dimensions (see Chapter 3). One large-scale study of over 190 000 employees in 32 countries and regions suggested that justice perceptions are most important to people in countries with individualistic, feminine, uncertainty avoidance, and low power-distance values.[119] Organizations can tailor programs to meet these justice expectations. For example, in countries that are highest in individualism, such as Australia and the United States, competitive pay plans and rewards for superior individual performance will enhance feelings of justice. In countries dominated by uncertainty avoidance, such as France, fixed pay compensation and employee participation may help employees feel more secure. The dominant dimension in Sweden is femininity, so relational concerns are considered important. Swedish organizations may therefore want to provide work–life balance initiatives and social recognition. Austria, in contrast, strongly values low power-distance. Ethical concerns may be foremost to individuals in perceiving justice in Austrian organizations, so it will be important for organizations to justify inequality between leaders and workers and provide symbols of ethical leadership.

Intrinsic and Extrinsic Motivation

A recent study found interesting differences in managers' perceptions of employee motivation.[120] The study examined managers from three distinct cultural regions: North America, Asia, and Latin America. The results of the study revealed that North American managers perceive their employees as being motivated more by extrinsic factors (for example, pay) than intrinsic factors (for example, doing meaningful work). Asian managers perceive their employees as being motivated by both extrinsic and intrinsic factors, while Latin American managers perceive their employees as being motivated by intrinsic factors.

Even more interesting, these differences affected evaluations of employee performance. As expected, Asian managers focused on both types of motivation when evaluating their employees' performance, and Latin American managers focused on intrinsic motivation. Oddly, North American managers, though believing that employees are motivated primarily by extrinsic factors, actually focused more on intrinsic factors when evaluating employee performance. Why the paradox? One explanation is that North Americans value uniqueness, so any deviation from the norm—such as being perceived as being unusually high in intrinsic motivation—is rewarded.

Latin American managers' focus on intrinsic motivation when evaluating employees may be related to a cultural norm termed *simpatía*, a tradition that compels employees to display their internal feelings. Consequently, Latin American managers are more sensitized to these displays and can more easily notice their employees' intrinsic motivation.

Cross-Cultural Consistencies

Don't assume that there are *no* cross-cultural consistencies. The desire for interesting work seems important to almost all employees, regardless of their national culture. In a study of seven countries, employees in Belgium, Britain, Israel, and the United States ranked work number one among 11 work goals, and employees in Japan, the Netherlands, and Germany ranked it either second or third.[121] In a study comparing job-preference outcomes among graduate students in the United States, Canada, Australia, and Singapore, growth, achievement, and responsibility had identical rankings as the top three.[122] Meta-analytic evidence shows that individuals in both individualistic and collectivistic cultures prefer an equitable distribution of rewards (the most effective employees get paid the most) over an equal division (everyone gets paid the same regardless of performance).[123] Across nations, the same basic principles of procedural justice are respected, and employees around the world prefer rewards based on performance and skills over rewards based on seniority.[124]

LESSONS LEARNED

- Recognize individual differences.
- Goals and feedback help motivate individuals.
- Rewards signal what is important to the employer (or leader).

Summary

The motivation theories in this chapter differ in their predictive strength. Maslow's hierarchy of needs, Herzberg's two-factor theory, and McClelland's theory of needs focus on needs. None of these theories has found widespread support, although support for McClelland's is the strongest, particularly regarding the relationship between achievement and productivity. Expectancy theory can be helpful, but it assumes that employees have few constraints on decision making, such as bias or incomplete information, which limits its applicability. Goal-setting theory can be helpful but does not cover absenteeism, turnover, or job satisfaction. Reinforcement theory can be helpful, but not regarding employee satisfaction or the decision to quit. Equity theory's strongest legacy is that it provided the spark for research on organizational justice, which has more support in the literature. Self-determination theory and cognitive evaluation theory have merits to consider.

SNAPSHOT SUMMARY

What Is Motivation?

Needs Theories of Motivation
- Maslow's Hierarchy of Needs Theory
- Two-Factor Theory
- McClelland's Theory of Needs
- Summarizing Needs Theories

Process Theories of Motivation
- Expectancy Theory
- Goal-Setting Theory
- Self-Efficacy Theory
- Reinforcement Theory

Responses to the Reward System
- Equity Theory

- Fair Process and Treatment
- Self-Determination Theory
- Increasing Intrinsic Motivation

Motivation for Whom?
- Job Engagement
- Putting It All Together

MyLab Management

 PERSONAL INVENTORY ASSESSMENT

Study, practise, and explore real business situations with these helpful resources:
- **Study Plan:** Check your understanding of chapter concepts with self-study quizzes.
- **Online Lesson Presentations:** Study key chapter topics and work through interactive assessments to test your knowledge and master management concepts.
- **Videos:** Learn more about the management practices and strategies of real companies.
- **Simulations:** Practise management decision-making in simulated business environments.

OB at Work

for **Review**

1. What are the three key elements of motivation?

2. What are some early theories of motivation? How applicable are they today?

3. What are the key tenets of expectancy theory?

4. What are the key principles of goal-setting theory, self-efficacy theory, and reinforcement theory?

5. Why do equity and fairness matter in the workplace?

6. How is organizational justice a refinement of equity theory?

7. How do the predictions of self-determination theory apply to intrinsic and extrinsic rewards?

8. What are some of the ethical issues with motivation theories?

9. What is the essence of what we know about motivating employees?

for **Managers**

- Consider goal-setting theory: Clear and difficult goals often lead to higher levels of employee productivity.

- Consider how reinforcement theory applies to the quality and quantity of work, persistence of effort, absenteeism, tardiness, and accident rates.

- Consult equity theory to help you understand productivity, satisfaction, absence, and turnover variables.

- Expectancy theory offers a powerful explanation of performance variables such as employee productivity, absenteeism, and turnover.

- Make sure extrinsic rewards for employees are not viewed as coercive, but instead provide information about competence and relatedness.

for **You**

- Don't think of motivation as something that should be done for you. Think about motivating others and yourself as well. How can you motivate yourself? After finishing a particularly long and dry chapter in a text, you could take a snack break. Or you might buy yourself a new album once that major accounting assignment is finished.

- Be aware of the kinds of things that motivate you, so you can choose jobs and activities that suit you best.

- When working in a group, keep in mind that you and the other members can think of ways to make sure everyone feels motivated throughout the project.

GOALS GET YOU TO WHERE YOU WANT TO BE

POINT

Of course this is a true statement.[125] Goal-setting theory is one of *the* best-supported theories in all the motivation literature. Study after study has consistently shown the benefits of goals. Want to excel on a test, lose a certain amount of weight, obtain a job with a particular income level, or improve your golf game? If you want to be a high performer, merely set a specific, difficult goal and let nature take its course. That goal will dominate your attention, cause you to focus, and make you try harder.

All too often, people are told by others to simply "do their best." Could anything be more vague? What does "do your best" actually mean? Maybe you feel that your "best" on one day is to muster a grade of 50 percent on an exam, while your "best" on another day is an 80. But if you were given a more difficult goal—say, to score a 95 on the exam—and you were committed to that goal, you would ultimately perform better.

Edwin Locke and Gary Latham, the researchers best known for goal-setting theory, put it best when they said: "The effects of goal setting are very reliable." In short, goal-setting theory is among the most valid and practical theories of motivation in organizational psychology.

COUNTERPOINT

Sure, a lot of research has shown the benefits of goal setting, but those studies ignore the harm that is often done by it. For one, how often have you set a "stretch" goal, only to see yourself fail later? Goals create anxiety and worry about reaching them, and they often create unrealistic expectations as well. Imagine those who had set a goal to earn a promotion in a certain period of time (a specific, difficult goal), only to find themselves laid off once the recession hit. Or how about those who envisioned a retirement of leisure yet had to take on a part-time job or delay retirement altogether in order to continue to make ends meet. When too many things are out of our control, our difficult goals become impossible.

Consider this: Goals can lead to unethical behaviour and poorer performance. How many reports have you heard over the years about teachers who "fudged" students' test scores in order to achieve educational standards? Another example: When Ken O'Brien, as a professional quarterback for the New York Jets, was penalized for every interception he threw, he achieved his goal of fewer interceptions quite easily—by refusing to throw the ball even when he should have.

In addition to this anecdotal evidence, research has directly linked goal setting to cheating. We should heed the warning of Professor Maurice E. Schweitzer—"Goal-setting is like a powerful medication"—before blindly accepting that specific, difficult goal.

BREAKOUT **GROUP** EXERCISES

Form small groups to discuss the following topics, as assigned by your instructor:

1. One of the members of your team continually arrives late for meetings and does not turn drafts of assignments in on time. Choose one of the available theories and indicate how the theory explains the member's current behaviour and how the theory could be used to motivate the group member to perform more responsibly.

2. You are unhappy with the performance of one of your instructors and would like to encourage the instructor to present more lively classes. Choose one of the available theories and indicate how the theory explains the instructor's current behaviour. How could you as a student use the theory to motivate the instructor to present more lively classes?

3. Harvard University recently changed its grading policy to recommend to instructors that the average course mark should be a B. This was the result of a study showing that more than 50 percent of students were receiving an A or A– for coursework. Harvard students are often referred to as "the best and the brightest," and they pay over US$36 000 per academic year for their education, so they expect high grades. Discuss the impact of this change in policy on the motivation of Harvard students to study harder.

EXPERIENTIAL EXERCISE

Organizational Justice

Task Purpose
This exercise will highlight the four primary sources of organizational justice and help you understand what managers can do to ensure fairness in the workplace.

Time
Approximately 20 to 30 minutes.

Instructions
Break into groups of 3 or 4.

1. Each person should recall an instance in which he or she was (a) treated especially fairly and (b) treated especially unfairly. Work-related instances are preferable, but nonwork examples are fine too. What do the stories have in common?

2. Spend several minutes discussing whether the instance was more distributive, procedural, informational, or interpersonal in nature. What was the source of the fair/unfair treatment? How did you feel, and how did you respond?

3. Each group should develop a set of recommendations for handling the unfair situations in a fairer manner. Select a leader for your group who will briefly summarize the unfair instances, along with the group's recommendations for handling them better. The discussion should reflect the four types of justice discussed in this chapter (distributive, procedural, informational, and interpersonal).

ETHICAL **DILEMMA**

The New GPA

In college and university classrooms, is an A the new B?[126] Grade inflation is of particular concern in graduate programs, where it is not uncommon for 75 percent of grades to be As. In fact, the most frequent grade given in US universities is an A, by 43 percent. This percentage has risen from 30 percent 20 years ago, representing a significant increase. At Harvard, the average grade is an A–. While this may sound great to students, there is a powerful downside to grade inflation. If an A– is the new class average, the crowding of grades at the top end of the scale can sap students' motivation to work hard. Organizations also find it harder to evaluate candidates' transcripts if grades are inflated. This means they must rely more on results of standardized tests, which were often taken in high school and may not reflect a student's current or best capabilities. Professors, too, may be less motivated to accurately assess and teach students through strong grading feedback that would help students learn.

There is no easy solution to the phenomenon of grade inflation. In a culture where "everyone does it," schools that take a stand against grade inflation produce students with potentially lower grades—but no less education— than their peers. These students may not be able to stand out in the increasingly competitive job market even when they are equally prepared. Over time, their schools will not be able to boast of the accomplishments of their graduates in terms of grades and employment placements. No longer will these schools look as attractive to potential students, so enrolment and thus revenue will suffer,

endangering the institution's ability to teach. Therefore, eliminating grade inflation poses powerful disincentives, and few (if any) post-secondary schools have successfully tried it. There is much more motivation for organizations, schools, professors, and students to continue grade inflation practices, even though they may be wrong.

Questions

1. How might forcing equitable grade distributions with C as average motivate students?

2. If around 75 percent of grades in graduate programs are As, have grades become meaningless as motivators?

3. Provincial funding of many post-secondary schools has decreased dramatically over the years, increasing the pressure on administrators to generate revenue through tuition increases, recruiting more international students, and other means. How might this pressure create ethical tensions among the competing needs of generating revenue, retaining students, and providing accurate grading?

CASE INCIDENTS

Equity and Executive Pay

Few topics in the business press grab headlines and ignite the public like the compensation packages received by top management, which continue to rise.[127] CEOs in Canada's 100 largest companies earned a median compensation of $5.6 million in 2013, a level of compensation just under that received before the economic downturn.

How do compensation committees set executive compensation? In many cases, it comes down to equity theory and depends on the referent others to which the CEO is compared. To determine a "fair" level of pay for a given CEO, members of a compensation board find out how much CEOs with similar levels of experience in similar firms (similar inputs) are being paid and attempt to adjust compensation (outcomes) to be similar. So, CEOs in large tech firms are paid similarly to CEOs in other large tech firms, CEOs in small marketing companies are paid similarly to CEOs in other small marketing companies, and so forth. Proponents of this practice consider it to be "fair" because it achieves equity.

However, critics of high CEO pay want to change the perspective by comparing the CEO's pay to the pay of

the average employee. For example, Canada's 100 highest paid CEOs are paid 171 times more than the average employee. From this perspective, CEO pay is grossly inequitable and thus "unfair."

In response, many CEOs, such as Mark Zuckerberg of Facebook and Larry Page of Google, have taken $1 annual salaries, though they still earn substantial compensation by exercising their stock options. In addition, shareholders of some companies, such as Verizon, are playing a greater role in setting CEO compensation by reducing awards when the company underperforms.

Questions

1. How does the executive compensation issue relate to equity theory? How should we determine what is a "fair" level of pay for top executives?

2. Individuals generally think performance should be essential or very important in deciding pay. What might be the positive motivational consequences for average employees if CEO pay is tied to performance?

Wage Reduction Proposal

The following proposal was made to employees of Montreal-based Quebecor's Vidéotron cable division:[128]

> Employees are asked to increase the number of hours worked per week to 40 from 35, while receiving the same pay as working the shorter workweek. In addition, they are asked to accept less paid holiday time.

Quebecor spokesman Luc Lavoie justified the request made to the employees by saying, "They have the richest work contract in the country, including eight weeks of holiday and high absenteeism."

The company made it clear that if this proposal were not accepted, it would sell its cable television and Internet installation and repair operations to Entourage Technology Solutions.

The employees, members of Canadian Union of Public Employees (CUPE) Local 2815, were reluctant to agree to these conditions. If they accepted, 300 to 400 employees were likely to be laid off, and the company could still consider outsourcing the work later.

Questions

1. Analyze this proposal in terms of motivation concepts.

2. As an employee, how would you respond if you received this proposal?

3. If you were the executive vice-president of the company, and a number of your non-unionized employees asked you for a holiday cash gift, would you have responded differently? Why or why not?

FROM CONCEPTS TO SKILLS

Setting Goals

You can be more effective at setting goals if you use the following eight suggestions:[129]

1. *Identify your key tasks.* Goal setting begins by defining what it is that you want to accomplish.

2. *Establish specific and challenging goals for each key task.* Identify the level of performance expected. Specify the target toward which you will work.

3. *Specify the deadlines for each goal.* Putting deadlines on each goal reduces ambiguity. Deadlines, however, should not be set arbitrarily. Rather, they need to be realistic, given the tasks to be completed.

4. *Allow the employee to participate actively.* When employees participate in goal setting, they are more likely to accept the goals. However, it must be sincere participation. That is, employees must perceive that you are truly seeking their input, not just going through the motions.

5. *Prioritize goals.* When you have more than one goal, it's important for you to rank the goals in order of importance. The purpose of prioritizing is to encourage you to take action and expend effort on each goal in proportion to its importance.

6. *Rate goals for difficulty and importance.* Goal setting should not encourage people to choose easy goals. Instead, goals should be rated for their difficulty and importance. When goals are rated, individuals can be given credit for trying difficult goals, even if they don't fully achieve them.

7. *Build in feedback mechanisms to assess goal progress.* Feedback lets you know whether your level of effort is sufficient to attain the goal. Feedback should be frequent and recurring.

8. *Link rewards to goal attainment.* Linking rewards to the achievement of goals will help motivate you.

. . . .

You worked your way through college while holding down a part-time job bagging groceries at the Food Town supermarket chain. You liked working in the food industry, and when you graduated, you accepted a position with Food Town as a management trainee. Three years have passed, and you have gained experience in the grocery store industry and in operating a large supermarket. About a year ago, you received a promotion to store manager at one of the chain's locations. One of the things you have liked about Food Town is that it gives store managers a great deal of autonomy in running their stores. The company provides very general guidelines to its managers. Top management is concerned with the bottom line; for the most part, how you get there is up to you. Now that you are finally a store manager, you want to establish an MBO-type program in your store. You like the idea that everyone should have clear goals to work toward and then be evaluated against those goals.

Your store employs 70 people, although except for the managers, most work only 20 to 30 hours per week. You have 6 people reporting to you: an assistant manager; a weekend manager; and grocery, produce, meat, and bakery managers. The only highly skilled jobs belong to the butchers, who have strict training and regulatory guidelines. Other less-skilled jobs include cashier, shelf stocker, maintenance worker, and grocery bagger.

Specifically describe how you would go about setting goals in your new position. Include examples of goals for the jobs of butcher, cashier, and bakery manager.

. . . .

1. Set personal and academic goals you want to achieve by the end of this term. Prioritize and rate them for difficulty.

2. Where do you want to be in five years? Do you have specific five-year goals? Establish three goals you want to achieve in five years. Make sure these goals are specific, challenging, and measurable.

Practising Skills

Reinforcing Skills

Motivation in Action

How can a global travel company keep its workforce motivated? It starts with freedom, happiness, and community.

LEARNING OUTCOMES

After studying this chapter, you should be able to:

1. Demonstrate how the different types of variable-pay programs can increase employee motivation.
2. Show how flexible benefits can be used to motivate.
3. Identify the motivational benefits of intrinsic rewards.
4. Describe the job characteristics model and the way it motivates.
5. Compare the main ways jobs can be redesigned.
6. Explain how specific alternative work arrangements can motivate employees.
7. Describe how employee involvement programs can motivate employees.
8. Describe how knowledge of what motivates people can be used to make organizations more motivating.

Jennifer Roberts/Contour/Getty Images

Toronto-based G Adventures' founder and CEO Bruce Poon Tip has spent nearly 30 years building an international adventure tourism company where employees would be happy and motivated, and strive to do a good job every day.[1] The company was named a platinum winner in 2017 for being one of Canada's Best Managed Companies. To earn platinum, companies must have been named to the list for at least eight years in a row.

G Adventures' 2017 award was in part due to a program it developed on a small island in Belize over the previous few years. However, local authorities complained that students there had dropped out of school and taken jobs in the tourism industry, most often to lead bicycle tours for G Adventures. Critics in Belize scolded Poon Tip: "As your company grows, fewer and fewer kids are going to school." This was not Poon Tip's intent at all. This problem also conflicted with the company's desire to be a "great social enterprise." Poon Tip promised the students a job and the loan of a bike to lead G Adventures tours if they stayed in school. It took some time for the students to believe this promise, but the local school attendance rate has gone from 35 percent to 90 percent.

Poon Tip takes equally innovative approaches to motivation when he is dealing with employees at corporate headquarters. The company's core values are freedom, happiness, and community, which are put into practice by seeking employees who share the company's desire to do good in the world while also assisting people with their adventure travel visions. "Tourism could be the greatest form of wealth distribution that the world has ever seen," says Poon Tip.

In this chapter, we focus on how to apply motivation concepts. We review a number of reward programs and consider whether rewards are overrated. We also discuss how to create more motivating jobs and workplaces, both of which have been shown to be alternatives to rewards in motivating individuals.

OB IS FOR EVERYONE

- Ever wonder why employees do some strange things?
- When might job redesign be most appropriate?
- Do employers really like flexible arrangements?
- Would you find telecommuting motivating?
- How do employees become more involved in the workplace?

THE BIG IDEA

Organizations can use piece-rate wages, merit-based pay, bonuses, profit sharing, and stock options to motivate employees. However, making jobs more motivating is more effective.

From Theory to Practice: The Role of Money

Money can be an extremely powerful motivator. For most individuals, though, pay is not the only motivator. It is a central means of motivation, but what you are actually doing for the money matters, too. A 2017 study found that 40 percent of Canadian employees would take a pay cut to work for an employer who would give them more professional development opportunities. About a quarter said they would take a 5 percent cut, and 17 percent said they would take a pay cut of 10 percent or more.[2] The process of motivating employees is complex, and people feel strongly about the implications of changes to their extrinsic or intrinsic benefits.

The motivation theories we have presented only give us vague ideas of how money relates to individual motivation. For instance, Theory X suggests that individuals need to be extrinsically motivated. Money is certainly one such extrinsic motivator. According to Maslow's hierarchy of needs, individuals' basic needs must be met, including food, shelter, and safety. Generally, money can be used to satisfy those needs. Herzberg's motivation–hygiene theory, on the other hand, suggests that money (and other extrinsic motivators) are necessary but not sufficient conditions for individuals to be motivated. Process theories are relatively silent about the role of money specifically, indicating more how rewards motivate, without specifying particular types of rewards. Expectancy theory does note that individuals need to value the reward, or it will not be very motivational. In this chapter, we apply motivation concepts to practices.

Creating Effective Reward Systems

G Adventures' headquarters is an office workplace that is fun,[3] because fun is something founder Bruce Poon Tip wants for his employees. The company provides foosball tables, a ping-pong table, and popcorn machines, among other perks. Meeting rooms are creatively decorated. On Friday afternoons there is beer, wine, and cider. There is a 2000-square-foot rooftop patio where employees can go to meet, relax, think, or work. All of these benefits are meant to help employees be creative in their work. Poon Tip believes employees are much more productive if they are not feeling pressured all of the time.

One of the really nice perks of working at G Adventures is the opportunity to travel for free (or nearly so). After being employed there for a year, employees can choose annually one of the tours offered by the company. The company will pay up to $3000 for trips up to 17 days, and $750 for flights. All of these actions signal to employees that they are valued as important contributors to the company's success. What else can a company do to make sure its employees feel valued?

As we saw in Chapter 3, pay is not a primary factor driving job satisfaction. However, it does motivate people, and companies often underestimate the importance of pay in keeping top talent. One study found that although only 45 percent of employers thought that pay was a key factor in losing top talent, 71 percent of top performers called it a top reason.[4]

Given that pay is so important, will the organization lead, match, or lag the market in pay? How will individual contributions be recognized? In this section, we consider (1) what to pay employees (which is decided by establishing a pay structure) and (2) how to pay individual employees (for example, through variable-pay programs).

What to Pay: Establishing a Pay Structure

There are many ways to pay employees. The process of initially setting pay levels entails balancing *internal equity*—the worth of the job to the organization (usually established through a technical process called *job evaluation*)—and *external equity*—the competitiveness of an organization's pay relative to pay in its industry (usually established through pay surveys). Obviously, the best pay system reflects what the job is worth internally while also staying competitive relative to the labour market. The *Ethical Dilemma* on page 193 discusses competitive compensation for top-level executives.

Some organizations prefer to pay above the market, while some may lag the market because they cannot afford to pay market rates, or they are willing to bear the costs of paying below market (namely, higher turnover as people are lured to better-paying jobs). Some companies that have realized impressive gains in income and profit margins have done so in part by holding down employee wages, such as Walt Disney and McDonald's.[5]

Pay more, and you may get better-qualified, more highly motivated employees who will stay with the organization longer. A study covering 126 large organizations found employees who believed that they were receiving a competitive pay level had higher morale and were more productive, and customers were more satisfied as well.[6] But pay is often the highest single operating cost for an organization, which means paying too much can make the organization's products or services too expensive. It's a strategic decision an organization must make, with clear trade-offs.

In the case of Walmart, it appears that its strategic decision to keep wages low has not worked. Sales at Canadian stores open for more than a year, an important barometer of retail health known as same-store sales, fell 1.3 percent and customer traffic at those stores declined 1.8 percent in 2013.[7] In 2015, Walmart Canada increased its base wage to $9/hour, and raised the base wage again to $10/hour in 2016.[8,9] Sales growth over that period increased, although not as quickly as that of one of Walmart's larger competitors, Costco. The average employee at Costco makes approximately two-and-a-half times what the average employee at Walmart earns. Costco's strategy is that they will get more if they pay more—higher wages have resulted in increased employee productivity and reduced turnover. Perhaps the recent Walmart decision to increase employee wages will help bring it closer in line with Costco's growth.

How to Pay: Rewarding Individuals through Variable-Pay Programs

"Why should I put any extra effort into this job?" asks a frustrated grade 4 teacher. "I can excel or I can do the bare minimum. It makes no difference. I get paid the same. Why do anything above the minimum to get by?" Similar comments have been voiced by schoolteachers (and some other unionized employees) for decades because pay increases are tied to seniority. The effect of pay increases is discussed in *Case Incident— Pay Raises Every Day* on pages 194–195.

A number of organizations are moving away from paying people based solely on credentials or length of service. Piece-rate, merit-based, bonuses, and employee stock ownership plans are all forms of a **variable-pay program** (also known as *pay for performance*) that bases a portion of an employee's pay on some individual, group, and/or organizational measure of performance. Earnings therefore fluctuate up and down with the measure of performance,[10] as Jason Easton, director of Strategy and Business Transformation at Toronto-based GM Canada, explains: "In any given year the variable pay can actually be zero, below the target, or above the target, depending on how the company has performed."[11] When GM Canada gave performance-based bonuses to its salaried employees, it generated discontent among union employees who had no such provision in their collective agreement.[12] The variable portion may be all or part of the paycheque, and it may be paid annually or upon attainment of benchmarks. It can also be either optional for the employee or an accepted condition of employment.[13] Variable-pay plans have long been used to compensate salespeople and executives, but the scope of variable-pay jobs has broadened.

Unfortunately, not all employees see a strong connection between pay and performance. The results of pay-for-performance plans are mixed; the context and receptivity of the individual to the plans play a large role. For instance, a study by researchers at the

1 Demonstrate how the different types of variable-pay programs can increase employee motivation.

variable-pay program A pay plan that bases a portion of an employee's pay on some individual and/or organizational measure of performance.

Université du Québec à Montréal indicated that variable-pay plans increase job satisfaction only if employee *effort* is rewarded as well as performance.[14] On the other hand, one study of 415 companies in South Korea suggested that group-based pay-for-performance plans may have a strong positive effect on organizational performance.[15] Finally, secrecy pays a role in the motivational success of variable-pay plans. Although in some government and not-for-profit agencies pay amounts are either specifically or generally made public, many organizations encourage or require pay secrecy.[16] Is this good or bad? Unfortunately, it's bad: Pay secrecy has a detrimental effect on job performance. Even worse, it adversely affects high performers more than other employees. It very likely increases employees' perception that pay is subjective, which can be demotivating. While individual pay amounts may not need to be broadcast to restore the balance, if general pay categories are made public and employees feel variable pay is linked objectively to their performance, the motivational effects of variable pay can be retained.[17]

The fluctuation in variable pay is what makes these programs attractive to management. It turns part of an organization's fixed labour costs into a variable cost, thus reducing expenses when performance declines. When the economy falters, as in 2008, companies with variable pay are able to reduce their labour costs much faster than others.[18] When pay is tied to performance, the employee's earnings reflect their contributions rather than become a form of entitlement. Low performers find, over time, that their pay stagnates, while high performers enjoy pay increases commensurate with their contributions.

Let's examine the different types of variable-pay programs in more detail.

Individual-Based Incentives

There are three major forms of individual-based variable-pay programs: piece-rate wages, merit-based pay, and bonuses.

Piece-Rate Wages The **piece-rate pay plan** has long been popular as a means for compensating production employees with a fixed sum for each unit of production completed, but it can be used in any organizational setting where the outputs are similar enough to be evaluated by quantity. A pure piece-rate plan provides no base salary and pays the employee only for what he or she produces.

Ballpark workers selling peanuts and soft drinks frequently are paid piece-rate. If they sell 40 bags of peanuts at $1 each for their earnings, their take is $40. The more peanuts they sell, the more they earn. Alternatively, piece-rate plans are sometimes distributed to sales teams, so a ballpark worker makes money on a portion of the total number of bags of peanuts sold by the group during a game.

Piece-rate plans are known to produce higher productivity and wages, so they can be attractive to organizations and motivating for employees.[19] In fact, one major Chinese university increased its piece-rate pay for articles by professors and realized 50 percent increased research productivity.[20] In the workplace, employees most likely to be motivated by piece-rate plans are managers and more tenured employees. Low-performing employees are generally not interested in piece-rate pay for obvious reasons—they will not get paid much!

The chief concern of both individual and team piece-rate employees is financial risk. A recent experiment in Germany found that 68 percent of risk-averse individuals prefer an individual piece-rate system, and that lower performers prefer team piece-rate pay. Why? The authors suggested risk-averse and high-performing individuals would rather take their chances on pay based on what they can control (their own work) because they are concerned others will slack off in a team setting.[21] This is a valid concern, as we will discuss in the next chapter. Organizations, on the other hand, should verify that their piece-rate plans are indeed motivating to individuals. European research has suggested that when the pace of work is determined by uncontrollable outside factors such as customer requests, rather than internal factors such as co-workers, targets, and machines, a piece-rate plan is not motivating.[22] Either way, managers must be mindful

piece-rate pay plan An individual-based incentive plan in which employees are paid a fixed sum for each unit of production completed.

of the motivation for workers to decrease quality in order to increase their speed of output. They should also be aware that by rewarding volume, piece-rate plans increase the probability of workplace injuries.[23]

Thus, while piece-rate plans can be a powerful motivator in many organizational settings, an obvious limitation is that they are not feasible for many jobs. An emergency room (ER) doctor and nurse can earn significant salaries regardless of their patients' outcomes. Would it be better to pay them only if their patients fully recover? It seems unlikely that most would accept such a deal, and it might cause unanticipated consequences as well (such as ERs turning away patients with terminal diseases or life-threatening injuries). So, although incentives are motivating and relevant for some jobs, it is unrealistic to think they work universally.

Merit-Based Pay   A **merit-based pay plan** pays for individual performance based on performance appraisal ratings. A main advantage is that high performers can get bigger raises. If designed correctly, merit-based pay plans let individuals perceive a strong relationship between their performance and their rewards.[24]

Most large organizations have merit-based pay plans, especially for salaried employees. Merit pay is slowly taking hold in the public sector. For example, most Canadian government employees are unionized, and the unions that represent them have usually demanded that pay raises be based solely on seniority.

A move away from merit pay is coming from some organizations that don't feel it separates high and low performers enough. "There's a very strong belief and there's evidence and academic research that shows that variable pay does create focus among employees," said Ken Abosch, a compensation manager at human-resource consulting firm Aon Hewitt. But when the annual review and raise are months away, the motivation of this reward for high performers diminishes. Even companies that have retained merit pay are rethinking the allocation.[25]

Although you might think a person's average level of performance is the key factor in merit pay decisions, recent research indicates that the projected level of future performance also plays a role. One study found that National Basketball Association (NBA)

Keita Wen sz/ICHPL Imaginechina/AP Images

Chinese Internet firm Tencent Holdings rewards employees with attractive incentives that include cash bonuses for lower-ranking employees. The young men shown here were among 5000 employees who received a special bonus tucked in red envelopes and personally handed out by Tencent's CEO and co-founder Pony Ma.

merit-based pay plan An individual-based incentive plan based on performance appraisal ratings.

players whose performance was on an upward trend were paid more than their average performance would have predicted. Managers of all organizations may unknowingly be basing merit pay decisions on how they *expect* employees will perform, which may result in overly optimistic (or pessimistic) pay decisions.[26]

Despite their intuitive appeal, merit-based pay plans have several limitations. One is that they are typically based on an annual performance appraisal and thus are only as valid as the performance ratings, which are often subjective. This brings up issues of discrimination. Research indicates that African American employees receive lower performance ratings than white employees, women's ratings are higher than men's, and there are demographic differences in the distribution of salary increases, even with all other factors equal.[27] Another limitation is that the pay-raise pool of available funds fluctuates based on economic or other conditions that have little to do with an individual employee's performance. For instance, a colleague at a top university who performed very well in teaching and research was given a pay raise of $300. Why? Because the budget for pay raises was very small. Yet that amount is hardly pay for performance. Lastly, unions typically resist merit-based pay plans. Relatively few teachers are covered by merit pay for this reason. Instead, seniority-based pay, which gives all employees the same raises, predominates.

The concept and intention of merit pay—that employees are paid for performance—is sound. For employee motivation purposes, however, merit pay should be only one part of a performance recognition program.

Bonuses An annual **bonus** is a significant component of total compensation for many jobs.[28] But bonus plans increasingly include lower-ranking employees; many companies now routinely reward production employees with bonuses in the thousands of dollars when profits improve. The incentive effects should be higher because, rather than paying for previous performance now rolled into base pay, bonuses reward only recent performance (merit pay is cumulative, but the increases are generally much smaller than bonus amounts). Moreover, when times are bad, firms can cut bonuses to reduce compensation costs.

Bonuses are not free from organizational politics (which we discuss in Chapter 8), and they can sometimes result in employees engaging in negative behaviours to ensure they will receive bonuses. *Focus on Ethics* raises the possibility that part of the US financial crisis that began in September 2008 was due to the way bonuses were awarded to executives.

FOCUS ON ETHICS

Huge Bonuses, Disastrous Results for the United States

Did bonuses help fuel a financial meltdown? During a two-week period in September 2008, the American economy almost looked to be in free fall.[29] The US government bought up the assets of mortgage insurers Freddie Mac and Fannie Mae. Global financial services firm Merrill Lynch, founded in 1914, agreed to be bought by Bank of America for very little money. Global financial services firm Lehman Brothers, founded in 1850, went into bankruptcy. Morgan Stanley was in merger discussions. Major American insurance corporation AIG received an $85-billion bailout from the US government. Independent investment banks Goldman Sachs, founded in 1869, and Morgan Stanley, founded in 1935, announced that they would become bank holding companies. Investment banks issue and sell securities and provide advice on mergers and acquisitions. By becoming bank holding companies, the two companies became subjected to greater regulation than they had been previously.

bonus An individual-based incentive plan that rewards employees for recent performance rather than historical performance.

There is no simple answer to why all of these corporations faced collapse or near collapse all at once, but the role that bonuses played in the financial meltdown has been raised. The trigger for the economic crisis was the collapse of many subprime mortgages during 2007 and 2008. In the preceding years, numerous Americans had been given mortgages for homes, even though they had no down payments and sometimes did not even have jobs. The loan payments were low at the beginning, but eventually many of those given subprime mortgages started to default on their loans.

Why would someone give out a loan to an individual who did not have a job or did not provide clear evidence of earnings? The banking industry rewarded mortgage brokers for making loans, giving out bonus payments based on the size of loans. The loans were then bundled together to make new financial instruments. These resulted in commissions and bonuses for those packaging the instruments. Several Wall Street CEOs who lost their jobs because of the fallout from subprime loans earned "tens of millions in bonuses during the heady days of 2005 and 2006." . . . .

The collapse of so many financial institutions at once suggests that rewarding individuals based on financial performance can cause problems.

This example also highlights the downside of bonuses: Employees' pay is more vulnerable to cuts. This is problematic when bonuses are a large percentage of total pay or when employees take bonuses for granted. "People have begun to live as if bonuses were not bonuses at all but part of their expected annual income," said Jay Lorsch, a Harvard Business School professor.

The way bonuses and rewards are categorized also affects people's motivation. Although it is a bit manipulative, splitting rewards and bonuses into categories—even if the categories are meaningless—may increase motivation.[30] Why? Because people are more likely to feel they missed out on a reward if they don't receive one from each category, and then work harder to earn rewards from more categories.

Organizational-Based Incentives

There are two major forms of organizational-based pay-for-performance programs: profit-sharing and stock option plans, which include employee stock ownership plans.

Profit-Sharing Plans   A **profit-sharing plan** distributes compensation based on some established formula designed around a company's profitability. Compensation can be direct cash outlays or, particularly for top managers, allocations of stock options. When you read about executives like Mark Zuckerberg, who accepts an absurdly modest $1 salary, remember that many executives are granted generous stock options. In fact, Zuckerberg has made as much as $2.3 billion after cashing out some of his stock options.[31] Although senior executives are most likely to be rewarded through profit-sharing plans, employees at any level can be recipients. Burlington, Ontario-based O.C. Tanner Canada pays all of its employees bonuses twice a year based on profits.

Studies generally support the idea that organizations with profit-sharing plans have higher levels of profitability than those without them.[32] These plans have also been linked to higher levels of employee commitment, especially in small organizations.[33] Profit-sharing at the organizational level appears to have positive impacts on employee attitudes; employees report a greater feeling of psychological ownership.[34] Recent research in Canada indicates that profit-sharing plans motivate individuals to higher job performance when they are used in combination with other pay-for-performance plans.[35] Obviously, profit-sharing does not work when there is no reported profit per se, such as in nonprofit organizations, or often in the public sector. However, profit-sharing may make sense for many organizations, large or small.

profit-sharing plan An organization-wide incentive plan in which the employer shares profits with employees based on a predetermined formula.

Employee Stock Ownership Plans An **employee stock ownership plan (ESOP)** is a company-established benefit plan in which employees acquire stock as part of their benefits. Research on ESOPs indicates they increase employee satisfaction and innovation.[36] ESOPs have the potential to increase job satisfaction only when employees psychologically experience ownership.[37] Even so, ESOPs may not inspire lower absenteeism or greater motivation,[38] perhaps because the employee's actual monetary benefit comes with cashing in the stock at a later date. Thus, employees need to be kept regularly informed of the status of the business and have the opportunity to positively influence it in order to feel motivated toward higher personal performance.[39]

Canadian companies lag far behind the United States in the use of ESOPs because Canada's tax environment is less conducive to such plans. Nevertheless, a significant number of employees at Winnipeg-based FWS Group of Companies, an integrated design-build construction services company founded 65 years ago, participate in the company's ESOP plan. Brent Clegg, CEO of FWS, explains the importance of this participation: "We strongly believe that broad employee ownership through an ESOP encourages a high performance culture which leads to operational excellence and the creation of outstanding value for all of our stakeholders."[40] Calgary-based WestJet, Toronto-based I Love Rewards, Edmonton-based Cybertech Automation, and Winnipeg-based Great-West Life are other examples of companies that have employee stock ownership plans.

ESOPs for top management can reduce unethical behaviour. For instance, CEOs are less likely to manipulate firm earnings reports to make themselves look good in the short run when they have an ownership share.[41] Of course, not all companies want ESOPs, and they won't work in all situations, but they can be an important part of an organization's motivational strategy.

[[🖼]] RESEARCH FINDINGS: Variable-Pay Programs

Do variable-pay programs work? Generally yes, but that does not mean everyone is equally motivated by them.[42] Many organizations have more than one variable-pay element in operation, such as an ESOP and bonuses, so managers should evaluate the effectiveness of the overall plan in terms of the employee motivation gained from each element separately and from all elements together. Managers should monitor their employees' performance–reward expectancy, since a combination of elements that makes employees feel that their greater performance will yield them greater rewards will be the most motivating.[43]

2 Show how flexible benefits can be used to motivate.

Flexible Benefits: Developing a Benefits Package

Now that we have discussed what and how to pay employees, let's discuss two other motivating factors organizations must decide: (1) what benefits and choices to offer (such as flexible benefits), and (2) how to construct employee recognition programs. Like pay, benefits are both a provision and a motivator. Whereas organizations of yesteryear issued a standard package to every employee, contemporary leaders understand that each employee values benefits differently. A flexible program turns the benefits package into a motivational tool.

Alain Boudreau and Yasmin Murphy have very different needs in terms of employee benefits. Alain is married and has three young children and a wife who is at home full time. His colleague Yasmin, too, is married, but her husband has a high-paying job with the federal government, and they have no children. Alain is concerned about having a good dental plan and enough life insurance to support his family in case it's needed. In contrast, Yasmin's husband already has her dental needs covered on his plan, and life insurance is a low priority for both Yasmin and her husband. Yasmin is more interested in extra vacation time and long-term financial benefits such as a tax-deferred savings plan.

employee stock ownership plan (ESOP) A company-established benefit plan in which employees acquire stock as part of their benefits.

A standardized benefits package for all employees at an organization would be unlikely to satisfactorily meet the needs of both Alain and Yasmin. The organization they work for could cover both sets of needs by offering flexible benefits.

Consistent with expectancy theory's thesis that organizational rewards should be linked to each employee's personal goals, **flexible benefits** individualize rewards by allowing each employee to choose the compensation package that best satisfies his or her current needs. Flexible benefits can be uniquely tailored to accommodate differences in employee needs based on age, marital status, partner's benefit status, and number and age of dependants.

Benefits in general can be a motivator for a person to go to work, and for a person to choose one organization over another. But are flexible benefits more motivating than traditional plans? It's difficult to tell. Some organizations that have moved to flexible plans report increased employee retention, job satisfaction, and productivity. However, flexible benefits may not substitute for higher salaries when it comes to motivation.[44] Furthermore, as more organizations worldwide adopt flexible benefits, the individual motivation they produce will likely decrease (the plans will be seen as a standard work provision). The downsides of flexible benefit plans may be obvious: They may be more costly to administrate, and identifying the motivational impact of different provisions is challenging. A recent survey of 211 Canadian organizations found that 60 percent offer flexible benefits, up from 41 percent in 2005.[45] They are becoming the norm in other countries, too. *Case Incident—Motivation for Leisure* on page 194 demonstrates the trade-off between different benefits.

Intrinsic Rewards: Employee Recognition Programs

We have discussed motivating employees through job design and by the extrinsic rewards of pay and benefits. On an organizational level, are those the only ways to motivate employees? Not at all! We would be remiss if we overlooked intrinsic rewards organizations can provide.

Laura makes only $11.60 per hour working at her fast-food job, and the job is not very challenging or interesting. Yet Laura talks enthusiastically about the job, her boss, and the company that employs her. "What I like is the fact that Guy [her supervisor] appreciates the effort I make. He compliments me regularly in front of the other people on my shift, and I've been chosen Employee of the Month twice in the past six months. Did you see my picture on that plaque on the wall?"

Organizations are increasingly realizing what Laura knows: Recognition programs and other ways of increasing an employee's intrinsic motivation work. An employee recognition program is a plan to encourage specific behaviours by formally appreciating specific employee contributions. Employee recognition programs range from a spontaneous and private "thank you" to widely publicized formal programs in which the procedures for attaining recognition are clearly identified.

A 2016 study by the Conference Board of Canada found that recognition programs are common in Canadian firms.[46] Recognition takes the form of both monetary and non-monetary rewards. The most prevalent recognition reward is for long service at an organization. Unfortunately, this is not a motivator for millennials, who on average work for five different employers in a 10-year period. The survey also found that only a third of organizations consider the different generations in the workplace when designing recognition programs. It found only 37 percent of organizations take today's multigenerational workforce into account when designing their rewards and recognition programs.

Brian Scudamore, CEO of Vancouver-based 1-800-GOT-JUNK?, understands the importance of showing employees that they are appreciated. "I believe that the best way to engage someone is with heartfelt thanks. We have created a culture of peer recognition, and 'thank yous' have become contagious. Whether it's a card, kudos at the

Identify the motivational benefits of intrinsic rewards.

flexible benefits A benefits plan that allows each employee to put together a benefits package individually tailored to his or her own needs and situation.

huddle, or basic one-on-one thanks, gratitude goes a long way toward building team engagement, loyalty and, of course, happiness."[47] Scudamore says that actions like these keep the company growing, and employees having fun.

Some Canadian firms recognize individual or group achievements with cash or merchandise. For example, Toronto-based software developer RL Solutions developed a formal program for employees to recognize co-workers who go above and beyond in working with clients or in other aspects of their work. Those recognized by their co-workers receive cash and/or other rewards. Employees are also recognized with bonuses when they refer good job candidates to the company.[48]

Other ways of recognizing performance include sending employees personal thank-you notes or emails for good performance, putting employees on prestigious committees, sending employees for training, and giving an employee an assistant for a day to help clear backlogs. Recognition and praise, however, need to be meaningful.[49]

[[🖐️]] RESEARCH FINDINGS: Incentives

Research suggests financial incentives may be more motivating in the short term, but in the long run nonfinancial incentives work best.[50] Surprisingly, there is not a lot of research on the motivational outcomes or global usage of employee recognition programs. However, recent studies indicate that employee recognition programs are associated with self-esteem, self-efficacy, and job satisfaction,[51] and the broader outcomes from intrinsic motivation are well documented.

With or without financial rewards, recognition programs can be highly motivating to employees. Despite the increased popularity of such programs, though, critics argue they are highly susceptible to political manipulation by management. When applied to jobs for which performance factors are relatively objective, such as sales, recognition programs are likely to be perceived by employees as fair. In most jobs, however, performance criteria are not self-evident, which allows managers to manipulate the system and recognize their favourites. Abuse can undermine the value of recognition programs and demoralize employees. Therefore, where formal recognition programs are used, care must be taken to ensure fairness. Where they are not, it is important to motivate employees by consistently recognizing their performance efforts.

Beware the Signals That Are Sent by Rewards

Perhaps more often than we would like, organizations engage in what has been called "the folly of rewarding A, while hoping for B";[52] in other words, managers may hope employees will engage in one type of behaviour, but they reward another. Expectancy theory suggests that individuals will generally perform in ways that raise the probability of receiving the rewards offered. Exhibit 5-1 provides examples of common management reward follies. By signalling what gets rewarded, organizations implicitly determine whether employees engage in organizational citizenship behaviour

> Ever wonder why employees do some strange things?

Research suggests that there are three major obstacles to ending these follies:[53]

1. *Individuals are unable to break out of old ways of thinking about reward and recognition practices.* Management often emphasizes quantifiable behaviours to the exclusion of nonquantifiable behaviours, management is sometimes reluctant to change the existing performance system, and employees sometimes have an entitlement mentality (they don't want change because they are comfortable with the current system for rewards).

EXHIBIT 5-1 Management Reward Follies

We hope for ...	But we reward ...
Teamwork and collaboration	The best team members
Innovative thinking and risk-taking	Proven methods and not making mistakes
Development of people skills	Technical achievements and accomplishments
Employee involvement and empowerment	Tight control over operations and resources
High achievement	Another year's effort
Long-term growth; environmental responsibility	Quarterly earnings
Commitment to total quality	Shipping on schedule, even with defects
Candour; surfacing bad news early	Reporting good news, whether it's true or not; agreeing with the manager, whether or not (s)he is right

Sources: Constructed from S. Kerr, "On the Folly of Rewarding A, While Hoping for B," *Academy of Management Executive* 9, no. 1 (1995), pp. 7–14; and "More on the Folly," *Academy of Management Executive* 9, no. 1 (1995), pp. 15–16. Copyright © Academy of Management, 1990.

2. *Organizations often don't look at the big picture of their performance system.* Consequently, rewards are allocated at subunit levels, with the result that units often compete against each other.

3. *Both management and shareholders often focus on short-term results.* They don't reward employees for longer-range planning.

Organizations would do well to ensure that they do not send the wrong message when offering rewards. When organizations outline an organizational objective of "team performance," for example, but reward each employee according to individual productivity, this does not send a message that teams are valued. When a retailer tells commissioned employees that they are responsible for monitoring and replacing stock, those employees will nevertheless concentrate on making sales. Employees motivated by the promise of rewards will do those things that earn them the rewards they value.

OB in the Street offers additional evidence that what is rewarded guides people's focus of activity.

OB IN THE STREET

Rewarding Gym Attendance While Wanting Weight Loss

Will offering incentives for going to the gym prevent first-year university students from gaining weight? University students are notorious for gaining several kilograms in their first year, as they adjust to living away from home and being more responsible for food choices while trying to keep up with their studies.[54] Researchers wondered if providing monetary incentives for students to go to the gym would help them keep off weight.

Students were assigned to experimental or control groups. In the experimental group, students were paid between $10 and $38.75 weekly if they met the goals researchers set for going to the fitness centre. Student activity was monitored through ID cards used to check in and check out of the centre.

The monetary incentives did make a difference in whether students went to the fitness centre weekly: 63 percent of those receiving incentives met the weekly goals on average, while only 13 percent of those in the control group did so. However, the rate of quitting going to the fitness centre dropped off at about the same rate for both

(continued)

the control and incentive groups. While the control group gained a bit more weight than did the group receiving incentives for going to the fitness centre, the difference was not significant.

The results indicate that the monetary rewards did in fact increase the likelihood that students would meet their weekly goals for going to the fitness centre. However, the students were not given rewards for maintaining or losing weight over the same period. The researchers had assumed that a link existed between going to the fitness centre and weight fluctuations. The students might have been more successful at minding their weight had the researchers rewarded weight loss rather than going to the fitness centre. ....

As we have seen from this discussion, understanding what motivates individuals is ultimately key to organizational performance. Employees whose differences are recognized, who feel valued, and who have the opportunity to work in jobs tailored to their strengths and interests will be motivated to perform at the highest levels. Employee participation also can increase employee productivity, commitment to work goals, motivation, and job satisfaction. However, we cannot overlook the powerful role of organizational rewards in influencing motivation. Pay, benefits, and intrinsic rewards must be carefully and thoughtfully designed in order to enhance employee motivation toward positive organizational outcomes.

4 Describe the job characteristics model and the way it motivates.

Motivating by Job Redesign

The way work is structured has a bigger impact on an individual's motivation than might first appear. **Job design** suggests that the way elements in a job are organized can influence employee effort, and the job characteristics model, discussed next, can serve as a framework to identify opportunities for changes to those elements

The Job Characteristics Model

Developed by OB researchers J. Richard Hackman from Harvard University and Greg Oldham from the University of Illinois, the **job characteristics model (JCM)** describes jobs in terms of five core job dimensions:[55]

- **Skill variety.** The degree to which the job requires a variety of different activities so the employee can use specialized skills and talents.

- **Task identity.** The degree to which the job requires completion of a whole and identifiable piece of work.

- **Task significance.** The degree to which the job has an impact on the lives or work of other people.

- **Autonomy.** The degree to which the job provides the employee freedom, independence, and discretion in scheduling work each day and determining the procedures for carrying it out.

- **Feedback.** The degree to which carrying out work activities generates direct and clear information about the employee's own performance.

Jobs can be rated as high or low on these dimensions. Examples of jobs with high and low ratings appear in Exhibit 5-2.

Exhibit 5-3 presents the job characteristics model (JCM). Note how the first three dimensions—skill variety, task identity, and task significance—combine to create meaningful work the employee will view as important, valuable, and worthwhile. A recent study found that religious workers, social workers, counsellors, and medical professionals rated their jobs as highly meaningful, while those who held jobs as food service and

job design The way the elements in a job are organized.

job characteristics model (JCM) A model that proposes that any job can be described in terms of five core job dimensions: skill variety, task identity, task significance, autonomy, and feedback.

skill variety The degree to which the job requires a variety of different activities.

task identity The degree to which the job requires completion of a whole and identifiable piece of work.

task significance The degree to which the job has a substantial impact on the lives or work of other people.

autonomy The degree to which the job provides substantial freedom, independence, and discretion to the individual in scheduling the work and determining the procedures to be used in carrying it out.

feedback The degree to which carrying out the work activities required by the job results in the individual obtaining direct and clear information about the effectiveness of his or her performance.

EXHIBIT 5-2 Examples of High and Low Job Characteristics

Skill Variety

High variety	The owner-operator of a garage who does electrical repair, rebuilds engines, does body work, and interacts with customers
Low variety	A body shop worker who sprays paint eight hours a day

Task Identity

High identity	A cabinet maker who designs a piece of furniture, selects the wood, builds the object, and finishes it to perfection
Low identity	A worker in a furniture factory who operates a lathe solely to make table legs

Task Significance

High significance	A nurse who cares for the sick in a hospital intensive care unit
Low significance	A custodian who sweeps hospital floors

Autonomy

High autonomy	A salesperson who schedules his or her own work each day, and decides on the sales approach for each customer without supervision
Low autonomy	A salesperson who is given a set of leads each day and is required to follow a standardized sales script with potential customers

Feedback

High feedback	A factory employee who assembles iPads and tests them to see whether they operate properly
Low feedback	A factory employee who assembles iPads and then routes them to a quality-control inspector for testing and adjustments

Source: Based on G. Johns, *Organizational Behavior: Understanding and Managing Life at Work*, 4th ed. Copyright © 1997. Adapted by permission of Pearson Education, Inc. Upper Saddle River, NJ.

EXHIBIT 5-3 The Job Characteristics Model

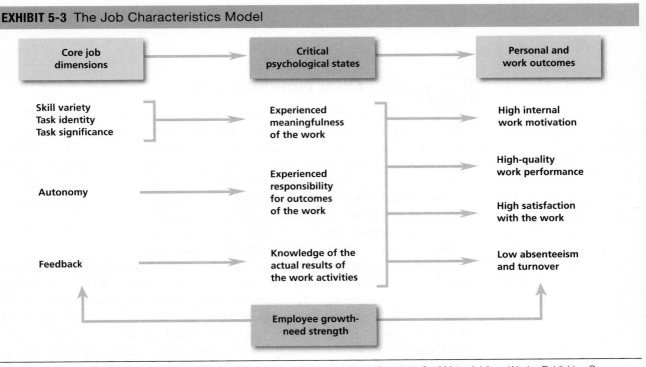

Source: J. R. Hackman, G. R. Oldham, *Work Redesign* (excerpted from pages 78–80). Copyright © 1980 by Addison-Wesley Publishing Co. ISBN: 978-0201027792.

hospitality workers rated them as being very low in meaningfulness. Fast-food cooks were at the bottom of the list of meaningfulness.[56]

Jobs with high autonomy give employees a feeling of personal responsibility for results; feedback will show them how effectively they are performing. The JCM proposes that individuals obtain internal rewards when they learn (knowledge of results) that they personally have performed well (experienced responsibility) on a task they care about (experienced meaningfulness).[57] The more these three psychological states are present, the greater will be employees' motivation, performance, and satisfaction, and the lower their absenteeism and likelihood of leaving. As Exhibit 5-3 indicates, individuals with a high growth need are more likely to experience the critical psychological states when their jobs are enriched—and respond to them more positively—than are their counterparts with a low growth need. Autonomy does not mean the same thing to every person, as *Focus on Research* shows.

FOCUS ON RESEARCH
Autonomy and Productivity

Can autonomy really make a difference? Research published by professors Marylène Gagné and Devasheesh Bhave of Concordia's John Molson School of Business found that every culture values autonomy, and that the perception of autonomy has a positive impact on employees.[58] "However, managers can't simply export North American methods of granting autonomy anywhere and expect them to work. Even in Canada, approaches to giving workers more autonomy need to be constantly rethought as the country becomes more multicultural," says Gagné.

The researchers found that how autonomy is applied makes a difference in how it is perceived. In some cultures, too much freedom in the workplace can be viewed as management disorganization. However, if employees feel they have some control over their activities, they generally show more commitment and productivity, particularly when the work is complex or demands creativity.

RESEARCH FINDINGS: JCM

Much evidence supports the JCM concept that the presence of these job characteristics generates higher job satisfaction and organizational commitment through increased motivation.[59] In general, research concurs with the theory behind the JCM, although studies have introduced potential modifiers. One study suggested that when employees were "other oriented" (concerned with the welfare of others at work), the relationship between intrinsic job characteristics and job satisfaction was weaker,[60] meaning that our job satisfaction comes less from these characteristics when we care about others. Another study proposed that the degree of psychological ownership we feel toward our work enhances our motivation, particularly if the feelings of ownership are shared among a work group.[61] Other research has explored the JCM in unique settings such as in virtual work situations, finding that if individuals work together online but not in person, their experience of meaningfulness, responsibility, and knowledge of results can suffer. Thankfully, managers can mitigate these for employees by consciously developing personal relationships with them and increasing their sense of task significance, autonomy, and feedback.[62]

> When might
> job redesign
> be most
> appropriate?

Motivating Potential Score

We can combine the core dimensions of the JCM into a single predictive index, called the **motivating potential score (MPS)**, which is calculated as follows:

$$\text{Motivating Potential Score (MPS)} = \left[\frac{\text{Skill variety} + \text{Task identity} + \text{Task significance}}{3}\right] \times \text{Autonomy} \times \text{Feedback}$$

To be high on motivating potential, jobs must be high on at least one of the three factors that lead to experienced meaningfulness and high on both autonomy and feedback. If jobs score high on motivating potential, the model predicts motivation, performance, and satisfaction will improve, while absence and turnover will be reduced. But we can better calculate motivating potential by simply adding characteristics rather than using the formula. Think about your job. Do you have the opportunity to work on different tasks, or is your day routine? Are you able to work independently, or do you constantly have a supervisor or co-worker looking over your shoulder? Your answers indicate your job's motivating potential.

The first part of the *Experiential Exercise* on page 192 provides an opportunity for you to apply the JCM to a job of your choice. You will also calculate the job's MPS. In the second part of the *Experiential Exercise*, you can redesign the job to show how you might increase its motivating potential. *From Concepts to Skills* on pages 195–196 provides specific guidelines on the kinds of changes that can help increase the motivating potential of jobs.

Job Redesign in the Canadian Context: The Role of Unions

Labour unions have been largely resistant to participating in discussions with management over job redesign issues. Redesigns often result in loss of jobs, and labour unions try to prevent job loss.[63] Union head offices, however, can sometimes be at odds with their membership over the acceptance of job redesign. Some members value the opportunity for skill development and more interesting work.

While managers may regard job redesign as more difficult under a collective agreement, the reality is that for change to be effective in the workplace, management must gain employees' acceptance of the plan whether or not they are unionized.

How Can Jobs Be Redesigned?

⑤ Compare the main ways jobs can be redesigned.

"Every day was the same thing," Frank said. "Stand on that assembly line. Wait for an instrument panel to be moved into place. Unlock the mechanism and drop the panel into the Jeep Liberty as it moved by on the line. Then I plugged in the harnessing wires. I repeated that for eight hours a day. I don't care that they were paying me $24 an hour. I was going crazy. Finally, I just said this isn't going to be the way I'm going to spend the rest of my life. My brain was turning to JELL-O. So I quit. Now I work in a print shop and I make less than $15 an hour. But let me tell you, the work I do is really interesting. The job changes all the time, I'm continually learning new things, and the work really challenges me! I look forward every morning to going to work again."

The repetitive tasks in Frank's job at the Jeep plant provided little variety, autonomy, or motivation. In contrast, his job in the print shop is challenging and stimulating. From an organizational perspective, the failure of Frank's first employer to redesign his job into a more satisfying one led to increased turnover. Redesigning jobs therefore has important practical implications—reduced turnover and increased job satisfaction among them. Let's look at some of the ways to put JCM into practice to make jobs more motivating.

motivating potential score (MPS) A predictive index suggesting the motivation potential in a job.

Job Rotation

If employees suffer from overroutinization, one alternative is **job rotation**, or the periodic shifting of an employee from one task to another with similar skill requirements at the same organizational level (also called *cross-training*). Manufacturers also use job rotation as needed to respond more flexibly to the volume of incoming orders. New managers are sometimes rotated through jobs, too, to help them get a picture of the whole organization.[64] For these reasons, job rotation can be applied in any setting where cross-training is feasible, from manufacturing floors to hospital wards. At Singapore Airlines, for instance, a ticket agent may temporarily take on the duties of a baggage handler, both to be cross-trained and get exposure to different aspects of the organization. Extensive job rotation is among the reasons Singapore Airlines is rated one of the best airlines in the world.[65] At McDonald's, this approach is used as a way to make sure that the new employees learn all of the tasks associated with making, packaging, and serving hamburgers and other items.

International evidence from Italy, Britain, and Turkey shows that job rotation is associated with higher levels of organizational performance in manufacturing settings.[66] It reduces boredom, increases motivation, and helps employees understand how their work contributes to the organization. It may also increase safety and reduce repetitive-based work injuries, but this is currently a topic of much study and debate, with mixed findings.[67]

Job rotation does have drawbacks. First, training costs increase when each rotation necessitates a round of training. Second, moving a worker into a new position reduces overall productivity for that role. Third, job rotation creates disruptions when members of the work group have to adjust to new employees. Finally, a manager may have to spend more time answering questions and monitoring the work of the recently rotated employee.

Relational Job Design

While redesigning jobs on the basis of job characteristics theory is likely to make work more intrinsically motivating, research is focusing on how to make jobs more pro-socially motivating to people. In other words, how can managers design work so employees are motivated to promote the well-being of the organization's beneficiaries (customers, clients, patients, and employees). This view of **relational job design** shifts the spotlight from the employee to those whose lives are affected by the job that the employee performs.[68] It also motivates individuals toward increased job performance.[69]

One way to make jobs more pro-socially motivating is to better connect employees with the beneficiaries of their work by relating stories from customers who have found the company's products or services to be helpful. Medical device manufacturer Medtronic invites people to describe how its products have improved, or even saved, their lives and shares these stories with employees during annual meetings, providing the employees a powerful reminder of the impact of their work. For another example, researchers found that when university fundraisers briefly interacted with the undergraduates who would receive the scholarship money they raised, they persisted 42 percent longer than and raised nearly twice as much money as fundraisers who did not interact with potential recipients.[70] The positive impact was apparent even when fundraisers met with just a single scholarship recipient.

Personal contact with beneficiaries may not always be necessary. One study found that radiologists who saw photographs of patients whose scans they were examining made more accurate diagnoses of their medical problems. Why? Seeing the photos made it more personal, which elicited feelings of empathy in the radiologists.[71]

Why do these connections have such positive consequences? Meeting beneficiaries first-hand—or even just seeing pictures of them—allows employees to see that their actions affect a real person and that their jobs have tangible consequences. It

job rotation The periodic shifting of an employee from one task to another.

relational job design Constructing jobs so employees see the positive difference they can make in the lives of others directly through their work.

Jeff Schear/Getty Images

Research suggests that half the organizations in Canada actively encourage employee volunteering. As a result, fully one-quarter of all the volunteer work in the country is done by employee volunteers. Here we see employees from Lowe's and Bank of Montreal working together to build social housing for people living in poverty.

makes customers or clients more memorable and emotionally vivid, which leads employees to consider the effects of their work actions more. Finally, connections allow employees to easily take the perspective of beneficiaries, which fosters higher levels of commitment.

You might be wondering whether connecting employees with the beneficiaries of their work is already covered by the idea of task significance in the JCM. However, some differences make beneficiary contact unique. For one, many jobs might be perceived to be high in significance, yet employees in those jobs never meet the individuals affected by their work. Second, beneficiary contact seems to have a distinct relationship with prosocial behaviours such as helping others. For example, one study found that life-guards who read stories about how their actions benefited swimmers were rated as more helpful by their bosses; this was not the case for lifeguards who read stories about the personal benefits of their work for themselves.[72] The upshot? There are many ways you can design jobs to be more motivating, and your choice should depend on the outcomes you would like to achieve.

Relational job design, with its focus on prosocial motivation, is an especially salient topic for organizations with corporate social responsibility (CSR) initiatives. As we discussed in earlier chapters, CSR efforts often include invitations for employees to volunteer their time and effort, sometimes using the skills they gained on the job (like Home Depot employees when they help rebuild homes) but often not (such as when bank employees help rebuild homes with groups like Habitat for Humanity). In both cases, the employees may be able to interact with the beneficiaries of their efforts, and research indicates that corporate-sponsored volunteer programs enhanced in the JCM dimensions of meaningfulness and task significance motivate employees to volunteer.[73] But while this motivation for prosocial behaviour is noteworthy, it is not the same as relational job design: For one, the CSR efforts are through volunteering (not on the job); and for another, the work they are providing is not usually the same work they do at their jobs (Home Depot workers do not build homes on the job). However, relational job design holds intriguing possibilities for CSR initiatives.

6 Explain how specific alternative work arrangements can motivate employees.

Alternative Work Arrangements

As you surely know, there are many approaches toward motivating people, and we have discussed some of them. Another approach to motivation is to consider alternative work arrangements such as flextime, job sharing, or tele-commuting. These are likely to be especially important for a diverse workforce of dual-earner couples, single parents, and employees caring for a sick or aging relative.

Do employers really like flexible arrangements?

Flextime

Flextime is short for "flexible work time." Flextime employees must work a specific number of hours a week, but they may vary the hours of work within certain limits. As shown in Exhibit 5-4, each day consists of a common core, usually six hours, with a flexibility band surrounding it. The core may be 9 a.m. to 3 p.m., with the office actually opening at 6 a.m. and closing at 6 p.m. Employees must be at their jobs during the common core period, but they may accumulate their other two hours before and/or after the core time. Some flextime programs allow employees to accumulate extra hours and turn them into days off.

EXHIBIT 5-4 Examples of Flextime Schedules

Schedule 1

Percent Time:	100% = 40 hours per week
Core Hours:	9:00 a.m.–5:00 p.m., Monday through Friday (1 hour lunch)
Work Start Time:	Between 8:00 a.m. and 9:00 a.m.
Work End Time:	Between 5:00 p.m. and 6:00 p.m.

Schedule 2

Percent Time:	100% = 40 hours per week
Work Hours:	8:00 a.m.–6:30 p.m., Monday through Thursday (1/2 hour lunch)
	Friday off
Work Start Time:	8:00 a.m.
Work End Time:	6:30 p.m.

Schedule 3

Percent Time:	90% = 36 hours per week
Work Hours:	8:30 a.m.–5:00 p.m., Monday through Thursday (1/2 hour lunch)
	8:00 a.m.–Noon Friday (no lunch)
Work Start Time:	8:30 a.m. (Monday–Thursday); 8:00 a.m. (Friday)
Work End Time:	5:00 p.m. (Monday–Thursday); Noon (Friday)

Schedule 4

Percent Time:	80% = 32 hours per week
Work Hours:	8:00 a.m.–6:00 p.m., Monday through Wednesday (1/2 hour lunch)
	8:00 a.m.–11:30 a.m. Thursday (no lunch)
	Friday off
Work Start Time:	Between 8:00 a.m. and 9:00 a.m.
Work End Time:	Between 5:00 p.m. and 6:00 p.m.

---

flextime Flexible work hours.

Canadian employees do not have much access to flextime, however. According to the results of a survey of 25 000 Canadians employed full time conducted by professor Linda Duxbury of the Sprott School of Business, Carleton University, only 15 percent of employees said they had access to flextime schedules. Employees did report some flexibility in determining some of their work hours, however, with 69 percent indicating high or moderate flexibility for work hours and location.[74] According to a recent survey, a majority (60 percent) of US organizations offer some form of flextime.[75] In Germany, 73 percent of businesses offer flextime, and such practices are becoming more widespread in Japan as well.[76] In Germany, Belgium, the Netherlands, and France, by law, employers are not allowed to refuse an employee's request for either a part-time or a flexible work schedule as long as the request is reasonable, such as to care for an infant child.[77]

Benefits of flextime include reduced absenteeism, increased productivity, reduced overtime expenses, reduced hostility toward management, reduced traffic congestion,[78] elimination of tardiness, and increased autonomy and responsibility for employees—any of which may increase employee job satisfaction.[79] But what is flextime's actual record?

Most of the evidence stacks up in favour of flextime. Perhaps most important from the organization's perspective, flextime increases profitability. Interestingly, though, this effect seems to occur only when flextime is promoted as a work–life balance strategy (not when it is for the organization's gain).[80] Flextime also tends to reduce absenteeism and frequently improves employee productivity and satisfaction,[81] probably for several reasons. Employees can schedule their work hours to align with personal demands, reducing tardiness and absences, and they can work when they are most productive. Flextime can also help employees balance work and family life.

A study by University of Toronto researchers found that flextime can lead to longer hours of work overall and more multi-tasking. These effects in turn lead to greater work–life conflict and stress.[82] So the management of flextime is an important issue for employees. Flextime's other major drawback is that it's not applicable to every job or every employee. It works well for clerical tasks where an employee's interaction with people outside the department is limited. It's not a viable option for receptionists, salespeople in retail stores, or anyone whose service job requires being at a workstation at predetermined times. It also appears that people who have a strong desire to separate their work and family lives are less apt to want flextime, so it's not a motivator for everyone.[83] Those who ask for it are often stigmatized, which can be avoided only if the majority of the organization's leaders adopt flexible hours to signal that flextime is acceptable.[84] Finally, research in the United Kingdom indicated that employees in organizations with flextime do not realize a reduction in their levels of stress, suggesting that this option may not truly improve work–life balance.[85] Since flextime is intuitively a worthwhile business practice, these findings suggest additional research is needed to determine the motivational aspects of flextime.

Job Sharing

Job sharing allows two or more people to split a full-time job. One might perform the job from 8:00 a.m. to noon, perhaps and the other from 1:00 p.m. to 5:00 p.m., or the two could work full but alternate days. While it's popular in Europe, it's not a common arrangement in Canada. About 14 percent of Canadian employers offer this arrangement.[86] The reasons it's not more widely adopted are likely the difficulty of finding compatible partners to share a job and the historically negative perceptions of individuals not completely committed to their jobs and employers.

However, eliminating job sharing for these reasons might be short-sighted. Job sharing allows the organization to draw upon the talents of more than one individual in a given job. It also opens up the opportunity to acquire skilled employees—for instance, parents with young children, retirees, and others desiring flexibility—who might not be available on a full-time basis.[87]

job sharing The practice of having two or more people split a 40-hour-a-week job.

From the employee's perspective, job sharing can increase motivation and satisfaction. An employer's decision to use job sharing is often based on economics. Two part-time employees sharing a job can be less expensive than one full-time employee, but experts suggest this is not the case because training, coordination, and administrative costs can be high. In Canada, benefits do not have to be paid for those working less than half, which may create an incentive for companies to increase job-sharing arrangements.

Ideally, employers should consider each employee and job separately, seeking to match the skills, personality, and needs of the employee with the tasks required for the job, taking into account that individual's motivating factors.

Telecommuting

Telecommuting (sometimes called *teleworking*) might be close to the ideal job for many people: no rush-hour traffic, flexible hours, freedom to dress as you please, and few interruptions. Telecommuting refers to working at home— or anywhere else the employee chooses that is outside the workplace—at least two days a week on a computer linked to the employer's office.[88] (A closely related concept— working from a *virtual office*—describes working outside the workplace on a relatively permanent basis.) A sales manager working from home is telecommuting, but a sales manager working from her car on a business trip is not. Despite the benefits of telecommuting, large organizations such as Yahoo! and Best Buy have eliminated it.[89] Yahoo! CEO Marissa Mayer discussed how telecommuting may undermine corporate culture, noting, "People are more productive when they're alone, but they're more collaborative and innovative when they're together."[90]

> Would you find telecommuting motivating?

A recent BMO poll found that about 23 percent of Canadian companies offer telecommuting,[91] which was down from about 40 percent of Canadian companies in 2008.[92]

What kinds of jobs lend themselves to telecommuting? Writers, attorneys, analysts, and employees who spend the majority of their time on computers or the phone—telemarketers, customer-service representatives, reservation agents, and product-support specialists—are candidates for telecommuting. As telecommuters, they can access information on their computer screens at home as easily as on the company screen in any office.

Aaron Harris/Bloomberg/Getty Images

telecommuting Working from home at least two days a week on a computer that is linked to the employer's office.

Vancouver-based TELUS involves many of its employees in its Work Styles program. Employees are encouraged to work from home or the office, whichever best fits the needs of getting work done. The program has led to increased morale and decreased turnover.

CAREER OBJECTIVES

How Can I Get Flextime?

My job is great, but I can't understand why management won't allow flextime. After all, I often work on a laptop in the office! I could just as easily be working on the same laptop at home without interruptions from my colleagues. I know I'd be more productive. How can I convince them to let me?

—*Sophia*

Dear Sophia:

We can't help but wonder two things: (1) is the ban on working from home a company policy, or your manager's policy; and (2) do you want flextime, or telecommuting? If you work for Yahoo!, for instance, you may not be able to convince anyone to let you work from home after CEO Marissa Mayer's very public decree against the policy. If the ban is your manager's policy—or even your division's policy—in an organization open to alternative work arrangements, you just may be able to get your way.

That leads us to the second question, about flextime vs. telecommuting. If you want flextime as you stated and just want to work from home during some non-core hours (say, work in the office for six hours a day and work another two hours a day from home), your employer may be more likely to grant your wish than if you want to completely telecommute (work all your hours from home).

Research indicates that employees are most likely to be granted work-from-home privileges as a result of a direct sympathetic relationship with their managers (not as a result of a company policy). Employees are also more likely to gain acceptance for partial than for full telecommuting (either flextime or by alternating days). It helps if you have a legitimate need to be home and if you do knowledge-based work. Jared Dalton, for instance, telecommutes two days a week as a manager for accounting firm Ernst & Young, and his wife Christina telecommutes on two different days, so they can oversee the care of their infant.

If it sounds like flextime depends on favouritism, you might be right. It's also, however, a reflection of the state of telecommuting: Only 38 percent of US organizations permit *some* of their employees to regularly work from home. To be one of the lucky few:

- *Check your organization's flexible options policies.*
- *Develop a plan for working from home to show your manager.* Include how many hours/week, which days/week, and where you will work, and explain how your manager can retain oversight of you.
- *Assemble evidence on your productivity.* Have you worked from home before? If so, show how much you achieved. You stated you would be more productive at home: How much more?

- *Outline your reasons for working from home.* Do you need to help care for an aging relative, for instance? Would working from home save you commuting time you could use for work?
- *Address management's concerns.* Research indicates the biggest ones are the possibility of abuse of the system and issues of fairness.
- *Consider your relationship with your manager.* Has he or she been supportive of you in the past? Is your manager approachable?

When you're ready, discuss your request with your manager. Remember, pitching the idea of telecommuting is the same as pitching any idea—you have got to think about what is in it for your employer, not for yourself.

Sources: "The 2015 Workplace Flexibility Study," *WorkplaceTrends.com,* February 3, 2015, https://workplacetrends.com/the-2015-workplace-flexibility-study/; T. S. Bernard, "For Workers, Less Flexible Companies," *New York Times,* May 20, 2014, pp. B1, B7; and C. C. Miller and L. Alderman, "The Flexibility Gap," *New York Times,* December 14, 2014, pp. 1, 5.

RESEARCH FINDINGS: Telecommuting

Telecommuting has several potential benefits. These include a larger labour pool from which to select (some people can/will only work by telecommuting), higher productivity, improved morale, and reduced office-space costs. A positive relationship exists between telecommuting and supervisor performance ratings,[93] but a relationship between telecommuting and potentially lower turnover intentions has not been substantiated in research to date.[94] Beyond the benefits to organizations and its employees, telecommuting has potential benefits to society. One study estimated that if people in the United States telecommuted half the time, carbon emissions would be reduced by approximately 51 metric tons per year. Environmental savings could come about from lower office energy consumption, fewer traffic jams that emit greenhouse gases, and a reduced need for road repairs.[95]

Telecommuting has several downsides too. The major one for management is less direct supervision. In today's team-focused workplace, telecommuting may also make it more difficult for managers to coordinate teamwork and it can reduce knowledge transfer in organizations.[96] Managers are also challenged to handle the demotivation of office workers who feel they are unfairly denied the freedom of telecommuters.[97] Contrary to Mayer's conclusions for Yahoo!, research indicates that more creative tasks may actually be best suited for telecommuting, whereas dull repetitive tasks like data entry decrease motivation and thus performance for remote workers.[98]

From the employee's standpoint, telecommuting can increase feelings of isolation and reduce job satisfaction. Research indicates it does not reduce work–family conflicts, perhaps because it often increases work hours beyond the contracted workweek.[99] Telecommuters are also vulnerable to the "out of sight, out of mind" effect. Employees who are not at their desks, miss meetings, and don't share in day-to-day informal workplace interactions may be at a disadvantage when it comes to raises and promotions because they are perceived as not putting in the requisite "face-time."[100] *Point/Counterpoint* on page 191 considers whether face-time actually matters. As for a CSR benefit of reducing car emissions by allowing telecommuting, research indicates that employees actually drive over 45 miles more per day, due to increased personal trips, when they telecommute![101]

Telecommuting is a contemporary reality, particularly in the minds of employees. The success of telecommuting will always depend on the quality of communications in order to establish good, though remote, working relationships. Telecommuting certainly does appear to make sense given changes in technology, the nature of work, and preferences of younger workers. Yet as the Yahoo! experience shows, some leaders do not think those benefits outweigh the costs.

Employee Involvement and Participation

Bruce Poon Tip wants his employees to be happy, and therefore encourages them to embrace the four pillars of happiness. The pillars are being able to grow, being connected, being part of something bigger than yourself, and having freedom.[102]

Poon Tip explains this code in his book, *Looptail*, which is about G Adventures:

I believe that if businesses want to be both sustainable and successful, they have to infuse their organizations with *passion* and *purpose*, as a way to engage the people inside the business, which will in turn engage people outside of it.

"Mayor" Dave Holmes is an integral part of encouraging employee involvement and participation at G Adventures. Holmes has to keep the company's more than 1500+ employees in over 100 countries informed and engaged. He does this by creating biweekly newscasts, and by travelling to meet with them. "Creating community, that's a huge part of my role," says Holmes.

Poon Tip and Holmes very much share the belief that happy workplaces are productive workplaces. Says Poon Tip:

Happy people do more, they think more, they're more creative, they're more free. And, ultimately, it's a very sound business decision in all aspects, whether it's attracting the best people or retaining the best people or giving the best customer service on the planet to your customers. Happy people deliver performance.

Holmes adds, "We see the results from it. We see double-digit growth as a company every year. Our happiness model is working for us."

What other ways can companies encourage employee involvement?

Employee involvement and participation (EIP)[103] are participative and use employees' input to increase their commitment to organizational success. If employees are engaged in decisions that increase their autonomy and control over their work lives, they will become more motivated, more committed to the organization, more productive, and more satisfied with their jobs. These benefits don't stop with individuals—when teams are given more control over their work, morale and performance increase as well.[104]

> How do employees become more involved in the workplace?

Examples of Employee Involvement Programs

Let's look at two major forms of employee involvement—participative management and representative participation—in more detail.

7 Describe how employee involvement programs can motivate employees.

Participative Management

The distinct characteristic common to all **participative management** programs is joint decision making, in which subordinates share a significant degree of decision-making power with their immediate superiors. This sharing can occur either formally through, say, briefings or surveys, or informally through daily consultations as a way to enhance motivation through trust and commitment.[105] Participative management has, at times, been considered as the solution for poor morale and low productivity. In reality, for participative management to be effective, followers must have trust and confidence in their leaders. Leaders should avoid coercive techniques and instead stress the organizational consequences of decision making to their followers.[106]

Studies of the participation–performance relationship have yielded mixed findings.[107] Organizations that institute participative management may realize higher stock returns, lower turnover rates, and higher labour productivity, although these effects are typically not large.[108] Research at the individual level indicates participation typically has only a modest influence on employee productivity, motivation, and job satisfaction. This does not mean participative management is not beneficial. However, it's not a sure means for improving performance.

Representative Participation

Most countries in western Europe require companies to practise **representative participation**. Representative participation redistributes power within an organization, putting labour's interests on a more equal footing with the interests of management and stockholders by including a small group of employees as participants in decision making. In the United Kingdom, Ireland, Australia, and New Zealand, representative participation was originally the only EIP program, formed to allow employee representatives to discuss issues outside union agreements, and the representatives were all from the union. However, representative groups are now increasingly a mix of union and nonunion, or separate from the union arrangement.[109]

The two most common forms of representation are works councils and board representatives.[110] Works councils are groups of nominated or elected employees who must be consulted when management makes decisions about employees. Board representatives are employees who sit on a company's board of directors and represent the employees' interests.

The influence of representative participation on working employees seems to be mixed, but generally an employee would need to feel his or her interests are well represented and make a difference to the organization in order for motivation to increase. Thus representative participation as a motivational tool is surpassed by more direct participation methods.

In sum, EIP programs clearly have the potential to increase employees' intrinsic motivation. The opportunity to make and implement decisions—and then see them

employee involvement and participation (EIP) Participative processes that use the input of employees and are intended to increase employee commitment to an organization's success.

participative management A process in which subordinates share a significant degree of decision-making power with their immediate superiors.

representative participation A system in which employees participate in organizational decision making through a small group of representative employees.

work out—can contribute to all desirable organizational outcomes. Giving employees control over key decisions, along with ensuring that their interests are represented, can enhance feelings of procedural justice. But, like any other initiatives, EIP programs must be carefully designed.

Linking Employee Involvement Programs and Motivation Theories

Employee involvement draws on a number of the motivation theories we discussed in Chapter 4. Theory Y is consistent with participative management, and Theory X is consistent with the more traditional autocratic style of managing people. In terms of Herzberg's two-factor theory, employee involvement programs could provide intrinsic motivation by increasing opportunities for growth, responsibility, and involvement in the work itself. The opportunity to make and implement decisions—and then see them work out—can help satisfy an employee's needs for responsibility, achievement, recognition, growth, and enhanced self-esteem. Extensive employee involvement programs clearly have the potential to increase employee intrinsic motivation in work tasks. Giving employees control over key decisions, along with ensuring that their interests are represented, can enhance feelings of procedural justice.

8 Describe how knowledge of what motivates people can be used to make organizations more motivating.

Motivation: Putting It All Together

In Chapter 4, we reviewed basic theories of motivation, considering such factors as how needs affect motivation, the importance of linking performance to rewards, and the need for fair processes. In this chapter, we considered various ways to pay and recognize people, and looked at job design and creating more flexible workplaces. Three Harvard University professors completed two studies that suggest a way to put all of these ideas together to understand (1) what motivates people and (2) how to use this knowledge to make sure that organizational processes motivate.[111]

According to the study authors, research suggests that four basic emotional drives (needs) guide individuals.[112] These are the drive to acquire; the drive to bond; the drive to comprehend; and the drive to defend. People want to acquire any number of scarce goods, both tangible and intangible (such as social status). They want to bond with other individuals and groups. They want to understand the world around them. As well, they want to protect against external threats to themselves and others, and want to ensure justice occurs.

Understanding these different drives makes it possible to motivate individuals more effectively. As the study authors point out, "each drive is best met by a distinct organizational lever." The drive to acquire is met through organizational rewards. The drive to bond can be met by "creat[ing] a culture that promotes teamwork, collaboration, openness, and friendship." The drive to comprehend is best met through job design and creating jobs that are "meaningful, interesting, and challenging." The drive to defend can be accomplished through an organization's performance management and resource allocation processes; this includes fair and transparent processes for managing performance and adequate resources to do one's job. Exhibit 5-5 indicates concrete ways that organizational characteristics can address individual drives.

GLOBAL IMPLICATIONS

Do the motivational approaches we have discussed vary by culture? Because we have covered some very different approaches in this chapter, let's break down our analysis by approach. Not every approach has been studied by cross-cultural researchers, so we consider cross-cultural differences in (1) variable pay, (2) flexible benefits, (3) job characteristics and job enrichment, (4) telecommuting, and (5) employee involvement.

EXHIBIT 5-5 How to Fulfill the Drives That Motivate Employees

DRIVE	PRIMARY LEVER	ACTIONS
1 Acquire	**Reward System**	• Sharply differentiate good performers from average and poor performers • Tie rewards clearly to performance • Pay as well as your competitors
2 Bond	**Culture**	• Foster mutual reliance and friendship among co-workers • Value collaboration and teamwork • Encourage sharing of best practices
3 Comprehend	**Job Design**	• Design jobs that have distinct and important roles in the organization • Design jobs that are meaningful and foster a sense of contribution to the organization
4 Defend	**Performance Management and Resource Allocation Processes**	• Increase the transparency of all processes • Emphasize their fairness • Build trust by being just and transparent in granting rewards, assignments, and other forms of recognition

Source: N. Nohria, B. Groysberg, and L.-E. Lee, "Employee Motivation: A Powerful New Model," *Harvard Business Review* 86, no. 7–8 (July–August 2008), p. 82.

Variable Pay

Globally, around 80 percent of companies offer some form of variable-pay plan. In Latin America, more than 90 percent of companies offer some form of variable-pay plan. In the United States, 91 percent of companies offer a variable-pay program.[113] In Latin America, companies also have the highest percentage of total payroll allocated to variable pay, at nearly 18 percent. European and US companies are at about 12 percent.[114] When it comes to executive compensation, Asian companies outpace Western companies in their use of variable pay.[115]

Flexible Benefits

Given the intuitive motivational appeal of flexible benefits, it may be surprising that their usage is not yet global. In China, only a limited percentage of companies offer flexible plans,[116] as in other Asian countries.[117] Almost all major corporations in the United States offer them. A similar survey of firms in the United Kingdom found that nearly all major organizations were offering flexible benefits programs, with options ranging from supplemental medical insurance to holiday trading (with co-workers), discounted bus travel, and child-care assistance.[118]

Job Characteristics and Job Enrichment

A few studies have tested the JCM in different cultures, but the results are not very consistent.[119] The fact that the model is relatively individualistic (it considers the relationship between the employee and his or her work) suggests job enrichment strategies may not have the same effects in collectivistic cultures as in individualistic cultures (such as the United States). Indeed, one study in Niger found that while the MPS was highly influenced by job dimensions, the correlations were different than the general data gathered from predominately individualist countries.[120] In contrast, another study suggests that the degree to which jobs have intrinsic job characteristics predicted job satisfaction and job involvement equally well for American, Japanese, and Hungarian employees.[121]

Telecommuting

While the movement away from telecommuting by some companies made headlines, it appears that for most organizations, it remains popular. Almost 50 percent of managers in Germany, the United Kingdom, and the United States are permitted telecommuting options. In developing countries, this percentage is between 10 and 20 percent.[122] Telecommuting is less practised in China, but there, too, it is growing.[123]

Employee Involvement

To be successful, EIP programs should be tailored to local and national norms.[124] A study of four countries, including the United States and India, confirmed the importance of modifying practices to reflect national culture.[125] While US employees readily accepted EIP programs, managers in India who tried to empower their employees through employee involvement programs were rated low by those employees. These reactions are consistent with India's high power-distance culture, which accepts and expects differences in authority. The work culture in India may not be in as much transition as in China, where some employees are becoming less high power-distance oriented. Chinese employees who were very accepting of traditional Chinese cultural values showed few benefits from participative decision making. However, Chinese employees who were less traditional were more satisfied and had higher performance ratings under participative management.[126] Another study conducted in China, however, showed that involvement increased employees' thoughts and feelings of job security, enhancing their well-being.[127] These differences within China may well reflect the current transitional nature of that culture. For example, research in urban China indicated that some aspects of EIP programs, namely those that favour consultation and expression but not participation in decision making, yield higher job satisfaction.[128]

Summary

As we have seen in this chapter, understanding what motivates individuals is ultimately the key to organizational performance. Employees whose differences are recognized, who feel valued, and who have the opportunity to work in jobs tailored to their strengths and interests will be motivated to perform at the highest levels. Employee participation also can increase employee productivity, commitment to work goals, motivation, and job satisfaction. However, we cannot overlook the powerful role of organizational rewards in influencing motivation. Pay, benefits, and intrinsic rewards must be carefully and thoughtfully designed in order to enhance employee motivation toward positive organizational outcomes.

SNAPSHOT SUMMARY

From Theory to Practice: The Role of Money

Creating Effective Reward Systems
- What to Pay: Establishing a Pay Structure
- How to Pay: Rewarding Individuals through Variable-Pay Programs
- Flexible Benefits: Developing a Benefits Package
- Intrinsic Rewards: Employee Recognition Programs

- Beware the Signals That Are Sent by Rewards

Motivating by Job Redesign
- The Job Characteristics Model
- Job Redesign in the Canadian Context: The Role of Unions
- How Can Jobs Be Redesigned?
- Relational Job Design
- Alternative Work Arrangements
- Flextime

Employee Involvement and Participation
- Examples of Employee Involvement Programs
- Linking Employee Involvement Programs and Motivation Theories

Motivation: Putting It All Together

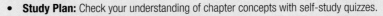
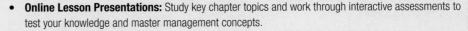

MyLab Management

   PERSONAL INVENTORY ASSESSMENT

Study, practise, and explore real business situations with these helpful resources:
- **Study Plan:** Check your understanding of chapter concepts with self-study quizzes.
- **Online Lesson Presentations:** Study key chapter topics and work through interactive assessments to test your knowledge and master management concepts.
- **Videos:** Learn more about the management practices and strategies of real companies.
- **Simulations:** Practise management decision-making in simulated business environments.

OB at Work

for Review

1. What is variable pay? What variable-pay programs are used to motivate employees? What are their advantages and disadvantages?

2. How can flexible benefits motivate employees?

3. What are the motivational benefits of intrinsic rewards?

4. What is the job characteristics model? How does it motivate employees?

5. What are the main ways that jobs can be redesigned? In your view, in what situations would one of the methods be favoured over the others?

6. What are the three alternative work arrangements of flextime, job sharing, and telecommuting? What are the advantages and disadvantages of each?

7. What are employee involvement programs? How might they increase employee motivation?

8. How can motivation theories be used to create more motivating work environments?

for Managers

- Recognize individual differences: Spend the time necessary to understand what is important to each employee. Design jobs to align with individual needs and maximize their motivation potential.

- Use goals and feedback. Give employees firm, specific goals, and provide them with feedback on how well they are doing in pursuit of those goals.

- Allow employees to participate in decisions that affect them. Employees can contribute to setting work goals, choosing their own benefits packages, and solving productivity and quality problems.

- Link rewards to performance and ensure that employees perceive the link between the two.

- Check the system for equity. Employees should perceive that individual effort and outcomes explain differences in pay and other rewards.

for You

- Because the people you interact with appreciate recognition, consider including a brief note on a nice card to show thanks for a job well done. Or you might send a basket of flowers. Sometimes just sending a pleasant, thankful email is enough to make a person feel valued. All of these things are easy enough to do, and appreciated greatly by the recipient.

- If you are working on a team or in a volunteer organization, try to find ways to motivate co-workers using the job characteristics model. For instance, make sure that everyone has some tasks over which they have autonomy, and make sure people get feedback on their work.

- When you are working on a team project, think about whether everyone on the team should get the same reward, or whether rewards should be allocated according to performance. Individual-based performance rewards may decrease team cohesiveness if individuals do not cooperate with one another.

"FACE-TIME" MATTERS

POINT	COUNTERPOINT

Although allowing people to work from home is gaining popularity, telecommuting will only hurt them and their employers.[129] Sure, employees say they are happier when their organization allows them the flexibility to work wherever they choose, but who would not like to hang around at home in their pyjamas pretending to work? I know plenty of colleagues who say, with a wink, that they are taking off to "work from home" the rest of the day. Who knows whether they are really contributing?

The bigger problem is the lack of face-to-face interaction between employees. Studies have shown that great ideas are born through interdependence, not independence. It's during those informal interactions around the water cooler or during coffee breaks that some of the most creative ideas arise. If you take that away, you stifle the organization's creative potential.

Trust is another problem. Have you ever trusted someone you have not met? Probably not. Again, face-to-face interactions allow people to establish trusting relationships more quickly, which fosters smoother social interactions and allows the company to perform better.

But enough about employers. Employees also benefit when they are at the office. If you are out of sight, you are out of mind. Want that big raise or promotion? You are not going to get it if your supervisor does not even know who you are.

So think twice the next time you either want to leave the office early or not bother coming in at all, to "work from home."

Please. So-called face-time is overrated. If all managers do is reward employees who hang around the office the longest, they are not being very good managers. Those who brag about the 80 hours they put in at the office (being sure to point out they were there on weekends) are not necessarily the top performers. Being present is not the same thing as being efficient.

Besides, there are all sorts of benefits for employees and employers who take advantage of telecommuting practices. For one, telecommuting is seen as an attractive perk companies can offer. With so many dual-career earners, the flexibility to work from home on some days can go a long way toward achieving a better balance between work and family. That translates into better recruiting and better retention. In other words, you will get and keep better employees if you offer the ability to work from home.

Plus, studies have shown that productivity is *higher*, not lower, when people work from home. This result is not limited to the United States. For example, one study found that Chinese call centre employees who worked from home outproduced their "face-time" counterparts by 13 percent.

You say all these earth-shattering ideas would pour forth if people interacted. I say consider that one of the biggest workplace distractions is chatty co-workers. So, although I concede that there are times when "face-time" is beneficial, the benefits of telecommuting far outweigh the drawbacks.

BREAKOUT **GROUP** EXERCISES

Form small groups to discuss the following topics, as assigned by your instructor:

1. How might the job of student be redesigned to make it more motivating?

2. What is your ideal job? To what extent does it match up with the elements of the JCM?

3. Would you prefer working from home or working at the office? Why?

EXPERIENTIAL EXERCISE

Analyzing and Redesigning Jobs

Break into groups of 5 to 7 members each.[130] Each student should describe the worst job he or she has ever had. Use any criteria you want to select 1 of these jobs for analysis by the group.

Members of the group will analyze the job selected by determining how well it scores on the job characteristics model. Use the following scale for your analysis of each job dimension:

7 = Very high

6 = High

5 = Somewhat high

4 = Moderate

3 = Somewhat low

2 = Low

1 = Very low

The following sample questions can guide the group in its analysis of the job in question:

- *Skill variety.* Describe the different identifiable skills required to do this job. What is the nature of the oral, written, and/or quantitative skills needed? What physical skills are required? Does the job holder get the opportunity to use all of his or her skills?

- *Task identity.* What is the product that the job holder creates? Is he or she involved in its production from beginning to end? If not, is he or she involved in a particular phase of its production from beginning to end?

- *Task significance.* How important is the product? How important is the job holder's role in producing it? How important is the job holder's contribution to the people he or she works with? If the job holder's job were eliminated, how inferior would the product be?

- *Autonomy.* How much independence does the job holder have? Does he or she have to follow a strict schedule? How closely is he or she supervised?

- *Feedback.* Does the job holder get regular feedback from his or her manager? From peers? From his or her staff? From customers? How about intrinsic performance feedback when doing the job?

Using the formula found on page 177, calculate the job's motivating potential score. Discuss whether you think this score accurately reflects your perceptions of the motivating potential of these professions.

Using the suggestions offered in the chapter for redesigning jobs, describe specific actions that management could take to increase this job's motivating potential.

Calculate the costs to management of redesigning the job in question. Do the benefits exceed the costs?

Conclude the exercise by having a representative of each group share his or her group's analysis and redesign suggestions with the entire class. Possible topics for class discussion might include similarities in the jobs chosen, problems in rating job dimensions, and the cost–benefit assessment of design changes.

ETHICAL **DILEMMA**

Are CEOs Paid Too Much?

Critics have described the astronomical pay packages given to Canadian and American CEOs as "rampant greed."[131] In 2015, the average annual compensation of CEOs in Canada's 100 largest companies was $9.5 million, up from $8.86 million in 2014. The 2015 CEO compensation was 193 times what the average full-time Canadian employee earned in 2015 ($49 510). Canadian CEOs may feel they are underpaid, though, if they compare themselves with a similar group of American CEOs, whose median pay was US$13.1 million in 2016, and 347 times that of the average pay for US employees.

How do you explain such large pay packages for CEOs? Some say that executive compensation represents a classic economic response to a situation in which the demand is great for high-quality top-executive talent, and the supply is low. Other arguments in favour of paying executives millions a year are the need to compensate people for the tremendous responsibilities and stress that go with such jobs; the motivating potential that seven- and eight-figure annual incomes provide to senior executives and those who might aspire to be; and the influence of senior executives on the company's bottom line.

Critics of executive pay practices in Canada and the United States argue that CEOs choose board members whom they can count on to support ever-increasing pay for top management. If board members fail to "play along," they risk losing their positions, their fees, and the prestige and power inherent in board membership.

In addition, it's not clear that executive compensation is tied to firm performance. For example, a 2014 analysis of compensation data by Equilar showed little correlation between CEO pay and company performance. Consider the data in Exhibit 5-6, which illustrates the disconnect that can sometimes happen between CEO compensation and firm performance. *Financial Post Magazine* uses a "Bang for the Buck" formula to calculate which CEOs were overpaid (or underpaid), based on their company's performance.

Is high compensation of CEOs a problem? If so, does the blame for the problem lie with CEOs or with the shareholders and boards that knowingly allow the practice? Are Canadian and American CEOs greedy? Are these CEOs acting unethically? Should their pay reflect more closely some multiple of their employees' wages? What do you think?

EXHIBIT 5-6 2017 Compensation of Canada's Most Overpaid CEOs*

CEO(s)	Pay Received (2-Year Avg.)	Pay Deserved	Amount Overpaid
1. Darren Enthistle, Joe Natale, TELUS, Vancouver, British Columbia	$14 680 000	$5 894 000	$8 786 000
2. Brendan Bell, Robert Gannicott, Dominion Diamond, Toronto, Ontario	$8 765 000	$1 564 000	$7 201 000
3. Bradley Shaw, Shaw Communications, Calgary, Alberta	$10 144 000	$3 508 000	$6 636 000
4. Geoffrey Martin, CCL Industries, Toronto, Ontario	$9 950 000	$4 923 000	$5 026 000
5. Sean Boyd, Agnico Eagle Mines, Toronto, Ontario	$9 688 000	$4 876 000	$4 812 000

Financial Post Magazine uses a "Bang for the Buck" formula to calculate the amount overpaid, taking into account CEO performance variables.

Source: "How Much Do They Make? Which Canadian CEOs Are Overpaid and Who Deserves More," *Financial Post Magazine*, November 9, 2017. http://business.financialpost.com/financial-post-magazine/from-biggest-bank-for-the-buck-to-most-overpaid-how-canadas-top-business-leaders-stack-up.

CASE INCIDENTS

Motivation for Leisure

"When I have time I don't have money. When I have money I don't have time," says Glenn Kelman, CEO of Redfin.[132] He is not alone. While many employees find themselves faced with 60-, 70-, or 80-hour weeks (and sometimes more), others who are unemployed can find themselves with too much time on their hands. Take Dennis Lee, a sales associate whose girlfriend is unemployed. She has time to spare, but he says her unemployment makes it "financially impossible for me to support the both of us, even if we just go on a small trip, and get a small hotel and stay for a couple of days."

Those who are employed and who may have the financial means to take a vacation often leave those vacation days on the table. The average Canadian employee receives almost four weeks of vacation time a year, and 76 percent take their full vacation time. The average US employee gets 2.6 weeks of vacation a year, yet only 43 percent take that time.

The challenge of taking leisure time does not seem to be a problem for employees in many European countries. Take the French, who get 30 days of vacation and say they take all of them. Employees in Spain, Italy, and Germany get about the same time off. Moreover, if you work in the European Union and get sick on vacation, the European Court of Justice states that you are entitled to take a make-up vacation.

Questions

1. Do you think North American employees are less motivated by vacation time than employees in other countries?

2. Why do you think Canadian workers often do not take all of their allotted vacation time, even when they may lose the benefit?

3. If many unemployed people spend around two hours per day looking for work, as some research indicates, how would you evaluate the impact of unemployment on work motivation? How would you spend your days if you were unemployed?

Pay Raises Every Day

How do you feel when you get a raise?[133] Happy? Rewarded? Motivated to work harder for that next raise? The hope of an increase in pay, followed by a raise, can increase employee motivation. However, the effect may not last. In fact, the "warm fuzzies" from a raise last less than a month, according to a recent study. If raises are distributed annually, performance motivation can dip for many months in between evaluations.

Some organizations have tried to keep the motivation going by increasing the frequency of raises. Currently, only about 5 percent of organizations give raises more than annually, but some larger employers like discount website retailer Zulily, Inc., assess pay quarterly. Zulily CEO Darrell Cavens would like to do so even more frequently. "If it wasn't a big burden, you'd almost want to work on it on a weekly basis," he said. That's because raises increase employee focus, happiness, engagement, and retention.

Jeffrey Housenbold, CEO of online photo publisher Shutterfly, Inc., also advocates frequent pay assessments, but for a different reason. The company gives bonuses four times a year to supplement its biannual raise structure as part of a review of employee concerns. "You can resolve problems early versus letting them fester," he said. Another reason is to increase feedback. Phone app designer Solstice Mobile gives promotions and salary increases six times a year; with this structure, Kelly O'Reagan climbed from $10/hour to $47.50/hour in four years. The company's CEO, John Schwan, said that young workers are especially motivated by the near-constant feedback. O'Reagan said, "Seeing that increase was like, 'Wow, this is quite different than what I had ever dreamed of.'"

You might be wondering how organizations can keep the dollar increases to employees flowing. Organizations are wondering, too. One tactic is to start employees at a low pay rate. Ensilon, a marketing services company, has coupled low starting salaries with twice-yearly salary reviews. Initial job candidates are skeptical, but most of the new hires earn at least 20 percent more after two years than they would with a typical annual raise structure.

No one is saying frequent pay raises are cheap, or easy to administrate. Pay itself is a complex issue, and maintaining pay equity adds another level of difficulty. Frequent pay reviews are motivating, but only for the people receiving them—for the others, it's a struggle to stay engaged. If a person has a track record of raises and then pay levels off, it can feel like a loss of identity as a strong performer rather than a natural consequence of achieving a higher level of pay. The frustration can lead to lower performance and increased turnover for high performers. CEO Schwan acknowledged, "It's definitely a risk."

Questions

1. Do you think frequent, small raises or annual, larger raises are more motivating? Why?

2. Do you think you would personally be more motivated by more frequent raises or by performance bonuses if the annual amounts were the same?

3. Annual pay raises in the United States are expected to be around 3 percent during the next few years. Do you think this percentage is motivating to employees? Why or why not?

FROM CONCEPTS TO SKILLS

1. *Combine tasks.* Managers should seek to take existing and fractionalized tasks and put them back together to form a new and larger module of work. This increases skill variety and task identity.

2. *Create natural work units.* The creation of natural work units means that the tasks an employee does form an identifiable and meaningful whole. This increases employee "ownership" of the work and improves the likelihood that employees will view their work as meaningful and important rather than as irrelevant and boring.

3. *Establish client relationships.* The client (who may be an "internal customer" or someone outside the organization) is the user of the product or service that the employee works on. Wherever possible, managers should try to establish direct relationships between employees and their clients. This increases skill variety, autonomy, and feedback for the employee.

4. *Expand jobs vertically.* Vertical expansion gives employees responsibilities and control that were formerly reserved for management. It seeks to partially close the gap between the "doing" and the "controlling" aspects of the job, and it increases employee autonomy.

Designing Enriched Jobs

How does management enrich an employee's job? The following suggestions, based on the JCM, specify the types of changes in jobs that are most likely to lead to improving their motivating potential (also see Exhibit 5-7).[134]

EXHIBIT 5-7 Guidelines for Enriching a Job

Suggested Action	Core Job Dimensions
Combine tasks	Skill variety
Form natural work units	Task identity
Establish client relationships	Task significance
Expand jobs vertically	Autonomy
Open feedback channels	Feedback

Source: HACKMAN, J.R., IMPROVING LIFE AT WORK, 1st Ed., ©1977. Reprinted and Electronically reproduced by permission of Pearson Education, Inc., Upper Saddle River, New Jersey.

5. *Open feedback channels.* By increasing feedback, employees not only learn how well they are performing their jobs, but also whether their performance is improving, deteriorating, or remaining at a constant level. Ideally, this feedback about performance should be received directly as the employee does the job, rather than from management on an occasional basis. For instance, at many restaurants you can find feedback cards on the table to indicate the quality of service received during the meal.

Practising Skills

You own and manage Sunrise Deliveries, a small freight transportation company that makes local deliveries of products for your customers. You have a total of nine employees—an administrative assistant, two warehouse personnel, and six delivery drivers.

The drivers' job is pretty straightforward. Each morning they come in at 7:30 a.m., pick up their daily schedule, and then drive off in their pre-loaded trucks to make their stops. They occasionally will also pick up packages and return them to the Sunrise warehouse, where they will be unloaded and redirected by the warehouse workers.

You have become very concerned with the high turnover among your drivers. Of your current six drivers, three have been working for you less than two months and only one's tenure exceeds six months. This is frustrating because you are paying your drivers more than many of the larger delivery companies like UPS and FedEx. This turnover is getting expensive because you constantly have to spend time finding and training replacements. It's also hard to develop a quality customer-service program when customers constantly see new faces. When you have asked departing drivers why they are quitting, common complaints include: "There's no room for advancement," "The job is boring," and "All we do is drive." What should you do to solve this problem?

Reinforcing Skills

1. Think of the worst job you have ever had. Analyze the job according to the five dimensions identified in the JCM. Redesign the job to make it more satisfying and motivating.

2. Spend one to three hours at various times observing employees in your college dining hall. What actions would you recommend to make these jobs more motivating?

6 Groups and Teamwork

How can
a team come
together and learn how
to serve lunch to
youngsters in summer
camp in just
a week?

1. Define *group* and *team*.
2. Analyze the growing popularity of teams in organizations.
3. Contrast the five types of teams.
4. Show how role requirements change in different situations.
5. Demonstrate how norms exert influence on an individual's behaviour.
6. Identify the five stages of group development.
7. Identify the characteristics of effective teams.
8. Explain the implications of diversity for group effectiveness.
9. Show how group size affects group performance.
10. Decide when to use individuals instead of teams.

Susan Wright

S usan Wright launched Toronto-based Summerlunch+ as a charity in the summer of 2016, after developing plans and raising funds during the previous eight months.[1] She had recognized for a number of years that lunch is not available in the summer for many children who receive subsidized lunches at school during the regular school year. Summerlunch+ provides healthy lunches and nutrition information through several summer camps in the Thornhill area of Toronto. This is an area where children are less likely to have access to healthy food. "There's so much benefit to eating well," she notes. "There is a ton of good research that supports that kids who eat a healthy meal do better in school and they do, overall, better in life."

Wright's challenge in launching the program was to create something that could run efficiently each summer without a lot of start-up costs. She relies on both secondary and post-secondary students to work in the program (in this photo, Wright [top right] appears with one of her teams). The Toronto District School Board provides local students through one of its volunteer programs, and has permitted the use of several of the area's public school kitchens. Canada Summer Jobs grants have allowed Wright to hire university students studying nutrition.

The students are all young, and there is often a difference in the maturity level of secondary and post-secondary students, yet Wright needs them to work together, and to start doing it quickly. The high school students help prepare the lunches and the university students need to earn their respect quickly. The program runs for six to eight weeks, delivering lunches to several of the summer camps in the area.

Developing teamwork among the student volunteers and leaders is one of the most important things Wright needs to do. For teams to excel, a number of conditions need to be met. Effective teams need wise leadership, a variety of resources, and a way to solve problems. Team members need to be dedicated and they need to build trust. In this chapter, we examine when it's best to have a team, how to create effective teams, and how to deal with diversity on teams.

OB IS FOR EVERYONE

- Ever wonder what causes flurries of activity in groups?
- Should individuals be paid for their teamwork or their individual performance?
- Why do some team members seem to get along better than others?
- Why don't some team members pull their weight?

THE BIG IDEA

Effective teams do not simply happen. They require attention to process, team composition, and rewards.

1 Define *group* and *team*.

Teams vs. Groups: What Is the Difference?

There is some debate whether groups and teams are really separate concepts or whether the two terms can be used interchangeably. We think that there is a subtle difference between the terms. A **group** is two or more people with a common relationship. Thus a group could be co-workers, or people meeting for lunch or standing at the bus stop. Unlike teams, groups do not necessarily engage in collective work that requires interdependent effort.

A **team**, on the other hand, generates positive synergy through coordination. The individual efforts result in a level of performance greater than the sum of the individual inputs. Groups become teams when they meet the following conditions:[2]

- Team members share *leadership*.

- Both individuals and the team as a whole share *accountability* for the work of the team.

- The team develops its own *purpose* or *mission*.

- The team works on *problem solving* continuously, rather than just at scheduled meeting times.

- The team's measure of *effectiveness* is the team's outcomes and goals, not individual outcomes and goals.

Thus, while not all groups are teams, all teams can be considered groups. Much of what we discuss in this chapter applies equally well to both, even though there are some important distinctions between the two.

2 Analyze the growing popularity of teams in organizations.

Why Have Teams Become So Popular?

The organization that *does not* use teams has become newsworthy. Teams are everywhere. How much time is spent working in teams? One study found that "the time spent by managers and employees in collaborative activities has ballooned by 50 percent or more" over the last two decades. It is not unusual at some companies for employees to spend three-quarters of their day communicating with co-workers.[3]

As organizations have restructured themselves to compete more effectively and efficiently, they have turned to teams as a better way to use employee talents. Management has found that teams are more flexible and responsive to changing events than are traditional departments or other forms of permanent groupings. Teams have the capability to quickly assemble, deploy, refocus, and disband. Teams also can be more motivational. Recall from the job characteristics model discussed in Chapter 5 that having greater task identity is one way of increasing motivation. Teams allow for greater task identity, with team members working on tasks together. However, teams are not necessarily appropriate in every situation. Are teams truly effective? What conditions affect their potential? How do members work together? These are some of the questions we will answer in this chapter.

3 Contrast the five types of teams.

Types of Teams

Teams can make products, provide services, negotiate deals, coordinate projects, offer advice, and make decisions.[4] In this section, first we describe the four most common kinds of teams you are likely to find in organizations:

- Problem-solving (or process-improvement) teams

- Self-managed (or self-directed) teams

- Cross-functional (or project) teams

- Virtual teams

group Two or more people with a common relationship.

team A group whose individual efforts result in performance that is greater than the sum of the individual inputs.

EXHIBIT 6-1 Four Types of Teams

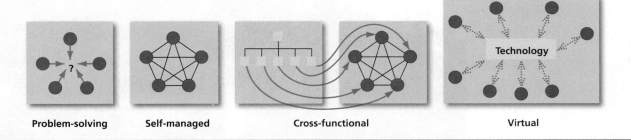

| Problem-solving | Self-managed | Cross-functional | Virtual |

The types of relationships that members within each team have to one another are shown in Exhibit 6-1. Later in this section, we also describe *multiteam systems*, which use a "team of teams" and are becoming increasingly widespread as work increases in complexity.

Problem-Solving Teams

Quality-control teams have been in use for many years. Originally seen most often in manufacturing plants, these were permanent teams that generally met at a regular time, sometimes weekly or daily, to address quality standards and any problems with the products made. The medical field in particular has recently implemented quality teams to improve their services in patient care. **Problem-solving teams** like these rarely have the authority to unilaterally implement their suggestions, but if their recommendations are paired with implementation processes, some significant improvements can be realized.

Self-Managed Teams

Problem-solving teams only make recommendations. Some organizations have gone further and created teams that also implement solutions and take responsibility for outcomes.

A **self-managed (or self-directed) team** is typically made up of 10 to 15 employees. The employees perform highly related or interdependent jobs; these teams take on some supervisory responsibilities.[5] Typically, the responsibilities include planning and scheduling of work, assigning tasks to members, making operating decisions, taking action on problems, and working with suppliers and customers. Fully self-managed teams even select their own members who evaluate one another's performance. When these teams are established, former supervisory positions can take on decreased importance and may even be eliminated.

Research results on the effectiveness of self-managed work teams have not been uniformly positive.[6] Some research indicates that self-managed teams may be more or less effective based on the degree to which team-promoting behaviours are rewarded. For example, one study of 45 self-managing teams of factory employees found that when team members perceived that economic rewards such as pay were dependent on input from their teammates, performance improved for both individuals and the team as a whole.[7]

A second area of research focus has been the impact of conflict on self-managed work team effectiveness. Some research indicates that self-managed teams are not effective when there is conflict. When disputes arise, members often stop cooperating and power struggles ensue, which lead to lower group performance.[8] However, other research indicates that when members feel confident they can speak up without being embarrassed, rejected, or punished by other team members—in other words,

problem-solving (or process-improvement) team A group of 5 to 12 employees from the same department who meet for a few hours each week to discuss ways of improving quality, efficiency, and the work environment.

self-managed (or self-directed) team A group of 10 to 15 employees who take on many of the responsibilities of their former managers.

Justin Lane/EPA/Newscom

Harley-Davidson Motor Company uses cross-functional teams at all levels of its organization in creating new products, such as its first electric motorcycle, shown here. From product conception to launch, cross-functional teams include Harley employees from product planning, engineering, design, marketing, manufacturing, and purchasing.

when they feel psychologically safe—conflict can be beneficial and boost team performance.[9]

Thirdly, research has explored the effect of self-managed work teams on member behaviour. Here again the findings are mixed. Although individuals on teams report higher levels of job satisfaction compared with other individuals, studies indicate they sometimes have higher absenteeism and turnover rates. One large-scale study of labour productivity in British establishments found that, although using teams improved individual (and overall) labour productivity, no evidence supported the claim that self-managed teams performed better than traditional teams with less decision-making authority.[10] On the whole, it appears that for self-managing teams to be advantageous, a number of facilitating factors must be in place. *Point/Counterpoint* on page 234 considers whether empowerment is key to effective teams.

Cross-Functional Teams

Starbucks created a team of individuals from production, global PR, global communications, and marketing to develop its VIA brand of instant coffee. The team's suggestions resulted in a product that would be cost-effective to produce and distribute and that was marketed with a tightly integrated, multifaceted strategy.[11] This example illustrates the use of **cross-functional (or project) teams**, made up of employees from about the same hierarchical level but different work areas, who come together to accomplish a task.

Cross-functional teams are an effective means for allowing people from diverse areas within an organization (or even between organizations) to exchange information, develop new ideas, solve problems, and coordinate complex projects. However, due to the high need for coordination, cross-functional teams are not easy to manage. First, it makes sense for power shifts to occur as different expertise is needed because

cross-functional (or project) team A group of employees at about the same hierarchical level, but from different work areas, who come together to accomplish a task.

the members are at roughly the same level in the organization, which creates leadership ambiguity. A climate of trust thus needs to be developed before shifts can happen without undue conflict.[12] Second, the early stages of development are often time-consuming as members learn to work with diversity and complexity. Third, it takes time to build trust and teamwork, especially among people from varying backgrounds with different experiences and perspectives.

In sum, the strength of traditional cross-functional teams is the collaborative effort of individuals with diverse skills from a variety of disciplines. When the unique perspectives of these members are considered, these teams can be very effective.

Virtual Teams

Problem-solving, self-managed, and cross-functional teams do their work face to face, whereas **virtual teams** use computer technology to tie together physically dispersed members in order to achieve a common goal.[13] They collaborate online—using communication links such as wide-area networks, corporate social media, videoconferencing, and email—whether members are nearby or continents apart. Nearly all teams today do at least some of their work remotely.

Virtual teams should be managed differently than face-to-face teams in an office, partially because virtual team members may not interact along traditional hierarchical patterns. Because of the complexity of interactions, research indicates that shared leadership of virtual teams may significantly enhance team performance, although the concept is still in development.[14] For virtual teams to be effective, management should ensure that (1) trust is established among team members (one inflammatory remark in a team-member email can severely undermine team trust); (2) team progress is monitored closely (so the team does not lose sight of its goals and no team member "disappears"); and (3) the efforts and products of the virtual team are publicized throughout

Lisa Brophy-Gervais

Queen's School of Business started an innovative executive MBA program in 2011 that relies on a virtual team of students. While there are three residential sessions during the program, most courses are taught in virtual boardroom sessions with students participating from home. "The program offers the same real-time connectivity and interactivity as our boardroom learning centres, but offers more accessibility to a top-ranked program to participants who wouldn't otherwise have the time or be able to physically be in a boardroom location on weekends," said Gloria Saccon, director of the executive MBA program.[15]

virtual team A team that uses computer technology to tie together physically dispersed members in order to achieve a common goal.

OB IN ACTION

Managing Virtual Teams

Establishing trust and commitment, encouraging communication, and assessing team members pose tremendous challenges for virtual team managers. Here are a few tips to make the process easier:

→ Establish **regular times** for group interaction.

→ Set up **firm rules** for communication.

→ Use **visual forms of communication** where possible.

→ **Copy the style of face-to-face teams**. For example, allow time for informal chitchat and socializing, and celebrate achievements.

→ **Give and receive feedback** and offer assistance on a regular basis. Be persistent with people who are not communicating with you or one another.

→ Agree on **standard technology** so all team members can work together easily.

→ Consider using **360-degree feedback** to better understand and evaluate team members.

→ Provide a **virtual meeting room** via an intranet, website, or bulletin board.

→ Note which employees **effectively use email** to build team rapport.

→ **Smooth the way for the next assignment** if membership on the team, or the team itself, is not permanent.

→ **Be available** to employees, but don't wait for them to seek you out.

→ Encourage **informal, off-line conversation** between team members.[16]

the organization (so the team does not become invisible).[17] For even more tips, see *OB in Action—Managing Virtual Teams*.

It would be a mistake to think virtual teams are an easy substitute for face-to-face teams. While the geographical reach and immediacy of online communication make virtual teams a natural development, and while virtual teams can contribute to environmental sustainability, as *Focus on Ethics* shows, managers must make certain this type of team is the optimal choice for the desired outcome and then maintain an oversight role throughout the collaboration.

Multiteam Systems

The types of teams we have described so far are typically smaller, standalone teams, although their activities relate to the broader objectives of the organization. As tasks become more complex, teams often grow in size. Increases in team size are accompanied by higher coordination demands, creating a tipping point at which the addition of another member does more harm than good. To solve this problem, organizations use **multiteam systems**, collections of two or more interdependent teams that share a superordinate goal. In other words, multiteam systems are a "team of teams."[19]

To picture a multiteam system, imagine the coordination of response needed after a major car accident. There is the emergency medical services team, which responds first and transports the injured to the hospital. An emergency room team then takes over, providing medical care, followed by a recovery team. Although the emergency services team, the emergency room team, and the recovery team are technically independent, their activities are interdependent, and the success of one depends on the success of the others. Why? Because they all share the higher goal of saving lives.

Some factors that make smaller, more traditional teams effective do not necessarily apply to multiteam systems and can even hinder their performance. One study showed that multiteam systems performed better when they had "boundary spanners" whose jobs were to coordinate with members of the other subteams. This reduced the need for some team member communication, which was helpful because it reduced coordination demands.[20] Leadership of multiteam systems is also much different than for standalone teams. While leadership of all teams affects team performance, a multiteam leader must both facilitate coordination among teams and lead each team. Research indicated teams that received more attention and engagement from the organization's leaders felt more empowered, which made them more effective as they sought to solve their own problems.[21]

In general, a multiteam system is the best choice either when a team has become too large to be effective, or when teams with distinct functions need to be highly coordinated.

From Individual to Team Member

multiteam system A collection of two or more interdependent teams that share a superordinate goal; a team of teams.

To make sure Summerlunch+ starts off well on the first day of summer camp, Susan Wright hires the university students a few weeks before the program begins. This lets the leaders and the students share in an orientation, have fun, and get on the same page.[22] The high school students receive their orientation on the first day of the program, and are given clear directions about what needs to be done. The university students make sure that the high school students are kept busy, so that they are not distracted by their phones.

While the meals are being prepared, everyone is expected to be focused on one another and the job at hand. Clear instructions are given:

- Phones must be put away.
- Individuals can work with their best friend but only if both are working productively.
- Everyone must follow safe food handling practices.
- Everyone is expected to share the responsibility, and to give feedback at day's end to help everyone figure out what could be done better next time.

During the first few weeks of team building, Wright makes sure that everyone understands their mission. The students know that they are making lives better for young people in their community by ensuring they don't go hungry. "Charitable work is generally mission-driven and our students are all working for minimum wage. We believe it helps them to understand the big picture of their work and the impact they are having within their own community."

For either a group or a team to function, individuals have to achieve some balance between their own needs and the needs of the group. When individuals come together to form groups and teams, they bring with them their personalities and all their previous experiences. They also bring their tendencies to act in different ways at different times, depending on the effects that different situations and different people have on them.

One way to think of these differences is in terms of possible pressures that individual group members put on one another through roles, norms, and status expectations, as *OB in the Workplace* indicates. As we consider the process of how individuals learn to work in

FOCUS ON ETHICS
Virtual Teams Leave a Smaller Carbon Footprint

Should virtual teams be used even more? Despite being in different countries, or even on different continents, many teams in geographically dispersed locations are able to communicate effectively without meeting face to face, thanks to technology such as videoconferencing, instant messaging, and email.[18] In fact, members of some of these virtual teams may never meet each other in person. Although the merits of face-to-face vs. electronic communication have been debated, there may be a strong ethical argument for virtual teams. Keeping team members where they are, as opposed to having them travel every time they need to meet, may be a more environmentally responsible choice. A very large proportion of airline, rail, and car transport is for business purposes and contributes greatly to global carbon dioxide emissions. When teams are able to meet virtually rather than face to face, they dramatically reduce their carbon footprint.

Here are several ways that virtual teams can be harnessed for greater sustainability:

1. Encourage all team members to think about whether a face-to-face meeting is really necessary and to try to use alternative communication methods whenever possible.
2. Communicate as much information as possible through virtual means, including email, telephone calls, and videoconferencing.
3. When travelling to team meetings, choose the most environmentally responsible methods possible. Also, check the environmental profile of hotels before booking rooms.
4. If the environmental savings are not enough motivation to reduce travel, consider the financial savings. According to a recent survey, businesses spend about 8 to 12 percent of their entire budget on travel. Communicating electronically can therefore result in two benefits: (a) It's cheaper and (b) it's good for the environment. . . . .

groups and teams, we will use the terms interchangeably. Many of the processes that each go through are the same, with the major difference being that teams within the workplace are often set up on a nonpermanent basis in order to accomplish projects.

OB IN THE WORKPLACE

Turning Around a Losing Team

Can one star performer make a team successful? The Winnipeg Blue Bombers won 3 games in 2013 and 9 of 36 from 2012 to 2013.[23] By early August 2014, though, fans thought maybe the team had turned its fate around, with a 5 to 1 winning record on August 6, the best in the West Division.

The Bombers hired quarterback Drew Willy before the 2014 season started, and he received some of the credit for making a difference, earning two CFL Offensive Player of the Week titles playing for the Bombers. With the early winning streak, head coach Mike O'Shea praised Willy for his leadership and his confidence. "He knows he can do it . . . his belief in himself, his knowledge that he can get the job done spills over to his teammates. They recognize that he believes they are going to get it done."

Willy's skills and leadership were not enough to lead the Bombers to a winning season, however. The team won just one more game after August 6, losing 12 during the season. Despite the dismal record, sportswriter Gary Lawless noted that "Willy is the future in Winnipeg and this off-season will all be about giving him what he needs to succeed." The general view was that Willy had done all that he could do, but he needed a better team. O'Shea noted, as the team was headed into the last game of the season, that even with a losing record, team members were still expected to give their all in the final game. "They need to come and play. . . . If we've got the right group of guys who love to play football, then this is another opportunity for them to do what they love to do." ....

4 Show how role requirements change in different situations.

Roles

Shakespeare said, "All the world's a stage, and all the men and women merely players." Using the same metaphor, all group members are actors, each playing a **role**, a set of expected behaviour patterns of a person in a given position in a social unit. We are required to play a number of diverse roles, both on and off our jobs.

As we will see, one of the tasks in understanding behaviour is grasping the role that a person is currently playing. For example, on the job a person might have the roles of electrical engineer, member of middle management, and primary company spokesperson in the community. Off the job, there are still more roles: spouse, parent, church member, food bank volunteer, and coach of the softball team. Many of these roles are compatible; some create conflicts. For instance, how does one's religious involvement influence managerial decisions regarding meeting with clients on the Sabbath? We address role conflict below.

Role Conflict

Most roles are governed by **role expectations**, that is, how others believe a person should act in a given situation. For instance, there are certain expectations about how a manager should act while at work. However, if the manager is also a parent, and that manager's child woke up sick in the morning, the manager may be confronted by conflicting role expectations: go to work or remain with the sick child. This dilemma is role conflict. **Role conflict** arises when an individual finds that complying with one role requirement may make it more difficult to comply with another.[24] At the extreme, it can include situations in which two or more role expectations are mutually contradictory! A great deal of research demonstrates that work–family conflict is one of the most significant sources of stress for most employees.[25]

role A set of expected behaviours of a person in a given position in a social unit.

role expectations How others believe a person should act in a given situation.

role conflict A situation in which an individual finds that complying with one role requirement may make it more difficult to comply with another.

Within organizations, most employees are simultaneously in occupations, work groups, divisions, and demographic groups, and these identities can conflict when the expectations of one clash with the expectations of another.[26] During mergers and acquisitions, employees can be torn between their identities as members of their original organization and of the new parent company.[27] Multinational organizations also have been shown to lead to dual identification, with the local division and with the international organization.[28]

Role Ambiguity

Role ambiguity exists when a person is unclear about the expectations of his or her role. In teams, role ambiguity can lead to confusion, stress, and even bad feelings. For instance, suppose two group members each think that the other one is responsible for preparing the first draft of a report. At the next group meeting, neither brings a draft report, and both are annoyed that the other person did not do the work.

Groups benefit when individuals know their roles. Roles within groups and teams should be balanced. Edgar Schein, professor emeritus of the MIT Sloan School of Management, suggests that **role overload** occurs when what is expected of a person "far exceeds what he or she is able to do."[29] **Role underload** occurs when too little is expected of someone, and that person feels that he or she is not contributing to the group.

Norms

Have you ever noticed that golfers don't speak while their partners are putting? Why? The answer is "norms"!

Norms are acceptable standards of behaviour shared by group members that express what they ought and ought not to do under certain circumstances. It's not enough for group leaders to share their opinions—even if members adopt the leaders' views, the effect may last only three days![30] When agreed to by the group, norms influence behaviour with a minimum of external controls. Different groups, communities, and societies have different norms, but they all have them.[31]

5 Demonstrate how norms exert influence on an individual's behaviour.

Getty Images/Noah Graham

A study of 23 National Basketball Association teams found that "shared experience"—tenure on the team and time on court—tended to improve turnover and boost win–loss performance significantly. Why do you think teams that stay together longer tend to play better?

role ambiguity A person is unclear about his or her role.

role overload Too much is expected of someone.

role underload Too little is expected of someone, and that person feels that he or she is not contributing to the group.

norms Acceptable standards of behaviour within a group that are shared by the group's members.

OB IN ACTION

Creating a Team Charter

When you form a new team, you may want to develop a team charter, so that everyone agrees on the basic norms for group performance. Consider including answers to the following in your charter:

→ What are team members' **names and contact information** (e.g., phone, email)?

→ How will **communication** among team members take place (e.g., phone, email)?

→ What will the **team ground rules** be (e.g., where and when to meet, attendance expectations, workload expectations)?

→ How will **decisions** be made (e.g., consensus, majority vote, leader rules)?

→ What **potential conflicts** may arise in the team? Among team members?

→ How will **conflicts be resolved** by the group?[33]

Formalized norms are written up in organizational manuals that set out rules and procedures for employees to follow. But, by far, most norms in organizations are informal. You don't need someone to tell you that throwing paper airplanes or engaging in prolonged gossip sessions at the water cooler is an unacceptable behaviour when the "big boss from Toronto" is touring the office. Similarly, we all know that when we are in an employment interview discussing what we did not like about our previous job, there are certain things we should not talk about (such as difficulty in getting along with co-workers or our manager). There are other things it's appropriate to talk about (inadequate opportunities for advancement, or unimportant and meaningless work).

Norms can cover virtually any aspect of group behaviour.[32] Some of the most common norms have to do with issues such as

- *Performance.* How hard to work, the level of output, what kind of quality, levels of tardiness

- *Appearance.* Dress codes, when to look busy, when to "goof off," how to show loyalty

- *Social arrangement.* With whom to eat lunch, whether to form friendships on and off the job

- *Allocation of resources.* Pay, assignments, allocation of tools and equipment

OB in Action—Creating a Team Charter presents a way for teams to develop norms when the team first forms.

The "How" and "Why" of Norms

How do norms develop? Why are they enforced? A review of the research allows us to answer these questions.[34]

Norms typically develop gradually as group members learn what behaviours are necessary for the team to function effectively. Of course, critical events in the group might short-circuit the process and quickly prompt new norms. Most norms develop in one or more of the following four ways:

- *Explicit statements made by a group member.* Often, instructions from the group's supervisor or a powerful member establish norms. The team leader might specifically say that no personal phone calls are allowed during working hours or that coffee breaks must be no longer than 10 minutes.

- *Critical events in the group's history.* These set important precedents. A bystander is injured while standing too close to a machine and, from that point on, members of the work group regularly monitor one another to ensure that no one other than the operator gets within two metres of any machine.

- *Primacy.* The first behavioural pattern that emerges in a group frequently sets team expectations. Groups of students who are friends often choose seats near one another on the first day of class and become upset if an outsider takes "their" seats in a later class.

- *Carry-over behaviours from past situations.* Group members bring expectations with them from other groups to which they have belonged. Thus, work groups typically prefer to add new members who are similar to current ones in background and experience. This is likely to increase the probability that the expectations they bring are consistent with those already held by the group.

Groups don't establish or enforce norms for every conceivable situation, however. The norms that the groups will enforce tend to be those that are important to them.[35] What makes a norm important?

- *It facilitates the group's survival.* Groups don't like to fail, so they seek to enforce any norm that increases their chances for success. This means that groups try to protect themselves from interference from other groups or individuals.

- *It increases the predictability of group members' behaviours.* Norms that increase predictability enable group members to anticipate one another's actions and to prepare appropriate responses.

- *It reduces embarrassing interpersonal problems for group members.* Norms are important if they ensure the satisfaction of their members and prevent as much interpersonal discomfort as possible.

- *It allows members to express the central values of the group and clarify what is distinctive about the group's identity.* Norms that encourage expression of the group's values and distinctive identity help solidify and maintain the group.

Conformity

As a group member, you desire acceptance by the group. Thus, you are susceptible to conforming to the group's norms. Considerable evidence shows that the group can place strong pressures on individual members to change their attitudes and behaviours to conform to the group's standard.[36] There are numerous reasons for **conformity**, with recent research highlighting the importance of a desire to form accurate perceptions of reality based on group consensus, to develop meaningful social relationships with others, and to maintain a favourable self-concept.

The impact that group pressures for conformity can have on an individual member's judgment and attitudes was demonstrated in studies by psychologist Solomon Asch.[37] Asch found that subjects gave answers that they knew were wrong, but that were consistent with the replies of other group members, about 35 percent of the time. The results suggest that group norms can pressure us toward conformity. We desire to be one of the group and avoid being visibly different.

Research by University of British Columbia professor Sandra Robinson and colleague Anne O'Leary-Kelly indicates that conformity may explain why some work groups are more prone to antisocial behaviour than others.[38] Individuals working with others who exhibited antisocial behaviour at work were more likely to engage in antisocial behaviour themselves. Of course, not all conformity leads to negative behaviour. Other research has indicated that work groups can have more positive influences, leading to more prosocial behaviour in the workplace.[39]

Overall, research continues to indicate that conformity to norms is a powerful force in groups and teams.

Positive Norms and Group Outcomes

One goal of every organization with corporate social responsibility (CSR) initiatives is for its values to hold normative sway over employees. After all, if employees aligned their thinking with positive norms, these norms would become stronger and the probability of positive impact would grow exponentially. We might expect the same outcomes from political correctness (PC) norms. But what *is* the effect of strong positive norms on group outcomes? The popular thinking is that to increase creativity in groups, for instance, norms should be loosened. However, research on gender-diverse groups indicates that strong PC norms increase group creativity. Why? Clear expectations about male-female interactions reduce uncertainty about group expectations,[40]

conformity Adjusting one's behaviour to align with the norms of the group.

which allows the members to more easily express their creative ideas without combatting stereotype norms.

Positive group norms may well beget positive outcomes, but only if other factors are present, too. For instance, in a recent study, a high level of group extraversion predicted helping behaviours more strongly when there were positive cooperation norms.[41] As powerful as norms can be, though, not everyone is equally susceptible to positive group norms. Individual personalities factor in, too, as well as the level of a person's social identity with the group. Also, a recent study in Germany indicated that the more satisfied people were with their groups, the more closely they followed group norms.[42]

Negative Norms and Group Outcomes

Matthew is frustrated by a co-worker who constantly spreads malicious and unsubstantiated rumours about him. Aisha is tired of a member of her work group who, when confronted with a problem, takes out his frustration by yelling and screaming at her and other members. Mi-Cha recently quit her job as a dental hygienist after being sexually harassed by her employer.

What do these illustrations have in common? They represent employees exposed to acts of deviant workplace behaviour.[43] As we discussed in Chapter 3, counterproductive work behaviour (CWB) or **deviant workplace behaviour** (also called *antisocial behaviour* or *workplace incivility*) is voluntary behaviour that violates significant organizational norms and, in so doing, threatens the well-being of the organization or its members. Exhibit 6-2 provides a typology of deviant workplace behaviours, with examples of each.

Few organizations will admit to creating or condoning conditions that encourage and maintain deviant behaviours. Yet they exist. For one, as we discussed before, a work group can become characterized by positive or negative attributes. When those attributes are negative, such as when a work group is high in psychopathy and aggression, the characteristics of deceit, amorality, and intent to harm others are pronounced.[44] Second, employees have been reporting an increase in rudeness and disregard toward others by bosses and co-workers in recent years. Workplace incivility, like many other deviant behaviours, has many negative outcomes for the victims.[45] Nearly half of employees who have suffered this incivility say it has led them to think about changing jobs; 12 percent actually quit because of it.[46] Also, a study of nearly 1500 respondents found that in addition to increasing turnover intentions, incivility at work increased reports of psychological stress and physical illness.[47] Third, research suggests that a lack of sleep,

EXHIBIT 6-2 Typology of Deviant Workplace Behaviour

Category	Examples
Production	Leaving early Intentionally working slowly Wasting resources
Property	Sabotage Lying about hours worked Stealing from the organization
Political	Showing favouritism Gossiping and spreading rumours Blaming co-workers
Personal aggression	Sexual harassment Verbal abuse Stealing from co-workers

Sources: S. H. Appelbaum, G. D. Iaconi, and A. Matousek, "Positive and Negative Deviant Workplace Behaviors: Causes, Impacts, and Solutions," *Corporate Governance* 7, no. 5 (2007), pp. 586–598; and R. W. Griffin, and A. O'Leary-Kelly, *The Dark Side of Organizational Behavior* (New York: Wiley, 2004).

deviant workplace behaviour
Voluntary behaviour that violates significant organizational norms and, in so doing, threatens the well-being of the organization or its members. Also called *antisocial behaviour* or *workplace incivility*.

which is often caused by heightened work demands and which hinders a person's ability to regulate emotions and behaviours, can lead to deviant behaviour. As organizations have tried to do more with less, pushing their employees to work extra hours, they may indirectly be facilitating deviant behaviour.[48]

Like norms in general, employees' antisocial actions are shaped by the group context within which they work. Evidence demonstrates deviant workplace behaviour is likely to flourish where it's supported by group norms.[49] For example, workers who socialize either at or outside work with people who are frequently absent from work are more likely to be absent themselves.[50] Thus, when deviant workplace norms surface, employee cooperation, commitment, and motivation are likely to suffer.

What are the consequences of workplace deviance for groups? Some research suggests a chain reaction occurs in groups with high levels of dysfunctional behaviour.[51] The process begins with negative behaviours like shirking, undermining co-workers, or being generally uncooperative. As a result of these behaviours, the group collectively starts to have negative moods. These negative moods then result in poor coordination of effort and lower levels of group performance.

Stages of Group and Team Development

> As the student workers at Summerlunch+ prepared to meet the youngsters they would be feeding, they faced a number of questions. What would the work be like? Would everyone like the food? Who would really be in charge? Would the program be successful? To build a successful team that produces high-quality work, the employees of Summerlunch+ had to go through several stages. What stages do teams go through as they develop?

When people get together for the first time with the purpose of achieving some objective, they discover that acting as a team is not something simple, easy, or genetically programmed. Working in a group or team is often difficult, particularly in the initial stages, when people don't necessarily know one another. As time passes, groups and teams go through various stages of development, although the stages are not necessarily exactly the same for each group or team. In this section, we discuss two models of group development. The five-stage model describes the standardized sequence of stages groups pass through. The punctuated-equilibrium model describes the pattern of development specific to temporary groups with deadlines. These models can be applied equally to groups and teams.

The Five-Stage Model

As shown in Exhibit 6-3, the five-stage group-development model has groups proceeding through the distinct stages of *forming, storming, norming, performing,* and *adjourning.*[52] Although we now know that not all groups pass through these stages in a linear fashion, the five-stage model of group development can still help in addressing any anxieties you might have about working in groups and teams. The model shows how individuals move from being independent to working interdependently with group members.

- *Stage I: Forming.* Think about the first time you met with a new team. Do you remember how some people seemed silent and others felt confused about the task you were to accomplish? Those feelings arise during the first stage of group development, known as **forming**. Forming is characterized by a great deal of uncertainty about the team's purpose, structure, and leadership. Members are "testing the waters" to determine what types of behaviour are acceptable. This stage is complete when members have begun to think of themselves as part of a team.

- *Stage II: Storming.* Do you remember how some people in your team just did not seem to get along, and sometimes power struggles even emerged? These

6 Identify the five stages of group development.

forming The first stage in group development, characterized by much uncertainty.

EXHIBIT 6-3 Stages of Group Development and Accompanying Issues

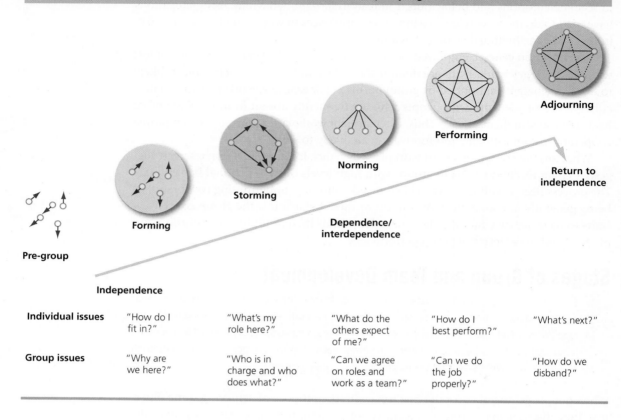

Individual issues	"How do I fit in?"	"What's my role here?"	"What do the others expect of me?"	"How do I best perform?"	"What's next?"
Group issues	"Why are we here?"	"Who is in charge and who does what?"	"Can we agree on roles and work as a team?"	"Can we do the job properly?"	"How do we disband?"

reactions are typical of the **storming** stage, which is one of intragroup conflict. Members accept the existence of the team, but resist the constraints that the team imposes on individuality. Furthermore, there is conflict over who will control the team. When this stage is complete, a relatively clear hierarchy of leadership will emerge within the team.

Some teams never really emerge from the storming stage, or they move back and forth through storming and the other stages. A team that remains forever planted in the storming stage may have less ability to complete the task because of all the interpersonal problems.

- *Stage III: Norming.* Many teams resolve the interpersonal conflict and reach the third stage, in which close relationships develop and the team demonstrates cohesiveness. There is now a strong sense of team identity and camaraderie. This **norming** stage is complete when the team structure solidifies, and the team has assimilated a common set of expectations of what defines correct member behaviour.

- *Stage IV: Performing.* Next, and you may have noticed this in some of your own team interactions, some teams just seem to come together well and start to do their work. This fourth stage, when significant task progress is being made, is called **performing**. The structure at this point is fully functional and accepted. Team energy has moved from getting to know and understand one another to performing the task at hand.

- *Stage V: Adjourning.* For permanent work groups and teams, performing is the last stage in their development. However, for temporary committees, teams, task forces, and similar groups that have a limited task to perform, there is an **adjourning** stage. In this stage, the group prepares for its disbandment. High

storming The second stage in group development, characterized by intragroup conflict.

norming The third stage in group development, characterized by close relationships and cohesiveness.

performing The fourth stage in group development, when the group is fully functional.

adjourning The final stage in group development for temporary groups, where attention is directed toward wrapping up activities rather than task performance.

task performance is no longer the group's top priority. Instead, attention is directed toward wrapping up activities. Group members' responses vary at this stage. Some members are upbeat, basking in the group's accomplishments. Others may be depressed over the loss of camaraderie and friendships gained during the work group's life.

For some teams, the end of one project may mean the beginning of another. In this case, a team has to transform itself in order to get on with a new project that may need a different focus and different skills, and may need to take on new members. Thus the adjourning stage may lead to renewal of the team to get the next project started.

Putting the Five-Stage Model into Perspective

Many interpreters of the five-stage model have assumed that a group becomes more effective as it progresses through the first four stages. This assumption may be generally true, but what makes a group effective is actually more complex.[53] First, groups proceed through the stages of group development at different rates. Those with a strong sense of purpose and strategy rapidly achieve high performance and improve over time, whereas those with less sense of purpose actually see their performance worsen over time. Similarly, groups that begin with a positive social focus appear to achieve the "performing" stage more rapidly. Nor do groups always proceed clearly from one stage to the next. Storming and performing can occur simultaneously, and groups can even regress to previous stages.

The five-stage model also ignores organizational context.[54] For instance, a study of a cockpit crew in an airliner found that, within 10 minutes, three strangers assigned to fly together for the first time had become a high-performing team. How could a team come together so quickly? The answer lies in the strong organizational context surrounding the tasks of the cockpit crew. This context provided the rules, task definitions, information, and resources needed for the team to perform. They did not need to develop plans, assign roles, determine and allocate resources, resolve conflicts, and set norms the way the five-stage model predicts. Nevertheless, a recent review of 40 years of research looking at this model suggests that it is still a good place to start when discussing group development.[55]

The Punctuated-Equilibrium Model

Temporary groups with deadlines don't seem to follow the previous model. Studies indicate that temporary groups with deadlines have their own unique sequence of action (or inaction):[56]

- The first meeting sets the group's direction.
- The first phase of group activity is one of inertia and thus slower progress.
- A transition takes place exactly when the group has used up half its allotted time.
- This transition initiates major changes.
- A second phase of inertia follows the transition.
- The group's last meeting is characterized by markedly accelerated activity.

This pattern, called the **punctuated-equilibrium model**, is shown in Exhibit 6-4. It's important for you to understand these shifts in group behaviour, if for no other reason than when you are in a group that is not working well or one that has got off to a slow start, you can start to think of ways to help the group move to a more productive phase.

Ever wonder what causes flurries of activity in groups?

punctuated-equilibrium model A set of phases that temporary groups go through that involves transitions between inertia and activity.

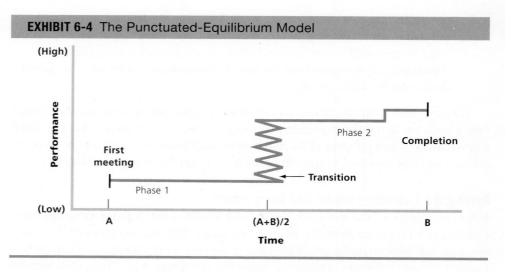

EXHIBIT 6-4 The Punctuated-Equilibrium Model

Phase 1

As both a team member and possibly a team leader, it's important that you recognize that the first meeting sets the team's direction. At the first meeting, the group's general purpose and direction is established, and then a framework of behavioural patterns and assumptions through which the team will approach its project emerges, sometimes in the first few seconds of the team's life. This is especially challenging when some team members are reluctant to speak up in meetings, as discussed in *Case Incident—Tongue-Tied in Teams* on page 236.

Once set, the team's direction becomes "written in stone" and is unlikely to be re-examined throughout the first half of the team's life. This is a period of inertia—that is, the team tends to stand still or become locked into a fixed course of action. Even if it gains new insights that challenge initial patterns and assumptions, the team is incapable of acting on these new insights in Phase 1. You may recognize that in some teams, during the early period of trying to get things accomplished, no one really did his or her assigned tasks. You may also recognize this phase as one where everyone carries out the tasks, but not in a very coordinated fashion. Thus, the team is performing at a relatively low state. This does not necessarily mean that it's doing nothing at all, however.

Phase 2

One of the more interesting discoveries made in work team studies was that teams experienced their transition precisely halfway between the first meeting and the official deadline, whether members spent an hour on their project or six months.[57] The midpoint appears to work like an alarm clock, heightening members' awareness that their time is limited and that they need to "get moving." When you work on your next team project, you might want to examine when your team starts to "get moving."

This transition ends Phase 1 and is characterized by a concentrated burst of changes, dropping of old patterns, and adoption of new perspectives. The transition sets a revised direction for Phase 2, which is a new equilibrium or period of inertia. In this phase, the team executes plans created during the transition period. The team's last meeting is characterized by a final burst of activity to finish its work. A number of studies support the basic premise of punctuated equilibrium, though not all of them found that the transition in the team occurred exactly at the midpoint.[58]

Applying the Punctuated-Equilibrium Model

We can use this model to describe typical experiences of student teams created for doing group term projects. At the first meeting, a basic timetable is established. Members size up one another. They agree they have nine weeks to do their project. The instructor's requirements are discussed and debated. From that point, the group meets regularly to carry out its activities. About four or five weeks into the project, however, problems are confronted. Criticism begins to be taken seriously. Discussion becomes more open. The group reassesses where it has been and aggressively moves to make necessary changes. If the right changes are made, the next four or five weeks find the group developing a first-rate project. The group's last meeting, which will probably occur just before the project is due, lasts longer than the others. In it, all final issues are discussed and details resolved.

In summary, the punctuated-equilibrium model characterizes deadline-oriented teams as exhibiting long periods of inertia, interspersed with brief revolutionary changes triggered primarily by their members' awareness of time and deadlines. To use the terminology of the five-stage model, the team begins by combining the *forming* and *norming* stages, then goes through a period of *low performing*, followed by *storming*, then a period of *high performing*, and, finally, *adjourning*.

This is not the only model of group stages by far, but it is a dominant theory with strong support. Keep in mind, however, that this model does not apply to all groups but is suited to the finite quality of temporary task groups working under a time deadline.[59]

CAREER OBJECTIVES

Can I Fudge the Numbers and Not Take the Blame?

I've got a great work group, except for one thing: The others make me omit negative information about our group's success that I'm in charge of as the treasurer. They gang up on me, insult me, and threaten me, so in the end I report what they want. They say omitting the negative information is not really wrong, and it doesn't violate our organization's rules, but on my own I would report everything. I need to stay in the group or I'll lose my job. If we are called out on the numbers, can I just put the blame on the whole group?

—Jean-Claude

Dear Jean-Claude:
The short answer is that, since you are in a leadership role in the group, you may not have the option of blaming the others. Further, you may be held individually accountable as a leader for the outcomes of this situation.

Your dilemma is not unusual. Once we think of ourselves as part of a collective, we want to stay in the group and can become vulnerable to pressures to conform. The pressure you are getting from multiple members can make you aware that you are in the minority in the group, and taunting can make you feel like an outsider or lesser member; therefore threats to harm your group standing may feel powerful.

So you have a choice: Submit to the pressure and continue misrepresenting your group's success, or adhere to the responsibility you have as the treasurer and come clean. From an ethical standpoint, we hope you don't consider the first option an acceptable choice. To make a change, you may be able to use social identification to your advantage. Rather than challenging the group as a whole, try meeting with individual group members to build trust, talking to each as fellow members of a worthy group that can succeed without any ethical quandaries. Don't try to build a coalition; instead,

build trust with individuals and change the climate of the group to value ethical behaviour. Then the next time you need to report the numbers, you can call upon the group's increased ethical awareness to gain support for your leadership decisions.

Sources: M. Cikara and J. J. Van Bavel, "The Neuroscience of Intergroup Relations: An Integrative Review," *Perspectives on Psychological Science* 9, no. 3 (2014), pp. 245–274; M. A. Korsgaard, H. H. Brower, and S. W. Lester, "It Isn't Always Mutual: A Critical Review of Dyadic Trust," *Journal of Management* 41, no. 1 (2015), pp. 47–70; R. L. Priem and P. C. Nystrom, "Exploring the Dynamics of Workgroup Fracture: Common Ground, Trust-With-Trepidation, and Warranted Distrust," *Journal of Management* 40, no. 3 (2014), pp. 674–795.

Creating Effective Teams

Building an effective team requires solid groundwork, which Susan Wright did with her Summerlunch+ student employees by explaining the norms, making sure there was enough supervision, and letting the employees develop confidence in their work.[60] After several weeks, Wright added more things to help the team develop.

Recognition and rewards can be part of building a solid team. Wright learned that the students wanted to go to Canada's Wonderland together. "In the background, we worked on getting tickets for the team. Once the students saw that we were listening and wanted to show our gratitude, we felt an immediate increase in commitment and energy."

By the fourth week, Wright and the others in charge expanded the roles of the student employees to bring them closer together. Students found their responsibility, creativity, and autonomy increased, unless a student seemed unable to handle these additional items. That way, students were not overwhelmed by changes, but the team could grow as a whole.

Finally, during the last week of camp, Wright sought more feedback from the students, asking them to tell the leaders about their roles and how they felt about their experience with Summerlunch+. Students were proud to have been part of this endeavour.

7 Identify the characteristics of effective teams.

When we consider team effectiveness, we refer to such objective measures as the team's productivity, managers' ratings of the team's performance, and aggregate measures of member satisfaction. Some of the considerations necessary to create effective teams are outlined next. However, we are also interested in team process. Exhibit 6-5 lists the characteristics of an effective team.

EXHIBIT 6-5 Characteristics of an Effective Team

1. **Clear purpose**	The vision, mission, goal, or task of the team has been defined and is now accepted by everyone. There is an action plan.
2. **Informality**	The climate tends to be informal, comfortable, and relaxed. There are no obvious tensions or signs of boredom.
3. **Participation**	There is much discussion, and everyone is encouraged to participate.
4. **Listening**	The members use effective listening techniques such as questioning, paraphrasing, and summarizing to get out ideas.
5. **Civilized disagreement**	There is disagreement, but the team is comfortable with this and shows no signs of avoiding, smoothing over, or suppressing conflict.
6. **Consensus decisions**	For important decisions, the goal is substantial but not necessarily unanimous agreement through open discussion of everyone's ideas, avoidance of formal voting, or easy compromises.
7. **Open communication**	Team members feel free to express their feelings on the tasks as well as on the group's operation. There are few hidden agendas. Communication takes place outside of meetings.
8. **Clear rules and work assignments**	There are clear expectations about the roles played by each team member. When action is taken, clear assignments are made, accepted, and carried out. Work is distributed among team members.
9. **Shared leadership**	While the team has a formal leader, leadership functions shift from time to time depending on the circumstances, the needs of the group, and the skills of the members. The formal leader models the appropriate behaviour and helps establish positive norms.
10. **External relations**	The team spends time developing key outside relationships, mobilizing resources, and building credibility with important players in other parts of the organization.
11. **Style diversity**	The team has a broad spectrum of team-player types including members who emphasize attention to task, goal setting, focus on process, and questions about how the team is functioning.
12. **Self-assessment**	Periodically, the team stops to examine how well it is functioning and what may be interfering with its effectiveness.

Source: Team players and teamwork: The new competitive business strategy by PARKER, GLENN M. Reproduced with permission of JOHN WILEY & SONS, INCORPORATED in the format Republish in a book via Copyright Clearance Center.

EXHIBIT 6-6 A Model of Team Effectiveness

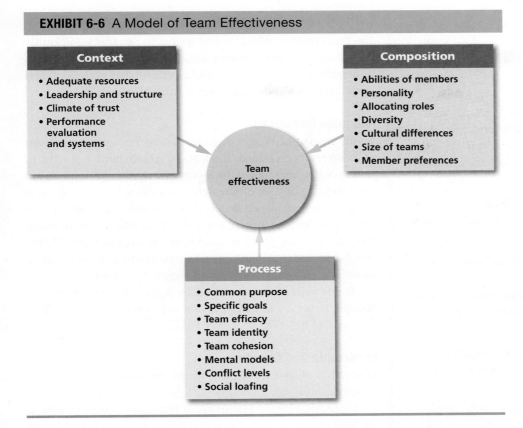

Context
- Adequate resources
- Leadership and structure
- Climate of trust
- Performance evaluation and systems

Composition
- Abilities of members
- Personality
- Allocating roles
- Diversity
- Cultural differences
- Size of teams
- Member preferences

Team effectiveness

Process
- Common purpose
- Specific goals
- Team efficacy
- Team identity
- Team cohesion
- Mental models
- Conflict levels
- Social loafing

There is no shortage of efforts that try to identify the factors that lead to team effectiveness. However, studies have taken what was once a large list of characteristics into a relatively focused model.[61] Exhibit 6-6 summarizes what we currently know about what makes teams effective.

Keep in mind two caveats as you review the issues that lead to effective teams:

- First, teams differ in form and structure. Since the model we present attempts to generalize across all varieties of teams, you need to be careful not to rigidly apply the model's predictions to all teams.[62] The model should be used as a guide, not as an inflexible prescription.

- Second, the model assumes that it's already been determined that teamwork is preferable over individual work. Creating "effective" teams in situations where individuals can do the job better is equivalent to solving the wrong problem perfectly.

What does *team effectiveness* mean in this model? Typically, it includes objective measures of the team's productivity, managers' ratings of the team's performance, and aggregate measures of member satisfaction. We can organize the key components of effective teams into three general categories. First are the resources and other *contextual* influences that make teams effective. The second relates to the team's *composition*. Finally, *process* variables are events within the team that influence effectiveness. We will explore each of these components next. *OB in Action—Harming Your Team* presents activities that can make a team ineffective. You might want to evaluate your own team experience against this checklist to give you some idea of how well your team is functioning, or to understand what might be causing problems for your team. Then consider the factors that lead to more effective teams below. For an applied look at the process of building an effective team, see the *Experiential Exercise* on page 235 which asks you to build a paper tower with teammates and then analyze how the team performed.

OB IN ACTION

Harming Your Team

→ **Refuse to share** issues and concerns. Team members refuse to share information and engage in silence, avoidance, and meetings behind closed doors where not all members are included.

→ **Depend** too much **on the leader**. Members rely too much on the leader and do not carry out their responsibilities.

→ **Fail to follow through** on decisions. Teams do not take action after decision making, showing that the needs of the team have low priority, or that members are not committed to the decisions that were made.

→ **Hide conflict**. Team members do not reveal that they have a difference of opinion, and this causes tension.

→ **Fail at conflict resolution**. Infighting, put-downs, and attempts to hurt other members damage the team.

→ **Form subgroups**. The team breaks up into smaller groups that put their needs ahead of the team as a whole.[63]

Context

The four contextual factors that appear to be most significantly related to team performance are adequate resources, effective leadership, a climate of trust, and a performance evaluation and reward system that reflects team contributions.

Adequate Resources

Teams are part of a larger organization system; every work team relies on resources outside the team to sustain itself. A scarcity of resources directly reduces the ability of a team to perform its job effectively. As one set of researchers concluded, after looking at 13 factors potentially related to team performance, "perhaps one of the most important characteristics of an effective work group is the support the group receives from the organization."[64] This support includes technology, adequate staffing, administrative assistance, encouragement, and timely information.

Teams must receive the necessary support from management and the larger organization if they are to succeed in achieving their goals.

Leadership and Structure

Leadership plays a crucial role in the development and success of teams.

Professor Richard Hackman of Harvard University, who is the leading expert on teams, suggests that the role of team leader involves the following:[66]

- Creating a real team rather than a team in name only

- Setting a clear and meaningful direction for the team's work

- Making sure that the team structure will support working effectively

Wadood Ibrahim (centre), CEO of Winnipeg-based Protegra, a management consulting firm, strongly believes in engaged teams. "We give Protegrans the autonomy and responsibility to do their own work, and as a result, they take on the challenge to do what they need to without strict hierarchical management structures in place."[65]

- Ensuring that the team operates within a supportive organizational context

- Providing expert coaching

Teams can't function if they can't agree on who is to do what and ensure all members share the workload. Agreeing on the specifics of work and how they fit together to integrate individual skills requires leadership and structure, either from management or from team members themselves. In self-managed teams, members absorb many of the duties typically assumed by managers. A manager's job then becomes managing *outside* (rather than inside) the team.

Leadership is especially important in multiteam systems. Here, leaders need to delegate responsibilities to teams and play the role of facilitator, making sure the teams work together rather than against one another.[67]

Recent research suggests that women may make better team leaders than men, as *Focus on Research* shows.

FOCUS ON RESEARCH
A Leader's Gender Can Affect Team Performance

Do men's and women's approaches to team leadership lead to different outcomes? "The more women participating equally in a project, the better the outcome," suggests Professor Jennifer Berdahl of the Sauder School of Business at the University of British Columbia.[68] Berdahl's research looked at 169 students enrolled in her organizational behaviour courses. She found that all of the teams started out with one person taking a leadership role. However, if the groups were predominantly male, the same person stayed in charge the entire time. In predominantly female teams, women shared leadership roles, and were more egalitarian in how they worked. Male-led teams, whether they were predominantly male groups or mixed-gender groups, received poorer grades on their projects than teams where women shared leadership roles.

Berdahl gives this advice to students: "In a creative project team, it's really important to ensure there is equal opportunity for participation." . . . .

Climate of Trust

Trust is the foundation of leadership; it allows a team to accept and commit to the leader's goals and decisions. Members of effective teams exhibit trust in their leaders.[69] They also trust one another. Interpersonal trust among team members facilitates cooperation, reduces the need to monitor one another's behaviour, and bonds individuals through the belief that members won't take advantage of them. Members are more likely to take risks and expose vulnerabilities when they can trust others on their team. Trust allows a team to accept and commit to its leader's goals and decisions. The overall level of trust in a team is important, but the way trust is dispersed among team members also matters. Trust levels that are asymmetric and imbalanced between team members can mitigate the performance advantages of a high overall level of trust—in such cases, coalitions form that often undermine the team as a whole.[70] *OB in Action—Building Trust* shows the dimensions that underlie the concept of trust. *Focus on Diversity* examines how trust varies across cultures.

OB IN ACTION
Building Trust

The following actions, in order of importance, help build one's trustworthiness.

→ **Integrity**—built through **honesty** and **truthfulness**.

→ **Competence**—demonstrated by technical and interpersonal **knowledge** and **skills**.

→ **Consistency**—shown by **reliability**, **predictability**, and **good judgment** in handling situations.

→ **Loyalty**—one's willingness to **protect** and **stand up** for another person.

→ **Openness**—one's willingness to **share ideas** and **information** freely.[71]

FOCUS ON DIVERSITY

Developing Team Members' Trust across Cultures

How do you develop trust on multicultural teams? The development of trust is critical in any work situation, but especially in multicultural teams, where differences in communication and interaction styles may lead to misunderstandings, eroding members' trust in one another.[72]

Some studies have shown that overall levels of trust differ across cultures. For example, Germans have been found to be less trusting of people from other countries, such as Mexicans and Czechs. Japanese employees have been found to be more trusting of their North American counterparts than the other way around, but only in long-lasting relationships. Chinese and US employees seem to trust each other equally.

There is some evidence that people from different cultures pay attention to different factors when deciding whether someone is trustworthy. Risk taking appears to be more critical to building trust for US and Canadian employees than for Japanese employees, perhaps reflecting that Canada and the United States are lower in uncertainty avoidance than Japan. Both Chinese and Mexican employees appear to rely more than US employees on emotional cues such as mutual understanding, openness, and social bonding, and less on cognitive cues such as reliability, professionalism, and economic cooperation.

When interacting with others from different cultures, whether in a formal team setting or not, it seems that what drives you to trust your colleagues may differ from what drives your colleagues to trust you, and recognizing these differences can help to facilitate higher levels of trust.

Trust is a perception that can be vulnerable to shifting conditions in a team environment. Also, trust is not unequivocally desirable. For instance, recent research in Singapore found that, in high-trust teams, individuals are less likely to claim and defend personal ownership of their ideas, but individuals who do still claim personal ownership are rated as lower contributors *by team members*.[73] This "punishment" by the team may reflect resentments that create negative relationships, increased conflicts, and reduced performance. For additional information on what leaders can do to improve the climate of trust in their organization, see *OB on the Edge—Trust*, on pages 240–245.

Performance Evaluation and Rewards

How do you get team members to be both individually and jointly accountable? Individual performance evaluations and incentives are not consistent with the development of high-performance teams. So in addition to evaluating and rewarding employees for their individual contributions, management should utilize hybrid performance systems that incorporate an individual member component to recognize individual contributions and a group to recognize positive team outcomes.[74] Some research has found that when team members did not trust their colleagues' ability, honesty, and dependability, they preferred individual-based rewards rather than team-based rewards. Even when trust improved over time from working together, there was still a preference for individual-based rewards, suggesting that "teams must have a very high level of trust for members to truly embrace group-based pay."[75]

> Should individuals be paid for their teamwork or their individual performance?

One additional consideration when deciding whether and how to reward team members is the effect of pay dispersion on team performance. Research by Nancy Langton, your Vancouver-based author, shows that when there is a large discrepancy in wages among group members, collaboration is lowered.[76] A study of baseball player salaries also found that teams where players were paid more similarly often outperformed teams with highly paid "stars" and lowly paid "scrubs."[77] How teams are structured and rewarded is the topic of *Focus on Research*.

FOCUS ON RESEARCH
The Impact of Rewards on Team Functioning

Can competitive teams learn to cooperate? Researchers at Michigan State University composed 80 four-person teams from undergraduate business students.[78] In a command-and-control computer simulation developed for the US Department of Defense, each team's mission was to monitor a geographic area, keep unfriendly forces from moving in, and support friendly forces. Team members played on networked computers, and performance was measured by both speed (how quickly they identified targets and friendly forces) and accuracy (the number of friendly fire errors and missed opportunities).

Teams were rewarded either cooperatively (in which case team members shared rewards equally) or competitively (in which case team members were rewarded based on their individual contributions). After playing a few rounds, the reward structures were switched so that the cooperatively rewarded teams were given competitive rewards and the competitively rewarded teams were now cooperatively rewarded.

The researchers found the initially cooperatively rewarded teams easily adapted to the competitive reward conditions and learned to excel. However, the formerly competitively rewarded teams could not adapt to cooperative rewards. It seems teams that start out being cooperative can learn to be competitive, but competitive teams find it much harder to learn to cooperate.

In a follow-up study, researchers found the same results: Cooperative teams more easily adapted to competitive conditions than competitive teams did to cooperative conditions. However, they also found competitive teams could adapt to cooperative conditions when given freedom to allocate their roles (as opposed to having the roles assigned). That freedom may lead to intrateam cooperation, and thus the process of structuring team roles helps the formerly competitive team learn to be cooperative. ....

Composition

The team composition category includes variables that relate to how teams should be staffed—the abilities and personalities of team members, the allocation of roles, diversity, cultural differences, size of the team, and members' preferences for teamwork. As you can expect, opinions vary widely about the type of members leaders want on their teams. Google tried to find a formula for building the perfect team, as *Focus on Research* notes.

Abilities of Members

It's true that we occasionally read about an athletic team of mediocre players who, because of excellent coaching, determination, and precision teamwork, beat a far more talented group. But such cases make the news precisely because they are unusual. A team's performance depends on part on the knowledge, skills, and abilities of its individual members.[80] Abilities set limits on what members can do and how effectively they will perform on a team.

Research reveals insights into team composition and performance. First, when solving a complex problem such as re-engineering an assembly line, high-ability teams—composed of mostly intelligent members—do better than lower-ability teams.

FOCUS ON RESEARCH
Building Teams

Is it possible to build the perfect team? HR people at Google set up a task force called Project Aristotle to find the secret to perfect teams.[79] The team thought an algorithm was out there, if they just studied enough teams. The task force studied 180 of the company's active teams and interviewed hundreds of employees.

"Who is on a team matters less than how the team members interact, structure their work, and view their contributions," said people operations analyst Julia Rozovsky. "Essentially, the best teams are made up of people who respect one another's emotions, can depend on each other, and actually care about what they're doing."

Rozovsky and the task force did find one important norm that seemed to apply to effective teams. This was the notion of psychological safety. For example, one engineer described his team leader as "direct and straightforward, which creates a safe space for you to take risks." Another engineer noted that his "team leader had poor emotional control," and this made him feel uneasy. Rozovsky concluded that in order to optimize teamwork, "We had to get people to establish psychologically safe environments." . . . . . .

High-ability teams are also more adaptable to changing situations; they can more effectively apply existing knowledge to new problems.

Finally, the ability of the team's leader matters. Smart team leaders help less-intelligent team members when they struggle with a task. A less intelligent leader can conversely neutralize the effect of a high-ability team.[81]

Exhibit 6-7 identifies some important skills that all team members can apply to help teams function well.

EXHIBIT 6-7 Teamwork Skills	
Orients team to problem-solving situation	Assists the team in arriving at a common understanding of the situation or problem. Determines the important elements of a problem situation. Seeks out relevant data related to the situation or problem.
Organizes and manages team performance	Helps team establish specific, challenging, and accepted team goals. Monitors, evaluates, and provides feedback on team performance. Identifies alternative strategies or reallocates resources to address feedback on team performance.
Promotes a positive team environment	Assists in creating and reinforcing norms of tolerance, respect, and excellence. Recognizes and praises other team members' efforts. Helps and supports other team members. Models desirable team member behaviour.
Facilitates and manages task conflict	Encourages desirable and discourages undesirable team conflict. Recognizes the type and source of conflict confronting the team and implements an appropriate resolution strategy. Employs "win-win" negotiation strategies to resolve team conflicts.
Appropriately promotes perspective	Defends stated preferences, argues for a particular point of view, and withstands pressure to change position for another that is not supported by logical or knowledge-based arguments. Changes or modifies position if a defensible argument is made by another team member. Projects courtesy and friendliness to others while arguing position.

Source: G. Chen, L. M. Donahue, and R. J. Klimoski, "Training Undergraduates to Work in Organizational Teams," *Academy of Management Learning & Education* 3, no. 1 (March 2004), p. 40.

Personality of Members

Teams have different needs, and people should be selected for the team on the basis of their personalities and preferences, as well as the team's needs for diversity and specific roles. We demonstrated in Chapter 2 that personality significantly influences individual behaviour. This assertion can also be extended to team behaviour.

> Why do some team members seem to get along better than others?

Some dimensions identified in the Big Five Personality Model are particularly relevant to team effectiveness.[82]

Conscientiousness is especially important to teams. Conscientious people are good at backing up other team members, and they are also good at sensing when their support is truly needed. Conscientious teams also have other advantages—one study found that behavioural tendencies such as organization, achievement orientation, and endurance were all related to higher levels of team performance.[83]

Team composition can be based on individual personalities to good effect. Suppose an organization needs to create 20 teams of 4 people each and has 40 highly conscientious people and 40 who score low on conscientiousness. Would the organization be better off (a) putting all the conscientious people together (forming 10 teams with the highly conscientious people and 10 teams of members low on conscientiousness) or (b) "seeding" each team with 2 people who scored high and 2 who scored low on conscientiousness?

Perhaps surprisingly, the evidence tends to suggest that option (a) is the best choice; performance across the teams will be higher if the organization forms 10 highly conscientious teams and 10 teams low in conscientiousness. The reason is that a team with varying conscientiousness levels will not work to the peak performance of its highly conscientious members. Instead, a group normalization dynamic (or simple resentment) will complicate interactions and force the highly conscientious members to lower their expectations, thus reducing the group's performance.[84]

What about the other traits? Teams with a high level of openness to experience tend to perform better, and research indicates that constructive task conflict *enhances* the effect. Open team members communicate better with one another and throw out more ideas, which makes teams composed of open people more creative and innovative.[85] Task conflict also enhances performance for teams with high levels of emotional stability.[86] It's not so much that the conflict itself improves performance for these teams, but that teams characterized by openness and emotional stability are able to handle conflict and leverage it to improve performance. The minimum level of team member agreeableness matters, too: Teams do worse when they have one or more highly disagreeable members, and a wide span in individual levels of agreeableness can lower productivity. Research is not clear on the outcomes of extraversion, but a recent study indicated that a high mean level of extraversion in a team can increase the level of helping behaviours, particularly in a climate of cooperation.[87] Thus the personality traits of individuals are as important to teams as the overall personality characteristics of the team.

Allocation of Roles

Teams have different needs, and members should be selected to ensure all the various roles are filled. A study of 778 major league baseball teams over a 21-year period highlights the importance of assigning roles appropriately.[88] As you might expect, teams with more experienced and skilled members performed better. However, the experience and skill of those in core roles who handled more of the workflow of the team, and were central to all work processes (in this case, pitchers and catchers), were especially vital. In other words, put your most able, experienced, and conscientious employees in the most central roles in a team.

EXHIBIT 6-8 Key Roles of Teams

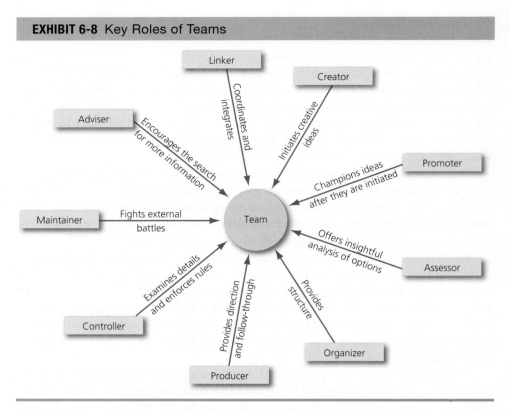

We can identify nine potential team roles (see Exhibit 6-8). Successful work teams have selected people to play all these roles based on their skills and preferences.[89] (On many teams, individuals will play multiple roles.) To increase the likelihood team members will work well together, managers need to understand the individual strengths each person can bring to a team, select members with their strengths in mind, and allocate work assignments that fit with members' preferred styles.

8 Explain the implications of diversity for group effectiveness.

Diversity of Members

Group diversity refers to the presence of a heterogeneous mix of individuals within a group. The degree to which members of a work unit (group, team, or department) share a common demographic attribute, such as age, gender, race, educational level, or length of service in the organization, is the subject of **organizational demography**. Organizational demography suggests that attributes such as age or the date of joining should help us predict turnover. The logic goes like this: Turnover will be greater among those with dissimilar experiences because communication is more difficult and conflict is more likely. Increased conflict makes membership less attractive, so employees are more likely to quit. Similarly, the losers of a conflict are more apt to leave voluntarily or be forced out.[90] The conclusion is that diversity negatively affects team performance.

Many of us hold the optimistic view that diversity should be a good thing—diverse teams should benefit from differing perspectives and do better. Two meta-analytic reviews show, however, that demographic diversity is essentially unrelated to team performance overall, while a third review suggests that race and gender diversity are actually negatively related to team performance.[91] Other research findings are mixed. One qualifier is that gender and ethnic diversity have more negative effects in occupations dominated by white or male employees, but in more demographically balanced

group diversity The presence of a heterogeneous mix of individuals within a group.

organizational demography The degree to which members of a work unit share a common demographic attribute, such as age, gender, race, educational level, or length of service in an organization, and the impact of this attribute on turnover.

occupations, diversity is less of a problem. Diversity in function, education, and expertise are positively related to team performance, but these effects are quite small and depend on the situation.

Proper leadership can improve the performance of diverse teams.[92] For example, one study of 68 teams in China found that teams diverse in terms of knowledge, skills, and ways of approaching problems were more creative, but only when their leaders were transformational and inspiring.[93]

Cultural Differences

We have discussed research on team diversity in race or gender. But what about diversity created by national differences? Like the earlier research, evidence here indicates that these elements of diversity interfere with team processes, at least in the short term,[94] but let's dig a little deeper: What about differences in cultural status? Though it's debatable, people with higher cultural status are usually in the majority or ruling race group of their nations. Researchers in the United Kingdom found that cultural-status differences affected team performance, whereby individuals in teams with more high cultural-status members than low cultural-status members realized improved performance . . . for *every* member.[95] This suggests not that diverse teams should be filled with individuals who have high cultural status in their countries, but that we should be aware of how people identify with their cultural status even in diverse group settings.

In general, cultural diversity seems to be an asset for tasks that call for a variety of viewpoints. But culturally heterogeneous teams have more difficulty learning to work with each other and solving problems. The good news is that these difficulties seem to dissipate with time.

Size of Teams

Most experts agree that keeping teams small is key to improving group effectiveness.[96] Amazon CEO Jeff Bezos uses the "two-pizza" rule, saying, "If it takes more than two pizzas to feed the team, the team is too big."[97] Psychologist George Miller claimed "the magical number [is] seven, plus or minus two," as the ideal team size.[98] Author and *Forbes* publisher Rich Karlgaard writes, "Bigger teams almost never correlate with a greater chance of success" because the potential connections between people grow exponentially as team size increases, complicating communications.[99]

Generally speaking, the most effective teams have five to nine members. Experts suggest using the smallest number of people who can do the task. Unfortunately, there is a pervasive tendency for managers to err on the side of making teams too large. While a minimum of four or five may be necessary to develop diversity of views and skills, managers seem to seriously underestimate how coordination problems can increase dramatically as team members are added. When teams have excess members, cohesiveness and mutual accountability decline, social loafing increases, and people communicate less. Members of large teams have trouble coordinating with one another, especially under time pressure. When a natural work unit is larger and you want a team effort, consider breaking the unit into subteams.[100]

Members' Preference for Teamwork

Not every employee is a team player. Given the option, many employees will select themselves *out* of team participation. When people who would prefer to work alone are required to team up, there is a direct threat to the team's morale.[101] This suggests that, when selecting team members, individual preferences should be considered, as well as abilities, personalities, and skills. High-performing teams are likely to be composed of people who prefer working as part of a team.

9 Show how group size affects group performance.

Han Chuanhao Xinhua News Agency/Newscom

Young employees of Alibaba's Tmall online shopping site celebrate their group's achievement of increasing the volume of sales orders during China's "Singles' Day" shopping event. Although social loafing is consistent with individualistic cultures, in collectivist societies such as China, employees are motivated by group goals and perform better when working in groups.

Team Processes

Process variables make up the final component of team effectiveness. The process category includes member commitment to a common purpose, establishment of specific goals, team efficacy, team identity, team cohesion, shared mental models, a managed level of conflict, and minimized social loafing. These will be especially important in larger teams, and in teams that are highly interdependent.[102]

Why are processes important to team effectiveness? Teams should create outputs greater than the sum of their inputs. Exhibit 6-9 illustrates how group processes can have an impact on a group's actual effectiveness.[103] Scientists often work in teams because they can draw on the diverse skills of various individuals to produce more meaningful research than researchers working independently—that is, they produce positive synergy, and their process gains exceed their process losses.

Common Plan and Purpose

Effective teams begin by analyzing the team's mission, developing goals to achieve that mission, and creating strategies for achieving the goals. Teams that consistently perform better have established a clear sense of what needs to be done and how.[104] This sounds obvious, but many teams ignore this fundamental process.

Members of successful teams put a tremendous amount of time and effort into discussing, shaping, and agreeing upon a purpose that belongs to them collectively and

EXHIBIT 6-9 Effects of Group Processes

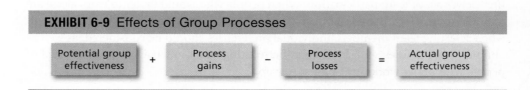

Potential group effectiveness + Process gains − Process losses = Actual group effectiveness

Courtesy of Freshii

Matthew Corrin, CEO of Toronto-based Freshii, a chain of healthy eating restaurants, is proud of the fact that more than 50 percent of his leadership team are women (Freshii's Jenny Hoshoian, Melissa Gallagher, and Ashley Dalziel are shown here). However, he didn't deliberately plan it that way. "We hire wicked smart people who align with our culture and mission, have experience in brands that we admire and share our passion for helping citizens of the world live better."[105]

individually. This common purpose, when accepted by the team, becomes the equivalent of what GPS is to a ship captain—it provides direction and guidance under any conditions. Like a ship following the wrong course, teams that don't have good planning skills are doomed, executing the wrong plan.[106] Teams should agree on whether their purpose is to learn about and master a task or simply to perform the task; evidence suggests that differing perspectives on learning vs. performance lead to lower levels of team performance overall.[107]

Effective teams show **reflexivity**, meaning that they reflect on and adjust their purpose when necessary. A team must have a good plan, but it needs to be willing and able to adapt when conditions call for it.[108] Interestingly, some evidence suggests that teams high in reflexivity are better able to adapt to conflicting plans and goals among team members.[109]

Specific Goals

Successful teams translate their common purpose into specific, measurable, and realistic performance goals. Just as goals can lead individuals to higher performance (see Chapter 4), they can also energize teams. Specific goals facilitate clear communication. They also help teams maintain their focus on achieving results.

Consistent with the research on individual goals, team goals should be challenging. Difficult but achievable goals have been found to raise team performance on those criteria for which they are set. So, for instance, goals for quantity tend to increase quantity, goals for speed tend to increase speed, goals for accuracy tend to increase accuracy, and so on.[110]

Team Efficacy

Effective teams have confidence in themselves. They believe they can succeed. We call this **team efficacy**.[111] Teams that have been successful raise their beliefs about future

reflexivity A team characteristic of reflecting on and adjusting the master plan when necessary.

team efficacy A team's collective belief that they can succeed at their tasks.

success, which, in turn, motivates them to work harder. In addition, teams that have a shared knowledge of individual capabilities can strengthen the link between team members' self-efficacy and their individual creativity because members can more effectively solicit informed opinions from their teammates.[112]

What, if anything, can management do to increase team efficacy? Two possible options are helping the team to achieve small successes and providing skills training. Small successes build team confidence. As a team develops an increasingly stronger performance record, it also increases the collective belief that future efforts will lead to success. In addition, managers should consider providing training to improve members' technical and interpersonal skills. The greater the abilities of team members, the greater the likelihood that the team will develop confidence and the capability to deliver on that confidence.

Team Identity

When people connect emotionally with the teams they are in, they are more likely to invest in their relationship with those teams. For example, research with soldiers in the Netherlands indicated that individuals who felt included and respected by team members became more willing to work hard for their teams, even though as soldiers they were already called upon to be dedicated to their units. Therefore, by recognizing individuals' specific skills and abilities, as well as creating a climate of respect and inclusion, leaders and members can foster positive **team identity** and improved team outcomes.[113]

Organizational identity is important, too. Rarely do teams operate in a vacuum—more often teams interact with other teams, requiring interteam coordination. Individuals with a positive team identity but without a positive organizational identity can become fixed to their teams and unwilling to coordinate with other teams within the organization.[114]

Team Cohesion

Have you ever been a member of a team that really "gelled," one in which team members felt connected? The term **team cohesion** means members are emotionally attached to one another and motivated toward the team because of their attachment. Team cohesion is a useful tool to predict team outcomes. For example, a large study in China recently indicated that if team cohesion is high and tasks are complex, costly investments in promotions, rewards, training, and so forth yield greater profitable team creativity. Teams with low cohesion and simple tasks, on the other hand, are not likely to respond to incentives with greater creativity.[115] Working as a cohesive team can be a matter of survival, as described in *Case Incident—Intragroup Trust and Survival* on page 237.

Team cohesion is a strong predictor of team performance such that when cohesion is harmed, performance may be, too. Negative relationships are one driver of reduced cohesion. To mitigate this effect, teams can foster high levels of interdependence and high-quality interpersonal interactions. *OB in Action—Increasing Group Cohesiveness* indicates how to increase both socio-emotional and instrumental cohesiveness.

Mental Models

Effective teams share accurate **mental models**—organized mental representations of the key elements within a team's environment that team members share.[116] (If team mission and goals pertain to *what* a team needs to be effective, mental models pertain to *how* a team does its work.) If team members have the wrong mental models, which is particularly likely to happen with teams under acute stress, their

team identity A team member's affinity for and sense of belongingness to his or her team.

team cohesion A situation when team members are emotionally attached to one another and motivated toward the team because of their attachment.

mental models Team members' knowledge and beliefs about how the work gets done by the team.

performance suffers.[117] One review of 65 independent studies found that teams with shared mental models engaged in more frequent interactions with one another, were more motivated, had more positive attitudes toward their work, and had higher levels of objectively rated performance.[118] If team members have different ideas about how to do things, however, the team will fight over methods rather than focus on what needs to be done.[119]

Conflict Levels

Conflict has a complex relationship with performance, and it's not necessarily bad. *Relationship conflicts*—those based on interpersonal incompatibility, tension, and animosity toward others—are almost always dysfunctional.[120] However, when teams are performing nonroutine activities, disagreements about task content (called *task conflicts*) stimulate discussion, promote critical assessment of problems and options, and can lead to better team decisions. A study conducted in China found that moderate levels of task conflict during the initial phases of team performance were positively related to team creativity, but both very low and very high levels of task conflict were negatively related to team performance.[121] In other words, both too much and too little disagreement about how a team should initially perform a creative task can inhibit performance.

The way conflicts are resolved can also make the difference between effective and ineffective teams. A study of ongoing comments made by 37 autonomous work groups showed that effective teams resolved conflicts by explicitly discussing the issues, whereas ineffective teams had unresolved conflicts that were focused more on personalities and the way things were said.[122]

Which teams are more likely to have conflicts than others? It's not a simple answer. While we may presume that diversity increases conflicts, the answer is likely to be much more subtle than that. For example, recent research in Spain found that when individual team members varied greatly in their perceptions of organizational support, task conflict increased, communication decreased, and ultimately team performance suffered.[123] If the researchers had instead compared only the average level of organizational support given to the team, rather than how members perceived the support, they would have missed the correct causal links. Thus we need to be careful not to overgeneralize. *OB in Action—Reducing Team Conflict* presents tactics that can be used to manage interpersonal conflict.

Social Loafing

As we noted earlier, individuals can engage in social loafing and coast on the group's effort when their particular contributions (or lack thereof) can't be identified. Effective teams undermine this tendency by making members individually

OB IN ACTION

Increasing Group Cohesiveness

To increase socio-emotional cohesiveness:

→ Keep the group relatively **small**.

→ Strive for a **favourable public image** to increase the status and prestige of belonging.

→ Encourage **interaction** and **cooperation**.

→ Emphasize members' **common characteristics** and interests.

→ **Point out environmental threats** (e.g., competitors' achievements) to rally the group.

To increase instrumental cohesiveness:

→ Regularly update and **clarify the group's goal(s)**.

→ Give every group member a **vital "piece of the action."**

→ Channel each group member's special talents toward the **common goal(s)**.

→ **Recognize** and equitably reinforce **every member's contributions**.

→ Frequently remind group members they **need one another** to get the job done.[124]

OB IN Action

Reducing Team Conflict

→ Work with **more, rather than less, information**, and debate on the basis of facts.

→ Develop **multiple alternatives** to enrich the level of debate.

→ Develop commonly agreed-upon **goals**.

→ Use **humour** when making tough decisions.

→ Maintain a **balanced power** structure.

→ Resolve issues **without forcing consensus**.[125]

and jointly accountable for the team's purpose, goals, and approach.[126] Therefore, members should be clear on what they are individually and jointly responsible for on the team. *From Concepts to Skills* on pages 238–239 discusses how to conduct effective team meetings. For more about social loafing, read the *Ethical Dilemma* on pages 235–236.

Why don't some team members pull their weight?

10 Decide when to use individuals instead of teams.

Beware! Teams Are Not Always the Answer

Despite considerable success in the use of teams, they are not necessarily appropriate in all situations. Teamwork takes more time and often more resources than individual work. Teams have increased communication demands, conflicts to be managed, and meetings to be run. So the benefits of using teams have to exceed the costs, and that is not always the case.[127] A study done by Statistics Canada found that the introduction of teamwork lowered turnover in the service industries, for both high- and low-skilled employees. However, manufacturing companies experienced higher turnover if they introduced teamwork and formal teamwork training, compared with not doing so (15.8 percent vs. 10.7 percent).[128]

How do you know if the work of your group would be better done in teams? It's been suggested that three tests be applied to see if a team fits the situation:[129]

- *Can the work be done better by more than one person?* Simple tasks that don't require diverse input are probably better left to individuals.

- *Does the work create a common purpose or set of goals for the people in the group that is more than the sum of individual goals?* For instance, the service departments of many new-car dealers have introduced teams that link customer service personnel, mechanics, parts specialists, and sales representatives. Such teams can better manage collective responsibility for ensuring that customers' needs are properly met.

- *Are the members of the group interdependent?* Teams make sense where there is interdependence among tasks—where the success of the whole depends on the success of each one, *and* the success of each one depends on the success of the others. Soccer, for instance, is an obvious *team* sport because of the interdependence of the players. Swim teams, by contrast, except for relays, rely heavily on individual performance to win a meet. They are groups of individuals performing individually, whose total performance is merely the aggregate summation of their individual performances.

GLOBAL IMPLICATIONS

Below we consider global research on two themes: team cultural diversity and group cohesiveness.

Team Cultural Diversity and Team Performance

How do teams composed of members from different countries perform? The evidence indicates that the cultural diversity of team members interferes with team processes, at least in the short term.[130] However, cultural diversity does seem to be an asset for tasks that call for a variety of viewpoints. But culturally heterogeneous team members have more difficulty learning to work with one another and solving problems.

Researchers in the United Kingdom found that cultural-status differences affected team performance, whereby individuals in teams with more high cultural-status members than low cultural-status members realized improved performance . . . for *every* member.[131] Another study found that teams in the European Union made up of members from collectivistic and individualistic countries benefited equally from group goals.[132]

Group Cohesiveness

Researchers studied teams from an international bank with branches in the United States (an individualistic culture) and in Hong Kong (a collectivistic culture) to determine the factors that affected group cohesiveness.[133] Teams were entirely composed of individuals from the branch country. The results showed that, regardless of what culture the teams were from, giving teams difficult tasks and more freedom to accomplish those tasks created a more tight-knit group. Consequently, team performance was enhanced.

However, the teams differed in the extent to which increases in task complexity and autonomy resulted in greater group cohesiveness. Teams in individualistic cultures responded more strongly than did teams in collectivistic cultures, became more united and committed, and, as a result, received higher performance ratings from their supervisors than did teams from collectivistic cultures.

A large study in China recently indicated that if team cohesion is high and tasks are complex, costly investments in promotions, rewards, training, and so forth yield greater profitable team creativity. Teams with low cohesion and simple tasks, on the other hand, are not likely to respond to incentives with greater creativity.[134]

These findings suggest that individuals from collectivistic cultures already have a strong predisposition to work together as a group, so there is less need for increased cohesiveness. However, if cohesion is low, teams will not perform as well. Managers in individualistic cultures may need to work harder to increase team cohesiveness. One way to do this is to give teams more challenging assignments and provide them with more independence.

Summary

We can draw several implications from our discussion of groups. First, norms control behaviour by establishing standards of right and wrong. Second, cohesiveness may influence a group's level of productivity, depending on the group's performance-related norms. Third, role conflict is associated with job-induced tension and job dissatisfaction.[135] Groups can be carefully managed toward positive organizational outcomes and optimal decision-making.

Few trends have influenced jobs as much as the massive movement of teams into the workplace. Working on teams requires employees to cooperate with others, share information, confront differences, and sublimate personal interests for the greater good of the team. Understanding the distinctions between problem-solving, self-managed, cross-functional, and virtual teams as well as multiteam systems helps determine the appropriate applications for team-based work. Concepts such as reflexivity, team efficacy, team identity, team cohesion, and mental models bring to light important issues relating to team context, composition, and processes. For teams to function optimally, careful attention must be given to hiring, creating, and rewarding team players. Still, effective organizations recognize that teams are not always the best method for getting the work done efficiently. Careful discernment and an understanding of organizational behaviour are needed.

LESSONS LEARNED

- A good team will achieve balance between individual needs and team needs.
- To create effective teams, members should be rewarded for engaging in team behaviour rather than individual behaviour.
- Teams should not be created for tasks that could be better done by individuals.

SNAPSHOT SUMMARY

Teams vs. Groups: What Is the Difference?
- Why Have Teams Become So Popular?
- Types of Teams

From Individual to Team Member
- Roles
- Norms

Stages of Group and Team Development
- The Five-Stage Model
- The Punctuated-Equilibrium Model

Creating Effective Teams
- Context
- Composition
- Team Processes

Beware! Teams Are Not Always the Answer

MyLab Management

 PERSONAL INVENTORY ASSESSMENT

Study, practise, and explore real business situations with these helpful resources:

- **Study Plan:** Check your understanding of chapter concepts with self-study quizzes.
- **Online Lesson Presentations:** Study key chapter topics and work through interactive assessments to test your knowledge and master management concepts.
- **Videos:** Learn more about the management practices and strategies of real companies.
- **Simulations:** Practise management decision-making in simulated business environments.

OB at Work

for **Review**

1. Define *group* and *team*.

2. How do you explain the growing popularity of teams in organizations?

3. What are the five types of teams?

4. Do role requirements change in different situations? If so, how?

5. How do group norms influence an individual's behaviour?

6. What are the five stages of group development?

7. What characteristics contribute to the effectiveness of a team?

8. What are the implications of diversity for group effectiveness?

9. How does group size affect group performance?

10. When is work performed by individuals preferred over work performed by teams?

for **Managers**

■ Recognize that groups can dramatically affect individual behaviour in organizations, to either positive or negative effect. Therefore, pay special attention to roles, norms, and cohesion—to understand how these are operating within a group is to understand how the group is likely to behave.

■ Effective teams have adequate resources, effective leadership, a climate of trust, and a performance evaluation and reward system that reflects team contributions. These teams have individuals with technical expertise as well as problem-solving, decision-making, and interpersonal skills and the right traits and skills.

■ Effective teams also tend to be small. They have members who fill role demands and who prefer to be part of a group.

■ Effective teams have members who believe in the team's capabilities and are committed to a common plan and purpose and have an accurate shared mental model of what is to be accomplished.

■ Select individuals who have the interpersonal skills to be effective team players, provide training to develop teamwork skills, and reward individuals for cooperative efforts.

for **You**

■ Know that you will be asked to work on teams and groups both during your undergraduate years and later on in life, so understanding how teams work is an important skill to have.

■ Think about the roles that you play on teams. Teams need task-oriented people to get the job done, but they also need maintenance-oriented people who help keep people working together and feeling committed to the team.

■ Help your team set specific, measurable, and realistic goals, as this leads to more successful outcomes.

TO GET THE MOST OUT OF TEAMS, EMPOWER THEM

POINT

If you want high-performing teams with members who like one another and their jobs, here is a simple solution: Remove the leash tied to them by management and let them make their own decisions.[136] In other words, empower them. This trend started a long time ago, when organizations realized that creating layers of bureaucracy thwarts innovation, slows progress to a trickle, and merely provides hoops for people to jump through in order to get anything done.

You can empower teams in two ways. One way is structurally, by transferring decision making from managers to team members and giving teams the official power to develop their own strategies. The other way is psychologically, by enhancing team members' beliefs that they have more authority, even though legitimate authority still rests with the organization's leaders. Structural empowerment leads to heightened feelings of psychological empowerment, giving teams (and organizations) the best of both worlds.

Research suggests that empowered teams benefit in a number of ways. Members are more motivated. They exhibit higher levels of commitment to the team and to the organization. They also perform much better. Empowerment sends a signal to the team that it's trusted and does not have to be constantly micromanaged by upper leadership. When teams get the freedom to make their own choices, they accept more responsibility for and take ownership of both the good and the bad.

Granted, that responsibility also means empowered teams must take the initiative to foster their ongoing learning and development, but teams entrusted with the authority to guide their own destiny do just that. So, do yourself (and your company) a favour and make sure that teams, rather than needless layers of middle managers, are the ones making the decisions that count.

COUNTERPOINT

Empowerment can do some good in certain circumstances, but it's certainly not a cure-all.

Yes, organizations have become flatter over the past several decades, paving the way for decision-making authority to seep into the lower levels of the organization. But consider that many teams are "empowered" simply because the management ranks have been so thinned that there is no one left to make the key calls. Empowerment is then just an excuse to ask teams to take on more responsibility without an accompanying increase in tangible benefits like pay.

In addition, the organization's leadership already has a good idea of what it would like its teams (and individual employees) to accomplish. If managers leave teams to their own devices, how likely is it that those teams will always choose what the manager wanted? Even if the manager offers suggestions about how the team might proceed, empowered teams can easily ignore that advice. Instead, they need direction on what goals to pursue and how to pursue them. That is what effective leadership is all about.

When decision-making authority is distributed among team members, each member's role is less clear, and members lack a leader to whom they can go for advice. Finally, when teams are self-managed, they become like silos, disconnected from the rest of the organization and its mission. Simply handing people authority is no guarantee they will use it effectively. So, leave the power to make decisions in the hands of those who have assigned leadership roles. After all, they got to be leaders for a reason, and they can best guide the team to stay focused and perform at top levels to maximize organizational outcomes.

BREAKOUT **GROUP** EXERCISES

Form small groups to discuss the following topics, as assigned by your instructor:

1. One of the members of your team continually arrives late for meetings and does not turn drafts of assignments in on time. In general, this group member is engaging in social loafing. What can the members of your group do to reduce social loafing?

2. Consider a team with which you have worked. Was there more emphasis on task-oriented or maintenance-oriented roles? What impact did this have on the group's performance?

3. Identify 4 or 5 norms that a team could put into place near the beginning of its life that might help the team function better over time.

EXPERIENTIAL EXERCISE

The Paper Tower Exercise

Step 1   Each group will receive 20 index cards, 12 paper clips, and 2 marking pens. Groups have 10 minutes to plan a paper tower that will be judged on the basis of 3 criteria: height, stability, and beauty. No physical work (building) is allowed during this planning period.

Step 2   Each group has 15 minutes for the actual construction of the paper tower.

Step 3   Each tower will be identified by a number assigned by your instructor. Each student is to individually examine all the paper towers. Your group is then to come to a consensus as to which tower is the winner (5 minutes). A spokesperson from your group should report its decision and the criteria the group used in reaching it.

Step 4   In your small groups, discuss the following questions (your instructor may choose to have you discuss only a subset of these questions):

   a. What percentage of the plan did each member of your group contribute, on average?

   b. Did your group have a leader? Why or why not?

   c. How did the group generally respond to the ideas that were expressed during the planning period?

   d. To what extent did your group follow the five-stage model of group development?

   e. List specific behaviours exhibited during the planning and building sessions that you felt were helpful to the group. Explain why you found them to be helpful.

   f. List specific behaviours exhibited during the planning and building sessions that you felt were dysfunctional to the group. Explain why you found them dysfunctional.

Source: This exercise is based on *The Paper Tower Exercise: Experiencing Leadership and Group Dynamics*, by Phillip L. Hunsaker and Johanna S. Hunsaker, unpublished manuscript. A brief description is included in "Exchange," *Organizational Behavior Teaching Journal* 4, no. 2 (1979), p. 49. Reprinted by permission of the authors. The materials list was suggested by Professor Sally Maitlis, Sauder School of Business, University of British Columbia.

ETHICAL **DILEMMA**

Dealing with Shirkers

As we discussed in this chapter, social loafing is one potential downside of working in groups. Research suggests that regardless of the type of task, when working in a group, most individuals contribute less than if they were working on their own. Sometimes these people are labelled shirkers because they don't fulfill their responsibilities as group members. Other times, social loafing is overlooked, and industrious employees do the work to meet the group's performance goals. Either way, social loafing creates an ethical dilemma.

Whether in class projects or in jobs we have held, most of us have experienced social loafing in groups. We may even have been guilty ourselves. Although limiting group size, holding individuals responsible for their contributions, setting group goals, and rewarding both individual and group performance might help reduce the occurrence of social loafing, in many cases people just try to work around shirkers rather than motivate them to perform at higher levels.

Managers must determine what level of social loafing for groups and for individual employees will be tolerated in terms of nonproductive meetings, performance expectations, and counterproductive work behaviours. Employees must decide what limits to social loafing they will impose on themselves and what tolerance they have for social loafers in their work groups.

Questions

1. Do group members have an ethical responsibility to report shirkers to leadership? If you were working on a group project for a class and a group member was loafing, would you communicate this information to the instructor? Why or why not?

2. Do you think social loafing is always shirking (failing to live up to your responsibilities)? Are there times when shirking is ethical or even justified?

3. Social loafing has been found to be higher in individualistic nations than in other countries. Do you think this means we should tolerate shirking by North American students and employees to a greater degree than if someone else does it?

CASE INCIDENTS

Tongue-Tied in Teams

Thirty-one-year-old Robert Murphy has the best intentions to participate in team meetings, but when it's "game time," he chokes.[137] An online marketing representative, Robert cannot be criticized for lack of preparation. After being invited to a business meeting with six of his co-workers and his supervisor, Robert began doing his research on the meeting's subject matter. He compiled notes, and arranged them neatly. As soon as the meeting began, "I just sat there like a lump, fixated on the fact that I was quiet." The entire meeting passed without Robert contributing a word.

Robert is certainly not the first person to fail to speak up during meetings, and he won't be the last. While some silent employees may not have any new ideas to contribute, the highly intelligent also freeze. One study found that if we believe our peers are smarter, we experience anxiety that temporarily blocks our ability to think effectively. In other words, worrying about what the group thinks of you makes you dumber. The study also found the effect was worse for women, perhaps because they can be more socially attuned to what others may think.

In other cases, failing to speak up may be attributed to personality. While the extraverted tend to be assertive and assured in group settings, the more introverted prefer to collect their thoughts before speaking—if they speak at all. But again, even those who are extraverted can remain quiet, especially when they feel they cannot contribute.

You may be wondering whether it is important for everyone to speak up. Collaboration (the word comes from "labouring together" in Latin) is at the heart of organizational transformation, so yes, the more participation, the more likely the collaboration will result in higher trust, increased productivity, and enhanced creativity. Furthermore, collaboration works best when individuals know their ideas are taken seriously.

The message from research is clear: Give free speech a try!

Questions

1. Recall a time when you failed to speak up during a group meeting. What were the reasons for your silence? Are they similar to or different from the reasons discussed here?

2. Can you think of other strategies that can help the tongue-tied?

3. Imagine that you are leading a team meeting and you notice that a couple of team members are not contributing. What specific steps might you take to try to increase their contributions?

Intragroup Trust and Survival

When 10 British Army soldiers on a 10-day training exercise descended into Low's Gully, a narrow chasm that cuts through Mt. Kinabalu in Borneo, each knew "the golden rule for such expeditions—never split up."[138] Yet the fittest three struggled out of the jungle with a concussion, malaria, and infected wounds 19 days later; two more terribly ill soldiers found a village the next day; and the remaining five emaciated and injured men were rescued from a cave by a helicopter on day 33. What happened?

On a surface level, the near-tragic fracturing of the group began with a logical division of labour, according to the training's initiators, Lieutenant Colonel Neill and Major Foster:

> Because the group would be one of mixed abilities, and the young British and NCOs [non-commissioned officers] were likely to be fitter and more experienced than the Hong Kong soldiers, the team would work in two halves on the harder phases of the descent. The British, taking advantage of Mayfield's expertise (in rock climbing), would set up ropes on the difficult sections, while he [Neill] and Foster would concentrate on bringing the Hong Kong soldiers down. Every now and then the recce (reconnaissance) party would report back, and the expedition would go on down in one unit until another reconnaissance party became necessary.

The men reported that from then on, perilous climbing conditions, debilitating sickness, and monsoon rains permanently divided the group. A review board found differently, blaming Neill's and Foster's leadership and their decision to take some less-experienced soldiers on the exercise.

No rulings were made about the near-catastrophic decision to divide the group, but closer inquiries show that this temporary work group of diverse members who were not previously acquainted started out with a high level of intragroup trust that dissolved over time. The resulting fault lines, based on members' similarities and differences and the establishment of ad hoc leaders, may have been inevitable.

Initially, all group members shared the common ground of soldier training, clear roles, and voluntary commitment to the mission. When the leaders ignored the soldiers' concerns about the severity of conditions, lack of preparation, and low level of communication, however, trust issues divided the group into subgroups. The initial reconnaissance party established common ground and trust that allowed them to complete the mission and reach safety, even though they divided yet again. Meanwhile, the main group that stayed with the leaders in the cave under conditions of active distrust fractured further.

We will never know whether it would have been better to keep the group together. However, we do know that this small group of soldiers trained to stay together for survival fractured into at least four subgroups because they did not trust their leaders or their group, endangering all their lives.

Questions

1. How was the common ground established by the reconnaissance subgroups different from the common ground established by the cave subgroups? See the leaders' description.

2. Do you think the group should have fractured as it did? Why or why not?

3. When the exercise was designed, Neill created a buddy system based on similarity of soldiers' backgrounds (rank, unit, age, fitness, skill level). The first group out of the jungle were assigned buddies and one other: two lance corporals and one corporal from the same unit (regular army); ages 24–26 with good fitness levels; all top roping and abseiling (TR&A) instructors. The second group out were assigned buddies: a sergeant and a lance corporal from the same unit (elite regular army); ages 25 and 37; good fitness levels; both with Commando Brigade skills. The group left in the cave split into a lieutenant colonel and a major (buddies); one from the regular army and one from the part-time territorial army; ages 46 and 54; fair fitness level; one TR&A and one ski instructor. The second faction was the three from the Hong Kong unit—a lance corporal and two privates, all from the Hong Kong unit; ages 24–32; fair to good fitness levels; one with jungle training and two novices. Would you have set up the buddy system as Neill did? Why or why not? If not, what would you have changed?

OB at Work

FROM CONCEPTS TO SKILLS

Conducting a Team Meeting

Team meetings have a reputation for inefficiency. For instance, noted Canadian-born economist John Kenneth Galbraith said, "Meetings are indispensable when you don't want to do anything."

When you are responsible for conducting a meeting, what can you do to make it more efficient and effective? Follow these 12 steps:[139]

1. *Prepare a meeting agenda.* An agenda defines what you hope to accomplish at the meeting. It should state the meeting's purpose; who will attend; what, if any, preparation is required of each participant; a detailed list of items to be covered; the specific time and location of the meeting; and a specific finishing time.

2. *Distribute the agenda in advance.* Participants should have the agenda sufficiently in advance so they can adequately prepare for the meeting.

3. *Consult with participants before the meeting.* An unprepared participant cannot contribute to his or her full potential. It's your responsibility to ensure that members are prepared, so check with them ahead of time.

4. *Get participants to go over the agenda.* The first thing to do at the meeting is to have participants review the agenda, make any changes, then approve the final agenda.

5. *Establish specific time parameters.* Meetings should begin on time and have a specific time for completion. It's your responsibility to specify these time parameters and to hold to them.

6. *Maintain focused discussion.* It's your responsibility to give direction to the discussion; to keep it focused on the issues; and to minimize interruptions, disruptions, and irrelevant comments.

7. *Encourage and support participation of all members.* To maximize the effectiveness of problem-oriented meetings, each participant must be encouraged to contribute. Quiet or reserved personalities need to be drawn out so their ideas can be heard.

8. *Maintain a balanced style.* The effective group leader pushes when necessary and is passive when need be.

9. *Encourage the clash of ideas.* You need to encourage different points of view, critical thinking, and constructive disagreement.

10. *Discourage the clash of personalities.* An effective meeting is characterized by the critical assessment of ideas, not attacks on people. When running a meeting, you must quickly intercede to stop personal attacks or other forms of verbal insult.

11. *Be an effective listener.* You need to listen with intensity, empathy, and objectivity, and do whatever is necessary to get the full intended meaning of each participant's comments.

12. *Bring proper closure.* You should close a meeting by summarizing the group's accomplishments. Clarify what actions, if any, need to follow the meeting, and allocate follow-up assignments. If any decisions are made, you also need to determine who will be responsible for communicating and implementing them.

OB at Work

Practising Skills

Jameel Saumur is the leader of a five-member project team that has been assigned the task of moving his engineering firm into the booming area of high-speed intercity rail construction. Saumur and his team members have been researching the field, identifying specific business opportunities, negotiating alliances with equipment vendors, and evaluating high-speed rail experts and consultants from around the world. Throughout the process, Tonya Eckler, a highly qualified and respected engineer, has challenged a number of things Saumur said during team meetings and in the workplace. For example, at a meeting two weeks ago, Saumur presented the team with a list of 10 possible high-speed rail projects and started evaluating the company's ability to compete for them. Eckler contradicted virtually all of Saumur's comments, questioned his statistics, and was quite pessimistic about the possibility of getting contracts on these projects. After this latest display of displeasure, two other group members, Bryan Worth and Maggie Ames, are complaining that Eckler's actions are damaging the team's effectiveness. Eckler was originally assigned to the team for her unique expertise and insight. If you had to advise this team, what suggestions would you make to get the team on the right track to achieve its fullest potential?

Reinforcing Skills

1. Interview three managers at different organizations. Ask them about their experiences in managing teams. Have each describe teams that they thought were effective and why they succeeded. Have each also describe teams that they thought were ineffective and the reasons that might have caused this.

2. Contrast a team you have been in where members trusted one another with another team you have been in where members lacked trust in one another. How did the conditions in each team develop? What were the consequences in terms of interaction patterns and performance?

OB ON THE EDGE

Paul and Chris Bennett/Environics Communications, Inc./Newscom

Trust

Bruce MacLellan, president and CEO of Toronto-based Environics Communications, finds that building trust in the workplace has a high payoff.[1] In fact, he believes that trust is a crucial element of his public relations firm's success. "Build trust [because] everything you say and do will be watched. . . . Building a stable and trusting atmosphere is essential to other success. People may not always agree, but if they see transparency, consistency and candour, it helps."

Employees (pictured above at a recent company retreat) look forward to the annual ESRA (read it backward) award. The award goes to the person who made the biggest blooper of the year in front of a client or colleague. One employee won for recommending a "suitable" parking spot from which the client got towed. Another employee was caught on a television interview looking like she was falling asleep. "She didn't realize she was on camera and looked like she was falling asleep while our client was speaking," MacLellan says. The award ensures that employees feel safe when they make mistakes and that they can trust their colleagues.

MacLellan also builds trust at Environics by helping employees achieve work–life balance. After working at the firm for four years, Steve Acken, vice-president of digital services, wanted to travel the world and requested four months of unpaid leave. "They held my job for four months and that was everything," said Acken. This made him even more committed to the firm.

Trust, or lack of trust, is an increasingly important leadership issue in today's organizations.[2] Trust is fragile. It takes a long time to build, can be easily destroyed, and is hard to regain.[3]

A 2017 survey of Canadians conducted by Environics Communications found that only 51 percent of Canadians trusted their senior leaders.[4] It's not just senior leaders who get a failing grade for communication. Internal communications are also dissatisfying: Only 46 percent of Canadian employees are satisfied.[5]

According to a recent survey by Edmonton-based David Aplin Recruiting, managers and human resources professionals are not aware that a trust deficit exists in the workplace and think that employees quit due to insufficient pay. Likely, this is because employees "aren't going to cite lack of trust as their reason for leaving. It would be experienced by many as burning a bridge on the way out the door," Aplin says.[6]

What Is Trust?

Trust is a psychological state that exists when you agree to make yourself vulnerable to another person because you have positive expectations about how things are going to turn out.[7] Although you aren't completely in control of the situation, you are willing to take a chance that the other person will come through for you. Trust is a primary attribute associated with leadership; breaking it can have serious adverse effects on a group's performance.[8] Trust is a history-dependent process based on relevant but limited samples of experience.[9] It takes time to form, building incrementally and accumulating. Most of us find it hard, if not impossible, to trust someone immediately if we don't know anything about them. At the extreme, in the case of total ignorance, we can gamble, but we cannot trust.[10] But as we get to know someone and the relationship matures, we gain confidence in our ability to form a positive expectation.

There is inherent risk and vulnerability in any trusting relationship. Trust involves making oneself vulnerable, as when, for example, we disclose intimate information or rely on another's promises.[11] By its very nature, trust provides the opportunity for disappointment or to be taken advantage of.[12] But trust is not taking risk per se; rather, it is a willingness to take risk.[13] So when I trust someone, I expect that he or she will not take advantage of me. This willingness to take risk is common to all trust situations.[14]

What Determines Trust?

What are the key characteristics leading us to believe a person is trustworthy? Research has identified three: integrity, benevolence, and ability.[15]

- *Integrity.* Integrity refers to honesty and truthfulness. When 570 white-collar employees were given a list of 28 attributes related to leadership, honesty was rated the most important by far.[16] Integrity also means having consistency between what you do and say.

- *Benevolence.* Benevolence means the trusted person has your interests at heart, even if your interests are not necessarily in line with his or hers. Caring and supportive behaviour is part of the emotional bond between leaders and followers.

- *Ability.* Ability encompasses an individual's technical and interpersonal knowledge and skills. You are unlikely to depend on someone whose abilities you do not believe in even if the person is highly principled and has the best intentions. Trust can be won in the ability domain by demonstrating competence.

Time is another component for building trust. We come to trust people based on observing their behaviour over a period of time.[17] The inset *What Are the Consequences of Trust* on page 242 illustrates the importance of developing trust in the workplace.

Basic Principles of Trust

Research offers a few principles that help us better understand how trust and mistrust are created:[18]

- *Mistrust drives out trust.* People who are trusting demonstrate their trust by increasing their openness to others, disclosing relevant information, and expressing their true intentions. People who mistrust conceal information and act opportunistically to take advantage of others. A few mistrusting people can poison an entire organization.

- *Trust begets trust.* Exhibiting trust in others tends to encourage reciprocity.

- *Trust can be regained (sometimes).* Leaders who betray trust are especially likely to be evaluated negatively by followers if there is already a low level of leader–member exchange.[19] Once it is violated, trust can be regained, but only in certain situations.[20] If the cause is lack of ability, it's usually best to apologize and recognize you should have done better. When lack of integrity is the problem, apologies don't do much good. Regardless of the violation, saying nothing or refusing to confirm or deny guilt is never an effective strategy for regaining trust. Trust can be restored when the individual observes a consistent

What Are the Consequences of Trust?

Trust between managers and employees has a number of advantages. Here are just a few that research has shown:[21]

- *Trust encourages taking risks.* Whenever employees decide to deviate from the usual way of doing things, or to take their managers' word on a new direction, they are taking a risk. In both cases, a trusting relationship can facilitate that leap.

- *Trust facilitates information sharing.* One big reason employees fail to express concerns at work is that they don't feel psychologically safe revealing their views. When managers demonstrate they will give employees' ideas a fair hearing and actively make changes, employees are more willing to speak out.[22]

- *Trusting groups are more effective.* When a leader sets a trusting tone in a group, members are more willing to help each other and exert extra effort, which increases trust. Members of mistrusting groups tend to be suspicious of each other, constantly guard against exploitation, and restrict communication with others in the group. These actions tend to undermine and eventually destroy the group.

- *Trust enhances productivity.* The bottom-line interest of companies appears to be positively influenced by trust. Employees who trust their supervisors tend to receive higher performance ratings, indicating higher productivity.[23] People respond to mistrust by concealing information and secretly pursuing their own interests.

pattern of trustworthy behaviours by the transgressor. However, if the transgressor used deception, trust never fully recovers, even when the person deceived is given apologies, promises, or a consistent pattern of trustworthy actions.[24]

- *Mistrusting groups self-destruct.* The corollary to the previous principle is that when group members mistrust one another, they rebel and separate. They pursue their own interests rather than the group's interests. Members of mistrusting groups tend to be suspicious of one another, are constantly on guard against exploitation, and restrict communication with others in the group.

- *Trust increases cohesion.* Trust holds people together.[25] If one person needs help or falters, that person knows that the others will be there to fill in.

- *Mistrust generally reduces productivity.* Leaders who break the psychological contract with workers, demonstrating they are not trustworthy, will find that employees are less satisfied and less committed, have a higher intent toward turnover, engage in less citizenship behaviour, and have lower levels of task performance.[26]

What Can Leaders Do to Increase Trust?

A review of the findings for the effects of leadership on building trust indicates that several characteristics of leadership are most likely to build trust. Leaders who engage in procedural justice (ensuring fair procedures and outcomes) and interactional justice (treating people fairly when procedures are carried out), encourage participative decision making, and use a transformational leadership style are most successful at building trust.[27]

Research with 100 companies around the world suggests that leaders can build trust by shifting their communication style from top-down commands to ongoing organizational dialogue. Lastly, when leaders regularly create interpersonal conversations with their employees that are intimate, interactive, and inclusive and that intentionally follow an agenda, followers demonstrate trust with high levels of engagement.[28] The inset *Increasing Organizational Candour* indicates ways that organizations can increase the level of trust available internally.

Building Team Trust

To improve the climate of trust in an organization, it is important to build team trust. One study examined the effect of trust in one's coach on team

Increasing Organizational Candour

To develop a culture of candour in your organization, start with yourself and consider these tips.[29]

- *Tell the truth.* Develop a reputation for straight talk.
- *Encourage people to speak truth to power.* People higher up in the organization need to know the truth. Encourage people lower down to be courageous and speak up.
- *Reward contrarians.* Recognize and challenge your own assumptions. Find colleagues to help you do that.
- *Practise having unpleasant conversations.* Deliver bad news kindly so that people do not get hurt unnecessarily.
- *Diversify your sources of information.* Communicate regularly with different groups of employees, customers, and competitors.
- *Admit your mistakes.* If you do so, others will do the same.
- *Build organizational support for transparency.* Hire people who have a reputation for candour elsewhere. Protect whistle-blowers.
- *Set information free.* Share information—unless there is a clear reason not to.

FACTBOX

Compared with people in low-trust companies, people in high-trust companies report:

- 74% less stress
- 106% more energy at work
- 50% higher productivity
- 13% fewer sick days
- 76% more engagement
- 29% more satisfaction with their lives
- 40% less burnout[30]

performance during basketball season for 30 teams in Division I and Division III of the NCAA (National Collegiate Athletic Association).[31] The findings show that basketball players' trust in their coach improves team performance. The two teams with the highest level of trust in their coach had outstanding records for the season studied. The team with the lowest level of trust won only 10 percent of its games, and the coach was fired at the end of the season.

As these results indicate, leaders have a significant impact on a team's trust climate. The following points summarize ways to build team trust:[32]

- *Recognize excellence.* Public recognition both celebrates successes and inspires others to aim for excellence.

- *Induce "challenge stress."* Assign difficult but achievable tasks that require team members to work together.

- *Give people discretion in how they do their work.* Feeling that they are trusted motivates employees.

- *Enable job crafting.* Give employees the opportunity to choose their projects, as this will focus energy on things employees care about. Then, hold them accountable for their work.

- *Share information broadly.* Uncertainty about the company's direction can cause stress and undermine teamwork.

- *Intentionally build relationships.* Completing tasks is important in the workplace, but so is time for making friends. Studies show that when people intentionally build social ties at work, performance improves.

- *Facilitate whole-person growth.* High-trust workplaces help people develop personally as well as professionally.

- *Show vulnerability.* Leaders in high-trust workplaces ask for help from colleagues instead of just telling them to do things.

High-performance teams are characterized by high mutual trust among members. That is, members believe in the integrity, character, and ability of one another. Since trust begets trust and distrust begets distrust, maintaining trust requires careful attention by leaders and team members.[33] High trust can have a downside, though, if it inspires team members to not pay attention to one another's work. Team members with high trust may not monitor one another, and if the low monitoring is accompanied by high individual autonomy, the team can perform poorly.[35]

The Need to Prevent Lying

If a liar is merely someone who lies, we are all liars. We lie to ourselves, and we lie to others. We lie consciously and unconsciously. We tell big lies and create small deceptions.

One of the reasons people lie is because lying is difficult for others to detect. In more than 200 studies, individuals correctly identified people who were lying only 47 percent of the time, which is less than random picking.[36] This seems to be true no matter what lie-detection technique is employed.

Lying is deadly to trust and decision making, whether or not lies can be detected. Managers—and organizations—simply cannot make good decisions when facts are misrepresented and people give false motives for their behaviours. Lying is a big

ethical problem as well. From an organizational perspective, using fancy lie-detection techniques and entrapping liars when possible yield unreliable results.[37] The most lasting solution comes from organizational behaviour, which studies ways to prevent lying by working with our natural propensities to create environments that are not conducive to lying. Research conducted by behavioural scientists suggests some steps to reduce lying in organizations.

- *Stop lying to ourselves.* Many studies reveal that we deem ourselves much less likely to lie than we judge others to be. At a collective level, this is impossible—everyone can't be below above average in their propensity to lie. So step 1 is to admit the truth: We lie much more than we should.

- *Trust, but verify.* Lying is learned at a very young age. Why do people learn to lie? Because they often get away with it. Negotiation research shows that individuals are more likely to lie in the future when their lies have succeeded or gone undetected in the past. Managers need to eliminate situations in which lying is available to employees.

- *Reward honesty.* If we want more honesty, we have to provide greater incentives for the truth, and more disincentives for lying and cheating.

The inset *The Rules for Trusting Wisely* presents some tips for starting on "a lifelong process of learning how to trust wisely and well."[38]

FACE OFF

Trust in others can be dangerous. If you get too close to someone else, that person could take advantage of you, and possibly hurt your chances to get ahead.

Trust improves relationships among individuals. Through trust, productivity can be increased and more creative ideas are likely to come forward.

WANT TO KNOW MORE?

P. J. Zak, "The Neuroscience Of Trust," *Harvard Business Review*, January–February 2017, pp. 84–90; D. DeSteno, "Who Can You Trust?" *Harvard Business Review*, March 2014, pp. 22–23; and A. J. C. Cuddy, M. Kohut, and J. Neffinger, "Connect, Then Lead," *Harvard Business Review*, July–August 2013, pp. 54–61.

RESEARCH EXERCISES

1. Look for data on the extent to which companies in other countries are trusted by the citizens of those countries. How do they compare with the extent to which Canadians trust companies? Can you draw any inferences about what leads to greater or less trust of corporations?

2. Identify three Canadian organizations that are trying to improve their image to be more trustworthy. What effect is this new image having on the organizations' bottom lines?

YOUR PERSPECTIVE

1. Why might corporations be willing to neglect the importance of trust and instead engage in behaviours such as those that could lead to corporate scandals?

2. What steps can organizations take to make sure that they are seen as trustworthy by the rest of society?

7 Communication

PART 3

INTERACTING EFFECTIVELY

Would communication
in the workplace
be more efficient
and less stressful
without email?

LEARNING OUTCOMES

After studying this chapter, you should be able to:

1. Describe the communication process and formal and informal communication.
2. Show how channel richness underlies the choice of communication channel.
3. Identify common barriers to effective communication.
4. Contrast downward, upward, and lateral communication.
5. Compare and contrast formal small-group networks and the grapevine.
6. Contrast oral, written, and nonverbal communication.
7. Show how to overcome the potential problems in cross-cultural communication.

After selling his first company, Flickr, to Yahoo! in 2005, Vancouver-based entrepreneur Stewart Butterfield moved on to his next venture, a multi-player, online game called Glitch.[1]

Tobias Hase/DPA Picture Alliance/Alamy Stock Photo

The Glitch team was spread out in different cities across North America, and members needed a more efficient way to communicate and share files. To meet this challenge, they developed a platform that used Internet Relay Chat (IRC), which supports a number of communication tools including discussion forums, private messaging, and data exchange. The system was easy, transparent, and kept all of their communications organized.

When it became clear that their game, in which players could cultivate plants, talk to rocks, and meditate, was not going anywhere, Butterfield reluctantly acknowledged that it was time to call it quits. When the company shut down, it had 45 employees and had been in operation for three-and-a-half-years, yet there were only 50 messages in the company-wide email system. In a time when employees are drowning in the deluge of emails they receive every day (roughly 111 per day, according to a 2017 study),[2] this really struck Butterfield and inspired him to take the system the company had developed and create a new communication tool for the business world called Slack. Clearly filling an untapped need, Slack is now one of the fastest-growing companies in the world and one of the fastest-growing business applications available. Within a month of launching, Slack was valued at $1 billion. It was number three on the Forbes Cloud 100 list for 2017. Just three years from its start in 2014, it had 5 million daily users of its messaging function that allows users in the same workplace to communicate with each other.

Good communication makes organizations successful. Communication is powerful: No group or organization can exist without sharing meaning among its members. In this chapter, we will analyze communication and ways we can make it more effective.

OB IS FOR EVERYONE

- Ever notice that communicating via email can lead to misunderstandings?
- Does body language really make a difference?
- How can you improve cross-cultural communication?

THE BIG IDEA

Real communication requires feedback (both giving it and seeking it).

① Describe the communication process and formal and informal communication.

The Communication Process

Communication is the *transfer* and *understanding* of a message between two or more people. Communicating is more than merely saying something; the meaning of what was said must also be understood.

Exhibit 7-1 depicts this **communication process**. The key parts of this model are (1) the sender, (2) encoding, (3) the message, (4) the channel, (5) decoding, (6) the receiver, (7) noise, and (8) feedback. The *sender* initiates a message by encoding a thought. The *message* is the actual physical product of the sender's *encoding*. When we speak, the speech is the message. When we write, the writing is the message. When we gesture, the movements of our arms and the expressions on our faces are the message. The *channel* is the medium through which the message travels. The sender selects it, determining whether to use a formal or informal channel. **Formal channels** are established by the organization and transmit messages related to the professional activities of members. They traditionally follow the authority chain within the organization. Other forms of messages, such as personal or social messages, follow **informal channels**, which are spontaneous and subject to individual choice.[3] The *receiver* is the person(s) to whom the message is directed, who must first translate the symbols into understandable form. This step is the *decoding* of the message. *Noise* represents communication barriers that distort the clarity of the message, such as perceptual problems, information overload, semantic difficulties, or cultural differences. The final link in the communication process is a feedback loop. *Feedback* is the check on how successful we have been in transferring our messages as originally intended. It determines whether understanding has been achieved.

The model indicates that communication is both an interactive and iterative process. The sender has to keep in mind the receiver (or audience), and in finalizing the communication may decide to revisit decisions about the message, the encoding, and/or the feedback.

② Show how channel richness underlies the choice of communication channel.

Choosing a Channel

Why do people choose one **channel** of communication over another; for instance, a phone call instead of a face-to-face talk? One answer might be anxiety! An estimated 5 to 20 percent of the population[4] suffers from debilitating **communication apprehension**, or social anxiety. These people experience undue tension and anxiety about oral communication, written communication, or both.[5] They may find it extremely difficult to talk with others face to face or become extremely anxious when they have to use the telephone. As a result, they may rely on memos, letters, or email to convey messages when a phone call would be not only faster but also more appropriate.

But what about the 80 to 95 percent of the population who don't suffer from this problem? Is there any general insight we might be able to provide regarding choice of

communication process The steps between a source and a receiver that result in the transfer and understanding of meaning.

formal channels Communication channels established by an organization to transmit messages related to the professional activities of members.

informal channels Communication channels that are created spontaneously and that emerge as responses to individual choices.

channel The medium through which a message travels.

communication apprehension Undue tension and anxiety about oral communication, written communication, or both.

EXHIBIT 7-1 The Communication Process Model

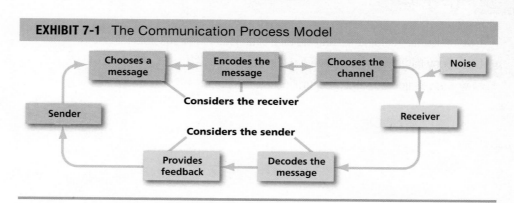

EXHIBIT 7-2 Information Richness of Communication Channels

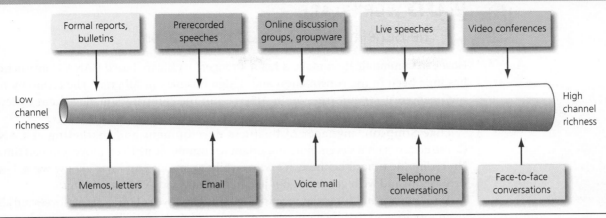

Source: R. H. Lengel and R. L. Daft, "The Selection of Communication Media as an Executive Skill," *Academy of Management Executive*, August 1988, pp. 225–232; and R. L. Daft and R. H. Lengel, "Organizational Information Requirements, Media Richness, and Structural Design," *Managerial Science*, May 1996, pp. 554–572. Reproduced from R. L. Daft and R. A. Noe, *Organizational Behavior* (Fort Worth, TX: Harcourt, 2001), p. 311. ISBN: 978-0030316814.

communication channel? A model of media richness has been developed to explain channel selection among managers.[6]

Channels differ in their capacity to convey information. Some are *rich* in that they have the ability to (1) handle multiple cues simultaneously, (2) facilitate rapid feedback, and (3) be very personal. Others are *lean* in that they score low on these three factors. As Exhibit 7-2 illustrates, face-to-face conversation scores highest in terms of **channel richness** because it transmits the most information per communication episode—multiple information cues (words, postures, facial expressions, gestures, intonations), immediate feedback (both verbal and nonverbal), and the personal touch of being present. *Focus on Research* explains why face-to-face meetings are so important.

FOCUS ON RESEARCH
Communicating in Bad Times

Can communication really make a difference during bad economic times? A recent study found that when economic times are bad, it is particularly important for management to create an atmosphere of trust.[7] They can do this by communicating directly with employees—bulletin boards, intranets, newsletters, and email can all be effective. However, face-to-face communication is the most important way of communicating. . . . .

Impersonal written media such as formal reports and bulletins rate lowest in richness.

The choice of one channel over another depends on whether the message is routine. Routine messages tend to be straightforward and have a minimum of ambiguity. Nonroutine messages are likely to be complicated and have the potential for misunderstanding. Individuals can communicate nonroutine messages more effectively by selecting rich channels.

channel richness The amount of information that can be transmitted during a communication episode.

OB IN THE WORKPLACE
The Benefits of Effective Communication

How can communication make a team stronger? Calgary-based CANA Construction has long been in the construction and design business in Alberta.[8] The economy has not been great for construction in Alberta, but the company's management believes communicating its situation with employees is good management.

Luke Simpson, manager of business development and marketing at CANA Construction, says it's even more important to communicate to employees in bad times. "In economic times like these, it's worthwhile to let our employees know we've been here before and we'll get through it just like we always have," he explains.

The company holds regular meetings with its employees. Younger employees are also given mentors, so that they can ask questions and make sure they know what is going on with the company. Management routinely visits construction sites to make sure that communication flows freely, and the culture is one where everyone is expected to be included in that communication. Simpson notes, "We have a culture that says, regardless of your position, everyone has a seat at the table when it comes to discussing everything from current projects to where the company is going."

CANA must be doing something right. It was named one of Canada's Best Managed Companies for 2016.

Channel richness is a helpful framework for choosing your mode of communication. It's not always easy to know when to choose oral rather than written communication, for instance. Experts say oral communication or "face-time" with co-workers, clients, and upper management is key to success. However, if you seek out the CEO just to say hello, you may be remembered as an annoyance rather than a star, and signing

Trevor Adeline/caia image/Alamy Stock Photo

According to Fabrizio Carinelli, president of CANA Construction, face-to-face meetings make good business sense. Supervisor and management meetings are held monthly at different construction sites. "We invite everybody from the company to come out, and we basically have a roundtable discussion," he explains. "It really enables everyone to get to know other people in the company and to know what's happening in different areas."[9]

up for every meeting on the calendar to increase your face-time is counterproductive to getting the work of the organization done. Your communication choice is worth a moment's thought: Is the message you need to communicate better suited to a discussion, or a diagram?

Whenever you need to gauge the receiver's receptivity, *oral communication* is usually the better choice. *Written communication* is generally the most reliable mode for complex and lengthy communications, and it can be the most efficient method for short messages when, for instance, a two-sentence text can take the place of a 10-minute phone call. But keep in mind that written communication can be limited in its emotional expression. Choose written communication when you want the information to be tangible, verifiable, and "on the record."

It's important to be alert to *nonverbal* aspects of communication and look for these cues as well as the literal meaning of a sender's words. You should particularly be aware of contradictions between the messages. Someone who frequently glances at her wristwatch is giving the message that she would prefer to terminate the conversation no matter what she actually says, for instance. We misinform others when we express one message verbally, such as trust, but nonverbally communicate a contradictory message that reads, "I don't have confidence in you."

Barriers to Effective Communication

3 Identify common barriers to effective communication.

> One of the features of Slack is that it tries to help users overcome information overload by organizing information and making it easy to find.[10] Stewart Butterfield, co-founder of Slack, hates email. "If someone I worked with emailed me, I'd probably fire them," he says. He acknowledges the frustrations many people feel about email. "With email, there's a constant tension between, 'Please copy me, I want to be in the loop' and 'Don't, because I get too much damn email,'" Butterfield explains.
>
> He and his team use Slack because it's a way to bring together all of the different ways people communicate with each other. As one business writer explains, "It replaces the electronic cacophony of messages sent through email, text, phone, video- and voice-conferencing, [with] Dropbox, group calendars, Facebook, LinkedIn, and Twitter."

While Slack tries to address information overload, a number of barriers can slow or distort effective communication, barriers that we need to recognize and reduce. This section presents the most prominent ones.

Filtering

Filtering refers to a sender purposely manipulating information so the receiver will see it more favourably. A manager who tells his boss what he feels the boss wants to hear is filtering information.

The more vertical levels in the organization's hierarchy, the more opportunities there are for filtering. Some filtering will occur wherever there are status differences. Factors such as fear of conveying bad news and the desire to please the boss often lead employees to tell their superiors what they think superiors want to hear, thus distorting upward communications.

Selective Perception

Selective perception is important because the receivers in the communication process selectively see and hear based on their needs, motivations, experience, background, and other personal characteristics. Receivers also project their interests and expectations into communications as they decode them. For example, an employment interviewer who believes that young people are more interested in spending time on leisure and social activities than working extra hours to further their careers is likely to be influenced by

filtering A sender's manipulation of information so that it will be seen more favourably by the receiver.

that stereotype when interviewing young job applicants. As we discussed in Chapter 2, we don't see reality; rather, we interpret what we see and call it "reality." A recent study found that people perceived that they communicated better with people with whom they were close (friends and partners) than with strangers. However, in ambiguous conversations, it turned out that their ability to communicate with close friends was no better than their ability to communicate with strangers.[11]

Information Overload

Individuals have a finite capacity for processing data. When the information we have to work with exceeds our processing capacity, the result is **information overload**. With emails, phone calls, text messages, meetings, and the need to keep current in one's field, more and more employees say that they are suffering from too much information.

What happens when individuals have more information than they can sort and use? They tend to select, ignore, pass over, or forget it. Or they may put off further processing until the overload situation ends. Consider what happens in a poorly planned PowerPoint presentation (see *Case Incident—PowerPoint Purgatory* on pages 271–272). In any case, lost information and less effective communication results, making it all the more important to deal well with overload.

To deal with information overload, it may make sense to connect to technology less frequently. By creating breaks for yourself, you may be better able to prioritize, think about the big picture, and thereby be more effective.

As information technology and immediate communication have become a more prevalent component of modern organizational life, more employees find they are never able to get offline. For example, some business travellers were disappointed when airlines began offering wireless Internet connections in flight because they could no longer use their travel time as a rare opportunity to relax without a constant barrage of organizational communications. The negative impacts of these communication devices can spill over into employees' personal lives as well. Both workers and their spouses relate the use of electronic communication technologies outside work to higher levels of work–life conflict.[12] Employees must balance the need for constant communication with their own personal need for breaks from work or they risk burnout from being on call 24 hours a day.

Emotions

You may interpret the same message differently when you are angry or distraught than when you are happy. For example, individuals in positive moods are more confident about their opinions after reading a persuasive message, so well-designed arguments have a stronger impact on their opinions.[13] People in negative moods are more likely to scrutinize messages in greater detail, whereas those in positive moods tend to accept communications at face value.[14] Extreme emotions such as jubilation or depression are most likely to hinder effective communication. In such instances, we are most prone to disregard our rational and objective thinking processes and substitute emotional judgments.

Language

Even when we are communicating in the same language, words mean different things to different people. Age and context are two of the biggest factors that influence such differences. For example, when business consultant Michael Schiller asked his 15-year-old daughter where she was going with friends, he told her, "You need to recognize your ARAs and measure against them." Schiller said that in response, his daughter "looked at him like he was from outer space." (*ARA* stands for accountability, responsibility, and authority.) Those new to corporate lingo may find acronyms such as *ARA*, words such as *deliverables* (verifiable outcomes of a project), and phrases such as *get the low-hanging*

information overload A condition in which information inflow exceeds an individual's processing capacity.

fruit (deal with the easiest parts first) bewildering, in the same way parents may be mystified by teen slang.[15]

Our use of language is far from uniform. If we knew how each of us modifies language, we could minimize communication difficulties, but we usually don't know. Senders tend to incorrectly assume that the words and terms they use mean the same to the receivers as to themselves.

Silence

It's easy to ignore silence or lack of communication because it is defined by the absence of information. This is often a mistake—silence itself can be the message to communicate non-interest or inability to deal with a topic. Silence can also be a simple outcome of information overload, or a delaying period for considering a response. For whatever reasons, research suggests using silence and withholding communication are common and problematic.[16] One survey found that more than 85 percent of managers reported remaining silent about at least one issue of significant concern.[17] The impact of silence can be organizationally detrimental. Employee silence can mean managers lack information about ongoing operational problems; management silence can leave employees bewildered. Silence regarding discrimination, harassment, corruption, and misconduct means top management cannot take action to eliminate problematic behaviour.

Silence is less likely when minority opinions are treated with respect, work group identification is high, and high procedural justice prevails.[18] Practically, this means managers must make sure they behave in a supportive manner when employees voice divergent opinions or concerns, and they must take these under advisement. One act of ignoring or belittling an employee for expressing concerns may well lead the employee to withhold important information in the future.

Effective listening skills are discussed in *From Concepts to Skills* on pages 272–273.

Lying

The final barrier to effective communication is outright misrepresentation of information, or lying. People differ in their definition of a lie. For example, is deliberately

Communication barriers exist between these call centre employees in Manila, Philippines, and their Canadian customers even though they all communicate in English. Training in pronunciation, intonation, vocabulary, and grammar helps employees to get messages across effectively to their customers.

Dondi Tawatao/Getty Images

withholding information about a mistake a lie, or do you have to actively deny your role in the mistake to pass the threshold? While the definition of a lie befuddles ethicists and social scientists, there is no denying the prevalence of lying. People may tell one to two lies per day, with some individuals telling considerably more.[19] Compounded across a large organization, this is an enormous amount of deception happening every day. Evidence shows people are more comfortable lying over the phone than face to face, and more comfortable lying in emails than when they have to write with pen and paper.[20]

Can you detect liars? Research suggests most people are not very good at detecting deception in others.[21] The problem is there are no nonverbal or verbal cues unique to lying—averting your gaze, pausing, and shifting your posture can also be signals of nervousness, shyness, or doubt. Most people who lie take steps to guard against being detected, so they might look a person in the eye when lying because they know that direct eye contact is (incorrectly) assumed to be a sign of truthfulness. Finally, many lies are embedded in truths; liars usually give a somewhat true account with just enough details changed to avoid detection.

In sum, the frequency of lying and the difficulty in detecting liars make this an especially strong barrier to effective communication.

Organizational Communication

Communication within organizations can be difficult.[22] There is email, but email simply piles up, making it difficult to distinguish between important and less important messages. Slack uses different channels of communication that help companies reduce the number of emails employees need to send. For instance, if you want to find someone to go to lunch with, you don't email. You go to the "lunch" channel to see who's looking for a lunch buddy. Stewart Butterfield, Slack's co-founder, notes that "a lot of the value in Slack is in transparency. It's easy to duck into channels and get a sense of what's going on all over the company, without having to read every email."

Slack is just one of several apps that make organizational communication more fluid. What else can an organization do to make communication more effective?

In this section, we explore ways that communication occurs in organizations, including the direction of communication, formal small-group networks, the grapevine, and electronic communications.

4 Contrast downward, upward, and lateral communication.

Direction of Communication

Communication can flow vertically and/or laterally in organizations through formal small-group networks or the informal grapevine.[23] We will explore each of these directional flows and their implications.

Downward Communication

Communication that flows from one level of a group or organization to a lower level is *downward communication*. Group leaders and managers use this approach to assign goals, provide job instructions, inform employees of policies and procedures, identify problems that need attention, and offer feedback.

In downward communication, managers must explain the reasons *why* a decision was made. Although this finding may seem like common sense, many managers feel they are too busy to explain things, or that explanations will raise too many questions. Evidence clearly indicates, though, that explanations increase employee commitment and support of decisions.[24] Managers might think that sending a message one time is enough to get through to lower-level employees, but research suggests that managerial communications must be repeated several times and through a variety of different media to be truly effective.[25] Moreover, for employees to actually listen to a manager's message, they must believe what is being said. Sentis' recent Canadian Employee Benchmark survey found that "40 percent [of employees] don't believe that their organization's senior leaders communicate honestly with employees."[26]

Another problem in downward communication is its one-way nature; generally, managers inform employees but rarely solicit their advice or opinions. Research revealed that nearly two-thirds of employees said their boss rarely or never asks their advice. The study noted, "Organizations are always striving for higher employee engagement, but evidence indicates they unnecessarily create fundamental mistakes. People need to be respected and listened to."[27] The way advice is solicited also matters. Employees will not provide input, even when conditions are favourable, if doing so seems against their best interests.[28]

The best communicators explain the reasons behind their downward communications but also solicit communication from the employees they supervise. That leads us to the next direction: upward communication.

Upward Communication

Upward communication flows to a higher level in the group or organization. It's used to provide feedback to higher-ups, inform them of progress toward goals, and relay current problems. Upward communication keeps managers aware of how employees feel about their jobs, co-workers, and the organization in general. Managers also rely on upward communication for ideas on how things can be improved.

Given that most managers' job responsibilities have expanded, upward communication is increasingly difficult because managers can be overwhelmed and easily distracted. As well, sometimes managers subtly (or not so subtly) discourage employees from speaking up.[29] To engage in effective upward communication, communicate in short summaries rather than long explanations, support your summaries with actionable items, and prepare an agenda to make sure you use your boss' attention well.[30] And watch what you say, especially if you are communicating something to your manager that will be unwelcome. If you are turning down an assignment, for example, be sure to project a "can do" attitude while asking advice about your workload dilemma or inexperience with the assignment.[31] Your delivery can be as important as the content of your communication.

Lateral Communication

When communication occurs among members of the same work group, members at the same level, or among any horizontally equivalent employees, we describe it as lateral (or horizontal) communication.

Horizontal communication saves time and eases coordination. Some lateral relationships are formally sanctioned. Often, they are informally created to short-circuit the vertical hierarchy and speed up action. So from management's perspective, lateral communication can be good or bad. Because strict adherence to the formal vertical structure for all communications can be inefficient, lateral communication occurring with the knowledge and support of managers can be beneficial. But dysfunctional conflict can result when formal vertical channels are breached, when members go above or around their managers, or when employers find out that actions have been taken or decisions made without their knowledge.

Small-Group Networks

Formal communication networks can be complicated, including hundreds of people and a half-dozen or more hierarchical levels. We have condensed these networks into three common small groups of five people each (see Exhibit 7-3): chain, wheel, and all-channel.

The *chain* rigidly follows the formal chain of command; this network approximates the communication channels you might find in a rigid three-level organization. The

5 Compare and contrast formal small-group networks and the grapevine.

formal communication networks
Task-related communications that follow the authority chain.

EXHIBIT 7-3 Three Common Small-Group Networks and Their Effectiveness

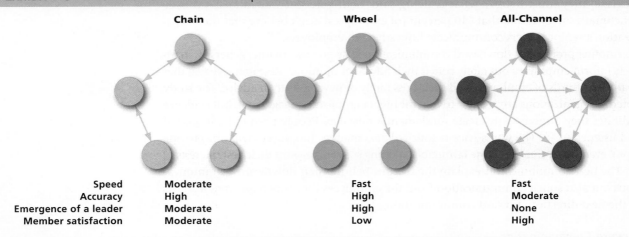

	Chain	Wheel	All-Channel
Speed	Moderate	Fast	Fast
Accuracy	High	High	Moderate
Emergence of a leader	Moderate	High	None
Member satisfaction	Moderate	Low	High

wheel relies on the leader to act as the central conduit for all group communication; it simulates the communication network you would find on a team with a strong leader. The *all-channel* network permits group members to actively communicate with one another; it's most often characterized in practice by self-managed teams, in which group members are free to contribute and no one person takes on a leadership role. Many organizations today like to consider themselves all-channel, meaning that anyone can communicate with anyone (but sometimes they shouldn't).

As Exhibit 7-3 illustrates, the effectiveness of each network is determined by the variable that concerns you. For instance, the structure of the wheel network facilitates the emergence of a leader, the all-channel network is best if high member satisfaction is most important, and the chain network is best if accuracy is most important. Exhibit 7-3 leads us to the conclusion that no single network is appropriate for all occasions.

The Grapevine

The most common **informal communication network** in a group or organization is the **grapevine**.[32] Although rumours and gossip transmitted through the grapevine may be informal, it's still an important source of information for employees and candidates. Grapevine or word-of-mouth information from peers about a company has important effects on whether job applicants join an organization.[33]

The grapevine is an important part of any group or organization communication network. It serves employees' needs: Small talk creates a sense of closeness and friendship among those who share information, although research suggests it often does so at the expense of those in the outgroup.[34] It also gives managers a feel for the morale of their organization, identifies issues employees consider important, and helps them tap into employee anxieties. Evidence indicates that managers can study the gossip driven largely by employee social networks to learn more about how positive and negative information is flowing through the organization.[35] Managers can furthermore identify influencers (highly networked people trusted by their co-workers[36]) by noting which individuals are small talkers (those who regularly communicate about insignificant, unrelated issues). Small talkers tend to be influencers. One study found that small talkers are so influential that they were significantly more likely to retain their jobs during layoffs.[37] Thus, while the grapevine may not be sanctioned or controlled by the organization, it can be understood and leveraged a bit.

Could managers entirely eliminate the gossip and rumours common to the grapevine if they so chose? No. Should they want to? Maybe not; in addition to the

informal communication networks
Communications that flow along social and relational lines.

grapevine The organization's most common informal network.

opportunities for managers to learn from the grapevine, some forms of gossip provide prosocial motivation for employees to help each other achieve organizational goals.[38] What managers should do is minimize the negative consequences of rumours by limiting their range and impact. *OB in Action—Reducing Rumours* gives some tips for reducing the negative consequences of rumours.

OB IN ACTION

Reducing Rumours

→ **Provide information**: Rumours tend to thrive in the absence of formal communication.

→ **Explain actions** and **decisions** that seem problematic.

→ **Do not shoot** the **messenger**: Respond to rumours calmly and rationally.

→ **Maintain open** communication **channels:** Encourage people to talk about their concerns and ideas.[39]

Modes of Communication

> Stewart Butterfield, co-founder of Slack, an organizational communication application that consolidates messaging of all sorts, realizes the value of downtime.[40] Though Slack can keep people connected 24/7, that is not what he expects of his own employees. "Most people will have a small number of effective hours to work, and to the extent those hours can overlap with other people's, the net effect will be more impact," Butterfield says. He encourages his employees to meet face to face during work hours, even if their work is on perfecting an online communication app.

How do group members transfer meaning among each other? They rely on oral, written, and nonverbal communication. This much is obvious, but as we will discuss, the choice between modes can greatly enhance or detract from the way the perceiver reacts to the message. Certain modes are highly preferred for specific types of communication. We will cover the latest thinking and practical applications.

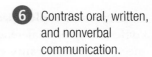

6 Contrast oral, written, and nonverbal communication.

Oral Communication

A primary means of conveying messages is oral communication. Speeches, formal one-on-one and group discussions, and the informal rumour mill or grapevine are popular forms of oral communication.

The advantages of oral communication are speed, feedback, and exchange. We can convey a verbal message and receive a response in minimal time. As one professional put it, "Face-to-face communication on a consistent basis is still the best way to get information to and from employees."[41] If the receiver is unsure of the message, rapid feedback allows the sender to quickly detect and correct it. The feedback we receive includes information and emotional content; however, we should acknowledge that we are usually bad listeners. Researchers indicate that we are prone to "listener burnout" in which we tune the other person out and rush to offer advice. "Good listeners overcome their natural inclination to fix the other's problems and to keep the conversation brief," said professor Graham Bodie.

One major disadvantage of oral communication surfaces whenever a message has to pass through a number of people: The more people, the greater the potential distortion. Therefore, oral communication "chains" are generally more of a liability than an effective tool in organizations. Let's discuss some popular oral communication applications.

Meetings

Meetings can be formal or informal, include two or more people, and take place in almost any venue. Some people hate meetings, so it's important to make them effective.

Good interpersonal communication is key to making meetings effective. Some experts recommend using humour as an ice breaker; public relations firm Peppercomm even offers stand-up comedy workshops to help businesses teach people how to use

OB IN ACTION

Solving the Pitfalls of Videoconferencing and Conference Calls

1. Set more **explicit agendas** and **firmer rules** than for face-to-face meetings.

2. Have callers begin by **introducing themselves**, their **roles** in the project, and **what they are looking for** in the meeting.

3. **Distribute discussion questions before the meeting**, and note the responses of each participant during the meeting.

4. **Assign a moderator** for the meeting (not the leader) **and a secretary** (again, not the leader).

5. **Understand people's preferences** for videoconferencing vs. conference calling before the meeting and **make sure everyone understands the technology**.[47]

humour.[42] But what if you don't have a voice in meetings? *Voice* refers to the ability to contribute words of value to the meeting.[43] By definition, voice challenges the status quo, supports others' viewpoints, adds constructively, or is defensive/destructive.[44] As you can see, voice refers to the input and reactions of a person within the meeting. A person without voice may have nothing to say, but research indicates that women in particular don't speak up in meetings even when they are in leadership positions, suggesting that certain group dynamics inhibit equal participation.[45] Without equitable participation, the benefits of meetings are questionable.

Videoconferencing and Conference Calling

Videoconferencing permits employees and clients to conduct real-time meetings with people at different locations. Live audio and video images let us see, hear, and talk with each other without being physically in the same location. *Conference calling* is generally limited to telephone exchanges where some people may gather around one speaker phone, and others call in through a secure line. There may be some shared files or videos everyone can see on their computers. Both modes are used selectively, according to the application.

You might assume people prefer videoconferencing to conference calling since video offers a more "live" experience, but 65 percent of all remote meetings are done via audio only. For reasons not clearly understood besides some people's reluctance to be on camera, the time people spend on audio-only calls may be growing almost 10 percent per year.[46] *OB in Action—Solving the Pitfalls of Videoconferencing and Conference Calls* offers some suggestions about using these mechanisms.

Telephone

The telephone has been around so long that we can overlook its efficiency as a mode of communication. Communication by telephone is fast, effective, and less ambiguous than email. However, telephone messages can be easily overlooked, and a lack of functions has made the phone difficult to use without electronic follow-up. Fortunately there are a number of software options to make phoning more versatile.

Written Communication

Written communication includes letters, email, instant messaging, organizational periodicals, and any other method that conveys written words or symbols. Written business communication today is usually conducted via letters, PowerPoint, email, instant messaging, text messaging, social media, apps, and blogs. We are all familiar with these methods, but let's consider the unique current business communication applications of them.

Letters

With all the technology available, why would anyone write and send a letter? Of all the forms of written communication, letter writing is the oldest—and the most enduring. Letter writing can be used to great effect in business, adding a personal touch to a communication or, alternately, creating a lasting document to signal an official communication. Interestingly, research indicates that when we write by hand, the content is much more memorable to us than when we type.[48]

CAREER OBJECTIVES

Isn't This Disability Too Much to Accommodate?

I thought it was a good, responsible move when my manager hired a guy who is hearing-impaired . . . but now I'm not so sure. We do okay in communicating with him, mostly thanks to email and texting. None of us knows sign language but sometimes we spell out words with our hands. But sometimes this can get frustrating for my co-workers and me. Why should we have to do so much accommodation?

—Jackie

Dear Jackie:

In short: Workplace accommodation means more than simply tolerating a disabled worker's presence. Perhaps you might consider this from your deaf co-worker's point of view (by the way, "deaf" is the preferred term, according to the National Association of the Deaf):

- *How are the communication conditions for him to work?* Are you being sure to include him in discussions by, say, assigning one of you to write down the important points for him and ask his opinions in meetings? Search for "10 Annoying Habits of Hearing People" online to get a glimpse of his perspective.

- *Do you know what he thinks about your "hand spelling?"* You may not know that American Sign Language (ASL) is not simply using one's hands to signal words and grammar. Your co-worker may be offended by your attempts at what you imagine "sign language" to be, but he would likely appreciate an effort for the group to actually learn some ASL and/or use a translator. There are apps and online translators where you can type in a phrase and see someone sign your words on the screen, for instance. Similarly, technology from MotionSavvy translates sign language into written speech.

If you can get past the barrier of thinking about how he should accommodate himself to your environment and instead show him how your group is willing to work to communicate with him, you may begin to develop an understanding of one another. In other words, search the Internet for tips on communicating with the deaf, and show him some respect.

———————

C. Swinbourne, "The 10 Annoying Habits of Hearing People," *The Huffington Post*, September 17, 2013, http://www.huffingtonpost.com/charlie-swinbourne/the-10-annoying-habits-of_b_3618327.html; National Association of the Deaf website, www.nad.org, accessed June 30, 2015; and R. Walker, "An Office Distraction," *New York Times*, March 22, 2015, p. 8.

The opinions provided here are of the managers and authors only and do not necessarily reflect those of their organizations. The authors or managers are not responsible for any errors or omissions, or for the results obtained from the use of this information. In no event will the authors or managers, or their related partnerships or corporations thereof, be liable to you or anyone else for any decision made or action taken in reliance on the opinions provided here.

PowerPoint

PowerPoint and other slide formats like Prezi can be an excellent mode of communication because slide-generating software combines words with visual elements to engage the reader and help explain complex ideas. PowerPoint is often used in conjunction with oral presentations, but its appeal is so intuitive that it can serve as a primary mode of communication. It is not without its detractors, however, who argue that it is too impersonal, disengaging, and frequently hard to follow.

Email

The growth of email since its inception nearly 50 years ago has been spectacular, and its use is so pervasive it's hard to imagine life without it. There are more than 3.1 billion active email accounts worldwide, and according to a 2017 study, the typical Canadian knowledge worker sends or receives 86 work-related emails at work and 25 at home.[49] Exhibit 7-4 shows the time managers and professionals spend daily on various tasks. Many managers report they spend too much time on email. See the *Ethical Dilemma* on pages 269—270 to consider some ethical challenges technology presents.

> Ever notice that communicating via email can lead to misunderstandings?

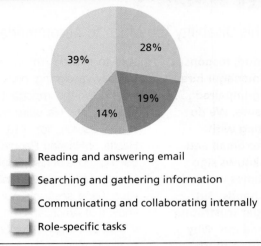

EXHIBIT 7-4 Allocation of Time at Work for Managers and Professionals

- Reading and answering email
- Searching and gathering information
- Communicating and collaborating internally
- Role-specific tasks

Source: Based on M. Chui et al., "The Social Economy: Unlocking Value and Productivity through Social Technologies," McKinsey & Company, July 2012, http://www.mckinsey.com/insights/high_tech_telecoms_internet/the_social_economy.

The business benefits of email messages are obvious: They can be quickly and cheaply written, edited, sent, and stored. Email is not without cost, however. One study indicated that people focus longer on tasks and are less stressed when they are cut off from checking email.[50] Canadians divert 42 percent of their email directly to "junk mail" folders, according to an Ipsos Reid study.[51] Over one-third of the survey respondents said they had trouble handling all of their email, and only 43 percent thought that email increased efficiency at work. Even though he and his business partner are located many plane hours apart, Damien Veran, co-founder of SlimCut Media (with offices in Toronto and Paris) does not think email is the answer for communicating with his co-founder, as *OB in the Workplace* demonstrates.

OB IN THE WORKPLACE

Asleep in Paris, Busy Working in Toronto

What is the best way to communicate when business partners are on different continents? Toronto-based Damien Veran and Paris-based Thomas Davy launched SlimCut Media in 2011.[52] The two, who have been friends since childhood, have only seen each other in person a handful of times since the company launched. To bridge the communication gap, they use the telephone and Skype. "Emails can be tricky," Mr. Veran says. "You need to be careful to make the amount of connecting [in real time] very regular."

Veran is still working hard at 4 p.m. in Toronto, while Davy's day is ending. Veran admits the two sacrifice personal time to keep the communication flowing. "He has to be there for the team at 9 a.m., but he also has to answer my emails from Canada at 11 p.m." ....

Despite the costs, email is likely here to stay, and is "often the first impression that others get of you," according to executive coach and etiquette expert Jacqueline Whitmore.[53] Still, even seasoned email users struggle with striking the proper tone in their communications.

Whitmore offers the following advice:

1. **Don't skip the subject line, but make it short and topic-related.**

2. **Give a greeting/salutation.** "Dear" and "hello" are good starting points. In later exchanges, "hi" may be appropriate. Use the person's name. "Err on the side of being more formal" in your greeting and the body of the email, Whitmore advises. Same for your closing; "Best regards" is more formal.

3. **Keep sentences, paragraphs, and thoughts short.** Use bullet points when possible.

4. **However, don't be curt.** "No one can see your facial expressions or hear your tone of voice, so the only way they're gauging your emotions is the tone that you use in that email," she said.

5. **Don't use text language.** "Even if you've just graduated from college and you're now out in the workforce," Whitmore observed, "remember that a lot of your clients may be Baby Boomers. It's important for you to stay professional."

6. **Check your spelling.** Check it again.

7. **When people write back, reply within 24 hours.** "Even if you don't have an answer for someone, reply anyway," she said.[54]

Instant Messaging

There are distinct pros and cons to instant messaging (IM), but mostly negatives for business interactions. If you are present when the IM comes in, you can respond in real time to engage in online typed dialogue, but the conversation will not be saved for later reference. If you miss the incoming IM, you may be alerted when you next log on that a person tried to reach you, which may be long after a response was needed.

Text Messaging

Text messaging may be a little bit better than IM but has many of the same pitfalls in business usage. The guidelines for the business use of texting are still evolving, but experts continually caution that business text language should be as formal as any other business communication. The level of informality and abbreviations we use in personal text messages are usually not advisable at work.[55]

Social Media

Nowhere has online communication been more transformed than in the rise of social networks like Facebook and LinkedIn, and business is taking advantage of the opportunities these social media present. Many organizations have developed their own in-house social networking applications, known as *enterprise social software*, and most have their own Facebook pages and Twitter feeds.[56] Social networking has become a tool for prospective employees, hiring managers, employees, and human resource divisions. See *Case Incident—Organizational Leveraging of Social Media* on pages 270–271 on how social media blurs the lines between work and personal lives.

Facebook has more than 1.44 billion active users per month,[57] and it's important to remember in business that users can send messages to other users either by posting on their walls (public), sending messages, or setting up chats (private). Some of the modes of communication may be appropriate for business application (such as an organization's Facebook page) but many are not. Research has found that none of the world's 50 most profitable companies' CEOs use Facebook.[58] This represents a dramatic shift from 2010, when these CEOs were using Facebook, LinkedIn, and Twitter quite equally. Privacy remains a high concern for many Facebook users, and some regions of the world do not have access to it.[59]

Unlike many social media venues, LinkedIn was created as an online business network and now has 187 million active users per month.[60] User profiles on the site are like virtual résumés. Communication is sometimes limited to endorsements of others' skills and establishment of business connections, though direct private communication is available and users can form and belong to groups. LinkedIn is used increasingly by top CEOs and is the top popular network for them (22 percent of the top 50 companies' CEOs use LinkedIn).[61]

Twitter is a hybrid social networking service for users to post "micro-blog" entries of 140 characters to their subscribers about any topic, including work. Twitter has 236 million active users monthly on average[62] and is growing as a business venue. American President Donald Trump may be its most famous user. While only 10 percent of the top companies' CEOs are on Twitter,[63] some have many followers, such as Richard Branson of Virgin Group, who has 5.99 million. Having many followers can be an advantage to a firm or a manager, but a huge liability when posts (tweets) are badly written or negative, something Trump does not seem to have figured out.

Apps

LinkedIn and Twitter are two of the most widely used social media platforms for businesses, but they are not the only ones. Apps—easily accessed mobile-friendly platforms—are increasingly the forum of choice for the public. Some websites have apps, while other apps exist without corresponding websites. One of the biggest apps is WhatsApp, at 450 million active monthly users. Apps are most popular in regions where mobile phone usage is primary.[64] Asia has the world's largest number of social media users, and apps are a big part of that through Line (Japan), WeChat (China), and Kakao Talk (South Korea).[65]

Blogs

A *blog* (short for web log) is a website about a single person or company. Experts see blogging as a business necessity for organizations, so it should not be overlooked as a vital form of communication to employees and customers, who can post feedback if they choose.[66] However, outdated blogs look bad to employees, customers, and the public, so new ones must be continually added to maintain relevancy.

Others

Flickr, Pinterest, Google+, YouTube, Wikis, Jive, Socialtext, and Social Cast are just a few of the many public and industry-specific platforms, with new ones launching daily. Some are designed for only one type of posting: YouTube accepts only videos, for instance, and Flickr only videos and images. Other sites have a particular culture, such as Pinterest's informal posts sharing recipes or decorating tips. The business applications have not been fully realized yet, but soon there will probably be at least one social media site tailored to every type of business communication.

To help you find a balance between your desire to engage in social media and to behave ethically toward the company in which you are employed, *OB in Action—Using Social Media Responsibly* summarizes rules established by IBM. Should managers care about employees' social media presence? *Point/ Counterpoint* on page 268 addresses this question.

Nonverbal Communication

Every time we deliver a verbal message, we also impart an unspoken message.[68] Sometimes the nonverbal component may stand alone as a powerful message of our business communication. No discussion of communication would thus be complete without

OB IN ACTION

Using Social Media Responsibly

➔ **Don't write** anything you would be **uncomfortable** having your employer read.

➔ Keep in mind that **what you publish** could be public for a **long time**.

➔ If you are writing about your company, **be transparent about your role** in the organization.

➔ **Get approval** from the organization before posting **private** or internal **conversations**.

➔ **Be upfront** about correcting errors and updating previous posts.[67]

consideration of **nonverbal communication**—which includes body movements, the intonations or emphasis we give to words, facial expressions, and the physical distance between the sender and receiver.

We could argue that *every body movement* has meaning, and no movement is accidental (though some are unconscious). We act out our state of being with nonverbal body language. For example, we smile to project trustworthiness, uncross our arms to appear approachable, and stand to signal authority.[69]

> Does body language really make a difference?

Body language can convey status, level of engagement, and emotional state.[70] Body language adds to, and often complicates, verbal communication. In fact, studies indicate that people read much more about another's attitude and emotions from their nonverbal cues than their words! If nonverbal cues conflict with the speaker's verbal message, the cues are sometimes more likely to be believed by the listener.[71]

If you read the minutes of a meeting, you would not grasp the impact of what was said the same way as if you had been there or could see the meeting on video. Why not? There is no record of nonverbal communication, and the emphasis given to words or phrases is missing. *Facial expressions* also convey meaning. Facial expressions, along with intonations, can show arrogance, aggressiveness, fear, shyness, and other characteristics.

The way individuals space themselves in terms of *physical distance*, commonly called **proxemics**, also has meaning. For instance individuals from "contact" cultures (for example, Arabs, Latin Americans, southern Europeans) are more comfortable with body closeness and touch than those from "noncontact" cultures (for example, Asians, North Americans, northern Europeans). If someone stands closer to you than is considered appropriate, it may indicate aggressiveness or sexual interest; if farther away, it may signal disinterest or displeasure with what is being said.

GLOBAL IMPLICATIONS

Effective communication is difficult under the best of conditions. Cross-cultural factors clearly create the potential for increased communication problems.

Cultural Barriers to Communication

There are a number of problems related to language difficulties in cross-cultural communication. First, there are *barriers caused by semantics*. Words mean different things to different people. Some words don't translate between cultures. For instance, the Finnish word *sisu* means something akin to "guts" or "dogged persistence" but is essentially untranslatable in English. Similarly, capitalists in Russia may have difficulty communicating with British or Canadian counterparts because English terms such as *efficiency*, *free market*, and *regulation* have no direct Russian equivalents.

Second, there are *barriers caused by word connotations*. Words imply different things in different languages. The Japanese word *hai* translates as "yes," but its connotation may be "yes, I'm listening," rather than "yes, I agree." Western executives may be hampered in their negotiations if they don't understand this connotation.

Third, there are *barriers caused by tone differences*. In some cultures, language is formal; in others, it's informal. In some cultures, the tone changes depending on the context: People speak differently at home, in social situations, and at work. Using a personal, informal style in a situation where a more formal style is expected can be inappropriate.

Fourth, there are *differences in tolerance for conflict and methods for resolving conflicts*. People from individualistic cultures tend to be more comfortable with direct conflicts and will make the source of their disagreements overt. Collectivists are more likely to

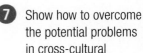

7 Show how to overcome the potential problems in cross-cultural communication.

---

nonverbal communication Messages conveyed through body movements, facial expressions, and the physical distance between the sender and receiver.

proxemics The study of physical space in interpersonal relationships.

acknowledge conflict only implicitly and avoid emotionally charged disputes. They may attribute conflicts to the situation more than to the individuals and therefore may not require explicit apologies to repair relationships, whereas individualists prefer explicit statements accepting responsibility for conflicts and public apologies to restore relationships.

Cultural Context

Cultures tend to differ in the degree to which context influences the meaning individuals take from communication.[72] In **high-context cultures** such as China, Korea, Japan, and Vietnam, people rely heavily on nonverbal and subtle situational cues when communicating with others, and a person's official status, place in society, and reputation carry considerable weight. What is *not* said may be more significant than what *is* said. In contrast, people from Europe and North America reflect their **low-context cultures**. They rely essentially on spoken and written words to convey meaning; body language or formal titles are secondary (see Exhibit 7-5).

Contextual differences mean quite a lot in terms of communication. Communication in high-context cultures implies considerably more trust by both parties. What may appear, to an outsider, as a casual and insignificant conversation is important because it reflects the desire to build a relationship and create trust. Oral agreements imply strong commitments in high-context cultures. Also, who you are—your age, seniority, rank in the organization—is highly valued and heavily influences your credibility. Managers can therefore "make suggestions" rather than give orders. But in low-context cultures, enforceable contracts will tend to be in writing, precisely worded, and highly legalistic. Similarly, low-context cultures value directness. Managers are expected to be explicit and precise in conveying intended meaning.

A Cultural Guide

There is much to be gained from business intercultural communications. It is safe to assume that every one of us has a different viewpoint that is culturally shaped. Because we do have differences, we have an opportunity to reach the most creative solutions possible with the help of others if we communicate effectively.

According to Fred Casmir, a leading expert in intercultural communication research, we often don't communicate well with people outside of our culture because we tend to generalize from only their cultural origin.[73] Doing so can be insensitive and potentially disastrous, especially when we make assumptions based on observable characteristics. Many of us have a richly varied ethnic background and would be offended if someone addressed us according to what culture our physical features might favour, for instance.

high-context cultures Cultures that rely heavily on nonverbal and subtle situational cues in communication.

low-context cultures Cultures that rely heavily on words to convey meaning in communication.

EXHIBIT 7-5 High- vs. Low-Context Cultures

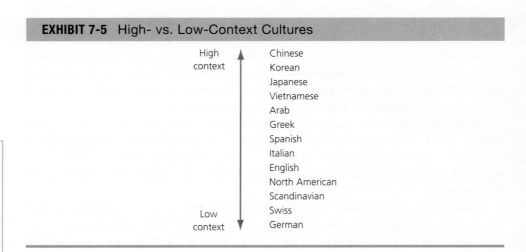

High context	Chinese
	Korean
	Japanese
	Vietnamese
	Arab
	Greek
	Spanish
	Italian
	English
	North American
	Scandinavian
Low context	Swiss
	German

Kiyoshi Ota/Bloomberg/Getty Images

Globalization has changed the way Toyota Motor Corporation provides employees with the information they need for decision making. In the past, Toyota transferred employee knowledge on the job from generation to generation through "tacit understanding," a common communication method used in the conformist and subdued Japanese culture. Today, however, as a global organization, Toyota transfers knowledge of its production methods to overseas employees by bringing them to its training centre in Japan, shown here, to teach them production methods by using how-to manuals, practice drills, and lectures.

Also, attempts to be culturally sensitive to another person are often based on stereotypes propagated by the media. These stereotypes usually don't have a correct or current relevance.

Casmir noted that because there are far too many cultures for anyone to understand completely, and individuals interpret their own cultures differently, intercultural communication should be based on sensitivity and the pursuit of common goals. He found the ideal condition is an ad

How can you improve cross-cultural communication?

hoc "third culture" a group can form when they seek to incorporate aspects of each member's cultural communication preferences. The norms this subculture establishes through appreciating individual differences create a common ground for effective communication. Intercultural groups that communicate effectively can be highly productive and innovative.

When communicating with people from a different culture, what can you do to reduce misinterpretations? Casmir and other experts offer the following suggestions:[74]

- *Know yourself.* Recognizing your own cultural identity and biases is critical to then understanding the unique viewpoint of other people.

- *Foster a climate of mutual respect, fairness, and democracy.* Clearly establish an environment of equality and mutual concern. This will be your "third culture" context for effective intercultural communication that transcends each person's cultural norms.

- *State facts, not your interpretation.* Interpreting or evaluating what someone has said or done, in contrast with describing, is based more on the observer's

Old Faithful Shop

Savannah Olsen, a Cree from Saddle Lake, Alberta, is the co-owner of Old Faithful Shop, located in Vancouver's historic Gastown district. When she received the National Aboriginal Entrepreneur of the Year by the Canadian Council for Aboriginal Business several years ago, the Council noted that her business is a model for helping "Canadians see Aboriginal people as net contributors to the Canadian economy and shared prosperity." Because of the store's location, she takes a unique approach to developing her customer base. Olsen says that she "[holds] in-store craft workshops and mini farmers' markets featuring growers and other local vendors. These events provide an opportunity to get to know our customers and establish a feeling of neighbourliness."[75]

culture and background than on the observed situation. If you state only facts, you will have the opportunity to benefit from the other person's interpretation. Delay judgment until you have had sufficient time to observe and interpret the situation from the differing perspectives of all the cultures involved.

- *Consider the other person's viewpoint.* Before sending a message, put yourself in the recipient's shoes. What are his or her values, experiences, and frames of reference? What do you know about his or her education, upbringing, and background that can give you added insight? Try to see the people in the group as they really are first, and take a collaborative problem-solving approach whenever potential conflicts arise.

- *Proactively maintain the identity of the group.* Like any culture, the establishment of a common-ground "third culture" for effective intercultural communication takes time and nurturing. Remind members of the group of your common goals, mutual respect, and need to adapt to individual communication preferences.

Summary

You have probably discovered the link between communication and employee satisfaction in this chapter: The less uncertainty, the greater the satisfaction. Distortions, ambiguities, and incongruities between verbal and nonverbal messages all increase uncertainty and reduce effective communication. Careful attention to the methods and modes for each communication better ensures that the message is properly interpreted by the receiver.

LESSONS LEARNED

- Just because something is said, it does not mean that it was heard.
- Communication is rarely "objective." Both the sender's and receiver's realities affect the framing and understanding of the message.
- Information overload is a serious problem for most individuals.

SNAPSHOT SUMMARY

The Communication Process
- Choosing a Channel

Barriers to Effective Communication
- Filtering
- Selective Perception
- Information Overload

- Emotions
- Language
- Silence
- Lying

Organizational Communication
- Direction of Communication

- Small-Group Networks
- The Grapevine

Modes of Communication
- Oral Communication
- Written Communication
- Nonverbal Communication

MyLab Management

 PERSONAL INVENTORY ASSESSMENT

Study, practise, and explore real business situations with these helpful resources:

- **Study Plan:** Check your understanding of chapter concepts with self-study quizzes.
- **Online Lesson Presentations:** Study key chapter topics and work through interactive assessments to test your knowledge and master management concepts.
- **Videos:** Learn more about the management practices and strategies of real companies.
- **Simulations:** Practise management decision-making in simulated business environments.

OB at Work

for Review

1. What are the key parts of the communication process, and how do you distinguish formal from informal communication?

2. How does channel richness underlie the choice of communication channel?

3. What are some common barriers to effective communication?

4. What are the differences among downward, upward, and lateral communication?

5. What are the differences between formal small-group networks and the grapevine?

6. How do oral communication, written communication, and nonverbal communication differ?

7. How do you overcome the potential problems of cross-cultural communication?

for Managers

- Remember that your communication mode will partly determine your communication effectiveness.

- Obtain feedback to make certain your messages—however they are communicated—are understood.

- Remember that written communication creates more misunderstandings than oral communication; communicate with employees through in-person meetings when possible.

- Make sure you use communication strategies appropriate to your audience and the type of message you are sending.

- Keep in mind that culture can be a communication barrier.

for You

- If you are having difficulty communicating with someone, you might consider that both you and the other person are contributing something to that breakdown. This tends to be true even if you are inclined to believe that the other person is the party more responsible for the breakdown.

- Often, either selective perception or defensiveness gets in the way of communication. As you work in your groups on student projects, try to observe communication flows more critically to help you understand ways that communication can be improved and dysfunctional conflict avoided.

EMPLOYEES' SOCIAL MEDIA PRESENCE SHOULD MATTER TO MANAGERS

POINT

Everyone uses social media.[76] Well, almost everyone: A Pew research study found that the highest percentage of adults who use social networking sites was in Israel at 53 percent, followed by 50 percent in the United States, 43 percent in Russia and Great Britain, and 42 percent in Spain. Canada was not included in the 20 countries studied.

Business is social, and using employees' social contacts to increase business has always been a facet of marketing. Organizations that don't follow their employees' social media presence are missing an opportunity to expand their business and strengthen their workforce. For example, the Honda employee who once told 30 friends that Honda is best can now tell 300 Facebook friends and 500 Twitter followers about the latest model. Employees' savvy about social media can have a substantial positive effect on the bottom line.

Monitoring employees' social media presence can also strengthen the workforce by identifying the best talent. Managers can look for potential online celebrities—frequent bloggers and Twitter users with many followers—to approach for co-branding partnerships. Scrutiny can also help employers spot problems. For example, consider the employee who is fired one day and turns violent. A manager who had been monitoring the employee's social media posts may have been able to detect warning signs. A human resources department monitoring employees' social media activity may be able to identify a substance abuse problem and provide help for the employee through the company's intervention policies.

A job candidate's social media presence provides one more input to hiring and retention decisions that many organizations already take advantage of. In reality, there is no difference between the employee and the person.

Employers that monitor social media can also identify employees who use their platforms to send out bad press or who leak proprietary information. For this reason, managers may someday be *required* to monitor employees' social media postings and to act upon infringements of company policies. Many do so already.

Managers should therefore develop enforceable social media policies and create a corporate infrastructure to regularly research and monitor social media activity. The potential increase in business and limit on liability is ample return for dedicating staff and work hours to building a successful social program.

COUNTERPOINT

There is little to be gained and much to be lost when organizations follow candidates' and employees' presence on social media. Managers may be able to learn more about individuals through their online activity, and organizations may be able to catch some good press from employee postings, but the risk of liability for this intrusion on privacy is inescapable. Managers are ill-equipped to monitor, interpret, and act upon employees' social media postings, and few have any experience with relating the medium to business use.

Managers may also easily misinterpret information they find. Few companies have training programs for the proper use of social media; only 40 percent have social media policies of any kind. Those that do are skating on thin ice because monitoring policies can conflict with privacy regulations.

An employee's online image does not reveal much that is relevant to the job, certainly not enough to warrant the time and money a business would spend on monitoring. Most users view social media as a private, recreational venue, and their membership on Facebook and other sites should be regarded with the same respect as would membership in a club. In this light, monitoring employees' social media accounts is an unethical violation of their right to privacy.

Federal and provincial laws require companies to not discriminate against women, people with disabilities, Indigenous peoples, and visible minorities. But managers who check into candidates' social media postings often find out more than the candidate wanted to share, and then there is no way to keep that information from affecting the hiring decision. Searching through social media can, therefore, expose a company to a costly discrimination claim.

Using employees' personal social media presence as a marketing tool through company-supportive postings is unethical from many standpoints. First, it's unethical to expect employees to expand the company's client base through their personal contacts. Second, it's unreasonable to expect them to endorse the company after working hours. The practice of asking employees for their social media passwords is an obvious intrusion into their personal lives.

In sum, people have a right to a professional and a private image. Unless the employee is offering to "friend" the company in a social media partnership, there is no question that employers should stay out of their personal business.

BREAKOUT **GROUP** EXERCISES

Form small groups to discuss the following topics, as assigned by your instructor:

1. What differences have you observed in the ways that men and women communicate?
2. How do you know when a person is listening to you? When someone is ignoring you?
3. Describe a situation in which you ignored someone. What impact did it have on that person's subsequent communication behaviours?

EXPERIENTIAL EXERCISE

An Absence of Nonverbal Communication

This exercise will help you see the value of nonverbal communication in interpersonal relations.

1. The class is to divide into pairs (Party A and Party B).
2. Party A is to select a topic from the following list:
   a. Managing in the Middle East is significantly different from managing in North America.
   b. Employee turnover in an organization can be functional.
   c. Some conflict in an organization is good.
   d. Whistle-blowers do more harm than good for an organization.
   e. An employer has a responsibility to provide every employee with an interesting and challenging job.
   f. Everyone should register to vote.
   g. Organizations should require all employees to undergo regular drug testing.
   h. Individuals who have majored in business or economics make better employees than those who have majored in history or English.
   i. The place where you get your college or university degree is more important in determining career success than what you learn while you are there.
   j. It's unethical for a manager to purposely distort communications to get a favourable outcome.
3. Party B is to choose his or her position on this topic (for example, arguing *against* the view that "an employer has a responsibility to provide every employee with an interesting and challenging job"). Party A now must take the opposite position.
4. The 2 parties have 10 minutes in which to debate their topic. The catch is that individuals can only communicate verbally. They may *not* use gestures, facial movements, body movements, or any other nonverbal communication. It may help for both parties to sit on their hands to remind them of these restrictions and to maintain an expressionless look.
5. After the debate is over, the class should discuss the following:
   a. How effective was communication during these debates?
   b. What barriers to communication existed?
   c. What purposes does nonverbal communication serve?
   d. Relate the lessons learned in this exercise to problems that might occur when communicating on the telephone or through email.

ETHICAL **DILEMMA**

BYOD

"What's your cell phone number? Good, I'll call you about the meeting."[77] If you're like many people in the world who have used a smartphone for years, or one of the 1.3 billion people who bought one recently, chances are you've used it for work. In fact, your employer may have even invited—or asked—you to use your smartphone, tablet, or laptop in your job. Such is the bring-your-own-device (BYOD) trend, which started out of friendly convenience but now carries major ethical issues. For instance:

- *Did you know your employer can wipe your personal devices clean?* Remotely? With no warning? It happens, and not just at the 21 percent of organizations that erase devices when employees are terminated. Any time an organization has a privacy concern, it may wipe all devices clean to prevent a further breach of its cyber-defences. Health-care consultant Michael Irvin lost his personal email accounts, apps, music, contacts, and photos suddenly one day, leaving his multi-use iPhone "like it came straight from the factory." Another individual lost pictures of a relative who had died.

- *Is your device part of your employment contract, either explicitly or by understanding?* If so, who pays for the device? Well, you did, and you continue to pay for the service. If the device breaks, then . . . who pays for the replacement device? Can you lose your job if you can't afford the device and service?

- *Can you use your device for all work-related communications?* The cloud has brought opportunities for people to send classified work information anywhere, anytime. Organizations are concerned about what social media, collaboration, and file-sharing applications are in use, which is fair, but some policies can limit how you use your own device.

- *Once you use your personal device for work, where are the boundaries between work and home life?* Research indicates that intensive smartphone users, for instance, need to disengage in their off-hours to prevent work–home stress and burnout. Yet not everyone can do this

even if they are allowed to; research indicated a significant proportion of smartphone users felt pressured to access their devices around the clock, whether or not that pressure was warranted.

The clear dilemma for employees is whether to acknowledge they own a smart device, and whether to offer its use for their employer's convenience. Put that way, it seems obvious to say no (why would you risk the possibility of later losing everything to a corporate swipe?), but having just one phone for both personal and professional use is more convenient. However, some people think it's just better to carry two phones—one for work, another for personal use. Attorney Luke Cocalis tried it and concluded, "It frankly keeps me saner."

Questions

1. Do you use your smartphone or other personal devices for work? If so, do you think this adds to your stress level or helps you by providing convenience?

2. Cocalis likes the two-phone lifestyle and says his boss has his personal phone number only for emergencies. But assistant talent manager Chloe Ifshin reports it doesn't work so well in practice. "I have friends who are clients and clients who are friends," she says, so work contacts end up on her personal phone and friends call her work phone. How does this consideration affect your thinking about BYOD?

3. Organizations are taking steps to protect themselves from what employees might be doing on their BYOD devices through allowing only approved computer programs and stricter policies, but no federal regulations protect employees from these. What ethical initiatives might organizations adopt to make this situation fair for everyone?

CASE INCIDENTS

Organizational Leveraging of Social Media

As you know, social media have transformed the way we interact.[78] The transparent, rapid-fire communication they make possible means people can spread information about companies more rapidly than ever.

Do organizations understand yet how to use social media effectively? Perhaps not. Only 3 of 10 CEOs in the *Fortune* 500 have any presence on national social media sites. Many executives are wary of these new technologies because they cannot always control the outcomes of

their communications. However, whether they are directly involved with social media or not, companies should recognize that messages are out there, so it benefits them to make their voices heard. Some experts say social media tools improve productivity because they keep employees connected to their companies during non-office hours. As well, social media can be an important way to learn about emerging trends. For example, André Schneider, chairman of World Climate Ltd., uses feedback from LinkedIn discussion groups and Facebook friends to discover emerging trends and issues worldwide. Padmasree Warrior, former chief technology officer of Cisco, has used social media to refine her presentations before a "test" audience.

The first step in developing a social media strategy is establishing a brand for your communications—after you define what you want your social media presence to express. Experts recommend that organizations first leverage their internal corporate networks to test their strategy in a medium that's easier to control. Most companies have the technology to use social media through their corporate websites and may use these platforms for communicating with employees and facilitating social networks for general information sharing. As social networking expert Soumitra Dutta of Cornell University notes, "My advice is to build your audience slowly and be selective about your contacts."

Despite the potential advantages, organizations also need to be aware of significant drawbacks for them. First, it's very difficult to control social media communications. Microsoft found this out when the professional blogger it hired spent more time promoting himself than getting posi-

tive information out about the company. Second, important intellectual capital might leak out. Companies need to establish strong policies and procedures to ensure that sensitive information about ongoing corporate strategies is not disseminated via social media. Finally, managers must be committed to monitoring motivation and interest beyond their initial forays into social media. A site that is rarely updated can send a very negative message about the organization's level of engagement with the world.

Questions

1. Are the drawbacks of the corporate leveraging of social media sufficient to make you think it's better for organizations to avoid certain media? If so, which media?

2. What features would you look for in a social media outlet? What types of information would you avoid making part of your social media strategy?

3. What do you think is the future direction of social media in business? How might emerging technologies change your forecast?

PowerPoint Purgatory

We have all been there, done that: 10 minutes, 20 PowerPoint slides.[79] Whether you have been the harried presenter racing through the slides or the hapless listener choosing between reading the slides or listening to the talk, it's miserable. In all, 350 PowerPoint presentations are given per second worldwide, and the program commands 95 percent of the presentation software market. Why do we do this to ourselves?

The short answer seems to be because we know how, or at least we think we do. Joel Ingersoll of Lorton Data, a Minneapolis database company, said, "You say to yourself, 'I'll start vomiting information I found on my hard drive until I hit, oh, about 20 slides, and then I'll wing the talking-to-people part.'" Bombarding audiences with stark phrases is only one possible pitfall, says Rick Altman, author of *Why Most PowerPoint Presentations Suck*. Another is to overdesign your presentation. Most of us spend 36 percent of our prep time on design, according to a study, yet we fail to remember that "less is more." The poor choices that sometimes result (such as using cartoonish typefaces for a serious presentation) can undermine your intended message. Altman cautions against using layer after layer of bullet points to write out what you should say instead, and he recommends making sparing

use of holograms, 3D, and live Twitter feeds that only detract from your message.

Successful talks are about a story and an interaction. "Even if you're a middle manager delivering financials to your department in slides, you're telling a story. A manager is constantly trying to persuade," says Nancy Duarte, owner of a presentation design company. Equally important is the audience. "Everyone is sick of the one-way diatribe," Duarte notes, and Altman recommends engaging people animatedly "as if they're in preschool waiting to get picked up by their parents." According to Keith Yamashita, founder of SYPartners communications, this may mean ditching PowerPoint altogether. "There are endless techniques that are more appropriate than PowerPoint," he contends. Like what?

Experts suggest fewer visual aids and more live interaction with the audience. High tech does not guarantee better storytelling. "Pin up butcher paper on the walls, draw a map of your thinking, and hand that out," Yamashita says, or use a white board. The results can amaze you. When sales engineer Jason Jones had trouble launching his two-hour slide presentation to a dozen clients, buddy Dave Eagle stepped in. "All right, I got two presentations for y'all," Eagle told the clients. He said one presentation was with slides, and the other just spoken. The clients chose the latter, and Jones and Eagle won the account.

Questions

1. What are some of the ways people misuse PowerPoint? What are the potential consequences?

2. In what presentations of yours have you found PowerPoint most effective in communicating your message? In what presentations did PowerPoint hinder your successful communication?

3. List the pros and cons you see for managers who avoid PowerPoint as a mode of communication.

FROM CONCEPTS TO SKILLS

Effective Listening

Too many people take listening skills for granted.[80] They confuse hearing with listening. What is the difference?

Hearing is merely picking up sound vibrations. Listening is making sense out of what we hear. That is, listening requires paying attention, interpreting, and remembering sound stimuli.

The average person normally speaks at a rate of 125 to 200 words per minute. However, the average listener can comprehend up to 400 words per minute. This leaves a lot of time for idle mind-wandering while listening. For most people, it also means they have acquired a number of bad listening habits to fill in the "idle time."

The following eight behaviours are associated with effective listening skills. If you want to improve your listening skills, look to these behaviours as guides:

1. *Make eye contact.* How do you feel when somebody doesn't look at you when you are speaking? If you are like most people, you are likely to interpret this behaviour as aloofness or lack of interest. We may listen with our ears, but others tend to judge whether we are really listening by looking at our eyes.

2. *Exhibit affirmative head nods and appropriate facial expressions.* The effective listener shows interest in what is being said. How? Through nonverbal signals. Affirmative head nods and appropriate facial expressions, when added to good eye contact, convey to the speaker that you are listening.

3. *Avoid distracting actions or gestures.* The other side of showing interest is avoiding actions that suggest your mind is somewhere else. When listening, don't look at your watch, shuffle papers, play with your pencil, or engage in similar distractions. They make the speaker feel that you are bored or uninterested. Maybe more important, they indicate that you are not fully attentive and may be missing part of the message that the speaker wants to convey.

4. *Ask questions.* The critical listener analyzes what he or she hears and asks questions. This behaviour provides clarification, ensures understanding, and assures the speaker that you are listening.

5. *Paraphrase.* Paraphrasing means restating what the speaker has said in your own words. The effective listener uses phrases such as "What I hear you saying is . . ." or "Do you mean . . . ?" Why rephrase what has already been said? Two reasons! First, it's an excellent control device to check whether you are listening carefully. You cannot paraphrase accurately if your mind is wandering or if you are thinking about what you are going to say next. Second, it's a control for accuracy. By rephrasing what the speaker has said in your own words and feeding it back to the speaker, you verify the accuracy of your understanding.

6. *Avoid interrupting the speaker.* Let the speaker complete his or her thought before you try to respond. Don't try to second-guess where the speaker's thoughts are going. When the speaker is finished, you will know!

7. *Don't overtalk.* Most of us would rather voice our own ideas than listen to what someone else says. Too many of us listen only because it's the price we have to pay to get people to let us talk. While talking may be more fun and silence may be uncomfortable, you cannot talk and listen at the same time. The good listener recognizes this fact and does not overtalk.

8. *Make smooth transitions between the roles of speaker and listener.* When you are a student sitting in a lecture hall, you find it relatively easy to get into an effective listening frame of mind. Why? Because communication is essentially one way: The teacher talks and you listen. But the teacher-student dyad is not typical. In most work situations, you are continually shifting back and forth between the roles of speaker and listener. The effective listener, therefore, makes transitions smoothly from speaker to listener and back to speaker. From a listening perspective, this means concentrating on what a speaker has to say and practising not thinking about what you are going to say as soon as you get an opportunity.

. . . .

Practising Skills

Form groups of 2. This exercise is a debate. Person A can choose any contemporary issue. Some examples include business ethics, the value of unions, stiffer grading policies, same-sex marriage, and money as a motivator. Person B then selects a position on this issue. Person A must automatically take the counter-position. The debate is to proceed for 8 to 10 minutes, with only one catch. After each person speaks, the other must summarize, in his or her own words and without notes, what the other person has said. If the summary does not satisfy the speaker, it must be corrected until it does. What impact do the summaries have on the quality of the debate?

. . . .

Reinforcing Skills

1. In another class—preferably one with a lecture format—practise active listening. Ask questions, paraphrase, exhibit affirming nonverbal behaviours. Then ask yourself: Was this harder for me than a normal lecture? Did it affect my note taking? Did I ask more questions? Did it improve my understanding of the lecture's content? What was the instructor's response?

2. Spend an entire day fighting your urge to talk. Listen as carefully as you can to everyone you talk to, and respond as appropriately as possible to understand, not to make your own point. What, if anything, did you learn from this exercise?

8 Power and Politics

Can a popular radio show host get away with sexual harassment? Power and politics tell much of the story.

Jian Ghomeshi, former host of the CBC radio show *Q with Jian Ghomeshi*, was fired by the CBC in 2014 after it saw "graphic evidence" of him physically injuring a woman.[1] Ghomeshi referred to it as "rough consensual sex," but that did not make a difference to the CBC. Ghomeshi and his lawyer tried to present evidence of consent with texts, emails, and photos of Ghomeshi's sexual encounters.

The CBC fired Ghomeshi because the evidence showed behaviour that "was far more aggressive and physical than anything they had been led to believe during months of discussions." Months earlier Ghomeshi had been accused of sexual assault, but the CBC kept Ghomeshi on the air while they conducted an investigation and examined the charges.

After viewing this new evidence, the CBC felt that it would not be able to defend itself once viewers found out about it. The CBC put Ghomeshi on indefinite leave on October 24, 2014, suggested that he think about whether he had anything more he wanted to say, and met with him again on October 26. People with knowledge of that meeting suggest that had Ghomeshi expressed remorse, or said he would seek treatment, that might have factored into the CBC's thinking. However, Ghomeshi refused to accept responsibility for the situation, which prompted his firing.

One reason the CBC acted as slowly as it did after the first allegations were made is that Ghomeshi was a very popular radio host. His show had very high ratings. This gave him both expert and referent power, which allowed him to keep his job when rumours about sexual misconduct first started to arise. The fact that he kept his job caused employees to feel their complaints to management about his behaviour were being ignored. CBC worried about the fallout from Ghomeshi's fans.

WENN Ltd / Alamy Stock Photo

In both research and practice, *power* and *politics* have been described as dirty words. It's easier for most of us to talk about sex or money than about power or political behaviour. Power is seductive. People who have power deny it, people who want it try not to look like they are seeking it, and those who are good at getting it are secretive about how they do so.[2]

A major theme in this chapter is that power and politics occur naturally in any group or organization. Although you might have heard the saying "Power corrupts, and absolute power corrupts absolutely," power is not always bad.

Power and politics are realities of organizational life, and they will not go away. Understanding how to use power and politics effectively makes organizational life more manageable, because it can help you gain the support you need to do your job effectively.

OB IS FOR EVERYONE

- Have you ever wondered how you might increase your power?
- What do you need to be truly empowered?
- Why do some people seem to engage in politics more than others?
- In what situations does impression management work best?

THE BIG IDEA

Power is not necessarily a zero–sum game. Sharing power may in fact increase everyone's power.

1 Define *power*.

A Definition of Power

Power refers to the capacity that A has to influence the behaviour of B, so that B acts in accordance with A's wishes.[3] This definition implies that there is a *potential* for power if someone is dependent on another. But one can have power and not impose it.[4]

Probably the most important aspect of power is that it's a function of **dependence**. The greater B's dependence on A, the greater A's power in the relationship. Dependence, in turn, is based on the alternatives that B perceives and the importance that B places on the alternative(s) that A controls. A person can have power over you only if he or she controls something you desire. If you are attending college or university on funds totally provided by your parents, you probably recognize the power that your parents hold over you. You are dependent on them for financial support. But once you are out of school, have a job, and are making a good income, your parents' power is reduced significantly. Who among us has not known or heard of the rich relative who is able to control a large number of family members merely through the implicit or explicit threat of "writing them out of the will"?

Power makes people uncomfortable.[5] Part of the discomfort about power may have to do with how people perceive those in power. A recent study found that people who behave rudely—putting their feet up on a chair, ordering a meal brusquely—were believed by those watching this behaviour to be more likely to "get to make decisions" and able to "get people to listen to what [they] say" than people who behave politely. The researchers concluded that "norm violators are perceived as having the capacity to act as they please."[6] As a result, they seem more powerful. Another study found that people who have power judged others much more negatively for speeding, dodging taxes, and keeping a stolen bike than if they engaged in this behaviour themselves. The study also found that those who had legitimate power were even more likely to indulge in moral hypocrisy (the attempt to appear moral without actually being moral) than those who did not feel personally entitled to their power.[7]

Power should not be considered a bad thing, however. *Focus on Research* provides insight into the dynamics of power, choice, and personal control.

Everyone wants power. Or do they? *Point/Counterpoint* on page 303 considers this question.

FOCUS ON RESEARCH
Power: It's All about Control

Why is choice less important when you have a sense of personal power?   A recent study examining how people think about power suggests that the desire for power is directly related to control.[8] In one of the experiments that was part of the study, subjects were asked to think about their feelings about being in the role of a boss or an employee after reading a description of the role. Subjects in the employee role read about being in a powerless situation, while those in the boss role read about being in a powerful situation. Afterward, subjects were asked to choose whether to "buy eyeglasses or ice cream from a store that had three options or a store that had fifteen options." Subjects in the powerless employee situation chose the scenario with more options, even if it meant driving farther or waiting longer.

In other words, people who have power do not feel the need for as much choice, and people who lack power demand to have more choice. This research suggests that "power satisfies the thirst for choice and choice quenches the desire for power because each replenishes a sense of control."

"People instinctively prefer high to low power positions," says Ena Inesi, one of the researchers from the London Business School. For those in low power positions, "it feels good when you have choice, and it doesn't feel good when choice is taken away." . . . . . .

power The capacity that A has to influence the behaviour of B, so that B acts in accordance with A's wishes.

dependence B's relationship to A when A possesses something that B requires.

Bases of Power

❷ Explain the three bases of formal power and the two bases of personal power.

Jian Ghomeshi's radio show was very popular.[9] When the show was still on the air, the CBC website indicated that the show had "the highest-ever ratings in its time slot in CBC history." The show also had an American following, with 180 US radio stations carrying the program. Because of this, Ghomeshi had both expertise power and referent power.

A report written after an independent investigation suggested that "host culture" at CBC enabled Ghomeshi. Host culture, according to the report, is "A belief that people who occupy the role of an on-air host inevitably have big personalities, big egos, and big demands. . . . Because this personality type is considered necessary for the job, certain host behaviour was generally tolerated despite the feeling that their egos and behaviour were problematic as there is general fear to stand up to the talent." One senior manager quoted in the report said "there tends to be a belief that bad behaviour is excused by results."

How do bases of power affect how individuals are treated and evaluated? Where does power come from? What is it that gives an individual or a group influence over others?[10]

Formal Power

Formal power is based on an individual's position in an organization. It can come from the ability to coerce or reward, or from formal authority.

Coercive Power

At the organizational level, A has **coercive power** over B if A can dismiss, suspend, or demote B, assuming B values her job. If A can assign B work activities B finds unpleasant, or treat B in a manner B finds embarrassing, A possesses coercive power over B. Coercive power comes also from withholding key information. People in an organization who have data or knowledge others need can make others dependent on them.

Reward Power

The opposite of coercive power is **reward power**. People will go along with the wishes or directives of another if doing so produces positive benefits; therefore, someone who can distribute rewards that others view as valuable will have power over those others. These rewards can be financial—such as controlling pay rates, raises, and bonuses—or nonfinancial, including offering recognition, promotions, interesting work assignments, friendly colleagues, and preferred work shifts or sales territories.[11]

Legitimate Power

In formal groups and organizations, probably the most frequent access to one or more of the bases of power is through a person's structural position. This is called **legitimate power**. It represents the power a person receives as a result of his or her position in the formal hierarchy of an organization.

Legitimate power is broader than the power to coerce and reward. Specifically, it includes acceptance by members of an organization of the authority of a hierarchical position. We associate power so closely with the concept of hierarchy that just drawing longer lines in an organization chart leads people to infer that the leaders are especially powerful.[12] When school principals, bank presidents, or government department heads speak, teachers, tellers, and civil servants listen and usually comply.

The *Ethical Dilemma* on pages 304–305 asks you to think about how much you should defer to those in power. The Milgram experiment, discussed in *Focus on Research*, looks at the extremes individuals sometimes go to in order to comply with authority figures.

coercive power A power base that is dependent on fear of the negative results from failing to comply.

reward power Power that achieves compliance based on the ability to distribute rewards that others view as valuable.

legitimate power Power that a person receives as a result of his or her position in the formal hierarchy of an organization.

FOCUS ON RESEARCH
A Shocking Experiment

Would you shock someone if you were told to do so?   A classic experiment conducted by Stanley Milgram studied the extent to which people are willing to obey those in authority.[13] Subjects were recruited for an experiment that asked them to administer electric shocks to a "student" who was supposed to learn a list of words. The experiments were conducted at Yale University, and subjects were assured by the experimenter, who was dressed in a white lab coat, that punishment was an effective way to learn. The subjects were placed in front of an instrument panel that indicated the shocks could go from 15 volts to 450 volts. With each wrong answer, subjects were to administer the next-highest shock level. After the shocks reached a middle level, the "student" started to cry out in pain. The experimenter would instruct the subject to continue administering shocks. The experimenter was trying to find out at what level the subjects would stop administering the electric shock. No subject stopped before 300 volts, and 65 percent of the subjects continued to the end of the experiment, even though, at the upper levels, the instrument panel was marked "Danger XXX." It should be noted that subjects were not actually administering shocks, and that the "student" was actually a confederate and was simply acting as if in pain. However, the subjects believed that they were administering electric shocks. This experiment suggests that many people will obey those who appear to have legitimate authority, even in questionable circumstances.

Personal Power

It is possible to have power, as do competent and productive chip designers in technology firms, without having the formal power that comes with being a manager. Some people have *personal power*, which comes from an individual's unique characteristics. There are two bases of personal power: expertise and the respect and admiration of others. Personal power is not mutually exclusive of formal power, but it can be independent.

Expert Power

Expert power is influence based on expertise, special skills, or knowledge. As jobs become more specialized, we become dependent on experts to achieve goals. It is generally acknowledged that physicians have expertise and hence expert power—most of us follow the advice that our doctor gives us. Computer specialists, tax accountants, economists, and other specialists can have power as a result of their expertise.

Referent Power

Referent power is based on identification with a person who has desirable resources or personal traits. If I like, respect, and admire you, you can exercise power over me because I want to please you. Referent power develops out of admiration of another and a desire to be like that person. It helps explain why celebrities are paid millions of dollars to endorse products in commercials, such as Drake for OVO Jordan brand sneakers, Eugenie Bouchard for Coca-Cola Canada, Gwen Stefani for L'Oréal, and Justin Timberlake for Sauza tequila. Some people who are not in formal leadership positions nonetheless have referent power and exert influence over others because of their charismatic dynamism, likeability, and emotional appeal.

The *Experiential Exercise* on page 304 gives you the opportunity to explore the effectiveness of different bases of power in changing someone's behaviour.

expert power Influence based on special skills or knowledge.

referent power Influence based on possession by an individual of desirable resources or personal traits.

Internet entrepreneur Mark Zuckerberg, co-founder and CEO of Facebook, has expert power. Shown here talking with employees, Zuckerberg earned the title "software guy" during college because of his expertise in computer programming. Today, Facebook depends on his expertise to achieve company goals.

Which Bases of Power Are Most Effective?

Of the three bases of formal power (coercive, reward, legitimate) and two bases of personal power (expert, referent), which are most important? Research suggests the personal sources of power are most effective. Both expert and referent power are positively related to employees' satisfaction with supervision, their organizational commitment, and their performance, whereas reward and legitimate power seem to be unrelated to these outcomes. One source of formal power—coercive power—can be damaging.

Generally, people will respond in one of three ways when faced with those who use the bases of power described above:

- *Commitment.* The person is enthusiastic about the request and shows initiative and persistence in carrying it out.

- *Compliance.* The person goes along with the request grudgingly, puts in minimal effort, and takes little initiative in carrying out the request.

- *Resistance.* The person is opposed to the request and tries to avoid it with such tactics as refusing, stalling, or arguing about it.[14]

A review of the research on the effectiveness of these forms of power finds that they differ in their impact on a person's performance.[15] Exhibit 8-1 summarizes some of this research. Coercive power leads to resistance from individuals, increases mistrust, and is negatively related to employee satisfaction and commitment. Reward power results in compliance if the rewards are consistent with what individuals want as rewards. Legitimate power also results in compliance, but it does not generally result in increased commitment. In other words, legitimate power does not inspire individuals to act beyond the basic level. Expert and referent powers are the most likely to lead to commitment from individuals and are positively related to employees' satisfaction with supervision, their organizational commitment, and their performance. Ironically, the least effective bases of power for improving commitment—coercive, reward, and legitimate—are the ones most often used by managers, perhaps because they are the easiest to introduce.[16] Research shows that deadline pressure increases group members' reliance on individuals with expert power.[17]

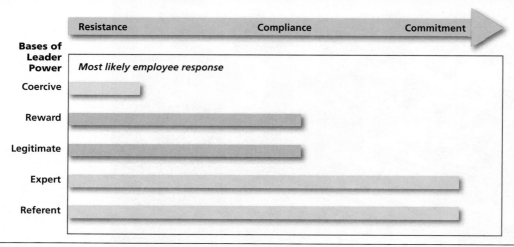

EXHIBIT 8-1 Continuum of Responses to Power

Source: STEERS, RICHARD M.; BLACK, J. STEWART, ORGANIZATIONAL BEHAVIOR, 5th Ed., ©1994. Reprinted and Electronically reproduced by permission of Pearson Education, Inc., Upper Saddle River, New Jersey.

3 Explain the role of dependence in power relationships.

Dependence: The Key to Power

Allegations about Ghomeshi's sexual misconduct started swirling in the spring of 2014.[18] He learned from friends that reporters and a former girlfriend were investigating his sex life. Specifically they were wondering whether there was any evidence he engaged in nonconsensual and/or violent sex.

Ghomeshi worried that this information might enter the public sphere, so he alerted senior management to these rumours to make sure they heard this information from him first. The CBC did not press Ghomeshi to give clear and detailed accounts, and he did not. Instead, the corporation decided to stand by him. There was a long history between Ghomeshi and the CBC, his accounts of what had happened were somewhat vague, and he was a CBC star. In other words, Ghomeshi had made the CBC dependent on him. So the corporation stood by him until it felt it could no longer do so. In a memo sent to employees, the CBC said "Jian's conduct in causing physical injury to a woman was inconsistent with the character of the public broadcaster, was fundamentally unacceptable for any employee, was likely to bring the reputation of his fellow employees and CBC into disrepute and could not be defended by CBC." What factors might lead one party (a person or an organization) to have greater power over another?

The most important aspect of power is that it is a function of dependence. In this section, we show how an understanding of dependence helps us understand the degrees of power.

The General Dependence Postulate

Let's begin with a general postulate: *The greater B's dependence on A, the greater the power A has over B.* When you possess anything that others require but that you alone control, you make them dependent upon you and, therefore, you gain power over them.[19] Another way to frame dependence is to think about a relationship in terms of "who needs whom?" The person who has the most need is the one most dependent on the relationship.[20]

Dependence is inversely proportional to the alternative sources of supply. If something is plentiful, possession of it will not increase your power. If everyone is intelligent, intelligence gives no special advantage. But if you can create a monopoly by controlling information, prestige, or anything that others crave, they become dependent on you. Alternatively, the more options you have, the less power you place in the hands of others. This explains, for example, why most organizations develop multiple suppliers rather than give their business to only one. It also explains why so many people aspire to financial independence. Independence reduces the power others can wield to limit our access to opportunities and resources.

What Creates Dependence?

Dependence is increased when the resource you control is important, scarce, and cannot be substituted.[21]

Importance

If nobody wants what you have, there is no dependence. To create dependence, the thing(s) you control must be perceived as important. However, note that there are many degrees of importance, from needing the resource for survival to wanting a resource that is in fashion or adds to convenience.

> Have you ever wondered how you might increase your power?

Scarcity

As noted previously, if something is plentiful, possession of it will not increase your power. A resource must be perceived as scarce to create dependence.

The scarcity–dependence relationship can further be seen in the power situation of employment. Where the supply of labour is low relative to demand, workers can negotiate compensation and benefits packages far more attractive than those in occupations with an abundance of candidates. For example, college and university administrators have no problem finding English instructors to staff classes. There are more individuals who have degrees enabling them to work as English instructors than there are positions available in Canada. The market for corporate finance professors, by contrast, is extremely tight, with the demand high and the supply limited. The result is that the bargaining power of finance faculty allows them to negotiate higher salaries, lighter teaching loads, and other benefits.

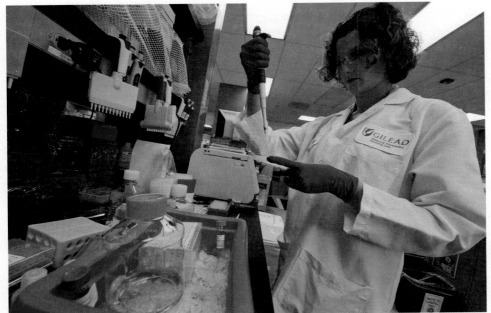

David Paul Morris/Bloomberg/Getty Images

Scientist Maria Kovalenko is in a position of power at Gilead Sciences, a research-based biopharmaceutical firm. Scientists are in a powerful occupational group at Gilead because they discover and develop medicines that improve the lives of patients and contribute to Gilead's growth and success.

Nonsubstitutability

The fewer substitutes there are for a resource, the more power the person controlling that resource has. For example, most universities value faculty publishing, so the more recognition the faculty member receives through publication, the more control that person has because other universities want faculty who are highly published and visible.

4 Identify power or influence tactics and their contingencies.

Influence Tactics

How do individuals translate their bases of power into specific, desired actions? Individuals use influence to try and get the desired actions they want from others. Research has identified 10 distinct **influence tactics**, which are described in Exhibit 8-2:[22]

EXHIBIT 8-2 Influence Tactics	
Influence Tactic	**Definition**
Rational Persuasion	Person A uses logical arguments and factual evidence to persuade person B that a proposal or request is viable and likely to result in the attainment of task objectives.
Inspirational Appeals	Person A makes an emotional request or proposal that arouses enthusiasm by appealing to person B's values and ideals, or by increasing person B's confidence that person B can do it.
Consultation	Person A seeks person B's participation in making a decision or planning how to implement a proposed policy, strategy, or change.
Ingratiation	Person A seeks to get person B in a good mood or to think favourably of person A before asking person B to do something.
Exchange	Person A makes an explicit or implicit promise that person B will receive rewards or tangible benefits if person B complies with a request or supports a proposal, or reminds person B of a prior favour to be reciprocated.
Personal Appeal	Person A appeals to person B's feelings of loyalty and friendship toward person A before asking person B to do something.
Coalition	Person A seeks the aid of others to persuade person B to do something or uses the support of others as an argument for person B to agree also.
Legitimating	Person A seeks to establish the legitimacy of a request by claiming the authority or right to make it or by verifying that it is consistent with organizational policies, rules, practices, or traditions.
Upward Appeals	Person A seeks to persuade person B that the request is approved by higher management, or appeals to higher management for assistance in gaining person B's compliance with the request.
Pressure	Person A uses demands, threats, or intimidation to convince person B to comply with a request or to support a proposal.

Source: G. Yukl and J. B. Tracey, "Consequences of Influence Tactics Used with Subordinates, Peers, and the Boss," *Journal of Applied Psychology* 77, no. 4 (1992) pp. 525–535.

influence tactics Ways in which individuals translate power bases into specific actions.

EXHIBIT 8-3 Preferred Tactics by Influence Direction

Upward Influence	Downward Influence	Lateral Influence
Rational persuasion	Rational persuasion	Rational persuasion
	Inspirational appeals	Consultation
	Pressure	Ingratiation
	Consultation	Exchange
	Ingratiation	Legitimacy
	Exchange	Personal appeals
	Legitimacy	Coalitions

About Influence Tactics

Some influence tactics are more effective than others. Rational persuasion, inspirational appeals, and consultation tend to be the most effective, especially when the audience is highly interested in the outcomes of a decision process. Pressure tends to frequently backfire and is typically the least effective of the 10 tactics.[23] You can increase your chance of success by using two or more tactics together, as long as your choices are compatible.[24] Using ingratiation and legitimacy together can lessen the negative reactions, but only when the audience does not really care about the outcome of a decision process or the policy is routine.[25]

The effectiveness of some influence tactics depends on the direction of influence,[26] and on the audience. As Exhibit 8-3 shows, rational persuasion is the only tactic that is effective across organizational levels. Inspirational appeals work best as a downward-influencing tactic with subordinates. When pressure works, it's generally only to achieve downward influence. The use of personal appeals and coalitions is most effective with lateral influence attempts. In addition to the direction of influence, a number of other factors affect which tactics work best. These include the sequencing of tactics, a person's skill in using the tactic, and the organizational culture.

In general, you are more likely to be effective if you begin with "softer" influence tactics that rely on personal power such as personal and inspirational appeals, rational persuasion, and consultation. If these fail, you can move to "harder" tactics (which emphasize formal power and involve greater costs and risks), such as exchange, coalitions, and pressure.[27] A single soft tactic is more effective than using a single hard tactic, and combining two soft tactics or a soft tactic and rational persuasion is more effective than any single tactic or a combination of hard tactics.[28]

The effectiveness of influence tactics depends on the audience.[29] People especially likely to comply with soft influence tactics tend to be more reflective and intrinsically motivated; they have high self-esteem and greater desire for control. Those likely to comply with hard influence tactics are more action oriented and extrinsically motivated and are more focused on getting along with others than on getting their own way.

Applying Influence Tactics

People differ in their **political skill**, or the ability to influence others in such a way as to enhance their own objectives. The politically skilled are more effective users of all of the influence tactics. Political skill is also more effective when the stakes are high—such as when the individual is accountable for important organizational outcomes. Finally, the politically skilled are able to exert their influence without others detecting it, a key element of its effectiveness (it's damaging to be labelled political).[30] These individuals are able to use their political skills in environments with low levels of procedural and distributive justice. In organizations that apply rules fairly, without favouritism or biases, political skill is negatively related to job performance ratings.[31]

Finally, we know that cultures within organizations differ markedly—some are warm, relaxed, and supportive; others are formal and conservative. Some encourage

political skill The ability to influence others in such a way as to enhance one's objectives.

participation and consultation, some encourage reason, and still others rely on pressure. People who fit the culture of the organization tend to obtain more influence.[32] Specifically, extraverts tend to be more influential in team-oriented organizations, and highly conscientious people are more influential in organizations that value working alone on technical tasks. People who fit the culture are influential because they can perform especially well in the domains deemed most important for success. Thus, the organization itself will influence which subset of influence tactics is viewed as acceptable for use.

How Power Affects People

> Ghomeshi's star power, which came from *Q*, also affected the way that he worked with his employees.[33] Some people in positions of power make demands on others so that they can protect their own reputations. Matt Tunnacliffe, who was a *Q* producer and director, said that Gomeshi "had a vision for the show and he made it happen . . . and he wasn't accepting of things that got in the way of that vision. That included subpar work, headphone settings, script work. It was a tough place to work sometimes."
>
> Staff reported that as the show grew in stature, it became more about Ghomeshi, and the staff felt that they received no credit for the show's success.
>
> Kathryn Borel, founding producer of *Q*, described being sexually assaulted by Ghomeshi for three years. Rather than face a trial, Ghomeshi entered a plea bargain in May 2016, and explained his behaviour as follows: "I now recognize that I crossed boundaries inappropriately. I didn't appreciate the damage that I caused . . . the incident was thoughtless and I was insensitive to her perspective and how demeaning my conduct was towards her." It is likely that, because he was in a position of power, he had little need to consider her perspective.
>
> What leads people to use power either selfishly or wisely?

Studies indicate that when someone is in a position of power, he or she may be more willing to exert that power.[34] *Focus on Research* shows how this idea played out in one particular study.

FOCUS ON RESEARCH
The Cookie Experiment

Who eats the fourth cookie? In a study known as the "cookie experiment," three psychologists instructed teams of three students to write a short paper during a meeting.[35] Two of the team members (the "subordinates") were to do the actual writing, and the third team member (the "boss") was assigned to evaluate the work and determine the pay the two writers would receive. Part way through the meeting, experimenters brought in a plate of five cookies. As expected, no one ate the fifth cookie (rules of etiquette suggest that one should not eat the last item on a plate). The researchers were interested, then, in who ate the fourth cookie, given that it was extra. "Bosses" were far more likely to take the fourth cookie than "subordinates," and were much more likely to chew with their mouths open and scatter crumbs widely, signs that their power enabled them to act in less-inhibited ways.

The authors concluded that people with power behave very differently than those without it. Powerful people are generally less inhibited and sometimes act in counternormative ways. Powerless people "are more likely to feel negative moods and emotions; to attend to punishment and threat; to make more careful, controlled judgments about others' intentions, attitudes, and actions; and to inhibit their own behaviours and act contingently upon others."

To this point, we have discussed what power is and how it is acquired. But we have not yet answered one important question: Does power corrupt?

Power does appear to have corrupting aspects. Power can lead people to place their own interests ahead of those of others' needs or goals. Why does this happen? Interestingly, research suggests that power not only leads people to focus on their self-interests because they can, it also liberates them to focus inward and thus come to place greater weight on their own aims and interests. Power also appears to lead individuals to "objectify" others (to see them as tools to obtain their instrumental goals), and to see relationships as more peripheral.[36] Powerful people react (especially negatively) to any threats to their competence. People in positions of power hold on to it when they can, and individuals who face threats to their power are exceptionally willing to take actions to retain it whether their actions harm others or not. One need only think of the many tweets US President Donald Trump made during his presidential campaign and afterward attacking people he thought had slighted him. Those given power are more likely to make self-interested decisions when faced with a moral hazard, which is lack of incentive to guard against risk where one is protected from its consequences. An example is hedge fund managers taking more risks with other people's money because they are rewarded for gains but less often punished for losses. People in power are more willing to denigrate others. Power also leads to overconfident decision making.[37]

Power Variables

As we have discussed, power does appear to have some important disturbing effects on us. But that is hardly the whole story—power is more complicated than that. It does not affect everyone in the same way, and there are even positive effects of power. Let's consider each of these in turn.

First, the toxic effects of power depend on the wielder's personality. Research suggests that if we have an anxious personality, power does not corrupt us because we are less likely to think that using power benefits us.[38] Second, the corrosive effect of power can be contained by organizational systems. One study found, for example, that while power made people behave in a self-serving manner, when accountability for this behaviour was initiated, the self-serving behaviour stopped. Third, we have the means to blunt the negative effects of power. One study showed that simply expressing gratitude toward powerful others makes them less likely to act aggressively against us.[39] Finally, consider the saying that those with little power abuse what little they have. There appears to be some truth to this in that the people most likely to abuse power are those who start low in status and gain power. Why is this the case? It appears that having low status is threatening, and the fear this creates is used in negative ways if power is later given.[40]

As you can see, some factors can moderate the negative effects of power. But there can be general positive effects. Power can energize and lead to increased motivation to achieve goals. It can also enhance our motivation to help others. One study found, for example, that desire to help others translated into actual work behaviour when people felt a sense of power.[41]

This study points to an important insight about power: It's not so much that power corrupts as it *reveals what we value*. Supporting this line of reasoning, another study found that power led to self-interested behaviour only in those with a weak moral identity (the degree to which morals are core to someone's identity). In those with a strong moral identity, power enhanced their moral awareness and willingness to act.[42]

Harassment: Unequal Power in the Workplace

People who engage in harassment in the workplace are typically abusing their power position. The manager–employee relationship best characterizes an unequal power

 Identify the causes and consequences of abuse of power.

relationship, where position power gives the manager the capacity to reward and coerce. Managers give employees their assignments, evaluate their performance, make recommendations for salary adjustments and promotions, and even decide whether employees retain their job. These decisions give a manager power. Since employees want favourable performance reviews, salary increases, and the like, it's clear that managers control the resources that most employees consider important and scarce.

Although co-workers do not have position power, they can have influence and use it to harass peers. In fact, although co-workers appear to engage in somewhat less severe forms of harassment than do managers, co-workers are the most frequent perpetrators of harassment, particularly sexual harassment, in organizations. How do co-workers exercise power? Most often they provide or withhold information, cooperation, and support.

We focus here on two types of harassment that have received considerable attention in the press: workplace bullying and sexual harassment.

Workplace Bullying

Many of us are aware, anecdotally if not personally, of managers who harass employees, demanding overtime without pay or excessive work performance. Further, some of the recent stories of workplace violence have reportedly been the result of an employee feeling intimidated at work. In research conducted in the private and public sector in southern Saskatchewan, Céleste Brotheridge, a professor at the Université du Québec à Montréal, found that bullying was prevalent and has a negative effect in the workplace: "Given bullying's deleterious effects on employee health, it is reason for concern."[43]

There is no clear definition of workplace bullying, and Marilyn Noble, a Fredericton-based adult educator, remarks that in some instances a fine line exists between managing and bullying. However, recent research suggests that bosses who feel inadequate or overwhelmed are more likely to bully.[44] As one of the study's co-authors explained: "The combination of having a high-power role and fearing that one is not up to the task . . . causes power holders to lash out."[45] A recent study by researchers at Université du Québec à Montréal looking at the effects of bullying on nurses showed that it decreases satisfaction and increases burnout.[46]

Quebec introduced the first anti-bullying labour legislation in North America on June 1, 2004. The legislation defines psychological harassment as "any vexatious behaviour in the form of repeated and hostile or unwanted conduct, verbal comments, actions or gestures that affects an employee's dignity or psychological or physical integrity and that results in a harmful work environment for the employee."[47] A number of other provinces have introduced workplace legislation addressing bullying and harassment issues, though not all provinces have done so. Most provinces do have a requirement in their Occupational Health and Safety Legislation to protect the health and safety of employees, which provides some protection. *OB on the Edge—Workplace Bullying* on pages 344–349 looks at this matter more closely.

Sexual Harassment

The Supreme Court of Canada defines **sexual harassment** as unwelcome behaviour of a sexual nature in the workplace that negatively affects the work environment or leads to adverse job-related consequences for the employee.[48] Despite the legal framework for defining sexual harassment, disagreement continues as to what *specifically* constitutes sexual harassment. Sexual harassment includes unwanted physical touching, recurring requests for dates when it is made clear the person is not interested, and coercive threats that a person will lose her or his job if she or he refuses a sexual proposition. The problems of interpreting sexual harassment often surface around some of its more subtle forms—unwanted looks or comments, off-colour jokes, sexual artifacts such as nude calendars in the workplace, sexual innuendo,

sexual harassment Unwelcome behaviour of a sexual nature in the workplace that negatively affects the work environment or leads to adverse job-related consequences for the employee.

or different interpretations of where the line between "being friendly" ends and "harassment" begins.

Most studies confirm that power is central to understanding sexual harassment.[49] This seems true whether the harassment comes from a supervisor, a co-worker, or an employee. Sexual harassment is more likely to occur when there are large power differentials. The supervisor–employee dyad best characterizes an unequal power relationship, where formal power gives the supervisor the capacity to reward and coerce. Because employees want favourable performance reviews, salary increases, and the like, supervisors control resources most employees consider important and scarce. Inadequate controls to detect and prevent sexual harassment by a manager typically create the greatest difficulty for those being harassed. If there are no witnesses, abusers are more likely to act. For example, male respondents in one study in Switzerland who were high in hostile sexism reported higher intentions to sexually harass in organizations that had low levels of justice, suggesting that failure to have consistent policies and procedures for all employees might increase levels of sexual harassment.[50]

Employers in Canada are expected to protect their employees with sexual harassment policies. Some employers have developed sexual harassment policies, and some go further, either banning workplace romances or requiring them to be reported to management. Lying about a workplace affair got one manager fired, as *OB in the Workplace* shows.

In addition to its legal repercussions, sexual harassment obviously has a negative impact on the work environment. Sexual harassment negatively affects job attitudes and leads those who feel harassed to withdraw from work (for example, avoiding work, failing to attend scheduled meetings). In fact, perceptions of sexual harassment are more likely than workplace bullying to lead to work withdrawal.[51] It also appears that sexual harassment has health consequences. Women exposed to workplace sexual harassment reported psychological distress two years after the harassment occurred.[52]

Workplaces are not the only place where sexual harassment occurs. While nonconsensual sex between professors and students is rape and subject to criminal charges, it's harder to evaluate apparently consensual relationships that occur outside the classroom. There is some argument over whether truly consensual sex is ever possible between students and professors and some universities have considered outright bans between

OB IN THE WORKPLACE

It's Not About the Affair, It's About the Coverup

Should an employee be fired for lying about a workplace affair? Bryan Reichard, a 41-year-old married manager at Kitchener-based Kuntz Electroplating, had an affair with one of the company's administrative assistants.[53] She was single and 26.

In order to prevent sexual harassment lawsuits, Kuntz implemented a non-fraternization policy, which specified that employees in romantic relationships needed to notify their manager. Reichard was repeatedly asked if he was having an affair with the administrative assistant, but he denied it. Kuntz did not forbid office relationships, so Reichard would not have been disciplined for having a workplace affair.

However, Reichard was eventually terminated for lying about the affair. The decision was appealed, and Kuntz's decision to terminate Reichard was upheld. The judge hearing the case gave his reasoning in his December 2011 judgment: "Kuntz had every right to consider that Reichard's wilful misconduct seriously called into question the trust, integrity and honesty required for him to perform his duties as a manager and that Kuntz's lack of trust in Reichard was sufficient to terminate him for cause." . . . .

professors and students engaging in intimate relationships. Most universities have been unwilling to adopt such an extreme stance, and it's not clear that in Canada such a policy would stand up in the courts. Carleton University does not prohibit relationships between individuals in authority and those who are not, but does include the following statement in its sexual harassment policy: "No individual in a position of authority is permitted to grade or supervise the performance of any student, or evaluate an employee or a colleague, with whom they are sexually involved or have been within the past five years."[54]

A recent study of five of Quebec's French-speaking universities found that almost 37 percent of the respondents (which included students, faculty, and staff) reported that they had experienced some form of sexual violence. Only 15 percent of that group reported the activities to the authorities, and more than 30 percent never told anyone, not even a friend, about the episode(s).[55] However, much of this harassment comes from student-on-student incidents. Iain Boekhoff, the editor-in-chief of Western University's Frosh issue of the *Gazette*, came under fire for publishing an article telling first-year students how to sexually harass their teaching assistants (TAs). Boekhoff defended the article as being relatively tame. "Two years ago it was just straight, 'How to have sex with your TA,' as one of the 50 or 100 things to do before you leave Western," he said.[56]

Sexual harassment can have a negative impact on the organizations and the victims themselves. But it can be avoided. The manager's role in preventing sexual harassment is critical. Managers can protect themselves and their employees from sexual harassment in the following ways:

- Make sure an active policy defines what constitutes sexual harassment, informs employees that they can be fired for inappropriate behaviour, and establishes procedures for making complaints.

- Reassure employees that they will not encounter retaliation if they issue a complaint.

- Investigate every complaint and inform the legal and human resource departments.

- Make sure that offenders are disciplined or terminated.

- Set up in-house seminars to raise employee awareness of sexual harassment issues.

Should workplaces ban all forms of sexual behaviour as a way of preventing harassment? *Focus on Ethics* considers this question.

The bottom line is that managers have a responsibility to protect their employees from a hostile work environment. They may easily be unaware that one of their employees is being sexually harassed, but being unaware does not protect them or their organization. If investigators believe a manager could have known about the harassment, both the manager and the company can be held liable.

6 Explain what empowerment is, and the factors that lead to it.

Empowerment: Giving Power to Employees

Thus far, our discussion has implied—to some extent, at least—that power is something that is more likely to reside in the hands of managers, to be used as part of their interaction with employees. However, in today's workplace, there is a movement toward sharing more power with employees by putting them in teams and also by making them responsible for some of the decisions regarding their jobs. For instance, at Vancouver-based iQmetrix Software Development, employees are part of a results-only workplace, where they are encouraged to make their own decisions.[57] Organizational specialists refer to this increasing responsibility as *empowerment*.

FOCUS ON ETHICS
Sex at Work

Should romantic relationships be prohibited at work?   The difficulty in monitoring and defining sexual harassment at work has led some organizations to go beyond discouraging overt sexually harassing behaviours.[58] Companies ranging from Walmart to Staples to Xerox have disciplined employees for workplace romances and upheld policies that ban hierarchical romantic relationships, such as between a supervisor and a subordinate. The idea is that such relationships are so fraught with potential for abuse of power that they cannot possibly be consensual for extended periods of time. Surveys by the Society of Human Resource Management suggest that concerns about both potential sexual harassment and lowered productivity have motivated prohibitions on workplace romances. However, ethicists and legal scholars have thrown some "no romance" policies into question on the grounds they are patronizing or invade employee privacy.

What does organizational behaviour research have to say about *consensual* sexual behaviour at work? One study of more than 1000 respondents found that 40 percent were exposed to sexual behaviour in some form in the past year. Counter to the idea that all sexual behaviour at work is negative, some female and many male respondents reported enjoying the experience. However, exposure to sexual behaviour at work was negatively related to performance and psychological well-being. People may report enjoying it, but it might be hurting their productivity and well-being anyway. ....

Definition of Empowerment

The definition of *empowerment* that we use here refers to the freedom and the ability of employees to make decisions and commitments.[59] Unfortunately, neither managers nor researchers agree on the definition of empowerment. One study found that executives were split about 50–50 in their definition.[60] One group of executives "believed that empowerment was about delegating decision making within a set of clear boundaries." Empowerment would start at the top, specific goals and tasks would be assigned, responsibility would be delegated, and people would be held accountable for their results. The other group believed that empowerment was "a process of risk taking and personal growth." This type of empowerment starts at the bottom, with considering the employees' needs, showing them what empowered behaviour looks like, building teams, encouraging risk-taking, and demonstrating trust in employees' ability to perform. *Case Incident—Delegate Power, or Keep It Close?* on page 305 considers the tension between delegating and remaining in charge.

One difficulty with empowerment is that managers often give lip service to the idea,[61] with organizations telling employees that they have decision-making responsibility, but not giving them the authority to carry out their decisions. The result is a great deal of cynicism in many workplaces, particularly when "empowered" employees are micromanaged. For an employee to be fully empowered, he or she needs access to the information required to make decisions; rewards for acting in appropriate, responsible ways; and the authority to make the necessary decisions. Empowerment means that employees understand how their job fits into the organization and are able to make decisions regarding job action guided by the organization's purpose and mission.

> What do you need to be truly empowered?

EXHIBIT 8-4 Characteristics of Empowered People

Robert E. Quinn and Gretchen M. Spreitzer, in their research on the characteristics of empowered people, found four characteristics that most empowered people have in common:

- *Self-determination:* They choose how to do their work (they are not micromanaged).
- *Sense of meaning:* They care about what they do because they consider what they do has an important purpose.
- *Sense of competence:* They believe that they have the ability to perform their work well.
- *Sense of impact:* They believe that their ideas are listened to and that they can influence work outcomes.

Source: Based on R. E. Quinn and G. M. Spreitzer, "The Road to Empowerment: Seven Questions Every Leader Should Consider," *Organizational Dynamics*, Autumn 1997, p. 41.

Not every employee appreciates being empowered, however. One study found that sometimes empowerment can make employees ill if they are put in charge at work but lack the confidence to handle their responsibilities.[62] The study authors suggested that employers who seek to increase employees' control over their work should also promote employees' sense of self-efficacy. Doing so is more likely to support employee well-being.

Exhibit 8-4 outlines what two researchers discovered in studying the characteristics of empowered people.

Courtesy of Steam Whistle Brewing

Managers at Toronto-based Steam Whistle Brewing must face their employees to ask what needs to be fixed if there are complaints about the managers. The company encourages its younger employees (a few of whom are shown here, congregating after work on the staff patio) to speak up. Co-founder Greg Taylor explains the rationale: "In many organizations, younger employees feel they won't be heard until they're established in their careers. We think that we're in the business of selling beer to young people, so we should listen to what they have to say."[63]

Great Little Box Company

At Vancouver-based Great Little Box Company (GLBC), which designs and manufactures corrugated containers, employees are given the freedom to do whatever they feel is necessary and appropriate to make customers happy. If a customer is dissatisfied with the product, the employee can say, "OK, I'll bring this product back and return it for you," without having to get prior authorization.

Politics: Power in Action

Whenever people get together in groups, power will be exerted. People want to carve out a niche to exert influence, to earn awards, and to advance their careers.[64] If they convert their power into action, we describe them as being engaged in politics. Those with good political skills have the ability to use their bases of power effectively.[65] In this section, we look at political behaviour, including the types of political activity people use to try to influence others, and impression management. Political skills are not confined to adults, of course. Even young children are quite adept at waging careful, deliberate campaigns to wear their parents down, so that they can get things that they want.

7 Describe how politics work in organizations.

Definition of Political Behaviour

There is no shortage of definitions for *organizational politics*. Essentially, this type of politics focuses on the use of power to affect decision making in an organization, sometimes for self-serving and organizationally unsanctioned behaviours.[66]

For our purposes, we will define **political behaviour** in organizations as those activities that are outside one's formal role and that influence, or attempt to influence, the distribution of advantages and disadvantages within the organization.[67]

This definition encompasses what most people mean when they talk about organizational politics. Political behaviour is outside one's specified job requirements. The behaviour requires some attempt to use one's bases of power. Our definition also encompasses efforts to influence the goals, criteria, or processes used for decision making when we state that politics is concerned with "the distribution of advantages and disadvantages within the organization." Our definition is broad enough to include such varied political behaviours as withholding key information from decision makers, joining a coalition, whistle-blowing, spreading rumours, leaking confidential information about organizational activities to the media, exchanging favours with others for mutual benefit, and lobbying on behalf of or against a particular individual or decision alternative. In this way, political behaviour is often negative, but not always. Exhibit 8-5 provides a quick measure to help you assess how political your workplace is.

political behaviour Those activities that influence, or attempt to influence, the distribution of advantages and disadvantages within the organization.

EXHIBIT 8-5 A Quick Measure of How Political Your Workplace Is

How political is your workplace? Answer the 12 questions using the following scale:

SD = Strongly disagree
D = Disagree
U = Uncertain
A = Agree
SA = Strongly agree

1. Managers often use the selection system to hire only people who can help them in their future. _____

2. The rules and policies concerning promotion and pay are fair; it's how managers carry out the policies that is unfair and self-serving. _____

3. The performance ratings people receive from their managers reflect more of the managers' "own agenda" than the actual performance of the employee. _____

4. Although a lot of what my manager does around here appears to be directed at helping employees, it's actually intended to protect my manager. _____

5. There are cliques or "in-groups" that hinder effectiveness around here. _____

6. My co-workers help themselves, not others. _____

7. I have seen people deliberately distort information requested by others for purposes of personal gain, either by withholding it or by selectively reporting it. _____

8. If co-workers offer to lend some assistance, it is because they expect to get something out of it. _____

9. Favouritism rather than merit determines who gets ahead around here. _____

10. You can usually get what you want around here if you know the right person to ask. _____

11. Overall, the rules and policies concerning promotion and pay are specific and well-defined. _____

12. Pay and promotion policies are generally clearly communicated in this organization. _____

This questionnaire taps the three salient dimensions that have been found to be related to perceptions of politics: manager behaviour; co-worker behaviour; and organizational policies and practices. To calculate your score for items 1–10, give yourself 1 point for Strongly disagree; 2 points for Disagree; and so forth (through 5 points for Strongly agree). For items 11 and 12, reverse the score (that is, 1 point for Strongly agree, etc.). Sum up the total: The higher the total score, the greater the degree of perceived organizational politics.

Source: G. R. Ferris, D. D. Frink, D. P. S. Bhawuk, J. Zhou, and D. C. Gilmore, "Reactions of Diverse Groups to Politics in the Workplace," *Journal of Management* 22, no. 1 (1996), pp. 32–33.

The Reality of Politics

Interviews with experienced managers show most believe political behaviour is a major part of organizational life.[68] Many managers report some use of political behaviour is ethical, as long as it doesn't directly harm anyone else. They describe politics as necessary and believe someone who never uses political behaviour will have a hard time getting things done. Most also indicate they have never been trained to use political behaviour effectively. But why, you may wonder, must politics exist? Isn't it possible for an organization to be politics-free? It's *possible*, but most unlikely.

Organizations have individuals and groups with different values, goals, and interests.[69] This sets up the potential for conflict over the allocation of limited resources, such as budgets, work space, and salary and bonus pools. If resources were abundant, then all constituencies within the organization could satisfy their goals. But because they are limited, not everyone's interests can be satisfied. Furthermore, gains by one individual or group are often *perceived* as coming at the expense of others within the organization (whether they are or not). These forces create competition among members for the organization's limited resources.

CAREER OBJECTIVES
Should I Become Political?

My office is so political! Everyone is just looking for ways to get ahead by plotting and scheming rather than doing the job. Should I just go along with it and develop my own political strategy?

—Julia

Dear Julia:

There's definitely a temptation to join in when other people are behaving politically. If you want to advance your career, you need to think about social relationships and how to work with other people in a smart and diplomatic way. But that doesn't mean you have to give in to pressure to engage in organizational politics.

Of course, in many workplaces, hard work and achievement aren't recognized, which heightens politicking and lowers performance. But politics aren't just potentially bad for the company. People who are seen as political can be gradually excluded from social networks and informal communication. Co-workers can sabotage a person with a reputation for dishonesty or manipulation so they don't have to deal with him or her. It's also likely that a political person will be the direct target of revenge from those who feel they've been wronged.

If you want to provide a positive alternative to political behaviour in your workplace, there are a few steps you can take:

- *Document your work efforts, and find data to back up your accomplishments.* Political behaviour thrives in an ambiguous environment where standards for success are subjective and open to manipulation. The best way to shortcut politics is to move the focus toward clear, objective markers of work performance.
- *Call out political behaviour when you see it.* Political behaviour is, by its very nature, secretive and underhanded. By bringing politics to light, you limit this capacity to manipulate people against one another.
- *Try to develop a network with only those individuals who are interested in performing well together.* This makes it hard for a very political person to get a lot done. On the other hand, trustworthy and cooperative people will be able to find many allies who are genuinely supportive. These support networks will result in performance levels that a lone political person simply cannot match.

Remember, in the long run a good reputation can be your greatest asset!

Based on: A. Lavoie "How to Get Rid of Toxic Office Politics," *Fast Company,* April 10, 2014, http://www.fastcompany.com/3028856/work-smart/how-to-make-office-politicking-a-lame-duck; C. Conner, "Office Politics: Must You Play?" *Forbes,* April 14, 2013, http://www.forbes.com/sites/cherylsnappconner/2013/04/14/office-politics-must-you-play-a-handbook-for-survivalsuccess/; and J. A. Colquitt and J. B. Rodell "Justice, Trust, and Trustworthiness: A Longitudinal Analysis Integrating Three Theoretical Perspectives," *Academy of Management Journal* 54 (2011), pp. 1183–1206.

The opinions provided here are of the managers and authors only and do not necessarily reflect those of their organizations. The authors or managers are not responsible for any errors or omissions, or for the results obtained from the use of this information. In no event will the authors or managers, or their related partnerships or corporations thereof, be liable to you or anyone else for any decision made or action taken in reliance on the opinions provided here.

Maybe the most important factor behind politics within organizations is the realization that most of the "facts" that are used to allocate the limited resources are open to interpretation. What, for instance, is *good* performance? What is an *adequate* improvement? What constitutes an *unsatisfactory* job? It's in this large and ambiguous middle ground of organizational life—where the facts *don't* speak for themselves—that politics flourish.

Finally, because most decisions must be made in a climate of ambiguity—where facts are rarely fully objective, and thus are open to interpretation—people within organizations will use whatever influence they can to support their goals and interests. That, of course, creates the activities we call *politicking*. For more about how one engages in politicking, see *From Concepts to Skills* on pages 306–308.

Therefore, to answer the earlier question about whether it is possible for an organization to be politics-free, we can say "yes"—but only if all the members of that organization hold the same goals and interests, organizational resources are not scarce, and performance outcomes are completely clear and objective. However, that does not describe the organizational world in which most of us live.

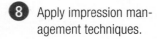

RESEARCH FINDINGS: Politicking

Individuals who successfully engage in politicking can achieve favourable outcomes. But for most people—who have modest political skills or are unwilling to play the politics game—outcomes tend to be predominantly negative.[70] There is, for instance, very strong evidence indicating that perceptions of organizational politics are negatively related to job satisfaction.[71] Politics may lead to self-reported declines in employee performance, perhaps because employees perceive political environments to be unfair, which demotivates them.[72] Not surprisingly, when politicking becomes too much to handle, it can lead employees to quit.[73]

> Why do some people seem to engage in politics more than others?

There are some qualifiers. First, the politics–performance relationship appears to be moderated by an individual's understanding of the "hows" and "whys" of organizational politics. Researchers noted, "An individual who has a clear understanding of who is responsible for making decisions and why they were selected to be the decision makers would have a better understanding of how and why things happen the way they do than someone who does not understand the decision-making process in the organization."[74] When both politics and understanding are high, performance is likely to increase because the individual will see political activity as an opportunity. This is consistent with what you might expect among individuals with well-honed political skills. But when understanding is low, individuals are more likely to see politics as a threat, which can have a negative effect on job performance.[75]

Second, perceptions of political behaviour at work influence the extent to which ethical leadership affects organizational citizenship behaviour.[76] One study found that male employees were more responsive to ethical leadership and showed the most organizational citizenship behaviour when levels of both politics and ethical leadership were high. Women, on the other hand, appear most likely to engage in organizational citizenship behaviour when the environment is consistently ethical and apolitical.

Third, when employees see politics as a threat, they often respond with defensive behaviours—reactive and protective behaviours to avoid action, blame, or change.[77] (Exhibit 8-6 provides some examples.) In the short run, employees may find that defensiveness protects their self-interest, but in the long run it wears them down. People who consistently rely on defensiveness find that eventually it is the only way they know how to behave. At that point, they lose the trust and support of their peers, bosses, employees, and clients.

Individuals use political activities for different purposes. Some of these activities (such as attacking or blaming others) are more likely to be used to defend one's position, while other activities (such as building support for ideas and managing impressions) are meant to enhance one's image. Evidence suggests that keeping your enemies close to you makes some sense politically, as *Focus on Research* indicates.

---

8 Apply impression management techniques.

Impression Management

The process by which individuals attempt to control the impression others form of them is called **impression management** (IM).[78] Being perceived positively by others has benefits for people in an organizational setting. It might, for instance, help them initially to get the jobs they want in an organization and, once hired, to get favourable evaluations, superior salary increases, and more rapid promotions.

Who might we predict will engage in impression management? No surprise here. It's our old friend, the high self-monitor (see Chapter 2).[79] Low self-monitors tend to present images of themselves that are consistent with their personalities, regardless of

impression management The process by which individuals attempt to control the impression others form of them.

EXHIBIT 8-6 Defensive Behaviours

Avoiding Action

Overconforming. Strictly interpreting your responsibility by saying things like "The rules clearly state . . ."or "This is the way we've always done it."

Buck passing. Transferring responsibility for the execution of a task or decision to someone else.

Playing dumb. Avoiding an unwanted task by falsely pleading ignorance or inability.

Stretching. Prolonging a task so that a person appears to be occupied—for example, turning a two-week task into a four-month job.

Stalling. Appearing to be more or less supportive publicly while doing little or nothing privately.

Avoiding Blame

Bluffing. Rigorously documenting activity to project an image of competence and thoroughness, known as "covering your rear."

Playing safe. Evading situations that may reflect unfavourably. It includes taking on only projects with a high probability of success, having risky decisions approved by superiors, qualifying expressions of judgment, and taking neutral positions in conflicts.

Justifying. Developing explanations that lessen one's responsibility for a negative outcome and/or apologizing to demonstrate remorse, or both.

Scapegoating. Placing the blame for a negative outcome on external factors that are not entirely blameworthy.

Misrepresenting. Manipulation of information by distortion, embellishment, deception, selective presentation, or obfuscation.

Avoiding Change

Prevention. Trying to prevent a threatening change from occurring.

Self-protection. Acting in ways to protect one's self-interest during change by guarding information or other resources.

FOCUS ON RESEARCH
Powerful Leaders Keep Their (Fr)Enemies Close

Is it really wise to keep your enemies close? We have all heard the term "frenemies" used to describe friends who are also rivals or people who act like friends but secretly dislike each other.[80] Some observers have argued that frenemies are increasing at work due to the "abundance of very close, intertwined relationships that bridge people's professional and personal lives."

Recent research based on three experimental studies found that a dominant leader chose to work in the same room with a rival in-group member, even when instructed that they would probably perform better apart; to sit closer to the rival when working together; and to express an explicit preference to be closer to the rival. The primary reason dominant leaders wanted to be closer to rivals was to monitor the rivals' behaviour and performance and protect their own power.

The research also found that the "keeping enemies closer" effect was strong under certain conditions—when a rival was socially dominant, when a dominant leader felt competition from the rival, and when the rewards and ability to serve as a dominant leader were dependent on the rival's performance.

These results suggest that the concept of frenemies is very real and that we choose to keep our rivals close so we can keep an eye on the competition they provide. . . . .

EXHIBIT 8-7 Impression Management Techniques

Conformity

Agreeing with someone else's opinion to gain his or her approval is a *form of ingratiation.*

Example: A manager tells his boss, "You're absolutely right on your reorganization plan for the western regional office. I couldn't agree with you more."

Favours

Doing something nice for someone to gain that person's approval is a *form of ingratiation.*

Example: A salesperson says to a prospective client, "I've got two tickets to the theatre tonight that I can't use. Take them. Consider it a thank-you for taking the time to talk with me."

Excuses

Explaining a predicament-creating event aimed at minimizing the apparent severity of the predicament is a *defensive IM technique.*

Example: A sales manager says to her boss, "We failed to get the ad in the paper on time, but no one responds to those ads anyway."

Apologies

Admitting responsibility for an undesirable event and simultaneously seeking to get a pardon for the action is a *defensive IM technique.*

Example: An employee says to his boss, "I'm sorry I made a mistake on the report. Please forgive me."

Self-Promotion

Highlighting your best qualities, downplaying your deficits, and calling attention to your achievements is a *self-focused IM technique.*

Example: A salesperson tells his boss, "Matt worked unsuccessfully for three years to try to get that account. I sewed it up in six weeks. I'm the best closer this company has."

Enhancement

Claiming that something you did is more valuable than most other members of the organization would think is a *self-focused IM technique.*

Example: A journalist tells his editor, "My work on this celebrity divorce story was really a major boost to our sales" (even though the story only made it to page 3 in the entertainment section).

Flattery

Complimenting others about their virtues in an effort to make yourself appear perceptive and likeable is an *assertive IM technique.*

Example: A new sales trainee says to her peer, "You handled that client's complaint so tactfully! I could never have handled that as well as you did."

Exemplification

Doing more than you need to in an effort to show how dedicated and hard-working you are is an *assertive IM technique.*

Example: An employee sends emails from his work computer when he works late so that his supervisor will know how long he has been working.

Sources: Based on M. C. Bolino, K. M. Kacmar, W. H. Turnley, and J. B. Gilstrap, "A Multi-Level Review of Impression Management Motives and Behaviors, *Journal of Management* 34, no. 6 (2008), pp. 1080–1109.

the beneficial or detrimental effects for them. In contrast, high self-monitors are good at reading situations and moulding their appearances and behaviour to fit each situation. If you want to control the impression others form of you, what IM techniques can you use? Exhibit 8-7 summarizes some of the most popular with examples.

Keep in mind that when people engage in impression management, they are sending a false message that might be true under other circumstances.[81] Excuses, for instance, may be offered with great sincerity. You may *actually* believe that ads contribute little to sales in your region. But misrepresentation can have a high cost.[82] So the impression manager must be cautious not to be perceived as insincere or manipulative.[83]

RESEARCH FINDINGS: Impression Management Techniques

One study found that when managers attributed an employee's organizational citizenship behaviour to impression management, they actually felt angry (probably because they felt manipulated) and gave subordinates lower performance ratings. When managers attributed the same behaviours to prosocial values and concern about the organization, they felt happy and gave higher performance ratings.[84] In sum, people don't like to feel others are manipulating them through impression management, so such tactics should be employed with caution. Not all

> In what situations does impression management work best?

impression management consists of talking yourself up, either. Recent research suggests modesty, in the form of generously providing credit to others and understating your own contributions to success, may create a more positive impression on others.[85]

The evidence indicates that most job applicants use impression management techniques in interviews[86] and that, when impression management behaviour is used, it works.[87] To develop a sense of how effective different IM techniques are in interviews, one study grouped data from thousands of recruiting and selection interviews into appearance-oriented efforts (like looking professional), explicit tactics (like flattering the interviewer or talking up your own accomplishments), and verbal cues (like using positive terms and showing general enthusiasm).[88] Across all the dimensions, it was clear that IM was a powerful predictor of how well people did.

However, there was a twist. When interviews were highly structured, meaning the interviewer's questions were written out in advance and focused on applicant qualifications, the effects of IM were substantially weaker. Manipulative behaviours like IM are more likely to have an effect in ambiguous and unstructured interviews.

In terms of performance evaluations, the picture is quite different. Ingratiation is positively related to performance ratings, meaning that those who ingratiate with their supervisors get higher performance evaluations. However, self-promotion appears to backfire: Those who self-promote actually may receive *lower* performance ratings.[89] There is an important qualifier to this general result. It appears that individuals high in political skill are able to translate impression management into higher performance appraisals, whereas those lower in political skill are more likely to be hurt by their attempts at impression management.[90]

Another study of 760 boards of directors found that individuals who ingratiated themselves to current board members (expressed agreement with the director, pointed out shared attitudes and opinions, complimented the director) increased their chances of landing on a board.[91] Finally, interns who attempted to use ingratiation with their supervisors in one study were usually disliked—unless they had high levels of political skill. For those who had this ability, ingratiation led to higher levels of liking from supervisors, and higher performance ratings.[92]

What explains these consistent results across multiple studies and contexts? If you think about them, they make sense. Ingratiating always works because everyone—both interviewers and supervisors—likes to be treated nicely. However, self-promotion may work only in interviews and backfire on the job because, whereas the interviewer has little idea whether you are blowing smoke about your accomplishments, the supervisor

FOCUS ON ETHICS

Impression Management during a Job Interview

How much impression management is ethical? Almost everyone agrees that dressing professionally, highlighting previous accomplishments, and expressing interest in the job are reasonable impression management tactics to improve your presentation in an interview.[93] Strategies like flattering the interviewer and using positive nonverbal cues like smiling and nodding are also often advised.

Is there an upside to such impression management? Research generally shows there is. The more effort applicants put into highlighting their skills, motivation, and admiration for the organization, the more likely they are to be hired. A recent study in Taiwan examined this relationship, finding that interviewers saw applicants who talked confidently about their qualifications as a better fit for the job, and applicants who said positive things about the organization as a better fit for the organization. Positive nonverbal cues improved interviewer moods, which also improved the applicant's ratings.

Despite evidence that making an effort to impress an interviewer can pay off, you can go too far. Evidence that a person misrepresented qualifications in the hiring process is usually grounds for immediate termination.

So what does an ethical, effective interview strategy entail? The key is to find a positive but truthful way to manage impressions. Don't be afraid to let an employer know about your skills and accomplishments, and be sure to show your enthusiasm for the job. At the same time, keep your statements as accurate as possible, and be careful not to overstate your abilities. In the long run, you are much more likely to be happy and successful in a job where both you and the interviewer can assess fit honestly. . . . .

knows because it's his or her job to observe you. *Focus on Ethics* considers the ethics of impression management during a job interview. *OB in Action* shows there are things that you can do to reduce the need for politics once in the workplace.

⑨ Identify the causes, consequences, and ethics of political behaviour.

The Ethics of Behaving Politically

Although there are no clear-cut ways to differentiate ethical from unethical politicking, there are questions you should consider. For example, what is the utility of engaging in politicking? Sometimes we do it for little good reason. Louis LaPierre, the former head of the New Brunswick Energy Institute, had his Order of Canada taken away from him in June 2014 after it came to light that he had lied about his academic record. LaPierre, who had been a professor at the University of Moncton for 30 years, had long claimed he earned a PhD in ecology from the University of Maine, when, in fact, he had earned a PhD in education from Walden University in Minnesota. LaPierre likely had a lot to gain by claiming he had a degree in science, rather than in education.[95] Outright lies like this may be a rather extreme example of impression management, but many of us have at least distorted information to make a favourable impression. One thing to keep in mind is whether it's really worth the risk. For LaPierre, in the end, it really was not. Another question to ask is this: How does the utility of engaging in the political behaviour balance out any harm (or potential harm) it will do to others? Complimenting a supervisor on his or her appearance in order to gain favour is probably

OB IN ACTION

Positive Alternatives to Political Behaviour

Document your work efforts, and find data to back up your accomplishments.

Call out political behaviour when you see it.

Try to *develop a network* with only those individuals who are interested in *performing well together*.[94]

Robert Pratta/Reuters

Organizations foster politicking when they reduce resources in order to improve performance. After announcing plans to downsize its global workforce of 100 000 employees to increase its competitiveness, French pharmaceutical firm Sanofi stimulated political activity among employees, who organized protests against the job cuts.

much less harmful than grabbing credit that you don't deserve for a project, as *Case Incident—Barry's Peer Becomes His Boss* on page 306 indicates.

Finally, does the political activity conform to standards of equity and justice? Sometimes it's difficult to weigh the costs and benefits of a political action, but its ethicality is clear. The department head who inflates the performance evaluation of a favoured employee and deflates the evaluation of a disfavoured employee—and then uses these evaluations to justify giving the former a big raise and the latter nothing—has treated the disfavoured employee unfairly.

Unfortunately, powerful people can become very good at explaining self-serving behaviours in terms of the organization's best interests. They can persuasively argue that unfair actions are really fair and just. Those who are powerful, articulate, and persuasive are most vulnerable to ethical lapses because they are more likely to get away with them. When faced with an ethical dilemma regarding organizational politics, try to consider whether playing politics is worth the risk and whether others might be harmed in the process. If you have a strong power base, recognize the ability of power to corrupt. Remember that it's a lot easier for the powerless to act ethically, if for no other reason than they typically have very little political discretion to exploit.

GLOBAL IMPLICATIONS

Although culture might enter any of the topics we have covered to this point, two questions are particularly important: (1) Does culture influence views on empowerment? (2) Does culture affect the influence tactics people prefer to use?

Views on Empowerment

Four US researchers investigated the effects of empowerment on employees of a multinational firm by looking at four of the company's comparable plants: one in the Midwestern United States, one in central Mexico, one in west-central India, and one in the south of Poland.[96] These four locations were chosen because they differed on power distance and individualism (concepts we discussed in Chapter 3). India and Mexico are considered high in power distance, and the United States is considered the lowest in power distance. Mexico and India are high in collectivity, the United States is highly individualistic, and Poland is moderately individualistic.

The findings showed that Indian employees gave their supervisors low ratings when empowerment was high, while employees in the other three countries rated their supervisors favourably when empowerment was high. In both the United States and Mexico, empowerment had no effect on satisfaction with co-workers. However, satisfaction with co-workers was higher when employees were empowered in Poland. In India, empowerment led to lower satisfaction with co-workers.

Similar findings in a study comparing empowerment in the United States, Brazil, and Argentina suggest that in hierarchical societies, empowerment may need to be introduced with care.[97] Employees in those countries may be more used to working in teams, but they also expect their manager to be the person with all the answers. Professor Marylène Gagné of Concordia's John Molson School of Business, who has studied empowerment cross-culturally,[98] notes that "in some cultures, bosses can't ask the opinion of subordinates, because it makes them appear weak. So managers in these environments have to find other ways to make people feel autonomous. There is no simple recipe."[99]

Preference for Influence Tactics

Preference for influence tactics varies across cultures.[100] Those from individualist countries tend to see power in personalized terms and as a legitimate means of advancing their personal ends, whereas those in collectivist countries see power in social terms and as a legitimate means of helping others.[101] A study comparing managers in the United States and China found US managers preferred rational appeal, whereas Chinese managers preferred coalition tactics. Reason-based tactics are consistent with the US preference for direct confrontation and rational persuasion to influence others and resolve differences, while coalition tactics align with the Chinese preference for meeting difficult or controversial requests with indirect approaches.

A study of Swedish, German, Czech, Polish, and Finnish managers found that Swedish managers saw mere differences in opinion as conflicts, so they adopted a conflict-avoidant strategy that emphasized more passive forms of persuasion.[102] German managers, on the other hand, saw disagreement as a useful opportunity to gain new knowledge and fostered some rational discussion as an influence technique. Finnish managers preferred discussion-oriented influence tactics as well. Czech and Polish managers believed managers were under pressure to halt conflicts quickly when they arose, since conflict resolution is time consuming. Therefore, the Czech and Polish managers switched to more autocratic, power-oriented influence styles.

Another study of managers in US culture and three Chinese cultures (People's Republic of China, Hong Kong, and Taiwan) found that US managers evaluated "gentle persuasion" tactics such as consultation and inspirational appeal as more effective than did their Chinese counterparts.[103] Other research suggests that effective US leaders achieve influence by focusing on personal goals of group members and the tasks at hand (an analytical approach), whereas influential East Asian leaders focus on relationships among group members and meeting the demands of the people around them (a holistic approach).[104]

Summary

Few employees relish being powerless in their jobs and organizations. People respond differently to the various power bases. Expert and referent power are derived from an individual's personal qualities. In contrast, coercion, reward, and legitimate power are essentially organizationally granted. Competence especially appears to offer wide appeal, and its use as a power base results in high performance by group members.

An effective manager accepts the political nature of organizations. Some people are more politically astute than others, meaning they are aware of the underlying politics and can manage impressions. Those who are good at playing politics can be expected to get higher performance evaluations and, hence, larger salary increases and more promotions than the politically naive or inept. The politically astute are also likely to exhibit higher job satisfaction and be better able to neutralize job stressors.

SNAPSHOT SUMMARY

A Definition of Power

Bases of Power
- Formal Power
- Personal Power
- Which Bases of Power Are Most Effective?

Dependence: The Key to Power
- The General Dependence Postulate
- What Creates Dependence?

Influence Tactics
- About Influence Tactics
- Applying Influence Tactics

How Power Affects People
- Power Variables
- Harassment: Unequal Power in the Workplace

Empowerment: Giving Power to Employees
- Definition of Empowerment

Politics: Power in Action
- Definition of Political Behaviour
- The Reality of Politics
- Impression Management
- The Ethics of Behaving Politically

MyLab Management

P I A PERSONAL INVENTORY ASSESSMENT

Study, practise, and explore real business situations with these helpful resources:

- **Study Plan:** Check your understanding of chapter concepts with self-study quizzes.
- **Online Lesson Presentations:** Study key chapter topics and work through interactive assessments to test your knowledge and master management concepts.
- **Videos:** Learn more about the management practices and strategies of real companies.
- **Simulations:** Practise management decision-making in simulated business environments.

OB at Work

for **Review**

1. What is power?
2. What are the five bases of power?
3. What is the role of dependence in power relationships?
4. What are the 10 most often identified power or influence tactics and their contingencies?
5. What is the connection between harassment and the abuse of power?
6. What does it mean to be empowered? What factors lead to empowerment?
7. How do politics work in organizations?
8. What are some examples of impression management techniques?
9. What standards can you use to determine whether a political action is ethical?

for **Managers**

- To maximize your power, increase others' dependence on you. For instance, increase your power in relation to your boss by developing a needed knowledge or skill for which there is no ready substitute.
- You will not be alone in attempting to build your power bases. Others, particularly employees and peers, will be seeking to increase your dependence on them, while you are trying to minimize it and increase their dependence on you.
- Try to avoid putting others in a position where they feel they have no power.
- An effective manager accepts the political nature of organizations. By assessing behaviour in a political framework, you can better predict the actions of others and use that information to formulate political strategies that will gain advantages for you and your work unit.
- Consider that employees who have poor political skills or are unwilling to play the politics game generally relate perceived organizational politics to lower job satisfaction and self-reported performance, increased anxiety, and higher turnover. Therefore, if you are good at organizational politics, help others understand the importance of becoming politically savvy.

for **You**

- Power and politics should not simply be viewed as a win–lose situation. Through power and politics, one builds coalitions to work together effectively. It's possible to make sure that everyone is included.
- There are a variety of ways to increase your power in an organization. As an example, you could acquire more knowledge about a situation and then use that information to negotiate a bonus with your employer. Even if you don't get the bonus, the knowledge may help you in other ways.
- To increase your power, consider how dependent others are on you. Dependence is affected by your importance and substitutability and by the scarcity of options. If you have needed skills that no one else has, you will have more power.
- Politics is a reality of most organizations. Being comfortable with politics is important. Politics is often about making deals with other people for mutual gain.
- Political skills can be developed. Taking time to join in an office birthday celebration for someone is part of developing the skill of working with others effectively.

EVERYONE WANTS POWER

POINT

We don't admit to wanting everything that we secretly want.[105] For instance, one psychologist found people would seldom admit to wanting money, but they thought everyone else wanted it. They were half right—everyone wants money; and everyone wants power.

Harvard psychologist David McClelland was justifiably famous for his study of underlying motives. McClelland measured people's motivation for power based on how they described pictures (this method is called the Thematic Apperception Test, or TAT). Why didn't he simply ask people how much they wanted power? Because he believed that many more people really wanted power than would admit, or even consciously realized. That is exactly what he found.

Why do we want power? Because it's good for us. It gives us more control over our own lives. It gives us more freedom to do as we wish. There are few things worse in life than feeling helpless, and few better than feeling in charge of your destiny. Research shows that people with power and status command more respect from others, have higher self-esteem (no surprise there), and enjoy better health than those of less stature.

Usually, people who tell you power does not matter are those who have no hope of getting it. Wanting power, like being jealous, can be one of those secrets people just will not admit to.

COUNTERPOINT

Of course it's true that some people desire power—and often behave ruthlessly to get it. For most of us, however, power is not high on our list of priorities, and for some, power is actually undesirable.

Research shows that most individuals feel uncomfortable when placed in powerful positions. One study asked individuals, before they began work in a four-person team, to "rank, from 1 [highest] to 4 [lowest], in terms of status and influence within the group, what rank you like to achieve." You know what? Only about one-third (34 percent) of participants chose the highest rank. In a second study, researchers focused on employees participating in Amazon's Mechanical Turk online service. They found that the main reason was to gain power to earn respect. If they could get respect without gaining power, that was preferred. In a third study, researchers found individuals desired power only when they had high ability—that is, when their influence helped their groups.

These studies suggest that we often confuse the desire for power with other things—like the desire to be respected and to help our groups and organizations succeed. In these cases, power is something most of us seek for more benevolent ends—and only when we think it does good.

Another study confirmed that most people want respect from their peers, not power. Cameron Anderson, the author of this research, sums it up nicely: "You don't have to be rich to be happy, but instead be a valuable contributing member to your groups. What makes a person high in status in a group is being engaged, generous with others, and making self-sacrifices for the greater good."

BREAKOUT **GROUP** EXERCISES

Form small groups to discuss the following topics, as assigned by your instructor:

1. Describe an incident where you tried to use political behaviour in order to get something you wanted. What influence tactics did you use?

2. In thinking about the incident described above, were your influence tactics effective? Why?

3. Describe an incident where you saw someone engaging in politics. What was your reaction to observing the political behaviour? Under what circumstances do you think political behaviour is appropriate?

EXPERIENTIAL EXERCISE

Comparing Influence Tactics

Students working in groups of three are each assigned to a role. One person is the influencer, one will be influenced, and one is the observer. These roles can be randomly determined.

To begin, students create a deck of cards for the seven *tactics* to be used in the exercise. These are legitimacy, rational persuasion, inspirational appeals, consultation, exchange, ingratiation, and pressure (defined in the chapter). Only the influencer draws cards from the set, and no one else may see what has been drawn.

The influencer draws a card and quickly formulates and acts out a strategy to use this tactic on the party being influenced. The person being influenced reacts realistically in a back-and-forth exchange over a brief period and states whether or not the tactic was effective. The observer attempts to determine which tactic is being used and which power base (coercive, reward, legitimate, expert, or referent) would reinforce this tactic. The influencer confirms or denies the approach used.

Change the roles and cards throughout the rounds. Afterward, the class discusses:

1. Based on your observations, which influence situation would probably have resulted in the best outcome for the person doing the influencing?

2. Was there a good match between the tactics drawn and the specific role each person took? In other words, was the tactic useful for the influencer given his or her base of power relative to the person being influenced?

3. What lessons about power and influence does this exercise teach us?

ETHICAL **DILEMMA**

How Much Should You Defer to Those in Power?

Although it's not always easy to admit it to ourselves, often we adapt our behaviour to suit those in power.[106] To some degree, it's important for organizational success that we do so. After all, people are in positions of authority for a reason, and if no one paid attention to the rules these people put in place, chaos would rule. But is it always ethical for us to defer to the powerful?

More often than we acknowledge, powerful individuals in organizations push our actions into ethical grey areas, or worse.

In Stanley Milgram's famous experiments, most individuals delivered what they thought were severe shocks only because an authority figure directed them to do so.

More recently, managers of restaurants and stores (including McDonald's, Taco Bell, and others) were persuaded to strip search customers or employees when an individual impersonating a police officer phoned in and instructed them to do so. What would you do if you thought a police officer, definitely a symbol of power, ordered you to do something you would never choose to do as a manager?

Outright abuses aside, power is wielded over us in more prosaic ways. For example, many stock analysts report pressure from their bosses to promote funds from which the organization profits most (a fact that is not disclosed to their clients). These might be good funds that the analysts would promote anyway. But what if they are not? Should the analyst ever promote the funds without discussing the conflict of interest with the client?

Few of us might think we would perform strip searches. But these examples, as well as the hazing incidents that took place in Dalhousie University's men's rugby team and women's hockey team in 2014, highlight the disturbing tendency for many of us to conform to the wishes of those in power. Knowing that blindly deferring to those in power might cause us to cross ethical lines is enough to keep each one of us thinking.

Questions

1. Do you think people tailor their behaviour to suit those in power more than they admit? Is that something you do?

2. One writer commented that bending behaviour to suit those in power reminds "anyone who is under pressure to carry out orders from 'above' to constantly question the validity and prudence of what they're being asked to do." Why don't we question this more often?

3. Why might some individuals resist the effects of power more strongly than others?

CASE INCIDENTS

Delegate Power, or Keep It Close?

Samantha Parks is the owner and CEO of Sparks, a small agency that develops advertising, promotions, and marketing materials for high-fashion firms.[107] Parks has tended to keep a tight rein on her business, overseeing most projects from start to finish. However, as the firm has grown, she has found it necessary to delegate more and more decisions to her associates. She was recently approached by a hairstyling chain that wants a comprehensive redefinition of its entire marketing and promotions look. Should Samantha try to manage this project in her traditional way, or should she delegate major parts to her employees?

Most managers confront this question at some point in their careers. Some experts propose that top executives need to stay very close to the creative core of their business, which means that even if their primary responsibility is to manage, CEOs should never cede too much control to committees of creative individuals or they can lose sight of the firm's overall future direction. Moreover, executives who do fall out of touch with the creative process risk being passed over by a new generation of "plugged-in" employees who better understand how the business really works.

Others offer the opposite advice, saying it's not a good idea for a CEO to "sweat the small stuff" such as managing individual client accounts or projects. These experts advise executives to identify everything they can "outsource" to other employees and to delegate as much as possible. By eliminating trivial tasks, executives will be better able to focus their attention on the most important decision-making and control aspects of their jobs, which will help the business and also ensure that the top executive maintains control over the functions that really matter.

These pieces of advice are not necessarily in conflict with one another. The real challenge is to identify what you can delegate effectively without ceding too much power and control away from the person with the unifying vision. That is certainly easier said than done, though.

Questions

1. If you were Samantha Parks, how would you prioritize which projects or parts of projects to delegate?

2. In explaining what makes her decisions hard, Parks said, "I hire good people, creative people, to run these projects, and I worry that they will see my oversight and authority as interfering with their creative process." How can she deal with these concerns without giving up too much control?

3. Should executives try to control projects to maintain their position of authority? Do they have a right to control projects and stay in the loop on important decisions just so they can remain in charge?

Barry's Peer Becomes His Boss

As Barry looked out the window of his office in Toronto, the gloomy October skies obscured his usual view of CN Tower.[108] "That figures," Barry thought to himself—his mood was just as gloomy.

Five months ago, Barry's company, CTM, a relatively small but growing technology company, reorganized itself. Although such reorganizations often imperil careers, Barry felt the change only improved his position. Barry's co-worker, Raphael, was promoted to a different department, which made sense because Raphael had been with the company for a few more years and had worked with the CEO on a successful project. Because Raphael was promoted and their past work roles were so similar, Barry thought his own promotion was soon to come.

However, six weeks ago, Barry's boss left. Raphael was transferred back to the same department and became Barry's boss. Although Barry felt a bit overlooked, he knew he was still relatively junior in the company and felt that his good past relationship with Raphael would bode well for his future prospects.

The previous six weeks, however, had brought nothing but disappointment. Although Raphael often told Barry he was doing a great job, drawing from several observations, Barry felt that opinion was not being shared with the higher-ups. Worse, a couple of Barry's friends in the company showed Barry several emails where Raphael had taken credit for Barry's work.

"Raphael is not the person I thought he was," thought Barry.

What was his future in the company if no one saw the outcomes of his hard work? How would it affect his career to work for someone who apparently was willing to do anything to get ahead, even at others' expense? He thought about looking for another job, but that prospect only darkened his mood further. He liked the company. He felt he did good work there.

As Barry looked again out his window, a light rain began to fall. The CN Tower was no more visible than before. He just did not know what to do.

Questions

1. Should Barry complain about his treatment by Raphael? To whom? If he did complain, what influence tactics should Barry use?

2. Studies have shown that those prone to complaining or "whining" tend to have less power in an organization. Do you think whining leads to diminished power and influence, or the other way around? How can Barry avoid appearing to be a whiner?

3. Do you think Barry should look for another job? Why or why not?

FROM CONCEPTS TO SKILLS

Politicking

Forget, for a moment, about the ethics of politicking and any negative impressions you may have of people who engage in organizational politics.[109] If you wanted to be more politically adept in your organization, what could you do? The following eight suggestions are likely to improve your political effectiveness:

1. *Frame arguments in terms of organizational goals.* Effective politicking requires camouflaging your self-interest. No matter that your objective is self-serving; all the arguments you marshal in support of it must be framed in terms of the benefits that the organization will gain. People whose actions appear to blatantly further their own interests at the expense of the organization's are almost universally denounced, are likely to lose influence, and often suffer the ultimate penalty of being expelled from the organization.

2. *Develop the right image.* If you know your organization's culture, you understand what the organization wants and values from its employees—in terms of dress; associates to cultivate and those to avoid; whether to appear risk-taking or risk-averse; the preferred leadership style; the importance placed on getting along well with others; and so forth. Then you are equipped to project the appropriate image. Because the assessment of your performance is not a fully objective process, both style and substance must be addressed.

3. *Gain control of organizational resources.* The control of organizational resources that are scarce and important is a source of power. Knowledge and expertise are particularly effective resources to control. They make you more valuable to the organization and, therefore, more likely to gain security, advancement, and a receptive audience for your ideas.

4. *Make yourself appear indispensable.* Because we are dealing with appearances rather than objective facts, you can enhance your power by appearing to be indispensable. That is, you don't have to really be indispensable as long as key people in the organization believe that you are. If the organization's prime decision makers believe there is no ready substitute for what you are giving the organization, they are likely to go to great lengths to ensure that your desires are satisfied.

5. *Be visible.* Because performance evaluation has a substantial subjective component, it's important that your manager and those in power in the organization be made aware of your contribution. If you are fortunate enough to have a job that brings your accomplishments to the attention of others, it may not be necessary to take direct measures to increase your visibility. But your job may require you to handle activities that are low in visibility, or your specific contribution may be indistinguishable because you are part of a team endeavour. In such cases, without appearing to be tooting your own horn, you will want to call attention to yourself by highlighting your successes in routine reports, having satisfied customers relay their appreciation to senior executives, being seen at social functions, being active in professional associations, developing powerful allies who speak positively about your accomplishments, and similar tactics. Of course, the skilled politician actively lobbies to get those projects that will increase his or her visibility.

6. *Develop powerful allies.* It helps to have powerful people in your camp. Cultivate contacts with potentially influential people above you, at your own level, and in the lower ranks. They can provide you with important information that may not be available through normal channels. There will be times, too, when decisions will be made in favour of those with the greatest support. Having powerful allies can provide you with a coalition of support if and when you need it.

7. *Avoid "tainted" members.* In almost every organization, there are fringe members whose status is questionable. Their performance and/or loyalty is suspect. Keep your distance from such individuals. Given the reality that effectiveness has a large subjective component, your own effectiveness might be called into question if you are perceived as being too closely associated with tainted members.

8. *Support your manager.* Since he or she evaluates your performance, you will typically want to do whatever is necessary to have your manager on your side. You should make every effort to help your manager succeed and look good, support your manager if under siege, and spend the time to find out what criteria will be used to assess your effectiveness. Do not undermine your manager, and do not speak negatively of your manager to others.

Practising Skills

You used to be the star marketing manager for Hilton Electronics Corporation. But for the past year, you have been outpaced again and again by Sean, a new manager in the design department who has been accomplishing everything expected of him and more. Meanwhile, your best efforts to do your job well have been sabotaged and undercut by Maria, who manages you and Sean. For example, before last year's international consumer electronics show, Maria moved $30 000 from your budget to Sean's. Despite your best efforts, your marketing team could not complete all the marketing materials normally developed to showcase all of your organization's new products at this important industry show. Also, Maria has chipped away at your staff and budget ever since. Although you have been able to meet most of your goals with less staff and budget, Maria has continued to slice away resources from your group. Just last week, she eliminated two positions in your team of eight marketing specialists to make room for a new designer and some extra equipment for Sean. Maria is clearly taking away your resources while giving Sean whatever he wants and more. You think it's time to do something, or soon you will not have any team or resources left. What do you need to do to make sure your division has the resources to survive and grow?

Reinforcing Skills

1. Keep a one-week journal of your behaviour, describing incidents when you tried to influence others around you. Assess each incident by asking: Were you successful at these attempts to influence them? Why or why not? What could you have done differently?

2. Outline a specific action plan, based on concepts in this module, that would improve your career progression in the organization in which you currently work or in which you would like to be employed.

9 Conflict and Negotiation

GM Canada and Unifor needed to negotiate a new collective bargaining agreement. Could the two sides reach an agreement with employees worried that the Oshawa plant might shut down?

LEARNING OUTCOMES

After studying this chapter, you should be able to:

1. Define *conflict*.
2. Describe the three types of conflict.
3. Describe the three loci of conflict.
4. Identify the conditions that lead to conflict.
5. Contrast distributive and integrative bargaining.
6. Show how individual differences influence negotiations.
7. Assess the roles and functions of third-party negotiations.

The canadian press

I n the fall of 2016, GM Canada and its employees' union, Unifor, were about to enter into negotiations for a new contract.[1] Before the parties even met together at the bargaining table, they were practically at an impasse. The future of two Oshawa plants was in question. One plant only had work scheduled in it until 2017, while the other had no work scheduled beyond 2019. GM Canada insisted that a labour agreement had to be reached before it made a decision about investing in the plant, while Unifor said a decision on the plant had to be made before an agreement could be reached.

Jerry Dias, national president of Unifor, underscored the position of the union: "I'm convinced that they have no interest in investing, therefore to sign an agreement without forcing it would be irresponsible. I'm convinced that if we do not secure Oshawa in this set of negotiations, we're going to have a closure."

Meanwhile, GM presented the issue as a business problem. Production in Canada had fallen as competition with China, India, and Mexico had increased because of those countries' lower costs of production. One union executive emphasized what he saw as the problem: "We look at the union negotiations as a first hurdle in making our business case, but the business case would also require us to address a number of macroeconomic factors, public-policy factors, supply-base issues . . . to be able to make a final decision (on Oshawa)." Would the parties be able to come to a satisfactory agreement without a strike?

In this chapter, we look at sources of conflict and strategies for resolving conflict, including negotiation.

OB IS FOR EVERYONE

- Is conflict always bad?
- Should you try to win at any cost when you bargain?
- How does anxiety affect negotiating outcomes?
- Do men and women negotiate differently?

THE BIG IDEA

Resolving conflicts and engaging in successful negotiations requires understanding your objectives and the objectives of the other party.

❶ Define *conflict*.

Conflict Defined

Several common themes underlie most definitions of conflict.[2] Conflict must be *perceived* by the parties to it; if no one is aware of a conflict, then it's generally agreed that no conflict exists. Conflict also involves opposition or incompatibility, and interaction between the parties.[3] These factors set the conditions that determine the beginning point of the conflict process. We can define **conflict** broadly as a process that begins when one party perceives that another party has negatively affected or is about to negatively affect something that the first party cares about.[4]

Conflict describes the point when an interaction becomes disagreement. People experience a wide range of conflicts in groups and organizations—incompatibility of goals, differences over interpretations of facts, disagreements based on behavioural expectations, and the like. Our definition covers the full range of conflict levels—from subtle forms of disagreement to overt and violent acts.

Conflict has positive and negative effects, which we will discuss further when we cover functional and dysfunctional conflict.

Functional vs. Dysfunctional Conflict

Contemporary perspectives differentiate types of conflict based on their effects. **Functional conflict** supports the goals of the group, improves its performance, and is thus a constructive form of conflict. For example, a debate among members of a work team about the most efficient way to improve production can be functional if unique points of view are discussed and compared openly. Conflict that hinders group performance is destructive or **dysfunctional conflict**. A highly personal struggle for control in a team

Is conflict always bad?

that distracts from the task at hand is dysfunctional. Exhibit 9-1 provides an overview depicting the effect of levels of conflict. To understand different types of conflict, we will discuss next the *types* of conflict and the *loci* of conflict.

Stimulating functional conflict can be productive, as *Case Incident—Disorderly Conduct* on pages 340–341 shows.

❷ Describe the three types of conflict.

Types of Conflict

One means of understanding conflict is to identify the *type* of disagreement, or what the conflict is about. Is it a disagreement about goals? Is it about people who just rub one another the wrong way? Or is it about the best way to get things done? Although each conflict is unique, researchers have classified conflicts into three categories: task, relationship, and process.

Task conflict relates to the content and goals of the work. **Relationship conflict** focuses on interpersonal relationships. **Process conflict** is about how the work gets done. Studies demonstrate that relationship conflicts, at least in work settings, are almost always dysfunctional.[5] Why? It appears that the friction and interpersonal hostilities inherent in relationship conflicts increase personality clashes and decrease mutual understanding, which hinders the completion of organizational tasks. Of the three types, relationship conflicts also appear to be the most psychologically exhausting to individuals.[6] Because they tend to revolve around personalities, you can see how relationship conflicts can become destructive. After all, we cannot expect to change our co-workers' personalities, and we would generally take offence at criticisms directed at who we are as opposed to how we behave.

While scholars agree that relationship conflict is dysfunctional, considerably less agreement exists as to whether task and process conflicts are functional. Early research suggested that task conflict within groups was associated with higher group

---

conflict A process that begins when one party perceives that another party has negatively affected or is about to negatively affect something that the first party cares about.

functional conflict Conflict that supports the goals of the group and improves its performance.

dysfunctional conflict Conflict that hinders group performance.

task conflict Conflict over content and goals of the work.

relationship conflict Conflict based on interpersonal relationships.

process conflict Conflict over how work gets done.

EXHIBIT 9-1 Conflict and Unit Performance

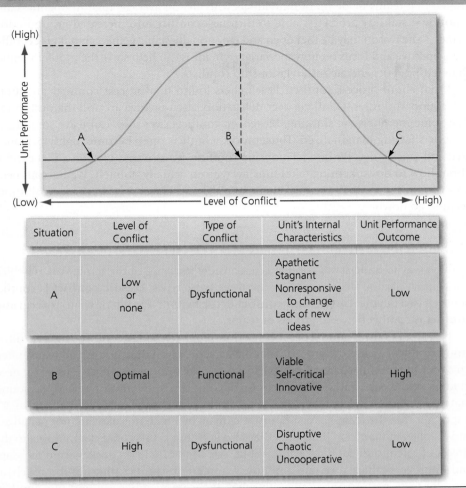

Situation	Level of Conflict	Type of Conflict	Unit's Internal Characteristics	Unit Performance Outcome
A	Low or none	Dysfunctional	Apathetic Stagnant Nonresponsive to change Lack of new ideas	Low
B	Optimal	Functional	Viable Self-critical Innovative	High
C	High	Dysfunctional	Disruptive Chaotic Uncooperative	Low

Sources: Based on S. P. Robbins, *Managing Organizational Conflict: A Nontraditional Approach* (Upper Saddle River, NJ: Prentice Hall, 1974), pp. 93–97; and F. Glasl, "The Process of Conflict Escalation and the Roles of Third Parties," in *Conflict Management and Industrial Relations,* ed. G. B. J. Bomers and R. Peterson (Boston: Kluwer-Nijhoff, 1982), pp. 119–140.

performance, but a recent review of 116 studies found that generalized task conflict was essentially unrelated to group performance. However, the research found that the relationship between conflict and performance depends on a number of mediating factors.[7]

One factor is whether the conflict includes top management or occurs at a lower hierarchical level in the organization. Task conflict among top management teams was positively associated with their performance, whereas conflict lower in the organization was negatively associated with their performance, perhaps because people in top positions may not feel as threatened in their organizational roles by conflict. The review also found that it matters whether other types of conflict are occurring at the same time. If task and relationship conflict occurred together, task conflict was more likely negative, whereas if task conflict occurs by itself, it was more likely positive. Some scholars have argued that the strength of conflict is important—if task conflict is very low, people are not really engaged or addressing the important issues. If task conflict is too high, however, infighting will quickly degenerate into relationship conflict. Moderate levels of task conflict may thus be optimal. Supporting this argument, one study in China found that moderate levels of task conflict in the early development stage increased creativity in groups, but high levels decreased team performance.[8]

Finally, the personalities of team members appear to matter. One study demonstrated that teams made up of individuals who are, on average, high in openness and emotional stability are better able to turn task conflict into increased group performance.[9] The reason may be that open and emotionally stable teams can put task conflict in perspective and focus on how the variance in ideas can help solve the problem, rather than letting it degenerate into relationship conflicts.

What about process conflict? Researchers found that process conflicts are about delegation and roles. Conflicts over delegation often revolve around the perception that some members are shirking. Moreover, conflicts over roles can leave some team members feeling marginalized. Thus, process conflicts often become highly personalized and quickly devolve into relationship conflicts. It's also true, of course, that arguing about how to do something takes time away from actually doing it. We have all been part of groups in which the arguments and debates about roles and responsibilities seem to go nowhere.

Loci of Conflict

3 Describe the three loci of conflict.

Another way to understand conflict is to consider its locus, or the framework in which the conflict occurs. Here, too, there are three basic types. **Dyadic conflict** is conflict between two people. **Intragroup conflict** occurs within a group or team. **Intergroup conflict** is conflict between groups or teams.

Nearly all of the literature on task, relationship, and process conflict considers intragroup conflict (within the group). That makes sense given that groups and teams often exist only to perform a particular task. However, it does not necessarily tell us all we need to know about the context and outcomes of conflict. For example, research has found that for intragroup task conflict to positively influence performance within the team, it's important that the team has a supportive climate in which mistakes are not penalized and every team member "[has] the other's back."[10] But is this concept applicable to the effects of intergroup conflict? Think about, say, the NHL. For a hockey team to adapt and improve, perhaps a certain amount of intragroup conflict (but not too much) is good for team performance, especially when the team members support one another. But would we care whether members from one team supported members from another team? Probably not. In fact, if teams are competing with one another so that only one team can "win," interteam conflict seems almost inevitable. Still, it must be managed. Intense intergroup conflict can be quite stressful to group members and might well affect the way they interact. One study found, for example, that high levels of conflict between teams caused individuals to focus on complying with norms within their teams.[11]

It may surprise you that individuals become most important in intergroup conflicts. One study that focused on intergroup conflict found an interplay between an individual's position within a group and the way that individual managed conflict between groups. Group members who were relatively peripheral in their own group were better at resolving conflicts between their group and another one. But this happened only when those peripheral members were still accountable to their group.[12] Thus, being at the core of your work group does not necessarily make you the best person to manage conflict with other groups.

Another intriguing question about loci is whether conflicts interact with or buffer one another. Assume, for example, that Jia and Alain are on the same team. What happens if they do not get along interpersonally (dyadic conflict) and their team also has high task conflict? Progress might be halted. What happens to their team if two other team members, Shawna and Justin, do get along well? The team might still be dysfunctional, or the positive relationship might prevail.

Thus, understanding functional and dysfunctional conflict requires not only that we identify the type of conflict; we also need to know where it occurs. It's possible that while the concepts of task, relationship, and process conflict are useful in

dyadic conflict Conflict that occurs between two people.

intragroup conflict Conflict that occurs within a group or team.

intergroup conflict Conflict between different groups or teams.

IBM encourages employees to engage in functional conflict that results in innovations, such as the Watson supercomputer designed to learn through the same process human brains use. For innovation to flourish, IBM relies on the creative tension from employees' different ideas and skills and provides a work environment that promotes risk-taking and outside-the-box thinking.

understanding intragroup or even dyadic conflict, they are less useful in explaining the effects of intergroup conflict.

Thinking about conflict in terms of type and locus helps us realize that it's probably inevitable in most organizations, and when it does occur, we can attempt to make it as productive as possible.

Sources of Conflict

A number of conditions can give rise to conflict. They *need not* lead directly to conflict, but at least one of these conditions is necessary if conflict is to surface. For simplicity's sake, these conditions (which we can also look at as causes or sources of conflict) have been condensed into three general categories: communication, structure, and personal variables.

4 Identify the conditions that lead to conflict.

Communication

As we saw in Chapter 7, communication can be a source of conflict through semantic difficulties, misunderstandings, and "noise" in the communication channels.[13]

A review of the research suggests that differing word connotations, jargon, insufficient exchange of information, and noise in the communication channel are all barriers to communication and potential antecedent conditions to conflict. Research has further demonstrated a surprising finding: The potential for conflict increases when either too little or too much communication takes place. Apparently, an increase in communication is functional up to a point, whereupon it's possible to overcommunicate, with a resultant increase in the potential for conflict.

Structure

Conflicts between two people can be structural in nature; that is, they can be the consequence of the requirements of the job or the workplace more than personality. For instance, it's not uncommon for the sales department to be in conflict with the production department, if sales perceives that products will be delivered late to customers. The term *structure* in this context includes variables such as size of the group, degree of specialization in the tasks assigned to group members, composition of the group, jurisdictional clarity, reward systems, leadership style, goal compatibility, and the degree of dependence between groups.

A review of structural variables that can lead to conflict in the workplace suggests the following:[14]

- *Size, specialization, and composition* of the group act as forces to stimulate conflict. The larger the group and the more specialized its activities, the greater the likelihood of conflict. The potential for conflict tends to be greatest where group members are younger and where turnover is high.

- *The greater the ambiguity* in precisely defining where responsibility for actions lies, the greater the potential for conflict to emerge. Such jurisdictional ambiguities increase intergroup fighting for control of resources and territory.

- *Reward systems* create conflict when one member's gain is at another's expense. Similarly, the performance evaluation process can create conflict when individuals feel that they are unfairly evaluated, or when managers and employees have differing ideas about the employees' job responsibilities.

- *Leadership style* can create conflict if managers tightly control and oversee the work of employees, allowing employees little discretion in how they carry out tasks.

- *The diversity of goals* among groups is a major source of conflict. When groups within an organization seek diverse ends, some of which are inherently at odds—such as when the sales team promises products that the development team has not yet finalized—opportunities for conflict increase.

- *If one group is dependent on another* (in contrast to the two being mutually independent), or if interdependence allows one group to gain at another's expense, opposing forces are stimulated.

Personal Variables

Have you ever met people to whom you take an immediate dislike? You disagree with most of their opinions. The sound of their voice, their smirk when they smile, and their personality annoy you. We have all met people like that. When you have to work with such individuals, there is often the potential for conflict.

Our last category of potential sources of conflict is personal variables, which include personality, emotions, and values. People high in the personality traits of disagreeableness, neuroticism, or self-monitoring are prone to tangle with other people more often, and to react poorly when conflicts occur.[15] Emotions can also cause conflict even when they are not directed at others. An employee who shows up to work irate from her hectic morning commute may carry that anger into her workday, which can result in a tension-filled meeting.[16] Furthermore, differences in preferences and values can generate higher levels of conflict. For example, a study in South Korea found that when group members didn't agree about their desired achievement levels, there was more task conflict; when group members didn't agree about their desired interpersonal closeness, there was more relationship conflict; and when group members didn't have similar desires for power, there was more conflict over status.[17]

Conflict Resolution

In the Unifor–GM negotiations, both parties looked for ways to meet the needs of the other, while making sure that they accomplished their own goals.[18] When the negotiations ended, it appeared that this did happen. While neither party achieved all that they might have hoped for, each side regarded the negotiation as a win. GM said that the deal would "enable significant new product, technology, and process investments" at two Ontario plants.

Jerry Dias, the president of Unifor, meanwhile, announced his happiness with the agreement. "Ultimately, we were not walking away from the table until we had a solution . . . we all knew we were going to be successful right from the beginning because we were determined." The union had managed to get guarantees for one of the Oshawa plants to stay open with increased wages and no layoffs.

Conflict in the workplace can affect the effectiveness of individuals, teams, and the entire organization.[19] One study found that 20 percent of managers' time is spent managing conflict.[20]

Once conflict arises, what can be done to resolve it? The way a conflict is defined goes a long way toward establishing the sort of outcomes that might settle it. For instance, if I define our salary disagreement as a zero-sum or *win–lose situation*—that is, if you get the increase in pay you want, there will be exactly that amount less for me—I am going to be far less willing to look for mutual solutions than if I frame the conflict as a potential *win–win situation*. So individual attitudes toward a conflict are important, because attitudes typically define the set of possible settlements.

Conflict Management Strategies Based on Dual Concern Theory

Conflict researchers often use *dual concern theory* to describe people's conflict management strategies.[21] Dual concern theory considers how one's degree of *cooperativeness* (the degree to which one tries to satisfy the other person's concerns) and *assertiveness* (the degree to which one tries to satisfy one's own concerns) determine how a conflict is handled.[22] The five conflict-handling strategies identified by the theory are as follows:

- *Forcing.* Imposing one's will on the other party.

- *Problem solving.* Trying to reach an agreement that satisfies both one's own and the other party's aspirations as much as possible.

- *Avoiding.* Ignoring or minimizing the importance of the issues creating the conflict.

- *Yielding.* Accepting and incorporating the will of the other party.

- *Compromising.* Balancing concern for oneself with concern for the other party in order to reach a solution.

Forcing is a win–lose solution, as is yielding, while problem solving seeks a win–win solution. Avoiding conflict and pretending it does not exist, and compromising, so that neither person gets what they want, can yield lose–lose solutions. Exhibit 9-2 illustrates these five strategies, along with specific actions that one might take when using them.

Choosing a particular strategy for resolving conflict depends on a variety of factors. *Forcing* brings out active attempts to contend with team members, and more individual effort to achieve ends without working together. *Problem solving* creates investigation of multiple solutions with other members of the team and tries to find a solution that satisfies all parties as much as possible. *Avoiding* is seen in behaviour like refusals to discuss issues and reductions in effort toward group goals. People who *yield* put their relationships ahead of the issues in the conflict, deferring to others' opinions and sometimes acting as a subgroup with them. Finally, when people *compromise*, they both expect to (and do) sacrifice parts of their interests, hoping that if everyone does the same, an agreement will sift out.

EXHIBIT 9-2 Conflict-Handling Strategies and Accompanying Behaviours

Sources: Based on K. W. Thomas, "Conflict and Negotiation Processes in Organizations," in *Handbook of Industrial and Organizational Psychology*, vol. 3, 2nd ed., ed. M. D. Dunnette and L. M. Hough (Palo Alto, CA: Consulting Psychologists Press, 1992), p. 668; C. K. W. De Dreu, A. Evers, B. Beersma, E. S. Kluwer, and A. Nauta, "A Theory-Based Measure of Conflict Management Strategies in the Workplace," *Journal of Organizational Behavior* 22, no. 6 (September 2001), pp. 645–668; and D. G. Pruitt and J. Rubin, *Social Conflict: Escalation, Stalemate and Settlement* (New York: Random House, 1986).

A review that examined the effects of these behaviours across multiple studies found that openness and problem solving were both associated with superior group performance, whereas avoiding and forcing strategies were associated with significantly worse group performance.[23] These effects were nearly as large as the effects of relationship conflict. This further demonstrates that it is not just the existence of conflict or even the type of conflict that creates problems, but also the ways people respond to conflict and manage the process once conflicts arise.

Research shows that while people may choose among the strategies, they have an underlying disposition to handle conflicts in certain ways.[24] In addition, some situations call for particular strategies. For instance, when a small child insists on trying to run into the street, a parent may need a forcing strategy to restrain the child. Co-workers who are having a conflict over setting deadlines to complete a project on time may decide that problem solving is the best strategy to use.

OB in Action—Choosing Strategies to Deal with Conflicts indicates the situations in which each strategy is best used.

What Can Individuals Do to Manage Conflict?

Individuals can use a number of conflict resolution techniques to try to defuse conflict inside and outside of the workplace. These include the following:[25]

- *Problem solving.* Requesting a face-to-face meeting to identify the problem and resolve it through open discussion.

OB IN ACTION

Choosing Strategies to Deal with Conflicts

Forcing

→ In **emergencies**

→ On **important** but unpopular **issues**

→ On **vital issues** when you know you are right

→ Against **people who take advantage** of noncompetitive behaviour

Problem solving

→ If both sets of concerns are **too important for compromise**

→ To **merge different perspectives**

→ To **gain commitment** through a consensus

→ To **mend a relationship**

Avoiding

→ When an issue is **trivial**

→ When your **concerns won't be met**

→ When potential **disruption outweighs the benefits** of resolution

→ To let people **cool down** and regain perspective

Yielding

→ When you find **you are wrong**

→ To show your **reasonableness**

→ When **issues are more important to others** than yourself

→ To **build social credits** for later issues

→ When **harmony and stability** are especially important

Compromising

→ When **goals are important but not worth more assertive approaches**

→ When opponents are committed to **mutually exclusive goals**

→ To achieve **temporary settlements** to complex issues

→ To arrive at **expedient solutions** under time pressure[26]

- *Developing overarching goals.* Creating a shared goal that requires both parties to work together, and motivates them to do so.

- *Smoothing.* Playing down differences while emphasizing common interests with the other party.

- *Compromising.* Agreeing with the other party that each will give up something of value to reach an accord.

- *Avoiding.* Withdrawing from or suppressing the conflict.

The choice of technique may depend on how serious the issue is to you, whether you take a win–win or a win–lose approach, and your preferred conflict management style. When the conflict is specifically work-related, additional techniques might be used:

- *Expansion of resources.* The scarcity of a resource—say, money, promotion opportunities, office space—can create conflict. Expansion of the resource can create a win–win solution. (Money is often the issue in pro sports strikes, as *Point/Counterpoint* on page 338 shows.)

- *Authoritative command.* Management can use its formal authority to resolve the conflict and then communicate its desires to the parties involved.

- *Altering the human variable.* Behavioural change techniques such as human relations training can alter attitudes and behaviours that cause conflict.

Handling Personality Conflicts

Tips for employees having a personality conflict
→ **Communicate directly** with the other person to resolve the perceived conflict (emphasize problem solving and common objectives, not personalities).

→ **Avoid dragging** co-workers into the conflict.

→ If dysfunctional conflict persists, **seek help** from direct supervisors or human resource specialists.

Tips for third-party observers of a personality conflict
→ **Do not take sides** in someone else's personality conflict.

→ **Suggest the parties work things out** themselves in a constructive and positive way.

→ If dysfunctional conflict persists, **refer the problem** to parties' direct supervisors.

Tips for managers whose employees are having a personality conflict
→ **Investigate and document** conflict.

→ If appropriate, **take corrective action** (e.g., feedback or behaviour shaping).

→ If necessary, **attempt informal dispute resolution**.

→ **Refer difficult conflicts** to human resource specialists or hired counsellors for formal resolution attempts and other interventions.[27]

- *Altering the structural variables.* The formal organization structure and the interaction patterns of conflicting parties can be changed through job redesign, transfers, creation of coordinating positions, and the like.

Resolving Personality Conflicts

Personality conflicts are an everyday occurrence in the workplace. A recent study found that Canadian supervisors spend about 16 percent of their time handling disputes among employees.[28] A variety of factors lead to personality conflicts at work, including the following:[29]

- Misunderstandings based on age, race, or cultural differences

- Intolerance, prejudice, discrimination, or bigotry

- Perceived inequities

- Misunderstandings, rumours, or falsehoods about an individual or group

- Blaming for mistakes or mishaps (finger-pointing)

Personality conflicts can result in lowered productivity when people find it difficult to work together. The individuals experiencing the conflict may seek sympathy from other members of the work group, causing co-workers to take sides. The ideal solution would be for the two people having a conflict to work it out between themselves, without involving others, but this does not always happen. *OB in Action—Handling Personality Conflicts* suggests ways of dealing with personality conflicts in the workplace.

Conflict Outcomes

The action–reaction interplay between conflicting parties creates consequences that are *functional*, if the conflict improves the group's performance, or *dysfunctional*, if it hinders performance.

Conflict is constructive when it improves the quality of decisions, stimulates creativity and innovation, encourages interest and curiosity among group members, provides the medium for problems to be aired and tensions released, and fosters self-evaluation and change. Mild conflicts also may generate energizing emotions so members of groups become more active, energized, and engaged in their work.[30]

Dean Tjosvold of Lingnan University in Hong Kong suggests three desired outcomes for conflict:[31]

- *Agreement.* Equitable and fair agreements are the best outcome. If agreement means that one party feels exploited or defeated, this will likely lead to further conflict later.

- *Stronger relationships.* When conflict is resolved positively, this can lead to better relationships and greater trust. If the parties trust each other, they are more likely to keep the agreements they make.

- *Learning.* Handling conflict successfully teaches one how to do it better next time. It gives an opportunity to practise the skills one has learned about handling conflict.

RESEARCH FINDINGS: The Constructive Effects of Conflict

Research studies in diverse settings confirm that conflict can be functional and improve productivity. Team members with greater differences in work styles and experience also tend to share more information with one another.[32]

These observations lead us to predict benefits to organizations from the increasing cultural diversity of the workforce. That is what the evidence indicates, under most conditions. Heterogeneity among group and organization members can increase creativity, improve the quality of decisions, and facilitate change by enhancing member flexibility.[33] Researchers compared decision-making groups composed of all-Caucasian individuals with groups that also contained members from Asian, Hispanic, and Black ethnic groups. The ethnically diverse groups produced more effective and more feasible ideas, and the unique ideas they generated tended to be of higher quality than the unique ideas produced by the all-Caucasian group.

Below we examine what research tells us about the constructive effects of conflict.

The above research findings suggest that conflict within a group can lead to strength rather than weakness. However, factors such as personality, social support, and communication moderate how well groups can deal with internal conflict. At an individual level, both a person's personality (agreeableness) and his or her level of social support influence that person's response to conflict. Agreeable employees and those with lower levels of social support respond to conflict more negatively.[34]

Open communication is important to resolving conflict. Group members who discuss differences of opinion openly and are prepared to manage conflict when it arises resolve conflicts successfully.[35] Group members with cooperative conflict styles and a strong underlying identification to the overall group goals are more effective than those with a more competitive style.[36] Managers need to emphasize shared interests in resolving conflicts, so group members who disagree with one another don't become too entrenched in their points of view and start to take the conflicts personally.

The destructive consequences of conflict on the performance of a group or an organization are generally well known: Uncontrolled opposition breeds discontent, which acts to dissolve common ties and eventually leads to the destruction of the group. A substantial body of literature documents how dysfunctional conflicts can reduce group effectiveness.[37] Among the undesirable outcomes are poor communication, reduced group cohesiveness, and subordination of group goals due to infighting among members. All forms of conflict—even the functional varieties—appear to reduce group member satisfaction and trust.[38] When active discussions turn into open conflicts between members, information sharing between members decreases significantly.[39] At the extreme, conflict can bring group functioning to a halt and potentially threaten the group's survival.

Negotiation

In the Unifor-GM contract negotiations, both parties had things they wanted to achieve at the bargaining table.[40] GM wanted to keep its labour costs low, and in particular restructure the pension plan for employees to make it more affordable for the company. Unifor wanted guarantees about the Oshawa plants staying open, as well as higher wages and no concessions on the pension plan.

In negotiations, one side sometimes has a better BATNA (best alternative to a negotiated agreement). Unifor's BATNA, at least in the short term, was for members to go on strike, making it impossible for GM to produce cars. It is not clear what GM's BATNA was, although it could consider whether shutting down the Oshawa plants would be a desirable thing.

Dennis DesRosiers, an automotive industry consultant in the Toronto area, felt that Unifor was in a better overall position. Engines, transmissions, and powertrains are built at a St. Catharines plant. "If Canadians don't produce the engines, GM doesn't produce the cars in the United States," DesRosiers said. "There's going to be an awful lot of rhetoric at the table, but at the end of the day Unifor is going to be the perceived winner in all this."

How do perceptions of fairness influence the negotiation process?

Earlier in the chapter, we reviewed a number of conflict resolution strategies. One well-developed strategy is to negotiate a resolution. Negotiation permeates the interactions of almost everyone in groups and organizations: Labour bargains with management; managers negotiate with employees, peers, and senior management; salespeople negotiate with customers; purchasing agents negotiate with suppliers; employees agree to cover for one another for a few minutes in exchange for some past or future benefit. In today's loosely structured organizations, in which members work with colleagues over whom they have no direct authority and with whom they may not even share a common boss, negotiation skills are critical.

We define **negotiation** as a process in which two or more parties try to agree on the exchange rate for goods or services they are trading.[41] Although we commonly think of the outcomes of negotiation in one-shot economic terms, like negotiating over the price of a car, every negotiation in organizations also affects the relationship between negotiators and the way negotiators feel about themselves.[42] Depending on how much the parties are going to interact with one another, sometimes maintaining the social relationship and behaving ethically will be just as important as achieving an immediate outcome of bargaining. Note that we use the terms *negotiation* and *bargaining* interchangeably.

Within a negotiation, individuals have issues, positions, and interests. *Issues* are items that are specifically placed on the bargaining table for discussion. *Positions* are the individual's stand on the issues. For instance, salary may be an issue for discussion. The salary you hope to receive is your position. Finally, *interests* are the underlying concerns that are affected by the negotiation resolution. For instance, the reason that you

Kyodo/Newscom

negotiation A process in which two or more parties exchange goods or services and try to agree on the exchange rate for them.

In general, people negotiate more effectively within cultures than between them. Politeness and positivity characterize the typical conflict-avoidant negotiations in Japan such as those of labour union leader Hidekazu Kitagawa (right), shown here presenting wage and benefits demands to Ikuo Mori, president of Fuji Heavy Industries, maker of Subaru vehicles.

might want a six-figure salary is that you are trying to buy a house in Vancouver, and that salary is your only hope of being able to make mortgage payments.

Negotiators who recognize the underlying interests of themselves and the other party may have more flexibility in achieving a resolution. For instance, in the example just given, an employer who offers you a mortgage at a lower rate than the bank does, or who provides you with an interest-free loan that can be used against the mortgage, may be able to address your underlying interests without actually meeting your salary position. You may be satisfied with this alternative, if you understand what your interest is.

Below we discuss bargaining strategies and how to negotiate.

Bargaining Strategies

There are two general approaches to negotiation: *distributive bargaining* and *integrative bargaining*.[43] These are compared in Exhibit 9-3.

5 Contrast distributive and integrative bargaining.

Distributive Bargaining

Distributive bargaining is a negotiating strategy that operates under zero-sum (win–lose) conditions. That is, any gain I make is at your expense, and vice versa. You see a used car advertised for sale online. It appears to be just what you have been looking to buy. You go out to see the car. It's great, and you want it. The owner tells you the asking price. You don't want to pay that much. The two of you then negotiate over the price. Every dollar you can get the seller to cut from the car's price is a dollar you save, and

> Should you try to win at any cost when you bargain?

every dollar more the seller can get from you comes at your expense. So the essence of distributive bargaining is negotiating over who gets what share of a fixed pie. By **fixed pie**, we mean a set amount of goods or services to be divided up. When the pie is fixed, or the parties believe it is, they tend to bargain distributively.

A party engaged in distributive bargaining focuses on trying to get the opponent to agree to a specific target point, or to get as close to it as possible. Examples of this tactic are persuading your opponent of the impossibility of reaching his or her target point and the advisability of accepting a settlement near yours; arguing that your target is fair, while your opponent's is not; and attempting to get your opponent to feel emotionally generous toward you and thus accept an outcome close to your target point.

When engaged in distributive bargaining, one of the best things you can do is to make the first offer, and to make it an aggressive one. Making the first offer shows

EXHIBIT 9-3 Distributive vs. Integrative Bargaining

Bargaining Characteristic	Distributive Bargaining	Integrative Bargaining
Goal	Get as much of the pie as possible	Expand the pie so that both parties are satisfied
Motivation	Win–lose	Win–win
Focus	Positions ("I can't go beyond this point on this issue.")	Interests ("Can you explain why this issue is so important to you?")
Interests	Opposed	Congruent
Information sharing	Low (Sharing information will only allow other party to take advantage)	High (Sharing information will allow each party to find ways to satisfy interests of each party)
Duration of relationship	Short term	Long term

Source: Based on R. J. Lewicki and J. A. Litterer, *Negotiation* (Homewood, IL: Irwin, 1985), p. 280.

distributive bargaining Negotiation that seeks to divide up a fixed amount of resources; a win–lose solution.

fixed pie The belief that there is only a set amount of goods or services to be divided up between the parties.

power; individuals in power are much more likely to make initial offers, speak first at meetings, and thereby gain the advantage. Another reason this is a good strategy is the anchoring bias (the tendency for people to fixate on initial information). Once that anchoring point is set, people fail to adequately adjust it based on subsequent information. A savvy negotiator sets an anchor with the initial offer, and scores of negotiation studies show that such anchors greatly favour the person who sets them.[44]

For example, say you have a job offer, and your prospective employer asks you what sort of starting salary you would want. You have just been given a gift—you have a chance to set the anchor, meaning that you should ask for the highest salary that you think the employer could reasonably offer. For most of us, asking for a million dollars is only going to make us look ridiculous, which is why we suggest being on the high end of what you think is *reasonable*. Too often, we err on the side of caution, being afraid of scaring off the employer, and thus settle for far too little. It *is* possible to scare off an employer, and it's true that employers do not like candidates to be overly aggressive in salary negotiations, but liking is not the same as respecting or doing what it takes to hire or retain someone.[45] What happens much more often is that we ask for less than what we could have obtained, as the *Ethical Dilemma* on page 340 shows.

OB in the Street shows that in the context of eBay auctions, however, sellers who start with a low price on an item can end up getting a higher selling price.

OB IN THE STREET

A Low Anchor Value Can Reap Higher Returns on eBay

Should a seller use a high or a low starting bid in an eBay auction? In their analysis of auction results on eBay, a group of researchers found that *lower* starting bids generated higher final prices.[46] As just one example, Nikon digital cameras with ridiculously low starting bids (one penny) sold for an average of $312, whereas those with higher starting prices went for an average of $204.

What explains such a counterintuitive result? The researchers found that low starting bids attract more bidders, and this increased traffic generates more competing bidders, so in the end the price is higher. Although this may seem irrational, negotiation and bidding behaviour are not always rational, and as you have probably experienced first-hand, once you start bidding for something, you want to win, forgetting that for many auctions the one with the highest bid is often the loser (the so-called winner's curse).

If you are thinking of participating in an auction, consider the following two points. First, some buyers think sealed-bid auctions—where bidders submit a single bid in a concealed fashion—present an opportunity to get a "steal" because a price war cannot develop among bidders. However, evidence routinely indicates that sealed-bid auctions are bad for the winning bidder (and thus good for the seller) because the winning bid is higher than would otherwise be the case. Second, buyers sometimes think jumping bids—placing a bid higher than the auctioneer is asking—is a smart strategy because it drives away competing bidders early in the game. Again, this is a myth. Evidence indicates bid jumping is good at causing other bidders to follow suit, thus increasing the value of the winning bid. . . . . . .

Another distributive bargaining tactic is revealing a deadline. Negotiators who reveal deadlines speed concessions from their negotiating counterparts, making them reconsider their position. Even though negotiators don't *think* this tactic works, in reality, negotiators who reveal deadlines do better.[47]

Integrative Bargaining

In contrast to distributive bargaining, **integrative bargaining** is preferable to distributive bargaining because the former builds long-term relationships. Integrative bargaining bonds negotiators and allows them to leave the bargaining table feeling they have

integrative bargaining Negotiation that seeks one or more settlements that can create a win–win solution.

achieved a victory. Distributive bargaining, however, leaves one party a loser. It tends to build animosity and deepen divisions when people have to work together on an ongoing basis. For a discussion on the role of unions in labour–management negotiations, see *Case Incident—The Pros and Cons of Collective Bargaining* on pages 341–342.

Research shows that over repeated bargaining episodes, a "losing" party who feels positively about the negotiation outcome is much more likely to bargain cooperatively in subsequent negotiations.

Why, then, don't we see more integrative bargaining in organizations? The answer lies in the conditions necessary for this type of negotiation to succeed. These include parties who are open with information and candid about their concerns, sensitivity by both parties to the other's needs, the ability to trust one another, and a willingness by both parties to maintain flexibility.[48] Because these conditions often don't exist in organizations, negotiations often take a win-at-any-cost dynamic.

> How does anxiety affect negotiating outcomes?

Compromise may be your worst enemy in negotiating a win–win agreement. Compromising reduces the pressure to bargain integratively. After all, if you or your opponent caves in easily, no one needs to be creative to reach a settlement. People then settle for less than they could have obtained if they had been forced to consider the other party's interests, trade off issues, and be creative.[49] Consider a classic example where two siblings are arguing over who gets an orange. Unknown to them, one sibling wants the orange to drink the juice, whereas the other sibling wants the orange peel to bake a cake. If one sibling gives in and gives the other sibling the orange, then they will not be forced to explore their reasons for wanting the orange, and thus they will never find the win–win solution: They could *each* have the orange because they want different parts of it! A poor compromise may sometimes be the result of negotiation anxiety. A recent study found that negotiators who feel anxious "expect lower outcomes, make lower first offers, respond more quickly to offers, exit bargaining situations earlier, and ultimately obtain worse outcomes."[50] If self-efficacy is high, this will moderate some of the harmful effects of anxiety.[51] So it's important to feel prepared and do what you can to reduce anxiety before negotiating a deal.

How to Negotiate

Exhibit 9-4 provides a simplified model of the negotiation process. It views negotiation as made up of five steps: (1) developing a strategy; (2) defining ground rules; (3) clarifying and justifying; (4) bargaining and problem solving; and (5) attaining closure and implementation.[52]

Developing a Strategy

Before you start negotiating, you need to do your homework. What is the nature of the conflict? What is the history leading up to this negotiation? Who is involved, and what are their perceptions of the conflict? What do you want from the negotiation? What are *your* goals? If you are a supply manager at Dell Computer, for instance, and your goal is to get a significant cost reduction from your keyboard supplier, make sure this goal remains in focus in discussions and doesn't get overshadowed by other issues. It often helps to put your goals in writing and develop a range of outcomes—from "most hopeful" to "minimally acceptable"—to keep your attention focused.

You should also assess what you think are the other party's goals.[53] What are they likely to ask for? How entrenched are they likely to be in their position? What intangible or hidden interests may be important to them? On what terms might they be willing to settle? When you

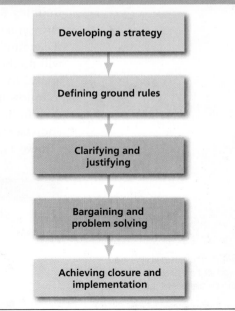

EXHIBIT 9-4 The Negotiation Process

- Developing a strategy
- Defining ground rules
- Clarifying and justifying
- Bargaining and problem solving
- Achieving closure and implementation

Source: Based on R. J. Lewicki, "Bargaining and Negotiation," *Exchange: The Organizational Behavior Teaching Journal* 6, no. 2 (1981), pp. 39–40.

can anticipate your opponent's position, you are better equipped to counter arguments with the facts and figures that support your position.

Relationships change as a result of negotiation, so take that into consideration. If you could "win" a negotiation but push the other side into resentment or animosity, it might be wiser to pursue a more compromising style. If preserving the relationship will make you seem easily exploited, you may consider a more aggressive style. As an example of how the tone of a relationship in negotiations matters, people who feel good about the *process* of a job offer negotiation are more satisfied with their jobs and less likely to turn over a year later regardless of their actual *outcomes* from these negotiations.[54]

In determining goals, parties are well advised to consider their "target and resistance" points, as well as their *best alternative to a negotiated agreement* (**BATNA**).[55] The buyer and the seller are examples of two negotiators. Each has a *target point* that defines what he or she would like to achieve. Each also has a *resistance point*, which marks the lowest outcome that is acceptable—the point below which each would break off negotiations rather than accept a less favourable settlement. The area between these two points makes up each negotiator's aspiration range. As long as there is some overlap between the buyer's and seller's aspiration ranges, a **bargaining zone** exists where each side's aspirations can be met. Referring to Exhibit 9-5, if the buyer's resistance point is $450, and the seller's resistance point is $500, then the two may not be able to reach agreement because there is no overlap in their aspiration ranges. Any offer you receive that is higher than your BATNA is better than an impasse.

In nearly all cases, the party with superior alternatives will do better in a negotiation, so experts advise negotiators to solidify their BATNA prior to any interaction.[56] There is an interesting exception to this general rule—negotiators with absolutely no alternative to a negotiated agreement sometimes "go for broke" since they don't even consider what would happen if the negotiation falls through.[57] Think carefully about what the other side is willing to give up. People who underestimate their opponent's willingness to give on key issues before the negotiation even starts end up with lower outcomes.[58] Conversely, you should not expect success in your negotiation effort unless you are able to make the other side an offer it finds more attractive than its BATNA.

You can practise your negotiating skills in the *Experiential Exercise* on page 339.

Defining Ground Rules

Once you have done your planning and developed a strategy, you are ready to define the ground rules and procedures with the other party over the negotiation itself. Who will do the negotiating? Where will it take place? What time constraints, if any, will apply? To what issues will negotiation be limited? Will there be a specific procedure to follow if an impasse is reached? During this phase, the parties will also exchange their initial proposals or demands. *From Concepts to Skills* on pages 342–343 directly addresses some of the actions you should take to improve the likelihood that you can achieve a good agreement.

BATNA The *best alternative to a negotiated agreement*; the outcome an individual faces if negotiations fail.

bargaining zone The zone between each party's resistance point, assuming that there is overlap in this range.

EXHIBIT 9-5 Staking Out the Bargaining Zone

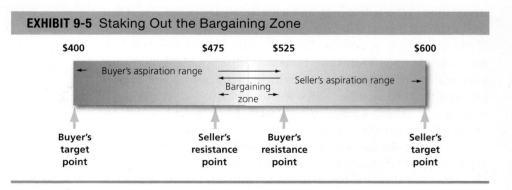

Clarifying and Justifying

After you have been presented your initial positions, you and the other party will explain, amplify, clarify, bolster, and justify your original demands. This step need not be confrontational. Rather, it's an opportunity for educating each other on the issues, why they are important, and how each arrived at their initial demands. Provide the other party with any documentation that helps support your position.

Bargaining and Problem Solving

The essence of the negotiation process is the actual give and take in trying to hash out an agreement. A recent study found that those who used competing and collaborating (essentially a combination of the forcing and problem solving conflict resolution styles discussed earlier in the chapter) as part of their strategy to gain a higher starting salary were more successful (and received higher increases) than those who used compromising and accommodating strategies.[59] The study looked at the influence of individual differences and negotiation strategies on starting salary outcomes based on a sample of 149 newly hired employees in various industry settings. Results indicated that those who chose to negotiate increased their starting salaries by an average of $5000. Individuals who negotiated by using competing and collaborating strategies, characterized by an open discussion of one's positions, issues, and perspectives, further increased their salaries as compared with those who used compromising and accommodating strategies. Individual differences, including risk aversion and integrative attitudes, played a significant role in predicting whether individuals negotiated, and if so, what strategies they used.

OB in Action—*Tips for Getting to Yes* gives you further ideas on how to make negotiating work for you, based on the popular book *Getting to Yes*.[60]

OB IN ACTION

Tips for Getting to Yes

R. Fisher and W. Ury present four principles for win–win negotiations in their book *Getting to Yes*:[62]

→ **Separate** the **people from** the **problem**. Work on the issues at hand, rather than getting involved in personality issues between the parties.

→ Focus on **interests, not positions**. Try to identify what each person needs or wants, rather than coming up with an unmovable position.

→ Look for ways to achieve **mutual gains**. Rather than focusing on one "right" solution for your position, brainstorm for solutions that will satisfy the needs of both parties.

→ Use **objective criteria** to achieve a fair solution. Try to focus on fair standards, such as market value, expert opinion, norms, or laws to help guide decision making.

Achieving Closure and Implementation

The final step in the negotiation process is formalizing your agreement and developing procedures for implementing and monitoring it. For major negotiations—from labour–management negotiations to bargaining over lease terms—this will require hammering out the specifics in a formal contract. For most cases, however, closure of the negotiation process is nothing more formal than a handshake.

Individual Differences in Negotiation Effectiveness

6 Show how individual differences influence negotiations.

Are some people better negotiators than others? The answer is more complex than you might think. Three factors influence how effectively individuals negotiate: personality, moods/emotions, and gender.

Personality Traits in Negotiation

Can you predict an opponent's negotiating tactics if you know something about his or her personality? Because personality and negotiation outcomes are related but only weakly, the answer is, at best, "sort of."[61] Most research has focused on the Big Five personality trait of agreeableness, for obvious reasons—agreeable individuals are cooperative, compliant, kind, and conflict-averse. We might think such characteristics make agreeable individuals easy prey in negotiations, especially distributive ones. The evidence suggests, however, that overall agreeableness is weakly related to negotiation outcomes. Why is this the case?

It appears that the degree to which agreeableness, and personality more generally, affects negotiation outcomes depends on the situation. The importance of being extraverted in negotiations, for example, will very much depend on how the other party reacts to someone who is assertive and enthusiastic. One complicating factor for agreeableness is that it has two facets: The tendency to be cooperative and compliant is one, but so is the tendency to be warm and empathetic.[63] It may be that while the former is a hindrance to negotiating favourable outcomes, the latter helps. Empathy, after all, is the ability to take the perspective of another person and to gain insight and understanding of them. We know perspective-taking benefits integrative negotiations, so perhaps the null effect for agreeableness is due to the two tendencies pulling against one another. If this is the case, then the best negotiator is a competitive but empathetic one, and the worst is a gentle but empathetic one. *Focus on Ethics* indicates how empathy can help you be a more ethical negotiator.

FOCUS ON ETHICS
Using Empathy to Negotiate More Ethically

How can empathy make you a more ethical negotiator?   You may have noticed that much of our advice for negotiating effectively depends on understanding the perspective and goals of the person with whom you are negotiating.[64] Preparing checklists of your negotiation partner's interests, likely tactics, and BATNA have all been shown to improve negotiation outcomes. Can these steps make you a more ethical negotiator as well? Studies suggest that they might.

Researchers asked respondents to indicate how much they tended to think about other people's feelings and emotions and to describe the types of tactics they engaged in during a negotiation exercise. More empathetic individuals consistently engaged in fewer unethical negotiation behaviours like making false promises and manipulating information and emotions.

When considering how to improve your ethical negotiation behaviour, follow these guidelines:

1. Try to understand your negotiation partner's perspective. This is not just understanding cognitively what the other person wants, but empathizing with the emotional reaction he or she will likely have to the possible outcomes.
2. Be aware of your own emotions, because many moral reactions are fundamentally emotional. One study found that engaging in unethical negotiation strategies increased feelings of guilt, so by extension, feeling guilty in a negotiation may mean that you are engaging in behaviour you will regret later.
3. Beware of empathizing so much that you work against your own interests. Just because you try to understand the motives and emotional reactions of the other side does not mean you have to assume that the other person is going to be honest and fair in return. So be on guard.

The type of negotiations may matter as well. In one study, agreeable individuals reacted more positively and felt less stress (measured by their cortisol levels) in integrative negotiations than in distributive ones. Low levels of stress, in turn, made for more effective negotiation outcomes.[65] Similarly, in "hard-edged" distributive negotiations, where giving away information leads to a disadvantage, extraverted negotiators do less well because they tend to share more information than they should.[66]

CAREER OBJECTIVES

How Can I Get a Better Job?

I feel like my career is at a standstill, and I want to talk to my boss about getting a more developmental assignment. How can I negotiate effectively for a better job position?

— *Wei*

Dear Wei:

You're certainly starting out on the right foot. A lot of people focus on a salary as a way to achieve success and negotiate for the best short-run offer. There is obviously an advantage to this strategy in the short run, but sustained career growth has better payoffs in the long run. Developing skills can help put you on track for multiple salary increases. A strong skill set from developmental assignments will also give you a better position for future negotiations because you will have more career options.

Long-term career negotiations based on developmental assignments are also easier to bring up with a supervisor. That is because salary negotiations are often a zero-sum situation, but career development negotiations can bring positive outcomes to both sides. When negotiating for a developmental assignment, make sure you emphasize a few points with your supervisor:

- *When it comes to salary negotiations, either you get the money, or the company keeps the money.* Given that, your interests and the interests of your managers are directly opposed. On the other hand, negotiating for developmental assignments usually means finding ways to improve not just your skills, but also your contribution to the company's bottom line. You can, in complete honesty, frame the discussion around these mutual benefits.

- *Let your supervisor know that you are interested in getting better at your job, and that you are motivated to improve through a developmental assignment.* Asking your supervisor for opportunities to grow is a clear sign that you are an employee worth investing in.

- *Be open to creative solutions.* It's possible that there are some idiosyncratic solutions (also called "I-deals") for enhancing both your interests and those of your supervisor. One of the best things about an integrative bargaining situation like this is that you and your negotiation partner can find novel solutions that neither would have imagined separately.

Think strategically about your career, and you will likely find you can negotiate not just for a better paycheque tomorrow, but for a paycheque that keeps increasing in the years to come.

Sources: Y. Rofcanin, T. Kiefer, and K. Strauss, "How I-Deals Build Resources to Facilitate Reciprocation: Mediating Role of Positive Affective States," *Academy of Management Proceedings,* August, 2014, DOI: 10.5465/AMBPP.2014.16096abstract; C. Liao, S. J. Wayne, and D. M. Rousseau, "Idiosyncratic Deals in Contemporary Organizations: A Qualitative and Meta-Analytical Review," *Journal of Organizational Behavior,* October 16, 2014, DOI: 10.1002/job.1959; and V. Brenninkmeijer and M. Hekkert-Koning "To Craft or Not to Craft," *Career Development International* 20 (2015): 147–62.

Self-efficacy is one individual-difference variable that consistently seems to relate to negotiation outcomes.[67] This is a fairly intuitive finding—it isn't too surprising to hear that those who believe they will be more successful in negotiation situations tend to perform more effectively. It may be that individuals who are more confident stake out stronger claims, are less likely to back down from their positions, and exhibit confidence that intimidates others. Although the exact mechanism is not yet clear, it does seem that negotiators may benefit from trying to get a boost in confidence before going to the bargaining table.

Research suggests that intelligence predicts negotiation effectiveness, but, as with personality, the effects are not especially strong.[68] In a sense, these weak links mean that you are not severely disadvantaged, even if you are an agreeable extravert, when it's time to negotiate. We can all learn to be better negotiators.[69]

Moods/Emotions in Negotiation

Do moods and emotions influence negotiation? They do, but the way they work depends on the emotions as well as the context. A negotiator who shows anger generally induces concessions from opponents, for instance, because the other negotiator believes no further concessions from the angry party are possible. One factor that governs this outcome, however, is power—you should show anger in negotiations only if you have at least as much power as your counterpart. If you have less, showing anger actually seems to provoke "hardball" reactions from the other side.[70] Another factor is how genuine your anger is—"faked" anger, or anger produced from so-called surface acting (see Chapter 2), is not effective, but showing anger that is genuine (so-called deep acting) is effective.[71] It also appears that having a history of showing anger, rather than sowing the seeds of revenge, actually induces more concessions because the other party perceives the negotiator as "tough."[72] Finally, culture seems to matter. For instance, one study found that when East Asian participants showed anger, it induced more concessions than if the negotiator expressing anger was from the United States or Europe, perhaps because of the stereotype of East Asians as refusing to show anger.[73]

Another relevant emotion is disappointment. Generally, a negotiator who perceives disappointment from his or her counterpart concedes more. In one study, Dutch students were given 100 chips to bargain over. Negotiators who expressed disappointment were offered 14 more chips than those who didn't. In a second study, showing disappointment yielded an average concession of 12 chips. Unlike a show of anger, the relative power of the negotiators made no difference in either study.[74]

Anxiety also appears to have an impact on negotiation. For example, one study found that individuals who experienced more anxiety about a negotiation used more deceptions in dealing with others.[75] Another study found that anxious negotiators expect lower outcomes, respond to offers more quickly, and exit the bargaining process more quickly, leading them to obtain worse outcomes.[76]

As you can see, emotions—especially negative ones—matter to negotiation. Even emotional unpredictability affects outcomes; researchers have found that negotiators who express positive and negative emotions in an unpredictable way extract more concessions because this behaviour makes the other party feel less in control.[77] As one negotiator put it, "Out of the blue, you may have to react to something you have been working on in one way, and then something entirely new is introduced, and you have to veer off and refocus."[78]

Gender Differences in Negotiation

Men and women behave similarly in many areas of organizational behaviour, but negotiation is not one of them. It seems fairly clear that men and women negotiate differently, men and women are treated differently by negotiation partners, and these differences affect outcomes.

A popular stereotype is that women are more cooperative and pleasant in negotiations than are men. Although this stereotype is controversial, it has some merit. Men tend to place a higher value on status, power, and recognition, whereas women tend to place a higher value on compassion and altruism. Moreover, women tend to value relationship outcomes more than men, and men tend to value economic outcomes more than women.[79]

> Do men and women negotiate differently?

These differences affect both negotiation behaviour and negotiation outcomes. Compared with men, women tend to behave in a less assertive, less self-interested, and more accommodating manner in negotiations. As a 2012 literature review concluded, women "are more reluctant to initiate negotiations, and when they do initiate negotiations, they ask for less, are more willing to accept [the] offer, and make more generous offers to their negotiation partners than men do."[80] A 2012 study of MBA students at Carnegie Mellon University found that male MBA students took the step of negotiating their first offer 57 percent of the time, compared with 4 percent for female MBA students. The net result? A $4000 difference in starting salaries.[81]

One comprehensive literature review suggests that the tendency for men to receive better negotiation outcomes in some situations does not cover *all* situations.[82] Indeed, evidence suggested women and men bargained more equally in certain situations, women sometimes outperformed men, and men and women obtained more nearly equal outcomes when negotiating on behalf of someone else. In other words, everyone was better at advocating for others than they were at advocating for themselves.

Factors that increased the predictability of negotiations also tended to reduce gender differences. When the range of negotiation settlements was well defined, men and women were more equal in outcomes. When more experienced negotiators were at the table, men and women were also more nearly equivalent. The study authors proposed that when situations are more ambiguous, with less well-defined terms and less experienced negotiators, stereotypes may have stronger effects, leading to larger gender differences in outcomes.

So what can be done to change this troublesome state of affairs? First, organizational culture plays a role. If an organization, even unwittingly, reinforces gender-stereotypical behaviours (men negotiating competitively, women negotiating cooperatively), it will negatively affect negotiations when anyone goes against stereotype. Men and women need to know that it's acceptable for each to show a full range of negotiating behaviours. Thus, a female negotiator who behaves competitively and a male negotiator who behaves cooperatively need to know that they are not violating expectations. Making sure negotiations are designed to focus on well-defined and work-related terms also has promise for reducing gender differences by minimizing the ambiguous space for stereotypes to operate. This focus on structure and work relevance also obviously helps focus negotiations on factors that will improve the organization's performance.

Research is less clear as to whether women can improve their outcomes by showing some gender-stereotypical behaviours. Researchers Laura Kray, professor at the

Chrystia Freeland, minister of Foreign Affairs in Justin Trudeau's Liberal government, is responsible for international diplomacy as well as trade relations with the United States. She is a seasoned journalist and a respected negotiator who is known for being likable, detail oriented, and tough.

Lars Hagberg/The Canadian Press

University of California, Berkeley, and colleagues suggested that female negotiators who were instructed to behave with "feminine charm" (be animated in body movements, make frequent eye contact with their partners, smile, laugh, be playful, and frequently compliment their partners) did better in negotiations than women not so instructed. These behaviours did not work for men.[83]

Other researchers disagree and argue that what can best benefit women is to break down gender stereotypes for the individuals who hold them.[84] It's possible this is a short-term/long-term situation: In the short term, women can gain an advantage in negotiation by being both assertive and flirtatious, but in the long term, their interests are best served by eliminating these sorts of sex role stereotypes.

Evidence also suggests that women's own attitudes and behaviours hurt them in negotiations. Managerial women demonstrate less confidence than men in anticipation of negotiating and are less satisfied with their performance afterward, even when their performance and the outcomes they achieve are similar to those of men.[85] Women are also less likely than men to see an ambiguous situation as an opportunity for negotiation. Women may unduly penalize themselves by failing to engage in negotiations that would be in their best interest. Some research suggests that women are less aggressive in negotiations because they are worried about backlash from others. A recent study by Professor Linda Schweitzer of the Sprott School of Business, Carleton University, and three colleagues found that women tend to have lower expectations about salaries and promotions as they enter the workforce, which may explain why they are less aggressive in salary negotiations.[86]

Negotiating in a Social Context

Jerry Dias, president of Unifor, was asked a few months after the Unifor-GM contract was ratified whether he had been optimistic or pessimistic when negotiations started.[87] He responded that he had felt confident that negotiations would get done, and noted, "I knew we were going to find solutions; I just didn't know that they would all happen prior to the strike deadlines." Knowing that keeping the Oshawa plants open was extremely important to the union likely affected his thoughts about the strike deadline.

Negotiations work better, generally, when the parties know each other. Dias noted that he spoke with Mary Barra (chairperson and CEO of GM) to let her know there would not be an agreement without a solution for Oshawa. Dias has known the chief negotiator of GM Canada for 20 years, and he says that helps when Dias makes strong points in the negotiations. That also enables GM's negotiator to go back to GM management to "say to the people at the top at GM, 'Listen, he's not kidding.'"

We have mostly been discussing negotiations that occur among parties that meet only once, and in isolation from other individuals. However, in organizations, many negotiations are open-ended and public. When you are trying to figure out who in a work group should do a tedious task, negotiating with your boss to get a chance to travel internationally, or asking for more money for a project, there is a social component to the negotiation. You are probably negotiating with someone you already know and will work with again, and the negotiation and its outcome are likely to be topics people will talk about. To really understand negotiations in practice, then, we must consider the social factors of reputation and relationships.

Reputation

Your reputation is the way other people think and talk about you. When it comes to negotiation, having a reputation for being trustworthy matters. In short, trust in a negotiation process opens the door to many forms of integrative negotiation strategies that benefit both parties.[88] The most effective way to build trust is to behave in an honest way across repeated interactions. Then, others feel more comfortable making open-ended offers with many different outcomes. This helps to achieve win–win outcomes, since both parties can work to achieve what is most important to themselves while still benefitting the other party.

Sometimes we either trust or distrust people based on word-of-mouth about a person's characteristics. What type of characteristics help a person develop a trustworthy reputation? A combination of competence and integrity.[89] Negotiators higher in self-confidence and cognitive ability are seen as more competent by negotiation partners.[90] They are also considered better able to accurately describe a situation and their own resources, and more credible when they make suggestions for creative solutions to impasses. Individuals who have a reputation for integrity can also be more effective in negotiations.[91] They are seen as more likely to keep their promises and present information accurately, so others are more willing to accept their promises as part of a bargain. This opens many options for the negotiator that would not be available to someone who is not seen as trustworthy. Finally, individuals who have higher reputations are better liked and have more friends and allies—in other words, they have more social resources, which may give them more understood power in negotiations.

Relationships

There is more to repeated negotiations than just reputation. The social, interpersonal component of relationships with repeated negotiations means that individuals go beyond valuing what is simply good for themselves and instead start to think about what is best for the other party and the relationship as a whole.[92] Repeated negotiations built on a foundation of trust also broaden the range of options, since a favour or concession today can be offered in return for some repayment further down the road.[93] Repeated negotiations also facilitate integrative problem solving. This occurs partly because people begin to see their negotiation partners in a more personal way over time and come to share emotional bonds.[94] Repeated negotiations also make integrative approaches more workable because a sense of trust and reliability has been built up.[95]

In sum, it's clear that an effective negotiator needs to think about more than just the outcomes of a single interaction. Negotiators who consistently act in a way that demonstrates competence, honesty, and integrity will usually have better outcomes in the long run.

Third-Party Negotiations

 Assess the roles and functions of third-party negotiations.

To this point, we have discussed bargaining in terms of direct negotiations. Occasionally, however, individuals or group representatives reach a stalemate and are unable to resolve their differences. In such cases, they may turn to alternative dispute resolution (ADR), where a third party helps both sides find a solution outside a courtroom. The three basic third-party roles are mediator, arbitrator, and conciliator.

Mediator

A **mediator** is a neutral third party who facilitates a negotiated solution by using reasoning and persuasion, suggesting alternatives, and the like. Mediators can be much more aggressive in proposing solutions than conciliators. Mediators are widely used in labour–management negotiations and in civil court disputes. British Columbia's Motor Vehicle Branch uses mediation to help settle accident claims. In Ontario, all disputes between companies and employees now go to mediation within 100 days.

mediator A neutral third party who facilitates a negotiated solution by using reasoning, persuasion, and suggestions for alternatives.

The overall effectiveness of mediated negotiations is fairly impressive. For example, a recent Mediate BC survey found that over 90 percent of mediations resolved all issues or helped the parties move toward resolution. The survey also found that the average satisfaction rate with the process was over 90 percent.[96] But the situation is the key to whether mediation will succeed; the conflicting parties must be motivated to bargain and resolve their conflict. Additionally, conflict intensity cannot be too high; mediation is most effective under moderate levels of conflict. Finally, perceptions of the mediator are important; to be effective, the mediator must be perceived as neutral and noncoercive.

Arbitrator

An **arbitrator** is a third party with the authority to dictate an agreement. Arbitration can be voluntary (requested by the parties) or compulsory (forced on the parties by law or contract).

The big advantage of arbitration over mediation is that it always results in a settlement. Whether there is a downside depends on how "heavy-handed" the arbitrator appears. If one party is left feeling overwhelmingly defeated, that party is certain to be dissatisfied and the conflict may resurface at a later time.

Conciliator

A **conciliator** is a trusted third party who provides an informal communication link between the negotiator and the opponent. Conciliation is used extensively in international, labour, family, and community disputes. In practice, conciliators typically act as more than mere communication conduits. They also engage in fact-finding, interpreting messages, and persuading disputants to develop agreements.

In Canada, the first step in trying to resolve a labour relations dispute can be to bring in a conciliation officer when agreement cannot be reached. This may be a good faith effort to resolve the dispute. Sometimes, however, a conciliator is used so that the union can reach a legal strike position or management can engage in a lockout. Provinces vary somewhat in how they set out the ability to engage in a strike after going through a conciliation process. For instance, in Nova Scotia, once the conciliation officer files a report that the dispute cannot be resolved through conciliation, there is a 14-day waiting period before either party can give 48 hours' notice of either a strike or a lockout.[97]

GLOBAL IMPLICATIONS

Below we consider (1) how conflict is handled in different cultures, (2) whether there are differences in negotiating styles across cultures, and (3) how the display of emotions affects negotiations in different cultures.

Conflict Resolution and Culture

Research suggests that differences across countries in conflict resolution strategies may be based on collectivistic tendencies and motives.[98] Collectivistic cultures see people as deeply embedded in social situations, whereas individualistic cultures see people as autonomous. As a result, collectivists are more likely to seek to preserve relationships and promote the good of the group as a whole. They will avoid direct expression of conflicts, preferring to use more indirect methods for resolving differences of opinion. Collectivists may also be more interested in demonstrations of concern and working through third parties to resolve disputes, whereas individualists will be more likely to confront differences of opinion directly and openly.

arbitrator A third party to a negotiation who has the authority to dictate an agreement.

conciliator A trusted third party who provides an informal communication link between the negotiator and the opponent.

Some research supports this theory. Compared to collectivistic Japanese negotiators, individualistic US negotiators are more likely to see offers as unfair and reject them. Another study revealed that while US managers were more likely to use competing tactics when faced with a conflict, Chinese managers were more likely to use compromising and avoiding.[99] Interview data, however, suggest top management teams in Chinese high-technology firms prefer integration even more than compromising and avoiding.[100]

Cross-cultural negotiations can also create issues of trust.[101] One study of Indian and US negotiators found that respondents reported having less trust in their cross-culture negotiation counterparts. The lower level of trust was associated with less discovery of common interests between parties, which occurred because cross-culture negotiators were less willing to disclose and solicit information. Another study found that both US and Chinese negotiators tended to have an ingroup bias, which led them to favour negotiating partners from their own cultures. For Chinese negotiators, this was particularly true when accountability requirements were high.

Cultural Differences in Negotiating Style

So what can we say about culture and negotiations? First, it appears that people generally negotiate more effectively within cultures than between them. For example, a Colombian is apt to do better negotiating with a Colombian than with a Sri Lankan. Second, it appears that in cross-cultural negotiations, it's especially important that the negotiators be high in openness. This point suggests that a good strategy is to choose cross-cultural negotiators who are high on openness to experience and to avoid factors such as time pressures that tend to inhibit learning about and understanding the other party.[102]

Culture, Negotiations, and Emotions

As a rule, no one likes to face an angry counterpart in negotiations. However, East Asian negotiators may respond less favourably to anger than people from other cultures.[103]

Two separate studies found that East Asian negotiators were less likely to accept offers from negotiators who displayed anger during negotiations. Another study explicitly compared how US and Chinese negotiators react to an angry counterpart. When confronted with an angry negotiator, Chinese negotiators increased their use of distributive negotiating tactics, whereas US negotiators capitulated somewhat in the face of angry demands.[104]

Why might East Asian and Chinese negotiators respond more negatively to angry negotiators? The authors of the research speculated that individuals from East Asian cultures may feel that using anger to get their way in a negotiation is not a legitimate tactic, so they refuse to cooperate when their opponents become upset.

Summary

While many people assume that conflict lowers group and organizational performance, this assumption is frequently incorrect. Conflict can be either constructive or destructive to the functioning of a group or unit. Levels of conflict can be either too high or too low to be constructive. Either extreme hinders performance. An optimal level is one that prevents stagnation, stimulates creativity, allows tensions to be released, and initiates the seeds of change without being disruptive or preventing coordination of activities.

LESSONS LEARNED

- A medium level of conflict often results in higher productivity than no conflict.
- Negotiators should identify their BATNA (*b*est *a*lternative *t*o a *n*egotiated *a*greement).
- In relationships with long-term consequences, it's best to use a win–win strategy in bargaining.

SNAPSHOT SUMMARY

Conflict Defined
- Functional vs. Dysfunctional Conflict
- Types of Conflict
- Loci of Conflict
- Sources of Conflict

Conflict Resolution
- Conflict Management Strategies Based on Dual Concern Theory
- What Can Individuals Do to Manage Conflict?

- Resolving Personality Conflicts

Conflict Outcomes

Negotiation
- Bargaining Strategies
- How to Negotiate

Individual Differences in Negotiation Effectiveness
- Personality Traits in Negotiation

- Moods/Emotions in Negotiation
- Gender Differences in Negotiation

Negotiating in a Social Context
- Reputation
- Relationships

Third-Party Negotiations
- Mediator
- Arbitrator
- Conciliator

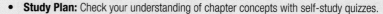
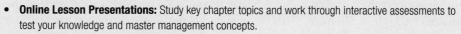
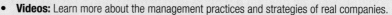

MyLab Management

Study, practise, and explore real business situations with these helpful resources:

- **Study Plan:** Check your understanding of chapter concepts with self-study quizzes.
- **Online Lesson Presentations:** Study key chapter topics and work through interactive assessments to test your knowledge and master management concepts.
- **Videos:** Learn more about the management practices and strategies of real companies.
- **Simulations:** Practise management decision-making in simulated business environments.

OB at Work

for Review

1. What is conflict?
2. What are the three types of conflict?
3. What are the three loci of conflict?
4. What are the conditions that lead to conflict?
5. What are the differences between distributive and integrative bargaining?
6. How do individual differences influence negotiations?
7. What are the roles and functions of third-party negotiations?

for Managers

- Seek integrative solutions when your objective is to learn, when you want to merge insights from people with different perspectives, when you need to gain commitment by incorporating concerns into a consensus, and when you need to work through feelings that have interfered with a relationship.
- You can build trust by accommodating others when you find you're wrong, when you need to demonstrate reasonableness, when other positions need to be heard, when issues are more important to others than to yourself, when you want to satisfy others and maintain cooperation, when you can build social credits for later issues, to minimize loss when you are outmatched and losing, and when others should learn from their own mistakes.
- Consider compromising when goals are important but not worth potential disruption, when opponents with equal power are committed to mutually exclusive goals, and when you need temporary settlements to complex issues.
- Distributive bargaining can resolve disputes, but it often reduces the satisfaction of one or more negotiators because it's confrontational and focused on the short term. Integrative bargaining, in contrast, tends to provide outcomes that satisfy all parties and build lasting relationships.
- Try to find creative ways to achieve the negotiating objectives of both parties, especially when you value the long-term relationship with the other party. That does not mean sacrificing your self-interest; rather, it means trying to find creative solutions that give both parties what they really want.

for You

- It may seem easier, but avoiding conflict does not necessarily have a more positive outcome than working with someone to resolve the conflict.
- Trying to achieve a win–win solution in a conflict situation tends to lead to better relationships and greater trust.
- It's not always possible to resolve conflict on one's own. There are alternative dispute resolution options, including having someone help mediate the conflict.
- It's better to focus more on interests rather than positions when engaged in a negotiation. Doing so gives you the ability to arrive at more flexible solutions.

PRO SPORTS STRIKES ARE CAUSED BY GREEDY OWNERS

POINT

It can be annoying to see the constant strikes, lockouts, and back-and-forth negotiations between sports teams and the players' unions.[105] Of the major pro sports leagues, Major League Baseball (MLB) is the only one without a strike since 1995—and it had eight in its history. You've got to wonder why this keeps happening. Here is why: Owners' greed knows no limit.

In nearly every recent strike or lockout, the main issue was money and how to divide it. When the National Hockey League (NHL) locked out the players during the 2012–2013 season, the owners were the instigators. They wanted to reduce the players' share of hockey revenues. They wanted to eliminate salary arbitration. They wanted to introduce term limits to contracts. They wanted to change free-agency rules and eliminate signing bonuses. On a philosophical level, some of these proposals are interesting because they reveal that owners want to restrict competition when it suits them and increase it when it benefits them.

While the owners were whining about the unfairness of long-term contracts, the Minnesota Wild's owner Craig Leipold signed Zach Parise and Ryan Suter to identical 13-year, $98 million contracts. Contracts like these suggest that owners want the players' union to save them from themselves.

Perhaps some of this behaviour would make sense if the owners were losing money, but that is hardly the case. The NHL has three teams worth over $1 billion each, and few are worth less than $200 million. The owners are not hurting, either. Most are millionaires many times over. N. Murray Edwards, co-owner of the Calgary Flames, had a net worth of $1.88 billion in 2017 and was ranked 23 of the 100 wealthiest Canadians.

In essence, what we have are rich owners trying to negotiate rules that keep them from competing with one another for players. It's a bald-faced and hypocritical attempt to use their own kind of union to negotiate favourable agreements, all the while criticizing the players' unions.

COUNTERPOINT

Major league owners are an easy target. But they have the most to lose from work stoppages. It's the players and their unions who push the envelope.

It's true that most major league players are well rewarded for their exceptional talents and the risks they take. It's also true that owners who are able to invest in teams are wealthy—investors usually are. But the fault for disputes lies with spoiled players—and the union leaders who burnish their credentials and garner the limelight by fanning the flames of discontent.

On this latter point, give all the credit in the world to the union negotiators (paid millions themselves), who do nothing if not hawk publicity and use hardball negotiating tactics. Take the NHL players' union boss Donald Fehr. For a "negotiation" set to begin at 10 a.m., he arrived at 11:15. At exactly 12:00, he announced he had a lunch meeting uptown and left.

Do we really need labour unions for workers whose average salaries for first team players in 2016–2017 are $2.9 million (NHL), $4.4 million (MLB), and $6.4 million (NBA)? NHL clubs spent 76 percent of their gross revenues on players' salaries and collectively lost $273 million the year before the most recent lockout. It's easy to argue that major league sports have an unusual number of labour disputes, but that is not necessarily accurate. Did you hear about the 2015 largest strike of oil refinery workers in decades or the ongoing worldwide strikes by low-paid workers in the fast-food industry? Somehow these strikes don't make the news or our collective consciousness as much as sports strikes. Sports strikes interest us, but we should not fall into the trap of blaming these on the owners.

BREAKOUT **GROUP** EXERCISES

Form small groups to discuss the following topics, as assigned by your instructor:

1. You and 2 other students carpool to class every day. The driver has recently taken to playing a new radio station quite loudly. You do not like the music, or the loudness. Using one of the conflict-handling strategies outlined in Exhibit 9-2, indicate how you might go about resolving this conflict.

2. Using the example above, identify a number of BATNAs (*best alternative to a negotiated agreement*) available to you, and then decide whether you should continue carpooling.

3. Which conflict-handling strategy is most consistent with how you deal with conflict? Is your strategy effective? Why or why not?

EXPERIENTIAL EXERCISE

A Negotiation Role Play

This role play is designed to help you develop your negotiating skills. The class is to break into pairs. One person will play the role of Alex, the department supervisor. The other person will play C.J., Alex's boss.

The situation: Alex and C.J. work for hockey-equipment manufacturer Bauer. Alex supervises a research laboratory. C.J. is the manager of R & D. Alex and C.J. are former skaters who have worked for Bauer for more than 6 years. C.J. has been Alex's boss for 2 years.

One of Alex's employees has greatly impressed Alex. This employee is Lisa Roland. Lisa was hired 11 months ago. She is 24 years old and holds a master's degree in mechanical engineering. Her entry-level salary was $57 500 a year. She was told by Alex that, in accordance with corporation policy, she would receive an initial performance evaluation at 6 months and a comprehensive review after 1 year. Based on her performance record, Lisa was told she could expect a salary adjustment at the time of the 1-year review.

Alex's evaluation of Lisa after 6 months was very positive. Alex commented on the long hours Lisa was working, her cooperative spirit, the fact that others in the lab enjoyed working with her, and her immediate positive impact on the project she had been assigned. Now that Lisa's first anniversary is coming up, Alex has again reviewed Lisa's performance. Alex thinks Lisa may be the best new person the R & D group has ever hired. After only a year, Alex has ranked Lisa as the number 3 performer in a department of 11.

Salaries in the department vary greatly. Alex, for instance, has a basic salary of $93 800, plus eligibility for a bonus that might add another $7000 to $11 000 a year. The salary range of the 11 department members is $48 400 to $79 000. The lowest salary is a recent hire with a bachelor's degree in physics. The 2 people whom Alex has rated above Lisa earn base salaries of $73 800 and $78 900. They are both 27 years old and have been at Bauer for 3 and 4 years, respectively. The median salary in Alex's department is $65 300.

Alex's role: You want to give Lisa a big raise. While she is young, she has proven to be an excellent addition to the department. You don't want to lose her. More important, she knows in general what other people in the department are earning, and she thinks she is underpaid. The company typically gives 1-year raises of 5 percent, although 10 percent is not unusual and 20 to 30 percent increases have been approved on occasion. You would like to get Lisa as large an increase as C.J. will approve.

C.J.'s role: All your supervisors typically try to squeeze you for as much money as they can for their people. You understand this because you did the same thing when you were a supervisor, but your boss wants to keep a lid on costs. He wants you to keep raises for recent hires generally in the range of 5 to 8 percent. In fact, he has sent a memo to all managers and supervisors stating this objective. However, your boss is also very concerned with equity and paying people what they are worth. You feel assured that he will support any salary recommendation you make, as long as it can be justified. Your goal, consistent with cost reduction, is to keep salary increases as low as possible.

The negotiation: Alex has a meeting scheduled with C.J. to discuss Lisa's performance review and salary adjustment. Take a couple of minutes to think through the facts in this exercise and to prepare a strategy. Then you have up to 15 minutes to conduct your negotiation. When your negotiation is complete, the class will compare the various strategies used and the outcomes that resulted.

ETHICAL DILEMMA

The Lowball Applicant

Consider this first-person account:

I am a human resources manager, so I interview people every day. Sometimes the managers in my company ask me to pre-screen candidates, which I do after discussing the job at length with the manager. I usually start the candidate screening with a few personality–job fit tests; then conduct an interview, following a list of job-specific questions the manager has given me; and finally discuss the job requirements, our company, and the pay/benefits. By that time in the process, the candidate usually has a good idea of the job and is eager to suggest a level of pay at the top of the advertised bracket or, often, above the pay bracket. However, this isn't always the case.

One time in particular, an excellent candidate with outstanding qualifications surprised me by saying that since she wanted flextime, she would accept a rate below the pay bracket. Confused, I asked her whether she wanted a reduction in hours below full time. She said no, she expected to work full time and only wanted to come in a little late and would leave a little late to make up the time. I guess she figured this was a concession worth slashing her salary for, but our company has flextime. In fact, she could have asked for five fewer hours per week, still have been considered full time by our company

policies, and negotiated for salary above the advertised pay grade.

I knew the manager would be highly interested in this candidate and that he could probably get her to work the longer full-time hours at a lower rate of pay. That outcome might be best for the company, or it might not. The candidate obviously didn't fully understand the company policies in her favour, and she was unsophisticated about her worth in the marketplace. What should I have done?

Questions

1. If the human resources manager were to coach the applicant to request a higher salary, would the coaching work against the interests of the organization? Is it the responsibility of the human resources manager to put the organization's financial interests first?

2. What do you see as the potential downside of the human resources manager abstaining from discussing the pay issue further with the candidate?

3. If the candidate were hired at the reduced rate she proposed, how might the situation play out over the next year when she gets to know the organization and its pay standards better?

CASE INCIDENTS

Disorderly Conduct

The sound of Matt and Peter's arguing is familiar to everyone in the office by now.[106] In an effort to make the best use of space and ensure a free flow of discussion and ideas, the founder of Markay Design had decided to convert the one-floor office of the company to an open plan with no walls between workers. The goal of such a layout

is to eliminate boundaries and enhance creativity. But for Matt and Peter, the new arrangement creates a growing sense of tension.

The argument boils down to the question of workspace order and organization. Peter prefers to keep his desk completely clean and clear, and he keeps a stack of cleaning wipes in a drawer to eliminate any dust or dirt. Matt, on the other hand, likes to keep all his work visible on his desk, so sketches, plans, magazines, and photos are scattered everywhere, alongside boxes of crackers and coffee cups. Peter finds it hard to concentrate when he sees Matt's piles of materials everywhere, while Matt feels he can be more creative and free flowing when he is not forced to clean and organize constantly. Many of Matt and Peter's co-workers wish they would just let the issue drop. The men enjoyed a good working relationship in the past, with Peter's attention to detail and thorough planning serving to rein in some of Matt's wild inspirations. But of late, their collaborations have been derailed in disputes.

Everyone knows it's not productive to engage in conflicts over every small irritant in the workplace. However, completely avoiding conflict can be equally negative. An emerging body of research has examined "conflict cultures" in organizations. The findings suggest having a culture that actively avoids and suppresses conflicts is associated with lower levels of creativity. Moreover, cultures that push conflict underground but do not succeed

in reducing the underlying tensions can become passive-aggressive, marked by underhanded behaviour against other co-workers.

Ultimately, finding a way through the clutter dispute is probably going to be an ongoing process to find a balance between perspectives. Both Matt and Peter worry that if they cannot find a solution, their usually positive work relationship will be too contentious to bear, and that would be a real mess.

Questions

1. Describe some of the factors that led this situation to become an open conflict.

2. Do you think this is an issue worth generating conflict over? What are the potential costs and benefits of Matt and Peter having an open discussion of the issues?

3. How can Matt and Peter develop an active problem-solving discussion to resolve this conflict? What could effectively be changed, and what is probably going to just remain a problem?

The Pros and Cons of Collective Bargaining

Fewer employees in the private sector are unionized, compared with those who work in the public sector (15.2 vs. 71.3 percent in 2014).[107] Does being in a labour union make a difference for optimal wages and benefits?

On the positive side, by negotiating as a collective, public-sector employees, who are more heavily unionized, are able to earn, on average, roughly 12 percent more than employees working in the mostly non-unionized private sector. Unions also can protect the rights of workers against capricious actions by employers. Consider the following example:

In a non-unionized workplace, Lydia criticized the work of five of her co-workers. They were not amused and posted angry messages on a Facebook page. Lydia complained to her supervisor that the postings violated the employer's "zero tolerance" policy against "bullying and harassment." The employer investigated and, agreeing that its policy had been violated, fired the five.

Most of us would probably prefer not to be fired for Facebook posts. This is a protection unions can provide.

On the negative side, public-sector unions at times have been able to negotiate employment arrangements

that are hard to sustain. According to the Fraser Institute, almost 89.3 percent of those employed by the Canadian government receive pension benefits as part of their total compensation. Only 23.8 percent of private-sector employees have these benefits. This allowed government employees to retire about 2.3 years earlier than private-sector employees.

Further, it's often more difficult to fire a member of a public-sector union, even if performance is exceptionally poor. A recent report by the Fraser Institute indicated that 3.8 percent of private-sector employees were fired compared to 0.6 percent of public-sector employees.

Reasonable people can disagree about the pros and cons of unions and whether they help or hinder an organization's ability to be successful. There is no dispute, however, that they often figure prominently in the study of workplace conflict and negotiation strategies.

Questions

1. Labour–management negotiations might be characterized as more distributive than integrative. Do you agree? Why do you think this is the case? What, if anything, would you do about it?

2. If unions have negotiated unreasonable agreements, what responsibility does management or the administration bear for agreeing to these terms? Why do you think they do agree?

3. If you were advising union and management representatives about how to negotiate an agreement, drawing from the concepts in this chapter, what would you tell them?

FROM CONCEPTS TO SKILLS

Negotiating

Once you have taken the time to assess your own goals, consider the other party's goals and interests, and develop a strategy, you are ready to begin actual negotiations.

The following five suggestions should improve your negotiating skills:[108]

1. *Begin with a positive overture.* Studies on negotiation show that concessions tend to be reciprocated and lead to agreements. As a result, begin bargaining with a positive overture—perhaps a small concession—and then reciprocate your opponent's concessions.

2. *Address problems, not personalities.* Concentrate on the negotiation issues, not on the personal characteristics of your opponent. When negotiations get tough, avoid the tendency to attack your opponent. It's your opponent's ideas or position that you disagree with, not him or her personally. Separate the people from the problem, and don't personalize differences.

3. *Pay little attention to initial offers.* Treat an initial offer as merely a point of departure. Everyone has to have an initial position. These initial offers tend to be extreme and idealistic. Treat them as such.

4. *Emphasize win–win solutions.* Inexperienced negotiators often assume that their gain must come at the expense of the other party. As noted with integrative bargaining, that need not be the case. There are often win–win solutions. Assuming a zero-sum game means missed opportunities for trade-offs that could benefit both sides. So if conditions are supportive, look for an integrative solution. Frame options in terms of your opponent's interests, and look for solutions that can allow your opponent, as well as yourself, to declare a victory.

5. *Create an open and trusting climate.* Skilled negotiators are better listeners, ask more questions, focus their arguments more directly, are less defensive, and have learned to avoid words and phrases that can irritate an opponent (for example, "generous offer," "fair price," "reasonable arrangement"). In other words, they are better at creating the open and trusting climate necessary for reaching an integrative settlement.

Practising Skills

As marketing director for Done Right, a regional home-repair chain, you have come up with a plan you believe has significant potential for future sales. Your plan involves a customer information service designed to help people make their homes more environmentally sensitive. Then, based on homeowners' assessments of their homes' environmental impact, your firm will be prepared to help them deal with problems or concerns they may uncover. You are really excited about the competitive potential of this new service. You envision pamphlets, in-store appearances by environmental experts, as well as contests for consumers and school kids. After several weeks of preparations, you make your pitch to your boss, Nick Castro. You point out how the market for environmentally sensitive products is growing and how this growing demand represents the perfect opportunity for Done Right. Nick seems impressed by your presentation, but he has expressed one major concern: He thinks your workload is already too heavy. He does not see how you are going to have enough time to start this new service and still be able to look after all of your other assigned marketing duties. You really want to start the new service. What strategy will you follow in your negotiation with Nick?

1. Negotiate with a team member or work colleague to handle a small section of work that you are not going to be able to get done in time for an important deadline.

2. The next time you purchase a relatively expensive item (such as an automobile, apartment lease, appliance, jewellery), attempt to negotiate a better price and gain some concessions such as an extended warranty, smaller down payment, maintenance services, or the like.

Reinforcing Skills

Dan Toulgoet

Workplace Bullying

Certain Vancouver School Board (VSB) trustees (Allen Wong, Joy Alexander, Mike Lombardi, and Patti Bacchus, shown above) and the VSB staff were at loggerheads for most of 2016.[1] The trustees were trying to stand up to the provincial government, which had ordered the VSB to produce a balanced budget by June 30, 2016. The board resisted doing this for months after the deadline, in part because producing a balanced budget would require more than $7 million in cuts and 12 school closures. School closures are always a difficult issue; parents do not want their child's school closed. Because the trustees are elected, they are more interested in what constituents want than what the provincial government wants.

It is the job of the VSB staff to recommend to the trustees how to make the cuts and which schools to close. The staff prepared recommendations on these matters for the trustees. Throughout 2016, while staff prepared recommendations, tensions between the staff and trustees escalated. Staff started to fear for their jobs. The tipping point came at a September 2016 public meeting where citizens could watch trustees question the staff. The meeting became heated.

WorkSafeBC was alerted to tensions between staff and trustees, and an investigation into alleged bullying behaviour began, with a report issued in March 2017. Among the conclusions of the report were:

- Many witnesses described a "culture of fear" in which staff felt vulnerable and at risk of personal attack and ridicule.

- There was evidence that the trustees' public attack of the work of the senior staff undermined the staff and publicly embarrassed and humiliated them.

- Individual trustees acted contrary to the VSB Code of Ethics and engaged in conduct that constituted bullying and harassment.

Because the trustees had been fired by the provincial government months before the report was issued, no disciplin-

ary action was taken; however the VSB has since put together guidelines against bullying for trustees and staff. Workplaces in many parts of Canada are required to address bullying. Bullying itself is not illegal, but some forms of it—for example, threats, assault, and harassment—are included in the Criminal Code.

What Is Happening in Our Workplaces?

Workplaces today receive highly critical reviews, being called everything from "uncivil" to "toxic." The trend has been growing over time. One study showed that one-quarter of those surveyed in 1998 reported rude treatment at work at least once a week. In 2005, nearly half reported experiencing that behaviour, while in 2011 just over half reported the same.

People are feeling more stressed at work, often as the result of heavier workloads due to layoffs of fellow employees, pressures for increased productivity, and managers who do not know how to manage. All of this has resulted in an increase in uncivil and aggressive workplace behaviours.[2]

What does *workplace civility* mean? Essentially it means acting politely and respectfully toward others.[3] *Workplace incivility* means being disrespectful and uncaring about how one treats others. Different workplaces have different norms for what demonstrates mutual respect; however, many provinces now require organizations to develop policies regarding workplace bullying and respectful workplace practices.

Some behaviour goes beyond incivility to workplace bullying. The Workplace Bullying Institute defines workplace bullying as

repeated, health-harming mistreatment of one or more persons (the targets) by one or more per-

petrators. It is abusive conduct that is:

- Threatening, humiliating, or intimidating
- Work interference —sabotage— which prevents work from getting done
- Verbal abuse[4]

What Do We Know about Workplace Bullying?

There are few statistics on workplace bullying in Canada. The Workplace Bullying Institute conducts the largest scientific study of bullying in the United States, and a recent study of 1000 adults found the following:[5]

- The percentage of respondents who have suffered abusive conduct at work is 27 percent.
- The percentage of respondents who have witnessed abusive conduct at work is 21 percent.
- A full 72 percent of respondents are aware that workplace bullying happens.
- Men are significantly more likely to engage in bullying behaviour than women (69 percent vs. 31 percent).
- Women who bully are significantly more likely to bully women rather than men (68 percent vs. 32 percent).
- Men who bully are more likely to target women rather than men (57 percent vs. 43 percent).
- Overall, 60 percent of bullying targets are women.

The evidence suggests that rudeness, bullying, and violence are all on the rise. The behaviours are harmful in the workplace.[7] The victims of these negative behaviours are not the only ones who suffer, however. Witnesses to bullying also suffer.[8]

Not all negative behaviour in the workplace is bullying. Yes, bullying is a workplace issue. However, it's sometimes hard to know if bullying is happening at the workplace. Many studies

FACTBOX

What happens when employees experience rudeness in the workplace?

- 48% decreased their work effort,
- 47% decreased their time at work,
- 38% decreased their work quality,
- 66% said their performance declined,
- 80% lost work time worrying about the incident,
- 63% lost time avoiding the offender, and
- 78% said their commitment to the organization declined.[6]

acknowledge that there is a "fine line" between strong management and bullying. Comments that are objective and are intended to provide constructive feedback are not usually considered bullying, but rather are intended to assist the employee with their work.

WorkSafeBC clarifies by noting that bullying and harassing behaviour does not include the following behaviours, if approached in an appropriate manner:[9]

- Expressing differences of opinion
- Offering constructive feedback, guidance, or advice about work-related behaviour
- Taking reasonable action related to the management and direction of workers or the place of employment (e.g., an employer or supervisor managing a worker's performance, taking reasonable disciplinary actions, assigning work)

Workplace Violence

Recently, researchers have suggested that incivility may be the beginning of more negative behaviours in the workplace, including aggression and violence.[10]

Kevin Douglas Addison chose a deadly way to exhibit the anger he felt toward his former employer. In April 2014, he took a shotgun and opened fire at his former place of employment, the Western Forest Products mill in Nanaimo, British Columbia, killing two employees (one of them a foreman) and injuring two others. The mill had closed in 2008 and had re-opened in a smaller capacity in 2010. Co-workers speculated that financial problems as well as not being rehired when the mill re-opened may have led Addison to engage in the shooting. Roy Robertson, a retired mill employee, called Addison "an absolutely super nice guy. But me, you, anyone else can crack under pressure. I don't know his situation."[11]

Workplace violence, according to the International Labour Organization (ILO), includes

any incident in which a person is abused, threatened or assaulted in circumstances relating to their work. These behaviours would originate from customers or co-workers at any level of the organization. This definition would include all forms of harassment, bullying, intimidation, physical threats, assaults, robbery and other intrusive behaviour.[12]

The numbers on workplace abuse vary by occupation. Overall, in a 2016 study by Vector Poll, 15 percent of Canadian employees reported experiencing workplace abuse, harassment, or assault during the previous 24 months.[13] In a 2016 Canadian Federation of Nurse Unions (CFNU) study, 61 percent of nurses reported experiencing those same behaviours in the previous 12 months.[14] A 2017 report from the Ontario English Catholic Teachers' Association found that "60 percent of [those] teachers have personally experienced violence in schools, while 70 percent have witnessed it."[15]

Glenn French, president and founder of the Toronto-based Canadian Initiative on Workplace Violence, acknowledges that there is less gun violence in the workplace here than in the United States: "We do it the Canadian way: we don't kill you, we'll just make your life a living hell by harassing and intimidating you on the job. The face of violence in Canada tends to be far more indirect than what we've seen [in the Western Forest Products mill in Nanaimo]."[16]

Sandra Robinson and Jennifer Berdahl, both professors at the Sauder School of Business at the University of British Columbia, have recently been looking at the effects of being ignored (ostracized) in the workplace. Their research found that while people tend to think that ostracism is less offensive than harassment, the people who are ostracized seem to suffer greater effects. "The experience of ostracism has a bigger impact on job dissatisfaction, on psychological well-being, on self-reported physical health, on intentions to quit the company," Robinson said.[17] The study found that ostracism was quite widespread: 71 percent of employees reported being ostracized in the previous six months, compared with 48 percent who reported being bullied.[18]

Those who are ostracized are more likely to quit their jobs within three years than those who have been bullied. Robinson concluded that because ostracism is less visible, it's harder to fight. "Victims of ostracism really feel they can't do anything about it. It's very difficult to call-out the absence of behaviour. A lot of people end up quitting for their own well-being."[19]

What Causes Incivility (and Worse) in the Workplace?

If employers and employees are acting with less civility toward each other, what is causing this to happen?

Managers and employees often have different views of the employee's role in the organization. Jeffrey Pfeffer, a professor of organizational behaviour at the Graduate School of Business at Stanford University, notes that many companies don't really value their employees: "Most managers, if they're being honest with themselves, will admit it: When they look at their people, they see costs, they see salaries, they see benefits, they see overhead. Very few companies look at their people and see assets."[20]

Most employees, however, like to think that they are assets to their organization. The realization that they are simply costs and not valued members of an organization can cause frustration for employees.

In addition, "employers' excessive demands and top-down style of management are contributing to the rise of 'work rage,'" claims Gerry Smith, author of Work Rage.[21] He cites demands coming from a variety of sources: "overtime, downsizing, rapid technological changes, company restructuring and difficulty balancing the demands of job and home."[22] Smith worries about the consequences of these demands: "If you push people too hard, set unrealistic expectations and cut back their benefits, they're going to strike back."[23]

Smith's work supports the findings of studies that report that the most common cause of anger and bullying is the actions of supervisors or managers.[24] Other common causes of anger identified by the researchers include lack of productivity by co-workers and others, tight deadlines, heavy workload, interaction with the public, and bad treatment. The inset *Do You Have a Bad Boss?* describes some of the bad behaviour of bosses.

One study found that how managers deal with displays of anger at work can do much to defuse tensions. Co-workers want to see the manager take some responsibility for a fellow employee's anger, rather than disciplining the employee, if the manager or the working conditions are the source of the anger.[25]

Some research on the psychological contract suggests that violations of implicit or explicit promises may not be necessary to affect employee intentions to stay with the organization and/or engage in citizenship behaviours. Professors Samantha Montes and David Zweig of the Rotman School of Management found that employees expect decent pay, developmental opportunities, and support (whether or not employers promise to deliver such); and when they don't receive those things, their behaviour toward the organization becomes negative.[29]

The Psychological Contract

Some researchers have looked at this frustration in terms of a breakdown of the psychological contract formed between employees and employers.

An employer and employee begin to develop psychological contracts as they are first introduced to each other in the hiring process. These contracts continue over time as the employer and the employee come to understand each other's expectations about the amounts and quality of work to be performed and the types of rewards to be given. For instance, when an employee is continually asked to work late and/or be available at all hours through pagers and email, the employee may assume that doing so will result in greater rewards or faster promotion down the line. The employer may have had no such intention, and may even be thinking that the employee should be grateful simply to have a job. Later, when the employee does not get expected (though never promised) rewards, he or she is disappointed.

Sandra Robinson, an organizational behaviour professor at the Sauder School of Business at the University of British Columbia, and her colleagues have found that when a psychological contract is violated (perceptually or actually), the relationship between the employee and the employer is damaged. The result can be a loss of trust.[27] The breakdown in trust can cause employees to be less ready to accept decisions or obey rules. The erosion of trust can also lead employees to take revenge on the employer. So they don't carry out their end of a task. Or they refuse to pass on messages. They engage in any number of subtle and not-so-subtle behaviours that affect the way work gets done—or prevents work from getting done. A recent study suggests that perceptions of the psychological contract vary by culture.[28]

The Toxic Organization

Pfeffer suggests that companies have become "toxic places to work."[30] He notes that companies, particularly in Silicon Valley, ask their employees to sign contracts on the first day of work indicating the employee's understanding that the company has the right to fire at will and for any reason. Some employers also ask their employees to choose between having a life and having a career. Pfeffer relates a joke people used to tell about Microsoft: "We offer flexible time—you can work any 18 hours you want."[31] This kind of attitude can be toxic to employees, although it does not imply that Microsoft is a toxic employer. The inset *How to Deal with a Toxic Boss* gives tips, should you find yourself in that situation.

What does it mean to be a toxic organization? The inset *What Does a Toxic Organization Look Like?* describes one. The late professor Peter Frost of the Sauder School of Business at the University of British Columbia noted that there will always be pain in organizations, but that sometimes it becomes so intense or prolonged that conditions within the organization begin to break down. In other words, the situation becomes toxic. This is not dissimilar to what the liver or kidneys do when toxins become too intense in a human body.[33]

What causes organizations to be toxic? Like Pfeffer, Robinson and colleagues identify a number of factors. Downsizing and organizational change are two main factors, particularly in recent years. Sometimes organizations experience unexpected events—such as the sudden death of a key manager, an unwise move by senior management, strong competition from a start-up company—that lead to toxicity. Other organizations are toxic throughout their system due to policies and practices that create distress. Such factors as unreasonable stretch goals or performance targets, or unrelenting internal competition, can create toxicity. There are also toxic managers who lead through insensitivity, vindictiveness, and failure to take responsibility, or they are control freaks or are unethical.

What Are the Effects of Incivility and Toxicity in the Workplace?

In general, researchers have found that the effects of workplace anger are sometimes subtle: a hostile work environment and the tendency to do only enough work to get by.[34]

Those who feel chronic anger in the workplace are more likely to report "feelings of betrayal by the organization, decreased feelings of loyalty, a decreased sense that respondent values and the organization's values are similar, a decreased sense that the employer treated the respondent with dignity and respect, and a decreased sense that employers had fulfilled promises made to respondents."[35] So do these feelings make a difference? Apparently so. Researchers have found that those who felt angry with their employers were less likely to put forth their best effort, more likely to be competitive toward other employees, and less likely to suggest "a quicker and better way to do their job."[36] All of these actions tend to decrease the productivity possible in the workplace.

It's not just those who work for an organization who are affected by incivility and toxicity. Poor service, from indifference to rudeness to outright hostility, characterizes many transactions in Canadian businesses. "Across the country, better business bureaus, provincial government consumer-help agencies and media ombudsmen report a lengthening litany of complaints about contractors, car dealers, repair shops, moving companies, airlines and department stores."[38] This suggests that customers and clients may well be feeling the impact of internal workplace dynamics.

FACTBOX

The effects of incivility on the workplace are high:

- 80% of workers lost work time worrying about an offending incident.
- 78% said their commitment to the organization declined.
- 66% reported their performance declined.
- 48% who had been on the receiving end of incivility intentionally decreased their work effort.
- 47% intentionally decreased the time spent at work.
- 80% of customers who witnessed rudeness among employees were unlikely to return to the business.[37]

What Does a Toxic Organization Look Like?

Toxic organizations have the following characteristics:[39]

- inability to achieve operation goals and commitments
- problem-solving processes driven by fear with few good decisions
- poor internal communication
- huge amounts of waste that result from poor decisions, and lots of rework
- interpersonal relationships driven by manipulative and self-centred agendas

FACE OFF

Manners are an over-romanticized concept. The big issue is not that employees need to be concerned about their manners. Rather, employers should be paying better wages.	The Golden Rule "Do unto others as you would have others do unto you," should still have a role in today's workplace. Being nice pays off.

The dynamics in the workplace may be starting to change. In 2016 the Faculty of Medicine at UBC circulated a video to its instructors that illustrated issues of student mistreatment. Viewers were asked to "avoid putting students on the spot with questions, to minimize 'cold and clinical' interactions, and to cultivate 'safe' learning environments for the young residents." Such a video would not have been made 10 years ago. But the current generation of students is demanding more respect and it has less tolerance for being exposed to bullying behaviour. This may turn out to be a good thing.[40]

Legislation to Prevent Bullying

The Canadian Criminal Code has no bullying offence, although depending on the circumstance, other charges could be made, such as criminal harassment, uttering threats, assault, and sexual assault. On a provincial level, only some provinces have adopted legislation directed at bullying. Others are still working out potential approaches.[41] But some aspects of bullying could be dealt with in some provinces through existing provincial violence and harassment legislation.

For instance, in 2012 WorkSafeBC started to accept mental disorder claims that were the results of "a cumulative series of significant work-related stressors." That was a major shift for the organization, which promotes workplace health and safety in British Columbia. Previously it had only processed claims for stress from traumatic events. Between 2012 and 2014, WorkSafeBC accepted 655 mental stress claims and paid out more than $10 million in damages. While the majority of claims were for traumatic incidents, about 30 percent were for workplace stress. "Forty-five to 50 people are applying for benefits every week. That's an indication that there are problems in the workplace," says Jennifer Leyen, director of special care services for WorkSafeBC.[42]

WorkSafeBC requires employers in the province to have a policy in place to prevent bullying and harassment. It also reminds employers and employees what bullying includes: insults, sabotage, threats. However, bullying does not include negative work evaluations, discipline, or firing. Some experts find that this new policy is not enough, however. "It overlooks other issues like the damage caused by a constant thrum of low-level incivility—the eye rolling, the interruptions, the dismissiveness."[43]

RESEARCH EXERCISES

1. Look for data on violence and anger in the workplace in other countries. How do these data compare with the Canadian and American data presented here? What might you conclude about how violence and anger in the workplace are expressed in different cultures?

2. Identify three Canadian organizations that are trying to foster better and/or less toxic environments for their employees. What kind of effect is this having on the organizations' bottom lines?

YOUR PERSPECTIVE

1. Is it reasonable to suggest, as some researchers have, that young people today have not learned to be civil to others or do not place a high priority on doing so? Do you see this as one of the causes of incivility in the workplace?

2. What should be done about managers who create toxicity in the workplace while being rewarded because they achieve bottom-line results? Should bottom-line results justify their behaviour?

WANT TO KNOW MORE?

If you would like to read more on this topic, see P. K. Jonason, S. Slomski, and J. Partyka, "The Dark Triad at Work: How Toxic Employees Get Their Way," *Personality and Individual Differences*, February 2012, pp. 449–453; B. Schyns and J. Schilling, "How Bad Are the Effects of Bad Leaders? A Meta-Analysis of Destructive Leadership and Its Outcomes," *The Leadership Quarterly*, February 2013, pp. 138–158; and Canadian Centre for Occupational Health and Safety, "Bullying in the Workplace," www.ccohs.ca/oshanswers/psychosocial/bullying.html.

10 Organizational Culture

PART 4

SHARING THE

ORGANIZATIONAL VISION

How can Hyatt Hotels effectively manage a global corporation with multiple hotel chains and thousands of employees? A strong organizational culture is part of the answer.

LEARNING OUTCOMES

After studying this chapter, you should be able to:

1 Describe the common characteristics of organizational culture.

2 Compare the functional and dysfunctional effects of organizational culture on people and the organization.

3 Identify the factors that create and sustain an organization's culture.

4 Show how culture is transmitted to employees.

5 Demonstrate how an ethical organizational culture can be created.

6 Describe a positive organizational culture.

As CEO of Hyatt Hotels Corporation, Mark Hoplamazian (pictured here) was concerned with how he was going to introduce change to his employees after the global hotel company experienced significant growth in 2013.[1] Hotels had been added to the brand, the organization was entering new areas of the hospitality industry, and he had to work with over 90 000 employees in 45 different countries. This presented significant implementation challenges. It was particularly vital for Hyatt, spread across the globe and highly decentralized, to make sure its associates understood and shared the mission of the

Richard Drew/AP Images

company. To get the message across, Hoplamazian wanted to create a uniform employment experience for each employee, starting with a cohesive orientation program for new hires.

Management at Hyatt had to determine how to socialize new employees into the company's culture, while being mindful that there could be some glitches, with perhaps not all aspects of the company's culture translating equally well in the 45 different countries on six continents Hyatt was in. Hyatt has multiple brands, including Hyatt, Park Hyatt, Andaz, Grand Hyatt, Hyatt Regency, Hyatt Place, and Hyatt House, and each services different parts of the hotel customer market. Park Hyatt is the organization's luxury brand. Andaz is a boutique category. Several of the other Hyatt brands are full-service hotels. Despite the differences in the needs they serve, the company's properties "share core values across the Hyatt brand: exceptional guest service, upscale amenities, popular food and beverage programs, and innovative interior designs that incorporate local art and style." These values need to be communicated to all employees for the company to do well.

In this chapter, we show that every organization has a culture. We examine how that culture reveals itself and the impact it has on the attitudes and behaviours of members of that organization. An understanding of what makes up an organization's culture and how it is created, sustained, and learned enhances our ability to explain and predict the behaviour of people at work.

OB IS FOR EVERYONE

- What does organizational culture do?
- Is culture the same as rules?
- What kind of organizational culture would work best for you?

THE BIG IDEA

A strong organizational culture can guide individual decisions and help everyone work together toward the same goals.

1 Describe the common characteristics of organizational culture.

What Is Organizational Culture?

When Henry Mintzberg, professor at McGill University and one of the world's leading management experts, was asked to compare organizational structure and corporate culture, he said, "Culture is the soul of the organization—the beliefs and values, and how they are manifested. I think of the structure as the skeleton, and as the flesh and blood. And culture is the soul that holds the thing together and gives it life force."[2]

Organizational culture refers to a system of shared meaning held by members that distinguishes the organization from other organizations.[3] Mintzberg's culture metaphor provides a clear image of how to think about culture. Culture provides stability to an organization and gives employees a clear understanding of "the way things are done around here." Culture sets the tone for how an organization operates and how individuals within the organization interact. Think of the different impressions you have when a receptionist tells you that "Ms. Dettweiler" will be available shortly, while at another organization you are told that "Emma" will be with you as soon as she gets off the phone. It's clear that in one organization the rules are more formal than in the other.

Seven primary characteristics capture the essence of an organization's culture:[4]

- *Innovation and risk-taking.* The degree to which employees are encouraged to be innovative and take risks

- *Attention to detail.* The degree to which employees are expected to work with precision, analysis, and attention to detail

- *Outcome orientation.* The degree to which management focuses on results, or outcomes, rather than on the techniques and processes used to achieve these outcomes

- *People orientation.* The degree to which management decisions take into consideration the effect of outcomes on people within the organization

- *Team orientation.* The degree to which work activities are organized around teams rather than individuals

- *Aggressiveness.* The degree to which people are aggressive and competitive rather than easygoing and supportive

- *Stability.* The degree to which organizational activities emphasize maintaining the status quo in contrast to growth

Each of these characteristics exists on a continuum from low to high.

When individuals consider their organization in terms of these seven characteristics, they get a composite picture of the organization's culture. This picture becomes the basis for feelings of shared understanding that members have about the organization, how things are done in it, and the way members are supposed to behave. Exhibit 10-1 demonstrates how these characteristics can be mixed to create highly diverse organizations. Organizational characteristics are even reflected in your classroom, as the *Experiential Exercise* on page 376 shows.

Culture Is a Descriptive Term

If you have ever been in an organization (certainly you have been in many!), you probably noticed a pervasive culture among the members. *Organizational culture* shows how employees perceive the characteristics of an organization, not whether they like them—that is, it's a descriptive term. Research on organizational culture has sought to measure how employees see their organization: Does it encourage teamwork? Does it reward innovation? Does it stifle initiative? In contrast, job satisfaction seeks to measure

organizational culture A system of shared meaning held by members that distinguishes the organization from other organizations.

EXHIBIT 10-1 Contrasting Organizational Cultures

Organization A	Organization B
• Managers must fully document all decisions.	• Management encourages and rewards risk-taking and change.
• Creative decisions, change, and risks are not encouraged.	• Employees are encouraged to "run with" ideas, and failures are treated as "learning experiences."
• Extensive rules and regulations exist for all employees.	• Employees have few rules and regulations to follow.
• Productivity is valued over employee morale.	• Productivity is balanced with treating its people right.
• Employees are encouraged to stay within their own department.	• Team members are encouraged to interact with people at all levels and functions.
• Individual effort is encouraged.	• Many rewards are team-based.

how employees feel about the organization's expectations, reward practices, and the like. Although the two terms have overlapping characteristics, keep in mind that *organizational culture* is descriptive, whereas *job satisfaction*, for example, is evaluative.

Do Organizations Have Uniform Cultures?

Organizational culture represents a perception of the organization that employees hold in common. Statements about organizational culture are valid only if individuals with different backgrounds or at different hierarchical levels describe their organization's culture in similar terms.[5] The purchasing department can have a subculture that includes the core values of the dominant culture, such as aggressiveness, plus additional values unique to members of that department, such as risk-taking. The **dominant culture** expresses the **core values** a majority of members share and that give an organization its distinct personality.[6] **Subcultures** tend to develop in large

Ronda Churchill/Bloomberg/Getty Images

Internet retailer Zappos understands how organizational behaviour affects an organization's performance. According to the Zappos Insights website, employees are encouraged "to create fun and a little weirdness," which helps the firm maintain a positive work environment.

dominant culture A system of shared meaning that expresses the core values shared by a majority of the organization's members.

core values The primary or dominant values that are accepted throughout the organization.

subcultures Mini-cultures within an organization, typically defined by department designations and geographical separation.

organizations to reflect common problems, situations, or experiences faced by groups of members in the same department or location. Most large organizations have a dominant culture and numerous subcultures.[7]

If organizations were composed only of a variety of subcultures, the dominant organizational culture would be significantly less powerful. It is the "shared meaning" aspect of culture that makes it such a potent device for guiding and shaping behaviour. This is what allows us to say that the Zappos culture values customer care and dedication over speed and efficiency, which directs the behaviour of Zappos executives and employees.[8]

Strong vs. Weak Cultures

It is possible to differentiate between strong and weak cultures.[9] If most employees (responding to surveys) have the same opinions about the organization's mission and values, the culture is strong; if opinions vary widely, the culture is weak.

In a **strong culture**, the organization's core values are both intensely held and widely shared.[10] The more members who accept the core values and the greater their commitment, the stronger the culture and the greater its influence on member behaviour. This is because the high degree of shared values and intensity create a climate of high behavioural control. For instance, Nordstrom employees know what is expected of them, and these expectations go a long way toward shaping their behaviour.

A strong culture should reduce employee turnover because it demonstrates high agreement about what the organization represents. Such unanimity of purpose builds cohesiveness, loyalty, and organizational commitment. These qualities, in turn, lessen employees' tendency to leave the organization.[11]

Culture vs. Formalization

We have seen in this text that high formalization creates predictability, orderliness, and consistency. A strong culture modifies behaviour similarly. Therefore, we should view formalization and culture as two different roads to a common destination. The stronger an organization's culture, the less management needs to be concerned with developing formal rules and regulations to guide employee behaviour. Those guides will be internalized in employees when they adopt the organization's culture.

2 Compare the functional and dysfunctional effects of organizational culture on people and the organization.

What Do Cultures Do?

Let's discuss the role culture performs and whether it can ever be a liability for an organization.

Culture's Functions

Culture defines the rules within an organization:

- It has a boundary-defining role because it creates distinction between organizations.
- It conveys a sense of identity to organization members.
- It helps create commitment to something larger than an individual's self-interest.
- It enhances stability; it is the social glue that helps hold the organization together by providing standards for what employees should say and do.
- It serves as a control mechanism that guides and shapes the attitudes and behaviour of employees, and helps them make sense of the organization.

strong culture A culture in which the core values are intensely held and widely shared.

This last function is of particular interest to us.[12] Culture defines the rules of the game.

A strong culture supported by formal rules and regulations ensures employees will act in a relatively uniform and predictable way. Today's trend toward decentralized organizations makes culture more important than ever, but ironically it also makes establishing a strong culture more difficult. When formal authority and control systems are reduced, culture's *shared meaning* can point everyone in the same direction. However, employees organized in teams may show greater allegiance to their team and its values than to the organization as a whole. In virtual organizations, the lack of frequent face-to-face contact makes establishing a common set of norms very difficult. Strong leadership that communicates frequently about common goals and priorities is especially important in innovative organizations.[13]

> What does organizational culture do?

Culture Creates Climate

If you have worked with someone whose positive attitude inspired you to do your best, or with a lacklustre team that drained your motivation, you have experienced the effects of climate. **Organizational climate** refers to the shared perceptions organizational members have about their organization and work environment.[14] This aspect of culture is like team spirit at the organizational level. When everyone has the same general feelings about what is important or how well things are working, the effect of these attitudes will be more than the sum of the individual parts. One meta-analysis found that across dozens of different samples, psychological climate was strongly related to individuals' level of job satisfaction, involvement, commitment, and motivation.[15] A positive workplace climate has been linked to higher customer satisfaction and organizational financial performance as well.[16] Read more about workplace climate in *Case Incident—Active Cultures* on pages 378–379.

Dozens of dimensions of climate have been studied, including innovation, creativity, communication, warmth and support, involvement, safety, justice, diversity, and customer service.[17] For example, someone who encounters a diverse climate will feel more comfortable collaborating with co-workers regardless of their demographic backgrounds. Climates can interact with one another to produce behaviour. For example, a climate of worker empowerment can lead to higher levels of performance in organizations that also have a climate of personal accountability.[18] Climate also influences the habits people adopt. If there is a climate of safety, everyone wears safety gear and follows safety procedures even if individually they would not normally think very often about being safe—indeed, many studies have shown that a safety climate decreases the number of documented injuries on the job.[19] WestJet sets the tone for its customers by making sure its employees have fun too, as *OB in the Workplace* shows.

The Ethical Dimension of Culture

Organizational cultures are not neutral in their ethical orientation, even when they are not openly pursuing ethical goals. Over time, the **ethical work climate (EWC)**, or the shared concept of right and wrong behaviour, develops as part of the organizational climate. The ethical climate reflects the true values of the organization and shapes the ethical decision-making of its members.

Researchers have developed *ethical climate theory (ECT)* and the *ethical climate index (ECI)* to categorize and measure the ethical dimensions of organizational cultures.[20] Of the nine identified ethical climate categories, five have been most prevalent in organizations: *instrumental*, *caring*, *independence*, *law and code*, and *rules*. Each explains the general mindset, expectations, and values of the managers and employees in relation

organizational climate The shared perceptions organizational members have about their organization and work environment.

ethical work climate (EWC) The shared concept of right and wrong behaviour in the workplace that reflects the true values of the organization and shapes the ethical decision-making of its members.

OB IN THE WORKPLACE
WestJet Brings on the Fun

How does a company ensure its cultural climate is maintained and supported? WestJet is a Canadian airline famous for its fun, customer-oriented corporate culture.[21] Both employees and guests are encouraged to actually enjoy flying—a goal that is reinforced by a casual working environment in which jokes and innocuous silliness are encouraged. Maintaining this positive and upbeat culture can be difficult, especially within a high-stress industry that experiences a great deal of uncertainty. WestJet management is well aware of the effects of the economy on its industry and ensures that, even in times of austerity, resources are provided to maintain its culture. WestJet has over 200 employee events a year that support and reinforce its culture. Employees who get it right are recognized through a "Kudos Corner"—an online program that allows peers and customers to acknowledge excellence when they see it.

Even WestJet's organizational structure supports its culture. For example, the company has a "WestJetters" committee of flight attendants who meet in order to, among other things, write jokes that can be used to amuse guests on flights. Devoting time and money to this sort of work may seem frivolous to some, but WestJet sees it as a crucial component of cultural maintenance. "Everybody's unique," says Don Bell, a WestJet founder and the airline's executive vice-president, "and if you embrace people's personalities rather than turn them into robots, and give them the guidelines and the working environment to blossom, it creates something that's very hard to reckon with."

WestJet has been able to demonstrate very clearly that a direct link exists between maintaining its fun, upbeat culture and high levels of customer satisfaction. Vince Molinaro, managing director of Leadership Solutions for Knightsbridge Human Capital Solutions, observed that "far too many organizations operate on the belief that you can have one set of principles and standards for employees, and another completely different set for customers. WestJet is demonstrating the power of alignment between employee and customer."

Charles Platiau/Reuters

Employees of French video game publisher Ubisoft are shown working on an upcoming version of the *Just Dance* game at the firm's creative studio near Paris. Imaginative employees who work in teams on challenging projects at Ubisoft's 26 creative studios around the world share the positive climate of creative collaboration that reflects the diversity of team members.

to their organization. For instance, in an *instrumental* ethical climate, managers may frame their decision making around the assumption that employees (and companies) are motivated by self-interest (egoistic). Conversely, in a *caring* climate, managers may operate under the expectation that their decisions will positively affect the greatest number of stakeholders (employees, customers, suppliers) possible.

Ethical climates of *independence* rely on each individual's personal moral ideas to dictate his or her workplace behaviour. *Law and code* climates require managers and employees to use an external standardized moral compass such as a professional code of conduct for norms, while *rules* climates tend to operate by internal standardized expectations from, perhaps, an organizational policy manual. Organizations often progress through different categories as they move through their business life cycle.

An organization's ethical climate powerfully influences the way its individual members feel they should behave, so much so that researchers have been able to predict organizational outcomes from the climate categories.[22] Instrumental climates are negatively associated with employee job satisfaction and organizational commitment, even though those climates appeal to self-interest (of the employee and the company). They are positively associated with turnover intentions, workplace bullying, and deviant behaviour. Caring and rules climates may bring greater job satisfaction. Caring, independence, rules, and law and code climates also reduce employee turnover intentions, workplace bullying, and dysfunctional behaviour. Research indicates that ethical cultures take a long-term perspective and balance the rights of multiple stakeholders including employees, stockholders, and the community. Managers are supported for taking risks and innovating, discouraged from engaging in unbridled competition, and guided to heed not just *what* goals are achieved but *how*.

Studies of ethical climates and workplace outcomes suggest that some ethical climate categories are likely to be found in certain organizations. Industries with exacting standards, such as engineering, accounting, and law, tend to have a rules or law and code climate. Industries that thrive on competitiveness, such as financial trading, often have an instrumental climate. Industries with missions of benevolence are likely to have a caring climate, even if they are for profit as in an environmental protection firm.

Research is exploring why organizations tend to fall into certain ethical climate categories by industry, especially successful organizations. We cannot conclude that instrumental climates are bad or that caring climates are good. Instrumental climates may foster the individual-level successes their companies need to thrive, for example, and they may help underperformers to recognize their self-interest is better served elsewhere. Managers in caring climates may be thwarted in making the best decisions when only choices that serve the greatest number of employees are acceptable.[23] The ECI, first introduced in 2010, is a new way researchers are seeking to understand the context of ethical drivers in organizations. By measuring the collective levels of moral sensitivity, judgment, motivation, and character of our organizations, we may be able to judge the strength of the influence our ethical climates have on us.[24]

Although ECT was first introduced more than 25 years ago, researchers have recently been studying ethics in organizations more closely to determine not only how ethical climates behave, but also how they might be fostered and even changed.[25] Eventually, we will be able to provide leaders with clear blueprints for designing effective ethical climates.

Culture and Sustainability

As the name implies, **sustainability** refers to practices that can be maintained over very long periods of time[26] because the tools or structures that support the practices are not damaged by the processes. One survey found that a great majority of executives saw sustainability as an important part of future success.[27] Concepts of sustainable management have their origins in the environmental movement, so processes that are in harmony with the natural environment are encouraged. *Social sustainability* practices

sustainability Organization practices that can be sustained over a long period of time because the tools or structures that support them are not damaged by the processes.

address the ways social systems are affected by an organization's actions over time and, in turn, how changing social systems may affect the organization.

Sustainable management doesn't need to be purely altruistic. Systematic reviews of the research literature show a generally positive relationship between sustainability and financial performance.[28] However, there is often a strong moral and ethical component that shapes organizational culture, and sustainability must be a core value in order for the relationship to exist.

To create a truly sustainable business, an organization must develop a long-term culture and put its values into practice.[29] In other words, there must be a sustainable system for creating sustainability! In one workplace study, a company seeking to reduce energy consumption found that soliciting group feedback reduced energy use significantly more than simply issuing reading materials about the importance of conservation.[30] Talking about energy conservation and building the value into the organizational culture results in positive employee behavioural changes. Like other cultural practices we have discussed, sustainability needs time and nurturing to grow.

Culture and Innovation

The most innovative companies are often characterized by their open, unconventional, collaborative, vision-driven, accelerating cultures.[31] Start-up firms often have innovative cultures by definition because they are usually small, agile, and focused on solving problems in order to survive and grow. Consider digital music leader The Echo Nest, recently bought by Spotify. As a start-up, the organization was unconventional, flexible, and open, hosting music app "hack" days for users and fostering a music culture.[32] All these are hallmarks of Spotify's culture, too, making the fit rather seamless.[33] Because of the similar organizational cultures, The Echo Nest and Spotify may be able to continue their start-up level of innovation.

Lee Jin-man

Founded in 1969, Samsung Electronics of South Korea is past the usual innovation life cycle stage, yet continues to foster a climate of creativity and idea generation. Samsung emulates a start-up culture through its Creative Labs, where employees like engineer Ki Yuhoon, shown here, take up to a year off from their regular jobs to work on innovative projects.

At the other end of the start-up spectrum, consider 30-year-old Intuit, one of the World's 100 Most Innovative Companies according to *Forbes*. Intuit employees attend workshops that teach them how to think creatively . . . and unconventionally. Sessions have led to managers talking through puppets and holding bake sales to sell prototype apps with their cupcakes. The culture stresses open accountability. "I saw one senior guy whose idea they'd been working on for nine months get disproved in a day because someone had a better way. He got up in front of everyone and said, 'This is my bad. I should have checked my hypothesis earlier,'" said Eric Ries, author of *The Lean Startup*. As a consultant for entrepreneurs, Ries considers the older software company equally innovative to start-ups because of its culture.[34]

Culture as a Liability

Culture can enhance organizational commitment and increase the consistency of employee behaviour, which clearly benefits an organization. Culture is valuable to employees too, because it spells out how things are done and what is important. But we should not ignore the potentially dysfunctional aspects of culture, especially a strong one, on an organization's effectiveness. Hewlett-Packard, once known as a premier computer manufacturer, rapidly lost market share and profits as dysfunction in its top management team trickled down, leaving employees disengaged, uncreative, unappreciated, and polarized.[35] Let's consider some of the major factors that signal a negative organizational culture, beginning with institutionalization.

Institutionalization

When an organization undergoes **institutionalization**—that is, it becomes valued for itself and not for the goods or services it produces—it takes on a life of its own, apart from its founders or members.[36] Institutionalized organizations often don't go out of business even if the original goals are no longer relevant. Acceptable modes of behaviour become largely self-evident to members, and although this isn't entirely negative, it does mean behaviours and habits go unquestioned, which can stifle innovation and make maintaining the organization's culture an end in itself.

Barriers to Change

Culture is a liability when shared values don't agree with those that further the organization's effectiveness. This is most likely when an organization's environment is undergoing rapid change, and its entrenched culture may no longer be appropriate.[37] Consistency of behaviour, an asset in a stable environment, may then burden the organization and make it difficult to respond to changes.

Barriers to Diversity

Hiring new employees who differ from the majority in race, age, gender, disability, or other characteristics creates a paradox:[38] Management wants to demonstrate support for the differences these employees bring to the workplace, but newcomers who wish to fit in must accept the organization's core culture. Second, because diverse behaviours and unique strengths are likely to diminish as people assimilate, strong cultures can become liabilities when they effectively eliminate the advantages of diversity. Third, a strong culture that condones prejudice, supports bias, or becomes insensitive to differences can undermine formal corporate diversity policies.

Strengthening Dysfunctions

In general, we have discussed cultures that cohere around a positive set of values and attitudes. This consensus can create powerful forward momentum. However, coherence around negativity and dysfunctional management systems in a corporation can produce downward forces that are equally powerful. One study of thousands of

institutionalization A condition that occurs when an organization takes on a life of its own, apart from any of its members, and acquires immortality.

hospitality-industry employees in hundreds of locations found that local organizational cultures marked by low or decreasing job satisfaction had higher levels of turnover.[39] As we know from this text, low job satisfaction and high turnover indicate dysfunction on the organization's part. Negative attitudes in groups add to negative outcomes, suggesting a powerful influence of culture on individuals.

Barriers to Acquisitions and Mergers

Historically, when management looked at acquisition or merger decisions, the key decision factors were potential financial advantage and product synergy. In recent years, cultural compatibility has become the primary concern.[40] All things being equal, whether the acquisition works seems to have much to do with how well the two organizations' cultures match up. When they don't mesh well, the organizational cultures of both become a liability to the whole new organization. A study conducted by Bain & Company found that 70 percent of mergers failed to increase shareholder values, and Hay Group found that more than 90 percent of mergers in Europe failed to reach financial goals. Considering this dismal rate of success, Lawrence Chia from Deloitte Consulting observed, "One of the biggest failings is people. The people at Company A have a different way of doing things from Company B . . . you can't find commonality in goals."[41] Culture clash was commonly argued to be one of the causes of AOL-Time Warner's problems.

3 Identify the factors that create and sustain an organization's culture.

Creating and Sustaining an Organization's Culture

> As Mark Hoplamazian, CEO of Hyatt Hotels, sought to give a better sense of the hotel's culture to employees, he recognized that to genuinely support the culture, some changes were needed.[42] Making meaningful and personal connections with guests, a core value, was difficult when associates had to divide their attention between the guest in front of them and the computer screen providing the information necessary to help that guest. Changing to a more user-friendly interface on various hotel operating systems allowed associates to engage more directly with guests.
>
> Hoplamazian also wanted Hyatt to be an employee-friendly workplace. One of the issues he found as he talked to employees was that scheduling of work hours was an annoyance. So the company developed an app so employees could schedule their work from their mobile phones.
>
> What role does culture play in creating high-performing organizations?

An organization's culture does not pop out of thin air, and once established, it rarely fades away. What influences the creation of a culture? What reinforces and sustains these forces once they are in place? Exhibit 10-2 summarizes how an organization's culture is established and sustained. We describe each part of this process next.

Is culture the same as rules?

EXHIBIT 10-2 How Organizational Cultures Form

How a Culture Begins

An organization's customs, traditions, and general way of doing things are largely due to what it has done before and how successful it was in doing it. This leads us to the ultimate source of an organization's culture: the founders.[43] Founders have a vision of what the organization should be, and the firm's initial small size makes it easy to impose that vision on all organizational members. In the case of the Calgary Stampede, early founders were willing to fight much larger political and legal systems, including the Indian Act itself, to ensure that Indigenous people could participate in the event. This philosophy would have sent a very strong message to Stampede workers and volunteers, reinforcing their culture of inclusion in a time period not known for tolerance in general and certainly not distinguished by any widespread inclusion of Indigenous cultures and people.

Culture creation occurs in three ways.[44] First, founders only hire and keep employees who think and feel the way they do. Second, they indoctrinate and socialize employees to their way of thinking and feeling. Finally, the founders' own behaviour encourages employees to identify with the founders and thereby internalize those beliefs, values, and assumptions. When the organization succeeds, the founders' personalities become embedded in the culture.

The culture at Toronto-based PCL, the largest general contracting organization in Canada, is still strongly influenced by the vision of Ernest Poole, who founded the company in 1906. "Poole's rules," which include "Employ highest grade people obtainable" and "Encourage integrity, loyalty and efficiencies," still influence the way the company hires and trains its employees long after the founder's death.[45] Other contemporary examples of founders who have had an immeasurable impact on their organizations' cultures are the late Ted Rogers of Toronto-based Rogers Communications, Frank Stronach of Aurora, Ontario-based Magna International, and Richard Branson of UK-based Virgin Group.

Keeping a Culture Alive

4 Show how culture is transmitted to employees.

Once a culture is in place, practices within the organization maintain it by giving employees a set of similar experiences.[46] The selection process, performance evaluation criteria, training and career development activities, and promotion procedures ensure that those hired fit in with the culture, that employees who support it are rewarded, and that those who challenge it are penalized (or even expelled). Three forces play a particularly important part in sustaining a culture: *selection* practices, the actions of *top management*, and *socialization* methods. Let's look at each.

Selection

The explicit goal of the selection process is to identify and hire individuals who have the knowledge, skills, and abilities to perform successfully.

The final decision, because it's significantly influenced by the decision maker's judgment of how well candidates will fit into the organization, identifies people whose values are consistent with at least a good portion of the organization.[47]

The selection process also provides information to applicants. Those who perceive a conflict between their values and those of the organization can remove themselves from the applicant pool. Selection thus becomes a two-way street, allowing employer and applicant to avoid a mismatch and sustaining an organization's culture by removing those who might attack or undermine its core values. Windsor, Ontario-based Windsor Family Credit Union makes job candidates go through a process that has as many as eight steps so that the organization and the employee can determine if they are a good fit for each other.[48] To signal that dignity and respect are important parts of Kitchener, Ontario-based Mennonite Savings and Credit Union's culture, job candidates are provided with interview questions in advance. The credit union encourages two-way communication throughout the hiring process.[49]

Top Management

The actions of top management have a major impact on the organization's culture.[50] Through words and behaviour, senior executives establish norms that filter through the organization about, for instance, whether risk-taking is desirable; how much freedom managers give their employees; appropriate dress; and what actions will pay off in terms of pay raises, promotions, and other rewards.

Socialization

No matter how effectively the organization recruits and selects new employees, they need help adapting to the prevailing culture. That help is **socialization**.[51] Socialization can help alleviate the problem many employees report that their new jobs are different than expected. Socialization done well will develop a new employee's self-efficacy, hope, optimism, and resilience.[52] *Case Incident—The Place Makes the People* on page 377–378 describes how even office space has socializing power.

New employees at the Japanese electronics company Sanyo are socialized through a particularly long training program. At their intensive five-month course, trainees eat and sleep together in company-subsidized dorms and are required to vacation together at company-owned resorts. They learn the Sanyo way of doing everything—from how to speak to managers to proper grooming and dress.[53] The company considers this program essential for transforming young employees, fresh out of school, into dedicated *kaisha senshi*, or corporate warriors.

Starbucks does not go to the extreme that Sanyo does, but it seeks the same outcome.[54] All new employees go through 24 hours of training. Classes cover everything necessary to transform new employees into brewing consultants. They learn the Starbucks philosophy, the company jargon, and even how to help customers make decisions about beans and grind, as well as about espresso machines. The result is employees who understand Starbucks' culture and who project an enthusiastic and knowledgeable image to customers.

We can think of socialization as a process composed of three stages: prearrival, encounter, and metamorphosis.[55] This process (illustrated in Exhibit 10-3) has an impact on the new employee's work productivity, commitment to the organization's objectives, and decision to stay with the organization. *OB in the Workplace* discusses how TELUS starts to socialize future employees from the time they visit the company's Careers web page.

The Prearrival Stage   The **prearrival stage** explicitly recognizes that each individual arrives with a set of values, attitudes, and expectations about both the work and the organization. One major purpose of a business school, for example, is to socialize students to the attitudes and behaviours companies want. Newcomers to high-profile organizations with strong market positions have their own assumptions about what it's like to work there.[56] How accurately people judge an organization's culture before they join the organization and how proactive their personalities are become critical predictors of how well they adjust.[57]

socialization The process that adapts new employees to an organization's culture.

prearrival stage The period of learning in the socialization process that occurs before a new employee joins the organization.

EXHIBIT 10-3 A Socialization Model

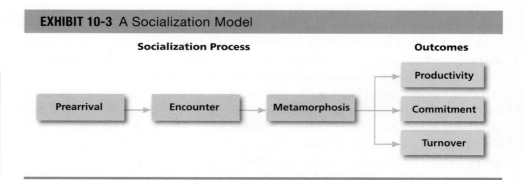

Fernando Morales/The Globe and Mail/The Canadian Press

Allen Lau, CEO of Toronto-based Wattpad, a mobile reading app, carefully considers who to hire for his company. The app's users form a diverse community and while Lau believes he should hire for cultural fit, his employees need to mirror his users in some way. "If a company is lacking diversity . . . because everyone has blind spots, and if the employee base is similar in terms of thinking and perspective, then naturally the blind spots will be larger."[58]

OB IN THE WORKPLACE

Making Culture Work

How early on should socialization take place? Leaders at Burnaby, BC-based TELUS recognize that in order for an organizational culture to work, that culture needs to be established early, preferably during the hiring process.[59] It also needs to be continually supported and reinforced.

TELUS prides itself on a culture focused on collaborative learning. This culture is heavily reinforced on its Careers web page. TELUS asks prospective candidates whether they build "spirited relationships." Prospective candidates are also informed that they should expect to "foster a strong collaborative network," and "continually drive their own learning." That learning is expected to begin immediately. Unlike most employers, TELUS offers job applicants tips about what specifically to include in their résumé and cover letter and how best to prepare for an interview with the company. It even offers a "Career Tools" page that helps job seekers identify their goals, outline their personal strengths, and match those goals and strengths with open positions within the organization.

This focus on learning is further reinforced after the hiring process. For example, collaboration tools and internal social networking sites are provided to all employees, and open-door policies encourage the free flow of information between staff and management. Regular webinars are offered on a variety of topics and mentors and coaches assist with the learning process. Dan Pontefract, chief envisioner at TELUS, explains the company's approach: "the more open and collaborative you are with people, the healthier your culture becomes." A healthy, established culture that emphasizes ongoing learning helps TELUS stay ahead of the curve in a highly competitive, innovation-focused industry.

One way to capitalize on prehire characteristics in socialization is to use the selection process to inform prospective employees about the organization as a whole. We have also seen how the selection process ensures the inclusion of the "right type"—those who will fit in.

The Encounter Stage Upon entry into the organization, the new employee begins the **encounter stage** and confronts the possibility that expectations—of the job, co-workers, boss, and organization in general—may differ from reality. If the expectations were fairly accurate, this stage merely reaffirms earlier perceptions.

However, this is often not the case. At the extreme, new members may become totally disillusioned with the realities of their job and resign. Proper recruiting and selection should significantly reduce the probability of this outcome, and so too should encouraging friendship ties in the organization—newcomers are more committed when friendly co-workers help them "learn the ropes."[60] A study by professor Alan Saks of the Rotman School of Management at the University of Toronto and professor Jamie Gruman of the School of Hospitality and Tourism Management at the University of Guelph demonstrates the benefits of orientation, training, and mentorship programs for new employees. These activities help employees adjust better because they make them feel happier, more confident that they will more likely fit with the organization, and therefore more engaged.[61]

The Metamorphosis Stage Finally, to work out any problems discovered during the encounter stage, the new employee changes or goes through the **metamorphosis stage**. The options presented in Exhibit 10-4 are designed to bring about metamorphosis. The more management relies on formal, collective, fixed, and serial socialization programs while emphasizing divestiture, the more likely newcomers' differences and perspectives will be stripped away and replaced by standardized and predictable behaviours.

encounter stage The stage in the socialization process in which a new employee sees what the organization is really like and confronts the possibility that expectations and reality may diverge.

metamorphosis stage The stage in the socialization process in which a new employee adjusts to the values and norms of the job, work group, and organization.

Dave Olecko/Bloomberg/Getty Images

In a study conducted by Peter B. Gustavson School of Business at the University of Victoria in 2015, Tim Hortons was rated the most trusted brand in Canada. However, franchisees do not believe that reputation will last much longer, now that the company is no longer private but is owned by Restaurant Brands, which is backed by the Brazilian investment firm 3G Capital.

EXHIBIT 10-4 Entry Socialization Options

Formal vs. Informal The more a new employee is segregated from the ongoing work setting and differentiated in some way to make explicit his or her newcomer's role, the more formal socialization is. Specific orientation and training programs are examples. Informal socialization puts the new employee directly into his or her job, with little or no special attention.

Individual vs. Collective New members can be socialized individually. This describes how it's done in many professional offices. They can also be grouped together and processed through an identical set of experiences, as in military boot camp.

Fixed vs. Variable This refers to the time schedule in which newcomers make the transition from outsider to insider. A fixed schedule establishes standardized stages of transition. This characterizes rotational training programs. It also includes probationary periods, such as the 8- to 10-year "associate" status accounting and law firms use before deciding whether to name a candidate as a partner. Variable schedules give no advance notice of their transition timetable. Variable schedules describe the typical promotion system, where individuals are not advanced to the next stage until they are "ready."

Serial vs. Random Serial socialization is characterized by the use of role models who train and encourage the newcomer. Apprenticeship and mentoring programs are examples. In random socialization, role models are deliberately withheld. The new employee is left on his or her own to figure things out.

Investiture vs. Divestiture Investiture socialization assumes that the newcomer's qualities and qualifications are the necessary ingredients for job success, so these qualities and qualifications are confirmed and supported. Divestiture socialization tries to strip away certain characteristics of the recruit. Fraternity and sorority "pledges" go through divestiture socialization to shape them into the proper role.

Sources: Based on J. Van Maanen, "People Processing: Strategies of Organizational Socialization," *Organizational Dynamics*, Summer 1978, pp. 19–36; and E. H. Schein, "Organizational Culture," *American Psychologist*, February 1990, p. 116.

These *institutional* practices are common in police departments, fire departments, and other organizations that value rule following and order. Programs that are informal, individual, variable, and random while emphasizing investiture are more likely to give newcomers an innovative sense of their role and methods of working. Creative fields, such as research and development, advertising, and filmmaking, rely on these *individual* practices. Most research suggests that high levels of institutional practices encourage person–organization fit and high levels of commitment, whereas individual practices produce more role innovation.[62]

The three-part entry socialization process is complete when

- The new employee has become comfortable with the organization and his or her job

- The new employee has internalized the norms of the organization and the work group, and understands and accepts these norms

- The new employee feels accepted by his or her peers as a trusted and valued individual, is self-confident that he or she has the competence to complete the job successfully, and understands the system—not only his or her own tasks but also the rules, procedures, and informally accepted practices

- The new employee understands how he or she will be evaluated and knows what criteria will be used to measure and appraise his or her work; he or she knows what is expected and what constitutes a job "well done"

As Exhibit 10-5 shows, successful metamorphosis should have a positive impact on the new employee's productivity and commitment to the organization. It should also reduce the tendency to leave the organization (turnover).

Researchers examine how employee attitudes change during socialization by measuring those attitudes at several points over the first few months. Several studies have now documented patterns of "honeymoons" and "hangovers" for new workers, showing that the period of initial adjustment is often marked by decreases in job satisfaction as idealized hopes come into contact with the reality of organizational life.[63] Newcomers

EXHIBIT 10-5 How Organizational Cultures Have an Impact on Employee Performance and Satisfaction

may find that the level of social support they receive from supervisors and co-workers is gradually withdrawn over the first few weeks on the job, as everyone returns to "business as usual."[64] Role conflict and role overload may rise for newcomers over time, and employees with the largest increases in these role problems experience the largest decreases in commitment and satisfaction.[65] It may be that the initial adjustment period for newcomers presents increasing demands and difficulties, at least in the short term.

How Employees Learn Culture

As Hyatt Hotels CEO Mark Hoplamazian talked to employees about how they learned the company culture, he began to rethink how culture was implemented at Hyatt.[66] He felt the company already hired great people. He talked to associates (as Hyatt's employees are known) to learn more about what happened when people joined the company, and how policies and procedures played a role in the working and private lives of those in the Hyatt family. He looked at the situation from different perspectives to see where things were not connecting. One employee who had previously worked for a hotel in Mexico that Hyatt acquired was asked what her first day at work for Hyatt was like. Hoplamazian found it was difficult for her to say anything more than "it was great." He wanted her to be more explicit, so he kept talking with her. Finally, she burst into tears. "In the first 48 hours of our management, she had learned mostly about how she could get fired! The onboarding/orientation program was all about compliance and policies and rules and regulations—like it is at so many companies. And the result was that it had terrified her," said Hoplamazian. He was dismayed that employees saw orientation, a foundational part of introducing employees to an organization's culture, as a negative experience. He went to work immediately to take orientation out of the hands of HR and legal, and make it a more welcoming experience. "We went back and redesigned the entire orientation process. The entirety of the first day of onboarding is now about what we stand for, what it means to be part of the Hyatt family—viewed and presented from an *emotional* perspective. Not from a left-brain, commercial perspective but from a right-brain experiential perspective."

Why does culture have such a strong influence on people's behaviour?

Culture is transmitted to employees in a number of forms, the most potent being stories, rituals, material symbols, and language. These forms enable both employees and the outside world to read the organization's culture. *From Concepts to Skills* on pages 379–381 offers additional ideas on how to read an organization's culture.

What kind of organizational culture would work best for you?

Stories

When Toronto-based Bank of Montreal (BMO) decided several years ago to become a leader in customer service in the banking industry, it needed a way of communicating this message to the bank's employees. The decision: "Every meeting starts with a customer story." No matter what kind of meeting is being held, one staff member has to tell a recent story about an interaction with a customer—ranging from feel-good stories to horror stories of something that went wrong for the customer. By focusing on customer stories, employees know they need to pay attention to interactions so that they can share the stories. Susan Brown, a senior vice-president with BMO, explains the importance of the story focus for the bank: "If you want to change culture, a great way to do it is the customer story. It's part of the evolution of developing a customer-centric culture."[67]

Stories circulate through many organizations, anchoring the present in the past and legitimating current practices. They typically include narratives about the organization's founders, rule breaking, rags-to-riches successes, workforce reductions, relocations of employees, reactions to past mistakes, and organizational coping.[68] Employees also create their own narratives about how they came to either fit or not fit with the organization during the process of socialization, including first days on the job, early interactions with others, and first impressions of organizational life.[69]

Rituals

Rituals are repetitive sequences of activities that express and reinforce the key values of the organization; what goals are most important; and/or which people are important vs. which are expendable.[70]

One well-known corporate ritual is Walmart's company chant. Begun by the company's founder, Sam Walton, as a way to motivate and unite his workforce, "Gimme a W, gimme an A, gimme an L, give me an M, A, R, T!" has become a company ritual that bonds Walmart employees and reinforces Walton's belief in the importance of his employees to the company's success. Similar corporate chants are used by IBM, Ericsson, Novell, Deutsche Bank, and PricewaterhouseCoopers.[71]

Material Symbols

The layout of corporate headquarters, the types of cars given to top executives, and the presence or absence of corporate aircraft are a few examples of **material symbols**. Others include the size of offices, the elegance of furnishings, executive perks, and dress code.[72] In addition, corporate logos, signs, brochures, and advertisements reveal aspects of the organization's culture.[73] These material symbols convey to employees, customers, and clients who is important, the degree of egalitarianism top management desires, and the kinds of behaviour that are appropriate (such as risk-taking, conservative, authoritarian, participative, individualistic, social).

Some cultures are known for the perks in their environments, such as Google's bocce courts, SAS's free health care clinic, and Microsoft's organic spa. At Bolton, Ontario-based Husky Injection Molding Systems, a more egalitarian culture is favoured. Employees and management share the parking lot, dining room, and even washrooms.

Language

Many organizations and subunits within them use language to help members identify with the culture, show their acceptance of it, and help preserve it. Unique terms describe equipment, offices, key individuals, suppliers, customers, or products that relate to the business. New employees may at first be overwhelmed by acronyms and jargon that, once assimilated, act as a common denominator to unite members of a

rituals Repetitive sequences of activities that express and reinforce the key values of the organization; what goals are most important; and which people are important and which are expendable.

material symbols What conveys to employees who is important, the degree of egalitarianism top management desires, and the kinds of behaviour that are appropriate.

Baidu, a Chinese web services firm, describes its culture as "simple"—meaning direct, open, and uncomplicated—and "reliable"—meaning trusting the competence of colleagues. Baidu's casual workplaces reflect this trust with lounges, gyms, yoga studios, and dome-shaped nap rooms employees may use at any time.

given culture or subculture. Baristas at Starbucks call drinks *short, tall, grande,* and *venti* instead of *small, medium, large,* and *extra-large,* and they know the difference between a half-decaf double tall almond skinny mocha and an iced short schizo skinny hazelnut cappuccino with wings. Students and employees at Grant MacEwan College are informed by the philosophy of the college's namesake. Dr. Grant MacEwan, historian, writer, politician, and environmentalist, was never a formal part of the management of the organization. However, many phrases from his writing and creed have found their way into formal college publications and calendars, as well as informal communications, including his most well known, "I have tried to leave things in the vineyard better than I found them."[74]

Changing Organizational Culture

One of the challenges Mark Hoplamazian, CEO of Hyatt, faced was how to communicate the company's commitment to the environment, one of Hyatt's global platforms, to the hotels.[75] The principle of thinking globally while acting locally was truly put to the test. Not all locations had the same resources or needs, and cities and countries had their own environmental regulations and policies. Hoplamazian wanted each hotel to contribute to Hyatt's corporate social responsibility (CSR) initiatives in a meaningful way, yet it would not be possible to implement one policy across the company. To address this, he decided to stop giving associates mapped-out plans for their decisions and instead "give them a compass and say 'You figure out how you want to bring yourself to bear.' A compass instead of a map is really one of the key concepts that we are moving towards." In providing a compass instead of a map, Hoplamazian communicated the need for change and new expectations for employees. Why has Hyatt been so successful in creating an organizational culture that enables change?

Changing an organization's culture is difficult and requires that many aspects of the organization change at the same time, especially the reward structure. Culture is such a challenge to change because it often represents the established mindset of employees and managers.

John Kotter, professor of leadership at Harvard Business School, has created a detailed approach to implementing change, which we discuss in Chapter 14.[76] Efforts directed at changing organizational culture do not usually yield immediate or dramatic results. Cultural change is actually a lengthy process—measured in years, not months. But we can ask the question, "Can culture be changed?" The answer is, "Yes!" The evidence suggests that cultural change is most likely to occur when most or all of the following conditions exist:

- *A dramatic crisis.* A shock that undermines the status quo calls into question the relevance of the current culture. Examples of a crisis might be a surprising financial setback, the loss of a major customer, or a dramatic technological breakthrough by a competitor.

- *Turnover in leadership.* New top leadership, who can provide an alternative set of key values, may be perceived as more capable of responding to the crisis. Top leadership definitely refers to the organization's chief executive, but also might need to include all senior management positions.

- *Young and small organization.* The younger the organization, the less entrenched its culture will be. It's also easier for management to communicate its new values when the organization is small.

- *Weak culture.* The more widely held a culture is, and the higher the agreement among members on its values, the more difficult it will be to change. Weak cultures are more open to change than strong ones.

Next we discuss two specific kinds of cultural change: creating an ethical organizational culture and creating a positive organizational culture.

Creating an Ethical Organizational Culture

Despite differences across industries and cultures, ethical organizational cultures share some common values and processes.[77] Therefore, managers can create a more ethical culture by adhering to the following principles:[78]

5 Demonstrate how an ethical organizational culture can be created.

- *Be a visible role model.* Employees will look to the actions of top management as a benchmark for appropriate behaviour, but everyone can be a role model to positively influence the ethical atmosphere. Senior managers who take the ethical high road send a positive message.

- *Communicate ethical expectations.* Whenever you serve in a leadership capacity, minimize ethical ambiguities by sharing a code of ethics that states the organization's primary values and the judgment rules that employees must follow.

- *Provide ethics training.* Set up seminars, workshops, and training programs to reinforce the organization's standards of conduct, to clarify what practices are permissible, and to address possible ethical dilemmas.

- *Visibly reward ethical acts and punish unethical ones.* Evaluate subordinates on how their decisions measured against the organization's code of ethics. Review the means taken to achieve goals, as well as the ends themselves. Visibly reward those who act ethically and conspicuously punish those who do not.

- *Provide protective mechanisms.* Provide formal mechanisms so everyone can discuss ethical dilemmas and report unethical behaviour without fear of reprimand. These might include identifying ethics counsellors, ombudspersons, or ethics officers for liaison roles.

The work of setting a positive ethical climate has to start at the top of the organization.[79] One study demonstrated that when top management emphasizes strong ethical values, supervisors are more likely to practise ethical leadership. Positive attitudes transfer down to line employees, who show lower levels of deviant behaviour and higher levels of cooperation and assistance. Several other studies have come to the same general conclusion: The values of top management are a good predictor of ethical behaviour among employees. One study involving auditors found perceived pressure from organizational leaders to behave unethically was associated with increased intentions to engage in unethical practices.[80] Clearly the wrong type of organizational culture can negatively influence employees' ethical behaviour. Finally, employees whose ethical values are similar to those of their department are more likely to be promoted, so we can think of ethical culture as flowing from the bottom up as well.[81] The *Ethical Dilemma* on page 377 discusses the importance of honesty as an ethical base.

6 Describe a positive organizational culture.

Creating a Positive Organizational Culture

At first blush, creating a positive culture may sound hopelessly naive, or like a Dilbert-style conspiracy. The one thing that makes us believe this trend is here to stay is that there are signs that management practice and OB research are converging.

A **positive organizational culture** emphasizes building on employee strengths, rewards more often than it punishes, and emphasizes individual vitality and growth.[82] Let's consider each of these areas.

Building on Employee Strengths

Although a positive organizational culture does not ignore problems, it emphasizes showing employees how they can capitalize on their strengths. As management guru Peter Drucker said, "Most [employees] do not know what their strengths are. When you ask them, they look at you with a blank stare, or they respond in terms of subject knowledge, which is the wrong answer." Wouldn't it be better to be in an organizational culture that helped you discover your strengths and how to make the most of them?

As CEO of Auglaize Provico, an agribusiness based in Ohio, Larry Hammond used this approach in the midst of the firm's worst financial struggles. When the organization had to lay off one-quarter of its workforce, he took advantage of what was right, rather than dwelling on what went wrong. "If you really want to [excel], you have to know yourself—you have to know what you're good at, and you have to know what you're not so good at," says Hammond. With the help of Gallup consultant Barry Conchie, Hammond focused on discovering and using employee strengths to help turn the company around. "You ask Larry [Hammond] what the difference is, and he'll say that it's individuals using their natural talents," says Conchie.[83]

Rewarding More Often Than Punishing

Although most organizations are sufficiently focused on extrinsic rewards such as pay and promotions, they often forget about the power of smaller (and cheaper) rewards like praise. Part of creating a positive organizational culture is "catching employees doing something right." Many managers withhold praise because they are afraid employees will coast or because they think praise is not valued. Employees generally don't ask for praise, and managers usually don't realize the costs of failing to give it.

Consider Elzbieta Górska-Kolodziejczyk, a plant manager for International Paper's facility in Kwidzyn, Poland. Employees worked in a bleak windowless basement. Staffing became roughly one-third of its prior level, while production tripled. These challenges had done in the previous three managers. So when she took over, at the top of her list was recognition and praise for staff. She initially found it difficult to give praise to those who were not used to it, especially men. "They were like cement at the beginning," she said. "Like cement." Over time, however, she found they valued and even

positive organizational culture
A culture that emphasizes building on employee strengths, rewards more than punishes, and emphasizes individual vitality and growth.

CAREER OBJECTIVES
How Do I Learn to Lead?

I'll be starting a new job in a few weeks. It's my first time working as a leader for a team, and I know I have a lot to learn. Is there any way I can be sure I'll achieve success as a leader?

—Gordon

Dear Gordon:

Learning about a new job is always complicated. Learning how to be a leader is doubly complicated. It's expected that you have the capacity to provide direction and purpose for employees, and that you will respect the existing culture of the group as well as the capacities of individual members. Here are a few key insights toward making your transition into leadership successful:

- *Ask questions.* New leaders are often anxious about asking questions of direct reports for fear of being seen as incompetent or weak. However, inquiring about how things have been done in the past and asking about individual goals signal that you are concerned about the team members. Familiarizing yourself with the group's culture and practices can also help you develop techniques to harness the team's strengths and overcome challenges.

- *Build relationships with other leaders.* Remember—you were put into this role for a reason, and the company wants to see you succeed, so make the most of the resources of others. Take detailed notes regarding specific activities and strategies that were successful, and schedule a check-in to discuss how these strategies have worked over time. If you can show you are truly engaged in the learning process, you will find others are more willing to provide you with assistance and advice.

- *Start small.* Much has been written about the importance of gaining small wins early on to build your reputation. The old saying "you never get a second chance to make a first impression" definitely holds true in the workplace. Try to develop new initiatives with clear outcomes that will allow you to demonstrate your leadership traits.

The best leadership transitions include learning what the situation calls for, and setting your team up for success from the start.

Be proactive!

Sources: Based on T. B. Harris, N. Li, W. R. Boswell, X. Zhang, and Z. Xie, "Getting What's New from Newcomers: Empowering Leadership, Creativity, and Adjustment in the Socialization Context," *Personnel Psychology* 67 (2014), pp. 567–604; Y. H. Ji, N. A. Cohen, A. Daly, K. Finnigan, and K. Klein, "The Dynamics of Voice Behavior and Leaders' Network Ties in Times of Leadership Successions," *Academy of Management Proceedings*, 2014, 16324; and B. Eckfeldt, "5 Things New CEOS Should Focus On," *Business Insider*, June 1, 2015, http://www.businessinsider.com/5-things-new-ceos-should-focus-on-2015-6.

reciprocated praise. One day a department supervisor pulled her over to tell her she was doing a good job. "This I do remember, yes," she said.[84]

Emphasizing Vitality and Growth

No organization will get the best out of employees who see themselves as cogs in the machine. A positive culture realizes the difference between a job and a career. It supports not only what the employee contributes to organizational effectiveness, but also how the organization can make the employee more effective personally and professionally.

Limits of Positive Culture

Is a positive culture the answer to all organizational problems? Although companies have embraced aspects of a positive organizational culture, it's a new enough area that there is some uncertainty about how and when it works best.

Not all national cultures value being positive as much as Canadian and US cultures do and, even within these countries, there surely are limits to how far organizations should go. For example, Admiral, a British insurance company, has established a Ministry of Fun in its call centres to organize poem writing, foosball, conkers (a British game involving chestnuts), and fancy dress days, which may clash with an industry value of more serious cultures. When does the pursuit of a positive culture start to seem coercive? As one critic notes, "Promoting a social orthodoxy of positiveness focuses on a particular constellation of desirable states and traits but, in so doing, can stigmatize those who fail to fit the template."[85] There may be benefits to establishing a positive culture, but an organization also needs to be objective and not pursue it past the point of effectiveness. See *Point/Counterpoint* on page 375 for additional thoughts on whether organizations should create a positive organizational culture.

GLOBAL IMPLICATIONS

We considered global cultural values (collectivism and individualism, power distance, and so on) in Chapter 3. Here, our focus is a bit narrower: How is organizational culture affected by a global context?

Organizational cultures often reflect national culture. The culture at AirAsia, a Malaysian-based airline, emphasizes openness and friendship. The carrier has a lot of parties, a participative management, and no private offices, reflecting Malaysia's relatively collectivistic culture. However, the culture of Air Canada does not reflect the same degree of informality. If Air Canada were to set up operations in Malaysia or merge with AirAsia, it would need to take these cultural differences into account. When an organization opens up operations in another country, it ignores the local culture at its own risk.

Three times a week, employees at the Canadian unit of Japanese video game maker Koei Tecmo begin the day by standing next to their desks, facing their boss, and saying "Good morning" in unison. Employees then deliver short speeches on topics that range from corporate principles to 3D game engines. Koei Tecmo also has employees punch a time clock and asks women to serve tea to top executive guests. Although these practices are consistent with Koei Tecmo's culture, they do not fit Canadian culture very well. "It's kind of like school," says one Canadian employee.[86]

The management of ethical behaviour is one area where national culture can rub against corporate culture.[87] Canadian managers tend to endorse the supremacy of anonymous market forces as a moral obligation for business organizations. This worldview sees bribery, nepotism, and favouring personal contacts as highly unethical. They also value profit maximization, so any action that deviates from profit maximization may suggest inappropriate or corrupt behaviour. In contrast, managers in developing economies are more likely to see ethical decisions as embedded in the social environment. That means doing special favours for family and friends is not only appropriate but possibly even an ethical responsibility. Managers in many nations view capitalism skeptically and believe the interests of employees should be put on a par with the interests of shareholders, which may limit profit maximization.

Creating a multinational organizational culture can initiate strife between employees of traditionally competing countries. When Swedish, Norwegian, Finnish, and Danish banks combined to form Nordea Bank AB, the stereotypes some employees held based on the countries' historical relationships created tensions. Finland had originally been a colony of Sweden, and Norway had been a part of Denmark and then of Sweden. The fact that none of the employees had yet been born when their countries were colonies didn't matter; complex alliances within Nordea formed along nationalistic lines. To bridge these gaps, Nordea employed storytelling to help employees identify with positive aspects of their shared geographical *region*. The organization reinforced the shared identity through press releases, corporate correspondence, equal country representation in top management, and championing of shared values. Although the organization continues to struggle with a multinational culture, the successes it has enjoyed can be attributed to careful attention to national differences.[88]

Because culture strongly affects performance, organizations that have units in different countries need to construct and clearly communicate a multinational culture that focuses on corporate values. These values should be unique and separate from identifiable country norms, emphasize respect and tolerance for cultural differences, and address the issue of cultural identity. Globalization can be an opportunity to positively change organizational culture.

Summary

Exhibit 10-5 depicts the impact of organizational culture. Employees form an overall subjective perception of the organization based on factors such as the degree of risk tolerance, team emphasis, and support of people. This overall perception represents, in effect, the organization's culture or personality and affects employee performance and satisfaction, with stronger cultures having greater impact.

SNAPSHOT SUMMARY

What Is Organizational Culture?
- Culture Is a Descriptive Term
- Do Organizations Have Uniform Cultures?
- Strong vs. Weak Cultures
- Culture vs. Formalization

What Do Cultures Do?
- Culture's Functions
- Culture Creates Climate
- The Ethical Dimension of Culture

- Culture and Sustainability
- Culture and Innovation
- Culture as a Liability

Creating and Sustaining an Organization's Culture
- How a Culture Begins
- Keeping a Culture Alive

How Employees Learn Culture
- Stories
- Rituals

- Material Symbols
- Language

Changing Organizational Culture
- Creating an Ethical Organizational Culture
- Creating a Positive Organizational Culture

MyLab Management

Study, practise, and explore real business situations with these helpful resources:

- **Study Plan:** Check your understanding of chapter concepts with self-study quizzes.
- **Online Lesson Presentations:** Study key chapter topics and work through interactive assessments to test your knowledge and master management concepts.
- **Videos:** Learn more about the management practices and strategies of real companies.
- **Simulations:** Practise management decision-making in simulated business environments.

OB at Work

OB at Work

for **Review**

1. What is organizational culture, and what are its common characteristics?

2. What are the functional and dysfunctional effects of organizational culture?

3. What factors create and sustain an organization's culture?

4. How is culture transmitted to employees?

5. How can an ethical organizational culture be created?

6. What is a positive organizational culture?

for **Managers**

- Realize that an organization's culture is relatively fixed in the short term. To effect change, involve top management and strategize a long-term plan.

- Hire individuals whose values align with those of the organization; these employees will tend to remain committed and satisfied. Not surprisingly, "misfits" have considerably higher turnover rates.

- Understand that employees' performance and socialization depend to a considerable degree on their knowing what to do and not do. Train your employees well and keep them informed of changes to their job roles.

- Be aware that your company's organizational culture may not be "transportable" to other countries. Understand the cultural relevance of your organization's norms before introducing new plans or initiatives overseas.

for **You**

- Increase your understanding of culture by looking for similarities and differences across groups and organizations. For instance, do you have two courses where the classroom environment differs considerably? What does this suggest about the underlying assumptions in teaching students? Similarly, compare customer service at two local coffee shops or sandwich shops. What does the employee behaviour suggest about each organization's culture?

- Carefully consider the culture of any organization at which you are thinking of being employed. You will feel more comfortable in cultures that share your values and expectations. You may find yourself reacting very negatively if an organization's culture (and values) does not match your own.

- Keep in mind that groups create mini-cultures of their own. When you work in a group on a student project, be aware of the values and norms that are being supported early on in the group's life. These will greatly influence the group's culture.

ORGANIZATIONS SHOULD STRIVE TO CREATE A POSITIVE ORGANIZATIONAL CULTURE

POINT

Organizations should do everything they can to establish a positive culture, because it works.[89] Scores of recent studies have shown that individuals who are in positive states of mind at work and in life lead happier, more productive, and more fulfilling lives. Given the accumulating evidence, researchers are now studying ways to make that happen.

A *Harvard Business Review* article discussed an interesting concept: *outsourcing inspiration*. What is meant by that? "A growing body of research shows that end users—customers, clients, patients, and others who benefit from a company's products and services—are surprisingly effective in motivating people to work harder, smarter, and more productively."

Some examples of how this might work:

- A "buddy program" that introduces Alzheimer's patients to scientists working to develop treatments for the disease

- Weekly team meetings that begin with stories about how the team has made a difference in customers' lives

- Health care workers coming face to face with a patient whose story deeply touches them

Of course, there are other ways of creating a positive organizational culture, including building on strengths and rewarding more than punishing.

Outsourcing inspiration is a great way for employees to feel appreciated, to experience empathy, and to see the impact of their work—all motivating outcomes that will lead organizations to be more effective and individuals more fulfilled in their work. Creating a positive organizational culture is not magic, but it tends to have extremely positive benefits for organizations that embrace it.

COUNTERPOINT

There are many unanswered questions about the merits of using positive organizational scholarship to build positive organizational cultures. Let's focus on three.

What is a positive culture? The employment relationship can be amicable and even mutually beneficial. However, glossing over natural differences in interests with the frosting of positive culture is intellectually dishonest and potentially harmful. From time to time, any organization needs to undertake unpopular actions. Can anyone dismiss an employee positively (and honestly), or explain to someone why others received a raise? There is a danger in trying to sugarcoat. Positive relationships will develop—or not—on their own. We would be better off preaching that people, and organizational cultures, should be honest and fair rather than unabashedly positive.

Is practice ahead of science? Before we start beseeching organizations to build positive cultures, we should make sure these initiatives work as expected. Many have unintended consequences, and we simply don't have enough research to support the claims. As one reviewer noted, "Everyone wants to believe they could have greater control over their lives by simply changing the way they think. Research that supports this idea gets promoted loudly and widely." But it's not based on a mountain of evidence.

Is building a positive culture manipulative? Psychologist Lisa Aspinwall writes of "saccharine terrorism," where employees are coerced into positive mindsets by happiness coaches. You may think this an exaggeration, but companies like UBS, American Express, KPMG, FedEx, Adobe, and IBM have used happiness coaches to do exactly that. As one critic noted, "Encouraging people to maintain a happy outlook in the face of less-than-ideal conditions is a good way of keeping citizens under control in spite of severe societal problems, or keeping employees productive while keeping pay and benefits low." Rather than insisting on positive cultures, how about promoting honest cultures as an idea?

OB at Work

Form small groups to discuss the following topics, as assigned by your instructor:

1. Choose 2 courses that you are taking this term, ideally in different faculties, and describe the culture of the classroom in each. What are the similarities and differences? What values about learning might you infer from your observations of culture?

2. Identify artifacts of culture in your current or previous workplace. From these artifacts, would you conclude that the organization had a strong or weak culture?

3. Have you or someone you know worked somewhere where the culture was strong? What was your reaction to that strong culture? Did you like that environment, or would you prefer to work where there is a weaker culture? Why?

EXPERIENTIAL EXERCISE

Greeting Newcomers

Divide into groups of 3–4 students. Discuss these four primary issues:

- *Describe your first impressions of the university when you applied.* This is important because it helps to identify assumptions other new students may have coming in.

- *Describe some of your early experiences in the new environment, and how they either reinforced or changed your pre-entry expectations.* Include activities officially sponsored by your school, as well as unplanned experiences that told you what the culture was like.

- *Identify key issues you wish you had learned more about when you arrived.* Think of the sorts of things that caused the most trouble for you, or that were difficult for you to figure out on your own.

- *Contrast your early experiences with your current knowledge of what the culture is like.* How has long-term interaction changed your ideas about the culture of the university?

After describing your school's culture as a whole, consider the same four issues as they relate to your major field of study.

Design a Program

Use the material from the chapter to develop an "ideal" program that could be used to introduce new students to the culture. This might closely resemble what you have experienced, or it may be very different. The goal should be to reduce student anxiety and stress during the transition, and to promote a culture that helps newcomers meet their goals as efficiently and effectively as possible. Your socialization program should include pre-entry messages, recruiting information, early orientation sessions, and long-term follow-up. You will want to determine, at each phase, who should be sending these messages so they have the most impact on newcomers.

Questions

1. Based on your observations and group discussion, what seem to be the most important elements of the culture that newcomers need to adjust to?

2. Do you think your school doesn't communicate some aspects of the culture to newcomers? If so, why?

3. How is the introduction to a business organizational culture and department similar to, or different from, introduction into a university and field of study?

ETHICAL **DILEMMA**

Culture of Deceit

We have noted throughout this chapter, and the text overall, that honesty is generally the best policy in managing OB.[90] But that doesn't mean honest dealing is always the rule in business.

Studies have found, in fact, that whole industries may encourage dishonesty. In one experiment, subjects were first asked either to think about their professional identities, or to complete a generic survey. They were then asked to report on a series of coin flips; they were told in advance that the more times the coin showed heads, the more money they would make. The bankers who took the generic survey were about as honest in reporting coin flips as people who worked in other fields. The bankers told to think about their professional identities, however, exaggerated how often the coin turned up heads. People in other professions didn't do so—the tie between professional identity and dishonesty was unique to those who worked in banking. These results are certainly not limited to the banking industry. Many other ways of priming people to think about financial transactions seem to generate more dishonesty. Studies have also found that many individuals feel pressured to engage in dishonest behaviour to meet the bottom line. Whenever money is under consideration, there are powerful motives.

Money motivations are strong in professional sports. For example, the number of top leaders in FIFA (world soccer's governing body) who were indicted in 2015 suggests that behaving dishonestly has been accepted within FIFA, and covering up for the dishonesty of others has been encouraged. Domenico Scala, FIFA's audit and compliance committee chair, noted, "To support the change we need a culture that censures inappropriate behaviour and enforces rules vigorously, fairly, and [is] responsive." There is general consensus that to overcome corruption, those in positions of authority must demonstrate commitment to an ethical culture. As Scala noted, "It is the leaders' tone that ensures it is embedded at all levels of the organization. This must be honest and communicated with sincerity in both words and actions." There may well be a tendency to become dishonest when there is money to be made, so leaders may need to be especially vigilant and communicate clear expectations for ethical behaviour.

Fortunately, evidence shows that asking people to focus on relationships and the way they spend their time can actually make them behave more honestly and helpfully. This suggests that a focus on the social consequences of our actions can indeed help to overcome corruption.

Questions

1. What are the negative effects of a culture that encourages dishonesty and corruption on its reputation and employees?

2. Why might some organizations push employees to behave in a dishonest or corrupt manner? Are there personal benefits to corruption that culture can counteract?

3. What actions can you take as a new employee if you are pressured to violate your own ethical standards at work? How might mid-level employees' responses to this question differ from those of more senior managers?

CASE INCIDENTS

The Place Makes the People

At Gerson Lehrman Group, you won't find an employee working in a cubicle day after day.[91] You also won't find an employee working in a free-form open-office area consistently either. The reason is that Gerson Lehrman is invested in "activity-based working." In this system, employees have access to cubicle spaces for privacy, conference rooms for group meetings, café seating for working with a laptop, and full open-office environments. Where you work on a particular day is entirely up to you.

It may be hard to remember, but office allocations were a uniform signal of hierarchical status and part of organizational culture until fairly recently. As organizations have become flatter and the need for creativity and flexibility has increased, the "open-office" plan has become a mainstay of the business world. The goal is to encourage free-flowing conversation and discussion, enhance creativity, and minimize hierarchy—in other words, to foster a creative and collaborative culture and remove office space from its status position.

Research on open offices, however, shows there is a downside. Open offices decrease the sense of privacy, reduce the feeling of owning your own space, and create a distracting level of background stimulation. As psychology writer Maria Konnikova noted, "When we're exposed to too many inputs at once—a computer screen, music, a colleague's conversation, the ping of an instant message—our senses become overloaded, and it requires more work to achieve a given result."

So is the activity-based hybrid described earlier a potential solution? With its constantly shifting workspace and lack of consistent locations, this may be an even less controlled environment than an open office. However, it does signal a culture that values the autonomy of individual workers to choose their own best environment at a particular time. The lack of consistency creates other problems, though. Workers cannot achieve even the modest level of personal control over any specific space that they had with the open design. Design expert Louis Lhoest notes that managers in an activity-based office "have to learn to cope with not having people within their line of sight." This is a difficult transition for many managers to make, especially if they are used to a command-and-control culture.

Whether a traditional, open, or activity-based design is best overall is obviously hard to say. Perhaps the better question is, which type will be appropriate for each organization?

Questions

1. How might different types of office design influence employee social interaction, collaboration, and creativity? Should these be encouraged even in organizations without an innovative culture?

2. Can the effects of a new office design be assessed objectively? How could you go about measuring whether new office designs are improving the organizational culture?

3. What types of jobs do you think might benefit most from the various forms of office design described above?

Active Cultures

Employees at many successful companies start the day by checking the economic forecast.[92] Patagonia's employees start the day by checking the weather forecast. The outdoor clothing company encourages its workforce to take time from the work day to get outside and get active. For Patagonia, linking employees with the natural environment is a major part of the culture.

New hires are introduced to this mindset very quickly. Soon after starting at Patagonia, marketing executive Joy Howard was immediately encouraged to go fly fishing, surfing, and rock climbing all around the world. She notes that all this vacationing is not just playing around—it's an important part of her job. "I needed to be familiar with the products we market," she said. Other practices support this outdoors-oriented, healthy culture. The company has an on-site organic café featuring locally grown produce. Employees at all levels are encouraged through an employee discount program to try out activewear in the field. Highly flexible hours ensure that employees feel free to take the occasional afternoon off to catch the waves or get out of town for a weekend hiking trip.

Are there bottom-line benefits to this organizational culture? Patagonia CEO Rose Marcario thinks so: "People recognize Patagonia as a company that's . . . looking at business through a more holistic lens other than profit." However, she is quick to add, "Profit is important; if it wasn't, you wouldn't be talking to me."

Patagonia's culture obviously makes for an ideal workplace for some people—but not for others who don't share its values. People who are just not outdoor types would likely feel excluded. While the unique mission and values of Patagonia may not be for everyone, for its specific niche in the product and employment market, the culture fits like a glove.

Questions

1. What key dimensions of its culture do you think make Patagonia successful? How does the organization help to foster this culture?

2. Does Patagonia use strategies to build its culture that you think could work for other companies? Is the company a useful model for others that are not so tied to a lifestyle? Why or why not?

3. What are the drawbacks of Patagonia's culture? Might it sometimes be a liability, and if so, in what situations?

FROM CONCEPTS TO SKILLS

How to "Read" an Organization's Culture

The ability to read and assess an organization's culture can be a valuable skill.[93]

If you are looking for a job, you will want to choose an employer whose culture is compatible with your values and in which you will feel comfortable. If you can accurately assess a prospective employer's culture before you make your decision, you may be able to save yourself a lot of grief and reduce the likelihood of making a poor choice. Similarly, you will undoubtedly have business transactions with numerous organizations during your professional career. You will be trying to sell a product or service, negotiate a contract, or arrange a joint venture, or you may merely be seeking out which individual in an organization controls certain decisions. The ability to assess another organization's culture can be a definite plus in successfully completing these pursuits.

For the sake of simplicity, we will approach the problem of reading an organization's culture from the point of view of a job applicant. We will assume you are interviewing for a job. Here is a list of things you can do to help learn about a potential employer's culture:

- Observe the physical surroundings. Pay attention to signs, pictures, style of dress, length of hair, degree of openness between offices, and office furnishings and arrangements.

- With whom did you meet? Just the person who would be your immediate manager? Or potential colleagues, managers from other departments, or senior executives? Based on what they revealed, to what degree do people other than the immediate manager have input into the hiring decision?

- How would you characterize the style of the people you met? Formal? Casual? Serious? Jovial?

- Does the organization have formal rules and regulations printed in a human resource policy manual? If so, how detailed are these policies?

- Ask questions of the people you meet. The most valid and reliable information tends to come from asking the same questions of many people (to see how closely their responses align) and by talking with boundary spanners. *Boundary spanners* are employees whose work links them to the external environment and includes jobs such as human resources interviewer, salesperson, purchasing agent, labour negotiator, public relations specialist, and company lawyer.

Questions that will give you insights into organizational processes and practices might include the following:

- What is the background of the founders?

- What is the background of current senior managers? What are their functional specializations? Were they promoted from within or hired from outside?

- How does the organization integrate new employees? Is there an orientation program? Training? If so, could you describe these features?

- How does your manager define his or her job success? (Amount of profit? Serving customers? Meeting deadlines? Acquiring budget increases?)

- How would you define fairness in terms of reward allocations?

- Can you identify some people here who are on the "fast track"? What do you think has put them on the fast track?

- Can you identify someone who seems to be considered a deviant in the organization? How has the organization responded to this person?

- Can you describe a decision that someone made here that was well received?

- Can you describe a decision that did not work out well? What were the consequences for the decision maker?

- Could you describe a crisis or critical event that has occurred recently in the organization? How did top management respond? What was learned from this experience?

Practising Skills

After spending your first three years after college graduation as a freelance graphic designer, you are looking at pursuing a job as an account executive at a graphic design firm. You feel that the scope of assignments and potential for technical training far exceed what you would be able to do on your own, and you are looking to expand your skills and meet a brand-new set of challenges. However, you want to make sure you "fit" into the organization where you are going to be spending more than eight hours every workday. What is the best way for you to find a place where you will be happy, and where your style and personality will be appreciated?

Reinforcing Skills

1. Do some comparisons of the atmosphere or feeling you get from various organizations. It will probably be easiest for you to do this exercise using restaurants, retail stores, or banks. Based on the atmosphere that you observe, what type of organizational culture do you think these organizations might have? If you can, interview three employees at each organization for their descriptions of their organization's culture.

2. Think about changes (major and minor) that you have dealt with over the past year. Perhaps these changes involved other people and perhaps they were personal. Did you resist the change? Did others resist the change? How did you overcome your resistance or the resistance of others to the change?

11 Leadership

Kelly Lovell has won many awards for her work with young entrepreneurs and helps business leaders better understand the needs of youth. What makes a successful leader?

LEARNING OUTCOMES

After studying this chapter, you should be able to:

1. Contrast leadership and management.
2. Summarize the conclusions of trait theories of leadership.
3. Identify the central tenets and main limitations of behavioural theories of leadership.
4. Assess contingency theories of leadership by their level of support.
5. Contrast inspirational and responsible leadership.
6. Identify the leadership roles available to nonmanagers.
7. Define *authentic leadership*.
8. Discuss the requirements of ethical leadership.
9. Define *servant leadership*.
10. Identify the challenges to our understanding of leadership.

Kelly Lovell, founder and CEO of Waterloo-based Lovell Corporation, is a 25-year-old entrepreneur who received her first recognition as a leader at age 19 when she earned the Ontario Ministry of Citizenship & Immigration's Newcomer Champion Award, the Rogers' Young Woman of the Year Award, Ontario's Change the World Youth Ambassador Award, and the Kitchener-Waterloo Community Caregiver and Service Award.[1] In 2016 Lovell was named Her Majesty Queen Elizabeth II's Young Leader of 2016—an award given to youth leaders from Commonwealth countries who have made a difference in their communities. In total she has won 15 awards for her leadership activities and has spoken at TEDx three times. She also did much of this while earning an honours degrees in biomedical science and in business administration from Western University.

Courtesy of Lovell Corporation

Lovell focuses on helping corporations develop effective youth marketing programs and guides them in how best to engage youth with their products and services. As well, she helps organizations develop employee retention strategies for Millennials and Generation Z. She also provides mentoring, skill development, and entrepreneurship coaching to young people.

Lovell is making a difference in the business community and the youth community, and she has travelled to a variety of places around the world to lend people her expertise. What kinds of leadership skills do people need to make a difference in the world?

In this chapter, we review leadership studies to determine what makes an effective leader. We consider factors that affect one's ability to lead and examine different leadership styles. Finally, we discuss challenges to our understanding of leadership.

OB IS FOR EVERYONE

- Have you ever wondered if there was one *right* way to lead?
- What are ways to practise leadership?
- Do perceptions of a leader matter?

THE BIG IDEA

Knowing how to lead well does not come naturally. Effective leadership requires an understanding of how to inspire individuals to achieve common goals.

① Contrast leadership and management.

What Is Leadership?

We define **leadership** as the ability to influence a group toward the achievement of a vision or set of goals. But not all leaders are managers, nor are all managers leaders. Just because an organization provides its managers with certain formal rights is no assurance they will lead effectively. Leaders can emerge from within a group as well as by formal appointment. Nonsanctioned leadership—the ability to influence that arises outside the formal structure of the organization—is often as important or more important than formal influence.

Organizations need strong leadership *and* strong management for optimal effectiveness. We need leaders to challenge the status quo, create visions of the future, and inspire organizational members to achieve the visions. We need managers to formulate detailed plans, create efficient organizational structures, and oversee day-to-day operations.

In our discussion of leadership, we will focus on two major tasks of those who lead in organizations: managing those around them to get the day-to-day tasks done, and inspiring others to do the extraordinary. It will become clear that successful leaders rely on a variety of interpersonal skills in order to encourage others to perform at their best. It will also become clear that, no matter the place in the hierarchy, from CEO to team leader, a variety of individuals can be called on to perform leadership roles. Think about your own definition of leadership as you participate in the *Experiential Exercise—What Is Leadership?* on page 409.

Leadership as Supervision

In this section, we discuss theories of leadership that were developed before 1980. These early theories focused on the supervisory nature of leadership—that is, how individuals managed the day-to-day functioning of employees. The theories took different approaches in understanding how best to lead in a supervisory capacity. The three general types of theories that emerged were (1) trait theories, which propose leaders have a particular set of traits that makes them different from nonleaders; (2) behavioural theories, which propose that particular behaviours make for better leaders; and (3) contingency theories, which propose the situation has an effect on leaders. When you think about these theories, remember that although they have been considered "theories of leadership," they rely on an older understanding of what "leadership" means, and don't convey a distinction between leadership and supervision.

② Summarize the conclusions of trait theories of leadership.

Trait Theories: Are Leaders Different from Others?

Have you ever wondered whether some fundamental personality difference makes some people "born leaders"? The search for personality, social, physical, or intellectual attributes that differentiate leaders from nonleaders goes back to the earliest stages of leadership research. **Trait theories of leadership** focus on personal qualities and characteristics. Leadership emergence and effectiveness are often evaluated separately vis-à-vis trait studies. Trait theory emerged in the hope that if it were possible to identify the traits of leaders, it would be easier to select people to fill leadership roles. Being able to select good leaders is important because not all people know how to be good leaders, as *Focus on Research* shows.

A comprehensive review of the leadership literature, organized around the Big Five framework, has found extraversion to be the most predictive trait of effective leadership.[2] However, extraversion is more strongly related to the way leaders emerge than to their effectiveness. Sociable and dominant people are more likely to assert themselves in group situations, which can help extraverts be identified as leaders, but effective leaders are not domineering. One study found that leaders who scored very high in

leadership The ability to influence a group toward the achievement of a vision or set of goals.

trait theories of leadership Theories that consider personal qualities and characteristics that differentiate leaders from nonleaders.

FOCUS ON RESEARCH
Bad Bosses Everywhere

Doesn't leadership come naturally? Although much is expected of leaders, what is surprising is how rarely they seem to meet the most basic definitions of effectiveness.[3] A recent study of 700 employees revealed that many believe their supervisors don't give credit when it's due, gossip about them behind their backs, and don't keep their word. The situation is so bad that for many employees, the study's lead author says, "They don't leave their company, they leave their boss."

Key findings of the study are as follows:

- 39 percent said their supervisor failed to keep promises.
- 37 percent said their supervisor failed to give credit when due.
- 31 percent said their supervisor gave them the "silent treatment" in the past year.
- 27 percent said their supervisor made negative comments about them to other employees or managers.
- 24 percent said their supervisor invaded their privacy.
- 23 percent said their supervisor blames others to cover up mistakes or minimize embarrassment.

Why do companies promote such people into leadership positions? One reason may be the Peter Principle. When people are promoted into one job (say, as a supervisor or coach) based on how well they did another (say, salesperson or player), that assumes that the skills of one role are the same as the other. The only time such people stop being promoted is when they reach their level of incompetence. Judging from the results of this study, that level of leadership incompetence is reached all too often.

A recent study found that lack of respect for a leader by employees—for instance, when employees feel that the leader is not the best person for the job—has a significant impact on whether employees will follow that leader. The researchers found that simply naming someone "the leader" did not by itself create effective leadership.[4] . . . .

assertiveness, a facet of extraversion, were less effective than those who scored moderately high.[5] So although extraversion can predict effective leadership, the relationship may be due to unique facets of the trait.

Unlike agreeableness and emotional stability, which do not seem to predict leadership, conscientiousness and openness to experience may predict leadership, especially leader effectiveness. For example, one recent study indicated that top management teams that were high in conscientiousness positively influenced organizational performance through their leadership.[6] Conscientiousness and extraversion are positively related to leaders' self-efficacy,[7] and people are more likely to follow someone who is confident he or she is going in the right direction, allowing these leaders to emerge.

In sum, leaders who like being around people and are able to assert themselves (extraverted), are disciplined and keep commitments they make (conscientious), and are creative and flexible (open) do have an advantage when it comes to leadership.

What about the Dark Triad personality traits of Machiavellianism, narcissism, and psychopathy (see Chapter 2)? Research indicates they are not all bad for leadership. A study in Europe and the United States found that normative (mid-range) scores on the Dark Triad personality traits were optimal, while low (and high) scores were associated with ineffective leadership. Furthermore, the study suggested that high emotional stability may actually accentuate the ineffective behaviours.[8] However, higher scores on Dark Triad traits and emotional stability can contribute to leadership emergence.

Thankfully, both this study and other international research indicate that building self-awareness and self-regulation skills may be helpful for leaders to control the effects of their Dark Triad traits.[9]

Another trait that may indicate effective leadership is emotional intelligence (EI), discussed in Chapter 2. A core component of EI is empathy. Empathetic leaders can sense others' needs, listen to what followers say (and don't say), and read the reactions of others. A leader who effectively displays and manages emotions will find it easier to influence the feelings of followers by expressing genuine sympathy and enthusiasm for good performance, and by showing irritation when employees fail to perform.[10]

The link between EI and leadership effectiveness may be worth investigating in greater detail.[11] Research has also demonstrated that people high in EI are more likely to emerge as leaders, even after taking cognitive ability and personality into account.[12] Based on the latest findings, we offer two conclusions. First, we can say that traits can predict leadership. Second, traits do a better job at predicting the emergence of leaders and the appearance of leadership than in distinguishing between *effective* and *ineffective* leaders.[13] The fact that an individual exhibits the right traits and that others consider that person to be a leader does not necessarily mean that the leader is successful at getting a group to achieve its goals.

❸ Identify the central tenets and main limitations of behavioural theories of leadership.

Behavioural Theories: Do Leaders Behave in Particular Ways?

Trait research provides a basis for *selecting* the right people for leadership. In contrast, **behavioural theories of leadership** imply we could *train* people to be leaders. *Case Incident—Leadership Mettle Forged in Battle* on page 410 talks about how leadership learned in one field can be applied elsewhere.

The Ohio State Studies

The most comprehensive behavioural theories resulted from the Ohio State Studies in the late 1940s,[14] which sought to identify independent dimensions of leader behaviour. Beginning with more than a thousand dimensions, the studies narrowed the list to two that substantially accounted for most of the leadership behaviour described by employees: *initiating structure* and *consideration*.

Initiating structure is the extent to which a leader is likely to define and structure his or her role and those of employees in order to attain goals; it includes behaviour that attempts to organize work, work relationships, and goals. A leader high in initiating structure is someone who assigns followers particular tasks, sets definite standards of performance, and emphasizes deadlines.

Consideration is the extent to which a leader's job relationships are characterized by mutual trust, respect for employees' ideas, and regard for their feelings. A leader high in consideration helps employees with personal problems, is friendly and approachable, treats all employees as equals, and expresses appreciation and support (is people-oriented). Most of us want to work for considerate leaders—when asked to indicate the factors that most motivated them at work, 66 percent of employees mentioned appreciation.[15]

The Michigan Studies

Leadership studies at the University of Michigan's Survey Research Center had similar objectives to the Ohio State Studies: to locate behavioural characteristics of leaders that appeared related to performance effectiveness.[16] The Michigan group identified two behavioural types: **employee-oriented leaders**, who emphasized interpersonal relations by taking a personal interest in the needs of employees and accepting individual differences among them; and **production-oriented leaders**, who emphasized the technical or task aspects of the job—focusing on accomplishing the group's task. These dimensions are closely related to the Ohio State dimensions. Employee-oriented

behavioural theories of leadership Theories that propose that specific behaviours differentiate leaders from nonleaders.

initiating structure The extent to which a leader is likely to define and structure his or her role and the roles of employees in order to attain goals.

consideration The extent to which a leader is likely to have job relationships characterized by mutual trust, respect for employees' ideas, and regard for their feelings.

employee-oriented leader A leader who emphasizes interpersonal relations.

production-oriented leader A leader who emphasizes the technical or task aspects of the job.

Indra Nooyi, CEO and board chairman of PepsiCo, is described as fun-loving, sociable, agreeable, conscientious, emotionally stable, and open to experiences. Recognized as one of the most powerful women in business, Nooyi's personal qualities and traits have contributed to her job performance and success.

leadership is similar to consideration, and production-oriented leadership is similar to initiating structure. In fact, most leadership researchers use the terms synonymously.[17]

The results of testing behavioural theory studies have been mixed. However, one review found the followers of leaders high in consideration were more satisfied with their jobs, were more motivated, and had more respect for their leaders. Initiating structure was more strongly related to higher levels of group and organization productivity and more positive performance evaluations.

RESEARCH FINDINGS: Behavioural Theories of Leadership

One study integrated the results of 59 previous studies in order to determine the impact of specific leader behaviours on leadership effectiveness, group performance, and employee job satisfaction.[18] Task-oriented behaviours explained 47.6 percent of the variance in group performance and 33.3 percent of the variance in overall leadership effectiveness. Change-oriented transformational leadership behaviours were also strongly associated with group performance and overall effectiveness, explaining 28.5 percent and 22.5 percent, respectively, of the variance in these areas. Consideration behaviours (such as providing emotional support) had a smaller but still significant impact on performance and leadership effectiveness (16.6 percent and 19.5 percent of total variance, respectively). Being supportive was associated with employee job satisfaction (21 percent of variance), but providing a reward structure had a greater impact, explaining 43.9 percent of the variance in employee job satisfaction. These results suggest that while all of these leader behaviours are important, task-oriented behaviours are essential to leadership effectiveness.

Summary of Trait Theories and Behavioural Theories

In general, research indicates there is validity for both the trait and behavioural theories. Parts of each theory can help explain facets of leadership emergence and effectiveness.

However, identifying the exact relationships is not a simple task. The first difficulty is in correctly identifying whether a trait or a behaviour predicts a certain outcome. The second is in exploring which combinations of traits and behaviours yield certain outcomes. The third challenge is to determine the causality of traits to behaviours so that predictions toward desirable leadership outcomes can be made.

Leaders who have certain traits desirable to their positions and who display culturally appropriate behaviours that initiate structure and show consideration do appear to be more effective. Beyond that, the determinations are less clear. For example, perhaps you are wondering whether conscientious leaders (trait) are more likely to be structuring (behaviour), and extraverted leaders (trait) are more considerate (behaviour). Unfortunately, we are not sure there is a connection. Future research is needed.

> Have you ever wondered if there was one *right* way to lead?

As important as traits and behaviours are in identifying effective or ineffective leaders, they do not guarantee success. Some leaders may have the right traits or display the right behaviours and still fail. Context matters too, which has given rise to the contingency theories we discuss next.

Contingency Theories: Does the Situation Matter?

4 Assess contingency theories of leadership by their level of support.

Some tough-minded leaders seem to gain a lot of admirers when they take over struggling companies and turn them around. However, predicting leadership success is more complex than finding a few hero examples. Also, the leadership style that works in very bad times does not necessarily translate into long-term success. When researchers looked at situational influences, it appeared that under condition *a*, leadership style *x* would be appropriate, whereas style *y* was more suitable for condition *b*, and style *z* for condition *c*. But what *were* conditions *a*, *b*, and *c*? We consider three situational theories: the Fiedler contingency model, Hersey and Blanchard's Situational Leadership®, and path-goal theory.

The Fiedler Contingency Model

Fred Fiedler developed the first comprehensive contingency model for leadership.[19] The **Fiedler contingency model** proposes that group performance depends on the proper match between the leader's style and the degree to which the situation gives the leader control. With the model, the individual's leadership style is assumed to be permanent. The **least preferred co-worker (LPC) questionnaire** identifies whether a person is *task-oriented* or *relationship-oriented* by asking respondents to think of all the co-workers they have ever had and describe the one they *least enjoyed* working with. If you describe this person in favourable terms (a high LPC score), you are relationship oriented. If you see your least preferred co-worker in unfavourable terms (a low LPC score), you are primarily interested in productivity and are task oriented.

After finding a score, a fit must be found between the organizational situation and the leader's style for there to be leadership effectiveness. We can assess the situation in terms of three contingency or situational dimensions:

- *Leader–member relations.* The degree of confidence, trust, and respect members have for their leader
- *Task structure.* The degree to which job assignments are procedurized (that is, structured or unstructured)
- *Position power.* The degree of influence a leader has over power-based activities such as hiring, firing, discipline, promotions, and salary increases

According to the model, the higher the task structure becomes, the more procedures are added; and the stronger the position power, the more control the leader has. A very

Fiedler contingency model A leadership theory that proposes that effective group performance depends on the proper match between the leader's style and the degree to which the situation gives the leader control.

least preferred co-worker (LPC) questionnaire An instrument that purports to measure whether a person is task or relationship oriented.

favourable situation (in which the leader has a great deal of control) might include a payroll manager who has the respect and confidence of his or her employees (good leader–member relations); activities that are clear and specific—such as wage computation, payroll processing, and report filing (high task structure); and considerable freedom to reward and punish employees (strong position power). The favourable situations are on the left side of the model in Exhibit 11-1. An unfavourable situation, to the right in the model, might be that of the disliked chairperson of a volunteer United Way fundraising team (low leader–member relations, low task structure, low position power). In this job, the leader has very little control.

When faced with a category I, II, III, VII, or VIII situation, task-oriented leaders perform better. Relationship-oriented leaders (represented by the solid line), however, perform better in moderately favourable situations—categories IV, V, and VI.

How would you apply Fiedler's findings? You would match leaders with the type of situation—in terms of leader–member relations, task structure, and position power—for which they were best suited. Because Fiedler views an individual's leadership style as fixed, there are only two ways to improve leader effectiveness.

First, you can change the leader to fit the situation—as a baseball manager puts a right- or left-handed pitcher into the game depending on the hitter. If a group situation rates as highly unfavourable but is currently led by a relationship-oriented manager, the group's performance could be improved under a manager who is task oriented. The second alternative is to change the situation to fit the leader, by restructuring tasks or increasing or decreasing the leader's power to control factors such as salary increases, promotions, and disciplinary actions.

Studies testing the overall validity of the Fiedler model were initially supportive, but the model has not been studied much in recent years. While it provides some insights we should consider, its strict practical application is problematic.

Hersey and Blanchard's Situational Leadership®

Situational Leadership® (SL) focuses on followers. SL says successful leadership depends on selecting the right leadership style contingent on the followers' *readiness*,

EXHIBIT 11-1 Findings from the Fiedler Model

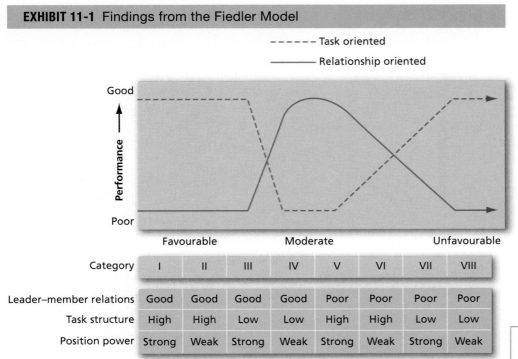

Category	I	II	III	IV	V	VI	VII	VIII
Leader–member relations	Good	Good	Good	Good	Poor	Poor	Poor	Poor
Task structure	High	High	Low	Low	High	High	Low	Low
Position power	Strong	Weak	Strong	Weak	Strong	Weak	Strong	Weak

Situational Leadership® (SL) A leadership theory that focuses on the readiness of followers.

or the extent to which they are willing and able to accomplish a specific task. A leader should choose one of four behaviours, depending on follower readiness. This idea is illustrated in Exhibit 11-2.

If followers are *unable* and *unwilling* to do a task, the leader needs to give clear and specific directions; if they are *unable* and *willing*, the leader needs to display high task orientation to compensate for followers' lack of ability and high relationship orientation to get them to "buy into" the leader's desires. If followers are *able* and *unwilling*, the leader needs to use a supportive and participative style; if they are both *able* and *willing*, the leader does not need to do much.

SL has intuitive appeal. It acknowledges the importance of followers and builds on the logic that leaders can compensate for followers' limited ability and motivation. Yet research efforts to test and support the theory have generally been disappointing.[20] Why? Possible explanations include internal ambiguities and inconsistencies in the model itself as well as problems with research methodology. So despite its intuitive appeal and wide popularity, any endorsement must be cautious for now.

Path-Goal Theory

Developed by University of Toronto professor Martin Evans in the late 1960s and subsequently expanded upon by Robert House (formerly at the University of Toronto, but now at the Wharton School of Business at the University of Pennsylvania), **path-goal theory** extracts elements from the Ohio State leadership research on initiating structure and consideration and the expectancy theory of motivation.[21] Path-goal theory suggests that it's the leader's job to provide followers with the information, support, or other resources necessary to achieve their goals. (The term *path-goal* implies effective leaders clarify followers' paths to their work goals and make the journey easier by reducing roadblocks.)

Path-goal theory identifies four leadership behaviours that might be used in different situations to motivate individuals:

- The *directive leader* lets followers know what is expected of them, schedules work to be done, and gives specific guidance as to how to accomplish tasks. This closely parallels the Ohio State dimension of initiating structure. This behaviour is best used when individuals have difficulty doing tasks or the

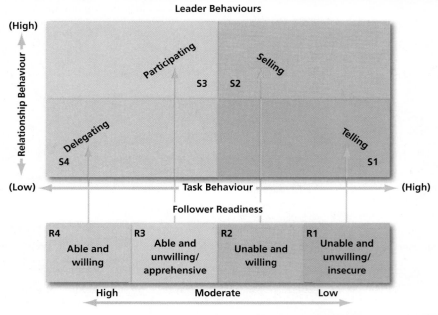

EXHIBIT 11-2 Hersey and Blanchard's Situational Leadership®

path-goal theory A leadership theory that says it is the leader's job to assist followers in attaining their goals and to provide the necessary direction and/or support to ensure that their goals are compatible with the overall objectives of the group or organization.

EXHIBIT 11-3 Path-Goal Theory

tasks are ambiguous. It would not be very helpful when used with individuals who are already highly motivated, have the skills and abilities to do the task, and understand the requirements of the task.

- The *supportive leader* is friendly and shows concern for the needs of followers. This is essentially synonymous with the Ohio State dimension of consideration. This behaviour is often recommended when individuals are under stress, or otherwise show that they need to be supported.

- The *participative leader* consults with followers and uses their suggestions before making a decision. This behaviour is most appropriate when individuals need to buy in to decisions.

- The *achievement-oriented leader* sets challenging goals and expects followers to perform at their highest level. This behaviour works well with individuals who like challenges and are highly motivated. It would be less effective with less capable individuals, or those who are highly stressed from overwork.

As Exhibit 11-3 illustrates, path-goal theory proposes two types of contingency variables that affect the leadership behaviour–outcome relationship: environmental variables that are outside the control of the employee and variables that are part of the personal characteristics of the employee. The theory proposes that employee performance and satisfaction are likely to be positively influenced when the leader compensates for what is lacking in either the employee or the work setting. However, the leader who spends time explaining tasks when those tasks are already clear or when the employee has the ability and experience to handle them without interference is likely to be ineffective because the employee will see such directive behaviour as redundant or even insulting.

RESEARCH FINDINGS: Path-Goal Theory

The match between leadership style and situation can be individualistic and mercurial. Some tasks might be both stressful and highly structured, and employees may have high ability or experience in some tasks and not others. Research has found that goal-focused leadership can lead to higher levels of emotional exhaustion for subordinates who are low in conscientiousness and emotional stability.[22] This suggests that leaders who set goals enable conscientious followers to achieve higher performance but may cause stress for employees who are low in conscientiousness.

Like SLT, path-goal theory has intuitive appeal, especially from a goal attainment perspective. Also like SLT, the theory can be only cautiously adopted for application, but it is a useful framework in examining the important role of leadership.[23]

Case Incident—Leadership by Algorithm on pages 410–411 explores ways to learn how to adapt your leadership style to better fit the situation.

⑤ Contrast inspirational and responsible leadership.

Inspirational Leadership

Kelly Lovell inspires young people by relating stories from her early teenage years.[24] She says that she struggled to find her voice, was bullied, and had poor self-esteem. She felt she was the butt of all jokes. Finally, she got involved in volunteer work.

Lovell attributes her success to her early experiences with volunteering and she encourages young people to follow her lead. "Volunteering equipped me with the experiences and skills I was missing to attract the supporters I needed. It was through volunteerism [that] I was able to understand my abilities because there is no pressure." Lovell's volunteer experience led her to develop an app to help other young people track their volunteer opportunities, and also the leadership skills that they learn from these activities.

Lovell won the Queen's Young Leaders Award for 2016, an award given to 60 youth from Commonwealth countries who are "taking the lead to transform the lives of others." Lovell was excited that this allowed her to meet the Queen, and she hopes the award will inspire the young people she reaches out to. "To make it to Buckingham Palace strengthens my message of what is possible with passion and drive, and how far a person can go if they take their own future into their hands."

What does it take to be an inspirational leader?

The leadership theories we have discussed so far ignore the importance of the leader as a communicator who inspires others to act beyond their immediate self-interests. In this section, we present two contemporary leadership theories with a common theme. They view leaders as individuals who inspire followers through their words, ideas, and behaviours. These theories are charismatic leadership and transformational leadership.

Charismatic Leadership

The following individuals are often cited as being charismatic leaders: Frank Stronach of Aurora, Ontario-based Magna International; Mogens Smed, CEO of Calgary-based DIRTT (Doing It Right This Time) Environmental Solutions; Pierre Trudeau, the late prime minister; Michaëlle Jean, former Governor General; and Craig Kielburger, founder of WE Charity (formerly Free the Children). So what do they have in common?

What Is Charismatic Leadership?

Max Weber, a sociologist, defined *charisma* (from the Greek word for "gift") as "a certain quality of an individual personality, by virtue of which he or she is set apart from ordinary people and treated as endowed with supernatural, superhuman, or at least specifically exceptional powers or qualities. These are not accessible to the ordinary person and are regarded as of divine origin or as exemplary, and on the basis of them the individual concerned is treated as a leader."[25]

The first researcher to consider charismatic leadership in terms of OB was Robert House. According to House's **charismatic leadership theory**, followers make attributions of heroic or extraordinary leadership abilities when they observe certain behaviours, and tend to give these leaders power.[26] A number of studies have attempted to identify the characteristics of the charismatic leader and have documented four—they have a vision, they are willing to take personal risks to achieve that vision, they are sensitive to followers' needs, and they exhibit extraordinary behaviours (see Exhibit 11-4).[27] Recent research in Greece suggested that charismatic leadership increases follower organizational identification

charismatic leadership theory
A leadership theory that states that followers make attributions of heroic or extraordinary leadership abilities when they observe certain behaviours.

EXHIBIT 11-4 Key Characteristics of Charismatic Leaders

1. *Vision and articulation.* Has a vision—expressed as an idealized goal—that proposes a future better than the status quo; and is able to clarify the importance of the vision in terms that are understandable to others.

2. *Personal risk.* Willing to take on high personal risk, incur high costs, and engage in self-sacrifice to achieve the vision.

3. *Sensitivity to followers' needs.* Perceptive of others' abilities and responsive to their needs and feelings.

4. *Unconventional behaviour.* Engages in behaviours that are perceived as novel and counter to norms.

Source: Based on J. A. Conger and R. N. Kanungo, *Charismatic Leadership in Organizations* (Thousand Oaks, CA: Sage, 1998), p. 94.

(commitment) by building a shared group identity among followers.[28] Other research indicates that charismatic leadership may predict follower job satisfaction.[29]

Are the heroic qualities ascribed to charismatic leaders part of their DNA? *Point/Counterpoint* on page 408 considers the question.

How Charismatic Leaders Influence Followers

How do charismatic leaders actually influence followers? They articulate an appealing **vision**—a long-term strategy for how to attain a goal by linking the present with a better future for the organization. Desirable visions fit the times and circumstances and reflect the uniqueness of the organization. Thus, followers are inspired not only by how passionately the leader communicates—there must be an underlying vision that appeals to followers as well.

A vision needs an accompanying **vision statement**, a formal articulation of an organization's vision or mission. Charismatic leaders may use vision statements to imprint on followers an overarching goal and purpose. These leaders also set a tone of cooperation and mutual support. They build followers' self-esteem and confidence with high performance expectations and the belief that followers can attain them. Through words and actions, the leader conveys a new set of values and sets an example for followers to imitate.

Finally, the charismatic leader engages in emotion-inducing and often unconventional behaviour to demonstrate courage and convictions about the vision.

RESEARCH FINDINGS: Charismatic Leadership

Charismatic leaders are able to reduce stress for their employees, perhaps because they help make work seem more meaningful and interesting.[30] Some personalities are especially susceptible to charismatic leadership.[31] For instance, an individual who lacks self-esteem and questions his or her self-worth is more likely to absorb a leader's direction rather than establish an individual way of leading or thinking. For these people, the situation may matter much less than the charismatic qualities of the leader. A recent study found that it is possible for a person to learn how to communicate charismatically, which would then cause that person to be perceived more as a leader. People who are perceived to be charismatic show empathy, enthusiasm, and self-confidence; have good speaking and listening skills; and make eye contact.[32]

Research indicates that charismatic leadership works as followers "catch" the emotions their leader is conveying.[33] One study found employees had a stronger sense of personal belonging at work when they had charismatic leaders, and increased their willingness to engage in helping and compliance-oriented behaviours.[34]

vision A long-term strategy for attaining a goal or goals.

vision statement A formal articulation of an organization's vision or mission.

Nick Woodman, founder and CEO of digital camcorder company GoPro, is a charismatic leader: energetic, enthusiastic, optimistic, confident, and extraverted. Woodman's charisma inspires his employees to work toward GoPro's vision of enabling people to share their lives through photos and videos.

The Dark Side of Charismatic Leadership

Unfortunately, charismatic leaders who are larger than life don't necessarily act in the best interests of their organizations.[35] Research has shown that individuals who are narcissistic are also higher in some behaviours associated with charismatic leadership.[36] Many charismatic—but corrupt—leaders have allowed their personal goals to override the goals of their organizations. Leaders at Enron, Tyco, WorldCom, and HealthSouth recklessly used organizational resources for their personal benefit and violated laws and ethics to inflate stock prices, and then cashed in millions of dollars in personal stock options. Some charismatic leaders—Hitler, for example—are all too successful at convincing their followers to pursue a disastrous vision. If charisma is power, then that power can be used for good—and for ill.

It's not that charismatic leadership isn't effective; overall, it is. But a charismatic leader isn't always the answer. Success depends, to some extent, on the situation and on the leader's vision, and on the organizational checks and balances in place to monitor the outcomes.

Transactional and Transformational Leadership

Fiedler's contingency model, situational leadership theory, and path-goal theory describe **transactional leaders**—those who guide their followers toward established goals by clarifying role and task requirements. A stream of research has focused on differentiating transactional from **transformational leaders**,[37] who inspire followers to transcend their self-interests for the good of the organization. Transformational leaders can have an extraordinary effect on their followers, who respond with increased levels of commitment.[38] Richard Branson of the Virgin Group is a good example of a transformational leader. He pays attention to the concerns and developmental needs of individual followers; changes followers' awareness of issues by helping them to look at old problems in new ways; and excites and inspires followers to put out extra effort to achieve group goals. Research suggests that transformational leaders are most effective

transactional leaders Leaders who guide or motivate their followers in the direction of established goals by clarifying role and task requirements.

transformational leaders Leaders who inspire followers to transcend their own self-interests and who are capable of having a profound and extraordinary effect on followers.

EXHIBIT 11-5 Characteristics of Transactional and Transformational Leaders

Transactional Leader

Contingent Reward: Contracts exchange of rewards for effort, promises rewards for good performance, recognizes accomplishments.

Management by Exception (active): Watches and searches for deviations from rules and standards, takes correct action.

Management by Exception (passive): Intervenes only if standards are not met.

Laissez-Faire: Abdicates responsibilities, avoids making decisions.

Transformational Leader

Idealized Influence: Provides vision and sense of mission, instills pride, gains respect and trust.

Inspirational Motivation: Communicates high expectations, uses symbols to focus efforts, expresses important purposes in simple ways.

Intellectual Stimulation: Promotes intelligence, rationality, and careful problem solving.

Individualized Consideration: Gives personal attention, treats each employee individually, coaches, advises.

Source: Republished with permission of Elsevier, from "Transactional to Transformational Leadership: Learning to Share the Vision", B. M. Bass, *Organizational Dynamics*, Winter 1990; permission conveyed through Copyright Clearance Center, Inc.

when their followers are able to see the positive impact of their work through direct interaction with customers or other beneficiaries.[39] Exhibit 11-5 briefly identifies and defines the characteristics that differentiate transactional from transformational leaders.

Transactional and transformational leadership complement each other; they are not opposing approaches to getting things done.[40] The best leaders are transactional *and* transformational. Transformational leadership *builds on* transactional leadership and produces levels of follower effort and performance that go beyond what transactional leadership alone can do. But the reverse is not true. So if you are a good transactional leader but do not have transformational qualities, you will likely only be a mediocre leader.

Full Range of Leadership Model

Exhibit 11-6 shows the **full range of leadership model**. Laissez-faire is the most passive and therefore the least effective of the leader behaviours.[41] Management by exception—active or passive—is slightly better than laissez-faire, but it's still considered ineffective. Management-by-exception leaders tend to be available only when there is a problem, which is often too late. Contingent reward leadership can be an effective style of leadership, but will not get employees to go above and beyond the call of duty.

Only with the four remaining leadership styles—all aspects of transformational leadership—are leaders able to motivate followers to perform above expectations and transcend their own self-interest for the sake of the organization. Individualized consideration, intellectual stimulation, inspirational motivation, and idealized influence (known as the "four *I*'s") all result in extra effort from employees, higher productivity, higher morale and satisfaction, higher organizational effectiveness, lower turnover, lower absenteeism, and greater organizational adaptability. Based on this model, leaders are generally most effective when they regularly use each of the four *I*'s.

How Transformational Leadership Works

Organizations with transformational leaders generally have greater decentralization of responsibility, managers with more propensity to take risks, and compensation plans

full range of leadership model A model that depicts seven management styles on a continuum: laissez-faire, management by exception, contingent reward leadership, individualized consideration, intellectual stimulation, inspirational motivation, and idealized influence.

EXHIBIT 11-6 Full Range of Leadership Model

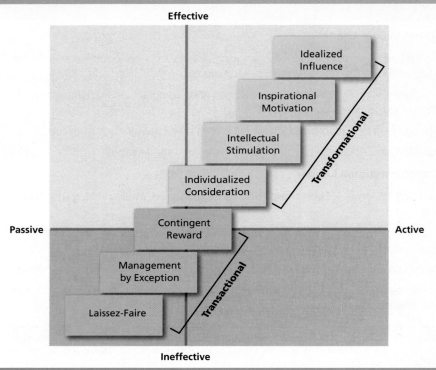

geared toward long-term results, all of which facilitate corporate entrepreneurship.[42] One study of information-technology workers in China found empowering leadership behaviour led to feelings of positive personal control among workers, which increased their creativity at work.[43] Other research in Germany found that transformational leadership positively influenced workers' creativity, but suggested leaders need to guard against dependent leader relationships, which lower employee creativity.[44]

Companies with transformational leaders often show greater agreement among top managers about the organization's goals, which yields superior organizational performance.[45] The Israeli military have seen similar results, showing that transformational leaders improve performance by building consensus among group members.[46]

RESEARCH FINDINGS: Transformational Leadership

Transformational leadership has been supported at diverse job levels and occupations (school principals, marine commanders, ministers, presidents of MBA associations, military cadets, union shop stewards, schoolteachers, sales reps). One study of research and development firms found that teams whose project leaders scored high on transformational leadership produced better-quality products as judged one year later and were more profitable five years later.[47] A review of 117 studies testing transformational leadership found that it was related to higher levels of individual follower performance, team performance, and organizational performance.[48]

The effect of transformational leadership on performance can vary by the situation. In general, transformational leadership has a greater impact on the bottom line in smaller, privately held firms than in more complex organizations.[49] Transformational leadership can also vary depending on whether work is evaluated at the team or the individual level.[50] Individual-focused transformational leadership is behaviour that empowers individual followers to develop ideas, enhance their abilities, and increase self-efficacy. Team-focused transformational leadership emphasizes group goals, shared values and beliefs, and unified efforts. However, research in China suggested that, in team situations, the members' identification with the group could override the effects of transformational leadership.[51]

Just as vision helps explain how charismatic leadership works, it also explains part of the effect of transformational leadership. The GLOBE study links a number of elements of transformational leadership with effective leadership, regardless of country.[52] The GLOBE team concluded that "effective business leaders in any country are expected by their subordinates to provide a powerful and proactive vision to guide the company into the future, strong motivational skills to stimulate all employees to fulfill the vision, and excellent planning skills to assist in implementing the vision."[53]

Although vision is important in any culture, the way it is formed and communicated may need to be adapted. Transformational leadership may be more effective when leaders can directly interact with the workforce to make decisions than when they report to an external board of directors or deal with a complex bureaucratic structure. One study showed transformational leaders were more effective in improving group potency in teams higher in power distance and collectivism.[54] Transformational leaders also obtain higher levels of trust, which reduces stress for followers.[55]

Transformational leaders are more effective not only because they are creative, but also because they encourage those who follow them to be creative, too.[56] Creativity and empowerment are key to organizational success, and transformational leaders are able to increase follower self-efficacy, giving the group a "can do" spirit.[57] One study looking at employee creativity and transformational leadership found employees with transformational leaders had more confidence in their ability to be creative at work and realized higher levels of creative performance.[58] Empowered followers are more likely to pursue ambitious goals, agree on the strategic goals of the organization, and believe the goals they are pursuing are personally important.[59]

A recent study also distinguished between an individual employee's perception of leadership behaviours and the collective perception shared by a group of followers. The researchers found that transformational leadership consistently increased the number of organizational citizenship behaviours engaged in by employees. That effect was significantly stronger when the group as a whole agreed that the leader's behaviours were empowering. If only some individuals felt empowered, the positive impact was lessened considerably.[60]

We have seen that transformational leadership yields many desirable organizational outcomes. When comparing transformational leadership with transactional leadership, research indicates transformational leadership is more strongly correlated than transactional leadership with lower turnover rates, higher productivity, lower employee stress and burnout, and higher employee satisfaction.[61] However, transformational leadership theory is not perfect. The full range of leadership model shows a clear division between transactional and transformational leadership that may not fully exist in effective leadership. Contrary to the full range of leadership model, the four *I*'s in transformational leadership are not always superior in effectiveness to transactional leadership; contingent reward leadership, in which leaders dole out rewards as certain goals are reached by employees, sometimes works as well as transformational leadership. More research is needed, but the general supportable conclusion is that transformational leadership is desirable and effective, given the right application.

Transformational vs. Charismatic Leadership

In considering transformational and charismatic leadership, you surely noticed some commonalities. There are differences, too. Charismatic leadership places somewhat more emphasis on the way leaders communicate (are they passionate and dynamic?), while transformational leadership focuses more on what they are communicating (is it a compelling vision?). Still, the theories are more alike than different. At their heart, both focus on the leader's ability to inspire followers, and sometimes they do so in the same way. Because of this, some researchers believe the concepts are somewhat interchangeable.

CAREER OBJECTIVES

How Can I Get My Boss to Be a Better Leader?

My boss is the CEO, and she's a gossipy, in-your-business over-sharer. She's always asking our top management team personal questions and sharing information with anyone. The other day, I caught her emailing my colleague about my salary and career prospects! What should I do about her poor leadership?

—Phil

Dear Phil:

Nobody likes an oversharer! Perhaps your boss isn't aware of the impact of her behaviour and thinks she is just being friendly. Assuming this is the case, you might be able to make her think first before sharing. If you're comfortable addressing her, you may suggest a private meeting to discuss your concerns. You should bring a list of the types of information she solicits and shares—with an example or two—and, if she is open to discussion, problem-solve with her about her habit. She may see that her "open book" approach is undermining her leadership effectiveness.

Another tactic might start with your researching the best privacy practices,

laws, and business guidelines. Be sure to source your organization's HR handbook for any mentions of privacy expectations. Then in your meeting you could present your research findings.

With both direct approaches, you run the risk of offending your boss, which may very well happen if she becomes embarrassed. Moreover, she may defend her behaviour if her over-sharing is actually strategic gossip and not see the problem, which could have ramifications for what she then thinks and says about you!

These approaches still might be worth trying, but from what you've said about her, it's highly unlikely she will change her general behaviour. Research indicates that her personal tendencies will prevail over time. It sounds like she is extraverted, for instance—you're not going to change that. She may be clever and manipulative, purposefully leveraging her information for personal gain without a concern for others (high-Machiavellian or narcissistic). In that case self-awareness can help, but her behaviour won't change unless she is willing to practise self-regulation.

Perhaps most importantly, it doesn't seem that you like your boss. This may be a real problem that you cannot surmount. How are you going to build a relationship of trust with her, trust that will be needed for you to continue to feel motivated and work hard? Unfortunately, if you cannot thrive in this environment, it may be best to move on.

Good luck for your best possible outcome!

———

Sources: Based on A. E. Colbert, M. R. Barrick, and B. H. Bradley, "Personality and Leadership Composition in Top Management Teams: Implications for Organizational Effectiveness," *Personnel Psychology* 67 (2014), pp. 351–387; R. B. Kaiser, J. M. LeBreton, and J. Hogan, "The Dark Side of Personality and Extreme Leader Behavior," *Applied Psychology: An International Review* 64, no. 1 (2015), pp. 55–92; and R. Walker, "A Boss Who Shares Too Much," *The New York Times*, December 28, 2014, p. 7.

 Identify the leadership roles available to nonmanagers.

Responsible Leadership

Kelly Lovell, who has dedicated her career to helping empower Millennials, explains what effective leadership means to her.[62] "If you want to make a change there is no better way to do so than doing it yourself. And with time, the attraction will all be organic. Stop listening to no; society is full of negativity. Your focus should be to use the doubts as a pivot. Hence, motivating yourself to make your plans work."

Lovell is an example of an authentic leader who knows who she is and what she believes and acts on her values and beliefs. How important is authentic leadership?

What is authentic leadership? Is there an ethical dimension to leadership? What is servant leadership? What is the leader's role in mentoring? In this section, we briefly address these contemporary issues in leadership.

Authentic Leadership

Campbell Soup's CEO Denise Morrison decided to lower sodium in the company's soup products simply because it was the right thing to do.[63] Kathleen Taylor, chair of the Royal Bank of Canada (RBC), believes that being a successful leader requires being authentic: "authentic leaders build meaningful relationships that yield far better results than command and control of the past."[64]

Authentic leadership focuses on the moral aspects of being a leader. **Authentic leaders** know who they are, know what they believe in, and act on those values and beliefs openly and candidly. Their followers consider them to be ethical people. The primary quality produced by authentic leadership is trust. Authentic leaders share information, encourage open communication, and stick to their

> What are ways to practise leadership?

ideals. The result: People come to have faith in them. Related to this behaviour is the concept of humbleness, another characteristic of being authentic. Research indicates that leaders who model humility help followers to understand the growth process for their own development.[65]

Authentic leadership, especially when shared among top management team members, creates a positive energizing effect that heightens firm performance.[66] Transformational or charismatic leaders can have a vision and communicate it persuasively, but sometimes the vision is wrong (as in the case of Hitler), or the leader is more concerned with his own needs or pleasures, as in the case of President Donald Trump.[67] Authentic leaders do not exhibit these behaviours. They may also be more likely to promote corporate social responsibility (CSR).

Ethical Leadership

Leadership is not value free. In assessing its effectiveness, we need to address the *means* a leader uses to achieve goals as well as the content of those goals. The role of the leader

7 Define *authentic leadership*.

8 Discuss the requirements of ethical leadership.

Tom Koene/ZUMApress/Newscom

Entrepreneur Grace Liu (third from the right, in the first row) is an authentic leader. Shown here with her employees, Liu is co-founder and managing director of Asianera, a maker of hand-painted bone china. She built her successful business of high-quality porcelain and innovative design based on her strong personal core values of respecting the individual and operating with integrity.

authentic leaders Leaders who know who they are, know what they believe in and value, and act on these values and beliefs openly and candidly. Their followers could consider them to be ethical people.

in creating the ethical expectations for all members is crucial.[68] Ethical top leadership influences not only direct followers but all the way down the command structure as well, because top leaders create an ethical culture and expect lower-level leaders to behave along ethical guidelines.[69] Leaders rated as highly ethical tend to have followers who engage in more organizational citizenship behaviours (OCBs) and who are more willing to bring problems to the leaders' attention.[70] Research also found that ethical leadership reduced interpersonal conflicts.[71]

Ethical and authentic leadership intersect at a number of junctures. Leaders who treat their followers ethically and authentically—with fairness, especially by providing honest, frequent, and accurate information—are seen as more effective.[72] Transformational leadership has ethical implications since these leaders change the way followers think. Charisma, too, has an ethical component. Unethical leaders use their charisma to enhance power over followers, directed toward self-serving ends. To integrate ethical and charismatic leadership, scholars have advanced the idea of **socialized charismatic leadership**—conveying other-centred (not self-centred) values through leaders who model ethical conduct.[73] Charismatic leaders are able to bring employee values in line with their own values through their words and actions.[74]

Although every member of an organization is responsible for ethical behaviour, many initiatives aimed at increasing organizational ethical behaviour are focused on the leaders. Because top executives set the moral tone for an organization, they need to set high ethical standards, demonstrate them through their own behaviour, and encourage and reward integrity in others while avoiding abuses of power. One recent research review found that role modelling by top leaders positively influenced managers throughout their organizations to behave ethically and fostered a climate that reinforced group-level ethical conduct. The findings suggest that organizations should invest in ethical leadership training programs, especially in industries with few ethical regulations. Leadership training programs that incorporate cultural values should be especially mandated for leaders who take foreign assignments or manage multicultural work teams.[75] Read the *Ethical Dilemma* on page 409 and consider how personal, work, and social values and work ethics intersect.

For ethical leadership to be effective, it's not enough for the leader to simply possess high moral character. After all, no universal standard for ethical behaviour exists, and ethical norms vary by culture, by industry, and even sometimes within an organization. Leaders must be willing to express their ethical beliefs and persuade others to follow their standards. Followers must believe in both the leader and the overlying principles, even if they don't personally agree with every minor stance.

To convey their beliefs, leaders should learn to express their moral convictions in statements that reflect values shared with their organization's members. Leaders can build on this foundation of trust to show their character, enhance a sense of unity, and create buy-in from followers. The leader's message should announce high goals and express confidence that they can be reached.

9 Define *servant leadership*.

socialized charismatic leadership A leadership concept that states that leaders convey values that are other-centred vs. self-centred and who model ethical conduct.

servant leadership A leadership style marked by going beyond the leader's own self-interest and instead focusing on opportunities to help followers grow and develop.

Servant Leadership

Scholars have recently considered ethical leadership from a new angle by examining **servant leadership**.[76] Servant leaders go beyond their self-interest and focus on opportunities to help followers grow and develop. Characteristic behaviours include listening, empathizing, persuading, accepting stewardship, and actively developing followers' potential. Because servant leadership focuses on serving the needs of others, research has focused on its outcomes for the well-being of followers. Perhaps not surprisingly, a study of 126 CEOs found that servant leadership is negatively correlated with the trait of narcissism.[77]

Arthur Mola/AP Images

Craig Kielburger was just 12 years old when he read about a young Pakistani boy of the same age who was murdered while engaged in child labour, and rallied his classmates to become involved in stopping the practice. This work eventually led to the creation of Free the Children (now *WE Charity*). WE Charity supports community development in nine countries where there is a high rate of child labour, child exploitation, and minimal opportunities for girls. Kielburger is an example of someone showing ethical leadership at a very early age.

What are the effects of servant leadership? One study of 123 supervisors found it resulted in higher levels of commitment to the supervisor, self-efficacy, and perceptions of justice, all of which were related to OCB.[78] This relationship between servant leadership and follower OCB appears to be stronger when followers are encouraged to focus on being dutiful and responsible.[79] Second, servant leadership increases team potency (a belief that one's team has above-average skills and abilities), which in turn leads to higher levels of group performance.[80] Third, a study with a nationally representative sample found higher levels of OCB were associated with a focus on growth and advancement, which in turn was associated with higher levels of creative performance.[81] Other research found that servant leadership and a resulting culture of serving increased employee job performance and creativity, while reducing turnover intentions.[82]

Mentoring

Many leaders take responsibility for developing future leaders through mentoring relationships. A **mentor** is often a senior employee who sponsors and supports a less-experienced employee (a mentee), but mentoring can happen much lower in the organization as well. The mentoring role includes coaching, counselling, and sponsorship to help mentees develop skills, to provide support and help bolster mentees' self-confidence, and to lobby so that mentees get good assignments, promotions, and salary increases.[83] At lower levels in the organization, mentors can help new employees learn to be successful. Successful mentors are good teachers. They present ideas clearly, listen well, and empathize with mentees' problems.

In formal mentoring relationships, protégé candidates are identified according to assessments of leadership potential, and then matched with leaders in corresponding organizational functions. Informal mentoring relationships develop when leaders

mentor An employee who sponsors and supports a less-experienced employee.

Chris Wattie/Reuters

Ed Clark (right), who stepped down as CEO of TD Bank in October 2014, spotted something in Bharat Masrani (left) the first time he met him in 2002. Clark soon became Masrani's mentor and champion, providing him with a variety of career opportunities. The mentoring paid off, as Masrani became Clark's successor.

identify a less experienced, lower-level employee who appears to have potential for future development.[84] The mentee will often be tested with a particularly challenging assignment. If he or she performs acceptably, the mentor will develop the relationship, informally showing the mentee how the organization *really* works outside its formal structures and procedures.

Are all employees in an organization equally likely to participate in a mentoring relationship? Unfortunately, no.[85] One study in South Korea found that mentors achieved higher levels of transformational leadership as a result of the process, while organizational commitment and well-being increased for both mentors and mentees.[86]

Although begun with the best intentions, formal relationships are not as effective as informal ones,[87] perhaps due to poor planning, design, and communication. Mentors must see the relationship as beneficial to themselves and the mentee, too, must have input into the relationship.[88] Formal mentoring programs are also most likely to succeed if they appropriately match the work style, needs, and skills of mentee and mentor.[89]

Mentors may be effective not because of the functions they provide, but because of the resources they can obtain; a mentor connected to a powerful network can build relationships that will help the protégé advance. Network ties, whether built through a mentor or not, are a significant predictor of career success.[90] If a mentor is not well connected or not a very strong performer, the best mentoring advice in the world will not be very beneficial.

You might assume that mentoring is valuable for objective outcomes such as compensation and job performance, but research suggests the gains are primarily psychological. Thus, while mentoring can have an impact on career success, it's not as much of a contributing factor as ability and personality. It may *feel* nice to have a mentor, but it does not appear that having a mentor, or even having a good mentor who provides both support and advice, is critical to one's career. The mentor is a boost to your confidence.

Challenges to Our Understanding of Leadership

> Kelly Lovell works with business leaders to help them understand Generation Z retention issues.[91] "Generation Z want to be spoken *with* versus *at* by companies. We want to be involved, have some sense our voice and opinion matters. We gravitate to opportunities with companies where our ideas can be recognized and heard," she says.
>
> Lovell recently wrote a book, *The Power of YOUth*, to help inspire young people to take action using stories of 200 young people who have taken action and made a difference. She hopes the book will help young people see their potential. "It is my hope that after reading a story, a youth can think, 'If they can overcome these challenges to make a difference, then I can, too,'" Lovell says.

"In the 1500s, people ascribed all events they didn't understand to God. Why did the crops fail? God. Why did someone die? God. Now our all-purpose explanation is leadership."[92] This may be an astute observation from management consulting, but of course much of an organization's success or failure is due to factors outside the influence of leadership. Sometimes it's a matter of being in the right or wrong place at a given time. In this section, we present challenges to the accepted beliefs about the value of leadership.

Leadership as an Attribution

As you may remember from Chapter 2, attribution theory examines how people try to make sense of cause-and-effect relationships. The **attribution theory of leadership** says leadership is merely an attribution people make about other individuals.[93] We attribute the following to leaders: intelligence, outgoing personality, strong verbal skills, aggressiveness, understanding, and industriousness.[94] At the organizational level, we tend, rightly or wrongly, to see leaders as responsible for both extremely negative and extremely positive performance.[95]

> Do perceptions of a leader matter?

Perceptions of leaders by their followers strongly affect leaders' ability to be effective. First, one study of 128 major US corporations found that whereas perceptions of CEO charisma did not lead to objectively better company performance, company performance did lead to perceptions of charisma.[96] Second, employee perceptions of leaders' behaviours are significant predictors of whether they blame the leader for failure, regardless of how the leader assesses him- or herself.[97] Third, a study of more than 3000 employees from Western Europe, the United States, and the Middle East found people who tended to "romanticize" leadership in general were more likely to believe their own leaders were transformational.[98]

We also make demographic assumptions about leaders. Respondents in a study assumed a leader described with no identifying racial information was white at a rate beyond the base rate of white employees in that company. Furthermore, where identical leadership situations are described but the leaders' race is manipulated, white leaders are rated as more effective than leaders of other racial groups.[99] One large-scale summary study (a meta-analysis) found that many individuals hold stereotypes of men as having more leadership characteristics than women, although, as you might expect, this tendency to equate leadership with masculinity has decreased over time.[100] Other data suggest women's perceived success as transformational leaders may be based on situations. Teams prefer male leaders when aggressively competing against other teams, but they prefer female leaders when the competition is within teams and calls for improving positive relationships within the group.[101]

Attribution theory suggests what is important is projecting the *appearance* of being a leader rather than focusing on *actual accomplishments*. Leader-wannabes who can shape the perception that they are smart, personable, verbally adept, aggressive, hard-working, and consistent in their style can increase the probability their bosses, colleagues, and employees will view them as effective leaders.

attribution theory of leadership A leadership theory that says that leadership is merely an attribution that people make about other individuals.

Substitutes for and Neutralizers of Leadership

One theory of leadership suggests that in many situations, leaders' actions are irrelevant.[102] Experience and training are among the **substitutes** that can replace the need for a leader's support or ability to create structure. Organizations such as videogame producer Valve Corporation, Gore-Tex maker W. L. Gore, and collaboration-software firm GitHub have experimented with eliminating leaders and management. Governance in the "bossless" work environment is achieved through accountability to co-workers, who determine team composition and sometimes even pay.[103] Organizational characteristics such as explicit formalized goals, rigid rules and procedures, and cohesive work groups can replace formal leadership, while indifference to organizational rewards can neutralize its effects. **Neutralizers** make it impossible for leader behaviour to make any difference to follower outcomes (see Exhibit 11-7).

Sometimes the difference between substitutes and neutralizers is fuzzy. If I am working on a task that is intrinsically enjoyable, theory predicts leadership will be less important because the task provides motivation. But does that mean intrinsically enjoyable tasks neutralize leadership effects, or substitute for them, or both? Another problem is that while substitutes for leadership (such as employee characteristics, the nature of the task, etc.) matter to performance, that doesn't necessarily mean leadership doesn't matter.[104] It's simplistic to think employees are guided to goal accomplishments solely by the actions of their leaders. We have introduced a number of variables—such as attitudes, personality, ability, and group norms—that affect employee performance and satisfaction. Leadership is simply another independent variable in our overall OB model.

Online Leadership

How do you lead people who are physically separated from you with whom you communicate electronically? This question needs attention from OB researchers.[105] Today's managers and their employees are increasingly being linked by networks rather than geographical proximity.

We propose that online leaders have to think carefully about what actions they want their digital messages to initiate. They confront unique challenges, the greatest of which appears to be developing and maintaining trust. **Identification-based trust,**

substitutes Attributes, such as experience and training, that can replace the need for a leader's support or ability to create structure.

neutralizers Attributes that make it impossible for leader behaviour to make any difference to follower outcomes.

identification-based trust Trust based on a mutual understanding of each other's intentions and appreciation of each other's wants and desires.

EXHIBIT 11-7 Substitutes for and Neutralizers of Leadership

Defining Characteristics	Relationship-Oriented Leadership	Task-Oriented Leadership
Individual		
Experience/training	No effect on	Substitutes for
Professionalism	Substitutes for	Substitutes for
Indifference to rewards	Neutralizes	Neutralizes
Job		
Highly structured task	No effect on	Substitutes for
Provides its own feedback	No effect on	Substitutes for
Intrinsically satisfying	Substitutes for	No effect on
Organization		
Explicit formalized goals	No effect on	Substitutes for
Rigid rules and procedures	No effect on	Substitutes for
Cohesive work groups	Substitutes for	Substitutes for

Source: Based on K. B. Lowe and W. L. Gardner, "Ten Years of the Leadership Quarterly: Contributions and Challenges for the Future," *Leadership Quarterly* 11, no. 4 (2000), pp. 459–514.

based on a mutual understanding of each other's intentions and appreciation of the other person's wants and desires, is particularly difficult to achieve without face-to-face interaction.[106] Online negotiations can also be hindered because parties tend to express lower levels of trust.[107]

We believe good leadership skills will soon include the ability to communicate support, trust, and inspiration through electronic communication and to accurately read emotions in others' messages. In electronic communication, writing skills are likely to become an extension of interpersonal skills in ways that are not yet defined.

GLOBAL IMPLICATIONS

We look at several topics from the chapter.

How to Lead

Most of the research discussed in this chapter was conducted in English-speaking countries. We know very little about how culture might influence the validity of the theories, particularly in Eastern cultures. However, a recent analysis of the GLOBE research program (see Chapter 3 for more details) has produced some useful preliminary insights about how to manage in Brazil, France, Egypt, and China.[108] Let's consider each.

- *Brazil.* Based on the values of Brazilian employees, a manager leading a team in Brazil would need to be team oriented, participative, and humane. Leaders high on consideration who emphasize participative decision making and have high LPC scores would be best suited to managing employees in this culture. As one Brazilian manager said in the study, "We do not prefer leaders who take self-governing decisions and act alone without engaging the group. That's part of who we are."

- *France.* French employees have a more bureaucratic view of leaders and are less likely to expect them to be humane and considerate than Canadian and American employees. A leader high on initiating structure (relatively task oriented) will do best and can make decisions in a relatively autocratic manner. A manager who scores high on consideration (people oriented) may find that style backfiring in France.

- *Egypt.* Employees in Egypt are more likely to value team-oriented and participative leadership than Canadian and American employees. However, Egypt is also a relatively high-power-distance culture, meaning status differences between leaders and followers are expected. To be participative yet demonstrate one's status, the leader should ask employees for their opinions, try to minimize conflicts, and not be afraid to take charge and make the final decision (after consulting team members).

- *China.* According to the GLOBE study, Chinese culture emphasizes being polite, considerate, and unselfish, but it also has a high performance orientation. These two factors suggest consideration and initiating structure may both be important. Although Chinese culture is relatively participative compared with the cultures of Canada and the United States, there are also status differences between leaders and employees. These findings suggest that a moderately participative style may work best with Chinese employees.

Servant Leadership

Servant leadership may be more prevalent and effective in certain cultures.[109] When asked to draw images of leaders, for example, US subjects tended to draw them in front of the group, giving orders to followers. Singaporeans tended to draw leaders at the back of the group, acting more to gather a group's opinions together and then unify them from the rear. This suggests the East Asian prototype is more like a servant leader, which might mean servant leadership is more effective in these cultures.

Summary

Leadership plays a central part in understanding group behaviour because it's the leader who usually directs us toward our goals. Knowing what makes a good leader should thus be valuable toward improving group performance. The Big Five Personality Model shows strong and consistent relationships between personality and leadership. The behavioural approach's major contribution was narrowing leadership into task-oriented (initiating structure) and people-oriented (consideration) styles. By considering the situation in which the leader operates, contingency theories promised to improve on the behavioural approach. Contemporary theories have made major contributions to our understanding of leadership effectiveness, and studies of ethics and positive leadership offer exciting promise.

LESSONS LEARNED

- Leaders provide vision and strategy; managers implement that vision and strategy.
- Leaders need to have a vision, they need to communicate that vision, and they must have followers.
- Leaders need to adjust their behaviours, depending on the situation and the needs of employees.

SNAPSHOT SUMMARY

What Is Leadership?

Leadership as Supervision
- Trait Theories: Are Leaders Different from Others?
- Behavioural Theories: Do Leaders Behave in Particular Ways?
- Summary of Trait Theories and Behavioural Theories

- Contingency Theories: Does the Situation Matter?

Inspirational Leadership
- Charismatic Leadership
- Transactional and Transformational Leadership

Responsible Leadership
- Authentic Leadership
- Ethical Leadership

- Servant Leadership
- Mentoring

Challenges to Our Understanding of Leadership
- Leadership as an Attribution
- Substitutes for and Neutralizers of Leadership
- Online Leadership

MyLab Management

 PERSONAL INVENTORY ASSESSMENT

Study, practise, and explore real business situations with these helpful resources:

- **Study Plan:** Check your understanding of chapter concepts with self-study quizzes.
- **Online Lesson Presentations:** Study key chapter topics and work through interactive assessments to test your knowledge and master management concepts.
- **Videos:** Learn more about the management practices and strategies of real companies.
- **Simulations:** Practise management decision-making in simulated business environments.

OB at Work

for **Review**

1. How are leadership and management different from one another?

2. What are the conclusions of trait theories of leadership?

3. What are the central tenets and main limitations of behavioural theories of leadership?

4. What are the contingency theories of leadership?

5. How do inspirational and responsible leadership compare and contrast?

6. What leadership roles are available to nonmanagers?

7. What is *authentic leadership*?

8. What are the requirements of ethical leadership?

9. What is *servant leadership*? How does it make a difference in organizations?

10. What challenges do we face in understanding leadership?

for **Managers**

- For maximum leadership effectiveness, ensure that your preferences on the initiating structure and consideration dimensions are a match for your work dynamics and culture.

- Hire candidates who exhibit transformational leadership qualities and who have demonstrated success in working through others to meet a long-term vision. Personality tests can reveal candidates higher in extraversion, conscientiousness, and openness, which may indicate leadership readiness.

- Hire candidates whom you believe are ethical and trustworthy for management roles, and train current managers in your organization's ethical standards in order to increase leadership effectiveness.

- Seek to develop trusting relationships with followers because, as organizations have become less stable and predictable, strong bonds of trust are replacing bureaucratic rules in defining expectations and relationships.

- Consider investing in leadership training such as formal courses, workshops, and mentoring.

for **You**

- It's easy to imagine that theories of leadership are more important to those who are leaders or who plan in the near future to become leaders. However, leadership opportunities occur throughout an organization. You have no doubt seen a student leader who did not have any formal authority be extremely successful.

- Leaders are not born, they learn how to lead by paying attention to the situation and what needs to be done.

- There is no one best way to lead. It's important to consider the situation and the needs of the people who will be led.

- Sometimes no leader is needed—the individuals in the group simply work well enough together that each takes turns at leadership without appointing a formal leader.

HEROES ARE MADE, NOT BORN

POINT

We often ascribe heroic qualities to our leaders.[110] They are courageous in the face of great risk. They persevere when few would. They take action when most sit by. Heroes are exceptional people who display exceptional behaviour.

But some social psychologists question this conventional wisdom. They note that heroism can be found in many spheres of life, including in the behaviour of whistle-blowers, explorers, religious leaders, scientists, Good Samaritans, and those who beat the odds. At some time in our lives, we all show heroism when the situation allows us to. If we want to see more heroic behaviour, we need to create more situations that produce it.

Stanford psychologist Philip Zimbardo goes even further to argue that our romantic view that heroes are born is misplaced:

> The banality of evil is matched by the banality of heroism. Neither is the consequence of dispositional tendencies. . . . Both emerge in particular situations at particular times, when situational forces play a compelling role in moving individuals across the line from inaction to action.

People exhibit brave behaviour every day. The workers who risked their lives to contain Japan's earthquake-ravaged nuclear reactors in 2011 are a great example. Thus, we err when we think leaders are uniquely positioned to behave heroically. We all can be heroes in the right situation.

COUNTERPOINT

Of course heroes are not like everyone else. That is what makes them heroes.

A generation of evidence from behavioural genetics reveals that "everything is genetic," meaning we have yet to discover an important human behaviour that does not have genetic origins. Although we are not aware of any such study with respect to heroism, it would be surprising if courageous behaviour were not at least partly genetic.

It's foolish to think courageous people are not exceptional because of who they are. Just as we know there is an entrepreneurial personality and a leader personality, there is a heroic personality. Research suggests, for example, that people who score high on conscientiousness are more likely to engage in courageous behaviour.

Not all leaders are heroes, but many have exhibited courageous behaviour. CEO Richard Branson may or may not be a hero, but when he launches his latest attempt to set the world record for an around-the-world balloon flight or sloop sailing, he exhibits the same courageous behaviour as when he is leading conglomerate Virgin Group. Virgin Group now includes more than 400 companies, including Virgin Galactic, a space tourism company, and Virgin Fuels, whose goal is to revolutionize the industry by providing sustainable fuels for automobiles and aircraft. Same leader, same heroic behaviour—in work and in life.

Are we really to believe that Richard Branson and other courageous leaders are just like everyone else?

BREAKOUT **GROUP** EXERCISES

Form small groups to discuss the following topics, as assigned by your instructor:

1. Identify an example of someone you think of as a good leader (currently or in the past). What traits did he or she have? How did these traits differ from those in someone you identify as a bad leader?

2. Identify a situation when you were in a leadership position (in a group, in the workplace, within your family, etc.). To what extent were you able to use a contingency approach to leadership? What made that easier or more difficult for you?

3. When you have worked in student groups, how frequently have leaders emerged in the groups? What difficulties occur when leaders are leading peers? Are there ways to overcome these difficulties?

EXPERIENTIAL EXERCISE

What Is Leadership?

Break the class into six groups: GROUP A: Government Leaders (prime minister, senator, premier, MLA, mayor); GROUP B: Business Leaders (CEO, president, leader in business); GROUP C: School Leaders (class president, informal leader); GROUP D: Sports Leaders (team captain, informal team leader, coach); GROUPS E and F: Effective Managers (manager who demonstrates competence/effectiveness in position).

1. Each group identifies *separately* the defining characteristics of leadership and management for the assigned role, not simply by brainstorming, but by deciding upon descriptors that most of the group agrees are the defining characteristics of leadership and management.

2. Reconvene the class. Draw six columns for each group and list the characteristics for each group. What similarities do you see between the lists? From the results of this exercise, does it appear that what it takes to be a good leader is different depending on the classification? Does it seem that the characteristics for leaders differ greatly from those needed for good managers?

ETHICAL **DILEMMA**

Smoking Success

"I've been high since I'm 13," Justin Hartfield observed, admitting that his résumé includes a stint as a high-school marijuana distributor and a member of a group of website hackers.[111] Now in his 30s, Hartfield is a successful entrepreneur and investor. So what if he is dealing in the same venues of his childhood passions—marijuana and websites? He says, "Marijuana is not going to be profitable to make in the long term, it's going to be a dollar a gram. And so someone . . . needs to step in and make it profitable to grow. I'm the best guy to do it." Hartfield envisions himself as the top leader of a newly legalized industry.

Obviously, he has no issue with the ethics of marijuana consumption or distribution. He created Weedmaps .com, a large directory for medical-marijuana users to find accessible doctors and dispensaries, and charges subscribers $295+ per month; his other business through Ghost Group invests in start-up marijuana operations. "I'm doing everything I can in this industry legally that isn't going to throw me in jail," he said.

Hartfield hopes recreational marijuana use is legalized everywhere soon. "I care about the least amount of people suffering under prohibition," he said, "and secondarily the more money I can make."

Questions

1. Hartfield is a leader in his industry, and he hopes to sell the most marijuana possible. Meanwhile, a study published by the National Academy of Sciences indicated that New Zealand teenagers who were heavy marijuana smokers lost up to 8 IQ points. Do you think that as a leader, Hartfield has a responsibility for the health of his customers?

2. How do you think the ethical responsibilities of leaders in this industry compare to those of leaders in, say, the tobacco and alcohol industries?

3. Would you take a leadership role in an organization if you had an ethical issue with its product or service? Why or why not?

CASE INCIDENTS

Leadership Mettle Forged in Battle

In 2008, facing a serious shortage of leadership-ready employees at the store management level, Walmart decided to recruit from the military.[112] The company sent recruiters to military job fairs and hired 150 junior military officers, pairing them with store mentors to learn on the job. The result: Walmart claims that it has been able to bring in world-class leaders who were ready to take over once they had learned the retail business. Other organizations that have heavily recruited from the military in recent years include Home Depot, Shell Canada, and Lowe's.

It is not really surprising to see companies turn to the military for leadership potential. A long tradition of books and seminars advises leaders to think like military leaders, ranging from Sun Tzu to Norman Schwarzkopf. Military veterans do have a variety of valuable skills learned through experience. General David Petraeus notes, "Tell me anywhere in the business world where a 22- or 23-year-old is responsible for 35 or 40 other individuals on missions that involve life and death. . . . They're under enormous scrutiny, on top of everything else. These are pretty formative experiences. It's a bit of a crucible-like experience that they go through." Military leaders are also accustomed to having to make do in less-than-optimal conditions, negotiate across cultures, be highly accountable, and operate under extreme stress.

However, veterans do have to relearn some lessons. Some may not be used to leading someone like an eccentric computer programmer who works strange hours and dresses like a slob, but brings more to the company's bottom line than a conventional employee. Indeed, in some companies, such as Google, there is nothing like the chain of command military leaders are used to. Still, there is an ample supply of battle-tested military leaders ready to report for corporate duty, and many companies are eager to have them.

Questions

1. Do you think leaders in military contexts exhibit the same qualities as organizational leaders? Why or why not?

2. In what ways not mentioned in the case would military leadership lessons *not* apply in the private sector? What might military leaders have to relearn to work in business?

3. Are specific types of work or situations more likely to benefit from the presence of "battle-tested" leaders? List a few examples.

Leadership by Algorithm

Is there one right way to lead?[113] Research suggests not, the methods explored in this chapter text suggest not, and common sense suggests a "one-size-fits-all" approach could be disastrous because organizations exist for diverse purposes and develop unique cultures. Leadership development programs generally teach a best-practices model, but experts suggest that individuals trained in leadership techniques that are contrary to their own natures risk losing the authenticity crucial to effective leadership. A promising path to leadership may thus lie in algorithms.

If you have ever taken a strengths-based assessment such as the Harrison Assessment or Gallup's Clifton StrengthsFinder, you know that surveys aimed at discovering your personality, skills, and preferences result in a personal profile. These tools are helpful, but algorithms can take your leadership development to the next level of personalization and application. They can take the results from each survey you complete, for instance, and use them to create a leadership program that matches your needs and abilities.

As the founder of management coaching organization TMBC and author of *StandOut*, Marcus Buckingham is an expert on creating leadership programs. He recommends the following steps:

Step 1. **Find or develop assessment tools.** These might include a personality component, such as a Big Five inventory test, and will include other tests companies can resource or create according to what leadership characteristics they are seeking to monitor.

Step 2. **Identify the top leaders in the organization and administer tests to them.** This step is not to determine what all the leaders have in common, but to group the top leaders into categories by their similar profiles.

Step 3. **Interview the leaders within each profile category to learn about the techniques they use that work.** Often these will be unique, unscripted, and

revealingly correlated to the strengths in their assessment profiles. Compile the techniques within each profile category.

Step 4. **The results of top leader profile categories and their techniques can be used to create an algorithm, or tailored method, for developing leaders.** Administer the assessment tests to developing leaders and determine their profile categories. The techniques from successful leaders can now be shared with the developing leaders who are most like them because they share the same profile category.

These steps provide a means for successful leaders to pass along to developing leaders techniques that are likely to feel authentic to the developing leaders and that encourage creativity. The techniques can be delivered in an ongoing process as short, personalized, interactive, and readily applicable tips and advice, yielding results no two-week leadership development course could achieve.

Questions

1. If you have participated in leadership development programs, how effective did you find them in (a) teaching you techniques and (b) giving you practical strategies you could use? What could they do better?

2. What are some potential negatives of using Buckingham's approach to leadership development?

3. Would you suggest applying Buckingham's steps to an organization in which you have worked? Why or why not?

FROM CONCEPTS TO SKILLS

Practising to be Charismatic

Not everyone is born charismatic. However, it's possible to develop this skill.

In order to be charismatic in your leadership style, you need to engage in the following behaviours:[114]

1. *Project a powerful, confident, and dynamic presence.* This has both verbal and nonverbal components. Use a captivating and engaging voice tone. Convey confidence. Talk directly to people, maintain direct eye contact, and hold your body posture in a way that says you are sure of yourself. Speak clearly, avoid stammering, and avoid sprinkling your sentences with noncontent phrases such as "ahhh" and "you know."

2. *Articulate an overarching goal.* You need to share a vision for the future, develop an unconventional way of achieving the vision, and have the ability to communicate the vision to others.

   The vision is a clear statement of where you want to go and how you are going to get there. You need to persuade others that the achievement of this vision is in their self-interest.

   You need to look for fresh and radically different approaches to problems. The road to achieving your vision should be seen as novel, but also appropriate to the context.

   Charismatic individuals not only have a vision, but they are also able to get others to buy into it. The real power of Martin Luther King Jr. was not that he had a dream, but that he could articulate it in terms that made it accessible to millions.

3. *Communicate high performance expectations and confidence in others' ability to meet these expectations.* You need to demonstrate your confidence in people by stating ambitious goals for them individually and as a group. You then convey absolute belief that they will achieve their expectations.

4. *Be sensitive to the needs of followers.* Charismatic leaders get to know their followers individually. You need to understand their individual needs and develop intensely personal relationships with each. This is done through encouraging followers to express their points of view, being approachable, genuinely listening to and caring about followers' concerns, and asking questions so that followers can learn what is really important to them.

Practising Skills

You are a manufacturing manager in a large electronics plant.[115] The company's management is always searching for ways to increase efficiency. They recently installed new machines and set up a new simplified work system, but to the surprise of everyone—including you—the expected increase in production was not realized. In fact, production has begun to drop, quality has fallen off, and the number of employee resignations has risen.

You do not think that there is anything wrong with the machines. You have had reports from other companies that are using them, and they confirm your opinion. You have also had representatives from the firm that built the machines go over them, and they report that the machines are operating at peak efficiency.

You know that some aspect of the new work system must be responsible for the change, but you are getting no help from your immediate team members—four first-line supervisors who report to you and who are each in charge of a section—or your supply manager. The drop in production has been variously attributed to poor training of the operators, lack of an adequate system of financial incentives, and poor morale. All of the individuals involved have deep feelings about this issue. Your team does not agree with you or with one another.

This morning you received a phone call from your division manager. He had just received your production figures for the past six months and was calling to express his concern. He indicated that the problem was yours to solve in any way that you think best, but that he would like to know within a week what steps you plan to take.

You share your division manager's concern with the falling productivity and know that your employees are also concerned. Using your knowledge of leadership concepts, which leadership style would you choose? Why?

. . . .

1. Think of a group or team to which you currently belong or of which you have been a part. What type of leadership style did the leader of this group appear to exhibit? Give some specific examples of the types of leadership behaviours he or she used. Evaluate the leadership style. Was it appropriate for the group? Why or why not? What would you have done differently? Why?

2. Observe two sports teams (either college/university or professional— one that you consider successful and the other unsuccessful). What leadership styles appear to be used in these team situations? Give some specific examples of the types of leadership behaviours you observe. How would you evaluate the leadership style? Was it appropriate for the team? Why or why not? To what degree do you think leadership style influenced the team's outcomes?

. . . .

Reinforcing Skills

12 Decision Making, Creativity, and Ethics

TD raised its sales targets and some of its employees felt pressured to meet goals. Can people act ethically while trying to save their jobs?

LEARNING OUTCOMES

After studying this chapter, you should be able to:

1. Contrast the rational model of decision making with bounded rationality and intuition.
2. Describe common decision biases and errors.
3. Contrast the strengths and weaknesses of group decision making.
4. Compare the effectiveness of interacting groups, brainstorming, and the nominal group technique.
5. Define *creativity*, and describe the three-stage model of creativity.
6. Describe the four criteria used in making ethical decisions.

Torontonian / Alamy Stock Photo

I n early 2017, Bev Beaton noticed a new $29.95 charge on her TD Bank statement.[1] When she called for an explanation, she was told that she was in a new account that required her to keep a minimum monthly balance of $5000 in the account. Beaton immediately disputed this change, saying she had not made a request to change her account type. The bank employee she was speaking to told her, "You must have."

Beaton was not alone in finding questionable charges and changes from TD. In spring of 2017, the CBC reported investigated the practice of upselling by TD employees. It heard from hundreds of current and former employees about how sales goals were driving some employees to engage in unethical behaviour. Employees said that sales goals were unreasonable and had tripled during the past three years.

The sales targets put the employees in an ethical bind. As one teller noted, "It's a choice between keeping my job and feeding my family . . . or doing what's right for the customer." Another teller, Dalisha Dyal, who worked at a Vancouver TD for four years, quit because of the pressure. "I was made to feel as if I was committing a huge wrong for looking out for the best interests of my customer over the interests of the bank," she said.

How do managers make decisions about sales targets? What governs employees' decisions about responding to these sales targets? What about the ethics of these decisions? In this chapter, we describe how decisions in organizations are made, as well as how creativity is linked to decision making. We also look at the ethical and socially responsible aspects of decision making. Decision making affects people at all levels of the organization, and it's engaged in by both individuals and groups. Therefore, we also consider the special characteristics of group decision making.

OB IS FOR EVERYONE

- Do people really consider every alternative when making a decision?
- Is it okay to use intuition when making decisions?
- Why is it that we sometimes make bad decisions?
- Why are some people more creative than others?
- How can people make more ethical decisions?

THE BIG IDEA

Decision making can be improved through systematic thinking and an awareness of common biases.

How Should Decisions Be Made?

A **decision** is the choice made from two or more alternatives. Decision making happens at all levels of an organization. Business schools train students to follow rational decision-making models. While models have merit, they don't always describe how people make decisions. There are decision-making errors people commit in addition to the perceptual errors we discussed in Chapter 2.

Knowing how to make decisions is an important part of everyday life. Below we consider various decision-making models that apply to both individual and group choices. (Later in the chapter, we discuss special aspects of group decision making.) We start with the rational decision-making model, which describes decision making in the ideal world, a situation that rarely exists. We then look at alternatives to the rational model, and how decisions actually get made.

① Contrast the rational model of decision making with bounded rationality and intuition.

The Rational Decision-Making Process

We often think that the best decision maker is the **rational** decision maker, who makes consistent, value-maximizing choices within specified constraints.[2] These choices are made following a six-step **rational decision-making model**.[3] Moreover, specific assumptions underlie this model.

The Six-Step Rational Model

The six steps in the rational decision-making model are presented in Exhibit 12-1.

First, the decision maker must *define the problem*. If you calculate your monthly expenses and find you are spending $50 more than your monthly earnings, you have defined a problem. Many poor decisions can be traced to the decision maker overlooking a problem or defining the wrong problem.

The decision maker then needs to *identify the criteria* that are relevant to making the decision. This step brings the decision maker's interests, values, and similar personal preferences into the process, because not all individuals will consider the same factors relevant for any particular decision.

EXHIBIT 12-1 Steps in the Rational Decision-Making Model

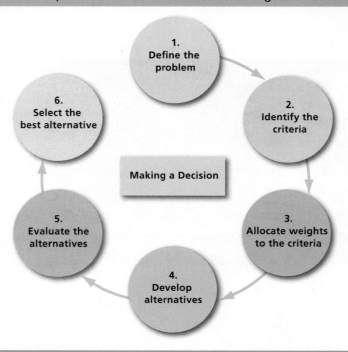

decision The choice made from two or more alternatives.

rational Refers to choices that are consistent and value-maximizing within specified constraints.

rational decision-making model A six-step decision-making model that describes how individuals should behave in order to maximize some outcome.

To understand the types of criteria that might be used to make a decision, consider how Toronto-based Canadian Imperial Bank of Commerce (CIBC) handles the many sponsorship requests it receives each year. When it makes a decision about whether to support a request, the bank takes into account a number of criteria. Specifically, to be eligible for funding, a request must

- Be aligned to the bank's commitment to Kids, Cures, or Community

- Be a Canadian registered charity or non-profit, using funds in Canada

- Have achievements and goals in line with CIBC's overall goals

- Address a community need and provide direct impact to the community served

- Include planned and measurable outcomes that can be evaluated

- Have audited financial statements, principled financial practices, and sustainable funding[4]

If the sponsorship request does not meet these criteria, it is not funded.

Because the criteria identified are rarely all equal in importance, the third step requires the decision maker to *allocate weights to the criteria*.

The fourth step requires the decision maker to *develop alternatives* that could succeed in resolving the problem.

The decision maker then critically *evaluates the alternatives*, using the previously established criteria and weights.

Finally, the decision maker *selects the best alternative* by evaluating each alternative against the weighted criteria and selecting the alternative with the highest total score.

Assumptions of the Model

The rational decision-making model assumes that the decision maker has complete information, is able to identify all the relevant options in an unbiased manner, and chooses the option with the highest utility.[5] Most decisions don't follow the rational model; people are usually content to find an acceptable or reasonable solution to a problem rather than an optimal one. Choices tend to be limited to the neighbourhood of the problem's symptom and the current alternative.

How Do Individuals Actually Make Decisions?

It can be difficult to make a rational decision if someone is pressuring you to make a different decision.[6] One TD teller on sick leave noted that her manager stood behind her three times a day to oversee her work. "They just really stress you out and say, 'You're not doing good. I need you to do double the amount you've been doing.' I couldn't sleep. I'd be thinking . . . 'What can I do tomorrow to try and get sales?'"

Another teller reported to CBC that she was put on a Performance Improvement Plan because she was falling below the sales targets. The plan involved coaching, and could result in discipline if her sales didn't increase. The pressure was so great that "I have invested clients' savings into funds which were not suitable, because of the SR [sales revenue] pressure," she said. "That's very difficult to admit. I didn't do this lightly."

The bank has a lot of information about its customers. When a customer goes to his or her branch and interacts with the teller, even for something as simple as to make a deposit, the computer screen in front of the teller makes suggestions about what products could be sold to the customer. This adds to the pressure tellers feel. Many of the longer-term employees did not envision a job as a sales clerk when they first started as tellers. Their fear of losing their jobs affects them on a daily basis.

What sorts of perceptual biases might affect the decisions people make?

CAREER OBJECTIVES

How Can I Make My Job Better?

Honestly, I hate my job. But there are reasons I should stay: This is my first job out of college, it pays pretty well, and it will establish my career. Is there any hope, or am I doomed until I quit?

—Taylor

Dear Taylor:

You're not doomed! You can work on your attitude to either improve your experience or find a positive perspective. In other words, if you can turn "I hate my job" into "this is what I'm doing to make my situation better," your job satisfaction is likely to improve. Try this:

- *Write down everything you hate about your job, but wait until you have a few days off so you can get a more objective viewpoint.* Be specific. Keep asking yourself why, as in, "Why do I dislike my office mate?" Also, consider your history: Was the job always a problem, or have circumstances changed?
- *Now write down everything you like about the job.* Again, be specific. Think about the environment, the people, and the work separately.

Find something positive, even if it's just the coffee in the break room.

- *Compare your lists for clues about your attitude and job satisfaction.* Look for mentions of the work or the people. Job satisfaction is generally more strongly related to how interesting your work is than it is to other factors. People, especially your supervisor, are important to your attitude toward work as well.
- *Read your lists aloud to a few trusted friends (you don't want to rant about your boss with your co-worker).* Ask them to help process your grievances. Are there deal-breakers like harassment?
- *Decide whether you can talk with your manager about this.* According to Roy L. Cohen, author of *The Wall Street Professional's Survival Guide*, "consider whether how you're being treated is unique to you or shared by your colleagues." If everyone has the same problem, especially if the problem is the boss, you probably should not approach your manager. But changes can be made in most situations.

Based on the sources of your grievances and your ability to make changes in the workplace, you may choose to address the issues, or develop skills for your next job. Meanwhile, don't sabotage yourself with sloppy performance and complaints. Instead, look for positive reinforcement, join a professional organization, or volunteer. Happy employees are healthier. You deserve to be one of them.

Sources: "Employee Engagement," *Workforce Management* (February 2013): 19; A. Hurst, "Being 'Good' Isn't the Only Way to Go," *New York Times,* April 20, 2014, 4; R. E. Silverman, "Work as Labor or Love?" *Wall Street Journal,* October 18, 2012, D3; H. J. Smith, T. F. Pettigrew, G. M. Pippin, and S. Bialosiewicz, "Relative Deprivation: A Theoretical and Meta-Analytic Review," *Personality and Social Psychology Review* 16 (2012): 203–32; and A. Tugend, "Survival Skills for a Job You Detest," *Wall Street Journal,* April 7, 2012, B5.

Most decisions in the real world don't follow the rational model. As one expert in decision making has concluded, "Most significant decisions are made by judgment, rather than by a defined prescriptive model."[7] What is more, people are remarkably unaware of making suboptimal decisions.[8]

In the following sections, we indicate areas where the reality of decision making conflicts with the rational model.[9] None of these ways of making decisions should be considered *irrational*; they simply depart from the rational model when information is unavailable or too costly to collect.

Bounded Rationality in Considering Alternatives

Our limited information-processing capability makes it impossible to assimilate all the information necessary to optimize decision making, even if the information is readily obtainable.[10] Many problems don't have an optimal solution because they are too complicated to fit the rational decision-making model, so people *satisfice*;

they seek solutions that are satisfactory and sufficient. We tend to reduce complex problems to a level we can readily understand.

When you considered which university or college to attend, did you look at *every* workable alternative? Did you carefully identify all the criteria that were important in your decision? Did you evaluate each alternative against the criteria in order to find the optimum school? The answer to these questions is probably no. But don't feel bad, because few people selected their educational institution this way.

> Do people really consider every alternative when making a decision?

Because the human mind cannot formulate and solve complex problems with full rationality, we operate within the confines of **bounded rationality**. We construct simplified models that extract the essential features from problems without capturing all their complexity. We can then behave rationally within the limits of the simple model.

How does bounded rationality work for the typical individual? Once we have identified a problem, we begin to search for criteria and alternatives. But the criteria are unlikely to be exhaustive. We identify alternatives that are highly visible and that usually represent familiar criteria and tried-and-true solutions. Next, we begin reviewing the alternatives, focusing on choices that differ little from the current state until we identify one that is "good enough"—that meets an acceptable level of performance. That ends our search. So the solution represents a **satisficing** choice—the first *acceptable* one we encounter—rather than an optimal one.

Satisficing is not always bad—a simple process may frequently be more sensible than the traditional rational decision-making model.[11] To use the rational model, you need to gather a great deal of information about all the options, compute applicable weights, and then calculate values across a huge number of criteria. All these processes can cost time, energy, and money. If there are many unknown weights and preferences, the fully rational model may not be any more accurate than a best guess. Sometimes a

Akio Kon/Bloomberg/Getty Images

Nintendo president Satoru Iwata (right) and DeNA president Isao Moriyasu operated within the confines of bounded rationality in deciding to form an alliance to develop and operate new game applications for mobile devices. The alliance brings Nintendo's games and characters to the mobile user market and strengthens DeNA's mobile gaming business.

bounded rationality Limitations on a person's ability to interpret, process, and act on information.

satisficing To provide a solution that is both satisfactory and sufficient.

fast-and-frugal process of solving problems might be your best option. Returning to your college or university choice, would it be best to fly around the country to visit dozens of potential campuses and pay application fees for all? It might be smarter to satisfice by finding a few colleges or universities that match most of your preferences and then focus your attention on differentiating among those.

Intuition

Perhaps the least rational way of making decisions is **intuitive decision making**, an unconscious process created from distilled experience.[12] Intuitive decision making occurs outside conscious thought; relies on holistic associations, or links between disparate pieces of information; is fast; and is affectively charged, meaning that it engages the emotions.[13]

While intuition is not rational, it's not necessarily wrong. Nor does it always contradict rational analysis; rather, the two can complement each other. Intuition can be a powerful force in decision making. Intuition is complex and based on years of experience and learning. *OB in the Street* shows how intuition applies to grand master chess players.

> Is it okay to use intuition when making decisions?

OB IN THE STREET

Intuition Comes to the Chessboard

Can intuition really help you win a chess game?   Apparently so.[14] Novice chess players and grand masters were shown an actual, but unfamiliar, chess game with about 25 pieces on the board. After 5 or 10 seconds, the pieces were removed, and each subject was asked to reconstruct the pieces by position. On average, the grand master could put 23 or 24 pieces in their correct squares, while the novice was able to replace only 6. Then the exercise was changed. This time, the pieces were placed randomly on the board. Again, the novice got only about 6 correct, but so did the grand master! The second exercise demonstrated that the grand master did not have a better memory than the novice. What the grand master *did* have was the ability, based on the experience of having played thousands of chess games, to recognize patterns and clusters of pieces that occur on chessboards in the course of games. Studies also show that chess professionals can play 50 or more games simultaneously, making decisions in seconds, and exhibit only a moderately lower level of skill than when playing one game under tournament conditions, where decisions take half an hour or longer. The expert's experience allows him or her to recognize the pattern in a situation and draw on previously learned information associated with that pattern to arrive at a decision quickly. The result is that the intuitive decision maker can decide rapidly based on what appears to be very limited information. ....

As the example of the chess players shows, those who use intuition effectively often rely on their experiences to help guide and assess their intuitions. That may be why senior managers are more likely to turn to intuition when they are lacking full information, as *Focus on Research* shows.

Does intuition contribute to effective decision making? Researchers are divided, but most experts are skeptical, in part because intuition is hard to measure and analyze. A recent study that examined people's ability to "use their gut" to make decisions found

intuitive decision making An unconscious process created out of a person's many experiences.

FOCUS ON RESEARCH
Putting Intuition to Work in the Workplace

How do senior managers use intuition in their decision making? A study of 57 Australian senior executives who make marketing sponsorship decisions found that almost all of them used intuition to help guide their decisions at least some of the time.[15] Organizations that placed a high value on trust when selecting sponsorship opportunities were more likely to have managers who based their decisions on intuition. Not surprisingly, managers at organizations with highly formalized decision-making processes reported less use of intuition, although even they reported using it moderately frequently. Managers were more likely to rely on their intuition when the factors under consideration were vague or complex, or the benefits of sponsorship were largely nonmonetary and intangible. Uncertainty in the environment, it seems, increased their reliance on "gut feel." While intuition can help us make better decisions if we have the appropriate tacit knowledge, it's worthwhile to double-check to ensure that perceptual errors are not biasing our thought processes. ....

that not everyone's gut is reliable. For some, the physiological feeling that one associates with intuition works, but for others it does not.[16] Probably the best advice from one expert is this: "Intuition can be very useful as a way of setting up a hypothesis but is unacceptable as 'proof.'"[17] Use hunches based on experience to speculate, yes, but always make sure to test those hunches with objective data and rational analysis.

As you can see, the more we use objective processes for decision making, the more likely we are to correct some of the problems with our perceptual process. Just as there are biases and errors in the perception process, it stands to reason there are identifiable biases and errors in our decision making, which we will outline next.

Judgment Shortcuts

Decision makers engage in bounded rationality, but they also allow systematic biases and errors to creep into their judgments.[18] To minimize effort and avoid trade-offs, people tend to rely too heavily on experience, impulses, gut feelings, and convenient rules of thumb. Shortcuts can distort rationality, as *OB in the Street* shows.

> Why is it that we sometimes make bad decisions?

2 Describe common decision biases and errors.

OB IN THE STREET
Penalty Kick Decisions

Should you stand still or leap into action? This is the classic question facing a goalie in a faceoff against a midfielder for a penalty kick.[19] Ofer H. Azar, a lecturer in the School of Management at Ben-Gurion University in Israel, finds that goalies often make the wrong decision.

Why? The goalie tries to anticipate where the ball will go after the kick. There is only a split second to do anything after the kick, so anticipating and acting seem like a good decision.

Azar became interested in studying goalie behaviour after realizing that the "incentives are huge" for the goalie to get it right. "Goalkeepers face penalty kicks regularly, so they are not only high-motivated decision makers, but also very experienced ones," he explains. That said, 80 percent of penalty kicks score, so goalies are in a difficult situation at that instant the kick goes off.

Azar's study found that goalies rarely stayed in the centre of the net as the ball was fired (just 6.3 percent of the time). But staying in the centre is actually the best strategy. Goalies halted penalty kicks when staying in the centre 33.3 percent of the time. They were successful only 14.2 percent of the time when they moved left and only 12.6 percent of the time when they moved right.

Azar argues that the results show that there is a "bias for action," explaining that goalies think they will feel worse if they do *nothing* and miss, than if they do *something* and miss. This bias then clouds their judgment, encouraging them to move to one side or the other, rather than just staying in the centre, where the odds are actually more in their favour. ....

In what follows, we discuss some of the most common judgment shortcuts to alert you to mistakes that are often made when making decisions.

Overconfidence Bias

We tend to be overconfident about our abilities and the abilities of others; also, we are usually not aware of this bias.[20] It's been said that "no problem in judgment and decision making is more prevalent and more potentially catastrophic than overconfidence."[21]

When we are given factual questions and asked to judge the probability that our answers are correct, we tend to be overly optimistic. This is known as **overconfidence bias**. In a study of confidence intervals (educated guesses about some characteristic of a population), when people said they were 90 percent confident that their answers were correct, their answers were correct only about 50 percent of the time—and experts were no more accurate in their estimation of confidence intervals than were novices.[22]

Individuals whose intellectual and interpersonal abilities are *weakest* are most likely to overestimate their performance and ability.[23] Also, a negative relationship exists between entrepreneurs' optimism and performance of their new ventures: The more optimistic, the less successful.[24] The tendency to be too confident about their ideas might keep some from planning how to avoid problems that arise.

Investor overconfidence operates in a variety of ways.[25] Finance professor Terrance Odean says, "People think they know more than they do, and it costs them." Investors, especially novices, overestimate not just their skill in processing information, but also the quality of the information. Most investors will do only as well as or just slightly better than the market.

Anchoring Bias

The **anchoring bias** is a tendency to fixate on initial information and fail to adequately adjust for subsequent information.[26] It occurs because the mind gives a disproportionate amount of emphasis to the first information it receives.[27] Anchors are widely used by people in professions where persuasion skills are important—such as advertising, management, politics, real estate, and law.

Any time a negotiation takes place, so does anchoring. As soon as someone states a number, your ability to ignore that number has been compromised. For instance, when a prospective employer asks how much you were making in your prior job, your answer typically anchors the employer's offer. You may want to keep this in mind when you negotiate your salary, but remember to set the anchor only as high as you realistically can. The more precise your anchor, the smaller the adjustment. Some research suggests that people think of making an adjustment after an anchor is set as rounding off a number. If you suggest a salary of $55 000, your boss will consider $50 000 to $60 000 a reasonable range for negotiation, but if you mention $55 650, your boss is more likely to consider $55 000 to $56 000 the range of likely values for negotiation.[28]

overconfidence bias Error in judgment that arises from being far too optimistic about one's own performance.

anchoring bias A tendency to fixate on initial information, from which one then fails to adequately adjust for subsequent information.

Confirmation Bias

The rational decision-making process assumes that we objectively gather information. But we don't. We *selectively* gather it. The **confirmation bias** represents a case of selective perception. We seek out information that reaffirms our past choices, and we discount information that contradicts them.[29] We also tend to accept at face value information that confirms our preconceived views, while we are skeptical of information that challenges these views. We even tend to seek out sources most likely to tell us what we want to hear, and give too much weight to supporting information and too little to contradictory information.[30] Fortunately, those who feel there is a strong need to be accurate in making a decision are less prone to confirmation bias.

Availability Bias

The **availability bias** is the tendency for people to base their judgments on readily available information. A combination of readily available information and our previous direct experience with similar information has a particularly strong impact on our decision making. Events that evoke emotions, that are particularly vivid, or that have occurred more recently tend to be more available in our memory. As a result, we tend to overestimate unlikely events, such as being in an airplane crash, suffering complications from medical treatment, or getting fired.[31] The availability bias can also explain why managers, when doing annual performance appraisals, tend to give more weight to the recent behaviour of an employee than to that of six or nine months ago.

Escalation of Commitment

Some decision makers escalate commitment to a failing course of action.[32] **Escalation of commitment** refers to staying with a decision even when there is clear evidence that it's wrong. For example, a friend has been dating someone for several years. Although she admits that things are not going well, she is determined to marry him anyway. Her justification: "I have a lot invested in the relationship!"

When is escalation of commitment most likely to occur? Evidence indicates that it tends to occur when individuals view themselves as responsible for the outcome. The fear of personal failure even biases the way we search for and evaluate information so that we choose only information that supports our dedication.[33]

It does not appear to matter whether we chose the failing course of action or it was assigned to us—we feel responsible and escalate commitment in either case. Also, the sharing of decision-making authority—as when others review the choice we made—can lead to higher escalation of commitment.[34] Finally, awareness of sunk costs associated with the decision reduces escalation of commitment when individuals feel responsible (it gives them an "escape clause").[35]

We usually think of escalation of commitment as ungrounded. However, persistence in the face of failure is responsible for a great many of history's greatest feats, the building of the Pyramids, the Great Wall of China, the Panama Canal, and the Empire State Building among them. Researchers suggest a balanced approach includes frequent evaluation of the spent costs and whether the next step is worth the anticipated costs.[36] What we want to combat is thus the tendency to *automatically* escalate commitment.

Randomness Error

Most of us like to think we have some control over our world and our destiny. Our tendency to believe we can predict the outcome of random events is the **randomness error**.

Decision making suffers when we try to create meaning in random events, particularly when we turn imaginary patterns into superstitions.[37] These can be completely contrived, such as "I never make important decisions on Friday the 13th." They can also evolve from a certain pattern of behaviour that has been reinforced previously. For example, Mikaël Kingsbury, a world champion in moguls who won a silver medal at the Sochi Olympics while representing Canada, wears the same T-shirt under his ski

confirmation bias The tendency to seek out information that reaffirms past choices and to discount information that contradicts past judgments.

availability bias The tendency for people to base their judgments on information that is readily available to them rather than complete data.

escalation of commitment An increased commitment to a previous decision despite negative information.

randomness error The tendency of individuals to believe that they can predict the outcome of random events.

OB IN ACTION

Reducing Biases and Errors in Decision Making

→ **Focus on goals.** Clear goals make decision making easier and help you eliminate options that are inconsistent with your interests.

→ **Look for information that disconfirms your beliefs.** When we deliberately consider various ways we could be wrong, we challenge our tendencies to think we are smarter than we actually are.

→ **Don't create meaning** out of random events. Ask yourself if patterns can be meaningfully explained or whether they are merely coincidence. Don't attempt to create meaning out of coincidence.

→ **Increase** your **options.** The more alternatives you can generate, and the more diverse those alternatives, the greater your chance of finding an outstanding one.[38]

clothing at every competition. The T-shirt says "It's good to be the King." He wore it the first time he won a medal in a World Cup event, and then started wearing it to every major competition. "Even if I do badly, it's still got some magic," he said.[39] Decisions based on random occurrences can handicap us when they affect our judgment or bias our major decisions.

Risk Aversion

Mathematically, we should find a 50–50 flip of a coin for $100 to be worth as much as a sure promise of $50. After all, the expected value of the gamble over a number of trials is $50. However, nearly everyone but committed gamblers would rather have the sure thing than a risky prospect.[40] For many people, a 50–50 flip of a coin even for $200 might not be worth as much as a sure promise of $50, even though the gamble is mathematically worth twice as much! This tendency to prefer a sure thing over a risky outcome is **risk aversion**.

Risk aversion has important implications. First, to offset the risks inherent in a commission-based wage, companies may pay commissioned employees considerably more than they do those on straight salaries. Second, risk-averse employees will stick with the established way of doing their jobs rather than take a chance on innovative methods. Continuing with a strategy that has worked in the past minimizes risk, but it will lead to stagnation. Third, ambitious people with power that can be taken away (most managers) appear to be especially risk averse, perhaps because they don't want to gamble everything they have worked so hard to achieve.[41] CEOs at risk of dismissal are also exceptionally risk averse, even when a riskier investment strategy is in their firms' best interests.[42]

Risk preference is sometimes reversed: People take chances when trying to prevent a negative outcome.[43] They may thus risk losing a lot of money at trial rather than settle for less out of court. Stressful situations can make risk preferences stronger. People under stress will more likely engage in risk-seeking behaviour to avoid negative outcomes, and risk-averse behaviour seeking positive outcomes.[44]

Hindsight Bias

The **hindsight bias** is the tendency to believe falsely, after the outcome of an event is actually known, that we could have accurately predicted that outcome.[45] When we have accurate feedback on the outcome, we seem to be pretty good at concluding that it was obvious.

For instance, the original home video rental industry, renting movies at brick-and-mortar stores, collapsed as online distribution outlets ate away at the market.[46] Some have suggested that if rental companies like Blockbuster had leveraged their brand to offer online streaming and kiosks, they could have avoided failure. While that seems obvious now in hindsight, tempting us to think we would have predicted it, many experts failed to predict industry trends in advance. Though criticisms of decision makers may have merit, as Malcolm Gladwell, author of *Blink* and *The Tipping Point*, writes, "What is clear in hindsight is rarely clear before the fact."[47]

We are all susceptible to biases like hindsight bias, but are we all susceptible to the same degree? It is not likely. Our individual differences play a significant role in our decision-making processes, while our organizations constrain the range of our available decision choices.

OB in Action—Reducing Biases and Errors in Decision Making provides you with some ideas for improving your decision making.

risk aversion The tendency to prefer a sure gain of a moderate amount over a riskier outcome, even if the riskier outcome might have a higher expected payoff.

hindsight bias The tendency to believe falsely, after an outcome of an event is actually known, that one could have accurately predicted that outcome.

Group Decision Making

The belief—characterized by juries—that two heads are better than one has long been accepted as a basic component of North American and many other countries' legal systems. Many decisions in organizations are made by groups, teams, or committees. In this section, we review group decision making and compare it with individual decision making.

3 Contrast the strengths and weaknesses of group decision making.

Groups vs. the Individual

Decision-making groups may be widely used in organizations, but are group decisions preferable to those made by an individual alone? The answer to this depends on a number of factors we consider below. See Exhibit 12-2 for a summary of our major points. *Point/Counterpoint* on page 443 also considers whether people are more creative when they work alone or with others.

Strengths of Group Decision Making

Groups generate *more complete information and knowledge*. By combining the resources of several individuals, groups bring more input into the decision-making process. They offer *increased diversity of views*, which opens up the opportunity to consider more approaches and alternatives. Finally, groups lead to *increased acceptance of a solution*. Group members who participate in making a decision are likely to support it enthusiastically and encourage others to accept it later.

Weaknesses of Group Decision Making

Group decisions are *time-consuming* because groups typically take more time to reach a solution. There are *conformity pressures*. The desire by group members to be accepted and considered an asset to the group can result in squashing any overt disagreement. Group discussion can be *dominated by one or a few members*. If they are low- and medium-ability members, the group's overall effectiveness will suffer. Finally, group decisions suffer from *ambiguous responsibility*. In an individual decision, it's clear who is accountable for the final outcome. In a group decision, the responsibility of any single member is watered down.

Effectiveness and Efficiency

Whether groups are more effective than individuals depends on how you define effectiveness. Group decisions are generally more *accurate* than the decisions of the average individual in a group, but they are less accurate than the judgments of the most accurate group member.[48] If decision effectiveness is defined in terms of *speed*, individuals are superior. If *creativity* is important, groups tend to be more effective than individuals. If effectiveness means the degree of *acceptance* the final solution achieves, the nod again goes to the group.[49]

But we cannot consider effectiveness without also assessing efficiency. With few exceptions, group decision making consumes more work hours than having an

EXHIBIT 12-2 Group vs. Individual Decision Making

Criteria of Effectiveness	Groups	Individuals
More complete information	✓	
Diversity of views	✓	
Decision quality	✓	
Accuracy	✓	
Creativity	✓	
Degree of acceptance	✓	
Speed		✓
Efficiency		✓

individual tackle the same problem. The exceptions tend to be the instances in which, to achieve comparable quantities of diverse input, the single decision maker must spend a great deal of time reviewing files and talking to other people. In deciding whether to use groups, then, consideration should be given to assessing whether increases in effectiveness are more than enough to offset the reductions in efficiency. The *Experiential Exercise* on pages 444–446 gives you an opportunity to assess the effectiveness and efficiency of group decision making vs. individual decision making.

In summary, groups are an excellent vehicle for performing many steps in the decision-making process and offer both breadth and depth of input for information gathering. If group members have diverse backgrounds, the alternatives generated should be more extensive and the analysis more critical. When the final solution is agreed on, there are more people in a group decision to support and implement it. These pluses, however, may be more than offset by the time consumed by group decisions, the internal conflicts they create, and the pressures they generate toward conformity. We must be careful to define the types of conflicts, however. Research in South Korea indicates that group conflicts about tasks may increase group performance, while conflicts in relationships may decrease performance.[50] In some cases, therefore, we can expect individuals to make better decisions than groups.

Groupthink and Groupshift

Two by-products of group decision making, groupthink and groupshift, can affect the group's ability to appraise alternatives objectively and achieve high-quality solutions.

Groupthink

Have you ever felt like speaking up in a meeting, classroom, or informal group, but decided against it? One reason may have been shyness. On the other hand, you may have been a victim of **groupthink**. Groupthink relates to norms. It describes situations in which group pressures for conformity deter the group from critically appraising unusual, minority, or unpopular views. Groupthink attacks many groups and can dramatically hinder their performance.

We have all seen the symptoms of the groupthink phenomenon:[51]

- *Illusion of invulnerability.* Group members become overconfident among themselves, allowing them to take extraordinary risks.

- *Assumption of morality.* Group members believe highly in the moral rightness of the group's objectives and do not feel the need to debate the ethics of their actions.

- *Rationalized resistance.* Group members rationalize any resistance to the assumptions they have made. No matter how strongly the evidence may contradict their basic assumptions, members behave so as to reinforce those assumptions continually.

- *Peer pressure.* Group members apply direct pressure on those who momentarily express doubts about any of the group's shared views or who question the validity of arguments supporting the alternative favoured by the majority.

- *Minimized doubts.* Those group members who have doubts or hold differing points of view seek to avoid deviating from what appears to be group consensus by keeping silent about misgivings and even minimizing to themselves the importance of their doubts.

- *Illusion of unanimity.* If someone does not speak, it's assumed that he or she is in full agreement. In other words, abstention becomes viewed as a yes vote.

groupthink A phenomenon in which group pressures for conformity prevent the group from critically appraising unusual, minority, or unpopular views.

Groupthink can also take place among strategic decision-makers, as *OB in the Street* shows.

OB IN THE STREET

Groupthink at Target Canada

Why did a large, experienced retailer make so many basic errors when launching its Canadian outlets? In 2013, US-based Target brought its mass-merchandise stores to Canada, opening over 100 stores in under a year.[52] Things did not go well over 2013 and 2014. The stores drastically underperformed, with customers complaining about poor selection, high prices, and empty store shelves. The retailer admits to poor planning, failing to research the prices charged by its Canadian competitors, and not making sure its supply chains would work properly.

Even with these difficulties, Target Chief Financial Officer John Mulligan said the retailer was in Canada for the long haul. Mulligan admitted that "we bit off way too much, too early. In retrospect we should've probably opened five to 10 stores [in 2013]—refined the operations, refined the supply chain, the technology, got our store teams trained. But again, that's all hindsight, we are where we are right now and we're focused on moving forward to fix this for our guests." Despite this statement, in 2015 the US parent company's CEO, Brian Cornell, announced that Target was pulling out of Canada and closing all 133 stores across the country.

Why did Target's Canadian management team choose to continue to open even more new stores in 2014 after its first stores opened with a strategy that was highly problematic? Groupthink is part of the answer. As one former employee stated: "[Key team members from the United States] were not guides or resources, as much as they were obstacles to progress. If it didn't come from/work in the U.S. then it was not a discussion point." The same employee added: "To . . . assume that the same 'playbook' used in the U.S. would work in Canada was incredible. The inability of the [key team members from the United States] to think and work beyond this led to us attempting to Xerox the U.S. store culture (for Team Members and Guests) instead of develop one that is tailored to Canadian tastes and attitudes." . . . .

Groupthink appears to be closely aligned with the conclusions psychologist Solomon Asch drew in his experiments with a lone dissenter, which we described in Chapter 6. Individuals who hold a position that is different from that of the dominant majority are under pressure to suppress, withhold, or modify their true feelings and beliefs. As members of a group, we find it more pleasant to be in agreement—to be a positive part of the group—than to be a disruptive force, even if disruption is necessary to improve the effectiveness of the group's decisions. Groups that are more focused on performance than on learning are especially likely to fall victim to groupthink and to suppress the opinions of those who do not agree with the majority.[53]

Do all groups suffer from groupthink? No. It seems to occur most often where there is a clear group identity; where members hold a positive image of their group, which they want to protect; and where the group perceives a collective threat to its positive image.[54] One study showed that those influenced by groupthink were more confident about their course of action early on.[55] Groups that believe too strongly in the correctness of their course of action are more likely to suppress dissent and encourage conformity than are groups that are more skeptical about their course of action.

What can managers do to minimize groupthink?[56]

- *Monitor group size.* People grow more intimidated and hesitant as group size increases, and, although there is no magic number that will eliminate group-think, individuals are likely to feel less personal responsibility when groups get larger than about 10.

- *Encourage group leaders to play an impartial role.* Leaders should actively seek input from all members and avoid expressing their own opinions, especially in the early stages of deliberation.

- *Appoint one group member to play the role of devil's advocate.* This member's role is to overtly challenge the majority position and offer divergent perspectives.

- *Stimulate active discussion of diverse alternatives to encourage dissenting views and more objective evaluations.* Group members might delay discussion of possible gains so they can first talk about the dangers or risks inherent in a decision. Requiring members to first focus on the negatives of an alternative makes the group less likely to stifle dissenting views and more likely to gain an objective evaluation.

Groupshift or Group Polarization

There are differences between group decisions and the individual decisions of group members.[57] In groups, discussion leads members toward a more extreme view of the position they already held. Conservative types become more cautious, and aggressive types take on more risk. Participants have engaged in **groupshift**, a phenomenon in which the initial positions of individual group members become exaggerated because of the interactions of the group.

Group polarization is a special type of groupthink. The group's decision reflects the dominant decision-making norm—toward greater caution or more risk—that develops during discussion.

The shift toward polarization has several explanations.[58] It has been argued, for instance, that the discussion makes members more comfortable with one another, and, thus, more willing to express extreme versions of their original positions. Another argument is that the group diffuses responsibility. Group decisions free any single member from accountability for the group's final choice, so greater risks can be taken.

Wenn Us/Alamy

groupshift A phenomenon in which the initial positions of individual group members become exaggerated because of the interactions of the group.

When Volkswagen was caught in a scandal for falsifying emission data, both groupthink and autocratic leadership may have been at play. One author describing the situation said, "Employees who had reservations about the illegal software—and there were some—had no place to turn."[59] Senior management refused to listen to engineers who complained.

It's also likely that people take on extreme positions because they want to demonstrate how different they are from the outgroup.[60] People on the fringes of political or social movements take on ever-more extreme positions just to prove they are really committed to the cause, whereas those who are more cautious tend to take moderate positions to demonstrate how reasonable they are.

How should you use the findings on groupshift? Recognize that group decisions exaggerate the initial position of the individual members, that the shift has been shown more often to be toward greater risk, and that the direction in which a group will shift is a function of the members' prediscussion inclinations. *Case Incident—If Two Heads Are Better Than One, Are Four Even Better?* on page 447 considers the impact of groupshift on investment decisions.

Group Decision-Making Techniques

Groups can use a variety of techniques to make decisions. We outline three of them below.

4 Compare the effectiveness of interacting groups, brainstorming, and the nominal group technique.

Interacting Groups

The most common form of group decision making takes place in **interacting groups**. Members meet face to face and rely on both verbal and nonverbal interaction to communicate with one another. But as our discussion of groupthink demonstrated, interacting groups often censor themselves and pressure individual members toward conformity of opinion. *Brainstorming* and the *nominal group technique* can reduce many of the problems inherent in the traditional interacting group.

Brainstorming

Brainstorming can overcome the pressures for conformity that dampen creativity[61] by encouraging any and all alternatives while withholding criticism.

In a typical brainstorming session, 6 to 12 people sit around a table. The group leader states the problem in a clear manner so that all participants understand it. Members then "free-wheel" as many alternatives as they can in a given period of time. To encourage group members to "think the unusual," no criticism is allowed, and all ideas are recorded for later discussion and analysis.

Brainstorming may indeed generate ideas—but not in a very efficient manner. Research consistently shows that individuals working alone generate more ideas than a group in a brainstorming session.[62] One reason for this is "production blocking." When people generate ideas in a group, many are talking at once, which blocks the individuals' thought process and eventually impedes the sharing of ideas.[63]

Nominal Group Technique

The **nominal group technique** may be more effective. This technique restricts discussion and interpersonal communication during the decision-making process, hence the term *nominal* (which means "in name only"). Group members are all physically present, as in a traditional committee meeting, but they operate independently. Specifically, a problem is presented and then the group takes the following steps:

- Before any discussion takes place, each member independently writes down his or her ideas on the problem.
- After this silent period, each member presents one idea to the group. No discussion takes place until all ideas have been recorded.
- The group discusses the ideas for clarity and evaluates them.
- Each group member silently and independently ranks the ideas. The idea with the highest aggregate ranking determines the final decision.

interacting groups Typical groups in which members interact with one another face to face.

brainstorming An idea-generation process that specifically encourages any and all alternatives, while withholding any criticism of those alternatives.

nominal group technique A group decision-making method in which individual members meet face to face to pool their judgments in a systematic but independent fashion.

EXHIBIT 12-3 Nominal Group Technique

	Individual Activity	Group Activity	Individual Activity
Team members receive description of problem.	Individuals silently write down possible solutions.	Individuals take turns describing solutions to each other; group then discusses and evaluates ideas.	Individuals silently rank (or vote on) each solution presented.

The steps of the nominal group technique are illustrated in Exhibit 12-3. The chief advantage of the technique is that it permits the group to meet formally but does not restrict independent thinking. Research generally shows that nominal groups outperform brainstorming groups.[64]

Each of these group decision techniques has its own strengths and weaknesses. The choice depends on what criteria you want to emphasize and the cost-benefit trade-off. As Exhibit 12-4 indicates, an interacting group is good for achieving commitment to a solution, brainstorming develops group cohesiveness, and the nominal group technique is an inexpensive means for generating a large number of ideas.

5 Define *creativity*, and describe the three-stage model of creativity.

Creativity in Organizational Decision Making

Although the rational decision-making model will often improve decisions, a decision maker also needs **creativity**; that is, the ability to produce novel and useful ideas.[65] Novel ideas are different from what has been done before but are appropriate for the problem presented.

Creativity allows the decision maker to fully appraise and understand problems, including seeing problems others cannot see. Such thinking is becoming more important. Although all aspects of organizational behaviour are complex, that is especially true for creativity. To simplify, Exhibit 12-5 provides a **three-stage model of creativity** in organizations. The core of the model is *creative behaviour*, which has both *causes* (predictors of creative behaviour) and *outcomes* (innovation). In this section, we discuss the three stages of creativity, starting with the centre, creative behaviour.

creativity The ability to produce novel and useful ideas.

three-stage model of creativity The proposition that creativity involves three stages: causes (creative potential and creative environment), creative behaviour, and creative outcomes (innovation).

EXHIBIT 12-4 Evaluating Group Effectiveness

Effectiveness Criteria	Type of Group			
	Interacting	Brainstorming	Nominal	Electronic
Number and quality of ideas	Low	Moderate	High	High
Social pressure	High	Low	Moderate	Low
Money costs	Low	Low	Low	High
Speed	Moderate	Moderate	Moderate	Moderate
Task orientation	Low	High	High	High
Potential for interpersonal conflict	High	Low	Moderate	Low
Commitment to solution	High	Not applicable	Moderate	Moderate
Development of group cohesiveness	High	High	Moderate	Low

Source: Based on C. Woodyard, "Toyota Brass Shakeup Aims to Give Regions More Control," *USA Today*, March 6, 2013, www.usatoday.com/story/money/cars/2013/03/06/toyota-shakeup/1966489/.

EXHIBIT 12-5 Three-Stage Model of Creativity in Organizations

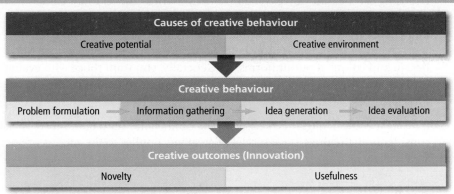

Creative Behaviour

Creative behaviour occurs in four steps, each of which leads to the next:

- *Problem formulation.* Any act of creativity begins with a problem that the behaviour is designed to solve. Thus, **problem formulation** is defined as the stage of creative behaviour in which we identify a problem or an opportunity that requires a solution as yet unknown. For example, Brendan Brazier believed at an early age that a plant-based diet could transform him into a professional athlete, so he set out to prove that by following such a diet. Brazier attributes "clean eating" to his seven-year career as an Ironman triathlete and two-time winner of the Canadian 50-kilometre Ultra Marathon. He is also the formulator of a line of plant-based nutritional products through his company, Vega, as well as a bestselling author.[66]

- *Information gathering.* Given a problem, the solution is rarely directly at hand. We need time to learn more and to process that learning. Thus, **information gathering** is the stage of creative behaviour when knowledge is sought and possible solutions to a problem incubate in an individual's mind. Information gathering leads us to identifying innovation opportunities.[67] Niklas Laninge of Hoa's Tool Shop, a Stockholm-based company that helps organizations become more innovative, argues that creative information gathering means thinking beyond usual routines and comfort zones. For example, have lunch with someone outside your field to discuss the problem. "It's so easy, and you're forced to speak about your business and the things that you want to accomplish in new terms. You can't use buzzwords because people don't know what you mean," Laninge says.[68]

- *Idea generation.* Once we have collected the relevant information, it's time to translate knowledge into ideas. Thus, **idea generation** is the process of creative behaviour in which we develop possible solutions to a problem from relevant information and knowledge. Sometimes we do this alone, when tricks like taking a walk[69] and doodling[70] can jumpstart the process. Increasingly, though, idea generation is collaborative. For example, when NASA engineers developed the idea for landing a spacecraft on Mars, they did so collaboratively. Before coming up with the Curiosity—an SUV-sized rover that lands on Mars from a sky crane—the team spent three days scribbling potential ideas on whiteboards.[71]

- *Idea evaluation.* Finally, it's time to choose from the ideas we have generated. Thus, **idea evaluation** is the process of creative behaviour in which we

---

problem formulation The stage of creative behaviour that involves identifying a problem or an opportunity that requires a solution as yet unknown.

information gathering The stage of creative behaviour when possible solutions to a problem incubate in an individual's mind.

idea generation The process of creative behaviour that involves developing possible solutions to a problem from relevant information and knowledge.

idea evaluation The process of creative behaviour involving the evaluation of potential solutions to problems to identify the best one.

evaluate potential solutions to identify the best one. Sometimes the method of choosing can be innovative. When Dallas Mavericks owner Mark Cuban was unhappy with the basketball team's uniforms, he asked fans to help design and choose the best uniform. Cuban said, "What's the best way to come up with creative ideas? You ask for them. So we are going to crowd source the design and colors of our uniforms."[72] Generally, you want those who evaluate ideas to be different from those who generate them, to eliminate the obvious biases.

Case Incident—The Youngest Female Self-Made Billionaire on pages 446–447 asks you to consider how the three-stage model of creativity applies to the success of Spanx owner Sara Blakely.

Causes of Creative Behaviour

Having defined creative behaviour, the main stage in the three-stage model, we now look back to the causes of creativity: creative potential and creative environment.

> Why are some people more creative than others?

Creative Potential

Is there such a thing as a creative personality? Indeed. While creative genius is rare—whether in science (Stephen Hawking), art (Pablo Picasso), or business (Steve Jobs)— most people have some of the characteristics shared by exceptionally creative people. The more of these characteristics we have, the higher our creative potential. Innovation is one of the top organizational goals for leaders. Consider these facets of potential:

Intelligence and Creativity   Intelligence is related to creativity. Smart people are more creative because they are better at solving complex problems. However, intelligent individuals may also be more creative because they have greater "working memory"; that is, they can recall more information that is related to the task at hand.[73] Along the same lines, recent research in the Netherlands indicates that an individual's high need for cognition (desire to learn) is correlated with greater creativity.[74]

Personality and Creativity   The Big Five personality trait of openness to experience (see Chapter 2) correlates with creativity, probably because open individuals are less conformist in action and more divergent in thinking.[75] Other traits of creative people include proactive personality, self-confidence, risk-taking, tolerance for ambiguity, and perseverance.[76] Hope, self-efficacy (belief in your capabilities), and positive affect also predict an individual's creativity.[77] Furthermore, research in China suggests that people with high core self-evaluations are better able than others to maintain creativity in negative situations.[78] Perhaps counterintuitively, some research supports the "mad genius" theory that some people with mental illness are wildly creative partially due to their psychopathology; history certainly provides examples, such as Vincent Van Gogh, John Forbes Nash, and others. However, the converse isn't true—people who are creative may have less psychopathology as a group than the general population.[79]

Expertise and Creativity   *Expertise* is the foundation for all creative work and thus is the single most important predictor of creative potential. Film writer, producer, and director Quentin Tarantino spent his youth working in a video rental store, where he built up an encyclopedic knowledge of movies. The potential for creativity is enhanced when individuals have abilities, knowledge, proficiencies, and similar expertise to their field of endeavour. For instance, you would not expect someone with minimal knowledge of programming to be very creative as a software engineer. The expertise of others is important, too. People with larger social networks have greater exposure to diverse ideas and informal access to the expertise and resources of others.[80]

Ethics and Creativity   Although creativity is linked to many desirable individual characteristics, it is not correlated with ethicality. People who cheat may actually be more creative than those who behave ethically, according to recent research. It may be that dishonesty and creativity can both stem from a rule-breaking desire.[81]

Creative Environment

Most of us have creative potential we can learn to apply, but as important as creative potential is, by itself it is not enough. We need to be in an environment where creative potential can be realized. What environmental factors affect whether creative potential translates into creative behaviours?

First and perhaps most important is *motivation*. If you are not motivated to be creative, it is unlikely that you will be. Intrinsic motivation, or the desire to work on something because it's interesting, exciting, satisfying, and challenging (discussed in more detail in Chapters 4 and 5), correlates fairly strongly with creative outcomes.[82]

It's also valuable to work in an environment that rewards and recognizes creative work. A study of health care teams found that team creativity translated into innovation only when the climate actively supported innovation.[83] The organization should foster the free flow of ideas, including providing fair and constructive judgment. Freedom from excessive rules encourages creativity; employees should have the freedom to decide what work is to be done and how to do it. One study in China revealed that both structural empowerment (in which the structure of the work unit allows sufficient employee freedom) and psychological empowerment (which lets the individual feel personally enabled to decide) were related to employee creativity.[84] However, research in Slovenia found that creating a competitive climate where achievement at any cost is valued will stymie creativity.[85]

Shahrzad Rafati, founder and CEO of Vancouver-based BroadbandTV, made *Fast Company*'s 2014 Most Creative People in Business 1000 list. When she was still an undergraduate computer science major at UBC, she came up with the idea of taking video uploaded to sites like YouTube and merging it with online advertising opportunities—bringing together both "pirates" and corporate content providers. Her company's MultiChannel Network (MCN) was ranked the third-largest on YouTube in 2014 with more than 1.6 billion monthly views.

You may be wondering about the link between organizational resources and creativity. While it is said that "necessity is the mother of invention," recent research indicates that creativity can be inspired by an abundance of resources as well. It appears that managers greatly affect the outcomes. They may be able to heighten innovation, when resources are limited, by encouraging employees to find resources for their novel ideas, and by giving direct attention to appropriate tools when resources are plentiful.[86] Managers also serve an important bridge role for knowledge transfer. When managers link teams to additional information and resources, radical creativity (introducing creative ideas that break the status quo) is more likely.[87] The weaker ties between team members and manager networks may actually have more impact on creativity than the direct, stronger ties that team members have with their own networks, because the weaker sources provide more divergent thinking.[88]

Good leadership matters to creativity. One study of more than 100 teams working in a large bank revealed that when the leader behaved in a punitive, unsupportive manner, the teams were less creative.[89] By contrast, when leaders are encouraging in tone, run their units in a transparent fashion, and encourage the development of their employees, the individuals they supervise are more creative.[90]

As we learned in Chapter 6, more work today is being done in teams, and many people believe diversity will increase team creativity. Past research has suggested that diverse teams are not more creative. More recently, however, a study of Dutch teams revealed that when team members were explicitly asked to understand and consider the point of view of the other team members (an exercise called perspective-taking), diverse teams *were* more creative than those with less diversity.[91] Leadership might make the difference. One study of 68 Chinese teams reported that diversity was positively related to team creativity only when the team's leader was inspirational and instilled members with confidence.[92]

There are other worthwhile findings regarding creativity. One study in a multinational pharmaceutical company found that teams that comprised members with diverse business functions were more creative when they shared knowledge of one another's areas of expertise.[93] However, if team members have a similar background, creativity may be heightened only when the members are sharing specific, detailed information,[94] since general information may be dismissed by members with the same expertise. As you might expect, newcomers to a team can be a rich source of creative ideas, although they are unfortunately often expected to contribute less early on.[95] Putting individuals who are resistant to change into teams that are supportive of change can increase total creativity,[96] perhaps because of the group's positive influence. Collectively, these studies show that diverse teams *can* be more creative, especially if they are intentionally led.

Creative Outcomes (Innovation)

The final stage in our model of creativity is the outcome. Creative behaviour does not always produce an innovative outcome. An employee might generate a creative idea and never share it. Management might reject a creative solution. Teams might squelch creative behaviours by isolating those who propose different ideas. A 2012 study showed that most people have a bias against accepting creative ideas because ideas create uncertainty. When people feel uncertain, their ability to see any idea as creative is blocked.[97]

We can define *creative outcomes* as ideas or solutions judged to be novel and useful by relevant stakeholders. Novelty itself does not generate a creative outcome if it is not useful. Thus, "off-the-wall" solutions are creative only if they help solve the problem. The usefulness of the solution might be self-evident (for example, the iPad), or it might be considered successful by only the stakeholders initially.[98]

An organization may harvest many creative ideas from its employees and call itself innovative. However, as one expert stated, "Ideas are useless unless used." Soft skills help translate ideas into results. One study found that in a large agribusiness company, creative ideas were most likely to be implemented when an individual was motivated to translate the idea into practice—and had strong networking ability.[99] These studies highlight an important fact: Creative ideas do not implement themselves; translating them into creative outcomes is a social process that requires use of other concepts addressed in this book, including power and politics (Chapter 8), leadership (Chapter 11), and motivation (Chapters 4 and 5).

From Concepts to Skills on pages 448–449 provides suggestions on how you can become more effective at solving problems creatively.

What About Ethics in Decision Making?

> TD's management, in response to the CBC report on the bank's aggressive sales goals, said that all employees are expected to follow the company's code of ethics.[100] TD spokesperson Daria Hill stated that every employee must "act ethically and . . . not allow a focus on business results to come before our focus on customers." Employees report that this makes it difficult to meet sales targets. "I've increased people's lines of credit by a couple thousand dollars, just to get SR [sales revenue] points," said a former teller from a Windsor, Ontario TD branch. Doing this violated the Federal Bank Act.
>
> How does ethics influence decision making?

6 Describe the four criteria used in making ethical decisions.

No contemporary examination of decision making would be complete without the discussion of ethics, because ethical considerations should be an important criterion in organizational decision making. **Ethics** is the study of moral values or principles that guide our behaviour and inform us whether actions are right or wrong. Ethical principles help us "do the right thing." In this section, we present four ways to ethically frame decisions and examine the factors that shape an individual's ethical decision-making behaviour. We also examine ways to encourage more ethical decisions. To learn more about your approach to ethical decision making, see the *Ethical Dilemma* on page 446.

Four Ethical Decision Criteria

An individual can use four criteria in making ethical choices. The first is **utilitarianism**, in which decisions are made solely on the basis of their outcomes, ideally to provide the greatest good for the greatest number.[101] This view dominates business decision making and is consistent with goals such as efficiency, productivity, and high profits. Keep in mind that utilitarianism is not always as objective as it sounds. A recent study indicated that the ethicality of utilitarianism is influenced in ways we don't realize. Participants were given a moral dilemma: The weight of five people bends a footbridge so it is low to some train tracks. A train is about to hit the bridge. The choice is to let all five people perish, or push the one heavy man off the bridge to save four people. In the United States, South Korea, France, and Israel, 20 percent of respondents chose to push the man off the bridge, in Spain, 18 percent, and in Korea, none. These might speak to cultural utilitarian values, but a minor change, asking people to answer in a non-native language they knew, caused more participants to push the man overboard: In one group, 33 percent pushed the man, and in another group 44 percent did.[102] The emotional distance of answering in a non-native language thus seemed to foster a utilitarian viewpoint. It appears that even our view of what we consider pragmatic is changeable.

A second ethical criterion is to make decisions consistent with fundamental liberties and privileges as set forth in documents such as the Canadian Charter of Rights and Freedoms. An emphasis on *rights* in decision making means respecting and protecting the basic rights of individuals, such as the rights to privacy, free speech, and due process. This criterion protects **whistle-blowers**[103] when they report unethical or illegal practices by their organizations to the media or to government agencies, using their right to free speech.

ethics The study of moral values or principles that guide our behaviour and inform us whether actions are right or wrong.

utilitarianism A decision focused on outcomes or consequences that emphasizes the greatest good for the greatest number.

whistle-blowers Individuals who report unethical practices by their employer to outsiders.

A third criterion is to impose and enforce rules fairly and impartially to ensure *justice* or an equitable distribution of benefits and costs.[104] Justice perspectives are sometimes used to justify paying people the same wage for a given job, regardless of performance differences, and using seniority as the primary determinant in making layoff decisions. A focus on justice protects the interests of the underrepresented and less powerful, but it can encourage a sense of entitlement that reduces risk-taking, innovation, and productivity.

A fourth ethical criterion is *care*. The ethics of care can be stated as follows: "The morally correct action is the one that expresses care in protecting the special relationships that individuals have with each other."[105] The care criterion suggests that we should be aware of the needs, desires, and well-being of those to whom we are closely connected. This perspective does remind us of the difficulty of being impartial in all decisions.

To summarize, a focus on *utilitarianism* promotes efficiency and productivity, but can sideline the rights of individuals with minority representation,. The use of *rights* protects individuals but can create a legalistic environment that hinders productivity and efficiency. A focus on *justice* protects the interests of the underrepresented and less powerful, but it can reduce risk-taking, innovation, and productivity.

Decision makers, particularly in for-profit organizations, feel comfortable with utilitarianism. The "best interests" of the organization and stockholders can justify a lot of questionable actions, such as large layoffs. But many critics feel this perspective needs to change. Public concern about individual rights and social justice suggests that managers should develop ethical standards based on nonutilitarian criteria. This presents a challenge because satisfying individual rights and social justice creates far more ambiguities than utilitarian effects on efficiency and profits. However, while raising prices, selling products with questionable effects on consumer health, closing down inefficient plants, laying off large numbers of employees, and moving production overseas to cut costs can be justified in utilitarian terms, there may no longer be a single measure by which good decisions are judged.

Lucas Jackson/Reuters

Murad Al-Katib, president of Regina-based AGT Food and Ingredients Inc., wanted to do good for Syrian refugees. Through his company, he got 700 million meals made from lentils, chickpeas, and wheat into the United Nations Syrian refugee program. For this he won the Oslo Business for Peace Award in 2017.[106]

This is where corporate social responsibility (CSR) comes in to effect a positive change. As we can see by looking at utilitarian ideals, organizations are not motivated to respond equitably when they are looking only at a balance sheet. However, public pressure on organizations to behave responsibly has meant sustainability issues now affect the bottom line: Consumers increasingly choose to purchase goods and services from organizations with effective CSR initiatives, high performers are attracted to work at CSR organizations, governments offer incentives to organizations for sustainability efforts, and so forth. CSR is now beginning to make good business sense, folding ethics into utilitarian computations.

Increasingly, researchers are turning to **behavioural ethics**—an area of study that analyzes how people behave when confronted with ethical dilemmas. Their research tells us that while ethical standards exist collectively in societies and organizations and individually in the form of personal ethics, we do not always follow ethical standards promoted by our organizations, and we sometimes violate our own standards. Our ethical behaviour varies widely from one situation to the next. *Focus on Research* considers why people cheat, and what organizations can do to limit cheating.

FOCUS ON RESEARCH
Why People Cheat

What makes individuals decide to cheat? We all have cheated at something.[107] We could assume that deciding to cheat is a product of cold hard calculus: Is the benefit of cheating worth the cost? Research shows, however, that cheating is less rational than expected. Several 2012 research projects yielded the following insights about how organizations can stem cheating and other unethical behaviour:

- *Cheating happens away from the cash.* One study found that people steal more when they are a couple of steps removed from the cash. For example, one gallery's gift shop was hemorrhaging money, but the reason was that volunteers were helping themselves to merchandise, not the cash drawer. Similarly, when researchers put six packs of Coke and six $1 bills in dorm fridges, every Coke was gone within 72 hours, but none of the cash.
- *Cheating is contagious.* A study of high school students in upper-middle-class communities revealed that among the 93 percent who admitted to cheating, the top reason was the pervasiveness of cheating by others. A recent study of accounting undergraduates revealed that cheating was most likely among students who reported having recently seen cheating and having friends who cheated.
- *Moods affect cheating.* Research shows that people cheat more when they are angry or tired. This insight reveals another positive dividend of trying to reduce negative moods at work.
- *Incentives matter.* Studies suggest that high-stakes outcomes create cheating as an inevitable consequence. Coaches, CEOs, and political leaders should still be held accountable, but it's helpful to understand circumstances in which expectations may seem attainable only by cheating. . . . .

Making Ethical Decisions

How might we increase ethical decision-making in organizations? First, sociologist James Q. Wilson proposed the *broken windows theory*—the idea that decayed and disorderly urban environments may facilitate criminal behaviour because they signal antisocial norms. Although controversial, the theory does fit with behavioural ethics research showing that seemingly superficial aspects of the environment—such as lighting, outward displays of wealth and status, and cleanliness—can affect ethical behaviour in organizations.[108] Managers must first realize that ethical behaviour can be affected by signals;

behavioural ethics Analyzing how people actually behave when confronted with ethical dilemmas.

for example, if signs of status and money are everywhere, an employee may perceive those, rather than ethical standards, to be of the highest importance. Second, managers should encourage conversations about moral issues; they may serve as a reminder and increase ethical decision making. One study found that simply asking business school students to think of an ethical situation had powerful effects when they were making ethical choices later.[109] Finally, we should be aware of our own moral "blind spots"—the tendency to see ourselves as more moral than we are and others as less moral than they are. An environment that encourages open discussions and does not penalize people for coming forward is key to overcoming blind spots and increasing the ethicality of decision making.[110]

> How can people make more ethical decisions?

Behavioural ethics research stresses the importance of culture to ethical decision making. There are few global standards for ethical decision making,[111] as contrasts between Asia and the West illustrate. For example, because bribery is more common in countries such as China, a Canadian working in China might face a dilemma: Should I pay a bribe to secure business if it's an accepted part of that country's culture? Although some companies such as IBM explicitly address this issue, many don't. Without sensitivity to cultural differences as part of the definition of ethical conduct, organizations may encourage unethical conduct without even knowing it.

While the difference between an ethical and unethical decision is not always clear-cut, there are some questions you should consider. Exhibit 12-6 illustrates a decision tree to guide ethical decision making.[112] This tree is built on three of the ethical decision criteria—utilitarianism, rights, and justice—presented earlier. The first question you need to answer addresses self-interest vs. organizational goals.

Hannah Yoon/The Canadian Press

Some retailers refused to carry Ivanka Trump clothes, and Silicon Valley executives have spoken out against Donald Trump. But Ottawa-based Shopify has resisted calls to not allow Breitbart News to use their platform to sell political merchandise. Breitbart had been one of the most outspoken supporters of Donald Trump before the election, and continues to be so. Shopify co-founder Tobias Lütke calls it a free speech matter. "This means protecting the right of organizations to use our platform even if they are unpopular or if we disagree with their premise, as long as they are within the law. That being said, if Breitbart calls us tomorrow and tells us that they are going to switch to another platform, we would be delighted."[113] Lütke's choice shows that ethical decision making is not easy, and different people can make different choices.

EXHIBIT 12-6 Is a Decision Ethical?

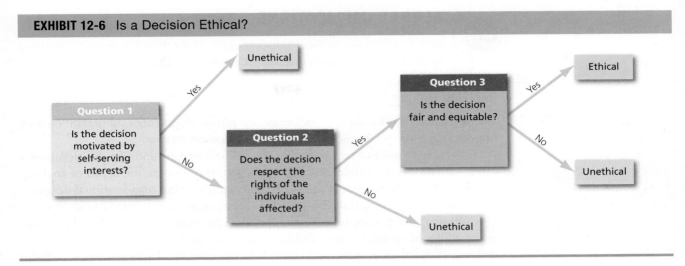

The second question concerns the rights of other parties. If the decision violates the rights of someone else (the person's right to privacy, for instance), then the decision is unethical.

The final question that needs to be addressed relates to whether the decision conforms to standards of fairness and equity. The department head who inflates the performance evaluation of a favoured employee and deflates the evaluation of a disfavoured employee—and then uses these evaluations to justify giving the former a big raise and nothing to the latter—has treated the disfavoured employee unfairly.

Unfortunately, the answers to the questions in Exhibit 12-6 are often argued in ways to make unethical decisions seem ethical. Powerful people, for example, can become very adept at explaining self-serving behaviours in terms of the organization's best interests. Similarly, they can persuasively argue that unfair actions are really fair and just. Our point is that immoral people can justify almost any behaviour. Those who are powerful, articulate, and persuasive are the most likely to be able to get away with unethical actions successfully. When faced with an ethical dilemma, try to answer the questions in Exhibit 12-6 truthfully. Organizations that don't foster a strong culture of ethics may find themselves facing disaster, as the story of now-bankrupt Montreal, Maine and Atlantic Railway (MMA), discussed in *OB in the Workplace*, shows.

OB IN THE WORKPLACE

The Ethics of Fostering a "Culture of Shortcuts"

How can an organization's culture contribute to a deadly disaster? The Transportation Safety Board of Canada's report about the Lac-Mégantic, Quebec, derailment that killed 47 people and obliterated part of the town indicated that MMA's lax attitude toward safety contributed to the disaster.[114] "The TSB found MMA was a company with a weak safety culture that did not have a functioning safety management system to manage risks," the agency said. The company's approach to safety represents a significant breach of ethics given the threat posed by a lack of appropriate standards in the rail industry. Gaps in training, employee monitoring, and maintenance were noted. One such gap, a failure to properly test the air brake system, contributed directly to the tragic events of July 6, 2013. From all indications, this "culture of shortcuts" was well established. Management's decision to let this culture flourish ultimately led MMA to disaster, bankruptcy, and ruin.

GLOBAL IMPLICATIONS

In this section, we consider global research on the three key areas we discussed in this chapter: decision making, creativity, and ethics.

Decision Making

The rational decision-making model makes no acknowledgment of cultural differences, nor does the bulk of OB research literature on decision making.

However, we need to recognize that the cultural background of a decision maker can have a significant influence on the selection of problems, the depth of analysis, the importance placed on logic and rationality, and whether organizational decisions should be made autocratically by an individual manager or collectively in groups.

Cultures differ in their time orientation, the importance of rationality, their belief in the ability of people to solve problems, and their preference for collective decision making. Differences in time orientation help us understand why managers in Egypt make decisions at a much slower and more deliberate pace than their US counterparts. While rationality is valued in North America, that is not true elsewhere in the world. A North American manager might make an important decision intuitively but know it's important to appear to proceed in a rational fashion because rationality is highly valued in the West. In countries such as Iran, where rationality is not as paramount as other factors, efforts to appear rational are not necessary.

Some cultures emphasize solving problems, while others focus on accepting situations as they are. Canada falls in the first category; Thailand and Indonesia are examples of the second. Because problem-solving managers believe they can and should change situations to their benefit, Canadian managers might identify a problem long before their Thai or Indonesian counterparts would choose to recognize it as such. Decision making by Japanese managers is much more group-oriented than in Canada. The Japanese value conformity and cooperation. So before Japanese CEOs make an important decision, they collect a large amount of information, which they use to form consensus when making group decisions.

In short, there are probably important cultural differences in decision making, but unfortunately not yet much research to identify them.

Creativity

One study suggests that countries scoring high on Hofstede's culture dimension of individuality (discussed in Chapter 3) are more creative.[115] Western countries such as the United States, Italy, and Belgium score high on individuality, and South American and Eastern countries such as China, Colombia, and Pakistan score low. Do these findings mean that Western cultures are more creative? Some evidence suggests that this is true. Another study compared the creative projects of German and Chinese college students, some of whom were studying in their homeland, and some of whom were studying abroad. An independent panel of Chinese and German judges determined that the German students were most creative and that Asian German students were more creative than domestic Chinese students. These results suggested that the German culture was more creative.[116] However, even if some cultures are more creative on average, strong variations always occur within cultures. Put another way, millions of Chinese are more creative than their US counterparts.

Ethics

Although ethical standards may seem ambiguous in the West, criteria defining right and wrong are actually much clearer there than in Asia, where few issues are black and white and most are grey. In Japan, people doing business together often exchange gifts, even expensive ones. This is part of Japanese tradition. When North American and European companies started doing business in Japan, most North American executives were not aware of the Japanese tradition of exchanging gifts and wondered whether this was a form of bribery. Most have come to accept this tradition now, and have even set different limits on gift giving in Japan than in other countries.

Global organizations must establish ethical principles for decision makers in countries such as India and China and modify them to reflect cultural norms if they want to uphold high standards and consistent practices. Having agreements among countries to police bribery may not be enough, however. The 34 countries of the Organisation for Economic Co-operation and Development (OECD) entered into an agreement to tackle corporate bribery in 1997. However, a study by Berlin-based Transparency International found that 21 of the OECD countries are "doing little or nothing" to enforce the agreement. Canada came under strong criticism for being "the only G7 country in the little or no enforcement category." The United States and Germany rated highest on number of cases filed. Transparency International noted that Canada needed to enforce more of its laws in this area.[117]

Summary

An understanding of the way people make decisions can help us explain and predict behaviour, but few important decisions are simple or unambiguous enough for the rational decision-making model's assumptions to apply. We find individuals looking for solutions that satisfice rather than optimize, injecting biases into the decision process, and relying on intuition. Managers should encourage creativity in employees and teams to create a route to innovative decision-making. Individuals are more likely to make ethical decisions when the culture in which they work supports ethical decision making.

LESSONS LEARNED

- Individuals often short-cut the decision-making process and do not consider all options.
- Intuition leads to better results when supplemented with evidence and good judgment.
- Exceptional creativity is rare, but expertise in a subject and a creative environment encourage novel and useful creative outcomes.

SNAPSHOT SUMMARY

How Should Decisions Be Made?
- The Rational Decision-Making Process

How Do Individuals Actually Make Decisions?
- Bounded Rationality in Considering Alternatives
- Intuition
- Judgment Shortcuts

Group Decision Making
- Groups vs. the Individual
- Groupthink and Groupshift
- Group Decision-Making Techniques

Creativity in Organizational Decision Making
- Creative Behaviour
- Causes of Creative Behaviour

- Creative Outcomes (Innovation)

What About Ethics in Decision Making?
- Four Ethical Decision Criteria
- Making Ethical Decisions

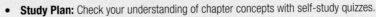

MyLab Management

PERSONAL INVENTORY ASSESSMENT

Study, practise, and explore real business situations with these helpful resources:

- **Study Plan:** Check your understanding of chapter concepts with self-study quizzes.
- **Online Lesson Presentations:** Study key chapter topics and work through interactive assessments to test your knowledge and master management concepts.
- **Videos:** Learn more about the management practices and strategies of real companies.
- **Simulations:** Practise management decision-making in simulated business environments.

OB at Work

1. What is the rational model of decision making? How is it different from bounded rationality and intuition?

2. What are some common decision biases or errors people make?

3. What are the strengths and weaknesses of group (vs. individual) decision making?

4. How effective are interacting groups, brainstorming, and the nominal group technique?

5. What is *creativity*, and what is the three-stage model of creativity?

6. What are the four criteria used in making ethical decisions, and how do they differ?

- Make better decisions by recognizing perceptual biases and decision-making errors we tend to commit. Learning about these problems doesn't always prevent us from making mistakes, but it does help.

- Adjust your decision-making approach to the national culture you are operating in and to the criteria your organization values. If you operate in a country that does not value rationality, don't feel compelled to follow the rational decision-making model or to try to make your decisions appear rational. Adjust your decision-making approach to ensure compatibility with the organizational culture.

- Combine rational analysis with intuition. These are not conflicting approaches to decision making. By using both, you can actually improve your decision-making effectiveness.

- Try to enhance your creativity. Actively look for novel solutions to problems, attempt to see problems in new ways, use analogies, and hire creative talent. Try to remove work and organizational barriers that might impede your creativity.

- In some decision situations, consider following the rational decision-making model. Doing so will ensure that you review a wider variety of options before committing to a particular decision.

- Analyze the decision situation and be aware of your biases. We all bring biases to the decisions we make.

- Combine rational analysis with intuition. As you gain experience, you should feel increasingly confident in imposing your intuitive processes on top of your rational analysis.

- Use creativity-stimulation techniques. You can improve your overall decision-making effectiveness by searching for innovative solutions to problems. This can be as basic as telling yourself to think creatively and to look specifically for unique alternatives.

- When making decisions, think about their ethical implications. A quick way to do this is to ask yourself: Would I be embarrassed if this action were printed on the front page of the newspaper?

PEOPLE ARE MORE CREATIVE WHEN THEY WORK ALONE

POINT

I know groups are all the rage.[118] Businesses are knocking down walls and cubicles to create more open, "collaborative" environments. "Self-managing teams" are replacing the traditional middle manager. Students in universities are constantly working on group projects, and even young children are finding themselves learning in small groups.

I also know *why* groups are all the rage. Work, they say, has become too complex for individuals to perform alone. Groups are better at brainstorming and coming up with creative solutions to complicated problems. Groups also produce higher levels of commitment and satisfaction—so long as group members develop feelings of cohesiveness and trust one another.

For every group that comes up with a creative solution, I'll show you twice as many individuals who would come up with a better solution had they only been left alone. Consider creative geniuses like Leonardo DaVinci, Isaac Newton, and Pablo Picasso—or, more recently, Steve Wozniak, the co-founder of Apple Computer. All were introverts who toiled by themselves. Wozniak has been quoted as saying "Work alone . . . not on a committee. Not on a team."

Enough anecdotal evidence. Research has also shown that groups can kill creativity. One study found that computer programmers at companies that give them privacy and freedom from interruptions outperformed their counterparts at companies that forced more openness and collaboration. Or consider Adrian Furnham, an organizational psychologist whose research led him to conclude that "business people must be insane to use brainstorming groups." People slack off in groups, and they are afraid to communicate any ideas that might make them sound dumb. These problems don't exist when people work alone. So take Picasso's advice: "Without great solitude, no serious work is possible."

COUNTERPOINT

I will grant your point that there are circumstances in which groups can hinder creative progress, but if the right conditions are put in place, groups are simply much better at coming up with novel solutions to problems than are individuals. Using strategies such as the nominal group technique, generating ideas electronically rather than face to face, and ensuring that individuals do not evaluate others' ideas until all have been generated are just a few ways you can set up groups for creative success.

The fact of the matter is that problems *are* too complex these days for individuals to effectively perform alone. Consider the Rovers launched by NASA to roam around Mars collecting data. An accomplishment like that is made possible only by a group, not a lone individual. Steve Wozniak's collaboration with Steve Jobs is what really made Apple sail as a company.

In addition, the most influential research is conducted by teams of academics, rather than individuals. Indeed, if you look at recent Nobel Prize winners in areas such as economics, physics, and chemistry, the majority have been academics who collaborated on the research.

So if you want creativity, two heads are in fact better than one.

BREAKOUT **GROUP** EXERCISES

Form small groups to discuss the following topics, as assigned by your instructor:

1. Apply the rational decision-making model to deciding where your group might eat dinner this evening. How closely were you able to follow the rational model in making this decision?

2. The company that makes your favourite snack product has been accused of being weak in its social responsibility efforts. What impact will this have on your purchase of any more products from that company?

3. You have seen a classmate cheat on an exam or an assignment. Do you do something about this or ignore it?

EXPERIENTIAL EXERCISE

Wilderness Survival

You are a member of a hiking party. After reaching base camp on the first day, you decide to take a quick sunset hike by yourself. After a few exhilarating miles, you decide to return to camp. On your way back, you realize that you are lost. You have shouted for help, to no avail. It is now dark and getting cold.

Your Task

Without communicating with anyone else in your group, read the following scenarios and choose the best answer. Keep track of your answers on a sheet of paper. You have 10 minutes to answer the 10 questions.

1. The first thing you decide to do is to build a fire. However, you have no matches, so you use the bow and drill method. What is the bow and drill method?

   a. A dry, soft stick is rubbed between one's hands against a board of supple green wood.

   b. A soft green stick is rubbed between one's hands against a hardwood board.

   c. A straight stick of wood is quickly rubbed back and forth against a dead tree.

   d. Two sticks (one being the bow, the other the drill) are struck to create a spark.

2. It occurs to you that you can also use the fire as a distress signal. How do you form the international distress signal?

   a. 2 fires

   b. 4 fires in a square

   c. 4 fires in a cross

   d. 3 fires in a triangle

3. You are very thirsty. You go to a nearby stream and collect some water in the small metal cup you have in your backpack. How long should you boil the water?

   a. 15 minutes

   b. 1 minute

   c. A few seconds

   d. It depends on the altitude.

4. You are very hungry, so you decide to eat what appear to be edible berries. When performing the universal edibility test, what should you do?

   a. Do not eat for 2 hours before the test.

   b. If the plant stings your lip, confirm the sting by holding it under your tongue for 15 minutes.

   c. If nothing bad has happened 2 hours after digestion, eat half a cup of the plant and wait again.

   d. Separate the plant into its basic components and eat each component, one at a time.

5. Next, you decide to build a shelter for the evening. In selecting a site, what do you *not* have to consider?

   a. It must contain material to make the type of shelter you need.

   b. It must be free of insects, reptiles, and poisonous plants.

   c. It must be large enough and level enough for you to lie down comfortably.

   d. It must be on a hill so you can signal rescuers and keep an eye on your surroundings.

6. In the shelter that you built, you notice a spider. You heard from a fellow hiker that black widow spiders populate the area. How do you identify a black widow spider?

   a. Its head and abdomen are black; its thorax is red.

   b. It is attracted to light.

   c. It runs away from light.

   d. It is dark with a red or orange marking on the female's abdomen.

7. After getting some sleep, you notice that the night sky has cleared, so you decide to try to find your way back to base camp. You believe you should travel north and can use the North Star for navigation. How do you locate the North Star?

   a. Hold your right hand up as far as you can and look between your index and middle fingers.

   b. Find Sirius and look 60 degrees above it and to the right.

   c. Look for the Big Dipper and follow the line created by its cup end.

   d. Follow the line of Orion's belt.

8. You come across a fast-moving stream. What is the best way to cross it?

   a. Find a spot downstream from a sandbar, where the water will be calmer.

   b. Build a bridge.

   c. Find a rocky area, because the water will be shallow and you will have hand- and footholds.

   d. Find a level stretch where it breaks into a few channels.

9. After walking for about an hour, you feel several spiders in your clothes. You don't feel any pain, but you know some spider bites are painless. Which of these spider bites is painless?

   a. Black widow

   b. Brown recluse

   c. Wolf spider

   d. Harvestman (daddy longlegs)

10. You decide to eat some insects. Which insects should you avoid?

    a. Adults that sting or bite

    b. Caterpillars and insects that have a pungent odour

    c. Hairy or brightly coloured ones

    d. All the above

Group Task

Break into groups of 5 or 6 people. Now imagine that your whole group is lost. Having written down your own answers first, compile your group's answers using consensus to reach each decision. Once the group comes to an agreement, write the group decisions down on the same sheet of paper that you used for your individual answers. You will have approximately 20 minutes for the group task.

Scoring Your Answers

Your instructor will provide you with the correct answers, which are based on expert judgments in these situations. Once you have received the answers, calculate (A) your individual score; (B) your group's score; (C) the average individual score in the group; and (D) the best individual score in the group. Write these down and consult with your group to ensure that these scores are accurate.

(A) Your individual score _____

(B) Your group's score _____

(C) Average individual score in group _____

(D) Best individual score in group _____

Discussion Questions

1. How did your group (B) perform relative to yourself (A)?

2. How did your group (B) perform relative to the average individual score in the group (C)?

3. How did your group (B) perform relative to the best individual score in the group (D)?

4. Compare your results with those of other groups. Did some groups do a better job of outperforming individuals than others?

5. What do these results tell you about the effectiveness of group decision making?

6. What can groups do to make group decision making more effective?

7. What circumstances might cause a group to perform worse than its best individual?

ETHICAL **DILEMMA**

Five Ethical Decisions: What Would You Do?

Assume that you are a middle manager in a company with about 1000 employees. How would you respond to each of the following situations?[119]

1. You are negotiating a contract with a potentially very large customer whose representative has hinted that you could almost certainly be assured of getting his business if you gave him and his wife an all-expenses-paid cruise to the Caribbean. You know the representative's employer would not approve of such a "payoff," but you have the discretion to authorize such an expenditure. What would you do?

2. You have an autographed CD by Sam Roberts and put it up for sale on eBay. So far, the highest bid is $74.50. A friend has offered you $100 for the CD, commenting that he could get $150 for it on eBay in a year. You know this is highly unlikely. Should you sell your friend the CD for what he offered ($100)? Do you have an obligation to tell your friend you have listed your CD on eBay?

3. Your company policy on reimbursement for meals while travelling on company business is that you will be repaid for your out-of-pocket costs, which are not to exceed $80 a day. You don't need receipts for these expenses—the company will take your word. When travelling, you tend to eat at fast-food places and rarely spend in excess of $20 a day. Most of your colleagues submit reimbursement requests in the range of $55 to $60 a day regardless of what their actual expenses are. How much would you request for your meal reimbursements?

4. You are the manager at a gaming company, and you are responsible for hiring a group to outsource the production of a highly anticipated new game. Because your company is a giant in the industry, numerous companies are trying to get the bid. One of them offers you some kickbacks if you give that firm the bid, but ultimately, it is up to your bosses to decide on the company. You don't mention the incentive, but you push upper management to give the bid to the company that offered you the kickback. Is withholding the truth as bad as lying? Why or why not?

5. You have discovered that one of your closest friends at work has stolen a large sum of money from the company. Would you do nothing? Go directly to an executive to report the incident before talking about it with the offender? Confront the individual before taking action? Make contact with the individual with the goal of persuading that person to return the money?

CASE INCIDENTS

The Youngest Female Self-Made Billionaire

Picture this:[120] The billionaire owner and founder stands in the conference room trying on bras while the CEO stands behind her, adjusting the straps. The floor is littered with underwear. The owner takes off one bra and puts on another. Five executives in the conference room barely blink.

Welcome to Sara Blakely's company, Spanx. In just a few years, Spanx became to slimming underwear what JELL-O is to gelatin and Kleenex is to facial tissue: So dominant that its name is synonymous with the industry.

At 45, Blakely is one of the youngest billionaires in the world. Like many stories of entrepreneurial success, hers is part gritty determination, part inspiration, and part circumstance. The grit was easy to see early on. As a child she lured friends into doing her chores by setting up a competition. At 16, Blakely was so intent on success that she listened to self-help guru Wayne Dyer's recordings incessantly. Friends refused to ride in her car. "No! She's going to make us listen to that motivational crap!" Blakely recalls they said.

After twice failing to get into law school, Blakely started her first business in 1990, running a kids' club at the Clearwater Beach Hilton. It worked until the Hilton's general manager found out. Later, while working full-time in sales, Blakely began learning how to start a more viable business. Her inspiration for Spanx came while she was cold-calling customers as a sales manager for an office supply company. She hated pantyhose. "It's Florida, it's hot, I'm carrying copy machines," she noted.

At the library, Blakely researched every pantyhose patent ever filed. She wrote her patent application by following a textbook she read in Barnes & Noble. Then she worked on marketing, manufacturing, and financing, treating each as its own project. After numerous rejections, she finally found mill owners in North Carolina willing to finance the manufacturing. "At the end of the day, the guy ended up just wanting to help me," Blakely said. "He didn't even believe in the idea."

For a time, Blakely relied on US stores such as Neiman Marcus to set up her table and on word-of-mouth to get the news out to the public. Her big break came when she sent samples to Oprah Winfrey's stylist. Harpo Productions called to say that Winfrey would name Spanx her favourite product of the year and warned Blakely to get her website ready. She did not have a website.

Billions of dollars in sales later, Blakely has no plans to slow down. Spanx is sold in 55 countries, and Blakely wants to double international sales. She says: "The biggest risk in life is not risking. Every risk you take in life is in direct proportion to the reward. If I'm afraid of something, it's the next thing I have to go do. That's just the way I've been."

Questions

1. Does hindsight bias affect the factors to which you might attribute Blakely's success? Why or why not?

2. Use the three-stage model of creativity to analyze Blakely's decision making. What can you learn from her story that might help you be more creative in the future?

If Two Heads Are Better Than One, Are Four Even Better?

Maggie Becker, age 24, is a marketing manager for a small chain of shops in Halifax. Recently, Maggie's wealthy uncle passed away and left her, his only niece, $100 000. Maggie considers her current salary adequate to meet her current living expenses, so she would like to invest the money so that when she buys a house she will have a nice nest egg on which to draw.

One of Maggie's neighbours, Brian, is a financial adviser. Brian told Maggie that the array of investment options is virtually endless. She asked him to present her with two of the best options, and this is what he offered her:

1. A very low-risk AAA bond fund. With this option, based on the information Brian provided, Maggie estimates that after five years she stands virtually zero chance of losing money, with an expected gain of approximately $7000.

2. A moderate-risk mutual fund. Based on the information Brian provided her, Maggie estimates that with this option she stands a 50 percent chance of making $40 000 but also a 50 percent chance of losing $20 000.

Maggie prides herself on being rational and objective in her thinking. However, she is unsure of what to do in this case. Brian refuses to help her, telling her that she has already limited herself by asking for only two options. While driving to her parents' house for the weekend, Maggie finds herself vacillating between the two options. Her older brother is also visiting the folks this weekend, so Maggie decides to gather her family around the table after dinner, lay out the two options, and go with their decision. "You know the old saying—two heads are better than one," she says to herself, "so four heads should be even better."

Questions

1. Has Maggie made a good decision about the way she is going to make the decision?

2. Which investment would you choose? Why?

3. Which investment do you think most people would choose?

4. Based on what you have learned about groupshift, which investment do you think Maggie's family will choose?

FROM CONCEPTS TO SKILLS

Solving Problems Creatively

Reaching creative solutions to problems can improve one's decision-making abilities.

You can be more effective at solving problems creatively if you use the following 10 suggestions:[121]

1. *Think of yourself as creative.* Research shows that if you think you cannot be creative, you won't be. Believing in your ability to be creative is the first step in becoming more creative.

2. *Pay attention to your intuition.* Every individual has a subconscious mind that works well. Sometimes answers will come to you when you least expect them. Listen to that "inner voice." In fact, most creative people will keep a notepad near their bed and write down ideas when the thoughts come to them.

3. *Move away from your comfort zone.* Every individual has a comfort zone in which certainty exists. But creativity and the known often do not mix. To be creative, you need to move away from the status quo and focus your mind on something new.

4. *Determine what you want to do.* This includes such things as taking time to understand a problem before beginning to try to resolve it, getting all the facts in mind, and trying to identify the most important facts.

5. *Think outside the box.* Use analogies whenever possible (for example, could you approach your problem like a fish out of water and look at what the fish does to cope? Or can you use the things you have to do to find your way when it's foggy to help you solve your problem?). Use different problem-solving strategies, such as verbal, visual, mathematical, or theatrical. Look at your problem from a different perspective, or ask yourself what someone else, such as your grandmother, might do if faced with the same situation.

6. *Look for ways to do things better.* This may involve trying consciously to be original, not worrying about looking foolish, keeping an open mind, being alert to odd or puzzling facts, thinking of unconventional ways to use objects and the environment, discarding usual or habitual ways of doing things, and striving for objectivity by being as critical of your own ideas as you would be of someone else's.

7. *Find several right answers.* Being creative means continuing to look for other solutions even when you think you have solved the problem. A better, more creative solution just might be found.

8. *Believe in finding a workable solution.* Like believing in yourself, you also need to believe in your ideas. If you don't think you can find a solution, you probably won't.

9. *Brainstorm with others.* Creativity is not an isolated activity. Bouncing ideas off of others creates a synergistic effect.

10. *Turn creative ideas into action.* Coming up with creative ideas is only part of the process. Once the ideas are generated, they must be implemented. Keeping great ideas in your mind, or on papers that no one will read, does little to expand your creative abilities.

Practising Skills

Every time the phone rings, your stomach clenches and your palms start to sweat. And it's no wonder! As sales manager for Brinkers, a machine tool parts manufacturer, you are besieged by calls from customers who are upset about late deliveries. Your boss, Carter Hererra, acts as both production manager and scheduler. Every time your sales representatives negotiate a sale, it's up to Carter to determine whether production can actually meet the delivery date the customer specifies. Carter invariably says, "No problem." The good thing about this is that you make a lot of initial sales. The bad news is that production hardly ever meets the shipment dates that Carter authorizes. Moreover, he does not seem to be all that concerned about the aftermath of late deliveries. He says: "Our customers know they're getting outstanding quality at a great price. Just let them try to match that anywhere. It can't be done. So even if they have to wait a couple of extra days or weeks, they're still getting the best deal they can." Somehow the customers don't see it that way, and they let you know about their unhappiness. Then it's up to you to try to soothe the relationship. You know this problem has to be taken care of, but what possible solutions are there? After all, how are you going to keep from making your manager angry or making the customers angry? Use your knowledge of creative problem solving to come up with solutions.

Practising Skills

1. Take 20 minutes to list as many words as you can using the letters in the word *brainstorm.* (There are at least 95.) If you run out of listings before time is up, it's okay to quit early. But try to be as creative as you can.

2. List on a piece of paper some common terms that apply to both water and finance. How many were you able to come up with?

Reinforcing Skills

StockLite/Shutterstock

OB ON THE EDGE

Spirituality in the Workplace

Savannah Olsen won the National Youth Aboriginal Entrepreneur Award in 2014 for creating the Old Faithful store, located in Vancouver.[1] She has always been an entrepreneur, with lots of business ideas running around in her head. In 2016 she opened a new store in Vancouver, The Good Spirit, right next door to Old Faithful.

The award was developed by the Canadian Council for Aboriginal Business. CCAB board member and co-chair Erin Meehan congratulated Olsen by saying, "Your accomplishments are proof that when you dream, big things happen and lives change."

Olsen is back to dreaming about changing lives. The Good Spirit caters to the spiritual side of one's nature. "My vision was to conjure all those factors together in one store that would encourage younger people, and anyone really, to explore their own path of spirituality," she said.

Olsen's store sells carefully selected tools to help people in their personal spiritual development. There is also a tarot studio where customers can get readings. Olsen hopes what she has created with The Good Spirit will help her customers "approach spirituality in an easy, open and accessible way."

While it might not be common to find spirituality stores on every street corner, spirituality is also coming to the workplace.

What Is Spirituality?

Workplace spirituality is *not* about organized religious practices. It's not about God or theology. This point was made clear in a recent study of 275 natural and social scientists at elite universities. About 25 percent "said they have a spirituality that is consistent with science, although they are not formally religious."[2]

Workplace spirituality recognizes that people have an inner life that nourishes and is nourished by meaningful work in the context of community.[3] Organizations that support a spiritual culture recognize that people seek to find meaning and purpose in their work and desire to connect with other human beings as part of a community. Many of the topics we have discussed—ranging from job design to corporate social responsibility (CSR)—are well matched to the concept of organizational spirituality. When a company emphasizes its commitment to paying suppliers in developing countries a fair (above-market) price for their goods to facilitate community development—as do Vancouver-based Maiwa Handprints; Halifax-based Fibres of Life; Hudson, Quebec-based Pure Art; and Whitehorse-based Bean North Café—it encourages a more spiritual culture.[4]

workplace spirituality The recognition that people have an inner life that nourishes and is nourished by meaningful work that takes place in the context of community.

Blake Ashforth of Arizona State University and Michael Pratt of the University of Illinois propose that workplace spirituality has three major dimensions:

- *Transcendence of self:* a connection to something greater than one's self, and encompassing other people and things
- *Holism and harmony:* integration of self in such a way that it informs one's behaviour
- *Growth:* self-development, self-actualization, and achieving one's hopes and potential

When pursued together, these three dimensions lead to connection, coherence, and completeness.[5]

Why Spirituality Now?

As noted in our discussion of emotions in Chapter 3, there is controversy over whether feelings should be displayed in the workplace. At the same time, employers are showing more concern about an employee's inner life. Just as the study of emotions improves our understanding of organizational behaviour, an awareness of spirituality can help us better understand employee behaviour. Similarly, organizations that are concerned with spirituality are more likely to directly address problems created by conflicts that occur in everyday life.[6]

Reasons for the Growing Interest in Spirituality

- Spirituality acts as a counterbalance to the pressures and stress of a turbulent pace of life. Contemporary lifestyles—single-parent families, geographical mobility, the temporary nature of jobs, new technologies that create distance between people—underscore the lack of community many people feel and increase the need for involvement and connection.

- Formalized religion has not worked for many people, and they continue to look for anchors to replace lack of faith and to fill a growing feeling of emptiness.

- Job demands have made the workplace dominant in many people's lives, yet they continue to question the meaning of work.

- More people desire to integrate personal life values with their professional life.

- An increasing number of people are finding that the pursuit of more material acquisitions leaves them unfulfilled.

Of course, employees have always had an inner life. So why has the search for meaning and purposefulness in work surfaced now? We summarize the reasons in the inset *Reasons for the Growing Interest in Spirituality.*

Spirituality and Mindfulness

Recently, mindfulness has become part of the discussion on spirituality in the workplace. Ellen J. Langer, Harvard professor of psychology, has been studying mindfulness for much of her academic career. She defines mindfulness as "the process of actively noticing new things. When you do that, it puts you in the present. It makes you more sensitive to context and perspective. It's the essence of engagement."[7]

Mindfulness means staying aware in the present and not simply accepting that "this is the way we have always done things." Langer explains

how to make this possible: "When you're mindful, rules, routines, and goals guide you; they don't govern you."[9] The inset *Advantages to Mindfulness* presents Langer's reasons to be mindful.

What is Langer's advice about being mindful? "Life consists only of moments, nothing more than that. So if you make the moment matter, it all matters. You can be mindful, you can be mindless. You can win, you can lose. The worst case is to be mindless and lose. So when you're doing anything, be mindful, notice new things, make it meaningful to you, and you'll prosper."[10]

Meditation is one way to become more mindful. Professor Jamie Gruman, at the College of Business and Economics at the University of Guelph, who studies meditation in the workplace, notes that "research shows people who meditate suffer from less stress, are less rigid in their thinking and are less likely to have overly emotional reactions to difficulties. All of these things are qualities of effective

working and management decision making."[11]

Research also shows that engaging in meditation helps people be more creative;[12] and that just three successive days of 25 minutes of mindfulness meditation can effectively reduce stress.[13] Fifteen minutes of mindful meditation was found to be helpful in stopping individuals from thinking about sunk costs when making decisions, making them more able to focus on the present and make clearer decisions.[14]

Mindful meditation is easy to practice, "doesn't require a rigid schedule," and can easily become part of one's work routine, notes Maria Gonzalez, president of Toronto-based Argonauta Strategic Alliances Consulting.[15] Her clients include BMO Financial Group, Ontario's Hydro One, and the Conference Board of Canada. She is also the author of *Mindful Leadership.*[16] Business meetings are a good example of why mindfulness is needed. "In many conversations, neither side is fully there for the discussion. It's become a constant that people are trying to multitask and holding their BlackBerrys under the table at meetings and never focusing on the issue at hand," says Gonzalez.[17]

Studies on mindful meditation have shown positive results. One study found that "Mindfulness meditation has been reported to enhance numerous mental abilities, including rapid memory recall."[18] One meta-analysis (a study that examined a large number of previous studies), determined that mindful meditation can help ease psychological stresses like anxiety, depression, and pain.[19] Another study found that meditation and mindfulness lower levels of the stress hormone cortisol.[20]

Advantages to Mindfulness

- It's easier to pay attention.
- You remember more of what you've done.
- You're more creative.
- You're able to take advantage of opportunities when they present themselves.
- You avert the danger not yet arisen.
- You like people better, and people like you better, because you're less evaluative.
- You're more charismatic.[8]

Characteristics of a Spiritual Organization

Spiritual organizations are concerned with helping people develop and reach their full potential. This is analogous to Abraham Maslow's description of self-actualization that we discussed in relation to motivation in Chapter 4. Similarly, organizations concerned with spirituality are more likely to directly address problems created by work–life conflicts.[21]

The Vancouver Island Health Authority recognizes that spiritual care can be helpful to those faced with stressful health care decisions.[22] Consequently, Nanaimo Regional General Hospital offers staff, patients, and patients' families access to spiritual health services that match their belief perspectives.

London, Ontario-based 3M Canada also provides a quiet room for meditation and reflection, which was one of the factors cited in explaining why it was chosen as one of Canada's top 100 employers for 2014.[23] Calgary-based Shell Canada provides a meditation and reflection centre so that its employees can have a more mindful, calming experience at work.[24]

What differentiates spiritual organizations from their nonspiritual counterparts? Although research on this question is only preliminary, several cultural characteristics tend to be evident in spiritual organizations.[25]

Benevolence

Spiritual organizations value showing kindness toward others and promoting the happiness of employees and other organizational stakeholders.

Strong Sense of Purpose

Spiritual organizations build their cultures around a meaningful purpose. While profits may be important, they are not the primary value of these organizations. People want to be inspired by a purpose that they believe is important and worthwhile.

Charllotte Kwon, owner and CEO of Vancouver-based Maiwa Handprints, pays the artisans from developing countries who provide textiles for her retail stores substantially more than what others pay them. She wants to protect craftspeople so that they can continue to produce their artwork. She also wants to make sure that their traditional arts will survive. "I don't want to lose traditional dyes made with specific recipes that are rarely written down. Without care, that information could be lost forever."[26] She also notes that she does not need to pay the artisans minimum prices to survive: "I live okay. I don't need anything more."[27]

Trust and Respect

Spiritual organizations are characterized by mutual trust, honesty, and openness. Managers are not afraid to admit mistakes. Steve Reaume, dealer principal of Windsor-based Reaume Chevrolet Buick GMC, a company founded by his grandfather, attributes the success of the business to the trust his family has built in the community. The company displays "A Tradition of Trust ... since 1931" banner in its showroom and on its website. Reaume explains the company's approach: "Generation after generation we've been earning people's trust. Treating customers right, every time, is all it takes."[28] Trust is also a big part of how Reaume treats its workforce and fosters employee loyalty.

FACTBOX

- 64% of Canadians consider themselves spiritual.
- 71% of Canadians attend religious services at least sometimes.
- 50% of Canadians report that they are religious.
- 60% of Canadians think that public schools should be doctrine-free.[29]

Humanistic Work Practices

The practices embraced by spiritual organizations include flexible work schedules, group- and organization-based rewards, narrowing of pay and status differentials, guarantees of individual employee rights, employee empowerment, and job security. Hewlett-Packard, for instance, has handled temporary downturns through voluntary attrition and shortened workweeks (shared by all), and it has handled longer-term declines through early retirements and buyouts.

Toleration of Employee Expression

Finally, spiritual organizations don't stifle employee emotions. They allow people to be themselves—to express their moods and feelings without guilt or fear of reprimand. Employees at Calgary-based WestJet Airlines, for instance, are encouraged to express their sense of humour on the job, to act spontaneously, and to make their work fun.

Organizational Models for Fostering Spirituality

- *Religion-based organization:* The organization's practices are consistent with biblical teachings; there is an emphasis on prayer as a primary form of intrafirm communication; employees are expected to accept core Christian principles as guides to decision making.

- *Evolutionary organization:* Spiritual openness is encouraged; the guiding texts are a mixture of Christian scriptures and philosophical works (Kant, Niebuhr, Buber); there is an emphasis on serving the customer, preserving the environment, and respecting stakeholders.

- *Recovering organization:* The organization models itself after the 12-step program of Alcoholics Anonymous; the 12-step program spirituality is discussed in ways that are acceptable to the largest number of people. The 12-step program emphasizes confession (of failures), acceptance of God's will and guidance, and reliance on the help of others. This model is infrequently found in the business world.

- *Socially responsible organization:* Social concerns and values are part of everyday business activities; the organization emphasizes the expression of the individual's "whole person" and soul; customers, suppliers, and other stakeholders are expected to bond more readily to the firm; spirituality and soul are explicit core business principles.

- *Values-based organization:* The organization firmly rejects all notions of religious doctrine; it favours nonreligious and nonspiritual secular values or virtues (e.g., awareness, consciousness, dignity, honesty, openness, respect, integrity, and, above all, trust); values are guides for policy setting and decision making throughout the firm. The Golden Rule is the prime business principle.

- *Best-practice model:* The organization combines parts of all of the above models; it emphasizes values-based secular orientation; it adds an openly expressed spiritual dimension; it emphasizes the importance of "a higher power," periodic moral audits, and a broadly inclusive approach to stakeholders."[30]

The inset *Organizational Models for Fostering Spirituality* describes models for spiritually based organizations.

Achieving a Spiritual Organization

Many organizations have grown interested in spirituality but have experienced difficulty putting its principles into practice. Several types of practices can facilitate a spiritual workplace,[31] including those that support work–life balance. Leaders can demonstrate values, attitudes, and behaviours that trigger intrinsic motivation and a sense of fulfilling a calling through work. Second, encouraging employees to consider how their work provides a sense of purpose can also help achieve a spiritual workplace. Often this is done through group counselling and organizational development. Third, a growing number of companies offer employees the counselling services of corporate chaplains. Many chaplains are employed by agencies, such as Marketplace Chaplains USA, while some corporations, such as R. J. Reynolds Tobacco and Tyson Foods, employ chaplains directly. The workplace presence of corporate chaplains, who are often ordained Christian ministers, is obviously controversial, although their role is not to increase spirituality but to help human resources departments serve the employees who already have Christian beliefs.[32] Similar roles for leaders of other faiths certainly must be encouraged.

Criticisms of Spirituality

Critics of organizations that embrace spiritual values have focused on three issues. First is the question of scientific foundation. What, really, is workplace spirituality? Is it just a new management buzzword? Second, are spiritual organizations legitimate? Specifically, do organizations have the right to claim spiritual values? Third is the question of economics: Are spirituality and profits compatible?

First, as you might imagine, comparatively little research exists on workplace spirituality. Spirituality has been defined so broadly in some sources that practices from job rotation to corporate retreats at meditation centres have been identified as spiritual. Questions need to be answered before the concept gains full credibility.

Second, an emphasis on spirituality can clearly make some employees uneasy. Critics have argued that secular institutions, especially business firms, have no business imposing spiritual values on employees. This criticism is undoubtedly valid when spirituality is defined as bringing religion and God into the workplace.[33] However, it seems less stinging when the goal is limited to helping employees find meaning and purpose in their work lives.

Finally, whether spirituality and profits are compatible objectives is a relevant concern for managers and investors in business. The evidence, although limited, indicates that they are. In one study, organizations that provided their employees with opportunities for spiritual development outperformed those that did not.[34] Other studies reported that spirituality in organizations was positively related to creativity, employee satisfaction, team performance, and organizational commitment.[35]

The cynic will say that all of this caring stuff is in fact merely good public relations. Even so, the results at WestJet suggest that a caring organization is good for the bottom line. WestJet is strongly committed to providing the lowest airfares, on-time service, and a pleasant experience for customers. WestJet employees have one of the lowest turnover rates in the airline industry, the company consistently has the lowest labour costs per miles flown of any major airline, and it has proven itself to be the most consistently profitable airline in Canada.[36]

13 Organizational Structure

Precision Nutrition is a fitness and nutrition coaching company with a flattened organizational structure. How has this organizational structure contributed to the company's success?

LEARNING OUTCOMES

After studying this chapter, you should be able to:

1 Identify seven elements of an organization's structure.

2 Describe the characteristics of a bureaucracy.

3 Describe the characteristics of a matrix organization.

4 Describe the characteristics of virtual, team, and circular structures.

5 Describe the effects of downsizing on organizational structures and employees.

6 Contrast the reasons for mechanistic and organic structural models.

7 Analyze the behavioural implications of different organizational designs.

In 2015, Toronto-based Precision Nutrition, a fitness and nutrition coaching company, was named one of Canada's most innovative fitness companies.[1] The company was started in 2005 by Phil Caravaggio (in the centre of the photo). His interest was in coaching and developing strategies for the company. When he grew from 8 to 50 employees, he found almost all of his time was spent managing employees, rather than getting his work done. He wanted a new organizational structure to make things more efficient. "I want to be a leader," he says. "I don't want to be a manager."

Courtesy of Precision Nutrition

Caravaggio put in place a management system called *holacracy*, developed by Brian Robertson. Holacracy promotes a flatter organizational structure, empowering individuals to make more decisions for the work that they do. As described on the HolacracyOne website, "In Holacracy, people have multiple roles, often on different teams, and those role descriptions are constantly updated by the team actually doing the work. This allows people a lot more freedom to express their creative talents, and the company can take advantage of those skills in a way it couldn't before. Since roles are not directly tied to the people filling them, people can hand-off and pick up new roles fairly easily."

Organizations are looking for new ways to structure. Not all are going as far as holacracy, though Zappos, with 4000 employees, is one of the largest using the system. Other organizations are flattening themselves to have fewer layers of bureaucracy.

Choosing an organizational structure requires far more than simply deciding who is the boss and how many employees are needed. The organization's structure will determine what relationships form, the formality of those relationships, and many work outcomes. The structure may also change as organizations grow and shrink, as management trends dictate, and as research uncovers better ways of maximizing productivity.

Structural decisions are arguably the most fundamental ones a leader has to make toward sustaining organizational growth.[2] In this chapter, we will explore how structure affects employee behaviour and the organization as a whole.

OB IS FOR EVERYONE

- What happens when a person performs the same task over and over again?
- What happens when a person reports to two bosses?
- What does *technology* mean?

THE BIG IDEA

Organizational structure determines what gets done in an organization, and who does it.

1 Identify the seven elements of an organization's structure.

What Is Organizational Structure?

An **organizational structure** defines how job tasks are formally divided, grouped, and coordinated. Managers should address seven key elements when they design their organization's structure: work specialization, departmentalization, chain of command, span of control, centralization and decentralization, formalization, and boundary spanning.[3] Exhibit 13-1 presents each element as the answer to an important structural question, and the following sections describe them.

Work Specialization

Work specialization, or *division of labour*, describes the degree to which tasks in the organization are subdivided into separate jobs. The essence of work specialization is that, rather than an entire job being completed by one individual, it's broken down into a number of steps, with each step being completed by a separate individual. Specialization is a means of making the most efficient use of employees' skills and even successfully improving them through repetition. Less time is spent changing tasks, putting away tools and equipment from a prior step, and getting ready for another.

> What happens when a person performs the same task over and over again?

Specialization can be efficient. It's easier and less costly to find and train employees to do specific and repetitive tasks. This is especially true of highly sophisticated and complex operations. For example, could Montreal-based Bombardier produce even one Canadian regional jet a year if one person had to build the entire plane alone? Not likely! Finally, work specialization increases efficiency and productivity by encouraging the creation of special inventions and machinery.

However, specialization can lead to boredom, fatigue, stress, low productivity, poor quality, increased absenteeism, and high turnover, so it is not always the best way to organize employees. Giving employees a variety of activities to do, allowing them to do a whole and complete job, and putting them into teams with interchangeable skills can result in significantly higher output and increased employee satisfaction.

Most managers today recognize that specialization provides economies in certain types of jobs but problems when it's carried too far. High work specialization helps McDonald's make and sell hamburgers and fries efficiently, and aids medical specialists working in hospitals. Wherever job roles can be broken down into specific tasks or projects, specialization is possible. Specialization may still confer advantages outside manufacturing, particularly where job sharing and part-time work are prevalent.[4]

EXHIBIT 13-1 Seven Key Questions That Managers Need to Answer in Designing the Proper Organizational Structure	
The Key Question	**The Answer Is Provided By**
1. To what degree are tasks subdivided into separate jobs?	*Work specialization*
2. On what basis will jobs be grouped together?	*Departmentalization*
3. To whom do individuals and groups report?	*Chain of command*
4. How many individuals can a manager efficiently and effectively direct?	*Span of control*
5. Where does decision-making authority lie?	*Centralization and decentralization*
6. To what degree will there be rules and regulations to direct employees and managers?	*Formalization*
7. Do individuals from different areas need to regularly interact?	*Boundary spanning*

organizational structure How job tasks are formally divided, grouped, and coordinated.

work specialization The degree to which tasks in the organization are subdivided into separate jobs.

SPUTNIK / Alamy Stock Photo

Work is specialized at the Russian factories that manufacture the wooden nesting dolls called *matryosh-kas*. At this factory outside Moscow, individuals specialize in doing part of the doll production, from the craftsmen who carve the dolls to the painters who decorate them. Work specialization brings efficiency to doll production, as some 50 employees can make 100 *matryoshkas* every two days.

Amazon's Mechanical Turk program, TopCoder, and others like it have facilitated a new trend in microspecialization in which extremely small pieces of programming, data processing, or evaluation tasks are delegated to a global network of individuals by a program manager who then assembles the results.[5] Program specialization allows employers to use online platforms to specialize—to assign multiple employees to tasks in a broad functional role like marketing.[6] Whereas specialization of yesteryear focused on breaking manufacturing tasks into specific duties within the same plant, today's specialization judiciously breaks complex tasks into specific elements by technology, by expertise, and region. Yet the core principle is the same.

Departmentalization

Once jobs are divided through work specialization, they must be grouped so that common tasks can be coordinated. The basis on which jobs are grouped together is called **departmentalization**. One of the concerns related to departmental groups is that they can become *silos* within an organization. Often, departments start protecting their own turf and not interacting well with other departments, which can lead to a narrow vision with respect to organizational goals.

Functional Departmentalization
One of the most popular ways to group activities is by *functions* performed. For example, a manufacturing company might separate engineering, accounting, manufacturing, human resources, and purchasing specialists into common departments. Similarly, a hospital might have departments devoted to research, patient care, accounting, and so forth. The major advantage to functional groupings is obtaining efficiencies from putting people with common skills and orientations together into common units.

departmentalization The basis on which jobs are grouped together.

Product Departmentalization

Tasks can also be departmentalized by the type of *product* the organization produces. Procter & Gamble groups each major product—such as Tide, Pampers, Charmin, and Pringles—under an executive who has complete global responsibility for it. The major advantage to this type of grouping is increased accountability for product performance, since all activities related to a specific product line are under the direction of a single manager.

Geographical Departmentalization

Another way to departmentalize is on the basis of geography, or territory. The sales function, for instance, may be divided regionally with departments for British Columbia, the Prairies, Central Canada, and Atlantic Canada. If an organization's customers are scattered over a large geographical area and have similar needs based on their location, then this form of departmentalization can be valuable. Toyota changed its management structure into geographic regions "so that they may develop and deliver ever better products," said CEO Akio Toyoda.[7]

Process Departmentalization

Some companies organize departments by the processing that occurs. For example, an aluminum tubing manufacturer might have the following departments: casting; press; tubing; finishing; and inspecting, packing, and shipping. This is an example of process departmentalization, because each department specializes in one specific phase in the production of aluminum tubing. Since each process requires different skills, this method offers a basis for the homogeneous categorizing of activities.

Process departmentalization can be used for processing customers, as well as products. For example, in some provinces, you may go through a series of steps handled by several departments before receiving your driver's licence: (1) validation by a motor vehicles division; (2) processing by the licensing department; and (3) payment collection by the treasury department.

Graham Hughes/Canadian Press images

The Carillon Generating Station on the Ottawa River (shown here) is one of Montreal-based Hydro-Québec's hydroelectric power stations. Hydro-Québec organizes its operations by functions so that the company can be more responsive to growth outside Quebec. It has four divisions: Hydro-Québec Production, Hydro-Québec TransÉnergie, Hydro-Québec Distribution, and Hydro-Québec Équipement et services partagés/Société d'énergie de la Baie James.

Customer Departmentalization

Yet another way to departmentalize is on the basis of the particular type of customer the organization seeks to reach. Microsoft, for example, is organized around four customer markets: consumers, large corporations, software developers, and small businesses. Customers in each department have a common set of problems and needs best met by having specialists for each.

Large organizations may use all the forms of departmentalization we have described. A major Japanese electronics firm organizes each of its divisions along functional lines, its manufacturing units around processes, sales around seven geographical regions, and each sales region into four customer groupings. In a strong recent trend among organizations of all sizes, rigid functional departmentalization is increasingly complemented by teams that cross traditional departmental lines. As we described in Chapter 6, as tasks have become more complex, and more diverse skills are needed to accomplish those tasks, management has turned to cross-functional teams.

Chain of Command

While the chain of command was once a basic cornerstone in the design of organizations, it has far less importance today.[8] But contemporary managers should still consider its implications, particularly for industries that deal with potential life-or-death situations when people need to quickly rely on decision makers. The **chain of command** is an unbroken line of authority that extends from upper organizational levels to the lowest level and clarifies who reports to whom.

We cannot discuss the chain of command without also discussing authority and unity of command. **Authority** refers to the rights inherent in a managerial position to give orders and expect them to be obeyed. To facilitate coordination, each managerial position is given a place in the chain of command, and each manager is given a degree of authority in order to meet his or her responsibilities. The principle of **unity of command** helps preserve the concept of an unbroken line of authority. It says a person should have one and only one superior to whom he or she is directly responsible. If the unity of command is broken, an employee might have to cope with conflicting demands or priorities from several superiors, as is often the case in organization charts' dotted-line reporting relationships depicting an employee's accountability to multiple managers.

Because managers have limited time and knowledge, they may choose to delegate some of their responsibilities to other employees. **Delegation** is the assignment of authority to another person to carry out specific duties, allowing the employee to make some of the decisions. Delegation is an important part of a manager's job, as it can ensure that the right people are part of the decision-making process. Through delegation, employees are being empowered to make decisions that previously were reserved for management. *From Concepts to Skills* on pages 488–489 presents strategies to be a better delegator.

Times change, and so do the basic tenets of organizational design. A low-level employee today can access information in seconds that was available only to top managers a generation ago. Many employees are now empowered to make decisions previously reserved for management. Add the popularity of self-managed and cross-functional teams as well as the structural designs that include multiple bosses, and you can see why authority and unity of command may appear to hold less relevance. *Point/Counterpoint* on page 484 considers whether management as we know it is an outdated concept.

Many organizations still find they can be most productive by enforcing the chain of command. Indeed, one survey of more than 1000 managers found that 59 percent agreed with the statement, "There is an imaginary line in my company's organizational chart. Strategy is created by people above this line, while strategy is executed by people below the line."[9] However, this same survey found that lower-level employees' buy-in

chain of command The unbroken line of authority that extends from upper organizational levels to the lowest level and clarifies who reports to whom.

authority The rights inherent in a managerial position to give orders and to expect the orders to be obeyed.

unity of command The idea that a subordinate should have only one superior to whom he or she is directly responsible.

delegation Assignment of authority to another person to carry out specific duties, allowing the employee to make some of the decisions.

(agreement and active support) to the organization's strategy was inhibited because they did not participate in the setting of the overall, big picture strategy but relied on those at the top of the hierarchy to do so.

Sometimes lower-level employees don't follow the chain of command and engage in creative deviance that results in very successful ideas, as *Case Incident—Creative Deviance: Bucking the Hierarchy?* on page 486 shows.

Span of Control

Span of control refers to the number of employees who report to a manager. This number will vary by organization, and by unit within an organization, and is determined by the number of employees a manager can efficiently and effectively direct. In an assembly-line factory, a manager may be able to direct numerous employees, because the work is well defined and controlled by machinery. A sales manager, by contrast, might have to give one-on-one supervision to individual sales reps, and, therefore, fewer would report to the sales manager. All things being equal, the wider or larger the span, the fewer levels, the more employees at each level, and the more efficient the organization. An example can illustrate the validity of this statement.

Assume that we have two organizations, both of which have approximately 4100 operative-level employees. As Exhibit 13-2 illustrates, if one has a uniform span of 4 and the other a span of 8, the wider span would have 2 fewer levels and approximately 800 fewer managers. If the average manager earned $56 000 a year, the wider span would save about $45 million a year in management salaries. Obviously, wider spans are more efficient in terms of cost. However, at some point when supervisors no longer have time to provide subordinates with the necessary leadership and support, effectiveness declines and employee performance suffers.

Narrow or small spans have their advocates. By keeping the span of control to five or six employees, a manager can maintain close control.[10] But narrow spans have three major drawbacks. First, as already described, they are expensive because they add levels of management. Second, they make vertical communication in the organization more complex. The added levels of hierarchy slow down decision making and can isolate upper management. Third, narrow spans of control encourage overly tight supervision and discourage employee autonomy.

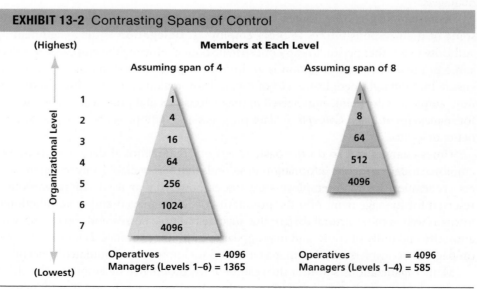

EXHIBIT 13-2 Contrasting Spans of Control

Source: Based on J. H. Gittell, "Supervisory Span, Relational Coordination, and Flight Departure Performance: A Reassessment of Postbureaucracy Theory," *Organization Science*, July–August 2001, 468–483.

span of control The number of employees who report to a manager.

The trend in recent years has been toward wider spans of control.[11] Wider spans of control are consistent with recent efforts by companies to reduce costs, cut overhead, speed up decision making, increase flexibility, get closer to customers, and empower employees. However, to ensure that performance does not suffer because of these wider spans, organizations have been investing heavily in employee training. Managers recognize that they can handle a wider span when employees know their jobs inside and out or can turn to their co-workers when they have questions.

Centralization and Decentralization

Centralization refers to the degree to which decision making is concentrated at a single point in the organization. In centralized organizations, top managers make all the decisions, and lower-level managers merely carry out their directives. In organizations at the other extreme, decentralized decision making is pushed down to the managers closest to the action or to work groups. The concept of centralization includes only formal authority—that is, the rights inherent to a position.

An organization characterized by centralization is inherently different structurally from one that is decentralized. In an organization characterized by **decentralization**, employees can act more quickly to solve problems, more people provide input into decisions, and employees are less likely to feel alienated from those who make decisions that affect their work lives. Decentralized departments make it easier to address customer concerns as well. The effects of centralization and decentralization can be predicted: Centralized organizations are better for avoiding commission errors (bad choices), while decentralized organizations are better for avoiding omission errors (lost opportunities).[12]

Management efforts to make organizations more flexible and responsive have produced a recent trend toward decentralized decision making by lower-level managers, who are closer to the action and typically have more detailed knowledge about problems than top managers. Big retailers such as Hudson's Bay have given store managers

David Carson/MCT/Landov

With more than 7000 neighbourhood and airport locations throughout North America and Europe, Enterprise Rent-A-Car empowers employees at the local level to make decisions that affect their work. Decentralization gives Enterprise a competitive advantage by enabling employees to provide personalized service that results in high customer satisfaction.

centralization The degree to which decision making is concentrated at a single point in the organization.

decentralization The degree to which decision making is distributed to lower-level employees.

considerably more discretion in choosing what merchandise to stock in individual stores. Doing so allows the stores to compete more effectively against local merchants. When Procter & Gamble empowered small groups of employees to make decisions about new-product development independent of the usual hierarchy, it was able to rapidly increase the proportion of new products ready for market.[13] Concerning creativity, research investigating a large number of Finnish organizations demonstrated that companies with decentralized research and development offices in multiple locations were better at producing innovation than companies that centralized all research and development in a single office.[14]

Decentralization is often necessary for companies with offshore sites because localized decision making is needed to respond to each region's profit opportunities, client base, and specific laws, while centralized oversight is needed to hold regional managers accountable. Failure to successfully balance these priorities can harm not only the organization, but also its relationships with foreign governments.[15]

Formalization

Formalization refers to the degree to which jobs within the organization are standardized. If a job is highly formalized, the employee has a minimal amount of discretion over what to do and when and how to do it, resulting in consistent and uniform output. There are explicit job descriptions, lots of organizational rules, and clearly defined procedures covering work processes. Formalization not only eliminates the possibility of employees engaging in alternative behaviours; it removes the need for them to consider alternatives. Conversely, where formalization is low, job behaviours are relatively nonprogrammed, and employees have a great deal of freedom to exercise discretion in their work.

McDonald's is an example of a company where employee routines are highly formalized. Employees are instructed in such things as how to greet the customer (smile, be sincere, make eye contact), ask for and receive payment (state amount of order clearly and loudly, announce the amount of money the customer gives to the employee, count change out loud and efficiently), and thank the customer (give a sincere thank you, make eye contact, ask customer to come again). McDonald's includes this information in training and employee handbooks, and managers are given a checklist of these behaviours so that they can observe their employees to ensure that the proper procedures are followed.[16]

The degree of formalization can vary widely among organizations and within organizations. In general, research from 94 high-technology Chinese firms indicated that formalization is a detriment to team flexibility in decentralized organization structures, suggesting that formalization does not work as well where duties are inherently interactive, or where there is a need to be flexible and innovative.[17] For example, publishing representatives who call on college and university professors to inform them of their company's new publications have a great deal of freedom in their jobs. They have only a general sales pitch, which they tailor as needed, and rules and procedures governing their behaviour may be little more than suggestions on what to emphasize about forthcoming titles and the requirement to submit a weekly sales report. At the other extreme, clerical and editorial employees in the same publishing houses may need to be at their desks by 8 a.m. and follow a set of precise procedures dictated by management.

Boundary Spanning

We have described ways that organizations create well-defined task structures and chains of authority. These systems facilitate control and coordination for specific tasks, but if there is too much division within an organization, attempts to coordinate across groups

formalization The degree to which jobs within the organization are standardized.

BMW encourages all employees, including this production worker at its plant in Jakarta, Indonesia, to build relationships throughout the global company. Boundary spanning at BMW links R & D, design, production, and marketing individuals to speed problem solving and innovation and to adapt to market fluctuations.

can be disastrous. One way to overcome compartmentalization and retain the positive elements of structure is to encourage or create boundary-spanning roles.

Within a single organization, **boundary spanning** occurs when individuals form relationships with people outside their formally assigned groups. An HR executive who frequently engages with the IT group is engaged in boundary spanning, as is a member of an R & D team who implements ideas from a production team. These activities help prevent formal structures from becoming too rigid and, not surprisingly, enhance organization and team creativity.[18]

Boundary-spanning activities occur not only within but also between organizations. Gathering information from external knowledge sources is especially advantageous in highly innovative industries where keeping up with the competition is challenging. Positive results are especially strong in organizations that encourage extensive internal communication; in other words, external boundary spanning is most effective when it is followed up with internal boundary spanning.[19]

Organizations can use formal mechanisms to facilitate boundary-spanning activities through their structures. One method is to assign formal liaison roles or develop committees of individuals from different areas of the organization. Development activities can also facilitate boundary spanning. Employees with experience in multiple functions, such as accounting and marketing, are more likely to engage in boundary spanning.[20] Many organizations try to set the stage for these sorts of positive relationships by creating job rotation programs so new hires get a better sense of different areas of the organization. A final method to encourage boundary spanning is to bring attention to overall organizational goals and shared identity concepts.

Common Organizational Designs

We now turn to describing some of the more common organizational designs: the *simple structure*, the *bureaucracy*, and the *matrix structure*.

boundary spanning When individuals form relationships outside their formally assigned groups.

The Simple Structure

What do a small retail store, a start-up electronics firm run by a hard-driving entrepreneur, and an airline "war room" in the midst of a company-wide pilots' strike have in common? They probably all use the **simple structure**.

The simple structure is said to be characterized most by what it is *not* rather than by what it is. The simple structure has a low degree of departmentalization, wide spans of control, authority centralized in a single person, and little formalization. It is a flat organization; it usually has only two or three vertical levels, a loose body of employees, and one individual with decision-making authority. Most companies start as a simple structure, and many innovative technology-based firms with short lifespans, like cellphone app development firms, remain compact by design.[21] The simple structure is most widely adopted in small businesses in which the manager and the owner are one and the same, such as the local corner grocery store.

The strength of the simple structure lies in its simplicity. It's fast, flexible, and inexpensive to maintain, and accountability is clear. One major weakness is that it's difficult to maintain in anything other than small organizations. It becomes increasingly inadequate as an organization grows because its low formalization and high centralization tend to create information overload at the top. Decision making typically becomes slower as the single executive continues trying to do it all. This proves to be the undoing of many small businesses. If the structure is not changed and made more elaborate, the firm often loses momentum and can eventually fail. The simple structure's other weakness is that it's risky—everything depends on one person. An illness at the top can literally halt the organization's information and decision-making capabilities.

❷ Describe the characteristics of a bureaucracy.

The Bureaucracy

Standardization! That is the key concept underlying all bureaucracies. Consider the bank where you keep your chequing account, the department store where you buy your clothes, or the government offices that collect your taxes, enforce health regulations, or provide local fire protection. They all rely on standardized work processes for coordination and control.

simple structure An organizational design characterized by a low degree of departmentalization, wide spans of control, authority centralized in a single person, and little formalization.

Hospitals benefit from standardized work processes and procedures common to bureaucratic structure because they help employees perform their jobs efficiently. The nursing staff in the maternity ward of a New Zealand hospital adhere to formal rules and regulations in providing care to moms and newborns.

A **bureaucracy** is characterized by highly routine operating tasks achieved through specialization, strictly formalized rules and regulations, tasks that are grouped into units, centralized authority, narrow spans of control, and decision making that follows the chain of command. Bureaucracy incorporates all the strongest degrees of departmentalization described earlier.

Bureaucracy is a dirty word in many people's minds. However, it does have advantages, primarily the ability to perform standardized activities in a highly efficient manner. Putting like specialties together in units results in economies of scale, minimum duplication of people and equipment, and a common language employees all share.

Strengths of Bureaucracy
German sociologist Max Weber, writing in the early 1900s, described bureaucracy as an alternative to the traditional administrative form. In the traditional model, leaders could be quite arbitrary, with authority based on personal relations. There were no general rules, and no separation between the leader's "private" and "public" business. Bureaucracy sometimes solved the problem of leaders who took advantage of their situation.

The primary strength of the bureaucracy lies in its ability to perform standardized activities in a highly efficient manner. Bureaucracies can get by nicely with less talented—and, hence, less costly—middle- and lower-level managers. Rules and regulations substitute for managerial discretion. Standardized operations, coupled with high formalization, allow decision making to be centralized. There is little need for innovative and experienced decision makers below the level of senior executives. In short, bureaucracy is an effective structure for ensuring consistent application of policies and practices and for ensuring accountability.

Weaknesses of Bureaucracy
Bureaucracy is not without its problems. Listen in on a dialogue among four executives in one company: "You know, nothing happens in this place until we *produce* something," said the production executive. "Wrong," commented the research and development manager. "Nothing happens until we *design* something!" "What are you talking about?" asked the marketing executive. "Nothing happens until we *sell* something!" The exasperated accounting manager responded, "It doesn't matter what you produce, design, or sell. No one knows what happens until we *tally up the results*!" This conversation highlights that bureaucratic specialization can create conflicts in which unit perspectives override the overall goals of the organization.

The other major weakness of a bureaucracy is something we have all experienced: obsessive concern with following the rules. When cases arise that don't precisely fit the rules, there is no room for modification. The bureaucracy is efficient only as long as employees confront problems that they have previously encountered and for which programmed decision rules have already been established. *Case Incident—"I Detest Bureaucracy"* on page 487 lets you consider alternatives to bureaucracy and how you might feel about these alternatives.

There are two aspects of bureaucracies we should explore: functional and divisional structures.

The Functional Structure
The **functional structure** groups employees by their similar specialties, roles, or tasks.[22] An organization organized into production, marketing, human resources, and accounting departments is an example. Many large organizations utilize this structure, although this is evolving to allow for quick changes in response to business opportunities. Still, there are advantages, including that the functional structure allows specialists to become experts more easily than if they worked in diversified units. Employees can also be motivated by a clear career path to the top of the organization chart specific to their specialties.

bureaucracy An organizational structure with highly routine operating tasks achieved through specialization, formalized rules and regulations, tasks that are grouped into units, centralized authority, narrow spans of control, and decision making that follows the chain of command.

functional structure An organizational structure that groups employees by their similar specialties, roles, or tasks.

The functional structure works well if the organization is focused on one product or service. Unfortunately it creates rigid, formal communications because the hierarchy dictates the communication protocol. Coordination among many units is a problem, and infighting in units and between units can lead to reduced motivation.

The Divisional Structure

The **divisional structure** groups employees into units by product, service, customer, or geographical market area.[23] It is highly departmentalized. Sometimes this structure is known by the type of division structure it uses: *product/service organizational structure* (like units for cat food, dog food, and bird food that report to an animal food producer), *customer organizational structure* (like units for outpatient care, inpatient care, and pharmacy that report to hospital administration), or *geographic organizational structure* (like units for Europe, Asia, and South America that report to corporate headquarters).[24]

The divisional structure has the opposite benefits and disadvantages of the functional structure. It facilitates coordination in units to achieve on-time completion, budget targets, and development and introduction of new products to market, while addressing the specific concerns of each unit. It provides clear responsibility for all activities related to a product, but with duplication of functions and costs. Sometimes this is helpful, say when the organization has a unit in Spain and another in China, very different markets, and a marketing strategy is needed for a new product. Marketing experts in both places can incorporate the appropriate cultural perspectives into their region's marketing campaign. However, the organization's marketing function employees in two places may represent an increased cost, in doing basically the same task in two different countries.

3 Describe the characteristics of a matrix organization.

The Matrix Structure

The **matrix structure** combines the functional and product structures, and we find it being used in advertising agencies, aerospace firms, research and development laboratories, construction companies, hospitals, government agencies, universities, management consulting firms, and entertainment companies.[25] It combines two forms of departmentalization: functional and product. Companies that use matrix-like structures include Boeing, BMW, IBM, and Procter & Gamble.

The most obvious structural characteristic of the matrix is that it breaks the unity-of-command concept. Employees in the matrix have two bosses—their functional department managers and their product managers.

Exhibit 13-3 shows the matrix structure used in a faculty of business administration. The academic departments of accounting, administrative studies, finance, and so forth are functional units. Specific programs (that is, products) are overlaid on the functions. Thus, members in a matrix structure have a dual chain of command: to their functional department and to their product groups. A professor of accounting who is teaching an undergraduate course reports to the director of undergraduate programs, as well as to the chair of the accounting department.

> What happens when a person reports to two bosses?

Advantages of a Matrix Structure

The strength of the matrix is its ability to foster coordination when the organization has a number of complex and interdependent activities. Information permeates the organization and more quickly reaches those people who need it. Furthermore, the matrix reduces "bureaupathologies"—its dual lines of authority limit people's tendency to protect their territories at the expense of the organization's goals.[26] A matrix also achieves economies of scale and facilitates the allocation of specialists by both providing the best resources and ensuring they are efficiently used.

divisional structure An organizational structure that groups employees into units by product, service, customer, or geographical market area.

matrix structure An organizational design that combines functional and product departmentalization; it has a dual chain of command.

EXHIBIT 13-3 Matrix Structure for a Faculty of Business Administration

Academic departments \ Programs	Undergraduate	Master's	PhD	Research	Executive development	Community service
Accounting						
Administrative studies						
Finance						
Information and decision sciences						
Marketing						
Organizational behaviour						
Quantitative methods						

Disadvantages of a Matrix Structure

The major disadvantages of the matrix lie in the confusion it creates, its tendency to foster power struggles, and the stress it places on individuals.[27] For individuals who desire security and absence of ambiguity, this work climate can be stressful. Reporting to more than one manager introduces role conflict, and unclear expectations introduce role ambiguity. Without the unity-of-command concept, ambiguity about who reports to whom is significantly increased and often leads to conflict and power struggles between functional and product managers.

Alternate Design Options

When Phil Caravaggio of Toronto-based Precision Nutrition talks about the organizational structure he has put in place, it sounds much like a team-based structure, which we describe below.[28] "It's a system for giving everyone real clear autonomy without everything devolving into chaos," he explains. There are few job titles, and no hierarchy. People are organized into circles and he refers to himself as the "lead link of the general company circle."

Holacracy generally groups people into autonomous circles based on projects. Each circle has a leader, but the leaders can change when necessary. Each circle also chooses a representative to sit in on meetings with other circles so that communication flows. This type of system requires a clear governance process so that everyone knows and understands the rules.

Caravaggio was able to test the system as Precision Nutrition undertook a big launch of a new certification program. He had to be out of town multiple times during the preparation, but said it was the smoothest launch they had ever had. He thought this signified that the structure could work for the company: "To me, it was the demarcation point between being a collection of heroic individuals, and having a system that is trusted by talented people to do what needs to be done."

In what situations could new forms of organization be effective?

Senior managers in a number of organizations have been developing new structural options with fewer layers of hierarchy and more emphasis on opening the boundaries of the organization.[29] In this section, we describe three such designs: the *virtual structure*, the *team structure*, and the *circular structure*. We also discuss how efforts to reduce bureaucracy and increase strategic focus have made downsizing routine.

The Virtual Structure

Why own when you can rent? That question captures the essence of the **virtual structure** (also sometimes called the *network* or *modular structure*), typically a small, core organization that outsources its major business functions.[30] The virtual structure is highly centralized, with little or no departmentalization.

The prototype of the virtual structure is today's film-making organization. In Hollywood's golden era, movies were made by huge, vertically integrated corporations. Studios such as MGM, Warner Brothers, and 20th Century Fox owned large movie lots and employed thousands of full-time specialists—set designers, camera people, film editors, directors, and even actors. Today, most movies are made by a collection of individuals and small companies who come together and make films project by project. This structural form allows each project to be staffed with the talent best suited to its demands, rather than just with the people employed by the studio. It minimizes bureaucratic overhead because there is no lasting organization to maintain. And it lessens long-term risks and their costs because there *is* no long term—a team is assembled for a finite period and then disbanded.

About one in nine Canadian companies engages in some sort of alliance. These alliances take many forms, ranging from precompetitive consortia to coproduction, cross-equity arrangements, and equity joint ventures with separate legal entities.[31] Amazon.ca partners with Canada Post in such an arrangement. Orders placed on Amazon.ca's website are fulfilled and shipped by Assured Logistics, which is part of Canada Post. Assured Logistics operates a Toronto-area warehouse that stores books, music, and movies so that they can be shipped when ordered, thus eliminating the need for Amazon to set up its own warehouse facility in Canada. Newman's Own, the food products company founded by Paul Newman, sells hundreds of millions of dollars in food every year yet employs only 28 people. This is possible because it outsources almost everything: manufacturing, procurement, shipping, and quality control.

Exhibit 13-4 shows a virtual organization in which management outsources all the primary functions of the business. The core of the organization is a small group of executives whose job is to oversee directly any activities done in house and to coordinate relationships with organizations that manufacture, distribute, and perform other crucial functions. The dotted lines represent the relationships typically maintained under contracts. In essence, managers in virtual structures spend most of their time coordinating and controlling external relations.

The major advantage of the virtual structure is its flexibility, which allows individuals with an innovative idea and little money to successfully compete against more established organizations. The structure also saves a great deal of money by eliminating permanent offices and hierarchical roles.[32]

EXHIBIT 13-4 A Virtual Organization

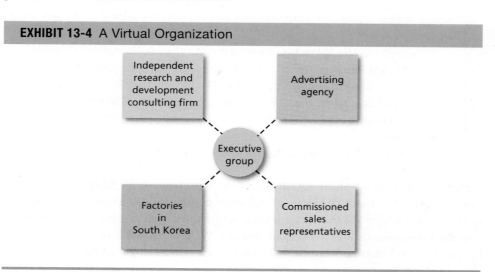

virtual structure A small core organization that outsources its major business functions.

The drawbacks of virtual structures have become increasingly clear as their popularity has grown.[33] They are in a state of perpetual flux and reorganization, which means roles, goals, and responsibilities are unclear, setting the stage for political behaviour. Cultural alignment and shared goals can be lost because of the low degree of interaction among members. Team members who are geographically dispersed and communicate infrequently find it difficult to share information and knowledge, which can limit innovation and slow response time. Sometimes—as with Vancouver-based Lululemon's shipments of unintentionally see-through yoga pants, where the deficiencies were not noticed until many had been sold—the consequences of having geographically remote managers can be embarrassing and even financially harmful to the company.[34] Ironically, some virtual organizations are less adaptable and innovative than those with well-established communication and collaboration networks. A leadership presence that reinforces the organization's purpose and facilitates communication is thus especially valuable.

OB in the Workplace explores some of the issues involved in creating a global virtual workplace.

OB IN THE WORKPLACE
The World Is My Corporate Headquarters

What does it mean to be a virtual company? Neither Automattic Inc., with 123 employees working in 26 countries nor Kalypso LP, with 150 employees around the globe, has a corporate headquarters or, truly, an office of any sort.[35] The implications of this new understanding of what it means to be a global virtual business are logistical, structural, and human.

On the logistics end of getting work done, office-less companies utilize every technology available, from Skype to blogs. Sensitive information is limited to phone discussions, though the difficulty of scheduling virtual meetings can be tricky across a number of time zones. When needed and at least annually, employees fly to designated intermediate spots for face-to-face time. Employees live where they want or where a strategic company presence for clients is desired.

The office-less company is not a good fit for every industry. The complete decentralization of the organization's physical structure dictates a nonhierarchical organization chart. High employee autonomy and empowerment to make decisions means supervision must be very light in order for the company to compete and take advantage of business opportunities specific to one employee's region, which the rest of the company cannot see.

With hiring possibilities worldwide, the company must also be clear about who can recruit new candidates and how to fit them into the organizational structure. Though the office-less company sounds like a good opportunity to maximize the worldwide talent pool, it presents challenges on a human level. According to Bill Poston, founding-partner of Kalypso, the office-less company does not work for people "who are uncomfortable with ambiguity." With the technology available, employees are not isolated, but the necessary lack of hierarchy means some employees may feel underappreciated.

The office-less company is still a rarity in the world, but its popularity is growing. It's very possible that truly global corporations of the future will need to consider a decentralization strategy that includes either many headquarters—or no headquarters at all. ......

The Team Structure

The **team structure** seeks to eliminate the chain of command and replace departments with empowered teams.[36] This structure removes vertical and horizontal

> **team structure** An organizational structure that replaces departments with empowered teams, and that eliminates horizontal boundaries and external barriers between customers and suppliers.

boundaries in addition to breaking down external barriers between the company and its customers and suppliers.

By removing vertical boundaries, management flattens the hierarchy and minimizes status and rank. Cross-hierarchical teams (which include top executives, middle managers, supervisors, and operative employees), participative decision-making practices, and 360-degree performance appraisals (in which peers and others evaluate performance) can be used. For example, at the Danish firm Oticon A/S, the world's largest hearing-aid manufacturer, all traces of hierarchy have disappeared. Everyone works at uniform mobile workstations, and project teams, not functions or departments, coordinate work.

As previously discussed, functional departments create horizontal boundaries between functions, product lines, and units. The way to reduce them is to replace functional departments with cross-functional teams and organize activities around processes. Xerox, for instance, develops new products through multidisciplinary teams that work on a single process instead of on narrow functional tasks.

When fully operational, the team structure may break down geographic barriers. Today, most large US companies see themselves as team-oriented global corporations; many, like Coca-Cola and McDonald's, do as much business overseas as in the United States, and some struggle to incorporate geographic regions into their structure. In other

CAREER OBJECTIVES

What Structure Should I Choose?

I'm running a small but growing business and need help figuring out how to keep positions flexible as we expand. What advice can you give me about designing job structures that will help combine my success today with growth for tomorrow?

—Anika

Dear Anika:

A surprising number of small businesses fail right at the point where they begin to grow. There are many reasons, including financing deficits and competitors that copy their good ideas. However, a common problem is that the structure the company began with is simply not right for a larger firm.

There are ways to meet the challenge. Start by looking at individual jobs and their responsibilities. Make a list for each job. When job roles and responsibilities are not defined, you do pick up a great deal of flexibility, assigning employees to tasks exactly when needed. Unfortunately, this flexibility also means it's hard to determine

which skills are available, or to identify gaps between planned strategy and available human resources.

Second, you may want to now define roles based on broad sets of competencies that span multiple levels of organizational functioning. In this *strategic competency model*, job roles and incentives are defined based on a clear structure. Here are the steps:

- *Look at the top level and think about the future.* In the competency model, you should use the mission statement and overall organizational strategies to evaluate your organization's future needs.
- *Once you've identified the organization's future needs, figure out a smart way to assign responsibilities to individuals.* You'll obviously need some specialization, but at the same time, consider general skills that will be useful for both growth and long-term sustainability.
- *As your business grows, identify applicants with the potential to meet future needs, and develop employee incentives to encourage broad skills profiles.* You'll want to

structure your plan so employees increase in competency as they move up the organization chart.

The most important thing to remember is that you aren't creating a job structure just for today—make sure it's ready to grow and change with your business.

Grow well!

Sources: Based on G. W. Stevens, "A Critical Review of the Science and Practice of Competency Modeling," *Human Resource Development Review* 12 (March 2013), pp. 86–107; P. Capelli and J. R. Keller, "Talent Management: Conceptual Approaches and Practical Challenges," *Annual Review of Organizational Psychology and Organizational Behavior* 1 (March 2014), pp. 305–331; and C. Fernández-Aráoz, "21st Century Talent Spotting," *Harvard Business Review*, June 2014, https://hbr.org/2014/06/21st-century-talent-spotting.

cases, the team approach is need-based. Such is the case with some Chinese companies, which made 93 acquisitions in the oil and gas industry in five years—incorporating each acquisition as a new team unit—to meet forecasted demand their resources in China could not meet.[37] The team structure provides a solution because it considers geography as more of a tactical, logistical issue than a structural one. In short, the goal may be to break down cultural barriers and open opportunities.

Some organizations create teams incorporating their employees and their customers or suppliers. For example, to ensure important product parts are reliably made to exacting specifications by its suppliers, Honeywell International partners some of its engineers with managers at those suppliers.

The Circular Structure

Picture the concentric rings of an archery target. In the centre are the executives, and radiating outward in rings grouped by function are the managers, then the specialists, then the workers. This is the **circular structure**.[38] Does it seem like organizational anarchy? Actually, there is still a hierarchy, but top management is at the very heart of the organization, with its vision spreading outward.

The circular structure has intuitive appeal for creative entrepreneurs, and some small innovative firms have claimed it. However, as in many of the current hybrid approaches, employees are apt to be unclear about whom they report to and who is running the show. We are still likely to see the popularity of the circular structure spread. The concept may have intuitive appeal for spreading a vision of corporate social responsibility (CSR), for instance.

The Leaner Organization: Downsizing

The goal of some organizational structures we have described is to improve agility by creating a lean, focused, and flexible organization. *Downsizing* is a systematic effort to make an organization leaner by closing locations, reducing staff, or selling off business units that do not add value. Downsizing does not necessarily mean physically shrinking the size of your office, although that has been happening too.

The radical shrinking of Toronto-based Sears Canada was a case of downsizing due to loss of market share and changes in consumer demand. Online shopping became a much bigger part of the retail landscape. The company sold off its biggest urban store properties in 2013, and has had mediocre results in recent years. In 2017 the company announced that it was closing 59 stores and eliminating 2900 jobs as part of a court-supervised restructuring. Sears did not develop a strong online presence, and that greatly affected its ability to meet the needs of consumers.[39]

Other firms downsize to direct all their efforts toward their core competencies. American Express claims to have been doing this in a series of layoffs over more than a decade: 7700 jobs in 2001; 6500 jobs in 2002; 7000 jobs (10 percent of its workforce) in 2008; and 4000 jobs in 2009. The 2013 cut of 5400 jobs (8.5 percent of the remaining workforce) represented "its biggest retrenchment in a decade."[40] An additional layoff of 4000 jobs was slated for 2015. Each layoff had been accompanied by a restructuring to reflect changing customer preferences, away from personal customer service and toward online customer service. According to CEO Ken Chenault, "Our business and industry continue to become transformed by technology. As a result of these changes, we have the need and the opportunity to evolve our organization and cost structure."[41]

Some companies focus on lean management techniques to reduce bureaucracy and speed decision making. For example, Starbucks adopted lean initiatives in 2009, which encompassed all levels of management and also focused on faster barista techniques and manufacturing processes. Customers have generally applauded the shortened wait

5 Describe the effects of downsizing on organizational structures and employees.

circular structure An organizational structure in which executives are at the centre, spreading their vision outward in rings grouped by function (managers, then specialists, then workers).

times and improved product consistency. Starbucks continues to reap returns from its lean initiatives, posting notable revenue gains each quarter.[42]

Despite the advantages of being a lean organization, the impact of downsizing on organizational performance is not without controversy. Reducing the size of the workforce has an immediately positive outcome in the form of lower wage costs. Companies downsizing to improve strategic focus often see positive effects on stock prices after the announcement. On the other hand, among companies that only cut employees but don't restructure, profits and stock prices usually decline. Part of the problem is the effect of downsizing on employee attitudes. Employees who remain often feel worried about future layoffs and may be less committed to the organization. Stress reactions can lead to increased sickness absences, lower concentration on the job, and lower creativity. Downsizing can also lead to more voluntary turnover, so vital human capital is lost. The result is a company that is more anemic than lean. The *Ethical Dilemma* on page 486 discusses the impact of job security on employee wellness and performance.

Companies can reduce negative impacts by preparing in advance, thus alleviating some employee stress and strengthening support for the new strategic direction.[43] The following are some effective strategies for downsizing. Most are closely linked to the principles for organizational justice we discussed in Chapter 4:

- *Invest.* Companies that downsize to focus on core competencies are more effective when they invest in high-involvement work practices afterward.

- *Communicate.* When employers make efforts to discuss downsizing with employees early, employees are less worried about the outcomes and feel the company is taking their perspective into account.

- *Participate.* Employees worry less if they can participate in the process in some way. In some companies, voluntary early retirement programs or severance packages can help achieve leanness without layoffs.

- *Assist.* Severance, extended health care benefits, and job search assistance demonstrate a company cares about its employees and honours their contributions.

Companies that make themselves lean can be more agile, efficient, and productive—but only if they make cuts carefully and help employees through the process.

---

6 Contrast the reasons for mechanistic and organic structural models.

Why Do Structures Differ?

One of the reasons why Phil Caravaggio put a new flattened organizational structure in place was that he didn't want to manage employees.[44] He thought his talents were better suited to leading and strategizing for the company. He was convinced that employees were capable of making decisions if they were empowered to do so. He also felt that roles could be stifling—that it might make more sense to have fluid roles where individuals helped with marketing on one project, but maybe dealt with managing the team on another project. Thus work at Precision Nutrition is organized into somewhat fluid project-based teams that form and disband as necessary.

Precision Nutrition's model is very much an organic model, which we discuss below.

mechanistic model A structure characterized by high specialization, rigid departmentalization, a clear chain of command, narrow spans of control, a limited information network, and centralization.

organic model A structure that is flat, uses cross-functional and cross-hierarchical teams, possesses a comprehensive information network, has wide spans of control, and has low formalization.

We have described many organizational design options. Exhibit 13-5 recaps our discussions by presenting two extreme models of organizational design. One we will call the **mechanistic model**. It's generally synonymous with the bureaucracy in that it has highly standardized processes for work, high formalization, and more managerial hierarchy. The other extreme is the **organic model**. It's flat, has fewer formal procedures for making decisions, has multiple decision makers, and favours flexible practices.[45]

EXHIBIT 13-5 Mechanistic vs. Organic Models

The Mechanistic Model　　　　　　**The Organic Model**

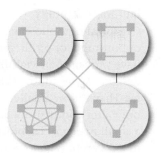

- High specialization
- Rigid departmentalization
- Clear chain of command
- Narrow spans of control
- Centralization
- High formalization

- Cross-functional teams
- Cross-hierarchical teams
- Free flow of information
- Wide spans of control
- Decentralization
- Low formalization

With these two models in mind, let's ask a few questions: Why are some organizations structured along more mechanistic lines, whereas others follow organic characteristics? What forces influence the choice of design? In the following pages, we present the major causes, or determinants, of an organization's structure: strategy, organizational size, technology, and environment.[46] The *Experiential Exercise* on page 485 gives you the opportunity to create different organizational structures and see how they can affect productivity.

Organizational Strategies

Because structure is a means to help management achieve its objectives, and objectives are derived from the organization's overall strategy, it's only logical that structure follow strategy. If management significantly changes the organization's strategy or its values, the structure must change to accommodate. For example, recent research indicates that aspects of organizational culture may influence the success of CSR initiatives.[47] If the culture is supported by the structure, the initiatives are more likely to have clear paths toward application. Most current strategy frameworks focus on three strategy dimensions—innovation, cost minimization, and imitation—and the structural design that works best with each.[48]

Innovation Strategy

To what degree does an organization introduce major new products or services? An **innovation strategy** strives to achieve meaningful and unique innovations. Obviously, not all firms pursue innovation. Apple and 3M do, but it certainly is not a strategy pursued by McDonald's. Innovative firms use competitive pay and benefits to attract top candidates and motivate employees to take risks. Some degree of the mechanistic structure can actually benefit innovation. Well-developed communication channels, policies for enhancing long-term commitment, and clear channels of authority all may make it easier for rapid change to occur smoothly.

Cost-Minimization Strategy

An organization pursuing a **cost-minimization strategy** tightly controls costs, refrains from incurring unnecessary innovation or marketing expenses, and cuts prices in selling a basic product. This would describe the strategy pursued by Walmart, as well as the

innovation strategy A strategy that emphasizes the introduction of major new products and services.

cost-minimization strategy A strategy that emphasizes tight cost controls, avoidance of unnecessary innovation or marketing expenses, and price cutting.

sellers of generic grocery products. Cost-minimizing organizations usually pursue fewer policies meant to develop commitment among their workforce.

Imitation Strategy

Organizations following an **imitation strategy** try to both minimize risk and maximize opportunity for profit, moving into new products or new markets only after innovators have proven their viability. Mass-market fashion manufacturers like H&M that copy designer styles follow this strategy, as do firms such as Hewlett-Packard and Caterpillar. They follow smaller and more innovative competitors with superior products, but only after competitors have demonstrated that the market is there. Italy's Moleskine, a small maker of fashionable notebooks, is another example of imitation strategy, but in a different way; looking to open more retail shops around the world, it imitates the expansion strategies of larger, successful fashion companies like Salvatore Ferragamo and Brunello Cucinelli.[49]

Exhibit 13-6 describes the structural option that best matches each strategy. Innovators need the flexibility of the organic structure (although, as we noted, they may use some elements of the mechanistic structure as well), while cost minimizers seek the efficiency and stability of the mechanistic structure. Imitators combine the two structures. They use a mechanistic structure in order to maintain tight controls and low costs in their current activities, but create organic subunits in which to pursue new undertakings.

Organizational Size

An organization's size significantly affects its structure. Organizations that employ 2000 or more people tend to have more specialization, more departmentalization, more vertical levels, and more rules and regulations than do small organizations. However, size becomes less important as an organization expands. Why is this? At around 2000 employees an organization is already fairly mechanistic. An additional 500 employees will not have much impact. But adding 500 employees to an organization that has only 300 members is likely to significantly shift it toward a more mechanistic structure.

Technology

Technology describes the way an organization transfers its inputs into outputs. Every organization has at least one technology for converting financial, human, and physical resources into products or services. For example, the Chinese consumer electronics company Haier uses an assembly-line process for mass-produced products, which is complemented by more flexible and innovative

What does *technology* mean?

EXHIBIT 13-6 The Strategy–Structure Relationship	
Strategy	**Structural Option**
Innovation	*Organic:* A loose structure; low specialization, low formalization, decentralized
Cost minimization	*Mechanistic:* Tight control; extensive work specialization, high formalization, high centralization
Imitation	*Mechanistic and organic:* Mix of loose with tight properties; tight controls over current activities and looser controls for new undertakings

imitation strategy A strategy of moving into new products or new markets only after their viability has already been proven.

technology The way in which an organization transfers its inputs into outputs.

structures to respond to customers and design new products.[50] Universities and colleges may use a number of instruction technologies to teach students—the formal lecture method, case analysis, experiential exercises, programmed learning, online instruction, and distance learning. Regardless, organizational structures adapt to their technology.

Variations in Technology

Numerous studies have examined the technology–structure relationship.[51] What differentiates technologies is their *degree of routineness*. Routine activities are characterized by automated and standardized operations, such as an assembly line, where one might affix a car door to a car at set intervals; automated transaction processing of sales transactions; and printing and binding of this book. Nonroutine activities are customized and require frequent revision and updating. They include furniture restoring, custom shoemaking, genetic research, and the writing and editing of this book. In general, organizations engaged in nonroutine activities tend to prefer organic structures, while those performing routine activities prefer mechanistic structures.

Environment

An organization's **environment** includes outside institutions or forces that can affect the organization's structure, such as suppliers, customers, competitors, and public pressure groups. Some organizations face dynamic environments—rapidly changing government regulations affecting their business, new competitors, difficulties in acquiring raw materials, continually changing product preferences by customers, and so on. Other organizations face relatively static environments—few forces in their environment are changing. Dynamic environments create significantly more uncertainty for managers than do static ones. To minimize uncertainty in key market arenas, managers may broaden their structure to sense and respond to threats. Most companies, including Pepsi and WestJet Airlines, have added social networking departments to their structure so as to respond to negative information posted on blogs. Or companies may form strategic alliances with other companies.

Any organization's environment has three dimensions: capacity, volatility, and complexity.[52]

The *capacity* of an environment refers to the degree to which it can support growth. Rich and growing environments generate excess resources, which can buffer the organization in times of relative scarcity.

Volatility describes the degree of instability in an environment. A dynamic environment with a high degree of unpredictable change makes it difficult for management to make accurate predictions. Because information technology changes at such a rapid pace, for instance, more organizations' environments are becoming volatile.

Finally, *complexity* is the degree of heterogeneity and concentration among environmental elements. Simple environments—like the tobacco industry, where the methods of production, competitive and regulatory pressures, and the like have not changed in quite some time—are homogeneous and concentrated. Environments characterized by heterogeneity and dispersion—like the broadband industry—are complex and diverse, with numerous competitors.

Exhibit 13-7 summarizes our definition of the environment along its three dimensions. The arrows in this figure are meant to indicate movement toward higher uncertainty. Organizations that operate in environments characterized as scarce, dynamic, and complex face the greatest degree of uncertainty because they have high unpredictability, little room for error, and a diverse set of elements in the environment to monitor constantly.

environment Those institutions or forces outside the organization that potentially affect the organization's performance.

EXHIBIT 13-7 Three-Dimensional Model of the Environment

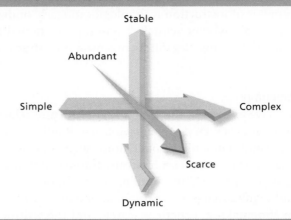

Given this three-dimensional definition of *environment*, we can offer some general conclusions about environmental uncertainty and structural arrangements. The more scarce, dynamic, and complex the environment, the more organic a structure should be. The more abundant, stable, and simple the environment, the more mechanistic a structure should be.

Institutions

Another factor that shapes organizational structure is **institutions**. These are cultural factors that act as guidelines for appropriate behaviour.[53] Institutional theory describes some of the forces that lead many organizations to have similar structures and, unlike the theories we've described so far, focuses on pressures that aren't necessarily adaptive. In fact, many institutional theorists try to highlight the ways corporate behaviours sometimes *seem* to be performance oriented but are actually guided by unquestioned social norms and conformity.

The most obvious institutional factors come from regulatory pressures; certain industries under government contracts, for instance, must have clear reporting relationships and strict information controls. Sometimes simple inertia determines an organizational form—companies can be structured in a particular way just because that's the way things have always been done. Organizations in countries with high power distance might have a structural form with strict authority relationships because it's seen as more legitimate in that culture. Some have attributed problems in adaptability in Japanese organizations to the institutional pressure to maintain authority relationships.

Sometimes organizations start to have a particular structure because of fads or trends. Organizations can try to copy other successful companies just to look good to investors, and not because they need that structure to perform better. Many companies have recently tried to copy the organic form of a company like Google only to find that such structures are a very poor fit with their operating environment. Institutional pressures are often difficult to see specifically because we take them for granted, but that doesn't mean they aren't powerful.

Organizational Designs and Employee Behaviour

institutions Cultural factors that lead many organizations to have similar structures, especially those factors that might not lead to adaptive consequences.

While Phil Caravaggio might find that holacracy has worked at Precision Nutrition, not everyone finds such a system a great way to work.[54] Zappos, the online shoe seller, had already introduced holacracy and decided to go a step further. In 2015, CEO Tony Hsieh announced that all management positions were going to be eliminated, and that employees needed to "either get on board with a bossless future or get out (with a generous severance)." Managers could keep their salaries, but were told to find themselves new roles in the company.

Many employees were confused, and by the end of 2015, 30 percent had resigned, which is a large number for an organization that had previously prided itself on employee engagement. Six months after Hsieh's announcement, some employees were still trying (unhappily) to figure out new roles for themselves.

We opened this chapter by implying that an organization's structure can have significant effects on its members. What might those effects be?

A review of the evidence leads to a pretty clear conclusion: You cannot generalize! Not everyone prefers the freedom and flexibility of organic structures. Different factors stand out in different structures as well. In highly formalized, heavily structured, mechanistic organizations, the level of fairness in formal policies and procedures (organizational justice) is a very important predictor of satisfaction. In more personal, individually adaptive organic organizations, employees value interpersonal justice more.[55] Some people are most productive and satisfied when work tasks are standardized and ambiguity minimized—that is, in mechanistic structures. So any discussion of the effect of organizational design on employee behaviour has to address individual differences. To do so, let's consider employee preferences for work specialization, span of control, and centralization.[56] *Focus on Research* looks at the impact of working from home on employee behaviour.

The evidence generally indicates that work specialization contributes to higher employee productivity—but at the price of job satisfaction. However, work specialization

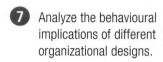

7 Analyze the behavioural implications of different organizational designs.

FOCUS ON RESEARCH
Working from Home

Are there advantages to companies that let employees work from home?   Employees who work from home even part of the time report they are happier, and as we saw in Chapter 3, happier employees are likely to be more productive than their dissatisfied counterparts.[57] From an organization's perspective, companies are realizing gains of five to seven extra work hours a week for each employee working from home. There are also cost savings, from reduced overhead for office space and utilities to elimination of unproductive social time. Employers of a home-based workforce can establish work teams and organizational reporting relationships with little attention to office politics, opening the potential to more objectively assign roles and responsibilities. These may be some of the reasons organizations have increasingly endorsed the concept of telecommuting.

Although we can all think of jobs that may never be conducive to working from home (such as many in the service industry), not all positions that *could* be based from home *should* be. Research indicates the success of a work-from-home position depends on the job's structure even more than on its tasks. The amount of interdependence needed between employees within a team or in a reporting relationship sometimes requires *epistemic interdependence*, which is each employee's ability to predict what other employees will do. Organization consultants pay attention to how employee roles relate in the *architecture* of the organization chart, realizing that intentional relationship building is key. Thus, while an employee may complete the tasks of a job well by working alone from home, the benefits of teamwork can be lost.

The success of a work-from-home program depends on the individual, the job, and the culture of the organization. Work from home can be satisfying for employees and efficient for organizations, but research suggests that there are limits. . . . .

is not an unending source of higher productivity. Problems start to surface, and productivity begins to suffer, when the human diseconomies of doing repetitive and narrow tasks overtake the economies of specialization. As the workforce has become more highly educated and desirous of jobs that are intrinsically rewarding, we seem to reach the point at which productivity begins to decline as a function of specialization more quickly than in the past. While decreased productivity often prompts companies to add oversight and inspection roles, the better answer may be to reorganize work functions and accountability.[58]

There is still a segment of the workforce that prefers the routine and repetitiveness of highly specialized jobs. Some individuals want work that makes minimal intellectual demands and provides the security of routine; for them, high work specialization is a source of job satisfaction. The question, of course, is whether they represent 2 percent of the workforce or 52 percent. Given that some self-selection operates in the choice of careers, we might conclude that negative behavioural outcomes from high specialization are most likely to surface in professional jobs occupied by individuals with high needs for personal growth and diversity.

It's probably safe to say that no evidence supports a relationship between span of control and employee satisfaction or performance. Although it's intuitively attractive to argue that large spans might lead to higher employee performance because they provide more distant supervision and more opportunity for personal initiative, the research fails to support this notion. Some people like to be left alone; others prefer the security of a boss who is quickly available at all times. Consistent with several of the contingency theories of leadership discussed in Chapter 11, we would expect factors such as employees' experiences and abilities and the degree of structure in their tasks to explain when wide or narrow spans of control are likely to contribute to their performance and job satisfaction. However, some evidence indicates that a manager's job satisfaction increases as the number of employees supervised increases.

We find fairly strong evidence linking centralization and job satisfaction. In general, less centralized organizations have a greater amount of autonomy. Autonomy appears positively related to job satisfaction. But, again, while one employee may value freedom, another may find autonomous environments frustratingly ambiguous.

We can draw one obvious insight: People don't select employers randomly. They are attracted to, are selected by, and stay with organizations that suit their personal characteristics.[59] Job candidates who prefer predictability are likely to seek out and take employment in mechanistic structures, and those who want autonomy are more likely to end up in organic structures. So the effect of structure on employee behaviour is undoubtedly reduced when the selection process facilitates proper matching of individual characteristics with organizational characteristics. Furthermore, companies should strive to establish, promote, and maintain the unique identity of their structures since skilled employees may quit as a result of dramatic changes.[60]

GLOBAL IMPLICATIONS

When we think about how culture influences how organizations are to be structured, several questions come to mind. First, does culture really matter to organizational structure? Second, do employees in different countries vary in their perceptions of different types of organizational structures? Finally, does downsizing have an effect for different cultures? Let's tackle each question in turn.

Culture and Organizational Structure

Does culture really affect organizational structure? The answer might seem obvious—yes!—but there are reasons it may not matter as much as you think. The US model of business has been very influential on organizational structures in other countries. Moreover, US and Canadian structures themselves have been influenced by structures in other countries (especially Japan, Great Britain, and Germany). However, cultural concerns still might be important. Bureaucratic structures still dominate in many parts of Europe and Asia. One management expert argues that US management often places too much emphasis on individual leadership, which may be jarring in countries where decision making is more decentralized.[61]

Culture and Employee Structure Preferences

Research suggests that national culture influences the preference for structure.[62] Organizations that operate with people from high power-distance cultures, such as Greece, France, and most of Latin America, find that their employees are much more accepting of mechanistic structures than are employees from low power-distance countries. So consider cultural differences along with individual differences when predicting how structure will affect employee performance and satisfaction.

Culture and the Impact of Downsizing

The changing landscape of organizational structure designs has implications for the individual progressing on a career path. Research with managers in Japan, the United Kingdom, and the United States indicated that employees who weathered downsizing and resulting hybrid organizational structures considered their future career prospects diminished. While this may or may not have been correct, their thinking shows that organizational structure does affect the employee and thus must be carefully designed.[63]

Summary

The theme of this chapter is that an organization's internal structure contributes to explaining and predicting behaviour. That is, in addition to individual and group factors, structural relationships in which people work have a bearing on employee attitudes. What is the basis for this argument? To the degree that an organization's structure reduces ambiguity for employees and clarifies concerns such as "What am I supposed to do?" "How am I supposed to do it?" "To whom do I report?" and "To whom do I go if I have a problem?" it shapes their attitudes and facilitates and motivates them to higher levels of performance. Exhibit 13-8 summarizes what we have discussed.

EXHIBIT 13-8 Organizational Structure: Its Determinants and Outcomes

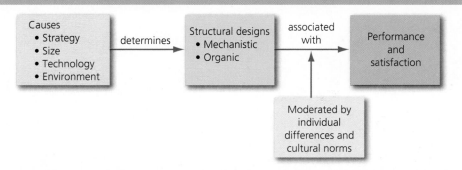

SNAPSHOT SUMMARY

What Is Organizational Structure?
- Work Specialization
- Departmentalization
- Chain of Command
- Span of Control
- Centralization and Decentralization
- Formalization
- Boundary Spanning

Common Organizational Designs
- The Simple Structure
- The Bureaucracy
- The Matrix Structure

Alternate Design Options
- The Virtual Structure
- The Team Structure
- The Circular Structure

- The Leaner Organization: Downsizing

Why Do Structures Differ?
- Organizational Strategies
- Organizational Size
- Technology
- Environment
- Institutions

Organizational Designs and Employee Behaviour

MyLab Management

 PERSONAL INVENTORY ASSESSMENT

Study, practise, and explore real business situations with these helpful resources:

- **Study Plan:** Check your understanding of chapter concepts with self-study quizzes.
- **Online Lesson Presentations:** Study key chapter topics and work through interactive assessments to test your knowledge and master management concepts.
- **Videos:** Learn more about the management practices and strategies of real companies.
- **Simulations:** Practise management decision-making in simulated business environments.

OB at Work

for **Review**

1. What seven key elements define an organization's structure?

2. What are the characteristics of a bureaucracy, and how does it differ from a simple structure?

3. What are the characteristics of a matrix organization?

4. What are the characteristics of virtual, team, and circular structures?

5. What are the effects of downsizing on organizational structures and employees?

6. What is the difference between a mechanistic structure and an organic structure?

7. What are the behavioural implications of different organizational designs?

for **Managers**

- Know that specialization can make operations more efficient, but excessive specialization can create employee dissatisfaction and reduce motivation.

- Avoid designing rigid hierarchies that overly limit employees' empowerment and autonomy.

- Balance the advantages of remote work against the potential pitfalls before adding flexible workplace options into the organization's structure.

- Downsize your organization to realize major cost savings, and focus the company around core competencies—if necessary. Downsizing can have a significant negative impact on employee morale.

- Consider the scarcity, dynamism, and complexity of the environment, and balance organic and mechanistic elements when designing an organizational structure.

for **You**

- Think about the type of organizational structure that suits you best when you look for a job. You may prefer a structured workplace, like that of a mechanistic organization. Or you may prefer a much less structured workplace, like that of an organic organization.

- If you decide to start your own company, know the different structural considerations so that you can create an organization that meets your needs as both a business person and a person with additional interests.

- As a manager or as an entrepreneur, consider how much responsibility (centralization/ decentralization) you want to take for yourself compared with how much you are willing to share with others in the organization.

OB at Work

THE END OF MANAGEMENT

POINT

Management—at least as we know it—is dying.[64] Formal organizational structures are giving way to flatter, less bureaucratic, less formal structures. And that's a good thing.

Innovative companies such as Apple, Google, Facebook, Twitter, and Groupon were born and now thrive thanks not to a multilayered bureaucracy, but to an innovative idea that was creatively executed by a flexible group of people freely collaborating. Management in those companies exists to facilitate, rather than control.

The scope of what managers do has broadened to include typing, taking notes, and managing their own files/schedules, while the scope of what administrative assistants do has broadened to include making social media posts and assuming technical duties. The most innovative firms have questioned whether they need job titles at all, instead emphasizing collaboration throughout the organization.

The best companies have eliminated offices altogether and encourage employees to mingle and form teams according to their project interests. This suits younger workers who aspire to work *with* the top players rather than *report to* them, and who value flexible hours and work-from-home options. Job titles are gone, roles are ambiguous, and reporting relationships morph by project.

The talent is ready for the elimination of management as we know it. The successful corporation of the future will have a flatter organizational structure and accountability based on performance.

COUNTERPOINT

There is no "one size fits all" approach to organizational structure. How flat, informal, and collaborative an organization should be depends on many factors, but no matter what, management structure is needed. Let's consider two cases.

People lauded how loosely and informally Warren Buffett structured his investment firm, Berkshire Hathaway, until it was discovered his CFO and heir apparent David Sokol was on the take. Wouldn't Buffett have known Sokol was compromised if he had supervised more closely or had structures in place to check such "freedom"? It's hard to argue with Berkshire Hathaway's past successes, but they don't prove the company is ideally structured.

At Honeywell International, CEO David Cote seems relaxed and fun-loving (he rides a Harley-Davidson and wears a leather bomber jacket to work), but his hard-hitting work ethic and firm hand on the reins are legendary. As the leader of a global technology and manufacturing conglomerate, Cote keeps a tight rein on the four industry divisions and 132 000 employees.

Cote's control focus does not end at the executive suite. At the factories, job titles are painted literally on the *floor* to indicate who needs to be present—and standing—at organizational meetings limited to 15 minutes. Is Cote a control freak? Maybe, but he successfully merged three disparate company cultures and more than 250 factories. The new Honeywell has climbed the *Fortune* 500 ranks and pulls in over $40 billion in annual sales. Profits have increased faster than sales, in part due to Cote's insistence on freezing raises and hiring only two to three employees for every four to five who exit.

Berkshire Hathaway and Honeywell illustrate the strong need for management structure in an ever-changing, diverse, worldwide marketplace.

BREAKOUT **GROUP** EXERCISES

Form small groups to discuss the following topics, as assigned by your instructor:

1. Describe the structure of an organization in which you worked. Was the structure appropriate for the tasks being done?

2. Have you ever worked in an organization with a structure that seemed inappropriate to the task? What would have improved the structure?

3. You are considering opening up a coffee bar with several of your friends. What kind of structure might you use? After the coffee bar becomes successful, you decide that expanding the number of branches might be a good idea. What changes to the structure might you make?

EXPERIENTIAL EXERCISE

The Sandwich Shop

Divide the class into groups of at least 4 individuals.

Background: The managers of a new chain of sandwich shops will need to determine what types of sandwiches consumers want and find recipes and ingredients. Ingredient sources, prices, and other logistical requirements (like refrigeration) will need to be determined, purchasing decisions will be ongoing, and supplier relationships will need to be managed. Financing must also be arranged at this early phase. With this groundwork, the company will move to the next stage of marketing, including pricing and the development of advertising materials. Finally, selecting and training workers will occur.

Each group creates the following:

A simple structure: Determine what a simple structure would look like for this organization. Recall that a simple structure is one in which there is little hierarchy, wide spans of control, and centralized decision making. To whom would the various tasks described above be assigned? What sort of delegation might take place? Who would coordinate the multiple operations? About how many people would be acting in an administrative role, and what sort of spans of control would they have? What challenges will the organization face as it grows?

A bureaucracy: Determine what a bureaucratic structure would look like for this organization. Bureaucracies are marked by more hierarchy, small spans of control, and specialized decision making. Again, you will want to establish task assignments, delegation, coordination, and the number of individuals required. Also consider possibilities for future growth with a bureaucratic system.

A virtual structure: Determine what a virtual structure would look like for this organization if many of the aspects of the business are outsourced. Consider which tasks can be adequately performed by individuals who do not work within the restaurant chain, and which should be kept in house.

Debriefing

After all groups have developed different structural options, convene for class discussion for groups to describe how they created responsibilities for different individuals. Then the class should talk about which system of organization seems most beneficial for this business.

ETHICAL **DILEMMA**

Post–Millennium Tensions in the Flexible Organization

The message from the business press has been consistent: Don't count on long-term employment.[65] For years, job seekers have been told they should expect to be responsible for their own careers and prepare for the possibility that they will be changing jobs frequently. A simple look at employment trends also confirms that highly routine and well-defined jobs have been decreasing in number.

The shift has often been described in fairly positive terms. Managers work to create organizations that have laudable characteristics like adaptability, flexibility, and creativity. Author Micha Kaufman notes that doing well in contemporary business environments means "having the flexibility to let go of the ideas of the past, the courage to constantly re-evaluate plans for the future, and the presence of mind to adapt to life, as it is, in the moment." There is a lot of appeal in creating your own future at work.

At the same time, many workers land in precarious positions. Researchers find that individuals who feel insecure or uncertain about future employment experience higher levels of psychological strain and worry. Insecure workers also get sick more frequently. Contrary to the positive image of the freelance worker with boundless energy and creativity, evidence shows that for many individuals, a lack of job security can result in exhaustion and an apprehensive approach to work problems.

Corporate leaders ask themselves what their role in creating job security should be. Some note that companies built around stability and security are less likely to compete successfully and may go out of business. Many organizations try to maintain flexibility *and* a certain level of security. For example, Scripps Health has maintained a pool of internal transfer opportunities and training assignments for individuals whose job functions are no longer needed. As a result, even within the highly volatile health care industry, it has been able to avoid layoffs. However, systems that provide job security do not come cheaply, nor are they feasible for all companies.

Questions

1. Do you think that stability is good or bad for employees?

2. Do employers have an ethical responsibility to provide security for employees or just a warning about a lack of security?

3. If long-term employment security is not feasible, what alternatives might employers provide to help employees make smoother transitions?

CASE INCIDENTS

Creative Deviance: Bucking the Hierarchy?

One of the major functions of an organizational hierarchy is to increase standardization and control for top managers.[66] Using the chain of command, managers can direct the activities of subordinates toward a common purpose. If the right person with a creative vision is in charge of a hierarchy, the results can be phenomenal. Until Steve Jobs's passing in October 2011, Apple had used a strongly top-down creative process in which most major decisions and innovations flowed directly through Jobs and were subsequently delegated to subteams as specific assignments to complete.

Then there is creative deviance, in which individuals create extremely successful products despite being told by senior management to stop working on them. The electrostatic displays used in more than half of Hewlett-Packard's instruments, the tape slitter that was one of the most important process innovations in 3M's history, and Nichia's development of multi-billion-dollar LED bright lighting technology were all officially rejected by the management hierarchy. In these cases, an approach like Apple's would have shut down some of the most successful products the companies ever produced. Doing "business as usual" can become such an imperative in a hierarchical organization that new ideas are seen as threats rather than opportunities for development.

It's not immediately apparent why top-down decision making works so well for one highly creative company like Apple, while hierarchy nearly ruined innovations at several other organizations. It may be that Apple's structure is actually quite simple, with relatively few layers and a great deal of responsibility placed on each individual for his or her own outcomes. Or it may be that Apple simply had a very unique leader who was able to rise above the conventional strictures of a CEO to create a culture of constant innovation.

Questions

1. Do you think it's possible for an organization to deliberately create an "anti-hierarchy" to encourage employees to engage in more acts of creative deviance? What steps might a company take to encourage creative deviance?

2. What are the dangers of an approach that encourages creative deviance?

3. Why do you think a company such as Apple is able to be creative with a strongly hierarchical structure, whereas other companies find hierarchy limiting?

4. Do you think Apple's success was entirely dependent upon Steve Jobs's role as head of the hierarchy? What are the potential liabilities of a company being so strongly connected to the decision making of a single individual?

"I Detest Bureaucracy"

Greg Strakosch, founder and executive chairman of interactive media company TechTarget, hates bureaucracy.[67] So he has created a workplace where his 600 employees are free to come and go as they please. There are no set policies mandating working hours or detailing sick, personal, or vacation days. Employees are free to take as much vacation as they want and to work the hours when they are most productive—even if it's between midnight and 4 a.m. What if you need a day off to take your kid to camp? No problem. Strakosch says ideas like setting a specific number of sick days "strike me as arbitrary and dumb." He trusts his employees to act responsibly.

Strakosch is quick to state that "this isn't a country club." A painstaking hiring process is designed to weed out all but the most autonomous. Managers set ambitious quarterly goals, and employees are given plenty of independence to achieve them. However, there is little tolerance for failure. As TechTarget's website states, there is a 100 percent focus on results. Employees are fired for underachieving.

Moreover, while hours are flexible, employees frequently put in at least 50 hours a week. In addition, regardless of hours worked, employees are required to remain accessible via email, cellphone, instant messaging, or laptop.

Strakosch's approach seems to be working. TechTarget became a public company in May 2007 with a $100 million IPO (initial public offering) and has grown to become the leading online media company for the technology sector. In May 2014, the company was recognized as one of the "Best Places to Work," the seventh time it has been so recognized.

Questions

1. What type of organizational structure does TechTarget have?

2. Why does this type of structure work at TechTarget?

3. How transferable is this structure to other organizations?

4. Would you want to work at TechTarget? Why or why not?

FROM CONCEPTS TO SKILLS

Delegating Authority

Managers get things done through other people. Because there are limits to any manager's time and knowledge, effective managers need to understand how to delegate. *Delegation* is the assignment of authority to another person to carry out specific duties. It allows an employee to make some of the decisions. Delegation should not be confused with participation. In participative decision making, there is a sharing of authority. In delegation, employees make decisions on their own.

A number of actions differentiate the effective delegator from the ineffective delegator. You can become a more effective delegator if you use the following five suggestions:[68]

1. *Clarify the assignment.* The place to begin is to determine what is to be delegated and to whom. You need to identify the person most capable of doing the task, then determine if he or she has the time and motivation to do the job.

   Assuming that you have a willing and able employee, it is your responsibility to provide clear information on what is being delegated, the results you expect, and any time or performance expectations you hold.

   Unless there is an overriding need to adhere to specific methods, you should delegate only the end results. That is, get agreement on what is to be done and the end results expected, but let the employee decide on the means.

2. *Specify the employee's range of discretion.* Every act of delegation comes with constraints. You are delegating authority to act, but not unlimited authority. What you are delegating is authority to act on certain issues and, on those issues, within certain parameters. You need to specify what those parameters are so employees know, in no uncertain terms, the range of their discretion.

3. *Allow the employee to participate.* One of the best sources for determining how much authority will be necessary to accomplish a task is the employee who will be held accountable for that task. If you allow employees to participate in determining what is delegated, how much authority is needed to get the job done, and the standards by which they will be judged, you increase employee motivation, satisfaction, and accountability for performance.

4. *Inform others that delegation has occurred.* Delegation should not occur in a vacuum. Not only do you and the employee need to know specifically what has been delegated and how much authority has been granted, but anyone else who may be affected by the delegation act also needs to be informed.

5. *Establish feedback controls.* The establishment of controls to monitor the employee's progress increases the likelihood that important problems will be identified early and that the task will be completed on time and to the desired specifications. For instance, agree on a specific time for completion of the task, and then set progress dates when the employee will report back on how well he or she is doing and any major problems that have surfaced. This can be supplemented with periodic spot checks to ensure that authority guidelines are not being abused, organization policies are being followed, and proper procedures are being met.

Practising Skills

You are the director of research and development for a large pharmaceutical manufacturer. Six people report directly to you: Sue (your secretary), Dale (laboratory manager), Todd (quality standards manager), Linda (patent coordination manager), Ruben (market coordination manager), and Marjorie (senior projects manager). Dale is the most senior of the five managers and is generally acknowledged as the chief candidate to replace you if you are promoted or leave.

You have received your annual instructions from the CEO to develop next year's budget for your area. The task is relatively routine, but takes quite a bit of time. In the past, you have always done the annual budget yourself. But this year, because your workload is exceptionally heavy, you have decided to try something different. You are going to assign budget preparation to one of your subordinate managers. The obvious choice is Dale. Dale has been with the company longest, is highly dependable, and, as your probable successor, is most likely to gain from the experience. The budget is due on your boss's desk in eight weeks. Last year it took you about 30 to 35 hours to complete. However, you have done a budget many times before. For a novice, it might take double that amount of time.

The budget process is generally straightforward. You start with last year's budget and modify it to reflect inflation and changes in departmental objectives. All the data that Dale will need are in your files, online, or can be obtained from your other managers.

You have just walked over to Dale's office and informed him of your decision. He seemed enthusiastic about doing the budget, but he also has a heavy workload. He told you, "I'm regularly coming in around 7 a.m. and it's unusual for me to leave before 7 p.m. For the past five weekends, I've even come in on Saturday mornings to get my work done. I can do my best to try to find time to do the budget." Specify exactly what you would say to Dale and the actions you would take if Dale agrees to do the budget.

Reinforcing Skills

1. Watch a classic movie that has examples of "managers" delegating assignments. Pay explicit attention to the incidence of delegation. Was delegating done effectively? What was good about the practice? How might it have been improved? Movies with delegation examples include *The Godfather*, *The Firm*, *Star Trek*, *Office Space*, *Nine-to-Five*, and *Working Girl*.

2. The next time you have to do a group project for a class, pay explicit attention to how tasks are delegated. Does someone assume a leadership role? If so, note how closely the delegation process is followed. Is delegation different in project or study groups than in typical work groups?

14 Organizational Change

Can Cirque du Soleil continue to adapt in order to deal with the challenges in the circus world that brought down the Ringling Bros. Circus?

LEARNING OUTCOMES

After studying this chapter, you should be able to:

1. Identify the forces for change.
2. Compare the four main approaches to managing organizational change.
3. Describe the sources of resistance to change.
4. Describe three ways to create a culture for change.

Sarah Edwards/IPA/WENN.com/Alamy

Montreal-based Cirque du Soleil has continued to reinvent itself, even while it faced financial difficulties during 2011–2013 that resulted in 600 layoffs.[1] Other circuses have been shuttered in recent years. Ringling Bros. and Barnum & Bailey Circus, the oldest circus in North America, closed down in May 2017 after 146 years. The circus experienced declining attendance, high costs, and battles with animal rights groups. It did not seem to have an idea for moving the circus in a different direction. Kenneth Feld, chairman and CEO of Feld Entertainment, which owns Ringling Bros., said times had changed too much to save the circus. "It's a different model that we can't see how it works in today's world to justify and maintain an affordable ticket price. So you've got all these things working against it."

By contrast, Cirque du Soleil seems to relish change. The circus had been privately owned since its start in 1984, but in 2015, 90 percent of the company was sold to investors, including a 20 percent stake to Chinese investment firm Fosun.

Cirque du Soleil is just one of many organizations that needs to reinvent itself to survive in a challenging business environment, something that Ringling Bros. was not able to do. Engaging in any kind of change in an organization is not easy. In this chapter, we examine the forces for change, managing change, and contemporary change issues.

OB IS FOR EVERYONE

- Are there positive approaches to change?
- How do you respond to change?
- What makes organizations resist change?

THE BIG IDEA

Change is inevitable, and being able to adapt to change will help the process go more smoothly.

① Identify the forces for change.

Forces for Change

No company today is in a particularly stable environment. Even those with dominant market share must change, sometimes radically. For example, the market for smartphones has been especially volatile.[2] During the fourth quarter of 2016, 78.29 million iPhones were sold, compared with 76.78 million Samsung phones. Contrast this with the fourth quarter of 2015, in which somewhat fewer (74.78 million) iPhones were sold, vs. somewhat more (81.3 million) Samsung phones. At the same time, the Chinese mobile phone company Xiaomi has been rapidly rising. A look just a few years further back shows formerly dominant players like Nokia or Research in Motion (RIM, makers of the BlackBerry) shrinking dramatically in size. RIM held zero percent market share at the end of 2016 for its smartphone, having reached its peak sales in 2011, with almost 52 million devices sold. In this and many markets, competitors are constantly entering and exiting the field, gaining and losing ground quickly.

"Change or die!" is the rallying cry among today's managers worldwide. Exhibit 14-1 summarizes six distinct forces that act as stimulants for change.

In a number of places in this book, we have discussed the changing *nature of the workforce*. Almost every organization must adjust to a multicultural environment, demographic changes, immigration, and outsourcing.

Technology is changing jobs and organizations. It is not hard to imagine the very idea of an office becoming an antiquated concept in the near future.

The Canadian housing and financial sectors have experienced extraordinary *economic shocks* in recent years, although not to the extent that they have in the United States. The financial turbulence that began in 2008 has eroded the average employee's retirement account considerably, forcing many employees to postpone their anticipated retirement date and, in some cases, making it harder for younger people to find jobs. Meanwhile, spending has dropped, and many Canadian retailers are still suffering the consequences today.

Competition has changed. Competitors are as likely to be across the ocean as across town. Successful organizations are fast on their feet, capable of developing new products

EXHIBIT 14-1 Forces for Change	
Force	**Examples**
Nature of the workforce	More cultural diversity
	Aging population
	Many new entrants with inadequate skills
Technology	Faster, cheaper, and more mobile computers
	Online music sharing
	Deciphering of the human genetic code
Economic shocks	Rise and fall of dot-com stocks
	Record low interest rates
	Turbulent financial markets
Competition	Global competitors
	Mergers and consolidations
	Growth of e-commerce
Social trends	Internet chat rooms
	Retirement of Baby Boomers
	Rise of discount and "big box" retailers
World politics	Global financial crises
	Opening of markets in China
	Government shakeups around the world
	Extreme weather

TIBOU/Maxppp/Landov

The transformational leadership of Netflix CEO Reed Hastings has helped the company grow from a small DVD rental service to an Internet streaming service with 53 million customers in 50 countries.

rapidly and getting them to market quickly. In other words, they are flexible and will require an equally flexible and responsive workforce.

Social trends don't remain static either. Consumers who are otherwise strangers now meet and share product information in chat rooms and blogs. Organizations must therefore continually adjust product and marketing strategies to be sensitive to changing social trends. For example, consumers, employees, and organizational leaders are increasingly sensitive to environmental concerns. As a result, "green" practices have quickly become expected rather than optional.

Not even globalization's strongest proponents could have imagined the changing *world politics* in recent years. We have seen a set of financial crises that rocked global markets; Japan's fall into recession in 2014; a dramatic rise in the power and influence of China; attempts by Russia to reinstate itself as a global power; intense shakeups in governments around the world, including the rise of Donald Trump; and the societal effects of extreme weather. Throughout the industrialized world, businesses— particularly in the banking and financial sectors—have come under new scrutiny.

Opportunities for Change

Organizations have many opportunities to engage in change. They can change their motivation structures or redesign jobs. They may engage in corporate social responsibility. They may organize more around teams or share more leadership by empowering employees. They may create flatter structures or move to more modular structures. Sometimes the entire culture of the organization needs to change for organizational change to be successful, as *Case Incident—Sprucing Up Walmart* on page 517 shows. Exhibit 14-2 summarizes the range of change targets available to organizations.

As we discussed the workplace in this book, and talked about possible change, we might have implied that change happens easily, perhaps overnight, and does not require careful thought or planning. This implication exists because we did not discuss how these changes actually happen in the workplace, what has to be done to achieve change, and how difficult change actually is. We wanted you to understand what changes were possible before we discussed how to carry them out.

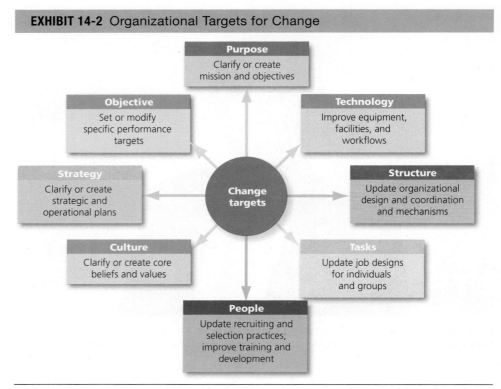

EXHIBIT 14-2 Organizational Targets for Change

Source: Organizational Behavior by Schermerhorn, John R.; Hunt, James G.; Osborn, Richard. Reproduced with permission of John Wiley in the format Republish in a book via Copyright Clearance Center.

Change Agents

Change agents manage change activities in an organization.[3] They see a future for the organization that others have not identified, and they are able to motivate, invent, and implement this vision. Change agents can be managers, nonmanagers, employees of the organization, or outside consultants.[4]

In some instances, internal management will hire outside consultants to provide advice and assistance with major change efforts. Because they are from the outside, these individuals can offer an objective perspective often unavailable to insiders. Outside consultants, however, are disadvantaged because they usually have an inadequate understanding of the organization's history, culture, operating procedures, and personnel. Outside consultants also may be prone to initiating more drastic changes—which can be a benefit or a disadvantage—because they don't have to live with the repercussions after the change is implemented. In contrast, internal staff specialists or managers, when acting as change agents, may be more thoughtful (and possibly more cautious) because they have to live with the consequences of their actions.

② Compare the four main approaches to managing organizational change.

Approaches to Managing Change

The creative teams at Cirque du Soleil are continually trying to improve their work.[5] In 2014, Dominic Champagne, the director, and Giles Martin, the creative director of Cirque du Soleil's "The Beatles LOVE," decided to refresh the show. It took them two years to remake the show. When asked why they did it, Cirque's director of creation, Chantal Tremblay, responded, "I think because we like the show so much and it's going really well, it's kind of giving back to the people after 10 years. We're adding more oomph to the wow that already existed." For organizations afraid of change, this would be a surprising answer. Instead, this creative team saw a positive challenge in reimagining "LOVE." What has made Cirque's approach to change successful?

change agents People who act as catalysts and assume the responsibility for managing change activities.

Photo by Jaime Hogge

A&W is growing its Millennial customers by opening more downtown locations and targeting Millennials' desire for quality ingredients (e.g., burgers are now made with hormone- and steroid-free beef). Attracting Millennial customers is half the battle. Convincing hundreds of franchisees to buy into the new focus is the other.

To this point, we have discussed the kinds of changes organizations can make. Assuming that an organization has uncovered a need for change, how does it engage in the change process? We turn to four approaches to managing change: Lewin's classic three-step model of the change process, Kotter's eight-step plan for implementing change, action research, and appreciative inquiry.

Lewin's Three-Step Model

Kurt Lewin argued that successful change in organizations should follow three steps, which are illustrated in Exhibit 14-3: **unfreezing** the status quo, **moving** to a new state, and **refreezing** the new change to make it permanent.[6]

By definition, the status quo is an equilibrium state. To move from this equilibrium—to overcome the pressures of both individual resistance and group conformity—unfreezing must happen in one of three ways (see Exhibit 14-4). The **driving forces**, which direct behaviour away from the status quo, can be increased. The **restraining forces**, which hinder movement from the existing equilibrium, can be decreased. A third alternative is to *combine the first two approaches*. Companies that have been successful in the past are likely to encounter restraining forces because people question the need for change.[7]

The value of this model can be seen through the example of a large oil company that decided to consolidate its three regional marketing offices in Winnipeg, Calgary, and Vancouver into a single regional office in Calgary. The decision was made in Toronto, and the people affected had no say whatsoever in the decision. The reorganization meant transferring more than 150 employees, eliminating some duplicate managerial positions, and instituting a new hierarchy of command.

unfreezing Change efforts to overcome the pressures of both individual resistance and group conformity.

moving Efforts to get employees involved in the change process.

refreezing Stabilizing a change intervention by balancing driving and restraining forces.

driving forces Forces that direct behaviour away from the status quo.

restraining forces Forces that hinder movement away from the status quo.

EXHIBIT 14-3 Lewin's Three-Step Change Model

Unfreezing → Moving → Refreezing

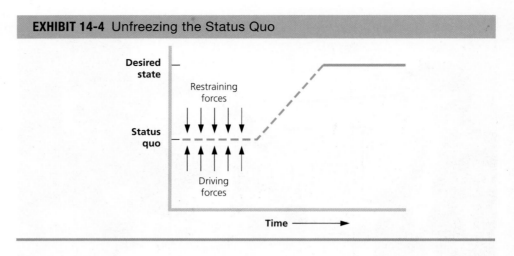

EXHIBIT 14-4 Unfreezing the Status Quo

The oil company's management expected employee resistance to the consolidation and outlined its alternatives. Those in Winnipeg or Vancouver might not want to transfer to another city, pull children out of school, make new friends, adapt to new co-workers, or undergo the reassignment of responsibilities. Positive incentives such as pay increases, liberal moving expenses, and low-cost mortgage funds for new homes in Calgary might encourage employees to accept the change. Management might also unfreeze acceptance of the status quo by removing restraining forces. It could counsel employees individually, hearing and clarifying each employee's specific concerns and apprehensions. Assuming that most of the fears were unjustified, the counsellor could assure the employees that there was nothing to fear and then demonstrate, through tangible evidence, that restraining forces were unwarranted. If resistance were extremely high, management might have to resort to both reducing resistance and increasing the attractiveness of the alternative if the unfreezing were to be successful.

Once the movement stage begins, it's important to keep the momentum going. Organizations that build up to change do less well than those that get to and through the moving stage quickly.

When change has been implemented, the new situation must be refrozen so that it can be sustained over time. Without this last step, change likely will be short-lived and employees will try to go back to the previous equilibrium state. The objective of refreezing, then, is to stabilize the new situation by balancing the driving and restraining forces.

How can the oil company's management refreeze its consolidation change? By systematically replacing temporary forces with permanent ones. Management might impose a new bonus system tied to the specific changes desired. The formal rules and regulations governing behaviour of those affected by the change should also be revised to reinforce the new situation. Over time, of course, the work group's own norms will evolve to sustain the new equilibrium. But until that point is reached, management should rely on more formal mechanisms.

A key feature of Lewin's three-step model is its conception of change as an episodic activity. For a debate about whether organizational change today is an episodic activity or an ongoing and at times chaotic process, see *Point/Counterpoint* on page 514.

Kotter's Eight-Step Plan for Implementing Change

John Kotter of Harvard Business School built on Lewin's three-step model to create a more detailed approach for implementing change.[8]

Kotter began by listing common failures that occur when managers try to initiate change. They may fail to create a sense of urgency about the need for change, a coalition for managing the change process, or a vision for change. They may not effectively communicate the vision or may not anchor the changes into the organization's culture. They

---

EXHIBIT 14-5 Kotter's Eight-Step Plan for Implementing Change

1. Establish a sense of urgency by creating a compelling reason for why change is needed.

2. Form a coalition with enough power to lead the change.

3. Create a new vision to direct the change and strategies for achieving the vision.

4. Communicate the vision throughout the organization.

5. Empower others to act on the vision by removing barriers to change and encouraging risk-taking and creative problem-solving.

6. Plan for, create, and reward short-term "wins" that move the organization toward the new vision.

7. Consolidate improvements, reassess changes, and make necessary adjustments in the new programs.

8. Reinforce the changes by demonstrating the relationship between new behaviours and organizational success.

Source: Based on J. P. Kotter, *Leading Change* (Boston: Harvard Business School Press, 1996).

---

also may fail to remove obstacles that could impede the vision's achievement or may not provide short-term and achievable goals. Finally, they may declare victory too soon.

Kotter then established eight sequential steps to overcome these problems. These steps are listed in Exhibit 14-5.

Notice how Exhibit 14-5 builds on Lewin's model. Kotter's first four steps essentially represent the "unfreezing" stage. Steps 5 through 7 represent "moving." The final step works on "refreezing." Kotter's contribution lies in providing managers and change agents with a more detailed guide for successfully implementing change.

Action Research

Action research refers to a change process based on the systematic collection of data and then selection of a change action based on what the analyzed data indicate.[9] Its value is in providing a scientific method for managing planned change. Action research consists of five steps: diagnosis, analysis, feedback, action, and evaluation.

The change agent, often an outside consultant in action research, begins by gathering information about problems, concerns, and needed changes from members of the organization. This *diagnosis* is analogous to the physician's search to find specifically what ails a patient. In action research, the change agent asks questions, reviews records, interviews employees, and actively listens to their concerns.

Diagnosis is followed by *analysis*. What problems do people key in on? What patterns do these problems seem to take? The change agent organizes this information into primary concerns, problem areas, and possible actions.

Action research requires the people who will participate in any change program to help identify the problem and determine the solution. So the third step—*feedback*—requires sharing with employees what has been found from the first and second steps. The employees, with the help of the change agent, develop action plans for bringing about any needed change.

Now the *action* part of action research is set in motion. The employees and the change agent carry out the specific actions they have identified to correct the problems.

The final step, consistent with the scientific underpinnings of action research, is *evaluation* of the action plan's effectiveness, using the initial data gathered as a benchmark.

Action research provides at least two specific benefits for an organization. First, it is problem focused. The change agent objectively looks for problems, and the type

action research A change process based on the systematic collection of data and then selection of a change action based on what the analyzed data indicate.

of problem determines the type of change action. This is a process that makes intuitive sense. Unfortunately, this too often does not happen in reality. Change activities can be solution-centred and therefore erroneously predetermined. The change agent has a favourite solution—for example, implementing flextime, teams, or a process re-engineering program—and then seeks out problems that his or her solution fits. A second benefit of action research is the lowering of resistance. Because action research involves employees so thoroughly in the process, it reduces resistance to change. Once employees have actively participated in the feedback stage, the change process typically takes on a momentum of its own.

Appreciative Inquiry

Most organizational change approaches are problem centred. They identify a problem or set of problems, then look for a solution. **Appreciative inquiry (AI)** accentuates the positive.[10] Rather than looking for problems to fix, this approach seeks to identify the unique qualities and special strengths of an organization, which can then be built on to improve performance. That is, it focuses on an organization's successes rather than on its problems.

> Are there positive approaches to change?

The AI process (see Exhibit 14-6) consists of four steps, or "Four D's," often played out in a large group meeting over two or three days, and overseen by a trained change agent:

- *Discovery.* Identify what people think are the strengths of the organization. Employees recount times they felt the organization worked best or when they specifically felt most satisfied with their jobs.

- *Dreaming.* Employees use information from the discovery phase to speculate on possible futures for the organization, such as what the organization will be like in five years.

- *Design.* Based on the dream articulation, participants focus on finding a common vision of how the organization will look, and agree on its unique qualities.

- *Destiny.* In this final step, participants define the organization's *destiny* or how to fulfill their dream, and they typically write action plans and develop implementation strategies.

AI has proven to be an effective change strategy in organizations such as Toronto-based Orchestras Canada; Ajax, Ontario-based Nokia Canada; Burnaby, BC-based TELUS; Calgary-based Encana; Toronto-based Parkinson Society Canada; and Toronto-based Toronto Western Hospital.

Professor Gervase Bushe of the Segal Graduate School of Business, Simon Fraser University, conducted a study at eight different sites of a Canadian school district to develop some understanding of factors that make AI successful in creating large-scale change. Of the eight sites, four showed transformational change, two showed incremental change, and two showed little or no change. The findings indicate that being able to

appreciative inquiry (AI) An approach to change that seeks to identify the unique qualities and special strengths of an organization, which can then be built on to improve performance.

EXHIBIT 14-6 The "Four *D*'s" of Appreciative Inquiry

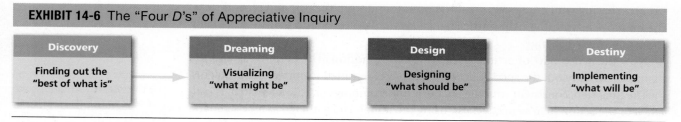

Discovery	Dreaming	Design	Destiny
Finding out the "best of what is"	Visualizing "what might be"	Designing "what should be"	Implementing "what will be"

Source: Based on D. L. Cooperrider and D. Whitney, *Collaborating for Change: Appreciative Inquiry* (San Francisco: Berrett-Koehler, 2000).

generate "new, compelling ideas" was critical to the success of the change project. The sites that were already reasonably happy with their schools and leadership showed less transformational change. It was in the schools with widely acknowledged problems, that participants tended to engage more, and generated many ideas that led to change.[11]

The use of AI in organizations is relatively recent, and it has not yet been determined when it is most appropriately used for organizational change.[12] More recently, scholars are finding that while it does give us the opportunity of viewing change from a much more positive perspective, in general AI has not lived up to its promises.[13] But researchers continue to study it.

CAREER OBJECTIVES

How Do I Fire Someone?

One of the people who reports to me really isn't living up to his job responsibilities, and I'm afraid that I have to let him go. I have no idea how to approach him so the meeting will turn out okay. What's the best way to terminate him?

—Ariana

Dear Ariana:

Most supervisors agree that terminating a problem employee can be one of the hardest parts of management. In general, the number-one way to reduce the stress of firing is to avoid giving surprises. A problem employee needs to be told as soon as possible that there are issues with performance. Be sure to document performance problems early, and let your employee know the consequences of failing to improve. It may even be the case that identifying problems can eliminate the need for firing through initiating development strategies and providing training that may improve his performance.

If you've decided the termination needs to proceed, then begin to plan the termination meeting. Good HR guidance can be one of your best resources in this process. It's natural to be worried about how your employee is going to react, but here are some strategies that may help you end the employment relationship in a way that minimizes conflicts:

- *Ask your HR representatives what alternatives and techniques they would recommend.* Many companies have established policies and procedures that will help you conduct this meeting in a professional manner.
- *Practise.* A chance to practise the meeting with a neutral party (*not* someone with connections to the person or your organization) will help you reduce stress and anticipate how the meeting will go.
- *Be sure to respect your employee during the process.* When possible, conduct the termination behind closed doors. Send a clear message that his employment is at an end. The last thing you want is a situation where he doesn't get the message or feels you are so indecisive that he can argue his way out of the termination. Attempts to "soften the blow" by providing positive feedback or working your way up to the bad news are often confusing and can create an opening for an extended, unpleasant, and unproductive argument.
- *Avoid going over past mistakes in detail.* At the point of termination, there is no reason to rehash old problems you've previously discussed—it's better to just make a clean statement that things aren't working out, and your documentation should have the details for later reference if needed. Going over the

reasons the relationship is over will make your employee feel insulted or offended.
- *Have an after-meeting plan.* What are your organization's policies? For instance, does your employee need to be escorted immediately out of the building? What are the policies for returning business property? Demonstrate adherence to the plan to keep the termination process objective.

Of course, none of this advice can remove all the stress of terminations, but a combination of preparation, respect, and clarity can help make the situation better than it would be otherwise.

Sources: S. R. McDonnell, "10 Steps Needed to Properly Fire Someone," *Entrepreneur,* May 26, 2015, http://www.entrepreneur.com/article/246573; E. Frauenheim, "Employee Crisis Communications 101," *Workforce,* November 13, 2013, http://www.workforce.com/articles/20036-employee-crisis-communications-101; and R. A. Mueller-Hanson and E. D. Pulakos, "Putting the 'Performance' Back in Performance Management," *SHRM-SIOP Science of HR White Paper Series,* 2015, http://www.shrm.org/Research/Documents/SHRM-SIOP%20Performance%20Management.pdf.

The opinions provided here are of the managers and authors only and do not necessarily reflect those of their organizations. The authors or managers are not responsible for any errors or omissions, or for the results obtained from the use of this information. In no event will the authors or managers, or their related partnerships or corporations thereof, be liable to you or anyone else for any decision made or action taken in reliance on the opinions provided here.

3 Describe the sources of resistance to change.

Resistance to Change

During the remaking of Cirque du Soleil's "The Beatles LOVE," many of the performers were acting each night in the older version of the show and then learning the new version (which entailed lengthy rehearsals) by day. For many employees, this could be a challenging task.[14] Change is hard enough without having to do your old job and your new job simultaneously. When creative director Giles Martin was asked whether this change was difficult on the performers, he replied that it was just the opposite:

> It's totally the reverse in the sense that they are so happy to be able to live through a little creation. . . . Now we're doing staging officially, so we're really in the mode of creation, and the artists love it because they have that chance to be there and listen to the direction of what he [Dominic Champagne, the director] wants in those numbers. . . . The performers and technical crew want to work and help to make changes for the show, which is going well.

> As we explore this section on resistance to change, you will see that Cirque du Soleil knows how to manage change effectively with its employees. The performers were encouraged to participate and be involved and they were kept in the communication loop. What other tactics might the directors have used to help prevent resistance to change?

Our egos are fragile, and we often see change as threatening. Even when employees are shown data that suggest they need to change, they latch on to whatever data they can find that suggest they are okay and don't need to change.[15] Employees who have negative feelings about a change cope by not thinking about it, increasing their use of sick time, or quitting. All these reactions can sap the organization of vital energy when it's most needed.[16] Resistance to change doesn't just come from lower levels of the organization. In many cases, higher-level managers will resist changes proposed by subordinates, especially if these leaders are focused on immediate performance.[17] Conversely, when leaders are more focused on mastery and exploration, they are more willing to hear and adopt subordinates' suggestions for change.

Resistance to change can be positive if it leads to open discussion and debate.[18] These responses are usually preferable to apathy or silence and can indicate that members of the organization are engaged in the process, providing change agents an opportunity to explain the change effort. Change agents can also monitor the resistance to modify the change to fit the preferences of members of the organization.

Resistance to change does not necessarily surface in standardized ways. It can be overt, implicit, immediate, or deferred. It is easiest for management to deal with resistance when it is overt and immediate, such as complaints, a work slowdown, or a strike threat. The greater challenge is managing resistance that is implicit or deferred because these responses—loss of loyalty or motivation, increased errors, or absenteeism—are more difficult to recognize. Deferred actions, sometimes surfacing weeks, months, or even years later, cloud the link between the change and the reaction to it. Or a single change that in and of itself might have little impact becomes the straw that breaks the camel's back because resistance to earlier changes has been deferred and stockpiled.

Let's look at the sources of resistance. For analytical purposes, we have categorized them by individual and organizational sources. In the real world, the sources often overlap.

Individual Resistance

Individual sources of resistance to change reside in basic human characteristics such as perceptions, personalities, and needs. Exhibit 14-7 summarizes four reasons why individuals may resist change:[19]

- *Self-interest.* People worry that they will lose something of value if change happens. Thus, they look after their own self-interest rather than that of the total organization.

- *Misunderstanding and lack of trust.* People resist change when they don't understand the nature of the change and fear that the cost of change will outweigh any potential gains for them. This often occurs when they don't trust those initiating the change.

- *Different assessments.* People resist change when they see it differently than their managers do and think the costs outweigh the benefits, even for the organization. Managers may assume that employees have the same information that they do, but this is not always the case.

- *Low tolerance for change.* People resist change because they worry that they do not have the skills and behaviour required of the new situation. They may feel that they are being asked to do too much, too quickly.

In addition to the reasons just outlined, individuals sometimes worry that being asked to change may indicate that what they have been doing in the past was somehow wrong. Managers should not overlook the effects of peer pressure on an individual's response to change. As well, the manager's attitude (positive or negative) toward the change and his or her relationship with employees will affect an individual's response to change.

> How do you respond to change?

The *Ethical Dilemma* on page 516 looks at one employee's resistance to a change in the workplace and asks you to consider whether the plan for implementing that change might have been part of the problem.

Organizational Resistance

Organizations, by their very nature, are conservative. They actively resist change. You don't have to look far to see evidence of this phenomenon. Government agencies want to continue doing what they have been doing for years, whether the need for their service changes or remains the same. Organized religions are deeply entrenched in their history. Attempts to change church doctrine require great persistence and patience. Educational institutions, which exist to open minds and challenge established ways

---

EXHIBIT 14-7 Sources of Individual Resistance to Change

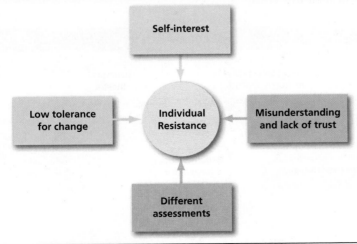

Source: Based on J. P. Kotter and L. A. Schlesinger, "Choosing Strategies for Change," *Harvard Business Review*, July–August 2008, pp. 107–109.

of thinking, are themselves extremely resistant to change. Most school systems are using essentially the same teaching technologies today as they were 50 years ago. Similarly, most business firms appear highly resistant to change. *Case Incident—When Companies Fail to Change* on page 517 considers how the failure to innovate has left a number of once leading-edge companies at the back of the pack.

What makes organizations resist change?

Six major sources of organizational resistance (shown in Exhibit 14-8) are as follows:

- *Structural inertia.* Organizations have built-in mechanisms—such as their selection processes and formalized regulations—to produce stability. When an organization is confronted with change, this structural inertia acts as a counterbalance.

- *Limited focus of change.* Organizations are made up of a number of interdependent subsystems. One cannot be changed without affecting the others. Limited changes in subsystems tend to be nullified by the larger system.

- *Group inertia.* Even if individuals want to change their behaviour, group norms may act as a constraint.

- *Threat to expertise.* Changes in organizational patterns may threaten the expertise of specialized groups.

- *Threat to established power relationships.* Any redistribution of decision-making authority can threaten long-established power relationships within the organization.

- *Threat to established resource allocations.* Groups in the organization that control sizable resources often see change as a threat. They tend to be content with the way things are.[20]

The *Experiential Exercise* on pages 515–516 asks you to identify and overcome resistance to organizational change.

Overcoming Resistance to Change

It's worth noting that not all change is good. Rapid, transformational change is risky, so change agents need to carefully think through the full implications. Speed can lead to bad decisions, and sometimes those initiating change fail to realize the full magnitude of the effects or their true costs.

EXHIBIT 14-8 Sources of Organizational Resistance to Change

Eight tactics can be used by change agents to deal with resistance to change.[21] Let's review them briefly.

- *Communication.* Communication is more important than ever in times of change. A study of German companies revealed that changes are most effective when a company communicates its rationale, balancing various stakeholder (shareholders, employees, community, customers) interests, compared to a rationale based on shareholder interests only.[22] Other research on a changing organization in the Philippines found that formal information sessions decreased employees' anxiety about the change, while providing high-quality information about the change increased their commitment to it.[23]

- *Participation.* It's difficult for individuals to resist a change decision in which they have participated. Assuming that the participants have the expertise to make a meaningful contribution, their involvement can reduce resistance, obtain commitment, and increase the quality of the change decision. However, against these advantages are the negatives: potential for a poor solution and great consumption of time.

- *Building support and commitment.* When managers or employees have low emotional commitment to change, they resist it and favour the status quo.[24] Employees are also more accepting of changes when they are committed to the organization as a whole.[25] So firing up employees and emphasizing their commitment to the organization overall can help them emotionally commit to the change rather than embrace the status quo. When employees' fear and anxiety are high, counselling and therapy, new-skills training, or a short paid leave of absence may facilitate adjustment to change.

- *Positive relationships.* People are more willing to accept changes if they trust the managers implementing them.[26] One study surveyed 235 employees from a large housing corporation in the Netherlands that was experiencing a merger. Those who had a more positive relationship with their supervisors, and who felt that the work environment supported development, were much more positive about the change process.[27] Underscoring the importance of social context, other research shows that even individuals who are generally resistant to change will be more willing to accept new and different ideas when they feel supported by their co-workers and believe the environment is safe for taking risks.[28] Another set of studies found that individuals whose dispositions made them more resistant to change felt more positive if they trusted the change agent.[29] This research suggests that if managers are able to facilitate positive relationships, they may be able to overcome resistance to change even among those who ordinarily don't like changes.

- *Implementing changes fairly.* One way organizations can minimize the negative impact of change is to make sure the change is implemented fairly. As we learned in Chapter 4, procedural fairness becomes especially important when employees perceive an outcome as negative, so it's crucial that employees see the reason for the change and perceive its implementation as consistent and fair.[30]

- *Manipulation and co-optation. Manipulation* refers to covert influence attempts. Twisting and distorting facts to make them more attractive, withholding undesirable information, and creating false rumours to get employees to accept a change are all examples of manipulation. If management threatens to close a manufacturing plant whose employees are resisting an across-the-board pay cut, and if the threat is unfounded, management is using manipulation. *Co-optation,* on the other hand, is a form of both manipulation and participation.

It seeks to buy off the leaders of a resistance group by giving them a key role, seeking their advice not to find a better solution but to get their endorsement. Both manipulation and co-optation are relatively inexpensive ways to gain the support of adversaries, but they can backfire if the targets become aware they are being tricked or used. Once that is discovered, the change agent's credibility may drop to zero.

- *Selecting people who accept change.* Research suggests that the ability to easily accept and adapt to change is related to personality—some people simply have more positive attitudes.[31] Individuals who are open to experience, take a positive attitude toward change, are willing to take risks, and are flexible in their behaviour are prime candidates. One study of managers in the United States, Europe, and Asia found that those with a positive self-concept and high risk tolerance coped better with organizational change. A study of 258 police officers found that those who were higher in the need for growth and who had an internal locus of control held more positive attitudes about organizational change efforts.[32] Individuals higher in general mental ability are also better able to learn and adapt to changes in the workplace.[33] In sum, an impressive body of evidence shows organizations can facilitate change by selecting people predisposed to accept it.

  Besides selecting individuals who are willing to accept changes, it is also possible to select teams that are more adaptable. In general, teams that are strongly motivated by learning about and mastering tasks are better able to adapt to changing environments.[34] It may be necessary to consider not only individual motivation but also group motivation when planning to implement changes.

- *Coercion.* Coercion is the application of direct threats or force upon the resisters. If management is determined to close a manufacturing plant whose employees do not accept a pay cut, the company is using coercion. Other examples include threatening employees with transfers, blocked promotions, negative performance evaluations, and poor letters of recommendation. Coercion is most effective when some force or pressure is enacted on at least some resisters—for instance, if an employee is publicly refused a transfer request, the threat of blocked promotions will become a real possibility in the minds of other employees. The advantages and drawbacks of coercion are approximately the same as those for manipulation and co-optation.

As you read *OB in the Workplace*, consider which of the above steps staff at Rockwood Institution used to help inmates introduce changes into their lives.

OB IN THE WORKPLACE

Habitat for Humanity and Rockwood Institution Partner to Change Lives

How can prison inmates be encouraged to learn new skills and influence their community in positive ways? Recidivism rates among released offenders are higher when those offenders don't perceive any other lifestyle options that would enable them to effectively support themselves and their loved ones.[35] At Rockwood Institution in Manitoba, Assistant Warden Shannon Plowman has found an effective formula to change recidivism rates by partnering with Linda Peters, the vice-president of Program Delivery for Habitat for Humanity. Their program, which is financially supported by Public Safety Canada and Human Resources and Skills Development Canada, gives minimum-security inmates with poor job prospects the opportunity to learn marketable construction skills in a safe and supportive environment.

At Rockwood, inmates who participate in the Habitat for Humanity specialized work program are provided with formal instruction on tool use and construction basics. Then, under professional supervision, they apply those skills to building a ready-to-transport house on the grounds of the correctional facility. The homes are then relocated to appropriate sites and are provided to needy families on the Habitat for Humanity waiting list. Eligible program "graduates" can also do supervised work in the broader community, receiving day passes to help on Habitat for Humanity builds in nearby Winnipeg and surrounding communities. These day passes are highly desirable, viewed as a privilege and reward. Upon release, some people even find transitional employment with Habitat for Humanity, working there for several months to develop an employment history and contacts in the construction industry.

This program manages change well. It focuses on providing education and fostering participation and direct involvement. Parole officers try to recommend new participants who are already open to changing their lives and most "graduates" advocate the program to other inmates. Support and commitment to the program are increased by allowing some participants to meet the families receiving the new homes, something that inmates report as being a transformative experience in their lives. One participant stated, "I never realized I could be proud for good things I was doing. Before I was always admired for being scary and fighting, it surprises me how proud I am of working on this house."

Rockwood officials and Habitat for Humanity staff work together to create an environment that enables, supports, and then reinforces and rewards positive change. It is a model many for-profit companies could learn from. ....

From Concepts to Skills on pages 518–519 provides additional tips for carrying out organizational change.

The Politics of Change

No discussion of resistance to change would be complete without a brief mention of the politics of change. Because change invariably threatens the status quo, it inherently implies political activity.

Politics suggests that the demand for change is more likely to come from outside change agents, employees who are new to the organization (who have less invested in the status quo), or managers who are slightly removed from the main power structure. Managers who have spent a long time with an organization and achieved a senior position in the hierarchy are often major impediments to change. For them, change can be a very real threat to their status and position, yet they may be expected to implement change to demonstrate that they are not merely caretakers. By acting as change agents, they can convey to stockholders, suppliers, employees, and customers that they are addressing problems and adapting to a dynamic environment. Of course, as you might guess, when forced to introduce change, these long-time power holders tend to implement incremental change. Radical change is often considered too threatening. This explains why boards of directors that recognize the need for rapid and radical change frequently turn to outside candidates for new leadership.[36] *OB in Action—How to Speed Up the Pace of Change* provides some tips for keeping up the pace of change.

OB IN ACTION

How to Speed Up the Pace of Change

→ Compel executives to **confront reality** and **agree on ground rules** for working together.

→ **Limit change initiatives** to two or three.

→ **Move ahead quickly** and dialogue with those not on board.

→ Get **all employees engaged**. Explain how changes are relevant to them personally.

→ Offer appropriate **rewards and incentives**.

→ **Celebrate milestones**.

→ **Anticipate** and **defuse** post-launch blues and midcourse overconfidence.[37]

4 Describe three ways to create a culture for change.

Creating a Culture for Change

Cirque du Soleil is an innovative organization.[38] Its employees are engaged and the company works on reinventing itself continuously. The investment of a Chinese company means that Cirque will be able to expand to China, giving it a large new audience—one that is already aware of Cirque.

Alma Derricks was hired to be one of Cirque's vice-presidents of sales and marketing shortly after the organization sold 90 percent of itself to outside investors. She noted the challenges of keeping ticket sales in Las Vegas while competing with shows by Celine Dion and Britney Spears. Still, Cirque performances can sell as many as 20 000 tickets in a night. "We have to always make the loudest noise in that environment and make sure that visitors are still aware that we're around, that we're exciting and that we're vital," Derricks says.

Cirque is investing in new product lines, including getting into the executive education business. SPARK, one of Cirque's new businesses, can be used as a learning laboratory for corporate teams (like Adobe and Google) to bring employees on retreat to learn about "trust, team building, operational excellence and customer service in a very tangible way."

The company introduced a new show, "Volta," in August 2017 that, besides the costumes, makeup, and characters that Cirque is known for, also includes extreme sports. "I think when people sat down to think not about how to reinvent Cirque du Soleil but to push the boundaries and try to do something different, extreme sports just came to the surface," said Johnny Kim, the show's assistant artistic director.

In summer 2017, Cirque also bought live entertainment company Blue Man Productions. Daniel Lamarre, president and CEO of Cirque du Soleil, explained the purchase: "We want to broaden our horizons, develop new forms of entertainment, reach out to new audiences and expand our own creative capabilities. Today, we are taking a decisive step towards materializing these ambitions."

Not many companies are this committed to reinventing themselves and expanding their horizons. What can be done to encourage more innovation in organizations?

We have considered how organizations can *adapt* to change. But recently, some OB scholars have focused on a more proactive approach—how organizations can *embrace* change by transforming their cultures. In this section we review three approaches: managing paradox, stimulating an innovative culture, and creating a learning organization.

Managing Paradox

In a *paradox* situation, we are required to balance tensions across various courses of action. There is a constant process of finding a balancing point, a dynamic equilibrium, among shifting priorities over time. Think of riding a bicycle: You must maintain forward momentum or you will fall over. From this perspective, there is no such thing as a separate discipline of "change management" because all management is dealing with constant change and adaptation.

The idea of paradox sounds abstract, but more specific concepts have begun to emerge from a growing body of research.[39] Several key paradoxes have been identified. *Learning* is a paradox because it requires building on the past while rejecting it at the same time. *Organizing* is a paradox because it calls for setting direction and leading while requiring empowerment and flexibility. *Performing* is a paradox between creating organization-wide goals to concentrate effort and recognizing the diverse goals of stakeholders inside and outside the organization. Finally, *belonging* is a paradox between establishing a sense of collective identity and acknowledging our desire to be recognized and accepted as unique individuals.

Managers can learn a few lessons from **paradox theory**,[40] which states the key paradox in management is that there is no final optimal status for an organization.[41]

paradox theory The theory that the key paradox in management is that there is no final optimal status for an organization.

The first lesson is that as the environment and members of the organization change, different elements take on more or less importance. For example, sometimes a company needs to acknowledge past success and learn how it worked, while at other times looking backward will only hinder progress. There is some evidence that managers who think holistically and recognize the importance of balancing paradoxical factors are more effective, especially in generating adaptive and creative behaviour in those they are managing.[42]

Stimulating a Culture of Innovation

How can an organization become more innovative? Although there is no guaranteed formula, structural, cultural, and human resource characteristics surface again and again when researchers study innovative organizations.[43] Change agents should consider introducing these characteristics into their organizations if they want to create an innovative climate. Let's start by clarifying what we mean by innovation.

Definition of *Innovation*

Change refers to making things different. **Innovation**, a specialized kind of change, is applied to initiating or improving a product, process, or service—a better solution.[44] All innovation involves change, but not all changes involve new ideas or lead to significant improvements. Innovations can range from incremental improvements, such as tablet computers, to radical breakthroughs, such as Nissan's electric Leaf car.

Sources of Innovation

Structural variables are one potential source of innovation.[45] A comprehensive review of the structure–innovation relationship leads to the following conclusions:[46]

- *Organic structures positively influence innovation.* Because they are lower in vertical differentiation, formalization, and centralization, organic organizations facilitate the flexibility, adaptation, and cross-fertilization that make the adoption of innovations easier.

- *Long tenure in management is associated with innovation.* Managerial tenure can provide the legitimacy and knowledge of how to accomplish tasks and obtain desired outcomes through creative methods.

- *Innovation is nurtured when there are slack resources.* Having an abundance of resources allows an organization to afford to purchase or develop innovations, bear the cost of instituting innovations, and absorb failures.

- *Interunit communication is high in innovative organizations.*[47] Innovative organizations are high users of committees, task forces, cross-functional teams, and other mechanisms that facilitate interaction across departmental lines.

Innovative organizations tend to have similar *cultures*. They encourage experimentation. They reward both successes and failures. They celebrate mistakes. Unfortunately, in too many organizations, people are rewarded for the absence of failures rather than for the presence of successes. Such cultures extinguish risk-taking and innovation. People will suggest and try new ideas only when they feel such behaviours exact no penalties. Managers in innovative organizations recognize that failures are a natural by-product of venturing into the unknown. W. L. Gore is known for its culture of innovation, as *OB in the Workplace* describes.

Within the *human resources* category, innovative organizations actively promote the training and development of their members so that they keep current, offer high

innovation A new idea applied to initiating or improving a product, process, or service.

Raina + Wilson/The Forbes Collection/Contour/Getty Images

Change is not always easy for an organization, but for CEO Mike McDerment of Toronto-based Fresh-Books, changes for his very successful business were spurred on by its success. He believes companies succeed when they make innovation a perpetual process, and not something that is engaged in out of necessity.

job security so employees don't fear getting fired for making mistakes, and encourage individuals to become champions of change. These practices should be mirrored for work groups as well. One study of 1059 individuals on over 200 different teams in a Chinese high-tech company found that work systems emphasizing commitment to

OB IN THE WORKPLACE

W. L. Gore Is a Leader in Innovation

What does it take to be a leader in innovation? An excellent model is W. L. Gore, the $2.6-billion-per-year global company best known as the maker of Gore-Tex fabric.[48] Gore has developed a reputation as one of the most innovative companies by developing a stream of diverse products—including guitar strings, vacuum cleaner filters, industrial sealants, and fuel cell components.

What is the secret of Gore's success? Gore continually thinks about innovation. It recently opened The Gore Innovation Center in Santa Clara, California, and has invited other organizations to come and explore Gore's inventions and discuss potential new products to develop. Gore's employees are given access to the innovation centre, filled with materials, so that they can develop their own ideas. There is a strong emphasis on teamwork, and individuals are encouraged to think about ways to make contributions to the company. Gore also believes in focusing on the long term: "Finally, *we believe in the long-term view*. Our decisions are based on long-term payoff, and we don't sacrifice our fundamental beliefs at Gore for short-term gain."

Gore pioneered a flat, unique lattice-type organizational structure (now termed an open allocation structure) run by employees (associates) working in self-organized project groups. What can other organizations do to duplicate Gore's track record for innovation?

employees increased creativity in teams.[49] These effects were even greater in teams where there was cohesion among co-workers.

Idea Champions and Innovation

Once a new idea is developed, **idea champions** actively and enthusiastically promote the idea, build support for it, overcome resistance to it, and ensure that it's implemented.[50] Champions often have similar personality characteristics: extremely high self-confidence, persistence, energy, and a tendency to take risks. They usually display traits associated with transformational leadership. They inspire and energize others with their vision of the potential of an innovation and through their strong personal conviction in their mission. Situations can also influence the extent to which idea champions are forces for change. For example, passion for change among entrepreneurs is greatest when work roles and the social environment encourage them to put their creative identities forward.[51] On the flip side, work roles that push creative individuals to do routine management and administration tasks will diminish both the passion for and implementation of change. Idea champions are good at gaining the commitment of others, and their jobs should provide considerable decision-making discretion. This autonomy helps them introduce and implement innovations in organizations when the context is supportive.[52]

Creating a Learning Organization

Another way an organization can proactively manage change is to make continuous growth part of its culture—to become a learning organization.[53]

What Is a Learning Organization?

Just as individuals learn, so too do organizations. A **learning organization** has developed the continuous capacity to adapt and change. The Dimensions of the Learning Organization Questionnaire (DLOQ) has been adopted and adapted internationally to assess the degree of commitment to learning organization principles.[54] Exhibit 14-9 describes what the DLOQ measures.

> **idea champions** Individuals who actively and enthusiastically promote an idea, build support for it, overcome resistance to it, and ensure that the idea is implemented.

> **learning organization** An organization that has developed the continuous capacity to adapt and change.

EXHIBIT 14-9 The Components of a Learning Organization Measured by the DLOQ

Dimension	Description
Continuous learning	Opportunities for ongoing education and growth are provided; learning is designed into work so that people can learn on the job.
Inquiry and dialogue	The organizational culture supports questioning, feedback, and experimentation; people gain productive reasoning skills to express their views and the capacity to listen to and inquire into the views of others.
Team learning	Work is designed to use teams to access different modes of thinking; collaboration is valued by the culture and rewarded; teams are expected to learn by working together.
Embedded system	Necessary systems to share learning are created, maintained, and integrated with work; employees have access to these high- and low-technology systems.
Empowerment	People are involved in setting and implementing a shared vision; responsibility is distributed so that people are motivated to learn what they are held accountable to do.
System connection	The organization is linked to its communities; people understand the overall environment and use information to adjust work practices; people are helped to see the effect of their work on the entire organization.
Strategic leadership	Leadership uses learning strategically for business results; leaders model, champion, and support learning.

Source: Based on V. J. Marsick and K. E. Watkins, "Demonstrating the Value of an Organization's Learning Culture," *Advances in Developing Human Resources 5*, no. 2 (2003), pp. 132–151. doi:10.1177/1523422303005002002.

Most organizations engage in what has been called **single-loop learning**. When errors are detected, the correction process relies on past routines and present policies. This type of learning has been likened to a thermostat, which, once set at 17°C, simply turns on and off to keep the room at the set temperature. It does not question whether the temperature should be set at 17°C. In contrast, learning organizations use **double-loop learning**. They correct errors by modifying the organization's objectives, policies, and standard routines. Double-loop learning challenges deeply rooted assumptions and norms within an organization. It provides opportunities for radically different solutions to problems and dramatic jumps in improvement. To draw on the thermostat analogy, a thermostat using double-loop learning would try to determine whether the correct policy is 17°C, and whether changes might be necessitated by a change in season.

Exhibit 14-10 summarizes the five basic characteristics of a learning organization. It's one in which people put aside their old ways of thinking, learn to be open with each other, understand how their organization really works, form a plan or vision on which everyone can agree, and then work together to achieve that vision.[55]

Proponents of the learning organization envision it as a remedy for three fundamental problems of traditional organizations: fragmentation, competition, and reactiveness.[56] First, *fragmentation* based on specialization creates "walls" and "chimneys" that separate different functions into independent and often warring fiefdoms. Second, an overemphasis on *competition* undermines collaboration. Managers compete to show who is right, who knows more, or who is more persuasive. Divisions compete when they ought to cooperate and share knowledge. Team leaders compete to show who the best manager is. Third, *reactiveness* misdirects management's attention to solving problems rather than being creative. The problem solver tries to make something go away, while a creator tries to bring something new into being. An emphasis on reactiveness to problems pushes out innovation and continuous improvement and, in its place, encourages people to constantly run around "putting out fires."

Managing Learning

What can managers do to make their firms learning organizations? Here are some suggestions:

- *Establish a strategy.* Managers need to make their commitment to change, innovation, and continuous improvement explicit.

- *Redesign the organization's structure.* The formal structure can be a serious impediment to learning. Flattening the structure, eliminating or combining

single-loop learning A process of correcting errors using past routines and present policies.

double-loop learning A process of correcting errors by modifying the organization's objectives, policies, and standard routines.

EXHIBIT 14-10 Characteristics of a Learning Organization

1. The organization has a shared vision that everyone agrees on.
2. People discard their old ways of thinking and the standard routines they use for solving problems or doing their jobs.
3. Members think of all organizational processes, activities, functions, and interactions with the environment as part of a system of interrelationships.
4. People openly communicate with each other (across vertical and horizontal boundaries) without fear of criticism or punishment.
5. People suppress their personal self-interest and fragmented departmental interests to work together to achieve the organization's shared vision.

Source: Based on P. M. Senge, *The Fifth Discipline: The Art and Practice of the Learning Organization* (New York: Doubleday, 2006).

departments, and increasing the use of cross-functional teams reinforce inter-dependence and reduce boundaries.

- *Reshape the organization's culture.* To become a learning organization, managers must demonstrate by their actions that taking risks and admitting failures are desirable traits. This means rewarding people who take chances and make mistakes. Managers also need to encourage functional conflict.

GLOBAL IMPLICATIONS

A number of change issues we have discussed in this chapter are culture-bound. To illustrate, let's briefly look at five questions:

- *Do people believe change is possible?* Remember that cultures vary in terms of beliefs about their ability to control their environment. In cultures in which people believe that they can dominate their environment, individuals will take a proactive view of change. This, for example, would describe Canada and the United States. In many other countries, such as Iran and Saudi Arabia, people see themselves as subjugated to their environment and thus will tend to take a passive approach toward change.

- *If change is possible, how long will it take to bring it about?* A culture's time orientation can help us answer this question. Societies that focus on the long term, such as Japan, will demonstrate considerable patience while waiting for positive outcomes from change efforts. In societies with a short-term focus, such as Canada and the United States, people expect quick improvements and will seek change programs that promise fast results.

- *Is resistance to change greater in some cultures than in others?* Resistance to change will be influenced by a society's reliance on tradition. Italians, as an example, focus on the past, whereas Canadians emphasize the present. Italians, therefore, should generally be more resistant to change efforts than their Canadian counterparts.

- *Does culture influence how change efforts will be implemented?* Power distance can help with this issue. In high power-distance cultures, such as Malaysia and Panama, change efforts will tend to be autocratically implemented by top management. In contrast, low power-distance cultures value democratic methods. We would predict, therefore, a greater use of participation in countries such as Austria and Denmark.

- *Do successful idea champions do things differently in different cultures?* The evidence indicates that the answer is yes.[57] People in collectivistic cultures, in contrast to individualistic cultures, prefer appeals for cross-functional support for innovation efforts; people in high power-distance cultures prefer champions to work closely with those in authority to approve innovative activities before work is conducted on them; and the higher the uncertainty avoidance of a society, the more champions should work within the organization's rules and procedures to develop the innovation. These findings suggest that effective managers will alter their organization's innovation strategies to reflect cultural values. So, for instance, while idea champions in Russia might succeed by ignoring budgetary limitations and working around confining procedures, idea champions in Greece, Portugal, Guatemala, and other cultures high in uncertainty avoidance will be more effective by closely following budgets and procedures.

Summary

The need for change has been implied throughout this text. For instance, think about attitudes, motivation, work teams, communication, leadership, organizational structures, and organizational cultures. Change was an integral part in our discussion of each. If environments were perfectly static, if employees' skills and abilities were always up to date, and if tomorrow were always exactly the same as today, organizational change would have little or no relevance to managers. But the real world is turbulent, requiring organizations and their members to undergo dynamic change if they are to perform at competitive levels. Coping with all these changes can be a source of stress, but with effective management, challenge can enhance engagement and fulfillment, leading to the high performance that, as you have discovered in this text, is one major goal of the study of organizational behaviour (OB).

LESSONS LEARNED

- Individuals resist change; breaking down that resistance is important.
- Change requires unfreezing the status quo, moving to a new state, and making the new change permanent.
- Innovative cultures reward both successes and failures so that people are not afraid to make mistakes.

SNAPSHOT SUMMARY

Forces for Change
- Opportunities for Change
- Change Agents

Approaches to Managing Change
- Lewin's Three-Step Model
- Kotter's Eight-Step Plan for Implementing Change

- Action Research
- Appreciative Inquiry

Resistance to Change
- Individual Resistance
- Organizational Resistance
- Overcoming Resistance to Change
- The Politics of Change

Creating a Culture for Change
- Managing Paradox
- Stimulating a Culture of Innovation
- Creating a Learning Organization

MyLab Management

Study, practise, and explore real business situations with these helpful resources:

- **Study Plan:** Check your understanding of chapter concepts with self-study quizzes.
- **Online Lesson Presentations:** Study key chapter topics and work through interactive assessments to test your knowledge and master management concepts.
- **Videos:** Learn more about the management practices and strategies of real companies.
- **Simulations:** Practise management decision-making in simulated business environments.

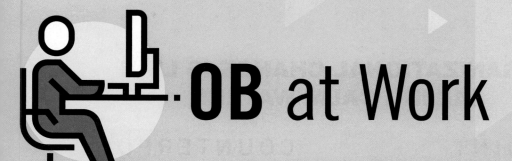

OB at Work

for **Review**

1. What are the forces for change?
2. What are the similarities and differences among the four main approaches to managing organizational change?
3. What forces act as sources of resistance to change?
4. How can managers create a culture for change?

for **Managers**

■ Consider that, as a manager, you are a change agent in your organization. The decisions you make and your role-modelling behaviour will help shape the organization's change culture.

■ Your management policies and practices will determine the degree to which the organization learns and adapts to changing environmental factors.

■ People resist change because change can be stressful. Low to moderate amounts of stress enable many people to perform their jobs better by increasing their work intensity, alertness, and ability to react. Therefore, don't hesitate to introduce change just because stress might be induced.

for **You**

■ Not everyone is comfortable with change, but you should realize that change is a fact of life. It is difficult to avoid and can result in negative consequences when it is avoided.

■ If you need to change something in yourself, be aware of the importance of creating new systems to replace the old. Saying you want to be healthier without specifying that you intend to go to the gym three times a week or eat five servings of fruits and vegetables a day means that change likely will not occur. It's important to specify goals and behaviours as part of change.

■ Consider focusing on positive aspects of change, rather than negative ones. For instance, instead of noting that you did not study hard enough, acknowledge the effort you put into studying and how that helped your performance, and then set positive goals as a result.

ORGANIZATIONAL CHANGE IS LIKE SAILING CALM WATERS

POINT

Organizational change is an episodic activity.[58] That is, it starts at some point, proceeds through a series of steps, and culminates in some outcome that those involved hope is an improvement over the starting point. It has a beginning, a middle, and an end.

Lewin's three-step model represents a classic illustration of this perspective. Change is seen as a break in the organization's equilibrium. The status quo has been disturbed, and change is necessary to establish a new equilibrium state. The objective of refreezing is to stabilize the new situation by balancing the driving and restraining forces.

Some experts have argued that organizational change should be thought of as balancing a system made up of five interacting variables within the organization— people, tasks, technology, structure, and strategy. A change in any one variable has repercussions on one or more of the others. This perspective is episodic in that it treats organizational change as essentially an effort to sustain an equilibrium. A change in one variable begins a chain of events that, if properly managed, requires adjustments in the other variables to achieve a new state of equilibrium.

Another way to conceptualize the episodic view of change is to think of managing change as analogous to captaining a ship. The organization is like a large ship travelling across the calm Mediterranean Sea to a local port. The ship's captain has made this exact trip hundreds of times before with the same crew. Every once in a while, however, a storm will appear, and the crew has to respond. The captain will make the appropriate adjustments—that is, implement changes—and, having manoeuvred through the storm, will return to calm waters. Like this ship's voyage, managing an organization should be seen as a journey with a beginning and an end, and implementing change as a response to a break in the status quo that is needed only occasionally.

COUNTERPOINT

The episodic approach for handling organizational change has become obsolete. Developed in the 1950s and 1960s, it reflects the environment of those times treating change as the occasional disturbance in an otherwise peaceful world. However, it bears little resemblance to today's environment of constant and chaotic change.

If you want to understand what it's like to manage change in today's organizations, think of it as equivalent to permanent whitewater rafting. The organization is not a large ship, but more akin to a 40-foot raft. Rather than sailing a calm sea, this raft must traverse a raging river made up of an uninterrupted flow of whitewater rapids. To make things worse, the raft is manned by 10 people who have never worked together or travelled the river before, much of the trip is in the dark, the river is dotted with unexpected turns and obstacles, the exact destination of the raft is not clear, and at irregular intervals the raft needs to pull to shore, where some new crew members are added and others leave. Change is a natural state, and managing it is a continual process. That is, managers never get the luxury of escaping the whitewater rapids.

The stability and predictability characterized by the episodic perspective no longer captures the world we live in. Disruptions in the status quo are not occasional, temporary, and followed by a return to an equilibrium state. There is, in fact, no equilibrium state. Managers today face constant change, bordering on chaos. They are being forced to play a game they have never played before, governed by rules that are created as the game progresses.

BREAKOUT **GROUP** EXERCISES

Form small groups to discuss the following topics, as assigned by your instructor:

1. Identify a local company that you think needs to undergo change. What factors suggest that change is necessary?

2. Have you ever tried to change the behaviour of someone you worked with (for instance, someone in one of your project groups)? How effective were you in getting change to occur? How would you explain this?

3. Identify a recent change that your college or university introduced, and its effects on the students. Did the students accept the change or fight it? How would you explain this?

EXPERIENTIAL EXERCISE

Strategizing Change

The Situation

TutorMe is a midsize company that employs 45 former teachers as tutors in public and private schools. The tutors work in the company's branches and corporate headquarters, and at home via phone and Internet.[59] The firm employs a support staff of 15. TutorMe used to be the only such company in the area, but two new tutoring chains recently opened branches nearby. Online tutoring firms have added competition as well.

TutorMe is beginning to struggle because of this increased competition. Its organizational culture could best be described as "lackadaisical" and its business practices as "loose." Although it provides a meaningful service to students, many of its tutors use their own methods instead of following the TutorMe manuals. Tutor pay is low and benefits are near zero. However, the tutors are skilled teachers who appreciate the opportunity to use their expertise in a flexible work situation, and turnover is low.

TutorMe's facilities look "tired" and are usually located in mostly abandoned strip malls far from well-travelled roads. The corporate headquarters is a bit nicer and in a more visible location. However, the managers often don't know what the tutors are doing, and billing practices are chaotic. There is no HR department, so the business staff handles both payments and employee issues, mostly by creating further problems that upper management must settle. The pay for the business staff is mid-range for the area with standard benefits, but high staff turnover has been an accepted part of TutorMe's business.

Upper management understands the company needs to change to survive, so its executives hired consultants to diagnose what TutorMe needs. The consultants believe the company should (1) eliminate some of its less-used branches, (2) relocate other branches to more visible locations, (3) train tutors with the TutorMe manuals and insist on standardization of teaching practices, (4) overhaul the organizational culture to reflect a commitment to tutoring excellence, and (5) train and set expectations for the business staff to raise performance levels and tighten accountability.

The consultants have warned TutorMe management that recent studies indicate only 30 to 43 percent of organizations achieve their goals for change initiatives. They have outlined the following specific obstacles and offered to help TutorMe be successful in its transformation:

1. Lack of adoption and commitment from top management

2. Employee resistance

3. Manager resistance

4. Insufficient communication

5. Budget overages and project delays

6. Employees and managers who ignore the new policies and procedures

The Procedure

Break into groups of three to four members. Each group will act as the consultants to guide TutorMe through the change process. Your group will need to come to a consensus, in writing, for each of the following assignments.

1. Gather all you know about TutorMe's current business practices. Write down the reasons tutors stay while staff turnover is high. Decide what is currently working for TutorMe. What is not working and needed to change even before competition came in?

2. Based on what you determine about TutorMe's business practices, do you agree or disagree with each of the consultants' five recommendations? Why or why not?

3. Consider the six obstacles the consultants identified, the five recommendations, and your answer to question 1. Which of the obstacles do you think will present problems for achieving the five recommendations? How? Make a list.

4. From your list in question 3, write down your targeted, informed recommendations for overcoming the obstacles. Also consider what further information you would like from the company.

5. Bring the class together and discuss your recommendations from question 4.

ETHICAL DILEMMA

Changes at the Television Station

A local television station had been experiencing a ratings decline for several years.[60] In 2014, the station switched some of its programming. That has explained some of the ratings decline. However, in recent months, the ratings have continued to slide. Eventually, the station manager, Lucien Stone, decided he had to make a change to the local newscast.

After meeting with the programming manager, Stone called a meeting of the employees and announced his intention to "spice things up" during the 5 p.m. and 10 p.m. local news. The 30-minute broadcasts would still include the traditional "top stories," "sports," and "weather" segments. However, on slow news days, more attention-getting material would be used. Stone also indicated some programming decisions would probably be revisited. "The days of *Little House on the Prairie* are over," he said.

Madison Devereaux, 29, had been the chief meteorologist since 2012. After receiving a degree in meteorology, she joined the station and quickly worked her way up the ranks, impressing viewers and management alike with her extensive knowledge and articulate, professional, mistake-free delivery.

Although she was religious, Devereaux was not one to express her religious beliefs in the newsroom. Most of those at the station were not even aware that she closely practised a religion.

Devereaux was troubled by the announced changes to the programming but did not speak up at the time. One Monday during a pre-production meeting, she learned that on Thursday of that week, one of the reporters, Sam Berkshow, would present a segment called "Dancing around the Economy," which would focus on how local strip clubs were doing well despite the sluggish economy.

Devereaux did not think it was appropriate to air the segment during the 5 p.m. newscast and asked both her producer and Stone to reconsider the piece, or at least air it in the 10 p.m. time slot. When they refused, she asked whether she could take the day off when the segment aired. Stone again refused. This was "sweeps week" (when ratings are calculated); Stone wanted to air the story, and Devereaux's contract prohibited her from taking time off during sweeps week.

When Devereaux did not show up for work that Thursday, the station fired her, arguing that she had breached her contract.

For her part, Devereaux said, "I'm not angry with the station, but I am sorry about the changes that have taken place."

Questions

1. Do you think either party behaved unethically in this case? If so, why?

2. How could Devereaux have handled the situation differently while still maintaining her personal integrity?

3. Drawing on Kotter's eight-step plan for implementing change, how might the station have handled its planned change differently?

Sprucing Up Walmart

For more than half a century, Walmart has prided itself on providing value to customers by being a low-price leader.[61] But the consumer mindset is changing. Now "value" also means convenience, ease of finding what you want, and the ability to get exactly what you want when you want it. Nationwide dollar-store chains often have lower prices than Walmart, so that point of competitive advantage is fading. Thanks to Amazon.com and other online retailers, consumers can shop from home whenever they like, compare prices, and know immediately what is available.

Contrast this with the experience many Walmart shoppers previously had when they entered a store—low inventory, disorganized aisles, unhelpful staff, and an overall depressing atmosphere. The company's online presence was about the same. The site was difficult to navigate and attempts to search for products were frustrating at best and more often fruitless.

Named Walmart's CEO in 2014, Doug McMillon set out to change this. "What people think about the company is important," he noted. At the moment, people were not thinking about value and low prices when they thought about Walmart. McMillon enacted a number of changes. First, since the company had earned a reputation of treating its store employees poorly—low wages, few benefits—while profits were in the billions of dollars, Walmart announced it would increase its minimum wage.

Second, the company asked for and paid more attention to employee feedback. Recurring issues included the dress code, store music, and even store temperatures.

So clothing rules were relaxed, more variety in music was introduced, and thermostats were adjusted. The company hopes improving employee morale will translate into a better experience for customers, thereby changing some of the negative images.

Walmart's web presence was another target for big changes. With Amazon as the store's biggest competitor, McMillon wanted to offer customers more items, pickup options, and ways to meet their needs and demands—like an online grocery-ordering service. This means a new way of thinking about marketing and inventory across the board.

McMillon was able to see how consumers have changed not only what they want, but also the way they want it—whether from the hands of happy employees or with the simple click of a button. The question remains: Will his actions be enough to change the way consumers see Walmart?

Questions

1. What key factors do you think prompted Walmart to change? Do they exemplify the change pressures discussed in the chapter? Why or why not?

2. What effects from Walmart's changes do you predict?

3. Describe how McMillon acted as a change agent in this situation.

When Companies Fail to Change

The Trinitron TV, transistor radio, Walkman, and VCR are the stuff of time capsules nowadays, but not long ago they were cutting-edge technology.[62] Japan was at the pinnacle of the home consumer electronics industry from the 1970s to the 1990s, introducing new innovations to the world each year. Now those same Japanese firms are at the back of the pack and struggling to stay in the game. Japanese electronics production has fallen by more than 41 percent, and Japan's global market share of electronics goods and services has decreased by more than half since 2000. Sony, for example, did not earn any profits

between 2008 and 2012, and then was falling behind again in 2014. What happened?

The simple answer is failure to innovate. While firms outside Japan pioneered digital technology and conquered the Internet, Japanese firms stuck to semiconductors and hardware. But the deeper issue is the refusal of Japanese managers to adapt to the global environment and to change their organizations accordingly. For instance, Sony mastered the technology needed for a digital music player years before Apple introduced the iPod in 2001, but its engineers resisted the change. Sony's divisions would not cooperate with one another fast enough to compete in this market or in the new market for flat-screen TVs. Even now, Sony has not managed to change its organization to reflect current global thinking in the industry. For instance, they and other Japanese firms make a larger number of products than most of their global competitors. Former Sony executive Yoshiaki Sakito said, "Sony makes too many models, and for none of them can they say, 'This contains our best, most cutting-edge technology.' Apple, on the other hand, makes one amazing phone in just two colors and says, 'This is the one.'" Sony was attempting to adjust its behaviour by fall 2014, realizing that it had too many models of smartphones. The plan is to focus on premium phones.

For Japanese electronics companies to survive, they must change. They were once able to structure their organizations around abundant, inexpensive labour to keep costs down and prices competitive, but that is no longer the case. One complicating factor is that Japan is an ancient country of many traditions, with a low birth rate and an aging population, so there will be an increasing shortage of workers. The country's culture will make it even more difficult to realign to globalization. It now must change to foster innovation, which may involve a cultural as much as an organizational transformation.

Questions

1. What made the Japanese electronics industry initially successful?

2. Why is the Japanese electronics industry no longer a success story?

3. What types of organizational changes would you advise Japanese electronics managers to consider?

FROM CONCEPTS TO SKILLS

Carrying Out Organizational Change

An After Action Review is a non-hierarchical team debriefing process that helps participants in and those responsible for a project understand what went well, what went wrong, and how performance can be improved.[63] Seven disciplines embedded in the After Action Review can help create effective change:

1. *Build an intricate understanding of the business.* Organizational members need to have the big picture revealed to them so they know why change is needed and what is happening in the industry. Let organizational members know what is expected of them as the change proceeds.

2. *Encourage uncompromising straight talk.* Communication cannot be based on hierarchy, but must allow everyone to contribute freely to the discussion.

3. *Manage from the future.* Rather than setting goals that are directed toward a specific future point in time (and thus encouraging everyone to stop when the goal is achieved), manage from the perspective of always looking toward the future and future needs.

4. *Harness setbacks.* When things do not go as planned, and there are setbacks, it's natural to blame yourself, others, or bad luck. Instead, teach everyone to view setbacks as learning opportunities and opportunities for improvement.

5. *Promote inventive accountability.* While employees know what the specific targets and goals are, they should also be encouraged in the change process to be inventive and take initiative when new opportunities arise.

6. *Understand the quid pro quo.* When organizations undergo change processes, employees are put under a lot of stress and strain. Organizations must ensure that employees are rewarded for their efforts. To build appropriate commitment, organizations must develop four levels of incentives:

   a. Reward and recognition for effort

   b. Training and skill development that will make the employee marketable

    c. Meaningful work that provides intrinsic satisfaction

    d. Communication about where the organization is going and some say in the process for employees

7. *Create relentless discomfort with the status quo.* People are more willing to change when the current situation looks less attractive than the new situation.

These points indicate that effective change is a comprehensive process, requiring a lot of commitment from both the organization's leaders and its members.

· ·

Practising Skills

You are the nursing supervisor at a local hospital that employs both emergency room and floor nurses. Each of these teams of nurses tends to work almost exclusively with others doing the same job. In your professional reading, you have come across the concept of cross-training nursing teams and giving them more varied responsibilities, which in turn has been shown to improve patient care while lowering costs. You call the two team leaders, Sue and Scott, into your office to explain that you want the nursing teams to move to this approach. To your surprise, they are both opposed to the idea. Sue says she and the other emergency room (ER) nurses feel they are needed in the ER, where they fill the most vital role in the hospital. They work special hours when needed, do whatever tasks are required, and often work in difficult and stressful circumstances. They think the floor nurses have relatively easy jobs for the pay they receive. Scott, the leader of the floor nurse team, tells you that his group believes the ER nurses lack the special training and extra experience that the floor nurses bring to the hospital. The floor nurses claim they have the heaviest responsibilities and do the most exacting work. Because they have ongoing contact with patients and families, they believe they should not be called away from vital floor duties to help the ER nurses complete their tasks. What should you do about your idea to introduce more cross-training for the nursing teams?

· ·

Reinforcing Skills

1. Think about a change (major and minor) that you have dealt with over the last year. Perhaps the change involved other people, and perhaps it was personal. Did you resist the change? Did others resist the change? How did you overcome your resistance or the resistance of others to the change?

2. Interview a manager at three different organizations about a change he or she implemented. What was the manager's experience in implementing the change? How did the manager manage resistance to the change?

ADDITIONAL CASES

The Additional Cases present key concepts examined in the text. The following table indicates the chapters that apply to the major topic areas addressed in each case.

Cases	Chapters													
	1	2	3	4	5	6	7	8	9	10	11	12	13	14
Case 1: The Personality Problem		✓	✓							✓				
Case 2: The Path to Fraud			✓									✓		
Case 3: Auditing, Attitudes, and Absenteeism			✓	✓	✓			✓		✓		✓	✓	
Case 4: Bad Faith Bargaining? Government Power and Negotiations with the Public Service								✓	✓			✓		
Case 5: Gender-Based Harassment among the Royal Canadian Mounted Police								✓		✓	✓			✓
Case 6: Disability Accommodations and Promotions at Bunco		✓								✓				
Case 7: Promotion from Within			✓	✓	✓		✓	✓						
Case 8: Repairing Jobs That Fail to Satisfy		✓	✓		✓									
Case 9: Virtual Organizations						✓				✓			✓	✓
Case 10: Trouble at City Zoo					✓		✓			✓	✓		✓	✓

Case 1: The Personality Problem

Learning Goals

In this case, you will have an opportunity to assess the positive and negative traits associated with a personality type that is often encountered in highly competitive, performance-oriented settings. You should consider the role of organizational culture in supporting and reinforcing behaviours associated with this personality type. Use that insight to suggest strategies that could help maximize the benefits of this personality type while minimizing its liabilities.

Major Topic Areas

- Personality (Chapter 2)
- Organizational culture (Chapter 10)
- Work attitudes (Chapter 3)

The Scenario

Jasmine Patel, director of Human Resources at Vertical Horizon, sits at her desk thinking about what to do next.[1] She is wondering how to handle the disruptive behaviour of a high-performing sales representative, Rhett Stark.

Vertical Horizon is a software company in the Kitchener-Waterloo high-tech corridor. It started out developing programming tools that help large teams of software developers work together effectively. Now it was moving into other areas such as web content management. Since the company was in the midst of adding to its product line, it was very important that the sales representatives support the transition. If sales of the new product line were too low, the entire company could fold.

The sales team consists of 12 outside (field) sales representatives and 6 inside representatives who provide support to the outside representatives. Each inside representative is responsible for generating leads and otherwise supporting the two outside sales representatives assigned to them. In addition, the sales team includes a sales manager who can be consulted on a daily basis for advice and a vice-president (VP) of Sales who is responsible for strategic initiatives.

Most of the sales representatives, as well as the sales manager and the VP of Sales, are relatively new to the organization. As a result, they often consult with Rhett for advice about the company's products, its customers, and sales strategies. Rhett is an outside sales representative who has been with the company for over eight years, a long time in the software world. His natural charisma combined with his strong product knowledge and excellent customer service has helped him exceed his sales quota quarter after quarter. Rhett is charming, bold, and highly self-confident. He is a gifted leader who has a natural ability to draw people to him. People feel special around Rhett. One co-worker says, "When he talks to you, he makes you feel like you are the most important and interesting person in the world." Although Rhett's personality has helped him become a successful sales representative, it has its downside.

Rhett is the ringleader of a group of sales representatives who often work late and then go out partying together. This behaviour has been supported by the VP of Sales, who feels that the time spent bonding after work makes for a strong team. The nights the sales representatives have spent together clubbing and bar hopping has created cohesion within the work group, but it has also had some negative effects. Jasmine overheard two male members of the sales team discussing marital problems that had arisen as a result of their late nights out. "What bothered me," one said to the other, "is that when I told Rhett that my wife was upset about it, he just laughed and walked away. I know it's my own responsibility, but you would think he would be more sympathetic."

A high-performing sales representative named Malcolm spoke to Jasmine privately about Rhett and made a similar point: "It's pretty clear that Rhett has a lot of informal power around here," he said. "Everyone, even management, listens to him and does what he says. I'm worried because I'm not part of his 'pack.' I don't drink or go out with Rhett's group. Rhett makes fun of me behind my back. He insults me in front of others, and no one dares say anything about it. Given his informal power in this department, how can I ever expect a fair chance at a promotion?"

Worrisome, too, is Rhett's behaviour with his inside sales representative, Aisha. Aisha recently asked to meet with Jasmine to discuss a few "issues." She told Jasmine: "Rhett

delegates work to me and then interferes by micro-managing it. When a project goes well, he takes the credit for it; when a project goes badly, he blames me publicly. I'm often asked to go beyond my duties to help Rhett; he even thinks it's okay to call me late at night and on weekends. If I don't do what Rhett asks, he says I'm being difficult and questioning his authority. Most of the time, I feel like I'm here only to meet his needs and not those of the other sales representative I'm assigned to. The thing is, Rhett's in charge of my performance review."

Jasmine has no authority to tell Rhett how to live his life outside the workplace, but it's clear that he is negatively affecting other employees in the department. He also appears to be completely unconcerned about his impact on other employees. Jasmine suspects that Rhett is a narcissist, and perhaps Machiavellian too. But he is the company's best sales representative by far. How can she manage this difficult personality and help create a healthier work environment?

Discussion Questions

1. Do you think that Rhett is Machiavellian and a narcissist? Why or why not?

2. Assuming that Rhett is Machiavellian and a narcissist, what is the most effective way to minimize the negative effect he can have on other employees?

3. How has the organization's culture contributed to the toxic subculture that seems to be developing in the sales department? What can management do to foster an organizational culture that is supportive of all employees, positive, and high performing?

Case 2: The Path to Fraud
Learning Goals

In this case, you will have an opportunity to evaluate a decision-making process that ultimately led to an employee engaging in unethical and illegal behaviour. Consider which factors contributed to Julie's decision to engage in fraud. How did organizational variables combine with external pressures to influence her decision? Use that insight to make recommendations about what the insurance company could, and should, do to prevent similar situations from unfolding in the future.

Major Topic Areas

- Decision making and ethics (Chapter 12)
- Work values and attitudes (Chapter 3)
- Corporate social responsibility (Chapter 12)

The Scenario

Julie Smith trembled uncontrollably as the judge ordered her to stand up for sentencing.[2] It was really happening. She would be sent to prison. All this time, no matter how many warnings she got from her lawyer, a part of her had never really believed that it would come to this. "A four-month sentence to be served in a minimum security facility followed by two years of probation," thundered the judge, "and you will pay full restitution." Julie fell back into her chair and began to cry. How would her six-year-old son cope while she was imprisoned? She had not even told anyone in her family what was happening because she was so embarrassed and humiliated. How had she ended up here?

In mid-2007, Julie started working as an accounts payable clerk for a large insurance company. Her job consisted primarily of processing invoices but as a member of the wider finance department she had many opportunities to observe and learn the company's audit procedures. Julie viewed the work in accounts payable as repetitive and tedious, and she was aware that she did not have the discretion or authority to make her own decisions. Everything at this company was done VERY strictly by the book. Despite these limitations, however, Julie enjoyed her job and the company of her co-workers and colleagues, and she felt that her employer treated her well.

In early 2008, Julie made a lateral move to the department that administered corporate commercial accounts. Large corporations bought insurance policies as protection from lawsuits and were required to pay a flat rate per term regardless of the number of claims made against them. Julie oversaw more than 500 corporate policies. When one of the corporate clients experienced a loss, Julie would process the claims for legal fees, compensation, and related incidentals. Examples of common losses included compensation paid out due to slips and falls, safety violations, and other lawsuits. Julie processed an average of 13 to 15 claims per week. When the compensation was less than $10 000, Julie simply created, signed, and issued the cheque herself. Claims over $10 000 required a second signature, but she could ask anybody in the office to sign, so this was rarely a problem.

After several months on the job, Julie noticed that the corporate clients did not receive reports about claims made against their accounts. Since corporate clients paid a flat fee regardless of how many cases were processed, the corporate clients had little incentive to actively monitor claims activities.

Although she enjoyed her job and her co-workers, Julie, a single mother with a toddler, struggled to make ends meet. She earned $24 000 per year. Her expenses had exceeded her income ever since her son was born. Daycare was so expensive, but she had no choice but to use it if she was planning to work full time. Worse, the small savings account that she inherited upon her mother's death a few years ago was nearly empty. She had only a high school education, and she had been very lucky to land the job at the insurance company in the first place. Her options for increasing her income were limited, and her son's father had never been involved in parenting or provided any type of financial support. In fact, Julie doubted she would be able to locate him, even if she tried. As she worried and considered her limited alternatives, Julie thought about her work tasks again, remembered that her company's internal audit process examined corporate commercial accounts only every six years, and came up with an idea for some relief.

Julie's son was enrolled in a private, at-home, daycare service. She was friends with Marie, the person who operated the home daycare, and they had shared a lot of laughs together. Julie usually paid for daycare on a bi-weekly basis using a personal cheque. Until the day she didn't. Three weeks after her initial flash of "inspiration," a different kind of cheque was handed over to Marie, one with the insurance company's name featured as payer instead of Julie's name. "That's weird," commented Marie, "what is up with this?" "Oh, I was embarrassed to tell you," said Julie, looking down at her feet. "I'm having some financial difficulties and my employer has decided to help me out, so the cheques for daycare will come from the company from now on." Although this sounded a little strange to Marie, she figured that the issue was personal, shrugged, and accepted Julie's cheque.

Julie left the daycare feeling euphoric. Her idea had actually worked! Three weeks previously, she had created a "loss" in the system with Marie's name ascribed to it. Julie selected one of the very large corporate commercial accounts against which to submit the claim, a company that was seldom, if ever, reviewed. She was well aware of the most common types of losses experienced, and so it was not difficult to come up with a scenario and dollar value that would not attract attention. She simply entered Marie's name as the claimant, approved the claim, and in due course a cheque was issued.

The plan had worked so well the first time that Julie executed it again. And again. And again. A little over eight months passed and, in that time, she created eight different claims under Marie's name. She added it up one day and realized that she had netted $12 000 from her "side activities." Julie reflected on how easy it had all been. She worried that she would be tempted to do it over and over again, and not just for daycare expenses. This was not the person she wanted to be. She decided that the only solution was to remove herself from temptation. She asked for, and received, a transfer to another department.

While Julie was celebrating her transfer and the fact that she would no longer be tempted, a problem emerged. The cheque for the last claim she had invented came back to her, because she had not filled in a field that coded the claim for the accounting system. Normally she could have fixed the oversight in a few seconds, but because she had been transferred, she no longer had access to the system. The person who replaced Julie asked her for a copy of the paperwork to back up the claim before filling in the missing information. Julie was unable to provide any. Not long after this incident, Julie arrived at work one morning to find herself called into a private room. Management informed her that they knew about the fraudulent claims, fired her, and advised her to get a lawyer. One month later, a police officer came to her home, and she was formally charged with fraud over $5000.

Now here she was, in court, being sentenced. She feared that her little boy would not understand why she would not return home that night. She had not told anybody about what was happening, in denial that she might actually go to jail. She felt numb all over and just prayed that her new boyfriend would be willing to take care of her son until she was released. If not, her son would become a ward of the state and be sent to a foster home; a thought that once again reduced Julie to despair. All she had ever wanted was to be able to look after her son properly. How had it come to this?

Discussion Questions

1. What does this case teach us about ethical decision-making behaviours?

2. Did the workplace environment or corporate culture contribute to Julie's ability to rationalize her fraudulent activities? Did these factors contribute to her decision to stop committing fraud? Based on your understanding of how work attitudes develop, explain how organizational factors may have contributed to her activities and subsequent decisions.

3. What can employers do to create an environment that encourages ethical behaviour?

Case 3: Auditing, Attitudes, and Absenteeism

Learning Goals

In this case, you will have an opportunity to evaluate whether an ethical lapse in an employee's behaviour should be considered as an isolated incident or a symptom of broader problems within the corporate culture. You will also be asked to consider which factors contributed to the decision by Peter's direct reports to simply go along with his directions. Other issues to consider include the following: How might factors such as poor socialization or communication have contributed to the behaviour of Peter's direct reports? What would theories of motivation suggest? Should the organization have used a more formalized structure? Use your own insight to make recommendations about what the organization could, and should, do to prevent similar situations from developing in the future.

Major Topic Areas

- Work attitudes (Chapter 3)
- Organizational culture and socialization (Chapter 10)
- Power (Chapter 8)
- Group dynamics (Chapter 6)
- Motivation (Chapters 4 and 5)
- Ethical decision-making (Chapter 12)
- Organizational structure (Chapter 13)

The Scenario

"You've got to be kidding," said Sanjay, shaking his head, "is he there right now?" "Yes," said Bianca, "if we drive over there you can see for yourself." "What the heck," exclaimed Sanjay, "let's go."[3] The pair left their office tower and drove the 10-minute distance to Peter's house. Bianca was right. Peter was supposed to be out at a client site overseeing an audit, but his car was parked in his driveway, and he could be seen clearly through his large, living room window. "Well, this is awkward," sighed Sanjay. "What do we do now?"

Sanjay and Bianca were senior managers at one of Canada's top four professional audit firms. Their team was responsible for performing audits for a broad range of corporate clients. The firm had a very traditional and formalized structure, like the other large players in their industry. Recent graduates were hired as "students in accounts," during which time they were expected to complete their professional exams and work toward their chartered accountant (CA) designation. Upon passing their CA exams, they could compete to become junior auditors in the firm. If they chose to stay with the firm, they could then expect to progress to a supervisory role and finally, in six to seven years, become a senior manager. The best and brightest auditors stood to become future partners in the firm. Many graduates, however, simply worked at the company long enough to achieve their CA designation, which requires a minimum of two years' experience working in an auditing firm. The culture this process created was coined "up or out," since that is exactly what happened. Employees moved up (i.e., they were promoted) or out (i.e., left the company). There was no shame in leaving, though; in fact, it was anticipated that most employees would remain only long enough to get their designations and then move on.

Peter had joined the firm a few years ago and had progressed to a supervisory role. Recently, Peter had come to the conclusion that the path to partner was not right for him, and he began applying for jobs with other companies. But his decision to apply for jobs elsewhere created a dilemma. He was not comfortable telling his employer he was looking for work elsewhere, and he was also concerned that if his employer knew that he was contemplating leaving the firm, his current assignments and standing would be negatively affected. To make matters worse, Peter had no idea how long it would take to find a new job, and he also had no idea how to manage organizing time off to participate in interviews.

Peter reviewed his work tasks and responsibilities and came up with what he perceived to be a viable solution to his dilemma. He began telling the people under his supervision that their current client did not require their presence on Fridays, and they should work at home instead. Peter encouraged them to use the time to work on things like file reviews or even just to relax. The members of Peter's team did not question his instructions, even though it was highly unusual to be allowed, and even encouraged, to work from home. Even full partners seldom worked from home. The clients themselves did not question the team's absence on Fridays either (one suspects that the average worker is not terribly disappointed when he or she discovers that the audit team is absent for a day). This arrangement allowed Peter to tell his manager that he was conducting on-site audits on Fridays, when he was actually scheduling and attending a series of job interviews on those days.

The situation continued for a couple of months before a few of Peter's direct reports became uncomfortable enough to say something. They approached Bianca, who drove past Peter's house the following Friday to see for herself whether or not he was there. When she confirmed that he was at home, instead of "on-site," she returned to the office to discuss the situation with Sanjay. Now here the two of them were, standing on Peter's front step, wondering how to handle the situation. Sanjay knocked on the door. Peter answered, but as soon as he saw Sanjay and Bianca, his face turned red. They asked him what was going on and were stunned when Peter began to cry.

After Peter regained his composure, the three of them returned to the office to discuss the situation. Sanjay and Bianca learned that the reason for the absences on Fridays was so that Peter could attend job interviews. Once Sanjay and Bianca heard all of the details, they asked Peter to step out of the office while they discussed the situation in more detail. "The irony," remarked Sanjay, once they were alone, "is that if Peter had just told us what was happening, we would have been happy to give him time off to go to interviews. We recently completed his performance evaluation, and although he is a solid accountant, he just isn't partner material. He doesn't have a future here anyway. It's not that he is a bad auditor, but others are better. I would have been happy to help him find a good placement." "That's all well and good," said Bianca, "but it isn't even Peter I'm worried about. He supervised several different teams over the couple of months he was doing this. Why did it take so long for any of them to let us know what he was doing? I know the work still got done and the clients were satisfied, and I know that everyone likes to be friendly around here and hang out together, but these people are auditors for goodness sake! I would have expected better. Do you think this might be a symptom of a bigger problem with our corporate culture? And if so, what should we do about it?"

Discussion Questions

1. Why do you think Peter's direct reports kept quiet about the "work from home" directive for as long as they did? Why did some of them eventually decide to inform management?

2. Do you think this situation would have happened if the organization had a more formal structure in place? Why or why not?

3. Do you think the lapse in Peter's ethical behaviour indicates a broader problem with the firm's corporate culture? Why or why not? If yes, what should management do now to try to change its corporate culture?

Case 4: Bad Faith Bargaining? Government Power and Negotiations with the Public Service

Learning Goals

In this case, you will have an opportunity to assess the impact of federal government policy on labour relations in the public sector. You will be asked to consider what strategies and tactics may contribute to the escalation of conflict and how the situation could be handled moving forward to lessen the intensity and emotional nature of the conflict. You will also be asked to consider issues of power and ethics. Do you believe the federal government is acting ethically in the case? What about the unions?

Major Topic Areas

- Power and politics (Chapter 8)
- Conflict and negotiation (Chapter 9)
- Ethics (Chapter 12)

The Scenario

Bargaining between unions and management in the public sector can be not only newsworthy but also highly controversial.[4]

In 1967, the Canadian government gave federal public servants collective bargaining rights. Those rights gave public-service unions the right to choose whether to settle contract disputes by arbitration or by strike.

Treasury Board President Tony Clement, who was responsible for federal labour issues, changed those rights in 2013 when he introduced sweeping reforms to the Public Service Labour Relations Act. The new rules for collective bargaining seem to favour the government.

In the federal public service, unions were once able to decide whether they wanted to settle their disputes by arbitration (a process in which an arbitrator imposes a decision on the parties in a dispute) or conciliation (a process in which a settlement is recommended and is backed by the right to strike). The new rules give the federal government, rather than the federal unions, the power to decide whether individual disputes are solved by arbitration or conciliation. Federal public service unions are concerned that the government can force them into conciliation (and a possible strike), even if their members believe arbitration would resolve a dispute. Ultimately, the new rules for collective bargaining have decreased the power of unions that represent federal public servants and make it more likely that affected union members will agree to concessions if they consider strike action undesirable.

The federal government has also placed limits on the factors that arbitrators and conciliation boards can consider when they provide decisions on disputes for federal unions. They are required to focus on two factors: the federal government's "fiscal circumstances relative to its budgetary policies" and the ability to recruit and retain employees. The labour board had previously concluded that those two preconditions favoured the federal government to an excessive degree; despite this conclusion, Clement made the preconditions law a few months later.

In 2014, Clement announced that the federal government would revamp the public service's sick leave policy.[5] Under the new collective bargaining rules, federal public service unions are seriously limited in resolving any disputes over sick leave.

Under the federal government's existing sick leave policy, federal public servants receive 15 days of paid sick leave per year. Unused days can be carried over to subsequent years (a process known as "banking") and then be used as needed. In some cases, employees may end up with many weeks "banked." This can help them get through a prolonged illness or major injuries, since it takes 65 days to become eligible for long-term disability payments. Clement points out that the existing sick leave policy creates significant liabilities on the government balance sheet, since the government needs to account for the potential use of banked sick days. In early 2014, banked sick leave was valued at $5.2 billion.[6] At the same time, a report by the Parliamentary Budget Office indicates that it costs the government very little to pay sick leave to federal servants. For example, "the report found that sick leave can range from a low of 0.16 percent of total [federal] departmental spending to 2.74 percent on the high end of the scale."[7]

Clement also cited absenteeism as an issue related to the existing sick leave policy, since workers with large amounts of banked sick leave time might use sick days for purposes other than those originally intended. Sick leave policy is also associated with an equity issue. Since employees need to wait 65 days to get long-term disability payments, the net effect is that long-term employees (ones who have had time to bank many days) have a much better safety net than junior employees. Clement believed that replacing the sick leave policy with a short-term disability plan would ensure that everyone's health needs are met in a consistent and fair manner, while mitigating the problems associated with the existing policy. He felt so strongly about it that he began negotiations with insurance providers before finalizing the new policy with the federal public service unions, a step that was very poorly received.

As a result, 17 federal public service unions signed a "solidarity pledge," agreeing that they would not surrender their current sick leave benefits. Many of those unions had three-year contracts that expired in December 2014, setting the stage for conflict and unrest over this (and likely other) issues. Will a bruising battle lie ahead?

Discussion Questions

1. Do the new collective bargaining rules for federal public service unions introduced by the federal government represent an abuse of government power? Why or why not?

2. Have any negotiation or communication errors been made by the government or by the unions in relation to federal sick leave reform? If yes, what are they?

3. How could the government, as an employer, proceed to develop a more trusting relationship with employees under the new rules for collective bargaining? What could they do to better manage labour relations moving forward?

Case 5: Gender–Based Harassment among the Royal Canadian Mounted Police

Learning Goals

In this case, you will have an opportunity to evaluate how organizational culture influences the way power is used and ethical decisions are made within the Royal Canadian Mounted Police (RCMP). Consider why the RCMP developed such a widespread problem with gender-based harassment allegations. Did the RCMP leadership contribute to the problem and, if so, how can they help to resolve it?

Major Topic Areas

- Workplace harassment and bullying (Chapter 8)

- Organizational culture (Chapter 10)

- Organizational change (Chapter 14)

- Leadership (Chapter 11)

The Scenario

In December 2006, the BC Court of Appeal upheld the decision by the BC Supreme Court to award Nancy Sulz $950 000 in damages for severe, long-term harassment experienced while she worked for Canada's RCMP.[8] The sexual harassment she endured starting in 1995 led to her request for a medical discharge from the RCMP in 2000, due to major depressive disorder. Her harasser, Staff Sergeant Donald Smith, has continued to enjoy a successful career with the force. Sulz was not the first person to complain about him; another female officer made similar allegations in the late 1980s but ultimately did not pursue them.

Four female RCMP officers alleged that they were sexually assaulted by Sergeant Robert Blundell during undercover operations that took place in Calgary between 1994 and 1997. Their internal complaints were dismissed and ignored, a problem that went all the way up to then-Commissioner Giuliano Zaccardelli. The officers reported that after filing complaints, they were "considered rats and whistle-blowers and subject to harassing ridicule."[9] The four officers felt that "the lack of response signalled to the rank and file of the RCMP that silence, cover-up, and minimization are the preferred method of dealing with harassment within the RCMP."[10]

The officers chose to file a lawsuit against the RCMP in Calgary's Court of Queen's Bench in September 2003 because of the RCMP's lack of response. "We have done everything we can do within the force to address the problems and issues," the four reported in a formal statement. "They have not been

satisfactorily resolved, and we've had to take this step as a last resort."[11] At the time of filing their case, two of the alleged victims were on stress leave and the other two reported losing career opportunities within the force. One lost her role as a hostage negotiator, and the other has not been assigned to undercover operations since making the allegations. The alleged perpetrator of the sexual assaults, meanwhile, lost one day of pay and was later promoted. The case was settled out of court in 2007, with the terms kept secret.[12] However, in December 2011, *The Fifth Estate* reported that two of the complainants continue to feel they were let down by the RCMP in the matter. "That seems to be the way of the RCMP, that's kind of like the toothless tiger. There's never any accountability," said Victoria Cliffe, one of the four complainants.[13]

Janet Merlo, of Nanaimo, BC, would no doubt understand the frustration the four Calgary RCMP officers experienced. She received a medical discharge from the RCMP due to post-traumatic stress disorder that was a direct result of ongoing workplace harassment and bullying. She was allegedly subjected to frequent sexual remarks and unwanted invitations from her immediate supervisor. Co-workers also left sex toys and pornography on her desk. It took two years after Merlo's initial complaint for the organization to respond. The response thanked Merlo for her letter and noted: "As you are aware the RCMP does not take these allegations lightly and, in fact, has an obligation to provide a harassment free environment for all of our employees."[14] Merlo was advised that the matter had been investigated but no action would be taken. Subsequently, Merlo initiated legal proceedings, but she was unable to continue due to the high costs involved.[15] Heli Kijanen, of Thunder Bay, Ontario, who quit her job with the RCMP in 2011 due to incessant harassment, has experienced the same challenges trying to get justice.

Other court cases are proceeding. Officer Elisabeth Couture, of Surrey, BC, made a claim through civilian courts against three male RCMP colleagues for systematically targeting her and creating a climate of fear in the workplace. Staff Sergeant Travis Pearson found himself in criminal court due to allegations that he raped Officer Susan Gastaldo, of Burnaby, BC, in his home and then actively stalked her children in order to intimidate her into silence. An unidentified former RCMP officer testified at his trial that Pearson had also attempted to rape her under very similar circumstances, but she was too intimidated to report it at the time.[16]

In November 2011, Corporal Catherine Galliford, of Langley, BC, another RCMP officer and victim of ongoing workplace sexual harassment, decided she had had enough. She used the media to give her voice weight and expose the extent and severity of the harassment experienced by many of the 2613 female RCMP officers, a small minority in a force of 22 000. It was not long before other women, inspired by Galliford, also came forward to tell their stories, resulting in the beginnings of a class action lawsuit against the RCMP for its failure to address widespread gender-based harassment and bullying. RCMP leadership has little reason to be surprised. An internal study conducted in 1996 found that 6 out of 10 female Mounties had been sexually harassed at work and that more than 10 percent reported unwanted touching by male colleagues.

Unfortunately, that same leadership has done a very poor job of responding to complaints or addressing the cultural issues that underlie them. Questioned after Galliford had gone public, Krista Carle, one of the four Calgary RCMP officers who filed a complaint against Blundell, said the following about her formal complaint: "there was an internal review and nothing came of it. There was a memo that went out to colleagues and staff about how there was an incident with someone placing inappropriate material on someone's desk. Everyone knew it was me, so it was almost like I got blamed for getting the guys in trouble. And they never found out who put the porn on my desk."[17] Carle was discharged from the RCMP with post-traumatic stress disorder that she attributes to 19 years of unremitting sexual harassment and general bullying.

Paul Champ, a lawyer who has been involved in RCMP cases, says that "the process often takes years because the RCMP often does not treat complaints as a priority. ... Most complaints are dismissed out of hand or dismissed with no remedy offered to the complainant other than 'we talked to him about it.'"[18]

Recognition of the scope of the problem led Bob Paulson, the new RCMP Commissioner, to make an unprecedented formal statement acknowledging that the continued existence of the force itself was at risk. He needed to "clear-cut problems that have taken root deeply. Too many Mounties believe their authority entitles them to misuse power. ... The Mounties are one or two more earth-shattering heartbreaks away from losing all credibility. I tell you, one day there is going to be the removal of the Stetson (the RCMP's emblematic hat and symbol of the force) if we don't get this right."[19]

Steps have been taken. An external labour relations expert was retained to review the RCMP's existing harassment policy, and a new code of conduct was introduced in April 2014.[20] Some are skeptical that these efforts will help to change a long-entrenched culture. Officer Elisabeth Couture believes that "management at the local level routinely turns a blind eye to harassment as it's occurring. You can have all the staff workshops on the issue that you want, but unless detachment supervisors deal with incidents in a forceful and unequivocal manner it won't matter."[21]

The RCMP's female officers who have experienced harassment, both past and present, are not waiting around to see if these efforts to effect change within the RCMP will be successful. By July 2014, a class action lawsuit was launched by over 330 women.[22] The lawyer representing Janet Merlo reports that "the stories are consistent. The stories are common in terms of harassment, bullying, and oftentimes, sexual issues. The calls are sad, hugely sad. The stories are terrible. Many serving members are unable to work because they are petrified in light of their experiences."[23] Lawyers are also quick to point out the impact that these gender-biased attitudes may have on perceived injustice in the broader community. For instance, a lack of perceived sensitivity may inhibit female members of the public from reporting sexual assaults or stalking incidents. With the class action lawsuit proceeding, the RCMP leadership will need to carefully consider how to restore its reputation and credibility among both female staff and the broader community.

Discussion Questions

1. What aspects of the organizational culture in the RCMP may have contributed to its problems with widespread sexual harassment allegations?

2. Do the alleged claims of sexual harassment point to a leadership problem? Why or why not?

3. Devise a plan to manage a culture change at the RCMP. What resistance might you encounter and how could you overcome it?

Case 6: Disability Accommodations and Promotions at Bunco

Learning Goals

In this case, you will have to decide whether to promote an employee who has a disability. You will need to consider whether the particular disability presents a legally and morally defensible reason against promotion to a management role. If you choose to promote the employee, what can you do to help ensure his success? If you do *not* promote him, how can you explain and justify your decision, while helping the person to maintain positive work attitudes?

Major Topic Areas

- Diversity (disability) (Chapter 3)
- Work attitudes (Chapter 3)
- Recruitment and selection (Chapter 10)

The Scenario

Nicholas, the director of finance at Bunco Canada, sat wearily at his desk, sighed deeply, and rubbed his eyes.[24] He wondered whether an external search for the company's newly created accounting manager role was the right choice. Had Nicholas's decision been reasonable and fair?

Paul had worked for Nicholas as a staff accountant for 14 years. Paul was a Certified Management Accountant (CMA) and was the senior accountant responsible for external financial reporting.

Paul was a consistent and reliable employee who, due to his long tenure, knew a lot about the organization. He had, at some point in his career, performed most accounting functions at Bunco, including plant costing, budgeting, analysis, and financial planning, and so he understood the details of each role extremely well. Paul got along well with the junior staff (most of whom had been with the company for more than 10 years) and was considered a key member of the accounting team. He frequently acted as an informal adviser to other members of his team, put in overtime, and engaged in special projects, including process improvements and database optimization. In fact, he had become the sole subject matter expert on some critical financial applications needed for monthly reporting. In the past four years, however, Paul had required special accommodations from Bunco for Crohn's disease.

Crohn's disease is an incurable inflammatory bowel disease that results in sporadic and unpredictable bouts of moderate to severe pain, fever, diarrhea, gas, vomiting, and rectal bleeding.[25] Sufferers of Crohn's may experience brief or extended remissions that last months or even years, and then relapse without obvious triggers, although many patients with Crohn's disease report that stress significantly worsens symptoms and can trigger flare-ups.[26] There is no cure for the disease, but anti-inflammatory and immune-modulator medication, surgery, and careful attention to diet can control symptoms and minimize relapses for some people.[27]

Canadian courts recognize Crohn's disease as a legitimate disability for employment-related purposes. Employers are required to accommodate Crohn's disease as long as that accommodation does not result in excessive hardship to them. "Duty to reasonably accommodate" means that an employer must take all reasonable measures to enable a disabled employee to keep working. In addition to making physical accommodations such as providing laptops, wheelchair ramps, etc., employers can also be required to revise job responsibilities and performance appraisal criteria.

When he was first diagnosed with Crohn's four years ago, Paul had discussed several concerns with Nicholas. "Nicholas, I don't know how long it will take me to get this under control. It's not like I can't work at all. I'll go for a couple hours and be fine, but then… I don't think anyone wants me running to the washrooms here. Besides it's humiliating. I need some privacy. When the pain flares up it's all I can focus on. Maybe I could just work from home on a laptop on my bad days, play it by ear a little bit?"

Nicholas replied: "Well I don't see a problem with you working from home sometimes, but are you sure that's what you want? I spoke to an HR representative about this yesterday, and she pointed out that we have a corporate policy that prohibits laptop use for everyone except senior management and sales, but under the circumstances, I'm pretty sure I can get one approved for you. I was wondering if going on long-term disability might be a better solution for you to get yourself well though, assuming that we can get the insurance company to support the claim. Your health has to be your first priority. That said, I don't really know what we'll do if you leave!"

Paul was reluctant to seek long-term disability, because he did not want to give up so much of his life to the disease. It was also unclear whether the claim would be accepted by Bunco's insurer. After another discussion with an HR representative, Nicholas decided that a laptop should be issued to Paul and that he should be permitted to work at home on his bad days. Nicholas trusted him not to abuse the privilege so felt no need to document the decision further. An informal "handshake agreement" was readily accepted by Paul.

Accommodation Implemented: The First Few Years

Paul and Nicholas explained the situation to co-workers in a regularly scheduled staff meeting, and, initially, everyone was supportive of the new arrangement. As more time passed, however, Nicholas became worried. He had anticipated the occasional absence, but over the first few months of the new arrangement, Paul consistently worked two days in the office and then had to go home for two to three days, meaning he was absent more than 50 percent of the time. Although Paul did respond to email, Nicholas felt that he had underestimated the ongoing impact that Paul's absence might have on the team over the long term. Nicholas was being inundated with daily questions from staff that would normally have been routed to Paul. Despite the difficulties adjusting, Nicholas felt strongly that accommodating Paul was the right thing to do, so he said nothing. About five months after the initial discussion and the purchase of a laptop for use by Paul, Paul's symptoms decreased, and he was able to work in the office about 85 percent of the time for the next 18 months.

About two years ago, Crohn's-related relapses and problems returned for Paul. At the same time, due to growth in market share and a new acquisition, the demands on the accounting department had increased significantly. Budget constraints did not allow for the hiring of additional staff. Everyone had to work a little harder and be willing to work significantly more overtime, often until 11:00 p.m. or midnight for several days in a row.

As previously mentioned, bouts of Crohn's disease are often triggered by stress. Since month's- and year's ends were particularly stressful times, Paul would often experience attacks then, just when he was needed most in the office. He was frequently absent during these key times, missing more than half of the month's ends over six months. Other accounting employees, who previously had supported Paul's accommodations, began to murmur their resentment among themselves.

One day Nicholas overheard several colleagues talk about him, when they did not realize he was in the area. "It would really make my life easier if I could work from home," one said. Another asked, "Couldn't he control his Crohn's with diet, if he really tried to? I think he just doesn't want to be stuck here all evening for a week like us suckers!" "I don't think he can control it *that* much," another voice chimed. A fourth person responded, "even so, it does make for a convenient excuse doesn't it; he could fake it on any given day, and nobody would even know the difference. I bet he took off this afternoon because he heard they're bringing in pizza for dinner AGAIN." "It's not even fair," a fifth voice complained. "If he can phone and email his work in why can't we? My ex is furious that I missed my night with the kids; I'll be paying for that one for a while."

Nicholas worried about the worsening morale among what had previously been a very close team. Furthermore, Paul had been significantly late submitting his external financial reports on several occasions, and his lack of availability had hampered other people's ability to complete interdependent tasks. Since his relapse began 18 months ago, the department had been late in submitting its monthly financial reports to head office seven times! The department still complied with deadlines imposed by the Securities and Exchange Commission (SEC), but it missed many internal deadlines. While not all of the department's late filings could be directly attributed to Paul's condition (and absences), he had certainly contributed to the problem.

That said, Nicholas knew that Paul had limited control over the Crohn's disease, so Nicholas did not mention his concerns to Paul or document performance problems. If anyone else said anything to Paul directly, Nicholas was unaware of it. Nicholas

ended up doing little more than hope that Paul would experience a remission and that the situation would improve.

The Accounting Manager Role

Meanwhile the changes continued apace at Bunco. Ongoing growth and further acquisitions-in-process meant that Nicholas acquired significant new responsibilities. Part of that transition included Nicholas taking on a more strategic role in financial management and physically relocating to the company's executive headquarters in Toronto. This meant that he would no longer be around day to day to manage the accounting department at the northern packaging facility. It was also no longer adequate for the department to adopt a flat organizational structure, with staff accountants formally reporting to the director. An accounting manager position would need to be created.

As director, Nicholas was responsible for financial strategy, identifying opportunities for cost reduction and revenue growth, foreign exchange strategy, ameliorating controls, and managing transition teams for new acquisitions. In turn, the new accounting manager would be responsible for much of what Nicholas had previously done. This included advising senior executives, including the CEO, about monthly financial results and projected year-end performance, as well as overall responsibility for costing and management accounting. This position required ongoing communication with various parts of the company, including occasional travel to the head office. The most important part of the accounting manager role, however, involved managing the team at the northern facility. This included assigning tasks and providing daily guidance, advice, and social support to junior staff.

Under normal circumstances, Paul would have been the natural choice for promotion to this new accounting manager position. He wanted it; indeed, he felt it was owed to him in return for his long years of service. He was the most senior person in the department and, other than Nicholas, Paul had the highest level of formal accounting education. The other members of the department did not qualify for the role, as they were not CMAs. Paul had also created many of the spreadsheets and systems that were an integral component of the company's financial reporting system. The new role, however, would come with a significantly increased stress load, since it involved management responsibilities and a much higher political profile in the organization. Could Paul really handle the stress, given his disability? Also, if he did experience a flare-up, how could he manage a team of people from home, when multiple questions came up each day? Reports to head office were already being sent late with alarming frequency, damaging the northern branch's reputation within the company. Would this situation become worse under Paul's direction?

Fourteen months earlier, Nicholas had carefully considered his options vis-à-vis filling the future account manager position. He tried to discuss his concerns with his HR department but discovered that promotions were legal and ethical grey areas when it came to disability accommodation. Under a subset of law regarding duty to accommodate, employers were not able to deny promotions based on inability to perform a job without first proving undue hardship, but what did that really mean? The concept was largely untested in the courtroom. An HR staff member suggested that Paul be asked to participate in a detailed medical assessment to prove that he could not complete the essential operational requirements of the job. This suggestion did not sit well with Nicholas. A medical assessment could be regarded as invasive, and the procedure would lead to Paul being expected to share a great deal of confidential medical information. Furthermore, as with any management job, it was hard to distinguish the *essential* aspects of the job from the secondary ones. Presenting and defending monthly financial reports, for example, was a key part of the job. It was also very stressful, as the reports were examined and questioned in detail by powerful senior executives. Since stress was a trigger for flare-ups of Crohn's disease, could Paul handle the pressure? What about travel to head office? This was also stressful, and travel might well prove impossible for Paul. Was it

fair to expect Paul to try, given his medical condition? Nicholas's biggest concern, however, was that Paul would not always be physically available to the staff. Nicholas felt that the physical presence of a manager in the office was central to the orderly flow of information, completion of daily tasks, and maintenance of a supportive and collegial environment. He did not know if he could truly justify calling that physical presence "essential," but his gut told him it was.

Under pressure to decide whether to fill the new position internally or externally, Nicholas was not sure that he was making the right choice, but he decided to launch an external search for an account manager, instead of promoting Paul.

Discussion Questions

1. Should Nicholas have promoted Paul? Why or why not?

2. **a.** What are Nicholas's legal responsibilities to Paul in this situation?

   b. What are Nicholas's ethical responsibilities to Paul in this situation? How does that balance with Nicholas's responsibilities to Paul's co-workers?

3. If Paul were to be promoted, what strategies could Nicholas use to help Paul achieve success in his new role?

Case 7: Promotion from Within

Learning Goals

This case will allow you to evaluate the impact of (in)effective employee relations on motivation and job performance. Pay particular attention to issues of perceived equity and also to expectation setting and how they each relate to motivation. Is this company's approach to internal recruitment likely to cause ongoing problems for them? If so, why?

Major Topic Areas

- Motivation (Chapters 4 and 5)
- Work attitudes (Chapter 3)
- Communication (Chapter 7)
- Politics (Chapter 8)

The Scenario

The two interviewers leaned forward across the table and looked at Elisa intently. "We are very impressed with your

résumé and your recently completed MBA," the HR manager stated, "but the client training role that we have available is entry level. With your 10 years of sales and training experience and your education, you seem rather overqualified and we are concerned."

Elisa shifted slightly in her seat then turned on her best smile as she answered the interviewer. "I do understand that I am overqualified for this job," she responded, "I have also heard that Kium Solutions is a really great place to work and I know your CEO has some really interesting ideas for moving the company forward. I think I could do a lot of good here and I am willing to start in an entry-level job to get in the door as long as there are other opportunities down the road." The interviewers glanced at each other and nodded. "Well that works for us," responded the HR manager. "You can start now and I am quite confident that something more challenging that better matches your qualifications will come up within a year or so." "That sounds great," said Elisa. "I look forward to coming on board."

Fifteen months later, Elisa was still in the entry-level training role, which saw her travelling to different client sites each day to train their new employees on how to use Kium's document management systems. Elisa was the first person with a degree in education who had served in the client trainer role. Her formal knowledge about teaching and learning had helped her make substantial improvements to the existing client training program. Elisa's manager had commented several times about the significant increases in client satisfaction ratings that they had observed. Clients were especially impressed that Elisa was so readily available to them—she even gave them her personal cellphone number. If they had a software question or problem at 9:00 p.m. or on a Saturday, Elisa would answer her phone and cheerfully help, something that was neither expected nor required. Elisa was sure that she had done everything she could to impress her new employers. As a result, she was particularly excited when her co-worker pointed out the new job that had been posted to the internal recruitment webpage (a special website for jobs posted internally with the intent of promoting from within).

The posting was for a newly created position, director of Training. Previously, the company only had client trainers (an entry-level job) and HR generalists who took care of all employee training. The new directorship would report to the VP of Sales, making it a highly prestigious position within the corporate hierarchy. The director would be responsible for improving initial staff orientation and the training received by new hires in the Sales department. Kium relied on its salesforce to grow its business. The director of Training would therefore be fulfilling an important role in the organization. Elisa could not be more delighted. After all, she had an MBA and a degree in adult education, plus she had over a decade of experience selling software solutions (although for companies other than Kium). In fact, it was her desire to get away from never-ending sales quotas and broaden her career choices that led her to pursue an MBA. Given her many qualifications and her record of strong performance, Elisa was confident that she would be a competitive candidate for the role.

Elisa sent in her résumé and, at the end of the application period, she was not the least bit surprised when she was called for an interview with the VP of Sales.

Elisa knew that she would have to explain why she was well qualified for the job. To prepare for the interview, she reread the strategic goals, vision, and mission of the company and thought carefully about how she could contribute. She even had her boyfriend ask her mock interview questions so that she could practise her answers. On the morning of her interview, although she felt prepared, she was also nervous. Then disappointment struck. The assistant to the VP of Sales called to say that the VP of Sales was no longer interested in interviewing her. After reviewing her résumé, he realized that she did not have enough direct experience in sales at Kium.

Elisa was stunned, wondering what on earth had happened. She could not believe that she would not even be given an opportunity to explain why she would be a good candidate for the job. She sent an email to the VP's assistant explaining her qualifications, but the assistant again confirmed that Elisa would not be permitted to interview for the job. Ultimately, Elisa went home an hour early that day, still distressed and bewildered. At 5:17 p.m. her cellphone rang. She saw that it was an important client who had recently purchased an expensive and complex solution from Kium. Just days ago, Elisa had promised the CEO at the client company that she would be there to answer questions and support their roll-out every step of the way. She looked again at the call display and at the time. She quietly looked away and let the call go to voicemail. The client could wait until Monday.

Discussion Questions

1. How would you explain the abrupt change in Elisa's customer service behaviour? Outline what has happened to her motivation using expectancy and equity theories.

2. Could Elisa's employer have anticipated the impact that cancelling the directorship interview might have on her future performance? What should her employer have done differently?

3. Elisa raised concern about being shut out of the directorship interview to the HR manager. What could the HR manager do now to help improve Elisa's motivation? Explain why your idea would be effective.

Case 8: Repairing Jobs That Fail to Satisfy

Learning Goals

Companies often divide up work as a way to improve efficiency, but specialization can lead to negative consequences. FlowFix is a company that for years has effectively used specialization to reduce costs relative to that of its competitors, but rising customer complaints suggest that the firm's strong position may be slipping. After reading the case, suggest some ways the company can create more interesting work for employees while improving customer satisfaction rates. You will also need to tackle the problem of how to find people qualified and ready to perform the multiple responsibilities required in FlowFix's jobs.

Major Topic Areas

- Job design (Chapter 5)

- Job satisfaction (Chapter 3)

- Personality (Chapter 2)

- Emotional labour (Chapter 2)

The Scenario

FlowFix is a mid-sized residential and commercial plumbing maintenance firm that operates in the Greater Vancouver area. It has been a major regional player in plumbing for decades. Tyron Johnson has been the senior executive at FlowFix for about two years. He used to work for a newer competing chain, Lightning Plumber, which has been drawing away more and more customers from FlowFix. Although his job at FlowFix pays more, Tyron is not happy with the way things are going. He has noticed the work environment is not as vital or energetic as the environment he saw at Lightning Plumber.

Tyron thinks the problem is that employees are not motivated to provide the type of customer service Lightning Plumber employees offer. He recently sent surveys to customers to collect information about customer service performance, and the data confirmed his fears. Although 60 percent of respondents said they were satisfied with their experience and would use FlowFix again, 40 percent felt their experience was not good, and 30 percent said they would use a competitor the next time they had a plumbing problem.

Tyron is wondering whether FlowFix's job design might be contributing to its problems in retaining customers. FlowFix has about 110 employees who are divided into one of four basic job categories: plumbers, plumber's assistants, order processors, and billing representatives. This structure is designed to keep costs as low as possible. Plumbers, who are licensed, make very high wages, whereas plumber's assistants make about one-quarter of what a licensed plumber makes. Using plumber's assistants is therefore a very cost-effective strategy that enables FlowFix to easily undercut the competition when it comes to price. Order processors make even less than plumber's assistants but about the same as billing processors. All work is specialized, but employees are often dependent on those in other job categories to perform at their most efficient level.

Like most plumbing companies, FlowFix gets a lot of residential business from people who consult the Internet. Corporate clients also use the company's online interface to make nonroutine maintenance requests. Customers either call in to describe a plumbing problem or submit an online request for plumbing services, receiving a return call within 24 hours with the information required to solve the problem. In both scenarios, FlowFix's order processors determine from the customer's description of the problem whether a plumber or a plumber's assistant should make the service call. The job is then assigned accordingly, and a service representative goes to the location. When the job has been completed, the information is relayed to a billing representative. The billing representative forwards the invoice to the service rep via cellphone, and the service rep then presents a bill to the customer for payment by credit card, debit card, or cash (corporate clients remit payment via monthly invoices rather than on-the-spot).

The Problem

Although specialization cuts costs significantly, Tyron is worried about customer dissatisfaction. According to his survey, about 25 percent of customer contacts ended in no service call because customers were confused by the diagnostic questions the order processors asked or because the order processors did not have sufficient knowledge or skill to explain the situation. That means fully one in four people who call FlowFix to hire a plumber were worse than dissatisfied: They did not become customers at all! The remaining 75 percent of calls that did end in a customer service encounter resulted in other problems.

The most frequent complaints, Tyron discovered via the customer surveys, were about response time and cost, especially when the wrong person was sent to a job. A plumber's assistant cannot complete a more technically complicated job. If a plumber's assistant arrives on site and cannot do the work, the appointment must be rescheduled (with a licensed plumber) and the customer's time and the staff's time have been wasted. The resulting delay often caused customers to decline further contact with FlowFix—many of them decided to move forward with Lightning Plumber instead.

"When I arrive at a job I can't take care of," says plumber's assistant Kiera Fritz, "the customer gets ticked off. They thought they were getting a licensed plumber, since they were calling for a plumber. Telling them they have to have someone else come out doesn't go over well."

On the other hand, when a plumber responds to a job easily handled by a plumber's assistant, the customer is still charged at the plumber's higher rate. Licensed plumber Philip Wong also does not like being in the position of giving customers bad news. "If I get called out to do something like snake a drain, the customer isn't expecting a hefty bill. I'm caught between a rock and a hard place—I don't set the rates or make the appointments, but I'm the one who gets it from the customer." Plumbers also resent being sent to do such simple work.

Louisa Gomez is one of FlowFix's order processors. She is also frustrated when the wrong person is sent to a job but feels she and the other order processors are doing the best they can. "We have a questionnaire we're supposed to follow with the calls to find out what the problem is and who needs to take the job," she explains. "The customers don't know that we have a standard form, so they think we can answer all their questions. Most of us don't know any more about plumbing than the caller. If they don't use the terms on the questionnaire, we don't understand what they're talking about. A plumber would, but we're not plumbers; we just take the calls."

Customer service issues also involve the billing representatives. They are the ones who are responsible for continuing to contact customers about payment. "It's not my fault the wrong guy was sent," says Susan MacArthur. "If two guys went out, that's two trips. If a plumber did the work, you pay plumber rates. Some of these customers don't get that I didn't take their first call, and so I get yelled at." The billing representatives also complain that they see only the tail end of the process, so they don't know what the original call entailed. The job is fairly impersonal, and much of the work involves recording customer complaints. Remember—40 percent of customers are not satisfied, and it's the billing representatives who take the brunt of customers' negative reactions on the phone.

All employees have to engage in emotional labour and it is not clear that they have the skills or personality traits to complete the customer interaction component of their jobs. FlowFix's employees are not trained to provide customer service, and they see their work mostly in technical, or mechanical, terms. Quite a few are actually anxious about speaking directly with customers. The order processors and billing representatives realize customer service is part of their job, but they also find dealing with negative feedback from customers and co-workers taxing.

A couple of months ago, a human resource management consultant was hired to survey FlowFix employees about their job attitudes. The results, shown below on a scale of 1 to 5, indicated that FlowFix employees were less satisfied than employees in comparable jobs. The table below provides a breakdown of respondents' satisfaction levels across a number of categories.

The Proposed Solution

The company is in trouble, and as revenues shrink and the cost savings that were supposed to be achieved by dividing up work fail to materialize, a change seems to be in order.

Tyron proposes using cash rewards to improve performance among employees. He thinks if employees were paid based on work outcomes, they would work harder to satisfy customers. Because it's not easy to measure how satisfied people are with the initial call-in, Tyron would like to give the order processors a small reward for every 20 calls successfully completed. For the hands-on work, he would like to have each billing representative collect information about customer satisfaction for each completed call. If no complaints are made and the job is handled promptly, a moderate cash reward would be given to the plumber or plumber's assistant. If the customer indicates real satisfaction with the service, a larger cash reward would be provided.

Tyron also wants to find a way to hire people who are a better fit with the company's new goals. The current hiring procedure relies on unstructured interviews, and Tyron has realized that he, his senior office manager, and his most experienced lead plumber are not very consistent when interviewing. Furthermore, they often rely on their gut instinct when making hiring decisions. Tyron thinks it would be better if hiring methods were standardized and customer service skills were evaluated during that process to help them identify recruits who can actually succeed in the job.

	FlowFix Plumbers	FlowFix Plumber's Assistants	FlowFix Office Employees	Average Plumber	Average Office Employees
I am satisfied with the work I am asked to do.	3.7	2.5	2.5	4.3	3.5
I am satisfied with my working conditions.	3.8	2.4	3.7	4.1	4.2
I am satisfied with my interactions with co-workers.	3.5	3.2	2.7	3.8	3.9
I am satisfied with my interactions with my supervisor.	2.5	2.3	2.2	3.5	3.4

The information that appears above about "average plumbers" and "average office employees" is taken from the consultant's records of similar companies and published industry data about skilled tradespeople. The comparatively low averages for FlowFix employees are not exactly surprising given some of the complaints FlowFix employees have made. Tyron is worried about these results, but has not been able to formulate a solution. The traditional FlowFix culture has been focused on minimizing costs, and the "soft stuff" like employee satisfaction has not been a major issue.

Discussion Questions

1. Although it's clear employees are not especially satisfied with their work, do you think this is a reason for concern? Does research suggest satisfied workers are actually better at their jobs? Are any other behavioural outcomes associated with job satisfaction?

2. Using the job characteristics model, explain why the present system of job design may be contributing to employee dissatisfaction. Describe some ways you could help employees feel more satisfied with their work by redesigning their jobs.

3. Tyron has a somewhat vague idea about how to implement the cash rewards system. Describe some of the specific ways you would make the reward system work better, while keeping morale high, based on the case.

4. Explain the advantages and disadvantages of using financial incentives in a program of this nature. What, if any, potential problems might arise if people are given money for achieving customer satisfaction goals? What other types of incentives might be considered?

5. Create a specific plan to assess whether the reward system is working. What are the dependent variables that should change if the system works? How will you go about measuring success?

6. What types of hiring recommendations would you make to find people better suited for these jobs? Which Big Five Personality Model traits would be useful for the customer service responsibilities and emotional labour?

Case 9: Virtual Organizations

Learning Goals

The multinational organization is an increasingly common and important part of the economy. This case takes you into the world of a cutting-edge music software business seeking success across three very different national and organizational cultures. Its managers need to make important decisions about how to structure work processes so that employees can be satisfied and productive doing very different tasks.

Major Topic Areas

- Organizational structure and virtual organizations (Chapter 13)

- Organizational culture (Chapter 10)

- Diversity and teams (Chapter 6)

- Organizational socialization (Chapter 10)

- Organizational change (Chapter 14)

The Scenario

Newskool Grooves is a transnational company that develops music software used to compose music, play recordings in clubs, and produce albums. Founder and CEO Gerd Finger is, understandably, the company's biggest fan. "I started this company from nothing, from just me, my ideas, and my computer. I love music—love playing music, love writing programs for making music, love listening to music—and the money is nice, too." Finger says he never wanted to work for someone else, to give away his ideas and let someone else profit from them. He wanted to keep control over them, and their image. "Newskool Grooves is always ahead of the pack. In this business, if you can't keep up, you're out. And we are the company everyone else must keep up with. Everyone knows when they get something from us, they're getting only the best and the newest."

The company headquarters are in Berlin, the nerve centre for the organization, where new products are developed and the organizational strategy is established. Newskool outsources a great deal of its coding work to programmers in Bangalore, India. Its marketing efforts are increasingly based in its Toronto offices. This division of labour is at least partially based on technical expertise and cost issues. The German team excels at design and production tasks. Because most of Newskool's customers are English speakers, the Toronto office has been the best group to write ads and market products. The Bangalore offices are filled with outstanding programmers who don't require the very high rates of compensation you would find in German or Canadian offices. The combination of high-tech software, rapid reorganization, and outsourcing makes Newskool the very definition of a virtual organization.

Finger also makes the final decision on all hiring for the company and places a heavy emphasis on independent work styles. "Why would I want to put my company in the hands of people I can't count on?" he asks with a laugh. "They have to believe in what we're doing here, really understand our direction and be able to go with it. I'm not the babysitter, I'm not the school master handing out homework. School time is over. This is the real world."

The Work Culture

Employees want to work at Newskool Grooves because it's cutting edge. Newskool's core market is dance musicians and DJs—people who appreciate that while relatively expensive, Newskool is a very high-quality and innovative brand. Newskool sees itself as a trendsetter, and this strategy has tended to pay off. While competitors develop similar products and therefore need to continually lower their prices to compete with one another, Newskool has kept revenues high by creating completely new products that don't face this type of price competition.

Unfortunately, computer piracy has eroded Newskool's ability to make money with just software-based music tools, and it has had to move into the production of hardware, such as drum machines and amplifiers that incorporate its computer technology. Making this massive market change might be challenging for some companies, but for an organization that reinvents itself every two to three years like Newskool does, the bigger fight is a constant war against stagnation and rigidity.

The organization has a very decentralized structure. With only 115 employees, the original management philosophy of allowing all employees to participate in decision making and innovation is still the lifeblood of the company's culture. One developer notes, "At Newskool, they want you to be part of the process. If you are a person who wants to do what you're told at work, you're in trouble. Most times, they can't tell you what they want you to do next—they don't even know what comes next! That's why they hire employees who are creative, people who can try to make the next thing happen. It's challenging, but a lot of us think it's very much an exciting environment."

The Virtual Environment

Because so much of the work can be performed on computers, Finger decided early to allow employees to work outside the office. The senior management in Berlin and Toronto are both quite happy with this arrangement. Because some marketing work does require face-to-face contact, the Toronto office has weekly in-person meetings. Employees who like Newskool are happiest when they can work through the night and sleep most of the day, firing up their computers to get work done at the drop of a hat. Project discussions often happen via social networking on the company's intranet.

The Bangalore offices have been less eager to work with the virtual model. Managers say their computer programmers find working with so little structure rather uncomfortable. They

are more used to the idea of a strong leadership structure and well-defined work processes. "When I started," says one manager, "Gerd said getting in touch with him would be no problem, getting in touch with Toronto would be no problem. We're small, we're family, he said. Well, it is a problem. When I call Toronto, they say to wait until their meeting day. I can't always wait until they decide to get together. I call Gerd—he says, 'Figure it out.' Then when I do, he says it isn't right and we have to start again. If he just told me in the first place, we would have done it."

Some recent events have also shaken up the company's usual way of doing business. Developers in the Berlin office had a major communications breakdown about their hardware DJ controller, which required many hours of discussion to resolve. It seems that people who seldom met face to face had all made progress—but had moved in opposite directions. To test and design the company's hardware products, employees apparently need to do more than send each other code; sometimes they need to collaborate face to face. Some spirited disagreements have been voiced within the organization about how to move forward in this new environment.

At the same time, the Toronto office was experiencing challenges in its ability to execute its marketing plans. According to Marketing Director Sandra Pelham, "Now that we were producing hardware—real instruments—we finally thought, 'All right, this is something we can work with!' We had a whole slate of musicians and DJs and producers to contact for endorsements, but Gerd said, 'No way.' He didn't want customers who only cared that a celebrity liked us. He scrapped the whole campaign. He says we're all about creativity and doing our own thing—until we don't want to do things his way."

Although the organization is not without problems, there is little question Newskool has been a standout success in the computer music software industry. While many companies are failing, Newskool is using its market power to push forward the next generation of electronic music-making tools. As Finger puts it, "Once the rest of the industry has gotten together and figured out how they're all going to cope with change, they'll look around and see that we're already three miles ahead of them down the road to the future."

Discussion Questions

1. Identify some of the problems likely to occur in a virtual organization such as Newskool Grooves. What are the advantages of virtual organizations?

2. Consider some of the cultural issues that will affect a company operating in various parts of the world. What actions would you take to ensure that Newskool's different offices work effectively with one another?

3. Based on what you know about motivation, personality, and organizational culture, what types of people are likely to be satisfied in each functional area of the company? Use concepts from the job characteristics model to describe what might need to change to increase employee satisfaction in all areas.

4. What types of human resources practices need to be implemented in this sort of organization? What principles of selection and hiring are likely to be effective? Which Big Five personality traits and abilities might Newskool supervisors want to use for selection?

Case 10: Trouble at City Zoo

Learning Goals

In this case, you will have an opportunity to assess how to restore trust among employees who have low morale. You should consider how organizational culture has led to the problems faced at the zoo. You will determine whether the organizational structure should be changed and also whether new reward systems should be put in place.

Major Topic Areas

- Communication (Chapter 7)
- Organizational design (Chapter 13)
- Leadership (Chapter 11)
- Organizational culture (Chapter 10)
- Job design (Chapter 5)
- Change management (Chapter 14)
- Resistance to change (Chapter 14)

The Scenario

City Zoo has been an important visitor destination for generations of children.[28] Locally, provincially, and nationally, City Zoo has had a remarkable reputation for providing a high-quality environment for its animals while enabling children of all ages to learn about animals and see them in natural environments. The zoo operates with a dedicated staff, as well as a large number of volunteers. Over half of its revenues come from a special tax levy on city property owners who vote on whether to renew the levy during city elections held every three years.

Despite its sterling reputation, the zoo went through a year of unpleasant publicity in 2017, after the board of directors dismissed head veterinarian Tim Bernardino. Newspaper reports of the dismissal suggested that Bernardino had been dismissed for speaking up about harm to some of the zoo's animals. The publicity forced zoo management to respond to many tough questions regarding its practices and operations regarding both animals and staff. City Council acted swiftly in the face of continued negative press coverage of the zoo, feeling a responsibility to the taxpayers. In order to answer all of the questions raised by the press, council created a special Citizens' Task Force to review the zoo's finances and operations, including animal care.

It is February 2018, and Emma Breslin has just been hired by the board of directors to take over as executive director of the zoo. She is reviewing the many concerns raised by the task force and wondering how she might restore employees' and the public's confidence in the zoo. She will be meeting with the board in two weeks to present her recommendations for moving forward. The board has asked her to act quickly because city residents will vote on the next tax levy in just three months. A "no" vote would substantially reduce the zoo's revenues for the next several years. (Exhibit 1 outlines the revenues and expenses of the zoo for fiscal year 2017.)

Background

The City Zoological Gardens got its start in 1905, when Samantha Fraser donated a hedgehog to the city's Parks Board. Building on that first donation, the zoo has grown to be one of the most comprehensive zoological institutions in the country. The zoo's African Savannah recreates the look of Africa's plains and jungles. The Savannah houses the world-famous Hippoquarium, the first natural hippo habitat to be created in a zoo. The zoo includes exhibits for Siberian tigers, Asian sloth bears, and the endangered African wild dogs. The zoo has also renovated the Aviary and the Primate Forest. More recent improvements include a new parking lot and gift shop. The zoo is a top tourist attraction for the city, and the number of annual visitors to the zoo has nearly tripled from 1982 (364 000 visitors) to 2016 (more than 1 million visitors). In the past five years, the zoo has twice been ranked as one of the top 10 zoos in North America for children and families. It was also voted one of the top five zoos in North America in the "North

EXHIBIT 1 City Zoo Revenues and Expenses, Fiscal Year 2017

Public Support

Property Tax Levy Receipts	$6 466 860
Grants	$174 780
Education Program Revenue	$344 110
Total Public Support	**$6 985 750**

Development Revenue

Membership	$3 903 420
Friends of the Zoo	$214 397
Annual Fundraising	$130 852
Corporate Support	$302 952
Development Events	$391 565
Total Development Revenue	**$4 943 186**

Earned Revenue

Admissions	$3 253 355
Advanced Sales	$337 908
Gross Revenue From Concessions and Gift Shop Operations	$7 153 483
Rides, Parking, and Tours	$1 560 727
Facility Rentals	$116 520
Total Earned Revenue	**$12 421 993**
Other Revenue	**$34 956**
Total Public Support and Revenue	**$24 385 885**

Expenses

Cost of Goods Sold	$2 448 164
Wages and Benefits	$13 900 524
Supplies, Maintenance, and Utilities	$4 387 642
Professional Services	$2 246 560
Other Expenses	$714 487
Conservation—Project Support	$45 093
Animal Purchases	$76 542
Special Exhibits	$293 630
Total Operating Expenses	**$24 112 642**
Excess (Deficit)	**$273 243**

America's Favorite Zoo" contest sponsored by Microsoft. The zoo's vision and mission statements (see Exhibit 2) are widely credited with helping the zoo achieve these awards.

Until 1982, the zoo was run by the city. That year, ownership was transferred to the City Zoological Society, a private nonprofit organization. Because of its dedication, the Society was able to introduce a number of improvements that the city had not been able to accomplish. The zoo has since doubled in size and now contributes significantly to the local economy.

A recent study by a local university found that the zoo generates almost $8 in local economic activity for each tax dollar it receives.

The zoo employs 157 full-time staff members and more than 550 part-time and seasonal employees. There are also more than 300 volunteers who assist with programs, events, and community outreach. Donors and members provide financial support for animal conservation and educational programming.

EXHIBIT 2 City Zoo Vision and Mission Statements

Vision Statement
To be one of the world's outstanding zoological institutions.

Mission Statement
Our mission is to provide excellent animal management, educational programs, and scientific activities and to provide visitors with an enjoyable, educational, and family-oriented experience.

Objectives to achieve mission statement:

- Animal exhibits that reflect natural habitats
- Educational programs to help visitors understand the relationships of wildlife and the environment
- Refuges for rare and endangered species to protect and propagate them
- Scientific programs that contribute to greater understanding of animals and their habitats
- A clean, safe, and pleasant facility for visitors and employees
- A broad base of community support and involvement
- Operating on a sound business basis

The Ministry of Natural Resources Inquiries

The 2013 Inquiry   In December 2012, Medusa, a female sloth bear mistakenly believed to be pregnant, was put into isolation, where it died. Zoo officials later admitted that they had misunderstood how to properly care for sloth bears. Tim French, the curator of large mammals at the time, made the decision to put the bear in isolation on his own, without reporting this to his supervisors. The bear's zookeeper, Melissa Fox, who reported to French, objected to his decision, but no one would listen to her, including acting head veterinarian Wynona Singh (who was in charge while Dr. Bernardino was away on research). Fox's daily notes, which she was required to file with her supervisor, described her worries about the bear. Fox finally became so upset with the bear's condition that she asked to be transferred to another part of the zoo. French resigned after the bear's death.

As a result of the investigation, the zoo was fined $1500 by the Ministry of Natural Resources for violating federal animal welfare regulations. The zoo also agreed to create an animal reporting system so that employees could raise any concerns they had about animal welfare, although nothing ever resulted from this agreement.

The 2016 Inquiry   In February 2016, the Ministry of Natural Resources began an investigation of animal deaths that had occurred at the zoo over the past several years:

- Cupid, a hippopotamus, died in the summer of 2015 at the age of 49. While the veterinary staff raised

some questionable circumstances concerning the death, zoo officials dismissed the animal's death as "old age."

- George, a 14-year-old giraffe, died in 2013 from tetanus three weeks after he was gored by a kudu when the two were put in an enclosure together.

- Medusa, the female sloth bear, died in December 2012.

Zoo officials were puzzled about why the Ministry of Natural Resources had decided to investigate these deaths. "Initially, my gut reaction was that the Ministry of Natural Resources was just stepping things up because of what had transpired at that other zoo," a zoo spokesperson said. The spokesperson was referring to several suspicious animal deaths, including an orangutan euthanized by mistake, at a large zoo in another part of the country.

As the Ministry of Natural Resources investigation progressed, however, many zoo staff became nervous about the way it was being conducted. Inspectors did not reveal the exact reason for their inspection, but they asked specific questions about the giraffe and the hippopotamus. The inspectors requested to speak to some employees, while refusing to speak with others. Zoo officials later said the surprise inspection was "unusual, unprecedented, and aggressive."

"As you can imagine, it was a very upsetting and confusing time. We've never had this kind of inspection, and the frustrating thing was they would not tell us what they were inspecting for," said William Lau, the zoo's executive director.

Before the Ministry of Natural Resources could issue a report, zoo officials decided to conduct their own internal investigation into the deaths of George, the giraffe, and Cupid, the hippopotamus. Officials were concerned that someone at the zoo had made a call to the Ministry of Natural Resources that led to the surprise inspection. Lau claimed that the investigation was not a "witch hunt," and that officials were not trying to find out if anyone had acted as a whistle-blower. "We simply want to understand what the Ministry of Natural Resources is worried about," he said.

The Ministry of Natural Resources issued a report on its investigation the following month. In it, the inspectors noted that the zoo had ignored the warnings of Dr. Tim Bernardino, City Zoo's head veterinarian, about animal care. "From the review of numerous documents and interviews, it is clear that these veterinary recommendations from the attending veterinarian [Dr. Bernardino] have not been addressed in a reasonable time. The licensee [the City Zoo] has failed to provide the attending veterinarian with adequate authority to ensure the provision of adequate veterinary care," the report stated.

Zoo Management

Board of Directors

The board of directors oversees City Zoo's business affairs and strategic plan, but day-to-day operations are left in the hands of the executive director. There are 18 people on the board. Each board member serves a three-year term. The term can be renewed up to two times, if the board member is nominated by the Nominating Committee and approved by the board of directors. The board in recent years has been mostly hands-off, allowing the executive director a great deal of latitude in running the zoo.

Executive Director

The executive director is effectively the CEO of the zoo, carrying out the strategic plan of the board. William (Bill) Lau was appointed executive director in 1993. Under his leadership, the zoo expanded considerably, won numerous awards, and significantly increased its revenues.

Lau did a good job of raising the zoo's profile externally, particularly in leading fundraising efforts that brought numerous exotic animals to the zoo. He was not necessarily seen as a good internal leader, however. The board's Executive Management Committee reported at a March 13, 2014, board meeting that the zoo's work environment was characterized by numerous disagreements. The minutes of this meeting showed that the board discussed "'open warfare' between managers; backbiting and rude behaviour during meetings; and problems in managers' relationships with Mr. Lau." The minutes also reported that "Working with Bill is experienced by some as difficult, intimidating, or scary." Some staff had complained that Lau frequently yelled at staff and failed to acknowledge their value. "There is a fear of repercussion, and some people are afraid they will be … seen as stupid, belittled in meetings, [and] blamed and shamed in front of others," the minutes state.

Chief Operating Officer

The chief operating officer (COO) is second in command at the zoo, reporting to the executive director. The COO responsibilities include most of the operational functions of the zoo: finance, human resources, maintenance and horticulture, interpretive services, and education. The Department of Veterinary Care was the only nonoperational function that also reported to the COO. All other animal-related departments, including the curators, reported to the executive director.

In early 2014, the zoo hired Robert (Bob) Stellenbosch to be the new COO. Unlike the COO he replaced, Stellenbosch had no animal-care experience in his previous positions. Before coming to the zoo, he had been executive director of the National Funeral Directors' Association for 14 years.

Prior to that, he had been executive director of the Provincial Bankers' Association. Nevertheless, veterinary care still fell under Stellenbosch's mandate, and the head veterinarian reported to him. Stellenbosch did not see this as a problem. As Stellenbosch pointed out, he often had to oversee "departments in areas I know very little about. The secret [is] having a strong line of communication with the people who report to you."

The zoo's executive director also did not see Stellenbosch's lack of animal-care experience as a problem. "We were looking for anybody with a background that could run a zoo on a day-to-day basis. We didn't find anybody with an animal background who could do that. We chose Bob Stellenbosch because he was the best candidate," Lau said.

Caring for the Animals

Three sets of employees work closely with the animals: veterinarians, curators, and zookeepers.

The Veterinarians

Dr. Tim Bernardino   Dr. Tim Bernardino, director of Animal Health and Nutrition at City Zoo, was the zoo's head veterinarian, and had been a zoo employee for over 20 years. Eight full- and part-time employees in the Animal Health and Nutrition department reported to him. Veterinarians are responsible for the health care program for the animals, and they also maintain all health records. Bernardino was also the "attending veterinarian" for the zoo, a position that carries with it the responsibility to communicate on a regular basis with the Ministry of Natural Resources. Part of this responsibility involved bringing questionable animal deaths to the attention of the Ministry of Natural Resources.

Bernardino was well respected by the international veterinarian community, and well-liked by the zookeepers. He was known to deeply care for all of the animals in the zoo, and kept up with the latest literature on the best ways to manage and display animals to maximize their comfort and well-being.

Bernardino's performance as head veterinarian was generally applauded by senior management. He had received glowing ratings in his annual performance reviews throughout his career. For instance, at the end of 2015, Bernardino received one of his best performance reviews ever. Robert Stellenbosch, his direct supervisor, wrote that Bernardino maintained "the highest quality of work!" He also wrote that "Tim is well respected throughout the zoo." Stellenbosch praised the veterinarian's technical skills, his dependability, and his tremendous work ethic.

There were occasional negative comments in his reviews, although these did not seem to weigh heavily in his overall evaluations. For instance, in his 2012 review, a former supervisor wrote, "Tim can be intense and inflexible, causing strained relations with fellow employees." Still, the supervisor noted that Bernardino "gets along reasonably well" with other zoo employees. In his 2014 review, the veterinarian was specifically asked to "focus more on people skills in the department and with curators." The review also noted that "Tim is strong in his beliefs, and sometimes needs to temper that once a final decision is made."

The negative performance appraisal comments were related to Bernardino's relationships with the curators and zookeepers. He was well respected by the zookeepers, and maintained good relations with them because their observations of the animals helped the animals stay healthy. However, some of the curators felt that Bernardino empowered the zookeepers too much, so that the zookeepers would sometimes go around their curators to make complaints about animal care. Bernardino worried that some of the zookeepers were disciplined by their curators when they spoke with him about their concerns regarding the animals. "People don't feel free to be open. Discussions don't happen. [There is] control of information, control of communications, control of decision making [by the curators]," he said.

Beth Else, curator of Conservation and Research, saw it differently. "I think he empowered the keepers to go around the supervisors and go to him when they didn't get the answer that they liked," she said, echoing comments of the other curators.

Despite his generally good reviews, Bernardino also felt that he was "alienated from the decision-making process ... with the curatorial staff and with other administrators." He sometimes complained the curators were given more weight than the veterinary staff in decision making about the animals, even when the health of the animals was in question. He also felt that his role as attending veterinarian, where he was accountable to the Ministry of Natural Resources, was "not well defined or understood by those in the zoo community."

Bernardino's reviews took a turn for the worse after the Ministry of Natural Resources released the report of its 2016 surprise investigation just three months later, in May 2016. Stellenbosch gave Bernardino, in writing, a reprimand about his performance. "We need to have team players, and you need to work through these issues in a more professional, less 'attacking' manner," the COO's warning stated. Bernardino was also told that he lacked "team attitude, professionalism, and judgment."

This warning was closely followed by the announcement that Bernardino would share the "attending veterinarian" position with two others: his subordinate, veterinarian Wynona Singh, and Mammals curator Randi Walker. Although Walker

was also a veterinarian, she was not licensed to practise as one in the province. In August 2016, Bernardino was told that he would no longer serve as an "attending veterinarian," and that Singh would be the sole "attending veterinarian." At about the same time, Bernardino received a written reprimand, in which he was accused of "steadily undermining animal curator Dr. Walker, poor communication skills, and intimidating other employees."

Dr. Wynona Singh   Dr. Wynona Singh, who reported to Dr. Bernardino, had been a full-time veterinarian at the zoo since 2005. She first joined the zoo in 2003 as a part-time veterinarian. Singh was the veterinarian on call when the giraffe died in 2013 and the sloth bear died in 2012, although she was not implicated in either death.

Bernardino and Singh often butted heads. In his 2015 evaluation of her, Bernardino recommended that she receive no salary increase. In January 2016, Bernardino told the zoo's human resources director that "if she doesn't improve and we keep her, I'm out of here."

Bernardino was reflecting on a survey of her performance he had conducted with the veterinary and animal food staff. Only 29 percent of them gave her favourable ratings, while 61 percent noted that she had big communication problems. The zookeepers specifically complained that Singh did not relate well to them and was not always open to their concerns. This led Bernardino to tell her that she "had to continue to improve some management skills, including communication." Despite negative reviews from her immediate staff and subordinates, Singh received high marks from the curators and associate curators, who indicated their full and unambiguous support of her.

The Curators and Zookeepers

Curators make recommendations such as what animals to acquire, whether animals should be bred, and whether animals should be lent to other zoos for either breeding or display purposes. Curators are also responsible for the designing and planning of animal exhibits, including coming up with ideas for new exhibits that might be of interest to the public. Although curators are responsible for the overall well-being of the animals, they are certainly aware of the marketing and public relations functions of animal exhibits.

The general curator at a zoo oversees the entire animal collection and animal management and is responsible for strategic collection planning. Zoos also have animal curators who manage a specific section of the animal collection. City Zoo had four area curators: curator of Fishes, curator of Reptiles, curator of Birds, and curator of Mammals. Some areas also had associate curators, such as the assistant curator of Large Mammals and the assistant curator of Small Mammals.

Senior zookeepers and zookeepers (also called *keepers*) report to the curators and work with individual animals, feeding them, handling them, keeping their cages clean, and looking after their welfare on a day-to-day basis. Keepers often work with the same animals for a number of years, so they can grow quite attached to their animals. Keepers can feel that they understand more about the welfare of their animals than the curators.

At City Zoo there was significant tension between the curators and the keepers. The keepers complained that curators did not listen to their concerns, and curators complained that the keepers often went around them to share concerns about animals with Dr. Bernardino. The curators felt that the keepers should raise all concerns with them, rather than with the veterinarian.

Randi Walker   Randi Walker was curator of Mammals at the zoo. The Mammals department's 22 full-time employees (including 14 zookeepers) took care of the zoo's apes, great cats, bears, elephants, and all hoofed animals. This was the largest animal department at the zoo, and was twice the size of the next largest department, the Birds department. All of the deaths investigated by the Ministry of Natural Resources had happened in Walker's unit.

The assistant curator of Large Mammals and the assistant curator of Small Mammals worked under Walker. The assistant curators were two of the most liked curators at the zoo. They had excellent animal-care backgrounds, were very aware of the zoo's communication problems, and knew how to work effectively with the other employees. They were also respected by the zookeepers and other curators.

Although curators do not usually have veterinary training, Walker had completed her veterinary studies. However, she was not licensed to practise veterinary medicine in the province. Her background may have led to her difficult relationship with Bernardino. Sometimes she tried to second-guess him, and other times she attempted to overrule his decisions.

Walker was particularly uncomfortable with the relationship that Bernardino had with the Mammals zookeepers. She felt that his close relationship to them undermined her. "There are communication problems with mammal keepers and [Mammals curator Randi Walker]," one keeper said. "Some people can talk; other people, if they open their mouth, she jumps on them. That's the underlying thing why people talk to Dr. Tim."

Gorilla keeper Dale Petiniot noted that while she had no problem discussing issues with Walker, sometimes keepers needed to discuss issues with a neutral third party. "It's not always that we're justified, but sometimes you need to talk about things, and you don't have a next step, other than the vet," Ms. Petiniot said.

When zoo officials, responding to the Ministry of Natural Resources' surprise investigation, tried to investigate the death of George the giraffe, they quickly discovered that most employees in the Mammals department would simply not talk about the event, saying that they feared retribution by Walker. Even though zoo officials offered immunity from any disciplinary action in exchange for clarification about what had happened, no one came forth to take responsibility for putting the two animals together. "Nobody claimed responsibility," Andy Yang, curator of Reptiles and head of the internal investigation, said.

The report of the internal investigation concluded, "The apparent failure of the mammal keeper staff to inform, discuss, and plan this introduction with the veterinary staff prior to any action was unacceptable and compromised the welfare of the giraffe." Yang's committee made a pointed observation regarding the Mammals department: "There are significant communication problems in the Mammals department that need attention. These communications problems have negatively affected animal welfare."

Xavier Tolson, a human resources consultant hired by the zoo at the end of 2016 to analyze workplace problems in the Mammals department, reached many of the same conclusions. "I do not believe I have ever seen a department as dysfunctional as the Mammals department [at the City Zoo]." He noted that there was a lot of conflict between the head curator and the zookeepers.

Tolson suggested that the keepers had a tendency to try to bully Walker into seeing their point of view about animal concerns.

Although most of her subordinates were critical of Walker's performance, managers at the most senior levels in the zoo were strongly supportive of her. She was always deferential to their views, and they felt she was right not to cave in to employee concerns.

The Biological Program Committee

In most zoos, the general curator oversees the work of the curators, zookeepers, and veterinarians and attempts to resolve any issue that might come up among the three groups. However, City Zoo had no general curator. When the zoo hired Robert Stellenbosch as COO in 2014, he was unable to serve as general curator, a role his predecessor had filled, because he had no previous animal experience.

Shortly after Stellenbosch was hired, Lau announced that the newly created Biological Program Committee (BPC) would perform the duties normally handled by the general curator. The committee consisted of the curators of Mammals, Birds, Reptiles, and Fishes, an animal behaviour specialist, and members of the zoo's veterinary staff. Only the four curators and the animal behaviour specialist had voting rights on the committee, however. The curators took turns chairing the monthly committee, rotating the position every few months. No one else was allowed to chair the committee.

Not everyone was happy with the new management committee meetings. Bernardino, who had had a very good relationship with the former general curator, felt that his authority was diminished because of the BPC structure. Bernardino also objected that he was not able to rotate into the role of committee chair. He complained that the curators did not pay enough attention to animal-care issues. He also complained that the curators treated members of the veterinary staff who were on the committee like second-class citizens. After trying to get along with the new management structure for about six months, Bernardino took his concerns about the BPC to the executive director. Lau dismissed the veterinarian's concerns, suggesting that communication among committee members was good, except for some "troublemakers," which Bernardino took to be a reference to himself.

Beth Else, curator of Conservation and Research at the zoo, noticed a change in Bernardino's demeanour after the creation of the BPC. "It seemed in the past that Tim relied on gentle persuasion to bring people over to his way of thinking. In recent years, particularly in the past year, Tim has been more of a disruptive influence at the zoo," Else said. "I don't want to give the impression that I think Tim is malicious, because I don't," Else said. "Tim, in his own mind, thinks he is doing what is right."

Other employees must have agreed with Else that Bernardino was trying to do the right things at the zoo. On February 23, 2017, the zoo staff voted on nominees for "Outstanding Employee" of the year. Bernardino received the most votes.

Shockwaves at the Zoo

Head Veterinarian Fired

On February 28, 2017, City Zoo dismissed Bernardino from his $102 000-a-year position as head veterinarian. The executive director said that the dismissal had nothing to do with the 2016 Ministry of Natural Resources inspection, or with issues about animal care. "There is no question in my mind that he raised the level of animal care here at the zoo," Lau explained. "And while I do have a problem with the way Bernardino dealt with the Ministry of Natural Resources in the past, the termination was a result of our concerns over Dr. Bernardino's administrative and management skills that we had worked with him to address over the last several years."

Bernardino's dismissal created shockwaves both inside and outside of the zoo. The local newspaper contacted several well-known veterinarians throughout the country to find out what they could do about Bernardino. All of the contacted veterinarians spoke with great regard for the dismissed veterinarian. Reporters also uncovered previous performance reviews of Bernardino, which indicated that Bernardino had performed exceptionally in his work with the animals. Reporters concluded from their investigation that "The firing of Dr. Bernardino in late February was the culmination of a year-long struggle between him and zoo administrators beginning, it appears, with the veterinarian's frank comments last year during a routine animal-care inspection by the Ministry of Natural Resources. Those comments led to an admonition by the Ministry of Natural Resources that the zoo failed to heed warnings about its animal-care practices."

The intense press coverage prompted the city to start its own investigation of zoo administration. City Council felt an obligation to protect taxpayers' money, and recognized that public confidence in the zoo was at an all-time low because of all the negative publicity. Council appointed a 14-member Citizens' Task Force in mid-March. The mandate of the task force was to review zoo finances and operations, including animal care, and to issue a report within 100 days.

As the task force was getting underway, more scandal struck the zoo. The local newspaper reported that Executive Director William Lau had traded in the Jeep he had been given at zoo expense for a luxury Volvo, also paid for by the zoo. Similarly, COO Robert Stellenbosch had traded in his Dodge for a luxury Volvo. The two Volvos were costing taxpayers $1200 per month.

Members of the public were outraged by this news, coming just two weeks after Bernardino's firing. One long-standing zoo member emailed the local newspaper that he was disgusted with zoo administrators: "The firing of the whistle-blowing vet is enough to make one wonder if the chimpanzees could not do a better job of running the place. If anything would make me stop supporting the zoo, it is the attitude of the zoo director and [chief operating officer]. To rent Volvos for themselves, to be so wasteful with the dollars of the taxpayers is tantamount to being part of the low-down reptile exhibit."

A Settlement and Resignations at the Top

After his dismissal, Bernardino approached the board of directors, requesting that they meet with him and give him back his job. The board was feeling under siege because of all the negative publicity. Bernardino's dismissal seemed to mobilize community sentiment toward the veterinarian, and against the zoo's senior management.

In an effort to quiet speculation by community members about zoo leadership, the board of directors made a settlement with Dr. Bernardino on May 1, 2017. The agreement reinstated him to his position of director of Animal Health and Nutrition of the zoo effective immediately, although he would serve in this role only as a "consultant," on an "as-needed basis." The agreement stated that Bernardino was not allowed to be on zoo grounds while performing his job, and could not enter the zoo as a private citizen for six months. The agreement prohibited him from discussing "his opinions as to the welfare of the animals at the Zoo, the circumstances of his termination or reinstatement of employment, his opinions regarding personnel at the Zoo, or any other matters pertaining to the Zoo" with anyone unless subpoenaed.

Bernardino's consulting position was to last for 18 months. He would be paid $105 000, plus health and retirement benefits during that time. Under the settlement, he would also receive $42 815 in back pay, benefits, and attorney's fees. The board agreed to remove all negative evaluations that were added to his file in 2016. Bernardino agreed that he would not file claims of wrongful discharge or breach of contract against the zoo.

Two weeks after the settlement with Bernardino, the zoo board announced that Executive Director William Lau would retire immediately, after 25 years at the zoo. The board also announced that COO Robert Stellenbosch would resign once a new management team was in place.

The Findings of the Citizens' Task Force

The Citizens' Task Force presented its findings to City Council at a public meeting held on July 8, 2017. The task force divided its presentation into three parts: a discussion of the employee survey they had commissioned; a presentation of what they had learned about the politics of zookeeping; and a discussion of other observations about how the zoo operated.

Employee Survey The Citizens' Task Force asked Maynard & Associates, a Toronto-based employee relations consulting firm, to determine employee morale. Exhibit 3 summarizes the results of the survey, including separate results for the Mammals department. Maynard & Associates have collected baseline data as a result of their many employee surveys, and those data are also included.

On many dimensions, City Zoo employees were more critical than the average employee in Maynard's surveys. Zoo employees complained about the lack of effective leadership, poor communication, and the scarcity of teamwork. Only half of the employees said there was open and honest communication at the zoo, and many employees noted that this lack of communication led to rumours and myths that spread throughout the zoo.

Employees said that they did not feel that they could talk freely to their supervisors about job-related problems, and they gave low marks to supervisors for resolving employee problems. Employees also gave low marks to supervisors for letting employees know what was expected of them. Supervisors were also criticized for not considering differing opinions, and a number of employees noted that they feared punishment if they expressed contrary opinions. Employees also expressed the expectation many employees placed on each other that "if you are not with us; you are against us," which created a lot of divisiveness across the zoo.

Despite the low morale uncovered by the survey, results indicated that employees loved working at the zoo, were fairly paid, and felt that they had been trained appropriately to do their jobs. However, they wanted to see an end to the political, communication, and leadership problems that dominated day-to-day work at the zoo.

The Politics of Zookeeping Three members of the Citizens' Task Force were asked to discuss the events that had occurred at City Zoo with respected members of the zoo community throughout North America. Dr. Christopher Bondar, the associate veterinarian at the Central Canada Zoo, suggested that it was not surprising that there were tensions between zoo management and the veterinarians. "The zoo business in general, because people's emotions tend to run high about animals and their welfare and because it is a small community, tends to have a lot of politics," said Dr. Bondar, who added that he has not encountered such problems at his own zoo. It can be hard to understand all of the politics at zoos because "so many businesses are about paperwork or industry or goods that don't spawn the type of passion people have for living animals."

Members of the task force spoke with Dr. Philip Robinson, a former director of veterinary services at the San Diego Zoo, and author of the book *Life at the Zoo: Behind the Scenes with the Animal Doctors*, and asked him about the relationship between curators and veterinarians. "The perception that [veterinarians] should stick to sick animals and leave the other issues to the other people on staff—traditionally, this is sort of a turf battle that has more to do with management style than anything that benefits the animals," he told them.

Other experts supported Dr. Robinson's position. They told the task force that it is crucial for veterinarians to interact with keepers to understand the needs of individual animals. "If the curator says to the keeper, 'You only tell me what's happening,' then the veterinarian is sort of between a rock and a hard place to know when the animal is on the road to a problem, or already is there and has the problem," said Randolph Stuart, the executive director of the Canadian Association of Zoo Veterinarians. "That's why most vets will keep a good rapport with keepers."

EXHIBIT 3 Employee Attitude Survey of City Zoo, and Some Comparisons

Category	Question	Percentage of Employees Who Agree or Strongly Agree with Statement			
		City Zoo	Mammals Department	Other Zoos	Other Organizations
Pay	My compensation is satisfactory and fair compared with that of other employees who work here.	80	81	82	75
	My compensation is satisfactory and fair compared with what I would earn at similar companies.	81	81	82	74
Recognition	My supervisor recognizes and provides positive feedback for work well done.	63	57	68	72
Supervision	My supervisor treats me fairly.	43	43	63	63
	My supervisor helps me perform my work effectively.	41	39	70	70
Communication	I feel comfortable expressing my ideas to my supervisor and other leaders in the company.	41	35	71	73
	Leaders communicate pertinent information to employees.	51	48	55	74
Empowerment	I am free to make decisions that affect my work without consulting with my supervisor.	55	45	67	69
	My ideas are used when managers make decisions that affect the company.	49	41	65	70
Job Satisfaction	Overall, the company is a good place to work.	68	60	70	77
Management	The managers here are honest, fair, and ethical.	45	39	76	79
Participation	Managers seek employee input into the way work is done here.	53	45	68	77
Teamwork	Employees work together as a team here.	59	53	79	79
	Teamwork is encouraged here.	55	50	75	75
Training	I receive adequate job-related training to do my job.	85	83	81	76
	There are plenty of opportunities here to learn additional skills.	85	78	81	74
Work Demands	The workload is fair and reasonable.	75	74	73	79

Experts in the area of zoo administration suggested that many zoo administrators don't appreciate the passion that veterinarians bring to their work. Veterinarians are chiefly concerned with animal welfare, while the zoo administration is also concerned with fundraising, providing an experience for zoo visitors, running successful gift shops and snack bars, and making sure parking lots are adequately designed for visitor load.

Dr. Mark Cornwall, the director of animal health and attending veterinarian at the Maple Leaf Zoo, stressed the need for good communication among all zoo employees. The Maple Leaf Zoo was sued by an employee under whistle-blower protection legislation. The employee was demoted and harassed after she complained to government officials about unsafe conditions at the zoo. "Everybody kind of learned something from

that," said Dr. Cornwall. "Animal welfare comes first," he said. "Zoo veterinarians are really the ones who are in charge of that. Veterinarians tend to champion those causes because that is what they are expected to do. You have different perspectives and opinions on those things, but the key is to sit down with all the folks." He added, "Zoos are complicated organisms and organizations. Open communication can improve the situation, however."

Other Issues Raised by the Task Force During its presentation, the Citizens' Task Force identified a number of other issues of concern, and they briefly reviewed these for council.

- *Organizational culture.* The task force found that lack of trust was a big issue among staff. They also found a "culture of fear" and noted that even though retaliation was often subtle, it was definitely there. In particular, keepers were afraid to admit actions or mistakes, even when immunity was offered. The task force expressed concern that many of the zookeepers were too focused on their own specific job duties and did not "see or support the 'big picture' of the zoo as both a wildlife conservation facility and a business."

- *Relationship among curators, veterinarians, and zookeepers.* Some curators were found to be good at managing animals but weak at managing people. The keepers complained that curators did not always respond in a timely manner to their proposals and suggestions for improving animal care. Veterinarians had some of the same complaints as the keepers— that curators did not always see the need to consult with veterinarians on animal management issues. The task force also noted that some keepers and curators held grudges that they might not be able to put behind them.

  Curators complained that veterinarians undermined them through direct contact with the keepers. However, the task force noted that there was no defined communication path for keepers to raise concern with the veterinary staff. Moreover, experts throughout the zoo veterinary world stressed the importance of open communication between keepers and veterinarians so that vets can fulfill their obligations under the Fish and Wildlife Conservation Act.

  The task force concluded that there was a lack of communication among keepers, veterinarians, and curators that led to questionable care standards for the animals. Because departments of the zoo did not work closely together, there was not a good system of checks and balances to maintain appropriate care.

- *The Biological Program Committee.* The Citizens' Task Force was particularly critical of the BPC, suggesting that many of the zoo's problems resulted from the creation of the BPC. The BPC created a mutual admiration society for the curators, and allowed the curators to overlook the concerns of keepers and the veterinarian staff. The board also found that there was no real accountability for decisions because of the committee structure.

- *Organizational structure.* The task force raised a number of questions about the current structure of the zoo, noting that communication issues, lack of teamwork, and lack of coordination were all factors that resulted in animal deaths, and were likely related to the current structure. During their investigation, they had asked Lau whether all individuals directly involved with animal

care had reported to him. He claimed they did, until a member of the task force, pointing to the organizational chart (see Exhibit 4), noted that the veterinarians and veterinarian technicians reported to the COO.

"It was largely the size of the group, and the number of people reporting to different people. We were trying to divide the zoo up so that neither Bob nor I [had too many]," Lau explained. "Money being what it is, we didn't want another high management position."

- *Employee conduct.* The task force found that there was a "lack of consistency, uniformity, accountability, and decisiveness in the enforcement of standards of conduct across departments" and that the Employee Relations department was not good at enforcing standards of conduct. A number of employees complained that those who worked hard were often expected to compensate for employees who underperformed.

  Employees are disciplined through a "five-step" process. An employee can be terminated if he or she receives five written infractions within a 12-month period. The task force found this process so burdensome that employees were almost never terminated. In fact, Jennifer Fisher, employee relations director, told the task force that "no animal keepers or other non-managerial employees had been fired in the past 20 years."

A New Executive Director Takes Over

Emma Breslin began her position as the new executive director last week, nine months after the previous executive director retired.

Breslin's previous position was as executive director for the past 10 years at Maritimes Zoo, a smaller zoo with 51 employees, a general curator, and two contract veterinarians. Breslin had been hired by Maritimes Zoo to reunite a divided staff. She is known as a consensus leader, and at Maritimes Zoo she increased communication, improved supervisory skills, and taught employees to value each other's contributions to the successful operation of the zoo. Breslin was also successful in raising awareness among the community about why financial support from the public was so important to the zoo.

Breslin faces a large public relations problem as she begins her new job. She knows that much of the zoo's revenue is dependent upon public support. The next tax levy vote is three months from now. The zoo also raises significant revenue through the "Friends of the Zoo" program, an annual subscription program where people donate money to the zoo. She

EXHIBIT 4 Organizational Chart of City Zoo, January 2014

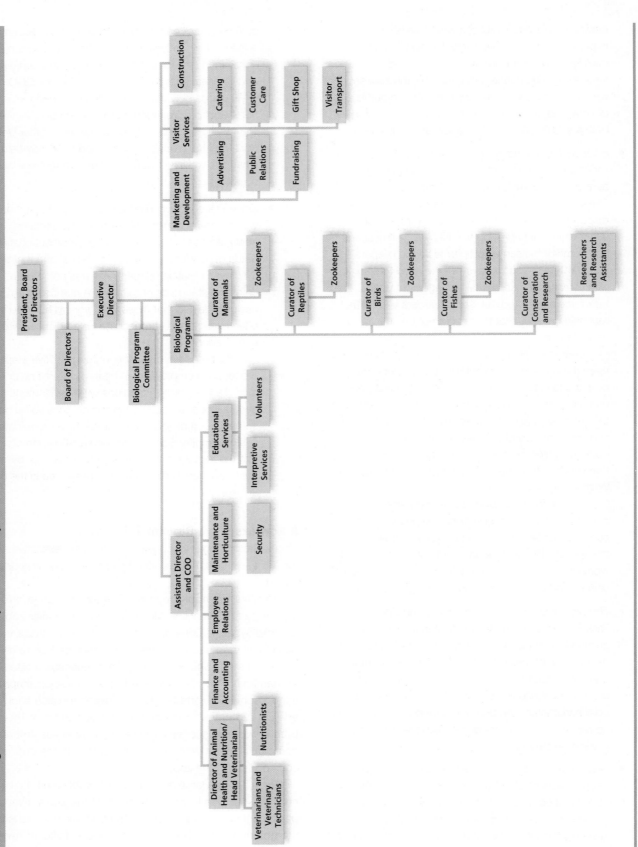

needs to restore community trust. At the same time, she needs to grow zoo attendance levels, which have fallen in the past six months, and develop a strategic plan for the zoo.

Breslin also faces a very divided and demoralized staff. She has reviewed what was written in the press and familiarized herself with the Citizens' Task Force review. She knows she needs to bring some peace and stability to employee relations. Her most difficult task will be to unite the staff. She needs to build staff morale and gain their trust. She wonders how she will accomplish these goals over the next year. The outline of what she intends to do over the next six months to get things back on track is to be presented to the board in two weeks.

Discussion Questions

1. What can Emma Breslin do to restore trust and morale among the employees?

2. Should Breslin promote Wynona Singh to head (and attending) veterinarian or hire someone from outside?

3. What changes to the organizational structure could Breslin make to help foster a more positive work environment?

4. How might trust be restored among community members so that a positive outcome for the tax levy might occur?

ENDNOTES

Chapter 1

1. Vignette based on J. Castaldo, "The Last Days of Target," *Canadian Business*, January 2016, http://www.canadianbusiness.com/the-last-days-of-target-canada/.

2. "Survey: Few CFOs Plan to Invest in Interpersonal Skills Development for Their Teams," Accountemps news release, June 19, 2013, http://accountemps.rhi.mediaroom.com/2013-06-19-Survey-Few-CFOs-Plan-to-Invest-in-Interpersonal-Skills-Development-for-Their-Teams.

3. These companies were named in the 100 Top Employers for 2017. See http://www.canadastop100.com/national/; http://www.canadastop100.com/atlantic/; and http://www.canadastop100.com/sk/.

4. I. S. Fulmer, B. Gerhart, and K. S. Scott, "Are the 100 Best Better? An Empirical Investigation of the Relationship between Being a 'Great Place to Work' and Firm Performance," *Personnel Psychology* (Winter 2003), pp. 965–993.

5. S. E. Humphrey, J. D. Nahrgang, and F. P. Morgeson, "Integrating Motivational, Social, and Contextual Work Design Features: A Meta-analytic Summary and Theoretical Extension of the Work Design Literature," *Journal of Applied Psychology* 92, no. 5 (2007), pp. 1332–1356.

6. E. R. Burris, "The Risks and Rewards of Speaking Up: Managerial Responses to Employee Voice," *Academy of Management Journal* 55, no. 4 (2012), pp. 851–875.

7. T. L. Miller, C. L. Wesley II, and D. E. Williams, "Educating the Minds of Caring Hearts: Comparing the Views of Practitioners and Educators on the Importance of Social Entrepreneurship Competencies," *Academy of Management Learning & Education* 2, no. 3 (2012), pp. 349–370.

8. H. Aguinis and A. Glavas, "What We Don't Know about Corporate Social Responsibility: A Review and Research Agenda," *Journal of Management* (July 2012), pp. 932–968.

9. Vignette based on J. Castaldo, "The Last Days of Target," *Canadian Business*, January 2016, http://www.canadianbusiness.com/the-last-days-of-target-canada/.

10. See, for example, C. Heath and S. B. Sitkin, "Big-B versus Big-O: What Is *Organizational* about Organizational Behavior?" *Journal of Organizational Behavior* 22 (2001), pp. 43–58. For a review of what one eminent researcher believes *should* be included in organizational behaviour, based on survey data, see J. B. Miner, "The Rated Importance, Scientific Validity, and Practical Usefulness of Organizational Behavior Theories: A Quantitative Review," *Academy of Management Learning & Education* 2, no. 3 (September 2003), pp. 250–268.

11. Statistics Canada, "Key Small Business Statistics—August 2013," modified September 10, 2013, https://www.ic.gc.ca/eic/site/061.nsf/eng/h_03018.html.

12. C. R. Farquhar and J. A. Longair, *Creating High-Performance Organizations with People*, Report R164–96 (Ottawa: The Conference Board of Canada, 1996).

13. D. M. Rousseau, *The Oxford Handbook of Evidence-Based Management* (Oxford Library of Psychology) (New York: Oxford University Press, 2014).

14. J. Surowiecki, "The Fatal-Flaw Myth," *New Yorker*, July 31, 2006, p. 25.

15. V. Monga, "What Is All That Data Worth?" *Wall Street Journal*, October 13, 2014, pp. B3, B6.

16. E. Dwoskin and Y. Koh, "Twitter Pushes Deeper into Data," *Wall Street Journal*, April 16, 2014, p. B2.

17. N. Bloom, R. Sadun, and J. Van Reenan, "How Three Essential Practices Can Address Even the Most Complex Global Practices," *Harvard Business Review*, November 2012, pp. 77–82.

18. C. Cole, "Changing Neurobiology with Behavior," *Association for Psychological Science Observer* 27, no. 6 (2014), pp. 29–32.

19. W. Isaacson, "Of Man and Machine," *Wall Street Journal*, September 27–28, 2015, pp. C1–C2.

20. Based on W. Chuang and B. Lee, "An Empirical Evaluation of the Overconfidence Hypothesis," *Journal of Banking and Finance*, September 2006, pp. 2489–2515; and A. R. Drake, J. Wong, and S. B. Salter, "Empowerment, Motivation, and Performance: Examining the Impact of Feedback and Incentives on Nonmanagement Employees," *Behavioral Research in Accounting* 19 (2007), pp. 71–89.

21. Vignette based on J. Castaldo, "The Last Days of Target," *Canadian Business*, January 2016, http://www.canadianbusiness.com/the-last-days-of-target-canada/.

22. Vignette based on J. Castaldo, "The Last Days of Target," *Canadian Business*, January 2016, http://www.canadianbusiness.com/the-last-days-of-target-canada/.

23. M. Strauss, "Lowe's Canada Looks To Build Brand Awareness Amid Rona Takeover," *Globe and Mail*, May 24, 2016, https://www.theglobeandmail.com/report-on-business/lowes-canada-looks-to-build-brand-awareness-amid-rona-takeover/article30132169/; D. Flavelle, "Rona Sees Growth Here: Home Reno Sales Flat during Make-or-Break Season but Canadian Retailer Keeps Faith in Diversification," *Toronto Star*, April 20, 2011, p. B1; and N. Van Praet, "Rona Shares Rise To Price Offered By Lowe's Two Years Ago," *Financial Post*, August 27, 2014.

24. See, for example, R. R. Thomas Jr., "From Affirmative Action to Affirming Diversity," *Harvard Business Review*, March–April 1990, pp. 107–117; B. Mandrell and S. Kohler-Gray, "Management Development That Values Diversity," *Personnel*, March 1990, pp. 41–47; J. Dreyfuss, "Get Ready for the New Work Force," *Fortune*, April 23, 1990, pp. 165–181; and I. Wielawski, "Diversity Makes Both Dollars and Sense," *Los Angeles Times*, May 16, 1994, p. II3.

25. Based on http://www.eluta.ca/jobs-at-sasktel#diversity:diversity-more; http://www.sasktel.com/wps/wcm/connect/content/home/about-sasktel/news/2012/sasktel-connects-8-more-first-nations-to-hs-internet; http://itac.ca/itaconline/aug09_online_full.html; and http://www.ammsa.com/publications/windspeaker/aboriginal-people-will-make-nearly-one-quarter-saskatchewan%E2%80%99s-population.

26. June 2011 figures, as reported at http://www.statcan.gc.ca/subjects-sujets/labour-travail/lfs-epa/t110708a2-eng.htm.

27. I. O. Karpen, "Service-Dominant Orientation: Measurement and Impact on Performance Outcomes," *Journal of Retailing* 91, no. 1 (2015), pp. 89–108.

28 E. Jaffe, "Using Technology to Scale the Scientific Mountain," *Association for Psychological Science Observer* 27, no. 6 (2014), pp. 17–19.

29 E. J. Hirst, "Burnout on the Rise," *Chicago Tribune*, October 19, 2012, http://articles.chicagotribune.com/2012-10-29/business/ct-biz-1029-employee-burnout-20121029_1_employee-burnout-herbert-freudenberger-employee-stress.

30 S. Shellenbarger, "Single and Off the Fast Track," *Wall Street Journal*, May 23, 2012, pp. D1, D3.

31 M. Mithel, "What Women Want," *Business Today*, March 8, 2013, http://businesstoday.intoday.in/story/careers-work-life-balance-women/1/193135.html.

32 Based on C. Atchison, "Secrets of Canada's Best Bosses," *PROFIT*, February 16, 2011, http://www.profitguide.com/manage-grow/leadership/secrets-of-canada%E2%80%99s-best-bosses-30084.

33 F. Luthans and C. M. Youssef, "Emerging Positive Organizational Behavior," *Journal of Management*, June 2007, pp. 321–349; C. M. Youssef and F. Luthans, "Positive Organizational Behavior in the Workplace: The Impact of Hope, Optimism, and Resilience," *Journal of Management* 33, no. 5 (2007), pp. 774–800; J. E. Dutton and S. Sonenshein, "Positive Organizational Scholarship," in *Encyclopedia of Positive Psychology*, ed. C. Cooper and J. Barling (Thousand Oaks, CA: Sage, 2007); A. M. Saks and J. A. Gruman, "Organizational Socialization and Positive Organizational Behaviour: Implications for Theory, Research, and Practice," *Canadian Journal of Administrative Sciences* 28, no. 1 (2011), pp. 4–16; and E. K. Loway, "Positive Organizational Scholarship," *Canadian Journal of Administrative Sciences* 28, no. 1 (2011), pp. 1–3.

34 L. M. Roberts, G. Spreitzer, J. Dutton, R. Quinn, E. Heaphy, and B. Barker, "How to Play to Your Strengths," *Harvard Business Review*, January 2005, pp. 1–6; and L. M. Roberts, J. E. Dutton, G. M. Spreitzer, E. D. Heaphy, and R. E. Quinn, "Composing the Reflected Best-Self Portrait: Becoming Extraordinary in Work Organizations," *Academy of Management Review* 30, no. 4 (2005), pp. 712–736.

35 "Five Jobs That Won't Exist in 10 Years … And One New Title You'll Start to See," *HR Magazine*, February 2014, p. 16.

36 D. M. Mayer, M. Kuenzi, R. Greenbaum, M. Bardes, and R. Salvador, "How Low Does Ethical Leadership Flow? Test of a Trickle-Down Model," *Organizational Behavior and Human Decision Processes* 108, no. 1 (2009), pp. 1–13; and A. Ardichvili, J. A. Mitchell, and D. Jondle, "Characteristics of Ethical Business Cultures," *Journal of Business Ethics* 85, no. 4 (2009), pp. 445–451.

37 D. Meinert, "Managers' Influence," *HR Magazine*, April 2014, p. 25.

38 See, for example, P. M. Podsakoff, S. B. MacKenzie, J. B. Paine, and D. G. Bachrach, "Organizational Citizenship Behaviors: A Critical Review of the Theoretical and Empirical Literature and Suggestions for Future Research," *Journal of Management* 26, no. 3 (2000), pp. 543–548; and S. W. Whiting, P. M. Podsakoff, and J. R. Pierce, "Effects of Task Performance, Helping, Voice, and Organizational Loyalty on Performance Appraisal Ratings," *Journal of Applied Psychology* 93, no. 1 (2008), pp. 125–139.

39 L. Nguyen, "Canadian Economy Loses $16.6B Annually Due to Absenteeism," *Toronto Star*, September 23, 2013.

40 W. Hoge, "Sweden's Cradle-to-Grave Welfare Starts to Get Ill," *International Herald Tribune*, September 25, 2002, p. 8.

41 T.-Y. Park and J. D. Shaw, "Turnover Rates and Organizational Performance: A Meta-analysis," *Journal of Applied Psychology* 98 (2013), pp. 268–309.

42 A. Adkins, "Millennials: The Job-Hopping Generation," *Business Journal*, May 12, 2016, http://www.gallup.com/businessjournal/191459/millennials-job-hopping-generation.aspx.

43 "Why This CEO Is Helping 20% Of His Employees Find New Jobs By Next Year," *Fast Company*, February 27, 2017, https://www.fastcompany.com/3068481/why-this-ceo-is-helping-20-of-his-employees-find-new-jobs-by-next-year.

44 M. Casey-Campbell and M. L. Martens, "Sticking It All Together: A Critical Assessment of the Group Cohesion-Performance Literature," *International Journal of Management Reviews* 11, no. 2 (2008), pp. 223–246.

45 X. Zhao and A. S. Mattila, "Examining the Spillover Effect of Frontline Employees' Work-Family Conflict on Their Affective Work Attitudes and Customer Satisfaction," *International Journal of Hospitality Management*, June 2013, pp. 310–315.

46 Based on B. X. Chen, "IPhone Sales in China Bolster Apple Earnings," *New York Times*, January 27, 2015, http://www.nytimes.com/2015/01/28/technology/apple-quarterly-earnings.html?_r=0; C. Duhigg and K. Bradsher, "How U.S. Lost Out on iPhone Work," *New York Times*, January 22, 2013, pp. A1, A22–A23; H. Gao, "How the Apple Confrontation Divides China," *Atlantic*, April 8, 2013, http://www.theatlantic.com/china/archive/2013/04/how-the-apple-confrontation-divides-china/274764/; and A. Satariano, "Apple Slowdown Threatens $30 Billion Global Supplier Web," *Bloomberg*, http://www.bloomberg.com/news/2013-04-18/apple-slowdown-threatens-30-billion-global-supplier-web-tech.html.

47 M. Taes, "If I Could Have More Data … ," *Wall Street Journal*, March 24, 2014, p. R5; S. Thurm, "It's a Whole New Data Game," *Wall Street Journal*, February 10, 2015, p. R6; and J. Willhite, "Getting Started in 'Big Data'," *Wall Street Journal*, February 4, 2014, p. B7.

48 R. E. Quinn, *Beyond Rational Management: Mastering the Paradoxes and Competing Demands of High Performance* (San Francisco: Jossey-Bass, 1991); R. E. Quinn, S. R. Faerman, M. P. Thompson, and M. R. McGrath, *Becoming a Master Manager: A Competency Framework* (New York: Wiley, 1990); and K. Cameron and R. E. Quinn, *Diagnosing and Changing Organizational Culture: Based on the Competing Values Framework* (Reading, MA: Addison Wesley Longman, 1999).

49 R. E. Quinn, S. R. Faerman, M. P. Thompson, and M. R. McGrath, *Becoming a Master Manager: A Competency Framework* (New York: Wiley, 1990).

50 D. Maley, "Canada's Top Women CEOs," *Maclean's*, October 20, 1997, pp. 52 passim.

51 Written by Nancy Langton and Joy Begley, copyright 1999. (The events described are based on an actual situation, although the participants, as well as the centre, have been disguised.)

Chapter 2

1 Vignette based on J. Vomiero, "On Her Second Dragon's Den Season, Michele Romanow Will Continue Bringing Tech The Forefront," *Mobilesyrup*, October 8, 2016, http://mobilesyrup.com/2016/10/08/on-her-second-dragons-den-season-michele-romanow-will-continue-bringing-tech-the-forefront/; J. Pachner, "Michele Romanow's Entrepreneurial Secret? Launch Now, Fix Later," *Canadian Business*, June 2, 2016, http://www.canadianbusiness.com/leadership/michele-romanow/.

2 E. Bernstein, "'Honey, You Never Said …,'" *Wall Street Journal*, March 24, 2015, pp. D1, D4.

3 K. C. Yam, R. Fehr, and C. M. Barnes, "Morning Employees Are Perceived as Better Employees: Employees' Start Times Influence Supervisor Performance Ratings," *Journal of Applied Psychology* 99, no. 6 (2014), pp. 1288–1299.

4 J. Dwyer, "Witness Accounts in Midtown Hammer Attack Show the Power of False Memory," *New York Times*, May 14, 2015, http://www.nytimes.com/2015/05/15/nyregion/witness-accounts-in-midtown-hammer-attack-show-the-power-of-false-memory.html?_r=1.

5 G. Fields and J. R. Emshwiller, "Long after Arrests, Records Live On," *Wall Street Journal*, December 26, 2014, pp. A1, A10.

6 S. S. Wang, "The Science of Standing Out," *Wall Street Journal*, March 18, 2014, pp. D1, D4.

7 E. Zell and Z. Krizan, "Do People Have Insight into Their Abilities? A Metasynthesis," *Perspectives on Psychological Science* 9, no. 2 (2014), pp. 111–125.

8 E. Demerouti, D. Xanthopoulou, I. Tsaousis, and A. B. Bakker, "Disentangling Task and Contextual Performance," *Journal of Personnel Psychology* 13, no. 2 (2014), pp. 59–69.

9 G. P. Goodwin, J. Piazza, and P. Rozin, "Moral Character Predominates in Person Perception and Evaluation," *Journal of Personality and Social Psychology* 106, no. 1 (2014), pp. 148–168.

10 P. Harvey, K. Madison, M. Martinko, T. R. Crook, and T. A. Crook, "Attribution Theory in the Organizational Sciences: The Road Traveled and the Path Ahead," *The Academy of Management Perspectives* 28, no. 2 (2014), pp. 128–146; and M. J. Martinko, P. Harvey, and M. T. Dasborough, "Attribution Theory in the Organizational Sciences: A Case of Unrealized Potential," *Journal of Organizational Behavior* 32, no. 1 (2011), pp. 144–149.

11 C. M. de Melo, P. J. Carnevale, S. J. Read, and J. Gratch, "Reading People's Minds from Emotion Expressions in Interdependent Decision Making," *Journal of Personality and Social Psychology* 106, no. 1 (2014), pp. 73–88.

12 J. M. Moran, E. Jolly, and J. P. Mitchell, "Spontaneous Mentalizing Predicts the Fundamental Attribution Error," *Journal of Cognitive Neuroscience* 26, no. 3 (2014), pp. 569–576; and D. R. Stadler, "Competing Roles for the Subfactors of Need for Closure in Committing the Fundamental Attribution Error," *Personality and Individual Differences* 47, no. 7 (2009), pp. 701–705.

13 See, for instance, N. Epley and D. Dunning, "Feeling 'Holier Than Thou': Are Self-Serving Assessments Produced by Errors in Self– or Social Prediction?" *Journal of Personality and Social Psychology* 79, no. 6 (2000), pp. 861–875; M. Goerke, J. Moller, S. Schulz-Hardt, U. Napiersky, and D. Frey, "'It's Not My Fault—But Only I Can Change It': Counterfactual and Prefactual Thoughts of Managers," *Journal of Applied Psychology* 89, no. 2 (2004), pp. 279–292; and E. G. Hepper, R. H. Gramzow, and C. Sedikides, "Individual Differences in Self-Enhancement and Self-Protection Strategies: An Integrative Analysis," *Journal of Personality* 78, no. 2 (2010), pp. 781–814.

14 N. Epley and D. Dunning, "Feeling 'Holier Than Thou': Are Self-Serving Assessments Produced by Errors in Self- or Social Prediction?" *Journal of Personality and Social Psychology* 79, no. 6 (2000), pp. 861–875.

15 Based on N. Hall, "Lawyer Awarded $100,000 by B.C. Human Rights Tribunal for Discrimination," *Vancouver Sun*, July 18, 2011; and *Gichuru v. The Law Society of British Columbia* (No. 9), 2011 BCHRT 185, https://www.canlii.org/en/bc/bchrt/doc/2011/2011bchrt185/2011bchrt185.html.

16 See P. Rosenzweig, *The Halo Effect* (New York: Free Press, 2007); I. Dennis, "Halo Effects in Grading Student Projects," *Journal of Applied Psychology* 92, no. 4 (2007), pp. 1169–1176; C. E. Naquin and R. O. Tynan, "The Team Halo Effect: Why Teams Are Not Blamed for Their Failures," *Journal of Applied Psychology*, April 2003, pp. 332–340; and T. M. Bechger, G. Maris, and Y. P. Hsiao, "Detecting Halo Effects in Performance-Based Evaluations," *Applied Psychological Measurement* 34, no. 8 (2010), pp. 607–619.

17 J. L. Eberhardt, P. G. Davies, V. J. Purdic-Vaughns, and S. L. Johnson, "Looking Deathworthy: Perceived Stereotypicality of Black Defendants Predicts Capital-Sentencing Outcomes," *Psychological Science* 17, no. 5 (2006), pp. 383–386.

18 A. S. Rosette, G. J. Leonardelli, and K. W. Phillips, "The White Standard: Racial Bias in Leader Categorization," *Journal of Applied Psychology* 93, no. 4 (2008), pp. 758–777.

19 Based on A. C. Kay, M. V. Day, M. P. Zanna, and A. D. Nussbaum, "The Insidious (and Ironic) Effects of Positive Stereotypes," *Journal of Experimental Social Psychology* 49 (2013), pp. 287–291; J. O. Sly and S. Cheryan, "When Compliments Fail to Flatter: American Individualism and Responses to Positive Stereotypes," *Journal of Personality and Social Psychology* 104 (2013), pp. 87–102; M. J. Tagler, "Choking Under the Pressure of a Positive Stereotype: Gender Identification and Self-Consciousness Moderate Men's Math Test Performance," *Journal of Social Psychology* 152 (2012), pp. 401–416; M. A. Beasley and M. J. Fischer, "Why They Leave: The Impact of Stereotype Threat on the Attrition of Women and Minorities from Science, Math and Engineering Majors," *Social Psychology of Education* 15 (2012), pp. 427–448; and A. Krendl, I. Gainsburg, and N. Ambady, "The Effects of Stereotypes and Observer Pressure on Athletic Performance," *Journal of Sport & Exercise Psychology* 34 (2012), pp. 3–15.

20 K. A. Martin, A. R. Sinden, and J. C. Fleming, "Inactivity May Be Hazardous to Your Image: The Effects of Exercise Participation on Impression Formation," *Journal of Sport & Exercise Psychology* 22, no. 4 (December 2000), pp. 283–291.

21 F. Yuan and R. W. Woodman, "Innovative Behavior in the Workplace: The Role of Performance and Image Outcome Expectations," *Academy of Management Journal* 53, no. 2 (2010), pp. 323–342.

22 J. K. Harter, F. L. Schmidt, J. W. Asplund, E. A. Killham, and S. Agrawal, "Causal Impact of Employee Work Perceptions on the Bottom Line of Organizations," *Perspectives on Psychological Science* 5, no. 4 (2010), pp. 378–389.

23 Y. H. Kim, C. Y. Chiu, and Z. Zou, "Know Thyself: Misperceptions of Actual Performance Undermine Achievement Motivation, Future Performance, and Subjective Well-Being," *Journal of Personality and Social Psychology* 99, no. 3 (2010), pp. 395–409.

24 H. G. Heneman III and T. A. Judge, *Staffing Organizations* (Middleton, WI: Mendota House, 2012).

25 J. Willis and A. Todorov, "First Impressions: Making Up Your Mind after a 100ms Exposure to a Face," *Psychological Science*, July 2006, pp. 592–598.

26 N. Eisenkraft, "Accurate by Way of Aggregation: Should You Trust Your Intuition-Based First Impressions?" *Journal of Experimental Social Psychology*, March 2013, pp. 277–279.

27 See, for example, K. F. E. Wong and J. Y. Y. Kwong, "Effects of Rater Goals on Rating Patterns: Evidence from an Experimental Field Study," *Journal of Applied Psychology* 92, no. 2 (2007), pp. 577–585; and S. E. DeVoe and S. S. Iyengar, "Managers' Theories of Subordinates: A Cross-Cultural Examination of Manager Perceptions of Motivation and Appraisal of Performance," *Organizational Behavior and Human Decision Processes*, January 2004, pp. 47–61.

28 D. B. McNatt and T. A. Judge, "Boundary Conditions of the Galatea Effect: A Field Experiment and Constructive Replication," *Academy of Management Journal*, August 2004, pp. 550–565; and X. M. Bezuijen, P. T. van den Berg, K. van Dam, and H. Thierry, "Pygmalion and Employee Learning: The Role of Leader Behaviors," *Journal of Management* 35 (2009), pp. 1248–1267.

29 See, for example, K. F. E. Wong and J. Y. Y. Kwong, "Effects of Rater Goals on Rating Patterns: Evidence from an Experimental Field Study," *Journal of Applied Psychology* 92, no. 2 (2007), pp. 577–585; and S. E. DeVoe and S. S. Iyengar, "Managers' Theories of Subordinates: A Cross-Cultural Examination of Manager Perceptions of Motivation and Appraisal of Performance," *Organizational Behavior and Human Decision Processes*, January 2004, pp. 47–61.

30 Vignette based on R. Faber, "Michele Romanow Wants to Be a Helpful Dragon," *Maclean's*, January 6, 2016, http://www.macleans.ca/education/michele-romanow-wants-to-be-a-helpful-dragon/.

31 D. Leising, J. Scharloth, O. Lohse, and D. Wood, "What Types of Terms Do People Use When Describing an Individual's

Personality?" *Psychological Science* 25, no. 9 (2014), pp. 1787–1794.

32 L. Weber, "To Get a Job, New Hires Are Put to the Test," *Wall Street Journal*, April 15, 2015, pp. A1, A10.

33 L. Weber and E. Dwoskin, "As Personality Tests Multiply, Employers Are Split," *Wall Street Journal*, September 30, 2014, pp. A1, A10.

34 D. Belkin, "Colleges Put the Emphasis on Personality," *Wall Street Journal*, January 9, 2015, p. A3.

35 M. J. W. McLarnona, M. G. Rothsteinb, R. D. Goffinc, M. J. Riederd, A. Poolec, H. T. Krajewskie, D. M. Powell, R. B. Jelley, and T. Mestdagh, "How Important Is Personality in the Selection of Medical School Students?" *Personality and Individual Differences* 104 (January 2017), pp. 442–447.

36 S. A. Birkeland, T. M. Manson, J. L. Kisamore, M. T. Brannick, and M. A. Smith, "A Meta-analytic Investigation of Job Applicant Faking on Personality Measures," *International Journal of Selection and Assessment* 14, no. 14 (2006), pp. 317–335.

37 D. H. Kluemper, B. D. McLarty, and M. N. Bing, "Acquaintance Ratings of the Big Five Personality Traits: Incremental Validity Beyond and Interactive Effects with Self-Reports in the Prediction of Workplace Deviance," *Journal of Applied Psychology* 100, no. 1 (2015), pp. 237–248; I. Oh, G. Wang, and M. K. Mount, "Validity of Observer Ratings of the Five-Factor Model of Personality Traits: A Meta-analysis," *Journal of Applied Psychology* 96, no. 4 (2011), pp. 762–773.

38 S. E. Hampson and L. R. Goldberg, "A First Large Cohort Study of Personality Trait Stability Over the 40 Years between Elementary School and Midlife," *Journal of Personality and Social Psychology* 91, no. 4 (2006), pp. 763–779.

39 See A. H. Buss, "Personality as Traits," *American Psychologist*, November 1989, pp. 1378–1388; and D. G. Winter, O. P. John, A. J. Stewart, E. C. Klohnen, and L. E. Duncan, "Traits and Motives: Toward an Integration of Two Traditions in Personality Research," *Psychological Review*, April 1998, pp. 230–250.

40 R. B. Kennedy and D. A. Kennedy, "Using the Myers-Briggs Type Indicator in Career Counseling," *Journal of Employment Counseling*, March 2004, pp. 38–44.

41 See, for instance, D. J. Pittenger, "Cautionary Comments Regarding the Myers-Briggs Type Indicator," *Consulting Psychology Journal: Practice and Research*, Summer 2005, pp. 210–221; L. Bess and R. J. Harvey, "Bimodal Score Distributions and the Myers-Briggs Type Indicator: Fact or Artifact?" *Journal of Personality Assessment*, February 2002, pp. 176–186; R. M. Capraro and M. M. Capraro, "Myers-Briggs Type Indicator Score Reliability across Studies: A Meta-analytic Reliability Generalization Study," *Educational and Psychological Measurement*, August 2002, pp. 590–602; and R. C. Arnau, B. A. Green, D. H. Rosen, D. H. Gleaves, and J. G. Melancon, "Are Jungian Preferences Really Categorical? An Empirical Investigation Using Taxometric Analysis," *Personality and Individual Differences*, January 2003, pp. 233–251.

42 M. R. Barrick and M. K. Mount, "Yes, Personality Matters: Moving On to More Important Matters," *Human Performance* 18, no. 4 (2005), pp. 359–372.

43 W. Fleeson and P. Gallagher, "The Implications of Big Five Standing for the Distribution of Trait Manifestation in Behavior: Fifteen Experience-Sampling Studies and a Meta-analysis," *Journal of Personality and Social Psychology* 97, no. 6 (2009), pp. 1097–1114.

44 T. A. Judge, L. S. Simon, C. Hurst, and K. Kelley, "What I Experienced Yesterday Is Who I Am Today: Relationship of Work Motivations and Behaviors to Within-Individual Variation in the Five-Factor Model of Personality," *Journal of Applied Psychology* 99, no. 2 (2014), pp. 199–221.

45 R. D. Zimmerman, W. R. Boswell, A. J. Shipp, B. B. Dunford, and J. W. Boudreau, "Explaining the Pathways between Approach-Avoidance Personality Traits and Employees' Job Search Behavior," *Journal of Management* 38, no. 5 (2012), pp. 1450–1475.

46 J. B. Hirsh and J. B. Peterson, "Predicting Creativity and Academic Success with a 'Fake-Proof' Measure of the Big Five," *Journal of Research in Personality* 42 (2008), pp. 1323–1333.

47 "New Fake-Proof Personality Test Created," *ScienceDaily*, October 8, 2008, https://www.sciencedaily.com/releases/2008/10/081007102849.htm.

48 See, for instance, I. Oh and C. M. Berry, "The Five-Factor Model of Personality and Managerial Performance: Validity Gains through the Use of 360 Degree Performance Ratings," *Journal of Applied Psychology* 94, no. 6 (2009), pp. 1498–1513; J. Hogan and B. Holland, "Using Theory to Evaluate Personality and Job-Performance Relations: A Socioanalytic Perspective," *Journal of Applied Psychology* 88, no. 1 (2003), pp. 100–112; and M. R. Barrick and M. K. Mount, "Select on Conscientiousness and Emotional Stability," in *Handbook of Principles of Organizational Behavior*, ed. E. A. Locke (Malden, MA: Blackwell, 2004), pp. 15–28.

49 P. R. Sackett and P. T. Walmsley, "Which Personality Attributes Are Most Important in the Workplace?" *Perspectives on Psychological Science* 9, no. 5 (2014), pp. 538–551.

50 S. J. Motowidlo, M. P. Martin, and A. E. Crook, "Relations between Personality, Knowledge, and Behavior in Professional Service Encounters," *Journal of Applied Social Psychology* 43, no. 9 (2013), pp. 1851–1861.

51 A. E. Poropat, "A Meta-analysis of the Five-Factor Model of Personality and Academic Performance," *Psychological Bulletin* 135, no. 2 (2009), pp. 322–338.

52 F. L. Schmidt and J. E. Hunter, "The Validity and Utility of Selection Methods in Personnel Psychology: Practical and Theoretical Implications of 85 Years of Research Findings," *Psychological Bulletin*, September 1998, p. 272.

53 A. K. Nandkeolyar, J. A. Shaffer, A. Li, S. Ekkirala, and J. Bagger, "Surviving an Abusive Supervisor: The Joint Roles of Conscientiousness and Coping Strategies," *Journal of Applied Psychology* 99, no. 1 (2014), pp. 138–150.

54 B. Wille, F. De Fruyt, and M. Feys, "Big Five Traits and Intrinsic Success in the New Career Era: A 15-Year Longitudinal Study on Employability and Work-Family Conflict," *Applied Psychology: An International Review* 62, no. 1 (2013), pp. 124–156.

55 M. K. Shoss, K. Callison, and L. A. Witt, "The Effects of Other-Oriented Perfectionism and Conscientiousness on Helping at Work," *Applied Psychology: An International Review* 64, no. 1 (2015), pp. 233–251.

56 G. J. Feist, "A Meta-analysis of Personality in Scientific and Artistic Creativity," *Personality and Social Psychology Review* 2, no. 4 (1998), pp. 290–309; C. Robert and Y. H. Cheung, "An Examination of the Relationship Between Conscientiousness and Group Performance on a Creative Task," *Journal of Research in Personality* 44, no. 2 (2010), pp. 222–231; and M. Batey, T. Chamorro-Premuzic, and A. Furnham, "Individual Differences in Ideational Behavior: Can the Big Five and Psychometric Intelligence Predict Creativity Scores?" *Creativity Research Journal* 22, no. 1 (2010), pp. 90–97.

57 J. L. Huang, A. M. Ryan, K. L. Zabel, and A. Palmer, "Personality and Adaptive Performance at Work: A Meta-analytic Investigation," *Journal of Applied Psychology* 99, no. 1 (2014), pp. 162–179.

58 R. D. Zimmerman, W. R. Boswell, A. J. Shipp, B. B. Dunford, and J. W. Boudreau, "Explaining the Pathways between Approach-Avoidance Personality Traits and Employees' Job Search Behavior," *Journal of Management* 38, no. 5 (2012), pp. 1450–1475.

59 B. Wille, F. De Fruyt, and M. Feys, "Big Five Traits and Intrinsic Success in the New Career Era: A 15-Year Longitudinal Study on Employability and Work-Family Conflict." *Applied Psychology: An International Review* 62, no. 1 (2013), pp. 124–156.

60 R. J. Foti and M. A. Hauenstein, "Pattern and Variable Approaches in Leadership Emergence and Effectiveness," *Journal of Applied Psychology*, March 2007, pp. 347–355.

61 B. Weiss and R. S. Feldman, "Looking Good and Lying to Do It: Deception as an Impression Management Strategy in Job Interviews," *Journal of Applied Social Psychology* 36, no. 4 (2006), pp. 1070–1086.

62 A. Minbashian, J. Earl, and J. E. H. Bright, "Openness to Experience as a Predictor of Job Performance Trajectories," *Applied Psychology: An International Review* 62, no. 1 (2013), pp. 1–12.

63 B. Wille, F. De Fruyt, and M. Feys, "Big Five Traits and Intrinsic Success in the New Career Era: A 15-Year Longitudinal Study on Employability and Work-Family Conflict." *Applied Psychology: An International Review* 62, no. 1 (2013), pp. 124–156.

64 R. Ilies, I. S. Fulmer, M. Spitzmuller, and M. D. Johnson, "Personality and Citizenship Behavior: The Mediating Role of Job Satisfaction," *Journal of Applied Psychology* 94, no. 4 (2009), pp. 945–959.

65 D. H. Kluemper, B. D. McLarty, and M. N. Bing, "Acquaintance Ratings of the Big Five Personality Traits: Incremental Validity Beyond and Interactive Effects with Self-Reports in the Prediction of Workplace Deviance," *Journal of Applied Psychology* 100, no. 1 (2015), pp. 237–248.

66 S. Clarke and I. Robertson, "An Examination of the Role of Personality in Accidents Using Meta-analysis," *Applied Psychology: An International Review* 57, no. 1 (2008), pp. 94–108.

67 B. Wille, F. De Fruyt, and M. Feys, "Big Five Traits and Intrinsic Success in the New Career Era: A 15-Year Longitudinal Study on Employability and Work-Family Conflict," *Applied Psychology: An International Review* 62, no. 1 (2013), pp. 124–156.

68 J. F. Rauthmann, "The Dark Triad and Interpersonal Perception: Similarities and Differences in the Social Consequences of Narcissism, Machiavellianism, and Psychopathy," *Social Psychological and Personality Science* 3 (2012), pp. 487–496.

69 P. D. Harms and S. M. Spain, "Beyond the Bright Side: Dark Personality at Work," *Applied Psychology: An International Review* 64, no. 1 (2015), pp. 15–24.

70 P. K. Jonason, S. Slomski, and J. Partyka, "The Dark Triad at Work: How Toxic Employees Get Their Way," *Personality and Individual Differences* 52 (2012), pp. 449–453.

71 E. H. O'Boyle, D. R. Forsyth, G. C. Banks, and M. A. McDaniel, "A Meta-analysis of the Dark Triad and Work Behavior: A Social Exchange Perspective," *Journal of Applied Psychology* 97 (2012), pp. 557–579.

72 L. Zhang, and M. A. Gowan, "Corporate Social Responsibility, Applicants' Individual Traits, and Organizational Attraction: A Person–Organization Fit Perspective," *Journal of Business and Psychology* 27 (2012), pp. 345–362.

73 D. N. Hartog and F. D. Belschak, "Work Engagement and Machiavellianism in the Ethical Leadership Process," *Journal of Business Ethics* 107 (2012), pp. 35–47.

74 E. Grijalva and P. D. Harms, "Narcissism: An Integrative Synthesis and Dominance Complementarity Model," *The Academy of Management Perspectives* 28, no. 2 (2014), pp. 108–127.

75 D. C. Maynard, E. M. Brondolo, C. E. Connelly, and C. E. Sauer, "I'm Too Good for This Job: Narcissism's Role in the Experience of Overqualification," *Applied Psychology: An International Review* 64, no. 1 (2015), pp. 208–232.

76 E. Grijalva and P. D. Harms, "Narcissism: An Integrative Synthesis and Dominance Complementarity Model," *The Academy of Management Perspectives* 28, no. 2 (2014), pp. 108–127.

77 B. J. Brummel and K. N. Parker, "Obligation and Entitlement in Society and the Workplace," *Applied Psychology: An International Review* 64, no. 1 (2015), pp. 127–160.

78 E. Grijalva and D. A. Newman, "Narcissism and Counterproductive Work Behavior (CWB): Meta-analysis and Consideration of Collectivist Culture, Big Five Personality, and Narcissism's Facet Structure," *Applied Psychology: An International Review* (2015), pp. 93–126.

79 D. C. Maynard, E. M. Brondolo, C. E. Connelly, and C. E. Sauer, "I'm Too Good for This Job: Narcissism's Role in the Experience of Overqualification," *Applied Psychology: An International Review* 64, no. 1 (2015), pp. 208–232.

80 E. Grijalva and P. D. Harms, "Narcissism: An Integrative Synthesis and Dominance Complementarity Model," *The Academy of Management Perspectives* 28, no. 2 (2014), pp. 108–127.

81 S. Konrath, B. P. Meier, and B. J. Bushman, "Development and Validation of the Single Item Narcissism Scale (SINS)." *PLoS ONE* (August 5, 2014), doi: 10.1371/journal.pone.0103469; and https://news.osu.edu/news/2014/08/05/just-one-simple-question-can-identify-narcissistic-people/.

82 J. J. Sosik, J. U. Chun, and W. Zhu, "Hang On to Your Ego: The Moderating Role of Leader Narcissism on Relationships between Leader Charisma and Follower Psychological Empowerment and Moral Identity," *Journal of Business Ethics*, February 12, 2013; B. M. Galvin, D. A. Waldman, and P. Balthazard, "Visionary Communication Qualities as Mediators of the Relationship between Narcissism and Attributions of Leader Charisma," *Personnel Psychology* 63, no. 3 (2010), pp. 509–537.

83 D. Meinert, "Narcissistic Bosses Aren't All Bad, Study Finds," *HR Magazine*, March 2014, p. 18.

84 K. A. Byrne and D. A. Worthy, "Do Narcissists Make Better Decisions? An Investigation of Narcissism and Dynamic Decision-Making Performance," *Personality and Individual Differences*, July 2013, pp. 112–117.

85 C. Andreassen, H. Ursin, H. Eriksen, and S. Pallesen, "The Relationship of Narcissism with Workaholism, Work Engagement, and Professional Position," *Social Behavior and Personality* 40, no. 6 (2012), pp. 881–890.

86 A. Chatterjee and D. C. Hambrick, "Executive Personality, Capability Cues, and Risk Taking: How Narcissistic CEOs React to Their Successes and Stumbles," *Administrative Science Quarterly* 56 (2011), pp. 202–237.

87 C. J. Resick, D. S. Whitman, S. M. Weingarden, and N. J. Hiller, "The Bright-Side and Dark-Side of CEO Personality: Examining Core Self-Evaluations, Narcissism, Transformational Leadership, and Strategic Influence," *Journal of Applied Psychology* 94, no. 6 (2009), pp. 1365–1381.

88 E. H. O'Boyle, D. R. Forsyth, G. C. Banks, and M. A. McDaniel, "A Meta-analysis of the Dark Triad and Work Behavior: A Social Exchange Perspective," *Journal of Applied Psychology* 97, no. 3 (2012), p. 558.

89 A. Reece, A. Girkan, and T. Chamorro-Premuzic, "Greed Is Good? Assessing the Relationship between Entrepreneurship and Subclinical Psychopathy," *Personality and Individual Differences* 54, no. 3 (2013), pp. 420–425.

90 B. Wille, F. De Fruyt, and B. De Clercq, "Expanding and Reconceptualizing Aberrant Personality at Work: Validity of Five-Factor Model Aberrant Personality Tendencies to Predict Career Outcomes," *Personnel Psychology* 66 (2013), pp. 173–223.

91 P. K. Jonason, S. Slomski, and J. Partyka, "The Dark Triad at Work: How Toxic Employees Get Their Way," *Personality and Individual Differences* 52 (2012), pp. 449–453; and H. M. Baughman, S. Dearing, E. Giammarco, and P. A. Vernon, "Relationships between Bullying Behaviours and the Dark Triad: A Study with Adults," *Personality and Individual Differences* 52 (2012), pp. 571–575.

92 U. Orth and R. W. Robins, "Understanding the Link between Low Self-Esteem and Depression," *Current Directions in Psychological Science* 22, no. 6 (2013), pp. 455–460.

93 B. Wille, F. De Fruyt, and B. De Clercq, "Expanding and Reconceptualizing Aberrant Personality at Work: Validity of Five-Factor Model Aberrant Personality Tendencies to Predict Career Outcomes," *Personnel Psychology* 66 (2013), pp. 173–223.

94 T. A. Judge and J. E. Bono, "A Rose by Any Other Name … Are Self-Esteem, Generalized Self-Efficacy, Neuroticism, and Locus of Control Indicators of a Common Construct?" in *Personality Psychology in the Workplace*, ed. B. W. Roberts and R. Hogan, (Washington, DC: American Psychological Association), pp. 93–118; and A. M. Grant and A. Wrzesniewski, "I Won't Let You Down … or Will I? Core Self-Evaluations, Other-Orientation, Anticipated Guilt and Gratitude, and Job Performance," *Journal of Applied Psychology* 95, no. 1 (2010), pp. 108–121.

95 A. N. Salvaggio, B. Schneider, L. H. Nishi, D. M. Mayer, A. Ramesh, and J. S. Lyon, "Manager Personality, Manager Service Quality Orientation, and Service Climate: Test of a Model," *Journal of Applied Psychology* 92, no. 6 (2007), pp. 1741–1750; B. A. Scott and T. A. Judge, "The Popularity Contest at Work: Who Wins, Why, and What Do They Receive?" *Journal of Applied Psychology* 94, no. 1 (2009), pp. 20–33; and T. A. Judge and C. Hurst, "How the Rich (and Happy) Get Richer (and Happier): Relationship of Core Self-Evaluations to Trajectories in Attaining Work Success," *Journal of Applied Psychology* 93, no. 4 (2008), pp. 849–863.

96 A. M. Grant and A. Wrzesniewksi, "I Won't Let You Down … or Will I? Core Self-Evaluations, Other-Orientation, Anticipated Guilt and Gratitude, and Job Performance," *Journal of Applied Psychology* 95, no. 1 (2010), pp. 108–121.

97 See M. Snyder, *Public Appearances/Private Realities: The Psychology of Self-Monitoring* (New York: W. H. Freeman, 1987); and S. W. Gangestad and M. Snyder, "Self-Monitoring: Appraisal and Reappraisal," *Psychological Bulletin*, July 2000, pp. 530–555.

98 F. J. Flynn and D. R. Ames, "What's Good for the Goose May Not Be as Good for the Gander: The Benefits of Self-Monitoring for Men and Women in Task Groups and Dyadic Conflicts," *Journal of Applied Psychology* 91, no. 2 (2006), pp. 272–281; and M. Snyder, *Public Appearances/Private Realities: The Psychology of Self-Monitoring* (New York: W. H. Freeman, 1987).

99 D. V. Day, D. J. Shleicher, A. L. Unckless, and N. J. Hiller, "Self-Monitoring Personality at Work: A Meta-analytic Investigation of Construct Validity," *Journal of Applied Psychology* 87, no. 2 (2002), pp. 390–401.

100 H. Oh and M. Kilduff, "The Ripple Effect of Personality on Social Structure: Self-monitoring Origins of Network Brokerage," *Journal of Applied Psychology* 93, no. 5 (2008), pp. 1155–1164; and A. Mehra, M. Kilduff, and D. J. Brass, "The Social Networks of High and Low Self-Monitors: Implications for Workplace Performance," *Administrative Science Quarterly*, March 2001, pp. 121–146.

101 A. Beer, "Comparative Personality Judgments: Replication and Extension of Robust Findings in Personality Perception Using an Alternative Method," *Journal of Personality Assessment* 96, no. 6 (2014), pp. 610–618; and S. Hirschmüller, B. Egloff, S. Nestler, and D. Mitja, "The Dual Lens Model: A Comprehensive Framework for Understanding Self–Other Agreement of Personality Judgments at Zero Acquaintance," *Journal of Personality and Social Psychology* 104 (2013), pp. 335–353.

102 S. Hirschmueller, B. Egloff, S. C. Schmukle, S. Nestler, and M. D. Back, "Accurate Judgments of Neuroticism at Zero Acquaintance: A Question of Relevance," *Journal of Personality* 83, no. 2 (2015), pp. 221–228.

103 M. D. Back, "Personality Expression and Impression Formation in Online Social Networks: An Integrative Approach to Understanding Processes of Accuracy, Impression Management, and Meta-accuracy," *European Journal of Personality* 28 (2014), pp. 73–94.

104 P.-Y. Liao, "The Role of Self-Concept in the Mechanism Linking Proactive Personality to Employee Work Outcomes," *Applied Psychology: An International Review* 64, no. 2 (2015), pp. 421–443.

105 K. Tornau and M. Frese, "Construct Clean-up in Proactivity Research: A Meta-analysis on the Nomological Net of Work-Related Proactivity Concepts and Their Incremental Values," *Applied Psychology: An International Review* 62, no. 1 (2013), pp. 44–96.

106 W.-D. Li, D. Fay, M. Frese, P. D. Harms, and X. Y. Gao, "Reciprocal Relationship between Proactive Personality and Work Characteristics: A Latent Change Score Approach," *Journal of Applied Psychology* 99, no. 5 (2014), pp. 948–965.

107 P. D. Converse, Patrick J. Pathak, A. M. DePaul-Haddock, T. Gotlib, and M. Merbedone, "Controlling Your Environment and Yourself: Implications for Career Success," *Journal of Vocational Behavior* 80 (2012), pp. 148–159.

108 G. Chen, J. Farh, E. M. Campbell-Bush, Z. Wu, and X. Wu, "Teams as Innovative Systems: Multilevel Motivational Antecedents of Innovation in R&D Teams," *Journal of Applied Psychology* 98 (2013), pp. 1018–1027.

109 Y. Gong, S.-Y. Cheung, M. Wang, and J.-C. Huang, "Unfolding the Proactive Process for Creativity: Integration of the Employee Proactivity, Information Exchange, and Psychological Safety Perspectives," *Journal of Management* 38, no. 5 (2012), pp. 1611–1633.

110 Z. Zhang, M. Wang, and S. Junqi, "Leader-Follower Congruence in Proactive Personality and Work Outcomes: The Mediating Role of Leader-Member Exchange," *Academy of Management Journal* 55 (2012), pp. 111–130.

111 G. Van Hoye and H. Lootens, "Coping with Unemployment: Personality, Role Demands, and Time Structure," *Journal of Vocational Behavior* 82 (2013), pp. 85–95.

112 R. D. Meyer, R. S. Dalal, and R. Hermida, "A Review and Synthesis of Situational Strength in the Organizational Sciences," *Journal of Management* 36 (2010), pp. 121–140.

113 R. D. Meyer, R. S. Dalal, I. J. Jose, R. Hermida, T. R. Chen, R. P. Vega, C. K. Brooks, V. P. Khare, "Measuring Job-Related Situational Strength and Assessing Its Interactive Effects with Personality on Voluntary Work Behavior," *Journal of Management* 40, no. 4 (2014), pp. 1010–1041.

114 A. M. Grant and N. P. Rothbard, "When in Doubt, Seize the Day? Security Values, Prosocial Values, and Proactivity under Ambiguity," *Journal of Applied Psychology*, 2013.

115 See, for instance, C. D. Fisher and N. M. Ashkanasy, "The Emerging Role of Emotions in Work Life: An Introduction," *Journal of Organizational Behavior*, Special Issue (2000), pp. 123–129; N. M. Ashkanasy, C. E. J. Hartel, and W. J. Zerbe, eds., *Emotions in the Workplace: Research, Theory, and Practice* (Westport, CT: Quorum Books, 2000); N. M. Ashkanasy and C. S. Daus, "Emotion in the Workplace: The New Challenge for Managers," *Academy of Management Executive*, February 2002, pp. 76–86; and N. M. Ashkanasy, C. E. J. Hartel, and C. S. Daus, "Diversity and Emotion: The New Frontiers in Organizational Behavior Research," *Journal of Management* 28, no. 3 (2002), pp. 307–338.

116 S. G. Barsade and D. E. Gibson, "Why Does Affect Matter in Organizations?" *Academy of Management Perspectives*, February 2007, pp. 36–59.

117 Emotion. *Oxford Advanced Learner's Dictionary*, http://www.oxforddictionaries.com/us/definition/american_english/emotion, retrieved July 1, 2017.

118 Mood. *The American Heritage Medical Dictionary* (2007), retrieved July 1, 2017 from http://medical-dictionary.thefreedictionary.com/mood.

119 Mood. *Farlex Partner Medical Dictionary* (2012), retrieved July, 2017, from http://medical-dictionary.thefreedictionary.com/mood.

120 Based on K. Sanford and A. J. Grace, "Emotion and Underlying Concerns during Couples' Conflict: An Investigation of within-Person Change," *Personal Relationships* 18, no. 1 (2011), pp. 96–109; and Baylor University, "Exploring How Partners Perceive Each Other's Emotion during a Relationship Fight," *ScienceDaily*, December 16, 2010, http://www.sciencedaily.com/releases/2010/12/101216161514.htm.

121 P. S. Russell and R. Giner-Sorolla, "Bodily Moral Disgust: What It Is, How It Is Different from Anger, and Why It Is an Unreasoned Emotion," *Psychological Bulletin* 139, no. 2 (2013), pp. 328–351.

122 H. A. Chapman and A. K. Anderson, "Things Rank and Gross in Nature: A Review and Synthesis of Moral Disgust," *Psychological Bulletin* 139, no. 2 (2013), pp. 300–327.

123 T. Krennenauer, J. B. Asendorpf, and G. Nunner-Winkler, "Moral Emotion Attributions and Personality Traits As Long-Term Predictors of Antisocial Conduct in Early Adulthood: Findings from a 20-Year Longitudinal Study," *International Journal of Behavioral Development*, May 2013, pp. 192–201.

124 See J. A. Morris and D. C. Feldman, "Managing Emotions in the Workplace," *Journal of Managerial Issues* 9, no. 3 (1997), pp. 257–274; S. Mann, *Hiding What We Feel, Faking What We Don't: Understanding the Role of Your Emotions at Work* (New York: HarperCollins, 1999); and S. M. Kruml and D. Geddes, "Catching Fire without Burning Out: Is There an Ideal Way to Perform Emotion Labor?" in *Emotions in the Workplace*, ed. N. M. Ashkanasy, C. E. J. Hartel, and W. J. Zerbe (New York: Quorum Books, 2000), pp. 177–188.

125 M. W. Kramer and J. A. Hess, "Communication Rules for the Display of Emotions in Organizational Settings," *Management Communication Quarterly*, August 2002, pp. 66–80; and J. M. Diefendorff and E. M. Richard, "Antecedents and Consequences of Emotional Display Rule Perceptions," *Journal of Applied Psychology*, April 2003, pp. 284–294.

126 P. S. Christoforou and B. E. Ashforth, "Revisiting the Debate on the Relationships between Display Rules and Performance: Considering the Explicitness of Display Rules," *Journal of Applied Psychology* 100, no. 1 (2015), pp. 249–261.

127 C. M. Brotheridge and R. T. Lee, "Development and Validation of the Emotional Labour Scale," *Journal of Occupational and Organizational Psychology* 76, no. 3 (September 2003), pp. 365–379.

128 U. R. Hulsheger, H. J. E. M. Alberts, A. Feinholdt, and J. W. B. Lang, "Benefits of Mindfulness at Work: The Role of Mindfulness in Emotion Regulation, Emotional Exhaustion, and Job Satisfaction," *Journal of Applied Psychology*, March 2013, pp. 310–325.

129 J. D. Kammeyer-Mueller, A. L. Rubenstein, D. M. Long, M. A. Odio, B. R. Buckman, Y. Zhang, and M. D. K. Halvorsen-Ganepola, "A Meta-analytic Structural Model of Dispositionally Affectivity and Emotional Labor," *Personnel Psychology* 66 (2013), pp. 47–90.

130 D. T. Wagner, C. M. Barnes, and B. A. Scott, "Driving It Home: How Workplace Emotional Labor Harms Employee Home Life," *Personnel Psychology* 67 (2014), pp. 487–516.

131 J. D. Kammeyer-Mueller, A. L. Rubenstein, D. M. Long, M. A. Odio, B. R. Buckman, Y. Zhang, and M. D. K. Halvorsen-Ganepola, "A Meta-analytic Structural Model of Dispositionally Affectivity and Emotional Labor," *Personnel Psychology* 66 (2013), pp. 47–90.

132 J. P. Trougakos, D. J. Beal, S. G. Green, and H. M. Weiss, "Making the Break Count: An Episodic Examination of Recovery Activities, Emotional Experiences, and Positive Affective Displays," *Academy of Management Journal* 51, no. 1 (2008), pp. 131–146.

133 J. M. Diefendorff, R. J. Erickson, A. A. Grandey, and J. J. Dahling, "Emotional Display Rules as Work Unit Norms: A Multilevel Analysis of Emotional Labor among Nurses," *Journal of Occupational Health Psychology* 16 (2011), pp. 170–186.

134 S. Brassen, M. Gamer, and C. Büchel, "Anterior Cingulate Activation Is Related to a Positivity Bias and Emotional Stability in Successful Aging," *Biological Psychiatry* 70, no. 2 (2011), pp. 131–137.

135 H. Guenter, I. J. H. van Emmerik, and B. Schreurs, "The Negative Effects of Delays in Information Exchange: Looking at Workplace Relationships from an Affective Events Perspective," *Human Resource Management Review* 24, no. 4 (December 2014), pp. 283–298; and F. K. Matta, H. T. Erol-Korkmaz, R. E. Johnson, and P. Biçaksiz, "Significant Work Events and Counterproductive Work Behavior: The Role of Fairness, Emotions, and Emotion Regulation," *Journal of Organizational Behavior* 35, no. 7 (2014), pp. 920–944.

136 C. D. Fisher, A. Minbashian, N. Beckmann, and R. E. Wood, "Task Appraisals, Emotions, and Performance Goal Orientations," *Journal of Applied Psychology* 98, no. 2 (2013), pp. 364–373.

137 N. M. Ashkanasy, C. E. J. Hartel, and C. S. Daus, "Diversity and Emotion: The New Frontiers in Organizational Behavior Research," *Journal of Management* 28, no. 3 (2002), p. 324.

138 Based on D. R. Caruso, J. D. Mayer, and P. Salovey, "Emotional Intelligence and Emotional Leadership," in *Multiple Intelligences and Leadership*, ed. R. E. Riggio, S. E. Murphy, and F. J. Pirozzolo (Mahwah, NJ: Lawrence Erlbaum, 2002), p. 70.

139 P. Salovey and D. Grewal, "The Science of Emotional Intelligence," *Current Directions in Psychological Science* 14, no. 6 (2005), pp. 281–285; and D. Geddes and R. R. Callister, "Crossing the Line(s): A Dual Threshold Model of Anger in Organizations," *Academy of Management Review* 32, no. 3 (2007), pp. 721–746.

140 Based on R. L. Hotz, "Too Important to Smile Back: The 'Boss Effect,'" *Wall Street Journal*, October 16, 2012, p. D2; E. Kim and D. J. Yoon, "Why Does Service with a Smile Make Employees Happy? A Social Interaction Model," *Journal of Applied Psychology* 97 (2012), pp. 1059–1967; and K. Weintraub, "But How Do You Really Feel? Someday the Computer May Know," *New York Times*, October 16, 2012, p. D3.

141 E. H. O'Boyle, R. H. Humphrey, J. M. Pollack, T. H. Hawver, and P. A. Story, "The Relation between Emotional Intelligence and Job Performance: A Meta-analysis," *Journal of Organizational Behavior* 32, no. 5 (2011), pp. 788–818.

142 R. Gilkey, R. Caceda, and C. Kilts, "When Emotional Reasoning Trumps IQ," *Harvard Business Review*, September 2010, p. 27.

143 M. Seo and L. F. Barrett, "Being Emotional During Decision Making—Good or Bad? An Empirical Investigation," *Academy of Management Journal* 50, no. 4 (2007), pp. 923–940.

144 Based on D. Iliescu, A. Ilie, D. Ispas, and A. Ion, "Emotional Intelligence in Personnel Selection: Applicant Reactions, Criterion, and Incremental Validity," *International Journal of Selection and Assessment*, September 2012, pp. 347–358; D. L. Joseph, J. Jin, D. A. Newman, and E. H. O'Boyle, "Why Does Self-Reported Emotional Intelligence Predict Job Performance? A Meta-analytic Investigation of Mixed EI," *Journal of Applied Psychology* 100, no. 2 (2015), pp. 298–342; R. Sharma, "Measuring Social and Emotional Intelligence Competencies in the Indian Context,"

Cross Cultural Management 19 (2012), pp. 30–47; and S. Sharma, M. Gangopadhyay, E. Austin, and M. K. Mandal, "Development and Validation of a Situational Judgment Test of Emotional Intelligence," *International Journal of Selection and Assessment*, March 2013, pp. 57–73.

145 See R. J. Bennett and S. L. Robinson, "Development of a Measure of Workplace Deviance," *Journal of Applied Psychology*, June 2000, pp. 349–360; see also P. R. Sackett and C. J. DeVore, "Counterproductive Behaviors at Work," in *Handbook of Industrial, Work & Organizational Psychology*, vol. 1, ed. N. Anderson, D. S. Ones, H. K. Sinangil, and C. Viswesvaran (Thousand Oaks, CA: Sage, 2001), pp. 145–164.

146 K. Lee and N. J. Allen, "Organizational Citizenship Behavior and Workplace Deviance: The Role of Affect and Cognition," *Journal of Applied Psychology* 87, no. 1 (2002), pp. 131–142; T. A. Judge, B. A. Scott, and R. Ilies, "Hostility, Job Attitudes, and Workplace Deviance: Test of a Multilevel Mode," *Journal of Applied Psychology* 91, no. 1 (2006), pp. 126–138; and S. Kaplan, J. C. Bradley, J. N. Luchman, and D. Haynes, "On the Role of Positive and Negative Affectivity in Job Performance: A Meta-analytic Investigation," *Journal of Applied Psychology* 94, no. 1 (2009), pp. 152–176.

147 S. C. Douglas, C. Kiewitz, M. Martinko, P. Harvey, Y. Kim, and J. U. Chun, "Cognitions, Emotions, and Evaluations: An Elaboration Likelihood Model for Workplace Aggression," *Academy of Management Review* 33, no. 2 (2008), pp. 425–451.

148 A. K. Khan, S. Ouratulain, and J. R. Crawshaw, "The Mediating Role of Discrete Emotions in the Relationship between Injustice and Counterproductive Work Behaviors: A Study in Pakistan," *Journal of Business and Psychology*, March 2013, pp. 49–61.

149 S. L. Koole, "The Psychology of Emotion Regulation: An Integrative Review," *Cognition and Emotion* 23 (2009), pp. 4–41; and H. A. Wadlinger and D. M. Isaacowitz, "Fixing Our Focus: Training Attention to Regulate Emotion," *Personality and Social Psychology Review* 15 (2011), pp. 75–102.

150 D. H. Kluemper, T. DeGroot, and S. Choi, "Emotion Management Ability: Predicting Task Performance, Citizenship, and Deviance," *Journal of Management*, May 2013, pp. 878–905.

151 J. P. Trougakos, D. J. Beal, B. H. Cheng, I. Hideg, and D. Zweig, "Too Drained to Help: A Resource Depletion Perspective on Daily Interpersonal Citizenship Behaviors," *Journal of Applied Psychology* 100, no. 1 (2015), pp. 227–236.

152 B. A. Scott, C. M. Barnes, and D. T. Wagner, "Chameleonic or Consistent? A Multilevel Investigation of Emotional Labor Variability and Self-Monitoring," *Academy of Management Journal* 55, no. 4 (2012), pp. 905–926.

153 U. R. Hülsheger, J. W. B. Lang, A. F. Schewe, and F. R. H. Zijlstra, "When Regulating Emotions at Work Pays Off: A Diary and an Intervention Study on Emotion Regulation and Customer Tips in Service Jobs," *Journal of Applied Psychology*, March 2015, pp. 263–277.

154 J. L. Jooa and G. Francesca, "Poker-Faced Morality: Concealing Emotions Leads to Utilitarian Decision Making," *Organizational Behavior and Human Decision Processes* 126 (January 2015), pp. 49–64.

155 J. L. Jooa and G. Francesca, "Poker-Faced Morality: Concealing Emotions Leads to Utilitarian Decision Making," *Organizational Behavior and Human Decision Processes* 126 (January 2015), pp. 49–64.

156 T. L. Webb, E. Miles, and P. Sheeran, "Dealing with Feeling: A Meta-analysis of the Effectiveness of Strategies Derived from the Process Model of Emotion Regulation," *Psychological Bulletin* 138, no. 4 (2012), pp. 775–808; S. Srivastava, M. Tamir, K. M. McGonigal, O. P. John, and J. J. Gross, "The Social Costs of Emotional Suppression: A Prospective Study of the Transition to College," *Journal of Personality and Social Psychology* 96 (2009), pp. 883–897; Y. Liu, L. M. Prati, P. L. Perrewé, and R. A. Brymer,

"Individual Differences in Emotion Regulation, Emotional Experiences at Work, and Work-Related Outcomes: A Two-Study Investigation," *Journal of Applied Social Psychology* 40 (2010), pp. 1515–1538; and H. A. Wadlinger and D. M. Isaacowitz, "Fixing our Focus: Training Attention to Regulate Emotion," *Personality and Social Psychology Review* 15 (2011), pp. 75–102.

157 J. J. Gross, E. Halperin, and R. Porat, "Emotion Regulation in Intractable Conflicts," *Current Directions in Psychological Science* 22, no. 6 (2013), pp. 423–429.

158 A. S. Troy, A. J. Shallcross, and I. B. Mauss, "A Person-by-Person Situation Approach to Emotion Regulation: Cognitive Reappraisal Can Either Help or Hurt, Depending on the Context," *Psychological Science* 24, no. 12 (2013), pp. 2505–2514.

159 E. Halperin, R. Porat, M. Tamir, and J. J. Gross, "Can Emotion Regulation Change Political Attitudes in Intractable Conflicts? From the Laboratory to the Field," *Psychological Science*, January 2013, pp. 106–111.

160 R. Teper, Z. V. Segal, and M. Inzlicht, "Inside the Mindful Mind: How Mindfulness Enhances Emotion Regulation through Improvements in Executive Control," *Current Directions in Psychological Science* 22, no. 6 (2013), pp. 449–454.

161 A. S. McCance, C. D. Nye, L. Wang, K. S. Jones, and C. Chiu, "Alleviating the Burden of Emotional Labor: The Role of Social Sharing," *Journal of Management* 39, no. 2 (2013), pp. 392–415.

162 F. Nils and B. Rimé, "Beyond the Myth of Venting: Social Sharing Modes Determine the Benefits of Emotional Disclosure," *European Journal of Social Psychology* 42 (2012), pp. 672–681; and J. D. Parlamis, "Venting as Emotion Regulation: The Influence of Venting Responses and Respondent Identity on Anger and Emotional Tone," *International Journal of Conflict Management* 23 (2012), pp. 77–96.

163 S.-C. S. Chi and S.-G. Liang, "When Do Subordinates' Emotion-Regulation Strategies Matter? Abusive Supervision, Subordinates' Emotional Exhaustion, and Work Withdrawal," *The Leadership Quarterly*, February 2013, pp. 125–137.

164 R. H. Humphrey, "How Do Leaders Use Emotional Labor?" *Journal of Organizational Behavior*, July 2012, pp. 740–744.

165 A. M. Grant, "Rocking the Boat but Keeping It Steady: The Role of Emotion Regulation in Employee Voice," *Academy of Management Journal* 56, no. 6 (2013), pp. 1703–1723.

166 Based on "Affective Computing," *MIT*, accessed October 1, 2014, http://affect.media.mit.edu/; "Affective Computing and Intelligent Interaction" (paper presented at IEEE Computer Society Annual Conference, Geneva, Switzerland, September 2013), http://ieeexplore.ieee.org/xpl/mostRecentIssue.jsp?reload=true&punumber=6679936; and K. Weintraub, "But How Do You Really Feel? Someday the Computer May Know," *New York Times*, October 16, 2012, p. D3.

167 C. West, "How Culture Affects the Way We Think," *APS Observer* 20, no. 7 (2007), pp. 25–26.

168 T. Masuda, R. Gonzalez, L. Kwan, and R. E. Nisbett, "Culture and Aesthetic Preference: Comparing the Attention to Context of East Asians and Americans," *Personality and Social Psychology Bulletin* 34, no. 9 (2008), pp. 1260–1275.

169 D. C. Park, "Developing a Cultural Cognitive Neuroscience of Aging," in *Handbook of Cognitive Aging*, ed. S. M. Hofer and D. F. Alwin (Thousand Oaks, CA: Sage, 2008), pp. 352–367.

170 Q. Wang, "On the Cultural Constitution of Collective Memory," *Memory* 16, no. 3 (2008), pp. 305–317.

171 See, for instance, A. H. Mezulis, L. Y. Abramson, J. S. Hyde, and B. L. Hankin, "Is There a Universal Positivity Bias in Attributions: A Meta-analytic Review of Individual, Developmental, and Cultural Differences in the Self-Serving Attributional Bias," *Psychological Bulletin* 130, no. 5 (2004), pp. 711–747; C. F. Falk, S. J. Heine, M. Yuki, and K. Takemura, "Why Do Westerners Self-Enhance More

Than East Asians?" *European Journal of Personality* 23, no. 3 (2009), pp. 183–203; and F. F. T. Chiang and T. A. Birtch, "Examining the Perceived Causes of Successful Employee Performance: An East–West Comparison," *International Journal of Human Resource Management* 18, no. 2 (2007), pp. 232–248.

172 R. Friedman, W. Liu, C. C. Chen, and S. S. Chi, "Causal Attribution for Interfirm Contract Violation: A Comparative Study of Chinese and American Commercial Arbitrators," *Journal of Applied Psychology* 92, no. 3 (2007), pp. 856–864.

173 J. Spencer-Rodgers, M. J. Williams, D. L. Hamilton, K. Peng, and L. Wang, "Culture and Group Perception: Dispositional and Stereotypic Inferences about Novel and National Groups," *Journal of Personality and Social Psychology* 93, no. 4 (2007), pp. 525–543.

174 J. D. Brown, "Across the (Not So) Great Divide: Cultural Similarities in Self-Evaluative Processes," *Social and Personality Psychology Compass* 4, no. 5 (2010), pp. 318–330.

175 A. Zhang, C. Reyna, Z. Qian, and G. Yu, "Interpersonal Attributions of Responsibility in the Chinese Workplace: A Test of Western Models in a Collectivistic Context," *Journal of Applied Social Psychology* 38, no. 9 (2008), pp. 2361–2377; and A. Zhang, F. Xia, and C. Li, "The Antecedents of Help Giving in Chinese Culture: Attribution, Judgment of Responsibility, Expectation Change and the Reaction of Affect," *Social Behavior and Personality* 35, no. 1 (2007), pp. 135–142.

176 See, for example, R. R. McCrae and P. T. Costa Jr., "Personality Trait Structure as a Human Universal," *American Psychologist*, May 1997, pp. 509–516; S. Yamagata, A. Suzuki, J. Ando, Y. Ono, K. Yutaka, N. Kijima, K. Yoshimura, F. Ostendorf, A. Angleitner, R. Riemann, F. M. Spinath, W. J. Livesley, and K. L. Jang, "Is the Genetic Structure of Human Personality Universal? A Cross-Cultural Twin Study from North America, Europe, and Asia," *Journal of Personality and Social Psychology* 90, no. 6 (2006), pp. 987–998; H. C. Triandis and E. M. Suh, "Cultural Influences on Personality," in *Annual Review of Psychology*, vol. 53, ed. S. T. Fiske, D. L. Schacter, and C. Zahn-Waxler (Palo Alto, CA: Annual Reviews, 2002), pp. 133–160; R. R. McCrae and J. Allik, *The Five-Factor Model of Personality across Cultures* (New York: Kluwer Academic/Plenum, 2002); and R. R. McCrae, P. T. Costa Jr., T. A. Martin, V. E. Oryol, A. A. Rukavishnikov, I. G. Senin, M. Hřebíčková, and T. Urbánek, "Consensual Validation of Personality Traits across Cultures," *Journal of Research in Personality* 38, no. 2 (2004), pp. 179–201.

177 M. Gurven, C. von Ruden, M. Massenkoff, H. Kaplan, and M. L. Vie, "How Universal Is the Big Five? Testing the Five-Factor Model of Personality Variation among Forager-Farmers in the Bolivian Amazon," *Journal of Personality and Social Psychology* 104, no. 2 (2013), pp. 354–370.

178 M. Eid and E. Diener, "Norms for Experiencing Emotions in Different Cultures: Inter- and Intranational Differences," *Journal of Personality and Social Psychology* 81, no. 5 (2001), pp. 869–885.

179 S. Oishi, E. Diener, and C. Napa Scollon, "Cross-Situational Consistency of Affective Experiences across Cultures," *Journal of Personality and Social Psychology* 86, no. 3 (2004), pp. 460–472; and J. Leu, J. Wang, and K. Koo, "Are Positive Emotions Just as 'Positive' across Cultures?" *Emotion* 11, no. 4 (2011).

180 M. Gendron, D. Roberson, J. M. van der Vyver, and L. F. Barrett, "Cultural Relativity of Perceiving Emotion from Vocalizations," *Psychological Science* 25, no. 4 (2014), pp. 911–920.

181 S. Nelton, "Emotions in the Workplace," *Nation's Business*, February 1996, p. 25.

182 B. Carey, "The Benefits of Blowing Your Top," *New York Times*, July 6, 2010, p. D1; R. Y. Cheung and I. J. Park, "Anger Suppression, Interdependent Self-Construal, and Depression among Asian American and European American College Students," *Cultural Diversity and Ethnic Minority Psychology* 16, no. 4 (2010), pp. 517–425; D. Geddes and L. T. Stickney, "The Trouble with Sanctions:

Organizational Responses to Deviant Anger Displays at Work," *Human Relations* 64, no. 2 (2011), pp. 201–230; J. Fairley, "Taking Control of Anger Management," *Workforce Management*, October 2010, p. 10; L. T. Stickney and D. Geddes, "Positive, Proactive, and Committed: The Surprising Connection Between Good Citizens and Expressed (vs. Suppressed) Anger at Work," *Negotiation and Conflict Management Research* 7, no. 4 (November 2014), pp. 243–264; and J. Whalen, "Angry Outbursts Really Do Hurt Your Health, Doctors Find," *Wall Street Journal*, March 24, 2015, pp. D1, D4.

183 Exercise based on M.-A. Reinard and N. Schwartz, "The Influence of Affective States on the Presence of Lie Detection," *Journal of Experimental Psychology* 18 (2012), pp. 377–389.

184 Based on S. Shellenbarger, "Thinking Happy Thoughts at Work," *Wall Street Journal*, January 27, 2010, p. D2; S. Sharma and D. Chatterjee, "Cos Are Keenly Listening to 'Happiness Coach,'" *Economic Times*, July 16, 2010, http://articles.economictimes.india-times.com; J. Smith, *The Executive Happiness Coach*, accessed May 3, 2011, http://www.lifewithhappiness.com; and S. Sonnentag and A. M. Grant, "Doing Good at Work Feels Good at Home, But Not Right Away: When and Why Perceived Prosocial Impact Predicts Positive Affect," *Personnel Psychology* 65 (2012), pp. 495–530.

185 Based on S. Cain, *Quiet: The Power of Introverts in a World That Can't Stop Talking* (New York: Random House/Broadway Paperbacks, 2013); G. Belojevic, V. Slepcevic, and B. Jakovljevic, "Mental Performance in Noise: The Role of Introversion," *Journal of Environmental Psychology* 21, no. 2 (2001), pp. 209–213; and P. Hills and M. Argyle, "Happiness, Introversion-Extraversion and Happy Introverts," *Personality and Individual Differences* 30, no. 4 (2001), pp. 595–608.

186 P. Hartcher, "Voters Now at Ease with Rich Pickings," *The Sydney Morning Herald*, July 30, 2013, http://www.smh.com.au/federal-politics/federal-election-2013/voters-now-at-ease-with-rich-pickings-20130729-2quvp.html; N. T. Feather, "Analyzing Relative Deprivation in Relation to Deservingness, Entitlement and Resentment," *Social Justice Research* 28 (2015), pp. 7–26; E. Kim and T. M. Glomb, "Victimization of High Performers: The Roles of Envy and Work Group Identification," *Journal of Applied Psychology* 99, no. 4 (2014), pp. 619–634; and K. Van Valkenburgh, *Investigating Tall Poppy Syndrome in United States Financial Institutions: An Attitude and Values Perspective*, doctoral dissertation, Alliant International University (2013), publication number 3595388.

187 Based on V. P. Richmond, J. C. McCroskey, and S. K. Payne, *Nonverbal Behavior in Interpersonal Relations*, 2nd ed. (Englewood Cliffs, NJ: Prentice Hall, 1991), pp. 117–138; and L. A. King, "Ambivalence over Emotional Expression and Reading Emotions in Situations and Faces," *Journal of Personality and Social Psychology*, March 1998, pp. 753–762.

Chapter 3

1 Vignette based on K. Porter, "Local Tech Companies Sign Open Letter Opposing Trump Travel Ban," *CBC News*, January 31, 2017, http://www.cbc.ca/news/canada/ottawa/tech-companies-oppose-trump-travel-ban-1.3954433; M. Braga, "Canadian Tech Companies Say They Value Diversity — But What Are They Doing About It?" *CBC News*, July 11, 2017, http://www.cbc.ca/news/technology/canada-tech-companies-diversity-reports-2017-1.4194556.

2 G. R. Maio, J. M. Olson, M. M. Bernard, and M. A. Luke, "Ideologies, Values, Attitudes, and Behavior," in *Handbook of Social Psychology*, ed. J. Delamater (New York, NY: Springer, 2003), pp. 283–308.

3 See, for example, B. Meglino and E. Ravlin, "Individual Values in Organizations," *Journal of Management* 24, no. 3 (1998), pp. 351–389.

4   See, for instance, A. Bardi, J. A. Lee, N. Hofmann-Towfigh, and G. Soutar, "The Structure of Intraindividual Value Change," *Journal of Personality and Social Psychology* 97, no. 5 (2009), pp. 913–929.

5   S. Roccas, L. Sagiv, S. H. Schwartz, and A. Knafo, "The Big Five Personality Factors and Personal Values," *Personality and Social Psychology Bulletin* 28, no. 6 (2002), pp. 789–801.

6   M. Rokeach, *The Nature of Human Values* (New York: Free Press, 1973), p. 56.

7   K. Hodgson, *A Rock and a Hard Place: How to Make Ethical Business Decisions When the Choices Are Tough* (New York: AMACOM, 1992), pp. 66–67.

8   K. Hodgson, "Adapting Ethical Decisions to a Global Marketplace," *Management Review* 81, no. 5 (May 1992), pp. 53–57. Reprinted by permission.

9   Vignette based on http://www.canadalearningcode.ca/.

10 G. Hofstede, *Culture's Consequences: International Differences in Work-Related Values* (Beverly Hills, CA: Sage, 1980); G. Hofstede, *Cultures and Organizations: Software of the Mind* (London: McGraw-Hill, 1991); G. Hofstede, "Cultural Constraints in Management Theories," *Academy of Management Executive* 7, no. 1 (1993), pp. 81–94; G. Hofstede and M. F. Peterson, "National Values and Organizational Practices," in *Handbook of Organizational Culture and Climate*, ed. N. M. Ashkanasy, C. M. Wilderom, and M. F. Peterson (Thousand Oaks, CA: Sage, 2000), pp. 401–416; and G. Hofstede, *Culture's Consequences: Comparing Values, Behaviors, Institutions, and Organizations across Nations*, 2nd ed. (Thousand Oaks, CA: Sage, 2001). For criticism of this research, see B. McSweeney, "Hofstede's Model of National Cultural Differences and Their Consequences: A Triumph of Faith—A Failure of Analysis," *Human Relations* 55, no. 1 (2002), pp. 89–118.

11 G. Hofstede, "Dimensionalizing Cultures: The Hofstede Model in Context," Online Readings in Psychology and Culture, Unit 2, 2011, http://scholarworks.gvsu.edu/orpc/vol2/iss1/8.

12 G. Hofstede, "Dimensionalizing Cultures: The Hofstede Model in Context," Online Readings in Psychology and Culture, Unit 2, 2011, http://scholarworks.gvsu.edu/orpc/vol2/iss1/8.

13 V. Taras, B. L. Kirkman, and P. Steel, "Examining the Impact of Culture's Consequences: A Three-Decade, Multilevel, Meta-analytic Review of Hofstede's Cultural Value Dimensions," *Journal of Applied Psychology* 95, no. 5 (2010), pp. 405–439.

14 M. Javidan and R. J. House, "Cultural Acumen for the Global Manager: Lessons from Project GLOBE," *Organizational Dynamics* 29, no. 4 (2001), pp. 289–305; and R. J. House, P. J. Hanges, M. Javidan, and P. W. Dorfman, eds., *Leadership, Culture, and Organizations: The GLOBE Study of 62 Societies* (Thousand Oaks, CA: Sage, 2004).

15 J. P. Meyer, D. J. Stanley, T. A. Jackson, K. J. McInnis, E. R. Maltin, and L. Sheppard, "Affective, Normative, and Continuance Commitment Levels Across Cultures: A Meta-analysis," *Journal of Vocational Behavior* 80, no. 2 (2012), pp. 225–245.

16 B. Meglino, E. C. Ravlin, and C. L. Adkins, "A Work Values Approach to Corporate Culture: A Field Test of the Value Congruence Process and Its Relationship to Individual Outcomes," *Journal of Applied Psychology* 74 (1989), pp. 424–432.

17 B. Z. Posner, J. M. Kouzes, and W. H. Schmidt, "Shared Values Make a Difference: An Empirical Test of Corporate Culture," *Human Resource Management* 24 (1985), pp. 293–310; and A. L. Balazas, "Value Congruency: The Case of the 'Socially Responsible' Firm," *Journal of Business Research* 20 (1990), pp. 171–181.

18 C. A. O'Reilly, J. Chatman, and D. Caldwell, "People and Organizational Culture: A Q-Sort Approach to Assessing Person-Organizational Fit," *Academy of Management Journal* 34 (1991), pp. 487–516.

19 C. Enz and C. K. Schwenk, "Performance and Sharing of Organizational Values" (paper presented at the annual meeting of the Academy of Management, Washington, DC, 1989).

20 See, for example, *The Multigenerational Workforce* (Alexandria, VA: Society for Human Resource Management, 2009); and M. Adams, *Sex in the Snow* (Toronto: Penguin, 1997).

21 J. Timm, "Leadership Q&A: Robert Dutton," *Canadian Business*, June 22, 2011.

22 K. W. Smola and C. D. Sutton, "Generational Differences: Revisiting Generational Work Values for the New Millennium," *Journal of Organizational Behavior* 23 (2002), pp. 363–382; and K. Mellahi and C. Guermat, "Does Age Matter? An Empirical Examination of the Effect of Age on Managerial Values and Practices in India," *Journal of World Business* 39, no. 2 (2004), pp. 199–215.

23 B. Malcolm, "Millennials Now Represent the Largest Generation in the Canadian Workforce," January 2, 2017, Ravenhill Group Incorporated, http://ravenhillgroup.com/millennials-canadian-workforce/.

24 E. Parry and P. Urwin, "Generational Differences in Work Values: A Review of Theory and Evidence," *International Journal of Management Reviews* 13, no. 1 (2011), pp. 79–96.

25 J. M. Twenge, S. M. Campbell, B. J. Hoffman, and C. E. Lance, "Generational Differences in Work Values: Leisure and Extrinsic Values Increasing, Social and Intrinsic Values Decreasing," *Journal of Management* 36, no. 5 (2010), pp. 1117–1142.

26 Based on P. Loriggio, "Teen Who Won Google Prize Juggles School Work with Science Fair," *Maclean's*, December 27, 2013; and A. Kingston, "Get Ready for Generation Z," *Maclean's*, July 15, 2014.

27 Statistics Canada, *Immigration and Ethnocultural Diversity in Canada* (Catalogue no. 99-010-X2011001) (Ottawa: Statistics Canada, 2013). Unfortunately these numbers have not been updated due to cutbacks in data collected by the Canadian government.

28 The source for projections in the paragraph is J.-D. Morency, É. C. Malenfant, and S. MacIsaac, *Immigration and Diversity: Population Projections for Canada and Its Regions, 2011 to 2036* (Catalogue Number 91-551-X) (Ottawa: Statistics Canada, 2017).

29 https://www.brookings.edu/blog/brookings-now/2013/10/03/what-percentage-of-u-s-population-is-foreign-born/.

30 Statistics Canada, *Immigration and Ethnocultural Diversity in Canada* (Catalogue no. 99-010-X2011001) (Ottawa: Statistics Canada, 2013).

31 Statistics Canada, "2011 Census of Population: Linguistic Characteristics of Canadians," *The Daily*, October 24, 2012.

32 Statistics Canada, "2011 Census of Population: Linguistic Characteristics of Canadians," *The Daily*, October 24, 2012.

33 B. Leber, "Police-Reported Hate Crime in Canada," Statistics Canada, *Juristat* (85-002-X), June 13, 2017.

34 M. Isaac, "Inside Uber's Aggressive, Unrestrained Workplace Culture," *New York Times*, February 22, 2017, p. A1.

35 A. Barsky, S. A. Kaplan, and D. J. Beal, "Just Feelings? The Role of Affect in the Formation of Organizational Fairness Judgments," *Journal of Management*, January 2011, pp. 248–279; J. A. Mikels, S. J. Maglio, A. E. Reed, and L. J. Kaplowitz, "Should I Go with My Gut? Investigating the Benefits of Emotion-Focused Decision Making," *Emotion*, August 2011, pp. 743–753; and A. J. Rojas Tejada, O. M. Lozano Rojas, M. Navas Luque, and P. J. Pérez Moreno, "Prejudiced Attitude Measurement Using the Rasch Scale Model," *Psychological Reports*, October 2011, pp. 553–572.

36 M. Riketta, "The Causal Relation between Job Attitudes and Performance: A Meta-analysis of Panel Studies," *Journal of Applied Psychology* 93, no. 2 (2008), pp. 472–481.

37 D. P. Moynihan and S. K. Pandey, "Finding Workable Levers over Work Motivation: Comparing Job Satisfaction, Job Involvement,

and Organizational Commitment," *Administration & Society* 39, no. 7 (2007), pp. 803–832.

38 For problems with the concept of job satisfaction, see R. Hodson, "Workplace Behaviors," *Work and Occupations*, August 1991, pp. 271–290; and H. M. Weiss and R. Cropanzano, "Affective Events Theory: A Theoretical Discussion of the Structure, Causes and Consequences of Affective Experiences at Work," in *Research in Organizational Behavior*, vol. 18, ed. B. M. Staw and L. L. Cummings (Greenwich, CT: JAI Press, 1996), pp. 1–3.

39 "One-half of Working Population Unhappy In Job: Survey," *Canadian HR Reporter*, May 2, 2016, http://www.hrreporter.com/article/27461-one-half-of-working-population-unhappy-in-job-survey/.

40 J. Barling, E. K. Kelloway, and R. D. Iverson, "High-Quality Work, Job Satisfaction, and Occupational Injuries," *Journal of Applied Psychology* 88, no. 2 (2003), pp. 276–283; and F. W. Bond and D. Bunce, "The Role of Acceptance and Job Control in Mental Health, Job Satisfaction, and Work Performance," *Journal of Applied Psychology* 88, no. 6 (2003), pp. 1057–1067.

41 Y. Georgellis and T. Lange, "Traditional versus Secular Values and the Job-Life Satisfaction Relationship across Europe," *British Journal of Management* 23 (2012), pp. 437–454.

42 S. E. Humphrey, J. D. Nahrgang, and F. P. Morgeson, "Integrating Motivational, Social, and Contextual Work Design Features: A Meta-analytic Summary and Theoretical Extension of the Work Design Literature," *Journal of Applied Psychology* 92, no. 5 (2007), pp. 1332–1356; and D. S. Chiaburu and D. A. Harrison, "Do Peers Make the Place? Conceptual Synthesis and Meta-analysis of Coworker Effect on Perceptions, Attitudes, OCBs, and Performance," *Journal of Applied Psychology* 93, no. 5 (2008), pp. 1082–1103.

43 K. H. Fong and E. Snape, "Empowering Leadership, Psychological Empowerment and Employee Outcomes: Testing a Multi-Level Mediating Model," *British Journal of Management* 26 (2015), pp. 126–138.

44 S. Ronen, M. Mikulincer, "Predicting Employees' Satisfaction and Burnout from Managers' Attachment and Caregiving Orientations," *European Journal of Work and Organizational Psychology* 21, no. 6 (2012), pp. 828–849.

45 A. Calvo-Salguero, J.-M. Salinas Martinez-de-Lecea, and A.-M. Carrasco-Gonzalez, "Work-Family and Family-Work Conflict: Does Intrinsic-Extrinsic Satisfaction Mediate the Prediction of General Job Satisfaction?" *The Journal of Psychology* 145, no. 5 (2011), pp. 435–461.

46 J. Zhang, Q. Wu, D. Miao, X. Yan, and J. Peng, "The Impact of Core Self-Evaluations on Job Satisfaction: The Mediator Role of Career Commitment," *Social Indicators Research* 116, no. 3 (2014), pp. 809–822.

47 T. A. Judge, C. J. Thoresen, J. E. Bono, and G. K. Patton, "The Job Satisfaction–Job Performance Relationship: A Qualitative and Quantitative Review," *Psychological Bulletin*, May 2001, pp. 376–407.

48 D. W. Organ, *Organizational Citizenship Behavior: The Good Soldier Syndrome* (Lexington, MA: Lexington Books, 1988), p. 4.

49 See P. M. Podsakoff, S. B. MacKenzie, J. B. Paine, and D. G. Bachrach, "Organizational Citizenship Behaviors: A Critical Review of the Theoretical and Empirical Literature and Suggestions for Future Research," *Journal of Management* 26, no. 3 (2000), pp. 513–563.

50 B. J. Hoffman, C. A. Blair, J. P. Maeriac, and D. J. Woehr, "Expanding the Criterion Domain? A Quantitative Review of the OCB Literature," *Journal of Applied Psychology* 92, no. 2 (2007), pp. 555–566.

51 B. B. Reiche et al., "Why Do Managers Engage in Trustworthy Behavior? A Multilevel Cross-Cultural Study in 18 Countries," *Personnel Psychology* 67 (2014), pp. 61–98.

52 D. S. Chiaburu and D. A. Harrison, "Do Peers Make the Place? Conceptual Synthesis and Meta-analysis of Coworker Effect on Perceptions, Attitudes, OCBs, and Performance," *Journal of Applied Psychology* 93, no. 5 (2008), pp. 1082–1103.

53 R. Ilies, I. S. Fulmer, M. Spitzmuller, and M. D. Johnson, "Personality and Citizenship Behavior: The Mediating Role of Job Satisfaction," *Journal of Applied Psychology* 94 (2009), pp. 945–959.

54 G. L. Lemoine, C. K. Parsons, and S. Kansara, "Above and Beyond, Again and Again: Self-Regulation in the Aftermath of Organizational Citizenship Behaviors," *Journal of Applied Psychology* 100, no. 1 (2015), pp. 40–55.

55 C. Vandenberghe, K. Bentein, R. Michon, J. Chebat, M. Tremblay, and J. Fils, "An Examination of the Role of Perceived Support and Employee Commitment in Employee-Customer Encounters," *Journal of Applied Psychology* 92, no. 4 (2007), pp. 1177–1187; and M. Schulte, C. Ostroff, S. Shmulyian, and A. Kinicki, "Organizational Climate Configurations: Relationships to Collective Attitudes, Customer Satisfaction, and Financial Performance," *Journal of Applied Psychology* 94 (2009), pp. 618–634.

56 B. Taylor, "Why Amazon Is Copying Zappos and Paying Employees to Quit," *Harvard Business Review*, April 14, 2014, https://hbr.org/2014/04/why-amazon-is-copying-zappos-and-paying-employees-to-quit/.

57 J. Barling, E. K. Kelloway, and R. D. Iverson, "High-Quality Work, Job Satisfaction, and Occupational Injuries," *Journal of Applied Psychology* 88, no. 2 (2003), pp. 276–283; and F. W. Bond and D. Bunce, "The Role of Acceptance and Job Control in Mental Health, Job Satisfaction, and Work Performance," *Journal of Applied Psychology* 88, no. 6 (2003), pp. 1057–1067.

58 Y. Georgellis and T. Lange, "Traditional versus Secular Values and the Job-Life Satisfaction Relationship across Europe," *British Journal of Management* 23 (2012), pp. 437–454.

59 O. Stavrova, T. Schlosser, and A. Baumert, "Life Satisfaction and Job-Seeking Behavior of the Unemployed: The Effect of Individual Differences in Justice Sensitivity," *Applied Psychology: An International Review* 64, no. 4 (2014), pp. 643–670.

60 J. Zhou and J. M. George, "When Job Dissatisfaction Leads to Creativity: Encouraging the Expression of Voice," *Academy of Management Journal*, August 2001, pp. 682–696; J. B. Olson-Buchanan and W. R. Boswell, "The Role of Employee Loyalty and Formality in Voicing Discontent," *Journal of Applied Psychology*, December 2002, pp. 1167–1174; and A. Davis-Blake, J. P. Broschak, and E. George, "Happy Together? How Using Nonstandard Workers Affects Exit, Voice, and Loyalty among Standard Employees," *Academy of Management Journal* 46, no. 4 (2003), pp. 475–485.

61 A. J. Nyberg and R. E. Ployhart, "Context-Emergent Turnover (CET) Theory: A Theory of Collective Turnover," *Academy of Management Review* 38 (2013), pp. 109–131.

62 P. E. Spector, S. Fox, L. M. Penney, K. Bruursema, A. Goh, and S. Kessler, "The Dimensionality of Counterproductivity: Are All Counterproductive Behaviors Created Equal?" *Journal of Vocational Behavior* 68, no. 3 (2006), pp. 446–460; and D. S. Chiaburu and D. A. Harrison, "Do Peers Make the Place? Conceptual Synthesis and Meta-analysis of Coworker Effect on Perceptions, Attitudes, OCBs, and Performance," *Journal of Applied Psychology* 93, no. 5 (2008), pp. 1082–1103.

63 P. A. O'Keefe, "Liking Work Really Does Matter," *New York Times*, September 7, 2014, p. 12.

64 D. Iliescu, D. Ispas, C. Sulea, and A. Ilie, "Vocational Fit and Counterproductive Work Behaviors: A Self-Regulation

Perspective," *Journal of Applied Psychology* 100, no. 1 (2015), pp. 21–39.

65 S. Gabriel, J. M. Diefendorff, M. M. Chandler, C. M. M. Pradco, and G. J. Greguras, "The Dynamic Relationships of Work Affect and Job Satisfaction with Perceptions of Fit," *Personnel Psychology* 67 (2014), pp. 389–420.

66 S. Diestel, J. Wegge, and K.-H. Schmidt, "The Impact of Social Context on the Relationship between Individual Job Satisfaction and Absenteeism: The Roles of Different Foci of Job Satisfaction and Work-Unit Absenteeism," *Academy of Management Journal* 57, no. 2 (2014), pp. 353–382.

67 H. Lian, D. L. Ferris, R. Morrison, and D. J. Brown, "Blame It on the Supervisor or the Subordinate? Reciprocal Relations between Abusive Supervision and Organizational Deviance," *Journal of Applied Psychology* 99, no. 4 (2014), pp. 651–664.

68 T. A. Beauregard, "Fairness Perceptions of Work–Life Balance Initiatives: Effects on Counterproductive Work Behavior," *British Journal of Management* 25 (2014), pp. 772–789.

69 D. Iliescu, D. Ispas, C. Sulea, and A. Ilie, "Vocational Fit and Counterproductive Work Behaviors: A Self-Regulation Perspective," *Journal of Applied Psychology* 100, no. 1 (2015), pp. 21–39.

70 S. Gabriel, J. M. Diefendorff, M. M. Chandler, C. M. M. Pradco, and G. J. Greguras, "The Dynamic Relationships of Work Affect and Job Satisfaction with Perceptions of Fit," *Personnel Psychology* 67 (2014), pp. 389–420.

71 S. Diestel, J. Wegge, and K.-H. Schmidt, "The Impact of Social Context on the Relationship between Individual Job Satisfaction and Absenteeism: The Roles of Different Foci of Job Satisfaction and Work-Unit Absenteeism," *Academy of Management Journal* 57, no. 2 (2014), pp. 353–382.

72 J. F. Ybema, P. G. W. Smulders, and P. M. Bongers, "Antecedents and Consequences of Employee Absenteeism: A Longitudinal Perspective on the Role of Job Satisfaction and Burnout," *European Journal of Work and Organizational Psychology* 19 (2010), pp. 102–124.

73 J. P. Hausknecht, N. J. Hiller, and R. J. Vance, "Work-Unit Absenteeism: Effects of Satisfaction, Commitment, Labor Market Conditions, and Time," *Academy of Management Journal* 51, no. 6 (2008), pp. 1123–1245.

74 G. Chen, R. E. Ployhart, H. C. Thomas, N. Anderson, and P. D. Bliese, "The Power of Momentum: A New Model of Dynamic Relationships between Job Satisfaction Change and Turnover Intentions," *Academy of Management Journal*, February 2011, pp. 159–181; and R. W. Griffeth, P. W. Hom, and S. Gaertner, "A Meta-analysis of Antecedents and Correlates of Employee Turnover: Update, Moderator Tests, and Research Implications for the Next Millennium," *Journal of Management* 26, no. 3 (2000), p. 479.

75 D. Liu, T. R. Mitchell, T. W. Lee, B. C. Holtom, and T. R. Hinkin, "When Employees Are Out of Step with Coworkers: How Job Satisfaction Trajectory and Dispersion Influence Individual- and Unit-Level Voluntary Turnover," *Academy of Management Journal* 55, no. 6 (2012), pp. 1360–1380.

76 T. H. Lee, B. Gerhart, I. Weller, and C. O. Trevor, "Understanding Voluntary Turnover: Path-Specific Job Satisfaction Effects and the Importance of Unsolicited Job Offers," *Academy of Management Journal* 51, no. 4 (2008), pp. 651–671.

77 K. Jiang, D. Liu, P. F. McKay, T. W. Lee, and T. R. Mitchell, "When and How Is Job Embeddedness Predictive of Turnover? A Meta-analytic Investigation," *Journal of Applied Psychology* 97 (2012), pp. 1077–1096.

78 G. J. Blau and K. R. Boal, "Conceptualizing How Job Involvement and Organizational Commitment Affect Turnover and Absenteeism," *Academy of Management Review*, April 1987, p. 290.

79 O. N. Solinger, W. van Olffen, and R. A. Roe, "Beyond the Three-Component Model of Organizational Commitment," *Journal of Applied Psychology* 93 (2008), pp. 70–83.

80 N. J. Allen and J. P Meyer, "The Measurement and Antecedents of Affective, Continuance, and Normative Commitment to the Organization," *Journal of Occupational Psychology* 63 (1990), pp. 1–18; and J. P. Meyer, N. J. Allen, and C. A. Smith, "Commitment to Organizations and Occupations: Extension and Test of a Three-Component Conceptualization," *Journal of Applied Psychology* 78 (1993), pp. 538–551.

81 M. Riketta, "Attitudinal Organizational Commitment and Job Performance: A Meta-analysis," *Journal of Organizational Behavior*, March 2002, pp. 257–266.

82 T. A. Wright and D. G. Bonett, "The Moderating Effects of Employee Tenure on the Relation between Organizational Commitment and Job Performance: A Meta-analysis," *Journal of Applied Psychology*, December 2002, pp. 1183–1190.

83 T. W. H. Ng, D. C. Feldman, and S. S. K. Lam, "Psychological Contract Breaches, Organizational Commitment, and Innovation-Related Behaviors: A Latent Growth Modeling Approach," *Journal of Applied Psychology* 95 (2010), pp. 744–751.

84 See, for example, W. Hom, R. Katerberg, and C. L. Hulin, "Comparative Examination of Three Approaches to the Prediction of Turnover," *Journal of Applied Psychology*, June 1979, pp. 280–290; H. Angle and J. Perry, "Organizational Commitment: Individual and Organizational Influence," *Work and Occupations*, May 1983, pp. 123–146; J. L. Pierce and R. B. Dunham, "Organizational Commitment: Pre-Employment Propensity and Initial Work Experiences," *Journal of Management*, Spring 1987, pp. 163–178; and T. Simons and Q. Roberson, "Why Managers Should Care about Fairness: The Effects of Aggregate Justice Perceptions on Organizational Outcomes," *Journal of Applied Psychology* 88, no. 3 (2003), pp. 432–443.

85 Y. Gong, K. S. Law, S. Chang, and K. R. Xin, "Human Resources Management and Firm Performance: The Differential Role of Managerial Affective and Continuance Commitment," *Journal of Applied Psychology* 94, no. 1 (2009), pp. 263–275.

86 A. A. Luchak and I. R. Gellatly, "A Comparison of Linear and Nonlinear Relations between Organizational Commitment and Work Outcomes," *Journal of Applied Psychology* 92, no. 3 (2007), pp. 786–793.

87 See, for example, J. M. Diefendorff, D. J. Brown, and A. M. Kamin, "Examining the Roles of Job Involvement and Work Centrality in Predicting Organizational Citizenship Behaviors and Job Performance," *Journal of Organizational Behavior*, February 2002, pp. 93–108.

88 Based on G. J. Blau and K. R. Boal, "Conceptualizing How Job Involvement and Organizational Commitment Affect Turnover and Absenteeism," *Academy of Management Review*, April 1987, p. 290.

89 G. Chen and R. J. Klimoski, "The Impact of Expectations on Newcomer Performance in Teams as Mediated by Work Characteristics, Social Exchanges, and Empowerment," *Academy of Management Journal* 46, no. 5 (2003), pp. 591–607; A. Ergeneli, G. Saglam, and S. Metin, "Psychological Empowerment and Its Relationship to Trust in Immediate Managers," *Journal of Business Research*, January 2007, pp. 41–49; and S. E. Seibert, S. R. Silver, and W. A. Randolph, "Taking Empowerment to the Next Level: A Multiple-Level Model of Empowerment, Performance, and Satisfaction," *Academy of Management Journal* 47, no. 3 (2004), pp. 332–349.

90 B. J. Avolio, W. Zhu, W. Koh, and P. Bhatia, "Transformational Leadership and Organizational Commitment: Mediating Role of Psychological Empowerment and Moderating Role of Structural Distance," *Journal of Organizational Behavior* 25, no. 8 (2004), pp. 951–968.

91 "100 Best Companies to Work For," *Fortune*, February 2015, http://www.fortune.com/best-companies/.

92 L. Rhoades, R. Eisenberger, and S. Armeli, "Affective Commitment to the Organization: The Contribution of Perceived Organizational Support," *Journal of Applied Psychology* 86, no. 5 (2001), pp. 825–836.

93 B. L. Rich, J. A. Lepine, and E. R. Crawford, "Job Engagement: Antecedents and Effects on Job Performance," *Academy of Management Journal* 53, no. 3 (2010), pp. 617–635.

94 B. L. Rich, J. A. Lepine, and E. R. Crawford, "Job Engagement: Antecedents and Effects on Job Performance," *Academy of Management Journal* 53, no. 3 (2010), pp. 617–635; and J. B. James, S. McKechnie, and J. Swanberg, "Predicting Employee Engagement in an Age-Diverse Retail Workforce," *Journal of Organizational Behavior* 32, no. 2 (2011), pp. 173–196.

95 "Building a Better Workforce," *PROFIT*, February 16, 2011, http://www.profitguide.com/manage-grow/human-resources/building-a-better-workforce-30073.

96 "Building a Better Workforce," *PROFIT*, February 16, 2011, http://www.profitguide.com/manage-grow/human-resources/building-a-better-workforce-30073.

97 T. Armstrong and R. Wright, "Employee Engagement: Leveraging the Science to Inspire Great Performance," *The Conference Board of Canada*, July 13, 2016.

98 S. Crabtree, "Worldwide, 13% of Employees Are Engaged at Work," *Gallup World*, October 8, 2013; and http://www.molson-coors.com/en/Responsibility/What%20Matters%20To%20Us/Employees%20Community/Our%20Employees/Engagement.aspx.

99 Based on C. Chase, "Butler Charles MacPherson Is Taking Ford of Canada's Service Advisors to School," *Driving*, August 8, 2014, http://driving.ca/ford/auto-news/how-a-butler-is-helping-to-improve-fords-customer-service; H. Kafoury, "Creating Customer Loyalty, One Employee at a Time: Engaging Workers Can Start with Mutual Respect between Management and Staff," *Gazette* (Montreal), January 21, 2014, p. B2; and J. Lofaro, "Charles the Butler in Ottawa to Train Ford Employees Proper Etiquette," *Metro* (Ottawa), August 6, 2014, http://metronews.ca/news/ottawa/1119408/charles-the-butler-in-ottawa-to-train-ford-employees-proper-etiquette/.

100 N. R. Lockwood, *Leveraging Employee Engagement for Competitive Advantage* (Alexandria, VA: Society for Human Resource Management, 2007); and R. J. Vance, *Employee Engagement and Commitment* (Alexandria, VA: Society for Human Resource Management, 2006).

101 N. R. Lockwood, *Leveraging Employee Engagement for Competitive Advantage* (Alexandria, VA: Society for Human Resource Management, 2007); and R. J. Vance, *Employee Engagement and Commitment* (Alexandria, VA: Society for Human Resource Management, 2006).

102 "Employee Engagement," *Workforce Management*, February 2013, p. 19; and "The Cornerstone OnDemand 2013 U.S. Employee Report," *Cornerstone OnDemand*, 2013, http://www.cornerstoneondemand.com/resources/research/survey-2013.

103 "Employee Engagement," *Workforce Management*, February 2013, p. 19; and "The Cornerstone OnDemand 2013 U.S. Employee Report," *Cornerstone OnDemand*, 2013, http://www.cornerstoneondemand.com/resources/research/survey-2013.

104 Y. Brunetto, S. T. T. Teo, K. Shacklock, and R. Farr-Wharton, "Emotional Intelligence, Job Satisfaction, Well-being and Engagement: Explaining Organisational Commitment and Turnover Intentions in Policing," *Human Resource Management Journal*, 2012, pp. 428–441.

105 P. Petrou, E. Demerouti, M. C. W. Peeters, W. B. Schaufeli, and J. Hetland, "Crafting a Job on a Daily Basis: Contextual Correlates and the Link to Work Engagement," *Journal of Organizational Behavior*, November 2012, pp. 1120–1141.

106 W. H. Macey and B. Schneider, "The Meaning of Employee Engagement," *Industrial and Organizational Psychology* 1 (2008), pp. 3–30; and A. Saks, "The Meaning and Bleeding of Employee Engagement: How Muddy Is the Water?" *Industrial and Organizational Psychology* 1 (2008), pp. 40–43.

107 J. M. George, "The Wider Context, Costs, and Benefits of Work Engagement," *European Journal of Work and Organizational Psychology* 20, no. 1 (2011), pp. 53–59; and J. R. B. Halbesleben, J. Harvey, and M. C. Bolino, "Too Engaged? A Conservation of Resources View of the Relationship between Work Engagement and Work Interference with Family," *Journal of Applied Psychology* 94, no. 6 (2009), pp. 1452–1465.

108 Vignette based on M. Braga, "Canadian Tech Companies Say They Value Diversity — But What Are They Doing About It?" *CBC News*, July 11, 2017, http://www.cbc.ca/news/technology/canada-tech-companies-diversity-reports-2017-1.4194556; and http://ladieslearningcode.com/annualreport2016/.

109 A. H. Eagly and J. L. Chin, "Are Memberships in Race, Ethnicity, and Gender Categories Merely Surface Characteristics?" *American Psychologist* 65 (2010), pp. 934–935.

110 W. J. Casper, J. H. Wayne, and J. G. Manegold, "Who Will We Recruit? Targeting Deep- and Surface-Level Diversity with Human Resource Policy Advertising," *Human Resource Management* 52, no. 3 (2013), pp. 311–332.

111 Corus Entertainment, "Accessibility & Diversity," accessed October, 2014, http://www.corusent.com/home/Corporate/AboutCorus/AccessibilityDiversity/tabid/2572/Default.aspx.

112 N. Girouard, D. Stack, and M. O'Neill-Gilbert, "Ethnic Differences during Social Interactions of Preschoolers in Same-Ethnic and Cross-Ethnic Dyads," *European Journal of Developmental Psychology* 8, no. 2 (2011), pp. 185–202.

113 A. Chapin, "Special Report: Diversity Knocks," *Canadian Business*, October 7, 2010.

114 D. A. Thomas and R. J. Ely, "Making Differences Matter: A New Paradigm for Managing Diversity," *Harvard Business Review*, September 1996, pp. 79–90; C. L. Holladay and M. A. Quiñones, "The Influence of Training Focus and Trainer Characteristics on Diversity Training Effectiveness," *Academy of Management Learning and Education* 7, no. 3 (2008), pp. 343–354; and R. Anand and M. Winters, "A Retrospective View of Corporate Diversity Training from 1964 to the Present," *Academy of Management Learning and Education* 7, no. 3 (2008), pp. 356–372.

115 L. Legault, J. Gutsell, and M. Inzlicht, "Ironic Effects of Anti-Prejudice Messages," *Psychological Science*, July 6, 2011, http://www.psychologicalscience.org/index.php/news/releases/ironic-effects-of-anti-prejudice-messages.html.

116 http://betakit.com/accessnow-founder-maayan-ziv-talks-business-benefits-of-accessibility-at-techto/.

117 A. Pomeroy, "Cultivating Female Leaders," *HR Magazine*, February 2007, pp. 44–50.

118 Based on P. Jeffery, "A Call to Action," *FP Magazine*, June 21, 2011.

119 Based on A. L. Molinsky, T. H. Davenport, B. Iyer, and C. Davidson, "3 Skills Every 21st-Century Manager Needs," *Harvard Business Review*, January/February 2012.

120 P. C. Earley and E. Mosakowski, "Cultural Intelligence," *Harvard Business Review*, October 2004, pp. 139–146.

121 S. S. Ramalu, R. C. Rose, N. Kumar, and J. Uli, "Doing Business in Global Arena: An Examination of the Relationship between Cultural Intelligence and Cross-Cultural Adjustment," *Asian Academy of Management Journal* 15, no. 1 (2010), pp. 79–97.

122 M. Gorji and H. Ghareseflo, "The Survey of Relationship between Cultural Intelligence and Emotional Intelligence with Employee's

Performance," *International Proceedings of Economics Development & Research* 25 (2011), p. 175.

123 J. Sanchez-Burks, F. Lee, R. Nisbett, I. Choi, S. Zhao, and J. Koo, "Conversing across Cultures: East-West Communication Styles in Work and Nonwork Contexts," *Journal of Personality and Social Psychology* 85, no. 2 (2003), pp. 363–372.

124 P. C. Earley and E. Mosakowski, "Cultural Intelligence," *Harvard Business Review*, October 2004, pp. 139–146.

125 A. L. Molinsky, T. H. Davenport, B. Iyer, and C. Davidson, "3 Skills Every 21st-Century Manager Needs," *Harvard Business Review*, January/February 2012.

126 World Business Culture, "Doing Business in South Korea," http://www.worldbusinessculture.com/Business-in-South-Korea.html.

127 C. Osborne, "South Korea Hits 100% Mark in Wireless Broadband," *CNET*, July 23, 2012, http://www.cnet.com/news/south-korea-hits-100-mark-in-wireless-broadband/.

128 Based on E. Snape, C. Lo, and T. Redman, "The Three-Component Model of Occupational Commitment: A Comparative Study of Chinese and British Accountants," *Journal of Cross-Cultural Psychology*, November 2008, pp. 765–781; and Y. Cheng and M. S. Stockdale, "The Validity of the Three-Component Model of Organizational Commitment in a Chinese Context," *Journal of Vocational Behavior*, June 2003, pp. 465–489.

129 J. M. Twenge, W. K. Campbell, and E. C. Freeman, "Generational Differences in Young Adults' Life Goals, Concern for Others, and Civic Orientation, 1966–2009," *Journal of Personality and Social Psychology* 102 (2012), pp. 1045–1062; M. Hartman, "Millennials at Work: Young and Callow, Like Their Parents," *New York Times*, March 25, 2014, p. F4; J. Jin and J. Rounds, "Stability and Change in Work Values: A Meta-analysis of Longitudinal Studies," *Journal of Vocational Behavior* 80 (2012), pp. 326–339; C. Lourosa-Ricardo, "How America Gives," *Wall Street Journal*, December 15, 2014, p. R3; "Millennials Rule," *New York Times Education Life*, April 12, 2015, p. 4; G. Ruffenach, "A Generational Gap: Giving to Charity," *Wall Street Journal*, January 20, 2015, p. R4; and S. W. Lester, R. L. Standifer, N. J. Schultz, and J. M. Windsor, "Actual versus Perceived Generational Differences at Work: An Empirical Examination," *Journal of Leadership & Organizational Studies* 19 (2012), pp. 341–354.

130 L. Gilman, "Memo App Lets Workers Vent Anonymously about the Boss," *Wall Street Journal*, January 21, 2015, p. B7; Glassdoor.com; A. S. McCance, C. D. Nye, L. Wang, K. S. Jones, and C. Chiu, "Alleviating the Burden of Emotional Labor: The Role of Social Sharing," *Journal of Management*, February 2013, pp. 392–415; R. E. Silverman, "Are You Happy in Your Job? Bosses Push Weekly Surveys," *Wall Street Journal*, December 3, 2014, pp. B1, B4; and R. E. Silverman, "Workers Really Do Put on a Happy Face for the Boss," *Wall Street Journal*, January 29, 2015.

131 A. B. Bakker, M. Tims, and D. Derks, "Proactive Personality and Job Performance: The Role of Job Crafting and Work Engagement," *Human Relations*, October 2012, pp. 1359–1178; A. Wrzesniewski, J. M. Berg, and J. E. Dutton, "Turn the Job You Have into the Job You Want," *Harvard Business Review*, June 2010, pp. 114–117; A. Wrzesniewski and J. E. Dutton, "Crafting a Job: Revisioning Employees as Active Crafters of Their Work," *Academy of Management Review* 26 (2010), pp. 179–201; and G. R. Slemp and D. A. Vella-Brodrick, "Optimising Employee Mental Health: The Relationship between Intrinsic Need Satisfaction, Job Crafting, and Employee Well-Being," *Journal of Happiness Studies* 15, no. 4 (2014), pp. 957–977.

132 S. Goldenberg, "Exposing Hidden Bias at Google," *New York Times*, September 25, 2014, pp. B1, B9; S. Lohr, "The Google Formula for Success," *New York Times*, September 29, 2014, p. B8; N. Wingfield, "Microsoft Chief Backpedals on Women's Pay," *New York Times*, October 10, 2014, pp. B7–B8; and E. Zell, Z. Krizan, and S. R.

Teeter, "Evaluating Gender Similarities and Differences Using Metasynthesis," *American Psychologist* 70 (2015), pp. 10–20.

OB on the Edge: Stress at Work

1 Based on W. Immen, "In This Office, Desks Are for Working, Not Eating Lunch," *Globe and Mail*, February 27, 2017, https://beta.theglobeandmail.com/report-on-business/industry-news/property-report/in-this-office-desks-are-for-working-not-eating-lunch/article34153148/; and A. O'Neill, "Doing Away With 'Dining al Desko.'" *Globe and Mail*, May 26, 2017, https://beta.theglobeandmail.com/report-on-business/careers/leadership-lab/doing-away-with-dining-al-desko/article35083814/.

2 Based on Statistics Canada, "Perceived Life Stress, Quite a Lot, by Sex, by Province and Territory," last modified June 12, 2014, http://www.statcan.gc.ca/tables-tableaux/sum-som/l01/cst01/health107b-eng.htm.

3 http://www.cbc.ca/news/business/canada-economy-depression-anixety-1.3744300.

4 J. O'Kane, "Canada's Work-Life Balance More Off-Kilter Than Ever," *Globe and Mail*, October 25, 2012.

5 J. O'Kane, "Canada's Work-Life Balance More Off-Kilter Than Ever," *Globe and Mail*, October 25, 2012.

6 Based on Statistics Canada, "Perceived Life Stress, Quite a Lot, by Sex, by Province and Territory," last modified June 12, 2014, http://www.statcan.gc.ca/tables-tableaux/sum-som/l01/cst01/health107b-eng.htm. Note: Statistics Canada has not collected more recent data due to cutbacks by the Harper government.

7 Adapted from R. S. Schuler, "Definition and Conceptualization of Stress in Organizations," *Organizational Behavior and Human Performance*, April 1980, p. 189. For an updated review of definitions, see C. L. Cooper, P. J. Dewe, and M. P. O'Driscoll, *Organizational Stress: A Review and Critique of Theory, Research, and Applications* (Thousand Oaks, CA: Sage, 2002).

8 See, for example, M. A. Cavanaugh, W. R. Boswell, M. V. Roehling, and J. W. Boudreau, "An Empirical Examination of Self-Reported Work Stress among U.S. Managers," *Journal of Applied Psychology*, February 2000, pp. 65–74.

9 S. Shellenbarger, "When Stress Is Good for You," *Wall Street Journal*, January 24, 2012, pp. D1, D5.

10 S. Shellenbarger, "When Stress Is Good for You," *Wall Street Journal*, January 24, 2012, pp. D1, D5.

11 N. P. Podsakoff, J. A. LePine, and M. A. LePine, "Differential Challenge-Hindrance Stressor Relationships with Job Attitudes, Turnover Intentions, Turnover, and Withdrawal Behavior: A Meta-analysis," *Journal of Applied Psychology* 92, no. 2 (2007), pp. 438–454; and J. A. LePine, M. A. LePine, and C. L. Jackson, "Challenge and Hindrance Stress: Relationships with Exhaustion, Motivation to Learn, and Learning Performance," *Journal of Applied Psychology*, October 2004, pp. 883–891.

12 L. W. Hunter and S. M. B. Thatcher, "Feeling the Heat: Effects of Stress, Commitment, and Job Experience on Job Performance," *Academy of Management Journal* 50, no. 4 (2007), pp. 953–968.

13 J. C. Wallace, B. D. Edwards, T. Arnold, M. L. Frazier, and D. M. Finch, "Work Stressors, Role-Based Performance, and the Moderating Influence of Organizational Support," *Journal of Applied Psychology* 94, no. 1 (2009), pp. 254–262.

14 "Most Stressful Jobs of 2017," http://www.careercast.com/jobs-rated/most-stressful-jobs-2017; and "Least Stressful Jobs of 2017," http://www.careercast.com/jobs-rated/least-stressful-jobs-2017.

15 "Stress in America: Paying with Our Health," *American Psychological Association*, February 4, 2015, p. 8.

16 J. de Jonge and C. Dormann, "Stressors, Resources, and Strain at Work: A Longitudinal Test of the Triple-Match Principle," *Journal of Applied Psychology* 91, no. 5 (2006), pp. 1359–1374;

K. Daniels, N. Beesley, A. Cheyne, and V. Wimalasiri, "Coping Processes Linking the Demands-Control-Support Model, Affect and Risky Decisions at Work," *Human Relations* 61, no. 6 (2008), pp. 845–874; and M. van den Tooren and J. de Jonge, "Managing Job Stress in Nursing: What Kind of Resources Do We Need?" *Journal of Advanced Nursing* 63, no. 1 (2008), pp. 75–84.

17 E. A. Rafferty and M. A. Griffin, "Perceptions of Organizational Change: A Stress and Coping Perspective," *Journal of Applied Psychology* 71, no. 5 (2007), pp. 1154–1162.

18 R. Ilies, N. Dimotakis, and I. E. De Pater, "Psychological and Physiological Reactions to High Workloads: Implications for Well-Being," *Personnel Psychology*, Summer 2010, pp. 407–436; A. B. Bakker, E. Demerouti, and A. I. Sanz-Vergel, "Burnout and Work Engagement: The JD–R Approach," *Annual Review of Organizational Psychology and Organizational Behavior* 1 (2014), pp. 389–411.

19 G. W. Evans and D. Johnson, "Stress and Open-Office Noise," *Journal of Applied Psychology*, October 2000, pp. 779–783.

20 T. M. Glomb, J. D. Kammeyer-Mueller, and M. Rotundo, "Emotional Labor Demands and Compensating Wage Differentials," *Journal of Applied Psychology*, August 2004, pp. 700–714; and A. A. Grandey, "When 'The Show Must Go On': Surface Acting and Deep Acting as Determinants of Emotional Exhaustion and Peer-Rated Service Delivery," *Academy of Management Journal*, February 2003, pp. 86–96.

21 S. Lim, L. M. Cortina, and V. J. Magley, "Personal and Workgroup Incivility: Impact on Work and Health Outcomes," *Journal of Applied Psychology* 93, no. 1 (2008), pp. 95–107; N. T. Buchanan and L. F. Fitzgerald, "Effects of Racial and Sexual Harassment on Work and the Psychological Well-Being of African American Women," *Journal of Occupational Health Psychology* 13, no. 2 (2008), pp. 137–151; C. R. Willness, P. Steel, and K. Lee, "A Meta-analysis of the Antecedents and Consequences of Workplace Sexual Harassment," *Personnel Psychology* 60, no. 1 (2007), pp. 127–162; and B. Moreno-Jiménez, A. Rodríguez-Muñoz, J. C. Pastor, A. I. Sanz-Vergel, and E. Garrosa, "The Moderating Effects of Psychological Detachment and Thoughts of Revenge in Workplace Bullying," *Personality and Individual Differences* 46, no. 3 (2009), pp. 359–364.

22 L. Yang, J. Bauer, R. E. Johnson, M. W. Groer, and K. Salomon, "Physiological Mechanisms That Underlie the Effects of Interactional Unfairness on Deviant Behavior: The Role of Cortisol Activity," *Journal of Applied Psychology* 99 (2014), pp. 310–321.

23 M. T. Schmitt, N. R. Branscombe, T. Postmes, and A. Garcia, "The Consequences of Perceived Discrimination for Psychological Well-Being: A Meta-analytic Review," *Psychological Bulletin* 140 (2014), pp. 921–948.

24 J. O'Reilly, S. L. Robinson, J. L. Berdahl, and S. Banki, "Is Negative Attention Better Than No Attention? The Comparative Effects of Ostracism and Harassment at Work," *Organization Science* (2014), pp. 774–793.

25 "Stress in America: Paying with Our Health," *American Psychological Association*, February 4, 2015, http://www.apa.org/news/press/releases/stress/2014/stress-report.pdf.

26 G. Livingston, "Survey Says: We're Stressed (and Not Loving It)," *Globe and Mail*, February 2, 2015, https://www.theglobeandmail.com/report-on-business/careers/career-advice/life-at-work/survey-says-were-stressed-and-not-loving-it/article22722102/.

27 Q. Hu, W. B. Schaufeli, and T. W. Taris, "The Job Demands–Resources Model: An Analysis of Additive and Joint Effects of Demands and Resources," *Journal of Vocational Behavior* 79, no. 1 (2011), pp. 181–190.

28 R. S. Schuler, "Definition and Conceptualization of Stress in Organizations," *Organizational Behavior and Human Performance*, April 1980, p. 191; and R. L. Kahn and P. Byosiere, "Stress in

Organizations," *Organizational Behavior and Human Performance*, April 1980, pp. 604–610.

29 M. Kivimäki, J. Head, J. E. Ferrie, E. Brunner, M. G. Marmot, J. Vahtera, and M. J. Shipley, "Why Is Evidence on Job Strain and Coronary Heart Disease Mixed? An Illustration of Measurement Challenges in the Whitehall II Study," *Psychosomatic Medicine* 68, no. 3 (2006), pp. 398–401.

30 M. Borritz, K. B. Christensen, U. Bültmann, R. Rugulies, T. Lund, I Andersen, E. Villadsen, F. Didreichsen, and T. S. Krisensen, "Impact on Burnout and Psychosocial Work Characteristics on Future Long-Term Sickness Absence, Prospective Results of the Danish PUMA Study among Human Service Workers," *Journal of Occupational and Environmental Medicine* 52, no. 10 (2010), pp. 964–970.

31 R. Ilies, N. Dimotakis, and I. E. DePater, "Psychological and Physiological Reactions to High Workloads: Implications for Well-Being," *Personnel Psychology* 63, no. 2 (2010), pp. 407–463.

32 D. Örtqvist and J. Wincent, "Prominent Consequences of Role Stress: A Meta-analytic Review," *International Journal of Stress Management* 13, no. 4 (2006), pp. 399–422.

33 J. J. Hakanen, A. B. Bakker, and M. Jokisaari, "A 35-Year Follow-Up Study on Burnout among Finnish Employees," *Journal of Occupational Health Psychology* 16, no. 3 (2011), pp. 345–360; E. R. Crawford, J. A. LePine, and B. L. Rich, "Linking Job Demands and Resources to Employee Engagement and Burnout: A Theoretical Extension and Meta-analytic Test," *Journal of Applied Psychology* 95, no. 5 (2010), pp. 834–848; and G. A. Chung-Yan, "The Nonlinear Effects of Job Complexity and Autonomy on Job Satisfaction, Turnover, and Psychological Well-Being," *Journal of Occupational Health Psychology* 15, no. 3 (2010), pp. 237–251.

34 L. L. Meier, N. K. Semmer, A. Elfering, and N. Jacobshagen, "The Double Meaning of Control: Three-Way Interactions between Internal Resources, Job Control, and Stressors at Work," *Journal of Occupational Health Psychology* 13, no. 3 (2008), pp. 244–258.

35 E. M. de Croon, J. K. Sluiter, R. W. B. Blonk, J. P. J. Broersen, and M. H. W. Frings-Dresen, "Stressful Work, Psychological Job Strain, and Turnover: A 2-Year Prospective Cohort Study of Truck Drivers," *Journal of Applied Psychology*, June 2004, pp. 442–454; R. Cropanzano, D. E. Rupp, and Z. S. Byrne, "The Relationship of Emotional Exhaustion to Work Attitudes, Job Performance, and Organizational Citizenship Behaviors," *Journal of Applied Psychology*, February 2003, pp. 160–169; and S. Diestel and K. Schmidt, "Costs of Simultaneous Coping with Emotional Dissonance and Self-Control Demands at Work: Results from Two German Samples," *Journal of Applied Psychology* 96, no. 3 (2011), pp. 643–653.

36 S. E. R. Crawford, J. A. LePine, and B. L. Rich, "Linking Job Demands and Resources to Employee Engagement and Burnout: A Theoretical Extension and Meta-analytic Test," *Journal of Applied Psychology* 95, no. 5 (2010), pp. 834–848.

37 See J. B. Halbesleben, "Sources of Social Support and Burnout: A Meta-analytic Test of the Conservation of Resources Model," *Journal of Applied Psychology* 91, no. 5 (2006), pp. 1134–1145; N. Bolger and D. Amarel, "Effects of Social Support Visibility on Adjustment to Stress: Experimental Evidence," *Journal of Applied Psychology* 92, no. 3 (2007), pp. 458–475; and C. Fernet, M. Gagné, and S. Austin, "When Does Quality of Relationships with Coworkers Predict Burnout over Time? The Moderating Role of Work Motivation," *Journal of Organizational Behavior* 31 (2010), pp. 1163–1180.

38 J. B. Avey, F. Luthans, and S. M. Jensen, "Psychological Capital: A Positive Resource for Combating Employee Stress and Turnover," *Human Resource Management*, September–October 2009, pp. 677–693.

39 See, for example, C. M. Middeldorp, D. C. Cath, A. L. Beem, G. Willemsen, and D. I. Boomsma, "Life Events, Anxious Depression, and Personality: A Prospective and Genetic Study," *Psychological*

Medicine 38, no. 11 (2008), pp. 1557–1565; and A. A. Uliaszek, R. E. Zinbarg, S. Mineka, M. G. Craske, J. M. Sutton, J. W. Griffith, R. Rose, A. Waters, and C. Hammen, "The Role of Neuroticism and Extraversion in the Stress-Anxiety and Stress-Depression Relationships," *Anxiety, Stress, and Coping* 23, no. 4 (2010), pp. 363–381.

40 J. D. Kammeyer-Mueller, T. A. Judge, and B. A. Scott, "The Role of Core Self-Evaluations in the Coping Process," *Journal of Applied Psychology* 94, no. 1 (2009), pp. 177–195.

41 R. J. Burke, A. M. Richardson, and M. Mortinussen, "Workaholism among Norwegian Managers: Work and Well-Being Outcomes," *Journal of Organizational Change Management* 7 (2004), pp. 459–470; and W. B. Schaufeli, T. W. Taris, and W. van Rhenen, "Workaholism, Burnout, and Work Engagement: Three of a Kind or Three Different Kinds of Employee Well-Being," *Applied Psychology: An International Review* 57, no. 2 (2008), pp. 173–203.

42 R. W. Renn, D. G. Allen, and T. M. Huning, "Empirical Examination of Individual-Level Personality-Based Theory of Self-Management Failure," *Journal of Organizational Behavior* 32, no. 1 (2011), pp. 25–43; and P. Gröpel and P. Steel, "A Mega-Trial Investigation of Goal Setting, Interest Enhancement, and Energy on Procrastination," *Personality and Individual Differences* 45, no. 5 (2008), pp. 406–411.

43 S. Klaperski, B. von Dawans, M. Heinrichs, and R. Fuchs, "Does the Level of Physical Exercise Affect Physiological and Psychological Responses to Psychosocial Stress in Women?" *Psychology of Sport and Exercise* 14, no. 2 (2013), pp. 266–274.

44 K. M. Richardson and H. R. Rothstein, "Effects of Occupational Stress Management Intervention Programs: A Meta-analysis," *Journal of Occupational Health Psychology* 13, no. 1 (2008), pp. 69–93.

45 V. C. Hahn, C. Binnewies, S. Sonnentag, and E. J. Mojza, "Learning How to Recover From Job Stress: Effects of a Recovery Training Program on Recovery, Recovery-Related Self-Efficacy, and Well-Being," *Journal of Occupational Health Psychology* 16, no. 2 (2011), pp. 202–216; and C. Binnewies, S. Sonnentag, and E. J. Mojza, "Recovery during the Weekend and Fluctuations in Weekly Job Performance: A Week-Level Study Examining Intra-Individual Relationships," *Journal of Occupational and Organizational Psychology* 83, no. 2 (2010), pp. 419–441.

46 "Three Canadian Companies Lauded for Employee Wellness Programs," hrreporter.com, December 9, 2016, http://www.hrreporter.com/article/31948-three-canadian-companies-lauded-for-employee-wellness-programs/.

47 N. Reese, "10 Simple Ways to Relieve Stress," July 1, 2016, https://www.healthline.com/health/10-ways-to-relieve-stress#1.

48 Sun Life Financial, *Sun Life-Buffett National Wellness Survey 2013*, 2013, http://www.sunlife.ca.

49 "Cdn Employers Not Measuring Wellness Outcomes: Survey," *Benefits Canada*, May 4, 2011, http://www.benefitscanada.com/news/cnd-employers-not-measuring-wellness-outcomes-survey-16510.

50 E. R. Greenglass and L. Fiksenbaum, "Proactive Coping, Positive Affect, and Well-Being: Testing for Mediation Using Path Analysis," *European Psychologist* 14, no. 1 (2009), pp. 29–39; and P. Miquelon and R. J. Vallerand, "Goal Motives, Well-Being, and Physical Health: Happiness and Self-Realization as Psychological Resources under Challenge," *Motivation and Emotion* 30, no. 4 (2006), pp. 259–272.

51 M. M. Butts, R. J. Vandenberg, D. M. DeJoy, B. S. Schaffer, and M. G. Wilson, "Individual Reactions to High Involvement Work Processes: Investigating the Role of Empowerment and Perceived Organizational Support," *Journal of Occupational Health Psychology* 14, no. 2 (2009), pp. 122–136.

52 L. Blue, "Making Good Health Easy," *Time*, November 12, 2009, http://www.time.com; and M. Andrews, "America's Best Health Plans," *US News and World Report*, November 5, 2007, pp. 54–60.

53 L. Blue, "Making Good Health Easy," *Time*, November 12, 2009, http://www.time.com; and M. Andrews, "America's Best Health Plans," *US News and World Report*, November 5, 2007, pp. 54–60.

54 K. M. Richardson and H. R. Rothstein, "Effects of Occupational Stress Management Intervention Programs: A Meta-analysis," *Journal of Occupational Health Psychology* 13, no. 1 (2008), pp. 69–93.

55 Based on S. Martin, "Money Is the Stressor for Americans," *Monitor on Psychology*, December 2008, pp. 28–29; *Helicobacter pylori and Peptic Ulcer Disease*, Centers for Disease Control and Prevention, U.S. Department of Health and Human Services; and M. Maynard, "Maybe the Toughest Job Aloft," *New York Times*, August 15, 2006, pp. C1, C6.

Chapter 4

1 Opening vignette based on R. Blackwell, "Lee Valley Tools Founder Leonard Lee Treated Customers as Friends," *Globe and Mail*, July 15, 2016.

2 See, for example, G. P. Latham and C. C. Pinder, "Work Motivation Theory and Research at the Dawn of the Twenty-First Century," *Annual Review of Psychology* 56 (2005), pp. 485–516; and C. C. Pinder, *Work Motivation in Organizational Behavior*, 2nd ed. (London, UK: Psychology Press, 2008).

3 S. Crabtree, "Worldwide, 13% of Employees Are Engaged at Work," *Gallup World*, October 8, 2013, http://www.gallup.com/poll/165269/worldwide-employees-engaged-work.aspx.

4 "The 2014 Wasting Time at Work Survey: Everything You've Always Wanted to Know about Wasting Time in the Office," *Salary.com*, accessed October 10, 2014, http://www.salary.com.

5 See, for example, T. R. Mitchell, "Matching Motivational Strategies with Organizational Contexts," in *Research in Organizational Behavior*, vol. 19, ed. L. L. Cummings and B. M. Staw (Greenwich, CT: JAI Press, 1997), pp. 60–62.

6 D. Gregor, *The Human Side of Enterprise* (New York: McGraw-Hill, 1960). For an updated analysis of Theory X and Theory Y constructs, see R. J. Summers and S. F. Cronshaw, "A Study of McGregor's Theory X, Theory Y and the Influence of Theory X, Theory Y Assumptions on Causal Attributions for Instances of Worker Poor Performance," in *Organizational Behavior*, ed. S. L. McShane, ASAC Conference Proceedings, vol. 9, part 5, Halifax, 1988, pp. 115–123.

7 K. W. Thomas, *Intrinsic Motivation at Work* (San Francisco: Berrett-Koehler, 2000); and K. W. Thomas, "Intrinsic Motivation and How It Works," *Training*, October 2000, pp. 130–135.

8 Based on D. Albarracin, I. Senay, and K. Noguchi, "Will We Succeed? The Science of Self-Motivation," *Psychological Science*, April 2010; and "Will We Succeed? The Science of Self-Motivation," *ScienceDaily*, June 1, 2010, http://www.sciencedaily.com/releases/2010/05/100528092021.htm.

9 Vignette based on R. Blackwell, "Lee Valley Tools Founder Leonard Lee Treated Customers as Friends," *Globe and Mail*, July 15, 2016.

10 A. H. Maslow, *Motivation and Personality* (New York: Harper and Row, 1954).

11 H. Skelsey, "Maslow's Hierarchy of Needs—The Sixth Level," *Psychologist* (2014), pp. 982–983.

12 C. Conley, *Peak: How Great Companies Get Their Mojo from Maslow* (San Francisco: Jossey-Bass, 2007).

13 H. Skelsey, "Maslow's Hierarchy of Needs—The Sixth Level," *Psychologist* (2014), pp. 982–983.

14 S. H. Mousavi and H. Dargahi, "Ethnic Differences and Motivation Based on Maslow's Theory on Iranian Employees," *Iranian Journal of Public Health* 42, no. 5 (2013), pp. 516–521.

15 D. Lester, "Measuring Maslow's Hierarchy of Needs," *Psychological Reports* 113, no. 1 (2013), pp. 127–129.

16 J.-K. Lee and J.-G. Choi, "Testing the Applicability of the Herzberg's Motivation-Hygiene Theory to the Hotel Industry," *Korean Journal of Business Administration* (2012), pp. 2091–2111.

17 See, for instance, C.-S. Park and K.-S. Ko, "A Study on Factors of Job Satisfaction of Caregivers in Home Care Facilities Based on Herzberg's Motivation-Hygiene Theory," *Church Social Work* (2012), pp. 123–158; and "Study on the Important Factors for Non-Commissioned Officer's Job Satisfaction in R.O.K. Army Based on Herzberg's Two Factor Theory," *Journal of Korean Public Police and Security Studies* (2012), pp. 217–238.

18 H. van Emmerick, W. L. Gardner, H. Wendt, and D. Fischer, "Associations of Culture and Personality with McClelland's Motives: A Cross-Cultural Study of Managers in 24 Countries," *Group and Organization Management* 35, no. 3 (2010), pp. 329–367.

19 D. C. McClelland, *The Achieving Society* (New York: Van Nostrand Reinhold, 1961).

20 D. G. Winter, "The Motivational Dimensions of Leadership: Power, Achievement, and Affiliation," in *Multiple Intelligences and Leadership*, ed. R. E. Riggio, S. E. Murphy, and F. J. Pirozzolo (Mahwah, NJ: Lawrence Erlbaum, 2002), pp. 119–138.

21 H. van Emmerick, W. L. Gardner, H. Wendt, and D. Fischer, "Associations of Culture and Personality with McClelland's Motives: A Cross-Cultural Study of Managers in 24 Countries." *Group and Organization Management* 35, no. 3 (2010), pp. 329–367.

22 See, for instance, F. Yang, J. E. Ramsay, O. C. Schultheiss, and J. S. Pang, "Need for Achievement Moderates the Effect of Motive-Relevant Challenge on Salivary Cortisol Changes," *Motivation and Emotion* (2015), pp. 321–334; M. S. Khan, R. J. Breitnecker, and E. J. Schwarz, "Adding Fuel to the Fire: Need for Achievement Diversity and Relationship Conflict in Entrepreneurial Teams," *Management Decision* 53, no. 1 (2015), pp. 75–79; M. G. Koellner and O. C. Schultheiss, "Meta-analytic Evidence of Low Convergence between Implicit and Explicit Measures of the Needs for Achievement, Affiliation, and Power," *Frontiers in Psychology* 5 (2014), article 826; and T. Bipp and K. van Dam, "Extending Hierarchical Achievement Motivation Models: The Role of Motivational Needs for Achievement Goals and Academic Performance," *Personality and Individual Differences* 64 (2014), pp. 157–162.

23 M. G. Koellner and O. C. Schultheiss, "Meta-analytic Evidence of Low Convergence between Implicit and Explicit Measures of the Needs for Achievement, Affiliation, and Power," *Frontiers in Psychology* 5 (2014), article 826.

24 J. Hofer, H. Busch, and C. Schneider, "The Effect of Motive-Trait Interaction on Satisfaction of the Implicit Need for Affiliation among German and Cameroonian Adults," *Journal of Personality* 83, no. 2 (2015), pp. 167–178.

25 Vignette based on V. Lu, "Leonard Lee, Founder of Lee Valley Tools, Was the Ultimate Craftsman," *thestar.com*, July 16, 2016, https://www.thestar.com/business/2016/07/16/leonard-lee-founder-of-lee-valley-tools-was-the-ultimate-craftsman.html.

26 R. L. Purvis, T. J. Zagenczyk, and G. E. McCray, "What's in It for Me? Using Expectancy Theory and Climate to Explain Stakeholder Participation, Its Direction and Intensity," *International Journal of Project Management* 33, no. 1 (2015), pp. 3–14.

27 M. Renko, K. G. Koeck, and A. Bullough, "Expectancy Theory and Nascent Entrepreneurship," *Small Business Economics* 39, no. 3 (2012), pp. 667–684; J. J. Donovan, "Work Motivation," in *Handbook of Industrial, Work & Organizational Psychology*, vol. 2, ed. N. Anderson, D. S. Ones, H. K. Sinangil, and C. Viswesvaran (Thousand Oaks, CA: Sage, 2001), pp. 56–59; and G. Yu and J. Guo, "Research on Employee Motivation Mechanism in Modern Enterprises Based on Victor H. Vroom's Expectancy Theory," in *Proceedings of the 9th International Conference on Innovation and Management*, ed. G. Duysters, A. DeHoyos, and K. Kaminishi, (2012), pp. 988–991.

28 Based on J. Nocera, "The Anguish of Being an Analyst," *New York Times*, March 4, 2006, pp. B1, B12.

29 See, for example, H. G. Heneman III and D. P. Schwab, "Evaluation of Research on Expectancy Theory Prediction of Employee Performance," *Psychological Bulletin*, July 1972, pp. 1–9; T. R. Mitchell, "Expectancy Models of Job Satisfaction, Occupational Preference and Effort: A Theoretical, Methodological and Empirical Appraisal," *Psychological Bulletin*, November 1974, pp. 1053–1077; and L. Reinharth and M. A. Wahba, "Expectancy Theory as a Predictor of Work Motivation, Effort Expenditure, and Job Performance," *Academy of Management Journal*, September 1975, pp. 502–537.

30 See, for example, L. W. Porter and E. E. Lawler III, *Managerial Attitudes and Performance* (Homewood, IL: Richard D. Irwin, 1968); D. F. Parker and L. Dyer, "Expectancy Theory as a Within-Person Behavioral Choice Model: An Empirical Test of Some Conceptual and Methodological Refinements," *Organizational Behavior and Human Performance*, October 1976, pp. 97–117; H. J. Arnold, "A Test of the Multiplicative Hypothesis of Expectancy-Valence Theories of Work Motivation," *Academy of Management Journal*, April 1981, pp. 128–141; and W. Van Eerde and H. Thierry, "Vroom's Expectancy Models and Work-Related Criteria: A Meta-analysis," *Journal of Applied Psychology*, October 1996, pp. 575–586.

31 P. C. Earley, *Face, Harmony, and Social Structure: An Analysis of Organizational Behavior across Cultures* (New York: Oxford University Press, 1997); R. M. Steers and C. Sanchez-Runde, "Culture, Motivation, and Work Behavior," in *Handbook of Cross-Cultural Management*, ed. M. Gannon and K. Newman (London: Blackwell, 2001), pp. 190–215; and H. C. Triandis, "Motivation and Achievement in Collectivist and Individualistic Cultures," in *Advances in Motivation and Achievement*, vol. 9, ed. M. Maehr and P. Pintrich (Greenwich, CT: JAI Press, 1995), pp. 1–30.

32 C. Gabelica, P. Van den Bossche, M. Segers, and W. Gijselaersa, "Feedback, a Powerful Lever in Teams: A Review," *Educational Research Review*, June 2012, pp. 123–144.

33 S. Huang, Y. Zhang, and S. M. Broniarczyk, "So Near and Yet So Far: The Mental Representation of Goal Progress," *Journal of Personality and Social Psychology* 103, no. 2 (2012), pp. 225–241.

34 B. D. Cawley, L. M. Keeping, and P. E. Levy, "Participation in the Performance Appraisal Process and Employee Reactions: A Meta-analytic Review of Field Investigations," *Journal of Applied Psychology*, August 1998, pp. 615–633; and P. E. Levy and J. R. Williams, "The Social Context of Performance Appraisal: A Review and Framework for the Future," *Journal of Management* 30, no. 6 (2004), pp. 881–905.

35 List directly quoted from R. Kreitner and A. Kinicki, *Organizational Behavior*, 6th ed. (New York: McGraw-Hill/Irwin, 2004), p. 335 (emphasis added).

36 E. A. Locke, "Toward a Theory of Task Motivation and Incentives," *Organizational Behavior and Human Performance*, May 1968, pp. 157–189.

37 P. C. Earley, P. Wojnaroski, and W. Prest, "Task Planning and Energy Expended: Exploration of How Goals Influence Performance," *Journal of Applied Psychology*, February 1987, pp. 107–114.

38 "KEYGroup Survey Finds Nearly Half of All Employees Have No Set Performance Goals," *IPMA-HR Bulletin*, March 10, 2006, p. 1; S. Hamm, "SAP Dangles a Big, Fat Carrot," *BusinessWeek*, May 22,

2006, pp. 67–68; and "P&G CEO Wields High Expectations but No Whip," *USA Today*, February 19, 2007, p. 3B.

39 See, for example, S. J. Carroll and H. L. Tosi, *Management by Objectives: Applications and Research* (New York: Macmillan, 1973); and R. Rodgers and J. E. Hunter, "Impact of Management by Objectives on Organizational Productivity," *Journal of Applied Psychology*, April 1991, pp. 322–336.

40 See, for instance, F. Ceresia, "A Model of Goal Dynamics in Organizations: Goal Setting, Goal Commitment, Training, and Management by Objectives," *Proceedings of 2009 Conference on Systems Science, Management Science & System Dynamics* 1 (2009), pp. 37–46; and H. Levinson, "Management by Whose Objectives?" *Harvard Business Review*, January 2003, pp. 107–116.

41 See, for example, E. Lindberg and T. L. Wilson, "Management by Objectives: The Swedish Experience in Upper Secondary Schools," *Journal of Educational Administration* 49, no. 1 (2011), pp. 62–75; and A. C. Spaulding, L. D. Gamm, and J. M. Griffith, "Studer Unplugged: Identifying Underlying Managerial Concepts," *Hospital Topics* 88, no. 1 (2010), pp. 1–9.

42 M. B. Kristiansen, "Management by Objectives and Results in the Nordic Countries: Continuity and Change, Differences and Similarities," *Public Performance and Management Review* 38, no. 3 (2015), pp. 542–569.

43 See, for instance, M. Tanikawa, "Fujitsu Decides to Backtrack on Performance-Based Pay," *New York Times*, March 22, 2001, p. W1; and W. F. Roth, "Is Management by Objectives Obsolete?" *Global Business and Organizational Excellence* 28 (May/June 2009), pp. 36–43.

44 E. A. Locke and G. P. Latham, *A Theory of Goal Setting and Task Performance* (Englewood Cliffs, NJ: Prentice Hall, 1980).

45 L. D. Ordóñez, M. E. Schweitzer, A. D. Galinsky, and M. Bazerman, "Goals Gone Wild: The Systematic Side Effects of Overprescribing Goal Setting," *Academy of Management Perspectives* 23, no. 1 (2009), pp. 6–16; and E. A. Locke and G. P. Latham, "Has Goal Setting Gone Wild, or Have Its Attackers Abandoned Good Scholarship?" *Academy of Management Perspectives* 23, no. 1 (2009), pp. 17–23.

46 C. P. Cerasoli, J. M. Nicklin, and M. T. Ford, "Intrinsic Motivation and Extrinsic Incentives Jointly Predict Performance: A 40-Year Meta-analysis," *Psychological Bulletin* 140, no. 4 (2014), pp. 980–1008.

47 K. Lanaj, C. D. Chang, and R. E. Johnson, "Regulatory Focus and Work-Related Outcomes: A Review and Meta-analysis," *Psychological Bulletin* 138, no. 5 (2012), pp. 998–1034.

48 K. Lanaj, C. D. Chang, and R. E. Johnson, "Regulatory Focus and Work-Related Outcomes: A Review and Meta-analysis," *Psychological Bulletin* 138, no. 5 (2012), pp. 998–1034.

49 D. L. Ferris, R. E. Johnson, C. C. Rosen, E. Djurdjevic, C.-H. Chang, and J. A. Tan, "When Is Success Not Satisfying? Integrating Regulatory Focus and Approach/Avoidance Motivation Theories to Explain the Relation between Core Self-Evaluation and Job Satisfaction," *Journal of Applied Psychology* 98, no. 2 (2013), pp. 342–353.

50 M. Roskes, A. J. Elliot, and C. K. W. De Dreu, "Why Is Avoidance Motivation Problematic, and What Can Be Done about It?" *Current Directions in Psychological Science* 23, no. 2 (2014), pp. 133–138.

51 J. R. Themanson and P. J. Rosen, "Examining the Relationships between Self-Efficacy, Task-Relevant Attentional Control, and Task Performance: Evidence from Event-Related Brain Potentials," *British Journal of Psychology* 106, no. 2 (2015), pp. 253–271.

52 A. Bandura, "Cultivate Self-Efficacy for Personal and Organizational Effectiveness," in *Handbook of Principles of Organizational Behavior*, ed. E. Locke (Malden, MA: Blackwell, 2004), pp. 120–136; and M. Ventura, M. Salanova, and S.

Llorens, "Professional Self-Efficacy as a Predictor of Burnout and Engagement: The Role of Challenge and Hindrance Demands," *Journal of Psychology* 149, no. 3 (2015), pp. 277–302.

53 M. Salanova, S. Llorens, and W. B. Schaufeli, "'Yes I Can, I Feel Good, and I Just Do It!' On Gain Cycles and Spirals of Efficacy Beliefs, Affect, and Engagement," *Applied Psychology: An International Review* 60, no. 2 (2011), pp. 255–285.

54 J. R. Themanson and P. J. Rosen, "Examining the Relationships between Self-Efficacy, Task-Relevant Attentional Control, and Task Performance: Evidence from Event-Related Brain Potentials," *British Journal of Psychology* 106, no. 2 (2015), pp. 253–271.

55 A. P. Tolli and A. M. Schmidt, "The Role of Feedback, Causal Attributions, and Self-Efficacy in Goal Revision," *Journal of Applied Psychology* 93, no. 3 (2008), pp. 692–701.

56 P. Tierney and S. M. Farmer, "Creative Self-Efficacy Development and Creative Performance over Time," *Journal of Applied Psychology* 96, no. 2 (2011), pp. 277–293.

57 A. Bandura, *Self-Efficacy: The Exercise of Control* (New York: Freeman, 1997).

58 T. A. Judge, C. L. Jackson, J. C. Shaw, B. Scott, and B. L. Rich, "Self-Efficacy and Work-Related Performance: The Integral Role of Individual Differences," *Journal of Applied Psychology* 92, no. 1 (2007), pp. 107–127.

59 T. A. Judge, C. L. Jackson, J. C. Shaw, B. Scott, and B. L. Rich, "Self-Efficacy and Work-Related Performance: The Integral Role of Individual Differences," *Journal of Applied Psychology* 92, no. 1 (2007), pp. 107–127.

60 A. M. Paul, "How to Use the 'Pygmalion' Effect," *Time*, April 1, 2013, http://ideas.time.com/2013/04/01/how-to-use-the-pygmalion-effect/.

61 A. Friedrich, B. Flunger, B. Nagengast, K. Jonkmann, and U. Trautwein, "Pygmalion Effects in the Classroom: Teacher Expectancy Effects on Students' Math Achievement," *Contemporary Educational Psychology* 41 (2015), pp. 1–12.

62 L. Karakowsky, N. DeGama, and K. McBey, "Facilitating the Pygmalion Effect: The Overlooked Role of Subordinate Perceptions of the Leader," *Journal of Occupational and Organizational Psychology* 85, no. 4 (2012), pp. 579–599; and P. Whiteley, T. Sy, and S. K. Johnson, "Leaders' Conceptions of Followers: Implications for Naturally Occurring Pygmalion Effects," *Leadership Quarterly* 23, no. 5 (2012), pp. 822–834.

63 A. Gegenfurtner, C. Quesada-Pallares, and M. Knogler, "Digital Simulation-Based Training: A Meta-analysis," *British Journal of Educational Technology* 45, no. 6 (2014), pp. 1097–1114.

64 E. C. Dierdorff, E. A. Surface, and K. G. Brown, "Frame-of-Reference Training Effectiveness: Effects of Goal Orientation and Self-Efficacy on Affective, Cognitive, Skill-Based, and Transfer Outcomes," *Journal of Applied Psychology* 95, no. 6 (2010), pp. 1181–1191; and R. Grossman, and E. Salas, "The Transfer of Training: What Really Matters," *International Journal of Training and Development* 15, no. 2 (2011), pp. 103–120.

65 K. M. Eddington, C. Majestic, and P. J. Silvia, "Contrasting Regulatory Focus and Reinforcement Sensitivity: A Daily Diary Study of Goal Pursuit and Emotion," *Personality and Individual Differences*, August 2012, pp. 335–340.

66 X. Zhu and M. Tian, "On the Incentive System for Chinese Local Governments' Work of Environmental Protection from the Perspective of Skinner's Reinforcement Theory," *Proceedings of the 2013 International Conference on Public Administration* (2013), pp. 271–277.

67 M. J. Goddard, "Critical Psychiatry, Critical Psychology, and the Behaviorism of B. F. Skinner," *Review of General Psychology* 18, no. 3 (2014), pp. 208–215.

68 F. Luthans and R. Kreitner, *Organizational Behavior Modification and Beyond*, 2nd ed. (Glenview, IL: Scott Foresman, 1985); and A. D. Stajkovic and F. Luthans, "A Meta-analysis of the Effects of Organizational Behavior Modification on Task Performance, 1975–95," *Academy of Management Journal*, October 1997, pp. 1122–1149.

69 Vignette based on R. Blackwell, "Lee Valley Tools Founder Leonard Lee Treated Customers as Friends," *Globe and Mail*, July 15, 2016; and T. O'Reilly, "Brand Envy: #Canada150," May 11, 2017, *CBC Radio*, http://www.cbc.ca/radio/undertheinfluence/brand-envy-canada150-1.4108158.

70 P. S. Goodman, "An Examination of Referents Used in the Evaluation of Pay," *Organizational Behavior and Human Performance*, October 1974, pp. 170–195; S. Ronen, "Equity Perception in Multiple Comparisons: A Field Study," *Human Relations*, April 1986, pp. 333–346; R. W. Scholl, E. A. Cooper, and J. F. McKenna, "Referent Selection in Determining Equity Perception: Differential Effects on Behavioral and Attitudinal Outcomes," *Personnel Psychology*, Spring 1987, pp. 113–127; T. P. Summers and A. S. DeNisi, "In Search of Adams' Other: Reexamination of Referents Used in the Evaluation of Pay," *Human Relations*, June 1990, pp. 497–511; S. Werner and N. P. Mero, "Fair or Foul? The Effects of External, Internal, and Employee Equity on Changes in Performance of Major League Baseball Players," *Human Relations*, October 1999, pp. 1291–1312; and R. W. Griffeth and S. Gaertner, "A Role for Equity Theory in the Turnover Process: An Empirical Test," *Journal of Applied Social Psychology*, May 2001, pp. 1017–1037.

71 See, for example, E. Walster, G. W. Walster, and W. G. Scott, *Equity: Theory and Research* (Boston: Allyn and Bacon, 1978); and J. Greenberg, "Cognitive Reevaluation of Outcomes in Response to Underpayment Inequity," *Academy of Management Journal*, March 1989, pp. 174–184.

72 J. Bai, "Analysis of Equity Theory in the Modern Enterprise Staff Motivation," *Proceedings of the 2012 International Conference on Management Innovation and Public Policy* (2012), pp. 165–167; C. Buzea, "Equity Theory Constructs in a Romanian Cultural Context," *Human Resource Development Quarterly* 25, no. 4 (2014), pp. 421–439; R. W. Griffeth and S. Gaertner, "A Role for Equity Theory in the Turnover Process: An Empirical Test," *Journal of Applied Social Psychology* 31, no. 5 (2001), pp. 1017–1037; and L. K. Scheer, N. Kumar, and J.-B. E. M. Steenkamp, "Reactions to Perceived Inequity in U.S. and Dutch Interorganizational Relationships," *Academy of Management* 46, no. 3 (2003), pp. 303–316.

73 B. K. Miller, "Entitlement and Conscientiousness in the Prediction of Organizational Deviance," *Personality and Individual Differences* 82 (2015), pp. 114–119; and H. J. R. Woodley and N. J. Allen, "The Dark Side of Equity Sensitivity," *Personality and Individual Differences* 67 (2014), pp. 103–108.

74 J. M. Jensen, P. C. Patel, and J. L. Raver, "Is It Better to Be Average? High and Low Performance as Predictors of Employee Victimization," *Journal of Applied Psychology* 99, no. 2 (2014), pp. 296–309.

75 C. O. Trevor, G. Reilly, and B. Gerhart, "Reconsidering Pay Dispersion's Effect on the Performance of Interdependent Work: Reconciling Sorting and Pay Inequality," *Academy of Management Journal*, June 2012, pp. 585–610.

76 C. O. Trevor, G. Reilly, and B. Gerhart, "Reconsidering Pay Dispersion's Effect on the Performance of Interdependent Work: Reconciling Sorting and Pay Inequality," *Academy of Management Journal*, June 2012, pp. 585–610.

77 See, for example, R. Cropanzano, J. H. Stein, and T. Nadisic, *Social Justice and the Experience of Emotion* (New York: Routledge/Taylor and Francis Group, 2011).

78 G. S. Leventhal, "What Should Be Done with Equity Theory? New Approaches to the Study of Fairness in Social Relationships," in *Social Exchange: Advances in Theory and Research*, ed. K. Gergen, M. Greenberg, and R. Willis (New York: Plenum, 1980), pp. 27–55.

79 J. Brockner and B. M. Wiesenfeld, "An Integrative Framework for Examining Reactions to Decisions: Interactive Effects of Outcomes and Procedures," *Psychological Bulletin* 120 (1996), pp. 189–208.

80 J. C. Shaw, E. Wild, and J. A. Colquitt, "To Justify or Excuse? A Meta-analytic Review of the Effects of Explanations," *Journal of Applied Psychology* 88, no. 3 (2003), pp. 444–458.

81 R. J. Bies, "Are Procedural and Interactional Justice Conceptually Distinct?" in *Handbook of Organizational Justice*, ed. J. Greenberg and J. A. Colquitt (Mahwah, NJ: Erlbaum, 2005), pp. 85–112; and B. A. Scott, J. A. Colquitt, and E. L. Paddock, "An Actor-Focused Model of Justice Rule Adherence and Violation: The Role of Managerial Motives and Discretion," *Journal of Applied Psychology* 94, no. 3 (2009), pp. 756–769.

82 G. A. Van Kleef, A. C. Homan, B. Beersma, D. V. Knippenberg, B. V. Knippenberg, and F. Damen, "Searing Sentiment or Cold Calculation? The Effects of Leader Emotional Displays on Team Performance Depend on Follower Epistemic Motivation," *Academy of Management Journal* 52, no. 3 (2009), pp. 562–580.

83 J. M. Robbins, M. T. Ford, and L. E. Tetrick, "Perceived Unfairness and Employee Health: A Meta-analytic Integration," *Journal of Applied Psychology* 97, no. 2 (2012), pp. 235–272.

84 J. A. Colquitt, B. A. Scott, J. B. Rodell, D. M. Long, C. P. Zapata, D. E. Conlon, and M. J. Wesson, "Justice at the Millennium, A Decade Later: A Meta-analytic Test of Social Exchange and Affect-Based Perspectives," *Journal of Applied Psychology* 98, no. 2 (2013), pp. 199–236.

85 K. Leung, K. Tong, and S. S. Ho, "Effects of Interactional Justice on Egocentric Bias in Resource Allocation Decisions," *Journal of Applied Psychology* 89, no. 3 (2004), pp. 405–415; and L. Francis-Gladney, N. R. Manger, and R. B. Welker, "Does Outcome Favorability Affect Procedural Fairness as a Result of Self-Serving Attributions," *Journal of Applied Social Psychology* 40, no. 1 (2010), pp. 182–194.

86 L. J. Barlcay and D. P. Skarlicki, "Healing the Wounds of Organizational Injustice: Examining the Benefits of Expressive Writing," *Journal of Applied Psychology* 94, no. 2 (2009), pp. 511–523.

87 This section is based on B. A. Scott, A. S. Garza, D. E. Conlon, and Y. J. Kim, "Why Do Managers Act Fairly in the First Place? A Daily Investigation of 'Hot' and 'Cold' Motives and Discretion," *Academy of Management Journal* 57, no. 6 (2014), pp. 1571–1591.

88 E. Deci and R. Ryan, eds., *Handbook of Self-Determination Research* (Rochester, NY: University of Rochester Press, 2002); R. Ryan and E. Deci, "Self-Determination Theory and the Facilitation of Intrinsic Motivation, Social Development, and Well-Being," *American Psychologist* 55, no. 1 (2000), pp. 68–78; and M. Gagné and E. L. Deci, "Self-Determination Theory and Work Motivation," *Journal of Organizational Behavior* 26, no. 4 (2005), pp. 331–362.

89 E. L. Deci, R. Koestner, and R. M. Ryan, "A Meta-analytic Review of Experiments Examining the Effects of Extrinsic Rewards on Intrinsic Motivation," *Psychological Bulletin* 125, no. 6 (1999), pp. 627–668; N. Houlfort, R. Koestner, M. Joussemet, A. Nantel-Vivier, and N. Lekes, "The Impact of Performance-Contingent Rewards on Perceived Autonomy and Competence," *Motivation & Emotion* 26, no. 4 (2002), pp. 279–295; G. J. Greguras and J. M. Diefendorff, "Different Fits Satisfy Different Needs: Linking Person-Environment Fit to Employee Commitment and Performance Using Self-Determination Theory," *Journal of Applied Psychology* 94, no. 2 (2009), pp. 465–477; and M. P. Moreno-Jiménez and M. C. H. Villodres, "Prediction of Burnout in Volunteers," *Journal of Applied Social Psychology* 40, no. 7 (2010), pp. 1798–1818. This work studies the personal experience of vol-

unteering and several antecedent and consequent variables. We studied the effect of the amount of time dedicated to the organization, motivation, social support, integration in the organization, self-efficacy, and characteristics of the work on a consequent variable of the volunteering experience; that is, burnout, with its three components of efficacy, cynicism, and exhaustion. The statistical analysis shows that the time dedicated to volunteering and the extrinsic motivations (that is, social and career) predicts higher levels of burnout, whereas intrinsic motivations (that is, values and understanding), life satisfaction, and integration in the organization are negatively related to burnout.

90 C. P. Cerasoli, J. M. Nicklin, and M. T. Ford, "Intrinsic Motivation and Extrinsic Incentives Jointly Predict Performance: A 40-Year Meta-analysis," *Psychological Bulletin* 140, no. 4 (2014), pp. 980–1008.

91 K. M. Sheldon, A. J. Elliot, and R. M. Ryan, "Self-Concordance and Subjective Well-Being in Four Cultures," *Journal of Cross-Cultural Psychology* 35, no. 2 (2004), pp. 209–223.

92 K. M. Sheldon, A. J. Elliot, and R. M. Ryan, "Self-Concordance and Subjective Well-being in Four Cultures," *Journal of Cross-Cultural Psychology* 35, no. 2 (2004), pp. 209–223.

93 L. M. Graves, M. N. Ruderman, P. J. Ohlott, and T. J. Webber, "Driven to Work and Enjoyment of Work: Effects on Managers' Outcomes," *Journal of Management* 38, no. 5 (2012), pp. 1655–1680.

94 K. M. Sheldon, A. J. Elliot, and R. M. Ryan, "Self-Concordance and Subjective Well-Being in Four Cultures," *Journal of Cross-Cultural Psychology* 35, no. 2 (2004), pp. 209–223.

95 J. P. Meyer, T. E. Becker, and C. Vandenberghe, "Employee Commitment and Motivation: A Conceptual Analysis and Integrative Model," *Journal of Applied Psychology* 89, no. 6 (2004), pp. 991–1007.

96 K. W. Thomas, E. Jansen, and W. G. Tymon Jr., "Navigating in the Realm of Theory: An Empowering View of Construct Development," in *Research in Organizational Change and Development*, vol. 10, ed. W. A. Pasmore and R. W. Woodman (Greenwich, CT: JAI Press, 1997), pp. 1–30.

97 This section based on C. Michaelson, "Meaningful Motivation for Work Motivation Theory," *Academy of Management Review* 30, no. 2 (2005), pp. 235–238; and R. M. Steers, R. T. Mowday, and D. L. Shapiro, "Response to Meaningful Motivation for Work Motivation Theory," *Academy of Management Review* 30, no. 2 (2005), p. 238.

98 C. Michaelson, "Meaningful Motivation for Work Motivation Theory," *Academy of Management Review* 30, no. 2 (2005), p. 237.

99 H.-T. Chang, H.-M. Hsu, J.-W. Liou, and C.-T. Tsai, "Psychological Contracts and Innovative Behavior: A Moderated Path Analysis of Work Engagement and Job Resources," *Journal of Applied Social Psychology* 43, no. 10 (2013), pp. 2021–2135.

100 See topics of employee engagement from Gallup on http://www.gallup.com/topic/employee_engagement.aspx.

101 M. S. Christian, A. S. Garza, and J. E. Slaughter, "Work Engagement: A Quantitative Review and Test of Its Relations with Task and Contextual Performance," *Personnel Psychology* 64, no. 1 (2011), pp. 89–136.

102 W. B. Schaufeli, A. B. Bakker, and W. van Rhenen, "How Changes in Job Demands and Resources Predict Burnout, Work Engagement, and Sickness Absenteeism," *Journal of Organizational Behavior* 30, no. 7 (2009), pp. 893–917; E. R. Crawford, J. A. LePine, and B. L. Rich, "Linking Job Demands and Resources to Employee Engagement and Burnout: A Theoretical Extension and Meta-analytic Test," *Journal of Applied Psychology* 95, no. 5 (2010), pp. 834–848; and D. Xanthopoulou, A. B. Bakker, E. Demerouti, and W. B. Schaufeli, "Reciprocal Relationships between Job Resources, Personal Resources, and Work Engagement," *Journal of Vocational Behavior* 74, no. 3 (2009), pp. 235–244.

103 B. L. Rich, J. A. LePine, and E. R. Crawford, "Job Engagement: Antecedents and Effects on Job Performance," *Academy of Management Journal* 53, no. 3 (2010), pp. 617–635.

104 M. Tims, A. B. Bakker, and D. Xanthopoulou, "Do Transformational Leaders Enhance Their Followers' Daily Work Engagement?" *Leadership Quarterly* 22, no. 1 (2011), pp. 121–131; and F. O. Walumbwa, P. Wang, H. Wang, J. Schaubroeck, and B. J. Avolio, "Psychological Processes Linking Authentic Leadership to Follower Behaviors," *Leadership Quarterly* 21, no. 5 (2010), pp. 901–914.

105 D. A. Newman and D. A. Harrison, "Been There, Bottled That: Are State and Behavioral Work Engagement New and Useful Construct 'Wines'?" *Industrial and Organizational Psychology* 1, no. 1 (2008), pp. 31–35; and A. J. Wefald and R. G. Downey, "Job Engagement in Organizations: Fad, Fashion, or Folderol," *Journal of Organizational Behavior* 30, no. 1 (2009), pp. 141–145.

106 See, for example, B. L. Rich, J. A. LePine, and E. R. Crawford, "Job Engagement: Antecedents and Effects on Job Performance," *Academy of Management Journal* 53, no. 3 (2010), pp. 617–635.

107 J. M. George, "The Wider Context, Costs, and Benefits of Work Engagement," *European Journal of Work and Organizational Psychology* 20, no. 1 (2011), pp. 53–59; and J. R. B. Halbesleben, J. Harvey, and M. C. Bolino, "Too Engaged? A Conservation of Resources View of the Relationship between Work Engagement and Work Interference with Family," *Journal of Applied Psychology* 94, no. 6 (2009), pp. 1452–1465.

108 N. J. Adler, *International Dimensions of Organizational Behavior*, 4th ed. (Cincinnati, OH: South-Western Publishing, 2002), p. 174.

109 G. Hofstede, "Motivation, Leadership, and Organization: Do American Theories Apply Abroad?" *Organizational Dynamics*, Summer 1980, p. 55.

110 G. Hofstede, "Motivation, Leadership, and Organization: Do American Theories Apply Abroad?" *Organizational Dynamics*, Summer 1980, p. 55.

111 D. F. Crown, "The Use of Group and Groupcentric Individual Goals for Culturally Heterogeneous and Homogeneous Task Groups: An Assessment of European Work Teams," *Small Group Research* 38, no. 4 (2007), pp. 489–508; J. Kurman, "Self-Regulation Strategies in Achievement Settings: Culture and Gender Differences," *Journal of Cross-Cultural Psychology* 32, no. 4 (2001), pp. 491–503; and M. Erez and P. C. Earley, "Comparative Analysis of Goal-Setting Strategies across Cultures," *Journal of Applied Psychology* 72, no. 4 (1987), pp. 658–665.

112 C. Sue-Chan and M. Ong, "Goal Assignment and Performance: Assessing the Mediating Roles of Goal Commitment and Self-Efficacy and the Moderating Role of Power Distance," *Organizational Behavior and Human Decision Processes* 89, no. 2 (2002), pp. 1140–1161.

113 R. Fischer and P. B. Smith, "Reward Allocation and Culture: A Meta-analysis," *Journal of Cross-Cultural Psychology* 34, no. 3 (2003), pp. 251–268.

114 F. F. T. Chiang and T. Birtch, "The Transferability of Management Practices: Examining Cross-National Differences in Reward Preferences," *Human Relations* 60, no. 9 (2007), pp. 1293–1330; A. E. Lind, T. R. Tyler, and Y. J. Huo, "Procedural Context and Culture: Variation in the Antecedents of Procedural Justice Judgments," *Journal of Personality and Social Psychology* 73, no. 4 (1997), pp. 767–780; and M. J. Gelfand, M. Erez, and Z. Aycan, "Cross-Cultural Organizational Behavior," *Annual Review of Psychology* 58 (2007), pp. 479–514.

115 J. K. Giacobbe-Miller, D. J. Miller, and V. I. Victorov, "A Comparison of Russian and U.S. Pay Allocation Decisions, Distributive Justice Judgments, and Productivity under Different

Payment Conditions," *Personnel Psychology* 51, no. 1 (1998), pp. 137–163.

116 M. C. Bolino and W. H. Turnley, "Old Faces, New Places: Equity Theory in Cross-Cultural Contexts," *Journal of Organizational Behavior* 29, no. 1 (2008), pp. 29–50.

117 F. F. T. Chiang and T. Birtch, "The Transferability of Management Practices: Examining Cross-National Differences in Reward Preferences," *Human Relations* 60, no. 9 (2007), pp. 1293–1330; and M. J. Gelfand, M. Erez, and Z. Aycan, "Cross-Cultural Organizational Behavior," *Annual Review of Psychology* 58 (2007), pp. 479–514.

118 M. C. Bolino and W. H. Turnley, "Old Faces, New Places: Equity Theory in Cross-Cultural Contexts," *Journal of Organizational Behavior* 29, no. 1 (2008), pp. 29–50.

119 R. Shao, D. E. Rupp, D. P. Skarlicki, and K. S. Jones, "Employee Justice across Cultures: A Meta-analytic Review," *Journal of Management* 39, no. 1 (2013), pp. 263–301.

120 Based on S. E. DeVoe and S. S. Iyengar, "Managers' Theories of Subordinates: A Cross-Cultural Examination of Manager Perceptions of Motivation and Appraisal of Performance," *Organizational Behavior and Human Decision Processes*, January 2004, pp. 47–61.

121 I. Harpaz, "The Importance of Work Goals: An International Perspective," *Journal of International Business Studies*, First Quarter 1990, pp. 75–93.

122 G. E. Popp, H. J. Davis, and T. T. Herbert, "An International Study of Intrinsic Motivation Composition," *Management International Review*, January 1986, pp. 28–35.

123 R. Fischer and P. B. Smith, "Reward Allocation and Culture: A Meta-analysis," *Journal of Cross-Cultural Psychology* 34, no. 3 (2003), pp. 251–268.

124 F. T. Chiang and T. Birtch, "The Transferability of Management Practices: Examining Cross-National Differences in Reward Preferences," *Human Relations* 60, no. 9 (2007), pp. 1293–1330; A. E. Lind, T. R. Tyler, and Y. J. Huo, "Procedural Context and Culture: Variation in the Antecedents of Procedural Justice Judgments," *Journal of Personality and Social Psychology* 73, no. 4 (1997), pp. 767–780; and M. J. Gelfand, M. Erez, and Z. Aycan, "Cross-Cultural Organizational Behavior," *Annual Review of Psychology* 58 (2007), pp. 479–514.

125 Based on E. A. Locke and G. P. Latham, "Building a Practically Useful Theory of Goal Setting and Task Motivation," *American Psychologist* 57 (2002), pp. 705–771; A. Tugend, "Expert's Advice to the Goal-Oriented: Don't Overdo It," *New York Times*, October 6, 2012, p. B5; and C. Richards, "Letting Go of Long-Term Goals," *New York Times*, August 4, 2012.

126 A. Ellin, "Failure Is Not an Option," *New York Times*, April 15, 2012, pp. 13–14; A. Massoia, "The New Normal: The Problem of Grade Inflation in American Schools," *Huffington Post*, January 12, 2015, http://www.huffingtonpost.com/angelina-massoia/the-new-normal-the-proble_b_6146236.html15; and S. Slavov, "How to Fix College Grade Inflation," *US News*, December 26, 2013, http://www.usnews.com/opinion/blogs/economic-intelligence/2013/12/26/why-college-grade-inflation-is-a-real-problem-and-how-to-fix-it.

127 Based on J. McFarland, "Major CEO Pay Increases in the Cards Again," *Globe and Mail*, June 1, 2014, http://www.theglobeandmail.com/report-on-business/careers/management/executive-compensation/pay-is-on-the-rise-for-canadas-top-executives/article18940701/; "CEO vs Average Pay in Canada: All in a Day's Work?" Canadian Centre for Policy Alternatives, January 2, 2014, https://www.policyalternatives.ca/ceo; J. Bizjak, M. Lemmon, and T. Nguyen, "Are All CEOs Above Average? An Empirical Analysis of Compensation Peer Groups and Pay Design," *Journal of Financial Economics* 100, no. 3 (2011), pp. 538–555; R. Foroohar, "Stuffing Their Pockets: For CEOs, A Lucrative Recession" *Newsweek*,

September 13, 2010; A. Kleinman, "Mark Zuckerberg $1 Salary Puts Him in Elite Group of $1 CEOs," *Huffington Post*, April 29, 2013; and G. Morgenson, "If Shareholders Say 'Enough Already,' the Board May Listen," *New York Times*, April 6, 2013.

128 Based on "Quebecor Plays Hardball with Defiant Union: Vidéotron 'Ready to Listen': Aims to Sell Cable Installation Operations," *Financial Post (National Post)*, March 5, 2002, p. FP6; and S. Silcoff, "Quebecor and Union in Showdown over Costs," *Financial Post (National Post)*, February 28, 2002, p. FP3.

129 Based on S. P. Robbins and D. A. DeCenzo, *Fundamentals of Management*, 4th ed. (Upper Saddle River, NJ: Prentice Hall, 2004), p. 85.

Chapter 5

1 "Secrets of Canada's Best Managed Companies," *Canadian Business*, May 9, 2017, http://www.canadianbusiness.com/best-managed-companies/#winners; C. McIntyre, "How G Adventures Made Social Good Part of Its Management Strategy," *Canadian Business*, May 9, 2017, http://www.macleans.ca/economy/business/how-g-adventures-made-social-good-part-of-its-management-strategy/.

2 ADP, "Many Canadian Workers Face a Growth Gap: ADP Canada Poll," March 15, 2017, https://www.adp.ca/en-ca/press-room/media-releases/2017/many-canadian-workers-face-a-growth-gap.aspx.

3 C. Weller, "10 Companies That Pay Employees Extra to Take Vacations," *Inc.*, October 3, 2016, https://www.inc.com/business-insider/10-companies-that-pay-employees-extra-for-vacations.html.

4 E. White, "Opportunity Knocks, and It Pays a Lot Better," *Wall Street Journal*, November 13, 2006, p. B3.

5 D. A. McIntyre and S. Weigley, "8 Companies That Most Owe Workers a Raise," *USA Today*, May 13, 2013, http://www.usatoday.com/story/money/business/2013/05/12/8-companies-that-most-owe-workers-a-raise/2144013/.

6 M. Sabramony, N. Krause, J. Norton, and G. N. Burns, "The Relationship between Human Resource Investments and Organizational Performance: A Firm-Level Examination of Equilibrium Theory," *Journal of Applied Psychology* 93, no. 4 (2008), pp. 778–788.

7 H. Shaw, "Walmart Canada Stung as Retail Competition Heats Up," *Financial Post*, November 14, 2013.

8 J. Sturgeon, "Meet the Big-Box Retailer That's Muscling in on Canadian Supermarkets," *Global News*, January 28, 2016, http://globalnews.ca/news/2483631/meet-the-big-box-retailer-thats-eating-canadian-supermarkets-lunch/.

9 J. Bowman, "Why Wal-Mart Will Never Pay Employees As Much As Costco," *Motley Fool*, November 6, 2016, https://www.fool.com/investing/2016/11/06/why-wal-mart-will-never-pay-employees-as-much-as-c.aspx.

10 Based on J. R. Schuster and P. K. Zingheim, "The New Variable Pay: Key Design Issues," *Compensation & Benefits Review*, March–April 1993, p. 28; K. S. Abosch, "Variable Pay: Do We Have the Basics in Place?" *Compensation & Benefits Review*, July–August 1998, pp. 12–22; and K. M. Kuhn and M. D. Yockey, "Variable Pay as a Risky Choice: Determinants of the Relative Attractiveness of Incentive Plans," *Organizational Behavior and Human Decision Processes*, March 2003, pp. 323–341.

11 "Canada's General Motors Workers to Get Up to 16 Per Cent of Salary in Bonuses," *Canadian Press*, February 14, 2011.

12 "Canada's General Motors Workers to Get Up to 16 Per Cent of Salary in Bonuses," *Canadian Press*, February 14, 2011.

13 See, for example, M. Damiani and A. Ricci, "Managers' Education and the Choice of Different Variable Pay Schemes: Evidence from

Italian Firms," *European Management Journal* 32, no. 6 (2014), pp. 891–902; and J. S. Heywood and U. Jirjahn, "Variable Pay, Industrial Relations and Foreign Ownership: Evidence from Germany," *British Journal of Industrial Relations* 52, no. 3 (2014), pp. 521–552.

14 J. Cloutier, D. Morin, and S. Renaud, "How Does Variable Pay Relate to Pay Satisfaction among Canadian Workers?" *International Journal of Manpower* 34, no. 5 (2013), pp. 465–485.

15 H. Kim, K. L. Sutton, and Y. Gong, "Group-Based Pay-for-Performance Plans and Firm Performance: The Moderating Role of Empowerment Practices," *Asia Pacific Journal of Management*, March 2013, pp. 31–52.

16 E. Belogolovsky and P. A. Bamberger, "Signaling in Secret: Pay for Performance and the Incentive and Sorting Effects of Pay Secrecy," *Academy of Management Journal* 57, no. 6 (2014), pp. 1706–1733.

17 E. Belogolovsky and P. A. Bamberger, "Signaling in Secret: Pay for Performance and the Incentive and Sorting Effects of Pay Secrecy," *Academy of Management Journal* 57, no. 6 (2014), pp. 1706–1733.

18 B. Wysocki, Jr., "Chilling Reality Awaits Even the Employed," *Wall Street Journal*, November 5, 2001, p. A1.

19 K. A. Bender, C. P. Green, and J. S. Heywood, "Piece Rates and Workplace Injury: Does Survey Evidence Support Adam Smith?" *Journal of Population Economics* 25, no. 2 (2012), pp. 569–590.

20 J. S. Heywood, X. Wei, and G. Ye, "Piece Rates for Professors," *Economics Letters* 113, no. 3 (2011), pp. 285–287.

21 A. Baker and V. Mertins, "Risk-Sorting and Preference for Team Piece Rates," *Journal of Economic Psychology* 34 (2013), pp. 285–300.

22 A. Clemens, "Pace of Work and Piece Rates," *Economics Letters* 115, no. 3 (2012), pp. 477–479.

23 K. A. Bender, C. P. Green, and J. S. Heywood, "Piece Rates and Workplace Injury: Does Survey Evidence Support Adam Smith?" *Journal of Population Economics* 25, no. 2 (2012), pp. 569–590.

24 S. L. Rynes, B. Gerhart, and L. Parks, "Personnel Psychology: Performance Evaluation and Pay for Performance," *Annual Review of Psychology* 56, no. 1 (2005), pp. 571–600.

25 S. Halzack, "Companies Look to Bonuses Instead of Salary Increases in an Uncertain Economy," *Washington Post*, November 6, 2012, http://www.washingtonpost.com/business/economy/companies-look-to-bonuses-instead-of-salary-increases-in-an-uncertain-economy/2012/11/06/52a7ec12-2751-11e2-9972-71bf64ea091c_story.html.

26 C. M. Barnes, J. Reb, and D. Ang, "More Than Just the Mean: Moving to a Dynamic View of Performance-Based Compensation," *Journal of Applied Psychology* 97, no. 3 (2012), pp. 711–718.

27 E. J. Castillo, "Gender, Race, and the New (Merit-Based) Employment Relationship," *Industrial Relations* 51, no. S1 (2012), pp. 528–562.

28 "Bonus Pay in Canada," *Manpower Argus*, September 1996, p. 5; E. White, "Employers Increasingly Favor Bonuses to Raises," *Wall Street Journal*, August 28, 2006, p. B3; and J. S. Lublin, "Boards Tie CEO Pay More Tightly to Performance," *Wall Street Journal*, February 21, 2006, pp. A1, A14.

29 Based on R. Curran, "Did Bonuses Help to Fuel Meltdown?" *Post. IE online*, September 21, 2008; and V. Bajaj, A. R. Sorkin, and M. J. de la Merced, "As Goldman and Morgan Shift, a Wall St. Era Ends," *New York Times*, September 21, 2008, http://dealbook.nytimes.com/2008/09/21/goldman-morgan-to-become-bank-holding-companies/.

30 S. S. Wiltermuth and F. Gino, "'I'll Have One of Each': How Separating Rewards into (Meaningless) Categories Increases Motivation," *Journal of Personality and Social Psychology*, January 2013, pp. 1–13.

31 "Mark Zuckerberg Reaped $2.3 Billion on Facebook Stock Options," *Huffington Post*, April 26, 2013, http://www.huffingtonpost.com.

32 D. D'Art and T. Turner, "Profit Sharing, Firm Performance, and Union Influence in Selected European Countries," *Personnel Review* 33, no. 3 (2004), pp. 335–350; and D. Kruse, R. Freeman, and J. Blasi, *Shared Capitalism at Work: Employee Ownership, Profit and Gain Sharing, and Broad-Based Stock Options* (Chicago: University of Chicago Press, 2010).

33 A. Bayo-Moriones and M. Larraza-Kintana, "Profit-Sharing Plans and Affective Commitment: Does the Context Matter?" *Human Resource Management* 48, no. 2 (2009), pp. 207–226.

34 N. Chi and T. Han, "Exploring the Linkages between Formal Ownership and Psychological Ownership for the Organization: The Mediating Role of Organizational Justice," *Journal of Occupational and Organizational Psychology* 81, no. 4 (2008), pp. 691–711.

35 J. H. Han, K. M. Barol, and S. Kim, "Tightening Up the Performance-Pay Linkage: Roles of Contingent Reward Leadership and Profit-Sharing in the Cross-Level Influence of Individual Pay-for-Performance," *Journal of Applied Psychology* 100, no. 2 (2015), pp. 417–430.

36 R. P. Garrett, "Does Employee Ownership Increase Innovation?" *New England Journal of Entrepreneurship* 13, no. 2, (2010), pp. 37–46.

37 D. McCarthy, E. Reeves, and T. Turner, "Can Employee Share-Ownership Improve Employee Attitudes and Behaviour?" *Employee Relations* 32, no. 4 (2010), pp. 382–395.

38 A. Pendleton, "Shared Capitalism at Work: Employee Ownership, Profit and Gain Sharing, and Broad-Based Stock Options," *Industrial & Labor Relations Review* 64, no. 3 (2011), pp. 621–622.

39 A. Pendleton and A. Robinson, "Employee Stock Ownership, Involvement, and Productivity: An Interaction-Based Approach," *Industrial and Labor Relations Review* 64, no. 1 (2010), pp. 3–29.

40 "Canada Celebrates First Employee Ownership Day," *ESOP Association Canada*, June 5, 2017, https://www.esopcanada.ca/single-post/2017/06/05/Canada-Celebrates-First-Employee-Ownership-Day.

41 X. Zhang, K. M. Bartol, K. G. Smith M. D. Pfarrer, and D. M. Khanin, "CEOs on the Edge: Earnings Manipulation and Stock-Based Incentive Misalignment," *Academy of Management Journal* 51, no. 2 (2008), pp. 241–258.

42 C. B. Cadsby, F. Song, and F. Tapon, "Sorting and Incentive Effects of Pay for Performance: An Experimental Investigation," *Academy of Management Journal* 50, no. 2 (2007), pp. 387–405.

43 J. H. Han, K. M. Barol, and S. Kim, "Tightening Up the Performance-Pay Linkage: Roles of Contingent Reward Leadership and Profit-Sharing in the Cross-Level Influence of Individual Pay-for-Performance." *Journal of Applied Psychology* 100, no. 2 (2015), pp. 417–430.

44 Z. Lin, J. Kelly, and L. Trenberth, "Antecedents and Consequences of the Introduction of Flexible Benefit Plans in China," *International Journal of Human Resource Management* 22, no. 5 (2011), pp. 1128–1145.

45 P. Stephens, "Flex Plans Gain in Popularity," *CA Magazine*, January/February 2010, p. 10.

46 N. Stewart, "The Power of Appreciation: Rewards and Recognition Practices in Canadian Organizations," *The Conference Board of Canada*, June 22, 2017.

47 B. Scudamore, "Pump up Employee Passion," *PROFIT*, October 13, 2010, http://www.profitguide.com/manage-grow/human-resources/pump-up-employee-passion-29964.

48 "Building a Better Workforce," *PROFIT*, February 16, 2011, http://www.profitguide.com/manage-grow/human-resources/building-a-better-workforce-30073.

49 See also D. A. Johnson and A. M. Dickinson, "Employee-of-the-Month Programs: Do They Really Work?" *Journal of Organizational Behavior Management* 30, no. 4 (2010), pp. 308–324.

50. S. E. Markham, K. D. Scott, and G. H. McKee, "Recognizing Good Attendance: A Longitudinal, Quasi-Experimental Field Study," *Personnel Psychology* 55, no. 3 (2002), p. 641; and S. J. Peterson and F. Luthans, "The Impact of Financial and Nonfinancial Incentives on Business Unit Outcomes over Time," *Journal of Applied Psychology* 91, no. 1 (2006), pp. 156–165.

51. C. Xu and C. Liang, "The Mechanisms Underlying an Employee Recognition Program," in *Proceedings of the International Conference on Public Human Resource Management and Innovation*, ed. L. Hale and J. Zhang Marietta, GA: American Scholars Press, 2013), pp. 28–35.

52. S. Kerr, "On the Folly of Rewarding A, While Hoping for B," *Academy of Management Executive* 9, no. 1 (1995), pp. 7–14.

53. "More on the Folly," *Academy of Management Executive* 9, no. 1 (1995), pp. 15–16.

54. Based on L. Pope and J. Harvey-Berino, "Burn and Earn: A Randomized Controlled Trial Incentivizing Exercise during Fall Semester for College First-Year Students," *Preventive Medicine* 56, no. 3–4 (March 2013), pp. 197–201.

55. C. B. Gibson, J. L. Gibbs, T. L. Stanko, P. Tesluk, and S. G. Cohen, "Including the 'I' in Virtuality and Modern Job Design: Extending the Job Characteristics Model to Include the Moderating Effect of Individual Experiences of Electronic Dependence and Copresence," *Organization Science* 22, no. 6 (2011), pp. 1481–1499.

56. Payscale, "The Most and Least Meaningful Jobs, 2014," accessed October 14, 2014, http://www.payscale.com/data-packages/most-and-least-meaningful-jobs/full-list.

57. J. R. Hackman, "Work Design," in *Improving Life at Work*, ed. J. R. Hackman and J. L. Suttle (Santa Monica, CA: Goodyear, 1977), p. 129.

58. Based on M. Gagné and D. Bhave, "Autonomy in the Workplace: An Essential Ingredient to Employee Engagement and Well-Being in Every Culture?" in *Human Autonomy in Cross-Cultural Context: Perspectives on the Psychology of Agency, Freedom, and Well-Being*, ed. V. I. Chirkov, R. M. Ryan, and K. M. Sheldon (Berlin, Germany: Springer, 2011); and "Freedom's Just Another Word for Employee Satisfaction," *Concordia University*, January 24, 2011, http://www.concordia.ca/cunews/main/releases/2011/01/24/freedoms-just-another-word-for-employee-satisfaction.html.

59. S. E. Humphrey, J. D. Nahrgang, and F. P. Morgeson, "Integrating Motivational, Social, and Contextual Work Design Features: A Meta-analytic Summary and Theoretical Extension of the Work Design Literature," *Journal of Applied Psychology* 92, no. 5 (2007), pp. 1332–1356.

60. B. M. Meglino and A. M. Korsgaard, "The Role of Other Orientation in Reactions to Job Characteristics," *Journal of Management* 33, no. 1 (2007), pp. 57–83.

61. J. L. Pierce, I. Jussila, and A. Cummings, "Psychological Ownership within the Job Design Context: Revision of the Job Characteristics Model," *Journal of Organizational Behavior* 30, no. 4 (2009), pp. 477–496.

62. C. B. Gibson, J. L. Gibbs, T. L. Stanko, P. Tesluk, and S. G. Cohen, "Including the 'I' in Virtuality and Modern Job Design: Extending the Job Characteristics Model to Include the Moderating Effect of Individual Experiences of Electronic Dependence and Copresence," *Organization Science* 22, no. 6 (2011), pp. 1481–1499.

63. B. Ingram, "Island Health Care Model Shift Criticized By Nurses," *Nanaimo Daily News*, January 15, 2014, p. A5.

64. T. Silver, "Rotate Your Way to Higher Value," *Baseline* March/April 2010, p. 12; and J. J. Salopek, "Coca-Cola Division Refreshes Its Talent with Diversity Push on Campus," *Workforce Management Online*, March 2011, http://www.workforce.com.

65. Skytrax website review of Singapore Airlines, accessed May 31, 2013, http://www.airlinequality.com/Airlines/SQ.htm.

66. A. Christini and D. Pozzoli, "Workplace Practices and Firm Performance in Manufacturing: A Comparative Study of Italy and Britain," *International Journal of Manpower* 31, no. 7 (2010), pp. 818–842; and K. Kaymaz, "The Effects of Job Rotation Practices on Motivation: A Research on Managers in the Automotive Organizations," *Business and Economics Research Journal* 1, no. 3 (2010), pp. 69–86.

67. S.-H. Huang and Y.-C. Pan, "Ergonomic Job Rotation Strategy Based on an Automated RGB-D Anthropometric Measuring System," *Journal of Manufacturing Systems* 33, no. 4 (2014), pp. 699–710; and P. C. Leider, J. S. Boschman, M. H. W. Frings-Dresen, and H. F. van der Molen, "Effects of Job Rotation on Musculoskeletal Complaints and Related Work Exposures: A Systematic Literature Review," *Ergonomics* 58, no. 1 (2015), pp. 18–32.

68. A. M. Grant, "Leading with Meaning: Beneficiary Contact, Prosocial Impact, and the Performance Effects of Transformational Leadership," *Academy of Management Journal* 55 (2012), pp. 458–476; and A. M. Grant and S. K. Parker, "Redesigning Work Design Theories: The Rise of Relational and Proactive Perspectives," *Annals of the Academy of Management* 3, no. 1 (2009), pp. 317–375.

69. J. Devaro, "A Theoretical Analysis of Relational Job Design and Compensation," *Journal of Organizational Behavior* 31 (2010), pp. 279–301.

70. A. M. Grant, E. M. Campbell, G. Chen, K. Cottone, D. Lapedis, and K. Lee, "Impact and the Art of Motivation Maintenance: The Effects of Contact with Beneficiaries on Persistence Behavior," *Organizational Behavior and Human Decision Processes* 103, no. 1 (2007), pp. 53–67.

71. Y. N. Turner, I. Hadas-Halperin, and D. Raveh, "Patient Photos Spur Radiologist Empathy and Eye for Detail" (paper presented at the annual meeting of the Radiological Society of North America, November 2008).

72. A. M. Grant, "The Significance of Task Significance: Job Performance Effects, Relational Mechanisms, and Boundary Conditions," *Journal of Applied Psychology* no. 93 (2008), pp. 108–124.

73. K. Pajo and L. Lee, "Corporate-Sponsored Volunteering: A Work Design Perspective," *Journal of Business Ethics* 99, no. 3 (2011), pp. 467–482.

74. L. Duxbury and C. Higgins, "Revisiting Work-Life Issues in Canada: The 2012 National Study on Balancing Work and Caregiving in Canada," accessed October 14, 2014, http://www.healthyworkplaces.info/wp-content/uploads/2012/11/2012-National-Work-Long-Summary.pdf.

75. K. Bal, "Does Flextime Penalize Night Owls?" *Human Resource Executive*, June 23, 2014, http://www.hreonline.com/HRE/view/story.jhtml?id=534357257.

76. T. Kato, "Work and Family Practices in Japanese Firms: Their Scope, Nature, and Impact on Employee Turnover," *International Journal of Human Resource Management* 20, no. 2 (2009), pp. 439–456; and P. Mourdoukoutas, "Why Do Women Fare Better in the German World of Work than in the US?" *Forbes*, March 25, 2013, http://www.forbes.com/sites/panosmourdoukoutas/2013/03/25/why-do-women-fare-better-in-the-german-world-of-work-than-in-the-us/.

77. R. Waring, "Sunday Dialogue: Flexible Work Hours," *New York Times*, January 19, 2013, http://www.nytimes.com/2013/01/20/opinion/sunday/sunday-dialogue-flexible-work-hours.html?pagewanted=all&_r=0.

78. S. Y. He, "Does Flextime Affect Choice of Departure Time for Morning Home-Based Commuting Trips? Evidence from Two Regions in California," *Transport Policy* 25 (2013), pp. 210–221.

79. S. Westcott, "Beyond Flextime: Trashing the Workweek," *Inc.*, August 2008, p. 30.

80 B. Y. Lee and S. E. DeVoe, "Flextime and Profitability," *Industrial Relations* 51, no. 2 (2012), pp. 298–316.

81 K. M. Shockley and T. D. Allen, "When Flexibility Helps: Another Look at the Availability of Flexible Work Arrangements and Work-Family Conflict," *Journal of Vocational Behavior* 71, no. 3 (2007), pp. 479–493; J. G. Grzywacz, D. S. Carlson, and S. Shulkin, "Schedule Flexibility and Stress: Linking Formal Flexible Arrangements and Perceived Flexibility to Employee Health," *Community, Work, and Family* 11, no. 2 (2008), pp. 199–214; and L. A. McNall, A. D. Masuda, and J. M. Nicklin, "Flexible Work Arrangements, Job Satisfaction, and Turnover Intentions: The Mediating Role of Work-to-Family Enrichment," *Journal of Psychology* 144, no. 1 (2010), pp. 61–81.

82 S. Schieman and M. Young, "Is There a Downside to Schedule Control for the Work-Family Interface?" *Journal of Family Issues* 31, no. 10 (2010), pp. 1391–1414.

83 K. M. Shockley and T. D. Allen, "Investigating the Missing Link in Flexible Work Arrangement Utilization: An Individual Difference Perspective," *Journal of Vocational Behavior* 76, no. 1 (2010), pp. 131–142.

84 C. L. Munsch, C. L. Ridgeway, and J. C. Williams, "Pluralistic Ignorance and the Flexibility Bias: Understanding and Mitigating Flextime and Flexplace Bias at Work," *Work and Occupations* 41, no. 1 (2014), pp. 40–62.

85 D. Eldridge and T. M. Nisar, "Employee and Organizational Impacts of Flextime Work Arrangements," *Industrial Relations* 66, no. 2 (2011), pp. 213–234.

86 T. Grant, "Job Sharing," *Globe and Mail*, May 16, 2009.

87 T. Grant, "Job Sharing," *Globe and Mail*, May 16, 2009.

88 See, for example, E. J. Hill, M. Ferris, and V. Martinson, "Does It Matter Where You Work? A Comparison of How Three Work Venues (Traditional Office, Virtual Office, and Home Office) Influence Aspects of Work and Personal/Family Life," *Journal of Vocational Behavior* 63, no. 2 (2003), pp. 220–241; B. Williamson, "Managing Virtual Workers," *Bloomberg Businessweek*, July 16, 2009, http://www.businessweek.com/stories/2009-07-15/managing-virtual-workers; and B. A. Lautsch and E. E. Kossek, "Managing a Blended Workforce: Telecommuters and Non-Telecommuters," *Organizational Dynamics* 40, no. 1 (2010), pp. 10–17.

89 B. Belton, "Best Buy Copies Yahoo, Reins in Telecommuting," *USA Today*, March 6, 2013, http://www.usatoday.com.

90 C. Tkaczyk, "Marissa Mayer Breaks Her Silence on Yahoo's Telecommuting Policy," *Fortune*, April 13, 2013, http://fortune.com/2013/04/19/marissa-mayer-breaks-her-silence-on-yahoos-telecommuting-policy/.

91 G. Karstens-Smith, "Remote Work an Escape When Trapped by Gridlock," *Toronto Star*, May 29, 2014, p. B1.

92 "Canadian Studies on Telework," *InnoVisions Canada*, http://www.ivc.ca/studies/canada/.

93 M. E. Roloff, "Why Teleworkers Are More Satisfied with Their Jobs Than Are Office-Based Workers: When Less Contact Is Beneficial," *Journal of Applied Communication Research* 38, no. 4 (2010), pp. 336–361.

94 E. E. Kossek, B. A. Lautsch, and S. C. Eaton, "Telecommuting, Control, and Boundary Management: Correlates of Policy Use and Practice, Job Control, and Work-Family Effectiveness," *Journal of Vocational Behavior* 68, no. 2 (2006), pp. 347–367.

95 J. Kotkin, "Marissa Mayer's Misstep and the Unstoppable Rise of Telecommuting," *Forbes*, March 26, 2013.

96 L. Taskin and F. Bridoux, "Telework: A Challenge to Knowledge Transfer in Organizations," *International Journal of Human Resource Management* 21, no. 13 (2010), pp. 2503–2520.

97 S. M. B. Thatcher and J. Bagger, "Working in Pajamas: Telecommuting, Unfairness Sources, and Unfairness Perceptions," *Negotiation and Conflict Management Research* 4, no. 3 (2011), pp. 248–276.

98 E. G. Dutcher, "The Effects of Telecommuting on Productivity: An Experimental Examination. The Role of Dull and Creative Tasks," *Journal of Economic Behavior & Organization* 84, no. 1 (2014), pp. 355–363.

99 M. C. Noonan and J. L. Glass, "The Hard Truth about Telecommuting," *Monthly Labor Review*, 2012, pp. 1459–1478.

100 J. Welch and S. Welch, "The Importance of Being There," *BusinessWeek*, April 16, 2007, p. 92; Z. I. Barsness, K. A. Diekmann, and M. L. Seidel, "Motivation and Opportunity: The Role of Remote Work, Demographic Dissimilarity, and Social Network Centrality in Impression Management," *Academy of Management Journal* 48, no. 3 (2005), pp. 401–419.

101 P. Zhu and S. G. Mason, "The Impact of Telecommuting on Personal Vehicle Usage and Environmental Sustainability," *International Journal of Environmental Science and Technology* 11, no. 8 (2014), pp. 2185–2200.

102 "Secrets of Canada's Best Managed Companies (2017)," *Canadian Business*, http://www.canadianbusiness.com/best-managed-companies/#winners; B. Poon Tip, *Looptail: How One Company Changed the World by Reinventing Business.* (Toronto: HarperCollins Canada, 2013); P. Hunter, "Meet the 'Mayor' of G Adventures, Whose Job Is to Make Employees Happy," *thestar.com*, June 6, 2015, https://www.thestar.com/news/insight/2015/06/06/meet-the-mayor-of-g-adventures-whose-job-is-to-make-employees-happy.html.

103 M. Marchington, "Analysing the Forces Shaping Employee Involvement and Participation (EIP) at Organisation Level in Liberal Market Economies (LMEs)," *Human Resource Management Journal* 25, no. 1 (2015), pp. 1–18.

104 See, for example, the increasing body of literature on empowerment, such as D. P. Ashmos, D. Duchon, R. R. McDaniel Jr., and J. W. Huonker, "What a Mess! Participation as a Simple Managerial Rule to 'Complexify' Organizations," *Journal of Management Studies* 39, no. 2 (2002), pp. 189–206; S. E. Seibert, S. R. Silver, and W. A. Randolph, "Taking Empowerment to the Next Level: A Multiple-Level Model of Empowerment, Performance, and Satisfaction," *Academy of Management Journal* 47, no. 3 (2004), pp. 332–349; M. M. Butts, R. J. Vandenberg, D. M. DeJoy, B. S. Schaffer, and M. G. Wilson, "Individual Reactions to High Involvement Work Processes: Investigating the Role of Empowerment and Perceived Organizational Support," *Journal of Occupational Health Psychology* 14, no. 2 (2009), pp. 122–136; R. Park, E. Applebaum, and D. Kruse, "Employee Involvement and Group Incentives in Manufacturing Companies: A Multi-Level Analysis," *Human Resource Management Journal* 20, no. 3 (2010), pp. 227–243; D. C. Jones, P. Kalmi, and A. Kauhanen, "How Does Employee Involvement Stack Up? The Effects of Human Resource Management Policies in a Retail Firm," *Industrial Relations* 49, no. 1 (2010), pp. 1–21; and M. T. Maynard, L. L. Gilson, and J. E. Mathieu, "Empowerment—Fad or Fab? A Multilevel Review of the Past Two Decades of Research," *Journal of Management* 38, no. 4 (2012), pp. 1231–1281.

105 M. Marchington, "Analysing the Forces Shaping Employee Involvement and Participation (EIP) at Organisation Level in Liberal Market Economies (LMEs)," *Human Resource Management Journal* 25, no. 1 (2015), pp. 1–18.

106 J. J. Caughron and M. D. Mumford, "Embedded Leadership: How Do a Leader's Superiors Impact Middle-Management Performance?" *Leadership Quarterly*, June 2012, pp. 342–353.

107 See, for example, K. L. Miller and P. R. Monge, "Participation, Satisfaction, and Productivity: A Meta-analytic Review," *Academy of Management Journal*, December 1986, pp. 727–753; J. A. Wagner III, "Participation's Effects on Performance and Satisfaction: A Reconsideration of Research Evidence," *Academy of Management*

Review, April 1994, pp. 312–330; C. Doucouliagos, "Worker Participation and Productivity in Labor-Managed and Participatory Capitalist Firms: A Meta-analysis," *Industrial and Labor Relations Review*, October 1995, pp. 58–77; J. A. Wagner III, C. R. Leana, E. A. Locke, and D. M. Schweiger, "Cognitive and Motivational Frameworks in U.S. Research on Participation: A Meta-analysis of Primary Effects," *Journal of Organizational Behavior* 18 (1997), pp. 49–65; E. A. Locke, M. Alavi, and J. A. Wagner III, "Participation in Decision Making: An Information Exchange Perspective," in *Research in Personnel and Human Resource Management*, vol. 15, ed. G. R. Ferris (Greenwich, CT: JAI Press, 1997), pp. 293–331; and J. A. Wagner III and J. A. LePine, "Effects of Participation on Performance and Satisfaction: Additional Meta-analytic Evidence," *Psychological Reports*, June 1999, pp. 719–725.

108 D. K. Datta, J. P. Guthrie, and P. M. Wright, "Human Resource Management and Labor Productivity: Does Industry Matter?" *Academy of Management Journal* 48, no. 1 (2005), pp. 135–145; C. M. Riordan, R. J. Vandenberg, and H. A. Richardson, "Employee Involvement Climate and Organizational Effectiveness," *Human Resource Management* 44, no. 4 (2005), pp. 471–488; and J. Kim, J. P. MacDuffie, and F. K. Pil, "Employee Voice and Organizational Performance: Team versus Representative Influence," *Human Relations* 63, no. 3 (2010), pp. 371–394.

109 M. Marchington, "Analysing the Forces Shaping Employee Involvement and Participation (EIP) at Organisation Level in Liberal Market Economies (LMEs)," *Human Resource Management Journal* 25, no. 1 (2015), pp. 1–18.

110 M. Marchington, "Analysing the Forces Shaping Employee Involvement and Participation (EIP) at Organisation Level in Liberal Market Economies (LMEs)," *Human Resource Management Journal* 25, no. 1 (2015), pp. 1–18.

111 N. Nohria, B. Groysberg, and L.-E. Lee, "Employee Motivation: A Powerful New Model," *Harvard Business Review*, July–August 2008, pp. 78–84.

112 P. R. Lawrence and N. Nohria, *Driven: How Human Nature Shapes Our Choices* (San Francisco: Jossey-Bass, 2002).

113 S. Miller, "Variable Pay Spending Spikes to Record High," *Society for Human Resource Management*, September 2, 2014, http://www.shrm.org/hrdisciplines/compensation/articles/pages/variable-pay-high.aspx.

114 S. Miller, "Companies Worldwide Rewarding Performance with Variable Pay," *Society for Human Resource Management*, March 1, 2010, http://www.shrm.org/hrdisciplines/compensation/articles/pages/variableworld.aspx.

115 S. Miller, "Asian Firms Offer More Variable Pay Than Western Firms," *Society for Human Resource Management*, March 28, 2012, http://www.shrm.org/hrdisciplines/compensation/articles/pages/asianvariablepay.aspx.

116 Z. Lin, J. Kellly, and L. Trenberth, "Antecedents and Consequences of the Introduction of Flexible Benefit Plans in China," *The International Journal of Human Resource Management* 22, no. 5 (2011), pp. 1128–1145.

117 R. C. Koo, "Global Added Value of Flexible Benefits," *Benefits Quarterly* 27, no. 4 (2011), pp. 17–20.

118 D. Lovewell, "Flexible Benefits: Benefits on Offer," *Employee Benefits*, March 2010, p. S15.

119 M. Erez, "Culture and Job Design," *Journal of Organizational Behavior* 31, no. 2/3 (2010), pp. 389–400.

120 B. M. Naba and L. Fan, "Employee Motivation and Satisfaction in Niger: An Application of the Job Characteristics Model," in *Proceedings of the 10th International Conference on Innovation and Management*, ed. A. de Hoyos, K. Kaminishi, and G. Duysters, (Wuhan, China: Wuhan University of Technology Press, 2013), pp. 523–527.

121 M. F. Peterson and S. A. Ruiz-Quintanilla, "Cultural Socialization as a Source of Intrinsic Work Motivation," *Group & Organization Management*, June 2003, pp. 188–216.

122 D. Wilkie, "Has the Telecommuting Bubble Burst?" *Society for Human Resource Management*, June 1, 2015, http://www.shrm.org/publications/hrmagazine/editorialcontent/2015/0615/pages/0615-telecommuting.aspx.

123 S. Raghuram and D. Fang, "Telecommuting and the Role of Supervisory Power in China," *Asia Pacific Journal of Management* 31, no. 2 (2014), pp. 523–547.

124 See, for instance, A. Sagie and Z. Aycan, "A Cross-Cultural Analysis of Participative Decision-Making in Organizations," *Human Relations* 56, no. 4 (2003), pp. 453–473; and J. Brockner, "Unpacking Country Effects: On the Need to Operationalize the Psychological Determinants of Cross-National Differences," in *Research in Organizational Behavior*, vol. 25, ed. R. M. Kramer and B. M. Staw (Oxford, UK: Elsevier, 2003), pp. 336–340.

125 C. Robert, T. M. Probst, J. J. Martocchio, R. Drasgow, and J. J. Lawler, "Empowerment and Continuous Improvement in the United States, Mexico, Poland, and India: Predicting Fit on the Basis of the Dimensions of Power Distance and Individualism," *Journal of Applied Psychology*, October 2000, pp. 643–658.

126 Z. X. Chen and S. Aryee, "Delegation and Employee Work Outcomes: An Examination of the Cultural Context of Mediating Processes in China," *Academy of Management Journal* 50, no. 1 (2007), pp. 226–238.

127 G. Huang, X. Niu, C. Lee, and S. J. Ashford, "Differentiating Cognitive and Affective Job Insecurity: Antecedents and Outcomes," *Journal of Organizational Behavior* 33, no. 6 (2012), pp. 752–769.

128 Z. Cheng, "The Effects of Employee Involvement and Participation on Subjective Wellbeing: Evidence from Urban China," *Social Indicators Research* 118, no. 2 (2014), pp. 457–483.

129 Based on J. Surowiecki, "Face Time," *New Yorker*, March 18, 2013, http://www.newyorker.com/magazine/2013/03/18/face-time; and L. Taskin and F. Bridoux, "Telework: A Challenge to Knowledge Transfer in Organizations," *International Journal of Human Resource Management* 21, no. 13 (2010), pp. 2503–2520.

130 This exercise is based on W. P. Ferris, "Enlivening the Job Characteristics Model," in *Proceedings of the 29th Annual Eastern Academy of Management Meeting*, ed. C. Harris and C. C. Lundberg (Baltimore, MD: May 1992), pp. 125–128.

131 Based on J. Hansen, "Canada's Top CEOs Earn 193 Times Average Worker's Salary," *cbcnews*, January 3, 2017, http://www.cbc.ca/news/business/top-ceo-pay-1.3907662; R. Kerber and P. Szekely, "CEO Pay Still Dwarfing Pay of U.S. Workers: Union Report, May 9, 2017, https://www.usnews.com/news/top-news/articles/2017-05-09/earnings-gap-over-us-workers-grows-for-s-p-500-ceos-union-report; J. McFarland, "Major CEO Pay Increases in the Cards Again," *Globe and Mail*, June 1, 2014, http://www.theglobeandmail.com/report-on-business/careers/management/executive-compensation/pay-is-on-the-rise-for-canadas-top-executives/article18940701/; T. Tedesco, "U.S. CEO Pay Leaves Canadians in Dust; Up 9% in a Year," *National Post*, May 30, 2014, p. A1; E. Chemi and A. Giorgi, "The Pay-for-Performance Myth," *Bloomberg Businessweek*, July 22, 2014, http://www.businessweek.com/articles/2014-07-22/for-ceos-correlation-between-pay-and-stock-performance-is-pretty-random; and "How They Performed," *Financial Post Magazine*, November 2013, p. 43.

132 Based on P. Coy, "The Leisure Gap," *Bloomberg Businessweek*, July 23–29, 2012, pp. 8–10; A. B. Krueger and A. I. Mueller, "Time Use, Emotional Well-Being, and Unemployment: Evidence from Longitudinal Data," *American Economic Review*, May 2012, pp. 594–599; and L. Kwoh, "More Firms Offer Option to Swap Cash for Time," *Wall Street Journal*, September 26, 2012, p. B6.

133 R. Feintzeig, "When the Annual Raise Isn't Enough," *Wall Street Journal*, July 16, 2014, pp. B1, B5; J. C. Marr and S. Thau, "Falling from Great (and Not-So-Great) Heights: How Initial Status Position Influences Performance after Status Loss," *Academy of Management Journal* 57, no. 1 (2014), pp. 223–248; and "Pay Equity & Discrimination," IWPR, http://www.iwpr.org/initiatives/pay-equity-and-discrimination.

134 Based on J. R. Hackman, "Work Design," in *Improving Life at Work*, ed. J. R. Hackman and J. L. Suttle (Santa Monica, CA: Goodyear, 1977), pp. 132–133.

Chapter 6

1 Opening vignette based on T. Hatherly, "New Summer Program in East York Helps Kids Bridge Nutrition Gap," *East York Mirror*, August 17, 2016; and personal interview notes, July 2017.

2 J. R. Katzenback and D. K. Smith, *The Wisdom of Teams: Creating the High-Performance Organization.* (Cambridge, MA: Harvard Business Review Press, 2015), p. 214.

3 R. Cross, R. Rebele, and A. Grant, "Collaborative Overload," *Harvard Business Review*, January–February 2016, pp. 74–79.

4 J. Mathieu, M. T. Maynard, T. Rapp, and L. Gilson, "Team Effectiveness 1997–2007: A Review of Recent Advancements and a Glimpse into the Future," *Journal of Management* 34, no. 3 (2008), pp. 410–476.

5 See, for example, A. Erez, J. A. LePine, and H. Elms, "Effects of Rotated Leadership and Peer Evaluation on the Functioning and Effectiveness of Self-Managed Teams: A Quasi-Experiment," *Personnel Psychology* (Winter 2002), pp. 929–948.

6 See, for example, A. Erez, J. A. LePine, and H. Elms, "Effects of Rotated Leadership and Peer Evaluation on the Functioning and Effectiveness of Self-Managed Teams: A Quasi-Experiment," *Personnel Psychology* (Winter 2002), pp. 929–948.

7 G. L. Stewart, S. H. Courtright, and M. R. Barrick, "Peer-Based Control in Self-Managing Teams: Linking Rational and Normative Influence with Individual and Group Performance," *Journal of Applied Psychology* 97, no. 2 (2012), pp. 435–447.

8 C. W. Langfred, "The Downside of Self-Management: A Longitudinal Study of the Effects of Conflict on Trust, Autonomy, and Task Interdependence in Self-Managing Teams," *Academy of Management Journal* 50, no. 4 (2007), pp. 885–900.

9 B. H. Bradley, B. E. Postlethwaite, A. C. Klotz, M. R. Hamdani, and K. G. Brown, "Reaping the Benefits of Task Conflict in Teams: The Critical Role of Team Psychological Safety Climate," *Journal of Applied Psychology* 97, no. 1 (2012), pp. 151–158.

10 J. Devaro, "The Effects of Self-Managed and Closely Managed Teams on Labor Productivity and Product Quality: An Empirical Analysis of a Cross-Section of Establishments," *Industrial Relations* 47, no. 4 (2008), pp. 659–698.

11 A. Shah, "Starbucks Strives for Instant Gratification with Via Launch," *PRWeek*, December 2009, p. 15.

12 F. Aime, S. Humphrey, D. S. DeRue, and J. B. Paul, "The Riddle of Heterarchy: Power Transitions in Cross-Functional Teams," *Academy of Management Journal* 57, no. 2 (2014), pp. 327–352.

13 See, for example, L. L. Martins, L. L. Gilson, and M. T. Maynard, "Virtual Teams: What Do We Know and Where Do We Go from Here?" *Journal of Management*, November 2004, pp. 805–835; and B. Leonard, "Managing Virtual Teams," *HR Magazine*, June 2011, pp. 39–42.

14 J. E. Hoch and S. W. J. Kozlowski, "Leading Virtual Teams: Hierarchical Leadership, Structural Supports, and Shared Team Leadership," *Journal of Applied Psychology* 99, no. 3 (2014), pp. 390–403.

15 "Virtual Teams a First in Canada," *Financial Post*, January 19, 2011, http://business.financialpost.com/2011/01/19/mba-virtual-teams-a-first-in-canada/. Material reprinted with the express permission of: National Post, a division of Postmedia Network Inc.

16 C. Joinson, "Managing Virtual Teams," *HR Magazine*, June 2002, p. 71. Reprinted with the permission of *HR Magazine*, published by the Society for Human Resource Management, Alexandria, VA.

17 A. Malhotra, A. Majchrzak, and B. Rosen, "Leading Virtual Teams," *Academy of Management Perspectives*, February 2007, pp. 60–70; and J. M. Wilson, S. S. Straus, and B. McEvily, "All in Due Time: The Development of Trust in Computer Mediated and Face-to-Face Teams," *Organizational Behavior and Human Decision Processes* 19 (2006), pp. 16–33.

18 Based on P. Tilstone, "Cut Carbon … and Bills," *Director*, May 2009, p. 54; L. C. Latimer, "6 Strategies for Sustainable Business Travel," *Greenbiz*, February 11, 2011, http://www.greenbiz.com/blog/2011/02/11/6-strategies-sustainable-business-travel; and F. Gebhart, "Travel Takes a Big Bite Out of Corporate Expenses," *Travel Market Report*, May 30, 2013, http://www.travelmarketreport.com/articles/Travel-Takes-Big-Bite-Out-of-Corporate-Expenses.

19 P. Balkundi and D. A. Harrison, "Ties, Leaders, and Time in Teams: Strong Inference about Network Structure's Effects on Team Viability and Performance," *Academy of Management Journal* 49, no. 1 (2006), pp. 49–68; G. Chen, B. L. Kirkman, R. Kanfer, D. Allen, and B. Rosen, "A Multilevel Study of Leadership, Empowerment, and Performance in Teams," *Journal of Applied Psychology* 92, no. 2 (2007), pp. 331–346; L. A. DeChurch and M. A. Marks, "Leadership in Multiteam Systems," *Journal of Applied Psychology* 91, no. 2 (2006), pp. 311–329; A. Srivastava, K. M. Bartol, and E. A. Locke, "Empowering Leadership in Management Teams: Effects on Knowledge Sharing, Efficacy, and Performance," *Academy of Management Journal* 49, no. 6 (2006), pp. 1239–1251; and J. E. Mathieu, K. K. Gilson, and T. M. Ruddy, "Empowerment and Team Effectiveness: An Empirical Test of an Integrated Model," *Journal of Applied Psychology* 91, no. 1 (2006), pp. 97–108.

20 R. B. Davison, J. R. Hollenbeck, C. M. Barnes, D. J. Sleesman, and D. R. Ilgen, "Coordinated Action in Multiteam Systems," *Journal of Applied Psychology* 97, no. 4 (2012), pp. 808–824.

21 M. M. Luciano, J. E. Mathieu, and T. M. Ruddy, "Leading Multiple Teams: Average and Relative External Leadership Influences on Team Empowerment and Effectiveness," *Journal of Applied Psychology* 99, no. 2 (2014), pp. 322–331.

22 Vignette based on personal interview notes, July 2017.

23 Based on Ed Tait, "Bombers Believe in Willy," *Winnipeg Free Press*, August 5, 2014, p. D1; "Talent, Teamwork Fuel Bombers Turnaround," *Brandon Sun*, August 6, 2014; G. Lawless, "They've Got a Marquee Man, Now Bombers' Task Is a Talent Hunt to Fill Supporting Roles," *Winnipeg Free Press*, October 29, 2014; and "Coach Will Keep Tabs On Players' Effort," *Winnipeg Free Press*, October 30, 2014, p. D3.

24 K. S. Wilson and H. M. Baumann, "Capturing a More Complete View of Employees' Lives Outside of Work: The Introduction and Development of New Interrole Conflict Constructs," *Personnel Psychology* 68, no. 2 (2015), pp. 235–282.

25 See, for example, F. T. Amstad, L. L. Meier, U. Fasel, A. Elfering, and N. K. Semmer, "A Meta-analysis of Work-Family Conflict and Various Outcomes with a Special Emphasis on Cross-Domain versus Matching-Domain Relations," *Journal of Occupational Health Psychology* 16, no. 2 (2011), pp. 151–169.

26 K. S. Wilson and H. M. Baumann, "Capturing a More Complete View of Employees' Lives Outside of Work: The Introduction and Development of New Interrole Conflict Constructs," *Personnel Psychology* 68, no. 2 (2015), pp. 235–282.

27 D. Vora and T. Kostova, "A Model of Dual Organizational Identification in the Context of the Multinational Enterprise," *Journal of Organizational Behavior* 28 (2007), pp. 327–350.

28 C. Reade, "Dual Identification in Multinational Corporations: Local Managers and Their Psychological Attachment to the Subsidiary versus the Global Organization," *International Journal of Human Resource Management* 12, no. 3 (2001), pp. 405–424.

29 E. H. Schein, *Organizational Psychology*, 3rd ed. (Englewood Cliffs, NJ: Prentice Hall, 1980), p. 145.

30 Y. Huang, K. M. Kendrick, and R. Yu, "Conformity to the Opinions of Other People Lasts for No More Than 3 Days," *Psychological Science* 25, no. 7 (2014), pp. 1388–1393.

31 M. S. Hagger, P. Rentzelas, and N. K. D. Chatzisrantis, "Effects of Individualist and Collectivist Group Norms and Choice on Intrinsic Motivation," *Motivation and Emotion* 38, no. 2 (2014), pp. 215–223; and M. G. Ehrhart and S. E. Naumann, "Organizational Citizenship Behavior in Work Groups: A Group Norms Approach," *Journal of Applied Psychology*, December 2004, pp. 960–974.

32 Adapted from P. S. Goodman, E. Ravlin, and M. Schminke, "Understanding Groups in Organizations," in *Research in Organizational Behavior*, vol. 9, ed. L. L. Cummings and B. M. Staw (Greenwich, CT: JAI Press, 1987), p. 159.

33 Submitted by Don Miskiman, Chair and U-C Professor of Management, Malaspina University College, Nanaimo, BC. With permission.

34 D. C. Feldman, "The Development and Enforcement of Group Norms," *Academy of Management Journal*, January 1984, pp. 47–53; and K. L. Bettenhausen and J. K. Murnighan, "The Development of an Intragroup Norm and the Effects of Interpersonal and Structural Challenges," *Administrative Science Quarterly*, March 1991, pp. 20–35.

35 D. C. Feldman, "The Development and Enforcement of Group Norms," *Academy of Management Journal*, January 1984, pp. 47–53; and K. L. Bettenhausen and J. K. Murnighan, "The Development of an Intragroup Norm and the Effects of Interpersonal and Structural Challenges," *Administrative Science Quarterly*, March 1991, pp. 20–35.

36 R. B. Cialdini and N. J. Goldstein, "Social Influence: Compliance and Conformity," *Annual Review of Psychology* 55 (2004), pp. 591–621.

37 S. E. Asch, "Effects of Group Pressure upon the Modification and Distortion of Judgments," in *Groups, Leadership and Men*, ed. H. Guetzkow (Pittsburgh, PA: Carnegie Press, 1951), pp. 177–190; and S. E. Asch, "Studies of Independence and Conformity: A Minority of One Against a Unanimous Majority," *Psychological Monographs: General and Applied* 70, no. 9 (1956), pp. 1–70.

38 S. L. Robinson and A. M. O'Leary-Kelly, "Monkey See, Monkey Do: The Influence of Work Groups on the Antisocial Behavior of Employees," *Academy of Management Journal* 41 (1998), pp. 658–672.

39 J. M. George, "Personality, Affect and Behavior in Groups," *Journal of Applied Psychology* 78 (1993), pp. 798–804; and J. M. George and L. R. James, "Personality, Affect, and Behavior in Groups Revisited: Comment on Aggregation, Levels of Analysis, and a Recent Application of Within and Between Analysis," *Journal of Applied Psychology* 78 (1993), pp. 798–804.

40 J. A. Goncalo, J. A. Chatman, M. M. Duguid, and J. A. Kennedy, "Creativity from Constraint? How the Political Correctness Norm Influences Creativity in Mixed-Sex Work Groups," *Administrative Science Quarterly* 60, no. 1 (2015), pp. 1–30.

41 E. Gonzalez-Mule, D. S. DeGeest, B. W. McCormick, J. Y. Seong, and K. G. Brown, "Can We Get Some Cooperation Around Here? The Mediating Role of Group Norms on the Relationship between Team Personality and Individual Helping Behaviors," *Journal of Applied Psychology* 99, no. 5 (2014), pp. 988–999.

42 T. Masson and I. Fritsche, "Adherence to Climate Change-Related Ingroup Norms: Do Dimensions of Group Identification Matter?" *European Journal of Social Psychology* 44, no. 5 (2014), pp. 455–465.

43 See R. J. Bennett and S. L. Robinson, "The Past, Present, and Future of Workplace Deviance," in *Organizational Behavior: The State of the Science*, 2nd ed., ed. J. Greenberg (Mahwah, NJ: Erlbaum, 2003), pp. 237–271; and C. M. Berry, D. S. Ones, and P. R. Sackett, "Interpersonal Deviance, Organizational Deviance, and Their Common Correlates: A Review and Meta-analysis," *Journal of Applied Psychology* 92, no. 2 (2007), pp. 410–424.

44 M. A. Baysinger, K. T. Scherer, and J. M. LeBreton, "Exploring the Disruptive Effects of Psychopathy and Aggression on Group Processes and Group Effectiveness," *Journal of Applied Psychology* 99, no. 1 (2014), pp. 48–65.

45 T. C. Reich and M. S. Hershcovis, "Observing Workplace Incivility," *Journal of Applied Psychology* 100, no. 1 (2015), pp. 203–215; and Z. E. Zhou, Y. Yan, X. X. Che, and L. L. Meier, "Effect of Workplace Incivility on End-of-Work Negative Affect: Examining Individual and Organizational Moderators in a Daily Diary Study," *Journal of Occupational Health Psychology* 20, no. 1 (2015), pp. 117–130.

46 See C. Pearson, L. M. Andersson, and C. L. Porath, "Workplace Incivility," in *Counterproductive Work Behavior: Investigations of Actors and Targets*, ed. S. Fox and P. E. Spector (Washington, DC: American Psychological Association, 2005), pp. 177–200.

47 S. Lim, L. M. Cortina, and V. J. Magley, "Personal and Workgroup Incivility: Impact on Work and Health Outcomes," *Journal of Applied Psychology* 93, no. 1 (2008), pp. 95–107.

48 M. S. Christian and A. P. J. Ellis, "Examining the Effects of Sleep Deprivation on Workplace Deviance: A Self-Regulatory Perspective," *Academy of Management Journal* 54, no. 5 (2011), pp. 913–934.

49 S. L. Robinson and A. M. O'Leary-Kelly, "Monkey See, Monkey Do: The Influence of Work Groups on the Antisocial Behavior of Employees," *Academy of Management Journal* 41 (1998), pp. 658–672; and T. M. Glomb and H. Liao, "Interpersonal Aggression in Workgroups: Social Influence, Reciprocal, and Individual Effects," *Academy of Management Journal* 46 (2003), pp. 486–496.

50 P. Bamberger and M. Biron, "Group Norms and Excessive Absenteeism: The Role of Peer Referent Others," *Organizational Behavior and Human Decision Processes* 103, no. 2 (2007), pp. 179–196; and A. Väänänen, N. Tordera, M. Kivimäki, A. Kouvonen, J. Pentti, A. Linna, and J. Vahtera, "The Role of Work Group in Individual Sickness Absence Behavior," *Journal of Health & Human Behavior* 49, no. 4 (2008), pp. 452–467.

51 M. S. Cole, F. Walter, and H. Bruch, "Affective Mechanisms Linking Dysfunctional Behavior to Performance in Work Teams: A Moderated Mediation Study," *Journal of Applied Psychology* 93, no. 5 (2008), pp. 945–958.

52 B. W. Tuckman, "Developmental Sequences in Small Groups," *Psychological Bulletin*, June 1965, pp. 384–399; B. W. Tuckman and M. C. Jensen, "Stages of Small-Group Development Revisited," *Group and Organizational Studies*, December 1977, pp. 419–427; and M. F. Maples, "Group Development: Extending Tuckman's Theory," *Journal for Specialists in Group Work*, Fall 1988, pp. 17–23.

53 J. K. Ito, C. M. Brotheridge, "Do Teams Grow Up One Stage at a Time?: Exploring the Complexity of Group Development Models," *Team Performance Management: An International Journal* 14, no. 5/6 (2008), pp. 214–232.

54 R. C. Ginnett, "The Airline Cockpit Crew," in *Groups That Work (and Those That Don't)*, ed. J. R. Hackman (San Francisco: Jossey-Bass, 1990).

55 D. A. Bonebright, "40 Years Of Storming: A Historical Review of Tuckman's Model of Small Group Development," *Human Resource Development International* 13, no. 1 (2010), pp. 111–120.

56 M. J. Garfield and A. R. Denis, "Toward an Integrated Model of Group Development: Disruption of Routines by Technology-Induced Change," *Journal of Management Information Systems* 29,

no. 3 (2012), pp. 43–86; M. J. Waller, J. M. Conte, C. B. Gibson, and M. A. Carpenter, "The Effect of Individual Perceptions of Deadlines on Team Performance," *Academy of Management Review*, October 2001, pp. 586–600; and A. Chang, P. Bordia, and J. Duck, "Punctuated Equilibrium and Linear Progression: Toward a New Understanding of Group Development," *Academy of Management Journal*, February 2003, pp. 106–117.

57 C. J. G. Gersick, "Time and Transition in Work Teams: Toward a New Model of Group Development," *Academy of Management Journal*, March 1988, pp. 9–41; and C. J. G. Gersick, "Marking Time: Predictable Transitions in Task Groups," *Academy of Management Journal*, June 1989, pp. 274–309.

58 M. M. Kazmer, "Disengaging from a Distributed Research Project: Refining a Model of Group Departures," *Journal of the American Society for Information Science and Technology*, April 2010, pp. 758–771.

59 M. M. Kazmer, "Disengaging from a Distributed Research Project: Refining a Model of Group Departures," *Journal of the American Society for Information Science and Technology*, April 2010, pp. 758–771.

60 Vignette based on personal interview notes, July 2017.

61 V. Gonzalez-Roma and A. Hernandez, "Climate Uniformity: Its Influence on Team Communication Quality, Task Conflict, and Team Performance," *Journal of Applied Psychology* 99, no. 6 (2014), pp. 1042–1058; C. F. Peralta, P. N. Lopes, L. L. Gilson, P. R. Lourenco, and L. Pais, "Innovation Processes and Team Effectiveness: The Role of Goal Clarity and Commitment, and Team Affective Tone," *Journal of Occupational and Organizational Psychology* 88, no. 1 (2015), pp. 80–107; L. Thompson, *Making the Team* (Upper Saddle River, NJ: Prentice Hall, 2000), pp. 18–33; and J. R. Hackman, *Leading Teams: Setting the Stage for Great Performance* (Boston: Harvard Business School Press, 2002).

62 See G. L. Stewart and M. R. Barrick, "Team Structure and Performance: Assessing the Mediating Role of Intrateam Process and the Moderating Role of Task Type," *Academy of Management Journal*, April 2000, pp. 135–148.

63 E. M. Stark, "Interdependence and Preference for Group Work: Main and Congruence Effects on the Satisfaction and Performance of Group Members," *Journal of Management* 26, no. 2 (2000), pp. 259–279; and J. W. Bishop, K. D. Scott, and S. M. Burroughs, "Support, Commitment, and Employee Outcomes in a Team Environment," *Journal of Management* 26, no. 6 (2000), pp. 1113–1132.

64 D. E. Hyatt and T. M. Ruddy, "An Examination of the Relationship between Work Group Characteristics and Performance," *Personnel Psychology* 50, no. 3 (1997), p. 577.

65 D. Aarts, "Canada's Smartest Employers 2014," *PROFIT*, November 7, 2013, http://www.profitguide.com/manage-grow/human-resources/meet-canadas-smartest-employers-2014-59150/2.

66 J. R. Hackman, *Leading Teams* (Boston: Harvard Business School Press, 2002).

67 P. Balkundi and D. A. Harrison, "Ties, Leaders, and Time in Teams: Strong Inference about Network Structure's Effects on Team Viability and Performance," *Academy of Management Journal* 49, no. 1 (2006), pp. 49–68; G. Chen, B. L. Kirkman, R. Kanfer, D. Allen, and B. Rosen, "A Multilevel Study of Leadership, Empowerment, and Performance in Teams," *Journal of Applied Psychology* 92, no. 2 (2007), pp. 331–346; L. A. DeChurch and M. A. Marks, "Leadership in Multiteam Systems," *Journal of Applied Psychology* 91, no. 2 (2006), pp. 311–329; A. Srivastava, K. M. Bartol, and E. A. Locke, "Empowering Leadership in Management Teams: Effects on Knowledge Sharing, Efficacy, and Performance," *Academy of Management Journal* 49, no. 6 (2006), pp. 1239–1251; and J. E. Mathieu, K. K. Gilson, and T. M. Ruddy, "Empowerment and Team Effectiveness: An Empirical Test of an Integrated Model," *Journal of Applied Psychology* 91, no. 1 (2006), pp. 97–108.

68 J. L. Berdahl and C. Anderson, "Men, Women, and Leadership Centralization in Groups over Time," *Group Dynamics: Theory, Research, and Practice* 9, no. 1 (2005), pp. 45–57; and W. Immen, "The More Women in Groups, the Better," *Globe and Mail*, April 27, 2005, p. C3.

69 K. T. Dirks, "Trust in Leadership and Team Performance: Evidence from NCAA Basketball," *Journal of Applied Psychology*, December 2000, pp. 1004–1012; M. Williams, "In Whom We Trust: Group Membership as an Affective Context for Trust Development," *Academy of Management Review*, July 2001, pp. 377–396; and J. Schaubroeck, S. S. K. Lam, and A. C. Peng, "Cognition-Based and Affect-Based Trust as Mediators of Leader Behavior Influences on Team Performance," *Journal of Applied Psychology*, Online First Publication, February 7, 2011, doi:10.1037/a0022625.

70 B. A. De Jong, and K. T. Dirks, "Beyond Shared Perceptions of Trust and Monitoring in Teams: Implications of Asymmetry and Dissensus," *Journal of Applied Psychology* 97, no. 2 (2012), pp. 391–406.

71 P. L. Schindler and C. C. Thomas, "The Structure of Interpersonal Trust in the Workplace," *Psychological Reports*, October 1993, pp. 563–573.

72 Based on D. L. Ferrin and N. Gillespie, "Trust Differences Across National-Societal Cultures: Much to Do, or Much Ado About Nothing," in *Organizational Trust: A Cultural Perspective*, ed. M. N. K. Sanders, D. Skinner, G. Dietz, N. Gillespie, and R. J. Lewicki (New York: Cambridge University Press, 2010), pp. 42–86; and J. Lauring and J. Selmer, "Openness to Diversity, Trust and Conflict in Multicultural Organizations," *Journal of Management & Organization*, November 2012, pp. 795–806.

73 G. Brown, C. Crossley, and S. L. Robinson, "Psychological Ownership, Territorial Behavior, and Being Perceived as a Team Contributor: The Critical Role of Trust in the Work Environment," *Personnel Psychology* 67 (2014), pp. 463–485.

74 See F. Aime, C. J. Meyer, and S. E. Humphrey, "Legitimacy of Team Rewards: Analyzing Legitimacy as a Condition for the Effectiveness of Team Incentive Designs," *Journal of Business Research* 63, no. 1 (2010), pp. 60–66; and P. A. Bamberger and R. Levi, "Team-Based Reward Allocation Structures and the Helping Behaviors of Outcome-Interdependent Team Members," *Journal of Managerial Psychology* 24, no. 4 (2009), pp. 300–327; and M. J. Pearsall, M. S. Christian, and A. P. J. Ellis, "Motivating Interdependent Teams: Individual Rewards, Shared Rewards, or Something in Between?" *Journal of Applied Psychology* 95, no. 1 (2010), pp. 183–191.

75 K. Merriman, "Low-Trust Teams Prefer Individualized Pay," *Harvard Business Review*, November 2008, p. 32.

76 J. Pfeffer and N. Langton, "The Effect of Wage Dispersion on Satisfaction, Productivity, and Working Collaboratively: Evidence from College and University Faculty," *Administrative Science Quarterly* 38 (1993), pp. 382–407.

77 M. Bloom, "The Performance Effects of Pay Dispersion on Individuals and Organizations," *Academy of Management Journal* 42 (1999), pp. 25–40.

78 B. Beersma, J. R. Hollenbeck, D. E. Conlon, S. E. Humphrey, H. Moon, and D. R. Ilgen, "Cutthroat Cooperation: The Effects of Team Role Decisions on Adaptation to Alternative Reward Structures," *Organizational Behavior and Human Decision Processes* 108, no. 1 (2009), pp. 131–142; and M. D. Johnson, S. E. Humphrey, D. R. Ilgen, D. Jundt, and C. J. Meyer, "Cutthroat Cooperation: Asymmetrical Adaptation to Changes in Team Reward Structures," *Academy of Management Journal* 49, no. 1 (2006), pp. 103–119.

79 N. Middlemiss, "'We Were Dead Wrong,' Admits Google HR Team," *HRD Canada*, March 7, 2016, http://www.hrmonline.ca/hr-news/we-were-dead-wrong-admits-google-hr-team-204028.aspx; and C. Duhigg, "What Google Learned from Its Quest to Build the Perfect

Team," *New York Times Magazine*, February 25, 2016, https://www.nytimes.com/2016/02/28/magazine/what-google-learned-from-its-quest-to-build-the-perfect-team.html?_r=0.

80 R. R. Hirschfeld, M. H. Jordan, H. S. Feild, W. F. Giles, and A. A. Armenakis, "Becoming Team Players: Team Members' Mastery of Teamwork Knowledge as a Predictor of Team Task Proficiency and Observed Teamwork Effectiveness," *Journal of Applied Psychology* 91, no. 2 (2006), pp. 467–474; and K. R. Randall, C. J. Resick, and L. A. DeChurch, "Building Team Adaptive Capacity: The Roles of Sensegiving and Team Composition," *Journal of Applied Psychology* 96, no. 3 (2011), pp. 525–540.

81 H. Moon, J. R. Hollenbeck, and S. E. Humphrey, "Asymmetric Adaptability: Dynamic Team Structures as One-Way Streets," *Academy of Management Journal* 47, no. 5 (October 2004), pp. 681–695; A. P. J. Ellis, J. R. Hollenbeck, and D. R. Ilgen, "Team Learning: Collectively Connecting the Dots," *Journal of Applied Psychology* 88, no. 5 (October 2003), pp. 821–835; C. L. Jackson and J. A. LePine, "Peer Responses to a Team's Weakest Link: A Test and Extension of LePine and Van Dyne's Model," *Journal of Applied Psychology* 88, no. 3 (June 2003), pp. 459–475; and J. A. LePine, "Team Adaptation and Postchange Performance: Effects of Team Composition in Terms of Members' Cognitive Ability and Personality," *Journal of Applied Psychology* 88, no. 1 (February 2003), pp. 27–39.

82 C. C. Cogliser, W. L. Gardner, M. B. Gavin, and J. C. Broberg, "Big Five Personality Factors and Leader Emergence in Virtual Teams: Relationships with Team Trustworthiness, Member Performance Contributions, and Team Performance," *Group & Organization Management* 37, no. 6 (2012), pp. 752–784; and "Deep-Level Composition Variables as Predictors of Team Performance: A Meta-analysis," *Journal of Applied Psychology* 92, no. 3 (2007), pp. 595–615.

83 T. A. O'Neill and N. J. Allen, "Personality and the Prediction of Team Performance," *European Journal of Personality* 25, no. 1 (2011), pp. 31–42.

84 S. E. Humphrey, J. R. Hollenbeck, C. J. Meyer, and D. R. Ilgen, "Personality Configurations in Self-Managed Teams: A Natural Experiment on the Effects of Maximizing and Minimizing Variance in Traits," *Journal of Applied Psychology* 41, no. 7 (2011), pp. 1701–1732.

85 A. P. J. Ellis, J. R. Hollenbeck, and D. R. Ilgen, "Team Learning: Collectively Connecting the Dots," *Journal of Applied Psychology* 88, no. 5 (October 2003), pp. 821–835; C. O. L. H. Porter, J. R. Hollenbeck, and D. R. Ilgen, "Backing Up Behaviors in Teams: The Role of Personality and Legitimacy of Need," *Journal of Applied Psychology* 88, no. 3 (June 2003), pp. 391–403; and J. A. Colquitt, J. R. Hollenbeck, and D. R. Ilgen, "Computer-Assisted Communication and Team Decision-Making Performance: The Moderating Effect of Openness to Experience," *Journal of Applied Psychology* 87, no. 2 (April 2002), pp. 402–410.

86 B. H. Bradley, B. E. Postlewaite, and K. G. Brown, "Ready to Rumble: How Team Personality Composition and Task Conflict Interact to Improve Performance," *Journal of Applied Psychology* 98, no. 2 (2013), pp. 385–392.

87 E. Gonzalez-Mule, D. S. DeGeest, B. W. McCormick, J. Y. Seong, and K. G. Brown, "Can We Get Some Cooperation around Here? The Mediating Role of Group Norms on the Relationship between Team Personality and Individual Helping Behaviors," *Journal of Applied Psychology* 99, no. 5 (2014), pp. 988–999.

88 S. E. Humphrey, F. P. Morgeson, and M. J. Mannor, "Developing a Theory of the Strategic Core of Teams: A Role Composition Model of Team Performance," *Journal of Applied Psychology* 94, no. 1 (2009), pp. 48–61.

89 C. Margerison and D. McCann, *Team Management: Practical New Approaches* (London: Mercury Books, 2000).

90 A. Joshi, "The Influence of Organizational Demography on the External Networking Behavior of Teams," *Academy of Management Review*, July 2006, pp. 583–595.

91 A. Joshi and H. Roh, "The Role of Context in Work Team Diversity Research: A Meta-analytic Review," *Academy of Management Journal* 52, no. 3 (2009), pp. 599–627; S. K. Horwitz and I. B. Horwitz, "The Effects of Team Diversity on Team Outcomes: A Meta-analytic Review of Team Demography," *Journal of Management* 33, no. 6 (2007), pp. 987–1015; and S. T. Bell, A. J. Villado, M. A. Lukasik, L. Belau, and A. L. Briggs, "Getting Specific about Demographic Diversity Variable and Team Performance Relationships: A Meta-analysis," *Journal of Management* 37, no. 3 (2011), pp. 709–743.

92 S. J. Shin and J. Zhou, "When Is Educational Specialization Heterogeneity Related to Creativity in Research and Development Teams? Transformational Leadership as a Moderator," *Journal of Applied Psychology* 92, no. 6 (2007), pp. 1709–1721; and K. J. Klein, A. P. Knight, J. C. Ziegert, B. C. Lim, and J. L. Saltz, "When Team Members' Values Differ: The Moderating Role of Team Leadership," *Organizational Behavior and Human Decision Processes* 114, no. 1 (2011), pp. 25–36.

93 J. Shin, T. Kim, J. Lee, and L. Bian, "Cognitive Team Diversity and Individual Team Member Creativity: A Cross-Level Interaction," *Academy of Management Journal* 55, no. 1 (2012), pp. 197–212.

94 W. E. Watson, K. Kumar, and L. K. Michaelsen, "Cultural Diversity's Impact on Interaction Process and Performance: Comparing Homogeneous and Diverse Task Groups," *Academy of Management Journal*, June 1993, pp. 590–602; P. C. Earley and E. Mosakowski, "Creating Hybrid Team Cultures: An Empirical Test of Transnational Team Functioning," *Academy of Management Journal*, February 2000, pp. 26–49; and S. Mohammed and L. C. Angell, "Surface- and Deep-Level Diversity in Workgroups: Examining the Moderating Effects of Team Orientation and Team Process on Relationship Conflict," *Journal of Organizational Behavior*, December 2004, pp. 1015–1039.

95 Y. F. Guillaume, D. van Knippenberg, and F. C. Brodebeck, "Nothing Succeeds Like Moderation: A Social Self-Regulation Perspective on Cultural Dissimilarity and Performance," *Academy of Management Journal* 57, no. 5 (2014), pp. 1284–1308.

96 D. Coutu, "Why Teams Don't Work," *Harvard Business Review*, May 2009, pp. 99–105. The evidence in this section is described in L. Thompson, *Making the Team* (Upper Saddle River, NJ: Prentice Hall, 2000), pp. 65–67. See also L. A. Curral, R. H. Forrester, and J. F. Dawson, "It's What You Do and the Way That You Do It: Team Task, Team Size, and Innovation-Related Group Processes," *European Journal of Work & Organizational Psychology* 10, no. 2 (June 2001), pp. 187–204; R. C. Liden, S. J. Wayne, and R. A. Jaworski, "Social Loafing: A Field Investigation," *Journal of Management* 30, no. 2 (2004), pp. 285–304; and J. A. Wagner, "Studies of Individualism–Collectivism: Effects on Cooperation in Groups," *Academy of Management Journal* 38, no. 1 (February 1995), pp. 152–172.

97 R. Karlgaard, "Think (Really!) Small," *Forbes*, April 13, 2015, p. 32.

98 R. Karlgaard, "Think (Really!) Small," *Forbes*, April 13, 2015, p. 32.

99 R. Karlgaard, "Think (Really!) Small," *Forbes*, April 13, 2015, p. 32.

100 "Is Your Team Too Big? Too Small? What's the Right Number?" *Knowledge@Wharton*, June 14, 2006, pp. 1–5; see also A. M. Carton and J. N. Cummings, "A Theory of Subgroups in Work Teams," *Academy of Management Review* 37, no. 3 (2012), pp. 441–470.

101 D. E. Hyatt and T. M. Ruddy, "An Examination of the Relationship between Work Group Characteristics and Performance: Once More into the Breech," *Personnel Psychology*, Autumn 1997, p. 555; and J. D. Shaw, M. K. Duffy, and E. M. Stark, "Interdependence and Preference for Group Work: Main and Congruence Effects on the Satisfaction and Performance of Group Members," *Journal of Management* 26, no. 2 (2000), pp. 259–279.

102 J. A. LePine, R. F. Piccolo, C. L. Jackson, J. E. Mathieu, and J. R. Saul, "A Meta-analysis of Teamwork Processes: Tests of a Multidimensional Model and Relationships with Team Effectiveness Criteria," *Personnel Psychology* 61 (2008), pp. 273–307.

103 J. F. Dovidio, "Bridging Intragroup Processes and Intergroup Relations: Needing the Twain to Meet," *British Journal of Social Psychology* 52, no. 1 (2013), pp. 1–24; and J. Zhou, J. Dovidio, and E. Wang, "How Affectively-Based and Cognitively-Based Attitudes Drive Intergroup Behaviours: The Moderating Role of Affective-Cognitive Consistency," *PloS ONE* 8, no. 11 (2013), article e82150.

104 J. A. LePine, R. F. Piccolo, C. L. Jackson, J. E. Mathieu, and J. R. Saul, "A Meta-analysis of Teamwork Processes: Tests of a Multidimensional Model and Relationships with Team Effectiveness Criteria," *Personnel Psychology* 61 (2008), pp. 273–307; and J. E. Mathieu and T. L. Rapp, "Laying the Foundation for Successful Team Performance Trajectories: The Roles of Team Charters and Performance Strategies," *Journal of Applied Psychology* 94, no. 1 (2009), pp. 90–103.

105 M. Corrin, "The Women Behind Freshii's Fast Growth," *Freshii*, March 8, 2017.

106 J. E. Mathieu and W. Schulze, "The Influence of Team Knowledge and Formal Plans on Episodic Team Process–Performance Relationships," *Academy of Management Journal* 49, no. 3 (2006), pp. 605–619.

107 A. N. Pieterse, D. van Knippenberg, and W. P. van Ginkel, "Diversity in Goal Orientation, Team Reflexivity, and Team Performance," *Organizational Behavior and Human Decision Processes* 114, no. 2 (2011), pp. 153–164.

108 A. Gurtner, F. Tschan, N. K. Semmer, and C. Nagele, "Getting Groups to Develop Good Strategies: Effects of Reflexivity Interventions on Team Process, Team Performance, and Shared Mental Models," *Organizational Behavior and Human Decision Processes* 102 (2007), pp. 127–142; M. C. Schippers, D. N. Den Hartog, and P. L. Koopman, "Reflexivity in Teams: A Measure and Correlates," *Applied Psychology: An International Review* 56, no. 2 (2007), pp. 189–211; and C. S. Burke, K. C. Stagl, E. Salas, L. Pierce, and D. Kendall, "Understanding Team Adaptation: A Conceptual Analysis and Model," *Journal of Applied Psychology* 91, no. 6 (2006), pp. 1189–1207.

109 A. N. Pieterse, D. van Knippenberg, and W. P. van Ginkel, "Diversity in Goal Orientation, Team Reflexivity, and Team Performance," *Organizational Behavior and Human Decision Processes* 114, no. 2 (2011), pp. 153–164.

110 See R. P. DeShon, S. W. J. Kozlowski, A. M. Schmidt, K. R. Milner, and D. Wiechmann, "A Multiple-Goal, Multilevel Model of Feedback Effects on the Regulation of Individual and Team Performance," *Journal of Applied Psychology*, December 2004, pp. 1035–1056.

111 K. Tasa, S. Taggar, and G. H. Seijts, "The Development of Collective Efficacy in Teams: A Multilevel and Longitudinal Perspective," *Journal of Applied Psychology* 92, no. 1 (2007), pp. 17–27; D. I. Jung and J. J. Sosik, "Group Potency and Collective Efficacy: Examining Their Predictive Validity, Level of Analysis, and Effects of Performance Feedback on Future Group Performance," *Group & Organization Management*, September 2003, pp. 366–391; and R. R. Hirschfeld and J. B. Bernerth, "Mental Efficacy and Physical Efficacy at the Team Level: Inputs and Outcomes among Newly Formed Action Teams," *Journal of Applied Psychology* 93, no. 6 (2008), pp. 1429–1437.

112 A. W. Richter, G. Hirst, D. van Knippenberg, and M. Baer, "Creative Self-Efficacy and Individual Creativity in Team Contexts: Cross-Level Interactions with Team Informational Resources," *Journal of Applied Psychology* 97, no. 6 (2012), pp. 1282–1290.

113 N. Ellemers, E. Sleebos, D. Stam, and D. de Gilder, "Feeling Included and Valued: How Perceived Respect Affects Positive Team Identity and Willingness to Invest in the Team," *British Journal of Management* 24 (2013), pp. 21–37.

114 T. A. De Vries, F. Walter, G. S. Van Der Vegt, and P. J. M. D. Essens, "Antecedents of Individuals' Interteam Coordination: Broad Functional Experiences as a Mixed Blessing," *Academy of Management Journal* 57, no. 5 (2014), pp. 1334–1359.

115 S. Chang, L. Jia, R. Takeuchi, and Y. Cai, "Do High-Commitment Work Systems Affect Creativity? A Multilevel Combinational Approach to Employee Creativity," *Journal of Applied Psychology* 99, no. 4 (2014), pp. 665–680.

116 S. Mohammed, L. Ferzandi, and K. Hamilton, "Metaphor No More: A 15-Year Review of the Team Mental Model Construct," *Journal of Management* 36, no. 4 (2010), pp. 876–910.

117 A. P. J. Ellis, "System Breakdown: The Role of Mental Models and Transactive Memory on the Relationships between Acute Stress and Team Performance," *Academy of Management Journal* 49, no. 3 (2006), pp. 576–589.

118 L. A. DeChurch and J. R. Mesmer-Magnus, "The Cognitive Underpinnings of Effective Teamwork: A Meta-analysis," *Journal of Applied Psychology* 95, no. 1 (2010), pp. 32–53.

119 S. W. J. Kozlowski and D. R. Ilgen, "Enhancing the Effectiveness of Work Groups and Teams," *Psychological Science in the Public Interest* (December 2006), pp. 77–124; and B. D. Edwards, E. A. Day, W. Arthur Jr., and S. T. Bell, "Relationships among Team Ability Composition, Team Mental Models, and Team Performance," *Journal of Applied Psychology* 91, no. 3 (2006), pp. 727–736.

120 K. M. Eisenhardt, J. L. Kahwajy, and L. J. Bourgeois III, "How Management Teams Can Have a Good Fight," *Harvard Business Review*, July–August 1997, p. 78.

121 J. Farh, C. Lee, and C. I. C. Farh, "Task Conflict and Team Creativity: A Question of How Much and When," *Journal of Applied Psychology* 95, no. 6 (2010), pp. 1173–1180.

122 K. J. Behfar, R. S. Peterson, E. A. Mannix, and W. M. K. Trochim, "The Critical Role of Conflict Resolution in Teams: A Close Look at the Links between Conflict Type, Conflict Management Strategies, and Team Outcomes," *Journal of Applied Psychology* 93, no. 1 (2008), pp. 170–188.

123 V. Gonzalez-Roma and A. Hernandez, "Climate Uniformity: Its Influence on Team Communication Quality, Task Conflict, and Team Performance," *Journal of Applied Psychology* 99, no. 6 (2014), pp. 1042–1058.

124 R. Kreitner and A. Kinicki, *Organizational Behavior*, 6th ed. (New York: Irwin, 2004), p. 460. Reprinted by permission of McGraw Hill Education.

125 K. Jehn, "A Multimethod Examination of the Benefits and Detriments of Intragroup Conflict," *Administrative Science Quarterly*, June 1995, pp. 256–282.

126 K. H. Price, D. A. Harrison, and J. H. Gavin, "Withholding Inputs in Team Contexts: Member Composition, Interaction Processes, Evaluation Structure, and Social Loafing," *Journal of Applied Psychology* 91, no. 6 (2006), pp. 1375–1384.

127 C. E. Naquin and R. O. Tynan, "The Team Halo Effect: Why Teams Are Not Blamed for Their Failures," *Journal of Applied Psychology*, April 2003, pp. 332–340.

128 D. Brown, "Innovative HR Ineffective in Manufacturing Firms," *Canadian HR Reporter*, April 7, 2003, pp. 1–2.

129 E. R. Crawford and J. A. LePine, "A Configural Theory of Team Processes: Accounting for the Structure of Taskwork and Teamwork," *Academy of Management Review*, January 2013, pp. 32–48.

130 W. E. Watson, K. Kumar, and L. K. Michaelsen, "Cultural Diversity's Impact on Interaction Process and Performance: Comparing Homogeneous and Diverse Task Groups," *Academy of Management Journal*, June 1993, pp. 590–602; P. C. Earley and

E. Mosakowski, "Creating Hybrid Team Cultures: An Empirical Test of Transnational Team Functioning," *Academy of Management Journal*, February 2000, pp. 26–49; and S. Mohammed and L. C. Angell, "Surface- and Deep-Level Diversity in Workgroups: Examining the Moderating Effects of Team Orientation and Team Process on Relationship Conflict," *Journal of Organizational Behavior*, December 2004, pp. 1015–1039.

131 Y. F. Guillaume, D. van Knippenberg, and F. C. Brodebeck, "Nothing Succeeds Like Moderation: A Social Self-Regulation Perspective on Cultural Dissimilarity and Performance," *Academy of Management Journal* 57, no. 5 (2014), pp. 1284–1308.

132 D. F. Crown, "The Use of Group and Groupcentric Individual Goals for Culturally Heterogeneous and Homogeneous Task Groups: An Assessment of European Work Teams," *Small Group Research* 38, no. 4 (2007), pp. 489–508.

133 Based on D. Man and S. S. K. Lam, "The Effects of Job Complexity and Autonomy on Cohesiveness in Collectivist and Individualistic Work Groups: A Cross-Cultural Analysis," *Journal of Organizational Behavior*, December 2003, pp. 979–1001.

134 S. Chang, L. Jia, R. Takeuchi, and Y. Cai, "Do High-Commitment Work Systems Affect Creativity? A Multilevel Combinational Approach to Employee Creativity," *Journal of Applied Psychology* 99, no. 4 (2014), pp. 665–680.

135 P. L. Perrewe, K. L. Zellars, G. R. Ferris, A. M. Rossi, C. J. Kacmar, and D. A. Ralston, "Neutralizing Job Stressors: Political Skill as an Antidote to the Dysfunctional Consequences of Role Conflict," *Academy of Management Journal*, February 2004, pp. 141–152.

136 Based on S. I. Tannenbaum, J. Mathieu, E. Salas, and D. Cohen, "Teams Are Changing: Are Research and Practice Evolving Fast Enough?" *Industrial and Organizational Psychology* 5 (2012), pp. 2–24; and R. Ashkenas, "How to Empower Your Team for Non-Negotiable Results," *Forbes*, April 24, 2013, http://www.forbes.com/sites/ronashkenas/2013/04/24/how-to-empower-your-team-with-non-negotiable-results/.

137 Based on E. Bernstein, "Speaking Up Is Hard to Do: Researchers Explain Why," *Wall Street Journal*, February 7, 2012, p. D1; M. Kashtan, "Want Teamwork? Promote Free Speech," New York Times, April 13, 2014, p. 8; and H. Leroy, B. Dierynck, F. Anseel, T. Simons, J. R. Halbesleben, D. McCaughey, G. T. Savage, and L. Sels, "Behavioral Integrity for Safety, Priority of Safety, Psychological Safety, and Patient Safety: A Team-Level Study," *Journal of Applied Psychology*, November 2012, pp. 1273–1281.

138 M. A. Korsgaard, H. H. Brower, and S. W. Lester, "It Isn't Always Mutual: A Critical Review of Dyadic Trust," *Journal of Management* 41, no. 1 (2014), pp. 47–70; R. L. Priem and P. C. Nystrom, "Exploring the Dynamics of Workgroup Fracture: Common Ground, Trust-with-Trepidation, and Warranted Distrust," *Journal of Management* 40, no. 3 (2014), pp. 764–795; and "The Call of Malaysia's 'Conquerable' Mount Kinabalu," *BBC*, June 5, 2015, http://www.bbc.com/news/world-asia-33020356.

139 Based on ROBBINS, STEPHEN P.; HUNSAKER, PHILLIP L., TRAINING IN INTERPERSONAL SKILLS: TIPS FOR MANAGING PEOPLE AT WORK, 2nd Ed., ©1996. Reprinted and Electronically reproduced by permission of Pearson Education, Inc., Upper Saddle River, New Jersey.

OB on the Edge: Trust

1 Based on B. MacLellan, "Turning 20, and Still a Young and Independent Agency," *Environics*, August 14, 2014, http://environicspr.com/us/2014/08/turning-20-still-young-independent-agency/; "Stitches of Laughter Help Create Tight-Knit Team," *Globe and Mail*, April 17, 2014; and G. Marr, "Sabbaticals Boost Job Satisfaction," *Gazette* (Montreal), August 18, 2012, p. F14.

2 See, for example, K. T. Dirks and D. L. Ferrin, "Trust in Leadership: Meta-analytic Findings and Implications for Research and Practice," *Journal of Applied Psychology*, August 2002, pp. 611–628; B. McEvily,

V. Perrone, A. Zaheer, guest editors, The special issue on trust in an organizational context, *Organization Science*, January–February 2003; and R. Galford and A. S. Drapeau, *The Trusted Leader* (New York: Free Press, 2003).

3 F. K. Sonnenberg, "Trust Me, Trust Me Not," *IndustryWeek*, August 16, 1993, pp. 22–28; and L. T. Hosmer, "Trust: the Connecting Link between Organizational Theory and Philosophical Ethics," *Academy of Management Review*, April 1995, pp. 379–403.

4 "A Lack of Trust and Confidence: Majority of Canadian Employees Don't Believe Their Senior Leaders," *CNW*, news release, October 18, 2012, http://www.hrvoice.org/wp-content/uploads/2013/05/BABW-Infographic.jpg.

5 http://environicspr.com/thinking/the-environics-communications-cantrust-index/.

6 J. Pollack, "Do Your Employees Trust You? Behaviour Survey Finds Lack of Trust in Senior Leaders as Top Reason for Quitting," *Telegraph-Journal*, May 30, 2009, p. E1.

7 D. M. Rousseau, S. B. Sitkin, R. S. Burt, and C. Camerer, "Not So Different After All: A Cross-Discipline View of Trust," *Academy of Management Review*, July 1998, pp. 393–404; and J. A. Simpson, "Psychological Foundations of Trust," *Current Directions in Psychological Science* 16, no. 5 (2007), pp. 264–268.

8 See, for instance, K. T. Dirks and D. L. Ferrin, "Trust in Leadership: Meta-analytic Findings and Implications for Research and Practice," *Journal of Applied Psychology* 87, no. 4, (2002), pp. 611–628; D. I. Jung and B. J. Avolio, "Opening the Black Box: An Experimental Investigation of the Mediating Effects of Trust and Value Congruence on Transformational and Transactional Leadership," *Journal of Organizational Behavior*, December 2000, pp. 949–964; and A. Zacharatos, J. Barling, and R. D. Iverson, "High-Performance Work Systems and Occupational Safety," *Journal of Applied Psychology*, January 2005, pp. 77–93.

9 J. B. Rotter, "Interpersonal Trust, Trustworthiness, and Gullibility," *American Psychologist*, January 1980, pp. 1–7.

10 J. D. Lewis and A. Weigert, "Trust as a Social Reality," *Social Forces*, June 1985, p. 970.

11 J. K. Rempel, J. G. Holmes, and M. P. Zanna, "Trust in Close Relationships," *Journal of Personality and Social Psychology*, July 1985, p. 96.

12 G. M. Granovetter, "Economic Action and Social Structure: The Problem of Embeddedness," *American Journal of Sociology*, November 1985, p. 491.

13 R. C. Mayer, J. H. Davis, and F. D. Schoorman, "An Integrative Model of Organizational Trust," *Academy of Management Review*, July 1995, p. 712.

14 C. Johnson-George and W. Swap, "Measurement of Specific Interpersonal Trust: Construction and Validation of a Scale to Assess Trust in a Specific Other," *Journal of Personality and Social Psychology*, September 1982, p. 1306.

15 J. A. Colquitt, B. A. Scott, and J. A. LePine, "Trust, Trustworthiness, and Trust Propensity: A Meta-analytic Test of Their Unique Relationships with Risk Taking and Job Performance," *Journal of Applied Psychology* 92, no. 4 (2007), pp. 909–927; and F. D. Schoorman, R. C. Mayer, and J. H. Davis, "An Integrative Model of Organizational Trust: Past, Present, and Future," *Academy of Management Review* 32, no. 2 (2007), pp. 344–354.

16 Cited in D. Jones, "Do You Trust Your CEO?" *USA Today*, February 12, 2003, p. 7B.

17 J. A. Simpson, "Foundations of Interpersonal Trust," in *Social Psychology: Handbook of Basic Principles*, 2nd ed., ed. A. W. Kruglanski and E. T. Higgins (New York: Guilford, 2007), pp. 587–607.

18 This section is based on D. E. Zand, *The Leadership Triad: Knowledge, Trust, and Power* (New York: Oxford University Press,

1997), pp. 122–134; and A. M. Zak, J. A. Gold, R. M. Ryckman, and E. Lenney, "Assessments of Trust in Intimate Relationships and the Self-Perception Process," *Journal of Social Psychology*, April 1998, pp. 217–228.

19 D. L. Shapiro, A. D. Boss, S. Salas, S. Tangirala, and M. A. Von Glinow, "When Are Transgressing *Leaders* Punitively Judged? An Empirical Test," *Journal of Applied Psychology* 96, no. 2 (2011), pp. 412–422.

20 D. L. Ferrin, P. H. Kim, C. D. Cooper, and K. T. Dirks, "Silence Speaks Volumes: The Effectiveness of Reticence in Comparison to Apology and Denial for Responding to Integrity- and Competence-Based Trust Violations," *Journal of Applied Psychology* 92, no. 4 (2007), pp. 893–908.

21 Based on J. R. Detert and E. R. Burris, "Leadership Behavior and Employee Voice: Is the Door Really Open?" *Academy of Management Journal* 50, no. 4 (2007), pp. 869–884; and J. A. Colquitt, B. A. Scott, and J. A. LePine, "Trust, Trustworthiness, and Trust Propensity: A Meta-analytic Test of Their Unique Relationships with Risk Taking and Job Performance," *Journal of Applied Psychology* 92, no. 4 (2007), pp. 909–927.

22 J. R. Detert and E. R. Burris, "Leadership Behavior and Employee Voice: Is the Door Really Open?" *Academy of Management Journal* 50, no. 4 (2007), pp. 869–884.

23 J. A. Colquitt, B. A. Scott, and J. A. LePine, "Trust, Trustworthiness, and Trust Propensity: A Meta-analytic Test of Their Unique Relationships with Risk Taking and Job Performance," *Journal of Applied Psychology* 92, no. 4 (2007), pp. 909–927.

24 M. E. Schweitzer, J. C. Hershey, and E. T. Bradlow, "Promises and Lies: Restoring Violated Trust," *Organizational Behavior and Human Decision Processes* 101 (2006), pp. 1–19.

25 B. A. De Jong and T. O. M. Elfring, "How Does Trust Affect the Performance of Ongoing Teams? The Mediating Role of Reflexivity, Monitoring, and Effort," *Academy of Management Journal* 53, no. 3 (2010), pp. 535–549.

26 H. Zhao, S. J. Wayne, B. C. Glibkowski, and J. Bravo, "The Impact of Psychological Contract Breach on Work-Related Outcomes: A Meta-analysis," *Personnel Psychology* 60 (2007), pp. 647–680.

27 K. T. Dirks and D. L. Ferrin, "Trust in Leadership: Meta-analytic Findings and Implications for Organizational Research," *Journal of Applied Psychology* 87 (2002), pp. 611–628.

28 B. Groysberg and M. Slind, "Leadership Is a Conversation," *Harvard Business Review*, June 2012, pp. 76–84.

29 Adapted from J. O'Toole and W. Bennis, "What's Needed Next: A Culture of Candor," *Harvard Business Review*, June 2009, pp. 54–61.

30 P. J. Zak, "The Neuroscience of Trust," *Harvard Business Review*, January–February 2017, pp. 84–90.

31 K. T. Dirks, "Trust in Leadership and Team Performance: Evidence from NCAA Basketball," *Journal of Applied Psychology* 85 (2000), pp. 1004–1012.

32 Based on P. J. Zak, "The Neuroscience Of Trust," *Harvard Business Review*, January–February 2017, pp. 84–90.

33 B. A. De Jong and T. O. M. Elfring, "How Does Trust Affect the Performance of Ongoing Teams? The Mediating Role of Reflexivity, Monitoring, and Effort," *Academy of Management Journal* 53, no. 3 (2010), pp. 535–549.

34 Adapted from R. M. Kramer, "Rethinking Trust," *Harvard Business Review*, June 2009, p. 71.

35 C. W. Langfred, "Too Much of a Good Thing? Negative Effects of High Trust and Individual Autonomy in Self-Managing Teams," *Academy of Management Journal* 47, no. 3 (June 2004), pp. 385–399.

36 N. Klein and H. Zhou, "Their Pants Aren't on Fire," *New York Times*, March 25, 2014, p. D3.

37 S. D. Levitt and S. J. Dubner, "Traponomics," *Wall Street Journal*, May 10–11, 2014, pp. C1, C2.

38 R. M. Kramer, "Rethinking Trust," *Harvard Business Review*, June 2009, p. 77.

Chapter 7

1   Opening vignette based on http://www.businessinsider.com/slack-ceo-stewart-butterfield-interview-2015-4; S. Stevenson, "Stewart Butterfield, Email Killer," *Wall Street Journal*, November 4, 2015, https://www.wsj.com/articles/slack-ceo-stewart-butterfield-on-changing-the-way-we-work-1446689564; J. Bercovici, "Slack Is Our Company of the Year. Here's Why Everybody's Talking about It," *Inc.*, December 2015/January 2016, https://www.inc.com/magazine/201512/jeff-bercovici/slack-company-of-the-year-2015.html; and A. Konrad, "Slack Moves Its App Store Front and Center, Backs Seven More Startups in Platform Push," *Forbes*, July 11, 2017, https://www.forbes.com/sites/alexkonrad/2017/07/11/slack-moves-app-store-invests-more-for-platform/#6588a2bf73ab.

2   "Carleton Study Finds People Spending a Third of Job Time on Email," *Carleton Newsroom*, April 20, 2017, http://newsroom.carleton.ca/2017/04/20/carleton-study-finds-people-spending-third-job-time-email/.

3   A. Tenhiaelae and F. Salvador, "Looking Inside Glitch Mitigation Capability: The Effect of Intraorganizational Communication Channels," *Decision Sciences* 45, no. 3 (2014), pp. 437–466.

4   L. A. Withers, and L. L. Vernon, "To Err Is Human: Embarrassment, Attachment, and Communication Apprehension," *Personality and Individual Differences* 40, no. 1 (2006), pp. 99–110.

5   See, for instance, S. K. Opt and D. A. Loffredo, "Rethinking Communication Apprehension: A Myers-Briggs Perspective," *Journal of Psychology*, September 2000, pp. 556–570; and B. D. Blume, G. F. Dreher, and T. T. Baldwin, "Examining the Effects of Communication Apprehension within Assessment Centres," *Journal of Occupational and Organizational Psychology* 83, no. 3 (2010), pp. 663–671.

6   See L. K. Trevino, J. Webster, and E. W. Stein, "Making Connections: Complementary Influences on Communication Media Choices, Attitudes, and Use," *Organization Science*, March–April 2000, pp. 163–182; and N. Kock, "The Psychobiological Model: Towards a New Theory of Computer-Mediated Communication Based on Darwinian Evolution," *Organization Science* 15, no. 3 (May–June 2004), pp. 327–348.

7   D. K. Denton, "Engaging Your Employees in Times of Uncertainty," *International Journal of Productivity and Quality Management* 7, no. 2 (2011), pp. 202–208.

8   Vignette based on S. Niedoba, "How CANA Group Focused on Communication to Build a Stronger Team," *Canadian Business*, December 28, 2016, http://www.canadianbusiness.com/lists-and-rankings/best-managed-companies/cana-group/.

9   S. Niedoba, "How CANA Group Focused on Communication to Build a Stronger Team," *Canadian Business*, December 28, 2016, http://www.canadianbusiness.com/lists-and-rankings/best-managed-companies/cana-group/.

10 Vignette based on A. Scott, "How Stewart Butterfield Built a Billion-Dollar Company in Eight Months," *Canadian Business*, January 5, 2015, http://www.canadianbusiness.com/innovation/stewart-butterfield-slack/.

11 K. Savitsky, B. Keysar, N. Epley, T. Carter, and A. Swanson, "The Closeness-Communication Bias: Increased Egocentrism among Friends versus Strangers," *Journal of Experimental Social Psychology* 47, no. 1 (2011), pp. 269–273.

12 D. Derks, D. van Duin, M. Tims, and A. B. Baker, "Smartphone Use and Work–Home Interference: The Moderating Role of Social Norms and Employee Work Engagement," *Journal of Occupational and Organizational Psychology* 88, no. 1 (2015), pp. 155–177.

13 P. Briñol, R. E. Petty, and J. Barden, "Happiness versus Sadness as a Determinant of Thought Confidence in Persuasion: A Self-Validation Analysis," *Journal of Personality and Social Psychology* 93, no. 5 (2007), pp. 711–727.

14 R. C. Sinclair, S. E. Moore, M. M. Mark, A. S. Soldat, and C. A. Lavis, "Incidental Moods, Source Likeability, and Persuasion: Liking Motivates Message Elaboration in Happy People," *Cognition and Emotion* 24, no. 6 (2010), pp. 940–961; and V. Griskevicius, M. N. Shiota, and S. L. Neufeld, "Influence of Different Positive Emotions on Persuasion Processing: A Functional Evolutionary Approach," *Emotion* 10, no. 2 (2010), pp. 190–206.

15 J. Sandberg, "The Jargon Jumble," *Wall Street Journal*, October 24, 2006, p. B1.

16 E. W. Morrison and F. J. Milliken, "Organizational Silence: A Barrier to Change and Development in a Pluralistic World," *Academy of Management Review* 25, no. 4 (2000), pp. 706–725; and B. E. Ashforth and V. Anand, "The Normalization of Corruption in Organizations," *Research in Organizational Behavior* 25 (2003), pp. 1–52.

17 F. J. Milliken, E. W. Morrison, and P. F. Hewlin, "An Exploratory Study of Employee Silence: Issues That Employees Don't Communicate Upward and Why," *Journal of Management Studies* 40, no. 6 (2003), pp. 1453–1476.

18 S. Tangirala and R. Ramunujam, "Employee Silence on Critical Work Issues: The Cross-Level Effects of Procedural Justice Climate," *Personnel Psychology* 61, no. 1 (2008), pp. 37–68; and F. Bowen and K. Blackmon, "Spirals of Silence: The Dynamic Effects of Diversity on Organizational Voice," *Journal of Management Studies* 40, no. 6 (2003), pp. 1393–1417.

19 K. B. Serota, T. R. Levine, and F. J. Boster, "The Prevalence of Lying in America: Three Studies of Self-Reported Lies," *Human Communication Research* 36, no. 1. (2010), pp. 2–25.

20 B. M. DePaulo, D. A. Kashy, S. E. Kirkendol, M. M. Wyer, and J. A. Epstein, "Lying in Everyday Life," *Journal of Personality and Social Psychology* 70, no. 5 (1996), pp. 979–995; and C. E. Naguin, T. R. Kurtzberg, and L. Y. Belkin, "The Finer Points of Lying Online: E-Mail versus Pen and Paper," *Journal of Applied Psychology* 95, no. 2 (2010), pp. 387–394.

21 A. Vrij, P. A. Granhag, and S. Porter, "Pitfalls and Opportunities in Nonverbal and Verbal Lie Detection," *Psychological Science in the Public Interest* 11, no. 3 (2010), pp. 89–121.

22 Vignette based on S. Stevenson, "Stewart Butterfield, Email Killer," *Wall Street Journal*, https://www.wsj.com/articles/slack-ceo-stewart-butterfield-on-changing-the-way-we-work-1446689564.

23 S. Jhun, Z.-T. Bae, and S.-Y. Rhee, "Performance Change of Managers in Two Different Uses of Upward Feedback: A Longitudinal Study in Korea," *International Journal of Human Resource Management* 23, no. 20 (2012), pp. 4246–4264; and J. W. Smither and A. G. Walker, "Are the Characteristics of Narrative Comments Related to Improvement in Multirater Feedback Ratings over Time?" *Journal of Applied Psychology* 89, no. 3 (June 2004), pp. 575–581.

24 P. Dvorak, "How Understanding the 'Why' of Decisions Matters," *Wall Street Journal*, March 19, 2007, p. B3.

25 T. Neeley and P. Leonardi, "Effective Managers Say the Same Thing Twice (or More)," *Harvard Business Review*, May 2011, pp. 38–39.

26 A. DiPaula, M. Bacica, and J. Winram, "To Be Believed Is to Be Heard," *Leadership*, Summer 2014, http://sentisresearch.com/wp-content/uploads/2014/07/BCHRMA-Summer-2014.pdf.

27 B. Amble, "Managers Ignoring the People Who Matter," Management-issues.com, September 18, 2006, http://www.management-issues.com/news/3593/manages-ignoring-the-people-who-matter/.

28 H. A. Richardson and S. G. Taylor, "Understanding Input Events: A Model of Employees' Responses to Requests for Their Input," *Academy of Management Review* 37 (2012), pp. 471–491.

29 J. R. Detert and L. K. Treviño, "Speaking Up to Higher-Ups: How Supervisors and Skip-Level Leaders Influence Employee Voice," *Organization Science* 21, no. 1 (2010), pp. 249–270.

30 E. Nichols, "Hyper-Speed Managers," *HR Magazine*, April 2007, pp. 107–110.

31 R. Walker, "Declining an Assignment, with Finesse," *New York Times*, August 24, 2014, p. 8.

32 See, for example, N. B. Kurland and L. H. Pelled, "Passing the Word: Toward a Model of Gossip and Power in the Workplace," *Academy of Management Review*, April 2000, pp. 428–438; and G. Michelson, A. van Iterson, and K. Waddington, "Gossip in Organizations: Contexts, Consequences, and Controversies," *Group and Organization Management* 35, no. 4 (2010), pp. 371–390.

33 G. Van Hoye and F. Lievens, "Tapping the Grapevine: A Closer Look at Word-of-Mouth as a Recruitment Source," *Journal of Applied Psychology* 94, no. 2 (2009), pp. 341–352.

34 J. K. Bosson, A. B. Johnson, K. Niederhoffer, and W. B. Swann Jr., "Interpersonal Chemistry through Negativity: Bonding by Sharing Negative Attitudes about Others," *Personal Relationships* 13 (2006), pp. 135–150.

35 T. J. Grosser, V. Lopez-Kidwell, and G. Labianca, "A Social Network Analysis of Positive and Negative Gossip in Organizational Life," *Group and Organization Management* 35, no. 2 (2010), pp. 177–212.

36 R. Feintzeig, "The Boss's Next Demand: Make Lots of Friends," *Wall Street Journal*, February 12, 2014, pp. B1, B6.

37 R. E. Silverman, "A Victory for Small Office Talkers," *Wall Street Journal*, October 28, 2014, p. D2.

38 M. Feinberg, R. Willer, J. Stellar, and D. Keltner, "The Virtues of Gossip: Reputational Information Sharing as Prosocial Behavior," *Journal of Personality and Social Psychology* 102 (2012), pp. 1015–1030.

39 L. Hirschhorn, "Managing Rumors," in *Cutting Back*, ed. L. Hirschhorn (San Francisco: Jossey-Bass, 1983), pp. 54–56; and D. K. Denton, "Engaging Your Employees in Times of Uncertainty," *International Journal of Productivity and Quality Management* 7, no. 2 (2011), pp. 202–208.

40 Vignette based on J. Bercovici, "Slack Is Our Company of the Year. Here's Why Everybody's Talking About It", *Inc.*, December 2015/January 2016, https://www.inc.com/magazine/201512/jeff-bercovici/slack-company-of-the-year-2015.html.

41 L. Dulye, "Get Out of Your Office," *HR Magazine*, July 2006, pp. 99–101.

42 M. Mihelich, "Bit by Bit: Stand-up Comedy as a Team-Building Exercise," *Workforce Management*, February 2013, p. 16; and "Comedy Experience," *Peppercomm*, accessed July 2, 2015, http://peppercomm.com/services/comedy-experience.

43 A. Bryant, "Finding, and Owning, Their Voice," *New York Times*, November 16, 2014, p. 6.

44 T. D. Maynes and P. M. Podsakoff, "Speaking More Broadly: An Examination of the Nature, Antecedents, and Consequences of an Expanded Set of Employee Voice Behaviors," *Journal of Applied Psychology* 99, no. 1 (2014), pp. 87–112.

45 J. Lipman, "A Guide for Men," *Wall Street Journal*, December 13–14, 2014, pp. C1, C2.

46 S. Shellenbarger, "Help! I'm on a Conference Call," *Wall Street Journal*, February 26, 2014, pp. D1, D2.

47 S. Shellenbarger, "Help! I'm on a Conference Call," *Wall Street Journal*, February 26, 2014, pp. D1, D2.

48 P. A. Mueller and D. M. Oppenheimer, "The Pen Is Mightier Than the Keyboard: Advantages of Longhand over Laptop Note Taking," *Psychological Science* 25, no. 6 (2014), pp. 1159–1168.

49 N. Bilton, "Disruptions: Life's Too Short for So Much E-mail," *New York Times*, July 8, 2012, http://bits.blogs.nytimes.

com/2012/07/08/life%E2%80%99s-too-short-for-so-much-e-mail/; and "Carleton Study Finds People Spending a Third of Job Time on Email," *Carleton Newsroom*, April 20, 2017, http://newsroom.carleton.ca/2017/04/20/carleton-study-finds-people-spending-third-job-time-email/.

50 G. J. Mark, S. Voida, and A. V. Cardello, "'A Pace Not Dictated by Electrons': An Empirical Study of Work without E-mail," *Proceedings of the SIGCHI Conference on Human Factors in Computing Systems*, 2012, pp. 555–564.

51 "Overloaded Canadians Trash 42% of All E-Mails: Study," *Ottawa Citizen*, June 26, 2008, p. D5.

52 Based on A. Anwar, "When Long Distance Makes the Startup More Complicated," *National Post*, August 5, 2014, p. FP6; and A. Seale, "SlimCut Media Proud of Its Dual Toronto-Paris Citizenship," *StartUp Toronto*, November 8, 2016.

53 C. L.-L. Tan, "Mind Your E-mail Manners: No 'XOXO' or 'LOL' Allowed," *Wall Street Journal*, April 21, 2015.

54 C. L.-L. Tan, "Mind Your E-mail Manners: No 'XOXO' or 'LOL' Allowed," *Wall Street Journal*, April 21, 2015.

55 E. Bernstein, "The Miscommunicators," *Wall Street Journal*, July 3, 2012, pp. D1, D3.

56 B. Roberts, "Social Media Gets Strategic," *HR Magazine*, October 2012, pp. 30–38.

57 "Number of Monthly Active Facebook Users Worldwide as of 1st Quarter 2015 (in Millions)," *Statista/Facebook*, accessed July 1, 2015, http://www.statista.com/statistics/264810/number-of-monthly-active-facebook-users-worldwide/.

58 K. Wagner, "The World's Top CEOs Are Tweeting More, Facebooking Less," *Re/Code*, May 17, 2015, http://recode.net/2015/05/17/the-worlds-top-ceos-are-tweeting-more-facebooking-less/.

59 P. Mozur, J. Osawa, and N. Purnell, "Facebook and WhatsApp a Tough Sell in Asia," *Wall Street Journal*, February 21, 2014, p. B4.

60 C. Smith, "By the Numbers: 125+ Amazing LinkedIn Statistics," *DMR*, June 6, 2015, http://expandedramblings.com/index.php/by-the-numbers-a-few-important-linkedin-stats/.

61 K. Wagner, "The World's Top CEOs Are Tweeting More, Facebooking Less." *Re/Code*, May 17, 2015, http://recode.net/2015/05/17/the-worlds-top-ceos-are-tweeting-more-face-booking-less/.

62 "Number of Monthly Active Twitter Users Worldwide from 1st Quarter 2010 to 1st Quarter 2015 (in Millions)," *Statista/Twitter*, accessed July 1, 2015 http://www.statista.com/statistics/282087/number-of-monthly-active-twitter-users/.

63 K. Wagner, "The World's Top CEOs Are Tweeting More, Facebooking Less." *Re/Code*, May 17, 2015, http://recode.net/2015/05/17/the-worlds-top-ceos-are-tweeting-more-facebooking-less/.

64 P. Mozur, J. Osawa, and N. Purnell, "Facebook and WhatsApp a Tough Sell in Asia," *Wall Street Journal*, February 21, 2014, p. B4.

65 P. Mozur, J. Osawa, and N. Purnell, "Facebook and WhatsApp a Tough Sell in Asia," *Wall Street Journal*, February 21, 2014, p. B4.

66 O. Allen, "6 Stats You Should Know about Business Blogging in 2015," *HubSpot Blogs*, March 11, 2015, http://blog.hubspot.com/marketing/business-blogging-in-2015.

67 M. Richtel, "Lost in E-mail, Tech Firms Face Self-Made Beast," *New York Times*, June 14, 2008, pp. A1, A14; and M. Johnson, "Quelling Distraction," *HR Magazine*, August 2008, pp. 43–46.

68 L. Talley and S. Temple, "How Leaders Influence Followers through the Use of Nonverbal Communication," *Leadership & Organizational Development Journal* 36, no. 1 (2015), pp. 69–80.

69 C. K. Goman, "5 Body Language Tips to Increase Your Curb Appeal," *Forbes*, March 4, 2013, http://www.forbes.com/sites/carolkinseygoman/2013/03/14/5-body-language-tips-to-increase-your-curb-appeal/.

70 A. Metallinou, A. Katsamanis, and S. Narayanan, "Tracking Continuous Emotional Trends of Participants During Affective Dyadic Interactions Using Body Language and Speech Information," *Image and Vision Computing*, February 2013, pp. 137–152.

71 J. Smith, "10 Nonverbal Cues That Convey Confidence at Work," *Forbes*, March 11, 2013, http://www.forbes.com/sites/jacquelynsmith/2013/03/11/10-nonverbal-cues-that-convey-confidence-at-work/.

72 See E. T. Hall, *Beyond Culture* (Garden City, NY: Anchor Press/Doubleday, 1976); W. L. Adair, "Integrative Sequences and Negotiation Outcome in Same- and Mixed-Culture Negotiations," *International Journal of Conflict Management* 14, no. 3–4 (2003), pp. 1359–1392; W. L. Adair and J. M. Brett, "The Negotiation Dance: Time, Culture, and Behavioral Sequences in Negotiation," *Organization Science* 16, no. 1 (2005), pp. 33–51; E. Giebels and P. J. Taylor, "Interaction Patterns in Crisis Negotiations: Persuasive Arguments and Cultural Differences," *Journal of Applied Psychology* 94, no. 1 (2009), pp. 5–19; and M. G. Kittler, D. Rygl, and A. Mackinnon, "Beyond Culture or Beyond Control? Reviewing the Use of Hall's High-/Low-Context Concept," *International Journal of Cross-Cultural Management* 11, no. 1 (2011), pp. 63–82.

73 M. C. Hopson, T. Hart, and G. C. Bell, "Meeting in the Middle: Fred L. Casmir's Contributions to the Field of Intercultural Communication," *International Journal of Intercultural Relations*, November 2012, pp. 789–797.

74 M. C. Hopson, T. Hart, and G. C. Bell, "Meeting in the Middle: Fred L. Casmir's Contributions to the Field of Intercultural Communication," *International Journal of Intercultural Relations*, November 2012, pp. 789–797.

75 "Charting a New Course," *National Post*, February 4, 2014.

76 Based on S. F. Gale, "Policies Must Score a Mutual Like," *Workforce Management*, August 2012; R. Huggins and S. Ward, "Countries with the Highest Percentage of Adults Who Use Social Networking Sites," *USA Today*, February 8, 2012, p. 1A; A. L. Kavanaugh, E. A. Fox, S. D. Sheetz, S. Yang, L. T. Li, D. J. Soemaker, A. Natsev, and L. Xie, "Social Media Use by Government: From the Routine to the Critical," *Government Information Quarterly*, October 2012, pp. 480–491; and S. Johnson, "Those Facebook Posts Could Cost You a Job," *San Jose Mercury News*, January 16, 2012, http://www.mercurynews.com/business/ci_19754451.

77 S. E. Ante, "Perilous Mix: Cloud, Devices from Home," *Wall Street Journal*, February 20, 2014, p. B4; D. Derks and A. B. Bakker, "Smartphone Use, Work–Home Interference, and Burnout: A Diary Study on the Role of Recovery," *Applied Psychology: An International Review* 63, no. 3 (2014), pp. 411–440; L. Duxbury, C. Higgins, R. Smart, and M. Stevenson, "Mobile Technology and Boundary Permeability," *British Journal of Management* 25 (2014), pp. 570–588; E. Holmes, "When One Phone Isn't Enough," *Wall Street Journal*, April 2, 2014, pp. D1, D2; C. Mims, "2014: The Year of Living Vulnerably," *Wall Street Journal*, December 22, 2014, pp. B1, B2; L. Weber, "Leaving a Job? Better Watch Your Cellphone," *Wall Street Journal*, January 22, 2014; and E. Yost, "Can an Employer Remotely Wipe an Employee's Cellphone?" *HR Magazine*, July 2014, p. 19.

78 Based on B. Acohido, "Social-Media Tools Boost Productivity," *USA Today*, August 13, 2012, p. 1B; H. Annabi and S. T. McGann, "Social Media as the Missing Links: Connecting Communities of Practice to Business Strategy," *Journal of Organizational Computing and Electronic Commerce* 23, no. 1–2 (2013), pp. 56–83; S. Dutta, "What's Your Personal Social Media Strategy," *Harvard Business Review*, November 2010, pp. 127–130; G. Connors, "10 Social Media Commandments for Employers," *Workforce Management*, February 2010, http://www.workforce.com/articles/10-social-media-commandments-for-employers; and L. Kwoh and M. Korn,

"140 Characters of Risk: CEOs on Twitter," *Wall Street Journal*, September 26, 2012, pp. B1, B8.

79 Based on A. A. Buchko, K. J. Buchko, and J. M Meyer, "Is There Power in PowerPoint? A Field Test of the Efficacy of PowerPoint on Memory and Recall of Religious Sermons," *Computers in Human Behavior*, March 2012, pp. 688–695; "Full Text of Iran's Proposals to Six World Powers in Moscow," *FARS News Agency* (Tehran), http://english.farsnews.com/newstext.php?nn=9103085486; and B. Parks, "Death to PowerPoint," *Bloomberg Businessweek*, September 3–9, 2012, pp. 83–85.

80 Based on S. P. Robbins and P. L. Hunsaker, *Training in Interpersonal Skills: TIPs for Managing People at Work*, 2nd ed. (Upper Saddle River, NJ: Prentice Hall, 1996), Chapter 3; and data in R. C. Huseman, J. M. Lahiff, and J. M. Penrose, *Business Communication: Strategies and Skills* (Chicago: Dryden Press, 1988), pp. 380, 425.

Chapter 8

1 Vignette based on "Ghomeshi Acquitted: Read the Verdict and Catch Up on What You Missed," *Globe and Mail*, January 5, 2017, https://www.theglobeandmail.com/news/national/jian-ghomeshi/article28476713/; J. Bradshaw and G. McArthur, "Behind the CBC's Decision To Fire Jian Ghomeshi," *Globe and Mail*, October 31, 2014, https://www.theglobeandmail.com/news/national/behind-the-cbcs-decision-to-fire-ghomeshi/article21396998/.

2 R. M. Kanter, "Power Failure in Management Circuits," *Harvard Business Review*, July–August 1979, p. 65.

3 Based on B. M. Bass, *Bass & Stogdill's Handbook of Leadership*, 3rd ed. (New York: Free Press, 1990).

4 B. Oc, M. R. Bashshur, and C. Moore, "Speaking Truth to Power: The Effect of Candid Feedback on How Individuals with Power Allocate Resources," *Journal of Applied Psychology* 100, no. 2 (2015), pp. 450–463.

5 D. H. Gruenfeld, M. E. Inesi, J. C. Magee, and A. D. Galinsky, "Power and the Objectification of Social Targets," *Journal of Personality and Social Psychology* 95, no. 1 (2008), pp. 111–127; A. D. Galinsky, J. C. Magee, D. H. Gruenfeld, J. A. Whitson, and K. A. Liljenquist, "Power Reduces the Press of the Situation: Implications for Creativity, Conformity, and Dissonance," *Journal of Personality and Social Psychology* 95, no. 6 (2008), pp. 1450–1466; and J. C. Magee and C. A. Langner, "How Personalized and Socialized Power Motivation Facilitate Antisocial and Prosocial Decision-Making," *Journal of Research in Personality* 42, no. 6 (2008), pp. 1547–1559.

6 G. A. Van Kleef, A. C. Homan, C. Finkenauer, S. Gundemir, and E. Stamkou, "Breaking the Rules to Rise to Power: How Norm Violators Gain Power in the Eyes of Others," *Social Psychological and Personality Science*, January 26, 2011, published online before print, http://selfteachingresources.pbworks.com/f/Breaking+the+Rules+to+Rise+to+Power+-+How+Norm+Violators+Gain+Power+in+the+Eyes+of+Others.pdf.

7 J. Lammers, D. A. Stapel, and A. Galinsky, "Power Increases Hypocrisy: Moralizing in Reasoning, Immunity and Behavior," *Psychological Science* 21, no. 5 (2010), pp. 737–744.

8 Based on E. Inesi, S. Botti, D. Dubois, D. D. Rucker, and A. D. Galinsky, "Power and Choice: Their Dynamic Interplay in Quenching the Thirst for Personal Control," *Psychological Science*, June 2011, published online before print; and Association for Psychological Science, "Power and Choice Are Interchangeable: It's All about Controlling Your Life," *ScienceDaily*, April 28, 2011, http://www.sciencedaily.com/releases/2011/04/110426111419.htm.

9 Vignette based on "Jian Ghomeshi Earned A Loyal Following With CBC's Q," Torstar News Service, October 26, 2014, http://www.metronews.ca/entertainment/2014/10/27/jian-ghomeshi-earned-a-loyal-following-with-cbcs-q.html; and A. Humpries, "'Troubling and Disappointing': CBC 'Severing Ties' with Executives in Ghomeshi Scandal," *National Post*, April 16, 2015, http://nationalpost.com/news/canada/cbc-severing-ties-with-executives-in-ghomeshi-scandal/wcm/8005c6c8-ffa2-40ed-8686-fb1ec2171f39.

10 E. Landells and S. L. Albrecht, "Organizational Political Climate: Shared Perceptions about the Building and Use of Power Bases," *Human Resource Management Review* 23, no. 4 (2013), pp. 357–365; P. Rylander, "Coaches' Bases of Power: Developing Some Initial Knowledge of Athletes' Compliance with Coaches in Team Sports," *Journal of Applied Sport Psychology* 27, no. 1 (2015), pp. 110–121; and G. Yukl, "Use Power Effectively," in *Handbook of Principles of Organizational Behavior*, ed. E. A. Locke (Malden, MA: Blackwell, 2004), pp. 242–247.

11 E. A. Ward, "Social Power Bases of Managers: Emergence of a New Factor," *Journal of Social Psychology*, February 2001, pp. 144–147.

12 S. R. Giessner and T. W. Schubert, "High in the Hierarchy: How Vertical Location and Judgments of Leaders' Power Are Interrelated," *Organizational Behavior and Human Decision Processes* 104, no. 1 (2007), pp. 30–44.

13 S. Milgram, *Obedience to Authority* (New York: Harper and Row, 1974).

14 G. Yukl, H. Kim, and C. M. Falbe, "Antecedents of Influence Outcomes," *Journal of Applied Psychology* 81, no. 3 (1996), pp. 309–317.

15 P. P. Carson, K. D. Carson, and C. W. Roe, "Social Power Bases: A Meta-analytic Examination of Interrelationships and Outcomes," *Journal of Applied Social Psychology* 23, no. 14 (1993), pp. 1150–1169.

16 C. M. Falbe and G. Yukl, "Consequences for Managers of Using Single Tactics and Combinations of Tactics," *Academy of Management Journal* 35 (1992), pp. 638–652.

17 Cited in J. R. Carlson, D. S. Carlson, and L. L. Wadsworth, "The Relationship between Individual Power Moves and Group Agreement Type: An Examination and Model," *SAM Advanced Management Journal* 65, no. 4 (2000), pp. 44–51.

18 Vignette based on J. Bradshaw and G. McArthur, "Behind the CBC's Decision To Fire Jian Ghomeshi," *Globe and Mail*, October 31, 2014, https://www.theglobeandmail.com/news/national/behind-the-cbcs-decision-to-fire-ghomeshi/article21396998/; and S. Houpt, "CBC Memo: Evidence of 'Physical Injury to a Woman' Spurred Ghomeshi Firing," *Globe and Mail*, October 31, 2014, https://www.theglobeandmail.com/news/national/cbc-fired-ghomeshi-after-seeing-graphic-evidence-of-physical-injury-to-a-woman-memo/article21412839/.

19 R. E. Sturm and J. Antonakis, "Interpersonal Power: A Review, Critique, and Research Agenda," *Journal of Management* 41, no. 1 (2015), pp. 136–163.

20 Thanks are due to an anonymous reviewer for supplying this insight.

21 M. C. J. Caniels and A. Roeleveld, "Power and Dependence Perspectives on Outsourcing Decisions," *European Management Journal* 27, no. 6 (2009), pp. 402–417; and R.-J. Bryan, D. Kim, and R. S. Sinkovics, "Drivers and Performance Outcomes of Supplier Innovation Generation in Customer-Supplier Relationships: The Role of Power-Dependence," *Decision Sciences*, 2012, pp. 1003–1038.

22 See, for example, D. M. Cable and T. A. Judge, "Managers' Upward Influence Tactic Strategies: The Role of Manager Personality and Supervisor Leadership Style," *Journal of Organizational Behavior* 24, no. 2 (2003), pp. 197–214; M. P. M. Chong, "Influence Behaviors and Organizational Commitment: A Comparative Study," *Leadership and Organization Development Journal* 35, no. 1 (2014), pp. 54–78; and G. Blickle, "Influence Tactics Used by Subordinates: An Empirical Analysis of the Kipnis and Schmidt Subscales," *Psychological Reports*, February 2000, pp. 143–154.

23 G. R. Ferris, W. A. Hochwarter, C. Douglas, F. R. Blass, R. W. Kolodinksy, and D. C. Treadway, "Social Influence Processes in Organizations and Human Resource Systems," in *Research in Personnel and Human Resources Management*, vol. 21, ed. G. R.

Ferris and J. J. Martocchio (Oxford, UK: JAI Press/Elsevier, 2003), pp. 65–127; and C. A. Higgins, T. A. Judge, and G. R. Ferris, "Influence Tactics and Work Outcomes: A Meta-analysis," *Journal of Organizational Behavior*, March 2003, pp. 89–106.

24 M. P. M. Chong, "Influence Behaviors and Organizational Commitment: A Comparative Study," *Leadership and Organization Development Journal* 35, no. 1 (2014), pp. 54–78.

25 R. E. Petty and P. Briñol, "Persuasion: From Single to Multiple to MetaCognitive Processes," *Perspectives on Psychological Science* 3, no. 2 (2008), pp. 137–147.

26 M. P. M. Chong, "Influence Behaviors and Organizational Commitment: A Comparative Study," *Leadership and Organization Development Journal* 35, no. 1 (2014), pp. 54–78.

27 M. P. M. Chong, "Influence Behaviors and Organizational Commitment: A Comparative Study," *Leadership and Organization Development Journal* 35, no. 1 (2014), pp. 54–78.

28 O. Epitropaki and R. Martin, "Transformational-Transactional Leadership and Upward Influence: The Role of Relative Leader-Member Exchanges (RLMX) and Perceived Organizational Support (POS)," *Leadership Quarterly* 24, no. 2 (2013), pp. 299–315.

29 A. W. Kruglanski, A. Pierro, and E. T. Higgins, "Regulatory Mode and Preferred Leadership Styles: How Fit Increases Job Satisfaction," *Basic and Applied Social Psychology* 29, no. 2 (2007), pp. 137–149; and A. Pierro, L. Cicero, and B. H. Raven, "Motivated Compliance with Bases of Social Power," *Journal of Applied Social Psychology* 38, no. 7 (2008), pp. 1921–1944.

30 G. R. Ferris, D. C. Treadway, P. L. Perrewé, R. L. Brouer, C. Douglas, and S. Lux, "Political Skill in Organizations," *Journal of Management*, June 2007, pp. 290–320; K. J. Harris, K. M. Kacmar, S. Zivnuska, and J. D. Shaw, "The Impact of Political Skill on Impression Management Effectiveness," *Journal of Applied Psychology* 92, no. 1 (2007), pp. 278–285; W. A. Hochwarter, G. R. Ferris, M. B. Gavin, P. L. Perrewé, A. T. Hall, and D. D. Frink, "Political Skill as Neutralizer of Felt Accountability–Job Tension Effects on Job Performance Ratings: A Longitudinal Investigation," *Organizational Behavior and Human Decision Processes* 102 (2007), pp. 226–239; and D. C. Treadway, G. R. Ferris, A. B. Duke, G. L. Adams, and J. B. Tatcher, "The Moderating Role of Subordinate Political Skill on Supervisors' Impressions of Subordinate Ingratiation and Ratings of Subordinate Interpersonal Facilitation," *Journal of Applied Psychology* 92, no. 3 (2007), pp. 848–855.

31 M. C. Andrews, K. M. Kacmar, and K. J. Harris, "Got Political Skill? The Impact of Justice on the Importance of Political Skills for Job Performance," *Journal of Applied Psychology* 94, no. 6 (2009), pp. 1427–1437.

32 C. Anderson, S. E. Spataro, and F. J. Flynn, "Personality and Organizational Culture as Determinants of Influence," *Journal of Applied Psychology* 93, no. 3 (2008), pp. 702–710.

33 Vignette based on J. Bradshaw and G. McArthur, "Behind the CBC's Decision To Fire Jian Ghomeshi," *Globe and Mail*, October 31, 2014, https://www.theglobeandmail.com/news/national/behind-the-cbcs-decision-to-fire-ghomeshi/article21396998/; and A. Hasham,"Jian Ghomeshi Apologizes In Court, Sex Assault Charge Withdrawn," *thestar.com*, May 11, 2016, https://www.thestar.com/news/crime/2016/05/11/jian-ghomeshi-trial.html.

34 R. Sutton, "How to Be a Good Boss in a Bad Economy," *Harvard Business Review*, June 2009, pp. 42–50.

35 D. Keltner, D. H. Gruenfeld, and C. Anderson, "Power, Approach, and Inhibition," *Psychological Review* 110, no. 2 (2003), pp. 265–284.

36 Y. Cho and N. J. Fast, "Power, Defensive Denigration, and the Assuaging Effect of Gratitude Expression," *Journal of Experimental Social Psychology* 48 (2012), pp. 778–782.

37 M. Pitesa and S. Thau, "Masters of the Universe: How Power and Accountability Influence Self-Serving Decisions under Moral Hazard," *Journal of Applied Psychology* 98 (2013), pp. 550–558; and N. J. Fast, N. Sivanathan, D. D. Mayer, and A. D. Galinsky, "Power and Overconfident Decision-Making," *Organizational Behavior and Human Decision Processes* 117 (2012), pp. 249–260.

38 J. K. Maner, M. T. Gaillot, A. J. Menzel, and J. W. Kunstman, "Dispositional Anxiety Blocks the Psychological Effects of Power," *Personality and Social Psychology Bulletin* 38 (2012), pp. 1383–1395.

39 J. Tierney, "A Serving of Gratitude May Save the Day," *International New York Times*, November 21, 2011, http://www.nytimes.com/2011/11/22/science/a-serving-of-gratitude-brings-healthy-dividends.html?_r=0.

40 N. J. Fast, N. Halevy, and A. D. Galinsky, "The Destructive Nature of Power without Status," *Journal of Experimental Social Psychology* 48 (2012), pp. 391–394.

41 T. Seppälä, J. Lipponen, A. Bardi, and A. Pirttilä-Backman, "Change-Oriented Organizational Citizenship Behaviour: An Interactive Product of Openness to Change Values, Work Unit Identification, and Sense of Power," *Journal of Occupational and Organizational Psychology* 85 (2012), pp. 136–155.

42 K. A. DeCelles, D. S. DeRue, J. D. Margolis, and T. L. Ceranic, "Does Power Corrupt or Enable? When and Why Power Facilitates Self-Interested Behavior," *Journal of Applied Psychology* 97 (2012), pp. 681–689.

43 T. Lee and C. M. Brotheridge, "When the Prey Becomes the Predator: Bullying as Predictor of Reciprocal Bullying, Coping, and Well-Being," working paper, University of Regina, 2005.

44 N. J. Fast and S. Chen, "When the Boss Feels Inadequate: Power, Incompetence, and Aggression," *Psychological Science* 20, no. 11 (2009), pp. 1406–1413.

45 University of California-Berkeley, "Bosses Who Feel Inadequate Are More Likely to Bully," *ScienceDaily*, October 15, 2009, http://www.sciencedaily.com/releases/2009/10/091014102209.htm.

46 S.-G. Trépanier, C. Fernet, and S. Austin, "A Longitudinal Investigation of Workplace Bullying, Basic Need Satisfaction, and Employee Functioning," *Journal of Occupational Health Psychology* 20, no.1 (2015), pp. 105–118.

47 Quebec Labour Standards, s. 81.18, "Psychological Harassment at Work."

48 *Janzen v. Platy Enterprises Ltd.*, [1989] 10 CHRR D/6205 SCC.

49 K. Jiang, Y. Hong, P. F. McKay, D. R. Avery, D. C. Wilson, and S. D. Volpone, "Retaining Employees through Anti-Sexual Harassment Practices: Exploring the Mediating Role of Psychological Distress and Employee Engagement," *Human Resource Management* 54, no. 1 (2015), pp. 1–21; J. W. Kunstman, "Sexual Overperception: Power, Mating Motives, and Biases in Social Judgment," *Journal of Personality and Social Psychology* 100, no. 2 (2011), pp. 282–294; and J. C. Quick and M. A. McFadyen, "Sexual Harassment: Have We Made Any Progress?" *Journal of Occupational Health Psychology* 22, no. 3 (2017), pp. 286–298.

50 F. Krings and S. Facchin, "Organizational Justice and Men's Likelihood to Sexually Harass: The Moderating Role of Sexism and Personality," *Journal of Applied Psychology* 94, no. 2 (2009), pp. 501–510.

51 A. M. Dionisi, J. Barling, and K. E. Dupré, "Revisiting the Comparative Outcomes of Workplace Aggression and Sexual Harassment," *Journal of Occupational Health Psychology* 17 (2012), pp. 398–408.

52 M. B. Nielsen and S. Einarsen, "Prospective Relationships between Workplace Sexual Harassment and Psychological Distress," *Occupational Medicine* 62 (2012), pp. 226–228.

53 Based on "The Dos and Don'ts of Office Romances," *Toronto Star*, August 2, 2012, http://www.thestar.com/life/2012/08/02/the_dos_and_donts_of_office_romances.html; H. Levitt, "What Tangled Webs We Weave," *Financial Post*, May 23, 2012, http://

business.financialpost.com/2012/05/23/what-tangled-webs-we-weave/; and *Reichard v. Kuntz*, [2011] ONSC 7460 (CanLII), para. 50.

54 "Human Rights Policies and Procedures, Part IV," *Carleton.ca*, accessed October 21, 2014, http://www.carleton.ca/equity/human-rights/policy/human-rights-policies-and-procedures-part-2/.

55 M. Lalonde, "Campus Culture: Crude, Degrading, Dangerous," *Montreal Gazette*, December 10, 2016.

56 "Western University Student Newspaper Pens 'Guide on How to Sexually Harass' TAs (TWEETS)," *Huffington Post*, August 26, 2014, http://www.huffingtonpost.ca/2014/08/26/western-university-gazette-seduce-ta_n_5718759.html.

57 "Building a Better Workforce," *PROFIT*, February 16, 2011, http://www.profitguide.com/manage-grow/human-resources/building-a-better-workforce-30073.

58 Based on J. L. Berdahl and K. Aquino, "Sexual Behavior at Work: Fun or Folly?" *Journal of Applied Psychology* 94, no. 1 (2009), pp. 34–47; and C. Boyd, "The Debate over the Prohibition of Romance in the Workplace," *Journal of Business Ethics* 97, no. 2 (2010), pp. 325–338.

59 This is the definition given by R. Forrester, "Empowerment: Rejuvenating a Potent Idea," *Academy of Management Executive*, August 2000, pp. 67–80.

60 R. E. Quinn and G. M. Spreitzer, "The Road to Empowerment: Seven Questions Every Leader Should Consider," *Organizational Dynamics*, Autumn 1997, p. 38.

61 C. Argyris, "Empowerment: The Emperor's New Clothes," *Harvard Business Review*, May–June 1998.

62 J. Schaubroeck, J. R. Jones, and J. L. Xie, "Individual Differences in Utilizing Control to Cope with Job Demands: Effects on Susceptibility to Infectious Disease," *Journal of Applied Psychology* 86, no. 2 (2001), pp. 265–278.

63 S. Niedoba, "How Singular Focus Made Steam Whistle Brewing One of Canada's Top Workplaces," *Canadian Business*, April 20, 2017, http://www.canadianbusiness.com/lists-and-rankings/best-managed-companies/steam-whistle-brewing/.

64 S. A. Culbert and J. J. McDonough, *The Invisible War: Pursuing Self-Interest at Work* (New York: Wiley, 1980), p. 6.

65 H. Mintzberg, *Power in and Around Organizations* (Englewood Cliffs, NJ: Prentice Hall, 1983), p. 26.

66 G. R. Ferris and W. A. Hochwarter, "Organizational Politics," in *APA Handbook of Industrial and Organizational Psychology*, vol. 3, ed. S. Zedeck (Washington, DC: American Psychological Association, 2011), pp. 435–459.

67 D. Farrell and J. C. Petersen, "Patterns of Political Behavior in Organizations," *Academy of Management Review*, July 1982, p. 405. For a thoughtful analysis of the academic controversies underlying any definition of organizational politics, see A. Drory and T. Romm, "The Definition of Organizational Politics: A Review," *Human Relations*, November 1990, pp. 1133–1154; and R. S. Cropanzano, K. M. Kacmar, and D. P. Bozeman, "Organizational Politics, Justice, and Support: Their Differences and Similarities," in *Organizational Politics, Justice and Support: Managing Social Climate at Work*, ed. R. S. Cropanzano and K. M. Kacmar (Westport, CT: Quorum Books, 1995), pp. 1–18.

68 D. A. Buchanan, "You Stab My Back, I'll Stab Yours: Management Experience and Perceptions of Organization Political Behavior," *British Journal of Management* 19, no. 1 (2008), pp. 49–64.

69 J. Pfeffer, *Power: Why Some People Have It—And Others Don't* (New York: Harper Collins, 2010).

70 G. R. Ferris, G. S. Russ, and P. M. Fandt, "Politics in Organizations," in *Impression Management in Organizations*, ed. R. A. Giacalone and P. Rosenfeld (Newbury Park, CA: Sage, 1989), pp. 143–170; and K. M. Kacmar, D. P. Bozeman, D. S. Carlson, and W. P. Anthony,

"An Examination of the Perceptions of Organizational Politics Model: Replication and Extension," *Human Relations*, March 1999, pp. 383–416.

71 K. M. Kacmar and R. A. Baron, "Organizational Politics: The State of the Field, Links to Related Processes, and an Agenda for Future Research," in *Research in Personnel and Human Resources Management*, vol. 17, ed. G. R. Ferris (Greenwich, CT: JAI Press, 1999); and M. Valle and L. A. Witt, "The Moderating Effect of Teamwork Perceptions on the Organizational Politics-Job Satisfaction Relationship," *Journal of Social Psychology*, June 2001, pp. 379–388.

72 S. Aryee, Z. Chen, and P. S. Budhwar, "Exchange Fairness and Employee Performance: An Examination of the Relationship between Organizational Politics and Procedural Justice," *Organizational Behavior & Human Decision Processes*, May 2004, pp. 1–14.

73 C. Kiewitz, W. A. Hochwarter, G. R. Ferris, and S. L. Castro, "The Role of Psychological Climate in Neutralizing the Effects of Organizational Politics on Work Outcomes," *Journal of Applied Social Psychology*, June 2002, pp. 1189–1207; and J. M. L. Poon, "Situational Antecedents and Outcomes of Organizational Politics Perceptions," *Journal of Managerial Psychology* 18, no. 2 (2003), pp. 138–155.

74 K. M. Kacmar, D. P. Bozeman, D. S. Carlson, and W. P. Anthony, "An Examination of the Perceptions of Organizational Politics Model," *Human Relations* 52, no. 3 (1999), p. 389.

75 K. M. Kacmar, M. C. Andrews, K. J. Harris, and B. Tepper, "Ethical Leadership and Subordinate Outcomes: The Mediating Role of Organizational Politics and the Moderating Role of Political Skill," *Journal of Business Ethics* 115, no. 1 (2013), pp. 33–44.

76 K. M. Kacmar, D. G. Bachrach, K. J. Harris, and S. Zivnuska, "Fostering Good Citizenship through Ethical Leadership: Exploring the Moderating Role of Gender and Organizational Politics," *Journal of Applied Psychology* 96 (2011), pp. 633–642.

77 C. Homburg and A. Fuerst, "See No Evil, Hear No Evil, Speak No Evil: A Study of Defensive Organizational Behavior towards Customer Complaints," *Journal of the Academy of Marketing Science* 35, no. 4 (2007), pp. 523–536.

78 See, for example, M. C. Bolino and W. H. Turnley, "More Than One Way to Make an Impression: Exploring Profiles of Impression Management," *Journal of Management* 29, no. 2 (2003), pp. 141–160; S. Zivnuska, K. M. Kacmar, L. A. Witt, D. S. Carlson, and V. K. Bratton, "Interactive Effects of Impression Management and Organizational Politics on Job Performance," *Journal of Organizational Behavior*, August 2004, pp. 627–640; and M. C. Bolino, K. M. Kacmar, W. H. Turnley, and J. B. Gilstrap, "A Multi-Level Review of Impression Management Motives and Behaviors," *Journal of Management* 34, no. 6 (2008), pp. 1080–1109.

79 D. J. Howard and R. A. Kerin, "Individual Differences in the Name Similarity Effect: The Role of Self-Monitoring," *Journal of Individual Differences* 35, no. 2 (2014), pp. 111–118.

80 Based on M. Thompson, "How to Work with Your Startup Frenemies," *VentureBeat*, December 22, 2012, http://venturebeat.com/; and N. L. Mead and J. K. Maner, "On Keeping Your Enemies Close: Powerful Leaders Seek Proximity to Ingroup Power Threats," *Journal of Personality and Social Psychology* 102 (2012), pp. 576–591.

81 M. R. Leary and R. M. Kowalski, "Impression Management: A Literature Review and Two-Component Model," *Psychological Bulletin*, January 1990, p. 40.

82 D. H. M. Chng, M. S. Rodgers, E. Shih, and X.-B. Song, "Leaders' Impression Management During Organizational Decline: The Roles of Publicity, Image Concerns, and Incentive Compensation," *Leadership Quarterly* 26, no. 2 (2015), pp. 270–285; and L. Uziel, "Life Seems Different with You Around: Differential Shifts in Cognitive Appraisal in the Mere Presence of Others

for Neuroticism and Impression Management," *Personality and Individual Differences* 73 (2015), pp. 39–43.

83 J. Ham and R. Vonk, "Impressions of Impression Management: Evidence of Spontaneous Suspicion of Ulterior Motivation," *Journal of Experimental Social Psychology* 47, no. 2 (2011), pp. 466–471; and W. M. Bowler, J. R. B. Halbesleben, and J. R. B. Paul, "If You're Close with the Leader, You Must Be a Brownnose: The Role of Leader–Member Relationships in Follower, Leader, and Coworker Attributions of Organizational Citizenship Behavior Motives," *Human Resource Management Review* 20, no. 4 (2010), pp. 309–316.

84 J. R. B. Halbesleben, W. M. Bowler, M. C. Bolino, and W. H Turnley, "Organizational Concern, Prosocial Values, or Impression Management? How Supervisors Attribute Motives to Organizational Citizenship Behavior," *Journal of Applied Social Psychology* 40, no. 6 (2010), pp. 1450–1489.

85 G. Blickle, C. Diekmann, P. B. Schneider, Y. Kalthöfer, and J. K. Summers, "When Modesty Wins: Impression Management through Modesty, Political Skill, and Career Success—A Two-Study Investigation," *European Journal of Work and Organizational Psychology*, December 1, 2012, pp. 899–922.

86 A. P. J. Ellis, B. J. West, A. M. Ryan, and R. P. DeShon, "The Use of Impression Management Tactics in Structural Interviews: A Function of Question Type?" *Journal of Applied Psychology*, December 2002, pp. 1200–1208.

87 C. K. Stevens and A. L. Kristof, "Making the Right Impression: A Field Study of Applicant Impression Management during Job Interviews," *Journal of Applied Psychology* 80 (1995), pp. 587–606; L. A. McFarland, A. M. Ryan, and S. D. Kriska, "Impression Management Use and Effectiveness across Assessment Methods," *Journal of Management* 29, no. 5 (2003), pp. 641–661; C. A. Higgins and T. A. Judge, "The Effect of Applicant Influence Tactics on Recruiter Perceptions of Fit and Hiring Recommendations: A Field Study," *Journal of Applied Psychology* 89, no. 4 (2004), pp. 622–632; and W. C. Tsai, C. C. Chen, and S. F. Chiu, "Exploring Boundaries of the Effects of Applicant Impression Management Tactics in Job Interviews," *Journal of Management*, February 2005, pp. 108–125.

88 M. R. Barrick, J. A. Shaffer, and S. W. DeGrassi. "What You See May Not Be What You Get: Relationships among Self-Presentation Tactics and Ratings of Interview and Job Performance," *Journal of Applied Psychology* 94, no. 6 (2009), pp. 1394–1411.

89 E. Molleman, B. Emans, and N. Turusbekova, "How to Control Self-Promotion among Performance-Oriented Employees: The Roles of Task Clarity and Personalized Responsibility," *Personnel Review* 41 (2012), pp. 88–105.

90 K. J. Harris, K. M. Kacmar, S. Zivnuska, and J. D. Shaw, "The Impact of Political Skill on Impression Management Effectiveness," *Journal of Applied Psychology* 92, no. 1 (2007), pp. 278–285; and D. C. Treadway, G. R. Ferris, A. B. Duke, G. L. Adams, and J. B. Thatcher, "The Moderating Role of Subordinate Political Skill on Supervisors' Impressions of Subordinate Ingratiation and Ratings of Subordinate Interpersonal Facilitation," *Journal of Applied Psychology* 92, no. 3 (2007), pp. 848–855.

91 J. D. Westphal and I. Stern, "Flattery Will Get You Everywhere (Especially if You Are a Male Caucasian): How Ingratiation, Boardroom Behavior, and Demographic Minority Status Affect Additional Board Appointments of U.S. Companies," *Academy of Management Journal* 50, no. 2 (2007), pp. 267–288.

92 Y. Liu, G. R. Ferris, J. Xu, B. A. Weitz, and P. L. Perrewé, "When Ingratiation Backfires: The Role of Political Skill in the Ingratiation–Internship Performance Relationship," *Academy of Management Learning and Education* 13 (2014), pp. 569–586.

93 C. Chen and M. Lin, "The Effect of Applicant Impression Management Tactics on Hiring Recommendations: Cognitive and Affective Processes," *Applied Psychology: An International Review*

63, no. 4, (2014), pp. 698–724; J. Levashina, C. J. Hartwell, F. P. Morgeson, and M. A. Campion, "The Structured Employment Interview: Narrative and Quantitative Review of the Research Literature," *Personnel Psychology*, Spring 2014, pp. 241–293; and M. Nemko, "The Effective, Ethical, and Less Stressful Job Interview," *Psychology Today*, March 25, 2014, https://www.psychologytoday.com/blog/how-do-life/201503/the-effective-ethical-and-less-stressful-job-interview.

94 Based on A. Lavoie, "How to Get Rid of Toxic Office Politics," *Fast Company*, April 10, 2014, http://www.fastcompany.com/3028856/work-smart/how-to-make-office-politicking-a-lame-duck; and C. Conner, "Office Politics: Must You Play?" *Forbes*, April 14, 2013, http://www.forbes.com/sites/cherylsnappconner/2013/04/14/office-politics-must-you-play-a-handbook-for-survivalsuccess/.

95 R. Westwood, "Order of Canada Winner Lied about Ph.D," *Maclean's*, September 26, 2013, http://www.macleans.ca/general/an-order-of-lies/; and "Louis LaPierre Stripped of Order of Canada," *CBC News*, June 13, 2014, http://www.cbc.ca/news/canada/new-brunswick/louis-lapierre-stripped-of-order-of-canada-1.2675141.

96 C. Robert, T. M. Probst, J. J. Martocchio, F. Drasgow, and J. J. Lawler, "Empowerment and Continuous Improvement in the United States, Mexico, Poland, and India: Predicting Fit on the Basis of the Dimensions of Power Distance and Individualism," *Journal of Applied Psychology* 85 (2000), pp. 643–658.

97 W. A. Randolph and M. Sashkin, "Can Organizational Empowerment Work in Multinational Settings?" *Academy of Management Executive*, February 2002, pp. 102–115.

98 M. Gagné and D. Bhave, "Autonomy in the Workplace: An Essential Ingredient to Employee Engagement and Well-Being in Every Culture?" in *Human Autonomy in Cross-Cultural Context: Perspectives on the Psychology of Agency, Freedom, and Well-Being*, ed. V. I. Chirkov, R. M. Ryan, and K. M. Sheldon (Berlin, Germany: Springer, 2011).

99 Concordia University, "Freedom's Just Another Word for Employee Satisfaction," *ScienceDaily*, January 24, 2011, http://www.concordia.ca/cunews/main/releases/2011/01/24/freedoms-just-another-word-for-employee-satisfaction.html.

100 P. P. Fu and G. Yukl, "Perceived Effectiveness of Influence Tactics in the United States and China," *Leadership Quarterly*, Summer 2000, pp. 251–266; O. Branzei, "Cultural Explanations of Individual Preferences for Influence Tactics in Cross-Cultural Encounters," *International Journal of Cross Cultural Management*, August 2002, pp. 203–218; G. Yukl, P. P. Fu, and R. McDonald, "Cross-Cultural Differences in Perceived Effectiveness of Influence Tactics for Initiating or Resisting Change," *Applied Psychology: An International Review*, January 2003, pp. 66–82; and P. P. Fu, T. K. Peng, J. C. Kennedy, and G. Yukl, "Examining the Preferences of Influence Tactics in Chinese Societies: A Comparison of Chinese Managers in Hong Kong, Taiwan, and Mainland China," *Organizational Dynamics* 33, no. 1 (2004), pp. 32–46.

101 C. J. Torelli and S. Shavitt, "Culture and Concepts of Power," *Journal of Personality and Social Psychology* 99, no. 4 (2010), pp. 703–723.

102 E. Szabo, "Meaning and Context of Participation in Five European Countries," *Management Decision* 44, no. 2 (2006), pp. 276–289.

103 J. L. T. Leong, M. H. Bond, and P. P. Fu, "Perceived Effectiveness of Influence Strategies in the United States and Three Chinese Societies," *International Journal of Cross Cultural Management*, May 2006, pp. 101–120.

104 Y. Miyamoto and B. Wilken, "Culturally Contingent Situated Cognition: Influencing Other People Fosters Analytic Perception in the United States but Not in Japan," *Psychological Science* 21, no. 11 (2010), pp. 1616–1622.

105 Based on B. Burrough and B. McLean, "The Hunt for Steve Cohen," *Vanity Fair*, June 2013, http://www.vanityfair.com/business/2013/06/steve-cohen-insider-trading-case; C. Anderson, R. Willer, G. J. Kilduff, and C. E. Brown, "The Origins of Deference: When Do People Prefer Lower Status?" *Journal of Personality and Social Psychology* 102 (2012), pp. 1077–1088; C. Anderson, M. W. Kraus, A. D. Galinsky, and D. Keltner, "The Local-Ladder Effect: Social Status and Subjective Well-Being," *Psychological Science* 23, no. 7 (2012), pp. 764–771; S. Kennelly, "Happiness Is About Respect, Not Riches," *Greater Good*, July 13, 2012, http://greatergood.berkeley.edu/article/item/happiness_is_about_respect_not_riches; and P. Lattman and B. Protess, "$1.2 Billion Fine for Hedge Fund SAC Capital in Insider Case," *New York Times Dealbook*, November 4, 2013, http://dealbook.nytimes.com/2013/11/04/sac-capital-agrees-to-plead-guilty-to-insider-trading/?_r=0.

106 Based on J. Sancton, "Milgram at McDonald's," *Bloomberg Businessweek*, September 2, 2012, pp. 74–75; and A. Wolfson, "'Compliance' Re-Creates McDonald's Strip-Search Ordeal," *USA Today*, September 1, 2012, http://usatoday30.usatoday.com/news/nation/story/2012-09-01/Compliance-strip-search-hoax/57509182/1.

107 Based on M. L. Tushman, W. K. Smith, and A. Binns, "The Ambidextrous CEO," *Harvard Business Review*, June 2011, pp. 74–79; and S. Bogan, "Find Your Focus," *Financial Planning*, February 2011, p. 72.

108 Based on M. G. McIntyre, "Disgruntlement Won't Advance Your Career," *Pittsburgh Post-Gazette*, September 23, 2012; and S. Shellenbarger, "What to Do with a Workplace Whiner," *Wall Street Journal*, September 12, 2012, pp. D1, D3.

109 Based on S. P. Robbins and P. L. Hunsaker, *Training in Interpersonal Skills: Tips for Managing People at Work*, 2nd ed. (Upper Saddle River, NJ: Prentice Hall, 1996), pp. 131–134.

Chapter 9

1 Vignette based on K. Owram, "Canadian Auto Industry Faces Biggest Existential Threat since 2009 Crisis As Labour Talks Begin," *Financial Post*, August 8, 2016, http://business.financialpost.com/transportation/canadian-auto-industry-faces-biggest-existential-threat-since-2009-as-labour-talks-begin; and K. Owram, "General Motors of Canada Ltd, Union 'Miles Apart' as Labour Negotiations Begin," *Financial Post*, August 10, 2016, http://business.financialpost.com/transportation/general-motors-of-canada-ltd-union-miles-apart-as-labour-negotiations-begin.

2 See, for instance, D. Tjosvold, A. S. H. Wong, and N. Y. F. Chen, "Constructively Managing Conflicts in Organizations," *Annual Review of Organizational Psychology and Organizational Behavior* 1 (March 2014), pp. 545–568; and M. A. Korsgaard, S. S. Jeong, D. M. Mahony, and A. H. Pitariu, "A Multilevel View of Intragroup Conflict," *Journal of Management* 34, no. 6 (2008), pp. 1222–1252.

3 L. L. Putnam and M. S. Poole, "Conflict and Negotiation," in *Handbook of Organizational Communication: An Interdisciplinary Perspective*, ed. F. M. Jablin, L. L. Putnam, K. H. Roberts, and L. W. Porter (Newbury Park, CA: Sage, 1987), pp. 549–599.

4 K. W. Thomas, "Conflict and Negotiation Processes in Organizations," in *Handbook of Industrial and Organizational Psychology*, 2nd ed., vol. 3, ed. M. D. Dunnette and L. M. Hough (Palo Alto, CA: Consulting Psychologists Press, 1992), pp. 651–717.

5 F. R. C. de Wit, L. L. Greer, and K. A. Jehn, "The Paradox of Intragroup Conflict: A Meta-analysis," *Journal of Applied Psychology* 97, no. 2 (2012), pp. 360–390; and N. Gamero, V. González-Romá, and J. M. Peiró, "The Influence of Intra-Team Conflict on Work Teams' Affective Climate: A Longitudinal Study," *Journal of Occupational and Organizational Psychology* 81, no. 1 (2008), pp. 47–69.

6 N. Halevy, E. Y. Chou, and A. D. Galinsky, "Exhausting or Exhilarating? Conflict as Threat to Interests, Relationships and Identities," *Journal of Experimental Social Psychology* 48 (2012), pp. 530–537.

7 F. R. C. de Wit, L. L. Greer, and K. A. Jehn, "The Paradox of Intragroup Conflict: A Meta-analysis," *Journal of Applied Psychology* 97 (2012), pp. 360–390.

8 J. Farh, C. Lee, and C. I. C. Farh, "Task Conflict and Team Creativity: A Question of How Much and When," *Journal of Applied Psychology* 95, no. 6 (2010), pp. 1173–1180.

9 B. H. Bradley, A. C. Klotz, B. F. Postlethwaite, and K. G. Brown, "Ready to Rumble: How Team Personality Composition and Task Conflict Interact to Improve Performance," *Journal of Applied Psychology* 98 (2013), pp. 385–392.

10 B. H. Bradley, B. F. Postlethwaite, A. C. Klotz, M. R. Hamdani, and K. G. Brown, "Reaping the Benefits of Task Conflict in Teams: The Critical Role of Team Psychological Safety Climate," *Journal of Applied Psychology* 97 (2012), pp. 151–158.

11 S. Benard, "Cohesion from Conflict: Does Intergroup Conflict Motivate Intragroup Norm Enforcement and Support for Centralized Leadership?" *Social Psychology Quarterly* 75 (2012), pp. 107–130.

12 G. A. Van Kleef, W. Steinel, and A. C. Homan, "On Being Peripheral and Paying Attention: Prototypicality and Information Processing in Intergroup Conflict," *Journal of Applied Psychology* 98 (2013), pp. 63–79.

13 R. S. Peterson and K. J. Behfar, "The Dynamic Relationship between Performance Feedback, Trust, and Conflict in Groups: A Longitudinal Study," *Organizational Behavior and Human Decision Processes*, September–November 2003, pp. 102–112.

14 See K. A. Jehn, "A Multimethod Examination of the Benefits and Detriments of Intragroup Conflict," *Administrative Science Quarterly*, June 1995, pp. 256–282.

15 T. M. Glomb and H. Liao, "Interpersonal Aggression in Work Groups: Social Influence, Reciprocal, and Individual Effects," *Academy of Management Journal* 46, no. 4 (2003), pp. 486–496; and V. Venkataramani and R. S. Dalal, "Who Helps and Who Harms? Relational Aspects of Interpersonal Helping and Harming in Organizations," *Journal of Applied Psychology* 92, no. 4 (2007), pp. 952–966.

16 R. Friedman, C. Anderson, J. Brett, M. Olekalns, N. Goates, and C. C. Lisco, "The Positive and Negative Effects of Anger on Dispute Resolution: Evidence from Electronically Mediated Disputes," *Journal of Applied Psychology*, April 2004, pp. 369–376.

17 J. S. Chun, and J. N. Choi, "Members' Needs, Intragroup Conflict, and Group Performance," *Journal of Applied Psychology* 99 (2014), pp. 437–450.

18 Vignette based on "Unifor Announces Tentative Deadline Deal with GM to Avert Strike," *CBCNews*, September 20, 2016, http://www.cbc.ca/news/business/unifor-tentative-deal-gm-strike-1.3770013; and General Motors of Canada Media Statement, 2016 Unifor Negotiations—September 20, 2016, http://media.gm.ca/media/ca/en/gm/home.detail.html/content/Pages/news/ca/en/2016/Sep/0920_MediaStatement.html.

19 D. Tjosvold, "Cooperative and Competitive Goal Approach to Conflict: Accomplishments and Challenges," *Applied Psychology: An International Review* 47, no. 3 (1998), pp. 285–342.

20 K. W. Thomas, "Conflict and Negotiation Processes in Organizations," in *Handbook of Industrial and Organizational Psychology*, 2nd ed., vol. 3, ed. M. D. Dunnette and L. M. Hough (Palo Alto, CA: Consulting Psychologists Press, 1992), pp. 651–717.

21 C. K. W. De Dreu, A. Evers, B. Beersma, E. S. Kluwer, and A. Nauta, "A Theory-Based Measure of Conflict Management Strategies in the Workplace," *Journal of Organizational Behavior* 22, no. 6 (September 2001), pp. 645–668. See also D. G. Pruitt and J.

Rubin, *Social Conflict: Escalation, Stalemate and Settlement* (New York: Random House, 1986).

22 C. K. W. De Dreu, A. Evers, B. Beersma, E. S. Kluwer, and A. Nauta, "A Theory-Based Measure of Conflict Management Strategies in the Workplace," *Journal of Organizational Behavior* 22, no. 6 (September 2001), pp. 645–668.

23 L. A. DeChurch, J. R. Mesmer-Magnus, and D. Doty, "Moving beyond Relationship and Task Conflict: Toward a Process-State Perspective," *Journal of Applied Psychology* 98 (2013), pp. 559–578.

24 R. A. Baron, "Personality and Organizational Conflict: Effects of the Type A Behavior Pattern and Self-Monitoring," *Organizational Behavior and Human Decision Processes*, October 1989, pp. 281–296; A. Drory and I. Ritov, "Effects of Work Experience and Opponent's Power on Conflict Management Styles," *International Journal of Conflict Management* 8 (1997), pp. 148–161; R. J. Sternberg and L. J. Soriano, "Styles of Conflict Resolution," *Journal of Personality and Social Psychology*, July 1984, pp. 115–126; and R. J. Volkema and T. J. Bergmann, "Conflict Styles as Indicators of Behavioral Patterns in Interpersonal Conflicts," *Journal of Social Psychology*, February 1995, pp. 5–15.

25 Based on S. P. Robbins, *Managing Organizational Conflict: A Nontraditional Approach* (Upper Saddle River, NJ: Prentice Hall, 1974), pp. 59–89.

26 Based on K. W. Thomas, "Toward Multidimensional Values in Teaching: The Example of Conflict Behaviors," *Academy of Management Review*, July 1977, p. 487; and C. K. W. De Dreu, A. Evers, B. Beersma, E. S. Kluwer, and A. Nauta, "A Theory-Based Measure of Conflict Management Strategies in the Workplace," *Journal of Organizational Behavior* 22, no. 6 (September 2001), pp. 645–668.

27 R. Kreitner and A. Kinicki, *Organizational Behavior*, 6th ed. (New York: McGraw-Hill, 2004), p. 492, Table 14-1. Reprinted by permission of McGraw Hill Education.

28 "Managers Spend More Than 6 Hours per Week Handling Staff Conflicts: Survey," *HR Reporter*, March 23, 2011.

29 R. D. Ramsey, "Interpersonal Conflicts," *SuperVision* 66, no. 4 (April 2005), pp. 14–17.

30 G. Todorova, J. B. Bear, and L. R. Weingart, "Can Conflict Be Energizing? A Study of Task Conflict, Positive Emotions, and Job Satisfaction," *Journal of Applied Psychology* 99 (2014), pp. 451–467.

31 Based on D. Tjosvold, *Learning to Manage Conflict: Getting People to Work Together Productively* (New York: Lexington Books, 1993), pp. 12–13.

32 M. E. Zellmer-Bruhn, M. M. Maloney, A. D. Bhappu, and R. Salvador, "When and How Do Differences Matter? An Exploration of Perceived Similarity in Teams," *Organizational Behavior and Human Decision Processes* 107, no. 1 (2008), pp. 41–59.

33 See T. H. Cox, S. A. Lobel, and P. L. McLeod, "Effects of Ethnic Group Cultural Differences on Cooperative Behavior on a Group Task," *Academy of Management Journal*, December 1991, pp. 827–847; and D. van Knippenberg, C. K. W. De Dreu, and A. C. Homan, "Work Group Diversity and Group Performance: An Integrative Model and Research Agenda," *Journal of Applied Psychology*, December 2004, pp. 1008–1022.

34 R. Ilies, M. D. Johnson, T. A. Judge, and J. Keeney, "A Within-Individual Study of Interpersonal Conflict as a Work Stressor: Dispositional and Situational Moderators," *Journal of Organizational Behavior* 32, no. 1 (2011), pp. 44–64.

35 K. J. Behfar, R. S. Peterson, E. A. Mannix, and W. M. K. Trochim, "The Critical Role of Conflict Resolution in Teams: A Close Look at the Links between Conflict Type, Conflict Management Strategies, and Team Outcomes," *Journal of Applied Psychology* 93, no. 1 (2008), pp. 170–188; A. G. Tekleab, N. R. Quigley, and P. E. Tesluk, "A Longitudinal Study of Team Conflict, Conflict Management, Cohesion, and Team Effectiveness," *Group and Organization Management* 34, no. 2 (2009), pp. 170–205; and E. Van de Vliert, M. C. Euwema, and S. E. Huismans, "Managing Conflict with a Subordinate or a Superior: Effectiveness of Conglomerated Behavior," *Journal of Applied Psychology* 80 (1995), pp. 271–281.

36 A. Somech, H. S. Desivilya, and H. Lidogoster, "Team Conflict Management and Team Effectiveness: The Effects of Task Interdependence and Team Identification," *Journal of Organizational Behavior* 30, no. 3 (2009), pp. 359–378.

37 P. J. Hinds and D. E. Bailey, "Out of Sight, Out of Sync: Understanding Conflict in Distributed Teams," *Organization Science*, November–December 2003, pp. 615–632.

38 K. A. Jehn, L. Greer, S. Levine, and G. Szulanski, "The Effects of Conflict Types, Dimensions, and Emergent States on Group Outcomes," *Group Decision and Negotiation* 17, no. 6 (2005), pp. 777–796.

39 M. E. Zellmer-Bruhn, M. M. Maloney, A. D. Bhappu, and R. Salvador, "When and How Do Differences Matter? An Exploration of Perceived Similarity in Teams," *Organizational Behavior and Human Decision Processes* 107, no. 1 (2008), pp. 41–59.

40 Vignette based on A. Brockman, "Auto Analysts Split on Unifor's Strength in GM Contract Talks," *CBCNews*, September 6, 2016, http://www.cbc.ca/news/canada/windsor/unifor-gm-contract-talks-bargaining-position-1.3750203.

41 M. H. Bazerman, J. R. Curhan, D. A. Moore, and K. L. Valley, "Negotiation," *Annual Review of Psychology* 51 (2000), pp. 279–314.

42 See, for example, D. R. Ames, "Assertiveness Expectancies: How Hard People Push Depends on the Consequences They Predict," *Journal of Personality and Social Psychology* 95, no. 6 (2008), pp. 1541–1557; and J. R. Curhan, H. A. Elfenbein, and H. Xu, "What Do People Value When They Negotiate? Mapping the Domain of Subjective Value in Negotiation," *Journal of Personality and Social Psychology* 91, no. 3 (2006), pp. 493–512.

43 This model is based on R. J. Lewicki, "Bargaining and Negotiation," *Exchange: The Organizational Behavior Teaching Journal* 6, no. 2 (1981), pp. 39–40; and B. S. Moskal, "The Art of the Deal," *IndustryWeek*, January 18, 1993, p. 23.

44 J. C. Magee, A. D. Galinsky, and D. H. Gruenfeld, "Power, Propensity to Negotiate, and Moving First in Competitive Interactions," *Personality and Social Psychology Bulletin*, February 2007, pp. 200–212.

45 H. R. Bowles, L. Babcock, and L. Lei, "Social Incentives for Gender Differences in the Propensity to Initiative Negotiations: Sometimes It Does Hurt to Ask," *Organizational Behavior and Human Decision Processes* 103 (2007), pp. 84–103.

46 Based on G. Ku, A. D. Galinsky, and J. K. Murnighan, "Starting Low but Ending High: A Reversal of the Anchoring Effect in Auctions," *Journal of Personality and Social Psychology* 90 (June 2006), pp. 975–986; K. Sherstyuk, "A Comparison of First Price Multi-Object Auctions," *Experimental Economics* 12, no. 1 (2009), pp. 42–64; and R. M. Isaac, T. C. Salmon, and A. Zillante, "A Theory of Jump Bidding in Ascending Auctions," *Journal of Economic Behavior & Organization* 62, no. 1 (2007), pp. 144–164.

47 D. A. Moore, "Myopic Prediction, Self-Destructive Secrecy, and the Unexpected Benefits of Revealing Final Deadlines in Negotiation," *Organizational Behavior and Human Decision Processes*, July 2004, pp. 125–139.

48 M. A. Rahim, *Managing Conflict in Organizations*, 4th ed. (New Brunswick, NJ: Transaction Publishers, 2011).

49 C. K. W. De Dreu, L. R. Weingart, and S. Kwon, "Influence of Social Motives on Integrative Negotiation: A Meta-analytic Review and Test of Two Theories," *Journal of Personality and Social Psychology*, May 2000, pp. 889–905.

50 A. W. Brooks and M. E. Schweitzer, "Can Nervous Nelly Negotiate? How Anxiety Causes Negotiators to Make Low First Offers,

Exit Early, and Earn Less Profit," *Organizational Behavior and Human Decision Processes* 115, no. 1 (2011), pp. 43–54. (Awarded Best Paper with a Student as First Author by the International Association for Conflict Management, 2010.), http://www.hbs.edu/faculty/Pages/item.aspx?num=45137.

51 A. W. Brooks and M. E. Schweitzer, "Can Nervous Nelly Negotiate? How Anxiety Causes Negotiators to Make Low First Offers, Exit Early, and Earn Less Profit," *Organizational Behavior and Human Decision Processes* 115, no. 1 (2011), pp. 43–54.

52 This model is based on R. J. Lewicki, D. Saunders, and B. Barry, *Negotiation*, 7th ed. (New York: McGraw Hill, 2014).

53 D. Malhotra and M. Bazerman, "Investigative Negotiation," *Harvard Business Review*, September 2007, pp. 72–78.

54 J. R. Curhan, H. A. Elfenbein, and G. J. Kilduff, "Getting off on the Right Foot: Subjective Value versus Economic Value in Predicting Longitudinal Job Outcomes from Job Offer Negotiations," *Journal of Applied Psychology* 94, no. 2 (2009), pp. 524–534.

55 R. Fisher and W. Ury, *Getting to Yes: Negotiating Agreement without Giving In*, 2nd ed. (New York: Penguin, 1991).

56 Based on L. L. Thompson, J. Wang, and B. C. Gunia. "Negotiation," *Annual Review of Psychology* 61 (2010), pp. 491–515.

57 M. Schaerer, R. I. Swaab, and A. D. Galinsky, "Anchors Weigh More Than Power: Why Absolute Powerlessness Liberates Negotiators to Achieve Better Outcomes," *Psychological Science*, December 2014, doi:10.1177/0956797614558718.

58 R. P. Larrick and G. Wu, "Claiming a Large Slice of a Small Pie: Asymmetric Disconfirmation in Negotiation," *Journal of Personality and Social Psychology* 93, no. 2 (2007), pp. 212–233.

59 M. Marks and C. Harold, "Who Asks and Who Receives in Salary Negotiation," *Journal of Organizational Behavior* 32, no. 3 (2011), pp. 371–394.

60 R. Fisher and W. Ury, *Getting to Yes; Negotiating Agreement without Giving In*, 2nd ed. (New York: Penguin, 1991).

61 H. A. Elfenbein, "Individual Difference in Negotiation: A Nearly Abandoned Pursuit Revived," *Current Directions in Psychological Science* 24 (2015), pp. 131–136.

62 R. Fisher and W. Ury, *Getting to Yes: Negotiating Agreement without Giving In*, 2nd ed. (New York: Penguin, 1991).

63 T. A. Judge, B. A. Livingston, and C. Hurst, "Do Nice Guys—and Gals—Really Finish Last? The Joint Effects of Sex and Agreeableness on Income," *Journal of Personality and Social Psychology* 102 (2012), pp. 390–407.

64 Based on T. R. Cohen, "Moral Emotions and Unethical Bargaining: The Differential Effects of Empathy and Perspective Taking in Deterring Deceitful Negotiation," *Journal of Business Ethics* 94, no. 4 (2010), pp. 569–579; and R. Volkema, D. Fleck, and A. Hofmeister, "Predicting Competitive-Unethical Negotiating Behavior and Its Consequences," *Negotiation Journal* 26, no. 3 (2010), pp. 263–286.

65 N. Dimotakis, D. E. Conlon, and R. Ilies, "The Mind and Heart (Literally) of the Negotiator: Personality and Contextual Determinants of Experiential Reactions and Economic Outcomes in Negotiation," *Journal of Applied Psychology* 97 (2012), pp. 183–193.

66 E. T. Amanatullah, M. W. Morris, and J. R. Curhan, "Negotiators Who Give Too Much: Unmitigated Communion, Relational Anxieties, and Economic Costs in Distributive and Integrative Bargaining," *Journal of Personality and Social Psychology* 95, no. 3 (2008), pp. 723–738; and D. S. DeRue, D. E. Conlon, H. Moon, and H. W. Willaby, "When Is Straightforwardness a Liability in Negotiations? The Role of Integrative Potential and Structural Power," *Journal of Applied Psychology* 94, no. 4 (2009), pp. 1032–1047.

67 S. Sharma, W. Bottom, and H. A. Elfenbein, "On the Role of Personality, Cognitive Ability, and Emotional Intelligence in Predicting Negotiation Outcomes: A Meta-analysis," *Organizational Psychology Review* 3 (2013), pp. 293–336.

68 H. A. Elfenbein, J. R. Curhan, N. Eisenkraft, A. Shirako, and L. Baccaro, "Are Some Negotiators Better Than Others? Individual Differences in Bargaining Outcomes," *Journal of Research in Personality*, December 2008, pp. 1463–1475.

69 A. Zerres, J. Hüffmeier, P. A. Freund, K. Backhaus, and G. Hertel, "Does It Take Two to Tango? Longitudinal Effects of Unilaterial and Bilateral Integrative Negotiation Training," *Journal of Applied Psychology* 98 (2013), pp. 478–491.

70 G. Lelieveld, E. Van Dijk, I. Van Beest, and G. A. Van Kleef, "Why Anger and Disappointment Affect Other's Bargaining Behavior Differently: The Moderating Role of Power and the Mediating Role of Reciprocal Complementary Emotions," *Personality and Social Psychology Bulletin* 38 (2012), pp. 1209–1221.

71 S. Côté, I. Hideg, and G. A. van Kleef, "The Consequences of Faking Anger in Negotiations," *Journal of Experimental Social Psychology* 49 (2013), pp. 453–463.

72 G. A. Van Kleef and C. K. W. De Dreu, "Longer-Term Consequences of Anger Expression in Negotiation: Retaliation or Spillover?" *Journal of Experimental Social Psychology* 46, no. 5 (2010), pp. 753–760.

73 H. Adam and A. Shirako, "Not All Anger Is Created Equal: The Impact of the Expresser's Culture on the Social Effects of Anger in Negotiations," *Journal of Applied Psychology* 98, no. 5 (2013), pp. 735–798.

74 G. Lelieveld, E. Van Dijk, I. Van Beest, and G. A. Van Kleef, "Why Anger and Disappointment Affect Other's Bargaining Behavior Differently," *Personality and Social Psychology Bulletin* 38 (2012), pp. 1209–1221.

75 M. Olekalns and P. L. Smith, "Mutually Dependent: Power, Trust, Affect, and the Use of Deception in Negotiation," *Journal of Business Ethics* 85, no. 3 (2009), pp. 347–365.

76 A. W. Brooks and M. E. Schweitzer, "Can Nervous Nellie Negotiate? How Anxiety Causes Negotiators to Make Low First Offers, Exit Early, and Earn Less Profit," *Organizational Behavior and Human Decision Processes* 115, no. 1 (2011), pp. 43–54.

77 M. Sinaceur, H. Adam, G. A. Van Kleef, and A. D. Galinsky, "The Advantages of Being Unpredictable: How Emotional Inconsistency Extracts Concessions in Negotiation," *Journal of Experimental Social Psychology* 49 (2013), pp. 498–508.

78 K. Leary, J. Pillemer, and M. Wheeler, "Negotiating with Emotion," *Harvard Business Review*, January–February 2013, pp. 96–103, https://hbr.org/2013/01/negotiating-with-emotion.

79 P. D. Trapnell and D. L. Paulhus, "Agentic and Communal Values: Their Scope and Measurement," *Journal of Personality Assessment* 94 (2012), pp. 39–52.

80 C. T. Kulik and M. Olekalns, "Negotiating the Gender Divide: Lessons from the Negotiation and Organizational Behavior Literatures," *Journal of Management* 38 (2012), pp. 1387–1415.

81 C. Suddath, "The Art of Haggling," *Bloomberg Businessweek*, November 26, 2012, p. 98.

82 J. Mazei, J. Hüffmeier, P. A. Freund, A. F. Stuhlmacher, L. Bilke, and G. Hertel, "A Meta-analysis on Gender Differences in Negotiation Outcomes and Their Moderators," *Psychological Bulletin* 141 (2015), pp. 85–104.

83 L. J. Kray, C. C. Locke, and A. B. Van Zant, "Feminine Charm: An Experimental Analysis of Its Costs and Benefits in Negotiations," *Personality and Social Psychology Bulletin* 38 (2012), pp. 1343–1357.

84 S. de Lemus, R. Spears, M. Bukowski, M. Moya, and J. Lupiáñez, "Reversing Implicit Gender Stereotype Activation as a Function of Exposure to Traditional Gender Roles," *Social Psychology* 44 (2013), pp. 109–116.

85 D. A. Small, M. Gelfand, L. Babcock, and H. Gettman, "Who Goes to the Bargaining Table? The Influence of Gender and Framing

on the Initiation of Negotiation," *Journal of Personality and Social Psychology* 93, no. 4 (2007), pp. 600–613; and C. K. Stevens, A. G. Bavetta, and M. E. Gist, "Gender Differences in the Acquisition of Salary Negotiation Skills: The Role of Goals, Self-Efficacy, and Perceived Control," *Journal of Applied Psychology* 78, no. 5 (October 1993), pp. 723–735.

86 L. Schweitzer, E. Ng, S. Lyons, and L. Kuron, "Exploring the Career Pipeline: Gender Differences in Pre-Career Expectations," *Relations Industrielles/Industrial Relations* 66, no. 3 (2011), pp. 422–444.

87 Based on N. McDonald, "Unifor President Dias Has Had Quite the Year," *thestar.com*, December 31, 2016, https://www.thestar.com/autos/2016/12/31/unifor-president-dias-has-had-quite-the-year.html.

88 D. T. Kong, K. T. Dirks, and D. L. Ferrin, "Interpersonal Trust within Negotiations: Meta-analytic Evidence, Critical Contingencies, and Directions for Future Research," *Academy of Management Journal* 57 (2014), pp. 1235–1255.

89 G. R. Ferris, J. N. Harris, Z. A. Russell, B. P. Ellen, A. D. Martinez, and F. R. Blass, "The Role of Reputation in the Organizational Sciences: A Multilevel Review, Construct Assessment, and Research Directions," *Research in Personnel and Human Resources Management* 32 (2014), pp. 241–303.

90 R. Zinko, G. R. Ferris, S. E. Humphrey, C. J. Meyer, and F. Aime, "Personal Reputation in Organizations: Two-Study Constructive Replication and Extension of Antecedents and Consequences," *Journal of Occupational and Organizational Psychology* 85 (2012), pp. 156–180.

91 A. Hinshaw, P. Reilly, and A. Kupfer Schneider, "Attorneys and Negotiation Ethics: A Material Misunderstanding?" *Negotiation Journal* 29 (2013), pp. 265–287; and N. A. Welsh, "The Reputational Advantages of Demonstrating Trustworthiness: Using the Reputation Index with Law Students," *Negotiation Journal* 28 (2012), pp. 117–145.

92 J. R. Curhan, H. A. Elfenbein, and X. Heng, "What Do People Value When They Negotiate? Mapping the Domain of Subjective Value in Negotiation," *Journal of Personality and Social Psychology* 91 (2006), pp. 493–512.

93 W. E. Baker and N. Bulkley, "Paying It Forward vs. Rewarding Reputation: Mechanisms of Generalized Reciprocity," *Organization Science* 25 (June 17, 2014), pp. 1493–1510.

94 G. A. Van Kleef, C. K. W. De Dreu, and A. S. R. Manstead, "An Interpersonal Approach to Emotion in Social Decision Making: The Emotions as Social Information Model," *Advances in Experimental Social Psychology* 42 (2010), pp. 45–96.

95 F. Lumineau and J. E. Henderson, "The Influence of Relational Experience and Contractual Governance on the Negotiation Strategy in Buyer–Supplier Disputes," *Journal of Operations Management* 30 (2012), pp. 382–395.

96 Mediate BC, "Mediator Survey 2014," *Mediate BC*, October 14, 2014, http://www.mediatebc.com/PDFs/MBC-Survey-Summary-Final.aspx.

97 Conciliation and Labour Tribunals Division, Nova Scotia Labour and Advanced Education, *Conciliation: A Guide for Employer and Union Committees* (Halifax: Author, 2012), http://novascotia.ca/lae/conciliation/docs/Conciliation_Guide_WEB.pdf.

98 H. R. Markus and S. Kitayama, "Culture and the Self: Implications for Cognition, Emotion, and Motivation," *Psychological Review* 98, no. 2 (1991), pp. 224–253; and H. Ren and B. Gray, "Repairing Relationship Conflict: How Violation Types and Culture Influence the Effectiveness of Restoration Rituals," *Academy of Management Review* 34, no. 1 (2009), pp. 105–126.

99 M. J. Gelfand, M. Higgins, L. H. Nishii, J. L. Raver, A. Dominguez, F. Murakami, S. Yamaguchi, and M. Toyama, "Culture and Egocentric Perceptions of Fairness in Conflict and Negotiation," *Journal of Applied Psychology*, October 2002, pp. 833–845; and

Z. Ma, "Chinese Conflict Management Styles and Negotiation Behaviours: An Empirical Test," *International Journal of Cross Cultural Management*, April 2007, pp. 101–119.

100 P. P. Fu, X. H. Yan, Y. Li, E. Wang, and S. Peng, "Examining Conflict-Handling Approaches by Chinese Top Management Teams in IT Firms," *International Journal of Conflict Management* 19, no. 3 (2008), pp. 188–209.

101 W. Liu, R. Friedman, and Y. Hong, "Culture and Accountability in Negotiation: Recognizing the Importance of In-Group Relations," *Organizational Behavior and Human Decision Processes* 117 (2012), pp. 221–234; and B. C. Gunia, J. M. Brett, A. K. Nandkeolyar, and D. Kamdar, "Paying a Price: Culture, Trust, and Negotiation Consequences," *Journal of Applied Psychology* 96, no. 4 (2010), pp. 774–789.

102 L. A. Liu, R. Friedman, B. Barry, M. J. Gelfand, and Z. Zhang, "The Dynamics of Consensus Building in Intracultural and Intercultural Negotiations," *Administrative Science Quarterly* 57 (2012), pp. 269–304.

103 Based on S. Kopelman and A. S. Rosette, "Cultural Variation in Response to Strategic Emotions in Negotiations," *Group Decision and Negotiation* 17, no. 1 (2008), pp. 65–77; and M. Liu, "The Intrapersonal and Interpersonal Effects of Anger on Negotiation Strategies: A Cross-Cultural Investigation," *Human Communication Research* 35, no. 1 (2009), pp. 148–169.

104 M. Liu, "The Intrapersonal and Interpersonal Effects of Anger on Negotiation Strategies: A Cross-Cultural Investigation," *Human Communication Research* 35, no. 1 (2009), pp. 148–169; and H. Adam, A. Shirako, and W. W. Maddux, "Cultural Variance in the Interpersonal Effects of Anger in Negotiations," *Psychological Science* 21, no. 6 (2010), pp. 882–889.

105 C. Gaines, "NBA Players Have The Highest-Average Salaries in the World But No League Spends More on Players Than the NFL," *Business Insider*, November. 14, 2016, http://www.businessinsider.com/nfl-mlb-nba-nhl-average-sports-salaries-2016-11; https://www.forbes.com/profile/n-murray-edwards/; J. Feinstein, "In the NHL Lockout, the Owners Have It All Wrong," *Washington Post*, December 25, 2012, http://articles.washingtonpost.com/; R. Cimini, "Geno Smith's Maturity Questioned," ESPN, May 3, 2013, http://espn.go.com/; K. Campbell, "Thanks to Donald Fehr, NHL Negotiating against Itself … and Losing," *The Hockey News*, December 29, 2012, http://sports.yahoo.com/; B. Murphy, "20 Years of Peace and Prosperity Have Followed MLB's Last Strike," *Twin Cities*, July 5, 2014, http://www.twincities.com/sports/ci_26095630/peace-that-lasts-since-1994-season-ending-strike; and E. Seba, "Oil Refinery Strike Widens to Largest U.S. Plant," *Huffington Post*, February 21, 2015, http://www.huffingtonpost.com/2015/02/21/us-refinery-strike-wide_n_6727736.html.

106 S. Shellenbarger, "Clashing over Office Clutter," *Wall Street Journal*, March 19, 2014, http://www.wsj.com/articles/SB10001424052702304747404579447331212245004; S. Shellenbarger, "To Fight or Not to Fight? When to Pick Workplace Battles," *Wall Street Journal*, December 17, 2014, http://www.wsj.com/articles/picking-your-workplace-battles-1418772621; and M. J. Gelfand, J. R. Harrington, and L. M. Leslie, "Conflict Cultures: A New Frontier for Conflict Management Research and Practice," in *Handbook of Conflict Management Research*, ed. N. M. Ashkanasy, O. B. Ayoko, and K. A. Jehn (Cheltenham, UK: Edward Elgar, 2014), pp. 109–135.

107 Based on http://www.mcmillan.ca/Canadian-Unionization-Rates-Continuing-to-Fall; and Fraser Institute, "Comparing Government and Private Sector Compensation in Canada," December 8, 2016, https://www.fraserinstitute.org/studies/comparing-government-and-private-sector-compensation-in-canada.

108 These suggestions are based on J. A. Wall Jr. and M. W. Blum, "Negotiations," *Journal of Management*, June 1991, pp. 278–282; and J. S. Pouliot, "Eight Steps to Success in Negotiating," *Nation's Business*, April 1999, pp. 40–42.

OB on the Edge: Workplace Bullying

1. Based on Y. Brend, "VSB Trustees Discuss Fate of 12 Schools on the Chopping Block," *CBC News*, September 15, 2016, http://www.cbc.ca/news/canada/british-columbia/vancouver-schools-closures-education-cuts-aging-infrastructure-1.3763993; and C. Pablo, "Independent Report Rips Sacked Vision Vancouver Trustees for Culture of Fear in School District," *Georgia Strait*, March 8, 2017, https://www.straight.com/news/878886/independent-report-rips-sacked-vision-vancouver-trustees-culture-fear-school-district.

2. L. M. Anderson and C. M. Pearson, "Tit for Tat? The Spiraling Effect of Incivility in the Workplace," *Academy of Management Review* 24, no. 3 (1999), pp. 452–471. For further discussion of this, see R. A. Baron and J. H. Neuman, "Workplace Violence and Workplace Aggression: Evidence on Their Relative Frequency and Potential Causes," *Aggressive Behavior* 22 (1996), pp. 161–173; C. C. Chen and W. Eastman, "Towards a Civic Culture for Multicultural Organizations," *Journal of Applied Behavioral Science* 33 (1997), pp. 454–470; and J. H. Neuman and R. A. Baron, "Aggression in the Workplace," in *Antisocial Behavior in Organizations*, ed. R. A. Giacalone and J. Greenberg (Thousand Oaks, CA: Sage, 1997), pp. 37–67.

3. L. M. Anderson and C. M. Pearson, "Tit for Tat? The Spiraling Effect of Incivility in the Workplace," *Academy of Management Review* 24, no. 3 (1999), pp. 452–471.

4. "Definition of Workplace Bullying," *Workforce Bullying Institute*, http://www.workplacebullying.org/individuals/problem/definition/.

5. "2014 WBI U.S. Workplace Bullying Survey," Workplace Bullying Institute, February 2014, http://www.workplacebullying.org/wbiresearch/wbi-2014-us-survey/.

6. C. Porath and C. Pearson, "The Price of Incivility: Lack of Respect Hurts Morale and the Bottom Line," *Harvard Business Review*, January–February 2013, p. 117.

7. M. Houshmand, J. O'Reilly, S. Robinson, and A. Wolff, "Escaping Bullying: The Simultaneous Impact of Individual and Unit-Level Bullying on Turnover Intentions," *Human Relations* 65, no. 7 (2012), pp. 901–918.

8. "Definition of Workplace Bullying," *Workforce Bullying Institute*, http://www.workplacebullying.org/individuals/problem/definition/.

9. https://www.worksafebc.com/en/health-safety/hazards-exposures/bullying-harassment.

10. R. A. Baron and J. H. Neuman, "Workplace Violence and Workplace Aggression: Evidence on Their Relative Frequency and Potential Causes," *Aggressive Behavior* 22 (1996), pp. 161–173; C. MacKinnon, *Only Words* (New York: Basic Books, 1994); J. Marks, "The American Uncivil Wars," *U.S. News & World Report*, April 22, 1996, pp. 66–72; and L. P. Spratlen, "Workplace Mistreatment: Its Relationship to Interpersonal Violence," *Journal of Psychosocial Nursing* 32, no. 12 (1994), pp. 5–6.

11. K. MacQueen and C. McKenna, "Workplace Rampage," *Maclean's*, May 8, 2014 , http://www.macleans.ca/news/canada/the-shootings-at-western-forest-in-nanaimo-point-to-a-bigger-problem/.

12. W. M. Glenn, "An Employee's Survival Guide: An ILO Survey of Workplaces in 32 Countries Ranked Argentina the Most Violent, Followed by Romania, France and Then, Surprisingly, Canada," *Occupational Health & Safety*, April–May 2002, p. 28 passim.

13. J. Lindzon, "Workplace Abuse Comes at Steep Cost for Nurses, Taxpayers," *Globe and Mail*, June 28, 2017, https://beta.theglobeandmail.com/report-on-business/careers/management/workplace-abuse-comes-at-steep-cost-for-nurses-taxpayers/article35461112.

14. J. Lindzon, "Workplace Abuse Comes at Steep Cost for Nurses, Taxpayers," *Globe and Mail*, June 28, 2017, https://beta.theglobeandmail.com/report-on-business/careers/management/workplace-abuse-comes-at-steep-cost-for-nurses-taxpayers/article35461112.

15. "Catholic School Board Raises Concerns with Report on Workplace Violence and Teachers," *CBC News*, June 29, 2017, http://www.cbc.ca/news/canada/windsor/catholic-school-board-raises-concerns-with-report-on-workplace-violence-and-teachers-1.4184017.

16. K. MacQueen and C. McKenna, "Workplace Rampage," *Maclean's*, May 8, 2014, http://www.macleans.ca/news/canada/the-shootings-at-western-forest-in-nanaimo-point-to-a-bigger-problem/.

17. E. Ellis, "Today's Jobs Can Be Hard on Your Head," *Vancouver Sun*, June 25, 2014, p. D1.

18. J. O'Reilly, S. L. Robinson, J. L. Berdahl, and S. Banki, "Is Negative Attention Better Than No Attention? The Comparative Effects of Ostracism and Harassment at Work," *Organizational Science*, April 4, 2014. Published online.

19. E. Ellis, "Today's Jobs Can Be Hard on Your Head," *Vancouver Sun*, June 25, 2014, p. D1.

20. A. M. Webber, "Danger: Toxic Company," *Fast Company*, November 1998, pp. 152–157.

21. D. Flavelle, "Managers Cited for Increase in 'Work Rage,'" *Vancouver Sun*, April 11, 2000, pp. D1, D11; and G. Smith, *Work Rage: Identify the Problems, Implement the Solutions* (Toronto: HarperCollins Canada, 2000).

22. "Work Rage," *BCBusiness Magazine*, January 2001, p. 23.

23. D. Flavelle, "Managers Cited for Increase in 'Work Rage,'" *Vancouver Sun*, April 11, 2000, pp. D1, D11.

24. A. Skogstad, T. Torsheim, S. Einarsen, and L. J. Hauge, "Testing the Work Environment Hypothesis of Bullying on a Group Level of Analysis: Psychosocial Factors as Precursors of Observed Workplace Bullying," *Applied Psychology: An International Review* 60, no. 3 (July 2011), pp. 475–495.

25. D. Geddes, and L. T. Stickney, "The Trouble with Sanctions: Organizational Responses to Deviant Anger Displays at Work," *Human Relations* 64, no. 2 (February 2011), pp. 201–230.

26. "7 Signs You Have a Terrible Boss," *Salary.com*, accessed December 21, 2017, https://www.salary.com/7-reasons-terrible-boss/.

27. S. L. Robinson and E. W. Morrison, "The Development of Psychological Contract Breach and Violation: A Longitudinal Study," *Journal of Organizational Behavior* 21, no. 5 (2000), pp. 525–546; and S. D. Salamon and S. L. Robinson, "Trust That Binds: The Impact of Collective Felt Trust on Organizational Performance," *Journal of Applied Psychology* 93, no. 3 (2008), pp. 593–601.

28. D. C. Thomas, S. R. Fitzsimmons, E. C. Ravlin, K. Au, B. Z. Ekelund, and C. Barzantny, "Psychological Contracts across Cultures," *Organization Studies* 31, no. 11 (2010), pp. 1437–1458.

29. S. Montes and D. Zweig, "Do Promises Matter? An Exploration of the Role of Promises in Psychological Contract Breach," *Journal of Applied Psychology* 94, no. 5 (2009), pp. 1243–1260.

30. A. M. Webber, "Danger: Toxic Company," *Fast Company*, November 1998, pp. 152–157.

31. A. M. Webber, "Danger: Toxic Company," *Fast Company*, November 1998, pp. 152–157.

32. Based on A. McKee, "Neutralize Your Toxic Boss," *HBR Blog Network*, September 24, 2008, http://blogs.hbr.org/2008/09/neutralize-your-toxic-boss/; and "Toxic Bosses: How to Live with the S.O.B.," *BusinessWeek*, August 13, 2008, http://www.businessweek.com/stories/2008-08-13/toxic-bosses-how-to-live-with-the-s-dot-o-dot-b-dot.

33. P. Frost, *Toxic Emotions at Work* (Cambridge, MA: Harvard Business School Press, 2003).

34. "Men More Likely to Be Rude in Workplace, Survey Shows," *Vancouver Sun*, August 16, 1999, p. B10.

35 D. E. Gibson and S. G. Barsade, "The Experience of Anger at Work: Lessons from the Chronically Angry" (paper presented at the annual meetings of the Academy of Management, Chicago, August 11, 1999).

36 D. E. Gibson and S. G. Barsade, "The Experience of Anger at Work: Lessons from the Chronically Angry" (paper presented at the annual meetings of the Academy of Management, Chicago, August 11, 1999).

37 C. Porath and C. Pearson, "The Price of Incivility," *Harvard Business Review*, January–February 2017, https://hbr.org/2013/01/the-price-of-incivility.

38 R. Corelli, "Dishing Out Rudeness: Complaints Abound as Customers Are Ignored, Berated," *Maclean's*, January 11, 1999, p. 44.

39 R. Bacal, "Toxic Organizations—Welcome to the Fire of an Unhealthy Workplace," *Work911.com*, 2000, http://work911.com/articles/toxicorgs.htm.

40 D. Aarts, "What Bosses Can Learn From Their Coddled Millennial Employees," *profitguide.com*, December 2, 2016, http://www.profitguide.com/manage-grow/human-resources/deborah-aarts-workplaces-should-adapt-to-coddled-millennials-107722.

41 L. Panjvani, "An Overview of Anti-Bullying Legislation and Alternatives in Canada," *LawNow*, July 1, 2013, http://www.lawnow.org/an-overview-of-anti-bullying-legislation-and-alternatives-in-canada.

42 E. Ellis, "Today's Jobs Can Be Hard on Your Head," *Vancouver Sun*, June 25, 2014, p. D1.

43 E. Ellis, "Today's Jobs Can Be Hard on Your Head," *Vancouver Sun*, June 25, 2014, p. D1.

Chapter 10

1 Vignette based on M. Solomon, "To Transform Your Company Culture, Change Your POV: Hyatt CEO's Perspective," *Forbes*, May 11, 2015, http://www.forbes.com/sites/micahsolomon/2015/05/11/transform-your-corporate-culture-by-changing-your-pov-the-hyatt-ceo-interview/; B. Witt, "Hyatt Hotels: Making CSR Work in a Decentralized Global Company," *Hotel Business Review*, May, 2015, http://hotelexecutive.com/business_review/3098/hyatt-hotels-making-csr-work-in-a-decentralized-global-company; S. Shankman, "How Hyatt's CEO Empowers Employees to Drive the Guest Experience," *Skift*, December 14, 2014, http://skift.com/2014/12/15/interview-how-hyatts-ceo-empowers-employees-to-drive-the-guest-experience/; "World of Hyatt," http://www.hyatttravelagents.com/cms.cfm?nPageNo=29694; and "Hyatt—About Our Brands," http://www.hyatttravelagents.com/cms.cfm?nPageNo=29694.

2 "Organization Man: Henry Mintzberg Has Some Common Sense Observations About the Ways We Run Companies," *Financial Post*, November 22/24, 1997, pp. 14–16.

3 See, for example, B. Schneider, M. G. Ehrhart, and W. H. Macey, "Organizational Climate and Culture," *Annual Review of Psychology*, 2013, pp. 361–388.

4 I. Borg, P. J. F. Groenen, K. A. Jehn, W. Bilsky, and S. H. Schwartz, "Embedding the Organizational Culture Profile into Schwartz's Theory of Universals in Values," *Journal of Personnel Psychology* 10 (2011), pp. 1–12.

5 See, for example, C. Ostroff, A. J. Kinicki, and M. M. Tamkins, "Organizational Culture and Climate," in *Handbook of Psychology: Industrial and Organizational Psychology*, ed. W.C. Borman, D. R. Ilgen, and R. J. Klimoski (New Jersey: Wiley, 2003), pp. 565–593.

6 D. A. Hoffman and L. M. Jones, "Leadership, Collective Personality, and Performance," *Journal of Applied Psychology* 90, no. 3 (2005), pp. 509–522.

7 P. Lok, R. Westwood, and J. Crawford, "Perceptions of Organisational Subculture and Their Significance for Organisational Commitment," *Applied Psychology: An International Review* 54, no. 4 (2005), pp. 490–514; and B. E. Ashforth, K. M. Rogers, and K. G. Corley, "Identity in Organizations: Exploring Cross-Level Dynamics," *Organization Science* 22 (2011), pp. 1144–1156.

8 T. Hsieh, "Zappos's CEO on Going to Extremes for Customers," *Harvard Business Review*, July/August 2010, pp. 41–45.

9 For discussions of how culture can be evaluated as a shared perception, see D. Chan, "Mutlilevel and Aggregation Issues in Climate and Culture Research," in *The Oxford Handbook of Organizational Climate and Culture*, ed. B. Schneider and K. M. Barbera (New York: Oxford University Press, 2014), pp. 484–495; and J. B. Sorensen, "The Strength of Corporate Culture and the Reliability of Firm Performance," *Administrative Science Quarterly*, March 2002, pp. 70–91.

10 B. Schneider, A. N. Salvaggio, and M. Subirats, "Climate Strength: A New Direction for Climate Research," *Journal of Applied Psychology* 87 (2002), pp. 220–229; L. M. Kotrba, M. A. Gillespie, A. M. Schmidt, R. E. Smerek, S. A. Ritchie, and D. R. Denison, "Do Consistent Corporate Cultures Have Better Business Performance: Exploring the Interaction Effects," *Human Relations* 65 (2012), pp. 241–262; and M. W. Dickson, C. J. Resick, and P. J. Hanges, "When Organizational Climate Is Unambiguous, It Is also Strong," *Journal of Applied Psychology* 91 (2006), pp. 351–364.

11 M. Schulte, C. Ostroff, S. Shmulyian, and A. Kinicki, "Organizational Climate Configurations: Relationships to Collective Attitudes, Customer Satisfaction, and Financial Performance," *Journal of Applied Psychology* 94, no. 3 (2009), pp. 618–634.

12 See S. Maitlis and M. Christianson, "Sensemaking in Organizations: Taking Stock and Moving Forward," *The Academy of Management Annals* 8 (2014), pp. 57–125; K. Weber and M. T. Dacin, "The Cultural Construction of Organizational Life," *Organization Science* 22 (2011), pp. 287–298.

13 Y. Ling, Z. Simsek, M. H. Lubatkin, and J. F. Veiga, "Transformational Leadership's Role in Promoting Corporate Entrepreneurship: Examining the CEO-TMT Interface," *Academy of Management Journal* 51, no. 3 (2008), pp. 557–576; and A. Malhotra, A. Majchrzak, and B. Rosen, "Leading Virtual Teams," *Academy of Management Perspectives* 21, no. 1 (2007), pp. 60–70.

14 L. R. James, C. C. Choi, C. E. Ko, P. K. McNeil, M. K. Minton, M. A. Wright, and K. Kim, "Organizational and Psychological Climate: A Review of Theory and Research," *European Journal of Work and Organizational Psychology* 17, no. 1 (2008), pp. 5–32; and B. Schneider and K. M. Barbera, "Introduction and Overview," in *The Oxford Handbook of Organizational Climate and Culture*, ed. B. Schneider and K. M Barbera (New York: Oxford University Press, 2014), pp. 3–22.

15 J. Z. Carr, A. M. Schmidt, J. K. Ford, and R. P. DeShon, "Climate Perceptions Matter: A Meta-analytic Path Analysis Relating Molar Climate, Cognitive and Affective States, and Individual Level Work Outcomes," *Journal of Applied Psychology* 88, no. 4 (2003), pp. 605–619.

16 M. Schulte, C. Ostroff, S. Shmulyian, and A. Kinicki, "Organizational Climate Configurations: Relationships to Collective Attitudes, Customer Satisfaction, and Financial Performance," *Journal of Applied Psychology* 94, no. 3 (2009), pp. 618–634.

17 D. S. Pugh, J. Dietz, A. P. Brief, and J. W. Wiley, "Looking Inside and Out: The Impact of Employee and Community Demographic Composition on Organizational Diversity Climate," *Journal of Applied Psychology* 93, no. 6 (2008), pp. 1422–1428; K. H. Ehrhart, L. A. Witt, B. Schneider, and S. J. Perry, "Service Employees Give as They Get: Internal Service as a Moderator of the Service Climate-Service Outcomes Link," *Journal of Applied Psychology* 96, no. 2 (2011), pp. 423–431; and A. Simha and J. B. Cullen, "Ethical Climates and Their Effects on Organizational Outcomes:

Implications from the Past and Prophecies for the Future," *Academy of Management Perspectives*, November 2011, pp. 20–34.

18 J. C. Wallace, P. D. Johnson, K. Mathe, and J. Paul, "Structural and Psychological Empowerment Climates, Performance, and the Moderating Role of Shared Felt Accountability: A Managerial Perspective," *Journal of Applied Psychology* 96, no. 3 (2011), pp. 840–850.

19 J. M. Beus, S. C. Payne, M. E. Bergman, and W. Arthur, "Safety Climate and Injuries: An Examination of Theoretical and Empirical Relationships," *Journal of Applied Psychology* 95, no. 4 (2010), pp. 713–727.

20 A. Simha and J. B. Cullen, "Ethical Climates and Their Effects on Organizational Outcomes: Implications from the Past and Prophecies for the Future," *Academy of Management*, November 2012, pp. 20–34.

21 Based on "West Jet, a True Example of Customer-Centric Culture," *Knightsbridge Thought Leadership Newsletter*, accessed August 15, 2014, http://www.knightsbridge.com/sitecore/content/Knightsbridge/home/ThoughtLeadership/onPeopleNewsletter/Articles/FEAT%201_Sept2011_WestJet.

22 A. Simha and J. B. Cullen, "Ethical Climates and Their Effects on Organizational Outcomes: Implications from the Past and Prophecies for the Future," *Academy of Management*, November 2012, pp. 20–34.

23 A. Simha and J. B. Cullen, "Ethical Climates and Their Effects on Organizational Outcomes: Implications from the Past and Prophecies for the Future," *Academy of Management*, November 2012, pp. 20–34.

24 A. Arnaud, "Conceptualizing and Measuring Ethical Work Climate: Development and Validation of the Ethical Climate Index," *Business & Society*, June 2010, pp. 345–458.

25 A. Arnaud and M. Schminke, "The Ethical Climate and Context of Organizations: A Comprehensive Model," *Organization Science*, November–December 2012, pp. 1767–1780.

26 J. Howard-Greenville, S. Bertels, and B. Lahneman, "Sustainability: How It Shapes Organizational Culture and Climate," in *The Oxford Handbook of Organizational Climate and Culture*, ed. B. Schneider and K. M. Barbera (New York: Oxford University Press, 2014), pp. 257–275.

27 P. Lacy, T. Cooper, R. Hayward, and L. Neuberger, "A New Era of Sustainability: UN Global Compact-Accenture CEO Study 2010," June 2010, http://www.uncsd2012.org/content/documents/Accenture_A_New_era_of_Sustainability_CEO_study.pdf.

28 H. R. Dixon-Fowler, D. J. Slater, J. L. Johnson, A. E. Ellstrand, and A. M. Romi, "Beyond 'Does It Pay to Be Green?' A Meta-analysis of Moderators of the CEP-CFP Relationship," *Journal of Business Ethics* 112 (2013), pp. 353–366.

29 P. Bansal, "From Issues to Actions: The Importance of Individual Concerns and Organizational Values in Responding to Natural Environmental Issues," *Organization Science* 14 (2003), pp. 510–527; P. Bansal, "Evolving Sustainably: A Longitudinal Study of Corporate Sustainable Development," *Strategic Management Journal* 26 (2005), pp. 197–218; and J. Howard-Grenville and A. J. Hoffman, "The Importance of Cultural Framing to the Success of Social Initiatives in Business," *Academy of Management Executive* 17 (2003), pp. 70–84.

30 A. R. Carrico and M. Riemer, "Motivating Energy Conservation in the Workplace: An Evaluation of the Use of Group-Level Feedback and Peer Education," *Journal of Environmental Psychology* 31 (2011), pp. 1–13.

31 J. P. Kotter, "Change Management: Accelerate!" *Harvard Business Review*, November 2012, pp. 44–58.

32 R. Walker, "Behind the Music," *Fortune*, October 29, 2012, pp. 57–58.

33 J. P. Titlow, "How Spotify's Music-Obsessed Culture Keeps Employees Hooked," *Fast Company*, August 20, 2014, http://www.fastcompany.com/3034617/how-spotifys-music-obsessed-culture-makes-the-company-rock.

34 "Why Intuit Is More Innovative Than Your Company," *Forbes*, https://www.forbes.com/sites/bruceupbin/2012/09/04/intuit-the-30-year-old-startup/3/#4ded43571a2c.

35 J. Bandler and D. Burke, "How HP Lost Its Way," *Fortune*, May 21, 2012, pp. 147–164.

36 G. F. Lanzara and G. Patriotta, "The Institutionalization of Knowledge in an Automotive Factory: Templates, Inscriptions, and the Problems of Durability," *Organization Studies* 28, no. 5 (2007), pp. 635–660; and T. B. Lawrence, M. K. Mauws, B. Dyck, and R. F. Kleysen, "The Politics of Organizational Learning: Integrating Power into the 4I Framework," *Academy of Management Review*, January 2005, pp. 180–191.

37 J. B. Sorensen, "The Strength of Corporate Culture and the Reliability of Firm Performance," *Administrative Science Quarterly*, March 2002, pp. 70–91.

38 See D. L. Stone, E. F. Stone-Romero, and K. M. Lukaszewski, "The Impact of Cultural Values on the Acceptance and Effectiveness of Human Resource Management Policies and Practices," *Human Resource Management Review* 17, no. 2 (2007), pp. 152–165; D. R. Avery, "Support for Diversity in Organizations: A Theoretical Exploration of Its Origins and Offshoots," *Organizational Psychology Review* 1 (2011), pp. 239–256; A. Groggins and A. M. Ryan, "Embracing Uniqueness: The Underpinnings of a Positive Climate for Diversity," *Journal of Occupational and Organizational Psychology* 86 (2013), pp. 264–282.

39 D. Liu, T. R. Mitchell, T. W. Lee, B. C. Holtom, and T. R. Hinkin, "When Employees Are out of Step with Coworkers: How Job Satisfaction Trajectory and Dispersion Influence Individual-and Unit-Level Voluntary Turnover," *Academy of Management Journal* 55 (2012), pp. 1360–1380.

40 R. A. Weber and C. F. Camerer, "Cultural Conflict and Merger Failure: An Experimental Approach," *Management Science*, April 2003, pp. 400–412; I. H. Gleibs, A. Mummendey, and P. Noack, "Predictors of Change in Postmerger Identification During a Merger Process: A Longitudinal Study," *Journal of Personality and Social Psychology* 95, no. 5 (2008), pp. 1095–1112; and F. Bauer and K. Matzler, "Antecedents of M&A Success: The Role of Strategic Complementarity, Cultural Fit, and Degree and Speed of Integration," *Strategic Management Journal* 35 (2014), pp. 269–291.

41 K. Voigt, "Mergers Fail More Often Than Marriages," CNN, May 22, 2009, http://edition.cnn.com/2009/BUSINESS/05/21/merger.marriage/.

42 Vignette based on S. Shankman, "How Hyatt's CEO Empowers Employees to Drive the Guest Experience," *Skift*, December 14, 2014, http://skift.com/2014/12/15/interview-how-hyatts-ceo-empowers-employees-to-drive-the-guest-experience/.

43 Y. L. Zhao, O. H. Erekson, T. Wang, and M. Song, "Pioneering Advantages and Entrepreneurs' First-Mover Decisions: An Empirical Investigation for the United States and China," *Journal of Product Innovation Management*, December 2012, pp. 190–210.

44 E. H. Schein, *Organizational Culture and Leadership*, Vol. 2. (New York: John Wiley & Sons, 2010).

45 "PCL's Biggest Investment: Its People," *National Post*, September 2, 2008, p. FP10.

46 See, for example, D. E. Bowen and C. Ostroff, "The 'Strength' of the HRM System, Organizational Climate Formation, and Firm Performance," *Academy of Management Review* 29 (2004), pp. 203–221.

47 W. Li, Y. Wang, P. Taylor, K. Shi, and D. He, "The Influence of Organizational Culture on Work-Related Personality Requirement Ratings: A Multilevel Analysis," *International Journal of Selection and*

Assessment 16, no. 4 (2008), pp. 366–384; I. Oh, K. S. Kim, and C. H. Van Iddekinge, "Taking It to Another Level: Do Personality-Based Human Capital Resources Matter to Firm Performance?" *Journal of Applied Psychology* 100 (2015), pp. 935–947; and A. Bardi, K. E. Buchanan, R. Goodwin, L. Slabu, and M. Robinson, "Value Stability and Change during Self-Chosen Life Transitions: Self-Selection versus Socialization Effects," *Journal of Personality and Social Psychology* 106 (2014), pp. 131–147.

48 "Building a Better Workforce," *PROFIT*, February 16, 2011, http://www.profitguide.com/manage-grow/human-resources/building-a-better-workforce-30073.

49 "Building a Better Workforce," *PROFIT*, February 16, 2011, http://www.profitguide.com/manage-grow/human-resources/building-a-better-workforce-30073.

50 D. C. Hambrick and P. A. Mason, "Upper Echelons: The Organization as a Reflection of Its Top Managers," *Academy of Management Review*, April 1984, pp. 193–206; M. A. Carpenter, M. A. Geletkanycz, and W. G. Sanders, "Upper Echelons Research Revisited: Antecedents, Elements, and Consequences of Top Management Team Composition," *Journal of Management* 30, no. 6 (2004), pp. 749–778; and H. Wang, A. S. Tsui, and K. R. Xin, "CEO Leadership Behaviors, Organizational Performance, and Employees' Attitudes," *The Leadership Quarterly* 22, no. 1 (2011), pp. 92–105.

51 D. M. Cable and C. K. Parsons, "Socialization Tactics and Person-Organization Fit," *Personnel Psychology*, Spring 2001, pp. 1–23; and T. N. Bauer, T. Bodner, B. Erdogan, D. M. Truxillo, and J. S. Tucker, "Newcomer Adjustment during Organizational Socialization: A Meta-analytic Review of Antecedents, Outcomes, and Methods," *Journal of Applied Psychology* 92, no. 3 (2007), pp. 707–721.

52 A. M. Saks and J. A. Gruman, "Organizational Socialization and Positive Organizational Behaviour: Implications for Theory, Research, and Practice," *Canadian Journal of Administrative Sciences* 28, no. 1 (2011), pp. 4–16.

53 J. Impoco, "Basic Training, Sanyo Style," *U.S. News & World Report*, July 13, 1992, pp. 46–48.

54 B. Filipczak, "Trained by Starbucks," *Training*, June 1995, pp. 73–79; and S. Gruner, "Lasting Impressions," *Inc.*, July 1998, p. 126.

55 D. M. Cable, F. Gino, and B. R. Staats, "Breaking Them In or Eliciting Their Best? Reframing Socialization around Newcomers' Authentic Self-Expression," *Administrative Science Quarterly* 58 (2013), pp. 1–36; and M. Tuttle, "A Review and Critique of Van Maanen and Schein's 'Toward a Theory of Organizational Socialization' and Implications for Human Resource Development," *Human Resource Development Review* 1 (2002), pp. 66–90.

56 C. J. Collins, "The Interactive Effects of Recruitment Practices and Product Awareness on Job Seekers' Employer Knowledge and Application Behaviors," *Journal of Applied Psychology* 92, no. 1 (2007), pp. 180–190.

57 J. D. Kammeyer-Mueller and C. R. Wanberg, "Unwrapping the Organizational Entry Process: Disentangling Multiple Antecedents and Their Pathways to Adjustment," *Journal of Applied Psychology* 88 (2003), pp. 779–794; E. W. Morrison, "Longitudinal Study of the Effects of Information Seeking on Newcomer Socialization," *Journal of Applied Psychology* 78 (2003), pp. 173–183; and M. Wangm, Y. Zhan, E. McCune, and D. Truxillo, "Understanding Newcomers' Adaptability and Work-Related Outcomes: Testing the Mediating Roles of Perceived P-E Fit Variables," *Personnel Psychology* 64, no. 1 (2011), pp. 163–189.

58 J. Galang, "As Wattpad Celebrates 10th Birthday CEO Allen Lau Shares Netflix-Like Ambitions," accesssed November 3, 2017, http://betakit.com/as-wattpad-celebrates-10th-birthday-ceo-allen-lau-shares-netflix-like-ambitions/.

59 Based on S. Dutton, "TELUS: A Pervasive Learning Culture," *Business to Community*, August 9, 2014, http://www.business2community.com/human-resources/telus-pervasive-learning-culture-keeps-employees-tuned-engaged-0967431#!bAwMv1;

"Why TELUS: Career Development," *TELUS*, accessed August 20, 2014, http://about.telus.com/community/english/careers/why_telus/career_development; and "Why TELUS: Culture," *TELUS*, accessed August 20, 2014, http://about.telus.com/community/english/careers/why_telus/culture.

60 E. W. Morrison, "Newcomers' Relationships: The Role of Social Network Ties During Socialization," *Academy of Management Journal* 45 (2002), pp. 1149–1160.

61 A. M. Saks and J. A. Gruman, "Getting Newcomers Engaged: The Role of Socialization Tactics," *Journal of Managerial Psychology* 26 (2011), pp. 383–402.

62 T. N. Bauer, T. Bodner, B. Erdogan, D. M. Truxillo, and J. S. Tucker, "Newcomer Adjustment during Organizational Socialization: A Meta-analytic Review of Antecedents, Outcomes, and Methods," *Journal of Applied Psychology* 92, no. 3 (2007), pp. 707–721.

63 W. R. Boswell, A. J. Shipp, S. C., Payne, and S. S. Culbertson, "Changes in Newcomer Job Satisfaction Over Time: Examining the Pattern of Honeymoons and Hangovers," *Journal of Applied Psychology* 94, no. 4 (2009), pp. 844–858; and W. R. Boswell, J. W. Boudreau, and J. Tichy, "The Relationship between Employee Job Change and Job Satisfaction: The Honeymoon-Hangover Effect," *Journal of Applied Psychology* 90 (2005), pp. 882–892.

64 J. D. Kammeyer-Mueller, C. R. Wanberg, A. L. Rubenstein, and Z. Song, "Support, Undermining, and Newcomer Socialization: Fitting in during the First 90 Days," *Academy of Management Journal* 56 (2013), pp. 1104–1124; and M. Jokisaari and J. Nurmi, "Change in Newcomers' Supervisor Support and Socialization Outcomes after Organizational Entry," *Academy of Management Journal* 52 (2009), pp. 527–544.

65 C. Vandenberghe, A. Panaccio, K. Bentein, K. Mignonac, and P. Roussel, "Assessing Longitudinal Change of and Dynamic Relationships among Role Stressors, Job Attitudes, Turnover Intention, and Well-Being in Neophyte Newcomers," *Journal of Organizational Behavior* 32, no. 4 (2011), pp. 652–671.

66 Vignette based on M. Solomon, "To Transform Your Company Culture, Change Your POV: Hyatt CEO's Perspective," *Forbes*, May 11, 2015, http://www.forbes.com/sites/micahsolomon/2015/05/11/transform-your-corporate-culture-by-changing-your-pov-the-hyatt-ceo-interview/; and S. Shankman, "How Hyatt's CEO Empowers Employees to Drive the Guest Experience," *Skift*, December 14, 2014, http://skift.com/2014/12/15/interview-how-hyatts-ceo-empowers-employees-to-drive-the-guest-experience/.

67 R. Spence, "Telling Stories Makes for Happy Endings," *National Post (Financial Post)*, April 20, 2009, p. FP4.

68 S. L. Dailey and L. Browning, "Retelling Stories in Organizations; Understanding the Functions of Narrative Repetition," *Academy of Management Review* 39 (2014), pp. 22–43.

69 A. J. Shipp and K. J. Jansen, "Reinterpreting Time in Fit Theory: Crafting and Recrafting Narratives of Fit in Medias Res," *Academy of Management Review* 36, no. 1 (2011), pp. 76–101.

70 See G. Islam and M. J. Zyphur, "Rituals in Organizations: A Review and Expansion of Current Theory," *Group and Organization Management* 34, no. 1 (2009), pp. 114–139.

71 V. Matthews, "Starting Every Day with a Shout and a Song," *Financial Times*, May 2, 2001, p. 11; and M. Gimein, "Sam Walton Made Us a Promise," *Fortune*, March 18, 2002, pp. 121–130.

72 M. G. Pratt and A. Rafaeli, "Artifacts and Organizations: Understanding Our Objective Reality," in *Artifacts and Organizations: Beyond Mere Symbolism*, ed. A. Rafaeli and M. G. Pratt (Mahwah, NJ: Lawrence Erlbaum, 2006), pp. 279–288.

73 Thanks to an anonymous reviewer for adding these.

74 Thanks to a reviewer for this story.

75 Based on S. Shankman, "How Hyatt's CEO Empowers Employees to Drive the Guest Experience," *Skift*, December 14, 2014, http://

skift.com/2014/12/15/interview-how-hyatts-ceo-empowers-employees-to-drive-the-guest-experience/.

76 J. P. Kotter, "Leading Changes: Why Transformation Efforts Fail," *Harvard Business Review*, March–April 1995, pp. 59–67; and J. P. Kotter, *Leading Change* (Boston: Harvard Business School Press, 1996).

77 A. Ardichvilli, J. A. Mitchell, and D. Jondle, "Characteristics of Ethical Business Cultures," *Journal of Business Ethics* 85, no. 4 (2009), pp. 445–451; and D. M. Mayer, "A Review of the Literature on Ethical Climate and Culture," in *The Oxford Handbook of Organizational Climate and Culture*, ed. B. Schneider and K. M. Barbera (New York: Oxford University Press, 2014), pp. 415–440.

78 Based on J. P. Mulki, J. F. Jaramillo, and W. B. Locander, "Critical Role of Leadership on Ethical Climate and Salesperson Behaviors," *Journal of Business Ethics* 86, no. 2 (2009), pp. 125–141; M. Schminke, M. L. Ambrose, and D. O. Neubaum, "The Effect of Leader Moral Development on Ethical Climate and Employee Attitudes," *Organizational Behavior and Human Decision Processes* 97, no. 2 (2005), pp. 135–151; and M. E. Brown, L. K. Treviño, and D. A. Harrison, "Ethical Leadership: A Social Learning Perspective for Construct Development and Testing," *Organizational Behavior and Human Decision Processes* 97, no. 2 (2005), pp. 117–134.

79 D. M. Mayer, M. Kuenzi, R. Greenbaum, M. Bardes, and S. Salvador, "How Low Does Ethical Leadership Flow? Test of a Trickle-Down Model," *Organizational Behavior and Human Decision Processes* 108, no. 1 (2009), pp. 1–13; and L. J. Christensen, A. Mackey, and D. Whetten, "Taking Responsibility for Corporate Social Responsibility: The Role of Leaders in Creating, Implementing, Sustaining, or Avoiding Socially Responsible Firm Behaviors," *Academy of Management Perspectives* 28 (2014), pp. 164–178.

80 B. Sweeney, D. Arnold, and B. Pierce, "The Impact of Perceived Ethical Culture of the Firm and Demographic Variables on Auditors' Ethical Evaluation and Intention to Act Decisions," *Journal of Business Ethics* 93, no. 4 (2010), pp. 531–551.

81 M. L. Gruys, S. M. Stewart, J. Goodstein, M. N. Bing, and A. C. Wicks, "Values Enactment in Organizations: A Multi-Level Examination," *Journal of Management* 34, no. 4 (2008), pp. 806–843.

82 D. L. Nelson and C. L. Cooper, eds., *Positive Organizational Behavior* (London, UK: Sage, 2007); K. S. Cameron, J. E. Dutton, and R. E. Quinn, eds., *Positive Organizational Scholarship: Foundations of a New Discipline* (San Francisco: Berrett-Koehler, 2003); and F. Luthans and C. M. Youssef, "Emerging Positive Organizational Behavior," *Journal of Management*, June 2007, pp. 321–349.

83 J. Robison, "Great Leadership under Fire," *Gallup Leadership Journal*, March 8, 2007, pp. 1–3.

84 R. Wagner and J. K. Harter, *12: The Elements of Great Managing* (New York: Gallup Press, 2006).

85 S. Fineman, "On Being Positive: Concerns and Counterpoints," *Academy of Management Review* 31, no. 2 (2006), pp. 270–291.

86 P. Dvorak, "A Firm's Culture Can Get Lost in Translation," *Wall Street Journal*, April 3, 2006, pp. B1, B3; K. Kranhold, "The Immelt Era, Five Years Old, Transforms GE," *Wall Street Journal*, September 11, 2006, pp. B1, B3; and S. McCartney, "Teaching Americans How to Behave Abroad," *Wall Street Journal*, April 11, 2006, pp. D1, D4.

87 D. J. McCarthy and S. M. Puffer, "Interpreting the Ethicality of Corporate Governance Decision in Russia: Utilizing Integrative Social Contracts Theory to Evaluate the Relevance of Agency Theory Norms," *Academy of Management Review* 33, no. 1 (2008), pp. 11–31.

88 P. Monin, N. Noorderhavin, E. Vaara, and D. Kroon, "Giving Sense to and Making Sense of Justice in Postmerger Integration," *Academy of Management Journal*, February 2013, pp. 256–284; A. Simha and J. B. Cullen, "Ethical Climates and Their Effects on Organizational Outcomes: Implications from the Past and Prophecies for the Future," *Academy of Management Perspectives*, November 2011, pp. 20–34; and E. Vaara and J. Tienari, "On the Narrative Construction of Multinational Corporations: An Antenarrative Analysis of Legitimation and Resistance in a Cross-Border Merger," *Organization Science*, March–April 2011, pp. 370–390.

89 Based on B. Azar, "Positive Psychology Advances, with Growing Pains," *Monitor on Psychology*, April 2011, pp. 32–36; A. Grant, "How Customers Can Rally Your Troops," *Harvard Business Review*, June 2011, http://hbr.org/2011/06/how-customers-can-rally-your-troops/ar/1; and J. McCarthy, "5 Big Problems with Positive Thinking (And Why You Should Do It Anyway)," *Positive Psychology*, October 5, 2010, http://psychologyofwellbeing.com/201010/5-big-problems-with-positive-thinking-and-why-you-should-do-it-anyway.html.

90 F. Gino, "Banking Culture Encourages Dishonesty," *Scientific American*, December 30, 2014, http://www.scientificamerican.com/article/banking-culture-encourages-dishonesty/; A. Cohn, E. Fehr, and M. A. Maréchal, "Business Culture and Dishonesty in the Banking Industry," *Nature*, 2014, doi:10.1038/nature13977; L. Geggel, "FIFA Scandal: The Complicated Science of Corruption," *Scientific American*, May 31, 2015, http://www.scientificamerican.com/article/fifa-scandal-the-complicated-science-of-corruption/; and K. Radnedge, "Culture Change Required If FIFA Is to Eliminate Wrongdoing," *World Soccer*, May 29, 2015, http://www.worldsoccer.com/columnists/keir-radnedge/culture-change-required-if-fifa-is-to-eliminate-wrongdoing-362278.

91 B. Lanks, "Don't Get Too Cozy," *Bloomberg Businessweek*, October 30, 2014, http://www.businessweekme.com/Bloomberg/newsmid/190/newsid/271; M. Konnikova, "The Open-Office Trap," *New Yorker*, January 7, 2014, http://www.newyorker.com/business/currency/the-open-office-trap; and N. Ashkanasy, O. B. Ayoko, and K. A. Jehn, "Understanding the Physical Environment of Work and Employee Behavior: An Affective Events Perspective," *Journal of Organizational Behavior* 35 (2014), pp. 1169–1184.

92 J. Murphy, "At Patagonia, Trying New Outdoor Adventures Is a Job Requirement," *Wall Street Journal*, March 10, 2015, http://www.wsj.com/articles/at-patagonia-trying-new-outdoor-adventures-is-a-job-requirement-1425918931; B. Schulte, "A Company That Profits as It Pampers Workers," *Washington Post*, October 25, 2014, http://www.washingtonpost.com/business/a-company-that-profits-as-it-pampers-workers/2014/10/22/d3321b34-4818-11e4-b72e-d60a9229cc10_story.html; and D. Baer, "Patagonia CEO: 'There's No Way I Should Make One Decision Based on Quarterly Results,'" *Business Insider*, November 19, 2014, http://www.businessinsider.com/patagonia-ceo-interview-2014-11.

93 Ideas in this feature were influenced by A. L. Wilkins, "The Culture Audit: A Tool for Understanding Organizations," *Organizational Dynamics*, Autumn 1983, pp. 24–38; H. M. Trice and J. M. Beyer, *The Cultures of Work Organizations* (Englewood Cliffs, NJ: Prentice Hall, 1993), pp. 358–362; H. Lancaster, "To Avoid a Job Failure, Learn the Culture of a Company First," *Wall Street Journal*, July 14, 1998, p. B1; and M. Belliveau, "4 Ways to Read a Company," *Fast Company*, October 1998, p. 158.

Chapter 11

1 Vignette based on http://kellyalovell.com/about-kellylovell/; J. Schroeder, "How Volunteerism Can Help Kickstart Your Career," *Forbes*, April 14, 2016, https://www.forbes.com/sites/julesschroeder/2016/04/14/how-volunteerism-can-help-kickstart-your-career/#481cbd131883; and M. Anderson, "Young and Restless," *IFP*, August 1, 2013, http://www.lfpress.com/2013/08/01/young-and-restless.

2 See T. A. Judge, J. E. Bono, R. Ilies, and M. W. Gerhardt, "Personality and Leadership: A Qualitative and Quantitative Review," *Journal of Applied Psychology*, August 2002, pp. 765–780.

3 Based on D. Fost, "Survey Finds Many Workers Mistrust Bosses," *San Francisco Chronicle*, January 3, 2007, http://www.sfgate.com; and T. Weiss, "The Narcissistic CEO," *Forbes*, August 29, 2006, http://www.forbes.com.

4 C. C. Eckel, E. Fatas, and R. Wilson, "Cooperation and Status in Organizations," *Journal of Public Economic Theory* 12, no. 4 (2010), pp. 737–762.

5 D. R. Ames and F. J. Flynn, "What Breaks a Leader: The Curvilinear Relation between Assertiveness and Leadership," *Journal of Personality and Social Psychology* 92, no. 2 (2007), pp. 307–324.

6 A. E. Colbert, M. R. Barrick, and B. H. Bradley, "Personality and Leadership Composition in Top Management Teams: Implications for Organizational Effectiveness," *Personnel Psychology* 67 (2014), pp. 351–387.

7 K.-Y. Ng, S. Ang, and K. Chan, "Personality and Leader Effectiveness: A Moderated Mediation Model of Leadership Self-Efficacy, Job Demands, and Job Autonomy," *Journal of Applied Psychology* 93, no. 4 (2008), pp. 733–743.

8 R. B. Kaiser, J. M. LeBreton, and J. Hogan, "The Dark Side of Personality and Extreme Leader Behavior," *Applied Psychology: An International Review* 64, no. 1 (2015), pp. 55–92.

9 B. H. Gaddis and J. L. Foster, "Meta-analysis of Dark Side Personality Characteristics and Critical Work Behaviors among Leaders across the Globe: Findings and Implications for Leadership Development and Executive Coaching," *Applied Psychology: An International Review* 64, no. 1 (2015), pp. 25–54.

10 R. H. Humphrey, J. M. Pollack, and T. H. Hawver, "Leading with Emotional Labor," *Journal of Managerial Psychology* 23 (2008), pp. 151–168.

11 F. Walter, M. S. Cole, and R. H. Humphrey, "Emotional Intelligence: Sine Qua Non of Leadership or Folderol?" *Academy of Management Perspectives*, February 2011, pp. 45–59.

12 S. Côté, P. N. Lopez, P. Salovey, and C. T. H. Miners, "Emotional Intelligence and Leadership Emergence in Small Groups," *Leadership Quarterly* 21 (2010), pp. 496–508.

13 N. Ensari, R. E. Riggio, J. Christian, and G. Carslaw, "Who Emerges as a Leader? Meta-analyses of Individual Differences as Predictors of Leadership Emergence," *Personality and Individual Differences*, September 2011, pp. 532–536.

14 This research is updated in T. A. Judge, R. F. Piccolo, and R. Ilies, "The Forgotten Ones? The Validity of Consideration and Initiating Structure in Leadership Research," *Journal of Applied Psychology*, February 2004, pp. 36–51.

15 D. Akst, "The Rewards of Recognizing a Job Well Done," *Wall Street Journal*, January 31, 2007, p. D9.

16 R. Kahn and D. Katz, "Leadership Practices in Relation to Productivity and Morale," in *Group Dynamics: Research and Theory*, 2nd ed., ed. D. Cartwright and A. Zander (Elmsford, NY: Row, Paterson, 1960).

17 T. A. Judge, R. F. Piccolo, and R. Ilies, "The Forgotten Ones? The Validity of Consideration and Initiating Structure in Leadership Research," *Journal of Applied Psychology*, February 2004, pp. 36–51.

18 S. Derue, J. Nahrgang, N. Wellman, and S. Humphrey. "Trait and Behavioral Theories of Leadership: An Integration and Meta-analytic Test of their Relative Validity," *Personnel Psychology* 64 (2011), pp. 7–52.

19 F. E. Fiedler, *A Theory of Leadership Effectiveness* (New York: McGraw-Hill, 1967).

20 See, for example, G. Thompson and R. P. Vecchio, "Situational Leadership Theory: A Test of Three Versions," *Leadership Quarterly* 20, no. 5 (2009), pp 837–848; and R. P. Vecchio, C. R. Bullis, and D. M. Brazil, "The Utility of Situational Leadership Theory—A Replication in a Military Setting," *Small Group Research* 37, no. 5 (2006), pp. 407–424.

21 R. Fehr, K. C. Yam, and C. Dang, "Moralized Leadership: The Construction and Consequences of Ethical Leader Perceptions," *Academy of Management Review* 40, no. 2 (2015), pp. 182–209; and M. Hernandez, C. P. Long, and S. B. Sitkin, "Cultivating Follower Trust: Are All Leader Behaviors Equally Influential?" *Organization Studies* 35, no. 12 (2014), pp. 1867–1892.

22 S. J. Perry, L. A. Witt, L. M. Penney, and L. Atwater, "The Downside of Goal-Focused Leadership: The Role of Personality in Subordinate Exhaustion," *Journal of Applied Psychology* 95, no. 6 (2010), pp. 1145–1153.

23 S. H. Malik, H. Sikandar, H. Hassan, and S. Aziz, "Path Goal Theory: A Study of Job Satisfaction in Telecom Sector," in C. Dan (ed.), *Management and Service Science* 8 (2001), pp. 127–134; and R. R. Vecchio, J. E. Justin, and C. L. Pearce, "The Utility of Transactional and Transformational Leadership for Predicting Performance and Satisfaction within a Path-Goal Theory Framework," *Journal of Occupational and Organizational Psychology* 81 (2008), pp. 71–82.

24 Vignette based on J. Schroeder, "How Volunteerism Can Help Kickstart Your Career," *Forbes*, April 14, 2016, https://www.forbes.com/sites/julesschroeder/2016/04/14/how-volunteerism-can-help-kickstart-your-career/#481cbd131883; C. Ip, "Kelly Lovell Helps Youth Discover their Voice," *Coldlakesun.com*, May 27, 2015, http://www.coldlakesun.com/2015/05/27/kelly-lovell-helps-youth-discover-their-voice; and B. Vrbanac, "Waterloo Youth Motivator Kelly Lovell Recognized by the Queen," *WaterlooChronicle.ca*, December 9, 2015, https://www.waterloochronicle.ca/news-story/6166021-waterloo-youth-motivator-kelly-lovell-recognized-by-the-queen/.

25 M. Weber, *The Theory of Social and Economic Organization*, trans. A. M. Henderson and T. Parsons (New York: The Free Press, 1947).

26 J. A. Conger and R. N. Kanungo, "Behavioral Dimensions of Charismatic Leadership," in *Charismatic Leadership*, ed. J. A. Conger and R. N. Kanungo (San Francisco: Jossey-Bass, 1988), p. 79; and A.-K. Samnani and P. Singh, "When Leaders Victimize: The Role of Charismatic Leaders in Facilitating Group Pressures," *Leadership Quarterly* 24, no. 1 (February 2013), pp. 189–202.

27 V. Seyranian and M. C. Bligh, "Presidential Charismatic Leadership: Exploring the Rhetoric of Social Change," *Leadership Quarterly* 19, no. 1 (2008), pp. 54–76.

28 A. Xenikou, "The Cognitive and Affective Components of Organisational Identification: The Role of Perceived Support Values and Charismatic Leadership," *Applied Psychology: An International Review* 63, no. 4 (2014), pp. 567–588.

29 P. A. Vlachos, N. G. Panagopoulos, and A. A. Rapp, "Feeling Good by Doing Good: Employee CSR-Induced Attributions, Job Satisfaction, and the Role of Charismatic Leadership," *Journal of Business Ethics* 118, no. 3 (2013), pp. 577–588.

30 A. H. B. De Hoogh and D. N. Den Hartog, "Neuroticism and Locus of Control as Moderators of the Relationships of Charismatic and Autocratic Leadership with Burnout," *Journal of Applied Psychology* 94, no. 4 (2009), pp. 1058–1067.

31 F. Cohen, S. Solomon, M. Maxfield, T. Pyszczynski, and J. Greenberg, "Fatal Attraction: The Effects of Mortality Salience on Evaluations of Charismatic, Task-Oriented, and Relationship-Oriented Leaders," *Psychological Science*, December 2004, pp. 846–851; and M. G. Ehrhart and K. J. Klein, "Predicting Followers' Preferences for Charismatic Leadership: The Influence of Follower Values and Personality," *Leadership Quarterly*, Summer 2001, pp. 153–179.

32 K. Levine, R. Muenchen, and A. Brooks, "Measuring Transformational and Charismatic Leadership: Why Isn't Charisma Measured?" *Communication Monographs* 77, no. 4 (2010), pp. 576–591.

33 A. Erez, V. F. Misangyi, D. E. Johnson, M. A. LePine, and K. C. Halverson, "Stirring the Hearts of Followers: Charismatic Leadership as the Transferal of Affect," *Journal of Applied Psychology* 93, no. 3 (2008), pp. 602–615. For reviews on the role of vision in leadership, see S. J. Zaccaro, "Visionary and Inspirational Models of Executive Leadership: Empirical Review and Evaluation," in

The Nature of Executive Leadership: A Conceptual and Empirical Analysis of Success, ed. S. J. Zaccaro (Washington, DC: American Psychological Association, 2001), pp. 259–278; and M. Hauser and R. J. House, "Lead Through Vision and Values," in *Handbook of Principles of Organizational Behavior*, ed. E. A. Locke (Malden, MA: Blackwell, 2004), pp. 257–273.

34 D. N. Den Hartog, A. H. B. De Hoogh, and A. E. Keegan, "The Interactive Effects of Belongingness and Charisma on Helping and Compliance," *Journal of Applied Psychology* 92, no. 4 (2007), pp. 1131–1139.

35 See, for instance, R. Khurana, *Searching for a Corporate Savior: The Irrational Quest for Charismatic CEOs* (Princeton, NJ: Princeton University Press, 2002); and J. A. Raelin, "The Myth of Charismatic Leaders," *Training & Development*, March 2003, pp. 47–54.

36 B. M. Galvin, D. A. Waldman, and P. Balthazard, "Visionary Communication Qualities as Mediators of the Relationship between Narcissism and Attributions of Leader Charisma," *Personnel Psychology* 63, no. 3 (2010), pp. 509–537.

37 See, for instance, D. Deichmann and D. Stam, "Leveraging Transformational and Transactional Leadership to Cultivate the Generation of Organization-Focused Ideas," *Leadership Quarterly* 26, no. 2 (2015), pp. 204–219; H.-J. Wolfram and L. Gratton, "Gender Role Self-Concept, Categorical Gender, and Transactional-Transformational Leadership: Implications for Perceived Workgroup Performance," *Journal of Leadership & Organizational Studies* 21, no. 4 (2014), pp. 338–353; and T. A. Judge and R. F. Piccolo, "Transformational and Transactional Leadership: A Meta-analytic Test of Their Relative Validity," *Journal of Applied Psychology*, October 2004, pp. 755–768.

38 A. E. Colbert, M. R. Barrick, and B. H. Bradley, "Personality and Leadership Composition in Top Management Teams: Implications for Organizational Effectiveness," *Personnel Psychology* 67 (2014), pp. 351–387.

39 A. M. Grant, "Leading with Meaning: Beneficiary Contact, Prosocial Impact, and the Performance Effects of Transformational Leadership," *Academy of Management Journal* 55 (2012), pp. 458–476.

40 D. Deichmann and D. Stam, "Leveraging Transformational and Transactional Leadership to Cultivate the Generation of Organization-Focused Ideas, " *Leadership Quarterly* 26, no. 2 (2015), pp. 204–219; and H.-J. Wolfram and L. Gratton, "Gender Role Self-Concept, Categorical Gender, and Transactional-Transformational Leadership: Implications for Perceived Workgroup Performance," *Journal of Leadership & Organizational Studies* 21, no. 4 (2014), pp. 338–353.

41 T. R. Hinkin and C. A. Schriesheim, "An Examination of 'Nonleadership': From Laissez-Faire Leadership to Leader Reward Omission and Punishment Omission," *Journal of Applied Psychology* 93, no. 6 (2008), pp. 1234–1248.

42 Y. Ling, Z. Simsek, M. H. Lubatkin, and J. F. Veiga, "Transformational Leadership's Role in Promoting Corporate Entrepreneurship: Examining the CEO-TMT Interface," *Academy of Management Journal* 51, no. 3 (2008), pp. 557–576.

43 X. Zhang and K. M. Bartol, "Linking Empowering Leadership and Employee Creativity: The Influence of Psychological Empowerment, Intrinsic Motivation, and Creative Process Engagement," *Academy of Management Journal* 53, no. 1 (2010), pp. 107–128.

44 S. A. Eisenbeiß and S. Boerner, "A Double-Edged Sword: Transformational Leadership and Individual Creativity," *British Journal of Management* 24 (2013), pp. 54–68.

45 A. E. Colbert, A. E. Kristof-Brown, B. H. Bradley, and M. R. Barrick, "CEO Transformational Leadership: The Role of Goal Importance Congruence in Top Management Teams," *Academy of Management Journal* 51, no. 1 (2008), pp. 81–96.

46 D. Zohar and O. Tenne-Gazit, "Transformational Leadership and Group Interaction as Climate Antecedents: A Social Network Analysis," *Journal of Applied Psychology* 93, no. 4 (2008), pp. 744–757.

47 R. T. Keller, "Transformational Leadership, Initiating Structure, and Substitutes for Leadership: A Longitudinal Study of Research and Development Project Team Performance," *Journal of Applied Psychology* 91, no. 1 (2006), pp. 202–210.

48 G. Wang, I. Oh, S. H. Courtright, and A. E. Colbert, "Transformational Leadership and Performance across Criteria and Levels: A Meta-analytic Review of 25 Years of Research," *Group and Organization Management* 36, no. 2 (2011), pp. 223–270.

49 Y. Ling, Z. Simsek, M. H. Lubatkin, and J. F. Veiga, "The Impact of Transformational CEOs on the Performance of Small- to Medium-Sized Firms: Does Organizational Context Matter?" *Journal of Applied Psychology* 93, no. 4 (2008), pp. 923–934.

50 X. Wang and J. M. Howell, "Exploring the Dual-Level Effects of Transformational Leadership on Followers," *Journal of Applied Psychology* 95, no. 6 (2010), pp. 1134–1144.

51 N. Li, D. S. Chiaburu, B. L. Kirkman, and Z. Xie, "Spotlight on the Followers: An Examination of Moderators of Relationships between Transformational Leadership and Subordinates' Citizenship and Taking Charge," *Personnel Psychology* 66 (2013), pp. 225–260.

52 R. J. House, M. Javidan, P. Hanges, and P. Dorfman, "Understanding Cultures and Implicit Leadership Theories across the Globe: An Introduction to Project GLOBE," *Journal of World Business*, Spring 2002, pp. 3–10.

53 D. E. Carl and M. Javidan, "Universality of Charismatic Leadership: A Multi-Nation Study" (paper presented at the National Academy of Management Conference, Washington, DC, August 2001), p. 29.

54 J. Schaubroeck, S. S. K. Lam, and S. E. Cha, "Embracing Transformational Leadership: Team Values and the Impact of Leader Behavior on Team Performance," *Journal of Applied Psychology* 92, no. 4 (2007), pp. 1020–1030.

55 J. Liu, O. Siu, and K. Shi, "Transformational Leadership and Employee Well-Being: The Mediating Role of Trust in the Leader and Self-Efficacy," *Applied Psychology: An International Review* 59, no. 3 (2010), pp. 454–479.

56 S. J. Shin and J. Zhou, "Transformational Leadership, Conservation, and Creativity: Evidence from Korea," *Academy of Management Journal*, December 2003, pp. 703–714; V. J. García-Morales, F. J. Lloréns-Montes, and A. J. Verdú-Jover, "The Effects of Transformational Leadership on Organizational Performance through Knowledge and Innovation," *British Journal of Management* 19, no. 4 (2008), pp. 299–313; and S. A. Eisenbeiß, D. van Knippenberg, and S. Boerner, "Transformational Leadership and Team Innovation: Integrating Team Climate Principles," *Journal of Applied Psychology* 93, no. 6 (2008), pp. 1438–1446.

57 F. O. Walumbwa, B. J. Avolio, and W. Zhu, "How Transformational Leadership Weaves Its Influence on Individual Job Performance: The Role of Identification and Efficacy Beliefs," *Personnel Psychology* 61, no. 4 (2008), pp. 793–825.

58 Y. Gong, J. Huang, and J. Farh, "Employee Learning Orientation, Transformational Leadership, and Employee Creativity: The Mediating Role of Employee Creative Self-Efficacy," *Academy of Management Journal* 52, no. 4 (2009), pp. 765–778.

59 J. E. Bono and T. A. Judge, "Self-Concordance at Work: Toward Understanding the Motivational Effects of Transformational Leaders," *Academy of Management Journal*, October 2003, pp. 554–571; Y. Berson and B. J. Avolio, "Transformational Leadership and the Dissemination of Organizational Goals: A Case Study of a Telecommunication Firm," *Leadership Quarterly*, October 2004, pp. 625–646; and J. Schaubroeck, S. S. K. Lam, and

S. E. Cha, "Embracing Transformational Leadership: Team Values and the Impact of Leader Behavior on Team Performance," *Journal of Applied Psychology* 92, no. 4 (2007), pp. 1020–1030.

60 S. Auh, B. Mengue, and Y. Jung, "Unpacking the Relationship between Empowering Leadership and Service-Oriented Citizenship Behaviors: A Multilevel Approach," *Journal of the Academy of Marketing Science* 42 (2014), pp. 558–579.

61 M. Birasnav, "Knowledge Management and Organizational Performance in the Service Industry: The Role of Transformational Leadership Beyond the Effects of Transactional Leadership," *Journal of Business Research* 67, no. 8 (2014), pp. 1622–1629; H. Hetland, G. M. Sandal, and T. B. Johnsen, "Burnout in the Information Technology Sector: Does Leadership Matter?" *European Journal of Work and Organizational Psychology* 16, no. 1 (2007), pp. 58–75; and A. K. Tyssen, A. Wald, and S. Heidenreich, "Leadership in the Context of Temporary Organizations: A Study on the Effects of Transactional and Transformational Leadership on Followers' Commitment in Projects," *Journal of Leadership & Organizational Studies* 21, no. 4 (2014), pp. 376–393.

62 Vignette based on "Startup Canada Podcast: Lovell Corp. CEO on Inspiring Young Entrepreneurs," *Betakit*, April 11, 2017, http://betakit.com/startup-canada-podcast-lovell-corp-ceo-on-inspiring-young-entrepreneurs/.

63 See B. J. Avolio, W. L. Gardner, F. O. Walumbwa, F. Luthans, and D. R. May, "Unlocking the Mask: A Look at the Process by Which Authentic Leaders Impact Follower Attitudes and Behaviors," *Leadership Quarterly*, December 2004, pp. 801–823; W. L. Gardner and J. R. Schermerhorn Jr., "Performance Gains through Positive Organizational Behavior and Authentic Leadership," *Organizational Dynamics*, August 2004, pp. 270–281; and M. M. Novicevic, M. G. Harvey, M. R. Buckley, J. A. Brown-Radford, and R. Evans, "Authentic Leadership: A Historical Perspective," *Journal of Leadership and Organizational Behavior* 13, no. 1 (2006), pp. 64–76.

64 "Expect to Make a Difference, Be an Authentic Leader and Have Integrity," York University, October 22, 2014, http://yfile.news.yorku.ca/2014/10/22/expect-to-make-a-difference-be-an-authentic-leader-have-integrity/.

65 B. P. Owens and D. R. Hekman, "Modeling How to Grow: An Inductive Examination of Humble Leader Behaviors, Contingencies, and Outcomes," *Academy of Management Journal* 55 (2012), pp. 787–818.

66 K. M. Hmieleski, M. S. Cole, and R. A. Baron, "Shared Authentic Leadership and New Venture Performance," *Journal of Management*, September 2012, pp. 1476–1499.

67 R. Ilies, F. P. Morgeson, and J. D. Nahrgang, "Authentic Leadership and Eudaemonic Wellbeing: Understanding Leader-Follower Outcomes," *Leadership Quarterly* 16 (2005), pp. 373–394.

68 J. Stouten, M. van Dijke, and D. De Cremer, "Ethical Leadership: An Overview and Future Perspectives," *Journal of Personnel Psychology* 11 (2012), pp. 1–6.

69 J. M. Schaubroeck, S. T. Hannah, B. J. Avolio, S. W. J. Kozlowski, R. G. Lord, L. K. Trevino, N. Dimotakis, and A. C. Peng, "Embedding Ethical Leadership within and across Organization Levels," *Academy of Management Journal* 55 (2012), pp. 1053–1078.

70 K. M. Kacmar, D. G. Bachrach, K. J. Harris, and S. Zivnuska, "Fostering Good Citizenship through Ethical Leadership: Exploring the Moderating Role of Gender and Organizational Politics," *Journal of Applied Psychology* 96, no. 3 (May 2011), pp. 633–642; and F. O. Walumbwa and J. Schaubroeck, "Leader Personality Traits and Employee Voice Behavior: Mediating Roles of Ethical Leadership and Work Group Psychological Safety," *Journal of Applied Psychology* 94, no. 5 (2009), pp. 1275–1286.

71 D. M. Mayer, K. Aquino, R. L. Greenbaum, and M. Kuenzi, "Who Displays Ethical Leadership, and Why Does It Matter? An Examination of Antecedents and Consequences of Ethical Leadership," *Academy of Management Journal* 55 (2012), pp. 151–171.

72 D. van Knippenberg, D. De Cremer, and B. van Knippenberg, "Leadership and Fairness: The State of the Art," *European Journal of Work and Organizational Psychology* 16, no. 2 (2007), pp. 113–140.

73 M. E. Brown and L. K. Treviño, "Socialized Charismatic Leadership, Values Congruence, and Deviance in Work Groups," *Journal of Applied Psychology* 91, no. 4 (2006), pp. 954–962.

74 M. E. Brown and L. K. Treviño, "Leader-Follower Values Congruence: Are Socialized Charismatic Leaders Better Able to Achieve It?" *Journal of Applied Psychology* 94, no. 2 (2009), pp. 478–490.

75 S. A. Eisenbeiß and S. R. Giessner, "The Emergence and Maintenance of Ethical Leadership in Organizations," *Journal of Personnel Psychology* 11 (2012), pp. 7–19.

76 D. van Dierendonck, "Servant Leadership: A Review and Synthesis," *Journal of Management* 37, no. 4 (2011), pp. 1228–1261.

77 S. J. Peterson, F. M. Galvin, and D. Lange, "CEO Servant Leadership: Exploring Executive Characteristics and Firm Performance," *Personnel Psychology* 65 (2012), pp. 565–596.

78 F. Walumbwa, C. A. Hartnell, and A. Oke, "Servant Leadership, Procedural Justice Climate, Service Climate, Employee Attitudes, and Organizational Citizenship Behavior: A Cross-Level Investigation," *Journal of Applied Psychology* 95, no. 3 (2010), pp. 517–529.

79 D. De Cremer, D. M. Mayer, M. van Dijke, B. C. Schouten, and M. Bardes, "When Does Self-Sacrificial Leadership Motivate Prosocial Behavior? It Depends on Followers' Prevention Focus," *Journal of Applied Psychology* 2009, no. 4 (2009), pp. 887–899.

80 J. Hu and R. C. Liden, "Antecedents of Team Potency and Team Effectiveness: An Examination of Goal and Process Clarity and Servant Leadership," *Journal of Applied Psychology*, 96, no. 4 (July 2011), pp. 851–862.

81 M. J. Neubert, K. M. Kacmar, D. S. Carlson, L. B. Chonko, and J. A. Roberts, "Regulatory Focus as a Mediator of the Influence of Initiating Structure and Servant Leadership on Employee Behavior," *Journal of Applied Psychology* 93, no. 6 (2008), pp. 1220–1233.

82 R. C. Liden, S. J. Wayne, C. Liao, and J. D. Meuser, "Servant Leadership and Serving Culture: Influence on Individual and Unit Performance," *Academy of Management Journal* 57, no. 5 (2014), pp. 1434–1452.

83 See, for example, L. J. Zachary, *The Mentor's Guide: Facilitating Effective Learning Relationships* (San Francisco: Jossey-Bass, 2000); M. Murray, *Beyond the Myths and Magic of Mentoring: How to Facilitate an Effective Mentoring Process*, rev. ed. (New York: Wiley, 2001); and F. Warner, "Inside Intel's Mentoring Movement," *Fast Company*, April 2002, pp. 116–120.

84 C. R. Wanberg, E. T. Welsh, and S. A. Hezlett, "Mentoring Research: A Review and Dynamic Process Model," in G. R. Ferris and J. J. Martocchio (eds.), *Research in Personnel and Human Resources Management*, vol. 22 (Greenwich, CT: Elsevier Science, 2003), pp. 39–124; and T. D. Allen, "Protégé Selection by Mentors: Contributing Individual and Organizational Factors," *Journal of Vocational Behavior* 65, no. 3 (2004), pp. 469–483.

85 See, for example, D. B. Turban T. W. Dougherty, and F. K. Lee, "Gender, Race, and Perceived Similarity Effects in Developmental Relationships: The Moderating Role of Relationship Duration," *Journal of Vocational Behavior*, October 2002, pp. 240–262.

86 J. U. Chun, J. J. Sosik, and N. Y. Yun, "A Longitudinal Study of Mentor and Protégé Outcomes in Formal Mentoring Relationships," *Journal of Organizational Behavior*, November 12, 2012, pp. 35–49.

87 B. R. Ragins and J. L. Cotton, "Mentor Functions and Outcomes: A Comparison of Men and Women in Formal and Informal Mentoring Relationships," *Journal of Applied Psychology*, August 1999, pp. 529–550; and C. M. Underhill, "The Effectiveness of Mentoring Programs in Corporate Settings: A Meta-analytical Review of the Literature," *Journal of Vocational Behavior* 68, no. 2 (2006), pp. 292–307.

88 T. D. Allen, E. T. Eby, and E. Lentz, "The Relationship between Formal Mentoring Program Characteristics and Perceived Program Effectiveness," *Personnel Psychology* 59 (2006), pp. 125–153; T. D. Allen, L. T. Eby, and E. Lentz, "Mentorship Behaviors and Mentorship Quality Associated with Formal Mentoring Programs: Closing the Gap between Research and Practice," *Journal of Applied Psychology* 91, no. 3 (2006), pp. 567–578; and M. R. Parise and M. L. Forret, "Formal Mentoring Programs: The Relationship of Program Design and Support to Mentors' Perceptions of Benefits and Costs," *Journal of Vocational Behavior* 72, no. 2 (2008), pp. 225–240.

89 L. T. Eby and A. Lockwood, "Protégés' and Mentors' Reactions to Participating in Formal Mentoring Programs: A Qualitative Investigation," *Journal of Vocational Behavior* 67, no. 3 (2005), pp. 441–458; G. T. Chao, "Formal Mentoring: Lessons Learned from Past Practice," *Professional Psychology: Research and Practice* 40, no. 3 (2009), pp. 314–320; and C. R. Wanberg, J. D. Kammeyer-Mueller, and M. Marchese, "Mentor and Protégé Predictors and Outcomes of Mentoring in a Formal Mentoring Program," *Journal of Vocational Behavior* 69 (2006), pp. 410–423.

90 M. K. Feeney and B. Bozeman, "Mentoring and Network Ties," Human Relations 61, no. 12 (2008), pp. 1651–1676; N. Bozionelos, "Intra-Organizational Network Resources: How They Relate to Career Success and Organizational Commitment," *Personnel Review* 37, no. 3 (2008), pp. 249–263; and S. A. Hezlett and S. K. Gibson, "Linking Mentoring and Social Capital: Implications for Career and Organization Development," *Advances in Developing Human Resources* 9, no. 3 (2007), pp. 384–412.

91 Based on B. Carmody, "Rethinking Youth Empowerment as Generation Z Blows Your Mind," *Inc.*, June 10, 2015, https://www.inc.com/bill-carmody/rethinking-youth-empowerment-as-generation-z-blows-your-mind.html; and http://www.lovellcorporation.com/lovell-corp-launches-global-youth-book-project-iyd-2017/.

92 The Jossey-Bass Reader on Educational Leadership, 2nd ed. (San Francisco: Wiley & Sons, 2007).

93 See, for instance, B. Schyns, J. Felfe, and H. Blank, "Is Charisma Hyper-Romanticism? Empirical Evidence from New Data and a Meta-analysis," *Applied Psychology: An International Review* 56, no. 4 (2007), pp. 505–527.

94 M. J. Martinko, P. Harvey, D. Sikora, and S. C. Douglas, "Perceptions of Abusive Supervision: The Role of Subordinates' Attribution Styles," *Leadership Quarterly*, August 2011, pp. 751–764.

95 M. C. Bligh, J. C. Kohles, C. L. Pearce J. E. Justin, and J. F. Stovall, "When the Romance Is Over: Follower Perspectives of Aversive Leadership," *Applied Psychology: An International Review* 56, no. 4 (2007), pp. 528–557.

96 B. R. Agle, N. J. Nagarajan, J. A. Sonnenfeld, and D. Srinivasan, "Does CEO Charisma Matter?" *Academy of Management Journal* 49, no. 1 (2006), pp. 161–174.

97 M. C. Bligh, J. C. Kohles, C. L. Pearce J. E. Justin, and J. F. Stovall, "When the Romance Is Over: Follower Perspectives of Aversive Leadership," *Applied Psychology: An International Review* 56, no. 4 (2007), pp. 528–557.

98 B. Schyns, J. Felfe, and H. Blank, "Is Charisma Hyper-Romanticism? Empirical Evidence from New Data and a Meta-analysis," *Applied Psychology: An International Review* 56, no. 4 (2007), pp. 505–527.

99 A. S. Rosette, G. J. Leonardelli, and K. W. Phillips, "The White Standard: Racial Bias in Leader Categorization," *Journal of Applied Psychology* 93, no. 4 (2008), pp. 758–777.

100 A. M. Koenig, A. H. Eagly, A. A. Mitchell, and T. Ristikari, "Are Leader Stereotypes Masculine? A Meta-analysis of Three Research Paradigms," *Psychological Bulletin* 137, no. 4 (2011), pp. 616–642.

101 M. Van Vugt and B. R. Spisak, "Sex Differences in the Emergence of Leadership during Competitions within and between Groups," *Psychological Science* 19, no. 9 (2008), pp. 854–858.

102 M. Van Vugt and B. R. Spisak, "Sex Differences in the Emergence of Leadership during Competitions within and between Groups," *Psychological Science* 19, no. 9 (2008), pp. 854–858.

103 R. E. Silverman, "Who's the Boss? There Isn't One," *Wall Street Journal*, June 20, 2012, pp. B1, B8.

104 S. D. Dionne, F. J. Yammarino, L. E. Atwater, and L. R. James, "Neutralizing Substitutes for Leadership Theory: Leadership Effects and Common-Source Bias," *Journal of Applied Psychology*, 87 (2002), pp. 454–464; and J. R. Villa, J. P. Howell, P. W. Dorfman, and D. L. Daniel, "Problems with Detecting Moderators in Leadership Research Using Moderated Multiple Regression," *Leadership Quarterly* 14 (2002), pp. 3–23.

105 L. A. Hambley, T. A. O'Neill, and T. J. B. Kline, "Virtual Team Leadership: The Effects of Leadership Style and Communication Medium on Team Interaction Styles and Outcomes," *Organizational Behavior and Human Decision Processes* 103 (2007), pp. 1–20; and B. J. Avolio and S. S. Kahai, "Adding the 'E' to E-Leadership: How It May Impact Your Leadership," *Organizational Dynamics* 31, no. 4 (2003), pp. 325–338.

106 S. J. Zaccaro and P. Bader, "E-Leadership and the Challenges of Leading E-Teams: Minimizing the Bad and Maximizing the Good," *Organizational Dynamics* 31, no. 4 (2003), pp. 381–385.

107 C. E. Naquin and G. D. Paulson, "Online Bargaining and Interpersonal Trust," *Journal of Applied Psychology*, February 2003, pp. 113–120.

108 M. Javidan, P. W. Dorfman, M. S. de Luque, and R. J. House, "In the Eye of the Beholder: Cross Cultural Lessons in Leadership from Project GLOBE," *Academy of Management Perspectives*, February 2006, pp. 67–90.

109 T. Menon, J. Sim, J. Ho-Ying Fu, C. Chiu, and Y. Hong, "Blazing the Trail versus Trailing the Group: Culture and Perceptions of the Leader's Position," *Organizational Behavior and Human Decision Processes* 113, no. 1 (2010), pp. 51–61.

110 Based on Z. E. Franco, K. Blau, and P. G. Zimbardo, "Heroism: A Conceptual Analysis and Differentiation Between Heroic Action and Altruism," *Review of General Psychology* 15, no. 2 (2011), pp. 99–113; O. Dorell, "At Nuke Plant, Heroes Emerge," *USA Today*, March 25, 2011, pp. 1A, 2A; G. R. Goethals and S. C. Allison, "Making Heroes: The Construction of Courage, Competence, and Virtue," *Advances in Experimental Psychology* 46 (2012), pp. 183–235; L. J. Walker, J. A. Frimer, and W. L. Dunlop, "Varieties of Moral Personality: Beyond the Banality of Heroism," *Journal of Personality* 78, no. 3 (2010), pp. 907–942; and J. Lehrer, "Are Heroes Born, or Can They Be Made?" *Wall Street Journal*, December 11, 2010, p. C12.

111 Justin Ross Hartfield website, http://www.justinhartfield.me; B. Weiss, "Thank You for Smoking—Marijuana," *Wall Street Journal*, March 15–16, 2014, A11; K. Wagner, "Weedmaps CEO Justin Hartfield May Soon Be America's Weed Guy," *Mashable*, May 16, 2014, http://www.mashable.com/2014/05/16/weedmaps-ceo-justin-hartfield/; and L. Phillips, "Drop in IQ Linked to Heavy Teenage Cannabis Use," *Nature*, August 28, 2012, https://www.nature.com/news/drop-in-iq-linked-to-heavy-teenage-cannabis-use-1.11278.

112 Based on B. O'Keefe, J. Birger, and D. Burke, "Battle Tested," *Fortune*, March 22, 2010, pp. 108–118; B. Whitmore, "Hiring Military Veterans Is Good Business," *Huntington WV Herald-Dispatch*, November 6, 2010, http://www.herald-dispatch.com;

B. Wansink, C. R. Payne, and K. van Ittersum, "Profiling the Heroic Leader: Empirical Lessons from Combat-Decorated Veterans of World War II," *Leadership Quarterly* 19, no. 5 (2008), pp. 547–555; and T. E. Ricks, "What Ever Happened to Accountability?" *Harvard Business Review*, October 2012, pp. 93–100.

113 Based on M. Buckingham, "Leadership Development in the Age of the Algorithm," *Harvard Business Review*, June 2012, pp. 86–94; M. D. Watkins, "How Managers Become Leaders," *Harvard Business Review*, June 2012, pp. 64–72; and J. M. Podolny, "A Conversation with James G. March on Learning About Leadership," *Academy of Management Learning & Education* 10 (2011), pp. 502–506.

114 Based on J. M. Howell and P. J. Frost, "A Laboratory Study of Charismatic Leadership," *Organizational Behavior and Human Decision Processes*, April 1989, pp. 243–269.

115 Based on V. H. Vroom, "A New Look at Managerial Decision Making," *Organizational Dynamics*, Spring 1973, pp. 66–80. With permission.

Chapter 12

1 Vignette based on E. Johnson, "'I Will Do Anything I Can to Make My Goal': TD Teller Says Customers Pay Price for 'Unrealistic' Sales Targets," *CBC News*, March 6, 2017, http://www.cbc.ca/news/canada/british-columbia/td-tellers-desperate-to-meet-increasing-sales-goals-1.4006743, and E. Johnson, "'We Do It because Our Jobs Are at Stake': TD Bank Employees Admit to Breaking the Law for Fear of Being Fired," *CBC News*, March 10, 2017, http://www.cbc.ca/news/business/td-bank-employees-admit-to-breaking-law-1.4016569.

2 E. Shafir and R. A. LeBoeuf, "Rationality," *Annual Review of Psychology* 53 (2002), pp. 491–517.

3 For a review of the rational decision-making model, see M. H. Bazerman and D. A. Moore, *Judgment in Managerial Decision Making*, 7th ed. (Hoboken, New Jersey: Wiley, 2008).

4 CIBC, "Donations and Sponsorship Funding Guidelines," accessed November, 2017, https://www.cibc.com/en/about-cibc/corporate-responsibility/community-and-sponsorship/funding-guidelines.html.

5 J. G. March, *A Primer on Decision Making* (New York: The Free Press, 2009); and D. Hardman and C. Harries, "How Rational Are We?" *Psychologist*, February 2002, pp. 76–79.

6 Vignette based on E. Johnson, "'I Will Do Anything I Can to Make My Goal': TD Teller Says Customers Pay Price for 'Unrealistic' Sales Targets," *CBC News*, March 6, 2017, http://www.cbc.ca/news/canada/british-columbia/td-tellers-desperate-to-meet-increasing-sales-goals-1.4006743, and M. King, "How Technology Has Turned Tellers into Sellers," *Globe and Mail*, March 14, 2017, https://beta.theglobeandmail.com/report-on-business/rob-commentary/how-technology-has-turned-tellers-into-sellers/article34297345/

7 M. H. Bazerman and D. A. Moore, *Judgment in Managerial Decision Making*, 7th ed. (Hoboken, NJ: Wiley, 2008).

8 J. E. Russo, K. A. Carlson, and M. G. Meloy, "Choosing an Inferior Alternative," *Psychological Science* 17, no. 10 (2006), pp. 899–904.

9 See, for example, L. R. Beach, *The Psychology of Decision Making* (Thousand Oaks, CA: Sage, 1997).

10 N. Halevy and E. Y. Chou, "How Decisions Happen: Focal Points and Blind Spots in Interdependent Decision Making," *Journal of Personality and Social Psychology* 106, no. 3 (2014), pp. 398–417; D. Kahneman, "Maps of Bounded Rationality: Psychology for Behavioral Economics," *The American Economic Review* 93, no. 5 (2003), pp. 1449–1475; and J. Zhang, C. K. Hsee, and Z. Xiao, "The Majority Rule in Individual Decision Making," *Organizational Behavior and Human Decision Processes* 99 (2006), pp. 102–111.

11 G. Gigerenzer, "Why Heuristics Work," *Perspectives on Psychological Science* 3, no. 1 (2008), pp. 20–29; and A. K. Shah and D. M. Oppenheimer, "Heuristics Made Easy: An Effort-Reduction Framework," *Psychological Bulletin* 134, no. 2 (2008), pp. 207–222.

12 See A. W. Kruglanski and G. Gigerenzer, "Intuitive and Deliberate Judgments Are Based on Common Principles," *Psychological Review* 118 (2011), pp. 97–109.

13 E. Dane and M. G. Pratt, "Exploring Intuition and Its Role in Managerial Decision Making," *Academy of Management Review* 32, no. 1 (2007), pp. 33–54; and J. A. Hicks, D. C. Cicero, J. Trent, C. M. Burton, and L. A. King, "Positive Affect, Intuition, and Feelings of Meaning," *Journal of Personality and Social Psychology* 98 (2010), pp. 967–979.

14 Based on P. D. Brown, "Some Hunches About Intuition," *New York Times*, November 17, 2007, p. B5.

15 Based on D. Delaney, C. Guilding, and L. McManus, "The Use of Intuition in the Sponsorship Decision Making Process," *Contemporary Management Research* 10, no. 1 (2014), pp. 33–60.

16 B. D. Dunn and H. C. Galton, "Listening to Your Heart: How Interoception Shapes Emotion Experience and Intuitive Decision Making," *Psychological Science* 21, no. 12 (December 2010), pp. 1835–1844.

17 C. Akinci and E. Sadler-Smith, "Intuition in Management Research: A Historical Review," *International Journal of Management Reviews* 14 (2012), pp. 104–122.

18 S. P. Robbins, *Decide & Conquer: Making Winning Decisions and Taking Control of Your Life* (Upper Saddle River, NJ: Financial Times/Prentice Hall, 2004), p. 13.

19 Based on P. Cohen, "Stand Still: Use Penalty-Kick Wisdom to Make Your Decisions," *National Post*, March 8, 2008, p. FW9.

20 S. Ludwig and J. Nafziger, "Beliefs about Overconfidence," *Theory and Decision*, April 2011, pp. 475–500.

21 S. Plous, *The Psychology of Judgment and Decision Making* (New York: McGraw-Hill, 1993), p. 217.

22 C. R. M. McKenzie, M. J. Liersch, and I. Yaniv, "Overconfidence in Interval Estimates: What Does Expertise Buy You," *Organizational Behavior and Human Decision Processes* 107 (2008), pp. 179–191.

23 R. P. Larrick, K. A. Burson, and J. B. Soll, "Social Comparison and Confidence: When Thinking You're Better Than Average Predicts Overconfidence (and When It Does Not)," *Organizational Behavior and Human Decision Processes* 102 (2007), pp. 76–94.

24 K. M. Hmieleski and R. A. Baron, "Entrepreneurs' Optimism and New Venture Performance: A Social Cognitive Perspective," *Academy of Management Journal* 52, no. 3 (2009), pp. 473–488.

25 R. Frick and A. K. Smith, "Overconfidence Game," *Kiplinger's Personal Finance* 64, no. 3 (2010), pp. 23.

26 See, for instance, J. P. Simmons, R. A. LeBoeuf, and L. D. Nelson, "The Effect of Accuracy Motivation on Anchoring and Adjustment: Do People Adjust from Their Provided Anchors?" *Journal of Personality and Social Psychology* 99 (2010), pp. 917–932.

27 J. S. Hammond, R. L. Keeney, and H. Raiffa, *Smart Choices* (Boston: HBS Press, 1999), p. 191.

28 C. Janiszewski and D. Uy, "Precision of the Anchor Influences the Amount of Adjustment," *Psychological Science* 19, no. 2 (2008), pp. 121–127.

29 See R. S. Nickerson, "Confirmation Bias: A Ubiquitous Phenomenon in Many Guises," *Review of General Psychology*, June 1998, pp. 175–220; and E. Jonas, S. Schultz-Hardt, D. Frey, and N. Thelen, "Confirmation Bias in Sequential Information Search after Preliminary Decisions," *Journal of Personality and Social Psychology*, April 2001, pp. 557–571.

30 B. Nyhan and J. Reifler, "When Corrections Fail: The Persistence of Political Misperceptions," *Political Behavior* 32, no. 2 (2010), pp. 303–330.

31 T. Pachur, R. Hertwig, and F. Steinmann, "How Do People Judge Risks: Availability Heuristic, Affect Heuristic, or Both?" *Journal of Experimental Psychology: Applied* 18 (2012), pp. 314–330.

32 See B. M. Staw, "The Escalation of Commitment to a Course of Action," *Academy of Management Review*, October 1981, pp. 577–587; and H. Moon, "Looking Forward and Looking Back: Integrating Completion and Sunk-Cost Effects within an Escalation-of-Commitment Progress Decision," *Journal of Applied Psychology*, February 2001, pp. 104–113.

33 T. Schultze, F. Pfeiffer, and S. Schulz-Hardt, "Biased Information Processing in the Escalation Paradigm: Information Search and Information Evaluation as Potential Mediators of Escalating Commitment," *Journal of Applied Psychology* 97 (2012), pp. 16–32.

34 D. J. Sleesman, D. E. Conlon, G. McNamara, and J. E. Miles, "Cleaning Up the Big Muddy: A Meta-analytic Review of the Determinants of Escalation of Commitment," *Academy of Management Journal* 55 (2012), pp. 541–562.

35 D. J. Sleesman, D. E. Conlon, G. McNamara, and J. E. Miles, "Cleaning Up the Big Muddy: A Meta-analytic Review of the Determinants of Escalation of Commitment," *Academy of Management Journal* 55 (2012), pp. 541–562.

36 H. Drummond, "Escalation of Commitment: When to Stay the Course?" *The Academy of Management Perspectives* 28, no. 4 (2014), pp. 430–446.

37 See, for example, A. James and A. Wells, "Death Beliefs, Superstitious Beliefs and Health Anxiety," *British Journal of Clinical Psychology*, March 2002, pp. 43–53.

38 S. P. Robbins, *Decide & Conquer: Making Winning Decisions and Taking Control of Your Life* (Upper Saddle River, NJ: Financial Times/Prentice Hall, 2004), pp. 164–168.

39 K. Gillespie, "Canadian Athletes' Superstitious Ways," *Toronto Star*, January 24, 2014.

40 See, for example, D. J. Keys and B. Schwartz, "Leaky Rationality: How Research on Behavioral Decision Making Challenges Normative Standards of Rationality," *Psychological Science* 2, no. 2 (2007), pp. 162–180; and U. Simonsohn, "Direct Risk Aversion: Evidence from Risky Prospects Valued Below Their Worst Outcome," *Psychological Science* 20, no. 6 (2009), pp. 686–692.

41 J. K. Maner, M. T. Gailliot, D. A. Butz, and B. M. Peruche, "Power, Risk, and the Status Quo: Does Power Promote Riskier or More Conservative Decision Making," *Personality and Social Psychology Bulletin* 33, no. 4 (2007), pp. 451–462.

42 A. Chakraborty, S. Sheikh, and N. Subramanian, "Termination Risk and Managerial Risk Taking," *Journal of Corporate Finance* 13 (2007), pp. 170–188.

43 P. Bryant and R. Dunford, "The Influence of Regulatory Focus on Risky Decision-Making," *Applied Psychology: An International Review* 57, no. 2 (2008), pp. 335–359.

44 A. J. Porcelli and M. R. Delgado, "Acute Stress Modulates Risk Taking in Financial Decision Making," *Psychological Science* 20, no. 3 (2009), pp. 278–283.

45 R. L. Guilbault, F. B. Bryant, J. H. Brockway, and E. J. Posavac, "A Meta-analysis of Research on Hindsight Bias," *Basic and Applied Social Psychology*, September 2004, pp. 103–117; and L. Werth, F. Strack, and J. Foerster, "Certainty and Uncertainty: The Two Faces of the Hindsight Bias," *Organizational Behavior and Human Decision Processes*, March 2002, pp. 323–341.

46 J. Bell, "The Final Cut?" *Oregon Business* 33, no. 5 (2010), p. 27.

47 M. Gladwell, "Connecting the Dots," *New Yorker*, March 10, 2003.

48 B. L. Bonner, S. D. Sillito, and M. R. Baumann, "Collective Estimation: Accuracy, Expertise, and Extroversion as Sources of Intra-Group Influence," *Organizational Behavior and Human Decision Processes* 103 (2007), pp. 121–133.

49 See, for example, W. C. Swap and Associates, *Group Decision Making* (Newbury Park, CA: Sage, 1984).

50 J. S. Chun and J. N. Choi, "Members' Needs, Intragroup Conflict, and Group Performance." *Journal of Applied Psychology* 99, no. 3 (2014), p. 437.

51 I. L. Janis, *Groupthink: Psychological Studies of Policy Decisions and Fiascoes*, 2nd ed. (Boston: Houghton Mifflin, 1982).

52 Based on L. Nguyen, "Target Corp. Regrets Opening So Many Stores So Quickly in Canada," *Canadian Press*, August 20, 2014, http://www.ctvnews.ca/business/target-corp-regrets-opening-so-many-stores-so-quickly-in-canada-1.1967662; M. Healy, "Same-Store Sales at Target Canada Tumble 11% in Second Quarter," *CBC News*, August 20, 2014, http://www.cbc.ca/news/business/same-store-sales-at-target-canada-tumble-11-in-second-quarter-1.2741617; "Why Was Target Canada Such a Disaster?" *Abbotsford Today*, May 26, 2014, http://www.abbotsfordtoday.ca/why-was-target-canada-such-a-disaster/; and P. Evans, "Target Closes All 133 Stores in Canada, Gets Creditor Protection," *CBC News*, January 15, 2015.

53 G. Park and R. P. DeShon, "A Multilevel Model of Minority Opinion Expression and Team Decision-Making Effectiveness," *Journal of Applied Psychology* 95, no. 5 (2010), pp. 824–833.

54 R. Benabou, "Groupthink: Collective Delusions in Organizations and Markets," *Review of Economic Studies*, April 2013, pp. 429–462.

55 J. A. Goncalo, E. Polman, and C. Maslach, "Can Confidence Come Too Soon? Collective Efficacy, Conflict, and Group Performance over Time," *Organizational Behavior and Human Decision Processes* 113, no. 1 (2010), pp. 13–24.

56 Based on See N. R. F. Maier, *Principles of Human Relations* (New York: Wiley, 1952); N. Richardson Ahlfinger and J. K. Esser, "Testing the Groupthink Model: Effects of Promotional Leadership and Conformity Predisposition," *Social Behavior & Personality* 29, no. 1 (2001), pp. 31–41; and S. Schultz-Hardt, F. C. Brodbeck, A. Mojzisch, R. Kerschreiter, and D. Frey, "Group Decision Making in Hidden Profile Situations: Dissent as a Facilitator for Decision Quality," *Journal of Personality and Social Psychology* 91, no. 6 (2006), pp. 1080–1093.

57 See D. J. Isenberg, "Group Polarization: A Critical Review and Meta-analysis," *Journal of Personality and Social Psychology*, December 1986, pp. 1141–1151; J. L. Hale and F. J. Boster, "Comparing Effect Coded Models of Choice Shifts," *Communication Research Reports*, April 1988, pp. 180–186; and P. W. Paese, M. Bieser, and M. E. Tubbs, "Framing Effects and Choice Shifts in Group Decision Making," *Organizational Behavior & Human Decision Processes*, October 1993, pp. 149–165.

58 M. P. Brady and S. Y. Wu, "The Aggregation of Preferences in Groups: Identity, Responsibility, and Polarization," *Journal of Economic Psychology* 31, no. 6 (2010), pp. 950–963.

59 J. Ewing, *Faster, Higher, Farther* (Norton & Company, 2017).

60 Z. Krizan and R. S. Baron, "Group Polarization and Choice-Dilemmas: How Important Is Self-Categorization?" *European Journal of Social Psychology* 37, no. 1 (2007), pp. 191–201.

61 See R. P. McGlynn, D. McGurk, V. S. Effland, N. L. Johll, and D. J. Harding, "Brainstorming and Task Performance in Groups Constrained by Evidence," *Organizational Behavior and Human Decision Processes*, January 2004, pp. 75–87; and R. C. Litchfield, "Brainstorming Reconsidered: A Goal-Based View," *Academy of Management Review* 33, no. 3 (2008), pp. 649–668.

62 N. W. Kohn and S. M. Smith, "Collaborative Fixation: Effects of Others' Ideas on Brainstorming," *Applied Cognitive Psychology* 25, no. 3 (May/June 2011), pp. 359–371.

63 N. L. Kerr and R. S. Tindale, "Group Performance and Decision-Making," *Annual Review of Psychology* 55 (2004), pp. 623–655.

64 C. Faure, "Beyond Brainstorming: Effects of Different Group Procedures on Selection of Ideas and Satisfaction with the Process," *Journal of Creative Behavior* 38 (2004), pp. 13–34.

65 T. M. Amabile, "A Model of Creativity and Innovation in Organizations," in *Research in Organizational Behavior*, vol. 10, ed. B. M. Staw and L. L. Cummings (Greenwich, CT: JAI Press, 1988), p. 126; and J. E. Perry-Smith and C. E. Shalley, "The Social Side of Creativity: A Static and Dynamic Social Network Perspective," *Academy of Management Review*, January 2003, pp. 89–106.

66 B. Brazier, "Brendan Brazier on Holistic Nutrition," *Ask Men*, n.d., http://ca.askmen.com/sports/foodcourt/brendan-brazier-on-holistic-nutrition.html; and "Is Your Art Killing You?" InvestorIdeas.com, May 13, 2013, http://www.investorideas.com/news/2013/renewable-energy/05134.asp.

67 M. M. Gielnik, A.-C. Kramer, B. Kappel, and M. Frese, "Antecedents of Business Opportunity Identification and Innovation: Investigating the Interplay of Information Processing and Information Acquisition," *Applied Psychology: An International Review* 63, no. 2 (2014), pp. 344–381.

68 G. Anderson, "Three Tips to Foster Creativity at Your Startup," *ArcticStartup*, May 8, 2013, http://www.arcticstartup.com/2013/05/08/three-tips-to-foster-creativity-at-your-startup.

69 G. Reynolds, "Want a Good Idea? Take a Walk," *New York Times*, May 6, 2014, p. D6.

70 S. Shellenbarger, "The Power of the Doodle: Improve Your Focus and Memory," *Wall Street Journal*, July 30, 2014, pp. D1, D3.

71 E. Millar, "How Do Finnish Kids Excel without Rote Learning and Standardized Testing?" *Globe and Mail*, May 9, 2013, http://www.theglobeandmail.com/report-on-business/economy/canada-competes/how-do-finnish-kids-excel-without-rote-learning-and-standardized-testing/article11810188/.

72 Z. Harper, "Mark Cuban Wants You to Design the New Dallas Mavericks Uniforms," *CBSSports.com*, May 13, 2013, http://www.cbssports.com/nba/eye-on-basketball/22230801/mark-cuban-wants-you-to-design-the-new-dallas-mavericks-uniforms.

73 C. K. W. De Dreu, B. A. Nijstad, M. Baas, I. Wolsink, and M. Roskes, "Working Memory Benefits Creative Insight, Musical Improvisation, and Original Ideation through Maintained Task-Focused Attention," *Personality and Social Psychology Bulletin* 38 (2012), pp. 656–669.

74 C.-H. Wu, S. K. Parker, and J. P. J. de Jong, "Need for Cognition as an Antecedent of Individual Innovation Behavior," *Journal of Management* 40, no. 6 (2014), pp. 1511–1534.

75 S. M. Wechsler, C. Vendramini, and T. Oakland, "Thinking and Creative Styles: A Validity Study," *Creativity Research Journal* 24 (April 2012), pp. 235–242.

76 Y. Gong, S. Cheung, M. Wang, and J. Huang, "Unfolding the Proactive Processes for Creativity: Integration of the Employee Proactivity, Information Exchange, and Psychological Safety Perspectives," *Journal of Management* 38 (2012), pp. 1611–1633.

77 A. Rego, F. Sousa, C. Marques, and M. P. E. Cunha, "Retail Employees' Self-Efficacy and Hope Predicting Their Positive Affect and Creativity," *European Journal of Work and Organizational Psychology* 21, no. 6 (2012), pp. 923–945.

78 H. Zhang, H. K. Kwan, X. Zhang, and L.-Z. Wu, "High Core Self-Evaluators Maintain Creativity: A Motivational Model of Abusive Supervision," *Journal of Management* 40, no. 4 (2012), pp. 1151–1174.

79 D. K. Simonton, "The Mad-Genius Paradox: Can Creative People Be More Mentally Healthy but Highly Creative People More Mentally Ill?" *Perspectives on Psychological Science* 9, no. 5 (2014), pp. 470–480.

80 C. Wang, S. Rodan, M. Fruin, and X. Xu, "Knowledge Networks, Collaboration Networks, and Exploratory Innovation," *Academy of Management Journal* 57, no. 2 (2014), pp. 484–514.

81 F. Gino and S. S. Wiltermuth, "Evil Genius? Dishonesty Can Lead to Greater Creativity," *Psychological Science* 25, no. 4 (2014), pp. 973–981.

82 S. N. de Jesus, C. L. Rus, W. Lens, and S. Imaginário, "Intrinsic Motivation and Creativity Related to Product: A Meta-analysis of the Studies Published Between 1990–2010," *Creativity Research Journal* 25 (2013), pp. 80–84.

83 A. Somech and A. Drach-Zahavy, "Translating Team Creativity to Innovation Implementation: The Role of Team Composition and Climate for Innovation," *Journal of Management* 39 (2013), pp. 684–708.

84 L. Sun, Z. Zhang, J. Qi, and Z. X. Chen, "Empowerment and Creativity: A Cross-Level Investigation," *Leadership Quarterly* 23 (2012), pp. 55–65.

85 M. Cerne, C. G. L. Nerstad, A. Dysvik, and M. Skerlavaj, "What Goes around Comes around: Knowledge Hiding, Perceived Motivational Climate, and Creativity," *Academy of Management Journal* 57, no. 1 (2014), pp. 172–192.

86 S. Sonnenshein, "How Organizations Foster the Creative Use of Resources," *Academy of Management Journal* 57, no. 3 (2014), pp. 814–848.

87 V. Venkataramani, A. W. Richter, and R. Clarke, "Creative Benefits from Well-Connected Leaders: Leader Social Network Ties as Facilitators of Employee Radical Creativity," *Journal of Applied Psychology* 99, no. 5 (2014), pp. 966–975.

88 J. E. Perry-Smith, "Social Network Ties beyond Nonredundancy: An Experimental Investigation of the Effect of Knowledge Content and Tie Strength on Creativity," *Journal of Applied Psychology* 99, no. 5 (2014), pp. 831–846.

89 D. Liu, H. Liao, and R. Loi, "The Dark Side of Leadership: A Three-Level Investigation of the Cascading Effect of Abusive Supervision on Employee Creativity," *Academy of Management Journal* 55 (2012), pp. 1187–1212.

90 J. B. Avey, F. L. Richmond, and D. R. Nixon, "Leader Positivity and Follower Creativity: An Experimental Analysis," *Journal of Creative Behavior* 46 (2012), pp. 99–118; and A. Rego, F. Sousa, C. Marques, and M. E. Cunha, "Authentic Leadership Promoting Employees' Psychological Capital and Creativity," *Journal of Business Research* 65 (2012), pp. 429–437.

91 I. J. Hoever, D. van Knippenberg, W. P. van Ginkel, and H. G. Barkema, "Fostering Team Creativity: Perspective Taking as Key to Unlocking Diversity's Potential," *Journal of Applied Psychology* 97 (2012), pp. 982–996.

92 S. J. Shin, T. Kim, J. Lee, and L. Bian, "Cognitive Team Diversity and Individual Team Member Creativity: A Cross-Level Interaction," *Academy of Management Journal* 55 (2012), pp. 197–212.

93 A. W. Richter, G. Hirst, D. van Knippenberg, and M. Baer, "Creative Self-Efficacy and Individual Creativity in Team Contexts: Cross-Level Interactions with Team Informational Resources," *Journal of Applied Psychology* 97 (2012), pp. 1282–1290.

94 X. Huang, J. J. Hsieh, and W. He, "Expertise Dissimilarity and Creativity: The Contingent Roles of Tacit and Explicit Knowledge Sharing," *Journal of Applied Psychology* 99, no. 5 (2014), pp. 816–830.

95 T. B. Harris, N. Li, W. R. Boswell, X.-A. Zhang, and Z. Xie, "Getting What's New from Newcomers: Empowering Leadership, Creativity, and Adjustment in the Socialization Context," *Personnel Psychology* 67 (2014), pp. 567–604.

96 A. H. Y. Hon, M. Bloom, and J. M. Crant, "Overcoming Resistance to Change and Enhancing Creative Performance," *Journal of Management* 40, no. 3 (2014), pp. 919–941.

97 J. S. Mueller, S. Melwani, and J. A. Goncalo, "The Bias against Creativity: Why People Desire but Reject Creative Ideas," *Psychological Science* 23 (2012), pp. 13–17.

98 T. Montag, C. P. Maertz, and M. Baer, "A Critical Analysis of the Workplace Creativity Criterion Space," *Journal of Management* 38 (2012), pp. 1362–1386.

99 M. Baer, "Putting Creativity to Work: The Implementation of Creative Ideas in Organizations," *Academy of Management Journal* 55 (2012), pp. 1102–1119.

100 Vignette based on E. Johnson, "'I Will Do Anything I Can to Make My Goal': TD Teller Says Customers Pay Price for 'Unrealistic' Sales Targets," *CBC News*, March 6, 2017, http://www.cbc.ca/news/canada/british-columbia/td-tellers-desperate-to-meet-increasing-sales-goals-1.4006743; and E. Johnson, "'We Do It because Our Jobs Are at Stake': TD Bank Employees Admit to Breaking the Law for Fear of Being Fired," *CBC News*, March 10, 2017, http://www.cbc.ca/news/business/td-bank-employees-admit-to-breaking-law-1.4016569.

101 K. V. Kortenkamp and C. F. Moore, "Ethics under Uncertainty: The Morality and Appropriateness of Utilitarianism When Outcomes Are Uncertain," *American Journal of Psychology* 127, no. 3 (2014), pp. 367–382.

102 A. Lukits, "Hello and Bonjour to Moral Dilemmas," *Wall Street Journal*, May 13, 2014, p. D4.

103 J. Hollings, "Let the Story Go: The Role of Emotion in the Decision-Making Process of the Reluctant, Vulnerable Witness or Whistle-Blower," *Journal of Business Ethics* 114, no. 3 (2013), pp. 501–512.

104 D. E. Rupp, P. M. Wright, S. Aryee, and Y. Luo, "Organizational Justice, Behavioral Ethics, and Corporate Social Responsibility: Finally the Three Shall Merge," *Management and Organization Review* 11 (2015), pp. 15–24.

105 P. L. Schumann, "A Moral Principles Framework for Human Resource Management Ethics," *Human Resource Management Review* 11 (Spring–Summer 2001), pp. 93–111.

106 J. Hazlewood, "AGT Food President Awarded International Prize by Nobel Laureates," *CBC News*, March 29, 2017, http://www.cbc.ca/news/canada/saskatoon/nobel-business-prize-al-katib-1.4045869.

107 Based on R. A. Bernardi, C. A. Banzhoff, A. M. Martino, and K. J. Savasta, "Challenges to Academic Integrity: Identifying the Factors Associated with the Cheating Chain," *Accounting Education* 21 (2012), pp. 247–263; M. K. Galloway, "Cheating in Advantaged High Schools: Prevalence, Justifications, and Possibilities for Change," *Ethics & Behavior* 22 (2012), pp. 378–399; and M. H. Bazerman and A. E. Tenbrunsel, *Blind Spots: Why We Fail to Do What's Right and What to Do about It* (Princeton, NJ: Princeton University Press, 2012).

108 L. L. Shu and F. Gino, "Sweeping Dishonesty Under the Rug: How Unethical Actions Lead to Forgetting of Moral Rules," *Journal of Personality and Social Psychology* 102 (2012), pp. 1164–1177.

109 B. C. Gunia, L. Wang, L. Huang, J. Wang, and J. K. Murnighan, "Contemplation and Conversation: Subtle Influences on Moral Decision Making," *Academy of Management Journal* 55 (2012), pp. 13–33.

110 R. F. West, R. J. Meserve, and K. E. Stanovich, "Cognitive Sophistication Does Not Attenuate the Bias Blind Spot," *Journal of Personality and Social Psychology* 103 (2012), pp. 506–519.

111 T. Jackson, "Cultural Values and Management Ethics: A 10-Nation Study," *Human Relations*, October 2001, pp. 1267–1302; see also J. B. Cullen, K. P. Parboteeah, and M. Hoegl, "Cross-National Differences in Managers' Willingness to Justify Ethically Suspect Behaviors: A Test of Institutional Anomie Theory," *Academy of Management Journal*, June 2004, pp. 411–421.

112 This discussion is based on G. F. Cavanagh, D. J. Moberg, and M. Valasquez, "The Ethics of Organizational Politics," *Academy of Management Journal*, June 1981, pp. 363–374.

113 J. Quittner, "Shopify Won't Remove Breitbart's Online Shop, Claiming Free Speech," *Fortune*, February 9, 2017, http://fortune.com/2017/02/09/shopify-wont-remove-breitbarts-online-shop-claiming-free-speech/.

114 Based on "Lac Mégantic: TSB Finds Company Had Weak Safety Culture," CBC.ca, August 19, 2014, http://www.cbc.ca/news/canada/montreal/lac-m%C3%A9gantic-tsb-finds-company-had-weak-safety-culture-1.2739921; and I. Peritz, "Lac-Mégantic Deaths Were Avoidable, Coroner's Report Says," *Globe and Mail*, October 8, 2014, http://www.theglobeandmail.com/news/national/lac-megantic-deaths-were-avoidable-coroners-report-says/article20982746/.

115 T. Rinne, D. G. Steel, and J. Fairweather, "The Role of Hofstede's Individualism in National-Level Creativity," *Creativity Research Journal* 25 (2013), pp. 129–136.

116 X. Yi, W. Hu, H. Scheithauer, and W. Niu, "Cultural and Bilingual Influences on Artistic Creativity Performances: Comparison of German and Chinese Students," *Creativity Research Journal* 25 (2013), pp. 97–108.

117 Transparency International, *Annual Report 2011* (Berlin, Germany: Author, 2012), http://www.transparency.org/content/download/61106/978536.

118 Based on S. Cain, "The Rise of the New Groupthink," *New York Times*, January 15, 2012, pp. 1, 6; and C. Faure, "Beyond Brainstorming: Effects of Different Group Procedures on Selection of Ideas and Satisfaction with the Process," *Journal of Creative Behavior* 38 (2004), pp. 13–34.

119 Several of these scenarios are based on D. R. Altany, "Torn between Halo and Horns," IndustryWeek, March 15, 1993, pp. 15–20.

120 Based on J. Mulkerrins, "All Spanx to Sara," *Daily Mail*, April 6, 2013, http://www.dailymail.co.uk/home/you/article-2303499/Meet-Spanx-creator-Sarah-Blakely.html; C. O'Connor, "American Booty," *Forbes*, March 26, 2012, pp. 172–178; and R. Tulshyan, "Spanx's Sara Blakely: Turning $5,000 into $1 Billion with Panties," *CNN.com*, December 5, 2012, http://www.cnn.com/2012/12/04/business/sara-blakely-spanx-underwear/.

121 Based on J. Calano and J. Salzman, "Ten Ways to Fire Up Your Creativity," *Working Woman*, July 1989, p. 94; J. V. Anderson, "Mind Mapping: A Tool for Creative Thinking," *Business Horizons*, January–February 1993, pp. 42–46; M. Loeb, "Ten Commandments for Managing Creative People," *Fortune*, January 16, 1995, pp. 135–136; and M. Henricks, "Good Thinking," *Entrepreneur*, May 1996, pp. 70–73.

OB on the Edge: Spirituality in the Workplace

1 A. Morrison, "'The Good Spirit' Metaphysical Shop Ready To Open In Gastown," *Scout Vancouver*, April 28, 2016, http://scoutmagazine.ca/2016/04/28/seen-in-vancouver-575-the-good-spirit-metaphysical-shop-ready-to-open-in-gastown/; H. A. Miller, "Inaugural Youth Entrepreneur Award Recognizes Unique Retail Effort," *Alberta Sweetgrass* 21, no. 3 (2014), http://www.ammsa.com/publications/alberta-sweetgrass/inaugural-youth-entrepreneur-award-recognizes-unique-retail-effort; and J. P. McGlynn, "Savannah Olsen and The Good Spirit," *Gastown*, June 7, 2016, http://gastown.org/savannah-olsen-and-the-good-spirit/.

2 Rice University, "More Than 20 Percent of Atheist Scientists Are 'Spiritual,' Study Finds," *ScienceDaily*, May 5, 2011, http://www.sciencedaily.com/releases/2011/05/110505124039.htm; and E. H. Ecklund and E. Long, "Scientists and Spirituality," *Sociology of Religion* 72, no. 3 (2011), pp. 253–274.

3 E. Poole, "Organisational Spirituality: A Literature Review," *Journal of Business Ethics* 84, no. 4 (2009), pp. 577–588.

4 L. W. Fry and J. W. Slocum, "Managing the Triple Bottom Line through Spiritual Leadership," *Organizational Dynamics* 37, no. 1 (2008), pp. 86–96.

5 B. E. Ashforth and M. G. Pratt, "Institutionalized Spirituality: An Oxymoron?" in *Handbook of Workplace Spirituality and Organizational Performance*, ed. R. A. Giacalone and C. L. Jurkiewicz (Armonk, NY: M. E. Sharpe, 2010), pp. 44–58; and A. M. Saks, "Workplace Spirituality and Employee Engagement," *Journal of Management, Spirituality & Religion* 8, no. 4 (2011), pp. 317–340.

6 V. Ligo, "Configuring a Christian Spirituality of Work," *Theology Today*, 2011, pp. 441–466.

7 A. Beard, "Mindfulness in the Age of Complexity," *Harvard Business Review*, March 2014, pp. 68–73, https://hbr.org/2014/03/mindfulness-in-the-age-of-complexity.

8 A. Beard, "Mindfulness in the Age of Complexity," *Harvard Business Review*, March 2014, pp. 68–73, https://hbr.org/2014/03/mindfulness-in-the-age-of-complexity.

9 A. Beard, "Mindfulness in the Age of Complexity," *Harvard Business Review*, March 2014, pp. 68–73, https://hbr.org/2014/03/mindfulness-in-the-age-of-complexity.

10 A. Beard, "Mindfulness in the Age of Complexity," *Harvard Business Review*, March 2014, pp. 68–73, https://hbr.org/2014/03/mindfulness-in-the-age-of-complexity.

11 W. Immen, "Meditation Finds an Ommm in the Office," *Globe and Mail*, November 27, 2012, http://www.theglobeandmail.com/report-on-business/small-business/sb-managing/human-resources/meditation-finds-an-ommm-in-the-office/article5684202/.

12 L. S. Colzato, A. Szapora, D. Lippelt, and B. Hommel, "Prior Meditation Practice Modulates Performance and Strategy Use in Convergent- and Divergent-Thinking Problems," *Mindfulness*, October 2014.

13 J. D. Creswell, L. E. Pacilio, E. K. Lindsay, and K. W. Brown, "Brief Mindfulness Meditation Training Alters Psychological and Neuroendocrine Responses to Social Evaluative Stress," *Psychoneuroendocrinology* 44 (June 2014), pp. 1–12.

14 A. C. Hafenbrack, Z. Kinias, and S. G. Barsade, "Debiasing the Mind through Meditation: Mindfulness and the Sunk-Cost Bias," *Psychological Science* 25, no. 2 (2013), pp. 369–376.

15 W. Immen, "Meditation Finds an Ommm in the Office," *Globe and Mail*, November 27, 2012, http://www.theglobeandmail.com/report-on-business/small-business/sb-managing/human-resources/meditation-finds-an-ommm-in-the-office/article5684202/.

16 M. Gonzalez, *Mindful Leadership: The 9 Ways to Self-Awareness, Transforming Yourself, and Inspiring Others* (Mississauga: John Wiley and Sons, 2012).

17 W. Immen, "Meditation Finds an Ommm in the Office," *Globe and Mail*, November 27, 2012, http://www.theglobeandmail.com/report-on-business/small-business/sb-managing/human-resources/meditation-finds-an-ommm-in-the-office/article5684202/.

18 S. McGreevey, "Turn Down the Volume," *Harvard Gazette*, April 22, 2011, http://news.harvard.edu/gazette/story/2011/04/%E2%80%98turn-down-the-volume%E2%80%99/.

19 M. Goyal, S. Singh, E. M. S. Sibinga, N. F. Gould, A. Rowland-Seymour, R. Sharma, Z. Berger, D. Sleicher, D. D. Maron, H. M. Shihab, P. D. Ranasinghe, S. Linn, S. Saha, E. B. Bass, and J. A. Haythornthwaite, "Meditation Programs for Psychological Stress and Well-Being: A Systematic Review and Meta-analysis," *JAMA Internal Medicine* 174, no. 3 (2014), pp. 357–368.

20 T. L. Jacobs, P. R. Shaver, E. S. Epel, A. P. Zanesco, S. R. Aichele, D. A. Bridwell, E. I. Rosenberg, B. G. King, K. A. Maclean, B. K. Sahdra, M. E. Kemeny, E. Ferrer, B. A. Wallace, and C. D. Saron, "Self-reported Mindfulness and Cortisol during a Shamatha Meditation Retreat," *Health Psychology* 32, no. 10 (October 2013), pp. 1104–1109.

21 W. Duggleby, D. Cooper, and K. Penz, "Hope, Self-Efficacy, Spiritual Well-Being and Job Satisfaction," *Journal of Advanced Nursing* 65, no. 11 (November 2009), pp. 2376–2385.

22 Information based on "About Us," *Vancouver Island Health Authority*, accessed November 27, 2014, http://www.viha.ca/spiritual_care/about/.

23 "The Best Canadian Companies to Work for in 2014," *Business Review Canada*, November 25, 2013, http://www.businessreviewcanada.ca/leadership/10/The-best-Canadian-companies-to-work-for-in-2014.

24 "Canadians Are Impatient, But Seek Serenity: Trend Part 1," *JWT Canada*, February 10, 2014, https://www.jwt.com/en/canada/thinking/canadiansareimpatientbutseekserenitytrendpart1/.

25 C. L. Jurkiewicz and R. A. Giacalone, "A Values Framework for Measuring the Impact of Workplace Spirituality on Organizational Performance," *Journal of Business Ethics* 49, no. 2 (2004), pp. 129–142.

26 D. McDonald, "A Colourful Commitment to Craft Leads to UFV Honorary Degree for Charllotte Kwon," *UFV Today*, June 11, 2014.

27 A. Daniels, "Textile Importer Defends Artisans' Rights," *Vancouver Sun*, May 1, 2000, pp. C8, C10.

28 "Get to Know Our Management Team," *Reaume Chev/Buick/GMC*, accessed November 27, 2014, http://www.reaumechev.com/contact-us-our-managers.

29 R. Johnson, "Polling Religion in Canada," *National Post*, December 21, 2012 (based on a 2012 Forum Research poll, commissioned exclusively for the *National Post*).

30 I. I. Mitroff and E. A. Denton, *A Spiritual Audit of Corporate America: A Hard Look at Spirituality, Religion, and Values in the Workplace* (San Francisco: Jossey-Bass, 1999).

31 See, for example, B. S. Pawar, "Workplace Spirituality Facilitation: A Comprehensive Model," *Journal of Business Ethics* 90, no. 3 (2009), pp. 375–386; and L. Lambert, *Spirituality Inc.: Religion in the American Workplace* (New York: New York University Press, 2009).

32 M. Oppenheimer, "The Rise of the Corporate Chaplain," *Bloomberg Businessweek*, August 23, 2012, pp. 58–61.

33 M. Lips-Miersma, K. L. Dean, and C. J. Fornaciari, "Theorizing the Dark Side of the Workplace Spirituality Movement," *Journal of Management Inquiry* 18, no. 4 (2009), pp. 288–300.

34 J.-C. Garcia-Zamor, "Workplace Spirituality and Organizational Performance," *Public Administration Review*, May–June 2003, pp. 355–363; and L. W. Fry, S. T. Hannah, M. Noel, and F. O. Walumbwa, "Impact of Spiritual Leadership on Unit Performance," *Leadership Quarterly* 22, no. 2 (2011), pp. 259–270.

35 A. Rego and M. Pina e Cunha, "Workplace Spirituality and Organizational Commitment: An Empirical Study," *Journal of Organizational Change Management* 21, no. 1 (2008), pp. 53–75; R. W. Kolodinsky, R. A. Giacalone, and C. L. Jurkiewicz, "Workplace Values and Outcomes: Exploring Personal, Organizational, and Interactive Workplace Spirituality," *Journal of Business Ethics* 81, no. 2 (2008), pp. 465–480; and M. Gupta, V. Kumar, and M. Singh, "Creating Satisfied Employees through Workplace Spirituality: A Study of the Private Insurance Sector in Punjab India," *Journal of Business Ethics* 122 (2014), pp. 79–88.

36 Cited in A. M. Saks, "Workplace Spirituality and Employee Engagement," *Journal of Management, Spirituality & Religion* 8, no. 4 (2011), pp. 317–340.

Chapter 13

1   Vignette based on https://www.holacracy.org/how-it-works/; and K. Wilkinson, "Holacracy Empowers Employees by Getting Rid of Bosses," *Canadian Business*, March 31, 2014, http://www.canadianbusiness.com/business-strategy/holacracy/.

2   L. Garicano and Y. Wu, "Knowledge, Communication, and Organizational Capabilities," *Organization Science*, September–October 2012, pp. 1382–1397.

3   See, for instance, R. L. Daft, *Organization Theory and Design*, 10th ed. (Cincinnati, OH: South-Western Publishing, 2010).

4   J. G. Miller, "The Real Women's Issue: Time," *Wall Street Journal*, March 9–10, 2013, p. C3.

5   T. W. Malone, R. J. Laubacher, and T. Johns, "The Age of Hyperspecialization," *Harvard Business Review*, July–August 2011, pp. 56–65.

6   J. Schramm, "A Cloud of Workers," *HR Magazine*, March 2013, p. 80.

7   C. Woodyard, "Toyota Brass Shakeup Aims to Give Regions More Control," *USA Today*, March 6, 2013, http://www.usatoday.com/story/money/cars/2013/03/06/toyota-shakeup/1966489/.

8   C. Hymowitz, "Managers Suddenly Have to Answer to a Crowd of Bosses," *Wall Street Journal*, August 12, 2003, p. B1.

9   "How Hierarchy Can Hurt Strategy Execution," *Harvard Business Review*, July–August 2010, pp. 74–75.

10 See, for example, J. H. Gittell, "Supervisory Span, Relational Coordination, and Flight Departure Performance: A Reassessment of Postbureaucracy Theory," *Organization Science*, July–August 2001, pp. 468–483.

11 J. Child and R. G. McGrath, "Organizations Unfettered: Organizational Form in an Information-Intensive Economy," *Academy of Management Journal*, December 2001, pp. 1135–1148.

12 F. A. Csascar, "Organizational Structure as a Determinant of Performance: Evidence from Mutual Funds," *Strategic Management Journal*, June 2013, pp. 611–632.

13 B. Brown and S. D. Anthony, "How P&G Tripled Its Innovation Success Rate," *Harvard Business Review*, June 2011, pp. 64–72.

14 A. Leiponen and C. E. Helfat, "Location, Decentralization, and Knowledge Sources for Innovation," *Organization Science* 22, no. 3 (2011), pp. 641–658.

15 K. Parks, "HSBC Unit Charged in Argentine Tax Case," *Wall Street Journal*, March 19, 2013, p. C2.

16 G. Morgan, *Images of Organization* (Newbury Park, CA: Sage, 1986), p. 21.

17 P. Hempel, Z.-X. Zhang, and Y. Han, "Team Empowerment and the Organizational Context: Decentralization and the Contrasting Effects of Formalization," *Journal of Management*, March 2012, pp. 475–501.

18 J. E. Perry-Smith and C. E. Shalley, "A Social Composition View of Team Creativity: The Role of Member Nationality-Heterogeneous Ties Outside of the Team," *Organization Science* 25 (2014), pp. 1434–1452; J. Han, J. Han, and D. J. Brass, "Human Capital Diversity in the Creation of Social Capital for Team Creativity," *Journal of Organizational Behavior* 35 (2014), pp. 54–71; and N. Sivasubramaniam, S. J. Liebowitz, and C. L. Lackman, "Determinants of New Product Development Team Performance: A Meta-analytic Review," *Journal of Product Innovation Management* 29 (2012), pp. 803–820.

19 N. J. Foss, K. Laursen, and T. Pedersen, "Linking Customer Interaction and Innovation: The Mediating Role of New Organizational Practices," *Organization Science* 22 (2011), pp. 980–999; N. J. Foss, J. Lyngsie, and S. A. Zahra, "The Role of External Knowledge Sources and Organizational Design in the Process of Opportunity Exploitation," *Strategic Management Journal* 34 (2013), pp. 1453–1471; A. Salter, P. Crisuolo, and A. L. J. Ter Wal, "Coping with Open Innovation: Responding to the Challenges of External Engagement in R&D," *California Management Review* 56 (Winter 2014), pp. 77–94.

20 T. A. de Vries, F. Walter, G. S. Van der Vegt, and P. J. M. D. Essens, "Antecedents of Individuals' Interteam Coordination: Broad Functional Experiences as a Mixed Blessing," *Academy of Management Journal* 57 (2014), pp. 1334–1359.

21 A. Murray, "Built Not to Last," *Wall Street Journal*, March 18, 2013, p. A11.

22 For a quick overview, see J. Davoren, "Functional Structure Organization Strength and Weakness," *Small Business Chronicle*, accessed June 25, 2015, http://smallbusiness.chron.com/functional-structure-organization-strength-weakness-60111.html.

23 See, for instance, A. Writing, "Different Types of Organizational Structure," *Small Business Chronicle*, accessed June 25, 2015, http://smallbusiness.chron.com/different-types-organizational-structure-723.html.

24 For a quick overview, see "Types of Business Organizational Structures," Pingboard, July 24, 2013, https://pingboard.com/blog/types-business-organizational-structures/.

25 J. R. Galbraith, *Designing Matrix Organizations That Actually Work: How IBM, Procter & Gamble, and Others Design for Success* (San Francisco: Jossey Bass, 2009); and E. Krell, "Managing the Matrix," *HR Magazine*, April 2011, pp. 69–71.

26 See, for instance, M. Bidwell, "Politics and Firm Boundaries: How Organizational Structure, Group Interests, and Resources Affect Outsourcing," *Organization Science*, November–December 2012, pp. 1622–1642.

27 See, for example, T. Sy and L. S. D'Annunzio, "Challenges and Strategies of Matrix Organizations: Top-Level and Mid-Level Managers' Perspectives," *Human Resource Planning* 28, no. 1 (2005), pp. 39–48; and T. Sy and S. Cote, "Emotional Intelligence: A Key Ability to Succeed in the Matrix Organization," *Journal of Management Development* 23, no. 5 (2004), pp. 437–455.

28 Based on I. Tossell, "Say Goodbye to Hierarchy, Hello to Holacracy," *Globe and Mail*, March 25, 2017, https://beta.theglobeandmail.com/report-on-business/rob-magazine/disruption-no-boss-needed-in-a-holacracy/article20198587/?ref=http://www.theglobeandmail.com&.

29 N. Anand and R. L. Daft, "What Is the Right Organization Design?" *Organizational Dynamics* 36, no. 4 (2007), pp. 329–344.

30 See, for example, N. S. Contractor, S. Wasserman, and K. Faust, "Testing Multitheoretical, Multilevel Hypotheses about Organizational Networks: An Analytic Framework and Empirical Example," *Academy of Management Review* 31, no. 3 (2006), pp. 681–703; and Y. Shin, "A Person-Environment Fit Model for Virtual Organizations," *Journal of Management*, October 2004, pp. 725–743.

31 "Why Do Canadian Companies Opt for Cooperative Ventures?" *Micro: The Micro-Economic Research Bulletin* 4, no. 2 (1997), pp. 3–5.

32 J. Schramm, "At Work in a Virtual World," *HR Magazine*, June 2010, p. 152.

33 C. B. Gibson and J. L. Gibbs, "Unpacking the Concept of Virtuality: The Effects of Geographic Dispersion, Electronic Dependence, Dynamic Structure, and National Diversity on Team Innovation," *Administrative Science Quarterly* 51, no. 3 (2006), pp. 451–495; H. M. Latapie and V. N. Tran, "Subculture Formation, Evolution, and Conflict Between Regional Teams in Virtual Organizations," *Business Review*, Summer 2007, pp. 189–193; and S. Davenport and U. Daellenbach, "'Belonging' to a Virtual Research Center: Exploring the Influence of Social Capital Formation Processes on Member Identification in a Virtual Organization," *British Journal of Management* 22, no. 1 (2011), pp. 54–76.

34 A. Poon and K. Tally, "Yoga-Pants Supplier Says Lululemon Stretches Truth," *Wall Street Journal*, March 20, 2013, p. B1.

35 Based on T. Johns and L. Gratton, "The Third Wave of Virtual Work," *Harvard Business Review*, January–February 2013, pp. 66–73; R. E. Silverman, "Step Into the Office-Less Company," *Wall Street Journal*, September 15, 2012, p. B6; and R. E. Silverman, "Tracking Sensors Invade the Workplace," *Wall Street Journal*, March 7, 2013, p. B1.

36 See, for instance, E. Devaney, "The Pros & Cons of 7 Popular Organizational Structures," accessed June 25, 2015, http://blog.hubspot.com/marketing/team-structure-diagrams.

37 J. Scheck, L. Moloney, and A. Flynn, "Eni, CNPC Link Up in Mozambique," *Wall Street Journal*, March 15, 2013, p. B3.

38 E. Devaney, "The Pros & Cons of 7 Popular Organizational Structures," accessed June 25, 2015, http://blog.hubspot.com/marketing/team-structure-diagrams.

39 P. Evans, "Sears Canada to Close 59 Stores, Lay Off 2,900 in Restructuring," *CBC News*, June 22, 2017, http://www.cbc.ca/news/business/sears-canada-ccaa-1.4172736.

40 S. Brady, "American Express Kicks Off 2013 with Biggest Layoffs in Four Years," *Brand Channel*, January 10, 2013, http://www.brandchannel.com/home/post/American-Express-Layoffs-011013.aspx.

41 L. Gensler, "American Express to Slash 4,000 Jobs on Heels of Strong Quarter," *Forbes*, January 21, 2015, http://www.forbes.com/sites/laurengensler/2015/01/21/american-express-earnings-rise-11-on-increased-cardholder-spending/.

42 C. Giammona, "Starbucks First-Quarter Profit Surges 82% as Food Sales Gain," *Bloomberg Business*, January 22, 2015, http://www.bloomberg.com/news/articles/2015-01-22/starbucks-first-quarter-profit-surges-82-as-food-sales-increase.

43 C. D. Zatzick and R. D. Iverson, "High-Involvement Management and Workforce Reduction: Competitive Advantage or Disadvantage?" *Academy of Management Journal* 49, no. 5 (2006), pp. 999–1015; A. Travaglione and B. Cross, "Diminishing the Social Network in Organizations: Does There Need to Be Such a Phenomenon as 'Survivor Syndrome' After Downsizing?" *Strategic Change* 15, no. 1 (2006), pp. 1–13; and J. D. Kammeyer-Mueller, H. Liao, and R. D. Arvey, "Downsizing and Organizational Performance: A Review of the Literature from a Stakeholder Perspective," *Research in Personnel and Human Resources Management* 20 (2001), pp. 269–329.

44 Vignette based on K. Wilkinson, "Holacracy Empowers Employees by Getting Rid of Bosses," *Canadian Business*, March 31, 2014, http://www.canadianbusiness.com/business-strategy/holacracy/.

45 K. Walker, N. Ni, and B. Dyck, "Recipes for Successful Sustainability: Empirical Organizational Configurations for Strong Corporate Environmental Performance," *Business Strategy and the Environment* 24, no. 1 (2015), pp. 40–57.

46 See, for instance, J. R. Hollenbeck, H. Moon, A. P. J. Ellis, B. J. West, D. R. Ilgen, L. Sheppard, C. O. L. H. Porter, and J. A. Wagner III, "Structural Contingency Theory and Individual Differences: Examination of External and Internal Person-Team Fit," *Journal of Applied Psychology*, June 2002, 599–606; and A. Drach-Zahavy and A. Freund, "Team Effectiveness Under Stress: A Structural Contingency Approach," *Journal of Organizational Behavior* 28, no. 4 (2007), pp. 423–450.

47 K. Walker, N. Ni, and B. Dyck, "Recipes for Successful Sustainability: Empirical Organizational Configurations for Strong Corporate Environmental Performance," *Business Strategy and the Environment* 24, no. 1 (2015), pp. 40–57.

48 See, for instance, S. M. Toh, F. P. Morgeson, and M. A. Campion, "Human Resource Configurations: Investigating Fit with the Organizational Context," *Journal of Applied Psychology* 93, no. 4 (2008), pp. 864–882.

49 M. Mesco, "Moleskine Tests Appetite for IPOs," *Wall Street Journal*, March 19, 2013, p. B8.

50 J. Backaler, "Haier: A Chinese Company that Innovates," *Forbes*, June 17, 2010, http://www.forbes.com/sites/china/2010/06/17/haier-a-chinese-company-that-innovates/.

51 See C. Perrow, "A Framework for the Comparative Analysis of Organizations," *American Sociological Review*, April 1967, pp. 194–208; J. Hage and M. Aiken, "Routine Technology, Social Structure, and Organizational Goals," *Administrative Science Quarterly*, September 1969, pp. 366–377; C. C. Miller, W. H. Glick, Y. Wang, and G. P. Huber, "Understanding Technology-Structure Relationships: Theory Development and Meta-analytic Theory Testing," *Academy of Management Journal*, June 1991, pp. 370–399; and W. D. Sine, H. Mitsuhashi, and D. A. Kirsch, "Revisiting Burns and Stalker: Formal Structure and New Venture Performance in Emerging Economic Sectors," *Academy of Management Journal* 49, no. 1 (2006), pp. 121–132.

52 See, for instance, J. A. Cogin and I. O. Williamson, "Standardize or Customize: The Interactive Effects of HRM and Environment Uncertainty on MNC Subsidiary Performance," *Human Resource Management* 53, no. 5 (2014), pp. 701–721; and G. Kim and M.-G. Huh, "Exploration and Organizational Longevity: The Moderating Role of Strategy and Environment," *Asia Pacific Journal of Management* 32, no. 2 (2015), pp. 389–414.

53 R. Greenwood, C. R. Hinings, and D. Whetten, "Rethinking Institutions and Organizations," *Journal of Management Studies* 51 (2014), pp. 1206–1220; and D. Chandler and H. Hwang, "Learning from Learning Theory: A Model of Organizational Adoption Strategies at the Microfoundations of Institutional Theory," *Journal of Management* 41 (2015), pp. 1446–1476.

54 Vignette based on D. Aarts, "The Utopian Dream of a 'Flat Hierarchy' is Actually a Nightmare," *Canadian Business*, May 2, 2016, http://www.canadianbusiness.com/blogs-and-comment/the-utopian-dream-of-a-flat-hierarchy-is-actually-a-nightmare/; and R. D. Hodge, "First, Let's Get Rid of All the Bosses," *New Republic*, October 4, 2015, https://newrepublic.com/article/122965/can-billion-dollar-corporation-zappos-be-self-organized.

55 C. S. Spell and T. J. Arnold, "A Multi-Level Analysis of Organizational Justice and Climate, Structure, and Employee Mental Health," *Journal of Management* 33, no. 5 (2007), pp. 724–751; and M. L. Ambrose and M. Schminke, "Organization Structure as a Moderator of the Relationship Between Procedural Justice, Interactional Justice, Perceived Organizational Support, and Supervisory Trust," *Journal of Applied Psychology* 88, no. 2 (2003), pp. 295–305.

56 See, for instance, C. S. Spell and T. J. Arnold, "A Multi-Level Analysis of Organizational Justice Climate, Structure, and Employee Mental Health," *Journal of Management* 33, no. 5 (2007), pp. 724–751; J. D. Shaw and N. Gupta, "Job Complexity, Performance, and Well-Being: When Does Supplies-Values Fit Matter?" *Personnel Psychology* 57, no. 4 (2004), pp. 847–879; and C. Anderson and C. E. Brown, "The Functions and Dysfunctions of Hierarchy," *Research in Organizational Behavior* 30 (2010), pp. 55–89.

57 Based on P. Puranam, M. Raveendran, and T. Knudsen, "Organization Design: The Epistemic Interdependence Perspective," *Academy of Management Review* 37, no. 3 (2012), pp. 419–440; and R. E. Silverman and Q. Fottrell, "The Home Office in the Spotlight," *Wall Street Journal*, February 27, 2013, p. B6.

58 T. Martin, "Pharmacies Feel More Heat," *Wall Street Journal*, March 16–17, 2013, p. A3.

59 See, for instance, R. E. Ployhart, J. A. Weekley, and K. Baughman, "The Structure and Function of Human Capital Emergence: A Multilevel Examination of the Attraction-Selection-Attrition Model," *Academy of Management Journal* 49, no. 4 (2006), pp. 661–677.

60   J. B. Stewart, "A Place to Play for Google Staff," *New York Times*, March 16, 2013, p. B1.

61   P. Dvorak, "Making U.S. Management Ideas Work Elsewhere," *Wall Street Journal*, May 22, 2006, p. B3.

62   See, for example, B. K. Park, J. A. Choi, M. Koo, S. Sul, and I. Choi, "Culture, Self, and Preference Structure: Transitivity and Context Independence Are Violated More by Interdependent People," *Social Cognition*, February 2013, pp. 106–118.

63   J. Hassard, J. Morris, and L. McCann, "'My Brilliant Career'? New Organizational Forms and Changing Managerial Careers in Japan, the UK, and USA," *Journal of Management Studies*, May 2012, pp. 571–599.

64   Based on A. Bryant, "Structure? The Flatter the Better," *New York Times*, January 17, 2010, p. BU2; "Honeywell International: From Bitter to Sweet," *Economist*, April 14, 2012, http://www.economist.com/node/21552631; A. Efrati and S. Morrison, "Chief Seeks More Agile Google," *Wall Street Journal*, January 22, 2011, pp. B1, B4; H. El Nasser, "What Office? Laptops Are Workspace," *USA Today*, June 6, 2012; *Fortune* 500 rankings, http://money.cnn.com/magazines/fortune/fortune500/2012/full_list/; "Honeywell | Company Structure Information from ICIS," ICIS.com, accessed November 12, 2014, http://www.icis.com/v2/companies/9145292/honeywell/structure.html; K. Linebaugh, "Honeywell's Hiring Is Bleak," *Wall Street Journal*, March 6, 2013, p. B3; A. Murray, "The End of Management," *Wall Street Journal*, August 21, 2010, p. W3; A. R. Sorkin, "Delegator in Chief," *New York Times*, April 24, 2011, p. B4; and S. Tully, "How Dave Cote Got Honeywell's Groove Back," *CNN Money*, May 14, 2012, http://management.fortune.cnn.com/2012/05/14/500-honeywell-cote/.

65   M. Kaufman, "The Wisdom of Job Insecurity," *Forbes*, October 3, 2014, http://www.forbes.com/sites/michakaufman/2014/10/03/the-wisdom-of-job-insecurity-dont-be-lulled-by-falling-unemployment/; C. Van Gorder, "A No-Layoffs Policy Can Work, Even in an Unpredictable Economy," *Harvard Business Review*, January 26, 2015, https://hbr.org/2015/01/a-no-layoffs-policy-can-work-even-in-an-unpredictable-economy; J. Zumbrun, "Is Your Job 'Routine'? If So, It's Probably Disappearing," *Wall Street Journal*, April 8, 2015, http://blogs.wsj.com/economics/2015/04/08/is-your-job-routine-if-so-its-probably-disappearing/; and U. Kinnunen, A. Mäkikangas, S. Mauno, N. De Cuyper, and H. De Witte, "Development of Perceived Job Insecurity across Two Years: Associations with Antecedents and Employee Outcomes," *Journal of Occupational Health Psychology* 19 (2014), pp. 243–258.

66   Based on C. Mainemelis, "Stealing Fire: Creative Deviance in the Evolution of New Ideas," *Academy of Management Review* 35, no. 4 (2010), pp. 558–578; and A. Lashinsky, "Inside Apple," *Fortune*, May 23, 2011, pp. 125–134.

67   Based on P. J. Sauer, "Open-Door Management," *Inc.*, June 2003, p. 44; and "Not Just Jobs. Opportunities," *TechTarget.com*, accessed November 12, 2014, http://www.techtarget.com/html/job_opps.htm.

68   Based on S. P. Robbins and P. L. Hunsaker, *Training in Interpersonal Skills*, 3rd ed. (Upper Saddle River, NJ: Prentice Hall, 2003), pp. 95–98.

Chapter 14

1   Vignette based on The Associated Press, "Ringling Bros. Closing Curtain on Namesake Circus After 146 years," *CBC News*, January 16, 2017, http://www.cbc.ca/news/world/ringling-bros-circus-ending-1.3936551; and R. Marowits, "Cirque du Soleil Founder Sells Company, Refuses to Pass It to His Children," *Canadian Business*, April 20, 2015, http://www.canadianbusiness.com/business-news/newsalert-cirque-du-soleil-sells-majority-stake-to-u-s-private-equity-firm/.

2   A. Chowdhry, "Apple Surpassed Samsung as Global Phone Market Leader, Says Report," *Forbes*, March 3, 2015, http://www.forbes.

com/sites/amitchowdhry/2015/03/04/apple-passes-samsung/; and https://www.statista.com/statistics/263401/global-apple-iphone-sales-since-3rd-quarter-2007/; https://www.digitaltrends.com/mobile/2016-smartphone-sales/; https://www.fastcompany.com/3056069/samsung-again-easily-sells-more-phones-than-apple-in-q4; and https://www.recode.net/2017/2/26/14742598/blackberry-sales-market-share-chart.

3   See, for example, K. H. Hammonds, "Practical Radicals," *Fast Company*, September 2000, pp. 162–174; and P. C. Judge, "Change Agents," *Fast Company*, November 2000, pp. 216–226.

4   A. Finder, P. D. Healy, and K. Zernike, "President of Harvard Resigns, Ending Stormy 5-Year Tenure," *New York Times*, February 22, 2006, pp. A1, A19.

5   Vignette based on D. Neisser, "How Cirque Du Soleil Contorts to Create Change," *Advertising Age*, December 14, 2016, http://adage.com/article/cmo-strategy/cirque-du-soleil-contorts-create-change/307141/; and R. Leach, "Major changes at Cirque's 'The Beatles Love' are two years in the making," *Las Vegas Sun*, February 16, 2016, https://lasvegassun.com/vegasdeluxe/2016/feb/16/major-changes-cirque-beatles-love-two-years-making/.

6   See, for instance, J. Manchester, D. L. Gray-Miceli, J. A. Metcalf, C. A. Paolini, A. H. Napier, C. L. Coogle, and M. G. Owens, "Facilitating Lewin's Change Model with Collaborative Evaluation in Promoting Evidence-Based Practices of Health Professionals," *Evaluation and Program Planning*, December 2014, pp. 82–90.

7   P. G. Audia, E. A. Locke, and K. G. Smith, "The Paradox of Success: An Archival and a Laboratory Study of Strategic Persistence Following Radical Environmental Change," *Academy of Management Journal*, October 2000, pp. 837–853; and P. G. Audia and S. Brion, "Reluctant to Change: Self-Enhancing Responses to Diverging Performance Measures," *Organizational Behavior and Human Decision Processes* 102, no. 2 (2007), pp. 255–269.

8   See, for instance, J. Kim, "Use of Kotter's Leading Change Model to Develop and Implement a Heart Failure Education Program for Certified Nursing Assistants in a Long-Term Care Facility," *Nursing Research* 64, no. 2 (2015), p. E35; and J. Pollack and R. Pollack, "Using Kotter's Eight Stage Process to Manage an Organisational Change Program: Presentation and Practice," *Systemic Practice and Action Research* 28, no. 1 (2015), pp. 41–66.

9   See, for example, L. S. Lüscher and M. W. Lewis, "Organizational Change and Managerial Sensemaking: Working through Paradox," *Academy of Management Journal* 51, no. 2 (2008), pp. 221–240.

10   See, for example, B. Verleysen, F. Lambrechts, and F. Van Acker, "Building Psychological Capital with Appreciative Inquiry: Investigating the Mediating Role of Basic Psychological Need Satisfaction," *Journal of Applied Behavioral Science* 51, no. 1 (2015), pp. 10–35; G. R. Bushe, "How Has AI Lived Up to Promises, What Is Its Future?" *AI Practitioner* 18, no. 1 (2016); and G. R. Bushe, "A Comparative Case Study of Appreciative Inquiries in One Organization: Implications for Practice," *Review of Research and Social Intervention* 29 (2010), pp. 7–24.

11   G. R. Bushe, "A Comparative Case Study of Appreciative Inquiries in One Organization: Implications for Practice," *Review of Research and Social Intervention* 29 (2010), pp. 7–24.

12   G. R. Bushe, "A Comparative Case Study of Appreciative Inquiries in One Organization: Implications for Practice," *Review of Research and Social Intervention* 29 (2010), pp. 7–24.

13   G. R. Bushe, "How Has AI Lived Up to Promises, What Is Its Future?" *AI Practitioner* 18, no. 1 (2016).

14   Vignette based on R. Leach, "Major Changes at Cirque's 'The Beatles Love' Are Two Years in the Making," *Las Vegas Sun*, February 16, 2016, https://lasvegassun.com/vegasdeluxe/2016/feb/16/major-changes-cirque-beatles-love-two-years-making/.

15 P. G. Audia and S. Brion, "Reluctant to Change: Self-Enhancing Responses to Diverging Performance Measures," *Organizational Behavior and Human Decision Processes* 102 (2007), pp. 255–269.

16 M. Fugate, A. J. Kinicki, and G. E. Prussia, "Employee Coping with Organizational Change: An Examination of Alternative Theoretical Perspectives and Models," *Personnel Psychology* 61, no. 1 (2008), pp. 1–36.

17 R. B. L. Sijbom, O. Janssen, and N. W. Van Yperen, "How to Get Radical Creative Ideas into a Leader's Mind? Leader's Achievement Goals and Subordinates' Voice of Creative Ideas," *European Journal of Work and Organizational Psychology* 24 (2015), pp. 279–296.

18 J. D. Ford, L. W. Ford, and A. D'Amelio, "Resistance to Change: The Rest of the Story," *Academy of Management Review* 33, no. 2 (2008), pp. 362–377.

19 Based on J. P. Kotter and L. A. Schlesinger, "Choosing Strategies for Change," *Harvard Business Review*, July–August 2008, pp. 130–139.

20 D. Katz and R. L. Kahn, *The Social Psychology of Organizations*, 2nd ed. (New York: Wiley, 1978), pp. 714–715.

21 J. P. Kotter and L. A. Schlesinger, "Choosing Strategies for Change," *Harvard Business Review*, March–April 1979, pp. 106–114.

22 P. C. Fiss and E. J. Zajac, "The Symbolic Management of Strategic Change: Sensegiving via Framing and Decoupling," *Academy of Management Journal* 49, no. 6 (2006), pp. 1173–1193.

23 A. E. Rafferty and S. L. D. Restubog, "The Impact of Change Process and Context on Change Reactions and Turnover during a Merger," *Journal of Management* 36, no. 5 (2010), pp. 1309–1338.

24 Q. N. Huy, "Emotional Balancing of Organizational Continuity and Radical Change: The Contribution of Middle Managers," *Administrative Science Quarterly*, March 2002, pp. 31–69; D. M. Herold, D. B. Fedor, and S. D. Caldwell, "Beyond Change Management: A Multilevel Investigation of Contextual and Personal Influences on Employees' Commitment to Change," *Journal of Applied Psychology* 92, no. 4 (2007), pp. 942–951; and G. B. Cunningham, "The Relationships among Commitment to Change, Coping with Change, and Turnover Intentions," *European Journal of Work and Organizational Psychology* 15, no. 1 (2006), pp. 29–45.

25 R. Peccei, A. Giangreco, and A. Sebastiano, "The Role of Organizational Commitment in the Analysis of Resistance to Change: Co-predictor and Moderator Effects," *Personnel Review* 40, no. 2 (2011), pp. 185–204.

26 J. P. Kotter, "Leading Change: Why Transformational Efforts Fail," *Harvard Business Review*, January 2007, pp. 96–103.

27 K. van Dam, S. Oreg, and B. Schyns, "Daily Work Contexts and Resistance to Organisational Change: The Role of Leader-Member Exchange, Development Climate, and Change Process Characteristics," *Applied Psychology: An International Review* 57, no. 2 (2008), pp. 313–334.

28 A. H. Y. Hon, M. Bloom, and J. M. Crant, "Overcoming Resistance to Change and Enhancing Creative Performance," *Journal of Management* 40 (2014), pp. 919–941.

29 S. Oreg and N. Sverdlik, "Ambivalence toward Imposed Change: The Conflict between Dispositional Resistance to Change and the Orientation toward the Change Agent," *Journal of Applied Psychology* 96, no. 2 (2011), pp. 337–349.

30 D. B. Fedor, S. Caldwell, and D. M. Herold, "The Effects of Organizational Changes on Employee Commitment: A Multilevel Investigation," *Personnel Psychology* 59 (2006), pp. 1–29.

31 S. Oreg, "Personality, Context, and Resistance to Organizational Change," *European Journal of Work and Organizational Psychology* 15, no. 1 (2006), pp. 73–101.

32 S. M. Elias, "Employee Commitment in Times of Change: Assessing the Importance of Attitudes toward Organizational Change," *Journal of Management* 35, no. 1 (2009), pp. 37–55.

33 J. W. B. Lang and P. D. Bliese, "General Mental Ability and Two Types of Adaptation to Unforeseen Change: Applying Discontinuous Growth Models to the Task-Change Paradigm," *Journal of Applied Psychology* 94, no. 2 (2009), pp. 411–428.

34 C. O. L. H. Porter, J. W. Webb, and C. I. Gogus, "When Goal Orientations Collide: Effects of Learning and Performance Orientation on Team Adaptability in Response to Workload Imbalance," *Journal of Applied Psychology* 95, no. 5 (2010), pp. 935–943.

35 Based on original research conducted by Dr. Katherine Breward, University of Winnipeg, as yet unpublished; and Habitat for Humanity, "Habitat for Humanity Manitoba Partners with Rockwood Institution to Build a Home in Winnipeg," news release, December 18, 2013, http://www.habitat.mb.ca/PDF/media/2013/Habitat%20Rockwood%20Home%20Dedication%20Press%20RELEASE.PDF.

36 See, for example, A. Karaevli, "Performance Consequences for New CEO 'Outsiderness': Moderating Effects of Pre- and Post-Succession Contexts," *Strategic Management Journal* 28, no. 7 (2007), pp. 681–706.

37 Based on R. H. Miles, "Accelerating Corporate Transformations (Don't Lose Your Nerve!)," *Harvard Business Review*, January/February 2010, pp. 68–75.

38 Vignette based on D. Neisser, "How Cirque Du Soleil Contorts to Create Change," *Advertising Age*, December 14, 2016, http://adage.com/article/cmo-strategy/cirque-du-soleil-contorts-create-change/307141/; and A. Woods, "Circus Meets Extreme Sports in Cirque du Soleil's Volta," *Toronto Star*, August 10, 2017, https://www.thestar.com/entertainment/2017/08/10/circus-meets-extreme-sports-in-cirque-du-soleils-volta.html.

39 W. K. Smith and M. W. Lewis, "Toward a Theory of Paradox: A Dynamic Equilibrium Model of Organizing," *Academy of Management Review* 36 (2011), pp. 381–403.

40 P. Jarzabkowski, J. Lê, and A. Van de Ven, "Responding to Competing Strategic Demands: How Organizing, Belonging, and Performing Paradoxes Coevolve," *Strategic Organization* 11 (2013), pp. 245–280; and W. K. Smith, "Dynamic Decision Making: A Model of Senior Leaders Managing Strategic Paradoxes," *Academy of Management Journal* 57 (2014), pp. 1592–1623.

41 J. Jay, "Navigating Paradox as a Mechanism of Change and Innovation in Hybrid Organizations," *Academy of Management Journal* 56 (2013), pp. 137–159.

42 Y. Zhang, D. A. Waldman, Y. Han, and X. Li, "Paradoxical Leader Behaviors in People Management: Antecedents and Consequences," *Academy of Management Journal* 58 (2015), pp. 538–466.

43 See, for example, F. Yuan and R. W. Woodman, "Innovative Behavior in the Workplace: The Role of Performance and Image Outcome Expectations," *Academy of Management Journal* 53, no. 2 (2010), pp. 323–342.

44 See, for instance, G. P. Pisano, "You Need an Innovation Strategy," *Harvard Business Review*, June 2015, pp. 44–54.

45 F. H. W. Volberda, F. A. J. Van den Bosch, and C. V. Heij, "Management Innovation: Management as Fertile Ground for Innovation," *European Management Review*, Spring 2013, pp. 1–15.

46 F. Damanpour, "Organizational Innovation: A Meta-analysis of Effects of Determinants and Moderators," *Academy of Management Journal*, September 1991, pp. 555–590; and G. Westerman, F. W. McFarlan, and M. Iansiti, "Organization Design and Effectiveness over the Innovation Life Cycle," *Organization Science* 17, no. 2 (2006), pp. 230–238.

47 See P. Schepers and P. T. van den Berg, "Social Factors of Work-Environment Creativity," *Journal of Business and Psychology* 21, no. 3 (2007), pp. 407–428.

48 Based on https://www.gore.com/innovation-center; A. Harrington, "Who's Afraid of a New Product?" *Fortune*, November 10, 2003,

pp. 189–192; C. C. Manz, F. Shipper, and G. L. Stewart, "Everyone a Team Leader: Shared Influence at W. L. Gore and Associates," *Organizational Dynamics* 38, no. 3 (2009), pp. 239–244; Gore, "A Team-Based, Flat Lattice Organization," accessed July 23, 2015, http://www.gore.com/en_xx/aboutus/culture/index.html; and S. Caulkin, "Gore-Text Gets Made without Managers," *The Observer*, November 1, 2008, http://www.theguardian.com/business/2008/nov/02/gore-tex-textiles-terri-kelly.

49 S. Chang, L. Jia, R. Takeuchi, and Y. Cai, "Do High-Commitment Work Systems Affect Creativity? A Multilevel Combinational Approach to Employee Creativity," *Journal of Applied Psychology* 99 (2014), pp. 665–680.

50 M. E. Mullins, S. W. J. Kozlowski, N. Schmitt, and A. W. Howell, "The Role of the Idea Champion in Innovation: The Case of the Internet in the Mid-1990s," *Computers in Human Behavior* 24, no. 2 (2008), pp. 451–467.

51 C. Y. Murnieks, E. Mosakowski, and M. S. Cardon, "Pathways of Passion: Identity Centrality, Passion, and Behavior among Entrepreneurs," *Journal of Management* 40 (2014), pp. 1583–1606.

52 S. C. Parker, "Intrapreneurship or Entrepreneurship?" *Journal of Business Venturing*, January 2011, pp. 19–34.

53 See, for example, T. B. Lawrence, M. K. Mauws, B. Dyck, and R. F. Kleysen, "The Politics of Organizational Learning: Integrating Power into the 4I Framework," *Academy of Management Review*, January 2005, pp. 180–191.

54 J. Kim, T. Egan, and H. Tolson, "Examining the Dimensions of the Learning Organization Questionnaire: A Review and Critique of Research Utilizing the DLOQ," *Human Resource Development Review*, March 2015, pp. 91–112.

55 L. Berghman, P. Matthyssens, S. Streukens, and K. Vandenbempt, "Deliberate Learning Mechanisms for Stimulating Strategic Innovation Capacity," *Long Range Planning*, February–April 2013, pp. 39–71.

56 R. Chiva and J. Habib, "A Framework for Organizational Learning: Zero, Adaptive, and Generative Learning," *Journal of Management & Organization* 21, no. 3 (2015), pp. 350–368; and J. Kim, T. Egan, and H. Tolson, "Examining the Dimensions of the Learning Organization Questionnaire: A Review and Critique of Research Utilizing the DLOQ," *Human Resource Development Review* 14, no. 1 (2015), pp. 91–112.

57 M. Cerne, M. Jaklic, and M. Skerlavaj, "Decoupling Management and Technological Innovations: Resolving the Individualism-Collectivism Controversy," *Journal of International Management*, June 2013, pp. 103–117.

58 For contrasting views on episodic and continuous change, see K. E. Weick and R. E. Quinn, "Organizational Change and Development," in *Annual Review of Psychology*, vol. 50, ed. J. T. Spence, J. M. Darley, and D. J. Foss (Palo Alto, CA: Annual Reviews, 1999), pp. 361–386. Counterpoint based on R. Thomas, D. S. Leisa, and C. Hardy, "Managing Organizational Change: Negotiating Meaning and Power-Resistance Relations," *Organization Science* 22, no. 1 (2011), pp. 22–41; and P. B. Vaill, *Managing as a Performing Art: New Ideas for a World of Chaotic Change* (San Francisco: Jossey-Bass, 1989).

59 D. Meinert, "Communicate Early and Often," *HR Magazine*, November 2012, p. 36; D. Meinert, "Define the Goals," *HR Magazine*, November 2012, pp. 32–33; and D. Meinert, "Wings of Change," *HR Magazine*, November 2012, pp. 30–32.

60 Based on C. Edelhart, "Weatherman's Stand Against Story Costs Job," *Californian*, May 16, 2011, http://www.bakersfieldcalifornian.com/local/x1898679505/Weathermans-stand-against-story-costs-job; and K. T. Phan, "ABC Affiliate Fires Christian over Strip Club Segment," *Fox News*, May 10, 2011, http://nation.foxnews.com/firing/2011/05/10/abc-affiliate-fires-christian-over-strip-club-segment.

61 S. Halzack, "Why Walmart Is Ditching Its Celine Dion Soundtrack and Getting a DJ," *Washington Post*, June 3, 2015, http://www.washingtonpost.com/news/business/wp/2015/06/03/why-Walmart-is-ditching-its-celine-dion-soundtrack-and-getting-a-deejay/; B. Ritholtz, "Walmart Learns to Live without Everyday Poverty Wages," *Bloomberg View*, June 11, 2015, http://www.bloombergview.com/articles/2015-06-11/Walmart-lives-without-everyday-poverty-wages; and B. O'Keefe, "The Man Who's Reinventing Walmart," *Fortune*, June 4, 2015, http://fortune.com/2015/06/04/walmart-ceo-doug-mcmillon/.

62 Based on A. Lawson, "Sony Issues New Profit Warning Hit By Massive Smartphone Losses," *Independent*, September 17, 2014; H. Hiyama, "Sony Break-Up Call Shines Light on Electronics Industry Problems," *Japan Today*, June 7, 2013, http://www.japantoday.com/category/opinions/view/sony-break-up-call-shines-light-on-electronic-industry-problems; R. Katz, "How Japan Blew Its Lead in Electronics," *Wall Street Journal*, March 23, 2012, p. A15; and H. Tabuchi, "How the Parade Passed Sony By," *New York Times*, April 15, 2012, pp. B1, B7.

63 Based on R. Pascale, M. Millemann, and L. Gioja, "Changing the Way We Change," *Harvard Business Review*, November–December 1997, pp. 127–139. The actual names of the points based on the After Action Review are taken from the article, although the summaries are provided by the authors of this book. See also "After Action Review," *Knowledge Sharing Tools and Methods Toolkit*, accessed November 26, 2014, http://www.kstoolkit.org/After+Action+Review.

Additional Cases

1 Note that this case is largely based on actual events occurring at a Canadian company. At the request of the individuals directly involved, however, the employee names and the company name have been disguised.

2 This is a true story about a female employee in a Canadian company. The names of the people involved have been disguised. However, the events are truthful and accurate. This case is based on an interview with "Julie" conducted after her release from jail. The interview took place on December 27, 2011.

3 This case is based on a real Canadian company. At the request of the owners, the employee names and the company name have been disguised.

4 This case is based largely on an extended feature news story written by K. More, "Public Service Bargaining: A Bruising Battle Lies Ahead," *Ottawa Citizen*, July 18, 2014, http://ottawacitizen.com/news/national/public-service-bargaining-a-bruising-battle-lies-ahead.

5 A. Thomson, "Tony Clement, Treasury Board President, Proposes Changes to Public Servants' Sick Leave," *Huffington Post Canada*, August 2, 2014, http://www.huffingtonpost.ca/2014/02/08/tony-clement-sick-leave_n_4752463.html.

6 K. May, "Tony Clement Wants to Cut Public Servants' Sick Days to Five," *Ottawa Citizen*, September 11, 2014, http://ottawacitizen.com/news/national/clement-wants-to-cut-public-servants-sick-days-to-five.

7 T. Pedwell, "PBO Sick Leave Report: No 'Incremental' Costs to Taxpayers," *Huffington Post Canada*, July 16, 2014, http://www.huffingtonpost.ca/2014/07/16/pbo-sick-leave-report_n_5590817.html.

8 S. Kari, "Ex-constable Must Again Prove RCMP Harassment," *Globe and Mail*, December 20, 2011, http://www.theglobeandmail.com/news/national/ex-constable-must-again-prove-rcmpharassment/article151366/.

9 S. Stewart, A. Hoffman, and P. Waldie, "Female Mounties Allege Harassment Not Investigated to Protect RCMP," *Canadian Press*, December 20, 2011, http://www.theglobeandmail.com/news/

national/female-mounties-allege-harassment-not-investigatedto-protect-rcmp/article1016726/.

10   S. Stewart, A. Hoffman, and P. Waldie, "Female Mounties Allege Harassment Not Investigated to Protect RCMP," *Canadian Press*, December 20, 2011, http://www.theglobeandmail.com/news/national/female-mounties-allege-harassment-not-investigatedto-protect-rcmp/article1016726/.

11   S. Stewart, A. Hoffman, and P. Waldie, "Female Mounties Allege Harassment Not Investigated to Protect RCMP," *Canadian Press*, December 20, 2011, http://www.theglobeandmail.com/news/national/female-mounties-allege-harassment-not-investigatedto-protect-rcmp/article1016726/.

12   "More B.C. Mounties Complain of Harassment," *CBC News*, November 8, 2011, http://www.cbc.ca/news/canada/britishcolumbia/story/2011/11/08/bc-rcmp-harassment.html.

13   "Lawyer 'Stunned' RCMP Brass Came in to Settle Harassment Case," *CBC News*, December 9, 2011, http://www.cbc.ca/news/canada/story/2011/12/09/rcmp-allegations-blundell.html.

14   G. Mason, "RCMP Took Two Years to Respond to Officer's Sexual Harassment Complaint," *Globe and Mail*, December 5, 2011, http://www.theglobeandmail.com/news/national/britishcolumbia/gary_mason/rcmp-took-two-years-to-respond-toofficers-sexual-harassment-complaint/article2261049/.

15   G. Mason, "Former Mountie Paints Picture of Near Daily Harassment," *Globe and Mail*, December 8, 2011, http://www.theglobeandmail.com/news/national/former-mountie-paintspicture-of-near-daily-harassment/article2259072/.

16   S. Cooper, "Alleged Mountie Harassment Made RCMP Staffer Fear for Family's Lives Court Hears," *National Post*, November 18, 2011, http://news.nationalpost.com/2011/11/18/allegedmountie-harassment-made-rcmp-staffer-fear-for-familys-livescourt-hears/.

17   V. Luk, "RCMP Sexual Harassment Claims Deepen after Second Female Mountie Comes Forward," *National Post*, November 10, 2011, http://news.nationalpost.com/2011/11/10/rcmp-sexualharassment-claims-deepen-after-second-female-mountie-slamsforce/. Material reprinted with the express permission of: Postmedia News, a division of Postmedia Network Inc.

18   V. Luk, "RCMP Sexual Harassment Claims Deepen after Second Female Mountie Comes Forward," *National Post*, November 10, 2011, http://news.nationalpost.com/2011/11/10/rcmp-sexualharassment-claims-deepen-after-second-female-mountie-slamsforce/. Material reprinted with the express permission of: Postmedia News, a division of Postmedia Network Inc.

19   C. Freeze, "Top Mountie Delivers Candid, Scathing View of Force at the Brink," *Globe and Mail*, December 20, 2011, http://www.theglobeandmail.com/news/politics/top-mountie-deliverscandid-scathing-view-of-force-at-the-brink/article2277241/.

20   D. Leblanc, "RCMP Introduce New Code of Conduct," *Globe and Mail*, April 26, 2014, http://www.theglobeandmail.com/news/politics/rcmp-introduce-new-code-of-conduct/article18237170/.

21   G. Mason, "RCMP Took Two Years to Respond to Officer's Sexual Harassment Complaint," *Globe and Mail*, December 5, 2011, http://www.theglobeandmail.com/news/national/britishcolumbia/gary_mason/rcmp-took-two-years-to-respond-toofficers-sexual-harassment-complaint/article2261049/.

22   A. Woo, "Sexual Harassment Claims against RCMP Reach 336," *Globe and Mail*, July 18, 2014, http://www.theglobeandmail.com/news/british-columbia/sexual-harassment-claims-against-rcmp-reach-336/article19669218/.

23   I. Bailey, "Lawyers Preparing Possible Class Action Lawsuit against RCMP," *Globe and Mail*, December 21, 2011, http://www.theglobeandmail.com/news/national/lawyers-preparingpossible-class-action-suit-against-rcmp/article2278817/.

24   Dr. Katherine Breward, "Disability Accommodations and Promotions at Bunco," *Case Research Journal* 30, no. 1 (2010), pp. 65–72. Reprinted with permission.

25   National Digestive Diseases Information Clearinghouse (NDDIC), Digestive Diseases *National Institute of Health*, publication number 06-3410 (Bethesda, MD: Author, 2006). http://digestive.niddk.nih.gov/ddiseases/pubs/crohns/#stress.

26   National Digestive Diseases Information Clearinghouse (NDDIC), Digestive Diseases *National Institute of Health*, publication number 06-3410 (Bethesda, MD: Author, 2006). http://digestive.niddk.nih.gov/ddiseases/pubs/crohns/#stress.

27   "Crohn's Disease," *MedicineNet.com*, accessed December 3, 2014, http://www.medicinenet.com/crohns_disease/article.htm.

28   This case was prepared by Nancy Langton, Sauder School of Business. This case is based on an actual set of events, although all names have been changed. © 2006 by Nancy Langton. Case sources: "Zoo Mulls Qualities Sought in Next Director," *toledoblade.com*, September 9, 2005, http://toledoblade.com; S. Eder, "Zoo Task Force Sets 100-Day Target for Submitting Investigation Report," *toledoblade.com*, March 25, 2005; S. Eder, "Experience with Animals Lacking for Operations Chief," *toledoblade.com*, March 13, 2005; S. Eder, "Reichard Held in High Esteem by Fellow Zoo Veterinarians," *toledoblade.com*, March 9, 2005; M Greenwell, "Zoo Sees New Job As Way to Fix Problems," *toledoblade.com*, June 23, 2005; J. Laidman, "Employee Relations Top Zoo Leaders' List," *toledoblade.com*, May 22, 2005; J. Laidman, "Embattled Zoo Leaders Quit," *toledoblade.com*, May 5, 2005; J. Laidman, "Clash of Philosophies, Loss of Animals Triggered Turmoil," *toledoblade.com*, March 13, 2005; J. Laidman, "Fired Zoo Veterinarian's File Mostly Positive, with a Few Concerns," *toledoblade.com*, March 9, 2005; J. Laidman, "Toledo Zoo Veterinarian Blames Firing on His Warnings to USDA," *toledoblade.com*, March 8, 2005; J. Laidman, "Feds Probe 2 Animal Deaths at Toledo Zoo," *toledoblade.com*, February 24, 2004; J. Laidman and T. Vezner, "Staff Offers Criticism, Praise in Zoo Survey," *toledoblade.com*, May 27, 2005; J. Laidman and T. Vezner, "Vet's Deal Isn't First to Silence Ex-Official," *toledoblade.com*, May 2, 2005; J. Laidman and T. Vezner, "Internal Battles Plunge Zoo into a Caldron of Discontent," *toledoblade.com*, March 20, 2005; S. H. Staelin, "Zoo Board Tackles Challenges," *toledoblade.com*, April 16, 2005; T. Vezner, "Zoo Names Chief Veterinarian, Ignoring Task Force's Proposal," *toledoblade.com*, December 17, 2005; T. Vezner, "Consultant Hired to Oversee Zoo Administration," *toledoblade.com*, July 20, 2005; T. Vezner, "Zoo's Ex-Vet on Hand for Report," *toledoblade.com*, July 9, 2005; T. Vezner, "Zoo Task Force Report Demands Broad Changes," *toledoblade.com*, July 7, 2005; T. Vezner and J. Laidman, "Flurry of Changes Leaves Workers Reeling," *toledoblade.com*, May 6, 2005; T. Vezner, "Settlement Bars Zoo Vet from Speaking to Panel," *toledoblade.com*, May 1, 2005; T. Vezner, "Zoo Task Force's Questions for Dennler Hit Time Limit," *toledoblade.com*, April 1, 2005; T. Vezner, "Inquiry in 2004 Disclosed Problems," *toledoblade.com*, March 27, 2005; Lucas County Commissioners Special Citizens Task Force for the Zoo, Final Report, July 8, 2005, http://www.co.lucas.oh.us/commissioners/Final_Report_Zoo_Task_Force.pdf; http://www.toledozoo.org, accessed January 17, 2006; and http://www.doctortim.org, accessed January 17, 2006.

GLOSSARY/SUBJECT INDEX

The page on which a key term is defined is printed in boldface.

NAME AND ORGANIZATION INDEX

LIST OF CANADIAN COMPANIES

Prince Edward Island

Quebec

Saskatchewan

Yukon